Media Comments

"...lighthouses, schoolhouses, stage coach stops, llama ranches ...There's lots to choose from and it should keep B&B fans happy for years." – Cathy Stapells, Toronto Sun.

"...helps you find the very best hideaways (many of the book's listings appear in the National Register of Historic Places.)" – Country Living.

"I love your book!" – Lydia Moss, Travel Editor, McCall's.

"Delightful, succinct, detailed and well-organized. Easy to follow style..."
– Don Wudke, Los Angeles Times.

"Pay for one night at a nearby country inn and get the second night free...Among them is the very fine L'Auberge Provencale...The goal of the program, sponsored by the Association of American Historic Inns, is to introduce first-timers to inn stays but frequent inn guests also are eligible for the bargain."
– James Yenckel, Washington Post.

"One of the better promotions we've seen." – Baton Rouge Advocate.

"...thoughtfully organized and look-ups are hassle-free...well-researched and accurate...put together by people who know the field. There is no other publication available that covers this particular segment of the bed & breakfast industry – a segment that has been gaining popularity among travelers by leaps and bounds. The information included is valuable and well thought out." – Morgan Directory Reviews.

"Readers will find this book easy to use and handy to have. An excellent, well-organized and comprehensive reference for inngoers and innkeepers alike."
– Inn Review, Kankakee, Illinois.

"This guide has become the favorite choice of travelers and specializes only in professionally operated inns and B&Bs rather than homestays (lodging in spare bedrooms)." – Laguna Magazine.

"This is the best bed and breakfast book out. It outshines them all!"
– Maggie Balitas, Rodale Book Clubs.

"Most of us military families have lived all over the world, so it takes an unusual book, service or trip to excite us! As I began to look through the book, my heart beat faster as I envisioned what a good time our readers could have visiting some of these very special historic bed and breakfast properties." – Ann Crawford, Military Living.

"Absolutely beautiful!" – KQIL talk show radio.

"This is a great book. It makes you want to card everything." – KBRT Los Angeles radio talk show.

"All our lines were tied up! We received calls from every one of our 40 stations (while discussing your book.)" – Business Radio Network.

"For a delightful change of scenery, visit one of these historical inns. (Excerpts from Bed & Breakfasts and Country Inns follow.) A certificate for one free consecutive night (minimum two nights stay) can be found in the book" – Shirley Howard, Good Housekeeping.

D1378219

Comments From Innkeepers

"The guests we receive from the Buy-One-Night-Get-One-Night-Free program are some of the most wonderful people. Most are first time inngoers and after their first taste of the inn experience they vow that this is the only way to travel." – Innkeeper, Mass.

"Guests that were staying here last night swear by your guide. They use it all the time. Please send us information about being in your guide." – Innkeeper, Port Angeles, Wash.

"The people are so nice! Please keep up the great program!"
– K. C, Avon Manor Inn, Avon-By-the-Sea, N.J.

"We would like to express our appreciation for the Free Night programs. We had an excellent response to the certificates. It has helped us fill our vacancies during the weekdays and in the slower time of the season. Keep up the good work!" – Hacienda Vargas, Sante Fe, N.M.

"Your book is so widely distributed that we booked up a room all the way from Japan!"
– Rose Inn, Ithaca, N.Y.

"We've just received the new edition. Congratulations on this magnificent book. You've done it again!" – Gilbert House, Charleston, W. V.

"We want to tell you how much we love your book. We have it out for guests to use. They love it! Each featured inn stands out so well. Thank you for the privilege of being in your book."
– Fairhaven Inn, Bath, Me.

"American Historic Inns is wonderful! We are proud and delighted to be included. Thank you for creating such a special guidebook." – The Heirloom, Ione, Calif.

"Your new edition has maintained the fine quality of previous editions and we are very pleased to be included." – The Victoriana 1898, Traverse City, Mich.

"Thanks so much for all your hard work. We receive the largest number of guidebook referrals from your book." – Saddle Rock Ranch, Sedona, Ariz.

"We are thrilled with your book. We appreciate your incredible traveling spirit captured in these pages!"
– Thorwood, Hastings, Minn.

"We tell all our guests about the Free Night promotion and how to participate. However, we also remind them to visit with us again. Almost 100% said they will–and do so! We must be doing something right. Thanks again for this unique opportunity." – House on the Hill, Lake George, N.Y.

"What a great deal for everyone involved. Thanks for the opportunity!"
– Victoria & Albert Inn, Abingdon, Va.

"We've had guests return two or three times after discovering us through your book. They have turned into wonderful guests and friends." – Port Townsend, Wash.

"The response to your book has been terrific and the guests equally terrific! Many are already returning. Thanks for all your hard work." – Rockport, Mass.

"We love your book and we also use it. Just went to New Orleans and had a great trip."
– Gettysburg, Pa.

"This has been one of the best B&B programs we have done and the guests have been delightful. Thanks!" – Eastern Shore, Md.

"We are grateful that so many of our old friends and new guests have found us through your book. We always recommend your publications to guests who wish to explore other fine country inns of New England." – Georgette & Albert Levis, Vermont innkeepers.

Comments About
Bed & Breakfasts and Country Inns

"Our office went crazy over this book. The quality of the inns and the quality of the book is phenomenal! Send us 52 books." – M. B., Westport, Conn.

"Outstanding! We were offering a variety of inn guide books, but yours was the only one guests bought." – J.A., White Oak Inn, Ohio

"My husband and I have really enjoyed our Bed & Breakfast free night for the past two summers. Such a good offer. Thanks!" – B.C., Houston, Texas

"The 300 women who attended my 'Better Cents' seminar went wild for the free-night book. I brought my copy and showed them the value of the free-night program. They all wanted to get involved. Thank you so much for offering such a great value." – R.R., Making Cents Seminars, Texas.

"Thank you for offering this special! It allowed us to get away even on a tight budget." – D.L., Pittsburgh, Pa.

"My husband and I enjoyed the ambiance and delicious breakfasts! This is a lovely inn and a great offer. Thanks for making it possible for us to enjoy." – J.D., Woodbury, N.J.

"This made our vacation a lot more reasonable. We got the best room in a beautiful top-drawer inn for half the price." – L.A., Irvine, Calif.

"I used your book and free night offer and took my 17-year-old daughter. It was our first B&B visit ever and we loved it. (We acted like friends instead of parent vs. teenager for the first time in a long time.) It was wonderful!" – B. F., Clinton, N.J.

"Thanks! Do we love your B&B offer! You betcha! The luxury of getting a two-day vacation for the cost of one is Christmas in July for sure. Keep up the good work." – R.R., Grapevine, Texas.

"What a great idea for gifts. I'm ordering five to use as birthday, housewarming and thank-you gifts." – J.R., Laguna Niguel, Calif.

"The best thing since ice cream – and I love ice cream!" – M. C., Cape May, N.J.

"Out of 25 products we presented to our fund raising committee your book was No. 1 and it generated the most excitement." – H. U., Detroit, Mich.

For my traveling kin,
Nancy, Marian, Dorothy & Wilma

೮೮೮೮

American Historic Inns™

Bed & Breakfasts
and
Country Inns

by Deborah Edwards Sakach

Published by

AMERICAN
HISTORIC
I N N S
INCORPORATED

PO Box 669
Dana Point
California
92629-0669

Bed & Breakfasts and Country Inns

Every effort has been made to produce a dependable reference guide based on information gathered from innkeepers. American Historic Inns, Inc. makes no representations or warranties with respect to the establishments listed herein and specifically disclaims any warranties of fitness for any particular purpose. We recommend that you contact each inn and B&B to verify information prior to making reservations. Although every attempt was made to be as accurate as possible, American Historic Inns, Inc. does not make any representation that this book is free from error. Information included in this publication has been checked for accuracy prior to publication. Since changes do occur, American Historic Inns, Inc. cannot be responsible for any variations from the information printed. No lodging establishment paid to be included in this book. The descriptions contained herein were based on information supplied by the establishments. American Historic Inns, Inc. will not be responsible if any establishment listed herein breaches its contract or refuses to accept the FREE-night certificate; however, we will attempt to secure compliance.

FRONT COVER:

Grand Victorian B&B Inn, Bellaire Michigan.
Photo by Don Rutt

BACK COVER:

The Keeper's House, Isle Au Haut, Maine
The Abbey, Cape May, N.J.
The White Oak Inn, Danville, Ohio
Scofield House B&B, Sturgeon Bay, Wis.
Photos by American Historic Inns
L'Auberge Provencale, White Post, Va.
Photo by Esther and Frank Schmidt

COVER DESIGN:
David Sakach

DATABASE MANAGER:
Sandy Imre

DATABASE ASSISTANTS:
Melanie Hackett, Joyce Roll, Elizabeth Spehart

EDITORIAL ASSISTANTS:
Tiffany Crosswy, Lucy Poshek, Joshua Prizer, Stephen Sakach

PROGRAMMING AND CARTOGRAPHY:
Tim Sakach

Publisher's Cataloging in Publication Data

Sakach, Deborah Edwards
American Historic Inns, Inc.
Bed & Breakfasts and Country Inns

1. Bed & Breakfast Accommodations - United States, Directories, Guide Books.
2. Travel - Bed & Breakfast Inns, Directories, Guide Books.
3. Bed & Breakfast Accommodations - Historic Inns, Directories, Guide Books.
4. Hotel Accommodations - Bed & Breakfast Inns, Directories, Guide Books.
5. Hotel Accommodations - United States, Directories, Guide Books.
I. Title. II Author. III Bed & Breakfast, Bed & Breakfasts and Country Inns.

American Historic Inns is a trademark of American Historic Inns, Inc.

ISBN: 0-9615481-9-3
Softcover
Printed in the United States of America.
10 9 8 7 6 5 4 3 2 1

Table Of Contents

How To Make A Reservation

1. **You must make ADVANCE reservations.** The FREE night offer is only valid by making reservations in advance directly with the participating lodging establishment AND when you identify yourself as having a Certificate from this guide.

2. **You must identify yourself FIRST as holding a Certificate from this guide, or the innkeeper is not obligated to honor the Certificate.**

3. All FREE nights are subject to availability. In some cases this may mean that the lodging establishment has rooms but is projecting that those rooms will be filled with full-fare customers. Most hotels consider they are at full occupancy when they are about 80% filled, and then cut off all reduced-fare programs at that time. Smaller properties such as Bed & Breakfast homes and Inns may use different formulas. Some set aside a specific number of rooms or suites for Certificate holders and then will not accept any more reservations for the promotion after those rooms are filled. Others will accept Certificate holders at the last minute when they project that they will have rooms available.

4. Try to obtain a confirmation number, confirmation letter or the name of the person taking your reservation.

5. If you have children or pets coming with you, or if you smoke, be sure to tell the innkeeper in advance. Most Bed & Breakfasts and Country Inns are non-smoking. Accommodations for children or pets may be limited or non-existent.

6. Understand the cancellation policy. A number of Bed & Breakfasts and Country Inns require a two-week or more notice of cancellation in order to refund your deposit. You should find out what the policy is at the same time you make your reservations.

7. **All holidays are excluded.** There may be other periods of time that are excluded as well.

8. This is a two-night minimum program and the two nights MUST BE CONSECUTIVE, i.e. "Monday and Tuesday," or "Sunday and Monday." You can stay longer, of course. Please read each inn's specific restrictions.

9. Always find out what meals, if any, are included in the rates and whether you will have to pay for meals. Not every establishment participating in this program provides a free breakfast.

10. Some locales require that bed tax be collected, even on FREE nights. If you have a question, check with the innkeeper, chamber of commerce or city hall serving the area in which you wish to stay.

11. For more information, request a brochure from participating Inns before you make your reservation.

12. Don't forget to take this book with the Certificate along with you.

The FREE night is given to you directly from the innkeeper in the hope that you or your friends will return and share your discovery with others. **The inns are not reimbursed by American Historic Inns, Inc.**

AMERICAN HISTORIC INNS
INCORPORATED

Certificate

ঙ *redeemable for* ও

One Free Night at a Bed & Breakfast or Country Inn

ঙ ঙ ঙ ঙ ও ও ও ও

Compliments of American Historic Inns, Inc. and participating Bed & Breakfasts and Country Inns.

This certificate entitles the bearer
to one free night at any one of the more
than 1,600 Bed & Breakfasts and Country Inns
included in this book when the bearer buys the
first night at the regular rate.
See back for requirements.

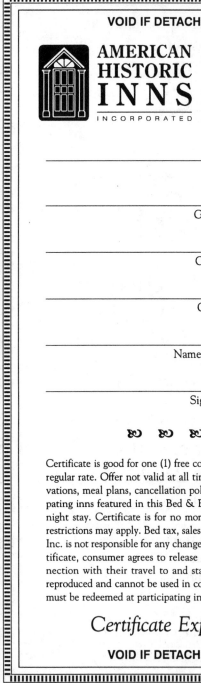

AMERICAN HISTORIC INNS
INCORPORATED

This section should be completed by the innkeeper when the certificate is redeemed.
MAIL COMPLETED CERTIFICATE TO:
AMERICAN HISTORIC INNS, INC.
PO BOX 669, DANA POINT, CA 92629-0669

_____
Name of Guest

_____
Guest Home Address

_____
Guest City/State/Zip

_____
Guest Home Phone

_____
Name of Bed & Breakfast/Inn

_____
Signature of Innkeeper

Certificate is good for one (1) free consecutive night when you purchase the first night at the regular rate. Offer not valid at all times. Contact inn in advance for availability, rates, reservations, meal plans, cancellation policies and other requirements. Offer valid only at participating inns featured in this Bed & Breakfast Guide. Not valid during holidays. Minimum 2-night stay. Certificate is for no more than two people and no more than one room. Other restrictions may apply. Bed tax, sales tax and gratuities not included. American Historic Inns, Inc. is not responsible for any changes in individual inn operation or policy. By use of this certificate, consumer agrees to release American Historic Inns, Inc. from any liability in connection with their travel to and stay at any participating Inn. This certificate may not be reproduced and cannot be used in conjunction with any other promotional offers. Certificate must be redeemed at participating inn by December 31, 1997. Void where prohibited.

Certificate Expires December 31, 1997

How To Use This Book

You hold in your hands a delightful selection of America's best Bed & Breakfasts and Country Inns. The innkeeper of each property has generously agreed to participate in our FREE night program. **They are not reimbursed for the second night, but make it available to you in the hope that you will return to their inn or tell others about your stay.**

Most knowledgeable innkeepers enjoy sharing regional attractions, local folklore, history, and pointing out favorite restaurants and other special features of their areas. They have invested much of themselves in creating an experience for you to long remember. Many have personally renovated historic buildings, saving them from deterioration and often, the bulldozer. Others have infused their inns with a unique style and personality to enliven your experience with a warm and elegant environment. Your innkeepers are a tremendous resource. Treat them kindly and you will be well rewarded.

Accommodations

You'll find Bed & Breakfasts and Country Inns in converted schoolhouses, stone castles, lighthouses, 18th-century farmhouses, Queen Anne Victorians, adobe lodges and more.

Many are listed in the National Register of Historic Places and have preserved the stories and memorabilia from their participation in historical events such as the Revolutionary or Civil wars.

The majority of inns included in this book were built in the 17th, 18th and 19th centuries. We have stated the date each building was constructed at the beginning of each description.

No inn paid to be featured in this guidebook. All costs for the production of the book have been absorbed by American Historic Inns. The selection of inns for this guidebook was made as carefully as possible from among the many that wanted to be included. American Historic Inns, as publishers, produced and financed the project. Inns did not pay advertising fees to be in the book.

They did, however, agree to honor the certificate for the free night when the first night is purchased. We hope you enjoy the choices we made and we encourage you to suggest new inns that you discover.

A Variety of Inns

A COUNTRY INN generally serves both breakfast and dinner and may have a restaurant associated with it. Many have been in operation for years; some, since the 18th century as you will note in our "Inns of Interest" section. Although primarily found on the East Coast, a few Country Inns are in other regions of the nation.

A BED & BREAKFAST facility's primary focus is lodging. It can have from three to 20 rooms or more. The innkeepers usually live on the premises. Breakfast is the only meal served and can be a full-course, gourmet breakfast or a simple buffet. Many B&B owners pride themselves on their culinary skills.

As with Country Inns, many B&Bs specialize in providing historic, romantic or gracious atmospheres with amenities such as canopied beds, fireplaces, spa tubs, afternoon tea in the library and scenic views.

Some give great attention to recapturing a specific historic period, such as the Victorian or Colonial eras. Many display antiques and other furnishings from family collections.

A HOMESTAY is a room available in a private home. It may be an elegant stone mansion in the best part of town or a charming country farm. Homestays have one to three guest rooms. Because homestays are often operated as a hobby-type business and open and close frequently, only a very few unique properties are included in this publication.

Baths

Not all Bed & Breakfasts and Country Inns provide a private bath for each guest room. We have included the number of rooms and the number of private baths in each facility. If you must have a private bath, make sure the room reserved for you provides this.

Beds

K, Q, D, T, indicates King, Queen, Double or Twin beds available at the inn.

Credit cards/Payments

MC	MasterCard
VISA	Visa
DC	Diner's Club
CB	Carte Blanche
AX	American Express
DS	Discover
TC	Traveler's checks
PC	Personal checks

Meals

Breakfasts/Teas

Continental breakfast: Coffee, juice, toast or pastry.

Continental-plus breakfast: A continental breakfast plus a variety of breads, cheeses and fruit.

Full breakfast: Coffee, juice, breads, fruit and an entree.

Gourmet breakfast: May be an elegant four-course candlelight offering or especially creative cuisine.

Teas: Usually served in the late afternoon with cookies, crackers or other in-between-meal offerings.

Meal Plans

AP: American Plan. All three meals may be included in the price of the room. Check to see if the rate quoted is for two people or per person.

MAP: Modified American Plan. Breakfast and dinner may be included in the price of the room.

EP: European Plan. No meals are included. We have listed only a few historic hotels that operate on an EP plan.

Always find out what meals, if any, are included in the rates. Not every establishment participating in this program provides breakfast, although most do. Inns offering the second night free may or may not include a complimentary lunch or dinner with the second night. Occasionally an innkeeper has indicated MAP and AP when she or he actually means that both programs are available and you must specify which program you are interested in.

Please do not assume meals are included in the rates featured in the book.

Rates

Rates are usually listed in ranges, i.e., $45-$105. The LOWEST rate is almost always available during off-peak periods and may only apply to the least expensive room. Rates are always subject to change and are not guaranteed. You should always confirm the rates when making the reservations. Rates for Canadian listings usually are listed in Canadian dollars. Rates are quoted for double occupancy for two people.

Breakfast and other meals MAY or MAY NOT be included in the rates and may not be included in the discount.

Smoking

The majority of Country Inns and B&Bs in historic buildings prohibit smoking; therefore, if you are a smoker we advise you to call and specifically check with each inn to see if and how they accommodate smokers.

Rooms

Under some listings, you will note that suites are available. We typically assume that suites include a private bath.

Additionally, under some listings, you will note a reference to cottages. A cottage may be a rustic cabin tucked in the woods, a seaside cottage or a private apartment-style accommodation.

Fireplaces

When fireplaces are mentioned in the listing they may be in guest rooms or in common areas. A few have fireplaces that are non-working because of city lodging requirements. Please verify this if you are looking forward to an intimate, fireside chat in your room.

State maps

The state maps have been designed to help travelers find an inn's location quickly and easily. Each city shown on the maps contains one or more inns.

As you browse through the guide, you will notice coordinates next to each city name, i.e. C3. The coordinates designate the location of inns on the state map.

Media coverage

Some inns have provided us with copies of magazine or newspaper articles written by travel writers about their establishments and we have indicated that in the listing. Articles written about the inns may be available either from the source as a reprint, through libraries or from the inn itself.

Comments from guests

Over the years, we have collected reams of guest comments about thousands of inns. Our files are filled with these documented comments. At the end of some descriptions, we have included a guest comment received about that inn.

Inspections

This book contains descriptions of more than 1,600 inns. Each year we travel across the country visiting hundreds of inns. Since 1981, we have had a happy, informal team of Inn travelers and prospective innkeepers who report to us about new Bed & Breakfast discoveries and repeat visits to favorite inns.

Although our staff usually sees hundreds of inns each year, inspecting inns is not the major focus of our travels. We visit as many as possible, photograph them and meet the innkeepers. Some inns are grand mansions filled with classic, museum-quality antiques. Others are rustic, such as reassembled log cabins or renovated barns or stables. We have enjoyed them all and cherish our memories of each establishment, pristine or rustic. Only rarely have we come across a truly disappointing inn poorly kept or poorly managed. This type of business usually does not survive because an inn's success depends upon repeat guests and enthusiastic word-of-mouth referrals from satisfied guests. We do not promote these types of establishments.

Traveler or tourist

Travel is an adventure into the unknown, full of surprises and rewards. A seasoned "traveler" learns that even after elaborate preparations and careful planning, travel provides the new and unexpected. The traveler learns to live with uncertainty and considers it part of the adventure.

To the "tourist," whether "accidental" or otherwise, new experiences are disconcerting. Tourists want no surprises. They expect things to be exactly as they had envisioned them. To tourists we recommend staying in a hotel or motel chain where the same formula is followed from one locale to another.

We have found that inngoers are travelers at heart. They relish the differences found at these unique Bed &

Breakfasts and Country Inns. This is the magic that makes traveling from Inn to Inn the delightful experience it is.

Minimum stays

Many inns require a two-night minimum stay on weekends. A three-night stay often is required during holiday periods.

Cancellations

Cancellation policies are individual for each Bed & Breakfast. It is not unusual to see 7- to 14-day cancellation periods or more. Please verify the inn's policy when making your reservation.

What if the Inn is full?

Ask the innkeeper for recommendations. They may know of an Inn that has recently opened or one nearby but off the beaten path. Call the local Chamber of Commerce in the town you hope to visit. They may also know of inns that have recently opened. Please let us know of any new discoveries you make.

We want to hear from you!

We've always enjoyed hearing from our readers and have carefully cataloged all letters and recommendations. If you wish to participate in evaluating your inn experiences, use the **Inn Evaluation Form** in the back of this book. You might want to make copies of this form prior to departing on your journey.

We hope you will enjoy this book so much that you will want to keep an extra copy or two on hand to offer to friends. Many readers have called to purchase our Free Night Certificate book for hostess gifts, birthday presents, or for seasonal celebrations. It's a great way to introduce your friends to America's enchanting Country Inns and Bed & Breakfasts.

Alabama

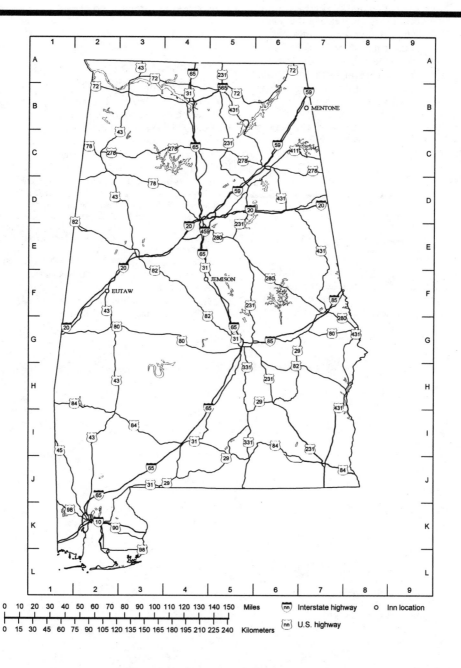

0 10 20 30 40 50 60 70 80 90 100 110 120 130 140 150 Miles

0 15 30 45 60 75 90 105 120 135 150 165 180 195 210 225 240 Kilometers

(nn) Interstate highway   o Inn location

(nn) U.S. highway

1

Eutaw   F2

Kirkwood Plantation
111 Kirkwood Dr, Eutaw, AL 35462-1101
(205)372-9009

Located on more than eight acres of green lawns,
pecan trees and azaleas, this is a stately antebellum
Greek Revival plantation house. There are eight
Ionic columns on the front and side of the house
and inside, Italian Carrara marble mantels adorn
the fireplaces. Massive mirrors and a Waterford crystal chandelier add to the elegance of the inn's furnishings, most of which are original to the house.
The innkeeper gives tours of the plantation along
with a mini history lesson on the Civil War and its
influence on Kirkwood Plantation.
Innkeeper(s): Mary Swayze. $75. 4 rooms. Breakfast included in rates.
Type of meal: full breakfast. Air conditioning in room.
Certificate may be used: Based upon availability.

Jemison   F4

The Jemison Inn
212 Hwy 191, Jemison, AL 35085
(205)688-2055

Circa 1930. Heirloom quality antiques fill this
gabled brick house. A Victorian decor predomi-
nates. Casseroles, sausage, cheese grits and muffins
comprise the inn's hearty breakfast.

Innkeeper(s): Nancy Ruzicka. $55-60. MC VISA AX DC CB DS. 3
rooms, 1 with PB, 1 with FP. Breakfast and afternoon tea included in
rates. Type of meal: full breakfast. Picnic lunch available. Beds: T.
Location: Midway between Birmingham and Montgomery in the heart of
horse country.
"I've never had a better breakfast anywhere."
Certificate may be used: January – December, Sunday – Thursday.

Mentone   B7

Mentone Inn
Hwy 117, PO Box 290,
Mentone, AL 35984
(205)634-4836 (800)455-7470

Circa 1927. Mentone is a refreshing stop for those
in search of the cool breezes and natural air conditioning of the mountains. Here antique treasures
mingle with modern-day conveniences. A sun deck
and spa complete the experience. Sequoyah
Caverns, Little River Canyon and DeSoto Falls are
moments away. The inn has its own hiking trails.
Innkeeper(s): Frances & Karl Waller. $60-125. MC VISA AX TC. 11
rooms with PB. Breakfast and afternoon tea included in rates. Types of
meals: continental breakfast, continental-plus breakfast, full breakfast
and early coffee/tea. Dinner, evening snack, picnic lunch, lunch, banquet service and catering service available. Beds: QT. Air conditioning
and ceiling fan in room. Cable TV, VCR, spa and bicycles on premises.
Antiques, fishing, parks, downhill skiing and watersports nearby.
Location: On Lookout Mountain in northeast Alabama.
Seen in: Birmingham News.
Certificate may be used: April 1-Aug. 31 (Monday-Thursday); Sept. 1-
Oct. 31 (subject to availability); Dec. 1-March 31 (Sunday-Saturday).

Alaska

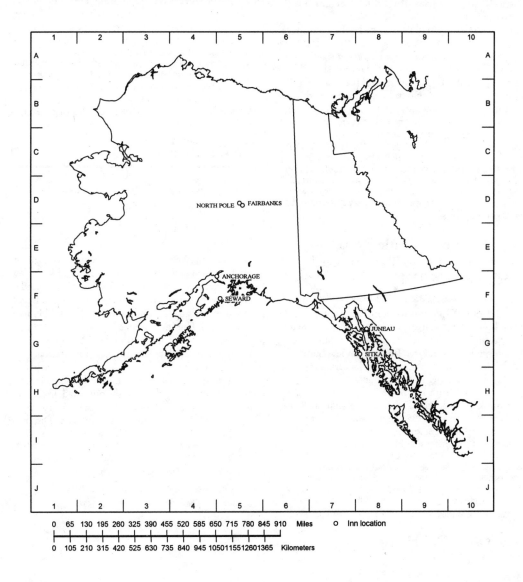

0 65 130 195 260 325 390 455 520 585 650 715 780 845 910   Miles   o   Inn location

0 105 210 315 420 525 630 735 840 945 1050 1155 1260 1365   Kilometers

Anchorage　　F5

Glacier Bear B&B

4814 Malibu Rd,
Anchorage, AK 99517-3274
(907)243-8818 Fax:(907)248-4532

Circa 1986. This cedar-sided contemporary home is located just a mile and a half from the world's largest float plane lake. The B&B is decorated with a mix of Oriental and Victorian pieces. One bedroom includes a pencil canopy bed, while another offers an antique king bed and a fireplace. The landscaped grounds include an eight-person spa surrounded by ferns, trees and wild berry bushes. The innkeepers offer both a hearty full breakfast or continental fare. Freshly ground coffee, tea, soft drinks and freshly baked cookies are available throughout the day. The innkeepers provide a courtesy van to and from the airport.

Innkeeper(s): Marge Brown & Georgia Taton. $59-95. MC VISA AX DS PC TC. 5 rooms, 3 with PB, 1 with FP. Breakfast included in rates. Types of meals: full breakfast, gourmet breakfast and early coffee/tea. Evening snack available. Beds: KQT. Cable TV, VCR, fax, spa, bicycles and library on premises. Antiques, fishing, parks, shopping, downhill skiing, cross-country skiing, sporting events and watersports nearby.

Certificate may be used: Oct. 1 to April 1.

North Country Castle B&B

PO Box 111876, 14600 Joanne Circle,
Anchorage, AK 99511
(907)345-7296 Fax:(907)345-7296

Circa 1986. While this modern, Victorian cottage-style home is not actually a castle, guests are treated like royalty. The innkeepers offer two rooms with mountain views, and the Turnagain View Suite, which features a fireplace, double Jacuzzi and private deck. The home, which is surrounded by woods, rests in the foothills of the Chugach Mountains. The innkeepers serve a hearty, traditional breakfast with muffins, French toast, egg dishes, fresh fruit, juice and reindeer sausage.

Innkeeper(s): Cindy & Wray Kinard. $70-125. PC TC. 3 rooms, 1 with PB, 1 with FP. 1 suite. Breakfast included in rates. Types of meals: continental breakfast, continental-plus breakfast, full breakfast and gourmet breakfast. Beds: QT. Turn-down service and ceiling fan in room. Fax, copier and library on premises. Fishing, parks, shopping, downhill skiing, cross-country skiing, sporting events and theater nearby.

Certificate may be used: April 1-May 15 and Oct. 1-Nov. 15.

The Oscar Gill House

1344 W 10th Ave,
Anchorage, AK 99501-3245
(907)258-1717 Fax:(907)258-6613

Circa 1913. This clapboard, Craftsman-style home was built in Knik, Alaska, but later disassembled

and moved to Anchorage a few years later. The home is one of the city's oldest, and the innkeepers have kept the decor simple and comfortable, with antiques here and there, as well as vintage furnishings from the '30s and '40s. Down comforters and bathrooms stocked with amenities are a few of the special touches guests will find. Breakfasts are served up in the cheery dining room, which features panoramic photos of Anchorage and the home in its original location. Innkeeper Susan Lutz prepares a variety of entrees for the morning meal, including items such as sourdough French toast Mexican egg casseroles accompanied by freshly ground coffee, a selection of teas and homemade hot chocolate.

Innkeeper(s): Mark & Susan Lutz. $65-95. MC VISA AX PC. 3 rooms, 1 with PB. Breakfast included in rates. Type of meal: full breakfast. Beds: QDT. Cable TV in room. Fax, bicycles and child care on premises. Fishing, parks, downhill skiing, cross-country skiing, sporting events and theater nearby.

Certificate may be used: Jan. 2-April 1, Oct. 1 through Nov. 22, Nov. 28 through Dec. 22.

Fairbanks　　D5

Chena River B&B

1001 Dolly Varden Dr,
Fairbanks, AK 99709-3229
(907)479-2532

Located on 10 acres along the Chena River, this inn offers spectacular views of the Northern Lights. Two of the rooms feature views of the river, woodlands and flower garden. (In the winter, moose are frequent visitors to the garden where they nibble its remnants.) The inn features hardwood floors, Oriental rugs and an enormous collection of books, many about Alaska. The innkeeper is a native Alaskan and has extensive knowledge about his home state. Breakfast features sourdough pancakes, bacon, sausage, eggs and fresh fruit salad. Guests are welcome to use the kitchen for snacks. Fairbanks is four miles. University museum, Riverboat Discovery and historic Chena Pump House are close-by.

Innkeeper(s): Steve Mease. $40-100. 5 rooms, 1 with PB. Breakfast included in rates. Type of meal: full breakfast. Beds: QDT.

Seen in: Washington Post, Northwest Living.

"Felt just like home, but the food was better."

Certificate may be used: September through May.

Juneau G8

Pearson's Pond Luxury Inn

4541 Sawa Cir, Juneau, AK 99801-8723
(907)789-3772 Fax:(907)789-6722

Circa 1985. View glaciers, visit museums and chance your luck at gold-panning streams, or simply soak in a hot tub surrounded by a lush forest and nestled next to a picturesque duck pond. Blueberries hang over the private decks of the guest rooms. A full, self-serve breakfast is provided each morning. Nearby trails offer excellent hiking, and the Medenhall Glacier is within walking distance. The sportsminded will enjoy river rafting or angling for world-class halibut and salmon.

Innkeeper(s): Steve & Diane Pearson. $79-165. MC VISA AX DC CB PC TC. 3 rooms with PB, 2 with FP. 2 suites. Breakfast, afternoon tea and evening snack included in rates. Types of meals: continental-plus breakfast and early coffee/tea. Beds: Q. Cable TV and VCR in room. Fax, copier, spa, bicycles and library on premises. Antiques, fishing, parks, shopping, downhill skiing, cross-country skiing, theater and watersports nearby.

Location: Three miles to airport and ferry terminal.

"A definite 10!"

Certificate may be used: October through April.

North Pole D5

Birch Tree B&B

3104 Dyke Rd,
North Pole, AK 99705-6801
(907)488-4667 Fax:(907)488-4667

Few people can boast that they've weathered the rugged North Pole country. At this modern-style B&B, however, visitors can enjoy the wilderness of Alaska in pleasant, inviting surroundings. The innkeepers offer four individually decorated rooms, one includes a hide-a-bed and separate dressing area. The den offers plenty of amenities, including a fireplace, books about Alaska and a pool table. Guests are invited to use the inn's barbecue grill and picnic table. The stunning Northern Lights often are visible from the home, and it's not unusual to see a moose or two roaming the grounds.

Innkeeper(s): Pat Albrecht. $45-70. MC VISA. 4 rooms. Breakfast included in rates. Type of meal: full breakfast.

Certificate may be used: October-April (anytime).

Seward F5

"The Farm" B&B

PO Box 305, Seward, AK 99664-0305
(907)224-5691 Fax:(907)224-2300

Circa 1906. This country home is located on 20 acres of farmlike setting with plenty of fields to enjoy. Rooms are spacious and comfortable, one includes a canopied waterbed. The innkeepers offer sleeping cottages and a three-room bungalow. Guests may use the laundry facilities. The home is three miles outside of Seward.

$45-85. MC VISA. 11 rooms, 7 with PB. 2 suites. Breakfast included in rates. Type of meal: continental-plus breakfast. Beds: KQT. Cable TV in room. VCR and fax on premises. Handicap access. Fishing, parks, shopping, cross-country skiing and watersports nearby.

Certificate may be used: September-May.

Sitka G8

Alaska Ocean View B&B

1101 Edgecumbe Dr,
Sitka, AK 99835-7122
(907)747-8310 Fax:(907)747-8310

Circa 1986. This Alaska-style all-cedar home is located in a quiet neighborhood just one block from the seashore and the Tongass National Forest. Witness the spectacular Alaska sunsets over Sitka Sound and surrounding islands. On clear days, view Mt. Edgecumbe, which is an extinct volcano located on Kruzoff Island and looks like Mt. Fuji. Binoculars are kept handy for guests who take a special treat in viewing whales and eagles.

Innkeeper(s): Carole & Bill Denkinger. $79-119. MC VISA AX PC TC. 3 rooms with PB. 2 suites. 1 conference room. Breakfast, afternoon tea and evening snack included in rates. Types of meals: continental-plus breakfast, full breakfast, gourmet breakfast and early coffee/tea. Beds: KQDT. Turn-down service, ceiling fan, cable TV and VCR in room. Fax, copier, spa and library on premises. Antiques, fishing, parks, shopping, theater and watersports nearby.

Certificate may be used: January, February, March and October, November, December.

Arizona

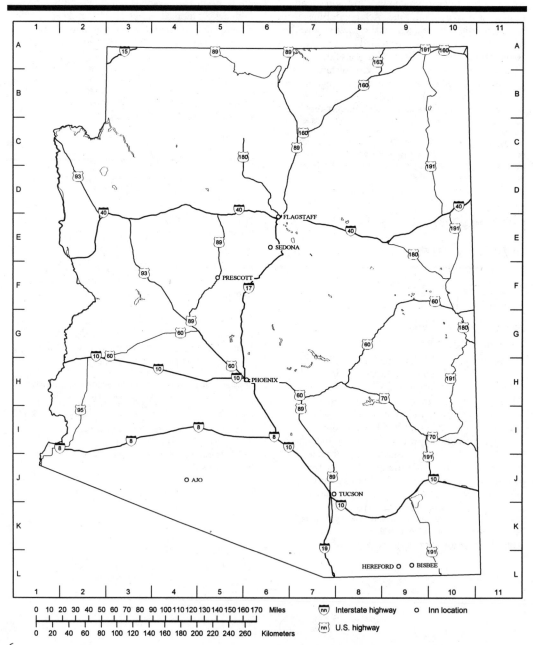

Interstate highway	o Inn location
U.S. highway	

Ajo   J4

The Mine Manager's House Inn B&B

1 W Greenway Dr, Ajo, AZ 85321-2713
(520)387-6505 Fax:(520)387-6508

Circa 1919. Overlooking the Southwestern Arizona desert and a mile-wide copper mine pit, the Mine Manager's is a large Craftsman home situated on three acres. Built by the local copper mining industry, it has 10-inch thick walls. A library, coin laundry and gift shop are on the premises. The Greenway Suite features a marble tub and shower and two other suites boast two queen-size beds each. A full breakfast is served in the formal dining room.

Innkeeper(s): Jean & Micheline Fournier. $69-105. MC VISA TC. 5 rooms with PB. 2 suites. Breakfast and evening snack included in rates. Type of meal: early coffee/tea. Beds: QT. Air conditioning and ceiling fan in room. Cable TV, VCR, fax and spa on premises. Handicap access. Parks and shopping nearby.

Seen in: Arizona Daily Star, Tucson Citizen, Catalina-Oracle, Arizona Sun, Arizona Highways-Sunset.

"The hospitality is what makes this place so inviting! A palace at the top of the hill with service to match."

Certificate may be used: May to July and September to Nov. 15.

Bisbee   L9

Bisbee Grand Hotel, A B&B Inn

61 Main Street, Box 825,
Bisbee, AZ 85603
(800)421-1909

Circa 1906. This National Register treasure is a stunning example of an elegant turn-of-the-century hotel. The hotel originally served as a stop for mining executives, and was restored back to its Old West Glory in the 1980s. Each of the rooms is decorated with Victorian furnishings and wall-coverings. The suites offer special items such as clawfoot tubs, an antique Chinese wedding bed, a fountain or four-poster bed. The Grand Western Salon boasts the back bar fixture from the Pony Saloon in Tombstone. After a full breakfast, enjoy a day touring the Bisbee area, which

includes mine tours, museums, shops, antiquing and a host of outdoor activities.

Innkeeper(s): Bill Thomas. $53-100. MC VISA AX DS. 11 rooms. Breakfast included in rates. Type of meal: full breakfast.

Certificate may be used: Excludes weekends and holidays. Two week advanced reservation required.

Flagstaff   E6

Comfi Cottages

1612 N Aztec St,
Flagstaff, AZ 86001-1106
(520)774-0731 Fax:(520)779-1008

Circa 1920. Each of the five cottages has been refurbished and features a variety of styles. One cottage is decorated in a Southwestern motif, while the others feature antiques and English Country decor.

Four cottages include fireplaces and all include kitchens stocked with equipment. Four have the added luxury of a washer and dryer. Bicycles are available for guest use, as well as picnic tables, a barbecue grill and picnic baskets. The Grand Canyon and national parks are close by, and the cottages are in the perfect location to enjoy all Flagstaff has to offer.

Innkeeper(s): Patricia Wiebe. $65-195. MC VISA DS. 5 cottages. Breakfast included in rates. Type of meal: full breakfast. Beds: KQDT. Ceiling fan, cable TV and VCR in room. Bicycles and tennis on premises. Antiques, fishing, parks, shopping, downhill skiing, cross-country skiing, sporting events, theater and watersports nearby.

"Beautiful and relaxing. A port in the storm."

Certificate may be used: November-February, Sunday-Thursday (no holidays or special events held locally).

Inn at Four Ten

410 N Leroux St,
Flagstaff, AZ 86001-4502
(520)774-0088 (800)774-2008
Fax:(520)774-6354

Circa 1894. Built by a wealthy banker, businessman and cattle rancher, this inn was first a stately family residence. Now fully renovated and elegantly decorated with antiques, stained glass and lace, the inn is a great home base for your Northern Arizona get-

away. It's an easy jaunt to the Grand Canyon, volcanic and meteor craters, ancient Pueblo ruins, Hopi and Navajo villages, the Painted Desert, the red rocks of Sedona and Oak Creek Canyon.
Innkeeper(s): Howard & Sally Krueger. $100-165. MC VISA PC TC. 9 rooms with PB, 7 with FP. 4 suites. 1 conference room. Breakfast and evening snack included in rates. Types of meals: full breakfast and gourmet breakfast. Beds: KQT. Air conditioning and ceiling fan in room. Library on premises. Handicap access. Antiques, parks, shopping, downhill skiing, cross-country skiing and theater nearby.
Seen in: Westways, Arizona Daily Sun.

"It was a joy to discover that the Inn embodied the finest qualities of what make a Bed and Breakfast our first choice when staying out of town."

Certificate may be used: Sunday-Thursday. November-February, excluding holidays.

Hereford L9

Ramsey Canyon Inn

31 E Ramsey Canyon Rd,
Hereford, AZ 85615-9613
(520)378-3010 Fax:(520)378-0487

Circa 1988. A stream winds its way through this 12-acre spread tucked up in the Huachuca mountains. The innkeepers offer accommodations in the rustic main house and in two creekside cottages. The cottages include a bedroom, sofa bed in the living room and fully stocked kitchen. Guests in the main house are treated to a full breakfast accompanied by home-baked breads and homemade jellies and jams from fruit in the inn's orchard. More than a dozen varieties of hummingbirds call

Ramsey Canyon their home and during a morning walk, guests are sure to find a few hummers and other wildlife.
Innkeeper(s): Ron & Shirlene DeSantis. $90-105. TC. 6 rooms with PB. Breakfast, afternoon tea and evening snack included in rates. Types of meals: gourmet breakfast and early coffee/tea. Beds: KQD. Ceiling fan in room. Antiques, parks and shopping nearby.
Certificate may be used: October-March 1, Sunday-Thursday

Phoenix H6

Maricopa Manor

15 W Pasadena Ave, Phoenix, AZ 85013
(602)274-6302 (800)292-6403
Fax:(602)266-3904

Circa 1928. The secluded Maricopa Manor stands amid palm trees on an acre of land. The Spanish-styled house features four graceful columns in the entry hall, an elegant living room with a marble mantel and a music room with a grand piano and an Irish harp. The spacious suites are decorated with satins, lace, antiques and leather-bound books. Guests may relax on the deck, on the patio or in the gazebo spa.
Innkeeper(s): Mary Ellen & Paul Kelley. $79-179. MC VISA AX DS PC TC. 5 suites, 2 with FP. Breakfast included in rates. Type of meal: continental-plus breakfast. Beds: KQ. Air conditioning, ceiling fan and cable TV in room. VCR, fax, copier, spa and swimming on premises. Handicap access. Antiques, parks, shopping, sporting events and theater nearby.
Location: North central Phoenix near museums, theaters.
Seen in: Arizona Business Journal, AAA Westways, San Francisco Chronicle, Focus, Sombrero.

"I've stayed 200+ nights at B&Bs around the world, yet have never before experienced the warmth and sincere friendliness of Maricopa Manor."

Certificate may be used: June 1 to Aug. 31.

Prescott F5

Juniper Well Ranch

PO Box 11083, Prescott, AZ 86304-1083
(520)442-3415

Circa 1991. A working horse ranch sits on the front 15 acres of this 50-acre, wooded property, which is surrounded by the Prescott National Forest. Guests are welcome to feed the horses, and children have been known to take a ride on a tractor with innkeeper David Bonham. Two log cabins and the ranch house sit farther back on the land where families can enjoy nature, "unlimited" hiking and seclusion. A summer house, which can be reserved by guests staying at the ranch, has no walls, a sloping roof with skylight, and an eight-foot hot tub. Guest pets, including horses, are welcome on an individual basis.

Innkeeper(s): David Bonham. $105. MC VISA AX DS PC TC. 3 cottages with PB, 3 with FP. Breakfast included in rates. Type of meal: full breakfast. Beds: QDT. Ceiling fan in room. Spa, stables and pet boarding on premises. Handicap access. Antiques, fishing, parks, shopping, cross-country skiing and theater nearby.

Certificate may be used: Sunday through Thursday.

Mount Vernon Inn

204 N Mount Vernon Ave,
Prescott, AZ 86301-3108
(520)778-0886 Fax:(520)778-7305

Circa 1900. The inn is nestled among towering shade trees in the center of the Mt. Vernon Historical District, Arizona's largest Victorian neighborhood. The architecture of this grand house

with its turret, gables, pediments and Greek Revival porch can best be described as whimsical. Cottages that once served as the carriage and tack houses also are available.

Innkeeper(s): Michele & Jerry Newman. $90-120. MC VISA DS TC. 4 rooms with PB. 3 cottages. Breakfast included in rates. Types of meals: full breakfast and early coffee/tea. Afternoon tea available. Beds: QDT. Ceiling fan in room. Cable TV, fax, copier and library on premises. Handicap access. Antiques, parks, shopping and theater nearby.

Certificate may be used: November through April. Sunday through Thursday only. Exclude holidays.

Pleasant Street Inn

142 S Pleasant St,
Prescott, AZ 86303-3811
(520)445-4774

Pleasant Street Inn was moved to its present site, in the heart of historic Prescott, in an effort to save the home from demolition. Rooms at this quaint, Victorian inn are decorated with a touch of whimsy with floral prints and chintz fabrics. The PineView Suite boasts a sitting room and fireplace. Another

suite includes a sitting room and private, covered deck. Guests are treated to a full breakfast and afternoon hors d'oeurves and refreshments are served. Prescott, which served twice as the state capital, offers a variety of museums and art galleries to explore, as well as the historic Court House Square. Nearby Prescott National Forest is a perfect place to enjoy hiking, climbing and other outdoor activities.

Innkeeper(s): Jean Urban. $80-120. MC VISA DS. 4 rooms. Breakfast included in rates. Type of meal: full breakfast.

Certificate may be used: Nov. 1 to April 30, Sunday through Thursday.

Prescott Pines Inn

901 White Spar Rd,
Prescott, AZ 86303-7231
(520)445-7270 (800)541-5374
Fax:(520)778-3665

Circa 1902. A white picket fence beckons guests to the veranda of this comfortably elegant country Victorian inn, originally the Haymore Dairy. There are masses of fragrant pink roses, lavenders and delphiniums, and stately ponderosa pines tower above the inn's four renovated cottages, which were once shelter for farmhands. The acre of grounds includes a garden fountain and romantic tree swing.

Innkeeper(s): Bruce & Margaret Sheldon. $59-199. EP. MC VISA PC. 13 rooms with PB, 3 with FP. 3 suites. 4 cottages. Breakfast included in rates. Types of meals: full breakfast and early coffee/tea. Beds: KQ. Air conditioning, ceiling fan and cable TV in room. Fax and copier on premises. Antiques, parks, shopping and theater nearby.

Location: One-and-a-third miles south of Courthouse Plaza.

Seen in: Sunset, Arizona Republic News.

"The ONLY place to stay in Prescott! Tremendous attention to detail."

Certificate may be used: Sunday-Thursday (except holidays); Oct. 15-May 15.

Victorian Inn of Prescott B&B

246 S Cortez St, Prescott, AZ 86303-3939
(520)778-2642 (800)704-2642

Circa 1893. The blue- and white-trimmed Victorian home with its tower and bay windows is a popular landmark of Prescott and is located one block from the historic town square. When it was constructed in the late 19th century, all the materials had to be brought in by train from the East Coast. Mauve and raspberry colors dominate the interior, which has been restored with many original fixtures. A favorite among the second-floor guest quarters is the spacious Victoriana Suite. Breakfast is a gourmet sit-down affair served on elegant china and linens.

Innkeeper(s): Tamia Thunstedt. $80-145. MC VISA AX DS. 4 rooms, 1 with PB, 1 with FP. 1 suite. Breakfast included in rates. Types of meals: full breakfast and early coffee/tea. Beds: Q. Ceiling fan in room. Antiques, fishing, parks, shopping, sporting events and theater nearby.
Seen in: Arizona Republic, Arizona Highways, Sunset, Home and Gardens.

Certificate may be used: Monday through Thursday nights.

Sedona   E6

The Graham B&B Inn

150 Canyon Circle Dr,
Sedona, AZ 86351-8676
(520)284-1425 (800)228-1425
Fax:(520)284-0767

Circa 1985. If the stunning Sedona scenery isn't enough to draw you to this popular Arizona getaway spot, this four-star, four-diamond bed & breakfast should do the trick. Guest rooms and suites are decorated in a variety of styles from Southwest to Victorian to Art Deco. Rooms and suites include amenities such as Jacuzzis, private balconies or patios and fireplaces. Bathrooms are stocked with bubble bath and lotions, and there are irons, hair dryers, curling irons and robes. The creative breakfast menus include items such as fanned pears with orange/almond sauce, a Southwestern green chili casserole, eight-grain toast with homemade jam, fresh juice and freshly brewed coffee. In the afternoon, refreshments are served.

Innkeeper(s): Roger & Carol Redenbaugh. $109-219. MC VISA DS PC TC. 6 rooms with PB, 4 with FP. 3 suites. 1 conference room. Breakfast, afternoon tea and evening snack included in rates. Types of meals: full breakfast, gourmet breakfast and early coffee/tea. Beds: KQT. Air conditioning, turn-down service, ceiling fan, cable TV and VCR in room. Fax, copier, spa, swimming, bicycles and library on premises. Antiques, fishing, parks, shopping and theater nearby.

Certificate may be used: Dec. 2-20 and Jan. 2-20, Monday through Thursday.

The Inn on Oak Creek

556 Highway 179,
Sedona, AZ 86336-6145
(520)282-7896 (800)499-7896
Fax:(520)282-0696

Circa 1973. With the red rocks of Oak Creek Canyon as its backdrop and the gentle sounds of water meandering down Oak Creek, guests enjoy a serene experience at this contemporary-style inn. Each room offers a fireplace. After a day of exploring Sedona or hiking through scenic canyons, guests can relax in a whirlpool tub. Many rooms also offer private decks with water views. Homemade pastries and granola, gourmet coffee, fresh fruit and creative entrees such as a spinach and cheese frittata, a Southwestern-style artichoke and salsa bake or German apple pancakes make waking up a treat. Guests may enjoy breakfast in bed if they prefer. The inn is within walking distance to galleries, shops and restaurants.

Innkeeper(s): Rick Morris & Pam Harrison. $130-225. MC VISA AX DS PC TC. 11 rooms with PB, 11 with FP. 1 suite. Breakfast and evening snack included in rates. Types of meals: gourmet breakfast and early coffee/tea. Picnic lunch available. Beds: KQDT. Air conditioning, cable TV and VCR in room. Fax, copier, swimming and library on premises. Handicap access. Antiques, fishing, parks, shopping, downhill skiing, theater and watersports nearby.

Certificate may be used: Dec. 1 to Feb. 13, Sunday-Thursday, holidays excluded.

Territorial House,
An Old West B&B

65 Piki Dr, Sedona, AZ 86336-4345
(520)204-2737 (800)801-2737
Fax:(520)204-2230

Circa 1970. This red rock and cedar two-story ranch home, nestled in the serene setting of Juniper and Cottonwood, is a nature lover's delight. Guests can see families of quail march through the landscape of cacti, plants and red rock or at night hear the call of coyotes. The territorial decor includes Charles Russell prints collected from taverns throughout the Southwest. More than 40 western movies were filmed in Sedona.

Innkeeper(s): John & Linda Steele. $95-155. MC VISA AX TC. 4 rooms with PB, 1 with FP. 1 suite. Breakfast and evening snack included in rates. Type of meal: full breakfast. Beds: KQ. Air conditioning, ceiling fan, cable TV and VCR in room. Fax, copier, spa and bicycles on premises. Antiques, fishing, parks, shopping, downhill skiing, theater and watersports nearby.

Certificate may be used: July-August, December, January, Feb. 1-15; Sunday-Thursday, no holidays.

Tucson   J7

Casa Alegre B&B
316 E Speedway Blvd,
Tucson, AZ 85705-7429
(520)628-1800 (800)628-5654
Fax:(520)792-1880

Circa 1915. Innkeeper Phyllis Florek decorated the interior of this Craftsman-style home with artifacts reflecting the history of Tucson, including Native American pieces and antique mining tools. Wake to

the aroma of fresh coffee and join other guests as you enjoy fresh muffins, fruit and other breakfast treats, such as succulent cheese pancakes with raspberry preserves. The Arizona sitting room opens onto serene gardens, a pool and a Jacuzzi. A two-bedroom suite, complete with kitchen privileges, is also available in the neighboring historic Buchanan House. An abundance of shopping and sightseeing are found nearby.

Innkeeper(s): Phyllis Florek. $55-95. MC VISA DS PC TC. 5 rooms with PB, 1 with FP. 1 conference room. Breakfast included in rates. Types of meals: full breakfast and gourmet breakfast. Beds: QT. Ceiling fan in room. VCR, fax, spa and swimming on premises. Antiques, parks, shopping, sporting events and theater nearby.

Location: West University Historic District.

Seen in: Arizona Times, Arizona Daily Star, Tucson Weekly.

"Enjoyed your excellent care."

Certificate may be used: May 15 through Dec. 20.

The Gable House
2324 N Madelyn Cir,
Tucson, AZ 85712-2621
(520)326-1150 (800)756-4846

Circa 1930. After his wife, actress Carole Lombard died in 1942, actor Clark Gable chose this rustic, Southwestern-style home as a place for solitude. Guests are sure to enjoy the same peace and tranquility Gable found within the walls of this bed & breakfast, which features Santa Fe Pueblo Indian

and Mexican influences. The guest rooms, named the Nina, Pinta and Santa Maria, are spacious and airy. The Santa Maria also includes a fireplace. The innkeepers prepare a continental-plus breakfast with a healthy touch.

Innkeeper(s): Al & Phyllis Cummings. $55-95. MC VISA AX. 3 rooms, 1 with PB, 1 with FP. Breakfast included in rates. Type of meal: continental-plus breakfast. Beds: K. Air conditioning, ceiling fan and VCR in room. Cable TV and spa on premises. Amusement parks, antiques, parks, shopping, downhill skiing, sporting events, theater and watersports nearby.

"You helped us with an immediate need. Gable House was wonderful, perfect, and better than we could have hoped."

Certificate may be used: Anytime except January-March, holidays.

Arkansas

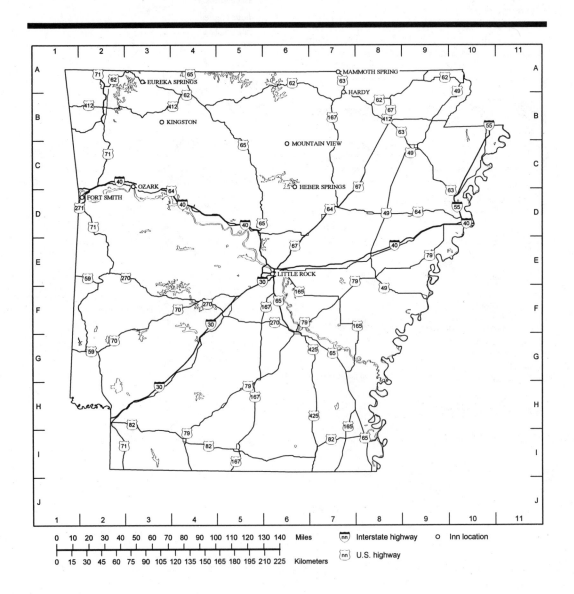

	1	2	3	4	5	6	7	8	9	10	11

MAMMOTH SPRING
EUREKA SPRINGS
HARDY
KINGSTON
MOUNTAIN VIEW
OZARK
FORT SMITH
HEBER SPRINGS
LITTLE ROCK

0 10 20 30 40 50 60 70 80 90 100 110 120 130 140 Miles

0 15 30 45 60 75 90 105 120 135 150 165 180 195 210 225 Kilometers

(nn) Interstate highway o Inn location

(nn) U.S. highway

Eureka Springs A3

Arsenic & Old Lace B&B Inn
60 Hillside Ave,
Eureka Springs, AR 72632-3133
(501)253-5454 (800)243-5223
Fax:(501)253-2246

Circa 1992. A new structure, but designed in the grand old Queen Anne Victorian style, this inn offers five guest rooms decorated with Victorian furnishings. Popular with honeymooners, the three upper-level guest rooms offer whirlpool tubs, as does one on the ground floor. The inn's gardens complement its attractive exterior, which includes a wraparound veranda and stone wall. Its location in the historic district makes it an excellent starting point for a sightseeing stroll.

Innkeeper(s): Gary & Phyllis Jones. $76-150. MC VISA AX DS PC TC. 5 rooms with PB, 2 with FP. 2 suites. Breakfast and evening snack included in rates. Type of meal: gourmet breakfast. Beds: KQT. Air conditioning, ceiling fan, cable TV and VCR in room. Fax on premises. Antiques, fishing, parks, shopping, theater and watersports nearby.

Certificate may be used: Jan. 15-Sept. 30, Sunday-Thursday. Nov. 1-Dec. 20, Sunday-Thursday.

Bridgeford House
263 Spring St,
Eureka Springs, AR 72632-3154
(501)253-7853 Fax:(501)253-5497

Circa 1884. This peach-colored Victorian delight is nestled in the heart of the Eureka Springs Historic District. Rooms feature antiques and are decorated

in a wonderfully charming Victorian style with private entrances. Guests will enjoy the fresh, hot coffee and selection of teas in their suites, and the large gourmet breakfast is the perfect way to start the day. Enjoy the horse-drawn carriage rides down Eureka Springs' famed boulevard with its stately homes.

Innkeeper(s): Denise McDonald. $85-95. MC VISA. 4 rooms, 3 with PB. 1 suite. Breakfast and afternoon tea included in rates. Types of meals: full breakfast, gourmet breakfast and early coffee/tea. Evening snack and room service available. Beds: QT. Air conditioning, ceiling fan and cable TV in room. VCR on premises. Antiques, fishing, shopping, theater and watersports nearby.

Location: North one mile on 62B in Eureka Springs Historic District.

Seen in: Times Echo Flashlight, Arkansas National Tour Guide, The American Country Inn & Bed and Breakfasts Cookbook, The Bed and Breakfast Cookbook.

"You have created an enchanting respite for weary people."

Certificate may be used: Jan. 1-Oct. 1; Nov. 1-Dec. 31, Sunday-Thursday.

Candlestick Cottage
6 Douglas St,
Eureka Springs, AR 72632-3416
(501)253-6813 (800)835-5184

Circa 1888. Woods and foliage surround this scenic country home, nestled just a few blocks from Eureka Springs' historic district. Guests are sure to discover a variety of wildlife strolling by the home, including an occasional deer. Breakfasts are served on the tree-top porch, which overlooks a waterfall and fish pond. The morning meal begins with freshly baked muffins and fresh fruit, followed by an entree. Innkeepers Bill and Patsy Brooks will prepare a basket of sparkling grape juice and wine glasses for those celebrating a special occasion. Guest rooms are decorated in Victorian style, and some include two-person Jacuzzis.

Innkeeper(s): Bill & Patsy Brooks. $55-99. MC VISA DS TC. 6 rooms with PB. Breakfast included in rates. Type of meal: full breakfast. Beds: QF. Air conditioning and cable TV in room. Antiques, fishing, parks and shopping nearby.

Certificate may be used: Monday through Thursday, April 1-Dec. 31. All week Jan. 1-March 31.

Cliff Cottage & The Place Next Door B&B
42 Armstrong St,
Eureka Springs, AR 72632-3608
(501)253-7409 (800)799-7409

Circa 1892. In the heart of Historic Downtown, this Painted Lady Eastlake Victorian is listed in the National Register of Historic Places. A favorite among honeymooners, accommodations also are available in a Victorian replica named The Place Next Door. Guest rooms include a double Jacuzzi, mini-refrigerator stocked with

complimentary champagne and beverages and private decks. The inn offers gourmet candlelight dinners and Victorian picnic lunches served aboard a 24-foot pontoon boat, which explores the area's romantic coves. Guests enjoy golf and tennis privileges at Holiday Island, which is located five miles away.

Innkeeper(s): Sandra Smith. $99-140. MC VISA PC. 7 rooms with PB. 3 suites. Breakfast included in rates. Types of meals: gourmet breakfast and early coffee/tea. Evening snack, picnic lunch and room service available. Beds: KQ. Air conditioning, ceiling fan, cable TV and VCR in room. Spa on premises. Antiques, fishing, parks, shopping, theater and watersports nearby.

Seen in: Arkansas Democrat Gazette, Country Inns

Certificate may be used: Jan. 2 to April 15, Monday to Thursday; Nov. 1 to Dec. 15, Monday to Thursday.

Crescent Cottage Inn

211 Spring St,
Eureka Springs, AR 72632-3153
(501)253-6022 (800)223-3246
Fax:(501)253-6234

Circa 1881. This Victorian inn was home to the first governor of Arkansas after the Civil War. Two long verandas overlook a breathtaking valley and two mountain ranges. The home is graced by a beautiful tower, spindlework and coffered ceilings. A huge arch joins the dining and living rooms, which, like the rest of the inn, are filled with antiques. Two of the guest rooms feature double whirlpool spas and one has a fireplace. The inn is situated on the quiet,

residential end of the historic loop. A five-minute walk into town takes guests past limestone cliffs, tall maple trees, gardens and refreshing springs. Try a ride on the steam engine train that departs nearby.

Innkeeper(s): Ralph & Phyllis Becker. $75-125. MC VISA DS PC TC. 4 rooms with PB, 1 with FP. 1 suite. Breakfast included in rates. Types of meals: full breakfast, and early coffee/tea. Room service available. Beds: Q. Air conditioning, ceiling fan, cable TV and VCR in room. Fax and copier on premises. Amusement parks, antiques, fishing, parks, shopping, sporting events, theater and watersports nearby.

Seen in: Country Homes, Country Inns, Minneapolis Tribune, Fort Lauderdale News, America's Painted Ladies.

"You gave us a piece of heaven we will never forget, what we dreamed of."

Certificate may be used: January-February (except Valentine's Day) to March 15.

Dairy Hollow House

515 Spring St,
Eureka Springs, AR 72632-3032
(501)253-7444 (800)562-8650
Fax:(501)253-7223

Circa 1888. Dairy Hollow House, the first of Eureka Springs' bed & breakfast inns, consists of a restored Ozark vernacular farmhouse and a 1940s bungalow-style cottage, both in a national historic district. Stenciled walls set off a collection of

Eastlake Victorian furnishings. Outstanding "Nouveau 'zarks" cuisine is available by reservation. Innkeeper Crescent Dragonwagon is the author of several books, including the award-winning Dairy Hollow House Cookbook and the new Soup and Bread Cookbook, and was called upon to cater President Clinton's inaugural brunch in Washington, D.C.

Innkeeper(s): Ned Shank & Crescent Dragonwagon. $135-195. MC VISA AX DC CB DS PC TC. 6 rooms with PB, 6 with FP. 3 suites. 1 conference room. Breakfast and evening snack included in rates. Types of meals: full breakfast and early coffee/tea. Restaurant on premises. Beds: KQD. Air conditioning and ceiling fan in room. Fax, copier and spa on premises. Handicap access. Amusement parks, antiques, fishing, parks, shopping, theater and watersports nearby.

Location: At the junction of Spring & Dairy Hollow Road.

Seen in: Innsider, Christian Science Monitor, Los Angeles Times, Gourmet, Southern Living, Bon Appetit, Country, Country Living.

"The height of unpretentious luxury."

Certificate may be used: Sunday-Thursday, February, March, November, December excluding any major holidays or inn special events.

Heart of The Hills Inn

5 Summit, Eureka Springs, AR 72632
(501)253-7468 (800)253-7468

Circa 1883. Three suites and a Victorian cottage comprise this antique-furnished homestead located just four blocks from downtown. The Victorian Room is furnished with a white iron bed, dresser, antique lamp and antique pedestal sink. Evening dessert is served. The honeymoon suite has a double Jacuzzi. The village trolley stops at the inn.

Innkeeper(s): Fred Janney. $64-109. MC VISA PC. 4 rooms, 3 with PB. 1 suite. 1 cottage. Breakfast and evening snack included in rates. Types of meals: gourmet breakfast and early coffee/tea. Beds: KQDT. Air conditioning, turn-down service, ceiling fan and cable TV in room. Library on premises. Handicap access. Antiques, fishing, shopping, theater and watersports nearby.

Location: On the historic loop.

Seen in: Carroll County Tribune's Peddler.

"It was delightful — the bed so comfortable, room gorgeous, food delicious and ohhh those chocolates."

Certificate may be used: November through September, Sunday through Thursday (may call at last minute).

The Heartstone Inn & Cottages

35 King's Hwy,
Eureka Springs, AR 72632-3534
(501)253-8916 (800)494-4921
Fax:(501)253-6821

Circa 1903. Described as a "pink and white confection," this handsomely restored Victorian with its wraparound verandas is located in the historic district. The award-winning inn is filled with antiques

and artwork from the innkeeper's native England. Live music is featured: in May a fine arts festival and in September, a jazz festival. Afternoon refreshments are available on the sunny deck overlooking a wooded ravine. Pink roses line the picket fence surrounding the inviting garden.

Innkeeper(s): Iris & Bill Simantel. $58-120. MC VISA AX DS PC TC. 12 rooms with PB, 1 with FP. 3 suites. 2 cottages. Breakfast included in

rates. Type of meal: gourmet breakfast. Beds: KQ. Air conditioning, ceiling fan and cable TV in room. Fax and spa on premises. Amusement parks, antiques, fishing, parks, shopping, theater and watersports nearby.

Location: Northwest Arkansas, Ozarks.

Seen in: Innsider, Arkansas Times, New York Times, Arkansas Gazette, Southern Living, Country Home, Country Inns.

"Extraordinary! Best breakfasts anywhere!"

Certificate may be used: Sunday through Wednesday arrivals during November through April. Other times, last minute only.

Sleepy Hollow Inn

92 S Main, Eureka Springs, AR 72632
(501)253-5561

Circa 1904. A three-story, Victorian cottage with gingerbread trim serves as an ideal accommodation for honeymooners or those in search of privacy and romance. There are two bedrooms, the main suite and a guest room with an antique bed. The cottage is rented to one group or couple at a time, so they are free to enjoy the home and relax. Guests can enjoy a soak in the antique clawfoot tub or snuggle up on the romantic porch swing. There is a well-equipped kitchen, stocked with beverages, pastries and other treats. Chilled champagne and fresh flowers can be arranged for those celebrating a special occasion. The one-acre grounds are dotted with gardens. There is a wrought iron table and chairs so guests can enjoy their morning coffee as well as singing birds and fragrant flowers. Restaurants, galleries and shops are just a short walk away, and the village's historical museum is across the street.

$110. MC VISA DS PC TC. 3 rooms, 1 with PB. 1 suite. Breakfast included in rates. Types of meals: continental breakfast and early coffee/tea. Evening snack available. Beds: D. Air conditioning, ceiling fan, cable TV and VCR in room. Antiques, fishing, parks, shopping, theater and watersports nearby.

Certificate may be used: Not available during town special events; reservations required; subject to availability.

Sunnyside Inn

5 Ridgeway Ave,
Eureka Springs, AR 72632-3024
(501)253-6638

Circa 1883. Beautifully renovated, this National Register Queen Anne Victorian is located three blocks from town. Traditional Victorian decor is especially outstanding in the Rose Room with a carved, high oak bed and original rose stained-glass windows. The Honeymoon Suite features an Abe Lincoln-era carved walnut bed with matching bureau. Country quiches, hot homemade cinnamon rolls and peach and blueberry cobblers are frequently served, sometimes on the deck overlooking the wilderness area. Gladys seems to love innkeeping; she owned an inn in Alaska before coming to Eureka Springs.

Innkeeper(s): Gladys R. Foris. $80-125. TC. 7 rooms with PB. 1 conference room. Breakfast included in rates. Beds: Q. Air conditioning in room. Cable TV and VCR on premises. Antiques, fishing, parks, shopping and theater nearby.

"The best weekend of our lives."

Certificate may be used: April 1 to Oct. 1, Monday-Thursday.

Taylor-Page Inn

33 Benton St,
Eureka Springs, AR 72632-3501
(501)253-7315

Within easy walking distance of downtown restaurants, shopping and trolley, this turn-of-the-century Square salt-box inn features Victorian and country decor in its three suites and rooms. Guests often enjoy relaxing in the inn's two sitting rooms. The suites offer ceiling fans, full kitchens and sundecks. The inn offers convenient access to antiquing, fishing, museums and parks.

Innkeeper(s): Jeanne Taylor. $60-80. MC VISA. 3 suites. Breakfast included in rates. Type of meal: continental breakfast. Air conditioning, ceiling fan and cable TV in room. Antiques and shopping nearby.

Certificate may be used: January-March, anytime. April through December, Monday through Thursday.

Fort Smith   D2

Beland Manor Inn B&B

1320 S Albert Pike Ave,
Fort Smith, AR 72903-2416
(501)782-3300 (800)334-5052

Circa 1950. Magnolia trees and pink and white azaleas surround this Colonial Revival mansion. Expansive lawns, hundreds of impatiens, a rose garden and patio adjoining a back garden gazebo, make the inn a popular setting for romantic weddings. Furnishings incorporate traditional pieces and antiques. A king-size, four-poster rice bed makes the Bridal Suite the option of choice. Best of all is the three-course Sunday breakfast, often featuring Eggs Benedict with strawberry crepes for dessert.

Innkeeper(s): Mike & Suzy Smith. $65-110. MAP. MC VISA AX DS PC TC. 6 rooms, 5 with PB. 1 suite. 1 conference room. Breakfast included in rates. Types of meals: gourmet breakfast and early coffee/tea. Dinner, evening snack, picnic lunch and banquet service available. Beds: KQTD. Air conditioning, ceiling fan and cable TV in room. VCR, fax and bicycles on premises. Handicap access. Antiques, parks, shopping and theater nearby.

Certificate may be used: September, November, December, January, February and March (excluding holidays).

Thomas Quinn Guest House

815 N B St, Fort Smith, AR 72901-2129
(501)782-0499

Circa 1863. Nine suites with kitchenettes are available at this inn, which in 1916 added a second story and stately columns to its original structure. Located on the perimeter of Fort Smith's historic district, it is close to the art center, historic sites, museums and restaurants. Several state parks are within easy driving distance. Early morning coffee and tea are served.

Innkeeper(s): Michael & Melody Conley. $59-79. EP. MC VISA AX DC CB DS TC. 9 suites. Type of meal: early coffee/tea. Beds: F. Air conditioning, cable TV and VCR in room. Amusement parks, antiques, fishing, parks, shopping and watersports nearby.

Certificate may be used: All year.

Hardy   A7

The Olde Stonehouse B&B Inn

511 Main St, Hardy, AR 72542-9034
(501)856-2983 (800)514-2983
Fax:(501)856-4036

Circa 1928. The stone fireplace which graces the comfortable living room of this former banker's home is set with fossils and unusual stones, including an Arkansas diamond. Lace tablecloths, china

and silver make breakfast a special occasion. Each room is decorated to keep the authentic feel of the roaring '20s. The bedrooms have antiques and ceiling fans. Aunt Jenny's room boasts a clawfoot tub and a white iron bed, while Uncle Buster's room is filled with Depression-era furniture. Spring River is only one block away and offers canoeing, boating and fishing. Old Hardy Town caters to antique and craft lovers. The innkeepers offer "Secret Suites," located in a nearby historic home. These romantic suites offer plenty of amenities, breakfasts in a basket are delivered to the door each morning.

Innkeeper(s): Peggy & David Johnson. $55-89. MC VISA AX DS PC TC. 9 rooms with PB, 2 with FP. 2 suites. 1 cottage. Breakfast and evening snack included in rates. Types of meals: full breakfast, gourmet breakfast and early coffee/tea. Picnic lunch available. Beds: QDT. Air conditioning, turn-down service, ceiling fan and VCR in room. Fax, copier, bicycles and library on premises. Amusement parks, antiques, fishing, parks, shopping, theater and watersports nearby.

Location: In a historic railroad town.

Seen in: Memphis Commercial Appeal, Jonesboro Sun, Vacations,

"For many years we had heard about 'Southern Hospitality' but never thought it to be this good … this was the best!"

Certificate may be used: November-April, anytime except special events. May-October, Sunday-Thursday.

Heber Springs   C6

The Anderson House Inn
201 E Main St,
Heber Springs, AR 72543-3116
(501)362-5266 (800)264-5279
Fax:(501)362-2326

Circa 1880. The original section of this welcoming two-story inn was built by one of Heber Springs' founding citizens. The main structure of the inn was built to house a theater, and the home also has enjoyed use as a schoolhouse, doctor's clinic and, when the second story was added, a hotel. Rooms are decorated in a cozy, country motif with bright colors and floral prints. Many of the antiques that fill each room are available for purchase. Historic Spring Park is just across the street offering pleasant scenery for the inn's guest as well as a variety of activities.

Innkeeper(s): Jim & Susan Hildebrand. $55-98. MC VISA AX DS PC TC. 16 rooms with PB, 1 with FP. 2 conference rooms. Breakfast included in rates. Types of meals: full breakfast and early coffee/tea. Afternoon tea, picnic lunch and banquet service available. Beds: QDT. Air conditioning, ceiling fan and cable TV in room. VCR, fax, spa and library on premises. Antiques, fishing, parks, shopping and watersports nearby.

Certificate may be used: Jan. 15 to Oct. 1, Sunday-Thursday.

Kingston   B3

Fool's Cove Ranch B&B
HCR 30 Box 198,
Kingston, AR 72742-9608
(501)665-2986 Fax:(501)665-2372

Circa 1979. Situated in the Ozarks' Boston Mountain range, this 6,000-square-foot farmhouse, part of a family farm, offers 160 acres of field, meadow, and forest. Guests who have had their horses test negative on a Coggins test may bring them along and utilize the farm's corrals. Guests may angle for bass or catfish in the pond. Favorite

gathering spots are the roomy parlor and the outdoor hot tub. Area attractions include the Buffalo River, Dogpatch USA and several fine fishing spots.

Innkeeper(s): Mary Jo & Bill Sullivan. $55-75. MC VISA AX DC CB DS PC TC. 4 rooms, 1 with PB. Breakfast and evening snack included in rates. Types of meals: full breakfast and early coffee/tea. Beds: QD. Air conditioning, turn-down service and ceiling fan in room. Cable TV, VCR, fax, copier, spa, library and pet boarding on premises. Handicap access. Amusement parks, antiques, fishing, parks, shopping, sporting events, theater and watersports nearby.

"We enjoyed the beauty and 'peace and quiet' but especially the good company."

Certificate may be used: Any day open, subject to availability.

Little Rock   E6

The Empress of Little Rock
2120 Louisiana St,
Little Rock, AR 72206-1522
(501)374-7966 Fax:(501)375-4537

Circa 1888. Day lilies, peonies and iris accent the old-fashioned garden of this elaborate, three-story Queen Anne Victorian. A grand center hall opens to a double staircase, lit by a stained-glass skylight. The 7,500 square feet include a sitting room at the top of the tower. The original owner kept a private poker game going here and the stained-glass windows allowed him to keep an eye out for local authorities, who might close down his gambling activities. The Hornibrook Room features a magnificent Renaissance Revival bedroom set with a high canopy. The Tower bedroom has an Austrian walnut bed. Gourmet breakfasts are served in the dining room.

Innkeeper(s): Sharon Welch-Blair. $85-125. MC VISA AX. 5 rooms. 1 suite. Breakfast included in rates. Types of meals: continental breakfast, full breakfast and early coffee/tea. Air conditioning, ceiling fan and cable TV in room. Antiques, shopping, sporting events and theater nearby.

Certificate may be used: May 1 through March 1, excluding Mystery weekends, football weekends and holidays.

Hotze House

1619 Louisiana St, Little Rock, AR 72216
(501)376-6563

Circa 1900. Upon its completion, this grand Neoclassical mansion was noted as one of the state's finest homes. Opulent, restored woodwork, a fireplace and a staircase carved from a South American mahogany tree grace the impressive front entrance. The home is filled with elegant, period pieces and traditional furnishings. Four of the guest rooms include fireplaces, and despite the turn-of-the-century authenticity, modern amenities of television, telephone and climate control are in each room. The innkeepers strive to make their National Register inn a place for both business travelers and those in search of romance or relaxation. Delectables such as frittatas, poached pears and Belgian waffles are served each morning either in the dining room or conservatory. The innkeepers keep a snack area stocked with hot water, soft drinks, beer, wine, cheese, fruit and the like.
Innkeeper(s): Peggy Tooker, Suzanne & Steve Gates. $80-100. MC VISA AX DS PC TC. 4 rooms with PB, 4 with FP. 2 conference rooms. Breakfast included in rates. Types of meals: full breakfast and early coffee/tea. Beds: KQ. Air conditioning, turn-down service, ceiling fan and cable TV in room. VCR, fax, copier and library on premises. Amusement parks, antiques, parks, shopping, sporting events and theater nearby.
Certificate may be used: Anytime, based on availability.

Mammoth Spring   A7

Roseland Inn B&B

570 Bethel, PO Box 4,
Mammoth Spring, AR 72554
(501)625-3378

Tucked away in a picturesque country town, this Colonial Revival home is just a stone's throw from one of the world's largest natural springs. Innkeeper Jean Pace, a former Mammoth Spring mayor, has decorated her National Register inn with antiques, collectibles and bright flower arrangements. With its reception hall, large front porch and gazebo, the home has served as a site for parties and weddings. Spring River and Mammoth Spring State Park are nearby, and Jean will refrigerate your daily catch.
Innkeeper(s): Jean Pace. $35-40. 4 rooms. Breakfast included in rates. Type of meal: full breakfast.
Certificate may be used: Year-round, Monday-Thursday, excluding weekends.

Mountain View   C6

Owl Hollow Country Inn

PO Box 1201,
Mountain View, AR 72560-1201
(501)269-8699 (800)379-8699

Circa 1906. This historic two-story Federal-style inn is located within a block of Courthouse Square and downtown eateries and shops. A full breakfast is served at 8 a.m. before guests head out to explore the many attractions offered in the surrounding area, including Blanchard Springs Caverns and the Ozark Folk Center.
Innkeeper(s): Glenna Watson. $55. MC VISA PC TC. 6 rooms with PB. Breakfast included in rates. Type of meal: full breakfast. Beds: QDT. Air conditioning and cable TV in room. VCR on premises. Antiques, fishing, parks, shopping, theater and watersports nearby.
"If you don't get them with kindness, of which you have plenty, you will get them with the great food."
Certificate may be used: March 1 to Dec. 1, Sunday through Thursday.

Wildflower B&B

100 Washington St, PO Box 72,
Mountain View, AR 72560
(501)269-4383 (800)591-4879

Circa 1918. The inn's wraparound porches are a gathering place for local musicians who often play old-time music. If you rock long enough, you're likely to see an impromptu hootenanny in the Courthouse Square across the street. Since there are no priceless antiques, children are welcome. However, you may have to watch them (and yourself) because there's a tempting first-floor bakery that's always "fixin' up" divinity cookies, macaroons and hot breads.
Innkeeper(s): Andrea Budy. $42-71. MC VISA AX DS. 8 rooms, 6 with PB. 3 suites. Breakfast included in rates. Types of meals: continental-plus breakfast and early coffee/tea. Picnic lunch and lunch available. Beds: DT. Air conditioning, turn-down service and ceiling fan in room. Antiques, fishing, parks, shopping, sporting events, theater and watersports nearby.
Location: In the Ozarks.
Seen in: New York Times, Dan Rather & CBS, Midwest Living, National Geographic Traveler, Travel Holiday.
"It's the kind of place you'll look forward to returning to."
Certificate may be used: Sunday through Thursday nights only, excluding special events.

Ozark C3

1887 Inn B&B
100 E Commercial St,
Ozark, AR 72949-3210
(501)667-1121

Circa 1885. At the foot of the Ozarks, this Queen Anne Victorian inn has been lovingly restored to its natural beauty. The inn's accommodations include a Honeymoon/Anniversary Suite, an intimate spot for a romantic candlelight dinner arranged by the innkeeper. Desks, fireplaces and queen beds can be found in the rooms. The decor features antique Victorian and country furnishings. Receptions, special events and weddings are popular here. Less than two blocks away is the Arkansas River.

Innkeeper(s): Karen Britting. $50-60. MC VISA. 4 rooms. 1 suite. Breakfast included in rates. Types of meals: full breakfast and early coffee/tea. Dinner, evening snack, picnic lunch, lunch, gourmet lunch, banquet service, catering service, catered breakfast and room service available. Air conditioning, turn-down service and ceiling fan in room. Cable TV and VCR on premises. Antiques and shopping nearby.

Certificate may be used: Anytime based on availability.

California

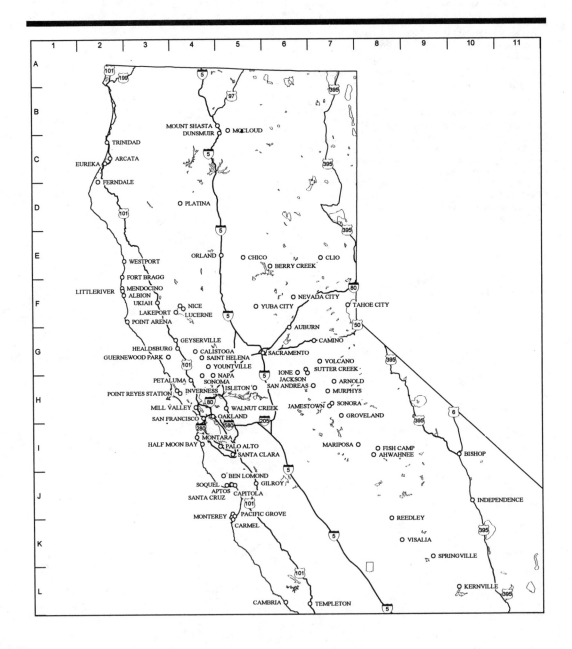

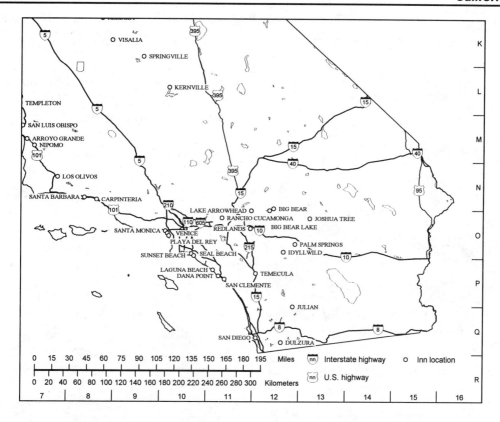

Ahwahnee
I8

Apple Blossom Inn B&B
44606 Silver Spur Tr,
Ahwahnee, CA 93601
(209)642-2001

Circa 1991. A bountiful organic apple orchard surrounds this inn, an attractive country cottage a short distance from Yosemite National Park. Visitors choose either the Red Delicious Room, with its two double beds and private entrance, or the Granny Smith Room, with queen bed and private balcony. Both rooms feature ceiling fans, private bath and sitting areas. Guests enjoy the inn's woodburning stove and the spa overlooking the woods.

Innkeeper(s): Lance, Lynn & Jenny Hays. $55-130. MC VISA AX DS TC. 3 rooms, 2 with PB. Breakfast, afternoon tea and evening snack included in rates. Types of meals: full breakfast and early coffee/tea. Beds: QD. Air conditioning, turn-down service, ceiling fan and VCR in room. Spa on premises. Antiques, fishing, parks, shopping, downhill skiing, cross-country skiing, theater and watersports nearby.

Certificate may be used: October-April, any days.

Albion
F2

Albion Ridge Huckleberry House
29381 Albion Ridge Rd,
Albion, CA 95410-9701
(707)937-2374 (800)482-5532
Fax:(707)937-1644

Circa 1995. Acres of Redwood and huckleberry bushes surround this romantic hideaway tucked just off the Mendocino coast. The grounds offer a pond stocked with rainbow trout. The suites include fireplaces and private decks, and the tower room affords a view of the pond. Each guest rooms is full of amenities, including coffee, tea and a refrigerator stocked with drinks. In the evening gaze at the stars or grab a movie from the house library. The innkeepers also offer a secluded cottage.

Innkeeper(s): Jon Geller. $95-130. MC VISA DS PC. 4 rooms, 3 with FP. 2 suites. 1 cottage. Breakfast included in rates. Types of meals: full breakfast, gourmet breakfast and early coffee/tea. Beds: Q. VCR in room. Fax on premises. Antiques, fishing, parks, shopping, theater and watersports nearby.

Certificate may be used: Dec. 1-14, Jan. 8-April 11, midweek (Sunday-Thursday).

Aptos

J5

Apple Lane Inn

6265 Soquel Dr, Aptos, CA 95003-3117
(408)475-6868 (800)649-8988
Fax:(408)464-5790

Circa 1870. Ancient apple trees border the lane that leads to this Victorian farmhouse set on two acres of gardens and fields. Built by the Porter

brothers, founding fathers of Aptos, the inn is decorated with Victorian wallpapers and hardwood floors. The original wine cellar still exists, as well as the old barn and apple-drying shed used for storage after harvesting the orchard. Miles of beaches are within walking distance. The innkeepers were married at the inn and later purchased it.
Innkeeper(s): Doug & Diana Groom. $95-150. TC. 5 rooms with PB. 3 suites. Breakfast and evening snack included in rates. Types of meals: full breakfast and early coffee/tea. Afternoon tea available. Beds: QDT. Turn-down service, ceiling fan and cable TV in room. Fax, copier, library and pet boarding on premises. Handicap access. Antiques, parks, shopping, sporting events, theater and watersports nearby.
Location: One mile from the beach, five minutes south of Santa Cruz.
Seen in: Santa Barbara Times, 1001 Decorating Ideas, New York Times.

"Our room was spotless and beautifully decorated."

Certificate may be used: All year, Sunday-Thursday except holidays.

Bayview Hotel

8041 Soquel Dr, Aptos, CA 95003-3928
(408)688-8654 (800)422-9843
Fax:(408)688-5128

Circa 1878. This Victorian hotel is the oldest operating inn on the Monterey Coast. Each of the rooms is decorated with local art, antiques, fireplaces and sitting areas. The inn is just a half a mile from beautiful beaches and a redwood forest is nearby. This inn is an ideal spot for those seeking relaxation or those on a coastal trip. Monterey and San Jose are less than an hour from the hotel, and San Francisco is 90 miles north. Hearty breakfasts are served in the inn's dining room, and the inn also has an on-site restaurant.
Innkeeper(s): Gwen Burkhard. $90-150. MC VISA AX TC. 11 rooms with PB, 2 with FP. 1 suite. 1 conference room. Breakfast included in rates. Types of meals: full breakfast, gourmet breakfast and early coffee/tea. Afternoon tea available. Beds: KQD. Turn-down service, cable TV and VCR in room. Fax and copier on premises. Amusement parks, antiques, parks, shopping and watersports nearby.
Location: Santa Cruz County.
Seen in: Mid-County Post, Santa Cruz Sentinel.

"Thank you so much for all of your tender loving care and great hospitality."

Certificate may be used: Sunday-Thursday nights, all year.

Mangels House

570 Aptos Creek Rd, PO Box 302,
Aptos, CA 95001
(408)688-7982

Circa 1886. Claus Mangels made his fortune in sugar beets and built this house in the style of a

Southern mansion. The inn, with its encircling veranda, stands on four acres of lawns and orchards. It is bounded by the Forest of Nisene Marks, 10,000 acres of redwood trees, creeks and trails. Monterey Bay is three-quarters of a mile away.
Innkeeper(s): Jacqueline Fisher. $105-145. MC VISA AX. 6 rooms with PB, 1 with FP. 1 conference room. Breakfast included in rates. Types of meals: full breakfast and early coffee/tea. Evening snack and catered breakfast available. Beds: KQT. Amusement parks, antiques, fishing, shopping, sporting events, theater and watersports nearby.
Location: Central Coast.
Seen in: Inn Serv, Innviews.

"Compliments on the lovely atmosphere. We look forward to sharing our discovery with friends and returning with them."

Certificate may be used: Midweek (Sunday-Thursday) holiday weekends excepted.

Arcata
C2

Hotel Arcata
708 9th St, Arcata, CA 95521-6206
(707)826-0217 (800)344-1221
Fax:(707)826-1737

Circa 1915. This historic landmark hotel is a fine example of Beaux Arts-style architecture. Several rooms overlook Arcata's downtown plaza, which is just across the way. A variety of rooms are available, each decorated in turn-of-the-century style. Some rooms include antiques or clawfoot tubs. The hotel offers a full-service restaurant with an old-fashioned saloon bar. Guests also enjoy free use of a nearby health club. The starting point of Arcata's architectural homes tour is within walking distance of the hotel.

Innkeeper(s): Virgil Moorehead. $90-142. MC VISA AX DC CB DS TC. 31 rooms with PB. 7 suites. 1 conference room. Breakfast included in rates. Dinner, lunch, banquet service, catering service and room service available. Beds: KQT. Cable TV in room. Fax and copier on premises. Handicap access. Amusement parks, antiques, fishing, parks, shopping, sporting events, theater and watersports nearby.

Certificate may be used: Subject to availability.

Arnold
H7

Lodge at Manuel Mill B&B
PO Box 998, Arnold, CA 95223-0998
(209)795-2622

Circa 1950. Overlooking a three-acre lake that comes right up to the wraparound deck, this log lodge was once the site of a 19th-century lumber mill. Some structures on the property are a century old. The 43 acres of woods include sugar cone pines, dogwoods, wild blackberries, and traces of the mill's gauge rail system. Sounds of the 24-foot waterfall that cascades over rocks may be heard from the rooms that open to the deck.The Lottie Crabtree Room, named for a spirited performer in the Gold Rush days, is a peaceful, cozy retreat. The Mr. Manual Room basks in 19th-century ambiance with an oak canopy bed and Victorian decor. The innkeepers prepare a hearty breakfast and present guests with a bottle of wine upon arrival. Calaveras Big Trees State Park is nearby

Innkeeper(s): Linda Johnson. $100-135. MC VISA. 5 rooms with PB. 1 suite. Breakfast included in rates. Type of meal: full breakfast. Picnic lunch and catering service available. Beds: KQD. Fishing, downhill skiing, cross-country skiing and watersports nearby.

Certificate may be used: Sunday-Thursday, November-April.

Arroyo Grande
M7

Arroyo Village Inn
407 El Camino Real,
Arroyo Grande, CA 93420-2647
(805)489-5926

Circa 1984. The travel section of the Los Angeles Times has featured many rare reviews of this country Victorian. Rooms feature extras such as balconies and window seats. Laura Ashley prints complement

the antiques. Day trips from the inn include Hearst Castle, wineries and mineral springs. Guests can test the water of local beaches on foot or ride up the coast on horseback. Breakfast features specialities such as homemade granola and breads, fresh fruit, omelets and French toast with caramel sauce and apple slices. A late afternoon tea provides wine and cheese or cookies and tea.

Innkeeper(s): Chuck & Louise Holden. $80-195. AP. MC VISA AX DS. 7 rooms, 2 with PB. 5 suites. Breakfast and evening snack included in rates. Type of meal: early coffee/tea. Beds: KQ. Air conditioning in room. Cable TV and fax on premises. Amusement parks, antiques, fishing, parks, shopping, sporting events, theater and watersports nearby.

Seen in: Los Angeles Times.

"Absolutely all the essentials of a great inn."

Certificate may be used: Sunday-Thursday, no holidays. January and February, includes weekends. Offer good only on $145+ suites.

Crystal Rose Inn
789 Valley Rd,
Arroyo Grande, CA 93420-4417
(805)481-1854 (800)767-3466
Fax:(805)481-9541

Circa 1895. Once the homestead for a large walnut farm, this picturesque Victorian inn features a tower that rises four stories, providing a view of meadows, sand dunes and the ocean. Surrounded by a white picket fence, the inn is decorated with authentic Victorian furnishings. A 30-foot-long rose arbor leads to a gazebo in the garden, a favorite setting for weddings.

Innkeeper(s): LaDona Nolan. $85-175. MAP. MC VISA AX. 9 rooms, 6 with PB. 3 suites. 1 conference room. Breakfast included in rates. Type of meal: full breakfast. Dinner, picnic lunch, lunch, catering service and room service available. Beds: KQDT. Handicap access. Antiques, fishing, theater and watersports nearby.

Location: Halfway between Los Angeles and San Francisco.

Seen in: Los Angeles Times, Daughters of Painted Ladies, Sunset, Travel, Five Cities Times-Press Recorder.

"Everything about the Crystal Rose is so quaint, homey and it takes you back in time! We will never forget our romantic interlude!"

Certificate may be used: Sunday through Thursday, year-round as available.

Auburn G6

Lincoln House B&B
191 Lincoln Way,
Auburn, CA 95603-4415
(916)885-8880

Circa 1933. In the heart of California's gold country travelers will find the Lincoln House, a captivating Bungalow home. The romantic Shenandoah Room offers a queen-size bed and a view of the inn's koi fish pond. A petrified wood fireplace beautifully complements the Southwest theme of the sitting room, and the dining room boasts a view of the Sierra Nevada mountains. When they are not exploring historic Old Town Auburn, guests may take a dip in the inn's swimming pool or relax on its covered porch.
Innkeeper(s): Leslie & Stan Fronczak. $69-85. MC VISA TC. 3 rooms with PB. 1 suite. Breakfast, afternoon tea and evening snack included in rates. Types of meals: full breakfast, gourmet breakfast and early coffee/tea. Beds: KQT. Air conditioning in room. Spa, swimming and library on premises. Antiques, fishing, parks, shopping, downhill skiing, cross-country skiing, sporting events, theater and watersports nearby.

Certificate may be used: May-October, Sunday through Thursday; October-May, every day except holidays.

Ben Lomond J5

Fairview Manor
245 Fairview Ave,
Ben Lomond, CA 95005-9347
(408)336-3355 (800)553-8840

Circa 1924. More than two acres of woods and foliage shroud this home, offering a private, tranquil setting for guests to enjoy. Follow the paths that wind through the grounds and you'll find lily ponds and the San Lorenzo River. The home rests on the former site of the Ben Lomond Hotel, which was destroyed by fire in 1906. A prominent San Francisco attorney chose this spot to build his summer home, and the manor stayed in the family until the 1980s when the current innkeepers purchased it. The cozy guest rooms are decorated with antiques.
Innkeeper(s): Nancy Glasson. $109-119. MC VISA. 7 rooms, 5 with PB. 1 conference room. Breakfast and evening snack included in rates. Type of meal: full breakfast. Beds: KQ. Handicap access. Antiques, fishing, parks, shopping and watersports nearby.

Certificate may be used: Sunday through Thursday, year-round.

Berry Creek E6

Lake Oroville Bed and Breakfast
240 Sunday Dr,
Berry Creek, CA 95916-9640
(916)589-0700 (800)455-5253
Fax:(916)589-5313

Circa 1991. Situated in the quiet foothills above Lake Oroville, this country inn features panoramic views from the private porches that extend from each guest room. Two favorite rooms are the Rose

Petal Room and the Victorian Room, both with lake views and whirlpool tubs. The inn's 40 acres are studded with oak and pine trees. Deer and songbirds abound.
Innkeeper(s): Cheryl Damberger. $75-125. AP. MC VISA AX DS. 6 rooms with PB. 1 conference room. Breakfast included in rates. Types of meals: full breakfast, gourmet breakfast and early coffee/tea. Afternoon tea, evening snack and catering service available. Beds: KQ. Air conditioning, ceiling fan and VCR in room. Fax, copier and child care on premises. Antiques, fishing, shopping, sporting events and theater nearby.

Location: Twenty minutes out of Oroville in the foothills above the lake.

Seen in: Oroville Mercury-Register.

Certificate may be used: Sunday-Thursday (except holidays). All year.

Big Bear   N12

Gold Mountain Manor Historic B&B
1117 Anita, PO Box 2027,
Big Bear, CA 92314
(909)585-6997 Fax:(909)585-0327

Circa 1928. This spectacular log mansion was once a hideaway for the rich and famous. Eight fireplaces provide a roaring fire in each room in fall and winter. The Lucky Baldwin Room offers a hearth made from stones of gold gathered in the famous Lucky Baldwin mine nearby. In the Clark Gable room is the fireplace Gable and Carole Lombard enjoyed on their honeymoon. Gourmet country breakfasts and afternoon hors d'oeuvres are served.
Innkeeper(s): Robert Angilella, Gloria Oren & Jose Tapia. $75-180. MC VISA DS. 7 rooms, 2 with PB, 6 with FP. 2 suites. 1 cottage. 1 conference room. Afternoon tea and evening snack included in rates. Types of meals: full breakfast, gourmet breakfast and early coffee/tea. Dinner, gourmet lunch and room service available. Beds: Q. Ceiling fan in room. Cable TV, VCR, fax, spa, bicycles and library on premises. Fishing, parks, downhill skiing, cross-country skiing, sporting events and watersports nearby.

Location: Two hours northeast of Los Angeles and Orange counties.

Seen in: Kenny G Holiday Album Cover.

"A majestic experience! In this magnificent house, history comes alive!"

Certificate may be used: January through Dec. 20, Monday through Thursday (excluding Wildcat room), non-holidays.

Big Bear Lake   O12

Truffles, A Special Place
PO Box 130649,
Big Bear Lake, CA 92315-8972
(909)585-2772

Romance abounds at this mountain inn, which is decorated in a whimsical, English country style. Rooms include four-poster or antique beds topped with luxurious feather mattresses. The Queen's Legacy room includes a soaking tub, while the Lady Rose offers a cozy alcove sitting area. Other rooms include special features such as a Palladian window or iron bed decorated with cherubs. Ever true to the inn's name, a truffle is placed on each pillow during the nightly turndown service. Those celebrating special occasions might find flowers or champagne in their rooms. The innkeepers deliver morning coffee or tea to their guests, and serve a lavish breakfast, afternoon tea and desserts in the evenings.

Innkeeper(s): Marilyn Kane. $110-140. MC VISA. 5 rooms. Breakfast included in rates. Type of meal: full breakfast.

Certificate may be used: March through June and September and October, Sunday through Thursday.

Wainwright Inn B&B
PO Box 130406,
Big Bear Lake, CA 92315-8962
(909)585-6914

Circa 1989. This Tudor-style B&B is located in a quiet, tree-filled residential area adjacent to Bear Mountain ski resort and golf course. The most popular accommodation is the Honeymoon Hideaway, with whirlpool for two, sleigh bed, fireplace, wet bar and private entrance. Canopy beds and English country antiques are found throughout the inn. Afternoon tea is served in the solarium and there's a massive brick fireplace in the Great Room.
Innkeeper(s): Sharon Berton. $95-175. AP. MC VISA AX DC CB. 4 rooms, 2 with PB, 1 with FP. 1 suite. 1 conference room. Breakfast included in rates. Types of meals: full breakfast and early coffee/tea. Picnic lunch available. Beds: Q. Turn-down service in room. Cable TV, VCR, spa and bicycles on premises. Antiques, fishing, parks, shopping, downhill skiing, cross-country skiing and theater nearby.

Location: Adjacent to Bear Mountain Ski Resort.

Seen in: Los Angeles Times, Gourmet Getaway.

Certificate may be used: Weekdays anytime except Dec. 15-Jan. 15. Seven days a week April 1-June 15.

Bishop   I10

The Matlick House
1313 Rowan Ln, Bishop, CA 93514-1937
(619)873-3133 (800)898-3133

Circa 1906. This lovely gray and pink home with a double veranda was built by Alan Matlick, one of the area's pioneers. The spacious parlor features a

clawfoot settee with massive curved arms, antique recliner, European burled-wood armoire and original cherry-wood fireplace. Rooms boast special pieces such as the white iron bed, Eastlake chair and quilted settee in the Lenna room. Guests will enjoy the home's views of both the Sierra Nevadas and the White Mountains. A hearty American breakfast with eggs, bacon and homemade biscuits is served in the dining room. The Eastern Sierras provide a wealth of activities, year-round catch-and-release fly fishing is within 20 minutes from the home.

Innkeeper(s): Ray & Barbara Showalter. $79-89. MC VISA AX DS TC. 5 rooms with PB. Breakfast and evening snack included in rates. Types of meals: continental-plus breakfast, full breakfast and early coffee/tea. Picnic lunch, lunch and catering service available. Beds: QT. Air conditioning, ceiling fan and cable TV in room. VCR and fax on premises. Antiques, fishing, parks, shopping, downhill skiing and cross-country skiing nearby.

Seen in: Inyo Register, Sunset.

"Like sleeping on a nice pink cloud after our Rock Creek Horse drive."

Certificate may be used: Anytime except last two weeks of May (Mule Days).

Calistoga   G4

Foothill House
3037 Foothill Blvd,
Calistoga, CA 94515-1225
(707)942-6933 (800)942-6933
Fax:(707)942-5692

Circa 1892. This country farmhouse overlooks the western foothills of Mount St. Helena. Graceful old California oaks and pockets of flowers greet guests. Each room features country antiques, a four-poster bed, a fireplace and a small refrigerator. Breakfast is served in the sun room or is delivered personally to your room in a basket. Three rooms offer private Jacuzzi tubs.

Innkeeper(s): Doris & Gus Beckert. $135-250. MC VISA AX DS PC TC. 4 suites, 4 with FP. Breakfast and evening snack included in rates. Types of meals: full breakfast, gourmet breakfast and early coffee/tea. Beds: KQT. Air conditioning, turn-down service, ceiling fan, cable TV and VCR in room. Fax, copier and library on premises. Amusement parks, antiques, fishing, parks, shopping and watersports nearby.

Location: Napa Valley.

Seen in: Herald Examiner, Baltimore Sun.

"Gourmet treats served in front of an open fire. Hospitality never for a moment flagged."

Certificate may be used: December-January, Sunday through Thursday, holidays excluded.

Cambria   L6

The J. Patrick House
2990 Burton Dr,
Cambria, CA 93428-4002
(805)927-3812 (800)341-5258

Circa 1983. This charming log cabin bed & breakfast is nestled in the woods overlooking Cambria's east village. The picturesque grounds include a garden area that separates the main house from the redwood cabin, where all but one of the guest rooms are located. Each of the guest rooms includes a wood-burning fireplace. Rooms are decorated in a romantic style with hand-stitched quilts and feather-filled duvet covers atop the beds. Wine and hors d'oeuvres are served each evening in the main house's fireplaced living room. Fresh fruits, homemade granola and freshly baked breads and muffins are among the fare during the morning meal. Be sure to request one of the innkeeper's "killer" chocolate chip cookies.

Innkeeper(s): Barbara & Mel Schwimmer. $110-160. MC VISA AX DS PC. 8 rooms with PB, 8 with FP. 1 suite. Breakfast and evening snack included in rates. Types of meals: continental-plus breakfast and early coffee/tea. Beds: KQ. Antiques, fishing, parks and shopping nearby.

Certificate may be used: Jan. 2-Dec. 19, Sunday-Thursday, excludes August, excludes weekends, excludes holiday periods.

Olallieberry Inn
2476 Main St, Cambria, CA 93428-3406
(805)927-3222 Fax:(805)927-0202

Circa 1873. This restored Greek Revival home features rooms decorated with fabrics and wall coverings and furnished with period antiques. Six of the guest rooms feature fireplaces. Butterfly and herb gardens and a 110-year-old redwood grace the front yard. The cheery gathering room boasts a view of the Santa Rosa Creek. Full breakfast with fresh breads, fruits and a special entree start off the day, and wine and hors d'oeurves are served in the afternoon. The inn is within walking distance to restaurants and shops.

Innkeeper(s): Peter & Carol Ann Irsfeld. $72-165. MC VISA PC TC. 9 rooms with PB, 6 with FP. 1 suite. Breakfast and evening snack included in rates. Types of meals: full breakfast, gourmet breakfast and early coffee/tea. Beds: KQ. Fax on premises. Handicap access. Antiques, fishing, shopping and watersports nearby.

Location: Central coast wine country.

Seen in: Los Angeles Times, Elmer Dills Radio Show.

"Our retreat turned into relaxation, romance and pure Victorian delight."

Certificate may be used: Sunday-Thursday, except May 1 through Oct. 31 and holidays.

Camino　　　G7

The Camino Hotel-Seven Mile House
4103 Carson Rd, PO Box 1197,
Camino, CA 95709
(916)644-7740 (800)200-7740
Fax:(916)644-7740

Circa 1888. Once a barracks for the area's loggers, this inn now caters to visitors in the state's famed gold country. Just east of Placerville, historic Camino is on the Old Carson Wagon Trail. Nine guest rooms are available, including the E.J. Barrett Room, a favorite with honeymooners. Other rooms feature names such as Pony Express, Stage Stop and Wagon Train. The family-oriented inn welcomes children, and a local park offers a handy site for their recreational needs. Popular area activities include antiquing, hot air ballooning and wine tasting.

Innkeeper(s): Paula Norbert & John Eddy. $65-95. AP. MC VISA AX DS PC TC. 9 rooms, 3 with PB. 1 conference room. Breakfast and evening snack included in rates. Types of meals: full breakfast and early coffee/tea. Afternoon tea, picnic lunch and banquet service available. Beds: QDT. Turn-down service and ceiling fan in room. Fax, copier and library on premises. Antiques, fishing, parks, shopping, downhill skiing, cross-country skiing, theater and watersports nearby.

Location: In the Apple Hill area of California's Gold Country.

Certificate may be used: Year-round except Friday, Saturday, Sunday in September, October, November.

Capitola-By-The-Sea　　　J5

The Inn at Depot Hill
250 Monterey Ave,
Capitola-By-The-Sea, CA 95010-3358
(408)462-3376 (800)572-2632
Fax:(408)462-3697

Circa 1901. Once a railroad depot, this inn offers rooms with themes to represent different parts of the world-a chic auberge in St. Tropez, a romantic hideaway in Paris, an Italian coastal villa, a summer home on the coast of Holland, and a traditional English garden room. Five rooms have garden patios boasting hot tubs. The rooms have many amenities which include a fireplace, white marble bathrooms and featherbeds. Guests are greeted with fresh flowers in their room.

Innkeeper(s): Suzie Lankes & Dan Floyd. $165-250. MC VISA AX TC. 8 rooms with PB, 8 with FP. 4 suites. Breakfast and evening snack included in rates. Types of meals: full breakfast and gourmet breakfast. Afternoon tea and room service available. Beds: KQ. Turn-down service, cable TV and VCR in room. Fax and spa on premises. Handicap

access. Amusement parks, antiques, fishing, parks, shopping, theater and watersports nearby.

Seen in: Country Inn, Santa Cruz Sentinel, McCalls, San Jose Mercury News, Fresno & Sacramento Bee, San Francisco Focus, American Airline Flight.

"The highlight of our honeymoon. Five stars in our book!"

Certificate may be used: Monday-Thursday, November through April. Excludes holidays and special events.

Carmel　　　K5

Cobblestone Inn
PO Box 3185, Carmel, CA 93921-3185
(408)625-5222 (800)833-8836
Fax:(408)625-0478

An exterior of wood and cobblestone gathered from the Carmel River provide a friendly facade for visitors to this bed & breakfast located two blocks from the heart of Carmel. Each guest room has its own cobblestone fireplace. The inn's country decor is enhanced with quilts, a colorful antique carousel horse and other early American antiques.

Innkeeper(s): Suzi Russo. $95-175. 24 rooms with PB, 24 with FP. Breakfast included in rates. Type of meal: early coffee/tea. Afternoon tea and picnic lunch available. Fax and copier on premises.

Seen in: Country Inns, Honeymoons.

Certificate may be used: December-January; Sunday-Thursday, holidays & special events excluded.

The Stonehouse Inn
PO Box 2517, Carmel, CA 93921-2517
(408)624-4569 (800)748-6618

Circa 1906. This quaint Carmel country house boasts a stone exterior, made from beach rocks collected and hand shaped by local Indians at the turn of the century. The original owner, "Nana" Foster, was hostess to notable artists and writers from the San Francisco area, including Sinclair Lewis, Jack London and Lotta Crabtree. The romantic Jack London room features a dramatic gabled ceiling, a brass bed and a stunning view of the ocean. Conveniently located, the inn is a short walk from Carmel Beach and two blocks from the village.

Innkeeper(s): Ad Navailles. $89-199. MC VISA AX. 6 rooms, 1 with PB. Breakfast included in rates. Type of meal: full breakfast. Beds: KQDT. Fishing, parks, shopping, theater and watersports nearby.

Location: Two blocks to downtown, 4 blocks to beach.

Seen in: Travel & Leisure, Country Living.

"First time stay at a B&B — GREAT!"

Certificate may be used: Nov. 1 through May 31, Sunday through Thursday, except special events such as Thanksgiving, Christmas, New Year, AT&T Golf Tournament.

Carpinteria   N8

Prufrock's Garden Inn
600 Linden Ave,
Carpinteria, CA 93013-2040
(805)566-9696

Circa 1904. A white picket fence surrounds this California-style cottage, which is just a few blocks from the beach. Five generations of the home's original family lived in this cozy inn. The bedrooms offer private sitting areas. Relax on the porch or stroll through the lush gardens. Carpinteria offers several antique shops and an open-air farmers' market.
Innkeeper(s): Judy, Jim, Julie & Jon Halversen. $66-139. MC VISA TC. 4 rooms, 2 with PB. Breakfast, afternoon tea and evening snack included in rates. Types of meals: full breakfast and early coffee/tea. Beds: Q. Turn-down service in room. VCR and bicycles on premises. Antiques, fishing, parks, shopping, sporting events, theater and watersports nearby.
Certificate may be used: Oct. 1-June 30, Sunday-Thursday.

Chico   E5

The Esplanade B&B
620 The Esplanade, Chico, CA 95926
(916)345-8084

Circa 1914. Each of the rooms at this comfortable bed & breakfast are named for someone special in innkeeper Lois Kloss' life. One room includes a Jacuzzi tub and stained-glass window. Others feature poster beds piled high with feather pillows. Lois serves a buffet-style breakfast in the morning, and treats guests to a glass of wine in the afternoons. The home is within walking distance from the university, downtown Chico and the Chico Museum.
Innkeeper(s): Lois I. Kloss. $45-65. MC VISA TC. 6 rooms with PB. Breakfast, afternoon tea and evening snack included in rates. Types of meals: full breakfast and early coffee/tea. Room service available. Beds: QDT. Air conditioning, ceiling fan and cable TV in room. Fax on premises. Amusement parks, antiques, fishing, parks, shopping, downhill skiing, cross-country skiing, sporting events, theater and watersports nearby.
Certificate may be used: All year, Sunday through Thursday.

Music Express Inn
1091 El Monte Ave,
Chico, CA 95928-9153
(916)345-8376 Fax:(916)893-8521

Circa 1977. Music lovers will delight in this inn's warmth and charm. Seven air-conditioned guest rooms, all with private bath and cable TV, provide country-style comfort to those visiting the college town of Chico. Guests will awake to the smell of homemade bread or rolls. Visitors are welcome to tickle the ivories of the inn's Steinway grand piano. The innkeeper, a music teacher, is adept at many instruments and plays mandolin in a local band. The inn's library also lures many guests, and those who explore the surrounding area will find plenty of opportunities for antiquing and fishing.
Innkeeper(s): Barney & Irene Cobeen. $55-85. MC VISA AX DS PC TC. 9 rooms with PB. 1 suite. 1 cottage. 2 conference rooms. Breakfast included in rates. Type of meal: full breakfast. Beds: KQDT. Air conditioning, ceiling fan, cable TV and VCR in room. Fax, copier and library on premises. Handicap access. Antiques, fishing, parks, shopping, sporting events, theater and watersports nearby.
Certificate may be used: All year.

Clio   E7

White Sulphur Springs Ranch
PO Box 136, Clio, CA 96106-0136
(916)836-2387 (800)854-1797
Fax:(916)836-2387

Circa 1857. Originally built by partners in the Jamison mine, this stage coach stop serviced the Truckee to Quincy stage. The inn has passed from relative to relative to friend and has not been sold since 1867 when it was purchased by George McLear. Elegantly restored, the rooms still retain many of the original furnishings, now embellished with colorful wallpapers and fabrics. The Marble Room features a moss green velvet fainting couch, marble topped antiques and a splendid view of the Mohawk Valley. Breakfast is served in the dining room. Mineral waters from five 85-degree springs fill the inn's swimming pool.
Innkeeper(s): Don & Karen Miller, Tom & Linda Vanella. $85-140. MC VISA DS TC. 9 rooms, 3 with PB. 2 conference rooms. Breakfast and afternoon tea included in rates. Types of meals: full breakfast and early coffee/tea. Picnic lunch available. Beds: KQD. Air conditioning in room. Cable TV, VCR, fax and copier on premises. Handicap access. Antiques, fishing, parks, shopping, downhill skiing, cross-country skiing and watersports nearby.

Seen in: Sacramento Union, Plumas-Sierra.

"White Sulphur Springs is alive with its past and its present."

Certificate may be used: Monday-Thursday, year-round, no holidays.

Dana Point
P11

Blue Lantern Inn
34343 Street of The Blue Lantern,
Dana Point, CA 92629
(714)661-1304 (800)950-1236
Fax:(714)496-1483

Circa 1990. The inn is situated high on a blufftop overlooking a stunning coastline and the blue waters of Dana Point harbor with its pleasure craft, fishing boats and the tall ship, Pilgrim. Each guest room features both a fireplace and a spa and there are private sundecks and mini-stereos. Afternoon tea, evening turndown service and bicycles are just a few of the amenities available.

Innkeeper(s): Lin McMahon. $135-350. MC VISA AX TC. 29 rooms with PB, 29 with FP. 1 suite. 1 conference room. Breakfast and afternoon tea included in rates. Types of meals: full breakfast, gourmet breakfast and early coffee/tea. Evening snack available. Beds: KQD. Turn-down service in room. Fax and bicycles on premises. Handicap access. Amusement parks, antiques, fishing, parks, shopping and watersports nearby.

Location: Overlooking yacht harbor near Laguna Beach.

Seen in: LA, Oregonian, Orange County Register.

Certificate may be used: Sunday-Thursday, holidays & events excluded. October-June (excluding July, August, September).

Dulzura
Q12

Brookside Farm
1373 Marron Valley Rd,
Dulzura, CA 91917-2113
(619)468-3043

Circa 1929. Ancient oaks shade terraces leading from the farmhouse to a murmuring brook. Behind a nearby stone barn, there is a grape arbor and beneath it, a spa. Each room in the inn and its two cottages is furnished with vintage pieces and handmade quilts. Adventurous hikers can explore mines nearby, which date from the gold rush of 1908. Innkeeper Edd Guishard is a former award-winning restaurant owner.

Innkeeper(s): Sally Guishard. $75-115. MC VISA AX DC CB DS. 11 rooms with PB, 4 with FP. 2 suites. 1 conference room. Breakfast and dinner included in rates. Type of meal: full breakfast. Beds: Q. Spa on premises. Handicap access.

Location: Thirty-five minutes southeast of San Diego.

Seen in: California, San Diego Home & Garden.

"Our stay at the farm was the most relaxing weekend we've had in a year."

Certificate may be used: Sunday-Thursday. Dinner (supper) not included.

Dunsmuir
B5

Dunsmuir Inn
5423 Dunsmuir Ave,
Dunsmuir, CA 96025-2011
(916)235-4543 (888)386-7684
Fax:(916)235-4154

Circa 1925. Set in the Sacramento River Valley, this country-style inn may serve as a base for an assortment of outdoor activities. At the end of the day, guests can enjoy the inn's own Rosie's Ice Cream Parlor for an old-fashioned soda or ice cream cone. Fishing, available in the crystal-clear waters of the Upper Sacramento River, is within walking distance. The innkeepers can suggest hiking trails and driving tours to mountain lakes, waterfalls, the Castle Crags State Park and Mt. Shasta.

Innkeeper(s): Jerry & Julie Iskra. $55-65. MC VISA AX DC CB DS PC TC. 4 rooms with PB. 1 suite. Breakfast included in rates. Types of meals: full breakfast and early coffee/tea. Evening snack and picnic lunch available. Beds: KDT. Air conditioning, turn-down service and ceiling fan in room. Cable TV, VCR and fax on premises. Antiques, fishing, parks, downhill skiing, cross-country skiing and watersports nearby.

Location: Sacramento River Valley.

Certificate may be used: January-April, October-December.

Eureka
C2

"An Elegant Victorian Mansion"
1406 C St, Eureka, CA 95501-1765
(707)444-3144 Fax:(707)442-5594

Circa 1888. One of Eureka's leading lumber barons built this picturesque home from 1,000-year-old virgin redwood. Original wallpapers, wood carpets and antique light fixtures create a wonderfully authentic Victorian ambiance. A tuxedoed butler and your hosts, decked in period attire, greet guests upon arrival. Croquet fields and Victorian gardens surround the inn. The hosts can arrange horse-drawn carriage rides or boat cruises. Old-fashioned ice cream sodas are served and to top it all off, each morning guests partake in a multi-course gourmet breakfast feast. The beds in the well-appointed guest quarters are topped with custom-made mattresses. There a video library of vintage silent films. The inn has been host to many historic personalities, including actresses Lillie Langtry and Sarah Bernhardt, and many senators and representatives. Innkeeper(s): Doug & Lily Vieyra. $95-185. EP. MC VISA. 4 rooms, 2 with PB. 1 suite. 1 conference room. Breakfast, afternoon tea and evening snack included in rates. Types of meals: gourmet breakfast and early coffee/tea. Beds: Q. Air conditioning and turn-down service in room. Cable TV, VCR, fax, copier, sauna, bicycles, tennis and library on premises. Amusement parks, antiques, fishing, parks, shopping, sporting events, theater and watersports nearby.

"A magnificent masterpiece, both in architecture and service. Four star service and regal opulence."

Certificate may be used: Van Gogh Room only, during months of January, February, during mid-week (Monday-Thursday). Excluding holidays and local special events. Subject to availability no earlier than two days prior to reservation date.

The Carter House Victorians

301 L St, Eureka, CA 95501
(707)444-8062 (800)404-1390
Fax:(707)444-8067

Circa 1884. The Carters found a pattern book in an antique shop and built this inn according to the architectural plans for an 1890 San Francisco Victorian. (The architect, Joseph Newsom, also designed the Carson House across the street.) Three open parlors with bay windows and marble fireplaces provide an elegant backdrop for relaxing. Guests are free to visit the kitchen in quest of coffee and views of the bay. The inn is

famous for its three-course breakfast, including an Apple Almond Tart featured in Gourmet magazine. Innkeeper(s): Mark & Christi Carter. $95-275. MAP, AP, EP. MC VISA AX DC CB DS PC TC. 31 rooms with PB, 15 with FP. 15 suites. 1 cottage. 2 conference rooms. Breakfast and afternoon tea included in rates. Types of meals: continental breakfast, continental-plus breakfast, full breakfast, gourmet breakfast and early coffee/tea. Dinner, evening snack and room service available. Beds: KQDT. Air conditioning, turn-down service, cable TV and VCR in room. Fax, copier and spa on premises. Handicap access. Antiques, fishing, parks, shopping, sporting events, theater and watersports nearby.

Location: Corner of Third & L streets in Old Town.

Seen in: Sunset, U.S. News & World Report, Country Home, Country Living, Bon Appetit, San Francisco Focus, Northwest Palate, Gourmet, Art Culinare, San Francisco Chronicle.

"We've traveled extensively throughout the U.S. and stayed in the finest hotels. You've got them all beat!!"

Certificate may be used: November-April 30, excluding holidays.

The Daly Inn

1125 H St, Eureka, CA 95501-1844
(707)445-3638 (800)321-9656
Fax:(707)444-3636

Circa 1905. This 6,000-square-foot Colonial Revival mansion is located in the historic section of Eureka. Enjoy the Belgian antique bedstead, fireplace and view of fish pond and garden from

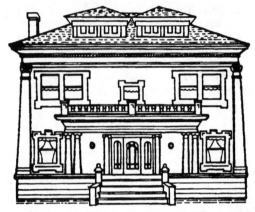

Annie Murphy's Room, or try the former nursery, Miss Martha's Room, with bleached pine antiques from Holland. Breakfast is served fireside in the inn's formal dining room or in the breakfast parlor or garden patio. Innkeeper(s): Sue & Gene Clinesmith. $70-135. MC VISA AX DS PC TC. 5 rooms, 3 with PB, 1 with FP. 2 suites. Breakfast and evening snack included in rates. Types of meals: gourmet breakfast and early coffee/tea. Beds: QT. Turn-down service in room. Cable TV, VCR, fax, copier and library on premises. Antiques, fishing, parks, shopping, sporting events and theater nearby.

Location: California's north coast.

"A genuine delight."

Certificate may be used: Nov. 1-May 1. Holidays & special event weekends excluded.

Ferndale   C2

Gingerbread Mansion Inn

PO Box 40, Ferndale, CA 95536-1380
(707)786-4000 (800)952-4136
Fax:(707)786-4381

Circa 1899. Built for Dr. H. J. Ring, the Gingerbread Mansion is now the most photographed of Northern California's inns. Near Eureka, it is in the fairy-tale Victorian village of Ferndale (a California Historical Landmark). Outside the inn are formal English gardens. Gingerbread Mansion is a unique combination of Queen Anne and Eastlake styles with elaborate

gingerbread trim. Inside are spacious and elegant rooms including two suites with "his" and "her" bathtubs. There are four parlors.

Innkeeper(s): Ken Torbert. $120-350. MC VISA AX PC TC. 10 rooms with PB, 5 with FP. 5 suites. Breakfast and afternoon tea included in rates. Types of meals: full breakfast and early coffee/tea. Beds: KQT. Turn-down service in room. Library on premises. Antiques, fishing, parks, shopping and theater nearby.

Location: Five miles west off Highway 101; 30 minutes south of Eureka.

Seen in: Stockton Record, San Francisco Focus, Los Angeles Times, Sunset.

"Absolutely the most charming, friendly and delightful place we have ever stayed."

Certificate may be used: Nov. 1-April 30, Sunday-Thursday, excluding holiday or special event periods.

Fish Camp I8

Karen's B&B Yosemite Inn
PO Box 8, Fish Camp, CA 93623-0008
(209)683-4550

Circa 1988. This contemporary home combines both modern and country decor. Pines and cedars surround the home, which is situated at 5,000 feet.

The three rooms, named Rose, Blue or Peach, are decorated in the corresponding color. Country breakfasts are served family style and include items such as homemade muffins, waffles or "pancrepes." The innkeeper's cottage fries are a specialty.

Innkeeper(s): Karen Bergh. $85. 3 rooms. Breakfast included in rates. Type of meal: full breakfast. Parks nearby.

Location: One mile south of Yosemite National Park.

Seen in: Contra Costa Times.

Certificate may be used: Oct. 15-Dec. 15, Jan. 1-March 31, void all holidays.

Fort Bragg E2

Glass Beach B&B
726 N Main St,
Fort Bragg, CA 95437-3017
(707)964-6774

Circa 1920. Each of the guest rooms at this Craftsman-style home is decorated in a different theme and named to reflect the decor. The Malaysian and Oriental Jade rooms reflect Asian artistry, while the Forget-Me-Not and Wild Flower rooms are bright, feminine rooms with walls decked in floral prints. Antiques are found throughout the home and the back cottage, which includes three of the inn's nine guest rooms. The inn also offers a hot tub for guest use. Breakfasts are served in the inn's dining room, but guests are free to fix up a tray and enjoy the meal in the privacy of their own room.

Innkeeper(s): Nancy Cardenas. $50-125. MC VISA DS TC. 9 rooms with PB, 4 with FP. 1 suite. Breakfast included in rates. Type of meal: full breakfast. Afternoon tea available. Beds: Q. Cable TV in room. Handicap access. Antiques, fishing, parks, shopping, theater and watersports nearby.

Certificate may be used: Oct. 1 through June 30, Sunday through Thursday, holiday periods excluded.

Grey Whale Inn
615 N Main St,
Fort Bragg, CA 95437-3240
(707)964-0640 (800)382-7244
Fax:(707)964-4408

Circa 1915. As the name implies, whales can be seen from many of the inn's vantage points during the creatures' migration season along the West Coast. The stately four-story redwood inn features airy and spacious guest rooms with ocean views. Some rooms include a fireplace, whirlpool tub for two or private deck. Near the heart of downtown Fort Bragg, it's an easy walk to the Skunk Train, shops, galleries and restaurants. There is also a fireside lounge, TV-VCR theater and a recreation area with pool table.

Innkeeper(s): John & Colette Bailey. $90-180. MC VISA AX DS PC TC. 14 rooms with PB, 3 with FP. 5 suites. 2 conference rooms. Breakfast included in rates. Type of meal: full breakfast. Beds: KQDT. Ceiling fan, cable TV and VCR in room. Fax, copier and library on premises. Handicap access. Antiques, fishing, parks, shopping, theater and watersports nearby.

Location: Almost in the heart of downtown Fort Bragg on the Mendocino Coast Highway.

Seen in: Inn Times, San Francisco Examiner, Travel, Fort Bragg Advocate News, Mendocino Beacon.

"We are going to return each year until we have tried each room. Sunrise room is excellent in the morning or evening."

Certificate may be used: October through June, Monday through Thursday.

Pudding Creek Inn

700 N Main St,
Fort Bragg, CA 95437-3017
(707)964-9529 (800)227-9529
Fax:(707)961-0282

Circa 1884. Originally constructed by a Russian count, the inn comprises two picturesque Victorian homes connected by an enclosed garden. There are mounds of begonias, fuchsias and ferns. The Count's Room, in seafoam green and cranberry accents, features inlaid redwood paneling, a stone fireplace and a brass bed. There is a TV/recreation room for guest use. A full buffet breakfast is provided and you can reserve ahead for a picnic

lunch. (Guests on a long coastal tour will appreciate the laundry service made available.)

Innkeeper(s): Carole Anloff. $65-125. MC VISA AX DS. 10 rooms with PB, 2 with FP. Breakfast and afternoon tea included in rates. Type of meal: full breakfast. Evening snack and picnic lunch available. Beds: KQDT. Fax on premises. Antiques, fishing and theater nearby.

Location: Corner of Bush and North Main.

Seen in: Evening Outlook.

"Best stop on our trip!"

Certificate may be used: November-June, midweek Sunday-Thursday only, no holidays.

The Rendezvous Inn & Restaurant

647 N Main St,
Fort Bragg, CA 95437-3219
(707)964-8142 (800)491-8142

Circa 1904. This turn-of-the-century inn offers visitors the convenience of lodging and dining. Six large guest rooms, all with private bath and queen beds, are designed with relaxation in mind, meaning television and phones are found elsewhere in the inn. Guests are encouraged to join others in the comfortable parlor for a glass or wine or beer, to watch TV, relax or socialize. Within walking distance are the Guest House Museum, Skunk Train and Glass and Pudding Creek beaches.

Innkeeper(s): Rose Jacobs. $55-110. MC VISA AX DS. 6 rooms. 2 suites. Breakfast included in rates. Types of meals: continental-plus breakfast and early coffee/tea. Dinner, lunch, banquet service and catering service available.

Certificate may be used: Sunday - Thursday, September through May.

Geyserville   G4

Hope-Merrill House

21253 Geyserville Ave,
Geyserville, CA 95441-9637
(707)857-3356 (800)825-4233
Fax:(707)857-4673

Circa 1885. The Hope-Merrill House is a classic example of the Eastlake Stick style that was so popular during Victorian times. Built entirely from redwood, the house features original wainscoting and silk-screened wallcoverings. A swimming pool, vineyard and gazebo are favorite spots for guests to relax. The Hope-Bosworth House, on the same street, was built in the Queen Anne style by an early Geyserville pioneer who lived in the home until the 1960s. The front picket fence is covered with roses. Period details include oak woodwork, sliding doors, polished fir floors and antique light fixtures. Guests will enjoy innkeeper Rosalie Hope's prize-winning breads with their full breakfasts.

Innkeeper(s): Rosalie Hope. $95-140. MC VISA AX PC TC. 12 rooms with PB, 3 with FP. 1 suite. Breakfast and picnic lunch included in rates.

Types of meals: full breakfast, gourmet breakfast and early coffee/tea. Beds: Q. Ceiling fan in room. Fax and copier on premises. Antiques, parks, shopping and watersports nearby.

Seen in: San Diego Union, Country Homes, Sunset, Sacramento Union.

"Innkeepers extraordinaire — Leisure and Outdoor Guide."

Certificate may be used: Sunday through Thursday. Holidays excluded.

Gilroy   J5

Country Rose Inn - B&B
PO Box 2500, Gilroy, CA 95021
(408)842-0441 Fax:(408)842-6646

Circa 1920. Amid five wooded acres, a half-hour's drive south of San Jose, sits the aptly named Country Rose Inn. A roomy Dutch Colonial manor, this inn was once a farmhouse on the Lucky Hereford Ranch. Every room features a rose theme, including wallpaper and quilted bedspreads. Each window offers a relaxing view of horses grazing, fertile fields, or the tranquil grounds, which boast magnificent 100-year-old oak trees.

Innkeeper(s): Rose Hernandez. $89-179. MC VISA AX PC. 5 rooms with PB, 2 with FP. 1 suite. 2 conference rooms. Breakfast and afternoon tea included in rates. Types of meals: full breakfast and early coffee/tea. Picnic lunch available. Beds: KQDT. Air conditioning and turn-down service in room. Fax and library on premises. Antiques, parks, shopping and theater nearby.

Location: Masten Avenue exit off Hwy 101 in San Martin, north of Gilroy.

"The quiet, serene country setting made our anniversary very special. Rose is a delightful, gracious hostess and cook."

Certificate may be used: October-May, anyday. June-September, Sunday-Thursday only.

Groveland   H7

The Groveland Hotel
18767 Main St, PO Box 481,
Groveland, CA 95321
(209)962-4000 (800)273-3314
Fax:(209)962-6674

Circa 1849. Located 25 miles from Yosemite National Park, the newly restored hotel features both an 1849 adobe building with 18-inch-thick walls constructed during the Gold Rush and a 1914

building erected to house workers for the Hetch Hetchy Dam. Both feature two-story balconies. There is a Victorian parlor, a gourmet restaurant and a Western saloon. Guest rooms feature European antiques and down comforters. The feeling is one of casual elegance.

Innkeeper(s): Peggy D. & Grover C. Mosley. $95-175. MC VISA AX DC CB DS PC TC. 17 rooms with PB, 3 with FP. 3 suites. 1 conference room. Breakfast included in rates. Types of meals: continental-plus breakfast and early coffee/tea. Picnic lunch, banquet service, catering service and room service available. Beds: QT. Air conditioning and ceiling fan in room. Cable TV, VCR, fax, copier, computer, library, pet boarding and child care on premises. Handicap access. Antiques, fishing, parks, shopping, downhill skiing, cross-country skiing and watersports nearby.

Seen in: Sonora Union Democrat, Peninsula, Sunset, Stockton Record, Country Inns.

"Hospitality is outstanding."

Certificate may be used: Oct. 15-April 15, Sunday through Thursday, excluding holidays.

Guernewood Park   G3

Fern Grove Inn
16650 River Rd,
Guernewood Park, CA 95446-9678
(707)869-9083 (800)347-9083
Fax:(707)869-2948

Clustered in a village-like atmosphere, these craftsman cottages have romantic fireplaces, private entrances and are decorated with freshly cut flowers. Your day starts with freshly brewed coffee and a leisurely buffet breakfast featuring renowned homemade muffins and pastries served in the relaxed atmosphere of the Common Room. The morning newspapers, soft classical music, warming fire and good conversation will stimulate your spirits. Innkeepers will provide you with concierge service throughout your stay.

Innkeeper(s): Dennis Ekstrom. $89-199. MC VISA AX DS. 17 rooms. 11 suites. Breakfast included in rates. Type of meal: continental-plus breakfast. Evening snack and picnic lunch available.

Certificate may be used: May 1-Oct. 31, Sunday-Thursday; Nov. 1-April 30, anyday; excludes holidays and special events.

Half Moon Bay   I4

Old Thyme Inn
779 Main St,
Half Moon Bay, CA 94019-1924
(415)726-1616

Circa 1899. Located on the historic Main Street of Old Town, this Queen Anne Victorian has a flower and herb garden surrounding it. Seven rooms are

named after various herbs that are found in the garden. Guests receive a complimentary book on herbs with each reservation. Most of the rooms have whirlpool baths and/or fireplaces. Resident teddy bears help keep guests in good company. The inn is within walking distance to beaches, restaurants, shops and art galleries.

Innkeeper(s): George & Maria Dempsey. $85-220. MC VISA PC. 7 rooms with PB, 4 with FP. 1 suite. 1 conference room. Breakfast included in rates. Beds: Q. Cable TV and VCR in room. Computer and spa on premises. Antiques, fishing, parks, shopping, sporting events, theater and watersports nearby.

Location: Five minutes from ocean.

Seen in: California Weekends, Los Angeles, San Mateo Times, San Jose Mercury News, Herb Companion, San Francisco Examiner.

"Furnishings, rooms and garden were absolutely wonderful. Delicious breakfast and great coffee … loved the peaceful neighborhood."

Certificate may be used: November-April, Monday-Thursday.

Healdsburg G4

Madrona Manor, A Country Inn
PO Box 818, Healdsburg, CA 95448-0818
(707)433-4231 (800)258-4003
Fax:(707)433-0703

Circa 1881. The inn is comprised of four historic structures in a national historic district. Surrounded by eight acres of manicured lawns and terraced flower and vegetable gardens, the stately mansion was built for John Paxton, a San Francisco businessman. Embellished with turrets, bay windows, porches, and a mansard roof, it provides a breathtaking view of surrounding vineyards. Elegant antique furnishings and a noteworthy restaurant add to the genuine country inn atmosphere. The Gothic-style Carriage House offers more casual lodging.

Innkeeper(s): John & Carol Muir. $140-240. MC VISA AX DC CB DS PC TC. 21 rooms with PB, 17 with FP. 3 suites. 1 cottage. 2 conference rooms. Breakfast included in rates. Type of meal: gourmet breakfast. Dinner and picnic lunch available. Beds: KQDT. Air conditioning in room.

Fax, copier, computer and swimming on premises. Handicap access. Antiques, fishing, parks, shopping, sporting events, theater and watersports nearby.

Location: In the heart of the wine country, Sonoma County.

Seen in: Gourmet, Woman's Day Home Decorating Ideas, Travel & Leisure, US News, Diversions, Money, Good Housekeeping.

"Our fourth visit and better every time."

Certificate may be used: Sunday through Thursday, all year.

Idyllwild O12

The Pine Cove Inn
23481 Hwy 243, PO Box 2181,
Idyllwild, CA 92549
(909)659-5033 Fax:(909)659-5034

Circa 1935. These rustic, A-frame cottages offer a variety of amenities in a natural, mountain setting. Refrigerators and microwaves have been placed in each unit, several of which include a wood-burning fireplace. A full breakfast is served in a separate lodge. The village of Idyllwild is three miles down the road, and the surrounding country offers a variety of activities.

Innkeeper(s): Bob & Michelle Bollmann. $70-90. MC VISA AX PC TC. 9 rooms with PB, 6 with FP. 3 suites. 1 conference room. Breakfast included in rates. Type of meal: full breakfast. Beds: QT. Ceiling fan in room. Cable TV, VCR and fax on premises. Antiques, fishing, parks, shopping, cross-country skiing and theater nearby.

Certificate may be used: Sunday through Thursday only, any dates except Dec. 15 through Jan. 4.

Wilkum Inn B&B
26770 Hwy 243 PO Box 1115,
Idyllwild, CA 92549-1115
(909)659-4087 (800)659-4086

Circa 1938. Situated among tall pines and oaks, this mountain village inn provides European-style hospitality. The Eaves is a two-room suite with queen bed, open-beam ceiling and a view of the pines. Nearby, the Idyllwild School of Music and the Arts hosts presentations and exhibitions year-round.

Innkeeper(s): Barbara Jones & Annamae Chambers. $75-100. PC TC. 6 rooms, 4 with PB, 2 with FP. 1 cottage. Breakfast and evening snack included in rates. Types of meals: continental-plus breakfast, gourmet breakfast and early coffee/tea. Beds: KQDT. Handicap access. Antiques, parks, shopping and theater nearby.

Location: Three-fourths of a mile south of village center.

Seen in: Los Angeles Times, Westways, Odyssey, Los Angeles.

"Your inn really defines the concept of country coziness and hospitality."

Certificate may be used: Sunday-Monday and/or Thursday-Friday. (B&B rooms only.)

Independence   J10

Winnedumah Inn
PO Box 147,
Independence, CA 93526-0147
(619)878-2040

Circa 1927. This old hotel was built in a Spanish Colonial style with arches, stucco and a front portico. Its location is at the foot of the Eastern Sierra in Owens Valley. Independence offers a trout-filled steam, majestic scenery and nearby hiking and fishing. The inn's restaurant will provide box lunches for these excursions.

Innkeeper(s): Marvey Chapman. $40-59. MC VISA. 22 rooms, 18 with PB. Breakfast included in rates. Types of meals: continental-plus breakfast and early coffee/tea. Banquet service and catering service available. Beds: QDT. Air conditioning in room. Cable TV, VCR, fax, copier, bicycles and library on premises. Handicap access. Fishing, downhill skiing, cross-country skiing and watersports nearby.

Certificate may be used: Feb. 1-July 1 except Memorial Day weekend Oct. 15-Dec. 30.

Inverness   H4

The Patterson House
PO Box 13, Inverness, CA 94937-0013
(415)669-1383 (800)690-1383
Fax:(415)669-1383

Circa 1916. Views of Tamales Bay with surrounding giant redwood trees, California oaks and Monterey pine trees await guests at this Craftsman-style inn perched on a hill. Guests are invited to read, sip port, plunk on the upright piano or just relax in front of the massive river rock fireplace. The breakfast room, which is next to the common room, has paned windows and French doors that open onto a wraparound deck.

Innkeeper(s): Rosalie Patterson. $113-145. MC VISA. 5 rooms with PB. Breakfast and afternoon tea included in rates. Type of meal: continental-plus breakfast. Beds: KQ. Antiques, fishing and watersports nearby.

Seen in: Country Inns.

"Understated elegance, nicest B&B we've ever stayed in."
Certificate may be used: Sunday through Thursday.

Rosemary Cottage
PO Box 273, Inverness, CA 94937-0273
(415)663-9338 (800)808-9338

Circa 1986. From the windows in this secluded cottage, guests enjoy views of a wooded canyon and hillside in the Pt. Reyes National Seashore Park. The cottage, which was designed by the host, is a cozy, self-contained hamlet with a well-equipped kitchen, bedroom and a living room with a wood-burning stove. The decor is French country, highlighting the beams, red oak floors and terra cotta tiles. The cottage's garden features a hot tub.

Innkeeper(s): Suzanne Storch. $150-160. PC TC. 3 cottages with PB, 3 with FP. Breakfast included in rates. Type of meal: full breakfast. Beds: QT. Spa on premises. Antiques, fishing, parks, shopping and watersports nearby.

Certificate may be used: Sunday-Friday, January-June, October-December, excluding holiday weeks.

Ten Inverness Way
10 Inverness Way, PO Box 63,
Inverness, CA 94937
(415)669-1648 Fax:(415)669-7403

Circa 1904. Shingled in redwood, this handsome bed & breakfast features a stone fireplace, good books, a player piano and access to a wonderful hiking area. The view from the breakfast room invites you to include a nature walk in your day's plans.

Innkeeper Mary Davies provides inside information on hiking the 100 square miles of wilderness and nearby beaches at Point Reyes National Seashore. She also offers a hot tub for weary travelers.

Innkeeper(s): Mary Davies & Barbara Searles. $110-160. MC VISA PC TC. 5 rooms with PB. Breakfast, afternoon tea and evening snack included in rates. Types of meals: full breakfast, gourmet breakfast and early coffee/tea. Beds: Q. Fax, spa and library on premises. Antiques, fishing, parks, shopping, theater and watersports nearby.

Location: Near Point Reyes National Seashore.

Seen in: Los Angeles Times, New York Times, Travel & Leisure, Sunset, Gourmet.

Certificate may be used: November-April, excluding holiday periods, Monday-Thursday.

Ione
G6

The Heirloom

214 Shakeley Ln, PO Box 322,
Ione, CA 95640-9572
(209)274-4468

Circa 1863. A two-story Colonial with columns, balconies and a private English garden, the antebellum Heirloom is true to its name. It has many family heirlooms and a square grand piano once owned by Lola Montez. The building was dedicated by the Native Sons of the Golden West as a historic site.

Innkeeper(s): Melisande Hubbs & Patricia Cross. $60-92. MC VISA AX PC TC. 6 rooms, 4 with PB, 3 with FP. 2 cottages. Breakfast and afternoon tea included in rates. Types of meals: full breakfast, gourmet breakfast and early coffee/tea. Room service available. Beds: KQDT. Air conditioning in room. Library on premises. Antiques, fishing, parks, shopping, cross-country skiing, theater and watersports nearby.
Location: California Gold Country - halfway between Yosemite and Lake Tahoe.
Seen in: San Francisco Chronicle, Country Living.

"Hospitality was amazing. Truly we've never had such a great time."
Certificate may be used: Sunday through Thursday, holidays excluded.

Isleton
H5

Delta Daze Inn

PO Box 607, Isleton, CA 95641-0607
(916)777-6794 (800)585-4667

Circa 1924. Once a bawdy house and gambling den, the Delta Daze Inn still retains its old Wild West flavor. A soda fountain area in the parlor relives the era when it was used as a front for more notorious prohibition activities. The Deltanental Room, used for breakfast and conferences, features an 18th-century, stained-glass archway that overlooks the Sacramento River Delta.
Innkeeper(s): Shirley & Frank Russell. $70-125. MC VISA PC. 12 rooms with PB. 1 suite. 1 conference room. Breakfast and afternoon tea

included in rates. Types of meals: full breakfast and early coffee/tea. Air conditioning and cable TV in room. Library on premises. Handicap access. Antiques, fishing, parks, shopping and watersports nearby.
Location: On the Sacramento River.

Seen in: Sunset.

"Fun, great inn, squeaky clean, quiet."

Certificate may be used: January through December.

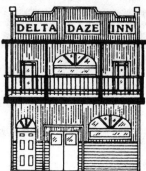

Jackson
G6

Court Street Inn

215 Court St, Jackson, CA 95642-2309
(209)223-0416 (800)200-0416
Fax:(209)223-5429

Circa 1872. This cheery yellow and white Victorian-era house is accentuated with green shutters and a porch stretching across the entire front. Behind the house, a two-story brick structure that once served as a Wells Fargo office and a museum for Indian artifacts now houses guests. Hors d'oeuvres and wine are served in the dining room under a pressed, carved tin ceiling. Guests relax in front of a marble fireplace in the parlor topped by a gilded mirror. Guest rooms are decorated in antiques. Downtown is only two blocks away.
Innkeeper(s): Gia & Scott Anderson. $75-180. MC VISA AX DS PC TC. 8 rooms, 7 with PB, 4 with FP. 1 suite. 1 cottage. Breakfast and afternoon tea included in rates. Types of meals: full breakfast and early coffee/tea. Evening snack available. Beds: KQD. Air conditioning, ceiling fan and cable TV in room. VCR, fax, copier and spa on premises. Antiques, fishing, parks, shopping, downhill skiing, cross-country skiing, theater and watersports nearby.
Location: In the center of the Gold Rush Highway 49.
Seen in: Amador Dispatch, Sunset, Brentwood News.

"Delightful! Thank you for the wonderful journey into yesteryear. Just what the doctor would have ordered. Keep the home fires burning. We'll be back soon."
Certificate may be used: Midweek, Sunday through Thursday, January through December.

Gate House Inn

1330 Jackson Gate Rd,
Jackson, CA 95642-9539
(209)223-3500 (800)841-1072
Fax:(209)223-1299

Circa 1902. This striking Victorian inn is listed in the National Register of Historic Places. Set on a hillside amid lovely gardens, the inn is within walk-

ing distance of a state historic park and several notable eateries. The inn's country setting, comfortable porches and swimming pool offer many opportunities for relaxation. Accommodations include three rooms, a suite and a romantic cottage with wood stove and whirlpool tub. All of the guest

rooms feature queen beds and elegant furnishings. Nearby are several lakes, wineries and golf courses. Innkeeper(s): Keith & Gail Sweet. $81-135. MC VISA AX DS PC TC. 5 rooms with PB, 3 with FP. 1 suite. 1 cottage. Breakfast included in rates. Types of meals: full breakfast and early coffee/tea. Afternoon tea available. Beds: Q. Air conditioning and ceiling fan in room. Fax, copier and swimming on premises. Antiques, fishing, parks, shopping, downhill skiing, cross-country skiing, theater and watersports nearby.

"Most gracious, warm hospitality."

Certificate may be used: Sunday-Thursday, holidays excluded. Weekends January only.

Wedgewood Inn

11941 Narcissus Rd,
Jackson, CA 95642-9600
(209)296-4300 (800)933-4393
Fax:(209)296-4301

Circa 1987. Located in the heart of Sierra gold country, this charming Victorian replica is crammed full of sentimental family heirlooms and antiques. Each room has been designed with careful attention to detail. A baby grand piano rests in the parlor. The carriage house is a separate cottage with its own private entrance. It boasts four generations of family heirlooms, a carved canopy bed, a wood-burning stove and a two-person Jacuzzi tub. The innkeepers' 1921 Model-T "Henry" is located in its own special showroom. Gourmet breakfasts are served on bone china and include specialties such as cheese-filled blintzes, fruit and baked goods. Afternoon cheese and beverages also are served each day.

Innkeeper(s): Vic & Jeannine Beltz. $90-155. MC VISA AX DS PC TC. 6 rooms with PB, 4 with FP. 1 suite. 1 cottage. Breakfast and evening snack included in rates. Types of meals: gourmet breakfast and early coffee/tea. Afternoon tea and room service available. Beds: Q. Air conditioning, turn-down service and ceiling fan in room. Copier, spa and library on premises. Antiques, fishing, parks, shopping, downhill skiing, cross-country skiing, theater and watersports nearby.

Certificate may be used: Sunday through Thursday inclusive, holiday weekends excluded. As available.

Jamestown H7

The Historic National Hotel B&B

77 Main St, PO Box 502,
Jamestown, CA 95327
(209)984-3446 (800)894-3446
Fax:(209)984-5620

Circa 1859. One of the 10 oldest continuously operating hotels in California, the inn maintains its original redwood bar where thousands of dollars in gold dust were spent. Electricity and plumbing were added for the first time when the inn was restored a few years ago. It is decorated with Gold Rush period antiques, brass beds and handmade quilts. The restaurant is considered to be one of the finest in the Mother Lode.

Innkeeper(s): Pamela & Stephen Willey. $80. MC VISA AX DC CB DS PC TC. 11 rooms, 5 with PB. 1 conference room. Breakfast included in rates. Types of meals: continental-plus breakfast and early coffee/tea. Dinner, evening snack, picnic lunch, lunch, gourmet lunch, banquet service and catering service available. Beds: QT. Air conditioning and cable TV in room. VCR and fax on premises. Antiques, fishing, parks, downhill skiing, cross-country skiing, theater and watersports nearby.

Location: Center of town.

Seen in: Bon Appetit, California, Focus, San Francisco, Gourmet.

"Excellent, wonderful place!"

Certificate may be used: Sunday through Thursday nights, holiday periods excluded. Based upon space availability.

Joshua Tree O13

Joshua Tree Inn

PO Box 340, Joshua Tree, CA 92252-0340
(619)366-1188 (800)366-1444
Fax:(619)366-3805

Circa 1950. The hacienda-style inn was once a '50s motel. It now offers Victorian-style rooms with king-size beds. Antiques and Old West memorabilia add to the decor. The inn is one mile from the gateway to the 467,000-acre Joshua Tree National Monument.

Innkeeper(s): Evelyn Shirbroun. $65-220. MAP. MC VISA AX. 11 rooms with PB. 2 suites. 1 conference room. Breakfast included in rates. Types of meals: full breakfast and early coffee/tea. Afternoon tea, evening snack, picnic lunch, lunch, gourmet lunch, banquet service,

catering service and room service available. Beds: K. Fax and copier on premises. Parks nearby.

Seen in: Los Angeles Times.

"Quiet, clean and charming."

Certificate may be used: Anytime, subject to availability.

Julian Q12

Julian Gold Rush Hotel
2032 Main St, PO Box 1856,
Julian, CA 92036
(619)765-0201 (800)734-5854

Circa 1897. The dream of a former slave and his wife lives today in this sole surviving hotel in Southern California's "Mother Lode of Gold Mining." This Victorian charmer is listed in the National Register of Historic Places and is a designated State of California Point of Historic Interest (#SDI-09). Guests enjoy the feeling of a visit to Grandma's and a tradition of genteel hospitality.

Innkeeper(s): Steve & Gig Ballinger. $72-160. MC VISA AX PC TC. 14 rooms with PB, 1 with FP. 1 suite. 2 cottages. 1 conference room. Breakfast and afternoon tea included in rates. Type of meal: full breakfast. Beds: QDT. Antiques, fishing, parks and theater nearby.

Location: Center of town.

Seen in: San Diego Union, PSA.

"Any thoughts you have about the 20th century will leave you when you walk into the lobby of this grand hotel- Westways Magazine."

Certificate may be used: Monday through Thursday, excluding holidays and weekends, shared baths only.

Julian White House
3014 Blue Jay Dr, PO Box 824, Julian,
CA 92036-9208
(619)765-1764 (800)948-4687

Circa 1979. Towering white pillars greet this inn's guests, who may feel they have traveled back in time to a Southern plantation. The attractive Colonial-style inn offers four luxurious guest rooms, including the Honeymoon Suite. The French Quarter Room features a New Orleans theme and Mardi Gras memorabilia, and the popular East Room boasts a goose down mattress and Laura Ashley linens on a queen-size Victorian-style brass bed. Guests often enjoy an evening at the Pine Hills Dinner Theatre, an easy walk from the inn.

Innkeeper(s): Mary & Alan Marvin. $90-135. MC VISA PC TC. 4 rooms with PB. 1 suite. Breakfast and evening snack included in rates. Types of meals: full breakfast and early coffee/tea. Beds: Q. Air conditioning and ceiling fan in room. Library on premises. Antiques, fishing, parks, cross-country skiing, theater and watersports nearby.

Seen in: San Diego Home/Garden, San Diego Union Tribune.

Certificate may be used: Monday-Thursday, except Easter and Christmas weeks.

Orchard Hill Country Inn
2502 Washington St, PO Box 425,
Julian, CA 92036-0425
(619)765-1700 Fax:(619)765-0290

Circa 1994. This charming Craftsman-style inn is a perfect country getaway for those seeking solace from the city lights. Expansive, individually appointed guest suites offer amenities such as fireplaces, whirlpool tubs, hand-knitted afghans and down comforters all surrounded by warm, country decor. Gourmet coffee, tea and cocoas also are provided in each suite, as are wet bars. The innkeepers also offer more than 100 games to help pass the time. Guests can enjoy a breakfast of fruits, muffins and a special egg dish on the porch or in the privacy of their room, and wine and hors d'oeuvres are provided each afternoon. The expansive grounds boast a variety of gardens highlighting native plants and flowers.

Innkeeper(s): Darrell & Pat Straube. $170-195. MC VISA AX PC TC. 22 rooms with PB, 11 with FP. 2 suites. 5 cottages. 2 conference rooms. Breakfast and evening snack included in rates. Types of meals: full breakfast and early coffee/tea. Dinner, picnic lunch, lunch, gourmet lunch, banquet service and catering service available. Restaurant on premises. Beds: KQ. Air conditioning, ceiling fan, cable TV and VCR in room. Fax, copier and library on premises. Handicap access. Antiques, fishing, parks, shopping, theater and watersports nearby.

Seen in: San Diego Union Tribune, Los Angeles Times, Orange County Register, Orange Coast, San Francisco Chronicle, San Bernardino Sun, Oceanside Blade-Citizen.

"The quality of the rooms, service and food were beyond our expectations."

Certificate may be used: January (excluding two weeks when closed) - December, Monday through Thursday, excluding holidays.

Random Oaks Ranch

3742 Pine Hills Rd, PO Box 454,
Julian, CA 92036
(619)765-1094 (800)262-4344
Fax:(619)765-0524

Guests at this inn, which doubles as a thoroughbred horse ranch, choose from two elegant cottages. The English Squire Cottage features a marble fireplace, Queen Anne furniture and a half-canopy queen bed. The Victorian Garden Cottage offers a custom-manteled fireplace, Queen Victorian cherry bed and sliding French doors. Both cottages sport private decks with spas, wet bars, microwave ovens and small refrigerators. Breakfast is served in the privacy of the cottages. The charming town of Julian is just two miles from the inn.

Innkeeper(s): Shari Foust-Helsel. $120-160. MC VISA. 2 suites. Breakfast included in rates. Types of meals: continental breakfast and full breakfast. Antiques, shopping and theater nearby.

Certificate may be used: Monday-Thursday, Jan. 2-Dec. 20 (holidays excluded).

Rockin' A B&B

1531 Orchard Ln, Julian, CA 92036-9607
(619)765-2820

Circa 1981. This contemporary woodsided ranch inn found in the countryside outside Julian offers a relaxing getaway for city folk. The inn boasts a private bass fishing facility and guests also visit the farm animals found on the grounds. The three guest rooms have private baths, and amenities include ceiling fans, a fireplace, spa and turndown service. The inn is a very popular anniversary and honeymoon destination. Visitors enjoy a full breakfast and evening snack and will find Julian a fun place to explore in their spare time.

Innkeeper(s): Gil & Dottie Archambeau. $89-145. MC VISA. 3 rooms with PB, 3 with FP. 1 suite. Breakfast and evening snack included in rates. Type of meal: full breakfast. Beds: QD. Turn-down service and ceiling fan in room. VCR and spa on premises. Antiques, fishing, parks, shopping, cross-country skiing and theater nearby.

Certificate may be used: Sunday through Thursday excluding holidays.

Kernville L10

Kern River Inn B&B

119 Kern River Dr, Kernville, CA 93238
(619)376-6750 (800)986-4382
Fax:(619)376-6643

Circa 1991. Located across from Riverside Park and the Kern River, this country-style inn boasts a wraparound porch with views and sounds of the river. The Whiskey Flat, Whitewater and Piute rooms include fireplaces. The Big Blue and

Greenhorn rooms offer whirlpool tubs. All rooms afford river views. Breakfasts at this AAA 3-diamond rated inn include the inn's renown, giant home-baked cinnamon rolls, egg and cheese dishes or sweetheart waffles.

Innkeeper(s): Jack & Carita Prestwich. $79-99. MC VISA AX PC TC. 6 rooms with PB, 3 with FP. Breakfast and afternoon tea included in rates. Types of meals: full breakfast and early coffee/tea. Beds: KQ. Air conditioning and ceiling fan in room. Cable TV, VCR, fax, copier and library on premises. Fishing, downhill skiing, cross-country skiing and watersports nearby.

Location: In the southern Sierra Nevada Mountains.

Seen in: Kern Valley Sun, Los Angeles Times, Valley News, Westaways

"For us, your place is the greatest. So romantic."

Certificate may be used: Nov. 1-March 31, Sunday-Thursday.

Laguna Beach P11

Carriage House

1322 Catalina,
Laguna Beach, CA 92651-3153
(714)494-8945

Circa 1922. A Laguna Beach historical landmark, this inn has a Cape Cod clapboard exterior. It housed an art gallery and a bakery before it was converted into apartments with large rooms and kitchens. Now as a cozy inn, each room has a private parlor. Outside, the courtyard fountain is shaded by a large carrotwood tree with hanging moss.

Innkeeper(s): Dee & Thom Taylor. $85-150. PC TC. 6 suites. Breakfast and evening snack included in rates. Type of meal: continental-plus breakfast. Beds: KQDT. Ceiling fan and cable TV in room. Antiques,

fishing, parks, shopping, theater and watersports nearby.

Location: Two & one-half blocks from the ocean.

Seen in: Glamour, Los Angeles Times, Orange County Register, Sunset.

"A true home away from home with all the extra touches added in. Reminds me of New Orleans."

Certificate may be used: Sunday through Thursday, September to June (as available).

Eiler's Inn

741 S Coast Hwy,
Laguna Beach, CA 92651-2722
(714)494-3004 Fax:(714)497-2215

Circa 1940. This New Orleans-style inn surrounds a lush courtyard and fountain. The rooms are decorated with antiques and wallpapers. Wine and cheese is served during the evening in front of the fireplace. Named after Eiler Larsen, famous town greeter of Laguna, the inn is just a stone's throw from the beach on the ocean side of Pacific Coast Highway.
Innkeeper(s): Henk & Annette Wirtz. $100-175. MC VISA AX. 12 rooms with PB, 1 with FP. 1 suite. Breakfast included in rates. Type of meal: continental-plus breakfast. Afternoon tea available. Beds: KQD.
Amusement parks, antiques, fishing, shopping and theater nearby.

Location: In the heart of the village.

Seen in: New York Times, Los Angeles Times, California Magazine, Home & Garden.

"Who could find a paradise more relaxing than an old-fashioned bed and breakfast with Mozart and Vivaldi, a charming fountain, wonderful fresh-baked bread, ocean air, and Henk's conversational wit?"

Certificate may be used: October-May, Sunday-Thursday.

Lake Arrowhead O11

Bracken Fern Manor

815 Arrowhead Villas Rd, PO Box 100,
Lake Arrowhead, CA 92352
(909)337-8557 Fax:(909)337-3323

Circa 1929. Opened during the height of the '20s as Lake Arrowhead's first membership resort, this country inn provided refuge to Silver Screen heroines, the wealthy and the prominent. Old letters

from the Gibson Girls found in the attic bespoke of elegant parties, dapper gentlemen, the Depression, Prohibition and homesick hearts. Each room is furnished with antiques collected from a lifetime of international travel. The Crestline Historical Society has its own museum and curator and a map of historical sites you can visit.
Innkeeper(s): Cheryl Weaver. $75-228. MC VISA AX. 10 rooms, 9 with PB. 3 suites. Breakfast and afternoon tea included in rates. Types of meals: continental-plus breakfast and early coffee/tea. Evening snack available. Beds: KQDT. Ceiling fan in room. Cable TV and VCR on premises. Antiques, fishing, shopping, downhill skiing, cross-country skiing, theater and watersports nearby.

Seen in: Mountain Shopper & Historic B&B, The Press Enterprise, Sun, Lava.

"My husband brought me here for my 25th birthday and it was everything I hoped it would be - peaceful, romantic and so relaxing ... Thank you for the wonderful memories I will hold close to my heart always."

Certificate may be used: Anytime except holidays.

Storybook Inn

28717 Hwy 18,
Lake Arrowhead, CA 92385
(909)336-1483

Circa 1942. Formerly known as the Fouch Estate, this 9,000-square-foot home illustrates Mr. Fouch's romantic flair. Its abundant mahogany paneling was bleached to match the color of his bride's hair! Two massive brick fireplaces dominate the main lobby. The three-story inn has enclosed solariums and porches. A hot tub nestled under ancient oaks provides a view of snow-capped mountains, forests and on clear days, the Pacific Ocean.
Innkeeper(s): John & Kathleen Wooley; Michelle Young. $75-185. MC VISA AX DS TC. 11 rooms with PB, 3 with FP. 6 suites. 1 conference room. Breakfast and evening snack included in rates. Types of meals: full breakfast, gourmet breakfast and early coffee/tea. Picnic lunch, catering service and room service available. Beds: KQD. Ceiling fan in room. Cable TV, VCR and spa on premises. Handicap access. Amusement parks, antiques, fishing, parks, shopping, downhill skiing, cross-country skiing, theater and watersports nearby.

Seen in: Los Angeles Times, Los Angeles, California, San Bernardino Sun, Orange County Register, Victorville Valley Press.

Certificate may be used: Year-round, Sunday through Thursday. Holidays excepted on rooms over $140.

Lakeport F4

Forbestown B&B Inn

825 Forbes St, Lakeport, CA 95453
(707)263-7858 Fax:(707)263-7878

Circa 1863. Located in the downtown area, this early California farmhouse is two blocks from the lake. Wisteria drape the front porch, overlooking the inn's yard. The dining room, where gourmet

breakfasts are served, has a wall of French windows looking out to the back garden with a tall redwood tree and handsome flagstone swimming pool. Clear Lake is fed by rain and underground sulfur and soda springs. The area has been acknowledged as having the cleanest air in California.

Innkeeper(s): Jack & Nancy Dunne. $75-150. MC VISA AX PC TC. 4 rooms, 1 with PB. 1 cottage. Breakfast, afternoon tea and evening snack included in rates. Types of meals: full breakfast, gourmet breakfast and early coffee/tea. Catered breakfast available. Beds: KQ. Turndown service and ceiling fan in room. Cable TV, VCR, fax, copier, spa, swimming and library on premises. Antiques, fishing, parks, shopping and watersports nearby.

Certificate may be used: Sunday through Thursday, year-round.

Little River   F2

The Victorian Farmhouse
7001 N Highway 1,
Little River, CA 95456
(707)937-0697 (800)264-4723

Circa 1877. Built as a private residence, this Victorian farmhouse is located on two-and-a-half acres in Little River. Two miles south of the historic village of Mendocino, the inn offers a relaxed country setting with deer, quail, flower gardens, an apple orchard and a running creek (School House Creek). A short walk will take you to the shoreline.

Innkeeper(s): Carole Molnar. $65-160. MC VISA AX. 10 rooms with PB. Breakfast and afternoon tea included in rates. Type of meal: full breakfast. Beds: KQT. Bicycles and tennis on premises. Amusement parks, antiques, fishing, parks, shopping, theater and watersports nearby.

"This morning when we woke up at home we really missed having George deliver breakfast. You have a lovely inn and you do a super job."

Certificate may be used: Sunday-Thursday, Sept. 15-June 30; holidays or holiday weeks excluded.

Los Olivos   N7

Los Olivos Grand Hotel
2860 Grand Ave, Los Olivos, CA 93441
(805)688-7788 (800)446-2455
Fax:(805)688-1942

Circa 1985. This four-star, four-diamond inn is ideally located in the Santa Ynez Valley, with its picturesque vineyards and rolling hills. Each guest room is decorated with the artwork of a different western or classic impressionist artist. There are fireplaces and many rooms also offer Jacuzzi tubs. Down comforters, room service, laundry service and in-room mini refrigerators are among the many amenities, and the hotel offers plenty of items to help business travelers. A full breakfast and afternoon tea are served daily, and the hotel's Remington Restaurant features an extensive dinner menu. Cocktails are available at Le Saloon, located in the lounge. There is a heated swimming pool and Jacuzzi on the premises, and arrangements can be made to rent bicycles and tour the countryside.

Innkeeper(s): Ken Mortensen. $160-325. MC VISA AX. 21 rooms with PB, 21 with FP. 1 suite. 3 conference rooms. Breakfast and afternoon tea included in rates. Types of meals: full breakfast, gourmet breakfast and early coffee/tea. Dinner, picnic lunch, lunch, gourmet lunch, banquet service, catering service, catered breakfast and room service available. Beds: KQ. Air conditioning, turn-down service, ceiling fan and cable TV in room. Fax, copier, spa, swimming and bicycles on premises. Antiques, fishing, parks, shopping and watersports nearby.

Certificate may be used: January-July; November-December (excluding August, September, October) Sunday-Thursday only - holidays & special events not included.

Lucerne   F4

Kristalberg B&B
PO Box 1629, Lucerne, CA 95458-1629
(707)274-8009

This country B&B affords a panoramic view of Clear Lake and surrounding mountain areas. Each of the guest rooms in furnished and decorated in a different period style. The master suite offers French Provencal design, other rooms feature 18th-century motifs. The parlor is decked in 18th-century Italian influences, while the dining area is pure Americana. The expansive breakfast is served in the home's formal dining room. German and Spanish are spoken at the B&B.

Innkeeper(s): Merv Myers. $55-150. MC VISA AX DS. 3 rooms. Breakfast included in rates. Type of meal: full breakfast.

Certificate may be used: November through March and weekdays (Sunday-Friday) April-October, also weekends on a stand-by basis.

Mariposa I8

Rockwood Gardens

5155 Tip Top Rd,
Mariposa, CA 95338-9003
(209)742-6817 (800)859-8862
Fax:(209)742-7400

Circa 1989. Nestled among the pines in the Sierra foothills, this contemporary Prairie-style inn was designed and built to complement the natural beauty found nearby. A creek, oaks, pond and wildflower meadow all are part of the inn's setting. Guests often use the inn as headquarters when exploring the many wonders of Yosemite National Park. Visitors select from the Rose, Duck and Manzanita rooms. Stroll the grounds and relish the fine view of evening stars.

Innkeeper(s): Gerald & Mary Ann Fuller. $65-95. TC. 3 rooms, 1 with FP. 1 suite. 1 conference room. Breakfast included in rates. Type of meal: continental-plus breakfast. Picnic lunch available. Beds: KQD. Air conditioning, ceiling fan and VCR in room. Cable TV, fax and copier on premises. Antiques, fishing, parks, shopping, downhill skiing, cross-country skiing and watersports nearby.

Certificate may be used: Jan. 2 to April 15 & Oct. 1 to Dec. 2, every day.

McCloud B5

McCloud Hotel B&B

PO Box 730, McCloud, CA 96057-0730
(916)964-2822 (800)964-2823
Fax:(916)964-2844

Circa 1915. Having once provided housing for mill workers and teachers, this inn is a nationally registered historic landmark. Guests may listen to music from the past in the lobby, which is furnished with an original registration desk, overstuffed honest

chair and a '30s style sofa. Board games, books and puzzles also can be found in the lobby. Guest rooms feature coordinated decorator fabrics and antique vanities and trunks.

Innkeeper(s): Marilyn & Lee Ogden. $68-130. MC VISA. 18 rooms with PB. 4 suites. 1 conference room. Breakfast and afternoon tea included in rates. Types of meals: full breakfast and early coffee/tea. Room service available. Beds: QT. Ceiling fan in room. Cable TV, fax and copier

on premises. Handicap access. Fishing, shopping, downhill skiing, cross-country skiing and watersports nearby.

Seen in: Redding Searchlight, Mount Shasta Herald, Siskiyou County Annual Progress Paper.

Certificate may be used: Anytime, no holidays.

Mendocino F2

Whitegate Inn

499 Howard St, Mendocino, CA 95460
(707)937-4892 (800)531-7282
Fax:(707)937-1131

Circa 1883. When it was first built, the local newspaper called Whitegate Inn "one of the most elegant and best appointed residences in town." It is resplendent with bay windows, a steep gabled roof, redwood siding and fishscale shingles. The house's

original wallpaper and candlelabras adorn the double parlors. There, an antique 1827 piano, at one time part of Alexander Graham Bell's collection, and inlaid pocket doors take you back to a simpler time. French and Victorian antique furnishings and a collection of early American cut glass add a crowning touch to the inn's elegant hospitality.

Innkeeper(s): Carol & George Bechtloff. $89-179. MC VISA AX DS TC. 6 rooms with PB, 6 with FP. 2 suites. 1 conference room. Breakfast and afternoon tea included in rates. Types of meals: full breakfast, gourmet breakfast and early coffee/tea. Beds: KQT. Cable TV in room. Fax on premises. Antiques, fishing, parks, shopping, theater and watersports nearby.

Location: One block from shopping in town & restaurants.

Seen in: Innsider, Country Inns, Country Home.

"Made our honeymoon a dream come true."

Certificate may be used: Dec. 1 through April 30 - Monday through Thursday only. No weekends, no holidays.

Mill Valley
H4

Mountain Home Inn

810 Panoramic Hwy,
Mill Valley, CA 94941-1765
(415)381-9000 Fax:(415)381-3615

Circa 1912. At one time the only way to get to
Mountain Home was by taking the train up Mount
Tamalpais. With 22 trestles and 281 curves, it was
called "the crookedest railroad in the world." Now
accessible by auto, the trip still provides a spectacular view of San Francisco Bay. Each guest room has
a view of the mountain, valley or bay.

Innkeeper(s): Lynn Saggese. $99-239. MC VISA AX PC TC. 10 rooms
with PB, 5 with FP. 1 conference room. Breakfast included in rates. Type
of meal: full breakfast. Picnic lunch and lunch available. Beds: QD. Fax
and copier on premises. Parks and shopping nearby.

Location: Mt. Tamalpais.

Seen in: San Francisco Examiner, California Magazine.

*"A luxurious retreat. Echoes the grand style and rustic
feeling of national park lodges — Ben Davidson, Travel
& Leisure."*

Certificate may be used: Nov. 1 to March 30, Monday-Thursday.
Holiday periods excluded.

Montara
I4

The Goose & Turrets B&B

835 George St, PO Box 937,
Montara, CA 94037-0937
(415)728-5451 Fax:(415)728-0141

Circa 1908. In the peaceful setting of horse ranches, strawflower farms and an art colony, this Italian
villa features beautiful gardens surrounded by a 20-
foot-high cypress hedge. The gardens include an
orchard, vegetable garden, herb garden, rose garden,
fountains, a hammock, swing and plenty of spots to
enjoy the surroundings. The large dining and living
room areas are filled with art, collectibles and classical music plays during afternoon tea. Among its
many previous uses, the Goose & Turrets once
served as Montara's first post office, the town hall, a
Sunday school and a grocery store.

Innkeeper(s): Raymond & Emily Hoche-Mong. $85-120. MC VISA AX
DS PC TC. 5 rooms with PB, 3 with FP. Breakfast and afternoon tea
included in rates. Beds: KQDT. Turn-down service in room. Library on
premises. Antiques, fishing, parks and watersports nearby.

Location: One-half mile from the Pacific Ocean, 20 minutes from San
Francisco airport.

Seen in: San Jose Mercury News, Half Moon Bay Review, Peninsula
Times Tribune, San Mateo Times, Los Angeles Times, Tri-Valley Herald,
Contra Costa Times.

*"Lots of special touches. Great Southern hospitality —
we'll be back."*

Certificate may be used: All year, Monday-Thursday.

Monterey
J5

The Jabberwock

598 Laine St, Monterey, CA 93940-1312
(408)372-4777 Fax:(408)655-2946

Circa 1911. Set in a half-acre of gardens, this
Victorian inn provides a fabulous view of Monterey
Bay and its famous barking seals. When you're ready

to settle in for the evening, you'll find huge Victorian
beds complete with lace-edged sheets and goose-
down comforters. Early evening hors d'oeuvres and
aperitifs are served in an enclosed veranda. After dinner, guests are tucked into bed with cookies and milk.

Innkeeper(s): Barbara Allen. $105-190. MC VISA. 7 rooms, 3 with PB, 1
with FP. 2 suites. Breakfast and afternoon tea included in rates. Types of
meals: gourmet breakfast and early coffee/tea. Evening snack available.
Beds: KQT. Fax, copier and library on premises. Amusement parks,
antiques, fishing, parks, shopping, theater and watersports nearby.

Location: Four blocks above Cannery Row, the beach and Monterey
Bay Aquarium.

Seen in: Sunset, Travel & Leisure, Sacramento Bee, San Francisco
Examiner, Los Angeles Times, Country Inns, San Francisco Chronicle,
Diablo, Elmer Dills KABC-Los Angeles TV.

*"Words are not enough to describe the ease and tran-
quility of the atmosphere of the house, rooms, owners
and staff of Jabberwock."*

Certificate may be used: November through April, Sunday-Thursday.

Mount Shasta
B5

Mount Shasta Ranch B&B

1008 W.A. Barr Rd,
Mount Shasta, CA 96067-9465
(916)926-3870 Fax:(916)926-6882

Circa 1923. This large two-story ranch house offers a full view of Mt. Shasta from its 60-foot-long redwood porch. Spaciousness abounds from the 1,500-square-foot living room with a massive rock fireplace to the large suites with private bathrooms that include large tubs and roomy showers. A full country breakfast may offer cream cheese-stuffed French toast or fresh, wild blackberry crepes. Just minutes away, Lake Siskiyou boasts superb fishing, sailing, swimming, and 18 hole golf course with public tennis courts.

Innkeeper(s): Bill & Mary Larsen. $50-95. MC VISA AX DS PC TC. 9 rooms, 4 with PB. 1 cottage. 1 conference room. Breakfast included in rates. Types of meals: full breakfast and early coffee/tea. Afternoon tea available. Beds: Q. Air conditioning, ceiling fan and cable TV in room. VCR, fax, copier, spa and library on premises. Antiques, fishing, parks, shopping, downhill skiing, cross-country skiing and watersports nearby.

Certificate may be used: Anytime.

Murphys
H7

Dunbar House, 1880

271 Jones St, PO Box 1375,
Murphys, CA 95247-9629
(209)728-2897 (800)692-6006
Fax:(209)728-1451

Circa 1880. A picket fence frames this Italianate home, built by Willis Dunbar for his bride. The porch, lined with rocking chairs, is the perfect place to take in the scenery of century-old gardens decorated by fountains, birdhouses and swings. A collection of antiques, family heirlooms and comfortable furnishings fill the interior. The two-room garden suite includes a bed dressed with fine linens and a down comforter and a two-person Jacuzzi spa. Guests can enjoy the morning fare in the dining room, garden or opt for breakfast in bed.

Innkeeper(s): Bob & Barbara Costa. $115-155. MC VISA AX PC TC. 4 rooms with PB, 4 with FP. 1 suite. Breakfast and afternoon tea included in rates. Types of meals: full breakfast, gourmet breakfast and early coffee/tea. Room service available. Beds: KQ. Air conditioning, turn-down service, ceiling fan, cable TV and VCR in room. Fax, copier and library on premises. Antiques, fishing, parks, shopping, downhill skiing, cross-country skiing, theater and watersports nearby.

Location: Two blocks from the center of town.

Seen in: Los Angeles Times, Gourmet, Victorian Homes, Country Inns, Travel & Leisure.

"Your beautiful gardens and gracious hospitality combine for a super bed & breakfast."

Certificate may be used: Sunday-Thursday only, excluding holidays.

Napa
H4

Beazley House

1910 1st St, Napa, CA 94559-2351
(707)257-1649 (800)559-1649
Fax:(707)257-1518

Circa 1902. Nestled in green lawns and gardens, this graceful shingled mansion is frosted with white trim on its bays and balustrades. Stained-glass windows and polished-wood floors set the atmosphere

in the parlor. There are six rooms in the main house and the carriage house features five more, many with fireplaces and whirlpool tubs. The venerable Beazley House was Napa's first bed & breakfast inn.

Innkeeper(s): Carol, Jim & Scott Beazley. $105-195. MC VISA. 11 rooms with PB, 6 with FP. 5 suites. 1 conference room. Breakfast and afternoon tea included in rates. Types of meals: full breakfast and early coffee/tea. Beds: KQDT. Air conditioning and ceiling fan in room. Fax on premises. Handicap access. Antiques, fishing, parks and shopping nearby.

Location: In the historic neighborhood of Old Town Napa, at the south end of Napa Valley.

Seen in: Los Angeles Times, USA Today, Emergo, Sacramento Bee.

"There's a sense of peace & tranquility that hovers over this house, sprinkling magical dream dust & kindness."

Certificate may be used: Dec. 1-23, Sunday through Thursday and Jan. 2-30, Sunday-Thursday.

Blue Violet Mansion

443 Brown St, Napa, CA 94559-3349
(707)253-2583 (800)959-2583
Fax:(707)257-8205

Circa 1886. English lampposts, a Victorian gazebo, and a rose garden welcome guests to this blue and white Queen Anne Victorian. Listed in the National Register, the house was originally built for a tannery executive. There are three-story bays, and from the balconies guests often view hot air balloons in the early morning. Three rooms feature

two-person spas and five have fireplaces. A full breakfast is served in the dining room. The innkeepers offer room service by request. Nearby is the wine train and restaurants.

Innkeeper(s): Kathy & Bob Morris. $145-285. MC VISA AX DC DS PC TC. 14 rooms with PB, 11 with FP. 3 suites. 1 conference room. Breakfast and evening snack included in rates. Types of meals: full breakfast and early coffee/tea. Dinner, picnic lunch, banquet service, catering service, catered breakfast and room service available. Beds: KQ. Air conditioning, turn-down service, ceiling fan and cable TV in room. VCR, fax, copier, spa and swimming on premises. Handicap access. Amusement parks, antiques, fishing, parks, shopping, theater and watersports nearby.

Seen in: America's Painted Ladies.

Certificate may be used: Sunday through Thursday, November through July.

The Hennessey House B&B

1727 Main St, Napa, CA 94559-1844
(707)226-3774 Fax:(707)226-2975

Circa 1889. This gracious Queen Anne Eastlake Victorian was once home to Dr. Edwin Hennessey, a Napa County physician. Pristinely renovated, the inn features stained-glass windows and a curving wraparound porch. A handsome hand-painted, stamped-tin ceiling graces the dining room. All rooms are furnished in antiques. The four guest rooms in the carriage house boast whirlpool baths, fireplaces or patios.

Innkeeper(s): Andrea LaMar. $80-155. MC VISA AX DS. 10 rooms with PB, 4 with FP. Breakfast included in rates. Type of meal: full breakfast. Beds: KQT. Air conditioning, ceiling fan and cable TV in room. Fax, spa and sauna on premises. Antiques and shopping nearby.

Location: One hour from San Francisco.
Seen in: AM-PM Magazine.

"Thank you for making our stay very pleasant."

Certificate may be used: November-June, Sunday-Thursday, non-holiday. Carriage House rooms only in winter months.

La Belle Epoque

1386 Calistoga Ave,
Napa, CA 94559-2552
(707)257-2161 (800)238-8070
Fax:(707)226-6314

This Queen Anne Victorian has a wine cellar and tasting room where guests can casually sip Napa Valley wines. The inn, which is one of the most unique architectural structures found in the wine country, is located in the heart of Napa's Calistoga Historic District. Beautiful original stained-glass windows include a window from an old church. A selection of fine restaurants and shops are within easy walking distance, as well as the riverfront, city parks and the Wine Train Depot. The train, which serves all meals, takes you just beyond St. Helena and back.

Innkeeper(s): Claudia Wedepohl. $110-145. MC VISA AX DS. 6 rooms. Breakfast included in rates. Types of meals: full breakfast and early coffee/tea. Air conditioning and ceiling fan in room. Cable TV and VCR on premises. Amusement parks, antiques, shopping, sporting events and theater nearby.

Certificate may be used: Dec. 1-23, Jan. 1-March 15, Monday-Thursday, holidays excluded.

Stahlecker House B&B
Country Inn & Garde

1042 Easum Dr, Napa, CA 94558-5525
(707)257-1588 (800)799-1588
Fax:(707)224-7429

Circa 1947. Situated on the banks of a tree-lined creek this ranch-style home, a former bakery, is on

one and a half acres. Antique tools hang on the wall of the Emerald Tool Room. Amy's Blue Rose Room is distinguished with rose wallpaper and a view of the rose garden. All have queen-size canopy beds. The Napa Wine Train station is five minutes away.

Innkeeper(s): Ron & Ethel Stahlecker. $95-185. MC VISA AX TC. 4 rooms with PB, 4 with FP. 1 suite. Breakfast and evening snack included in rates. Types of meals: full breakfast, gourmet breakfast and early coffee/tea. Afternoon tea, picnic lunch and catered breakfast available. Beds: QT. Air conditioning, turn-down service and ceiling fan in room. Fax, spa and library on premises. Antiques, fishing, parks, shopping, theater and watersports nearby.

Seen in: Napa Valley Traveller.

"Friendly hosts and beautiful gardens."

Certificate may be used: Feb. 28 to July 31, Oct. 1 to Dec. 20, Monday to Thursday (not Friday, Saturday or Sunday)

Nevada City   F6

Emma Nevada House

528 E Broad St,
Nevada City, CA 95959-2213
(916)265-4415 (800)916-3662
Fax:(916)265-4416

Circa 1856. What is considered the childhood home of 19th-century opera star Emma Nevada now serves as an attractive Queen Anne Victorian inn. English roses line the white picket fence in front,

and the forest-like back garden has a small stream with benches. The Empress' Chamber is the most romantic room with ivory Italian linens atop a French antique bed, a bay window and a massive French armoire. Some rooms have whirlpool baths. Guests enjoy relaxing in the hexagonal sunroom and on the inn's wraparound porches. Empire Mine State Historic Park is nearby.

Innkeeper(s): Ruth Ann Riese. $90-150. MC VISA AX PC TC. 6 rooms with PB, 1 with FP. Breakfast and afternoon tea included in rates. Types of meals: full breakfast and early coffee/tea. Beds: Q. Air conditioning in room. Cable TV, fax and library on premises. Antiques, fishing, parks, shopping, downhill skiing, theater and watersports nearby.

Seen in: The Union.

"A delightful experience: such airiness and hospitality in the midst of so much history. We were fascinated by the detail and the faithfulness of the restoration. This house is a quiet solace for city-weary travelers. There's a grace here."

Certificate may be used: Jan. 2-Nov. 22.

The Red Castle Inn

109 Prospect St,
Nevada City, CA 95959-2831
(916)265-5135 (800)761-4766

Circa 1860. The Smithsonian has lauded the restoration of this four-story brick Gothic Revival known as "The Castle" by townsfolk. Its roof is laced with wooden icicles and the balconies are adorned with gingerbread. Within, there are intricate moldings, antiques, Victorian wallpapers, canopy beds and woodstoves. Verandas provide views of the historic city through cedar, chestnut and walnut trees, and of terraced gardens with a fountain pond.

Innkeeper(s): Conley & Mary Louise Weaver. $100-125. MC VISA PC TC. 7 rooms with PB. 3 suites. Breakfast and afternoon tea included in rates. Types of meals: full breakfast, gourmet breakfast and early coffee/tea. Catering service available. Beds: QD. Air conditioning and turn-down service in room. Library on premises. Antiques, fishing, parks, shopping, downhill skiing, cross-country skiing, theater and watersports nearby.

Location: Within the Nevada City historic district overlooking the town.

Seen in: Sunset, Gourmet, Sacramento Bee, Los Angeles Times, Travel Holiday, Victorian

Homes, Innsider, San Francisco Focus 1992 Grand Hotel Award, US News and World Report, USAir, McCalls, New York Times.

"The Red Castle Inn would top my list of places to stay. Nothing else quite compares with it-Gourmet."

Certificate may be used: Sunday through Thursday, April 1 through Aug. 31 except Easter week and town special events; Sunday through Friday, Jan. 1-March 31 except town special events.

Nice
F4

Featherbed Railroad Company B&B
2870 Lakeshore Blvd, PO Box 4016,
Nice, CA 95464
(707)274-4434

Circa 1940. Located on five acres on Clear Lake, this unusual inn features guest rooms in five luxuriously renovated, painted, and papered cabooses. Each has its own featherbed and private bath. The Southern Pacific cabooses have a bay window alcove, while those from the Santa Fe feature small cupolas. Bicycles, canopied patio boats and jet skis are available for rent.

Innkeeper(s): Lorraine Bassignani. $90-140. MC VISA AX DS. 9 rooms, 5 with PB. Breakfast included in rates. Type of meal: full breakfast. Beds: DT. Spa on premises.
Seen in: Santa Rosa Press Democrat, Fairfield Daily Republic.
Certificate may be used: Sunday-Thursday, Oct. 15-April 15.

Nipomo
M7

The Kaleidoscope Inn
130 E Dana St, Nipomo, CA 93444-1297
(805)929-5444

Circa 1887. The sunlight that streams through the stained-glass windows of this charming Victorian creates a kaleidoscope effect and thus the name. The inn is surrounded by gardens. Each romantic guest room is decorated with antiques and the library offers a fireplace. Fresh flowers add a special touch. Breakfast is either served in the  dining room, or in the gardens or in your room.

Innkeeper(s): Pat Linane. $80. MC VISA AX. 3 rooms with PB. 1 conference room. Breakfast, afternoon tea and evening snack included in rates. Types of meals: full breakfast, gourmet breakfast and early coffee/tea. Room service available. Beds: KQ. Turn-down service and ceiling fan in room. Cable TV, VCR and library on premises. Antiques,

fishing, parks, shopping, theater and watersports nearby.
Location: Twenty miles south of San Luis Obispo, near Pismo Beach.
Seen in: Santa Maria Times, Los Angeles Times, Country.

"Beautiful room, chocolates, fresh flowers, peaceful night's rest, great breakfast."

Certificate may be used: Anytime other than three-day holidays.

Oakland
H4

Dockside Boat & Bed
77 Jack London Sq,
Oakland, CA 94607-3732
(510)444-5858 (800)436-2574
Fax:(510)444-0420

Enjoy views of San Francisco's skyline at this unique bed & breakfast, which offers dockside lodging aboard private motor or sailing yachts. The yachts vary in size from a cozy 35-foot vessel to a 60-foot yacht. Each boat includes staterooms, galleys, bathrooms and living/dining areas. A continental breakfast is served each morning. Private charters and catered, candlelight dinners can be arranged. The yachts are docked at Pier 39 in San Francisco and Jack London Square in Oakland. Both locations are convenient to restaurants, shops and other attractions.

Innkeeper(s): Rob & Mollie Harris. $95-275. MC VISA AX DS TC. 9 rooms, 6 with PB, 1 with FP. Breakfast included in rates. Type of meal: continental breakfast. Picnic lunch and catering service available. Beds: QDT. VCR in room. Fax and copier on premises. Antiques, fishing, parks, shopping, sporting events, theater and watersports nearby.
Location: On San Francisco Bay.
Seen in: People, San Jose Mercury News, San Francisco Chronicle, Portland Oregonian, Denver Post, Washington Post.
Certificate may be used: Sunday through Thursday evenings (maximum 12 nights per year), Nov. 1 through May 31.

Orland
E5

The Inn at Shallow Creek Farm
4712 County Road DD,
Orland, CA 95963-9336
(916)865-4093 (800)865-4093

Circa 1900. This vine-covered farmhouse was once the center of a well-known orchard and sheep ranch. The old barn, adjacent to the farmhouse, was a livery stop. The citrus orchard, now restored, blooms with 165 trees. Apples, pears, peaches, apricots, persimmons, walnuts, figs, and pomegranates are also grown here. Guests can meander to examine the Polish crested chickens, silver guinea fowl, Muscovy ducks, and African geese. The old caretaker's house is now a four-room guest cottage.

Hundreds of narcissus grow along the creek that flows through the property.

Innkeeper(s): Mary & Kurt Glaeseman. $55-75. MC VISA PC. 4 rooms, 2 with PB. 1 suite. Breakfast included in rates. Types of meals: continental-plus breakfast and early coffee/tea. Beds: QT. Air conditioning and ceiling fan in room. Library on premises. Antiques, fishing, parks and theater nearby.

Location: Northern California, 3 miles off Interstate 5.

Seen in: Adventure Road, Orland Press Register, Focus, Chico Enterprise Record.

"Now that we've discovered your country oasis, we hope to return as soon as possible."

Certificate may be used: Monday-Thursday, all year.

Pacific Grove   J5

Gatehouse Inn

225 Central Ave,
Pacific Grove, CA 93950-3017
(408)649-8436 (800)753-1881
Fax:(408)648-8044

Circa 1884. This Italianate Victorian seaside inn is just a block from the ocean and Monterey Bay. The inn is decorated with Victorian and 20th-century antiques and touches of Art Deco. Guest rooms

feature fireplaces, clawfoot tubs and down comforters. Some rooms have ocean views. The dining room boasts opulent Bradbury & Bradbury Victorian wallpapers as do some of the guest rooms. Afternoon hors d'oeuvres, wine and tea are served. The refrigerator is stocked for snacking.

Innkeeper(s): Lois Deford. $110-150. MC VISA AX DS PC TC. 9 rooms with PB, 5 with FP. Breakfast, afternoon tea and evening snack included in rates. Types of meals: full breakfast, gourmet breakfast and early coffee/tea. Beds: KQT. Turn-down service in room. Fax, copier and bicycles on premises. Handicap access. Antiques, fishing, parks, shopping, theater and watersports nearby.

Location: One block from the ocean.

Seen in: San Francisco Chronicle, Monterey Herald, Time, Newsweek, Inland Empire, Bon Appetit.

"Thank you for spoiling us."

Certificate may be used: Jan. 1-April 30, Sunday-Thursday.

Gosby House Inn

643 Lighthouse Ave,
Pacific Grove, CA 93950-2643
(408)375-1287 (800)527-8828
Fax:(408)655-9621

Circa 1887. Built as an upscale Victorian inn for those visiting the old Methodist retreat, this sunny yellow mansion features an abundance of gables, turrets and bays. During renovation the innkeeper slept in all the rooms to determine just what antiques were needed and how the beds should be

situated. Ten of the romantic rooms include fireplaces and many offer canopy beds. The Carriage House rooms include fireplaces, decks and spa tubs. Gosby House, which has been open to guests for more than a century, is in the National Register.

Innkeeper(s): Tess Arthur. $90-150. MC VISA AX TC. 22 rooms, 20 with PB, 11 with FP. Breakfast and afternoon tea included in rates.

Types of meals: full breakfast, gourmet breakfast and early coffee/tea. Beds: QD. Turn-down service in room. Fax, copier and bicycles on premises. Handicap access. Antiques and shopping nearby.

Location: Six blocks from the ocean.

Seen in: San Francisco Chronicle, Oregonian, Los Angeles Times, Travel & Leisure.

Certificate may be used: November-March Sunday-Thursday excluding holidays & special events.

Green Gables Inn

104 5th St,
Pacific Grove, CA 93950-2903
(408)375-2095 (800)722-1774
Fax:(408)375-5437

Circa 1888. This half-timbered Queen Anne Victorian appears as a fantasy of gables overlooking spectacular Monterey Bay. The parlor has stained-glass panels framing the fireplace and bay windows looking out to the sea. A favorite focal point is an

antique carousel horse. Most of the guest rooms have panoramic views of the ocean, fireplaces, gleaming woodwork, soft quilts, and flowers. Across the street is the Monterey Bay paved oceanfront cycling path. (Mountain bikes may be borrowed from the inn.)

Innkeeper(s): Emily Frew. $100-160. MC VISA AX TC. 11 rooms, 6 with PB, 6 with FP. 1 suite. Breakfast and afternoon tea included in rates. Types of meals: full breakfast, gourmet breakfast and early coffee/tea. Beds: KQD. Turn-down service in room. Fax, copier and bicycles on premises. Handicap access. Antiques, shopping and theater nearby.

Location: On Monterey Bay four blocks from Monterey Bay Aquarium.

Seen in: Travel & Leisure, Country Living.

Certificate may be used: December; January (excluding February-November) Sunday-Thursday no holidays, special events.

Old St. Angela Inn

321 Central Ave,
Pacific Grove, CA 93950-2934
(408)372-3246 (800)748-6306
Fax:(408)372-8560

Circa 1910. Formerly a convent, this Cape-style inn has been restored and includes a glass solarium

where breakfast is served. The ocean is a block away and it's just a short walk to the aquarium or fisherman's wharf.

Innkeeper(s): Lewis Shaefer & Susan Kuslis. $90-115. MC VISA DS PC TC. 8 rooms, 5 with PB. Breakfast, afternoon tea and evening snack included in rates. Types of meals: full breakfast, gourmet breakfast and early coffee/tea. Beds: QDT. Fax and spa on premises. Antiques, fishing, parks, shopping, theater and watersports nearby.

"Outstanding inn and outstanding hospitality."

Certificate may be used: Nov. 1-30, Jan. 1-April 30, Sunday-Thursday.

Palm Springs   O12

Casa Cody Country Inn

175 S Cahuilla Rd,
Palm Springs, CA 92262-6331
(619)320-9346 (800)231-2639
Fax:(619)325-8610

Circa 1920. Casa Cody, built by a relative of Wild Bill Cody and situated in the heart of Palm Springs, is the town's second-oldest operating inn. The San Jacinto Mountains provide a scenic background for the tree-shaded spa, the pink bougainvillea and the blue waters of the inn's two swimming pools. Each suite has a small kitchenette and features a soft-pink and turquoise Southwestern decor. Several have wood-burning fireplaces. There are Mexican pavers, French doors and private patios.

Innkeeper(s): Elissa Goforth. $49-185. MC VISA AX DC CB DS PC TC. 23 rooms, 25 with PB, 10 with FP. 8 suites. 2 cottages. Breakfast included in rates. Type of meal: continental-plus breakfast. Beds: KQT. Air conditioning, ceiling fan, cable TV and VCR in room. Fax, copier, spa, swimming and library on premises. Handicap access. Amusement parks, antiques, fishing, parks, shopping, cross-country skiing, theater and watersports nearby.

Seen in: New York Times, Washington Post, Los Angeles Times, San Diego Union Tribune, Seattle Times, Portland Oregonian, Los Angeles, San Diego, Pacific Northwest, Sunset, Westways, Alaska Airlines.

"Outstanding ambiance, friendly relaxed atmosphere."

Certificate may be used: Sunday through Thursday except February, March and April and holidays.

Sakura, Japanese B&B

1677 N Via Miraleste at Vista Chino,
Palm Springs, CA 92262
(619)327-0705 (800)200-0705
Fax:(619)327-6847

Circa 1945. An authentic Japanese experience awaits guests of this private home, distinctively decorated with Japanese artwork and antique kimonos. Guests are encouraged to leave their shoes at the door, grab kimonos and slippers and discover what real relaxation is all about. Guests may choose either American or Japanese breakfasts, and Japanese or vegetarian dinners also are available. The Palm Springs area is home to more than 70 golf courses and many fine shops. During the summer months, the innkeepers conduct tours in Japan.
Innkeeper(s): George & Fumiko Cebra. $45-75. 3 rooms, 2 with PB. 1 suite. Breakfast included in rates. Types of meals: full breakfast and early coffee/tea. Afternoon tea, dinner and picnic lunch available. Beds: Q. Air conditioning and cable TV in room. VCR, fax, spa and child care on premises. Amusement parks, antiques, fishing, parks, shopping, cross-country skiing, sporting events, theater and watersports nearby.
Certificate may be used: All year, Sunday through Thursday.

Palo Alto
15

Adella Villa

PO Box 4528, Palo Alto, CA 94309-4528
(415)321-5195 Fax:(415)325-5121

Circa 1923. This Italian villa is located in an area of one-acre estates five minutes from Stanford University. Two guest rooms feature whirlpool tubs, three guest rooms have showers. The music room boasts a 1920 mahogany Steinway grand piano. There is a solar-heated swimming pool set amid manicured gardens.

Innkeeper(s): Tricia Young. $110. MC VISA AX DC CB PC TC. 5 rooms with PB. 1 conference room. Breakfast and afternoon tea included in rates. Types of meals: full breakfast, gourmet breakfast and early coffee/tea. Evening snack available. Beds: KQT. Ceiling fan and cable TV in room. VCR, fax, copier, swimming, bicycles and library on premises. Amusement parks, antiques, fishing, parks, shopping, sporting events, theater and watersports nearby.
Location: Twenty-five miles south of San Francisco at the tip of Silicon Valley.
Seen in: Los Angeles Times.

"This place is as wonderful, gracious and beautiful as the people who own it!"
Certificate may be used: All year except June.

Petaluma
H4

Cavanagh Inn

10 Keller St, Petaluma, CA 94952-2939
(707)765-4657 Fax:(707)769-0466

Circa 1902. Embrace turn-of-the-century California at this picturesque Georgian Revival manor. The garden is filled with beautiful flowers, plants and fruit trees. Innkeeper Jeanne Farris is an award-winning chef and prepares the mouthwatering breakfasts. A typical meal might start off with butterscotch pears and fresh muffins with honey butter. This starter would be followed by an entree, perhaps eggs served with rosemary potatoes. The innkeepers also serve afternoon refreshments. The parlor and library, which boasts heart-of-redwood paneled walls, is an ideal place to relax. Cavanagh Inn is located at the edge of Petaluma's historic district, and close to shops and the riverfront, including the Petaluma Queen Riverboat.
Innkeeper(s): Ray & Jeanne Farris. $75-125. MC VISA AX PC. 7 rooms, 5 with PB. 1 conference room. Breakfast, afternoon tea and evening snack included in rates. Types of meals: gourmet breakfast and early coffee/tea. Beds: KQDT. Turn-down service in room. Cable TV, VCR, fax and library on premises. Antiques, parks, shopping and theater nearby.
Certificate may be used: Jan. 1 to May 1, Monday-Thursday.

Platina
D4

Living Spring Farm & Guest Ranch

HCR 1 Box 611, Platina, CA 96076-9600
(916)352-4338 (800)230-9567

Circa 1960. Anyone who has ever longed to visit a farm will enjoy this replica of an early 20th-century farm, which is dedicated to preserving the "old-fashioned" methods of farming. Visitors stay in an air-conditioned, farmstyle guest house, furnished in country decor and featuring private baths. Guests are encouraged to gain hands-on experience with as many farm tasks as they can manage, including cow milking, fruit picking, calf roping, crop harvesting and the processing of butter and cheese. Children enjoy arts and crafts and nature lessons. All meals, horseback riding and wagon rides are included in the rate.
Innkeeper(s): Mary Gibbs. $75-100. MC VISA AX DC CB DS. 8 rooms with PB. Breakfast, dinner and picnic lunch included in rates. Types of meals: full breakfast and early coffee/tea. Lunch and banquet service available. Beds: DT. Air conditioning in room. Child care on premises. Fishing nearby.

"Thank you for sharing your house, ranch, and selves with us. We came away in a daze of delightment. We think your accommodations are as close to perfect as can be."

Certificate may be used: Year-round excluding holiday weekends. Rates are per person, includes three meals and horseback riding.

Playa Del Rey   O10

Inn at Playa Del Rey
435 Culver Blvd,
Playa Del Rey, CA 90293-7705
(310)574-1920 Fax:(310)574-9920

Circa 1995. Relax and enjoy the view of a 350-acre bird sanctuary from this restful Cape Cod-style inn, located just a few blocks from the ocean. The individually appointed rooms are designed for relaxation. The hosts keep the bathrooms stocked with thick towels, fluffy robes and plenty of bubble bath. Some rooms include private decks, others offer fireplaces, Marina views or Jacuzzi tubs. Two of the rooms offer the romantic amenity of a fireplace in the bathroom. The third-floor suite, with its fireplace, private deck, Jacuzzi tub, living room and scenic view, is a perfect place to celebrate a romantic occasion. Guests are treated to a hearty breakfast, and after a day combing the beach, the guests are offered wine and cheese. There are bicycles available to tour the area, and a hot tub is located in the inn's private garden.

Innkeeper(s): Susan Zolla. $95-225. MC VISA AX DS PC. 22 rooms with PB, 9 with FP. 2 suites. Breakfast and afternoon tea included in rates. Types of meals: full breakfast and early coffee/tea. Beds: KQT. Air conditioning, cable TV and VCR in room. Fax, copier, spa, bicycles and library on premises. Handicap access. Amusement parks, antiques, fishing, parks, shopping, sporting events, theater and watersports nearby.

Certificate may be used: Sunday-Wednesday Sept. 8-Dec. 18, 1996, Jan. 5-Feb.3, 1997.

Point Arena   F3

Coast Guard House
695 Arena Cove, Point Arena, CA 95468
(707)882-2442 Fax:(707)882-2442

This National Register, Cape Cod-style home was built by the Lifesaving Service and later was used by the U.S. Coast Guard. The innkeepers have kept and preserved many of the lifeboats that were used throughout the home's 50-year service as a Coast Guard station. A collection of photographs and memorabilia also is displayed. Guest rooms are decorated in Arts and Crafts or Art Deco style, many afford ocean or canyon views. The Boathouse, a replica of the ground's original boathouse, is a romantic cabin with a woodburning stove, private

patio and spa with an ocean view. The Point Arena Lighthouse and Museum, as well as many shops and restaurants are just a few miles away.

Innkeeper(s): Mia & Kevin Gallagher. $75-175. MC VISA DC CB. 6 rooms. Breakfast included in rates. Type of meal: continental breakfast.

Certificate may be used: Monday through Thursday; November through April, holidays excluded.

Point Reyes Station   H4

Carriage House
325 Mesa Rd, PO Box 1239,
Point Reyes Station, CA 94956
(415)663-8627 Fax:(415)663-8431

Circa 1960. This recently remodeled inn boasts a view of Inverness Ridge. The two suites are furnished in antiques and folk art, and features a private parlor, television, VCR, a fireplace and a private entrance. Children are welcome and cribs and daybeds are available. Point Reyes National Seashore has 100 miles of trails for cycling, hiking or horseback riding. Photographers and nature lovers can enjoy watch whales and seals, birdwatch or simply enjoy the scenery.

Innkeeper(s): Felicity Kirsch. $130-160. 2 suites, 2 with FP. Breakfast included in rates. Type of meal: continental-plus breakfast. Beds: QT. Cable TV in room. Bicycles and child care on premises. Antiques, fishing, parks and shopping nearby.

Location: Near Point Reyes National Seashore and Tomales Bay State Park.

"What a rejuvenating getaway. We loved it. The smells, sounds and scenery were wonderful."

Certificate may be used: Sunday-Thursday, except holiday weeks.

The Tree House
PO Box 1075,
Point Reyes Station, CA 94956-1075
(415)663-8720

Circa 1970. This homestay offers an outstanding view of Point Reyes Station from the deck and some of the guest rooms. The King's Room features a king-size waterbed while Queen Quarter boasts its own fireplace. A hot tub is tucked away in a cozy spot of the garden.

Innkeeper(s): Lisa Patsel. $90-110. 3 rooms with PB, 2 with FP. 1 suite. Breakfast included in rates. Type of meal: continental-plus breakfast. Ceiling fan and VCR in room. Spa and pet boarding on premises. Antiques, parks and shopping nearby.

Certificate may be used: Sunday through Thursday.

Rancho Cucamonga O11

Christmas House B&B
9240 Archibald Ave,
Rancho Cucamonga, CA 91730-5236
(909)980-6450

Circa 1904. This Queen Anne Victorian has been renovated in period elegance, emphasizing its intricate wood carvings and red and green stained-glass windows. Once surrounded by 80 acres of citrus groves and vineyards, the home, with its wide, sweeping veranda, is still a favorite place for taking in the beautiful lawns and palm trees. The elegant atmosphere attracts the business traveler, romance-seeker and vacationer.

Innkeeper(s): Janice Ilsley. $85-185. MC VISA AX DS. 6 rooms, 4 with PB, 3 with FP. 1 suite. 1 conference room. Breakfast included in rates. Types of meals: full breakfast, gourmet breakfast and early coffee/tea. Beds: QD. Air conditioning, ceiling fan and VCR in room. Spa on premises. Antiques, fishing, shopping, downhill skiing, sporting events and theater nearby.

Location: East of downtown Los Angeles, three miles from Ontario Airport.

Seen in: Country Inns, Los Angeles Times, Elan.

"Coming to Christmas House is like stepping through a magic door into an enchanted land. Many words come to mind — warmth, serenity, peacefulness."

Certificate may be used: Any night except Saturday night.

Redlands O11

Morey Mansion
190 Terracina Blvd,
Redlands, CA 92373-4846
(909)793-7970 Fax:(909)793-7870

The exquisite exterior of this fanciful Victorian is like a fairy tale manor with its gingerbread trim and unique onion dome. David Morey, a shipbuilder and cabinet maker built the home for his wife, Sarah, using a variety of architectural styles. David also carved much of the ornate woodwork. The home has been featured in several movies and commercials. The current owner is an antique dealer and has filled the home with museum-quality pieces. Each room is dramatic, boasting many one-of-a-kind pieces. Carole Lombard once stayed in the home, and one of the rooms is named for her.

Innkeeper(s): Dolly Wimer. $109-185. MC VISA AX DC CB DS. 5 rooms. Breakfast included in rates. Type of meal: continental-plus breakfast.

Certificate may be used: Sunday through Thursday (Saturday and Sunday okay-Thursday and Friday okay).

Reedley K8

The Fairweather Inn B&B
259 S Reed Ave, Reedley, CA 93654-2845
(209)638-1918

Circa 1914. This Craftsman-style inn is situated on the bluffs of the Kings River, a half-hour's drive from Sequoia and Kings Canyon national parks. After a restful night in one of the inn's four guest rooms, all with queen beds, visitors will enjoy their gourmet breakfast in the dining room. The antique-filled inn is within walking distance of downtown restaurants and shops, and Reedley also offers a beautiful golf course near the river. Fresno and Visalia are 20 minutes away.

Innkeeper(s): Violet Demyan. $75-85. MC VISA AX. 4 rooms, 2 with PB. 1 suite. Breakfast included in rates. Type of meal: full breakfast. Beds: Q. Air conditioning in room. Antiques, fishing, downhill skiing, sporting events and watersports nearby.

"The Fairweather Inn is like an 'Oasis in the Desert'."

Certificate may be used: Sunday through Thursday.

Sacramento G6

Amber House
1315 22nd St,
Sacramento, CA 95816-5717
(916)552-6525 (800)755-6526
Fax:(916)552-6529

Circa 1905. This Craftsman-style bungalow on the city's Historic Preservation Register is in a neighborhood of fine old homes eight blocks from the

capitol. Each room is named for a famous poet and features stained glass, English antiques, selected volumes of poetry and fresh flowers. Ask for the Lord Byron Room where you can soak by candlelight in the whirlpool tub or enjoy one of the new rooms with marble baths and Jacuzzi tubs in the adjacent 1913 Mediterranean mansion.

Innkeeper(s): Michael & Jane Richardson. $99-249. MC VISA AX DC CB DS PC TC. 9 rooms with PB, 1 with FP. 1 suite. 1 conference room. Breakfast included in rates. Type of meal: early coffee/tea. Gourmet lunch and catering service available. Beds: KQ. Air conditioning, turn-down service, cable TV and VCR in room. Fax, bicycles and library on premises. Antiques, fishing, parks, shopping, downhill skiing, cross-country skiing, theater and watersports nearby.

Location: Eight blocks to the east of the State Capitol.

Seen in: Travel & Leisure, Village Crier.

"Your cordial hospitality, the relaxing atmosphere and delicious breakfast made our brief business/pleasure trip so much more enjoyable."

Certificate may be used: All year except holidays, subject to availability.

Saint Helena   G4

Cinnamon Bear B&B
1407 Kearney St,
Saint Helena, CA 94574-1822
(707)963-4653 (800)791-3020
Fax:(707)963-0251

Circa 1904. This Craftsman bungalow, originally home to a town mayor, has broad wraparound porches with inviting bent-willow furniture. The decor includes antiques, original light fixtures, hardwood floors, teddy bears and quilts. The innkeeper's husband is a local Napa Valley chef, so the gourmet breakfasts are a treat. There are plenty of restaurants nearby, and the inn is also near the West Coast campus of the famed Culinary Institute of America.

Innkeeper(s): Cathye Raneri. $115-155. MC VISA AX. 3 rooms with PB. Breakfast included in rates. Type of meal: gourmet breakfast. Evening snack and catering service available. Beds: Q. Air conditioning in room. Cable TV, VCR, fax and copier on premises. Antiques, parks and shopping nearby.

Location: Two blocks from town.

Seen in: Napa Register.

"Just like home, only better."

Certificate may be used: December-April, Sunday-Thursday holidays excluded.

Spanish Villa
474 Glass Mountain Rd,
Saint Helena, CA 94574-9669
(707)963-7483

Circa 1981. This contemporary Mission-style Spanish villa is nestled in a wooded valley in the Napa wine country, three miles from town. Guests will be charmed by the Tiffany lamp replicas found throughout the inn, including the guest rooms. A large sitting room and fireplace are favorite gathering spots. The quiet, country roads found in the area are popular for biking, jogging or walking. Don't miss the chance to visit nearby Calistoga, with its hang gliding and famous mud baths.

Innkeeper(s): Roy & Barbie Bissember. $115-175. 3 rooms with PB. Breakfast included in rates. Types of meals: continental breakfast and early coffee/tea. Beds: K. Cable TV and VCR on premises. Amusement

parks, antiques, fishing, parks, shopping, theater and watersports nearby.

Certificate may be used: Sunday-Thursday.

San Andreas   H7

Robin's Nest
PO Box 1408,
San Andreas, CA 95249-1408
(209)754-1076

Circa 1895. Guests are treated to lemonade and homemade cookies upon arrival to this three-story Queen Anne Victorian. Unique features include a round window in the formal parlor, 12-foot ceilings

throughout the main floor and double gables on the exterior. The guest rooms are decorated with antiques and the Snyder Suite features a four-poster bed with steps and an original seven-foot bathtub.

Innkeeper(s): George Jones. $55-95. MC VISA AX. 9 rooms, 7 with PB. 5 suites. Breakfast included in rates. Type of meal: full breakfast. Beds: QDT. Antiques, fishing, downhill skiing, cross-country skiing, theater and watersports nearby.

Seen in: Stockton Record, In Flight, Westways.

"An excellent job of making guests feel at home."

Certificate may be used: Anytime except holidays and Saturdays.

San Clemente   P11

Casa De Flores B&B
184 Ave La Cuesta,
San Clemente, CA 92672
(714)498-1344

Circa 1974. Located a mile from the Pacific, you can enjoy a 180-degree view of the ocean, harbor and hills from this home. In a residential area, it was designed by your hostess. The Private Patio room offers skylights, a private spa and an ocean

view. More than 1,000 orchid plants are grown on the grounds. Grab a sand chair and towel and head for your own stretch of the five miles of San Clemente beaches. Whale watching and fishing charters are available at the Dana Point Harbor, 10 minutes away.

Innkeeper(s): Marilee Arsenault. $75-100. PC. 2 suites, 1 with FP. Breakfast included in rates. Type of meal: gourmet breakfast. Beds: K. Cable TV and VCR in room. Library on premises. Amusement parks, antiques, fishing, parks, shopping and watersports nearby.

Location: South of the Dana Point Harbor.

Certificate may be used: Sunday through Thursday except holidays.

San Diego   Q12

Heritage Park Inn
2470 Heritage Park Row,
San Diego, CA 92110-2803
(619)299-6832 (800)995-2470
Fax:(619)299-9465

Circa 1889. Situated on a seven-acre Victorian park in the heart of Old Town, this inn two of seven preserved classic structures. The main house offers a variety of beautifully appointed guest rooms, decked in traditional Victorian furnishings and decor. The

opulent Manor Suite includes two bedrooms, a Jacuzzi tub and sitting room. Several rooms offer ocean views, and guest also can see the nightly fireworks show at nearby Sea World. A collection of classic movies is available, and a different movie is shown each night in the inn's parlor. Guests are treated to a light afternoon tea and the breakfast are served on fine china on candlelit tables. The home is within walking distance to the many sites, shops and restaurants in the historic Old Town. A small antique shop and Victorian toy store also are located in the next door to the inn.

Innkeeper(s): Nancy & Charles Helsper. $90-225. MAP. MC VISA TC. 10 rooms with PB. 1 suite. 1 conference room. Breakfast and afternoon tea included in rates. Types of meals: gourmet breakfast and early coffee/tea. Picnic lunch and catering service available. Beds: KQT. Turn-down service and ceiling fan in room. VCR, fax and copier on premises. Amusement parks, antiques, fishing, parks, shopping, sporting events, theater and watersports nearby.

Location: In historic Old Town.

Seen in: Los Angeles Herald Examiner, Innsider, Los Angeles Times, Orange County Register, San Diego Union, In-Flight, Glamour, Country Inns.

"A beautiful step back in time. Peaceful and gracious."

Certificate may be used: Call innkeeper for dates. Based on availability.

San Francisco   H4

Archbishop's Mansion
1000 Fulton St,
San Francisco, CA 94117-1608
(415)563-7872 (800)543-5820
Fax:(415)885-3193

Circa 1904. This French Empire-style manor was built for the Archbishop of San Francisco. It is designated as a San Francisco historic landmark. The grand stairway features redwood paneling, Corinthian columns and a stained-glass dome. The parlor has a hand-painted ceiling. Each of the guest rooms is named for an opera and decorated to reflect its spirit. Rooms have antiques, Victorian window treatments, fresh flowers, and embroidered linens. Breakfast is served in French picnic baskets.

Innkeeper(s): Rick Janvier. $129-385. MC VISA AX DC. 15 rooms with PB, 13 with FP. 5 suites. Breakfast included in rates. Types of meals: continental-plus breakfast and early coffee/tea. Beds: KQD. Turn-down service, cable TV and VCR in room. Fax and copier on premises. Parks nearby.

Seen in: Travel-Holiday, Travel & Leisure.

"The ultimate, romantic honeymoon spot."

Certificate may be used: Nov. 1 to April 15, Sunday-Thursday, holidays excluded.

No Name Victorian B&B

847 Fillmore St,
San Francisco, CA 94117-1703
(415)479-1913 Fax:(415)921-2273

Circa 1890. Located in the historic district of Alamo Square, this Second Empire Victorian sits close to the Civic Center, Opera House, Davies Symphony Hall and Union Square. An 1830s wedding bed from mainland China adorns the honeymoon room. The massive hand-carved bed is believed to bring good spirits and luck to the couple who spend their wedding night there. Chinese antiques, a wood-burning fireplace, a city view and Chinese robes also are included. There's a family accommodation with a private entrance, full kitchen and a crib.

Innkeeper(s): Eva Strakova. $69-125. MC VISA AX PC TC. 5 rooms, 3 with PB, 4 with FP. 1 suite. Breakfast included in rates. Types of meals: full breakfast and early coffee/tea. Afternoon tea available. Beds: QT. Cable TV, fax, spa and child care on premises. Parks, shopping, sporting events and theater nearby.

Location: In the heart of San Francisco.

Certificate may be used: Nov. 1-April 30.

Petite Auberge

863 Bush St,
San Francisco, CA 94108-3312
(415)928-6000 (800)365-3004
Fax:(415)775-5717

Circa 1917. This five-story hotel features an ornate baroque design with curved bay windows. Now

transformed to a French country inn, there are antiques, fresh flowers and country accessories. Most rooms also have working fireplaces. It's a short walk to the Powell Street cable car.

Innkeeper(s): Brian Asbill. $110-220. MC VISA AX TC. 26 rooms with PB, 17 with FP. 1 suite. Breakfast and afternoon tea included in rates. Types of meals: full breakfast, gourmet breakfast and early coffee/tea. Beds: KQ. Turn-down service and VCR in room. Fax and copier on premises. Handicap access. Antiques, parks, shopping, sporting events and theater nearby.

Location: Two-and-a-half blocks from Union Square.

Seen in: Travel & Leisure, Oregonian, Los Angeles Times, Brides.

"Breakfast was great, and even better in bed!"

Certificate may be used: November-March Sunday-Thursday. Holidays & special events excluded.

Victorian Inn on The Park

301 Lyon St,
San Francisco, CA 94117-2108
(415)931-1830 (800)435-1967
Fax:(415)931-1830

Circa 1897. This grand three-story Queen Anne inn, built by William Curlett, has an open belvedere turret with a teahouse roof and Victorian railings. Silk-screened wallpapers, created especially for the

inn, are accentuated by intricate mahogany and redwood paneling. The opulent Belvedere Suite features French doors opening to a Roman tub for two. Overlooking Golden Gate Park, the inn is 10 minutes from downtown.

Innkeeper(s): Lisa & William Benau. $89-164. MC VISA AX DC CB DS PC TC. 12 rooms with PB, 3 with FP. 2 suites. Breakfast included in rates. Types of meals: continental-plus breakfast and early coffee/tea. Beds: QT. Cable TV, fax, library and child care on premises. Antiques, parks, sporting events and theater nearby.

Location: Adjacent to Golden Gate Park.

Seen in: Innsider, Country Inns, Good Housekeeping, New York Times, Good Morning America, Country Inns USA, Great Country Inns of America.

"The excitement you have about your building comes from the care you have taken in restoring and maintaining your historic structure."

Certificate may be used: Both nights must be Sunday through Thursday. Holidays excluded, May 1-31 excluded, Aug. 1-31 excluded.

White Swan Inn

845 Bush St,
San Francisco, CA 94108-3300
(415)775-1755 (800)999-9570
Fax:(415)775-5717

Circa 1915. This four-story inn is near Union Square and the Powell Street cable car. Beveled-glass doors open to a reception area with granite floors, an antique carousel horse and English artwork. Bay windows and a rear deck contribute to the feeling of an English garden inn. The guest rooms are decorated with bold English wallpapers and prints. All rooms have fireplaces. Turndown service is provided. Innkeeper(s): Brian Larsen. $145-250. MC VISA AX TC. 26 rooms with PB, 26 with FP. 3 suites. 1 conference room. Breakfast and afternoon tea included in rates. Types of meals: full breakfast, gourmet breakfast and early coffee/tea. Beds: KQT. Turn-down service and VCR in room. Fax and copier on premises. Antiques, parks, shopping, sporting events and theater nearby.

Location: In the heart of downtown.

Seen in: Travel & Leisure, Victoria.

"Wonderfully accommodating. Absolutely perfect."

Certificate may be used: November-March, Sunday-Thursday. Holidays, special events excluded.

San Luis Obispo
M7

Garden Street Inn

1212 Garden St,
San Luis Obispo, CA 93401-3962
(805)545-9802 Fax:(805)545-9403

Circa 1887. Innkeepers Dan and Kathy Smith restored this elegant home, paying meticulous attention to detail. Each room has a special theme. The Field of Dreams room, dedicated to Kathy Smith's father, includes memorabilia from his sports reporting days, toy figures from various baseball teams and framed pictures of antique baseball cards. The Cocoon room diplays dozens of beautiful butterfly knickknacks. Situated downtown, the inn is within

walking distance of shops and restaurants and the San Luis Obispo Mission. Pismo Beach and Hearst Castle are also neaby attractions.

Innkeeper(s): Kathy Smith. $90-160. MC VISA AX. 13 rooms with PB, 5 with FP. 4 suites. 2 conference rooms. Breakfast and afternoon tea included in rates. Types of meals: full breakfast, gourmet breakfast and early coffee/tea. Beds: KQ. Air conditioning and turn-down service in room. Fax on premises. Handicap access. Antiques, fishing, parks, shopping, sporting events, theater and watersports nearby.

Seen in: Times-Press-Recorder, Telegram-Tribune, San Francisco Chronicle, Los Angeles Times, Orange County Register, Los Angeles Daily News.

"We appreciate your warmth and care."

Certificate may be used: Sunday-Thursday; suites only; October-May.

Santa Barbara
N8

Blue Dolphin Inn

420 W Montecito St,
Santa Barbara, CA 93101
(805)965-2333 Fax:(805)962-4907

Circa 1870. It's a short walk to the beach and harbor from this Victorian inn, which offers accommodations in the main house and adjacent carriage house. Guest rooms are decorated in period style with antiques. Brass beds, tapestry pillows, and fluffy comforters add a romantic touch. Several rooms include fireplaces, Jacuzzi tubs or private balconies and terraces. Fresh fruit salads, croissants, homemade breads and quiche highlight the breakfast fare. With prior notice and for an extra cost, the innkeepers can arrange in-room gourmet dinners. Innkeeper(s): Byria O'Hayon-Crosby. $65-185. EP. MC VISA AX DC DS PC TC. 9 rooms with PB, 6 with FP. 3 suites. Breakfast and afternoon tea included in rates. Types of meals: gourmet breakfast and early coffee/tea. Picnic lunch and room service available. Beds: KQT. Ceiling fan, cable TV and VCR in room. Fax and library on premises. Handicap access. Antiques, fishing, parks, shopping, sporting events, theater and watersports nearby.

Certificate may be used: At full tariff Sunday through Thursday, non holiday periods, Oct. 15 through May 15. No other discounts apply.

Cheshire Cat Inn

36 W Valerio St,
Santa Barbara, CA 93101-2524
(805)569-1610 Fax:(805)682-1876

Circa 1894. The Eberle family built two graceful houses side by side, one a Queen Anne, the other a Colonial Revival. President McKinley was entertained here on a visit to Santa Barbara. There is a pagoda-like porch, a square and a curved bay, rose gardens, grassy lawns and a gazebo. Laura Ashley wallpapers are featured here and in the owner's other inn, a 12th-century manor in Scotland. Large English flower gardens, new deck with sitting areas and fountains, were recently added.

Innkeeper(s): Christine Dunstan. $89-249. MC VISA. 14 rooms, 10 with PB. 4 suites. 1 conference room. Breakfast included in rates. Type of meal: full breakfast. Room service available. Beds: KQT. Ceiling fan and cable TV in room. Spa on premises. Amusement parks, antiques, fishing, shopping, sporting events, theater and watersports nearby.

Location: Downtown.

Seen in: Two on the Town, KABC, Los Angeles Times, Santa Barbara, American In Flight, Elmer Dills Recommends.

"Romantic and quaint."

Certificate may be used: October through May, Sunday through Thursday, excluding public holidays.

Glenborough Inn

1327 Bath St,
Santa Barbara, CA 93101-3623
(805)966-0589 (800)962-0589
Fax:(805)564-8610

Circa 1885. This Craftsman-style inn recreates a turn-of-the-century atmosphere in the Main house and White house. There is also an 1880s cottage reminiscent of the Victorian era. Inside are antiques, rich wood trim and elegant fireplace suites with canopy beds. There's always plenty of hospitality and an open invitation to the secluded garden hot tub. Breakfast is homemade and has been written up in "Bon Appetit" and "Chocolatier."

Innkeeper(s): Michael Diaz & Steve Ryan. $90-225. MC VISA AX DC CB DS PC TC. 11 rooms with PB, 6 with FP. 4 suites. 1 cottage. Breakfast included in rates. Types of meals: continental breakfast, continental-plus breakfast, full breakfast, gourmet breakfast and early coffee/tea. Dinner, picnic lunch and gourmet lunch available. Beds: KQD. Ceiling fan in room. Cable TV, fax and spa on premises. Antiques, fishing, parks, shopping, sporting events, theater and watersports nearby.

Seen in: Houston Post, Los Angeles Times, Horizon, Los Angeles, Pasadena Choice.

"A delightful, elegant and charming suite..."

Certificate may be used: October-June, Sunday-Thursday, except holidays.

The Old Yacht Club Inn

431 Corona Del Mar,
Santa Barbara, CA 93103-3601
(805)962-1277 (800)676-1676
Fax:(805)962-3989

Circa 1912. This California Craftsman house was the home of the Santa Barbara Yacht Club during the Roaring '20s. It was opened as Santa Barbara's first B&B and has become renowned for its gourmet food and superb hospitality. Innkeeper Nancy Donaldson is the author of The Old Yacht Club Inn Cookbook.

Innkeeper(s): Nancy Donaldson. $140-150. MC VISA AX DS. 9 rooms with PB. 1 conference room. Breakfast included in rates. Types of meals: full breakfast, gourmet breakfast and early coffee/tea. Dinner available. Beds: KQ. Ceiling fan and cable TV in room. Fax, copier, spa and bicycles on premises. Antiques, fishing, shopping, sporting events, theater and watersports nearby.

Location: East Beach.

Seen in: Los Angeles, Valley.

"Donaldson is one of Santa Barbara's better-kept culinary secrets."

Certificate may be used: November, December, January, February, Monday-Thursday only. Two week advanced reservations.

Secret Garden Inn and Cottages

1908 Bath St,
Santa Barbara, CA 93101-2813
(805)687-2300 (800)676-1622
Fax:(805)687-4576

Circa 1908. The main house and adjacent cottages surround the lovely gardens and are decorated in American and English-Country style. The Hummingbird is a large cottage guest room with a queen-size white iron bed and a private deck with a hot tub for your exclusive use. Wine and light hors d'oeuvres are served in the late afternoon, and hot apple cider is served each evening.

Innkeeper(s): Jack Greenwald, Christine Dunstan. $105-195. MC VISA AX PC TC. 9 rooms with PB, 1 with FP. 3 suites. 4 cottages. Breakfast, afternoon tea and evening snack included in rates. Types of meals: full breakfast and early coffee/tea. Beds: KQ. Ceiling fan and cable TV in room. Fax, copier and bicycles on premises. Antiques, fishing, shopping, theater and watersports nearby.

Location: Quiet residential area near town and the beach.

Seen in: Los Angeles Times, Santa Barbara, Independent

"Mahvolous, simply maaahvolous! Loved everything. And just think, I'm here on a business trip - boy, love this job! I'll be back for sure - business of course."

Certificate may be used: Sunday-Thursday only, except on national holidays.

The Upham Hotel & Garden Cottages

1404 De La Vina St,
Santa Barbara, CA 93101-3027
(805)962-0058 (800)727-0876
Fax:(805)963-2825

Circa 1871. Antiques and period furnishings decorate each of the inn's guest rooms and suites. The inn is the oldest continuously operating hostelry in Southern California. Situated on an acre of gardens

in the center of downtown, it's within easy walking distance of restaurants, shops, art galleries and museums. The staff is happy to assist guests in discovering Santa Barbara's varied attractions. Garden cottage units feature porches or secluded patios and several have gas fireplaces.

Innkeeper(s): Jan Martin Winn. $120-350. MC VISA AX DC CB DS TC. 50 rooms with PB, 8 with FP. 4 suites. 4 cottages. 4 conference rooms. Breakfast and evening snack included in rates. Types of meals: continental-plus breakfast and early coffee/tea. Banquet service available. Beds: KQD. Ceiling fan and cable TV in room. VCR, fax and copier on premises. Antiques, fishing, parks, shopping, sporting events, theater and watersports nearby.

Seen in: Los Angeles Times, Santa Barbara, Westways, Santa Barbara News-Press.

"Your hotel is truly a charm. Between the cozy gardens and the exquisitely comfortable appointments, The Upham is charm itself."

Certificate may be used: Sunday through Thursday, month of August excluded.

Santa Clara
I5

Madison Street Inn

1390 Madison St,
Santa Clara, CA 95050-4759
(408)249-5541 (800)491-5541
Fax:(408)249-6676

Circa 1890. This Queen Anne Victorian inn still boasts its original doors and locks, and "No Peddlers or Agents" is engraved in the cement of the original carriageway. Guests, however, always receive a warm and gracious welcome to high-ceilinged rooms furnished in antiques, Oriental rugs and Victorian wallpaper.

Innkeeper(s): Theresa & Ralph Wigginton. $60-85. MC VISA AX DC DS PC TC. 6 rooms, 4 with PB. Breakfast, afternoon tea and evening snack included in rates. Types of meals: continental breakfast, continental-plus breakfast, full breakfast, gourmet breakfast and early coffee/tea. Picnic lunch, gourmet lunch, banquet service, catering service and catered breakfast available. Beds: QD. Ceiling fan in room. Cable TV, VCR, fax, spa, swimming and bicycles on premises. Amusement parks, antiques, parks, sporting events, theater and watersports nearby.

Location: Ten minutes from San Jose.

Seen in: Discovery.

"We spend many nights in hotels that look and feel exactly alike whether they are in Houston or Boston. Your inn was delightful. It was wonderful to bask in your warm and gracious hospitality."
Certificate may be used: Anytime.

Santa Cruz
J5

The Darling House- A B&B Inn By The Sea

314 W Cliff Dr,
Santa Cruz, CA 95060-6145
(408)458-1958

Circa 1910. It's difficult to pick a room at this oceanside mansion. The Pacific Ocean Room features a fireplace and a wonderful ocean view. The Chinese Room might suit you as well with its silk-draped, hand-carved rosewood canopy wedding bed. Elegant oak, ebony, and walnut woodwork is enhanced by the antique decor of Tiffanys and Chippendales. Roses, beveled glass and libraries add to the atmosphere. Beyond the ocean-view veranda are landscaped gardens. Guests often walk to the wharf for dinner.

Innkeeper(s): Karen Darling. $125-150. MC VISA AX DS. 5 rooms. 1 conference room. Breakfast included in rates. Type of meal: continental breakfast. Beds: KQDT. Turn-down service in room. Spa on premises. Amusement parks, antiques, fishing, shopping, sporting events and theater nearby.

Location: A stone's throw from the Pacific Ocean.

Seen in: Modern Maturity, Pacific.

"So pretty, so sorry to leave."

Certificate may be used: November-April, Sunday-Thursday, holidays excluded.

Santa Monica   O10

Channel Road Inn
219 W Channel Rd,
Santa Monica, CA 90402-1105
(310)459-1920 Fax:(310)454-9920

Circa 1910. This shingle-clad building is a variation of the Colonial Revival Period, one of the few remaining in Los Angeles. The abandoned home was saved from the city's wrecking crew by Susan Zolla, with the encouragement of the local historical society. The rooms feature canopy beds, fine linens, custom mattresses and private porches. Chile Cheese Puff served with salsa, is a popular breakfast speciality. The Pacific Ocean is one block away, and guests often enjoy borrowing the inn's bicycles to pedal along the 30-mile coastal bike path. In the evening, the inn's spectacular cliffside spa is popular.

Innkeeper(s): Kathy Jensen. $95-225. MC VISA AX PC TC. 12 rooms with PB, 2 with FP. 2 suites. Breakfast, afternoon tea and evening snack included in rates. Types of meals: full breakfast and early coffee/tea. Room service available. Beds: KQDT. Ceiling fan, cable TV and VCR in room. Fax, copier, computer, spa and bicycles on premises. Handicap access. Amusement parks, antiques, fishing, parks, shopping, sporting events, theater and watersports nearby.

Location: One block from the ocean.

Seen in: Los Angeles, New York Times, Brides.

"One of the most romantic hotels in Los Angeles."

Certificate may be used: Sunday-Tuesday evenings, Sept. 10-Nov. 7, Jan. 7-May 1.

Seal Beach   O10

The Seal Beach Inn & Gardens
212 5th St, Seal Beach, CA 90740-6115
(310)493-2416 (800)433-3292
Fax:(310)799-0483

Circa 1923. This historic Southern California inn has lush gardens and the look of an oceanside estate. It's a short walk to the Seal Beach pier, shops and restaurants. Major attractions in Orange

County and the Los Angeles area are within short driving distances. Business travelers can plan meetings in rooms where 24 people can sit comfortably. The inn has a Mediterranean villa ambiance, and no two rooms are alike.

Innkeeper(s): Marjorie B. & Harty Schmael. $118-185. AP. MC VISA AX DC CB DS TC. 23 rooms with PB, 4 with FP. 11 suites. Breakfast and evening snack included in rates. Types of meals: full breakfast and early coffee/tea. Afternoon tea available. Beds: KQ. Turn-down service in room. Fax and copier on premises. Amusement parks, antiques, fishing, parks, shopping, sporting events, theater and watersports nearby.

Location: 300 yards from the ocean, five minutes from Long Beach.

Seen in: Brides, Country Inns, Glamour, Country, Long Beach Press Telegram, Orange County Register, Los Angeles Times.

"The closest thing to Europe since I left there. Delights the senses and restores the soul."

Certificate may be used: Sunday through Thursday; Thursday as second night. October to April, space available, no checks (personal). Stay charged at time of reservation. 72 hour (by noon) cancellation. Offer includes any suite, except Penthouse.

Sonoma   H4

Starwae Inn
21490 Broadway,
Sonoma, CA 95476-8204
(707)938-1374 (800)793-4792
Fax:(707)935-1159

Circa 1930. Two local artists host this bed & breakfast. Their home and studios are on the property, and guests will find sculptures tucked here and there. Rooms are decorated with original artwork and handmade pottery, and some of the furnishings have been created by the innkeeper. Items such as individual quiche, scones and fresh berry danish are served at breakfast.

Innkeeper(s): John Curry & Janice Crow. $90-125. EP. MC VISA TC. 4 rooms with PB, 1 with FP. 3 suites. 1 conference room. Breakfast included in rates. Types of meals: continental-plus breakfast and early coffee/tea. Beds: QD. Air conditioning and cable TV in room. Fax, copier and bicycles on premises. Antiques, fishing, parks, shopping and theater nearby.

Certificate may be used: Nov. 1 to March 1, Sunday through Thursday, holidays excluded.

Vineyard Inn

23000 Arnold Dr,
Sonoma, CA 95476-9748
(707)938-2350 (800)359-4667
Fax:(707)938-2353

Circa 1941. This Mission Revival-style inn is comprised of 12 adjoining bungalows decorated to reflect a sense of California's colorful history. The gardens, which surround the bungalows and main building, were created by a landscape designer who worked for Disneyland. The grounds offer a barbecue area, picnic tables and a hammock. The continental breakfasts can be enjoyed either in the Spanish-style ramada or in the privacy of your room. Conference facilities are available. The inn offers close access to the area's many wineries, including the oldest vineyard in the state.

Innkeeper(s): David & Jennifer Rose. $75-115. MC VISA AX TC. 14 rooms with PB. 6 suites. 1 conference room. Breakfast included in rates. Types of meals: continental breakfast and early coffee/tea. Beds: QT. Air conditioning and cable TV in room. Fax and copier on premises. Antiques nearby.

Certificate may be used: Jan. 10 to Dec. 20, Sunday-Thursday.

Sonora   H7

Lavender Hill B&B

683 Barretta St, Sonora, CA 95370-5132
(209)532-9024

In the historic Gold Rush town of Sonora is this Queen Anne Victorian inn. Its four guest rooms include the Lavender Room, which has a mini-suite with desk, sitting area and clawfoot tub. After a busy day fishing, biking, river rafting or exploring nearby Yosemite National Park, guests may relax in the antique-filled parlor or the sitting room. Admiring the inn's gardens from the wraparound porch is also a favorite activity. Be sure to ask about dinner theater packages.

Innkeeper(s): Charles Marinelli. $70-90. MC VISA AX. 4 rooms. Breakfast included in rates. Types of meals: full breakfast and early coffee/tea. Air conditioning, turn-down service and ceiling fan in room. Cable TV on premises. Antiques, shopping, downhill skiing,

cross-country skiing, sporting events and theater nearby.

Certificate may be used: April 1 through Dec. 31, Sunday through Thursday only. Jan. 1 through March 31, anytime.

Soquel   J5

Blue Spruce Inn

2815 S Main St, Soquel, CA 95073-2412
(408)464-1137 (800)559-1137
Fax:(408)475-0608

Circa 1875. Near the north coast of Monterey Bay, this old farmhouse has been freshly renovated and refitted with luxurious touches. The Seascape is a favorite room with its private entrance, wicker furnishings and bow-shaped Jacuzzi for two. The Carriage House offers skylights above the bed, while

a heart decor dominates Two Hearts. Local art, Amish quilts and featherbeds are featured throughout. Brunch enchiladas are the inn's speciality. Santa Cruz is four miles away.

Innkeeper(s): Patricia & Tom O'Brien. $85-135. MC VISA AX PC TC. 6 rooms with PB, 5 with FP. 1 conference room. Breakfast and evening snack included in rates. Types of meals: full breakfast, gourmet breakfast and early coffee/tea. Beds: QT. Turn-down service, cable TV and VCR in room. Fax and library on premises. Amusement parks, antiques, fishing, parks, shopping, theater and watersports nearby.

Location: At the edge of Soquel Village, mid-Santa Cruz County, north shore of the Monterey Bay.

Seen in: Village View, California Meetings.

"You offer such graciousness to your guests and a true sense of welcome."

Certificate may be used: Sunday-Thursday. Oct. 1 until May 15.

Springville K9

Annie's B&B
33024 Globe Dr,
Springville, CA 93265-9718
(209)539-3827 Fax:(209)539-2179

Circa 1903. Innkeepers Annie and John Bozanich nicknamed their country-style bed & breakfast "Hog Heaven," in honor of their bountiful sow, Blossom, and more petite potbellied pig, Boo. The five-acre grounds boast wonderful views of the Sierra Nevadas. The grounds also include John's custom saddle shop. In keeping with the swine theme, Annie has named one guest quarter Sows Room and another the Boars Room. The third room was named in honor of Annie's grandmother, Ode. Ode's Room features her grandmother's bedroom set and a bedspread crocheted by Ode. This room is located in the back house and has its own private entrance. Annie prepares the multitude of home-baked treats on an antique, woodburning cookstove. In addition to the ample breakfast, afternoon refreshments are served.

Innkeeper(s): Ann & John Bozanich. $75-85. MC VISA AX DC TC. 3 rooms with PB. Breakfast, afternoon tea and evening snack included in rates. Types of meals: full breakfast and early coffee/tea. Dinner available. Beds: DT. Ceiling fan in room. Cable TV, VCR and spa on premises. Antiques, fishing, parks, shopping, cross-country skiing, theater and watersports nearby.

Certificate may be used: Sunday-Thursday only, no holidays or special events days.

Sunset Beach O10

Harbour Inn
PO Box 1439,
Sunset Beach, CA 90742-1439
(310)592-4770 (800)596-4770
Fax:(310)592-3547

Circa 1989. This waterside inn offers relaxing accommodations in a setting convenient to the beach (it's just a block away) and many of Southern California's popular attractions. Situated midway between Huntington Beach and Long Beach, the inn is close to Disneyland, Knott's Berry Farm and many fine restaurants and shops. The simple, comfortable rooms are decorated in cheerful floral prints, and many afford ocean or harbor views. An expanded continental breakfast is served each morning, offering a variety of cereals, pastries, bagels and homemade breads.

Innkeeper(s): Joyce & Marion Dooley. $69-109. MC VISA AX DC CB DS TC. 25 rooms, 17 with PB. 8 suites. 1 conference room. Type of meal: continental-plus breakfast. Catering service and room service available. Beds: KQ. Air conditioning, cable TV and VCR in room. Fax and copier on premises. Handicap access. Amusement parks, antiques, fishing, parks, sporting events, theater and watersports nearby.

Certificate may be used: Oct. 1 to May 15, Sunday-Friday, holidays and special events excluded.

Sutter Creek G6

Grey Gables B&B Inn
161 Hanford St, PO Box 1687,
Sutter Creek, CA 95685-1687
(209)267-1039 (800)473-9422
Fax:(209)267-0998

Circa 1897. The innkeepers of this Victorian home offer poetic accommodations both in the delightful decor and by the names of their guest rooms. The Keats, Bronte and Tennyson rooms afford garden views, while the Byron and Browning rooms include clawfoot tubs. The Victorian Suite, which encompasses the top floor, affords views of the garden, as well as a historic churchyard. All of the guest rooms boast fireplaces. Stroll down brick pathways through the terraced garden or relax in the parlor. A proper English tea is served with cakes and scones. Hors d'oeuvres and libations are served in the evenings.

Innkeeper(s): Roger & Susan Garlick. $85-125. MC VISA AX DS PC TC. 8 rooms with PB, 8 with FP. Breakfast, afternoon tea and evening snack included in rates. Types of meals: gourmet breakfast and early coffee/tea. Beds: KQT. Air conditioning and ceiling fan in room. Fax and copier on premises. Handicap access. Antiques, fishing, parks, shopping, downhill skiing, cross-country skiing, theater and watersports nearby.

Certificate may be used: Year-round, Sunday-Thursday, holidays excluded.

The Hanford House
61 Hanford St, Hwy 49,
Sutter Creek, CA 95685
(209)267-0747 (800)871-5839
Fax:(209)267-1825

Circa 1929. When Karen and Bob Tierno purchased this unique Gold Country inn, they were determined to maintain the former innkeepers' standards for hospitality. Karen and Bob went a step further and added many new amenities for their guests, including a conference room, fax machine and providing computer access. While these touches are perfect for the business traveler, the inn is still a place for relaxation. The inn offers a shaded outdoor patio, charming parlor and a rooftop sundeck. Guests are greeted with freshly baked cookies upon check-in, treated to a homemade breakfast each morning and invited to partake in afternoon refreshments.

Innkeeper(s): Bob & Karen Tierno. $89-139. MC VISA DS TC. 9 rooms with PB, 1 with FP. 1 conference room. Breakfast, afternoon tea and evening snack included in rates. Types of meals: full breakfast, gourmet breakfast and early coffee/tea. Catering service available. Beds: Q. Air conditioning and ceiling fan in room. Fax on premises. Handicap access. Parks, downhill skiing and watersports nearby.

Certificate may be used: Sunday-Thursday (excluding holidays, all year).

Tahoe City   F7

Mayfield House
236 Grove St, PO Box 5999,
Tahoe City, CA 96145
(916)583-1001

Circa 1932. Norman Mayfield, Lake Tahoe's pioneer contractor, built this house of wood and stone, and Julia Morgan, architect of Hearst Castle, was a frequent guest. Dark-stained pine paneling, a beamed ceiling, and a large stone fireplace make an inviting living room. Many rooms have views of mountains, woods, or the golf course.

Innkeeper(s): Cynthia & Bruce Knauss. $75-150. MC VISA AX. 6 rooms, 3 with PB. Breakfast included in rates. Types of meals: full breakfast and early coffee/tea. Evening snack available. Beds: KQD. Cable TV on premises. Fishing, parks, shopping, downhill skiing, cross-country skiing and watersports nearby.

Location: Downtown on Highway 28.

Seen in: Sierra Heritage, Tahoe Today.

"The place is charming beyond words, complete with down comforters and wine upon checking in. The breakfast is superb."

Certificate may be used: Jan. 5-June 30, Sunday-Thursday, Oct. 1-Nov. 22, Sunday-Thursday.

Temecula   P12

Loma Vista B&B
33350 La Serena Way,
Temecula, CA 92591-5049
(909)676-7047 Fax:(909)676-0077

Circa 1987. This California Mission-style home offers vineyard views from its balconies. Each guest room is named for a variety of wine. The Fume Blanc, Zinfandel, Sauvignon Blanc and Chardonnay rooms include private balconies where guests can take in the view. Champagne breakfasts get the day off to a good start, and evening wine and cheese is served. After dinner, relax in the inn's hot tub. The area is full of activities, including winery tours, shopping and hot air ballooning. Temecula is an hour from San Diego and about 90 miles from Los Angeles.

Innkeeper(s): Betty & Dick Ryan. $95-125. MC VISA DS PC TC. 6 rooms with PB. Breakfast and evening snack included in rates. Types of meals: gourmet breakfast and early coffee/tea. Beds: KQT. Air conditioning and ceiling fan in room. Cable TV, fax, spa, bicycles and library on premises. Antiques, fishing and parks nearby.

Location: Wine country, 5 miles from Lake Skinner.

Seen in: Sunset, Bride's, Los Angeles Times, Los Angeles Magazine.

Certificate may be used: Monday-Thursday holidays excluded.

Templeton   L6

Country House Inn
91 S Main St, Templeton, CA 93465-8701
(805)434-1598 (800)362-6032

Circa 1886. This Victorian home, built by the founder of Templeton, is set off by rose-bordered gardens. It was designated as a historic site in San Luis Obispo County. All of the rooms are decorated with antiques and fresh flowers. Hearst Castle and six wineries are nearby.

Innkeeper(s): Dianne Garth. $85-95. MC VISA DS PC. 5 rooms with PB, 1 with FP. 1 suite. Breakfast included in rates. Types of meals: full breakfast, gourmet breakfast and early coffee/tea. Afternoon tea available. Beds: KQT. Ceiling fan in room. Antiques, fishing, parks, shopping, theater and watersports nearby.

Location: Twenty miles north of San Luis Obispo on Hwy 101.

"A feast for all the senses, an esthetic delight."

Certificate may be used: April-September, Sunday-Thursday; October-March, Sunday-Saturday.

Trinidad   C2

The Lost Whale Inn B&B
3452 Patricks Point Dr,
Trinidad, CA 95570-9782
(707)677-3425 (800)677-7859
Fax:(707)677-0284

Circa 1989. The view from this Cape Cod-style inn is one of the best in Northern California. Rugged coastline and an endless sea, dotted from time to time with whales, is what guest enjoy from the inn's relaxing porch. Several guest rooms offer ocean views. Innkeepers Susanne Lakin and Lee Miller are an artist and musician, respectively, and their creative energy has formed a wonderful sense of romance throughout the inn. However, there is a family atmosphere prevalent as well. The innkeepers offer several sleeping lofts for children, a playground area and a variety of animals to pet.

Innkeeper(s): Susanne Lakin & Lee Miller. $100-160. MC VISA AX DS PC TC. 8 rooms with PB. 2 cottages. 1 conference room. Breakfast and afternoon tea included in rates. Types of meals: gourmet breakfast and early coffee/tea. Beds: QDT. Fax, copier, spa and library on premises. Antiques, fishing, parks, shopping, cross-country skiing, sporting

events, theater and watersports nearby.
Certificate may be used: Jan. 1-March 30, excluding holidays.

Ukiah   F3

Vichy Hot Springs Resort & Inn
2605 Vichy Springs Rd,
Ukiah, CA 95482-3507
(707)462-9515 Fax:(707)462-9516

Circa 1864. This famous spa once attracted guests such as Jack London, Mark Twain and Teddy Roosevelt. Twelve rooms and two redwood cottages have been renovated for bed & breakfast, while the 1860s naturally sparkling mineral baths remain unchanged. A new hot spa and Olympic-size pool await your arrival. A magical waterfall is a 30-minute walk along a year-round stream.
Innkeeper(s): Gilbert & Marjorie Ashoff. $130-170. MC VISA AX DC CB DS PC TC. 15 rooms with PB, 3 with FP. 3 cottages. 2 conference rooms. Breakfast and picnic lunch included in rates. Types of meals: continental-plus breakfast and early coffee/tea. Catering service available. Beds: QT. Air conditioning in room. Fax, copier, computer, spa and swimming on premises. Handicap access. Antiques, fishing, parks, shopping, theater and watersports nearby.
Location: Three miles east of US Hwy 101 in Ukiah, Mendocino County.
Seen in: Sunset, Sacramento Bee, San Jose Mercury News, Gulliver (Japan), Oregonian, Contra Costa Times, New York Times, San Francisco Chronicle.

"Very beautiful grounds and comfortable accommodations. Thanks for your gracious hospitality and especially the opportunity to meet such good friends...and the water's great!- Attorney General State of California, Dan Lungren. Great place! Good for Presidents and everyone else.- Ex-Governor California, Jerry Brown."
Certificate may be used: Sunday-Thursday (May-October), Sunday-Friday (November-April), no holidays.

Venice   O10

Venice Beach House
15 30th Pl, Venice, CA 90291-0043
(310)823-1966 Fax:(310)823-1842

Circa 1911. This two-story cape boasts a beautiful garden and a veranda with an ocean view. Every room is specially decorated and guest quarters feature canopy beds and rockers. The inn has a swimming beach and is situated near the Venice Pier, which can be reached on foot or with the inn's bicycles. In the evening, refreshments are served by a fire or on the veranda, where guests can enjoy the sunset. The Pier Suite has an ocean view, sitting room and wood-burning fireplace. The James Peasgood suite has a Jacuzzi, a balcony and cathedral wood ceilings.

Innkeeper(s): Leslie Smith. $85-165. MC VISA AX PC TC. 9 rooms, 5 with PB, 1 with FP. 2 suites. Breakfast and afternoon tea included in rates. Type of meal: full breakfast. Beds: KQDT. Cable TV in room. Fax, swimming and library on premises. Amusement parks, antiques, fishing, parks, shopping, sporting events, theater and watersports nearby.
Location: One-half block from the famous Venice beach boardwalk.
Seen in: Independent Journal, Sunset, The Argaunant, Daily News, Herald Examiner.

"To stay at the Venice Beach House is to stay with a friendly family - a 'home away from home' (except the breakfasts are a lot better!) We've stayed in four different rooms, each better than the last."
Certificate may be used: September-May, Sunday-Monday.

Visalia   K8

Ben Maddox House B&B
601 N Encina St, Visalia, CA 93291-3603
(209)739-8381 (800)401-9800

Circa 1876. Just 40 minutes away from Sequoia National Park sits this late-19th-century home, constructed completely of gorgeous Sequoia redwood. The parlor, dining room and bedrooms remain in their original state. The house has been tastefully furnished with antiques from the 18th and 19th centuries. "Big Bertha," a coal-burning furnace that has been converted to gas, heats the home from her spot in the basement, so no fireplaces are necessary. Breakfasts are a delight, both to look at and to eat, with fresh fruit, a selection of homemade breads, eggs and meat. The meal is surrounded by crystal, gold, flowers and candlelight.
Innkeeper(s): Diane & Al Muro. $75-85. MC VISA AX. 4 rooms, 3 with PB. Breakfast and evening snack included in rates. Types of meals: full breakfast and early coffee/tea. Beds: KQ. Air conditioning, ceiling fan and cable TV in room. Spa and bicycles on premises. Antiques, fishing, parks, shopping, cross-country skiing, sporting events, theater and watersports nearby.
Seen in: Southland.

"Just a very gracious and delightful place and excellent breakfast, also comfortable and a warm and friendly hostess, a delightful experience in all."
Certificate may be used: March 1-Jan. 31, Sunday-Friday.

Volcano   G7

St. George Hotel
16104 Pine Grove,
Volcano, CA 95689-0009
(209)296-4458 Fax:(209)296-4458

Circa 1862. This handsome old three-story hotel in the National Register features a double-tiered wraparound porch. There is a dining room, full bar and lounge area with fireplace. It is situated on one acre of lawns. An annex built in 1961 provides rooms with private baths. Volcano is a Mother Lode town that has been untouched by supermarkets and modern motels and remains much as it was during the Gold Rush. Modified American Plan (breakfast and dinner) available.

Innkeeper(s): Marlene & Chuck Inman. $71-77. MAP. MC VISA AX. 20 rooms, 6 with PB. 1 conference room. Breakfast included in rates. Type of meal: full breakfast. Dinner available. Beds: QDT. Fax and copier on premises. Antiques, fishing, parks, shopping, downhill skiing, cross-country skiing, theater and watersports nearby.

Location: Sixty-one miles from Sacramento.

"What is so precious about the hotel is its combination of graciousness and simplicity."

Certificate may be used: Wednesday-Friday, except January and half of February, and subject to availability.

Walnut Creek   H5

The Mansion at Lakewood
1056 Hacienda Dr,
Walnut Creek, CA 94598-4740
(510)945-3600 (800)477-7898
Fax:(510)945-3608

Secluded acres with garden paths, fountains and a gazebo surround this Victorian hideaway. Guests are pampered with flowers, fluffy robes, bath salts and rooms scented with potpourri. Heart-shaped chocolates and poetry books restored many weary guests' tired spirits. The grounds were part of an old Spanish land grant, and the home was built by an early Walnut Creek settler. The old-fashioned chandeliers and antiques add to the historical charm. The Juliet Suite includes a balcony with a garden view. Another room offers a Jacuzzi tub, and still others include fireplaces, four-poster beds and canopies.

Innkeeper(s): Sharyn McCoy. $135-300. MC VISA AX DS. 7 rooms. Breakfast included in rates. Type of meal: continental-plus breakfast.

Certificate may be used: January through December, Sunday through Thursday (no Fridays or Saturdays).

Westport   E2

Howard Creek Ranch
40501 N Hwy One, PO Box 121,
Westport, CA 95488
(707)964-6725 Fax:(707)964-6725

Circa 1871. First settled as a land grant of thousands of acres, Howard Creek Ranch is now a 40-acre farm with sweeping views of the Pacific Ocean, sandy beaches and rolling mountains. A 75-foot

bridge spans a creek that flows past barns and outbuildings to the beach 200 yards away. The farmhouse is surrounded by green lawns, an award-winning flower garden, and grazing cows and horses. This rustic rural location offers antiques, a hot tub and sauna.

Innkeeper(s): Charles & Sally Grigg. $55-145. MC VISA AX. 11 rooms, 9 with PB, 5 with FP. 3 suites. 3 cottages. Breakfast included in rates. Types of meals: full breakfast, gourmet breakfast and early coffee/tea. Beds: KQD. Ceiling fan in room. Fax, spa, swimming, sauna and library on premises. Antiques, fishing, parks, shopping and theater nearby.

Location: Mendocino Coast on the ocean.

Seen in: California, Country, Vacations.

"Of the dozen or so inns on the West Coast we have visited, this is easily the most enchanting one."

Certificate may be used: Oct. 15-May15, Sunday-Thursday, excluding holiday periods.

Yountville   G4

Bordeaux House
6600 Washington St,
Yountville, CA 94599-1301
(707)944-2855 (800)677-6370

Circa 1980. Surrounded by some of California's most famous vineyards, this inn offers a variety of guest rooms, each appointed with modern-style decor and a woodburning fireplace. A majestic pine tree and unique, brick spiral staircase designate the front of this inn, which is set on nearly one acre of landscaped grounds. Guests are pampered with an afternoon tea. Aside from the famed wineries, the area is full of antique shops, galleries and boutiques to explore.

Innkeeper(s): Jean Lunney. $95-135. MC VISA TC. 7 rooms with PB, 6 with FP. 1 conference room. Breakfast and afternoon tea included in rates. Type of meal: continental-plus breakfast. Beds: QT. Air conditioning and cable TV in room. Antiques, parks, shopping and theater nearby.

Certificate may be used: November-April, Sunday through Thursday.

Maison Fleurie

6529 Yount St,
Yountville, CA 94599-1278
(707)944-2056 (800)788-0369
Fax:(707)944-9342

Circa 1894. Vines cover the two-foot thick brick walls of the Bakery, the Carriage House and the Main House of this French country inn. One of the Four Sisters Inns, it is reminiscent of a bucolic setting in Provence. Rooms are decorated in a pristine, romantic style, some with vineyard and garden views. Rooms in the Old Bakery have fireplaces. A pool and outdoor spa are available and you may borrow bicycles for wandering the countryside.

Innkeeper(s): Roger Asbill. $110-190. MC VISA AX TC. 13 rooms with PB, 6 with FP. Breakfast and afternoon tea included in rates. Types of meals: full breakfast, gourmet breakfast and early coffee/tea. Beds: KQD. Turn-down service in room. Fax, spa and bicycles on premises. Handicap access. Antiques and shopping nearby.

"Peaceful surroundings, friendly staff."

Certificate may be used: November-March, Sunday-Thursday holidays, special events excluded.

Yuba City   *F5*

Harkey House B&B

212 C St, Yuba City, CA 95991-5014
(916)674-1942

Circa 1875. An essence of romance fills this Victorian Gothic house set in a historic neighborhood. Every inch of the home has been given a special touch, from the knickknacks and photos in the sitting room to the quilts and furnishings in the guest quarters. The Harkey Suite features a brass bed with a down comforter and extras such as an adjoining library room and a pellet-burning stove. Breakfasts of muffins, fresh fruit, juice and freshly ground coffee are served in a glass-paned dining room or on the patio.

Innkeeper(s): Bob & Lee Jones. $75-100. MC VISA AX DS PC TC. 4 rooms with PB, 2 with FP. 1 suite. 1 conference room. Breakfast included in rates. Types of meals: full breakfast and early coffee/tea. Beds: Q. Air conditioning, turn-down service, ceiling fan and cable TV in room. VCR, spa, swimming and library on premises. Antiques, fishing, parks, shopping, theater and watersports nearby.

Seen in: Country.

"This place is simply marvelous...the most comfortable bed in travel."

Certificate may be used: Sunday through Saturday.

Colorado

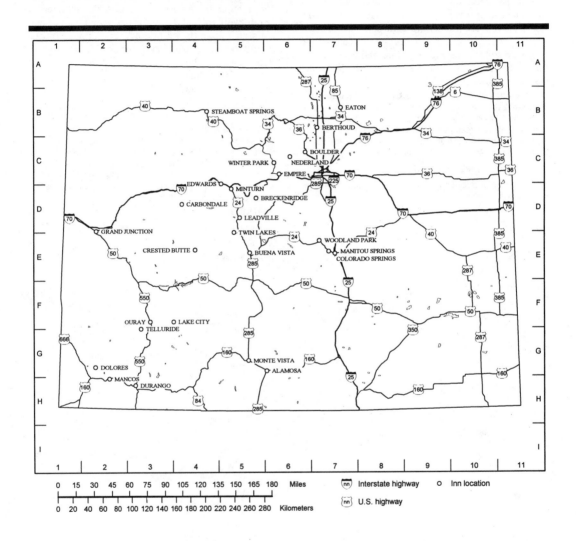

Miles: 0 15 30 45 60 75 90 105 120 135 150 165 180

Kilometers: 0 20 40 60 80 100 120 140 160 180 200 220 240 260 280

⬡nn Interstate highway   ○ Inn location

⬡nn U.S. highway

Alamosa   G6

Cottonwood Inn
123 San Juan Ave,
Alamosa, CO 81101-2547
(719)589-3882 (800)955-2623
Fax:(719)589-6437

Circa 1908. This refurbished Colorado bungalow is filled with antiques and paintings by local artists. The dining room set once belonged to Billy Adams, a Colorado governor in the 1920s. Blue-corn

blueberry pancakes and flaming Grand Marnier omelets are the inn's specialties. A favorite day trip is riding the Cumbres-Toltec Scenic Railroad over the La Magna Pass, site of an Indiana Jones movie.
Innkeeper(s): Julie Mordecai & George Sellman. $48-85. MC VISA AX DC CB DS PC TC. 7 rooms, 2 with PB. 3 suites. Breakfast and evening snack included in rates. Types of meals: full breakfast, gourmet breakfast and early coffee/tea. Afternoon tea and catered breakfast available. Beds: KQTD. Cable TV, VCR, fax and copier on premises. Antiques, parks and downhill skiing nearby.
Location: Close to Great Sand Dunes National Monument.
Seen in: Rocky Mountain News, Country Inns, Denver Post, Milwaukee Journal.

"My husband wants to come over every morning for blueberry pancakes and strawberry rhubarb sauce."
Certificate may be used: Nov. 1-April 31, excluding Crane Festival weekend.

Berthoud   B7

Berthoud B&B
444 N 1st St, Berthoud, CO 80513-1317
(970)532-4566 Fax:(970)532-4566

Circa 1895. With the Rocky Mountains as a backdrop and complete with a two-story turret and sweeping veranda, this inn reminds guests of a picture-perfect Victorian dollhouse. Tucked away in the turret is the Madame Pompadour Suite where Louis XV furniture graces the sitting area. The room is given a French country garden feel with its

sleeping alcove with lavender walls, violet floral wallpaper, curtains, bed cover and orchid carpet. A chandelier hangs from the turret ceiling above a huge, circular bed, and 11 windows offer a view of the yard and its tall evergreens.
Innkeeper(s): Janet & Gary. $95-135. MC VISA AX DS PC TC. 7 rooms with PB. 2 suites. 1 conference room. Breakfast included in rates. Types of meals: gourmet breakfast and early coffee/tea. Afternoon tea, dinner, evening snack, lunch, gourmet lunch, banquet service, catering service and room service available. Beds: KQ. Turn-down service, ceiling fan, cable TV and VCR in room. Fax, copier, spa, bicycles, library and pet boarding on premises. Handicap access. Amusement parks, antiques, fishing, parks, shopping, downhill skiing, cross-country skiing, sporting events, theater and watersports nearby.
Certificate may be used: January through May, September through December, Sunday-Thursday.

Boulder   C6

The Magpie Inn
1001 Spruce St, Boulder, CO 80302-4028
(303)449-6528

Circa 1899. The Magpie Inn employed nine local interior designers to refurbish the mansion. Each room was given special and unique attention, with the focus being romance with a Victorian theme. The result is a collection of antiques, custom furniture and softly hued fabrics to elicit memories of an elegant home. Visual delights abound from marble fireplaces and fine paintings to old photographs and prints of Boulder.
Innkeeper(s): Teresa Koby. $88-135. MC VISA. 7 rooms. 1 suite. Breakfast included in rates. Types of meals: continental breakfast and full breakfast. Cable TV on premises. Antiques, shopping, downhill skiing, cross-country skiing, sporting events and theater nearby.
Certificate may be used: September-April.

Breckenridge D5

Hunt Placer Inn
275 Ski Hill Rd, PO Box 4898,
Breckenridge, CO 80424-4898
(970)453-7573 (800)472-1430
Fax:(970)453-2335

Circa 1994. Set among woods in a historic, gold-mining town, this delightful mountain chalet is located on what was an actual mining claim. Guest rooms are decorated in a variety of styles, from Southwestern to European, each with an elegant flair. The room and suite names reflect the decor, such as the Bavaria Suite or the Gold Rush Room. The morning menu changes daily, offering items such as Swiss muesli, fresh fruit, pancakes topped with praline sauce, creme brulee and quiche. A free shuttle takes wintertime guests to the nearby ski slopes and alpine slide.

Innkeeper(s): Carl & Gwen Ray. $95-185. MC VISA AX DC CB DS PC TC. 8 rooms with PB, 3 with FP. 1 conference room. Breakfast and afternoon tea included in rates. Types0of meals: full breakfast, gourmet breakfast and early coffee/tea. Beds: QT. Cable TV, VCR and fax on premises. Handicap access. Antiques, fishing, parks, shopping, downhill skiing, cross-country skiing, theater and watersports nearby.

Certificate may be used: April, September through November, Sunday through Thursday.

Swan Mountain Inn
16172 Hwy 9,
Breckenridge, CO 80424
(303)453-7903 (800)578-3687

Circa 1986. Less than seven miles from the outstanding ski areas of Keystone, Breckenridge and Copper Mountain, this log home is a cozy, warm place to enjoy a mountain getaway. After a day enjoying nature, guests can dine by candlelight at the inn's dining room or enjoy a drink at the fireside bar. Relax on the glassed-inn sun porches, the decks or a comfortable hammock.

Innkeeper(s): Steve Gessner. $40-100. MC VISA DS PC TC. 4 rooms, 3 with PB. 1 suite. Breakfast and afternoon tea included in rates. Types of meals: full breakfast and gourmet breakfast. Dinner and gourmet lunch available. Cable TV and VCR in room. Spa on premises. Handicap access. Antiques, fishing, parks, shopping, downhill skiing, cross-country skiing and watersports nearby.

Certificate may be used: April 16-June 30, Sept. 15-Nov. 21, Sunday-Thursday.

Buena Vista E5

Trout City Inn
PO Box 431,
Buena Vista, CO 81211-0431
(719)495-0348

Guests at this unique inn can sleep in an elegant Victorian Pullman car or in the Drover's caboose. Located on 40 acres of the San Isabel National Forest, the inn's site is on the path of two famous mountain railroads. Although the historic narrow gauge train is stationary, the locomotive has been used for parades. The depot rooms are furnished in authentic Victorian style, but the berth mattresses are custom madeólonger and a bit firmer than those of a hundred years ago.

Innkeeper(s): Juel Kjeldsen. $35-40. MC VISA. 4 rooms. 1 conference room. Breakfast included in rates. Type of meal: full breakfast. VCR on premises. Antiques, shopping, downhill skiing, cross-country skiing and theater nearby.

Certificate may be used: June 15-Sept. 15, weekends only (Friday, Saturday, Sunday evenings).

Carbondale D4

Ambiance Inn
66 N 2nd St, Carbondale, CO 81623-2102
(970)963-3597 (800)350-1515

Circa 1976. This contemporary chalet-style home is located in the beautiful Crystal Valley between Aspen and Glenwood Springs. Year-round activities are numerous in the area, but ski buffs will be excited to know that Aspen and Snowmass are only a 30-minute drive away. Glenwood Springs and the world's largest hot springs are just 15 minutes away. Custom picnic baskets for outings are available with two days' advance notice. The New Orleans Library is adjacent to all three guest rooms on the second floor.

Innkeeper(s): Norma & Robert Morris. $60-80. MC DS PC. 4 rooms with PB. 1 suite. Breakfast and picnic lunch included in rates. Types of meals: full breakfast and early coffee/tea. Beds: Q. Ceiling fan and cable TV in room. VCR on premises. Antiques, fishing, parks, shopping, downhill skiing, cross-country skiing and sporting events nearby.

Seen in: Rocky Mountain News.

Certificate may be used: Excludes holidays and Christmas week. Midweek okay.

Colorado Springs E7

Black Forest B&B
11170 Black Forest Rd,
Colorado Springs, CO 80908-3986
(719)495-4208 (800)809-9901
Fax:(719)495-0688

Circa 1984. Ponderosa pines, golden aspens and fragrant meadows surround this massive log home built on the highest point east of the Rocky Mountains. This rustic mountain setting is complete with 20 acres of beautiful country to explore. If you want to fully experience mountain living, the innkeepers will be more than happy to share their

chores with you, which range from cutting firewood to planting Christmas trees on their tree farm. A greenhouse holds a indoor lap pool, sauna, fitness center and honeymoon suite.

Innkeeper(s): Robert & Susan Putnam. $75-125. MC VISA AX DS PC TC. 4 rooms with PB, 1 with FP. 3 suites. 2 cottages. 1 conference room. Breakfast and evening snack included in rates. Types of meals: continental-plus breakfast and early coffee/tea. Beds: KQDT. Ceiling fan in room. VCR, fax and copier on premises. Handicap access. Antiques, parks, shopping, cross-country skiing, sporting events and theater nearby.

Certificate may be used: November through April, except Christmas and Thanksgiving.

Cheyenne Canon Inn
2030 W Cheyenne Blvd, Colorado Springs, CO 80906
(719)633-0625 (800)633-0625
Fax:(800)633-8826

Circa 1921. World travelers Barbara and John Starr have filled this rustic home with interesting finds from their many visits to foreign lands. The home was built by the wife of a Manitou Springs sheriff and originally served as an upscale casino, and more infamously, a bordello. During the home's heyday as an inn, guests included the Marx Brothers and Lon Cheney. The massive home features more than 100 windows, all boasting beautiful views, original stained glass and silver wall sconces. Each of the seven guest rooms and two cottages captures an unique international flavor. The innkeepers recently added "Le Petit Chateau," a romantic cottage

tucked beneath 50-foot tall pines trees. Spend the night tucked away in a room reminiscent of a Swiss chalet or enjoy the atmosphere of an Oriental tea room in another guest quarter. The second-floor hot tub affords a view of Cheyenne Mountain. The innkeepers have created a relaxing retreat, but also offer many amenities for the business traveler including in-room phones and modem outlets.

Innkeeper(s): John, Barbara & Josh Starr. $75-175. MC VISA AX DS PC TC. 9 rooms with PB, 3 with FP. 3 suites. 1 cottage. 2 conference rooms. Types of meals: full breakfast and early coffee/tea. Beds: KQT. Turn-down service, ceiling fan, cable TV and VCR in room. Fax, copier, spa and library on premises. Antiques, fishing, parks, shopping, downhill skiing, cross-country skiing, sporting events and theater nearby.

Seen in: Denver Post, Colorado Source, Beacon.

"It truly was 'home away from home.' You have made it so welcoming and warm. Needless to say our breakfasts at home will never come close to the Cheyenne Canon Inn!!"

Certificate may be used: Nov. 1 to April 30, Sunday-Thursday. Holidays excluded.

The Painted Lady
1318 W Colorado Ave,
Colorado Springs, CO 80904-4023
(719)473-3165

Circa 1894. Once a popular restaurant in Old Colorado City, the Painted Lady has been remodeled into a bed & breakfast by its new owners. The three-story Victorian is decorated in a warm, romantic manner with lace and floral fabrics. Antique iron and four-poster beds, clawfoot tubs and brass fixtures fill the guest rooms. Hearty breakfasts, served on the veranda in summer, might include seafood quiche or souffles and homemade breads. Afternoon refreshments can be enjoyed in the parlor or on one of the porches.

Innkeeper(s): Valerie Maslowski. $70-115. MC VISA AX DS TC. 4 rooms, 3 with PB. 2 suites. Breakfast included in rates. Types of meals: full breakfast and early coffee/tea. Beds: QDT. Air conditioning, ceiling fan and cable TV in room. VCR on premises. Antiques, fishing, parks, shopping, downhill skiing, cross-country skiing, sporting events, theater and watersports nearby.

Location: In historic Old Colorado City.

"Calm, peaceful. Our first B&B, very memorable."

Certificate may be used: Nov. 1 to April 30, Sunday-Thursday.

Crested Butte E4

Crystal Inn
624 Gothic Ave, PO Box 125,
Crested Butte, CO 81224-0125
(970)349-1338 (800)390-1338
Fax:(970)349-1942

Circa 1993. This natural wood home is located on a quiet, residential street a block and a half from a ski shuttle stop. Antiques and country furnishings decorate the cozy guest rooms. Each of the parlors offers a warming fire. There is an indoor hot tub as well. Breakfasts are served family style with eggs, sausages, bacon, fruit, cereal and the like. Shops and restaurants are within walking distance.

Innkeeper(s): Dennis & Charlene Goree. $70-109. MC VISA AX DS PC TC. 5 rooms with PB. Breakfast included in rates. Beds: Q. Cable TV, VCR, fax and spa on premises. Fishing, parks, shopping, downhill skiing, cross-country skiing, theater and watersports nearby.

Certificate may be used: Dec. 22-Nov. 20, 1997; Sunday-Thursday.

Dolores G2

Mountain View B&B
28050 County Rd P, Dolores, CO 81323
(970)882-7861 (800)228-4592

Circa 1984. This sprawling ranch-type home has a magnificent view of the Mesa Verde National Park, which is 12 miles to its entrance. Besides spending a day or two touring the museum and

cliff dwellings in Mesa Verde, guests can step outside this inn to enjoy its 22 acres of trails, woods and a small canyon with creek. In each direction, a short drive will take you to mountains, desert, canyon lands, mesa, forest lakes and world famous archaeological settings.

Innkeeper(s): Brenda & Cecil Dunn. $49-79. MC VISA PC TC. 8 rooms with PB. 4 suites. 1 conference room. Breakfast and evening snack included in rates. Types of meals: continental-plus breakfast, full breakfast and early coffee/tea. Dinner available. Beds: QDT. Ceiling fan in room. Spa and library on premises. Handicap access. Fishing, parks, shopping, downhill skiing, cross-country skiing and watersports nearby.

Certificate may be used: Jan. 5-April 30.

Durango H3

Leland House
721 E 2nd Ave, Durango, CO 81301-5435
(970)385-1920 (800)664-1920
Fax:(970)385-1967

Circa 1927. Each room of this two-story brick building is named after a historic figure associated with the Leland House, which has ties to a well-known builder, lumber company magnate, wool merchant and railroad executive. Gourmet breakfasts include the inn specialties of home-cooked

granola and cranberry scones. Also, daily entrees include Southwestern burritos, filled French toast, pancakes or waffles topped with fresh fruit. Guests can tour the historic districts of Durango and browse through many fine shops, galleries and outlet stores.

Innkeeper(s): Kirk & Diane Komick. $85-135. MC VISA AX DS PC TC. 10 rooms with PB. 6 suites. Breakfast and afternoon tea included in rates. Types of meals: full breakfast and gourmet breakfast. Picnic lunch and catering service available. Restaurant on premises. Beds: QD. Air conditioning, ceiling fan and cable TV in room. VCR, fax and copier on premises. Antiques, fishing, parks, shopping, downhill skiing, cross-country skiing, theater and watersports nearby.

Certificate may be used: Oct. 15 through May 15, except holidays.

The Rochester Hotel

721 E Second, Durango, CO 81301
(970)385-1920 (800)664-1920
Fax:(970)385-1967

Circa 1892. This Federal-style inn's decor is inspired by many Western movies filmed in and around the town. The inn is located one block from the Historic Main Avenue District and three blocks

from the Durango-Silverton Narrow Gauge Railroad. Conveniently located in a beautifully landscaped downtown setting, the building is an authentically restored late-Victorian hotel, fully furnished with antiques from the period.

Innkeeper(s): Kirk & Diane Komick. $125-185. MC VISA AX DS PC TC. 15 rooms with PB. 2 suites. 2 conference rooms. Breakfast and afternoon tea included in rates. Types of meals: full breakfast and gourmet breakfast. Picnic lunch and catering service available. Beds: KQ. Air conditioning, ceiling fan and cable TV in room. VCR, fax and copier on premises. Handicap access. Antiques, fishing, parks, shopping, downhill skiing, cross-country skiing, theater and watersports nearby.

Seen in: Four Corners, Durango, Weekly.

"In a word — exceptional! Far exceeded expectations in every way."

Certificate may be used: Oct. 15 through May 15, excluding holidays.

Eaton
B7

The Victorian Veranda

515 Cheyenne Ave,
Eaton, CO 80615-3473
(970)454-3890

This Queen Anne Victorian boasts a view of the Rocky Mountains from the swings on its wraparound porch. The interior features a hand-carved oak staircase and century-old antiques. The innkeepers provide a tandem bicycle for guests who wish to partake in a tour of the town's historic areas. The West Room boasts a black marble fireplace. The East Room, which overlooks the lush grounds, includes an antique brass bed and whirlpool tub. During mild weather, breakfasts are served on the inn's veranda.

Innkeeper(s): Nadine White. $45-60. 3 rooms. Breakfast included in rates. Type of meal: full breakfast.

Certificate may be used: January to December, Monday through Thursday and excluding holidays.

Edwards
D5

The Lazy Ranch B&B

PO Box 404, Edwards, CO 81632-0404
(970)926-3876 (800)655-9343
Fax:(970)926-3876

Circa 1886. Enjoy a taste of the Old West at this working horse ranch. The Lazy Ranch is the only original homestead left in the Vail Valley. A variety of animals, including chickens, peacocks, rabbits, dogs and cats create the authentic farm atmosphere. Hearty country breakfasts are served with farm-fresh eggs. The innkeepers offer bonfires, barbecues and barn dances to make your country vacation complete. Couples might enjoy moonlight horseback rides accompanied by a romantic dinner. Innkeeper Buddy Calhoun's artwork is displayed in a converted bunk house, which now serves as a gallery.

Innkeeper(s): Buddy & Linda Calhoun. $60-100. MC VISA DS TC. 4 rooms, 1 with PB, 1 with FP. 1 suite. Breakfast and picnic lunch included in rates. Types of meals: full breakfast and early coffee/tea. Catering service and catered breakfast available. Beds: QD. Turn-down service and cable TV in room. VCR, fax, copier, stables and pet boarding on premises. Fishing, shopping, downhill skiing, cross-country skiing and watersports nearby.

"As weekends go, they just don't get any better than the one spent at Lazy Ranch. Thank you so much for the hospitality."

Certificate may be used: April 1-Nov. 1, excluding all holidays.

Empire
C6

Mad Creek B&B
PO Box 404, Empire, CO 80438-0404
(303)569-2003

Circa 1881. This mountain town cottage has just the right combination of Victorian decor with lace, flowers, antiques and gingerbread trim on the facade. Unique touches include door frames of old mineshaft wood, kerosene lamps, Eastlake antiques and complimentary cross-country ski gear and mountain bikes. Relax in front of the rock fireplace while watching a movie, peruse the library filled with local lore, or plan your next adventure with Colorado guides and maps. Empire, which was once a mining town, is conveniently located within 15 to 45 minutes of at least six major ski areas.

Innkeeper(s): Heather & Mike Lopez. $49-69. MC VISA TC. 3 rooms, 1 with PB. Breakfast, afternoon tea and evening snack included in rates. Types of meals: full breakfast and early coffee/tea. Beds: QD. Ceiling fan in room. Cable TV, VCR and bicycles on premises. Antiques, fishing, parks, shopping, downhill skiing, cross-country skiing, theater and watersports nearby.

Certificate may be used: Oct. 15-Nov. 20, Sunday-Thursday; April 16-May 20, Sunday-Thursday.

Grand Junction
D2

Junction Country Inn
861 Grand Ave,
Grand Junction, CO 81501-3424
(970)241-2817

Circa 1907. Innkeepers Karl and Theresa Bloom have created a haven of hospitality at this sturdy, brick inn, which is located in Grand Junction's historic area. The decor is a mix of Edwardian and Victorian with lacy curtains and quilts on the beds. Children are welcomed. Karl and Theresa have a variety of toys and an outdoor play area for little ones. Picnic lunches can be arranged, and the innkeepers serve home-baked treats for their guests each evening.

Innkeeper(s): Karl & Theresa Bloom. $35-79. MC VISA AX TC. 4 rooms, 1 with PB. 2 suites. Breakfast and evening snack included in rates. Picnic lunch available. Beds: QDT. Air conditioning in room. Cable TV, VCR, bicycles and child care on premises. Amusement parks, antiques, fishing, parks, shopping, cross-country skiing, sporting events, theater and watersports nearby.

Certificate may be used: January-December, any days.

Lake City
F4

Crystal Lodge
PO Box 246, Lake City, CO 81235-0246
(303)944-2201 (800)984-1234
Fax:(303)944-2503

With the San Juan Mountains as its backdrop, this rustic, log lodge offers a variety of comfortable accommodations. Aside from the lodge's nine bed-chambers, there are several apartments and cottages, which offer kitchens and sitting or living areas. An extensive country breakfast is available each morning in the lodge's restaurant. Lake City, which once was a booming mining town, boasts the state's largest collection of restored Victorians. Outdoor enthusiasts will have no trouble finding something to do, as Lake City is surrounded by 600,000 acres of public land, perfect for fishing, hiking, horseback riding and many other activities.

Innkeeper(s): Ann Udell. $45-95. MC VISA. 18 rooms. Breakfast included in rates.

Certificate may be used: Oct. 1-May 25.

Old Carson Inn
8401 County Rd 30, PO Box 144,
Lake City, CO 81235
(970)944-2511 (800)294-0608

Circa 1990. Located at an elevation of 9,400 feet, this massive log house provides a secluded mountain setting in a forest of aspens and spruce. The

Bonanza King Mine Room features a cathedral ceiling and soaring windows overlooking an aspen grove. Native American artifacts and antiques are sprinkled throughout the inn.

Innkeeper(s): Don & Judy Berry. $55-105. MC VISA DS. 7 rooms with PB. Breakfast included in rates. Type of meal: full breakfast. Picnic lunch available. Beds: KQ. Ceiling fan in room. VCR and spa on premises. Antiques, fishing, shopping and cross-country skiing nearby.

"Words are inadequate to express how very much we delighted in our stay at your beautiful home."

Certificate may be used: Oct. 1-June 1 excluding holidays.

Leadville

D5

The Ice Palace Inn & Antiques

813 Spruce St, Leadville, CO 80461-3555
(719)486-8272

Circa 1901. Innkeeper Kami Kolakowski was born in this historic Colorado town, and it was her dream to one day return and run a bed & breakfast. Now with husband Giles, she has created a restful retreat out of this turn-of-the-century home built with lumber from the famed Leadville Ice Palace. Giles and Kami have filled the home with antiques and pieces of history from the Ice Palace and the town. Guests are treated to a mouth-watering gourmet breakfast with treats such as stuffed French toast or German apple pancakes. As the name suggests, an antique shop is located on the premises.

Innkeeper(s): Giles & Kami Kolakowski. $69-129. PC TC. 3 rooms with PB. Breakfast, afternoon tea and evening snack included in rates. Types of meals: gourmet breakfast and early coffee/tea. Catering service and room service available. Beds: QDT. Turn-down service and ceiling fan in room. Cable TV, VCR and library on premises. Antiques, fishing, parks, shopping, downhill skiing, cross-country skiing, theater and watersports nearby.

Certificate may be used: Anytime upon availability. No holidays.

Peri & Ed's Mountain Hide Away

201 W 8th St, Leadville, CO 80461-3529
(719)486-0716 (800)933-3715
Fax:(719)486-2181

Circa 1879. This former boarding house was built during the boom days of Leadville. Families can picnic on the large lawn sprinkled with wildflowers under soaring pines. Shoppers and history buffs can enjoy exploring historic Main Street, one block away. The surrounding mountains are a natural playground offering a wide variety of activities, and the innkeepers will be happy to let you know their favorite spots and help with directions. The sunny Augusta Tabor room features a sprawling king-size bed with a warm view of the rugged peaks.

Innkeeper(s): Peri & Ed Solder. $45-85. MC VISA AX DS PC TC. 9 rooms, 5 with PB, 2 with FP. 2 suites. 2 cottages. Breakfast included in rates. Type of meal: full breakfast. Beds: KQDT. Ceiling fan in room. Cable TV, VCR and library on premises. Antiques, fishing, parks, shopping, downhill skiing, cross-country skiing and theater nearby.

Certificate may be used: Monday, Tuesday, Wednesday. October, November, April, May, June.

Wood Haven Manor

PO Box 1291, Leadville, CO 80461-1291
(719)486-0109 (800)748-2570
Fax:(719)486-0210

Circa 1898. Located on the town's Banker's Row, this Victorian inn is located in a winter wonderland, with cross-country and downhill skiing nearby,

snowmobiling and back country outings. Gourmet breakfasts include freshly baked bread, sourdough pancakes or eggs Santa Fe, in-season fruits and cool fruit smoothies.

Innkeeper(s): Bobby & Jolene Wood. $59-95. MC VISA AX DS PC TC. 8 rooms, 7 with PB. 2 suites. Breakfast, afternoon tea and evening snack included in rates. Types of meals: full breakfast, gourmet breakfast and early coffee/tea. Beds: QDT. Cable TV, VCR, fax, copier and library on premises. Amusement parks, antiques, fishing, parks, shopping, downhill skiing, cross-country skiing, theater and watersports nearby.

Location: Historic "Bankers Row."

Seen in: Country Traditional, Country Almanac, Country Decorating Ideas.

"The room, the food and the hospitality were truly wonderful."

Certificate may be used: Sunday through Thursday, except holidays. Excluding July, August, December and March.

Mancos

H2

Bauer House

100 Bauer Ave, PO Box 1049,
Mancos, CO 81328
(970)533-9707 (800)733-9707
Fax:(970)533-7022

Circa 1890. George Bauer, Mancos' town founder, built this three-story, brick Victorian. Several of the prominent family's possessions are on display, as well as old town newspapers, pictures and bank ledgers. The three guest rooms feature country decor, and there is a penthouse with a kitchen and bar. All of the guest quarters boast mountain views. There are porches to relax on and the innkeeper is in the process of adding a putting green and croquet lawn. Bobbi Black tries a new, creative menu for each day. Breakfast treats include stuffed pancakes, homemade waffles or stratas accompanied by fresh fruit, muffins and granola. The Mancos area offers many activities, including the more unusual stagecoach rides and llama backpack trips in addition to golfing, hiking and whitewater rafting.

Innkeeper(s): Bobbi Black. $75-125. MC VISA DS TC. 4 rooms with PB. 1 suite. Breakfast, afternoon tea and evening snack included in rates. Types of meals: full breakfast and early coffee/tea. Picnic lunch and catering service available. Beds: QT. Turn-down service and ceiling fan in room. Cable TV, VCR, fax and copier on premises. Antiques, fishing, parks, shopping, cross-country skiing, sporting events, theater and watersports nearby.

Certificate may be used: Sunday through Thursday, May 15-Oct. 15.

Manitou Springs E7

Red Crags B&B

302 El Paso Blvd,
Manitou Springs, CO 80829-2308
(719)685-1920 (800)721-2248
Fax:(719)685-1073

Circa 1870. Well-known in this part of Colorado, this unique, four-story Victorian mansion sits on a bluff with a combination of views that includes Pikes Peak, Manitou Valley, Garden of the Gods and the City of Colorado Springs. The formal dining room features a rare cherrywood Eastlake fireplace. Outside, guests can walk through beautifully landscaped gardens or enjoy a private picnic area with a barbecue pit and a spectacular view.

Innkeeper(s): Howard & Lynda Lerner. $75-150. MC VISA AX DS PC TC. 6 rooms with PB, 5 with FP. 3 suites. Breakfast, afternoon tea and evening snack included in rates. Types of meals: continental breakfast, gourmet breakfast and early coffee/tea. Beds: K. Fax, spa and bicycles on premises. Antiques, parks, shopping and theater nearby.

Seen in: Bridal Guide, Denver Post, Los Angeles Times, Springs Woman.

Certificate may be used: Oct. 15, to April 30; Sunday-Thursday; holidays excluded; subject to availability.

Minturn D5

Eagle River Inn

PO Box 100, Minturn, CO 81645-0100
(970)827-5761 (800)344-1750
Fax:(970)827-4020

Circa 1894. Earth red adobe walls, rambling riverside decks, mature willow trees and brilliant flowers enhance the secluded backyard of this Southwestern-style inn. Inside, the lobby features comfortable Santa Fe furniture, an authentic bee-

hive fireplace and a ceiling of traditional latilas and vegas. Baskets, rugs and weavings add warmth. Guest rooms found on two floors have views of the river or mountains. Minturn, which had its beginnings as a stop on the Rio Grande Railroad, is the home of increasingly popular restaurants, shops and galleries.

Innkeeper(s): Patty Bidez. $85-180. MC VISA AX PC TC. 12 rooms with PB. Breakfast and evening snack included in rates. Type of meal: full breakfast. Beds: KT. Cable TV in room. Fax, spa and bicycles on premises. Fishing, shopping, downhill skiing, cross-country skiing and sporting events nearby.

Location: Vail Valley.

Seen in: Rocky Mountain News, Country Accents, Travel Holiday, Vail Valley.

"We love this place and have decided to make it a yearly tradition!"

Certificate may be used: Sunday-Thursday nights, excluding holidays. All year.

Monte Vista G5

The Windmill B&B

4340 W Hwy 160,
Monte Vista, CO 81144
(719)852-0438 (800)467-3441

Circa 1959. This Southwestern-style inn affords panoramic views of the surrounding Sangre De Cristo and San Juan mountain ranges. The 22-acre grounds still include the namesake windmill that once was used to irrigate water in the yard and garden. A hot tub and "Frisbee Golf" course are other fun items found on the property. Each of the guest rooms is decorated in a different theme, with a few antiques placed here and there. The plentiful country breakfast are served in a dining room with mountain views.

Innkeeper(s): Sharon & Dennis Kay. $65-79. MC VISA PC. 4 rooms with PB. Breakfast and evening snack included in rates. Types of meals: full breakfast, gourmet breakfast and early coffee/tea. Beds: KQT. Turn-down service in room. VCR and spa on premises. Antiques, fishing, parks, shopping, downhill skiing, cross-country skiing and theater nearby.

Certificate may be used: Sept. 15 to June 1, Sunday-Friday.

Nederland C6

Goldminer Hotel

601 Klondike Ave,
Nederland, CO 80466-9542
(303)258-7770 (800)422-4629
Fax:(303)258-3850

Circa 1897. This turn-of-the-century hotel is a highlight in the Eldora National Historic District. Suites and rooms are decorated with period antiques.

The inn provides packages that include guided jeep, horseback, hiking and fishing tours in the summer and back-country ski tours in the winter.

Innkeeper(s): Scott Bruntjen. $69-129. MC VISA AX TC. 8 rooms, 4 with PB, 1 with FP. 1 suite. 1 cottage. 1 conference room. Breakfast included in rates. Types of meals: full breakfast and early coffee/tea. Beds: KDT. Cable TV, VCR, fax, copier, computer, spa and library on premises. Handicap access. Antiques, fishing, parks, shopping, downhill skiing, cross-country skiing and sporting events nearby.

Location: Eldora National Historic District.

Seen in: Daily Camera, Mountain Ear.

Certificate may be used: All except Dec. 18-Jan. 10, May 10-20; Friday-Saturday, June-October.

Ouray   F3

Damn Yankee B&B Inn
100 Sixth Ave, PO Box 709,
Ouray, CO 81427
(800)687-2926 (800)845-7512
Fax:(970)325-0502

Circa 1991. Nestled at the foot of mountains, this rustic hideaway affords glorious views from its second-story balcony and sitting room. The parlor boasts a baby grand piano and wood-burning fireplace, and guests will always find something to snack on in the sitting room, which is stocked with fruit, drinks and other treats. Guests planning to hit the nearby slopes will appreciate the inn's expansive, gourmet breakfast, which is served each morning. The innkeepers provide free admission to the Ouray Hot Springs, one of the area's popular attractions.
Innkeeper(s): Mike & Marj Manley. $68-165. MAP. MC VISA AX DS PC TC. 10 rooms with PB, 4 with FP. 2 suites. 1 cottage. 1 conference room. Breakfast, afternoon tea, dinner, evening snack and picnic lunch included in rates. Types of meals: full breakfast, gourmet breakfast and early coffee/tea. Beds: KQ. Ceiling fan, cable TV and VCR in room. Fax, copier, sauna and library on premises. Handicap access. Amusement

parks, antiques, fishing, parks, shopping, downhill skiing, cross-country skiing, theater and watersports nearby.

Certificate may be used: Weekdays April 1 through May 15 and weekdays Nov. 1 through Dec. 15.

Steamboat Springs   B4

Steamboat Valley Guest House
PO Box 773815,
Steamboat Springs, CO 80477-3815
(970)870-9017 (800)530-3866
Fax:(970)879-0361

Circa 1957. Enjoy a sleigh ride across snow-covered hills or take in the mountain view from the hot tub at this rustic Colorado home. Logs from the town mill and bricks from an old flour mill were used to construct the home, which features rooms with exposed wooden beams, high ceilings and country furnishings. Beds are covered with fluffy comforters, and several guest rooms afford magnificent views of this skiing resort town. The innkeepers prepare a varied breakfast menu with staples such as Irish oatmeal to the more gourmet, such as a puffy souffle. The home is located in the Steamboat Springs' historic Old Town area.
Innkeeper(s): George & Alice Lund. $73-148. MC VISA AX DC CB DS PC TC. 4 rooms with PB, 1 with FP. 1 suite. Breakfast and afternoon tea included in rates. Types of meals: full breakfast and early coffee/tea. Beds: QT. Cable TV, VCR, fax, copier, spa and library on premises. Fishing, parks, shopping, downhill skiing, cross-country skiing, theater and watersports nearby.

Certificate may be used: Monday-Thursday, year round. Excludes holidays.

Telluride   G3

New Sheridan Hotel
231 W Colorado Ave, PO Box 980,
Telluride, CO 81435
(970)728-4351 (800)200-1891
Fax:(970)728-5024

Circa 1895. This charming hotel reflects the Victorian ambiance of a historic mining town. The building was redecorated recently to its former glory and is the only remaining original Victorian hotel and bar in Telluride. The hotel combines Victorian luxury with the comfort of an alpine lodge. Guests can relax by a roaring fire in the library or in the privacy of their cozy guest room or suite. There is a rooftop Jacuzzi on premises. Hearty country breakfasts are served each morning, preparing guests for day enjoying Colorado's wilderness. The inn is just steps from shops and restaurants, and ski lifts are a five-minute walk.

Innkeeper(s): Tom Taylor. $65-285. MC VISA AX. 32 rooms, 24 with PB. 6 suites. Breakfast included in rates. Types of meals: full breakfast and early coffee/tea. Afternoon tea, picnic lunch and banquet service available. Beds: KQ. Turn-down service, ceiling fan and cable TV in room. Fax, copier and bicycles on premises. Handicap access. Antiques, fishing, parks, shopping, downhill skiing, cross-country skiing, theater and watersports nearby.

Certificate may be used: April-November, Sunday-Thursday, excluding holidays and special events.

Twin Lakes   E5

Twin Lakes Mountain Retreat
PO Box 175, Twin Lakes, CO 81251-0175
(719)486-2593

Circa 1886. Plenty of trees and wildlife surround this cozy, two-story Victorian farmhouse, which is decorated with country furnishings and antiques. Early morning coffee is served in the warm kitchen in front of an antique wood cook stove, which is still used to prepare meals. Floor-to-ceiling windows offer

lake and mountain views. The innkeepers provide special bath salts and soaps for guests who wish to take a long soak after a day exploring the outdoors.
Innkeeper(s): Roger & Denny Miller. $69-73. MC VISA PC TC. 5 rooms, 3 with PB. 1 cottage. Breakfast, afternoon tea and evening snack included in rates. Types of meals: full breakfast and early coffee/tea. Dinner available. Beds: QD. Turn-down service in room. Cable TV, VCR and library on premises. Antiques, fishing, shopping, downhill skiing, cross-country skiing, theater and watersports nearby.
Seen in: Denver Post.

"Your friendliness and hospitality were a pleasure."

Certificate may be used: Monday-Friday excluding holidays. May 1 through Oct. 15.

Winter Park   C6

Alpen Rose
244 Forest Trail, PO Box 769,
Winter Park, CO 80482
(970)726-5039 (800)531-1373
Fax:(970)726-0993

Circa 1960. The innkeepers of this European-style mountain B&B like to share their love of the mountains with guests. There is a superb view of the James and Perry Peaks from the large southern deck where you can witness spectacular sunrises and evening alpen glows. The view is enhanced by lofty pines, wildflowers and quaking aspens. Each of the bedrooms is decorated with treasures brought over from Austria, including traditional featherbeds for the queen-size beds. The town of Winter Park is a small, friendly community located 68 miles west of Denver.
Innkeeper(s): Robin & Rupert Sommerauer. $60-125. MC VISA AX DS PC TC. 6 rooms with PB, 1 with FP. Breakfast and afternoon tea included in rates. Types of meals: gourmet breakfast and early coffee/tea. Beds: KQT. Cable TV, VCR, fax, copier and spa on premises. Antiques, fishing, parks, shopping, downhill skiing, cross-country skiing and watersports nearby.

Certificate may be used: June 1 to Dec. 15, Sunday-Friday.

Candlelight Mountain Inn
148 Fern Way, PO Box 600,
Winter Park, CO 80482
(970)887-2877 (800)546-4846

Circa 1978. Stroll down a candlelit lane to reach this mountainside inn, surrounded by woods. Relax in a glider swing as you gaze at a campfire and mountain views, or soak in the hot tub as you watch shooting stars. The innkeepers have created a relaxing environment at their comfortable inn, which includes a common area with a recreation room, toy room, dining area and guest kitchen. The inn is a perfect place to relax after a busy day of skiing,

skating, biking, golfing or hiking. Other popular area activities include white-water rafting, jeep tours and taking in the scenery from a hot air balloon. The Rocky Mountain National Park is just 30 minutes from the inn.

Innkeeper(s): Kim & Tim Onnen. $45-85. PC TC. 4 rooms, 2 with PB. Breakfast and evening snack included in rates. Type of meal: full breakfast. Beds: QDT. VCR and pet boarding on premises. Antiques, fishing, parks, shopping, downhill skiing, cross-country skiing and theater nearby.

Certificate may be used: April 15 through June 15, excluding Memorial weekend, Sept. 1-Dec. 1, excluding Labor Day and Thanksgiving weekends.

Outpost B&B Inn

687 County Rd 517, PO Box 41,
Winter Park, CO 80482
(970)726-5346 (800)430-4538
Fax:(970)726-5346

Circa 1970. Rocky mountain peaks, woods and rolling pastures surround this 40-acre spread, which affords views of the Continental Divide. Guests stay in an antique-filled lodge inn. The inn's atrium includes a hot tub. The innkeepers serve a huge, multi-course feast for breakfast. During the winter months, the innkeepers offer free shuttle service to Winter Park and Mary Jane ski areas.

Innkeeper(s): Ken & Barbara Parker. $70-110. MC VISA AX DC DS PC TC. 7 rooms with PB. Breakfast and evening snack included in rates. Type of meal: gourmet breakfast. Beds: KQDT. VCR, fax and spa on premises. Fishing, parks, shopping, downhill skiing, cross-country skiing, theater and watersports nearby.

Certificate may be used: Anytime except Dec. 20-Jan. 2, April 16-May 31.

Woodland Park E7

Pikes Peak Paradise

236 Pinecrest Rd, PO Box 5760,
Woodland Park, CO 80863-8432
(719)687-6656 (800)728-8282
Fax:(719)687-9008

Circa 1987. This three-story Georgian Colonial with stately white columns rises unexpectedly from the wooded hills west of Colorado Springs. The entire

south wall of the inn is made of glass to enhance its splendid view of Pikes Peak. A sliding glass door opens from each room onto a patio. Eggs Benedict and Belgian waffles are favorite breakfast dishes.

Innkeeper(s): Priscilla, Martin & Tim. $95-195. MC VISA AX DS PC TC. 6 rooms, 2 with PB, 3 with FP. 4 suites. Breakfast included in rates. Type of meal: gourmet breakfast. Beds: KQ. Ceiling fan in room. VCR, fax and spa on premises. Handicap access. Amusement parks, antiques, fishing, parks, shopping, cross-country skiing, sporting events, theater and watersports nearby.

Location: West of Colorado Springs, 25 minutes.

Seen in: Rocky Mountain News.

Certificate may be used: Oct. 15 to May 15, Sunday-Thursday.

Connecticut

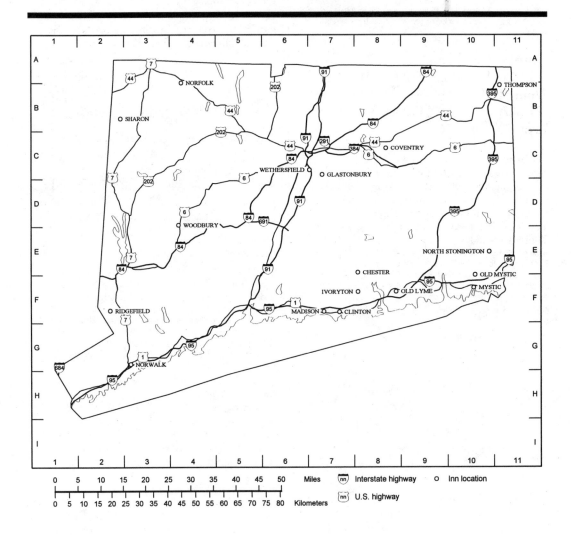

0 5 10 15 20 25 30 35 40 45 50   Miles

0 5 10 15 20 25 30 35 40 45 50 55 60 65 70 75 80   Kilometers

(nn) Interstate highway   o Inn location

(nn) U.S. highway

Chester
E8

The Inn at Chester
318 W Main St, Chester, CT 06412-1026
(203)526-9541 (800)949-7829
Fax:(203)526-4387

Circa 1778. More than 200 years ago, Jeremiah Parmelee built a clapboard farmhouse along a winding road named the Killingworth Turnpike. The Parmelee Homestead stands as a reflection of the past and is an inspiration for the Inn at Chester. Each of the rooms is individually appointed with Eldred Wheeler Reproductions. The Lincoln Suite has a sitting room with a fireplace. Enjoy lively conversation or live music while imbibing your favorite drink at the inn's tavern, Dunk's Landing. Outside Dunk's Landing a 30-foot fireplace soars into the rafters.
Innkeeper(s): Deborah Moore. $88-205. MC VISA AX TC. 42 rooms with PB, 2 with FP. 1 suite. 3 conference rooms. Breakfast included in rates. Type of meal: continental-plus breakfast. Dinner, lunch and banquet service available. Beds: KQDT. Air conditioning and cable TV in room. VCR, fax, copier, sauna, bicycles, tennis, library and pet boarding on premises. Handicap access. Antiques, fishing, parks, shopping, downhill skiing, cross-country skiing, theater and watersports nearby.
Seen in: Connecticut, New Haven Register, Hartford Courant, Pictorial Gazette, Discover Connecticut, Way, New York Times.

Certificate may be used: Nov. 1-April 1, Sunday-Thursday.

Clinton
F7

Captain Dibbell House
21 Commerce St,
Clinton, CT 06413-2054
(860)669-1646 Fax:(860)669-1646

Circa 1866. Built by a sea captain, this graceful Victorian house is only two blocks from the harbor where innkeeper Ellis Adams used to sail his own vessel. A ledger of household accounts dating from the 1800s is on display, and there are fresh flowers in each guest room.
Innkeeper(s): Helen & Ellis Adams. $60-95. MC VISA. 4 rooms with PB. Breakfast included in rates. Type of meal: full breakfast. Beds: KQT. Air conditioning, turn-down service and ceiling fan in room. Cable TV and bicycles on premises. Antiques, fishing, parks, shopping, theater and watersports nearby.
Location: Exit 63 & I-95, south on Rt. 81 to Rt. 1, east for 1 block, right on Commerce.
Seen in: Clinton Recorder, New Haven Register, Hartford Courant.

"This was our first experience with B&Bs and frankly, we didn't know what to expect. It was GREAT!"
Certificate may be used: Sunday through Thursday, holidays and special events weekends excluded.

Coventry
C8

Maple Hill Farm B&B
365 Goose Ln, Coventry, CT 06238-1215
(860)742-0635 (800)742-0635

Circa 1731. This historic farmhouse still possesses its original kitchen cupboards and a flour bin used for generations. Family heirlooms and the history of the former home owners are shared with guests.

There is a three-seat outhouse behind the inn. Visitors, of course, are provided with modern plumbing, as well as a screened porch and greenhouse in which to relax.
Innkeeper(s): Anthony Felice, Jr. & Marybeth Gorke-Felice. $55-75. MC VISA PC TC. 4 rooms, 1 with PB. Breakfast included in rates. Types of meals: full breakfast and early coffee/tea. Beds: DT. Turn-down service in room. VCR, fax, copier, spa, swimming, stables, bicycles and library on premises. Antiques, fishing, parks, shopping, cross-country skiing, sporting events, theater and watersports nearby.
Location: A good stopping point between Boston and New York.
Seen in: Journal Inquirer, Coventry Journal, Forbes, Hartford Courant, Yankee Traveler.

"Comfortable rooms and delightful country ambiance."
Certificate may be used: Feb. 1 through April 30, anytime except holidays. Balance of year, Sunday through Thursday nights, except holidays.

Glastonbury   C7

Butternut Farm
1654 Main St,
Glastonbury, CT 06033-2962
(860)633-7197 Fax:(860)659-1758

Circa 1720. This Colonial house sits on two acres of landscaped grounds amid trees and herb gardens. Prize-winning goats, pigeons and chickens are housed in the old barn on the property. Eighteenth-century Connecticut antiques, including a cherry highboy and cherry pencil-post canopy bed, are placed throughout the inn, enhancing the natural beauty of the pumpkin-pine floors and eight brick fireplaces.

Innkeeper(s): Don Reid. $68-88. AX TC. 5 rooms with PB, 3 with FP. 2 suites. Breakfast included in rates. Type of meal: full breakfast. Beds: DT. Air conditioning and VCR in room. Fax on premises. Antiques, fishing, parks, shopping, downhill skiing, cross-country skiing, sporting events and theater nearby.

Location: South of Glastonbury Center, 1.6 miles, 10 minutes to Hartford.

Seen in: New York Times, House Beautiful, Yankee, Antiques.

Certificate may be used: Year-round, Sunday-Thursday.

Ivoryton   F8

The Copper Beech Inn
46 Main St, Ivoryton, CT 06442-1004
(860)767-0330 Fax:(860)767-7840

Circa 1887. The Copper Beech Inn was once the home of ivory importer A.W. Comstock, one of the early owners of the Comstock Cheney Company, producer of ivory combs and keyboards. The village took its name from the ivory trade centered here. An enormous copper beech tree shades the property. Each room in the renovated Carriage House boasts a whirlpool bath and French doors opening onto a deck. The inn's restaurant has received numerous accolades.

Innkeeper(s): Eldon & Sally Senner. $118-190. MC VISA AX DC CB PC TC. 13 rooms with PB. 1 conference room. Breakfast included in rates. Type of meal: continental-plus breakfast. Banquet service available. Beds: KQDT. Air conditioning and cable TV in room. Library on premises. Handicap access. Antiques, fishing, parks, shopping, theater and watersports nearby.

Location: Lower Connecticut River valley.

Seen in: Los Angeles Times, Bon Appetit, Connecticut, Travel & Leisure, Discerning Traveler.

"The grounds are beautiful ... just breathtaking ... accommodations are wonderful."

Certificate may be used: Nov. 1-May 15, Sunday-Thursday. Holidays excluded.

Madison   F7

Madison Beach Hotel
PO Box 546, 94 W Wharf Rd,
Madison, CT 06443-2905
(203)245-1404 Fax:(203)245-0410

Circa 1800. Since most of Connecticut's shoreline is privately owned, the Madison is one of the few waterfront lodgings available. It was originally constructed as a stagecoach stop and later became a popular vacation spot for those who stayed for a month at a time with maids and chauffeurs. Art Carney is said to have driven a Madison Beach Hotel bus here when his brother was the manager. Rooms are furnished in a variety of antiques and wallpapers and many have splendid views of the lawn and the Long Island Sound from private porches.

Innkeeper(s): Lorraine Casula. $80-195. MC VISA AX DC DS TC. 35 rooms, 29 with PB. 6 suites. 2 conference rooms. Breakfast included in rates. Types of meals: continental breakfast, continental-plus breakfast and early coffee/tea. Dinner, picnic lunch, lunch, banquet service and room service available. Beds: QT. Air conditioning and cable TV in room. VCR, fax and copier on premises. Handicap access. Antiques, fishing, shopping, sporting events, theater and watersports nearby.

Seen in: New England Travel.

"The accommodations were wonderful and the service was truly exceptional."

Certificate may be used: Off season on weekend Nov. 1-May 15, Friday-Sunday; In season midweek May 15-Nov. 1, Sunday-Friday. Closed January & February.

Mystic   F10

The Whaler's Inn
20 E Main St, Mystic, CT 06355-2646
(860)536-1506 (800)243-2588
Fax:(860)572-1250

Circa 1901. This classical revival-style inn is built on the historical site of the Hoxie House, the Clinton House and the U.S. Hotel. Just as these famous 19th-century inns offered, the Whaler's Inn has the same charm and convenience for today's visitor to Mystic. Once a booming ship-building center, the town's connection to the sea is ongoing and the sailing schooners still pass beneath the Bascule Drawbridge in the center of town. The inn has indoor and outdoor dining available and more than 75 shops and restaurants are within walking distance.

Innkeeper(s): Richard Prisby. $69-135. MC VISA AX TC. 41 rooms with PB. 1 suite. 1 conference room. Type of meal: early coffee/tea. Dinner, lunch and gourmet lunch available. Beds: KQD. Air conditioning and cable TV in room. Fax, copier and child care on premises. Handicap access. Antiques, fishing, parks, shopping and watersports nearby.

Certificate may be used: Nov. 26-March 28.

Norfolk   B4

Manor House
69 Maple Avenue,
Norfolk, CT 06058-0447
(860)542-5690 Fax:(860)542-5690

Circa 1898. Charles Spofford, designer of London's subway, built this home with many gables, exquisite cherry paneling and grand staircase. There are Moorish arches and Tiffany windows. Guests can enjoy hot-mulled cider after a sleigh ride, hay ride,

or horse and carriage drive along the country lanes nearby. The inn was named by "Discerning Traveler" as Connecticut's most romantic hideaway.

Innkeeper(s): Hank & Diane Tremblay. $85-190. MC VISA AX DS PC TC. 8 rooms with PB, 2 with FP. 1 suite. 1 conference room. Breakfast and afternoon tea included in rates. Types of meals: full breakfast, gourmet breakfast and early coffee/tea. Catering service, catered breakfast and room service available. Beds: KQDT. Ceiling fan in room. Cable TV, fax, computer and library on premises. Antiques, fishing, parks, shopping, downhill skiing, cross-country skiing, sporting events, theater and watersports nearby.

Location: Close to the Berkshires.

Seen in: Boston Globe, Philadelphia Inquirer, Innsider, Rhode Island Monthly, Gourmet, National Geographic Traveler, Good Housekeeping.

"Queen Victoria, eat your heart out."

Certificate may be used: Weekdays, excluding holidays and month of October.

North Stonington   E10

Antiques & Accommodations
32 Main St,
North Stonington, CT 06359-1709
(203)535-1736 (800)554-7829

Circa 1861. Set among the backdrop of an acre of herb, edible flower, perennial and cutting gardens, this Victorian treasure offers a romantic location for a weekend getaway. Rooms filled with antiques

boast four-poster canopy beds and fresh flowers surrounded by a soft, pleasing decor. Honeymooners or couples celebrating an anniversary are presented with special amenities such as balloons, champagne and heart-shaped waffles for breakfast. Candlelit breakfasts include unique items such as edible flowers along with the delicious entrees.

Innkeeper(s): Ann & Tom Gray. $169-229. MC VISA. 5 rooms, 6 with PB. 2 suites. Breakfast included in rates. Type of meal: full breakfast. Beds: Q. Air conditioning, cable TV and VCR in room. Antiques and fishing nearby.

Seen in: Country Inns, Country Wagon Journal, Homesteader.

"The building's old-fashioned welcome-all decor made us feel comfortable the moment we stepped in."

Certificate may be used: Sunday-Thursday.

Norwalk   G3

Silvermine Tavern
194 Perry Ave, Norwalk, CT 06850-1123
(203)847-4558 Fax:(203)847-9171

Circa 1790. The Silvermine consists of the Old Mill, the Country Store, the Coach House and the Tavern itself. Primitive paintings and furnishings, as well as family heirlooms, decorate the inn. Guest rooms and dining rooms overlook the Old Mill, the waterfall and swans gliding across the millpond.

Innkeeper(s): Frank Whitman, Jr. $90-110. MC VISA AX DC PC TC. 10 rooms with PB. 2 conference rooms. Breakfast included in rates. Type of meal: continental breakfast. Dinner, lunch, banquet service and catering service available. Beds: DT. Air conditioning in room. VCR, fax and copier on premises. Antiques, fishing, parks, shopping and theater nearby.

Seen in: Advocate, Greenwich Time, U.S. Air.

Certificate may be used: All year except no October and no Friday arrival.

Old Lyme   F8

Bee and Thistle Inn
100 Lyme St, Old Lyme, CT 06371-1426
(860)434-1667 (800)622-4946
Fax:(860)434-3402

Circa 1756. This stately inn is situated along the banks of the Lieutenant River. There are five and one-half acres of trees, lawns and a sunken English garden. The inn is furnished with Chippendale antiques and reproductions. A guitar duo plays in the parlor on Friday and a harpist plays in the parlor on Saturday evenings. Bee and Thistle was recently voted the most romantic inn in the state, the most romantic dinner spot, and "Best Restaurant" in the state by readers of "Connecticut Magazine."

Innkeeper(s): Bob, Penny, Lori and Jeff Nelson. $69-195. EP. MC VISA AX DC PC TC. 11 rooms, 9 with PB, 1 with FP. 1 cottage. Type of meal: gourmet breakfast. Afternoon tea and lunch available. Beds: KQDT. Air conditioning and ceiling fan in room. Antiques, fishing, parks, shopping, theater and watersports nearby.

Location: Historic district next to Florence Griswold Museum.

Seen in: Countryside, Country Living, Money, New York, U.S. Air, New York Times, Country Traveler.

Certificate may be used: Sunday-Thursday, except not Sunday on holiday weekends.

Old Mystic   F10

Red Brook Inn
2800 Gold Star Hwy, PO Box 237,
Old Mystic, CT 06372-0237
(860)572-0349

Circa 1740. If there was no other reason to visit Old Mystic, a charming town brimming with activities, the Red Brook Inn would be reason enough. The Crary Homestead features two unique rooms, both with working fireplaces, while the Haley Tavern offers such amenities as mahogany or canopy beds and many of the tavern rooms also feature fireplaces. Innkeeper Ruth Keyes has selected a beautiful array of antiques to decorate her inn. Guests are sure to enjoy Keyes wonderful authentic Colonial meals. A special winter meal takes three days to

complete and Keyes prepares it over an open hearth. The aquarium, Mystic Seaport Museum, a cider mill and many charming shops are only minutes away.

Innkeeper(s): Ruth Keyes. $95-189. MC VISA AX DS PC TC. 10 rooms with PB, 7 with FP. 3 conference rooms. Breakfast, afternoon tea and evening snack included in rates. Types of meals: full breakfast, gourmet breakfast and early coffee/tea. Beds: QDT. Air conditioning in room. Cable TV, VCR and library on premises. Amusement parks, antiques, fishing, parks, shopping, sporting events, theater and watersports nearby.

Location: Off route 184 (Gold Star Highway).

Seen in: Travel & Leisure, Yankee, New York, Country Decorating, Philadelphia Inquirer, National Geographic Traveler, Discerning Traveler.

"The staff is wonderful. You made us feel at home. Thank you for you hospitality."

Certificate may be used: Spring and Winter, Jan. 10 to May 10 and Nov. 1 to Dec. 15.

Ridgefield   F2

West Lane Inn
22 West Ln, Ridgefield, CT 06877-4914
(203)438-7323 Fax:(203)438-7325

Circa 1849. This National Register Victorian mansion on two acres features an enormous front veranda filled with white whicker chairs and tables overlooking a manicured lawn. A polished oak staircase rises to a third-floor landing and lounge. Chandeliers, wall sconces and floral wallpapers help to establish an intimate atmosphere. Although the rooms do not have antiques, they feature amenities such as heated towel racks, extra-thick towels, air conditioning and desks. The inn holds a AAA four-diamond award.

Innkeeper(s): Maureen Mayer. $110-165. MC VISA AX DC CB. 20 rooms with PB, 2 with FP. Breakfast included in rates. Type of meal: continental breakfast. Evening snack and room service available. Beds: KQ. Air conditioning and ceiling fan in room. Handicap access. Antiques, fishing, shopping, cross-country skiing and theater nearby.

Seen in: Stanford-Advocate, Greenwich Times, Home & Away Connecticut.

"Thank you for the hospitality you showed us. The rooms are comfortable and quiet. I haven't slept this soundly in weeks."

Certificate may be used: Nov. 30 through April 30. Sunday through Thursday, exclude holidays.

Sharon B2

1890 Colonial B&B
Rt 41, PO Box 25, Sharon, CT 06069
(203)364-0436

Circa 1890. Summertime guests can find a cool place to sit on the screened porch of this center-hall Colonial home situated on five park-like acres. Guests visiting in the winter can warm up to any of the main floor fireplaces in the living room, dining room and den. Guest rooms are spacious and have high ceilings. A furnished apartment also is available with private entrance and kitchenette at special weekly rates.

Innkeeper(s): Carole "Kelly" Tangen. $85-109. 3 rooms with PB. 1 suite. Breakfast included in rates. Types of meals: full breakfast and early coffee/tea. Beds: QT. Turn-down service, ceiling fan and cable TV in room. VCR on premises. Antiques, fishing, parks, shopping, downhill skiing, cross-country skiing, theater and watersports nearby.

Certificate may be used: Sunday to Friday, all year, except May-June & September-October and holidays.

Thompson B11

Hickory Ridge Lakefront B&B
1084 Quaddick Town Farm Rd,
Thompson, CT 06277-2929
(203)928-9530

Circa 1990. Enjoy three wooded acres in the private rural setting of this spacious post-and-beam home. The inn's property includes a chunk of the Quaddick Lake shoreline and canoes are available for guests. There's plenty of hiking to do with 17 private acres and access to miles of state lands. Quaddick State Park is within walking or bicycling distance. Breakfasts of baked goods and entrees are served at your convenience.

Innkeeper(s): Birdie Olson. $40-85. 3 rooms, 1 with PB, 1 with FP. 1 suite. Breakfast included in rates. Types of meals: full breakfast and early coffee/tea. Picnic lunch available. Beds: DT. Turn-down service in room. Cable TV, VCR and child care on premises. Antiques, fishing,

shopping, cross-country skiing and theater nearby.

Certificate may be used: Sunday through Thursday, July 1-Oct. 30 (except holidays). Anytime Nov. 1-June 30 (except holidays and graduations).

Wethersfield C7

Chester Bulkley House B&B
184 Main St,
Wethersfield, CT 06109-2340
(203)563-4236

Circa 1830. Wide pine floors, hand-carved woodwork, working fireplaces and period pieces enhance the ambiance of this Greek Revival structure. Nestled in the historic village of Old Wethersfield and minutes from downtown Hartford, the inn offers a uniquely comfortable haven for business and holiday travelers. While visiting Hartford, guests may want to take in a performance of the opera, the symphony, the ballet or a Broadway show.

Innkeeper(s): Frank & Sophia Bottaro. $65-85. MC VISA AX DS TC. 12 rooms, 3 with PB. 1 suite. Breakfast included in rates. Types of meals: full breakfast and early coffee/tea. Afternoon tea and room service available. Beds: KQDT. Air conditioning and ceiling fan in room. Cable TV and fax on premises. Antiques, fishing, parks, shopping, downhill skiing, sporting events and theater nearby.

Certificate may be used: Jan. 2-May 23 all times; May 24-Oct. 30 weekdays only; Nov. 1-Dec. 30 all days except holidays.

Woodbury D4

Merryvale B&B
1204 Main St S,
Woodbury, CT 06798-3804
(203)266-0800 Fax:(203)263-4479

Circa 1789. Found in a town that has a reputation as the Antiques Capital of Connecticut, this B&B is a simple yet rambling Colonial. Guests can enjoy complimentary tea, coffee and biscuits throughout the day. A grand living room invites travelers to relax by the fireplace and enjoy a book from the extensive collection of classics and mysteries. Woodbury's charm, pride and determination to hold on to its way of life has been well publicized and many believe that this is where New England truly began.

Innkeeper(s): Gary & Pat Ubaldi Nurnberger. $80-130. MC VISA AX. 4 rooms with PB. 2 suites. Breakfast included in rates. Type of meal: full breakfast. Evening snack available. Beds: KQDT. Air conditioning in room. Cable TV and VCR on premises. Amusement parks, antiques, fishing, shopping, downhill skiing and cross-country skiing nearby.

Seen in: Voices, Yankee Traveler, Hartford Courant, Newtown Bee.

"Your hospitality will always be remembered."

Certificate may be used: Jan. 7-Feb. 28, Monday-Sunday.

Delaware

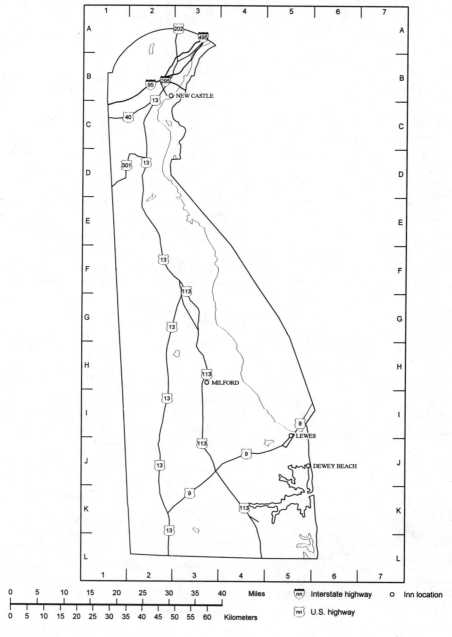

0   5   10   15   20   25   30   35   40   Miles

0 5 10 15 20 25 30 35 40 45 50 55 60   Kilometers

[nn] Interstate highway   o Inn location

[nn] U.S. highway

Dewey Beach

J5

Barry's Gull Cottage B&B

116 Chesapeake St,
Dewey Beach, DE 19971
(302)227-7000 Fax:(302)227-7000

Circa 1962. It's only a block to the beach from this Nantucket-style home, which also affords views of a lake. Rooms feature antiques, beds covered in quilts, wicker furnishings and stained glass. The innkeepers pamper guests with treats throughout the day, beginning with a healthy breakfast. Afternoon tea is served, and the evening is topped off with sherry, port wine, coffee and luscious chocolate cake. Relax in the hot tub illuminated by candlelight. The area offers plenty of shopping, from outlets to antiques, and good restaurants are close to this beach retreat.

Innkeeper(s): Vivian & Bob Barry. $75-135. PC TC. 6 rooms, 3 with PB. 1 suite. 1 cottage. Breakfast, afternoon tea and evening snack included in rates. Types of meals: full breakfast, gourmet breakfast and early coffee/tea. Beds: KQD. Air conditioning, turn-down service, ceiling fan and cable TV in room. VCR, fax, copier, spa, bicycles and library on premises. Amusement parks, antiques, fishing, parks, shopping, theater and watersports nearby.

Certificate may be used: Sunday-Thursday, May, June, after Sept. 15, October.

Lewes

I5

The Bay Moon B&B

128 Kings Hwy, Lewes, DE 19958-1418
(302)644-1802 Fax:(302)644-1802

Circa 1887. The exterior of this cedar Victorian is mysterious and unique. The front veranda is shrouded by the flowers and foliage that decorate the front walk. The custom-made, hand-crafted beds in the guest rooms are topped with feather pillows and down comforters. Cordials are placed in the room and there is a champagne turndown service. During a nightly cocktail hour, appetizers and wine are served. The innkeeper offers plenty of amenities. Each room is stocked with cable TV and a VCR and there's an extensive library as well. Beach supplies and an outdoor shower are helpful for guests who want to enjoy the ocean, which is about one mile from the inn.

Innkeeper(s): Laura Beth Kelly. $75-145. EP. MC VISA PC TC. 4 rooms with PB. 1 suite. Breakfast and evening snack included in rates. Types of meals: continental-plus breakfast and early coffee/tea. Beds: KQ. Turn-down service, ceiling fan and cable TV in room. VCR, fax, library and child care on premises. Handicap access. Antiques, fishing, parks, shopping, sporting events, theater and watersports nearby.

Certificate may be used: Weekdays only, Monday-Wednesday: all seasons, no holidays.

New Devon Inn

142 2nd St, Lewes, DE 19958-1324
(302)645-6466 (800)824-8754
Fax:(302)645-7196

Circa 1926. In the heart of the historic district, this inn has 24 individually decorated guest rooms. All rooms feature antique beds and turndown service. The inn, which prefers guests over the age of 16, also offers conference facilities, catering and convenient access to antiquing, beaches, dining and sightseeing. Two suites also are available. The shore is just a half-mile from the inn. Prime Hook National Wildlife Refuge and Cape Henlopen State Park are nearby.

Innkeeper(s): Suzanne Steele & Judith Henderson. $65-170. AP. MC VISA AX DC DS TC. 26 rooms with PB. 2 suites. 1 conference room. Type of meal: early coffee/tea. Beds: QDT. Air conditioning and turn-down service in room. Cable TV, fax and copier on premises. Handicap access. Antiques, fishing, parks, shopping and watersports nearby.

Seen in: New York Times, Mid-Atlantic Country, National Geographic.

Certificate may be used: Year-round, Sunday through Thursday, holidays excluded.

Wild Swan Inn

525 Kings Hwy, Lewes, DE 19958-1421
(302)645-8550 Fax:(302)645-8550

Circa 1905. This Queen Anne Victorian is a whimsical site, painted in pink with white, green and burgundy trim. The interior is dotted with antiques and dressed in Victorian style. A full, gourmet breakfast and freshly ground coffee are served each morning. The innkeepers have placed many musical treasures in their inn, including an early Edison phonograph and a Victrola. The 1915 player piano often serenades guests during breakfast. Lewes, which was founded in 1631, is the first town in the first state. Wild Swan is within walking distance of downtown where several fine restaurants

await you. The surrounding seascape and country-side are ideal for cycling, running and walking.

Innkeeper(s): Michael & Hope Tyler. $85-120. PC TC. 3 rooms with PB. Breakfast and evening snack included in rates. Types of meals: gourmet breakfast and early coffee/tea. Beds: KD. Air conditioning and turn-down service in room. Fax, swimming, bicycles and library on premises. Antiques, fishing, parks, shopping, theater and watersports nearby.

Certificate may be used: Nov. 1 through May 1, any day except holidays.

Milford   H3

The Towers

101 NW Front St, Milford, DE 19963
(302)422-3814 (800)366-3814

Circa 1783. Once a simple colonial house, this ornate Steamboat Gothic fantasy features every imaginable Victorian architectural detail, all added in 1891. There are 10 distinct styles of gingerbread as well as towers, turrets, gables, porches and bays.

Inside, chestnut and cherry woodwork, window seats and stained-glass windows are complemented with American and French antiques. The back garden boasts a gazebo, porch and swimming pool. Ask for the splendid Tower Room or Rapunzel Suite.

Innkeeper(s): Daniel Bond. $95-125. MC VISA. 6 rooms, 4 with PB. 2 suites. Breakfast included in rates. Beds: QD. Air conditioning and ceiling fan in room. Swimming and bicycles on premises. Antiques, fishing, parks, shopping, theater and watersports nearby.

Location: In the historic district and a short drive to Delaware Bay & the Atlantic Ocean.

Seen in: Washington Post, Baltimore Sun, Washingtonian, Mid-Atlantic Country.

"I felt as if I were inside a beautiful Victorian Christmas card, surrounded by all the things Christmas should be."

Certificate may be used: Any Friday or Saturday night throughout the year.

New Castle   B2

The Jefferson House B&B

5 The Strand,
New Castle, DE 19720-4825
(302)325-1025

Circa 1790. Overlooking the Strand and the Delaware River, The Jefferson House served as a hotel, a rooming house and a shipping-company office during Colonial times. On the side lawn is a "William Penn landed here" sign. The inn features heavy paneled doors, black marble mantels over the fireplaces and a fanlight on the third floor. There is private access to the river, and a spa beckons guests after a long day of sightseeing. Cobblestone streets add to the quaintness of the first capital city of the colonies.

Innkeeper(s): Brenda. $54-85. MC VISA PC TC. 3 rooms with PB, 1 with FP. 2 suites. Breakfast included in rates. Type of meal: continental breakfast. Beds: D. Air conditioning, ceiling fan and cable TV in room. Spa on premises. Antiques, fishing, parks, shopping, cross-country skiing, sporting events and watersports nearby.

Location: Mid-Atlantic region.

Seen in: Roll Call.

"I loved sleeping on an old brass bed, in a room filled with antiques and charm, just feet from where William Penn landed in New Castle."

Certificate may be used: Free night cannot be a Friday or Saturday night. Excludes holidays or special event times.

Florida

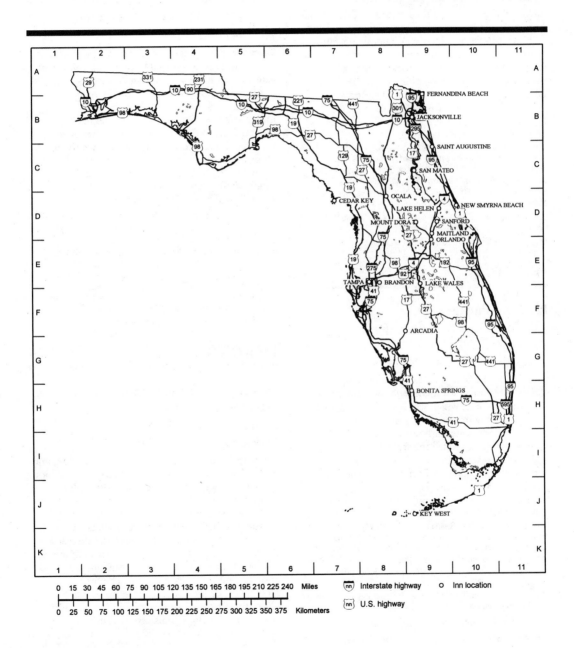

Amelia Island

Florida House Inn
PO Box 688, 22 S 3rd St,
Amelia Island, FL 32034-4207
(904)261-3300 Fax:(904)277-3831

Circa 1857. Located in the heart of a 50-block historic National Register area, the Florida House Inn is thought to be the oldest continuously operating tourist hotel in Florida. Recently renovated, the inn features a small pub, a guest parlor, a library and a New Orleans-style courtyard in which guests may enjoy the shade of 200-year-old oaks. Rooms are decorated with country pine and oak antiques, cheerful handmade rugs and quilts. The Carnegies and Rockefellers have been guests.

Innkeeper(s): Bob Warner. $70-130. MC VISA AX. 11 rooms with PB, 6 with FP. 1 suite. 1 conference room. Breakfast included in rates. Types of meals: full breakfast and early coffee/tea. Dinner, picnic lunch, lunch and catering service available. Beds: KQT. Air conditioning, ceiling fan and cable TV in room. Fax, copier and spa on premises. Handicap access. Antiques, fishing, sporting events and theater nearby.

Seen in: Amelia Now, Tampa Tribune, Miami Herald, Toronto Star, Country Living, Ft. Lauderdale Sun Sentinel.

Certificate may be used: Sunday through Thursday.

Arcadia   F9

Historic Parker House
427 W Hickory St,
Arcadia, FL 33821-3703
(941)494-2499 (800)969-2499

Circa 1895. Period antiques, including a wonderful clock collection, grace the interior of this turn-of-the-century home, which was built by a local cattle baron. Along with two charming rooms and a bright, "yellow" suite, innkeepers Shelly and Bob Baumann recently added the spacious Blue Room, which offers a white iron and brass bed and clawfoot bathtub. An expanded continental breakfast with pastries, fresh fruits, cereals, muffins and a variety of beverages is offered each morning, and afternoon teas can be prepared on request.

Innkeeper(s): Bob & Shelly Baumann. $60-75. MC VISA AX TC. 4 rooms, 2 with PB, 2 with FP. 1 conference room. Breakfast and afternoon tea included in rates. Types of meals: continental-plus breakfast and early coffee/tea. Room service available. Beds: QDT. Air conditioning, ceiling fan and cable TV in room. Antiques, fishing, parks, shopping and watersports nearby.

Seen in: Tampa Tribune, Desoto Sun Herald, Florida Travel & Life, Miami Herald (Palm Beach Edition), WINK-TV News.

"Everything was first class and very comfortable."

Certificate may be used: May 1 to Dec. 15, Sunday-Friday.

Bonita Springs   H9

Historic Shangri-La Inn & Health Spa
27580 Old 41 Rd,
Bonita Springs, FL 33923-5592
(941)992-3811 (800)279-3811
Fax:(941)947-9079

Circa 1918. Guests pamper both body and soul at this restful inn surrounded by more than eight lush acres, which include a river and mineral spring. The day is filled with activities, including relaxation, yoga and aerobics classes or aqua-aerobics in the inn's heated swimming pool. Massages, facials, tennis courts and a fitness center are further offerings. Lectures and entertainment stressing health are offered in the evenings. The cuisine is strictly vegetarian, but the creative choices will satisfy any palate. Fresh fruits and organic cereals start off the day, followed by afternoon refreshments. Dinner includes a variety of gourmet choices from the inn's award-winning chef. Fashionable rooms are appointed with artwork and Tiffany-style decor.

Innkeeper(s): Leo & Deborah Dahlmanns. $49-195. MC VISA. 58 rooms with PB. 16 suites. 2 conference rooms. Breakfast and dinner included in rates. Types of meals: full breakfast and early coffee/tea. Lunch available. Beds: KQT. Air conditioning, ceiling fan and cable TV in room. VCR, fax, copier, spa and sauna on premises. Fishing, parks, shopping and watersports nearby.

Certificate may be used: September to Nov. 30, April 15 to May 3.

Brandon   E8

Behind The Fence B&B Inn
1400 Viola Dr at Countryside,
Brandon, FL 33511-7327
(813)685-8201 (800)448-2672

Circa 1976. Experience the charm of New England on Florida's west coast at this secluded country inn surrounded by tall pines and oaks. Although the frame of the home was built in the mid-1970s, the innkeepers searched Hillsborough County for 19th century and turn-of-the-century artifacts, including old stairs, doors, windows, a pantry and the back porch. Guests can stay either in the main house or in a two-bedroom cottage. All rooms are filled with antique Amish-county furniture. The innkeepers serve fresh popcorn each night in front of the fireplace. Breakfast includes fresh fruit, cereals, juices, coffees and delicious Amish sweet rolls.

Innkeeper(s): Larry & Carolyn Yoss. $59-79. PC TC. 5 rooms, 3 with PB. 1 suite. 1 cottage. 1 conference room. Breakfast, afternoon tea and evening snack included in rates. Types of meals: continental-plus breakfast and early coffee/tea. Beds: DT. Air conditioning, cable TV and VCR in room. Swimming on premises. Amusement parks, antiques, fishing, parks, shopping, sporting events, theater and watersports nearby.

Seen in: Brandon News, Travel Host.

"One of the best kept secrets in all of Tampa! Thanks again!"

Certificate may be used: August-November, Monday-Thursday.

Cedar Key   D7

Island Hotel
2nd & B St, Cedar Key, FL 32625
(352)543-5111

Circa 1859. The history of Island Hotel begins at about the same time as the history of Cedar Key, which was developed in the hopes that the Florida railroad would bring prosperity to the area. After the Civil War, this prosperity was realized for Cedar Key and the Island Hotel's builder Major John Parsons. Current innkeepers Tom and Alison Sanders have worked to preserve the home's traditional beauty,

filling rooms with lovely furnishings and special items such as feather beds or clawfoot tubs. Some rooms boast views of the Gulf or Back Bayou. All rooms include access to the inn's balcony. A gourmet seafood restaurant is located on the premises promising a delightful array of local catch.

Innkeeper(s): Tom & Alison Sanders. $65-95. MC VISA AX DS. 10 rooms, 6 with PB. Breakfast included in rates. Types of meals: full breakfast and gourmet breakfast. Beds: QD. Air conditioning and ceiling fan in room. Antiques, fishing, parks, shopping, sporting events and watersports nearby.

"Always one of our favorites (year after year after year). Great food, hospitality, atmosphere, we'll return."

Certificate may be used: Anytime. Saturday nights not included.

Fernandina Beach   B9

The Taber House
PO Box 734,
Fernandina Beach, FL 32035-0734
(904)261-6391

Circa 1857. This inn offers three suites, all authentic replicas of Victorian architecture, complete with gingerbread woodwork. Fernandina Beach, in Florida's very northeast corner, boasts a charming historic district, of which the inn's cottages are at

the geographic center. The innkeepers, veteran world travelers, have furnished each cottage with just the right touches. Each cottage features one or two queen beds and in-room phones.

Innkeeper(s): Frances Taber. $95-135. 3 suites. Breakfast included in rates. Type of meal: continental-plus breakfast. Beds: Q. Air conditioning, turn-down service, cable TV and VCR in room. Pet boarding on premises. Antiques, fishing, shopping, sporting events, theater and watersports nearby.

Certificate may be used: Anytime.

Jacksonville   B9

House on Cherry St
1844 Cherry St,
Jacksonville, FL 32205-8702
(904)384-1999 Fax:(904)384-5013

Circa 1909. Seasonal blooms fill the pots that line the circular entry stairs to this Federal-style house on tree-lined Cherry Street. It was moved in two pieces to its present site on St. Johns River in the historic Riverside area. Traditionally decorated rooms include antiques, collections of hand-carved decoy ducks and old clocks that chime and tick. Most rooms overlook the river. Your hosts are a social worker and family doctor.

Innkeeper(s): Carol Anderson. $85. MC VISA PC TC. 4 suites. Breakfast and evening snack included in rates. Type of meal: gourmet breakfast. Beds: QT. Air conditioning and ceiling fan in room. Cable TV, VCR, fax, copier and bicycles on premises. Antiques, fishing, parks, shopping, sporting events, theater and watersports nearby.

Location: Historic Avondale.

Seen in: Florida Wayfarer, Tampa Tribune, New York Times.

Certificate may be used: June-October.

Key West
J9

Duval House

815 Duval St, Key West, FL 33040-7405
(305)294-1666 (800)223-8825
Fax:(305)292-1701

Circa 1890. The Duval House's seven Victorian houses surround a garden and a swimming pool. French doors open onto the tropical gardens. Guests may relax on the balconies. Continental Plus breakfast is served in the pool lounge. Rooms have wicker and antique furniture and Bahamian fans.

Innkeeper(s): Richard Kamradt. $70-260. MC VISA AX DC CB DS TC. 25 rooms. 4 suites. Breakfast included in rates. Beds: QD. Air conditioning, ceiling fan and cable TV in room. Fax and swimming on premises. Antiques, fishing, shopping and watersports nearby.

Seen in: Newsday, Palm Beach Post, Cleveland Plain-Dealer, Roanoke Times, Brides, Vacations.

"You certainly will see us again."

Certificate may be used: May 1 to Dec. 14, Sunday through Thursday only, subject to availability.

Lake Helen
D9

Clauser's B&B

201 E Kicklighter Rd,
Lake Helen, FL 32744-3514
(904)228-0310 (800)220-0310
Fax:(904)228-2337

Circa 1890. This three-story, turn-of-the-century vernacular Victorian inn is surrounded by a variety of trees in a quiet, country setting. The inn is listed in the national, state and local historic registers, and offers eight guest rooms, all with private bath. Each room features a different type of country decor, such as Americana, English and prairie. Guests enjoy hot tubbing in the Victorian gazebo or relaxing on the inn's porches, which feature rockers, a swing and cozy wicker furniture. Borrow a bike to take a closer look at the historic district. Stetson University, fine dining and several state parks are nearby.

Innkeeper(s): Tom & Marge Clauser, Janet Watson. $65-120. MC VISA AX DS PC TC. 8 rooms with PB, 1 with FP. Breakfast and evening snack included in rates. Types of meals: full breakfast and early coffee/tea. Beds: KQ. Air conditioning and ceiling fan in room. Cable TV, VCR, fax, copier, spa, bicycles and library on premises. Handicap access. Amusement parks, antiques, fishing, parks, sporting events, theater and watersports nearby.

Certificate may be used: April 1-Nov. 30, Sunday-Thursday.

Lake Wales
E9

Chalet Suzanne Country Inn & Restaurant

3800 Chalet Suzanne Dr,
Lake Wales, FL 33853-7060
(941)676-6011 (800)433-6011
Fax:(941)676-1814

Circa 1924. Situated on 70 acres adjacent to Lake Suzanne, this country inn's architecture includes gabled roofs, balconies, spires and steeples. The superb restaurant has a glowing reputation, and places of interest on the property include the Swiss

Room, Wine Dungeon, Gift Boutique, Autograph Garden, Chapel Antiques, Ceramic Salon, Airstrip and the Soup Cannery. The inn has been transformed into a village of cottages and miniature chateaux, one connected to the other seemingly with no particular order.

Innkeeper(s): Carl & Vita Hinshaw. $135-195. MC VISA AX DC CB DS TC. 30 rooms with PB. Breakfast included in rates. Types of meals: full breakfast and early coffee/tea. Lunch and room service available. Beds: KQDT. Air conditioning, ceiling fan and cable TV in room. VCR, fax, copier, swimming and library on premises. Handicap access. Amusement parks, antiques, fishing, parks, shopping, sporting events, theater and watersports nearby.

Location: Four miles north of Lake Wales. US Hwy 27 & County Road 17A.

Seen in: Southern Living, Country Inns, National Geographic Traveler. Uncle Ben's 1992 award.

"I now know why everyone always says, 'Wow!' when they come up from dinner. Please don't change a thing."

Certificate may be used: All year, Sunday through Thursday nights.

Maitland
D9

Thurston House

851 Lake Ave, Maitland, FL 32751-6306
(407)539-1911 (800)843-2721
Fax:(407)539-0365

Circa 1885. Just minutes from busy Orlando and the many attractions found nearby, this classic Queen Anne Victorian inn boasts a lakefront,

countryside setting. Two of the inn's three screened porches provide views of Lake Eulalia. Two parlors provide additional relaxing spots, and many guests like to stroll the grounds, which feature fruit trees and several bountiful gardens.
Innkeeper(s): Carole Ballard. $80-90. MC VISA AX. 4 rooms with PB. Breakfast and evening snack included in rates. Types of meals: continental-plus breakfast and early coffee/tea. Beds: Q. Air conditioning and ceiling fan in room. Cable TV, VCR, fax, copier and library on premises. Antiques, fishing, parks, shopping, sporting events and theater nearby.
Seen in: Fort Lauderdale Sun Sentinel, Orlando Sentinel, Florida Living, Country Almanac.

"Gracious hosts. What a jewel of a place. We couldn't have enjoyed ourselves more!"

Certificate may be used: June 1 through Sept. 30, Sunday-Thursday.

Mount Dora D9

Magnolia Inn
347 E 3rd Ave,
Mount Dora, FL 32757-5654
(352)735-3800 (800)776-2112
Fax:(352)735-0258

Circa 1926. This Mediterranean-style inn in Central Florida offers elegant accommodations to its guests, who will experience the Florida Boom

furnishings of the 1920s. Guests will enjoy the convenience of early coffee or tea before sitting down to the inn's full breakfasts. Be sure to borrow a bicycle for a relaxing ride or take a soak in the inn's spa. Lake Griffin State Recreational Area and Wekiwa Springs State Park are within easy driving distance. Just an hour from Disneyworld and the other Orlando major attractions, Mount Dora is the antique capital of Central Florida. Known as the Festival City, it is also recommended by "Money" Magazine as the best retirement location in Florida and is the site of Renninger's Winter Antique Extravaganzas.

Innkeeper(s): Gerry & Lolita Johnson. $120-160. MC VISA AX PC TC. 3 rooms with PB. 1 suite. Breakfast included in rates. Types of meals: full breakfast and early coffee/tea. Beds: QT. Air conditioning and ceiling fan in room. Cable TV, VCR, fax, copier and spa on premises. Amusement parks, antiques, fishing, parks, shopping, theater and watersports nearby.
Seen in: Mount Dora Topic.

"Most gracious hospitality."

Certificate may be used: Sunday through Thursday nights.

New Smyrna Beach D10

Night Swan Intracoastal B&B
512 S Riverside Dr,
New Smyrna Beach, FL 32168-7345
(904)423-4940 (800)465-4261
Fax:(904)427-2814

Circa 1906. From the 140-foot dock at this waterside bed & breakfast, guests can gaze at stars, watch as ships pass or perhaps catch site of dolphins. The turn-of-the-century home is decorated with period furnishings, including an antique baby grand piano, which guests are invited to use. Several guest rooms afford views of the Indian River or Atlantic Intracoastal Waterway. The innkeepers have created several special packages, featuring catered gourmet dinners, boat tours or romantic baskets with chocolate, wine and flowers.
Innkeeper(s): Martha & Chuck Nighswonger. $59-129. MC VISA AX DS TC. 8 rooms with PB. 4 suites. 1 conference room. Breakfast and evening snack included in rates. Types of meals: full breakfast and early coffee/tea. Catering service available. Beds: KQ. Air conditioning, ceiling fan, cable TV and VCR in room. Fax and library on premises. Antiques, fishing, parks, shopping, theater and watersports nearby.
Certificate may be used: June 1 to Jan. 30, Sunday-Thursday.

Ocala D8

Seven Sisters Inn
820 SE Fort King St,
Ocala, FL 34471-2320
(904)867-1170 Fax:(904)867-5266

Circa 1888. This highly acclaimed Queen Anne-style Victorian is located in the heart of the town's historic district. In 1986, the house was judged "Best Restoration Project" in the state by Florida Trust Historic Preservation Society. Guests may relax on the large covered porches or visit with other guests in the club room. A gourmet breakfast features a different entree daily which include blueberry French bread, three-cheese stuffed French toast, egg pesto and raspberry-oatmeal pancakes.
Innkeeper(s): Ken Oden & Bonnie Morehardt. $105-135. 8 rooms with PB, 3 with FP. 4 suites. 1 conference room. Breakfast, afternoon tea

and evening snack included in rates. Types of meals: full breakfast, gourmet breakfast and early coffee/tea. Dinner and picnic lunch available. Beds: KQT. Air conditioning, turn-down service, ceiling fan and cable TV in room. Fax, copier and pet boarding on premises. Amusement parks, antiques, fishing, parks, shopping, sporting events, theater and watersports nearby.

Seen in: Southern Living Feature, Glamour, Conde Nast Traveler, Country Inns (one of twelve best).

Certificate may be used: Sunday-Thursday, no holidays or weekends.

Orlando   E9

The Courtyard at Lake Lucerne
211 N Lucerne Cir East,
Orlando, FL 32801-3721
(407)648-5188 (800)444-5289
Fax:(407)246-1368

Circa 1885. Three different styles of homes comprise this award-winning inn. The Norment-Parry Inn, built in 1885, is Orlando's oldest house and is restored as a Victorian inn complete with American and English antiques. The Wellborn is an example of Art Deco architecture, dates to the 1940s and offers one-bedroom suites including living rooms

and kitchenettes. The I. W. Phillips House is an antebellum-style manor house and has three large rooms on the second floor, which overlook the courtyard and fountains below.

Innkeeper(s): Eleanor & Sam Meiner. $75-165. MC VISA AX DC. 21 rooms with PB, 2 with FP. 1 conference room. Breakfast included in

rates. Type of meal: continental-plus breakfast. Beds: KQD. Air conditioning, ceiling fan and cable TV in room. Copier, computer on premises. Amusement parks, antiques, fishing, shopping, sporting events, theater and watersports nearby.

Seen in: Florida Historic Homes, Country Inns, Miami Herald, Southern Living, Country Victorian.

"Best-kept secret in Orlando."

Certificate may be used: June, July August, Subject to availability.

Saint Augustine   C9

Carriage Way B&B
70 Cuna St,
Saint Augustine, FL 32084-3684
(904)829-2467 (800)908-9832
Fax:(904)826-1461

Circa 1883. A two-story veranda dominates the facade of this square Victorian. Painted creamy white with blue trim, the house is located in the heart of the historic district. It's within a four-block walk to restaurants and shops and the Intracoastal Waterway. Guest rooms reflect the charm of a light Victorian touch, with brass, canopy and four-poster beds. Many furnishings have been in the house for 60 years. On Saturday evenings the dining-room table is laden with scrumptious desserts and coffee. A full gourmet breakfast is provided in the morning.

Innkeeper(s): Bill & Diane Johnson. $69-115. MC VISA AX DS TC. 9 rooms with PB, 1 with FP. Breakfast and evening snack included in rates. Types of meals: full breakfast and early coffee/tea. Dinner and picnic lunch available. Beds: QD. Air conditioning and ceiling fan in room. Cable TV, fax, copier and bicycles on premises. Amusement parks, antiques, fishing, parks, shopping, sporting events, theater and watersports nearby.

Location: Heart of historic district.

Seen in: Miami Herald, Florida Times Union, Palm Beach Post, Sunday Oklahoman.

"Charming in every detail."

Certificate may be used: Monday through Thursday, Jan. 1 to Dec. 31, excluding holidays & holiday weeks.

Castle Garden B&B
15 Shenandoah St,
Saint Augustine, FL 32084-2817
(904)829-3839

Circa 1879. This restored Moorish Revival-style inn features a castle-like facade of coquina stone. Among the six guest rooms are two honeymoon suites with sunken bedrooms, Jacuzzi tubs, and cathedral ceilings. Special touches include pillow chocolates and complimentary wine. An indoor chapel serves as an occasional wedding site.

Innkeeper(s): Bruce Kloeckner. $55-150. MC VISA AX DS. 6 rooms with PB. 2 suites. Breakfast included in rates. Types of meals: full breakfast and early coffee/tea. Picnic lunch available. Beds: KQT. Air

conditioning, ceiling fan and cable TV in room. Antiques, fishing, shopping, theater and watersports nearby.

Certificate may be used: Monday through Thursday. Other times if available.

Old City House Inn & Restaurant

115 Cordova St,
Saint Augustine, FL 32084-4413
(904)826-0113 Fax:(904)829-3798

Circa 1873. Saint Augustine is a treasure bed of history and this inn is strategically located in the center. A red-tile roof covers this former stable, and a veranda and courtyard add to the Spanish atmosphere. Gourmet breakfasts are prepared by innkeeper

John Compton, whose recipes have been printed in Food Arts magazine. Inn guests are privy to the expansive breakfasts, but can join others for lunch and dinner in the restaurant. Appetizers include baked brie and Alligator Fritters. For lunch, unique salads, fresh fish and chicken create the menu, while dinner choices include gourmet standards such as Filet Mignon or a more unusual Seafood Strudel.

Innkeeper(s): Robert West. $65-145. MC VISA AX DC CB DS. 7 rooms with PB. Breakfast included in rates. Types of meals: full breakfast, gourmet breakfast and early coffee/tea. Dinner, lunch and catering service available. Beds: Q. Air conditioning, ceiling fan and cable TV in room. VCR, fax, copier and bicycles on premises. Handicap access. Antiques, fishing, shopping, theater and watersports nearby.

Location: In the heart of Saint Augustine, within walking distance of all the sights.

Seen in: Florida Times Union, Florida Trend, Ft. Lauderdale Sun Sentinel.
Certificate may be used: Sunday-Thursday.

Segui Inn

47 San Marco Ave,
Saint Augustine, FL 32084-3276
(904)825-2811 Fax:(904)824-3967

This inn is located on the edge of Saint Augustine's historic district. Marcie's Room features a king bed with handmade wedding-ring quilt, clawfoot tub, Victorian couch and private balcony. Martha Lee's Room boasts a queen bed and daybed in a separate sitting area. The full breakfasts feature homemade bread and jams, and may include George's pancakes or waffles. Be sure to inquire about discounts for senior citizens, members of the military and parents of Flagler College students.

Innkeeper(s): Nikki Lent. $65-110. MC VISA. 4 rooms. 1 suite. Breakfast included in rates. Types of meals: full breakfast and early coffee/tea. Air conditioning and ceiling fan in room. Cable TV and VCR on premises. Antiques, shopping, sporting events and theater nearby.

Certificate may be used: Sunday through Thursday, excluding all holidays.

St. Francis Inn

279 Saint George St,
Saint Augustine, FL 32084-5031
(904)824-6068 (800)824-6062
Fax:(904)810-5525

Circa 1791. Long noted for its hospitality, the St. Francis Inn is nearly the oldest house in town. A classic example of Old World architecture, it was built by Gaspar Garcia who received a Spanish grant to the plot of land. Coquina was the main building material. The city of Saint Augustine was founded in 1565.

Innkeeper(s): Joseph Finnegan, Jr. $55-115. MC VISA PC. 14 rooms, 8 with PB. 4 with FP. 6 suites. 1 cottage. 1 conference room. Breakfast included in rates. Types of meals: continental-plus breakfast and early coffee/tea. Beds: KQDT. Air conditioning, ceiling fan and cable TV in room. Fax, copier, swimming and bicycles on premises. Antiques, fishing, parks, shopping, sporting events and watersports nearby.

Location: In the Saint Augustine Historic District, the nation's oldest city.

Seen in: Orlando Sentinel.

"We have stayed at many nice hotels but nothing like this. We are really enjoying it."

Certificate may be used: Sunday through Thursday, September through May (excluding holiday periods).

Victorian House B&B

11 Cadiz St,
Saint Augustine, FL 32084-4431
(904)824-5214

Circa 1894. Enjoy the historic ambiance of Saint Augustine at this turn-of-the-century Victorian, decorate to reflect the grandeur of that gentile era. The heart-of-pine floors are topped with hand-hooked rugs, stenciling highlights the walls, and the innkeepers have filled the guest rooms with canopy beds and period furnishings. The expanded continental breakfast includes homemade granola, fruit and variety of freshly made breads and muffins.
Innkeeper(s): Daisy Morden. $70-95. MC VISA AX TC. 8 rooms with PB, 2 with FP. 2 suites. Breakfast included in rates. Type of meal: continental-plus breakfast. Beds: KQTD. Air conditioning, ceiling fan and cable TV in room. Antiques, fishing, parks, shopping, theater and watersports nearby.

Certificate may be used: May-June, Monday-Thursday, except holidays, September-October, Monday-Thursday.

San Mateo   C9

Ferncourt B&B

150 Central Ave, PO Box 758,
San Mateo, FL 32187
(904)329-9755

This Victorian "painted lady," is one of the few remaining relics from San Mateo's heyday in the early 1900s. Teddy Roosevelt once visited the elegant home. The current innkeepers have restored the Victorian atmosphere with rooms decorated with bright, floral

prints and gracious furnishings. Awake to the smells of brewing coffee and the sound of a rooster crowing before settling down to a full gourmet breakfast. Historic Saint Augustine is a quick, 25-mile drive.

Innkeeper(s): Erma Morgan. $45-75. MC VISA DS. 6 rooms. Breakfast included in rates. Type of meal: full breakfast.

Certificate may be used: Anytime, Sunday through Thursday, January through December. Jan. 3 through Feb. 10 and Aug. 1 through Sept. 30.

Sanford   D9

The Higgins House

420 S Oak Ave, Sanford, FL 32771-1826
(407)324-9238 (800)584-0014

Circa 1894. This inviting blue Queen Anne-style home features cross gables with patterned wood shingles, bay windows and a charming round window on the second floor. Pine floors, paddle fans and a piano in the parlor, which guests are encouraged to play, create Victorian ambiance. The second-story balcony affords views not only of a charming park and Sanford's oldest church, but of Space

Shuttle launches from nearby Cape Canaveral. The Queen Anne room looks out over a Victorian box garden, while the Wicker Room features a bay window sitting area. The Country Victorian room boasts a 19th-century brass bed. Guests also can opt to stay in Cochran's Cottage, which features two bedrooms and baths, a living room, kitchen and porch. Nature lovers will enjoy close access to Blue Spring State Park, Ocala National Forest, Lake Monroe and the Cape Canaveral Wildlife Refuge. And of course, Walt Disney World, Seaworld and Universal Studios aren't far away.
Innkeeper(s): Walter & Roberta Padgett. $85-145. MC VISA AX DS PC TC. 3 rooms. 1 cottage. Breakfast and evening snack included in rates. Types of meals: continental-plus breakfast and early coffee/tea. Picnic lunch available. Beds: QD. Air conditioning, turn-down service and ceiling fan in room. Cable TV, VCR, spa and bicycles on premises. Antiques, fishing, parks, shopping and watersports nearby.
Location: In the historic district.
Seen in: Southern Living, Sanford Herald, Connecticut Traveler, LifeTimes, Orlando Sentinel, Southern Accents.

"The Higgins House is warm and friendly, filled with such pleasant sounds, and if you love beauty and nature, you're certain to enjoy the grounds."
Certificate may be used: Sunday-Thursday.

Tampa E8

Gram's Place
3109 N Ola Ave, Tampa, FL 33603-5744
(813)221-0596 Fax:(813)221-0596

Circa 1945. These two cottage houses offer a variety of amenities, including lush grounds with a Jacuzzi, waterfall, sundeck and courtyard. The innkeepers named their relaxing home after singer Gram Parsons. The home and comfortable guest rooms feature a mix of European and modern decor with a few simple, country touches. The home is just a few miles from downtown Tampa.

Innkeeper(s): Mark Holland. $55-75. MC VISA AX TC. 7 rooms, 4 with PB. Breakfast included in rates. Types of meals: continental breakfast and continental-plus breakfast. Beds: QF. Air conditioning, ceiling fan, cable TV and VCR in room. Fax and spa on premises. Amusement parks, antiques, fishing, parks, shopping, sporting events, theater and watersports nearby.

Certificate may be used: Monday-Wednesday, June to August.

Georgia

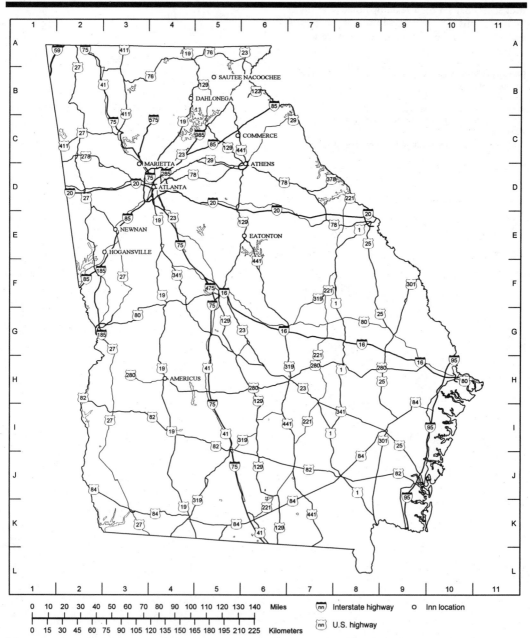

0 10 20 30 40 50 60 70 80 90 100 110 120 130 140 Miles

0 15 30 45 60 75 90 105 120 135 150 165 180 195 210 225 Kilometers

Interstate highway   ○ Inn location

U.S. highway

Americus   H4

The Pathway Inn B&B
501 S Lee St, Americus, GA 31709-3919
(912)928-2078 (800)889-1466
Fax:(912)928-2078

Circa 1906. This turn-of-the-century inn is located along the Andersonville Trail and not far from the city of Andersonville, a Civil War village. The gracious, wraparound porch is a perfect spot for relaxation. The innkeepers plan the breakfast times around their guests' schedules, serving up a country breakfast with freshly baked breads. The guest rooms offer romantic amenities such as whirlpools and snug down comforters. Two of the rooms are named in honor of Jimmy and Rosalynn Carter, whose hometown is just a short distance down the road. Late afternoons are reserved for wine and refreshments.
Innkeeper(s): Sheila & David Judah. $70-117. MC VISA AX DS PC TC. 5 rooms with PB, 2 with FP. 1 conference room. Breakfast included in rates. Types of meals: gourmet breakfast and early coffee/tea. Evening snack and room service available. Beds: KQ. Air conditioning, ceiling fan, cable TV and VCR in room. Fax and copier on premises. Antiques, parks and theater nearby.
Certificate may be used: Dec. 16 to Jan. 15, Sunday-Saturday. March 1-20, Sunday-Saturday.

Athens   D6

The Nicholson House
6295 Jefferson Rd,
Athens, GA 30607-1714
(706)353-2200

This unique home was built as a two-story log dwelling in the early 19th century, and it served as a stagecoach stop on Old Federal Road. In 1947, an extensive restoration by J.P. Nicholson altered the home into a Colonial Revival manor built around the log structure. The six-acre grounds boasts natural springs and a nature walk, and the innkeepers offer a rocking chair porch for relaxation.
Innkeeper(s): Stuart Kelley. $75-105. MC VISA AX DS. 5 rooms. Breakfast included in rates. Type of meal: continental-plus breakfast.
Certificate may be used: All periods except peak times i.e. event weekends, football home games, and bike races.

Atlanta   D4

Beverly Hills Inn
65 Sheridan Dr NE,
Atlanta, GA 30305-3121
(404)233-8520 (800)331-8520
Fax:(404)233-8659

Circa 1929. Period furniture and polished-wood floors decorate this inn located in the Buckhead neighborhood. There are private balconies, kitchens and a library with a collection of newspapers and

books. The governor's mansion, Neiman-Marcus, Saks and Lord & Taylor are five minutes away.
Innkeeper(s): Mit Amin. $90-160. MC AX DC DS PC TC. 18 suites. Breakfast included in rates. Type of meal: continental-plus breakfast. Beds: QD. Air conditioning and cable TV in room. Antiques, parks and shopping nearby.
Location: North on Peachtree 15 minutes then one-half block off Peachtree.
Seen in: Country Inns, Southern Living, Time.
"Our only regret is that we had so little time. Next stay we will plan to be here longer."
Certificate may be used: Anytime, subject to availability.

Oakwood House B&B
951 Edgewood Ave NE,
Atlanta, GA 30307-2582
(404)521-9320 Fax:(404)688-6034

Circa 1911. This post-Victorian house has seen duty as a boarding house, travel agency and psychologists' offices. The inviting interior includes original moldings, stained glass, exposed brick and traditional furnishings. A mantel, which once lived in an old-style movie theater, now makes its home at the inn. Bookworms will appreciate the innkeepers' large collection of books. The inn, located in Atlanta's charming Historic District, is full of beautiful old homes. Guests are only a few minutes from shopping in exclusive Buckhead to browsing downtown. The Jimmy Carter Library and Martin Luther King Jr. Tomb are nearby. A subway station is only one a one half blocks away.

Innkeeper(s): Judy & Robert Hotchkiss. $75-145. MC VISA AX PC TC. 5 rooms with PB, 1 with FP. 1 suite. 2 conference rooms. Breakfast included in rates. Types of meals: continental-plus breakfast and early coffee/tea. Beds: KQDT. Air conditioning, turn-down service and ceiling fan in room. Fax, copier, spa and library on premises. Handicap access. Amusement parks, antiques, parks, shopping, sporting events and theater nearby.

Location: Two miles east of downtown.

Seen in: CBS, Style, Inn Times.

"Thank you for a wonderful stay. We wish you the best."

Certificate may be used: Sunday-Thursday if available; some holidays and special events excluded.

Commerce   C5

The Pittman House B&B
81 Homer Rd,
Commerce, GA 30529-1806
(706)335-3823

Circa 1890. An hour's drive from Atlanta is this four-square Colonial inn, found in the rolling hills of Northeast Georgia. The inn has four guest rooms, furnished in country decor. The surrounding area offers many activities, including Lake Lanier, Lake Hartwell, Hurricane Shoals, Crawford W. Long Museum, an outlet mall, a winery and a championship golf course. Innkeeper Tom Tomberlin, a woodcarver, has items for sale in an antique shop next to the inn.

Innkeeper(s): Tom & Dot Tomberlin. $55-65. MC VISA PC TC. 4 rooms, 2 with PB. 1 suite. Breakfast included in rates. Types of meals: full breakfast and early coffee/tea. Beds: D. Air conditioning, ceiling fan and cable TV in room. VCR on premises. Antiques, fishing, parks, shopping, sporting events and watersports nearby.

Certificate may be used: Sunday through Thursday.

Dahlonega   B4

Cavender Castle Winery
Hwy19/60 at Crisson Gold Mine,
Dahlonega, GA 30533
(706)864-4759

This gothic-inspired castle is also home to a winery, and offers easy access to the many attractions of North Georgia's mountain country, including the Dahlonega Gold Museum. The inn sits atop Gold Hill, overlooking nine vine-covered acres. The Chardonnay Room boasts a mountain view and queen bed. Guests are welcome to play croquet or horseshoes, relax in the library, sample a taste of the Cavender's wines or explore the vineyards and gardens. The gourmet breakfast is served by candlelight.

Innkeeper(s): Linda Phillips. $65-85. MC VISA. 4 rooms. Breakfast included in rates. Types of meals: full breakfast and early coffee/tea. Dinner, picnic lunch, catering service and room service available. Air conditioning and ceiling fan in room. Antiques, shopping and theater nearby.

Certificate may be used: November through April.

Worley Homestead Inn
410 W Main St,
Dahlonega, GA 30533-1640
(404)864-7002

Circa 1845. Four blocks from the historic town square is this beautiful old Colonial Revival inn. Several guest rooms are equipped with fireplaces, adding to the romantic atmosphere and Victorian ambiance. All the rooms feature antique beds. A popular spot for honeymooners and couples

celebrating anniversaries, many guests take advantage of Dahlonega's proximity to the lures of the Chattahoochee National Forest.

Innkeeper(s): Mary Scott. $65-75. MC VISA. 8 rooms. Breakfast included in rates. Types of meals: full breakfast and early coffee/tea. Air conditioning and cable TV in room. Antiques and shopping nearby.

Certificate may be used: January through March, excluding holidays and special events.

Eatonton   E6

Crockett House
671 Madison Rd,
Eatonton, GA 31024-7830
(706)485-2248

Circa 1895. This 19th-century home is an alluring stop on the historic Antebellum Trail, which stretches from Athens to Macon. The sisters who built the home lived there without electricity or plumbing until the 1970s. Today, however, the home features these modern conveniences, but still maintains old-fashioned charm. Several guest rooms offer the added amenity of fireplaces. The balcony and wraparound porches are scenic places to relax.
Innkeeper(s): Christie & Peter Crockett. $65-85. MC VISA AX PC TC. 6 rooms with PB, 4 with FP. Breakfast included in rates. Types of meals: full breakfast, gourmet breakfast and early coffee/tea. Afternoon tea, dinner, picnic lunch, lunch, gourmet lunch, catering service and catered breakfast available. Beds: KQD. Air conditioning, ceiling fan and cable TV in room. VCR and library on premises. Antiques, fishing, parks, shopping, sporting events, theater and watersports nearby.

Certificate may be used: Anytime, based on availability.

Hogansville   E3

Fair Oaks Inn
703 E Main St,
Hogansville, GA 30230-1509
(706)637-8828

Circa 1901. This turn-of-the-century Victorian home is on the site of an original 1835 plantation. Each bedroom has a fireplace with authentic period mantels. There are a series of formal gardens with a swimming pool, and gazebo, lattice-covered swings and eight converted New Orleans street lights. The master suite has two fireplaces, a sitting room, bedroom with private bath, steam room and Jacuzzi. Breakfast is served in the formal dining room or on the sun porch.
Innkeeper(s): Ken Hammock & Wayne Jones. $75-125. MC VISA AX DC CB DS TC. 6 rooms, 2 with PB, 6 with FP. 2 suites. Breakfast included in rates. Type of meal: gourmet breakfast. Beds: KQ. Air conditioning and ceiling fan in room. Cable TV, VCR and bicycles on premises. Antiques and fishing nearby.

Certificate may be used: Sept. 15 to April 1, Sunday-Thursday.

Marietta   D3

Whitlock Inn
57 Whitlock Ave,
Marietta, GA 30064-2343
(770)428-1495 Fax:(770)919-9620

Circa 1900. This cherished Victorian has been recently restored and is in a National Register Historic District, located one block from the Marietta Square. To enjoy the best of Georgia's

past, including family recipes and preserved Southern accents, be sure to arrive for afternoon tea and snacks served in the antique-filled parlor. Amenities even the Ritz doesn't provide are in every room and you can rock on the front verandas. There is a ballroom grandly suitable for weddings and business meetings.
Innkeeper(s): Alexis Edwards. $85. MC VISA AX DS. 5 rooms with PB. 3 conference rooms. Breakfast included in rates. Type of meal: continental-plus breakfast. Beds: KQT. Air conditioning, ceiling fan and cable TV in room. Fax and copier on premises. Amusement parks, antiques, parks, shopping, sporting events and theater nearby.
Seen in: Marietta Daily Journal.

"Your inn is beautiful. It was a great experience. "

Certificate may be used: Anytime. Weekdays are best. Call for weekend availability.

Newnan   E3

Parrott Camp Soucy
Home & Gardens
155 Greenville St,
Newnan, GA 30263-2630
(404)502-0676 Fax:(404)253-4846

Circa 1884. Victorian touches were added to this stunning Second Empire home completing its wonderful exterior by 1886. Current innkeepers Helen and Rick Cousins patterned the interior after the famed Biltmore House, with its elegant, yet comfortable furnishings. Each unique room is filled with bright patterns, luxurious canopied beds and period antiques. Dark woodwork and high ceilings accent the decor. Guest quarters boast special amenities such as fireplaces, sitting areas, terrycloth robes and soft fluffy towels for guests who wish to relax in the spa or pool. For those preferring a soak in the tub, the Cousins provide bathtub pillows and bath foams. The library, which boasts a columned fireplace, includes a collection of books, classical music and classic movies. A full breakfast is served either in the dining room or on the veranda, which overlooks the home's four acres of gardens.

Innkeeper(s): Helen & Rick Cousins. $95-165. MC VISA. 4 rooms with PB. Breakfast included in rates. Type of meal: full breakfast. Afternoon tea available. Beds: Q. Antiques and theater nearby.

Seen in: Atlanta Constitution.

"Our weekend was absolutely delightful. It was extremely enjoyable to be totally pampered by both of you. All the elegant touches throughout the house and the warm conversations with you were appreciated. We'll be back, we loved it."

Certificate may be used: January through April, Sunday through Thursday.

Sautee B5

The Stovall House
1526 Hwy 255 N, Sautee, GA 30571
(706)878-3355

Circa 1837. This house, built by Moses Harshaw and restored in 1983 by Ham Schwartz, has received two state awards for its restoration. The handsome farmhouse has an extensive wraparound porch providing vistas of 28 acres of cow pastures, meadows and creeks. High ceilings, polished walnut woodwork and decorative stenciling provide a pleasant backdrop for the inn's collection of antiques. Victorian bathroom fixtures include pull-chain toilets and pedestal sinks. The inn has its own restaurant.

Innkeeper(s): Ham Schwartz. $60-75. MC VISA PC TC. 5 rooms with PB. Breakfast included in rates. Type of meal: continental breakfast. Dinner and catering service available. Beds: KQDT. Ceiling fan in room. Library on premises. Amusement parks, antiques, fishing, parks, shopping, theater and watersports nearby.

Seen in: Atlanta Journal.

"Great to be home again. Very nostalgic and hospitable."

Certificate may be used: November through September, Sunday through Thursday.

Hawaii

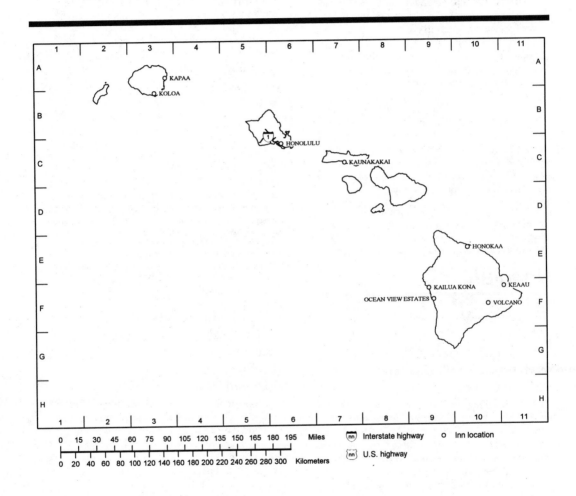

KAPAA
KOLOA

HONOLULU
KAUNAKAKAI

HONOKAA
KAILUA KONA   KEAAU
OCEAN VIEW ESTATES   VOLCANO

0 15 30 45 60 75 90 105 120 135 150 165 180 195 Miles

0 20 40 60 80 100 120 140 160 180 200 220 240 260 280 300 Kilometers

(nn) Interstate highway   o   Inn location

(nn) U.S. highway

Honokaa
E10

Hale Kukui

PO Box 5044, Honokaa, HI 96727-5044
(808)775-7130 (800)444-7130
Fax:(808)775-7130

Circa 1992. From the four-acre grounds that surround this snug cottage, guests can take in a 20-mile
view of spectacular Hawaii coastline. The grounds
feature a stream and a variety of tropical foliage,
including palms, plantains, bamboo and African
tulip trees. During the early months of the year,
humpback whales choose the waters below as a spot
to frolic. Half of the cottage is devoted to a two-
bedroom suite, which features a living room, kitchenette, bathroom and private lanai. The other section encompasses a smaller studio room, a compact
version of the suite. These rooms can be combined
for larger parties. As the nearest store is several
miles away, the hosts provide a variety of continental fare for the first morning's stay.

Innkeeper(s): Bill & Sarah McCowatt. $85-125. PC TC. 3 rooms. 2
suites. 1 cottage. Beds: Q. Ceiling fan and VCR in room. Fax and swimming on premises. Handicap access. Fishing, parks and watersports
nearby.

Certificate may be used: March 15-Dec. 15, all week.

Honolulu
C6

The Manoa Valley Inn

2001 Vancouver Dr,
Honolulu, HI 96822-2451
(808)947-6019 (800)535-0085
Fax:(808)946-6168

Circa 1915. This exquisite home offers the best of
two worlds, a beautiful, country home surrounded by
a tropical paradise. Each restored room features lavish decor with ornate beds, ceiling fans and period
furniture. Little amenities such as the his and her
robes create a romantic touch. Breakfasts with kona
coffee, juices and fresh fruits are served, and after a
day of sightseeing, evening wine and cheese are
served. The inn's common rooms offer unique
touches such as nickelodeon and antique Victrola.
The Manoa Valley is a perfect location to enjoy
Hawaii and is only blocks away from the University
of Hawaii.

Innkeeper(s): Herb Fukushima. $99-190. MC VISA AX DC TC. 8 rooms,
3 with PB. 1 suite. 1 cottage. Breakfast and evening snack included in
rates. Type of meal: continental breakfast. Beds: KQD. Ceiling fan in
room. Cable TV, fax, copier and library on premises. Fishing, parks,
shopping, sporting events, theater and watersports nearby.

Location: On the island of Oahu.

Seen in: Travel & Leisure, LA Style.

"A wonderful place!! Stepping back to a time of luxury!"

Certificate may be used: Year-round, based on availability, excluding
holidays.

Kailua Kona
F9

Adrienne's Casa Del Sol B&B Inn

77-6335 Alii Dr,
Kailua Kona, HI 96740-2405
(808)326-2272 (800)395-2272
Fax:(808)326-9492

Circa 1982. This Mediterranean-style inn is in the
heart of the famed Kona coast and between the
quaint and historic village of Kailua (three miles to
the north) and the modern Keahou Resort with its
acclaimed Kona country club (three miles to the
south). Breakfast is served at ocean or pool side and
includes an array of tropical fruits, Kona coffee,
homemade breads, muffins, local jellies and jams.
Enjoy the famous Kona sunsets with the scent of
fragrant citrus and exotic blossoms in the balmy air.

Innkeeper(s): Adrienne & Reg Batty. $50-200. MC VISA TC. 6 rooms, 3
with PB. 1 suite. 2 conference rooms. Breakfast included in rates.
Types of meals: continental-plus breakfast, gourmet breakfast and early
coffee/tea. Beds: KQDT. Ceiling fan and cable TV in room. VCR, fax,
copier and spa on premises. Antiques, fishing, parks, shopping, downhill skiing, theater and watersports nearby.

Certificate may be used: May 1-Nov. 15.

Hale Maluhia B&B

76-770 Hualalai Rd,
Kailua Kona, HI 96740-9776
(808)329-1123 (800)559-6627
Fax:(808)326-5487

This one-acre estate was lovingly designed as a
Hawaiian plantation-style home for many families
to enjoy. The estate (House of Peace) has a
Victorian and wicker interior with overstuffed sofas,
antiques and Oriental rugs. Banana, mango, papaya,
breadfruit and banyan trees edge and shade the
compound. The hillsides are terraced with flower
and vegetable gardens. Beach and snorkeling equipment are available at no charge, and the beaches are
within a 15-minute drive. Holualoa is a sleepy, old
coffee town on a mountain side above Kailua-Kona.

Innkeeper(s): N.K. Smith. $55-225. MC VISA AX DS. 5 rooms. 1 con-
ference room. Breakfast included in rates. Types of meals: full breakfast
and early coffee/tea. Cable TV in room. VCR on premises. Antiques,
shopping, downhill skiing and theater nearby.

Certificate may be used: July 15-Nov. 15.

Kapaa A3

Rosewood
872 Kamalu Rd, Kapaa, HI 96746-9701
(808)822-5216 Fax:(808)822-5478

Circa 1900. For a truly Polynesian experience, guests can stay at this inn's rustic Thatched Cottage, which appears as a dream from "Robinson Crusoe." The cottage includes sleeping, living and dining areas as well as a small kitchen. There is also a Victorian Cottage with a kitchen, two bedrooms, dining area and laundry facilities. Inside the turn-of-the-century, plantation-style house, there are two guest rooms featuring country decor. For those on a budget, the innkeepers also offer accommodations in the Bunkhouse. Guests in the main house or cottages are treated to breakfasts of tropical fruits, homemade granola with macadamia nuts, Kona coffee and entrees such as Hawaiian sweet bread served as French toast. The acre grounds are lush with flowers, tropical plants, a variety of fruit trees and ponds with waterfalls.

Innkeeper(s): Norbert & Rosemary Smith. $65-115. PC TC. 5 rooms, 2 with PB. 2 cottages. Breakfast included in rates. Type of meal: continental-plus breakfast. Ceiling fan in room. Cable TV, VCR, fax, copier and child care on premises. Fishing and watersports nearby.

Certificate may be used: Anytime.

Kaunakakai C7

Kamalo Plantation
HC 01, Box 300,
Kaunakakai, HI 96748-9606
(808)558-8236 Fax:(808)558-8236

Circa 1980. Ancient Hawaiian temple ruins built in the 13th and 14th century are found on the tropical, five-acre property of this Hawaiian Plantation-style home. A guest cottage is available away from the main house and surrounded by an acre of tropical garden. The ocean is only a five-minute walk away. The island of Molokai is known for its unique beauty and peaceful lifestyle. The innkeepers, who have lived and sailed in the islands for several years, can help you with information on shopping for local crafts, visiting museums and when festivals and special events take place.

Innkeeper(s): Akiko Shiotsu Foster. $55-75. 3 rooms, 1 with PB. Breakfast included in rates. Type of meal: continental-plus breakfast. Afternoon tea available. Beds: KTW. Fishing and shopping nearby.

Certificate may be used: April 1 to Oct. 31.

Keaau F11

Rainforest Retreat
HCR 1, Box 5655, 16-1891 37th Ave,
Keaau, HI 96749-9404
(808)982-9601 Fax:(808)966-6898

Circa 1988. The innkeepers at Rainforest Retreat offer two private, apartment-style accommodations, nestled on eight-acre of grounds, which include an orchid nursery. Each is furnished comfortably with modern decor. The Ohia House offers views of Mauna Kea, a complete kitchen, a bathroom and king and double beds. The Garden Studio has a kitchenette, king-size bed and bathroom. The innkeepers keep items such as Kona coffee, beverages, breads and eggs in the guest refrigerators. The retreat is 45 minutes from Volcanoes National Park and snorkeling, tide pools and beaches are less than 30 minutes away.

Innkeeper(s): Lori Campbell. $65-110. MC VISA AX DS TC. 2 rooms, 1 with PB. 1 cottage. Breakfast included in rates. Type of meal: full breakfast. Beds: KQ. Copier, spa and bicycles on premises. Parks, shopping and watersports nearby.

Certificate may be used: May to August, Monday-Thursday.

Koloa B3

Victoria Place B&B
3459 Lawailoa Ln, Koloa, HI 96756-9646
(808)332-9300 Fax:(808)332-9465

Circa 1970. Three guest rooms open out to a pool area surrounded by hibiscus, gardenia and bougainvillea. The light and cheerful rooms are tiny but filled with native plants and flowers such as ginger and bird of paradise. For more spacious accommodations request the apartment. Innkeeper Edee Seymour loves to share her island secrets with guests and can direct you to hidden beaches off the tourist track. (She has received an award for being the friendliest person on the island.)

Innkeeper(s): Edee Seymour. $60-111. PC TC. 4 rooms with PB. 1 suite. Breakfast included in rates. Type of meal: continental-plus breakfast. Beds: KQDT. Cable TV, VCR, fax, copier, swimming and library on premises. Handicap access. Parks, shopping, theater and watersports nearby.

Certificate may be used: When there is availability, Jan. 30-Dec. 1.

Ocean View · F9

Bougainvillea B&B
PO Box 6045,
Ocean View, HI 96737-6045
(808)929-7089 (800)688-1763
Fax:(808)929-7089

Circa 1980. Visitors to this Hawaiian Plantation-style home will be treated to the expertise of an innkeeper who has an extensive background in travel as the owner of an agency and as a teacher. All ground arrangements can be made through her. While using the inn as your base, you can enjoy the Hawaii of old as well as all the diversity the Big Island has to offer. The inn is located in a historic area near Volcano National Park.

Innkeeper(s): Martie Jean & Don Nitsche. $59. MC VISA AX DC CB DS PC TC. 4 rooms with PB. Breakfast included in rates. Types of meals: continental-plus breakfast and gourmet breakfast. Beds: Q. Ceiling fan and VCR in room. Fax, copier, spa, swimming and bicycles on premises. Fishing, parks, theater and watersports nearby.

Certificate may be used: Jan. 10-Dec. 15, Sunday to Friday.

Volcano · F10

Volcano Inn
PO Box 963, Volcano, HI 96785-0963
(808)967-7773 (800)628-3876
Fax:(808)967-8067

Circa 1989. These six cedar cabins are located on a lush, three-acre spread adjacent to Volcanoes National Park. Three of the cabins include a fireplace or wood-burning stove, and four have a kitchen stocked with coffee and tea. As several cabins can sleep five to seven guests, families and groups are welcome.

Innkeeper(s): Ron Ober & Joan Prescott. $55-80. MC VISA PC TC. 6 cottages. Beds: KQDT. VCR in room. Fax on premises. Shopping and watersports nearby.

Certificate may be used: May 1 to June 20, Aug. 25 to Dec. 20 except over Thanksgiving holidays.

Idaho

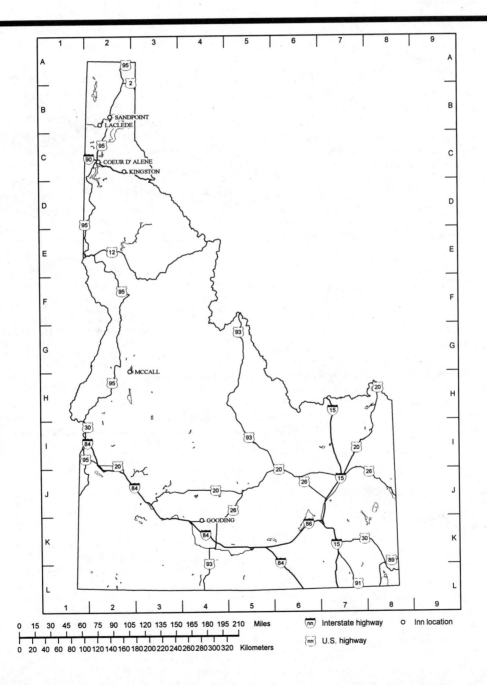

0 15 30 45 60 75 90 105 120 135 150 165 180 195 210   Miles

0 20 40 60 80 100 120 140 160 180 200 220 240 260 280 300 320   Kilometers

(nn) Interstate highway   o Inn location

(nn) U.S. highway

Coeur d'Alene   C2

The Country Ranch
1495 S Greenferry Rd,
Coeur d'Alene, ID 83814-7606
(208)664-1189 Fax:(208)664-1189

Surrounded by almost 30 acres of woods and rolling hills, this serene retreat is an ideal spot to escape from life's hectic pace. Explore the hillside on a nature walk and guests are sure to find a variety of birds and other wildlife, perhaps deer and elk. Each of the guest suites is decorated with a poster bed. The Valley View Room includes a sitting room with a mini-library. The Jacuzzi tub found in the Mountain View Room overlooks the ranch's orchard. The scent of freshly baked breads and gourmet coffee entices guests to the glass-enclosed morning room for full, gourmet breakfast.

Innkeeper(s): Ann & Harry Holmberg. $75-95. MC VISA PC TC. 2 suites. Breakfast and evening snack included in rates. Types of meals: full breakfast, gourmet breakfast and early coffee/tea. Beds: Q. Air conditioning, turn-down service and cable TV in room. VCR, fax and library on premises. Amusement parks, antiques, fishing, parks, shopping, downhill skiing, cross-country skiing, theater and watersports nearby.

Certificate may be used: May 1 to Sept. 1, Sunday-Thursday.

The Roosevelt Inn
105 E Wallace Ave,
Coeur d'Alene, ID 83814-2947
(208)765-5200 (800)290-3358
Fax:(208)664-4142

This turn-of-the-century, red brick home was named for President Theodore Roosevelt. As Roosevelt translates to Rosefield in Dutch, the innkeepers have kept a rosy theme running throughout the inn. Rooms feature turn-of-the-century furniture and some rooms afford a lake view. Coeur d'Alene boasts many activities such as the world's longest floating boardwalk, and a variety of shops and restaurants are within walking distance of the inn. The natural surrounds offer hiking, boating, skiing and many other outdoor activities.

Innkeeper(s): John Marias. $70-125. MC VISA AX DS. 17 rooms. Breakfast included in rates. Type of meal: full breakfast.

Certificate may be used: October-April, Sunday-Thursday.

Gooding   K4

Gooding Hotel B&B
112 Main St, Gooding, ID 83330-1102
(208)934-4374

Circa 1906. Travelers will appreciate the handy location of this Colonial Revival inn, between Boise and Twin Falls, just off Interstate 84. The historic hotel is listed in the National Register. Guests may avail themselves of the inn's two sitting rooms.

Many attractions are found within a one-hour drive of the inn, including Malad Gorge State Park, Shoshone Falls, Shoshone Ice Caves, Snake River Canyon and Sun Valley.

Innkeeper(s): Lauren & Elsa Freeman. $35-55. AP. MC VISA AX DS PC TC. 8 rooms, 1 with PB. Breakfast included in rates. Types of meals: continental breakfast, continental-plus breakfast, full breakfast, gourmet breakfast and early coffee/tea. Room service available. Beds: QDT. Air conditioning and ceiling fan in room. Cable TV, copier and bicycles on premises. Antiques, fishing, parks, shopping, downhill skiing and cross-country skiing nearby.

Certificate may be used: Year-round except Aug. 15-31.

Kingston   C2

Kingston 5 Ranch B&B
42297 Silver Valley Rd,
Kingston, ID 83839-0130
(208)682-4862 (800)583-4041
Fax:(208)682-4862

Circa 1930. With the Coeur d'Alene Mountains as its backdrop, this picturesque country farmhouse is a wonderful place to escape and relax. Lazy mornings begin as the scent of freshly ground coffee wafts through the home. Then a hearty country breakfast is served with cured ham, bacon, Belgian waffles topped with fresh fruit, omelets and plenty of other treats. Many of the ingredients are grown on the farm. The original owners built a garage on the property first and lived there until the Pennsylvania Dutch barn and the farmhouse were built. Innkeepers Walt and Pat Gentry have refurbished the home completely, filling the guest rooms with lace, down comforters and charming furnishings. Rooms also offer romantic amenities such as mountain views, a four-poster bed, private veranda, jetted tub or a private deck with an outdoor hot tub.

Innkeeper(s): Walter & Pat Gentry. $99-125. MC VISA PC TC. 2 rooms with PB, 1 with FP. 1 suite. Breakfast included in rates. Types of meals: full breakfast and early coffee/tea. Evening snack available. Beds: Q. Air conditioning, turn-down service, ceiling fan and cable TV in room. VCR, fax, copier, spa, stables and bicycles on premises. Amusement parks, antiques, fishing, parks, shopping, downhill skiing, cross-country skiing, theater and watersports nearby.

"The food was fabulous and so much!"

Certificate may be used: Sunday through Thursday, Jan. 2 to May 14 & Sept. 30 through Nov. 23.

Laclede
B2

Mountain View Farm B&B
PO Box 0150, Laclede, ID 83841-0150
(208)265-5768

The innkeepers spent five, painstaking years restoring this quaint farmhouse, which was built in 1900 on the grounds of what was a dairy farm and apple orchard. Relax in the common room in front of the wood stove or stroll through the eight-acre grounds, which boast gardens, trees and pastures that are home to a variety of farm animals. Guest rooms feature beautiful pieces such as antique iron beds, wicker, an Eastlake Victorian bed or a brass bed. Breakfasts, with farm-fresh eggs and baked goods, are served on china and crystal in the dining room.

Innkeeper(s): Toni Brown. $55-65. MC VISA. 4 rooms. Breakfast included in rates. Type of meal: full breakfast.

Certificate may be used: All times, except July and August.

McCall
G2

Northwest Passage
201 Rio Vista, PO Box 4208,
McCall, ID 83638
(208)634-5349 (800)597-6658
Fax:(208)634-4977

Circa 1938. This mountain country inn rests on five acres and offers four guest rooms, two of them suites. Guests enjoy the inn's two sitting rooms, fireplace and full breakfasts. There are horse corrals on the premises, and most pets can be accommodated when arrangements are made in advance. The inn is furnished in country decor and provides easy access

to a myriad of recreational opportunities found in the area. Payette Lake is just a short distance from the inn, and the Brundage Mountain Ski Area and Ponderosa State Park are nearby.

Innkeeper(s): Steve Schott. $60-80. MC VISA DS. 6 rooms, 5 with PB, 1 with FP. 2 suites. 1 conference room. Breakfast included in rates. Type of meal: full breakfast. VCR and fax on premises. Antiques, fishing, shopping, downhill skiing, cross-country skiing and theater nearby.

Certificate may be used: Year-round except holiday weekends and during winter carnival (first week in February).

Sandpoint
B2

The Inn at Angel on Lake B&B
410 Railroad Ave,
Sandpoint, ID 83864-1557
(208)263-0816 (800)872-0816

Circa 1895. Originally the home of Sandpoint's first mayor, this Queen Anne Victorian inn offers the feel of a bygone era and the picturesque setting of Lake Pend Oreille. The guest rooms, with their classic movie themes, will delight visitors, who select from the African Queen, Blazing Saddles, Casablanca and Gone With the Wind rooms, each offering its own special ambiance and amenities. Views of the lake and the Cabinet Mountains are enjoyed at the inn, and another special treat is an outdoor hot tub. The Schweitzer Mountain ski area is just minutes from the inn.

Innkeeper(s): Tracy & Grace Bowser. $55-85. MC VISA PC TC. 4 rooms, 2 with PB. Breakfast included in rates. Type of meal: full breakfast. Beds: KQ. Air conditioning and ceiling fan in room. Cable TV, VCR, fax, spa, swimming, bicycles, tennis and library on premises. Antiques, fishing, parks, shopping, downhill skiing, cross-country skiing, theater and watersports nearby.

Certificate may be used: Sept. 15-May 31 (except Dec. 15-31, Thanksgiving and other national holidays).

Illinois

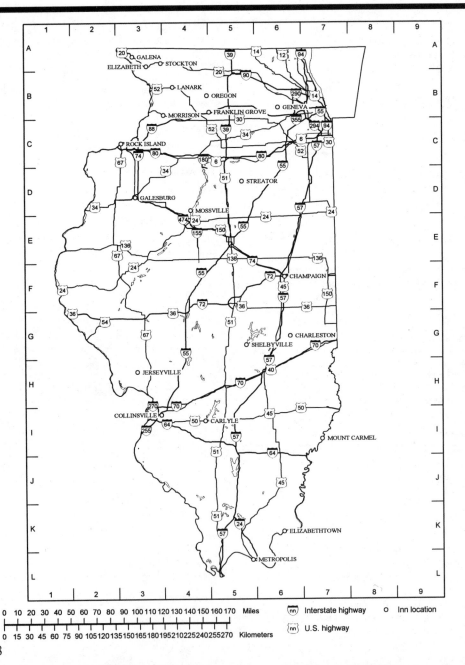

0 10 20 30 40 50 60 70 80 90 100 110 120 130 140 150 160 170 Miles

0 15 30 45 60 75 90 105 120 135 150 165 180 195 210 225 240 255 270 Kilometers

[nn] Interstate highway o Inn location

[nn] U.S. highway

Carlyle

I4

Victorian Inn

1111 Franklin St, Carlyle, IL 62231-1835
(618)594-8506

This Clinton County historic landmark was built in Queen Anne style with stained-glass windows, a curving staircase, ornate woodwork, oak floors and pocket doors. Each of six fireplaces features unique tile. After arriving, guests are treated to tea for two in the Victorian parlor, which has a turn-of-the-century pump organ. Bedchambers are full of special amenities, such as fluffy robes and slippers. The innkeepers offer a special child's room, which features antique toys and playthings.
Innkeeper(s): Mary Mincks. $55-70. MC VISA. 2 rooms. Breakfast included in rates. Type of meal: full breakfast.

Certificate may be used: Sunday through Thursday, September through March.

Champaign

F6

The Golds B&B

2065 CR 525 E,
Champaign, IL 61821-9521
(217)586-4345

Circa 1874. Visitors to the University of Illinois area may enjoy a restful experience at this inn, west of town in a peaceful farmhouse setting. Antique country furniture collected by the innkeepers over the past 25 years is showcased in the inn and is beautifully offset by early American stenciling on its walls. An apple tree and garden are on the grounds, and seasonal items are sometimes used as breakfast fare. Guests enjoy jogging and often come across pheasants, rabbits and other wildlife.
Innkeeper(s): Rita & Bob Gold. $45-50. PC TC. 3 rooms, 1 with PB. Breakfast included in rates. Types of meals: continental-plus breakfast and early coffee/tea. Beds: QDT. Air conditioning in room. Cable TV and VCR on premises. Antiques, fishing, parks, shopping, cross-country skiing, sporting events, theater and watersports nearby.

Location: near University of Illinois.

Seen in: News Gazette.

Certificate may be used: Anytime except special event weekends.

Charleston

G6

Charleston B&B

814 4th St, Charleston, IL 61920-2708
(217)345-6463 (800)832-3366
Circa 1863. This Italianate home, built during the turmoil of the Civil War, was constructed by a

Mexican War veteran and local brick mason. He created a sturdy home, with foot-thick walls made from clay taken from a local pond. The previous owner began the restoration process, using materials he salvaged during renovation of Charleston's Old Main. The oak banisters and wainscoting are some added items. The final restoration was completed by innkeepers Tom and Shirley Scism, who returned the home to its original luster. Rooms are filled with antiques and unique pieces from the Scism's world travels, including a remarkable collection of clocks. The one-acre grounds, sometimes referred to as Hickory Hills, are dotted with a variety of trees, highlighted by six massive hickories.
Innkeeper(s): Shirley & Tom Scism. $40-45. EP. MC VISA TC. 4 rooms, 1 with PB. 1 conference room. Breakfast included in rates. Types of meals: continental breakfast, continental-plus breakfast and early coffee/tea. Room service available. Beds: KQD. Air conditioning, turn-down service, ceiling fan and cable TV in room. Fax and copier on premises. Antiques, fishing, parks, shopping, sporting events and theater nearby.

Certificate may be used: Except first two weeks in August, Christmas week, and one week in November (college homecoming).

Collinsville

I3

Maggie's B&B

2102 N Keebler Ave, Collinsville, IL
62234-4713
(618)344-8283
Circa 1900. A rustic two-acre wooded area surrounds this friendly Victorian inn, once a boarding

house. Rooms with 14-foot ceilings are furnished with exquisite antiques and art objects collected on worldwide travels. Downtown St. Louis, the Gateway Arch and the Mississippi riverfront are just 10 minutes away.
Innkeeper(s): Maggie Leyda. $37-80. PC TC. 5 rooms, 3 with PB, 2 with FP. 1 suite. 1 conference room. Breakfast included in rates. Types of meals: full breakfast and early coffee/tea. Beds: QDT. Air conditioning, turn-down service, ceiling fan, cable TV and VCR in room. Spa and library on premises. Handicap access. Amusement parks, antiques, fishing, parks, shopping, sporting events and theater nearby.

Seen in: Collinsville Herald Journal, Innsider, Belleville News, Democrat, Saint Louis Homes & Gardens.

"We enjoyed a delightful stay. You've thought of everything. What fun!"

Certificate may be used: Sunday-Thursday, year-round except holidays.

Elizabeth A3

Ridgeview B&B
8833 S Massbach Rd,
Elizabeth, IL 61028-9714
(815)598-3150

Circa 1921. The unique combination of a country schoolhouse and former artist's home greets guests of the Ridgeview B&B, which overlooks the scenic Rush Creek Valley in the state's Northwest corner. Once the residence of artist Thomas Locker, the Swiss-influenced inn now houses three guest rooms and a suite in its loft area, furnished in country-Southwest decor. The School Room sports an authentic, old-fashioned effect, with blackboard, small school desks and a library with an 1882 math book. The Art Room was once Thomas Locker's bedroom. Chestnut Mountain Ski Resort is nearby.
Innkeeper(s): Elizabeth (Betty) A. Valy. $49-99. MC VISA. 4 rooms with PB. 1 suite. Breakfast included in rates. Types of meals: continental breakfast and full breakfast. Beds: KQ. Air conditioning and ceiling fan in room. Cable TV and VCR on premises. Antiques, fishing, parks, shopping, downhill skiing, cross-country skiing and theater nearby.
Certificate may be used: Jan. 1 to Dec. 30, holidays excluded.

Elizabethtown K6

River Rose Inn B&B
1 Main St PO Box 78,
Elizabethtown, IL 62931-0078
(618)287-8811

Circa 1914. Large, shade trees veil the front of this Greek Gothic home, nestled along the banks of the Ohio River. From the grand front entrance, guests look out to polished woodwork and a staircase leading to shelves of books. Rooms are cheerful and nostalgic, decorated with antiques. Each guest room offers something special. One has a four-poster bed, another offers a fireplace. The Scarlet Room has its own balcony, and the Rose Room has a private patio. The Magnolia Cottage is ideal for honeymooners and includes a whirlpool tub for two, fireplace and a deck that overlooks the river. Breakfasts are served either in the dining room or in the glass atrium room, where guests can enjoy the water views.

Innkeeper(s): Don & Elisabeth Phillips. $53-90. MC VISA PC TC. 5 rooms with PB, 1 with FP. 1 cottage. Breakfast included in rates. Types of meals: gourmet breakfast and early coffee/tea. Beds: Q. Air conditioning, ceiling fan and cable TV in room. VCR, swimming and library on premises. Antiques, fishing, parks, shopping and watersports nearby.
Certificate may be used: March 15 through Dec. 31, Sunday-Thursday.

Franklin Grove B5

Whitney House
1620 Whitney Rd,
Franklin Grove, IL 61031-9464
(815)456-2526

Circa 1856. This historic Italianate inn, located in a tranquil, countryside farm setting, provides an ideal getaway for busy Chicago or Milwaukee residents or a convenient stop for those traveling the upper Midwest. Recognized by historical registers at the national, state and local levels, the Whitney House B&B offers four guest rooms, many antique furnishings, feather beds and old-fashioned tubs. The inn's six acres are home to the Whitney #20 Crab Apple. Nearby are five state parks and the John Deere Home. Be sure to visit the non-alcoholic wine cellar and antique and collectibles shop.
Innkeeper(s): Jo Miller. $55-75. 4 rooms, 3 with PB. Breakfast included in rates. Type of meal: full breakfast. Lunch available. Beds: KQD. Ceiling fan in room. Cable TV and VCR on premises. Antiques, fishing, shopping and cross-country skiing nearby.

"It is beautiful!"

Certificate may be used: Anytime.

Galena A3

Cottage at Amber Creek
PO Box 5, Galena, IL 61036-0005
(815)777-9320 (800)781-9530
Fax:(815)777-9476

Circa 1840. This 300-acre farm offers a secluded cottage surrounded by the scenery of hilly countryside, woods and meadows. The cottage once served as the summer kitchen for the farm's main house, which was built in the 1840s. The cozy haven includes a small kitchen, fireplace, living room, bedroom and bathroom with a whirlpool tub. The bed is covered with down comforters and fluffy pillows. Firewood, towels and linens all are provided. For an extra charge, the hosts will provide flowers and champagne.
Innkeeper(s): Kate Freeman. $75-175. MC VISA AX DC DS PC TC. 1 room with PB. Breakfast included in rates. Type of meal: continental breakfast. Beds: Q. Air conditioning in room. Antiques, fishing, parks, shopping, downhill skiing, cross-country skiing and theater nearby.
Certificate may be used: Sunday through Thursday nights. All months except October.

Galesburg D3

Seacord House
624 N Cherry St,
Galesburg, IL 61401-2731
(309)342-4107

A former county sheriff and businessman built this Eastlake-style Victorian, which is located in the town's historic district. The home was named for its builder, William Seacord, a prominent local man whose family is mentioned in Carl Sandburg's autobiography. In keeping with the house's historical prominence, the innkeepers have tried to maintain its turn-of-the-century charm. Victorian wallpapers, lacy curtains and a collection of family antiques grace the guest rooms and living areas. The bedrooms, however, feature the modern amenity of waterbeds. For those celebrating romantic occasions, the innkeepers provide heart-shaped muffins along with regular morning fare.

Innkeeper(s): Gwendolyn D. Johnson. $40. MC VISA. 3 rooms.
Breakfast included in rates. Type of meal: continental-plus breakfast.

Certificate may be used: Any day between Nov. 1 and April 1.

Geneva B6

The Oscar Swan Country Inn
1800 W State St, Geneva, IL 60134-1002
(708)232-0173

Circa 1902. This turn-of-the-century Colonial Revival house rests on seven acres of trees and lawns. Its 6,000 square feet are filled with homey touches. There is a historic barn on the property and a gazebo on the front lawn. A pillared breezeway

connects the round garage to the house. The stone pool is round, as well. Nina is a home economics teacher and Hans speaks German and is a professor of business administration at Indiana University.

Innkeeper(s): Nina Heymann. $65-139. MC VISA AX. 8 rooms, 4 with PB. 1 conference room. Breakfast included in rates. Type of meal: full breakfast. Lunch and catering service available. Beds: KQD. Air conditioning and VCR in room. Antiques, shopping, cross-country skiing and theater nearby.

Seen in: Chicago Tribune, Windmill News.

"Thank you for making our wedding such a beautiful memory. The accommodations were wonderful, the food excellent."

Certificate may be used: January-July, November and December. Not Saturdays.

Jerseyville H3

The Homeridge B&B
1470 N State St,
Jerseyville, IL 62052-1127
(618)498-3442

Circa 1867. This red brick Italianate Victorian features ornate white trim, a stately front veranda and a cupola where guests often take in views of sunsets and the surrounding 18 acres. The home was constructed by Cornelius Fisher, just after the Civil War. In 1891, it was purchased by Senator Theodore Chapman and remained in his family until the 1960s. The innkeepers have filled the 14-room manor with traditional and Victorian furnishings, enhancing the high ceilings and ornate woodwork typical of the era. Guests are invited to take a relaxing dip in the inn's swimming pool or relax with a refreshment on the veranda. The inn is not appropriate for children younger than 14.

Innkeeper(s): Sue & Howard Landon. $85-95. MC VISA AX. 4 rooms with PB. Breakfast included in rates. Types of meals: full breakfast and early coffee/tea. Afternoon tea available. Beds: KDT. Air conditioning and ceiling fan in room. Cable TV, VCR, copier, swimming, bicycles and library on premises. Amusement parks, antiques, fishing, parks, shopping, cross-country skiing, sporting events, theater and watersports nearby.

Certificate may be used: Nov. 1 through April 30.

Lanark B4

Standish House
540 W Carroll St, Lanark, IL 61046-1026
(815)493-2307 (800)468-2307

Circa 1882. Four generations of Standishes are associated with this Queen Anne Victorian house. The current owner is Norman Standish, descendant of Captain Myles Standish. Furnishings include English antiques from the 17th and 18th centuries and canopy beds. The inn is closed during Thanksgiving week as the innkeepers sponsor a

series of lectures on early American history and Myles Standish for school groups. A full breakfast is served by candlelight in the formal dining room.

Innkeeper(s): Eve Engles. $60-70. MC VISA. 5 rooms, 1 with PB. Breakfast included in rates. Type of meal: full breakfast. Beds: Q. Antiques, fishing, downhill skiing, cross-country skiing, theater and watersports nearby.

Location: One hundred twenty miles west of Chicago on route 64.

Seen in: Northwestern Illinois Dispatch, Country, Midwest Living, Daily Telegraph, Daily Leader.

"Absolutely beautiful! Immaculate, enjoyable, comfortable, very refreshing."

Certificate may be used: Anytime, December to May, based on availability.

Metropolis   L5

Isle of View B&B
205 Metropolis St,
Metropolis, IL 62960-2213
(618)524-5838 Fax:(618)524-2978

Circa 1889. Metropolis, billed as the "home of Superman," is not a bustling concrete city, but a quaint, country town tucked along the Ohio River. The Isle of View, a stunning Italianate manor, is just a short walk from shops, restaurants and the Players Riverboat Casino. Several rooms offer river views. All the guest rooms are appointed in Victorian design with antiques. The Master Suite was originally the home's library and includes a unique coal-burning fireplace, canopy bed and two-person whirlpool tub.

Innkeeper(s): Kim & Gerald Offenburger. $55-115. MC VISA AX DC CB DS TC. 5 rooms with PB, 4 with FP. 1 conference room. Breakfast included in rates. Types of meals: gourmet breakfast and early coffee/tea. Banquet service and catering service available. Beds: KQD. Air conditioning, ceiling fan and cable TV in room. Antiques, fishing, parks, shopping, theater and watersports nearby.

"You may never want to leave."

Certificate may be used: November-March, Sunday-Friday.

Morrison   B4

Hillendale B&B
600 W Lincolnway,
Morrison, IL 61270-2058
(815)772-3454 (800)349-7702
Fax:(815)772-7023

Circa 1891. Guests at Hillendale don't simply spend the night in the quaint town of Morrison, Ill., they spend the night in France, Italy, Hawaii or Africa. Each of the guests rooms in this Tudor manor reflects a different theme from around the

world. Travelers and innkeepers Barb and Mike Winandy cleverly decorated each of the guest quarters. The Kimarrin room reflects Mayan culture with photographs of antiquities. The Outback, a private cottage, boasts a fireplace and whirlpool spa along with its Australian decor. The Failte room includes

a rococo Victorian antique highback bed, fireplace and Irish-themed decor. And these are just a few of the possibilities. Barb creates wonderful breakfasts full of muffins, breads and special entrees. Stroll the two-acre grounds and you will encounter a three-tier water pond, which sits in front of a teahouse, built by the original owner after a trip to Japan. One of the tiers houses Japanese Koi and another a water garden. The area has riverboat gambling and plenty of outdoor activities. Carriage, hay and sleigh rides can be arranged.

Innkeeper(s): Barb & Mike Winandy. $50-140. MC VISA AX DC DS TC. 10 rooms with PB. Breakfast included in rates. Type of meal: full breakfast. Beds: KQ. Air conditioning, ceiling fan, cable TV and VCR in room. Fax and copier on premises. Antiques, fishing, parks, cross-country skiing and theater nearby.

Seen in: New York Times, Sterling Gazette, Whiteside News Sentinel.

"We've never been any place else that made us feel so catered to and comfortable. Thank you for allowing us to stay in your beautiful home. We feel very privileged."

Certificate may be used: Sunday-Thursday.

Mossville   D4

Old Church House Inn
1416 E Mossville Rd, Mossville, IL 61552
(309)579-2300

Circa 1869. Once a church sanctuary, this restored Colonial-style home now features Victorian ambiance highlighted by the 18-foot wooden ceilings, arched windows and period furnishings. Each of the guest rooms offers something unique, such as an 1860s carved bedstead, featherbeds, handmade quilts and lacy curtains. Guests can enjoy a relaxing stroll through flower, herb and vegetable gardens, or sip afternoon tea.

Innkeeper(s): Dean & Holly Ramseyer. $69-99. MC VISA. 2 rooms, 1 with PB. Breakfast and afternoon tea included in rates. Types of meals: continental-plus breakfast and early coffee/tea. Picnic lunch and room service available. Beds: Q. Air conditioning and turn-down service in room. Bicycles on premises. Antiques, fishing, shopping, cross-country skiing, sporting events, theater and watersports nearby.

Location: Five miles north of Peoria.

Seen in: Chillicothe Bulletin, Journal Star.

"Your hospitality, thoughtfulness, the cleanliness, beauty, I should just say everything was the best."

Certificate may be used: Monday-Thursday, all year on private bath rate only.

Mount Carmel I7

Living Legacy Homestead
Box 146A, RR #2, Mount Carmel, IL 62863
(618)298-2476

Circa 1870. This turn-of-the-century German homestead features both farmhouse and log house settings. Antiques and period furniture abound, and visitors experience the unique sight of the log house's exposed interior walls and loft. The 10-acre grounds are home to flower, herb and vegetable gardens, and guests also are free to roam the meadows, barnyard and wildlife areas. Nearby are the Beall Woods State Natural Area and the Wabash River. A gift shop featuring antiques, crafts and collectibles is on the premises.

Innkeeper(s): Edna Schmidt Anderson. $50-70. TC. 4 rooms, 2 with PB. 1 cottage. 1 conference room. Breakfast included in rates. Types of meals: full breakfast and early coffee/tea. Dinner, evening snack, picnic lunch and lunch available. Beds: DT. Air conditioning and ceiling fan in room. Library on premises. Antiques, fishing and parks nearby.

Certificate may be used: April 1 to Nov. 30, Monday-Thursday.

The Poor Farm B&B
Poor Farm Rd,
Mount Carmel, IL 62863-9803
(618)262-4663 (800)646-3276
Fax:(618)262-8199

Circa 1915. This uniquely named inn served as a home for the homeless for more than a century. Today, the stately Federal-style structure hosts travelers and visitors to this area of Southeast Illinois. Fireplaces and VCRs in the rooms add to guests' comfort and the inn also has bicycles available for those wishing to explore the grounds. The Poor Farm B&B sits adjacent to a recreational park with a well-stocked lake and is within walking distance of an 18-hole golf course and driving range.

Innkeeper(s): Liz & John Stelzer. $45-85. MC VISA AX DS PC TC. 5 rooms with PB, 2 with FP. 2 suites. 2 conference rooms. Breakfast included in rates. Types of meals: full breakfast and early coffee/tea. Afternoon tea, dinner, evening snack, lunch, banquet service and catering service available. Beds: QDT. Air conditioning, turn-down service, ceiling fan and VCR in room. Fax, copier, bicycles and library on premises. Handicap access. Amusement parks, antiques, fishing, parks, shopping, cross-country skiing, sporting events, theater and watersports nearby.

"Delightful. Oatmeal supreme. Best in Illinois. Enjoyed every moment. Hi Yo Silver!"

Certificate may be used: Jan. 10-Nov. 15, Sunday-Thursday, holidays excluded.

Oregon B4

Pinehill B&B
400 Mix St, Oregon, IL 61061-1113
(815)732-2061

Circa 1874. This Italianate country villa is listed in the National Register. Ornate touches include guest rooms with Italian marble fireplaces and French silk-screened mural wallpaper. Outside, guests may enjoy porches, swings and century-old pine trees. Seasonal events include daily chocolate tea parties featuring the inn's own exotic homemade fudge collection.

Innkeeper(s): Sharon Burdick. $65-165. 5 rooms with PB, 3 with FP. 1 conference room. Breakfast and afternoon tea included in rates. Types of meals: full breakfast and early coffee/tea. Evening snack, picnic lunch and catering service available. Beds: KQD. Air conditioning and turn-down service in room. Antiques, fishing, shopping and watersports nearby.

Seen in: Fox Valley Living, Victorian Sampler, Freeport Journal.

"We enjoyed our stay at Pine Hill, your gracious hospitality and the peacefulness. Our thanks to you for a delightful stay. We may have to come again, if just to get some fudge."

Certificate may be used: January, March, and April on Sunday, Monday, Tuesday, and Wednesday.

Rock Island   C3

Victorian Inn
702 20th St, Rock Island, IL 61201-2638
(309)788-7068

Circa 1876. Built as a wedding present for the daughter of a Rock Island liquor baron, the inn's striking features include illuminated stained-glass tower windows. Other examples of the Victorian decor are the living room's beveled-plate-glass French doors and the dining room's Flemish Oak

ceiling beams and paneling, crowned by turn-of-the-century tapestries. Standing within sight of three other buildings listed in the National Register, the inn's wooded grounds are home to many songbirds from the area. A glassed-in Florida porch is perfect for relaxing during any season and a patio table in the gardens is a great place to enjoy a glass of pink lemonade on warm evenings.

Innkeeper(s): David & Barbara Parker. $65-120. MC VISA AX PC TC. 6 rooms with PB, 2 with FP. Breakfast and evening snack included in rates. Types of meals: continental breakfast, continental-plus breakfast, full breakfast, gourmet breakfast and early coffee/tea. Afternoon tea available. Beds: KQDT. Air conditioning and ceiling fan in room. Cable TV, copier and library on premises. Antiques, fishing, parks, cross-country skiing, sporting events, theater and watersports nearby.

Certificate may be used: Year-round, subject to availability.

Shelbyville   G5

The Shelby Historic House and Inn
816 W Main St,
Shelbyville, IL 62565-1354
(217)774-3991 (800)342-9978
Fax:(217)774-2224

This Queen Anne Victorian inn is listed in the National Register of Historic Places. The inn is well known for its conference facilities, and is less than a mile from Lake Shelbyville, one of the state's most popular boating and fishing spots. Guaranteed tee times are available at a neighboring championship golf course. Three state parks are nearby, and the Amish settlement near Arthur is within easy driving distance.

Innkeeper(s): Ken Fry. $52-78. MC VISA AX DC CB DS TC. 38 rooms. 6 suites. 1 conference room. Type of meal: continental breakfast. Beds: K. Air conditioning and cable TV in room. Fax on premises. Handicap access. Antiques, fishing, parks, shopping, theater and watersports nearby.

Certificate may be used: Nov. 1 through May 15.

Stockton   A3

Maple Lane Country Inn & Resort
3114 S Rush Creek Rd,
Stockton, IL 61085-9039
(815)947-3773 Fax:(815)947-3773

Circa 1838. The expansive grounds of this large Colonial Revival mansion feature a guest house, gazebo, and several farm buildings. The full gourmet breakfasts will delight guests. Historic Galena is within easy driving distance, as are several state parks.

Innkeeper(s): Rose & Bill Stout. $89-150. TC. 22 rooms with PB, 1 with FP. 6 suites. 2 conference rooms. Breakfast included in rates. Types of meals: full breakfast and gourmet breakfast. Banquet service and catering service available. Beds: QF. Air conditioning and VCR in room. Cable TV, fax, copier, spa and sauna on premises. Antiques, fishing, parks, shopping, downhill skiing, cross-country skiing, sporting events, theater and watersports nearby.

Certificate may be used: Sunday-Thursday, upon availability, except holidays, hunting season and special events.

Streator   **D5**

Dicus House B&B
609 E Broadway St,
Streator, IL 61364-2306
(815)672-6700 (800)262-1890

Circa 1890. A fine example of Stick/Eastlake Victorian architecture, this inn is recognized as a National Historic Place. The antique-filled inn regularly hosts Mystery Party weekends. Original woodwork, six marble fireplaces and the many antiques will impress guests, who are just a short drive from

the Illinois River and its many recreational settings, including Rock and Matheison state parks. The surrounding area offers an abundance of community festivals and antique/collectible auctions.

Innkeeper(s): Art & Felicia Bucholtz. $50-55. MC VISA AX DS. 4 rooms, 2 with PB. Breakfast included in rates. Types of meals: full breakfast and early coffee/tea. Catering service available. Beds: Q. Air conditioning in room. Cable TV and VCR on premises. Antiques, fishing, shopping, cross-country skiing and theater nearby.

Seen in: Illinois Cooks, Country Register, Times Press, Mary Macs Tea Times.

"Your place is beautiful. Everything was peaceful and private. Your breakfasts were delicious."

Certificate may be used: Anytime January through April. Sunday through Thursday, May to December excluding holidays and special events.

Indiana

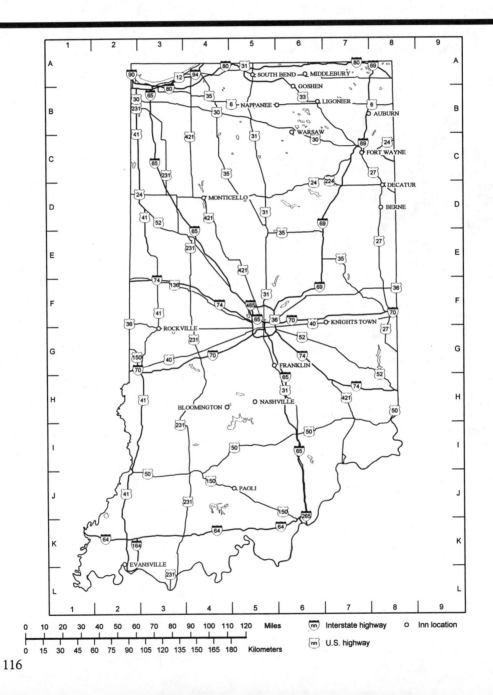

Auburn
B7

Hill Top Country Inn

1733 CR 28, Auburn, IN 46706
(219)281-2298

Circa 1860. Originally a pioneer log house, the Hill Top was also once a farmhouse before it was fashioned into the California Craftsman-style bungalow in the 1920s. Guests have their choice of the Front Parlour, Lavender & Lace or Country Slumber guest rooms, all with custom touches. A special feature of this inn is its Benny Bear Haven Room, where a single child will feel right at home and very grown up, while the child's parents enjoy the privacy of their own room. The Hill Top's antique-dominated kitchen is a favorite with many visitors.

Innkeeper(s): Chuck & Becky Derrow. $45-70. 10 rooms, 2 with PB. Breakfast, afternoon tea and evening snack included in rates. Type of meal: full breakfast. Beds: KDT. Air conditioning and ceiling fan in room. Bicycles on premises. Antiques, fishing, parks, shopping, cross-country skiing and watersports nearby.

Certificate may be used: All year if there is a vacancy.

Berne
D8

Schug House Inn

706 W Main St, Berne, IN 46711-1328
(219)589-2303

Circa 1907. This Queen Anne home was built in 1907 by Emanuel Wanner. It was constructed for the Schug family, who occupied the home for 25 years, and whom the innkeepers chose the name of their inn. Victorian features decorate the home, including inlaid floors, pocket doors and a wraparound porch. Guest rooms boast walnut, cherry and oak furnishings. Fruit, cheeses and pastries are served on antique china each morning in the dining room. Horse-drawn carriages from the nearby Old Order Amish community often pass on the street outside.

Innkeeper(s): John Minch. $35-40. MC VISA. 9 rooms, 8 with PB. 1 conference room. Breakfast included in rates. Type of meal: continental breakfast. Beds: KQDT.

Certificate may be used: Jan. 4-June 15 and Oct. 1-Dec. 31.

Bloomington
H4

The Bauer House B&B

4595 N Maple Grove Rd,
Bloomington, IN 47404-9083
(812)336-4383

Circa 1864. This red brick farmhouse B&B features a double-tiered, columned porch welcoming guests to a peaceful stay. It is located three miles from

downtown. A hearty Hoosier breakfast is served. Ask about the Hilly Hundred Bicycle Ride, Drum & Bugle competition and the Civil War reenactment days, all held nearby.

Innkeeper(s): Beverly Bauer. $45-55. 3 rooms, 2 with PB. Breakfast included in rates. Type of meal: continental-plus breakfast. Beds: D. Air conditioning in room. Antiques, shopping and sporting events nearby.

Location: Three miles from downtown.

Seen in: Herald Times.

"Your place is peaceful and quiet, a place to enjoy."

Certificate may be used: March through November, Sunday evening through Thursday evening.

Decatur
D8

Cragwood Inn B&B

303 N 2nd St, Decatur, IN 46733-1329
(219)728-2000

Circa 1900. This Queen Anne Victorian with four porches, gingerbread frosting, a turret and a graceful bay facade was built by a Decatur banker. Finely carved oak is magnificently displayed in the paneled ceilings, staircase and pillars of the parlor. Ornate tin ceilings, leaded-glass windows and a crystal chandelier are among other highlights. The wicker bed in the Garden Room looks out through a Palladian window. The Turret Suite and the Blue Room have their own fireplace.

Innkeeper(s): George & Nancy Craig. $60-65. MC VISA PC TC. 4 rooms, 2 with PB, 2 with FP. 1 conference room. Breakfast and evening snack included in rates. Types of meals: full breakfast, gourmet breakfast and early coffee/tea. Beds: QDT. Air conditioning in room. VCR, bicycles and library on premises. Antiques and parks nearby.

Location: South of Fort Wayne.

Seen in: Inside Chicago, Great Lakes Getaway, Christmas Victorian Craft.

"Your wonderful hospitality, beautiful home and company made my trip that much more enjoyable."

Certificate may be used: Sunday-Thursday and/or anytime Jan. 1-April 1, when available.

Evansville
K2

Coolbreeze Estate B&B
1240 SE 2nd St,
Evansville, IN 47713-1304
(812)422-9635

Circa 1906. Situated in a historic residential area, this Victorian inn is approached through a white picket fence. Built for a railroad executive, it is near

downtown and the river. British themes run throughout the guest quarters, from the tartan plaid Scottish Room to the yellow and green Irish Room. The parlor and library are open to guests.

Innkeeper(s): Katelin & David Hills. $75. AX DC CB DS PC TC. 4 rooms with PB. 2 suites. 2 conference rooms. Breakfast included in rates. Type of meal: full breakfast. Beds: QD. Air conditioning in room. Cable TV, VCR and library on premises. Handicap access. Antiques, parks, shopping, sporting events, theater and watersports nearby.

Location: Old Ohio River city.

Seen in: Evansville Courier, Midwest Living.

"Our stay here has brought a kind sweetness to our journey."

Certificate may be used: Anytime November-April; Sunday through Thursday, May-October.

Fort Wayne
C7

The Carole Lombard House B&B
704 Rockhill St,
Fort Wayne, IN 46802-5918
(219)426-9896

Circa 1895. Jane Alice Peters, a.k.a. Carole Lombard, spent her first six years in this turn-of-the-century home located in Ft. Wayne's historic West-Central neighborhood. The innkeepers named two guest rooms in honor of Lombard and her second husband, Clark Gable. Each of these rooms features memorabilia from the Gable-Lombard romance. A video library with a collection of classic movies is available, including many of Lombard's films. The innkeepers provide bicycles for exploring Fort Wayne and also provide information for a self-guided architectural tour of the historic area.

Innkeeper(s): Bev Fiandt. $55-65. MC VISA DS PC TC. 4 rooms with PB. Breakfast included in rates. Types of meals: full breakfast and early coffee/tea. Beds: KQDT. Air conditioning and cable TV in room. VCR and bicycles on premises. Antiques, parks, sporting events and theater nearby.

Certificate may be used: Sunday-Thursday all year.

Franklin
G5

Oak Haven B&B
4975 N 100 E, Franklin, IN 46131-7880
(317)535-9491

Circa 1913. Nestled under the shade of several large trees lies the Oak Haven B&B, a modified American four-square home. The tranquil country setting offers a peaceful change of pace from busy Indianapolis, less than a half-hour away. Handsome oak touches are featured, including a built-in coat rack and the furnishings in the Royal Oak Suite. Visitors are intrigued by the inn's "dumb waiter." A full country breakfast is served on fine china in the formal dining room.

Innkeeper(s): Alan & Brenda Smith. $45-75. MC VISA PC. 4 rooms, 2 with PB. Breakfast and evening snack included in rates. Types of meals: continental breakfast, full breakfast and early coffee/tea. Beds: QDT. Air conditioning and ceiling fan in room. VCR and library on premises. Antiques, shopping, sporting events and theater nearby.

Certificate may be used: November through April.

Goshen   B6

Waterford B&B
3004 S Main St, Goshen, IN 46526-5423
(219)533-6044

This Italianate inn, listed with the National Register, features all Midwest antiques in its furnishing schemes. The innkeeper, an avid antiquer, can provide tips on where to buy in the surrounding area. A full breakfast is served at the Waterford and guests also may relax in the sitting room or in front of the fireplace. The inn is a short distance from the state's chain of lakes, Amish country or famous South Bend, home of the University of Notre Dame.

Innkeeper(s): Judith Forbes. $55-60. 4 rooms. Breakfast included in rates. Type of meal: full breakfast. Antiques and shopping nearby.

Certificate may be used: Jan. 1 through March 31, reservations preferred.

Knightstown   F7

Old Hoosier House
7601 S Greensboro Pike,
Knightstown, IN 46148-9613
(317)345-2969 (800)775-5315

Circa 1840. The Old Hoosier House was owned by the Elisha Scovell family, who were friends of President Martin Van Buren, and the president stayed overnight in the home. Features of the Victorian house include tall, arched windows and a gabled entrance. Rooms are decorated with antiques and lace curtains. Hearty Hoosier breakfasts include such specialties as a breakfast pizza of egg, sausage

and cheese, and Melt-Away Puff Pancakes. The inn's eight acres are wooded, and the deck overlooks a pond on the fourth hole of the adjacent golf course.

Innkeeper(s): Jean & Tom Lewis. $60-70. PC. 4 rooms with PB, 1 with FP. 1 suite. Breakfast, afternoon tea and evening snack included in rates. Types of meals: full breakfast and early coffee/tea. Beds: KQT. Air conditioning, ceiling fan, cable TV and VCR in room. Library on premises. Handicap access. Antiques, fishing, parks, shopping, sporting events and theater nearby.

Location: Greensboro Pike & Rd. 750 S.

Seen in: Indianapolis Star News, New Castle Courier-Times, Indianapolis Monthly.

"We had such a wonderful time at your house. Very many thanks."

Certificate may be used: Anytime.

Ligonier   B6

Minuette
210 S Main St, Ligonier, IN 46767-1902
(219)894-4494

Circa 1899. This striking inn, with its Colonial Revival architecture and handcrafted interior, is listed in the National Register of Historic Places. Its guest rooms offer visitors a peaceful respite after

a day spent exploring Indiana's famous Amish country. Originally known as the Jacob Straus House, the inn was built by one of Ligonier's early Jewish immigrant settlers. The Minuette features many elegant Victorian touches, such as handlaid mosaic tile, stained glass, handcarved woodwork, crystal chandeliers and beamed ceiling. Guests also enjoy innkeeper Jan Yinger's miniaturia work, which includes doll houses.

Innkeeper(s): Ron & Jan Yinger. $55-60. MC VISA TC. 4 rooms with PB. Breakfast included in rates. Types of meals: continental breakfast, continental-plus breakfast, full breakfast, gourmet breakfast and early coffee/tea. Afternoon tea, dinner, evening snack, picnic lunch, banquet service, catering service and room service available. Beds: QT. Air conditioning and ceiling fan in room. VCR and bicycles on premises. Antiques, fishing, parks, shopping, cross-country skiing, theater and watersports nearby.

Certificate may be used: Anytime, Jan. 1 to Dec. 31.

Middlebury   A6

Bee Hive B&B

PO Box 1191, Middlebury, IN 46540-1191
(219)825-5023 Fax:(219)825-5023

Circa 1985. This comfortable home was built with native timber. Red oak beams and a special loft add ambiance and a homey feel. Rooms include country decor and snuggly quilts, which are handmade locally. Guests can spend the day relaxing or visit the nearby Amish communities. There are local craft shops and other attractions, which include flea markets and the Shipshewana auction. The bed & breakfast is only four miles from the oldest operating mill in Indiana.
Innkeeper(s): Herb & Treva Swarm. $52-68. MC VISA PC TC. 4 rooms, 1 with PB. 1 cottage. Breakfast and evening snack included in rates. Types of meals: full breakfast and early coffee/tea. Beds: QD. Air conditioning and ceiling fan in room. VCR, fax and copier on premises. Antiques, fishing, parks, shopping, downhill skiing, cross-country skiing, sporting events, theater and watersports nearby.
Location: In Amish Country.

"What a great place to rest the mind, body and soul."
Certificate may be used: Anytime.

Patchwork Quilt Country Inn

11748 CR 2, Middlebury, IN 46540
(219)825-2417 Fax:(219)825-5172

Located in the heart of Indiana's Amish country, this inn offers comfortable lodging and fine food. Some of the recipes are regionally famous, such as the award-winning Buttermilk Pecan Chicken. All guest rooms feature handsome quilts and country decor, and The Loft treats visitors to a whirlpool tub and kitchenette. Ask about the four-hour guided

tour of the surrounding Amish area. The alcohol- and smoke-free inn also is host to a gift shop.
Innkeeper(s): Maxine Zook. $51-100. MC VISA. 15 rooms. 2 suites. Breakfast included in rates. Types of meals: full breakfast and early coffee/tea. Dinner and lunch available. Air conditioning in room. VCR on premises. Antiques, shopping, downhill skiing, cross-country skiing and theater nearby.
Certificate may be used: November, Dec. 1-26, March and April.

Monticello   D4

The Victoria

206 S Bluff St, Monticello, IN 47960-2309
(219)583-3440

This Queen Anne Victorian was built by innkeeper Karen McClintock's grandfather. Karen and husband, Steve, have filled the home with family antiques and collectibles, including a whimsical cow collection in the breakfast room. A grand, hand-carved oak staircase greets guests as they arrive. Rooms are decorated in a Victorian country theme, setting off the high ceilings and polished wood floors. The grounds boasts old magnolia and maple trees and perennials planted by Karen's grandparents.
Innkeeper(s): Karen McClintock. $50-60. 3 rooms. Breakfast included in rates. Type of meal: continental-plus breakfast.
Certificate may be used: October through April; Monday through Thursday.

Nappanee   B6

The Victorian Guest House

302 E Market St,
Nappanee, IN 46550-2102
(217)773-4383

Circa 1887. Listed in the National Register, this three-story Queen Anne Victorian inn was built by Frank Coppes, one of America's first noted kitchen cabinet makers. Nappanee's location makes it an ideal stopping point for those exploring the heart of Amish country, or visiting the South Bend or chain of lakes areas. Visitors may choose from six guest rooms, including the Coppes Suite, with its original golden oak woodwork, antique tub and stained glass. Full breakfast is served at the antique 11-foot dining room table. Amish Acres is just one mile from the inn.

Innkeeper(s): Vickie Heinsberger. $75. MC VISA DS. 6 rooms with PB. Breakfast and afternoon tea included in rates. Types of meals: full breakfast and early coffee/tea. Evening snack, banquet service and catering service available. Beds: QDT. Air conditioning, turn-down service, ceiling fan and cable TV in room. Antiques, shopping, sporting events, theater and watersports nearby.

Seen in: Goshen News.

Certificate may be used: Dec. 1 through April 15, Monday-Thursday.

Nashville   H5

Wraylyn Knoll B&B
PO Box 481, Nashville, IN 47448-0481
(812)988-0733

The village of Nashville offers more than 250 specialty shops and restaurants, but guests need not look far from the 12 acres that surrounds Wraylyn Knoll to find activity. Set on top of a hill and surrounded by woods, the grounds include a swimming pool, nature trails and a fishing pond. Guests can opt to stay in the main house or Dove Cottage, which includes two bedrooms. Weekend guests are treated to a full, country breakfast.

Innkeeper(s): Marcia Peters Wray. $50-80. MC VISA. 6 rooms. Breakfast included in rates. Type of meal: continental-plus breakfast.

Certificate may be used: Sunday through Thursday, March through September.

Paoli   J5

Braxtan House Inn B&B
210 N Gospel St, SR 37,
Paoli, IN 47454-1410
(812)723-4677 (800)627-2982

Circa 1893. Thomas Braxtan, son of original Quaker settlers, was a business owner and stock trader who built this Victorian house. With 21 rooms, the inn became a hotel when nearby mineral springs lured guests to Paoli. Oak, cherry, chestnut and maple woodwork are featured. The inn is

furnished in antiques and highlighted with stained and leaded glass.

Innkeeper(s): Kate & Duane Wilhelmi. $60-65. MC VISA AX DS. 6 rooms with PB. 1 conference room. Breakfast and evening snack included in rates. Types of meals: full breakfast and early coffee/tea. Beds: QD. Air conditioning and ceiling fan in room. Cable TV and child care on premises. Antiques, fishing, parks, downhill skiing and watersports nearby.

Location: Downtown Paoli on state road 37N.

Seen in: Paoli News-Republican, Bloomington Herald Times, Courier-Journal.

"Wonderful. Lovely hospitality."

Certificate may be used: Any time except weekends during ski season (December-March) and all of Christmas week (Dec. 25-31).

Rockville   G3

Suits Us B&B
514 N College St,
Rockville, IN 47872-1511
(317)569-5660

Circa 1883. Sixty miles west of Indianapolis is this stately Colonial Revival inn, where Woodrow Wilson, Annie Oakley, and James Witcomb Riley were once guests of the Strause Family. The inn offers a fireplace and library, bicycles and an exercise room. Billie Creek Village is nearby and the Ernie Pyle State Historic Site and Raccoon State Recreation Area are within easy driving distance.

Innkeeper(s): Bob & Ann McCullough. $50-100. TC. 4 rooms with PB. 1 suite. Breakfast included in rates. Types of meals: continental-plus breakfast, full breakfast and early coffee/tea. Beds: KQD. Air conditioning, ceiling fan, cable TV and VCR in room. Bicycles on premises. Antiques, fishing, parks, shopping and watersports nearby.

Seen in: Touring America.

Certificate may be used: Sunday-Thursday (except special events), March 1-Nov. 30.

South Bend   A5

Oliver Inn
630 W Washington St, South Bend, IN 46601-1444
(219)232-4545 Fax:(219)288-9788

Circa 1886. This stately Queen Anne Victorian sits amid 30 towering maples and was once home to Josephine Oliver Ford, daughter of James Oliver, of chilled plow fame. Located in South Bend's historic district, this inn offers a comfortable library and eight inviting guest rooms, some with built-in fireplaces. The inn is within walking distance of downtown, and public transportation is available.

Innkeeper(s): Richard & Venera Monahan. $85-175. MC VISA AX DS TC. 8 rooms with PB, 2 with FP. 3 suites. 1 conference room. Breakfast

and evening snack included in rates. Types of meals: continental-plus breakfast and early coffee/tea. Beds: KQT. Air conditioning, turn-down service, ceiling fan and cable TV in room. Fax on premises. Handicap access. Antiques, fishing, parks, shopping, cross-country skiing, sporting events, theater and watersports nearby.

Certificate may be used: November-April, Sunday-Thursday.

Warsaw B6

Candlelight Inn

503 E Fort Wayne St,
Warsaw, IN 46580-3338
(219)267-2906 (800)352-0640
Fax:(219)269-4646

Circa 1860. Canopy beds, pedestal sinks, clawfoot tubs and period antiques carry out the inn's "Gone With the Wind" theme. Scarlet's Chamber features rose wallpaper, a queen bed and mauve carpeting, while Rhett Butler's Chamber boasts navy walls, hardwood floors, a walnut canopy bed, burgundy velvet sofa and a Jacuzzi tub.

Innkeeper(s): Deborah Hambyre. $74-129. MC VISA AX. 10 rooms, 6 with PB. Breakfast included in rates. Types of meals: full breakfast and early coffee/tea. Room service available. Air conditioning, turn-down service, ceiling fan and cable TV in room. Fax on premises. Antiques, fishing, shopping and theater nearby.

Location: Two miles south on State Road 15 off Highway 30.

Certificate may be used: Anytime rooms available.

White Hill Manor

2513 E Center St, Warsaw, IN 46580-3819
(219)269-6933 Fax:(219)268-2260

Circa 1934. This elegantly crafted 4,500-square-foot English Tudor was constructed during the Depression when fine artisans were available at low cost. Handsome arched entryways and ceilings, crown molding and mullioned windows create a gracious intimate atmosphere. The mansion has been carefully renovated and decorated with a combination of traditional furnishings and contemporary English fabrics.

Innkeeper(s): Gladys Deloe. $80-120. MC VISA AX DS. 8 rooms with PB. Breakfast included in rates. Type of meal: full breakfast. Beds: KQ. Handicap access. Fishing nearby.

Seen in: Indiana Business, USA Today.

"It's the perfect place for an at-home getaway."

Certificate may be used: September through April, any day of the week.

Iowa

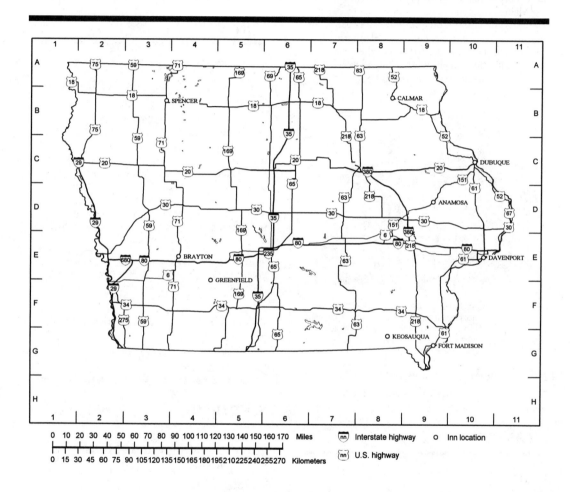

0 10 20 30 40 50 60 70 80 90 100 110 120 130 140 150 160 170 Miles

0 15 30 45 60 75 90 105 120 135 150 165 180 195 210 225 240 255 270 Kilometers

⬡ Interstate highway   ○ Inn location

⬡ U.S. highway

123

Anamosa

D9

The Shaw House

509 S Oak St, Anamosa, IA 52205-1537
(319)462-4485

Circa 1890. Framed by enormous old oak trees, this three-story Italianate mansion was built in the style of a Maine sea captain's house. Bordered by sweeping lawns and situated on a hillside on 45 acres, the inn provides views of graceful pastureland from the front porch swing and the tower. Polished oak, walnut and pine floors highlight the carved woodwork and antique furnishings. Guests can enjoy a short walk to downtown.

Innkeeper(s): Constance McKean. $70-85. 5 rooms, 2 with PB, 1 with FP. 1 suite. 1 conference room. Breakfast included in rates. Types of meals: full breakfast and early coffee/tea. Evening snack available. Beds: QDT. Air conditioning in room. Child care on premises. Antiques, fishing, shopping, downhill skiing, cross-country skiing, sporting events and theater nearby.

Seen in: Cedar Rapids Gazette, Anamosa Journal-Eureka.

"The views were fantastic as was the hospitality."

Certificate may be used: When available.

Brayton

E4

Hallock House B&B

PO Box 19, 3265 Jay Ave,
Brayton, IA 50042-7524
(712)549-2449 (800)945-0663

Circa 1882. Innkeeper Ruth Barton's great-great Uncle, Isaac Hallock, built this Queen Anne Victorian. The home is an architectural gem featuring high ceilings, ornate woodwork, carved pocket doors and a built-in china cupboard. And as is the Victorian tradition, several porches decorate the exterior. The home is across the street from the site of an old stagecoach stop, which brought an abundance of cattlemen into town, many of who stayed in the Hallock House. The innkeepers offer stable facilities and an exercise area for guests traveling with horses.

Innkeeper(s): Guy & Ruth Barton. $40. VISA TC. 2 rooms with PB. Breakfast included in rates. Type of meal: full breakfast. Beds: QD. Air conditioning and ceiling fan in room. VCR, bicycles and pet boarding on premises. Antiques, fishing, parks and shopping nearby.

Certificate may be used: Anytime except holidays, reservation required.

Calmar

B8

Calmar Guesthouse

RR 1 Box 206, Calmar, IA 52132-9801
(319)562-3851

Circa 1890. This beautifully restored Victorian home was built by John B. Kay, a lawyer and poet. Stained-glass windows, carved moldings, an oak-and-walnut staircase and gleaming woodwork highlight the gracious interior. A grandfather clock ticks in the living room. In the foyer, a friendship yellow rose is incorporated into the stained-glass window pane. Breakfast is served in the formal dining room. The Laura Ingalls Wilder Museum is nearby in Burr Oak. Smoking is not permitted.

Innkeeper(s): Lucile Kruse. $45-50. MC VISA PC TC. 5 rooms, 1 with PB. Breakfast included in rates. Types of meals: full breakfast and early coffee/tea. Beds: Q. Air conditioning and cable TV in room. VCR, bicycles and library on premises. Antiques, fishing, parks, shopping, downhill skiing, cross-country skiing, sporting events, theater and watersports nearby.

Seen in: Iowa Farmer Today, Calmar Courier, Minneapolis Star-Tribune, Home and Away, Iowan.

"What a delight it was to stay here. No one could have made our stay more welcome or enjoyable."

Certificate may be used: Monday to Thursday, April to October only.

Davenport

E10

Fulton's Landing Guest House

1206 E River Dr, Davenport,
IA 52803-5742
(319)322-4069 Fax:(319)322-8186

Circa 1871. Enjoy views of the Mississippi River from the porches of this brick, Italianate home, which is listed in the National Register. The guest rooms are decorated with antiques, including ceiling fans. After enjoying the morning meal, guests have a variety of activities to choose. Riverboat gambling, shopping and downtown Davenport all are nearby.

Innkeeper(s): Pat & Bill Schmidt. $60-125. MC VISA AX. 5 rooms, 3 with PB. 1 suite. 2 conference rooms. Breakfast included in rates. Types of meals: full breakfast and gourmet breakfast. Banquet service, catering service and room service available. Beds: Q. Air conditioning, ceiling fan and cable TV in room. Fax, copier and bicycles on premises. Antiques, fishing, parks, shopping, cross-country skiing, sporting events, theater and watersports nearby.

Certificate may be used: Nov. 1 through April 30.

Dubuque C10

The Mandolin Inn

199 Loras Blvd, Dubuque, IA 52001-4857
(319)556-0069 (800)524-7996
Fax:(319)556-0587

Circa 1908. This three-story brick Edwardian with Queen Anne wraparound veranda boasts a mosaic-tiled porch floor. Inside are in-laid mahogany and rosewood floors, bay windows and a turret that starts in the parlor and ascends to the second-floor Holly Marie Room, decorated in a wedding motif. This room features a seven-piece French Walnut

bedroom suite and a crystal chandelier. A three-course gourmet breakfast is served in the dining room with Italian tile depicting women's work at the turn-of-the-century. There is an herb garden outside the kitchen. A church is across the street and riverboat gambling is 12 blocks away.

Innkeeper(s): Jan Oswald. $60-110. MC VISA AX DS PC TC. 8 rooms, 4 with PB. 2 conference rooms. Breakfast included in rates. Types of meals: gourmet breakfast and early coffee/tea. Beds: KQD. Air conditioning, ceiling fan and cable TV in room. Fax on premises. Antiques, fishing, parks, shopping, downhill skiing, cross-country skiing, sporting events, theater and watersports nearby.

"From the moment we entered the Mandolin, we felt at home. I know we'll be back."

Certificate may be used: Sunday through Thursday. Year-round, except for holidays.

The Richards House

1492 Locust St, Dubuque, IA 52001-4714
(319)557-1492

Circa 1883. Owner David Stuart estimates that it will take several years to remove the concrete-based

brown paint applied by a bridge painter in the '60s to cover the 7,000-square-foot, Stick-Style Victorian house. The interior, however, only needed a tad of polish. The varnished cherry and bird's-eye maple woodwork is set aglow under electrified gaslights. Ninety stained-glass windows, eight pocket doors with stained glass and a magnificent entryway reward those who pass through.

Innkeeper(s): Michelle A. Delaney. $40-95. MC VISA AX DC CB DS TC. 6 rooms, 3 with PB, 5 with FP. 1 suite. 1 conference room. Breakfast included in rates. Types of meals: full breakfast and early coffee/tea. Afternoon tea and evening snack available. Beds: K. Cable TV in room. VCR and fax on premises. Antiques, fishing, parks, shopping, downhill skiing, cross-country skiing, theater and watersports nearby.

Location: In the Jackson Park National Register Historic District.

Seen in: Collectors Journal, Telegraph Herald.

"Although the guide at the door had warned us that the interior was incredible, we were still flabbergasted when we stepped into the foyer of this house."

Certificate may be used: Sunday through Thursday, all year. Very limited availability on Fridays (call).

Fort Madison G9

Kingsley Inn

707 Avenue H (Hwy 61),
Fort Madison, IA 52627
(319)372-7074 (800)441-2327
Fax:(319)372-7096

Circa 1858. Overlooking the Mississippi River, this century-old inn is located in downtown Fort Madison. Though furnished with antiques, all 14 rooms offer modern amenities and private baths (some with whirlpools) as well as river views. A riverboat casino

and a variety of shops are within a few blocks of the inn.

Innkeeper(s): Myrna Reinhard. $65-115. MC VISA AX DC DS. 14 rooms with PB. 1 conference room. Breakfast included in rates. Types of meals: continental-plus breakfast and early coffee/tea. Beds: KQD. Air conditioning and cable TV in room. Fax on premises. Handicap access. Antiques, fishing, shopping and theater nearby.

Location: US Highway 61 in downtown Fort Madison.

Seen in: The Hawkeye.

"Wow, how nice and relaxing quiet atmosphere, great innkeeper so personal kind and friendly."

Certificate may be used: November through March.

Mississippi Rose & Thistle Inn
532 Avenue F,
Fort Madison, IA 52627-2909
(319)372-7044

Circa 1881. Gourmet suppers and picnics are available to guests with advance reservations at this beautiful, red brick Victorian inn. Breakfast specialties cooked by the innkeeper, a gourmet chef,

include creamy scrambled eggs with sausage and vegetables in a buttery crustade and B.J.'s Sticky Buns. There are three parlors including a game room. The first fort built west of the Mississippi is two blocks away. Also, two blocks away is the Catfish Bend Casino River Boat and not too much farther is the longest swing-span bridge in the world.

Innkeeper(s): Bill & Bonnie Saunders. $65-90. MC VISA AX DS PC TC. 4 rooms with PB. 1 suite. 1 conference room. Breakfast included in rates. Types of meals: gourmet breakfast and early coffee/tea. Afternoon tea, dinner, picnic lunch, lunch and gourmet lunch available. Beds: KQ. Air conditioning and turn-down service in room. Cable TV, VCR and library on premises. Antiques, fishing, parks, shopping, sporting events, theater and watersports nearby.

Seen in: Daily Democrat.

"The very best, we've never been so pampered. Thanks for a memorable stay."

Certificate may be used: January-May, November-December, Sunday-Friday.

Greenfield F4

The Wilson Home
RR 2 Box 132-1,
Greenfield, IA 50849-9757
(515)743-2031

Circa 1918. Located on 20 acres, this B&B is highlighted by an indoor pool complex with a curving 40-foot pool. Guest rooms are above this building and feature Southwestern, country and traditional themes. The innkeepers are happy to guide hunters to private hunting lands known for excellent pheasant and quail hunting. Madison Country and its famous bridges are within a 20-minute drive.

Innkeeper(s): Wendy Wilson. $75-125. DS. 2 rooms with PB. Breakfast included in rates. Types of meals: full breakfast and early coffee/tea. Evening snack available. Beds: Q. Air conditioning in room. Cable TV, VCR and child care on premises. Antiques, fishing and shopping nearby.

Certificate may be used: Sunday-Thursday nights, October-May.

Keosauqua G8

Hotel Manning
100 Van Buren St, Keosauqua, IA 52565
(319)293-3232 (800)728-2718
Fax:(319)293-9960

Circa 1899. This historic riverfront inn offers a peek at bygone days. Its steamboat gothic exterior is joined by an interior that strives for historic authenticity. The Shimek State Forest and Lacey-Keosauqua State Park are within easy driving distance, and a picnic lunch prepared at the inn would be ideal to take along. Full dining services are also available.

Innkeeper(s): Ron & Connie Davenport. $35-67. MC VISA DS PC. 18 rooms, 10 with PB. 2 suites. 1 conference room. Breakfast included in rates. Types of meals: continental breakfast, full breakfast and early coffee/tea. Dinner, picnic lunch, lunch, banquet service, catering service and catered breakfast available. Beds: QD. Air conditioning and ceiling fan in room. VCR, fax and copier on premises. Antiques, fishing, parks, shopping and cross-country skiing nearby.

Certificate may be used: Sunday-Thursday, May-October; anytime, November-April.

Mason House Inn of Bentonsport
RR 2, Box 237, Keosauqua, IA 52565
(319)592-3133

Circa 1846. A Murphy-style copper bathtub folds down out of the wall at this unusual inn built by Mormon craftsmen, who stayed in Bentonsport for one year on their trek to Utah. More than half of the furniture is original to the home, including a nine-foot walnut headboard and a nine-foot mirror.

This is the only operating pre-Civil War steamboat inn in Iowa. Guests can imagine the days when steamboats made their way up and down the Des Moines River, while taking in the scenery. A full breakfast is served, but if guests crave a mid-morning snack, each room is equipped with its own stocked cookie jar.

Innkeeper(s): William McDermet III. $39-74. MC VISA. 9 rooms, 5 with PB. 1 conference room. Breakfast included in rates. Types of meals: full breakfast and early coffee/tea. Dinner, picnic lunch and lunch available. Beds: KQ. Air conditioning and ceiling fan in room. Bicycles on premises. Handicap access. Antiques, shopping and cross-country skiing nearby.

Location: In the historic village of Bentonsport.

Seen in: Des Moines Register, Fairfield Ledger, Friends.

"The attention to detail was fantastic, food was wonderful and the setting was fascinating."

Certificate may be used: Sunday through Thursday, all year.

Spencer
B3

The Hannah Marie Country Inn
4070 Highway 71,
Spencer, IA 51301-2033
(712)262-1286 (800)972-1286
Fax:(712)262-3294

Circa 1907. Two restored farmhouses grace the green lawns and golden fields of corn that surround it. Guest rooms are decorated with down comforters,

Iowa-made quilts, antiques and lace curtains. The Sweetheart Room has an in-room clawfoot tub. Guests are given walking sticks and parasols for strolling along the old creek. A bistro is located on the grounds. The innkeepers host themed tea parties, such as a Children's Etiquette lunch, Queen of Hearts tea or Queen Elizabeth's Garden Party.

Innkeeper(s): Mary Nichols. $69-105. MC VISA AX DS PC TC. 5 rooms with PB. 1 conference room. Breakfast and evening snack included in rates. Types of meals: continental breakfast, full breakfast, gourmet breakfast and early coffee/tea. Afternoon tea, dinner, lunch, gourmet lunch and banquet service available. Beds: Q. Air conditioning, turndown service and ceiling fan in room. VCR, fax and library on premises. Amusement parks, antiques, fishing, parks, shopping, cross-country skiing, theater and watersports nearby.

Location: Five miles south of Spencer.

Seen in: Innsider, Midwest Living, Brides, Des Moines Register, Sioux City Journal, Home and Away.

"Best bed & breakfast in Iowa.- Des Moines Register."

Certificate may be used: April, May, November, December.

Kansas

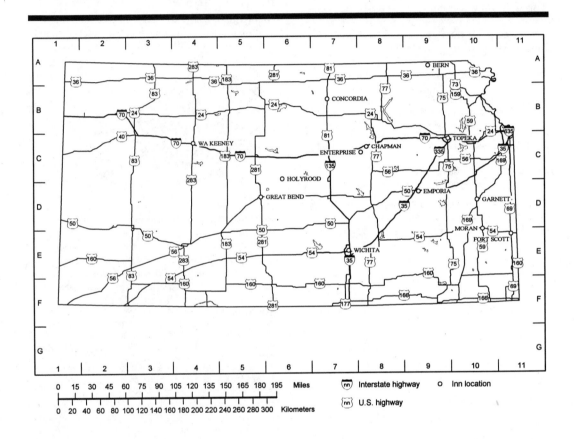

0 15 30 45 60 75 90 105 120 135 150 165 180 195   Miles

0 20 40 60 80 100 120 140 160 180 200 220 240 260 280 300   Kilometers

(nn) Interstate highway   o   Inn location

(nn) U.S. highway

Bern   A9

Lear Acres B&B

RR 1 Box 31, Bern, KS 66408-9715
(913)336-3903

Circa 1918. A working farm just south of the Nebraska border, Lear Acres is exactly the down-home setting it appears to be. The two-story farmhouse features three spacious guest rooms, all with views of the surrounding countryside. Many of the inn's furnishings are period pieces from the early 1900s. Guests will be greeted by a menagerie of farm pets and animals, adding to the distinctly country atmosphere. The full breakfast features food from the innkeepers' farm and garden. Fall or winter guests may ask for Grandma's cozy feather bed.

Innkeeper(s): Toby Lear. $35-38. 3 rooms. Breakfast included in rates. Type of meal: full breakfast. Air conditioning, turn-down service, ceiling fan and VCR in room. Antiques nearby.

Certificate may be used: Any weekend, except Memorial Day with minimum of 10-day advance reservation.

Chapman   C8

Windmill Inn B&B

1787 Rain Rd, Chapman, KS 67431-9317
(913)263-8755

The Windmill Inn is a place of memories. Many were created by the innkeepers grandparents who built the home, others are the happy remembrances guests take home. The home is filled with antiques, family heirlooms. Stained glass and a window seat add to the charm. For an extra charge, the innkeepers provide dinner or picnic lunches. The wrap-around porches offer a relaxing swing, and on starry nights, the outdoor spa is the place to be. Historic Abilene is just a few miles down the road, offering a glimpse of an authentic Old West town, located on the Chisolm Trail.

Innkeeper(s): Deb Sanders. $55-85. 4 rooms. Breakfast included in rates. Type of meal: full breakfast.

Certificate may be used: Sunday through Thursday.

Concordia   B7

Crystle's B&B

508 W 7th St, Concordia, KS 66901-2708
(913)243-2192 (800)889-6373

Circa 1880. This Queen Anne Victorian inn has been recognized by the city's historical society. The home has been in the owner's family for four generations. Three of the inn's five guest rooms showcase Crystle's impressive plate collection. The inn is filled with charming Victorian touches, and a favorite feature is the 1916 Steinway grand piano in the parlor. Guests may enjoy breakfast in their room, the inn's dining room or, weather permitting, on the sun-drenched front porch. Located in a famous grain-production area of the state, Concordia offers much of interest. Be sure to take in the impressive Brown Grand Theatre.

Innkeeper(s): Betty Suther. $35-50. MC VISA. 5 rooms, 1 with PB. 1 conference room. Breakfast included in rates. Types of meals: full breakfast and early coffee/tea. Beds: QD. Air conditioning in room. Cable TV and VCR on premises. Antiques, parks, shopping and theater nearby.

Seen in: Blade Empire, Innsider.

Certificate may be used: Off-season and during weekdays.

Emporia   D9

Plumb House B&B

628 Exchange St,
Emporia, KS 66801-3008
(316)342-6881

Circa 1910. Named for former owners of this restored Victorian Shingle home, the Plumb House offers elegant touches of that period's finery

throughout its attractive interior. Try the Rosalie Room, with its pink roses, white lace; the Horseless Carriage room with old-fashioned tub and rocking chair; or the Loft, a suite with not only a view, but all the amenities of home, including TV, refrigerator and microwave. Be sure to inquire about the inn's two-hour Tea Party, available for that extra-special occasion.

Innkeeper(s): Barbara Stoecklin. $65-80. MC VISA AX PC TC. 5 rooms, 3 with PB, 1 with FP. 1 suite. 1 conference room. Breakfast, afternoon tea and evening snack included in rates. Types of meals: continental breakfast, full breakfast, gourmet breakfast and early coffee/tea. Room service available. Beds: KQDT. Air conditioning, turn-down service and ceiling fan in room. Cable TV, VCR and spa on premises. Antiques, fishing, parks, shopping, sporting events and theater nearby.

Seen in: Emporia Gazette, KSNW-TV, Wichita, Kansas.

"This is the most elegant place I have ever had the pleasure to stay in. It's beautiful Victorian decor has refreshed my soul."

Certificate may be used: Anytime.

The White Rose Inn
901 Merchant St,
Emporia, KS 66801-2813
(316)343-6336

Circa 1902. Emporia is a Midwest college town, and the White Rose Inn is a mere three blocks from Emporia State University. This Queen Anne Victorian home offers three private suites for its guests, all with a sitting room and queen beds. Each morning, guests will be treated to a different and delicious menu, and every afternoon tea or espresso is served. Guests who so desire may have breakfast in bed, and the innkeepers will happily arrange for a massage, manicure or pedicure. The inn also hosts weddings and family reunions.

Innkeeper(s): Samuel & Lisa Tosti. $50-75. MC VISA AX DC DS TC. 4 suites. Breakfast and afternoon tea included in rates. Types of meals: full breakfast, gourmet breakfast and early coffee/tea. Dinner, evening snack, picnic lunch, lunch, gourmet lunch, banquet service, catering service, catered breakfast and room service available. Beds: Q. Air conditioning, turn-down service and cable TV in room. VCR on premises. Antiques, fishing, parks, sporting events and theater nearby.

Certificate may be used: Year-round based on availability.

Enterprise   C8

Ehrsam Place B&B
103 S Grant, Enterprise, KS 67441
(913)263-8747 (800)470-7774

Circa 1872. In its early days, this home and the family that lived in it were the talk of the town. The family held an abundance of well-attended parties, and many rumors were spread about why the Ehrsam company safe was kept in the home's basement. Rumors aside, the home features a variety of architectural styles, leaning toward Georgian, with columns gracing the front entrance. The 17-acre grounds are fun to explore, offering a windmill, silo, stables, a carriage house and creek. The innkeepers encourage guests to explore the home as well, which rises three stories. The basement still houses the illusive safe. Rooms are decorated in a variety of styles, from Art Deco to Victorian. Guest can enjoy breakfast in bed if they choose. With advance notice, the innkeepers will prepare hors d'oeuvres, picnic lunches and dinners for their guests.

Innkeeper(s): Reg & Jan Welser. $50-75. AP. TC. 4 rooms, 2 with PB. 1 suite. 1 conference room. Breakfast, afternoon tea and evening snack included in rates. Types of meals: continental-plus breakfast, full breakfast, gourmet breakfast and early coffee/tea. Dinner, picnic lunch, lunch, gourmet lunch, catered breakfast and room service available. Beds: QD. Air conditioning, ceiling fan, cable TV and VCR in room. Copier, spa, bicycles and pet boarding on premises. Antiques, fishing, parks, shopping, sporting events, theater and watersports nearby.

Certificate may be used: All year Sunday-Thursday nights.

Fort Scott   E11

The Chenault Mansion
820 S National Ave,
Fort Scott, KS 66701-1321
(316)223-6800

Curved-glass windows, stained glass, ornate woodwork, pocket doors and fireplaces have been refurbished in this gracious home, to reflect its beginnings in the late 19th century. Antiques and a large china and glass collection add ambiance to the elegant rooms. Full breakfasts are served in the well-appointed dining room. The David P. & Mary Josephine Thomas Suite, located in the tower room, boasts a sitting room and wicker furnishings. Other rooms feature special pieces such as a hand-carved walnut bed, and two of the rooms have fireplaces.

Innkeeper(s): Robert Schafer. $65-80. MC VISA DS. 5 rooms. Breakfast included in rates. Type of meal: full breakfast.

Certificate may be used: All year - if stay is on weekend, Thursday or Sunday night must be included.

Lyons' House
742 S National Ave,
Fort Scott, KS 66701-1319
(316)223-0779 (800)784-8378

This four-story, landmark Italianate manor is one of the first mansions built on the prairie. The home features original chandeliers, which highlight the polished wood floors, family heirlooms and antiques. Innkeeper Pat Lyons serves up an abundant, Southern-style breakfast with treats such as biscuits and gravy or French toast with custard filling. Snacks are always available, and Pat keeps rooms stocked with tea and coffee service. Afternoon teas are served by request, and turndown service is one of the many romantic touches guests will enjoy. Pat has created several special packages for her guests, including her Mystery in a Parlor event, which combines gourmet meals with a murder-mystery game.

Innkeeper(s): Pat Lyons. $60-70. 4 rooms. Breakfast included in rates. Type of meal: full breakfast.

Certificate may be used: Anytime, Jan. 1-April 30; Sunday-Thursday, May 1-Dec. 31.

Garnett   D10

Kirk House
145 W 4th Ave, Garnett, KS 66032-1313
(913)448-5813 Fax:(913)448-6478

Circa 1913. Those interested in the arts will love Kirk House. The innkeepers have backgrounds as art dealers, and count weaving and classical music among their other interests. Guests receive plenty of

KIRK HOUSE · 1913

pampering at this inn, located in eastern Kansas, south of Ottawa. Food preparation and presentation are stressed here, with visitors enjoying gourmet breakfasts, afternoon teas and evening snacks. The inn also offers turndown service and a sitting room and library for further relaxation.

Innkeeper(s): Robert Cugno & Robert Logan. $65-90. 5 rooms, 1 with PB. Breakfast included in rates. Types of meals: full breakfast and gourmet breakfast. Afternoon tea, evening snack and picnic lunch available. Beds: QDT. Turn-down service in room. Cable TV and VCR on premises. Antiques, fishing, shopping, sporting events, theater and watersports nearby.

Seen in: Metro News, Kansas, Topeka Capitol Journal, Wichita Eagle.

"What a nugget of class, beauty & culture in the middle of Kansas! A feast for the eyes & mouth, too much to absorb in one visit. Gracious, knowledgeable, sensitive innkeepers. We can't rate this wonderful spot too highly."

Certificate may be used: Sunday through Thursday, all year.

Great Bend   D5

Peaceful Acres B&B
RR 5 Box 153,
Great Bend, KS 67530-9805
(316)793-7527

Circa 1899. A casual country setting greets guests at Peaceful Acres, a comfortable farmhouse with plenty of sheep, chicken, dogs and cats to entertain all visitors, especially children, who are more than welcome here. Activities abound for the youngsters and they also will enjoy the zoo in Great Bend, five miles away. Cheyenne Bottoms and Pawnee Rock are within easy driving distance.

Innkeeper(s): Dale & Doris Nitzel. $30. 2 rooms. 1 conference room. Breakfast included in rates. Type of meal: full breakfast. Beds: QDT. Air conditioning and ceiling fan in room. VCR and library on premises. Antiques, fishing, parks and shopping nearby.

Certificate may be used: Anytime available.

Holyrood   C6

Hollyrood House
PO Box 280, Holyrood, KS 67450-0280
(913)252-3678

Circa 1884. The Hollyrood House offers a spacious living room with a fireplace. One guest room has a large bay window. Breakfast is served in the dining room or on the porch.

Innkeeper(s): Ronald & Rose Anne Schepmann. $30-50. MC VISA. 3 rooms. 1 cottage. Breakfast included in rates. Types of meals: continental breakfast and full breakfast. Evening snack available. Spa on premises. Antiques and fishing nearby.

Seen in: Ellsworth Reporter, Great Bend Tribune.

"Best place I have ever stayed."

Certificate may be used: All week, based upon availability.

Moran   E10

Hedgeapple Acres B&B
RR 2 Box 27, Moran, KS 66755-9500
(316)237-4646

Circa 1974. Nestled on 80-acres of farmland, this country home offers comfortable furnishings and plenty of places to relax. One of the bedchambers boasts a whirpool tub, while another includes a fireplace. Guests not only enjoy a hearty country breakfast, but supper as well. Spend the day exploring the area, which includes historic Fort Scott, or grab your rod and reel and try out the farm's two stocked ponds.

Innkeeper(s): Jack & Ann Donaldson. $58-65. MC VISA AX DS PC TC. 6 rooms with PB, 1 with FP. 1 conference room. Breakfast, dinner and evening snack included in rates. Types of meals: full breakfast and early coffee/tea. Banquet service and catering service available. Beds: K. Air conditioning and ceiling fan in room. Cable TV, VCR, fax and library on premises. Handicap access. Antiques, fishing, parks, shopping and theater nearby.

Certificate may be used: All year, Sunday through Thursday.

Topeka
C9

The Sunflower B&B
915 SW Munson Ave,
Topeka, KS 66604-1129
(913)357-7509

Circa 1887. This National Register home is a whimsical example of Queen Anne Victorian architecture with stained-glass windows, ornate plaster moldings, medallions and reproductions of period wallpapers. Antique Victorian furnishings and collectibles complete the look. The Giles Bedroom, named for the home's original builder and a founding Topeka citizen, includes an Eastlake-style fireplace, bay window and carved walnut bed. The Servants Quarters features a hand-painted bedroom set and a fainting couch. The breakfast menu varies from gourmet fare to homemade country goodies.
Innkeeper(s): Michael Stringer. $50-55. 2 rooms with PB. Breakfast included in rates. Types of meals: continental breakfast, full breakfast, gourmet breakfast and early coffee/tea. Evening snack available. Beds: D. Air conditioning, turn-down service and ceiling fan in room. Cable TV, VCR and bicycles on premises. Antiques, fishing, parks, shopping, sporting events, theater and watersports nearby.
Certificate may be used: Oct. 15-May 15, Sunday through Thursday.

Wakeeney
C4

Thistle Hill B&B
RR 1 Box 93, Wakeeney, KS 67672-9736
(913)743-2644

Circa 1950. This modern cedar farmhouse has a unique, "older" feel, aided mainly by its porch, which is reminiscent of the Old West. The interior features an oak-floored dining room and views of the inn's gardens, farm and prairie. The second-story guest rooms include the Prairie Room, with a queen-size bed; the Sunflower Room, which boasts a handmade Kansas sunflower quilt and a view of the farm's working windmill; and the Oak Room, which offers a queen-size handmade fence post bed and a

hide-a-bed for extra family members. Guests may explore a 60-acre prairie-wildflower restoration, which attracts many species of birds.
Innkeeper(s): Dave & Mary Hendricks. $55-65. MC VISA PC TC. 3 rooms with PB. Breakfast and afternoon tea included in rates. Types of meals: full breakfast, gourmet breakfast and early coffee/tea. Air conditioning and ceiling fan in room. VCR, stables and library on premises. Antiques, fishing, parks and shopping nearby.
Location: Half-way between Denver and Kansas City. Sternberg Museum, Cottonwood Ranch and Castle Rock nearby.
Seen in: Kansas Weekend Guide, Kansas City Star, Country.
Certificate may be used: September-April (except second weekend in November).

Wichita
E7

The Inn at The Park
3751 E Douglas Ave,
Wichita, KS 67218-1002
(316)652-0500 (800)258-1951
Fax:(316)652-0610

Circa 1910. This popular three-story brick mansion offers many special touches, including unique furnishings in each of its 11 guest rooms, three of which are suites. Some of the rooms feature fireplaces, refrigerators or hot tubs. The inn's convenient location makes it ideal for business travelers or those interested in exploring Wichita at length. The inn's parkside setting provides additional opportunities for relaxation or recreation. Ask for information about shops and restaurants in Wichita's Old Town.
Innkeeper(s): Lynda Weixelman. $75-135. MC VISA AX DS. 12 rooms with PB, 8 with FP. 3 suites. 1 conference room. Breakfast included in rates. Types of meals: continental-plus breakfast and early coffee/tea. Catering service available. Beds: KQ. Air conditioning, turn-down service, cable TV and VCR in room. Fax, copier, computer and spa on premises. Antiques, shopping and theater nearby.
Seen in: Wichita Business Journal.

"This is truly a distinctive hotel. Your attention to detail is surpassed only by your devotion to excellent service."
Certificate may be used: All the time.

Kentucky

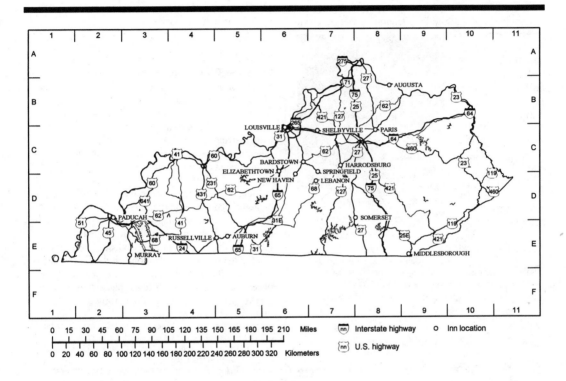

		Miles
0 15 30 45 60 75 90 105 120 135 150 165 180 195 210		
0 20 40 60 80 100 120 140 160 180 200 220 240 260 280 300 320		Kilometers

(nn) Interstate highway   ○ Inn location

{nn} U.S. highway

133

Auburn
E5

Auburn Guest House & Carriage House

421 W Main St, Auburn, KY 42206-5239
(502)542-6019

Circa 1938. This Southern Colonial mansion features mannequins dressed in vintage clothing. Guests may relax in the lounge, on the side porch or on the deck in the back of the house. The inn is furnished with antiques. The dressing room has an antique fainting couch. Guest rooms include the Primitive Room with chestnut pieces, the Maple Room, the Walnut Room, the Oak Room and the Cherry Room. The inn is listed in the National Register of Historical Places.

Innkeeper(s): David & Joy Williams. $55. 4 rooms, 2 with PB. Breakfast included in rates. Type of meal: full breakfast. Beds: D. Air conditioning and cable TV in room. Antiques and shopping nearby.

Location: On Highway 68 between Bowling Green and Russelville.

Seen in: Logan County News.

"I loved every second I spent in your beautiful home."
Certificate may be used: May 1-Dec. 1, Sunday-Friday.

Augusta
B8

Augusta Ayre

201 W 2nd St, Augusta, KY 41002-1004
(606)756-3228

Circa 1840. This Federal-style home was built by a freed slave and offers close access to the Ohio River and a city park. Each of the guest rooms includes a fireplace, and the sitting room is the perfect place to curl up and enjoy a book or old movie. Augusta offers many historic homes and antique shops to visit.

Innkeeper(s): Maynard Krum. $65-90. DS. 2 rooms, 2 with FP. Breakfast included in rates. Types of meals: full breakfast and early coffee/tea. Beds: D. Air conditioning and ceiling fan in room. Cable TV and VCR on premises. Antiques, fishing, parks and watersports nearby.

"Thank you for your generous hospitality and all the special touch surprises! A wonderful home away from home."
Certificate may be used: Sunday through Thursday, March to Aug. 30. Anytime, January & February, except holidays.

Bardstown
C6

Beautiful Dreamer B&B

440 E Stephen Foster Ave,
Bardstown, KY 40004-2202
(502)348-4004 (800)811-8312

Circa 1995. From one of the porches at this Federal-style inn, guests can view My Old Kentucky Home, the actual house which inspired the famous Stephen Foster song. Civil War troops camped in the vicinity of the home, which is located in a historic district. The home was built in 1995, yet reflects a grandeur of an earlier era. Rooms are furnished elegantly with antiques and reproductions fashioned from cherry wood. One guest room includes a fireplace, others have either a four-poster or sleigh bed. Guests are encouraged to relax on a porch or in the upstairs sitting area, where refreshments and snacks are available. Coffee and tea are served in this area prior to breakfast. The morning meal is hearty and served family style. Fresh fruit is always available, and home-baked cinnamon or sweet rolls, baked French toast, biscuits and gravy, bacon, grits and egg dishes are among the special treats which change daily.

Innkeeper(s): Lynell Ginter. $79-99. MC VISA PC. 4 rooms with PB, 1 with FP. Breakfast and evening snack included in rates. Types of meals: full breakfast and early coffee/tea. Beds: QD. Air conditioning, ceiling fan and cable TV in room. Handicap access. Amusement parks, antiques, fishing, parks, shopping, theater and watersports nearby.

Certificate may be used: Jan. 1 to May 1 & Sept. 1 to Dec. 30, Sunday through Thursday. Not valid May 2 through Aug. 31.

The Mansion Bed & Breakfast

1003 N 3rd St,
Bardstown, KY 40004-2616
(502)348-2586 (800)399-2586
Fax:(502)349-6098

Circa 1851. The Confederate flag was raised for the first time in Kentucky on this property. The beautifully crafted Greek Revival mansion is in the National Register of Historic Places. Period antiques and hand-crocheted bedspreads, dust ruffles and shams are featured in the guest rooms. There are more than three acres of tall trees and gardens. The Courthouse in historic Bardstown is nine blocks away.

Innkeeper(s): Joseph & Charmaine Downs. $85. MC VISA DS. 8 rooms with PB. 1 conference room. Breakfast included in rates. Type of meal: continental-plus breakfast. Beds: KD. Air conditioning and ceiling fan in room. Cable TV and VCR on premises. Antiques, fishing, shopping and theater nearby.

Certificate may be used: All year on stays beginning on Sunday night through Wednesday.

Elizabethtown   C6

Olde Bethlehem Academy Inn
7051 Saint John Rd,
Elizabethtown, KY 42701-8766
(502)862-9003 (800)662-5670

Circa 1818. Presidents and diplomats once were hosted at this Greek Revival mansion, originally the home of a Kentucky governor. The home later was used by the Sisters of Loretto as a chapel, school and home. The inn still includes the chapel, which is decorated by a large mural. The guest rooms are furnished with antiques and reproductions, and the innkeepers have won awards for their interior design, a mix of elegance and country styles. For guests in search of a relaxing spot, the covered veranda is lined with rockers and chairs.

Innkeeper(s): Michael Dooley. $75-85. MC VISA. 6 rooms with PB, 2 with FP. 1 conference room. Breakfast included in rates. Type of meal: full breakfast. Handicap access.

Location: Less than one hour from Mammoth Cave and Churchill Downs.

Certificate may be used: Subject to availability.

Harrodsburg   C7

Canaan Land Farm B&B
4355 Lexington Rd,
Harrodsburg, KY 40330-9220
(606)734-3984 (800)450-7607

Circa 1795. This National Register farmhouse, one of the oldest brick houses in Kentucky, is appointed with antiques, quilts and featherbeds. Your host is a shepherd/attorney and your hostess is a handspinner and artist. A large flock of sheep and other assorted barnyard creatures graze the pastures at this working farm. In 1995, the innkeepers

reconstructed an 1815, historic log house on the grounds. The log house includes three guestrooms and three working fireplaces.

Innkeeper(s): Theo & Fred Bee. $75-105. PC TC. 7 rooms with PB, 3 with FP. Breakfast included in rates. Types of meals: full breakfast and early coffee/tea. Beds: DT. Air conditioning in room. VCR, spa and swimming on premises. Antiques, fishing, parks, shopping and watersports nearby.

Location: Two miles from Shakertown.

Seen in: Danville Advocate, Lexington Herald Lodger.

"You truly have a gift for genuine hospitality."

Certificate may be used: Anytime of year, Sunday-Thursday.

Lebanon   D7

Myrtledene B&B
370 N Spalding Ave,
Lebanon, KY 40033-1563
(502)692-2223 (800)391-1721

Circa 1833. Once a Confederate general's headquarters at a point during the Civil War, this pink brick inn, located at a bend in the road, has greeted visitors entering Lebanon for more than 150 years. When General John Hunt Morgan returned in 1863 to destroy the town, the white flag hoisted to signal a truce was flown at 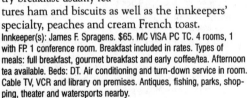 Myrtledene. A country breakfast usually features ham and biscuits as well as the innkeepers' specialty, peaches and cream French toast.

Innkeeper(s): James F. Spragens. $65. MC VISA PC TC. 4 rooms, 1 with FP. 1 conference room. Breakfast included in rates. Types of meals: full breakfast, gourmet breakfast and early coffee/tea. Afternoon tea available. Beds: DT. Air conditioning and turn-down service in room. Cable TV, VCR and library on premises. Antiques, fishing, parks, shopping, theater and watersports nearby.

Seen in: Lebanon Enterprise, Louisville Courier-Journal, Lebanon/Marion County Kentucky.

"Our night in the Cabbage Rose Room was an experience of another time, another culture. Your skill in preparing and presenting breakfast was equally elegant! We'll be back!"

Certificate may be used: Anytime except Sept. 22-25.

Louisville
C6

Rose Blossom

1353 S 4th St, Louisville, KY 40208-2349
(502)636-0295

This spacious Second Empire Victorian is listed in the National Register. Among its 18 rooms are seven guest rooms, three with private bath. An oak stairwell and leaded glass in the entry hall and stairwell add to the home's authentic old-time aura. Ten fireplaces are found, some with carved mantels and decorative tile. The first-floor bath boasts a whirlpool tub, and Mary has amassed an impressive collection of fine plates and china. The University of Louisville is within easy walking distance.
Innkeeper(s): Mary Ohlmann. $85-95. MC VISA AX DS. 7 rooms, 6 with PB. Breakfast included in rates. Types of meals: full breakfast and early coffee/tea. Catering service available. Air conditioning and turn-down service in room. Cable TV on premises. Antiques, shopping, sporting events and theater nearby.
Certificate may be used: Most of the time, except Derby time (May), St. James Art Fair (October).

The Inn at The Park

1332 S 4th St, Louisville, KY 40208-2314
(502)637-6930 (800)700-7275
Fax:(502)637-2796

Circa 1886. An impressive sweeping staircase is one of many highlights at this handsome Richardsonian Romanesque inn, in the historic district of Old Louisville. Guests also will appreciate the hardwood floors, 14-foot ceilings and stone balconies on the second and third floors. The six guest rooms offer a variety of amenities and a view of Central Park. Guests may enjoy breakfast in their rooms or in the well-appointed central dining area.
Innkeeper(s): John & Sandra Mullins. $79-119. MC VISA AX PC TC. 7 rooms, 6 with PB, 3 with FP. 1 suite. Breakfast included in rates. Types of meals: full breakfast and early coffee/tea. Beds: KQ. Air conditioning, ceiling fan and cable TV in room. VCR and fax on premises. Amusement parks, antiques, parks, shopping, sporting events and theater nearby.
Certificate may be used: Jan. 1 to Dec. 31, Sunday-Thursday.

Ashton's Victorian Secret B&B

1132 S 1st St, Louisville, KY 40203-2804
(502)581-1914 (800)449-4691

Circa 1883. This three-story Queen Anne Victorian has 11 fireplaces. Antiques and period furnishings are featured throughout the brick inn, located in Historic Old Louisville. Guest amenities include sundecks, washer-dryer facilities and a workout room with a bench press, rowing machine and stationary bicycle.

Innkeeper(s): Nan & Steve Roosa. $48-89. PC. 4 rooms, 1 with PB, 4 with FP. 1 suite. Breakfast included in rates. Type of meal: continental-plus breakfast. Beds: KQD. Air conditioning and ceiling fan in room. Amusement parks, antiques, parks, shopping, sporting events, theater and watersports nearby.
Certificate may be used: Jan. 2-Feb. 28.

Middlesborough
E9

The Ridge Runner B&B

208 Arthur Hts, Middlesborough, KY
40965-1728
(606)248-4299

Circa 1890. Bachelor buttons, lilacs and wildflowers line the white picket fence framing this 20-room brick Victorian mansion. Guests enjoy relaxing in its turn-of-the-century library and parlor filled with Victorian antiques. Ask for the President's Room and you'll enjoy the best view of the Cumberland Mountains. (The innkeeper's great, great-grandfather hosted Abe Lincoln the night before his Gettysburg address, and the inn boasts some heirlooms from that home.) A family-style breakfast is provided and special diets can be accommodated if notified in advance. Cumberland Gap National Park is five miles away.
Innkeeper(s): Susan Richards & Irma Gall. $55-65. PC. 4 rooms, 2 with PB. Breakfast and evening snack included in rates. Type of meal: early coffee/tea. Beds: DT. Turn-down service and ceiling fan in room. Antiques, parks and shopping nearby.
Seen in: Lexington Herald Leader, Blue Ridge Country, Indianapolis Star, Daily News, Courier Journal.
Certificate may be used: Sunday-Thursday, excluding month of October.

Murray
E3

The Diuguid House B&B

603 Main St, Murray, KY 42071-2034
(502)753-5470

Circa 1895. This Victorian house features eight-foot-wide hallways and a golden oak staircase with stained-glass window. There is a sitting area adjoining the portico. Guest rooms are generous in size.
Innkeeper(s): Karen & George Chapman. $40. MC VISA DC PC TC. 3 rooms. Breakfast included in rates. Types of meals: full breakfast and early coffee/tea. Beds: QT. Cable TV on premises. Antiques, fishing, parks, theater and watersports nearby.
Location: Downtown Murray, near state university.
Seen in: Murray State News.

"We enjoyed our visit in your beautiful home, and your hospitality was outstanding."

Certificate may be used: Anytime except university graduation, homecoming, parents weekends and last weekend in April.

New Haven D6

The Sherwood Inn
138 S Main St,
New Haven, KY 40051-6355
(502)549-3386

Circa 1914. Since 1875 the Johnson family has owned the Sherwood Inn. A week after the original building burned in 1913, construction for the current building began. In the National Register, the inn catered to passengers of the nearby L & N (Louisville and Nashville) Railroad. Antiques and

reproductions complement some of the inn's original furnishings. The restaurant is open for dinner Wednesday through Saturday. The inn's slogan, first advertised in 1875 remains, "first class table and good accommodations."

Innkeeper(s): Cecilia Johnson. $45-65. MC VISA DS. 5 rooms, 3 with PB. Breakfast included in rates. Type of meal: full breakfast. Beds: D. Air conditioning and ceiling fan in room. Cable TV on premises. Shopping nearby.

Location: Eleven miles south from Bardstown on US 31-E.

Seen in: Kentucky Standard.

"A memorable stop."

Certificate may be used: Upon availability.

Paducah D2

The 1857's B&B
PO Box 7771, Paducah, KY 42001-0789
(502)444-3960 (800)264-5607
Fax:(502)444-3960

Circa 1857. Paducah's thriving, history-rich commercial district is home to this Folk Victorian inn, located in Market House Square. Guests choose from the Master Bedroom, a suite featuring an antique queen four-poster bed, and a guest room highlighted by a Victorian highback bed. The popular third-floor game room boasts a hot tub and impressive mahogany billiard table. The Ohio River

is an easy walk from the inn, and guests also will enjoy an evening stroll along the gas-lit brick sidewalks. The inn occupies the second and third floors of a former clothing store, with an Italian restaurant at street level.

Innkeeper(s): Deborah Bohnert. $65-95. MC VISA PC TC. 3 rooms. 1 suite. Breakfast included in rates. Types of meals: continental-plus breakfast and early coffee/tea. Room service available. Beds: KQDT. Air conditioning, ceiling fan and cable TV in room. VCR, fax, copier and library on premises. Antiques, fishing, shopping, theater and watersports nearby.

Certificate may be used: January-March, October-November.

Paducah Harbor Plaza B&B
201 Broadway St,
Paducah, KY 42001-0711
(502)442-2698 (800)719-7799

This striking, five-story brick structure was known as the Hotel Belvedere at the turn of the century. Guests now choose from four guest rooms on the second floor, where they also will find the arch-windowed Broadway Room, with its views of the Market House District and the Ohio River, just a block away. Breakfast is served in this room, which also contains a 1911 player piano. The  guest rooms all feature different color schemes and each is furnished with antique furniture and handmade quilts.

Innkeeper(s): Beverly McKinley. $55-75. MC VISA AX. 4 rooms. Breakfast included in rates. Type of meal: continental-plus breakfast. Air conditioning, ceiling fan and cable TV in room. VCR on premises. Antiques, shopping and theater nearby.

Certificate may be used: January, February, March, November, December.

Paris C8

Rosedale B&B
1917 Cypress St, Paris, KY 40361-1220
(606)987-1845

Circa 1862. Once the home of Civil War General John Croxton, this low-roofed Italianate inn was voted prettiest B&B in the Bluegrass area by the Lexington Herald-Leader in 1994. The four decorated guest rooms feature Colonial touches and are filled with antiques and paintings. Fresh flowers, down comforters and ceiling fans add to the rooms' comfort and charm. The Henry Clay Room, with its twin four-poster beds, is one option for visitors. Guests may relax with a game of croquet, bocce, horseshoes or on one of the benches found on the inn's three-acre lawn. Duncan Tavern Historic Shrine is nearby, as well as beautiful horse farms.

Innkeeper(s): Katie & Jim Haag. $65-100. MC VISA PC TC. 4 rooms, 2 with PB. 2 suites. Breakfast and evening snack included in rates. Types of meals: full breakfast and early coffee/tea. Beds: DT. Air conditioning and ceiling fan in room. Cable TV, VCR and library on premises. Antiques, fishing, parks, shopping, sporting events and theater nearby.

Certificate may be used: January-December, Sunday-Thursday.

Russellville   E5

The Log House
2139 Franklin Rd, Russellville, KY 42276
(502)726-8483 Fax:(502)726-2270

Circa 1976. This ideal log cabin retreat was built from hand-hewn logs from old cabins and barns in the area. Rooms are full of quilts, early American furnishings and folk art from around the world. The log walls and hardwood floors create an unparalleled atmosphere of country warmth. An impressive kitchen is decorated with an old-fashioned stove and crammed with knickknacks. Innkeeper Allison Dennis creates hand-woven garments and accessories in an adjacent studio. Nashville and Opryland are about an hour's drive, and the local area boasts a number of antique shops.

Innkeeper(s): Allison & Richard Dennis. $85-95. MC VISA AX DS PC TC. 4 rooms with PB, 2 with FP. Breakfast included in rates. Type of meal: gourmet breakfast. Room service available. Beds: QDT. Air conditioning in room. VCR, fax, copier, spa and library on premises. Amusement parks, antiques, fishing, parks, shopping, sporting events, theater and watersports nearby.

Certificate may be used: Anytime, prior reservations are essential.

Shelbyville   C7

The Wallace House
813 Plainview St,
Shelbyville, KY 40065-1543
(502)633-4272

Circa 1804. This Federal-style inn, midway between Louisville and Frankfort, is listed in the National Register of Historic Places. Its five well-appointed guest suites all feature kitchenettes. The talented innkeepers (Donald is a physician, his wife a gifted pianist) enjoy golfing and gardening.

Innkeeper(s): Donald Chatham. $65-95. MC VISA. 7 rooms, 5 with PB. 5 suites. Breakfast included in rates. Type of meal: continental breakfast. Beds: KT. Air conditioning in room. Cable TV on premises. Antiques, fishing, shopping and theater nearby.

Certificate may be used: Weekdays, excluding May 1-10.

138

Somerset   D8

Shadwick House
411 S Main St, Somerset, KY 42501-2062
(606)678-4675

This two-story home was built as a boarding house by the innkeeper's great-grandmother, Nellie Stringer Shadwick. Nellie opened her home to guests for many years, and after her death, daughter Marie Carmichael took over. John Dillinger was rumored to have been a guest at one time. Today, it's Marie's grandchildren who have continued the legacy of hospitality. The first floor has been transformed into a boutique with a variety of antiques and crafts, many fashioned by native Kentuckians. The rooms are decorated with antiques, some of which are original to the house.

Innkeeper(s): Ann Epperson. $40-50. MC VISA. 4 rooms. Breakfast included in rates. Type of meal: full breakfast.

Certificate may be used: Monday-Thursday, except holidays.

Springfield   C7

Maple Hill Manor
2941 Perryville Rd,
Springfield, KY 40069-9611
(606)336-3075

Circa 1851. This brick Revival home with Italianate detail is a Kentucky Landmark home and is listed in the National Register of Historic Places. It features 13-1/2-foot ceilings, 10-foot doors, nine-foot windows, a cherry spiral staircase, stenciling in the foyer, a large parlor with a fireplace, hardwood floors  and period furnishings. The library has floor-to-ceiling mahogany bookcases and the Honeymoon Room features a canopy bed and Jacuzzi. A large patio area is set among old maple trees.

Innkeeper(s): Kathleen Carroll. $50-80. MC VISA. 7 rooms with PB. 1 conference room. Breakfast included in rates. Types of meals: full breakfast and early coffee/tea. Evening snack available. Beds: QT. Ceiling fan in room. VCR on premises. Antiques, fishing, shopping and theater nearby.

Seen in: Danville's Advocate-Messenger, Springfield Sun, Eastside Weekend, Courier Journal.

"Thank you again for your friendly and comfortable hospitality."

Certificate may be used: Sunday through Thursday.

Louisiana

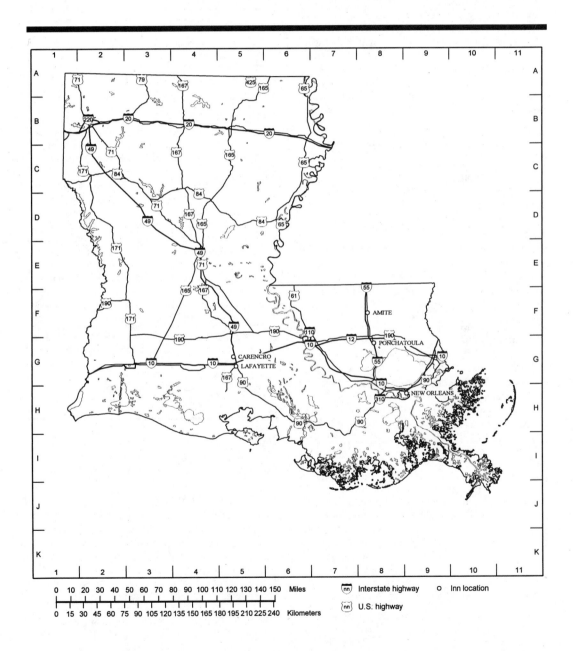

Amite
F8

Blythewood Plantation
PO Box 155, 400 Daniel St,
Amite, LA 70422-2318
(504)345-6419

Circa 1885. The grounds surrounding this majestic plantation home were part of a Spanish land grant. The original home, a pre-Civil War manor, burned, but was rebuilt in the late 19th century. The grand rooms include a gas chandelier, leaded-glass doors and walnut mantels, all original features. In true Louisiana style, guests are served a refreshing mint julep upon arrival. Candlelight dinners can be arranged, as can special teas, parties and weddings.
Innkeeper(s): Maxine, Ann, Diane. $79-189. TC. 9 rooms. 2 conference rooms. Breakfast and dinner included in rates. Types of meals: full breakfast and gourmet breakfast. Evening snack, picnic lunch, lunch, gourmet lunch, banquet service and catered breakfast available. Beds: D. Air conditioning and cable TV in room. VCR on premises. Handicap access. Antiques, parks and watersports nearby.
Certificate may be used: Based on availability.

Carencro
G5

La Maison De Campagne
825 Kidder Rd, Carencro, LA 70520-9119
(318)896-6529 (800)895-0235
Fax:(318)896-1494

Circa 1871. Built by a successful plantation owner, this turn-of-the-century Victorian has once again found a new life with innkeepers Fred and Joeann McLemore. The McLemores turned what was an almost dilapidated old home into a welcoming B&B, surrounded by nine acres of manicured lawns dotted with flowers and trees. The home is filled with antiques and treasures Joeann collected during Fred's three decades of military service, which took them around the world. Fine Victorian pieces are accented by lace and Oriental rugs. The innkeepers offer accommodations in the main house, or for longer stays, in an adjacent sharecropper's cottage. The cottage includes kitchen and laundry facilities. Joeann prepares the Cajun-style breakfasts. Several different homemade breads or pastries accompany items such as banana-strawberry soup, sweet potato biscuits, spicy Cajun eggs souffles or a potato and sausage quiche.
Innkeeper(s): Joeann & Fred McLemore. $95-125. AP. MC VISA AX DS PC TC. 4 rooms with PB. 1 cottage. Breakfast and evening snack included in rates. Types of meals: continental breakfast, gourmet breakfast and early coffee/tea. Beds: KQD. Air conditioning, turn-down service and ceiling fan in room. Cable TV, fax, copier and swimming on

premises. Antiques, fishing, parks, shopping, sporting events, theater and watersports nearby.
Location: Heart of Cajun Country.
Seen in: Los Angeles Times.
Certificate may be used: Jan. 1-Dec. 31, Sunday-Thursday except not honored during Mardi Gras, Crawfish Festival and Festival Internationale.

Lafayette
G5

Alida's, A B&B
2631 SE Evangeline Thruway,
Lafayette, LA 70508-2168
(318)264-1191 (800)922-5867
Fax:(318)264-1415

Circa 1902. This home is named for teacher Alida Martin, who along with once owning this Queen Anne house, was responsible for educating many Lafayette citizens, including a few civic leaders. Alida taught at the house until a one-room schoolhouse was constructed. The innkeepers named a room for Alida, decorated with a 19th-century walnut bed and matching armoire. The bath still features the original clawfoot tub. Other rooms include special antiques, Bavarian collectibles and clawfoot tubs. After breakfast, guest can trek to nearby sites such as the Tabasco Plant and Live Oak Gardens on Jefferson Island.
Innkeeper(s): Tanya & Doug Greenwald. $75-125. MC VISA AX DS PC TC. 4 rooms with PB. 1 conference room. Breakfast and evening snack included in rates. Types of meals: full breakfast and gourmet breakfast. Beds: QD. Air conditioning and ceiling fan in room. VCR, fax and copier on premises. Antiques, fishing, parks, shopping and sporting events nearby.
Certificate may be used: November-February.

New Orleans
H9

Fairchild House
1518 Prytania St,
New Orleans, LA 70130-4416
(504)524-0154 (800)256-8096
Fax:(504)568-0063

Circa 1841. Set in the oak-lined Lower Garden District of New Orleans, this Greek Revival home was built by architect L.H. Pilie. The most prominent owner was cotton broker Louis Fairchild. Having undergone a recent renovation, the home has retained its elegant 19th-century setting. Afternoon wine, cheese and tea are included. The innkeepers feature a special honeymoon package and can arrange a four-day tour package of New Orleans.

Innkeeper(s): Rita Olmo & Beatriz Aprigliano. $70-110. MC VISA AX TC. 6 rooms with PB. 1 suite. Breakfast included in rates. Type of meal: continental-plus breakfast. Beds: KQD. Air conditioning and ceiling fan in room. Fax and copier on premises. Antiques, shopping and theater nearby.

Location: Oak-lined lower garden district.

"We felt very comfortable and welcome."

Certificate may be used: June 1-Aug. 31, please call during other seasons.

Garden District B&B

2418 Magazine St,
New Orleans, LA 70130-5604
(504)895-4302 Fax:(504)895-4302

This restored Victorian home is nestled in New Orleans' Garden District and surrounded by gracious antebellum homes. The innkeepers have restored the pine floors and 12-foot ceilings to their original glory. Rooms include antiques, ceilings fans and Victorian decor. The patio is surrounded by a lush, tropical garden. Guests won't have to walk far to explore the hundreds of antique shops which line Magazine Street.

Innkeeper(s): Joseph Kinsella. $55-75. MC VISA. 6 rooms. Breakfast included in rates. Type of meal: continental breakfast.

Certificate may be used: June, July, August; other months on availability.

Lamothe House

621 Esplanade Ave,
New Orleans, LA 70116-2018
(504)947-1161 (800)367-5858
Fax:(504)943-6536

Circa 1830. A carriageway that formerly cut through the center of many French Quarter buildings was enclosed at the Lamothe House in 1866, and is now the foyer. Splendid Victorian furnishings enhance moldings, high ceilings, and hand-turned mahogany stairway railings. Gilded opulence goes unchecked in the Mallard and Lafayette suites. Registration takes place in the second-story salon above the courtyard.

Innkeeper(s): Carol Chauppette. $75-250. MC VISA AX PC TC. 20 rooms with PB, 1 with FP. 9 suites. 2 cottages. 1 conference room. Breakfast included in rates. Type of meal: continental-plus breakfast. Afternoon tea available. Beds: QTD. Air conditioning, turn-down service, ceiling fan and cable TV in room. VCR, fax, copier, swimming and child care on premises. Amusement parks, antiques, fishing, parks, shopping, sporting events and theater nearby.

Seen in: Houston Post, Travel & Leisure.

Certificate may be used: Sunday through Thursday except special events (Sugar Bowl, Super Bowl, Mardi Gras, Jazz Fest, etc.).

Maison Esplanade

1244 Esplanade Ave,
New Orleans, LA 70116-1978
(504)523-8080 (800)290-4233
Fax:(504)527-0040

Circa 1846. Experience the splendor of New Orleans in this Creole-style inn, which is located within walking distance of the French Quarter. Polished wood floors, ceiling fans and 13-foot ceilings highlight this historic district home, which is furnished with antiques and replicas. Bedchambers honor New Orleans' jazz tradition, bearing names such as the Jelly Roll Norton Suite or Count Basie Suite. Nightly turndown service is one of the many amenities provided for guests. Breakfast service begins about 7:30 a.m., but continues until nearly noon, a pleasure for late risers. The hosts welcome guests with a refreshment and are full of information about the myriad of tours available in the city, including tours of the French Quarter, plantation homes, swamps, historic homes or the city itself. They can also help arrange cooking classes and other outings.

Innkeeper(s): Norma Castaing & Delores Boeckl. $49-159. MC VISA AX DC DS TC. 9 rooms with PB. 2 suites. Breakfast included in rates. Type of meal: continental-plus breakfast. Beds: Q. Air conditioning, turn-down service and ceiling fan in room. Fax and copier on premises. Antiques, shopping and theater nearby.

Certificate may be used: Subject to availability.

The Olivier Estate, A B&B

1425 N Prieur St,
New Orleans, LA 70116-1744
(504)949-9600 Fax:(504)948-2219

Circa 1855. The expansive parlor at this Spanish Colonial boasts a hand-crafted, marble-topped bar with a roulette wheel embedded in it, which was made for gangster Al Capone. This eclectic room also includes a mahogany, three-slate pool table with leather pockets, a handmade Italian gaming table and a 1950s vintage quarter slot machine. The spacious bedchambers include private entrances, and some offer working fireplaces and marble baths. During the week, freshly baked croissants and a few other treats are the morning fare, while on the weekends, the innkeepers offer a full, Creole-style breakfast. An open bar, nightly turndown service, hot tub and fresh flowers are just a few of the amenities guest will enjoy during their stay.

Innkeeper(s): Richard Saucier. $125-325. MC VISA AX. 5 rooms with PB. 3 suites. Breakfast included in rates. Types of meals: continental breakfast and full breakfast. Beds: KQ. Antiques, fishing, theater and watersports nearby.

"The courtesy, hospitality and friendliness of the staff was incredible. We'll return again."

Certificate may be used: Non-special events.

The Prytania Park Hotel

1525 Prytania St,
New Orleans, LA 70130-4415
(504)524-0427 (800)862-1984
Fax:(504)522-2977

Circa 1850. This hotel consists of a Victorian building and a new building. Request the older rooms to enjoy the English Victorian reproduction furnishings, garden chintz fabrics and 14-foot ceilings. Some of these rooms have fireplaces. Rooms in the new section feature refrigerators, microwaves and contemporary furnishings. It is one-half block from the historic St. Charles Avenue streetcar.
Innkeeper(s): Edward Halpern. $99-229. MC VISA AX DC CB DS PC TC. 62 rooms with PB. 6 suites. Breakfast included in rates. Type of meal: continental-plus breakfast. Lunch available. Beds: KQDT. Air conditioning, ceiling fan and cable TV in room. Fax and copier on premises. Antiques, parks, shopping and sporting events nearby.
Location: Lower Garden District.

"A little jewel. Baton Rouge Advocate."

Certificate may be used: June 1-Aug. 31, based on space availability, not valid during special events, reservations required.

St. Peter House

1005 Saint Peter St,
New Orleans, LA 70116-3014
(504)524-9232 (800)535-7815
Fax:(504)523-5198

Circa 1800. The St. Peter House, which is ideally situated in the middle of the French Quarter, offers a delightful glance at New Orleans French heritage and 18th-century charm. From the lush courtyards to the gracious balconies, guests will enjoy the view of the busy quarter. Rooms are individually appointed with period antiques.
Innkeeper(s): Brent Kovach. $49-225. MC VISA AX PC TC. 28 rooms with PB. 11 suites. Breakfast included in rates. Type of meal: continental-plus breakfast. Beds: KQDT. Air conditioning, turn-down service, ceiling fan and cable TV in room. Fax on premises. Amusement parks, antiques, fishing, parks, shopping and theater nearby.

Certificate may be used: January, June, July, August, December, except special events.

Ponchatoula   G8

Bella Rose Mansion

225 N 8th St, Ponchatoula, LA 70454
(504)386-3857 Fax:(504)386-3857

Circa 1942. This Georgian-style mansion boasts a three-story spiral staircase which rises up to a stained-glass dome. Master craftsmen detailed this luxurious manor with mahogany paneling, parquet floors, Waterford crystal chandeliers and a marble-walled solarium with a fountain. Each of the guest rooms and suites boast a Jacuzzi and each has individual decor. The Veranda Suite features a Victoria's Secret-style decor, while the Mallard Room, has more masculine surroundings. The mansion includes an indoor terrazzo shuffleboard court, heated swimming pool and the innkeepers own a large collection of antique gaming equipment on permanent display in a first-floor museum. Gourmet breakfasts feature entrees such as Eggs Benedict complemented with fresh fruits and juices. Ponchatoula's many antique shops have earned its nickname as America's Antique City.
Innkeeper(s): Rose James & Michael-Ray Britton. $125-225. MC VISA. 4 rooms with PB. 2 suites. Breakfast included in rates. Type of meal: gourmet breakfast. Beds: KQ. Air conditioning and ceiling fan in room. VCR, fax, copier, swimming, bicycles and library on premises. Antiques, fishing, parks, shopping, sporting events, theater and watersports nearby.
Seen in: Houston Chronicle, Sunday Star.

"What a fabulous place! Your warmth is truly an asset. The peacefulness is just what we needed in our hectic lives."

Certificate may be used: July through December.

Maine

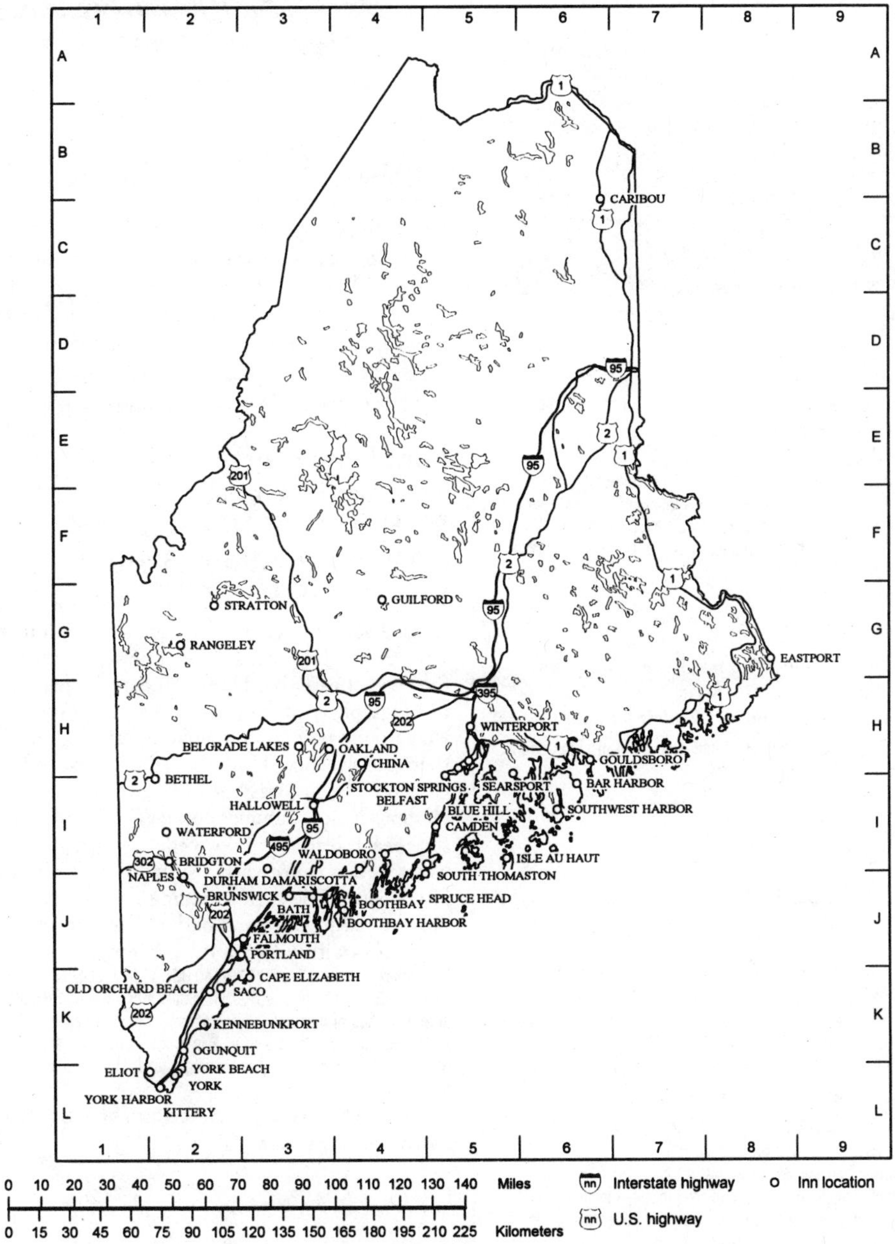

CARIBOU
STRATTON
GUILFORD
RANGELEY
EASTPORT
WINTERPORT
BELGRADE LAKES
OAKLAND
CHINA
GOULDSBORO
BETHEL
STOCKTON SPRINGS
SEARSPORT
BAR HARBOR
BELFAST
HALLOWELL
BLUE HILL
SOUTHWEST HARBOR
CAMDEN
WATERFORD
WALDOBORO
ISLE AU HAUT
BRIDGTON
NAPLES
DURHAM
DAMARISCOTTA
SOUTH THOMASTON
BRUNSWICK
SPRUCE HEAD
BATH
BOOTHBAY
BOOTHBAY HARBOR
FALMOUTH
PORTLAND
CAPE ELIZABETH
OLD ORCHARD BEACH
SACO
KENNEBUNKPORT
OGUNQUIT
ELIOT
YORK BEACH
YORK
YORK HARBOR
KITTERY
0 10 20 30 40 50 60 70 80 90 100 110 120 130 140 Miles
0 15 30 45 60 75 90 105 120 135 150 165 180 195 210 225 Kilometers
Interstate highway
U.S. highway
Inn location

Bar Harbor 16

Manor House Inn

106 West St, Bar Harbor, ME 04609-1856
(207)288-3759 (800)437-0088
Fax:(207)288-2974

Circa 1887. Colonel James Foster built this 22-room Victorian mansion, now in the National Register. It is an example of the tradition of gracious

summer living for which Bar Harbor was and is famous. In addition to the main house, there are several charming cottages situated in the extensive gardens on the property.

Innkeeper(s): Mac Noyes. $50-175. MC VISA. 14 rooms, 7 with PB, 6 with FP. 7 suites. Breakfast and afternoon tea included in rates. Types of meals: full breakfast and early coffee/tea. Beds: KQT. Ceiling fan in room. Cable TV, fax and copier on premises. Antiques, fishing, parks, shopping and watersports nearby.

Location: Close to Acadia National Park.

Seen in: Discerning Traveler.

"Wonderful honeymoon spot! Wonderful inn, elegant, delicious breakfasts, terrific innkeepers. We loved it all! It's our fourth time here and it's wonderful as always."

Certificate may be used: April through mid-June and Oct. 22 through mid-November. Sunday through Thursday.

The Maples Inn

16 Roberts Ave,
Bar Harbor, ME 04609-1820
(207)288-3443 Fax:(207)288-0356

Circa 1903. This 15-room Victorian "summer cottage" once served wealthy summer visitors to Mt. Desert Island. Located on a quiet residential street, away from Bar Harbor traffic, it has been tastefully restored and filled with Colonial and Victorian furnishings. The inn is within walking distance of shops, boutiques and restaurants. Acadia National Park is five minutes away.

Innkeeper(s): Susan Sinclair. $60-150. MC VISA DS PC TC. 6 rooms with PB, 1 with FP. 1 suite. Breakfast and afternoon tea included in rates. Types of meals: gourmet breakfast and early coffee/tea. Beds:

QT. Air conditioning in room. Cable TV, fax and library on premises. Antiques, fishing, parks, shopping, cross-country skiing, sporting events, theater and watersports nearby.

Location: Within two blocks of the ocean.

Seen in: San Diego Tribune, New York Times, Gourmet, Bon Appetit, Los Angeles Times.

"What a wonderful place this is. Warm, comfortable, friendly, terrific breakfasts, great tips for adventure around the island. I could go on and on."

Certificate may be used: Jan. 1-April 30, holidays excluded.

Mira Monte Inn & Suites

69 Mount Desert St,
Bar Harbor, ME 04609-1327
(207)288-4263 (800)553-5109
Fax:(207)288-3115

Circa 1864. A gracious 18-room Victorian mansion, the Mira Monte has been newly renovated in the style of early Bar Harbor. It features period furnishings, pleasant common rooms, a library and wraparound porches. Situated on estate grounds, there are sweeping lawns, paved terraces, and many gardens. The inn was one of the earliest of Bar Harbor's famous summer cottages. The two-room suites each feature canopy beds, two-person whirlpools, a parlor with a sleeper sofa, fireplace and kitchenette. The two-bedroom suite includes a full kitchen, dining area and parlor. The suites boast private decks with views of the gardens.

Innkeeper(s): Marian Burns. $75-180. MC VISA AX DS TC. 16 rooms, 15 with PB, 11 with FP. 3 suites. Breakfast and afternoon tea included in rates. Types of meals: full breakfast and early coffee/tea. Beds: KQT. Air conditioning, cable TV and VCR in room. Fax and library on premises. Handicap access. Antiques, fishing, parks, shopping and theater nearby.

Location: Five-minute walk from the waterfront, shops and restaurants.

Seen in: Los Angeles Times.

"On our third year at your wonderful inn in beautiful Bar Harbor. I think I enjoy it more each year. A perfect place to stay in a perfect environment."

Certificate may be used: May 1-June 14, Oct. 16-31, holidays excluded.

The Ridgeway Inn

11 High St, Bar Harbor, ME 04609-1816
(207)288-9682

Circa 1890. Located on a quiet, tree-lined street, this Victorian B&B is a welcome sight for weary travelers. Each of the guest rooms is individually decorated and named after the cottages of the wealthy who made Bar Harbor their summer vacation spot. Many of these homes were destroyed in a 1947 fire, but the innkeepers have preserved their memory. Beds are covered with down comforters. One rooms includes a Jacuzzi tub, while another offers a private deck. The innkeepers serve an expansive, multi-course breakfast on fireside tables illuminated by candlelight. Freshly baked breads, scones and muffins are followed by a fruit recipe, which all precedes the daily entree.

Innkeeper(s): Lucie Rioux Hollfelder. $60-150. MC VISA PC TC. 5 rooms with PB. 2 suites. Breakfast and afternoon tea included in rates. Types of meals: full breakfast, gourmet breakfast and early coffee/tea. Beds: KQ. Amusement parks, antiques, fishing, parks, shopping, cross-country skiing, theater and watersports nearby.

Certificate may be used: Oct. 15-Dec. 15 (excluding Veteran's Day); April 1-June 15 (excluding Memorial Day weekend).

Bath

Fairhaven Inn

RR 2 PO Box 85, N Bath Rd,
Bath, ME 04530
(207)443-4391

Circa 1790. With its view of the Kennebec River, this site was so attractive that Pimbleton Edgecomb built his Colonial house where a log cabin had previously stood. His descendants occupied it for the next 125 years. Antiques and country furniture fill the inn. Meadows and lawns, and woods of hemlock, birch and pine cover the inn's 27 acres.

Innkeeper(s): Susie & Dave Reed. $60-100. MC VISA DS PC TC. 8 rooms, 6 with PB. 1 suite. 1 cottage. 1 conference room. Breakfast included in rates. Types of meals: full breakfast and early coffee/tea. Beds: KQT. Cable TV, fax and library on premises. Antiques, parks, shopping, cross-country skiing, sporting events, theater and watersports nearby.

Seen in: The State, Coastal Journal.

"The Fairhaven is now marked in our book with a red star, definitely a place to remember and visit again."

Certificate may be used: Year-round, Sunday-Friday.

The Galen C. Moses House

1009 Washington St,
Bath, ME 04530-2759
(207)442-8771

Circa 1874. This Victorian mansion is filled with beautiful architectural items, including stained-glass windows, wood-carved and marble fireplaces and a grand staircase. The innkeepers have filled the library, a study, morning room and the parlor with antiques. A corner fireplace warms the dining room, overlooking the lawns and gardens. There is a formal drawing room where tea is presented.

Innkeeper(s): James Haught, Larry Kieft. $65-95. MC VISA PC TC. 19 rooms, 3 with PB. Breakfast and afternoon tea included in rates. Types of meals: continental breakfast and gourmet breakfast. Beds: QDT. Turn-down service and cable TV in room. VCR and library on premises. Antiques, fishing, parks, shopping, cross-country skiing, theater and watersports nearby.

Seen in: Philadelphia, Back Roads USA.

"For our first try at B&B lodgings, we've probably started at the top, and nothing else will ever measure up to this. Wonderful food, wonderful home, grounds and wonderful hostess!"

Certificate may be used: Nov. 1-April 30.

Belfast

The Jeweled Turret Inn

16 Pearl St, Belfast, ME 04915-1907
(207)338-2304 (800)696-2304

Circa 1898. This grand Victorian is named for the staircase that winds up the turret, lighted by stained- and leaded-glass panels and jewel-like embellishments. It was built for attorney James Harriman. Dark pine beams adorn the ceiling of the den, and the fireplace is constructed of bark and rocks from every state in the Union. Elegant antiques furnish the guest rooms. Guests can relax

in one of the inn's four parlors, which are furnished with period antiques, wallpapers, lace and boast fireplaces. The verandas feature wicker and iron bistro sets and views of the historic district. The inn is within walking distance of the town and its shops, restaurants and the harbor.

Innkeeper(s): Cathy & Carl Heffentrager. $65-95. MC VISA PC TC. 7 rooms with PB, 1 with FP. Breakfast and afternoon tea included in rates. Types of meals: full breakfast and early coffee/tea. Beds: QDT. Ceiling fan in room. Antiques, fishing, shopping, downhill skiing, cross-country skiing, theater and watersports nearby.

Seen in: Republican Journal, Waterville Sentinel, Los Angeles Times.

"The ambiance was so romantic that we felt like we were on our honeymoon."

Certificate may be used: April 1 to June 30, September, Oct. 16 to Nov. 30, (no holidays).

The Thomas Pitcher House B&B
19 Franklin St, Belfast, ME 04915-1105
(207)338-6454

Circa 1873. This richly appointed home was considered state-of-the-art back in 1873 for it was one of only a few homes offering central heat and hot or cold running water. Today, innkeepers have added plenty of modern amenities, but kept the ambiance

of the Victorian Era. Each room is unique, some vanities include original walnut and marble, while another bathroom includes tin ceilings and a step-down bath. Some rooms have cozy reading areas. Guests enjoy a full breakfast each morning with menus that feature specialties such as Maine blueberry buttermilk pancakes or a French toast puff made with homemade raisin bread.

Innkeeper(s): Fran & Ron Kresge. $60-80. MC VISA PC TC. 4 rooms with PB. Breakfast included in rates. Types of meals: full breakfast, gourmet breakfast and early coffee/tea. Beds: QD. Ceiling fan in room. Cable TV, VCR and library on premises. Antiques, fishing, parks, shopping, downhill skiing, cross-country skiing, theater and watersports nearby.

Seen in: Republican Journal.

"A home away from home."

Certificate may be used: Oct. 15-June 15 (Sunday through Saturday).

Belgrade Lakes   H3

Wings Hill
PO Box 386,
Belgrade Lakes, ME 04918-0386
(207)495-2400 (800)509-4647

Circa 1800. Antiques and original artwork grace the interior of this restored Cape-style farmhouse. The huge wraparound porch is screened in and an ideal place to relax. Many of the antiques and collectibles are available for sale. The innkeepers serve a country breakfast, which is prepared in the quaint kitchen, an inviting room warmed by a woodburning stove. The innkeepers will help guests plan activities, including rentals for skiing, boating and snowmobiling.

Innkeeper(s): Dick Hofmann. $95. MC VISA. 8 rooms with PB. Breakfast included in rates. Types of meals: full breakfast and early coffee/tea. Afternoon tea available. Cable TV and VCR on premises. Antiques, fishing, shopping, downhill skiing, cross-country skiing, sporting events, theater and watersports nearby.

Certificate may be used: Sunday-Thursday, May-October.

Bethel   I2

Abbott House
Rt 26, Bethel, ME 04217
(207)824-7600 (800)240-2377

Circa 1773. Guests at this 18th-century home are treated to a variety of soothing amenities. Innkeepers Joe Cardello and Penny Bohac-Cardello offer massage service, an outdoor hot tub and will set up goodies such as chocolates and flowers for guests celebrating a special occasion. Penny is an excellent baker and creates all the fresh breads for breakfast and afternoon tea. Her freshly baked treats, such as a succulent blueberry cake, complement Joe's array of breakfast fare. Joe serves up a hearty meal with meats, potatoes, egg dishes and fresh fruit, all garnished with edible flowers from the inn's garden. In warmer months, iced coffees and iced tea are served with the afternoon and evening refreshments.

Innkeeper(s): Joe Cardello, Penny Bohac-Cardello. $55-65. MC VISA AX. 5 rooms, 3 with PB. 1 suite. Breakfast, afternoon tea and evening snack included in rates. Types of meals: full breakfast and early coffee/tea. Dinner and catering service available. Beds: QDT. Cable TV and spa on premises. Antiques, fishing, parks, shopping, downhill skiing and cross-country skiing nearby.

Certificate may be used: All year, midweek (Sunday-Thursday), Spring-Summer-Fall, weekends.

L'Auberge Country Inn

Mill Hill Rd, PO Box 21,
Bethel, ME 04217
(207)824-2774 (800)760-2774
Fax:(207)824-2774

In the foothills of the White Mountains, surrounded by five acres of gardens and woods, this former carriage house was converted to a guest house in the 1920s. Among its seven guest rooms are two spacious suites. The Theater Suite offers a four-poster queen bed and dressing room. The Family Suite can accommodate up to six guests. Mount Abrahms and Sunday River ski areas are just minutes away.

Innkeeper(s): Werner Kohlmeyer. $55-115. MC VISA AX DS. 6 rooms. 2 suites. 1 conference room. Breakfast included in rates. Types of meals: continental-plus breakfast and early coffee/tea. Banquet service and catering service available. Cable TV, VCR and child care on premises. Antiques, shopping, downhill skiing and cross-country skiing nearby.

Certificate may be used: Midweek, non-holiday.

Blue Hill   H5

Arcady Down East

HC 64 Box 370, Blue Hill, ME 04614
(207)374-5576

Circa 1834. This attractive Victorian Shingle inn, listed in the National Register, offers many authentic touches, including period antiques and tin ceilings. The inn's seven guest rooms include the Celebration Suite, perfect for honeymooners with its cozy fireplace and sitting area. Another favorite with visitors is the Captain's Quarters, featuring a skylight to help highlight its unique furnishings. The impressive coastal beauty of Acadia National Park is a short drive from the inn.

Innkeeper(s): Gene & Bertha Wiseman. $85-110. MC VISA AX TC. 7 rooms, 5 with PB, 1 with FP. 1 suite. Breakfast included in rates. Types of meals: full breakfast and early coffee/tea. Beds: KQDT. Turn-down service and ceiling fan in room. Bicycles and child care on premises. Antiques, fishing, parks, shopping, cross-country skiing, theater and watersports nearby.

Certificate may be used: Every night except month of August.

Boothbay   J4

Kenniston Hill Inn

Rt 27, PO Box 125,
Boothbay, ME 04537-0125
(207)633-2159 (800)992-2915
Fax:(207)633-2159

Circa 1786. The elegant clapboard home is the oldest inn at Boothbay Harbor and was occupied by the Kenniston family for more than a century. Five

of the antique-filled bedrooms have fireplaces. After a walk through the beautiful gardens or woods, warm up in the parlor next to the elegant, open-hearthed fireplace. Candlelit dinners are available November through April and served in the parlor in front of a roaring fire. Boothbay Harbor offers something for everybody, including whale-watching excursions and dinner theaters.

Innkeeper(s): Susan & David Straight. $60-110. MC VISA DS PC TC. 10 rooms with PB, 5 with FP. 1 cottage. Breakfast and afternoon tea included in rates. Types of meals: full breakfast, gourmet breakfast and early coffee/tea. Beds: KQDT. Ceiling fan in room. Cable TV, VCR and fax on premises. Antiques, fishing, parks, shopping, downhill skiing, cross-country skiing, theater and watersports nearby.

Seen in: Boothbay Register.

"England may be the home of the original bed & breakfast, but Kenniston Hill Inn is where it has been perfected!"

Certificate may be used: January through June, November and December.

Boothbay Harbor   J4

Harbour Towne Inn
on The Waterfront

71 Townsend Ave,
Boothbay Harbor, ME 04538-1158
(207)633-4300 (800)722-4240
Fax:(207)633-4300

Circa 1890. This waterfront Victorian inn boasts 13 guest rooms and one suite. Many rooms offer a private deck and the Penthouse has an astonishing

view of the harbor. Breakfast is served in the inn's Sunroom, and guests also may relax in the parlor, which has a fireplace. The inn's meticulous grounds include flower gardens and well-kept shrubs and trees. It's an easy walk to the village and its art galleries, restaurants and shops. Special off-season packages are available. The Ft. William Henry Fisherman's Memorial is nearby.

Innkeeper(s): George Thomas. $69-250. MC VISA AX DS PC TC. 12 rooms with PB. 1 suite. 1 conference room. Breakfast included in rates. Type of meal: continental-plus breakfast. Beds: KQDT. Ceiling fan and cable TV in room. Fax and copier on premises. Handicap access. Antiques, fishing, parks, shopping, downhill skiing, cross-country skiing, theater and watersports nearby.

Certificate may be used: Off low season excluding Friday, Saturday nights; holiday, special events and the Penthouse.

Bridgton   I2

Tarry-A-While Resort
Box A, Highland Ridge Rd,
Bridgton, ME 04009
(207)647-2522

Circa 1900. The Tarry-a-While Resort brings the charm of Switzerland to the western hills of Maine. The dining room features weathered barnboard paneling, pine tables, Swiss cowbells, a giant alpenhorn

and a picture window looking down Highland Lake and across the White Mountains. Guests dine on gourmet Swiss cooking. The resort consists of a Victorian mansion, cottages and a social hall. Rooms have quaint old-world furnishings, including handmade furniture.

Innkeeper(s): Nancy Stretch. $70-130. MC VISA. 27 rooms, 26 with PB, 2 with FP. Breakfast included in rates. Type of meal: full breakfast. Beds: KQDT. Air conditioning in room. Bicycles on premises. Antiques, shopping and theater nearby.

Seen in: Down East, Yankee.

"The views, space, personal attention and laid-back ambiance is just what we needed on our precious vacation time."

Certificate may be used: Anytime May 30 to June 29 and Sept. 5 to Oct. 5.

Brunswick   J3

Brunswick B&B
165 Park Row, Brunswick, ME 04011-2000
(207)729-4914

Circa 1860. The Brunswick, a Greek Revival-style home, overlooks the town green. Guests often relax in one of the two front parlors, with their inviting fireplaces. Summertime guests enjoy the wraparound front porch. Rooms are filled with antiques, collectibles and quilts. In the years that the bed & breakfast served as a family home for law professor Daniel Stanwood, the home was host to an array of famed personalities, including Edna St. Vincent Millay, Thornton Wilder and Admiral Richard Byrd. Ice skating in the "mall" across the street is a popular winter activity. Freeport, only a 10-minute drive, is perfect for shoppers, and several state parks are nearby.

Innkeeper(s): Mercie & Steve Normand. $73-93. MC VISA. 5 rooms with PB. Breakfast included in rates. Types of meals: full breakfast and early coffee/tea. Beds: KQDT. Cable TV, fax and copier on premises. Antiques, fishing, parks, shopping, sporting events and theater nearby.

Seen in: Times Record, Coastal Journal, Atlanta Journal.

"Just as wonderful as we remembered!"

Certificate may be used: Nov. 1-April 30, Sunday-Thursday.

Samuel Newman House
7 South St, Brunswick, ME 04011-2514
(207)729-6959

This early 19th-century Federal-style manor, adjacent to Bowdoin College, was originally the home of Samuel Phillips Newman, an early Bowdoin professor and mentor to Hawthorne and Longfellow. Freshly baked muffins, pastries and homemade granola are served each morning at this historic home, which is open for guests only during the summer months.

Innkeeper(s): Guenter Rose. $55-85. MC VISA. 7 rooms. Breakfast included in rates. Type of meal: continental breakfast.

Certificate may be used: Weekdays in June (Monday-Thursday). Only open June-August.

Camden   I5

Blue Harbor House, A Village Inn
67 Elm St, Rt 1, Camden, ME 04843-1904
(207)236-3196 (800)248-3196
Fax:(207)236-6523

Circa 1810. James Richards, Camden's first settler, built this Cape house on a 1768 homesite. (The King granted him the land as the first person to fulfill all the conditions of a settler.) An 1810 carriage house has been refurbished to offer private suites,

some with whirlpool tubs. Breakfast is served on the sun porch overlooking the Camden Hills. Dinner, available by reservation, can be a gourmet affair or an authentic Maine lobster bake on the lawn. The bustling harbor is a five-minute walk away.
Innkeeper(s): Jody Schmoll & Dennis Hayden. $85-135. MAP. MC VISA AX DS PC TC. 10 rooms with PB. 2 suites. 1 conference room. Breakfast and afternoon tea included in rates. Types of meals: gourmet breakfast and early coffee/tea. Beds: KQDT. Air conditioning, turn-down service, cable TV and VCR in room. Fax, bicycles and library on premises. Antiques, fishing, parks, shopping, downhill skiing, cross-country skiing, theater and watersports nearby.

Location: Camden Village.

Seen in: Dallas Morning News, Discerning Traveler, Country Living.

"I don't know when I've enjoyed my stay in a country inn more."

Certificate may be used: Nov. 1 to May 15, excludes Carriage House Suites.

Elms B&B

84 Elm St, Rt 1, Camden, ME 04843-1907
(207)236-6250 (800)755-3567
Fax:(207)236-7330

Circa 1806. Captain Calvin Curtis built this Colonial a few minutes' stroll from the picturesque harbor. Candlelight shimmers year round from the inn's windows. A sitting room, library, and parlor are open for guests and tastefully appointed bed chambers scattered with antiques are available in both the main house and the carriage house. A cottage garden can be seen beside the carriage house.
Innkeeper(s): Ted & Jo Panayotoff. $65-95. MC VISA TC. 6 rooms, 4 with PB, 1 with FP. Breakfast and afternoon tea included in rates. Types of meals: continental breakfast, full breakfast and early coffee/tea. Beds: QD. Handicap access. Antiques, fishing, parks, shopping, downhill skiing, cross-country skiing and theater nearby.

"The warmth of your home is only exceeded by the warmth of yourself."

Certificate may be used: Oct. 16 to June 13 all days of the week.

Lord Camden Inn

24 Main St, Camden, ME 04843-1704
(207)236-4325 (800)336-4325
Fax:(207)236-7141

Circa 1893. Located in a restored brick building on the town's Main Street, the inn is decorated in American country antiques. A friendly staff will be happy to suggest some of the many activities in the area. Day sails and island picnics can be arranged and bicycle rentals are available for inland rides or to tour islands after a short ferry ride. Most guest rooms offer balconies with spectacular views of Camden Harbor, the village or the hills.
Innkeeper(s): Randall S. Hocking & Suzanne A. Brown. $88-175. MC VISA PC. 31 rooms with PB. 4 suites. 2 conference rooms. Breakfast included in rates. Types of meals: continental-plus breakfast and early coffee/tea. Beds: KQD. Air conditioning and cable TV in room. Fax and copier on premises. Antiques, fishing, parks, shopping, downhill skiing, cross-country skiing, theater and watersports nearby.

Certificate may be used: October through May.

Cape Elizabeth K3

Inn By The Sea

40 Bowery Beach Rd,
Cape Elizabeth, ME 04107-2514
(207)799-3134 (800)888-4287
Fax:(207)799-4779

Circa 1986. This cottage-style resort is like a modern version of the hotels and inns that dotted Maine's coast in its heyday as a summer spot. The inn has its own private boardwalk leading to Crescent Beach. Guests can enjoy swimming, tennis and shuffleboard without leaving the inn's grounds, which also offer a tea garden and gazebo. The well-appointed rooms are elegant, but not imposing, with Chippendale furnishings, wicker and floral chintz. Guests opting for one of the inn's cozy garden suites can grab a book from the inn's library and enjoy it from a rocker on their own private porch. Cuisine at the inn's gourmet Audubon Room is full of memorable items. In the summer months, the inn opens its outdoor West End Cafe and Pool Bar.
Innkeeper(s): Maureen McQuade. $100-390. EP. MC VISA AX DS TC. 43 suites, 6 with FP. 2 conference rooms. Type of meal: full breakfast. Dinner, picnic lunch, banquet service, catering service and room service available. Beds: KQD. Turn-down service, ceiling fan, cable TV and VCR in room. Fax, copier and bicycles on premises. Amusement parks, antiques, fishing, parks, shopping, downhill skiing, cross-country skiing, sporting events, theater and watersports nearby.

Certificate may be used: November-April, excluding holidays, Sunday-Friday.

Caribou   C6

The Old Iron Inn

155 High St, Caribou, ME 04736-1868
(207)492-4766

Circa 1900. Innkeepers Kate and Kevin McCartney
named their Arts and Crafts-style B&B after their
extensive collection of antique irons. Guests literally can follow the advancement of this necessary
appliance. Turn-of-the-century antiques and
Victorian flair decorate the rooms. The inn, located
in downtown Caribou, is within walking distance of
the town's shopping district.

Innkeeper(s): Kevin & Kate McCartney. $35-45. MC VISA AX DS TC. 4
rooms, 1 with PB. Breakfast included in rates. Types of meals: continental breakfast, continental-plus breakfast, full breakfast, gourmet
breakfast and early coffee/tea. Dinner, lunch and catered breakfast
available. Beds: D. Fax on premises. Amusement parks, fishing, downhill skiing, cross-country skiing and theater nearby.

Certificate may be used: No restrictions.

China   H4

Loons Call Inn

PO Box 342, China, ME 04926-0342
(207)968-2025 Fax:(207)968-2025

Circa 1974. Each year a variety of birds return to
this inn located by the banks of China Lake. The
innkeepers, both members of the Audubon Society,
enjoy keeping track of the eagles, blue herons,
ospreys and, of course, the namesake loons, that
land on the shore. Guests staying in the semi-
private library loft access the room via an oak spiral
staircase. The bed is situated under a skylight, perfect for stargazing. The Executive Suite includes a
reading area and whirlpool tub.

Innkeeper(s): Gary & Tera Coull. $75-99. MC VISA TC. 4 rooms, 3 with
PB. 2 suites. Breakfast included in rates. Types of meals: continental
breakfast, continental-plus breakfast, full breakfast, gourmet breakfast
and early coffee/tea. Evening snack, lunch and banquet service available. Beds: KQT. Cable TV, VCR, fax, copier, spa, bicycles and child
care on premises. Antiques, fishing, parks, shopping, downhill skiing,
cross-country skiing, sporting events, theater and watersports nearby.

Certificate may be used: All year with reservation 30 days in advance
if available.

Damariscotta   I4

Brannon-Bunker Inn

PO Box 045, HCR 64, Rt 129,
Damariscotta, ME 04543-0045
(207)563-5941

Circa 1820. This Cape-style house has been a
home to many generations of Maine residents, one
of whom was captain of a ship that sailed to the
Arctic. During the '20s, the barn served as a dance
hall. Later, it was converted into comfortable guest
rooms. Victorian and American antiques are featured and there are collections of military and
political memorabilia.

Innkeeper(s): Joe & Jeanne Hovance. $60-70. MC VISA AX PC TC. 8
rooms, 5 with PB. 1 suite. Breakfast included in rates. Type of meal:
continental-plus breakfast. Beds: QDT. VCR, library and child care on
premises. Handicap access. Antiques, fishing, parks, shopping, cross-
country skiing, theater and watersports nearby.

Seen in: Times-Beacon Newspaper.

*"Wonderful beds, your gracious hospitality and the very
best muffins anywhere made our stay a memorable one."*

Certificate may be used: April 1-June 15, Sunday-Thursday & Sept.
10-Dec. 1, Sunday-Thursday. No three-day holiday weekends.

Durham   I3

The Bagley House

1290 Royalsborough Rd,
Durham, ME 04222-5225
(207)865-6566 (800)765-1772
Fax:(207)353-5878

Circa 1772. Six acres of fields and woods surround
the Bagley House. Once an inn, a store, and a
schoolhouse, it is the oldest house in town. Guest
rooms are decorated with colonial furnishings and
hand-sewn Maine quilts. For breakfast, guests gather
in the country kitchen in front of a huge brick fireplace and beehive oven.

Innkeeper(s): Suzanne O'Connor. $70-
125. MC VISA AX DS. 5 rooms
with PB, 1 with FP. 1 conference
room. Breakfast and afternoon
tea included in rates. Types of
meals: full breakfast and early
coffee/tea. Evening snack
and picnic lunch avail-
able. Beds:
QDT. Fax
on premis-
es. Antiques,
shopping, downhill skiing, cross-
country skiing, sporting events and theater
nearby.

Location: Route 136, Durham.

Seen in: Los Angeles Times, New England Getaways, Lewiston Sun.

"I had the good fortune to stumble on the Bagley House. The rooms are well-appointed and the innkeeper is as charming a host as you'll find."

Certificate may be used: November-June, Sunday-Thursday.

Eastport   G8

The Milliken House
29 Washington St,
Eastport, ME 04631-1324
(207)853-2955

Circa 1846. Formerly known as the Artists Retreat, this stately Victorian is furnished with ornately carved, marble-topped furniture. The builder maintained a wharf on Eastport's waterfront from which he serviced the tall trading ships that used the harbor as a port of entry to the United States. Much of the furniture is original, brought to the United States for Benjamin Milliken's bride.
Innkeeper(s): Joyce Weber. $40-60. MC VISA AX PC TC. 5 rooms. 1 conference room. Breakfast included in rates. Type of meal: full breakfast. Beds: QT.
Certificate may be used: January-June, October-December. Any day.

Weston House
26 Boynton St, Eastport, ME 04631-1305
(207)853-2907 (800)853-2907

Circa 1810. Jonathan Weston, an 1802 Harvard graduate, built this Federal-style house on a hill overlooking Passamaquoddy Bay. John Audubon

stayed here as a guest of the Westons while awaiting passage to Labrador in 1833. Each of the guest rooms are furnished with antiques and Oriental rugs. The Weston and Audubon rooms boast views of the bay and gardens. Breakfast menus vary, including such delectables as heavenly pancakes with hot apricot syrup or freshly baked muffins and coddled eggs. Seasonal brunches are served on weekends and holidays. The area is full of outdoor activities,

including whale watching. Nearby Saint Andrews-by-the-Sea offers plenty of shops and restaurants.
Innkeeper(s): Jett & John Peterson. $55-70. TC. 5 rooms, 1 with FP. 1 suite. 1 conference room. Breakfast and afternoon tea included in rates. Type of meal: gourmet breakfast. Picnic lunch and catering service available. Beds: KQDT. Cable TV in room. Fishing, shopping and theater nearby.
Seen in: Downeast, Los Angeles Times, Boston Globe.

"The most memorable bed & breakfast experience we have ever had."

Certificate may be used: Subject to availability. All months with the exception of the month of August.

Eliot   L2

High Meadows B&B
Rt 101, Eliot, ME 03903
(207)439-0590

Circa 1740. A ship's captain built this house, now filled with remembrances of colonial days. At one point, it was raised and a floor added underneath, so the upstairs is older than the downstairs. It is conveniently located to factory outlets in Kittery, Maine, and great dining and historic museums in Portsmouth, New Hampshire. Smoking is permitted on the porch and terrace.
Innkeeper(s): Elaine & Ray. $60-80. MC VISA AX PC TC. 5 rooms, 4 with PB, 1 with FP. 1 conference room. Breakfast and afternoon tea included in rates. Types of meals: full breakfast and early coffee/tea. Beds: QDT. Turn-down service in room. Cable TV on premises. Antiques, fishing, shopping and watersports nearby.
Seen in: Portsmouth Herald, York County Focus.

"High Meadows was the highlight of our trip."
Certificate may be used: Monday-Thursday; April, May, June.

Moses Paul Inn
270 Goodwin Rd, Eliot, ME 03903-1204
(207)439-1861 (800)552-6058

Circa 1780. This Colonial farmhouse is charming and hard to miss, with its bright red exterior and white trim. The home is truly welcoming. Restored wood floors and woodwork gleam, and rooms, some with exposed beams, are decorated with treasures the innkeepers found at local auctions. Quilts, antiques and country furnishings are among the finds. Be sure to ask the innkeepers about a French soldier who may still inhabit the halls in ghostly form. Kittery Outlet Malls and historic Portsmouth are just a few minutes away, as is the coastline.
Innkeeper(s): Joanne Weiss & Larry James. $60-75. MC VISA DS PC TC. 5 rooms, 2 with PB. Breakfast included in rates. Type of meal: full breakfast. Beds: QDT. Ceiling fan in room. Cable TV, VCR, fax and library on premises. Amusement parks, antiques, fishing, parks, shopping, downhill skiing, cross-country skiing, sporting events, theater and watersports nearby.
Certificate may be used: Anytime, subject to availability.

Guilford   G4

Trebor Inn
Golda Ct, Guilford, ME 04443
(207)876-4070 (800)223-5509

Seven guest rooms are available at this stately, turreted Victorian inn, which overlooks Guilford from
high on a hill along the Moosehead Trail. Those
who enjoy hunting bear, deer, partridge and pheasant should inquire about the inn's special rates for
hunters. Meals are served family-style, and dinners
are available on request. The family-oriented inn
also accommodates business meetings, family
reunions and weddings. Within five minutes of the
inn, visitors will find basketball courts, a nine-hole
golf course and tennis courts. Peaks-Kenny State
Park and Sebec Lake are nearby.

Innkeeper(s): Lorraine Vernal. $38-65. MC VISA AX. 7 rooms. Breakfast
included in rates. Types of meals: full breakfast and early coffee/tea.
Dinner available. Cable TV and VCR on premises. Antiques, shopping,
downhill skiing and cross-country skiing nearby.

Certificate may be used: Jan. 2 to Oct. 30.

Hallowell   I3

Maple Hill Farm B&B Inn
RR 1 Box 1145, Hallowell, ME 04347
(207)622-2708 (800)622-2708
Fax:(207)622-0655

Circa 1890. Visitors to Maine's capital city have
the option of staying at this nearby inn, a peaceful
farm setting adjacent to a 550-acre state wildlife

management area that is available for canoeing,
fishing and hunting. This Victorian Shingle-style
inn was once a stagecoach stop and dairy farm.
Guests may borrow a bicycle for a relaxing ride, or
hop into a whirlpool tub after a busy day of sightseeing or other activities. The inn, with its 62-acre
grounds, easily accommodates conferences, parties
and receptions. Cobbossee Lake is a five-minute
drive from the inn.

Innkeeper(s): Scott Cowger. $50-90. MC VISA AX DC CB DS. 7 rooms,
4 with PB. 1 suite. 1 conference room. Breakfast and afternoon tea
included in rates. Types of meals: full breakfast and early coffee/tea.
Evening snack, picnic lunch, banquet service and catering service available. Beds: QD. VCR on premises. Handicap access. Antiques, fishing,
shopping, cross-country skiing, theater and watersports nearby.

Seen in: Family Fun, An Explorer's Guide to Maine, The Forecaster,
Portland Press Herald.

*"You add many thoughtful touches to your service that
set your B&B apart from others, and really make a
difference."*

Certificate may be used: May-October, Sunday-Wednesday.
November-April, anytime but cannot select both Friday and Saturday.

Isle Au Haut   I5

The Keeper's House
PO Box 26, Isle Au Haut, ME 04645-0026
(207)367-2261

Circa 1907. Designed and built by the U.S.
Lighthouse Service, the handsome 48-foot-high
Robinson Point Light guided vessels into this once-
bustling island fishing village. Guests arrive on the
mailboat. Innkeeper Judi Burke, whose father was a
keeper at the Highland Lighthouse on Cape Cod,
provides picnic lunches so guests may explore the
scenic island trails. Dinner is served in the keeper's

dining room. The lighthouse is adjacent to the most
remote section of Acadia National Park. It's not
uncommon to hear the cry of an osprey, see deer
approach the inn, or watch seals and porpoises
cavorting off the point. Guest rooms are comfortable and serene, with stunning views of the island's
ragged shore line, forests and Duck Harbor.

Innkeeper(s): Jeff & Judi Burke. $250. PC TC. 6 rooms. 1 cottage.
Breakfast, dinner and picnic lunch included in rates. Types of meals: full
breakfast, gourmet breakfast and early coffee/tea. Afternoon tea, lunch
and gourmet lunch available. Beds: D. Swimming, bicycles and library
on premises. Parks and shopping nearby.

Location: A small island six miles south of Stonington, reached by
mailboat.

Seen in: New York Times, USA Today, Los Angeles Times, Ladies Home

Journal, Christian Science Monitor, Down East, New York Woman, Philadelphia Inquirer, McCalls, Country, Men's Journal, Travel & Leisure.

"Simply one of the unique places on Earth."

Certificate may be used: May 1 through June 15 and Oct. 16-31.

Kennebunkport K2

Cove House
11 S Maine St,
Kennebunkport, ME 04046-6313
(207)967-3704

Circa 1793. This roomy Colonial Revival farmhouse overlooks Chick's Cove on the Kennebunk River. The inn's peaceful setting offers easy access to beaches, shops and the town. Three guest rooms serve visitors of this antique-filled home. Guests enjoy full breakfasts, which often include the inn's famous blueberry muffins, in the Flow Blue dining room. A popular gathering spot for guests is the book-lined living room/library. Bicycles may be borrowed for a leisurely ride around the town. A cozy, secluded cottage with a screened front porch is another lodging option.
Innkeeper(s): Katherine Jones. $70-90. MC VISA PC TC. 3 rooms with PB. 1 cottage. Breakfast and afternoon tea included in rates. Types of meals: full breakfast and early coffee/tea. Beds: QT. Cable TV, VCR, bicycles and library on premises. Antiques, fishing, parks, shopping, cross-country skiing, theater and watersports nearby.

Certificate may be used: Nov. 1-May 15.

English Meadows Inn
141 Port Rd, Kennebunkport, ME 04043
(207)967-5766 (800)272-0698
Fax:(207)967-5766

Circa 1860. Bordered by century-old lilac bushes, this Queen Anne Victorian inn and attached carriage house offer 11 guest rooms. The inn's well-tended grounds, which include apple trees, gardens and lush lawns, invite bird-lovers or those who

desire a relaxing stroll. Four-poster beds, afghans and handsewn quilts are found in many of the guest rooms, and visitors also will enjoy the talents of local artists, whose works are featured throughout the inn. Guests may eat breakfast in bed before heading out to explore Kennebunkport.

Innkeeper(s): Charles Doane. $75-108. MC VISA AX DS PC TC. 13 rooms with PB. 1 suite. 1 cottage. Breakfast and afternoon tea included in rates. Types of meals: full breakfast and early coffee/tea. Room service available. Beds: KQDT. Cable TV and fax on premises. Amusement parks, antiques, fishing, parks, shopping, cross-country skiing, theater and watersports nearby.

"Thanks for the memories! You have a warm Yankee hospitality here!"

Certificate may be used: November-May, Sunday through Thursday.

Kylemere House 1818
6 South St, PO Box 1333,
Kennebunkport, ME 04046-1333
(207)967-2780

Circa 1818. Located in Maine's largest historic district, this Federal-style house was built by Daniel Walker, a descendant of an original Kennebunkport family. Later, Maine artist and architect Abbot

Graves purchased the property and named it "Crosstrees" for its maple trees. The inn features New England antiques and brilliant flower gardens in view of the formal dining room in spring and summer. A full breakfast is provided. Art galleries, beaches, antiquing and golf are nearby.
Innkeeper(s): Ruth Toohey. $80-135. MC VISA. 4 rooms with PB, 1 with FP. Breakfast included in rates. Types of meals: full breakfast and early coffee/tea. Beds: KQT. Bicycles on premises. Antiques, fishing, shopping and theater nearby.
Seen in: Boston Globe, Glamour, Regis and Kathie Lee Show.

"Beautiful inn. Outstanding hospitality. Thanks for drying our sneakers, fixing our bikes. You are all a lot of fun!"

Certificate may be used: Sunday-Thursday, mid-May to mid-June and November.

Maine Stay Inn & Cottages
34 Maine St,
Kennebunkport, ME 04046-6174
(207)967-2117 (800)950-2117
Fax:(207)967-8757

Circa 1860. In the National Register, this is a square-block Italianate contoured in a low hip-roof design. Later additions reflecting the Queen Anne period include a suspended spiral staircase, crystal windows, ornately carved mantels and moldings, bay windows and porches. A sea captain built the handsome cupola that became a favorite spot for making taffy. In the '20s, the cupola was a place from which to spot offshore rumrunners. Guests enjoy afternoon tea with stories of the Maine Stay's heritage. One suite in the main building and five of the cottage rooms have working fireplaces.

Innkeeper(s): Carol & Lindsay Copeland. $85-210. MC VISA AX DS PC TC. 17 rooms with PB, 7 with FP. 4 suites. 11 cottages. Breakfast and afternoon tea included in rates. Types of meals: full breakfast and early coffee/tea. Beds: QDT. Air conditioning and cable TV in room. Fax, copier, computer and child care on premises. Amusement parks, antiques, fishing, shopping, cross-country skiing, theater and watersports nearby.

Location: In the Kennebunkport National Historic District.

Seen in: Boston Globe, Discerning Traveler, Montreal Gazette, Innsider, Tourist News, Down East, Staten Island Advance, Birmingham News, Delaware County Times, Family Travel Times.

"We have traveled the East Coast from Martha's Vineyard to Bar Harbor, and this is the only place we know we must return to."

Certificate may be used: Midweek, Monday through Thursday, late October through mid-June.

Kittery   L2

Enchanted Nights B&B
29 Wentworth St Rt 103,
Kittery, ME 03904-1720
(207)439-1489

Circa 1890. Feather beds, Victorian decor, handcarved Oak and other touches make this inn a pleasant place to stay. Two of the rooms boast double whirlpool tubs. One guest room is decked in Victorian style, while another offers the ambiance of a French country cottage. The Turret is a cozy, little hideaway with a 13-foot pointed ceiling and wrought-iron bed. Gourmet coffee, herbal teas, fresh fruits and delicious omelets are the fare for the expansive morning meal, which is served on fine, antique china.

Innkeeper(s): Peter T. Lamandis. $47-145. MC VISA AX DS. 6 rooms with PB. Breakfast included in rates. Types of meals: full breakfast and gourmet breakfast. Beds: QD. Air conditioning, ceiling fan, cable TV and VCR in room. Bicycles and pet boarding on premises. Handicap access. Fishing, parks, shopping, theater and watersports nearby.

"The atmosphere was great. Your breakfast was elegant. The breakfast room made us feel we had gone back in time. All in all it was a very enjoyable stay."

Certificate may be used: Nov. 1 to June 20, Sunday-Thursday.

Medomak

Roaring Brook B&B
Rt 32, Box 130, Medomak, ME 04551
(207)529-5467 (800)484-7229
Fax:(207)529-5467

Circa 1940. Innkeepers Don and Lorelei Eckert have brought hospitality back to this New England Cape-style home, which served as a guest house in the 1950s. Aside from the guest rooms, enhanced by the country Colonial furnishings and decor, Don and Lorelei offer an efficiency apartment during the summer months. German pancakes, homemade breads and omelets are some of the delectables that might highlight the morning meal. The B&B is only a few miles from Round Pond, and lighthouses, antiquing and restaurants await guests in nearby villages.

Innkeeper(s): Don & Lorelei Eckert. $50-90. MC VISA TC. 4 rooms, 2 with PB, 1 with FP. 1 suite. Breakfast included in rates. Types of meals: full breakfast and early coffee/tea. Beds: QDT. Turn-down service in room. Cable TV, VCR and fax on premises. Antiques, fishing, shopping, theater and watersports nearby.

Certificate may be used: Oct. 1-June 30, Sunday-Saturday.

Naples

J2

Augustus Bove House

Corner Rts 302 & 114, RR1 Box 501,
Naples, ME 04055
(207)693-6365 (800)693-6365

Circa 1830. A long front lawn nestles up against
the stone foundation and veranda of this house,
once known as the Hotel Naples, one of the area's
summer hotels in the 1800s. The guest rooms are
decorated in a Colonial style and modestly furnished with antiques. Many rooms provide a view of
Long Lake. A fancy country breakfast is provided.
Innkeeper(s): David & Arlene Stetson. $49-110. MC VISA AX DS PC
TC. 11 rooms, 7 with PB. 1 suite. Breakfast and afternoon tea included
in rates. Types of meals: full breakfast and early coffee/tea. Beds: KQT.
Air conditioning and cable TV in room. VCR and fax on premises.
Antiques, fishing, parks, shopping, downhill skiing, cross-country ski-
ing, theater and watersports nearby.
Location: Corner of routes 302 & 114.
Seen in: Brighton Times.

"Beautiful place, rooms, and people."

Certificate may be used: Void July and August, holidays and first week
of October.

The Inn at Long Lake

Lake House Rd, PO Box 806,
Naples, ME 04055
(207)693-6226 (800)437-0328

Circa 1906. Reopened in 1988, the inn housed the
overflow guests from the Lake House resort about 90
years ago. Guests traveled to the resort via the
Oxford-Cumberland Canal, and each room is
named for a historic canal boat. The cozy rooms

offer fluffy comforters and a warm, country decor in
a romantic atmosphere. Warm up in front of a
crackling fire in the great room, or enjoy a cool
Long Lake breeze on the veranda while watching
horses in nearby pastures. Murder-mystery weekends
offer a spooky alternative to your getaway plans.
Innkeeper(s): Maynard & Irene Hincks. $55-130. MC VISA DS PC TC.
16 rooms with PB. 2 suites. 1 conference room. Breakfast included in
rates. Types of meals: continental-plus breakfast and early coffee/tea.
Beds: QDT. Air conditioning in room. Library on premises. Antiques,

fishing, parks, shopping, downhill skiing, cross-country skiing and
watersports nearby.
Location: Sebago Lakes Region.
Seen in: Bridgton News, Portland Press Herald.

*"Convenient location, tastefully done and the prettiest
inn I've ever stayed in."*

Certificate may be used: Oct. 16-May 14.

Ogunquit

K2

Chestnut Tree Inn

PO Box 2201, Ogunquit, ME 03907-2201
(207)646-4529 (800)362-0757

Circa 1870. Gable roofs peak out from the top of
this Victorian inn, which has greeted guests for
more than a century. A smattering of antiques and
Victorian decor creates a 19th-century atmosphere.
Guests can relax on the porch or head out for a
stroll on Marginal Way, a mile-long path set along
Maine's scenic coastline. The beach, shops,
Ogunquit Playhouse and a variety of restaurants are
just a few minutes down the road.
Innkeeper(s): Cynthia Diana & Ronald St. Laurent. $35-125. MC VISA
AX TC. 33 rooms, 15 with PB. 1 suite. Types of meals: continental
breakfast and continental-plus breakfast. Beds: QDT. Air conditioning
and cable TV in room. Amusement parks, antiques, fishing, parks,
shopping, downhill skiing, cross-country skiing, sporting events, theater and watersports nearby.
Certificate may be used: Monday-Thursday, May 15-June 15 and Sept.
15-Oct. 15.

Hartwell House

118 Shore Rd, PO Box 393,
Ogunquit, ME 03907
(207)646-7210 (800)235-8883

Circa 1921. Hartwell House offers suites and guest
rooms furnished with distinctive Early American
and English antiques. Many rooms are available
with French doors opening to private balconies
overlooking sculpted flower gardens. Breakfast may
be enjoyed in the dining room or on the patio.
Afternoon tea is served daily.
Innkeeper(s): William & Anne Mozingo. $80-175. MC VISA AX DS TC.
16 rooms with PB. 3 suites. 4 conference rooms. Breakfast and afternoon tea included in rates. Types of meals: gourmet breakfast and early
coffee/tea. Catering service available. Beds: QT. Air conditioning and
ceiling fan in room. Cable TV and fax on premises. Amusement parks,
antiques, fishing, parks, shopping, cross-country skiing, sporting
events, theater and watersports nearby.
Seen in: Innsider.

*"This engaging country inn will be reserved for my spe-
cial clients. — Travel agent."*

Certificate may be used: Nov. 6 to April 26.

Old Orchard Beach K2

Atlantic Birches Inn
20 Portland Ave Rt 98,
Old Orchard Beach, ME 04064-2212
(207)934-5295 (800)486-1681

Circa 1903. The front porch of this Shingle-style Victorian is shaded by white birch trees. Badminton and croquet are set up on the lawn. The house is a place for relaxation and enjoyment, an uncluttered, simple haven filled with comfortable furnishings. The guest rooms are decorated with a few antiques and pastel wallcoverings. Maine's coast offers an endless amount of activities, from boating to whale watching.

Innkeeper(s): Dan & Cyndi Bolduc. $39-85. EP. MC VISA AX DS TC. 5 rooms with PB. Breakfast included in rates. Type of meal: continental-plus breakfast. Beds: KQDT. Air conditioning and ceiling fan in room. Cable TV, VCR, copier, swimming and library on premises. Amusement parks, antiques, fishing, parks, shopping, sporting events and watersports nearby.

Certificate may be used: Nov. 1 to May 1.

Portland J3

Andrews Lodging B&B
417 Auburn St, Portland, ME 04103-2109
(207)797-9157 Fax:(207)797-9040

Circa 1780. Innkeepers Douglas and Elizabeth Andrews offer plenty of activities to keep guests busy at their Colonial inn. The grounds include badminton, croquet and volleyball areas, and during winter months guests can use the inn's ice rink. Rooms are cozy, decorated with bright prints and a collection of antiques. The suite includes a whirlpool tub. There is a kitchen for guest use. Well-behaved pets are welcomed, as Douglas is also a veterinarian. The Freeport Factory Outlets and L.L. Bean store are just a few miles away, as is the coast.

Innkeeper(s): Douglas & Elizabeth Andrews. $55-125. MC VISA AX TC. 6 rooms, 1 with PB. 1 suite. Breakfast included in rates. Types of meals: continental-plus breakfast and early coffee/tea. Catered breakfast available. Beds: QT. Turn-down service and cable TV in room. VCR, fax, bicycles and pet boarding on premises. Antiques, fishing, parks, shopping, downhill skiing, cross-country skiing, sporting events, theater and watersports nearby.

Certificate may be used: Oct. 15 to Dec. 15 and Jan. 2 to June 30, anyday, Sunday through Saturday.

Rangeley G2

Northwoods
PO Box 79, Rangeley, ME 04970-0079
(207)864-2440 (800)295-4968

Circa 1912. This immaculate Colonial Revival home, which has all the original woodwork intact, has a magnificent view of Rangeley Lake. Inside, guests can find a doll house museum filled with porcelain dolls and antiques. Still largely unspoiled,

the surrounding mountain and lake region offers a variety of activities and moose can be seen grazing and walking through the area. The inn's formal and prominent character is part of the unique residential architecture of the town. Although centrally located in Rangeley Village, Northwoods has a peaceful and lofty quality.

Innkeeper(s): Janice Thorp. $60-90. MC VISA PC TC. 4 rooms, 3 with PB. Breakfast included in rates. Type of meal: full breakfast. Beds: QDT. Cable TV and VCR on premises. Antiques, fishing, downhill skiing, cross-country skiing, theater and watersports nearby.

Certificate may be used: Weekdays June and July, October-December, January-April. Only one weekend night included.

Saco K2

Crown 'N' Anchor Inn
121 North St, PO Box 228,
Saco, ME 04072-0228
(207)282-3829 (800)561-8865

Circa 1827. This Greek Revival house features both Victorian baroque and colonial antiques. A collection of British coronation memorabilia displayed throughout the inn includes 200 items. Guests gather in the Victorian parlor or the formal library. The innkeepers, two college librarians and an academic bookseller, lined the shelves with several thousand volumes, including extensive Civil War and British royal family collections and travel, theater and nautical books. The floor-to-ceiling windows of the Eliza Hitchcock Room overlook the

Damariscotta River. Royal Dalton china, crystal and fresh flowers create a festive breakfast setting.

Innkeeper(s): John Barclay & Martha Forester. $60-95. MC VISA AX PC TC. 5 rooms with PB, 3 with FP. Breakfast included in rates. Types of meals: full breakfast, gourmet breakfast and early coffee/tea. Afternoon tea available. Beds: KQDT. Cable TV in room. VCR and library on premises. Amusement parks, antiques, fishing, parks, shopping, downhill skiing, cross-country skiing, sporting events, theater and watersports nearby.

Seen in: Lincoln County News, Yankee, Saco, Bidd & Ford, Old Orchard Beach Courier, Portland Press Herald.

Certificate may be used: Year-round, Sunday through Thursday with the exception of July and August.

Searsport   H5

Brass Lantern Inn
PO Box 407, 81 W Main St,
Searsport, ME 04974-3501
(207)548-0150 (800)691-0150

Circa 1850. This Victorian inn is nestled at the edge of the woods on a rise overlooking Penobscot Bay. Showcased throughout the inn are many collectibles, antiques and family heirlooms, including an extensive doll collection. Enjoy breakfast in the dining room with its ornate tin ceiling, where you'll feast on Maine blueberry pancakes and other sumptuous treats. Centrally located between Camden and Bar Harbor, Searsport is known as the antique capital of Maine. There are many local attractions, including the Penobscot Marine Museum, fine shops and restaurants, as well as a public boat facility.

Innkeeper(s): Pat Gatto & Lee Anne Lee. $60-75. MC VISA PC TC. 4 rooms with PB. Breakfast included in rates. Type of meal: full breakfast. Beds: DT. Cable TV and library on premises. Antiques, fishing, parks, shopping, cross-country skiing and theater nearby.

Seen in: Country Extra, Republication Journal.

"Very elegant surrounding, cozy atmosphere. Truly caring, thoughtful, friendly, people sharing their house."

Certificate may be used: Monday-Thursday, September to June, no holidays.

Thurston House B&B
PO Box 686, 8 Elm St,
Searsport, ME 04974-3368
(207)548-2213 (800)240-2213

Circa 1831. The innkeepers of this Colonial home proudly serve their "Forget About Lunch" breakfast, which consists of three courses, fresh prepared fruit, baked hot breads and then a sumptuous entree course. Special diets are happily accommodated as well. Stephen Thurston was the pastor of the first Congregational Church in Searsport for the heart of the 19th century. He was one of the town's most

prominent citizens as well. In 1853, the 242-ton brig named after Thurston was launched.

Innkeeper(s): Carl Eppig. $40-65. MC VISA. 4 rooms, 2 with PB, 2 with FP. 1 suite. Breakfast included in rates. Types of meals: full breakfast and early coffee/tea. Afternoon tea available. Beds: DT. Antiques, fishing, shopping, downhill skiing, cross-country skiing, sporting events, theater and watersports nearby.

Seen in: Yankee, The Evening Times-Globe, The Great Hallowell-Searsport Antiques Rivalry.

"When we again travel in the Maine area, there is no doubt that we will make certain to stay at Thurston House. They deserve the best accolades!"

Certificate may be used: November through May.

Watchtide
190 W Main St,
Searsport, ME 04974-3514
(207)548-6575 (800)698-6575

Circa 1795. Built for a sea captain, this New England Cape-style inn with its nearly four acres of lawns and gardens, has a spectacular view of Penobscot Bay. Breakfast is served on the wicker furnished porch which overlooks the inn's bird sanctuary and the bay. An antique shop, with a large collection of angels made by a resident artist, is located in the adjacent barn. Guests can receive a discount at this shop.

Innkeeper(s): Nancy-Linn Nellis. $55-85. PC TC. 4 rooms, 2 with PB. Breakfast and afternoon tea included in rates. Types of meals: gourmet breakfast and early coffee/tea. Beds: DT. Turn-down service in room. Cable TV and library on premises. Antiques, fishing, parks, shopping, downhill skiing, cross-country skiing, sporting events, theater and watersports nearby.

Seen in: Republican Journal, Daily Item, Courier Weekend, Bangor Daily News, Pilot Tribune, Sunday Patriot News.

"We'd felt like being back to the 19th-century, with lovely furnished rooms and warm hospitality."

Certificate may be used: Oct. 15-May 15, Sunday through Thursday.

South Thomaston   I5

Weskeag at The Water
PO Box 213,
South Thomaston, ME 04858-0213
(207)596-6676 (800)596-5576

Circa 1830. The backyard of this three-story house stretches to the edge of Weskeag River and Ballyhac Cove. Fifty yards from the house, there's reversing white-water rapids, created by the 10-foot tide that narrows into the estuary. Guests often sit by the water's edge to watch the birds and the lobster fishermen. Sea kayakers can launch at the inn and explore the nearby coves and then paddle on to the ocean. The inn's furnishings include a mixture of comfortable antiques. Featherbed eggs are a house specialty.

Innkeeper(s): Lynne Smith. $50-85. 9 rooms, 4 with PB. Breakfast included in rates. Type of meal: full breakfast. Beds: QD. Ceiling fan in room. Cable TV and VCR on premises. Antiques, fishing, shopping, downhill skiing, cross-country skiing and theater nearby.

Location: Overlooking the reversing white-water rapids that connect the salty Weskeag River to the bay.

Certificate may be used: Anytime Nov. 1-June 15 and Sunday through Thursday Sept. 15-Oct. 31.

Southwest Harbor   I6

The Lamb's Ear B&B
60 Clark Point Rd, PO Box 30,
Southwest Harbor, ME 04679
(207)244-9828 Fax:(207)244-9924

Circa 1857. This stately colonial inn was built by Captain Mayo, one of the town's earliest settlers. Guests can view lobster boats, sailing ships and all

the other activities of Southwest Harbor. The harbor is surrounded by Acadia National Park with its pristine, pine forests, lakes and mountains. Breakfasts at the inn have been known to be "as artistic as they are excellent.

Innkeeper(s): Elizabeth, Monique & Darrell Hoke. $65-145. MC VISA PC TC. 8 rooms with PB, 2 with FP. 1 suite. Breakfast and afternoon tea included in rates. Types of meals: gourmet breakfast and early coffee/tea. Beds: QDT. Cable TV in room. Fax on premises. Amusement parks, antiques, fishing, parks, shopping, cross-country skiing, theater and watersports nearby.

"The food is delicious, the presentation is beautiful."

Certificate may be used: May 1-June 15.

Spruce Head   J5

Craignair Inn
533 Clark Island Rd,
Spruce Head, ME 04859
(207)594-7644 (800)320-9997
Fax:(207)596-7124

Circa 1930. Craignair originally was built to house stonecutters working in nearby granite quarries. Overlooking the docks of the Clark Island Quarry, where granite schooners once were loaded, this roomy, three-story inn is tastefully decorated with local antiques.

Innkeeper(s): Theresa E. Smith. $74-102. MC VISA AX PC TC. 24 rooms, 8 with PB. Breakfast included in rates. Types of meals: full breakfast and early coffee/tea. Banquet service, catering service and catered breakfast available. Beds: KDT. Ceiling fan in room. Fax, copier and swimming on premises. Antiques, fishing, parks, shopping, downhill skiing, cross-country skiing, theater and watersports nearby.

Location: Clark Island ocean view.

Seen in: Boston Globe, Free Press, Tribune.

"A coastal oasis of fine food and outstanding service with colonial maritime ambiance!"

Certificate may be used: Labor Day through June 30, excluding all holiday weekends.

Stockton Springs   H5

Whistlestop B&B
RR 1 Box 639,
Stockton Springs, ME 04981-9801
(207)567-3727

Circa 1957. This traditional Cape Cod-style home, located on the edge of the village of Stockton Springs, overlooks quiet Stockton Harbor. Guests can relax on the patio or in the living room with grand piano, classical music and perhaps a fire in the hearth on cool evenings. Stockton Springs is located on Penobscot Bay, midway between Camden and Mount Desert Island. Guests taking a

stroll down to one of the rocky beaches can find an abundance of wildlife and flowers along the shore.
Innkeeper(s): Katherine Christie Wilson. $50-70. MC VISA PC TC. 2 rooms. Breakfast included in rates. Types of meals: full breakfast and early coffee/tea. Beds: KDT. Cable TV, VCR and copier on premises. Antiques, fishing, parks, shopping, cross-country skiing, theater and watersports nearby.
Location: On Stockton Harbor (Penobscot Bay).
Certificate may be used: Anytime, except July, August and holiday weekends.

Waldoboro   I4

Broad Bay Inn & Gallery
PO Box 607, Waldoboro, ME 04572-0607
(207)832-6668 (800)736-6769

Circa 1830. This Colonial inn lies in the heart of an unspoiled coastal village. You'll find Victorian furnishings throughout and some guest rooms have canopy beds. Afternoon tea is served on the deck. An established art gallery displays works by renowned artists, as well as limited-edition prints. Television, games and an art library are available in the common room.
Innkeeper(s): Libby Hopkins. $45-75. MC VISA. 5 rooms. Breakfast included in rates. Types of meals: full breakfast and early coffee/tea. Beds: DT. Cable TV, VCR and copier on premises. Antiques, fishing, parks, shopping, downhill skiing, cross-country skiing, theater and watersports nearby.
Seen in: Boston Globe, Ford Times, Courier Gazette, Princeton Packet.

"Breakfast was so special - I ran to get my camera. Why, there were even flowers on my plate."
Certificate may be used: Year-round, Sunday-Thursday.

Waterford   I2

Kedarburn Inn
Rt 35 Box 61, Waterford, ME 04088
(207)583-6182 Fax:(207)583-6424

Circa 1858. The innkeepers of this Victorian establishment invite guests to try a taste of olde English hospitality and cuisine at their inn, nestled in the foothills of the White Mountains in Western Maine. Located in a historic village, the inn sits beside the flowing Kedar Brook, which runs to the shores of Lake Keoka. Each of the spacious rooms is decorated with handmade crocheted pillows, embroidered curtains, hand-sewn linens and arrangements of dried flowers. A variety of tea sandwiches, beverages, pastries, English biscuits and other tasty items are served for afternoon tea.
Innkeeper(s): Margaret & Derek Gibson. $71-125. MC VISA AX DS PC TC. 7 rooms, 3 with PB. 1 suite. 1 conference room. Breakfast included in rates. Types of meals: full breakfast and early coffee/tea. Afternoon tea, dinner, evening snack, banquet service, catering service, catered

breakfast and room service available. Restaurant on premises. Beds: KQDT. Air conditioning in room. Cable TV, VCR, fax and pet boarding on premises. Antiques, fishing, shopping, downhill skiing, cross-country skiing, theater and watersports nearby.
Location: In the White Mountains.
Seen in: Maine Times.
Certificate may be used: Jan. 1-Dec. 31.

West Gouldsboro   H6

Sunset House
Rt 186, HCR 60, Box 62,
West Gouldsboro, ME 04607
(207)963-7156 (800)233-7156

Circa 1898. This coastal country farm inn is situated near Acadia National Park. Naturalists can observe rare birds and other wildlife in an unspoiled setting. Seven spacious bedrooms are spread over

three floors. Four of the bedrooms have ocean views; a fifth overlooks a freshwater pond behind the house. During winter, guests can ice skate on the pond, while in summer it is used for swimming. The innkeepers have resident cats and poodle, and they also raise goats. Guests enjoy a full country breakfast cooked by Carl, who has been an executive chef for more than 20 years.
Innkeeper(s): Kathy & Carl Johnson. $69-79. MC VISA AX DC CB DS PC TC. 6 rooms, 3 with PB. Breakfast included in rates. Types of meals: full breakfast and early coffee/tea. Beds: KDT. VCR on premises. Antiques, fishing, parks, shopping and cross-country skiing nearby.
Location: Only 6.5 miles from the Schoodic Peninsula, which is the quiet side of Acadia National Park.
Certificate may be used: All year except August.

Winterport
H5

Colonial Winterport Inn
114 Main St, PO Box 525,
Winterport, ME 04496-3228
(207)223-5307

Circa 1833. In the 1800s, visitors to Maine knew this Federal-style inn as the Frankfort Commercial House. Innkeepers Judie and Duncan Macnab are full of stories about the history of their pre-Civil War treasure, which offers a view of the Penobscot River. The Macnabs have kept the decor simple with 19th-century antiques, and several rooms include fireplaces. Duncan, who handles the cooking, holds two degrees from the Cordon Bleu. He plans a different breakfast each day, accompanied by fresh fruits, breads and juices. Duncan also creates the five-course, gourmet dinners at the inn's restaurant.
Innkeeper(s): Duncan & Judie Macnab. $50-85. MC VISA AX DS TC. 6 rooms with PB, 3 with FP. 1 conference room. Breakfast included in rates. Types of meals: full breakfast and early coffee/tea. Dinner, picnic lunch, gourmet lunch, banquet service and catering service available. Antiques, parks, shopping and theater nearby.
Certificate may be used: All year.

York
L2

Dockside Guest Quarters
PO Box 205, York, ME 03909-0205
(207)363-2868 Fax:(207)363-1977

Circa 1900. This small, three-diamond rated resort provides a panoramic view of the Atlantic Ocean and harbor activities. Guest rooms are located in the classic large New England home, which is the

Maine House, and modern multi-unit cottages. Most rooms have private balconies or porches with unobstructed views of the water. Some suites have fireplaces. The resort is available for weddings. The on-premise restaurant is bi-level with floor to ceiling windows, affording each table a view of the harbor. Child care services are available.

Innkeeper(s): Lusty Family. $73-148. MC VISA DS PC. 21 rooms, 2 with FP. 6 suites. 1 conference room. Types of meals: continental-plus breakfast and early coffee/tea. Afternoon tea and lunch available. Beds: KQDT. Cable TV in room. Fax, bicycles, library and child care on premises. Amusement parks, antiques, fishing, parks, shopping, cross-country skiing, theater and watersports nearby.
Location: York Harbor, Maine Rt. 103.
Seen in: Boston Globe.

"We've been back many years. It's a paradise for us, the scenery, location, maintenance, living quarters."

Certificate may be used: May 1-June 19, Oct. 9-May 1, excluding weekends and holidays.

York Beach
L2

Homestead Inn B&B
8 S Main St (Rt 1A), PO Box 15,
York Beach, ME 03910
(207)363-8952

Circa 1905. This turn-of-the-century boarding house is next to Short Sands Beach. The original hard pine has been retained throughout. Bedrooms have a panoramic view of the ocean and hills. The house is kept cozy and warm by the heat of a wood-stove and fireplace. Guests enjoy the sound of the surf and seagulls. Continental breakfast is offered on the sun deck or in the family dining room.
Innkeeper(s): Daniel Duffy. $49-69. 4 rooms. Breakfast included in rates. Type of meal: continental-plus breakfast. Afternoon tea and evening snack available. Beds: TD. Ceiling fan in room. Bicycles on premises. Amusement parks, antiques, fishing, shopping, sporting events and theater nearby.
Certificate may be used: April-June; September and October, Sunday-Thursday (not applicable July-August).

York Harbor
L2

The Inn at Harmon Park
415 York St, York Harbor, ME 03911
(207)363-2031 Fax:(207)351-2948

Circa 1899. The innkeeper of this turn-of-the-century inn has worked hard to maintain the home's Victorian ambiance. Rooms are decorated with wicker furnishings and ceiling fans. Fresh flowers add extra color. The inn includes several fireplaces, one of which is found in a guest room. The inn is within walking distance of York Harbor Beach.
Innkeeper(s): Sue Antal. $49-99. PC TC. 5 rooms, 4 with PB, 1 with FP. 1 suite. Breakfast included in rates. Types of meals: full breakfast and early coffee/tea. Beds: KQDT. Ceiling fan in room. Cable TV, VCR, fax, copier, bicycles and library on premises. Amusement parks, antiques, fishing, parks, shopping, cross-country skiing, sporting events, theater and watersports nearby.
Location: Three-block walk to beaches and historic district.
Certificate may be used: Nov. 1 to May 1, Sunday-Friday.

York Harbor Inn

PO Box 573, Rt 1A,
York Harbor, ME 03911-0573
(207)363-5119 (800)343-3869
Fax:(207)363-3545

Circa 1800. The core building of the York Harbor Inn is a small log cabin constructed on the Isles of Shoals. Moved and reassembled at this dramatic location overlooking the entrance to York Harbor, the cabin is now a gathering room with a handsome

stone fireplace. There is an English-style pub in the cellar, a large ballroom and five meeting rooms. The dining room and some guest rooms overlook the ocean. Several guest rooms have ocean view decks, working fireplaces, and Jacuzzi spas. One three-room suite is available.

Innkeeper(s): Joseph & Garry Dominguez. $89-195. MAP. MC VISA AX DC CB PC TC. 33 rooms with PB, 4 with FP. 1 suite. 4 conference rooms. Breakfast included in rates. Types of meals: continental breakfast, continental-plus breakfast and early coffee/tea. Dinner, lunch, banquet service, catering service and room service available. Beds: KQD. Air conditioning and cable TV in room. VCR, fax, copier, spa, swimming and child care on premises. Amusement parks, antiques, fishing, parks, shopping, cross-country skiing, theater and watersports nearby.

Location: York Harbor's historic district.

Seen in: New York Times, Down East, Food & Wine.

"It's hard to decide where to stay when you're paging through a book of country inns. This time we chose well."

Certificate may be used: Year-round, except Friday and Saturday in July and August, based on availability.

Maryland

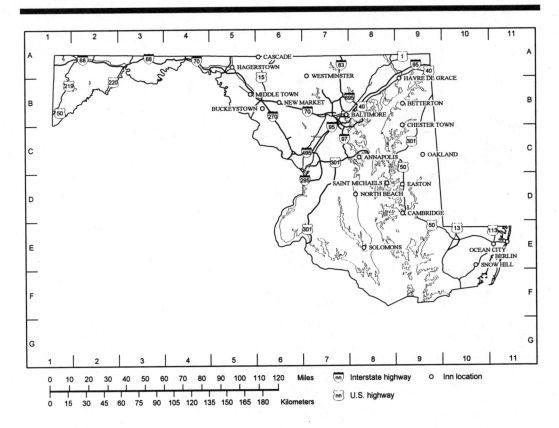

Miles: 0 10 20 30 40 50 60 70 80 90 100 110 120

Kilometers: 0 15 30 45 60 75 90 105 120 135 150 165 180

Interstate highway   ○ Inn location

U.S. highway

Annapolis C8

Chesapeake Bay Lighthouse B&B
1423 Sharps Point Rd,
Annapolis, MD 21401-6139
(410)757-0248

Circa 1926. Each of the guest rooms in this cottage-style replica lighthouse boasts water views of scenic Chesapeake Bay. The innkeepers built their unique B&B from designs found in the National Archives. Grab a pair of binoculars and enjoy the sites of the Bay Bridge, Thomas Point Lighthouse or Annapolis harbor entrance 300 foot pier. The lighthouse is only six miles from Annapolis, which is full of historic attractions, shops and restaurants.
Innkeeper(s): Janice & Bill Costello. $95-119. MC VISA AX. 3 rooms. Breakfast included in rates. Type of meal: continental-plus breakfast. Air conditioning in room.

Certificate may be used: Jan. 1 through March 31, Sunday through Thursday, holidays excluded.

Baltimore B7

Bauernschmidt Manor B&B
2316 Bauernschmidt Dr,
Baltimore, MD 21221-1713
(410)687-2233

This historic home was the summer residence of the son of George Bauernschmidt family, who started a beer brewing company in 1860. In its heyday, the brewery was one of the world's leading producers of beer. The turn-of-the-century home is believed to have been built from bricks from the Baltimore fire of 1904. The antique-filled home boasts four fireplaces and a fourth-floor cupola, which affords a beautiful view of the bay. One of the fireplaces is found in the charming Bauernschmidt Room, which also includes a Jacuzzi. The innkeepers offer special theater and boating packages.
Innkeeper(s): Suzanne Gerard. $75-125. 3 rooms. Breakfast included in rates. Type of meal: full breakfast.

Certificate may be used: Based upon availability.

Betsy's B&B
1428 Park Ave,
Baltimore, MD 21217-4230
(410)383-1274 (800)899-7533
Fax:(410)728-8957

Circa 1870. This four-story townhouse features many elegant touches, including a hallway floor laid with alternating strips of oak and walnut, ceiling medallions, large windows and a marble mantel.

Walls are decked with family heirlooms and other interesting collectibles. Breakfast is served in the elegant dining room, complete with its unique carved marble mantel. Each of the comfortably decorated guest rooms also features one of the B&Bs six mantels.
Innkeeper(s): Betsy Grater. $85. MC VISA AX DS PC TC. 3 rooms with PB. Breakfast included in rates. Type of meal: full breakfast. Beds: KQ. Air conditioning in room. Cable TV, VCR, fax, copier and computer on premises. Antiques, parks, shopping, sporting events and theater nearby.
Location: Inner Harbor, about 1.5 miles north.

Seen in: Peabody Reflector, Nation's Business, Times Herald, Baltimore Sun, Working Woman, WJZ-TV.

"What hotel room could ever compare to a large room in a 115-year-old house with 12-foot ceilings and a marble fireplace with hosts that could become dear longtime friends?"

Certificate may be used: Sunday through Thursday, except holiday weekends with Monday holiday.

Union Square House B&B
23 S Stricker St,
Baltimore, MD 21223-2423
(410)233-9064 Fax:(410)233-4046

Circa 1870. This restored Victorian Italianate townhouse is situated in "Millionaires' Row" of the Union Square Historic District. It faces Union Square Park with its gardens, trees, gracious domed gazebo and fountain. Rooms feature original plaster moldings, handsome woodwork and period furnishings. The University of Maryland, B&O Railroad Museum, Convention Center and the Inner Harbor are just a few blocks away.
Innkeeper(s): Joseph & Patrice Debes. $85-120. MC VISA AX DS TC. 3 rooms with PB, 2 with FP. 1 suite. 1 conference room. Breakfast and afternoon tea included in rates. Types of meals: continental-plus breakfast, full breakfast and early coffee/tea. Beds: D. Air conditioning in room. Fax on premises. Antiques, parks, shopping, sporting events, theater and watersports nearby.

"It is apparent that much care and thoughtfulness have gone into making your house a memorable and delightful place for your guests."

Certificate may be used: Oct. 15-Dec. 22, 1996 (includes weekends); Jan. 2-April 15, 1997 (includes weekends); Oct. 15-Dec. 22, 1997 (includes weekends). For the period of April 16-Oct. 14, second night free only Monday-Thursday, holidays excluded for 1996 and 1997.

Berlin
E11

Atlantic Hotel Inn & Restaurant
2 N Main St, Berlin, MD 21811-1043
(410)641-3589 (800)814-7672
Fax:(410)641-4928

Circa 1895. The exterior of this stunning Victorian hotel is a red brick wonder, decked with ornate trim. The hotel was built by Horace and Ginny Harmonson, and it was Ginny who ran the hotel until passing it on to her daughter. Through the years, the inn has had a succession of owners, the current of which refurbished the hotel back to its 19th-century glory. Rich fabrics cover the period antiques, which are set on polished wood floors and Oriental rugs. Bedchambers are awash in color with lacy touches and canopy or poster beds. The hotel has established a grand culinary tradition, carried on today by chef Stephen Jacques, a graduate of the Culinary Institute of America. Subtle lighting, linen tablecloths and soft decor create a romantic environment in the hotel dining room, where guests can choose from a variety of seasonal cuisine.

Innkeeper(s): Larry Wilgu. $55-135. MC VISA AX TC. 17 rooms, 16 with PB. 1 suite. 1 conference room. Breakfast included in rates. Type of meal: continental breakfast. Dinner, lunch and banquet service available. Beds: QD. Air conditioning and turn-down service in room. Amusement parks, antiques, fishing, parks and watersports nearby.

Certificate may be used: Oct. 1 to April 30, excluding holiday weekends.

Merry Sherwood Plantation
8909 Worcester Hwy,
Berlin, MD 21811-3016
(410)641-0358 (800)660-0358
Fax:(410)641-3605

Circa 1859. This magnificent pre-Civil War mansion is a tribute to Southern plantation architecture. The inn features antique period furniture, handwoven, Victorian era rugs and a square grand piano. The ballroom, now a parlor for guests, boasts twin fireplaces and pier mirrors. (Ask to see the hidden cupboards behind the fireside bookcases in the

library.) Nineteen acres of grounds are beautifully landscaped and feature azaleas, boxwoods and 125 varieties of trees.

Innkeeper(s): Kirk Burbage. $95-150. MC VISA. 8 rooms, 6 with PB, 4 with FP. 1 suite. Breakfast included in rates. Type of meal: full breakfast. Afternoon tea available. Beds: QD. Air conditioning in room. Cable TV on premises. Amusement parks, antiques, fishing, shopping and watersports nearby.

Seen in: Washington Post, Baltimore Sun, Southern Living.

"Pure elegance and privacy at its finest."

Certificate may be used: Advance reservations required. Sunday through Thursday only, year-round and available at the discretion of innkeeper at all other times, including weekends. Notify innkeeper of promotion when making reservation. Other times based on availability.

Betterton
B9

Lantern Inn B&B
115 Ericsson Ave, PO Box 29,
Betterton, MD 21610-9746
(410)348-5809 (800)499-7265

Circa 1904. Framed by a picket fence and a wide front porch, this four-story country inn is located one block from Betterton beach, a boating and fishing area. Simply furnished rooms are comfortable and air-conditioned. A hearty hunter's breakfast is served each morning. The surrounding area is world-famous for its hunting of Canadian geese and snow geese from the arctic tundra.

Innkeeper(s): Kenneth Washburn. $68-85. MC VISA. 13 rooms, 4 with PB. Breakfast included in rates. Type of meal: continental-plus breakfast. Beds: KDT. Antiques, fishing and watersports nearby.

Location: On the Chesapeake Bay.

Seen in: Richland Times-Dispatch, North Carolina Outdoorsman, Washingtonian, Mid-Atlantic Country.

"Thanks for your warm hospitality."

Certificate may be used: Sunday through Thursday, Jan. 15-Dec. 15, holidays excluded.

Buckeystown
B6

Catoctin Inn & Antiques
3613 Buckeystown Pike,
Buckeystown, MD 21717
(301)874-5555 (800)730-5550

Circa 1780. The inn's four acres of dogwood, magnolias, maples and sweeping lawns overlook the village and the Catoctin Mountains range. Some special features of the inn include a library with marble fireplaces and a handsome wraparound veranda. A gazebo marks the site for weddings, showers and receptions for up to 150 guests. An antique shop on the property is housed in a two-story Victorian carriage house. Nearby villages to visit include Harper's Ferry, Antietam and New Market. Buckeystown's Monocacy River provides canoeing and fishing.

Innkeeper(s): Terry & Sarah MacGillivray. $65-95. MC VISA AX DS PC. 5 rooms with PB. 1 suite. 3 conference rooms. Breakfast and afternoon tea included in rates. Type of meal: full breakfast. Catering service available. Beds: Q. Air conditioning, turn-down service, cable TV and VCR in room. Library and child care on premises. Antiques, fishing, shopping, downhill skiing, cross-country skiing, sporting events and theater nearby.

Certificate may be used: Sunday-Friday nights.

Cambridge   D9

Glasgow B&B Inn
1500 Hambrooks Blvd,
Cambridge, MD 21613
(410)228-0575

Circa 1760. Located along the Choptank River on seven acres, this brick colonial is reached by way of a long tree-lined driveway. The house was built by Dr. William Murray whose son was a friend to Thomas Jefferson and John Quincy Adams. (According to local legend, part of the U.S. Constitution was written here.) The inn is decorated with country colonial antiques and reproductions, enhanced by high ceilings, a mahogany staircase and deep-window seats.

Innkeeper(s): Martha Rayne. $85-125. MC VISA. 7 rooms, 3 with PB, 6 with FP. Breakfast included in rates. Type of meal: full breakfast. Beds: KQ.

Seen in: Mid-Atlantic Country, Tidewater Times.

Certificate may be used: Monday through Thursday.

Cascade   A6

Bluebird on The Mountain
14700 Eyler Ave,
Cascade, MD 21719-1938
(301)241-4161 (800)362-9526

Circa 1900. In the mountain village of Cascade, this gracious shuttered Georgian manor is situated on two acres of trees and wildflowers. Three suites have double whirlpool tubs. There is an outdoor hot tub as well. The Rose Garden Room and Mt. Magnolia suites have fireplaces and porches overlooking the back garden. The inn is appointed with antiques, lace and white linens, and white wicker.

Innkeeper(s): Eda Smith-Eley. $105-125. MC VISA AX PC. 5 rooms, 3 with PB, 3 with FP. 2 suites. Breakfast included in rates. Types of meals: continental-plus breakfast, full breakfast, gourmet breakfast and early coffee/tea. Room service available. Beds: KQT. Air conditioning, turn-down service, ceiling fan, cable TV and VCR in room. Spa on premises.

Antiques, fishing, parks, shopping, downhill skiing, sporting events, theater and watersports nearby.

Seen in: Warm Welcomes, Baltimore Sun, Frederick News.

"A wonderful balance of luxury and at-home comfort."

Certificate may be used: January-April, Monday-Thursday nights.

Chestertown   C9

Brampton Inn
25227 Chestertown Rd,
Chestertown, MD 21620-3944
(410)778-1860 Fax:(410)778-1805

Circa 1860. Situated on 35 acres of gardens, meadows and woodland on Maryland's Eastern Shore between the Chester River and Chesapeake Bay, Brampton is a graceful three-story brick, Greek Italianate Revival house. Swiss innkeeper Danielle Hanscom selected family antiques to furnish the parlor and dining room. A massive walnut staircase winds to the upstairs where spacious rooms feature canopied beds, antiques and reproductions. A full country breakfast is served.

Innkeeper(s): Michael & Danielle Hanscom. $95-155. MAP. MC VISA AX PC TC. 10 rooms, 8 with PB, 8 with FP. 2 suites. 2 cottages. Breakfast and afternoon tea included in rates. Types of meals: full breakfast, gourmet breakfast and early coffee/tea. Beds: KQDT. Air conditioning and ceiling fan in room. Fax, copier and library on premises. Handicap access. Antiques, shopping, theater and watersports nearby.

Seen in: Washington Post, New York Times.

"A stately beauty that exudes peace and tranquility."

Certificate may be used: All year, Sunday-Thursday.

Lauretum Inn B&B
954 High St,
Chestertown, MD 21620-3955
(410)778-3236 (800)742-3236
Fax:(410)778-1922

Circa 1870. At the end of a long winding driveway this massive Queen Anne Victorian commands a hilltop setting on six acres just outside of town. Inviting parlors and a porch are available to guests.

Spacious guest rooms overlook the inn's lawns, often visited by deer in the early morning. Peg, the mother of 16 children, once plied the intracoastal waters on her 40-foot boat and can help you plan your stay in the area.

Innkeeper(s): Peg Sites. $60-115. MC VISA AX DS PC. 5 rooms, 3 with PB. 2 suites. Breakfast, afternoon tea and evening snack included in rates. Types of meals: continental-plus breakfast and early coffee/tea. Beds: QDT. Air conditioning in room. VCR and fax on premises. Antiques, fishing, parks, shopping, sporting events, theater and watersports nearby.

Certificate may be used: Jan. 2-Feb. 28, Sunday-Saturday.

The Inn at Mitchell House
8796 Maryland Pkwy,
Chestertown, MD 21620-4209
(410)778-6500

Circa 1743. This pristine 18th-century manor house sits as a jewel on 12 acres overlooking Stoneybrook Pond. The guest rooms and the inn's several parlors are preserved and appointed in an authentic Colonial mood, heightened by handsome

polished wide-board floors. Eastern Neck Island National Wildlife Refuge, Remington Farms, St. Michaels, Annapolis and nearby Chestertown are all delightful to explore. The Inn at Mitchell House is a popular setting for romantic weddings and small corporate meetings.

Innkeeper(s): Tracy Stone. $75-110. MC VISA. 6 rooms, 5 with PB, 2 with FP. 2 suites. Breakfast included in rates. Types of meals: full breakfast and early coffee/tea. Afternoon tea and gourmet lunch available. Beds: KQ. Air conditioning and turn-down service in room. VCR on premises. Antiques, fishing, shopping, sporting events, theater and watersports nearby.

Seen in: Washingtonian, New York, Glamour, Philadelphia Inquirer, Baltimore Sun, Kent County News, Ten Best Inns in the Country.

Certificate may be used: Sunday through Thursday, excluding holidays.

Easton D9

Gross' Coate Plantation 1658
11300 Gross' Coate Rd,
Easton, MD 21601-5458
(410)819-0802 (800)580-0802
Fax:(410)819-0803

Circa 1760. Lord Baltimore granted this expansive property to Roger Gross in 1658, and the plantation home, a classic example of Georgian architecture, dates back to 1760. The innkeepers purchased the

home in 1983 and after extensive renovation have restored the manor and several other buildings to their original glory. The innkeepers also added a swimming pool and four ponds for waterfowl and wildlife conservation. The dining room floor was built in 1850 from walnut trees which fell during a hurricane. The south parlor still features the home's original mantel with hand-carved reeded pilasters, rope carving and tabour fluting.

Innkeeper(s): Jon & Molly Ginn. $295-495. MC VISA AX DS PC. 8 suites, 6 with FP. 1 conference room. Breakfast and afternoon tea included in rates. Types of meals: continental-plus breakfast, gourmet breakfast and early coffee/tea. Beds: KQDT. Turn-down service in room. VCR, fax, copier, swimming, bicycles, library and pet boarding on premises. Antiques, fishing, parks, shopping, sporting events, theater and watersports nearby.

Location: On Chesapeake Bay.

Seen in: Chesapeake Current, Garden Design, Mid Atlantic, Southern Living, Washingtonian, Washington Post Weekend, Homes of the Cavaliers.

"Your inn is beautiful and so peaceful, relaxing, we will most definitely return and look forward to your gracious hospitality in the future."

Certificate may be used: January-March, all days of the week, excluding holidays.

The McDaniel House

14 N Aurora St, Easton, MD 21601-3617
(410)822-3704 (800)787-4667

Circa 1840. A wide veranda wraps around this three-story white Queen Anne Victorian, complete with octagonal tower, dormers and a wraparound porch. Located in the historic district, considered to be the "Colonial Capital of the Eastern Shore," it's within walking distance to the Classic Avalon Theater, Academy of Art, many good restaurants and unique shops. A large barn on the property often is used by cyclists for storing their bicycles while visiting the inn.

Innkeeper(s): Debra Mughrabi. $75-110. MC VISA AX PC TC. 8 rooms, 6 with PB. Breakfast, afternoon tea and evening snack included in rates. Types of meals: continental breakfast and continental-plus breakfast. Room service available. Beds: KQD. Air conditioning and ceiling fan in room. Cable TV on premises. Antiques, fishing, parks, shopping and watersports nearby.

Certificate may be used: Nov. 30, 1996 - April 30, 1997.

Hagerstown   A5

Beaver Creek House B&B

20432 Beaver Creek Rd,
Hagerstown, MD 21740-1514
(301)797-4764

Circa 1905. History buffs enjoy this turn-of-the-century inn located minutes away from Antietam and Harpers Ferry National Historical Parks. The surrounding villages house antique shops and some hold weekend auctions. The inn features a courtyard with a fountain and a country garden. Innkeepers

Don and Shirley Day furnished the home with family antiques and memorabilia. Guests can sip afternoon tea or complimentary sherry in the elegant parlor or just relax on the porch and take in the view of South Mountain.

Innkeeper(s): Donald & Shirley Day. $75-95. MC VISA AX PC TC. 5 rooms with PB. 1 conference room. Breakfast included in rates. Types of meals: full breakfast, gourmet breakfast and early coffee/tea. Beds: DT. Air conditioning and ceiling fan in room. Copier on premises.

Amusement parks, antiques, fishing, parks, shopping, downhill skiing, cross-country skiing, sporting events, theater and watersports nearby.
Seen in: Baltimore Sun, Hagerstown Journal, Herald Mail, Washington Post, Frederick.

"Thanks so much for your hospitality. You're wonderful hosts and breakfast was delicious as usual. Don't change a thing."

Certificate may be used: Year-round, Monday through Thursday.

Sunday's B&B

39 Broadway,
Hagerstown, MD 21740-4019
(800)221-4828

Circa 1890. This Queen Anne Victorian is appropriately appointed with period antiques. Fresh flowers and fruit baskets are provided and guests are pampered with a full breakfast, afternoon tea, evening wine and cheese and for late evening, bedside cordials and truffles. Antietam, Harpers Ferry and the C&O Canal are nearby.

Innkeeper(s): Robert Ferrino. $95-105. 3 rooms with PB. Breakfast included in rates. Types of meals: full breakfast and early coffee/tea. Afternoon tea, dinner, picnic lunch and catering service available. Beds: QD. Air conditioning and cable TV in room. Antiques, fishing, parks, shopping, downhill skiing and theater nearby.

Location: Twenty minutes from Antietam Battlefields.

"You made a wedding night in heaven."

Certificate may be used: Anytime, seven days a week, year-round.

Havre De Grace   B9

Spencer Silver Mansion

200 S Union Ave,
Havre De Grace, MD 21078-3224
(410)939-1097 (800)780-1485

Circa 1896. This elegant granite Victorian mansion is graced with bays, gables, balconies, a turret and a gazebo veranda. The Victorian decor, with antiques and Oriental rugs, complements the house's carved-oak woodwork, fireplace mantels and parquet floors. The Concord Point Lighthouse (oldest continuously operated lighthouse in America) is only a walk

away. In addition to the four rooms in the main house, a romantic carriage house suite is available, featuring an in-room fireplace, TV, whirlpool bath and kitchenette.

Innkeeper(s): Carol & Jim Nemeth. $65-125. MC VISA AX DS PC TC. 5 rooms, 3 with PB, 1 with FP. 1 cottage. Breakfast included in rates. Types of meals: full breakfast and early coffee/tea. Beds: QDT. Air conditioning, turn-down service and cable TV in room. Antiques, fishing, parks, shopping and watersports nearby.

Location: In the heart of the historic district, 2 blocks from the waterfront.

Seen in: Mid-Atlantic Country, Maryland.

"A fabulous find. Beautiful house, excellent hostess. I've stayed at a lot of B&Bs, but this house is the best."

Certificate may be used: Monday through Thursday, all year.

Middletown B5

Stone Manor Country Club
5820 Carroll Boyer Rd,
Middletown, MD 21769-6315
(301)473-5454 Fax:(301)371-5622

Circa 1780. If you're searching for a romantic, secluded getaway and hope to be pampered with fine cuisine and elegant surroundings, head for this impressive stone estate house. Tucked between mountain ranges on 114 acres of picturesque farmland, the home often is the site of weddings and receptions. Despite the size of this manor home, the interior is intimate and inviting, filled with a variety of styles and furnishings. Each of the rooms, named for flowers, afford tranquil views of gardens, ponds or woods. A variety of drinks, fruit and cheese are placed in the guest rooms upon arrival. The inn hosts a variety of seminars, accompanied by gourmet buffets, with items such as chilled melon and lemon balm soup or pan roasted salmon with beurre blanc. The dinner menu is filled with equally impressive fare.

Innkeeper(s): Judith Harne. $125-250. MC VISA AX TC. 5 rooms with PB, 4 with FP. 4 suites. Breakfast included in rates. Types of meals: continental breakfast, continental-plus breakfast, full breakfast, gourmet breakfast and early coffee/tea. Afternoon tea, dinner, evening snack, picnic lunch, lunch, gourmet lunch, banquet service and catering service available. Beds: Q. Air conditioning, turn-down service and ceiling fan in room. VCR, fax, copier and child care on premises. Handicap access. Antiques, fishing, parks, shopping, downhill skiing, cross-country skiing, sporting events, theater and watersports nearby.

Certificate may be used: January, February, March, July, August, November; Tuesday, Wednesday & Thursday evenings.

New Market B6

National Pike Inn
PO Box 299,
New Market, MD 21774-0299
(301)865-5055

Circa 1796. This red shuttered brick Federal-style home is one of the few inns remaining on the National Pike, an old route that carried travelers from Baltimore to points west. The inn's Colonial decor includes wingback chairs, Oriental rugs and four-poster beds. Azalea gardens border a private courtyard and fountain. New Market, founded in 1793, offers more than 30 antique shops and other charming points of interest, including an old-fashion general store, all within walking distance of the inn.

Innkeeper(s): Tom & Terry Rimel. $75-125. MC VISA PC TC. 6 rooms, 4 with PB, 3 with FP. 1 suite. 1 conference room. Breakfast included in rates. Type of meal: full breakfast. Beds: QD. Air conditioning in room. Cable TV and VCR on premises. Antiques, shopping, sporting events and theater nearby.

Location: Exit 62 off interstate 70, 6 miles east of Frederick, Maryland.

Seen in: Mid-Atlantic Country, Country.

"A total joy! A relaxed, charming and romantic setting."

Certificate may be used: Monday-Thursday, two-night minimum. Excludes special events.

Oakland C9

Harley Farm B&B
16766 Garrett Hwy,
Oakland, MD 21550-4036
(301)387-9050 (888)231-3276
Fax:(301)387-9050

Circa 1990. From the drive, this B&B appears as an unassuming, albeit charming, farmhouse surrounded by acres of rolling hills. Inside, the innkeepers have added many elegant touches, transforming the home into a gracious retreat with Chinese carpets, tapestries and European furnishings. The innkeepers host a variety of classes and workshops throughout the year, with subjects ranging from yoga, art, leadership and management. Guests can sign up for seasonal programs as well, one workshop teaches guests how to create their own Williamsburg Christmas, while another instructs guests on how to prepare fresh apple and pumpkin butter. Croquet, badminton and volleyball courts are set up on the grounds, and summertime brings hay rides and barn dances.

Innkeeper(s): Wayne & Kam Gillespie. $70-100. MC VISA AX DS PC TC. 7 rooms with PB. 1 suite. Breakfast included in rates. Type of meal:

full breakfast. Beds: QD. Air conditioning and ceiling fan in room. Cable TV, VCR, spa, bicycles and library on premises. Antiques, fishing, parks, shopping, downhill skiing, cross-country skiing and watersports nearby.

Certificate may be used: April-June (Sunday-Thursday) not including holiday weekends, September, November (same terms).

Ocean City   E11

Atlantic House
501 N Baltimore Ave,
Ocean City, MD 21842-3926
(410)289-2333

Circa 1927. From the front porch of this bed & breakfast, guests can partake in ocean views. The rooms are decorated in a casual, beach style with simple furnishings. The morning breakfast buffet includes such items as freshly baked breads, fruit, cereals, egg casseroles and yogurt. In the afternoons, light refreshments also are served. The inn is a short walk to the beach, boardwalk and shopping.

Innkeeper(s): Paul & Debi Cook. $55-145. MC VISA AX DS TC. 14 rooms, 8 with PB. 1 suite. 1 conference room. Breakfast, afternoon tea and evening snack included in rates. Types of meals: full breakfast and early coffee/tea. Beds: QD. Air conditioning, ceiling fan and cable TV in room. Spa and swimming on premises. Amusement parks, antiques, fishing, parks, shopping, sporting events, theater and watersports nearby.

Certificate may be used: Labor Day to Memorial Day, Sunday-Thursday.

Saint Michaels   D8

Kemp House Inn
412 Talbot St, PO Box 638,
Saint Michaels, MD 21663
(410)745-2243

Circa 1807. This two-story Georgian house was built by Colonel Joseph Kemp, a shipwright and one of the town forefathers. The inn is appointed in period furnishings accentuated by candlelight. Guest rooms include patchwork quilts, a collection of four-poster rope beds and old-fashioned nightshirts. There are several working fireplaces. Robert E. Lee is said to have been a guest.

Innkeeper(s): Diane M. Cooper. $65-105. MC VISA DS. 8 rooms, 6 with PB, 4 with FP. Breakfast included in rates. Types of meals: continental breakfast and early coffee/tea. Catered breakfast available. Beds: QDT. Air conditioning in room. Antiques, fishing, shopping and watersports nearby.

Location: Historic town on the eastern shore of the Chesapeake.

Seen in: Gourmet, Philadelphia.

"It was wonderful. We've stayed in many B&Bs, and this was one of the nicest!"

Certificate may be used: Sunday through Thursday nights, excluding holidays. Year-round.

Parsonage Inn
210 N Talbot St,
Saint Michaels, MD 21663-2102
(410)745-5519 (800)394-5519

Circa 1883. A striking Victorian steeple rises next to the wide bay of this brick residence, once the home of Henry Clay Dodson, state senator, pharmacist and brickyard owner. The house features brick

detail in a variety of patterns and inlays, perhaps a design statement for brick customers. Porches are decorated with filigree and spindled columns. Laura Ashley linens, late Victorian furnishings, fireplaces and decks add to the creature comforts. Four bikes await guests who wish to ride to Tilghman Island or to the ferry that goes to Oxford. Gourmet breakfast is served in the dining room.

Innkeeper(s): Willard Workman. $90-145. MC VISA PC TC. 8 rooms with PB, 3 with FP. Breakfast included in rates. Types of meals: full breakfast and gourmet breakfast. Beds: KQD. Air conditioning and ceiling fan in room. Cable TV and bicycles on premises. Handicap access. Antiques, fishing, shopping and watersports nearby.

Location: In the historic district.

Seen in: Wilmington, Delaware News Journal, Philadelphia Inquirer.

"Striking, extensively renovated."

Certificate may be used: Sunday through Thursday, November until June.

Snow Hill   E10

Chanceford Hall Inn
209 W Federal St,
Snow Hill, MD 21863-1159
(410)632-2231

Circa 1759. This pre-Revolutionary War inn is listed in the National Register and Smithsonian's "Guide to Historic America." Rooms feature romantic, canopy beds and the home boasts 10 fireplaces and Oriental rugs throughout. Afternoon wine and

CIRCA 1769

hors d'oeuvres are served after guests check in, and a full breakfast is served each morning in the inn's formal dining room. Spend the day exploring the Snow Hill area, or simply relax by the pool. The innkeepers offer bicycles for their guests.

Innkeeper(s): Michael & Thelma C. Driscoll. $115-135. PC TC. 5 rooms with PB, 4 with FP. 1 suite. Breakfast included in rates. Types of meals: full breakfast, gourmet breakfast and early coffee/tea. Beds: Q. Air conditioning in room. Cable TV, VCR, copier, swimming and bicycles on premises. Antiques, fishing, parks, shopping and watersports nearby.

Certificate may be used: Monday through Thursday, December through May.

River House Inn
201 E Market St,
Snow Hill, MD 21863-2000
(410)632-2722 Fax:(410)632-2866

Circa 1860. This picturesque Gothic Revival house rests on the banks of the Pocomoke River and boasts its own dock. Its two acres roll down to the river over long tree-studded lawns. Lawn furniture and a hammock add to the invitation to relax as do

the inn's porches. Some guest rooms feature marble fireplaces. The 17th-century village of Snow Hill boasts old brick sidewalks and historic homes. Canoes can be rented a block from the inn or you may wish to take a river cruise on the innkeeper's pontoon boat.

Innkeeper(s): Larry & Susanne Knudsen. $92-152. MC VISA AX TC. 11 rooms, 9 with PB, 1 with FP. 2 suites. 1 cottage. Breakfast and evening snack included in rates. Types of meals: full breakfast and early coffee/tea. Beds: KQT. Air conditioning and ceiling fan in room. Cable TV, VCR, fax, copier, bicycles, library and child care on premises. Handicap access. Amusement parks, antiques, fishing, shopping and watersports nearby.

Seen in: Daily Times.

"Thank you for making our first B&B an exceptional one."

Certificate may be used: November-April except holiday weekends; May-October, Sunday-Thursday, except holidays.

Snow Hill Inn
104 E Market St,
Snow Hill, MD 21863-1067
(410)632-2102 Fax:(410)632-3623

Circa 1790. Gables, chimneys and blue shutters highlight the exterior of this Victorian country home. Two of the guest rooms include working fireplaces, and all are decorated with period furnishings. Plan on taking a picnic, because the innkeepers will pack up a box or basket filled with gourmet goodies from the inn's restaurant. Walking tours of Snow Hill's historic district, which features more than 100 homes and churches, are popular.

Innkeeper(s): Jim & Kathy Washington. $75. MC VISA AX TC. 3 rooms with PB, 1 with FP. Breakfast included in rates. Type of meal: continental-plus breakfast. Dinner and lunch available. Beds: QD. Air conditioning in room. Cable TV on premises. Antiques, fishing, parks, shopping and watersports nearby.

Certificate may be used: Sunday-Friday.

Solomons Island   E8

Solomons Victorian Inn
125 Charles Street,
Solomons Island, MD 20688-0759
(410)326-4811 Fax:(410)326-0133

Circa 1906. The Davis family, renowned for their shipbuilding talents, constructed this elegant Queen Anne Victorian at the turn of the century. Each of the inn's elegant common rooms and bedchambers boast special touches such as antiques, oriental rugs and lacy curtains. The home affords views of Solomons Harbor and its entrance into the picturesque Chesapeake Bay. Weekend guests are treated to an expansive breakfast in a dining room, which overlooks the harbor.

Innkeeper(s): Richard & Helen Bauer. $80-165. MC VISA PC. 6 rooms with PB. 1 suite. Breakfast and evening snack included in rates. Types of meals: full breakfast, gourmet breakfast and early coffee/tea. Beds: KQT. Air conditioning in room. Cable TV, fax and library on premises. Antiques, fishing, parks, shopping, theater and watersports nearby.

Certificate may be used: Sept. 15-May 15, Sunday-Thursday.

Westminster A7

The Winchester Country Inn
111 Stoner Ave,
Westminster, MD 21157-5451
(410)876-7373 (800)887-3950
Fax:(410)848-7409

Circa 1760. William Winchester, the founder of
Westminster, built this unusual English-style house.
It has a steeply slanted roof similar to those found in
the Tidewater area. A central fireplace opens to

both the parlor and the central hall. Colonial-
period furnishings prevail, with some items loaned
by the local historic society. Community volunteers,
historians, craftsmen and designers helped restore
the inn. A non-profit agency provides some of the
housekeeping and gardening staff from its develop-
mentally disabled program.

Innkeeper(s): Estella Williams. $40-75. AP. VISA. 5 rooms, 3 with PB.
Breakfast included in rates. Type of meal: full breakfast. Catering service
available. Beds: K. Air conditioning, cable TV and VCR in room.
Handicap access. Antiques, fishing, parks, shopping and theater nearby.

Seen in: Country Living, Evening Sun, Towson Flier, Itinerary, Cracker
Barrell, Carroll County Sun.

"We give your inn an A+. Our stay was perfect."

Certificate may be used: Jan. 1-May 31, Sunday-Saturday; Oct. 1-
Dec. 31, Sunday-Saturday.

Massachusetts

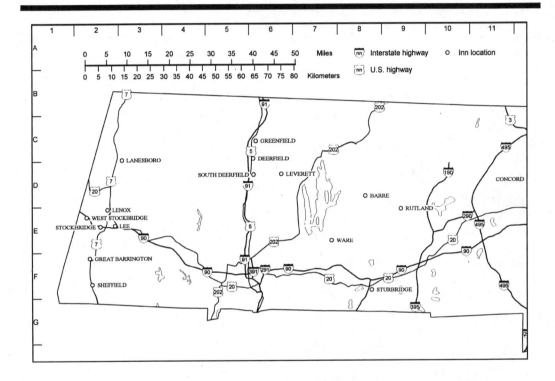

| | 1 | 2 | 3 | 4 | 5 | 6 | 7 | 8 | 9 | 10 | 11 |

0 5 10 15 20 25 30 35 40 45 50   Miles   (nn) Interstate highway   o Inn location

0 5 10 15 20 25 30 35 40 45 50 55 60 65 70 75 80   Kilometers   (nn) U.S. highway

GREENFIELD
LANESBORO
DEERFIELD
SOUTH DEERFIELD   LEVERETT
LENOX
WEST STOCKBRIDGE   BARRE
STOCKBRIDGE   LEE   RUTLAND
GREAT BARRINGTON   WARE
SHEFFIELD   STURBRIDGE
CONCORD

Barnstable   I17

Beechwood Inn
2839 Main St, Rt 6A,
Barnstable, MA 02630-1017
(508)362-6618 (800)609-6618
Fax:(508)362-0298

Circa 1853. Beechwood is a beautifully restored
Queen Anne Victorian offering period furnishings,
some rooms with fireplaces or ocean views. Its
warmth and elegance make it a favorite hideaway
for couples looking for a peaceful and romantic
return to the Victorian Era. The inn is named for
rare old beech trees that shade the veranda.
Innkeeper(s): Debbie & Ken Traugot. $90-150. MC VISA AX PC TC. 6
rooms with PB, 2 with FP. Breakfast and afternoon tea included in rates.

Type of meal: early coffee/tea. Beds: KQD. Fax, copier, bicycles and
library on premises. Antiques, fishing, parks, shopping, sporting
events, theater and watersports nearby.

Location: Cape Cod's historic North Shore.

Seen in: New England Weekends, Rhode Island Monthly.

*"Your inn is pristine in every detail. We concluded that
the innkeepers, who are most hospitable, are the best
part of Beechwood."*

Certificate may be used: November through April, anytime except holiday weekends.

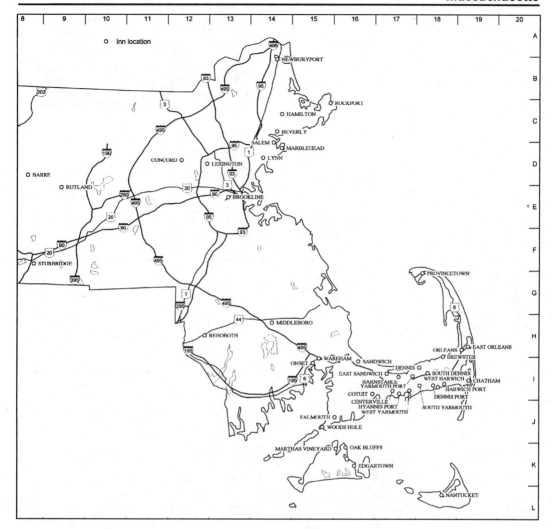

Crocker Tavern B&B

3095 Main St, Barnstable, MA 02630
(508)362-5115 (800)773-5359
Fax:(508)362-5562

Circa 1754. This historic Cape Cod inn once served as a headquarters for the Whigs during the Revolutionary Era. The inn is part of the Olde Kings Highway Historic District, and also is listed on the National Register. Visitors choose from five guest rooms in this two-story Georgian-style inn, each with a four-poster or canopy bed, sitting area and antiques. Several rooms include working fireplaces. Many of this homes Colonial elements have been beautifully restored, such as the wood plank floors, exposed beams, window seats and the elegant woodwork. The B&B is within walking distance to restaurants, antique shops, historic sites and the harbor, where guests sign up for whale-watching excursions.

Innkeeper(s): Sue & Jeff Carlson. $70-105. MC VISA PC TC. 5 rooms with PB, 2 with FP. Breakfast and evening snack included in rates. Types of meals: continental-plus breakfast and early coffee/tea. Afternoon tea available. Beds: QD. Air conditioning in room. Fax and library on premises. Handicap access. Antiques, fishing, parks, shopping, cross-country skiing, theater and watersports nearby.

Seen in: Cape Cod Times, Society for the Preservation of New England Antiquities.

Certificate may be used: Nov. 1-May 15, weekends.

Barre D8

The Jenkins House B&B Inn
Rt 122/32 at Barre Common,
Barre, MA 01005
(508)355-6444 (800)378-7373

Circa 1834. Five guest rooms await visitors at this handsome Gothic Revival inn. Three of the rooms feature private baths, and other amenities include air conditioning, ceiling fans, desks and turndown service. One guest room boasts a romantic fireplace. The full breakfast may include chocolate waffles and homemade muffins or scones. The Woods Memorial Library is just a few steps from the inn, and Rutland State Park is within easy driving distance.

Innkeeper(s): David Ward. $70-120. MC VISA AX DS. 5 rooms, 3 with PB, 1 with FP. Breakfast included in rates. Type of meal: full breakfast. Evening snack and room service available. Beds: KQDT. Air conditioning, turn-down service and ceiling fan in room. Pet boarding on premises. Antiques, fishing, shopping, downhill skiing, cross-country skiing and theater nearby.

Certificate may be used: Year-round, Monday through Thursday, excludes holidays, events and October.

Beverly C14

Bunny's B&B
17 Kernwood Hgts, Beverly, MA 01915
(508)922-2392

Circa 1940. This Dutch Colonial inn is located on a scenic route along the state's northeastern coast. One room features a decorative fireplace and a handmade Oriental rug. Breakfasts in the formal dining room always feature homemade muffins and the innkeepers will make every effort to meet special dietary needs if notified in advance.

Innkeeper(s): Bunny & Joe Stacey. $55-85. TC. 4 rooms, 2 with PB. Breakfast included in rates. Type of meal: continental-plus breakfast. Beds: QDT. Antiques, parks, shopping and theater nearby.

Certificate may be used: Nov. 19 to May 13, Sunday to Saturday.

Brewster H18

Old Sea Pines Inn
2553 Main St, PO Box 1026,
Brewster, MA 02631-1959
(508)896-6114 Fax:(508)896-8322

Circa 1900. This turn-of-the-century mansion on three-and-one-half acres of lawns and trees was formerly the Sea Pines School of Charm and Personality for Young Women, established in 1907. Recently renovated, the inn displays elegant

wallpapers and a grand sweeping stairway. It is located near beaches and bike paths, as well as village shops and restaurants.

Innkeeper(s): Michele Rowan. $45-105. MC VISA AX DC DS. 21 rooms, 14 with PB, 3 with FP. 2 suites. 1 conference room. Breakfast and afternoon tea included in rates. Types of meals: full breakfast and early coffee/tea. Evening snack, picnic lunch, banquet service, catering service and room service available. Beds: QDT. Air conditioning and cable TV in room. Handicap access. Antiques, fishing, shopping, theater and watersports nearby.

Location: Cape Cod.

Seen in: New York Times, Cape Cod Oracle, For Women First, Home Office, Entrepreneur.

"The loving care applied by Steve, Michele and staff is deeply appreciated."

Certificate may be used: Weekdays only March 31-May 31 and weekdays only Oct. 15-Dec. 21.

Brookline E13

The Bertram Inn
92 Sewall Ave, Brookline, MA 02146
(617)566-2234 (800)295-3822
Fax:(617)277-1887

Circa 1907. Antiques and authenticity are the rule at this turn-of-the-century Gothic Revival inn, found on a peaceful, tree-lined street. Innkeeper Bryan R. Austin is well-versed in the restoration of historical properties and furniture. That knowledge is evident at the Bertram Inn, with its old-English stylings and Victorian decor. Boston College, Boston University, Fenway Park and the F.L. Olmstead National Historic Site all are nearby. Shops and restaurants are within walking distance.

Innkeeper(s): Bryan Austin. $59-164. MC VISA PC TC. 13 rooms, 11 with PB, 2 with FP. Breakfast included in rates. Type of meal: continental-plus breakfast. Afternoon tea available. Beds: KQDT. Air conditioning, ceiling fan and cable TV in room. Fax on premises. Antiques, parks, shopping, sporting events and theater nearby.

Seen in: Where Boston.

"This B&B is just wonderful, I can't imagine a nicer place. Thank you for your warm generosity, a fine substitute for home."

Certificate may be used: Nov. 15 to April 15, Sunday-Friday.

Centerville 117

Copper Beech Inn of Cape Cod

497 Main St, Centerville, MA 02632
(508)771-5488 Fax:(508)775-2884

Circa 1830. Shaded by a massive European beech tree is this white clapboard house, listed in the National Register. It was built by Captain Hillman Crosby, a name long associated with boat builders and fast sailing ships. Preserved and restored, the inn is a walk away to Craigville Beach, considered one of the 10 best beaches in the United States. Summer theater and fine restaurants are also nearby.

Innkeeper(s): Joyce Diehl. $80-90. MAP. MC VISA AX DS PC TC. 3 rooms with PB. Breakfast included in rates. Types of meals: full breakfast and early coffee/tea. Beds: KQD. Air conditioning and turn-down service in room. Cable TV, VCR, fax, copier, bicycles and library on premises. Antiques, fishing, parks, shopping, sporting events, theater and watersports nearby.

Seen in: Innsider, Cape Cod Life, Cape Cod Times, Country.

"Everything we were looking for, clean and private, but best of all were our wonderful hosts."

Certificate may be used: Sunday through Thursday.

Chatham 119

Carriage House Inn

407 Old Harbor Rd,
Chatham, MA 02633-2322
(508)945-4688 (800)355-8868
Fax:(508)945-4688

Circa 1890. The charming Cape Cod resort town of Chatham is home to this Colonial Revival inn which features English and Traditional decor. Guests will enjoy the special touches, such as turn-down-service and fresh chocolates on the pillows

each night. The inn's garden helps furnish fresh flowers for its tasteful interior. Borrow a bike for a tour of the area, or relax in front of the fireplace. Beach towels are furnished for trips to the shore, just a quarter-mile mile away. The Monomoy National Wildlife Reserve also is nearby.

Innkeeper(s): Pam & Tom Patton. $85-165. MC VISA AX PC TC. 6 rooms with PB, 3 with FP. Breakfast and evening snack included in rates. Types of meals: continental-plus breakfast and early coffee/tea. Beds: Q. Air conditioning and ceiling fan in room. Cable TV, VCR, fax and bicycles on premises. Antiques, fishing, parks, shopping, theater and watersports nearby.

"This might well have been our best B&B experience ever. It was the hosts who made it so memorable."

Certificate may be used: November-April, Sunday-Thursday, excluding holidays. Subject to availability.

Cyrus Kent House

63 Cross St, Chatham, MA 02633-2207
(508)945-9104 (800)338-5368
Fax:(508)945-9104

Circa 1877. A former sea captain's home, the Cyrus Kent House was built in the Greek Revival style. The award-winning restoration retained many original features such as wide pine floorboards, ceiling rosettes, and marble fireplaces. Although furnished with antiques and reproductions, all modern amenities are available. Most bedrooms have four-poster beds. Suites feature sitting rooms with fireplaces. Chatham's historic district is a short stroll away.

Innkeeper(s): Sharon Mitchell-Swan. $85-175. MC VISA. 10 rooms with PB, 2 with FP. 3 suites. Breakfast and afternoon tea included in rates. Types of meals: continental-plus breakfast and early coffee/tea. Beds: QD. Cable TV in room. Fax on premises. Antiques, fishing, shopping and watersports nearby.

Location: Located on a quiet side street within easy walking distance of the historic village of Chatham.

Seen in: Country Inns.

Certificate may be used: November through April 15.

Old Harbor Inn

22 Old Harbor Rd, Chatham, MA 02633
(508)945-4434 (800)942-4434
Fax:(508)945-2492

Circa 1932. This pristine New England bed & breakfast was once the home of "Doc" Keene, a popular physician in the area. A meticulous renovation has created an elegant, beautifully appointed inn offering antique furnishings, designer linens and lavish amenities in an English country decor. A buffet breakfast, featuring Sharon's homemade scones, is served in the sunroom or on the deck. The beaches, boutiques and galleries are a walk away and there is an old grist mill, the Chatham Lighthouse, and a railroad museum. Band concerts are offered Friday nights in the summer at Kate Gould Park.

Innkeeper(s): Tom & Sharon Ferguson. $95-195. MC VISA DC CB DS PC TC. 8 rooms with PB, 2 with FP. 2 suites. 1 conference room. Breakfast included in rates. Types of meals: continental-plus breakfast and early coffee/tea. Afternoon tea and picnic lunch available. Beds: KQT. Air conditioning, turn-down service and ceiling fan in room. VCR, bicycles and library on premises. Antiques, fishing, parks, shopping, theater and watersports nearby.

Location: On the elbow of Cape Cod.

Seen in: Herald News, Traveler, Country Inns, Boston, Cape Cod Life, Country Inns, Cape Cod Travel Guide, Honeymoon.

"The Old Harbor Inn—what a delight! Muffins in the morning, serenity at night. The comforts of home—it does not lack. You can be sure that we'll be back."

Certificate may be used: Oct. 15 through June 15, Sunday through Thursday.

Concord D12

Colonel Roger Brown House

1694 Main St, Concord, MA 01742-2831
(508)369-9119 (800)292-1369
Fax:(508)369-1305

Circa 1775. This house was the home of Minuteman Roger Brown who fought the British at the Old North Bridge. The frame for this center-chimney Colonial was raised April 19, the day the battle took place. Some parts of the house were built as early as 1708. The adjacent Damon Mill houses a fitness club available to guests. Both buildings are in the National Register.

Innkeeper(s): Lauri Berlied. $75-90. MC VISA AX DC PC TC. 5 rooms with PB. 1 suite. Breakfast and afternoon tea included in rates. Type of meal: continental-plus breakfast. Beds: QT. Air conditioning in room. Fax, copier, computer, spa, swimming, sauna and library on premises. Antiques, fishing, parks, shopping, downhill skiing, cross-country skiing, theater and watersports nearby.

Seen in: Middlesex News, Concord Journal.

"The Colonel Roger Brown House makes coming to Concord even more of a treat! Many thanks for your warm hospitality."

Certificate may be used: November-May; June-August on availability.

Hawthorne Inn

462 Lexington Rd, Concord, MA 01742
(508)369-5610 Fax:(508)287-4949

Circa 1870. The Hawthorne Inn is situated on land that once belonged to Ralph Waldo Emerson, the Alcotts and Nathaniel Hawthorne. It was here that Bronson Alcott planted his fruit trees, made pathways to the Mill Brook, and erected his Bath House. Hawthorne purchased the land and repaired a path leading to his home with trees planted on either side. Two of these trees still stand. Across the road is Hawthorne's House, The Wayside. Next to it is the Alcott's Orchard House, and Grapevine Cottage where the Concord grape was developed. Nearby is Sleepy Hollow Cemetery

where Emerson, the Alcotts, the Thoreaus, and Hawthorne were laid to rest.

Innkeeper(s): Marilyn Mudry & Gregory Burch. $110-175. MC VISA AX DS PC TC. 7 rooms with PB. Breakfast and afternoon tea included in rates. Type of meal: continental-plus breakfast. Beds: QDT. Air conditioning in room. Fax and library on premises. Antiques, fishing, parks, shopping and cross-country skiing nearby.

Location: On the famed "Battle Road" of 1775. East of Town Green by eight-tenth of a mile.

Seen in: New York Times, Boston Globe, Yankee.

"Surely there couldn't be a better or more valuable location for a comfortable, old-fashioned country inn."

Certificate may be used: November-March, Saturday-Thursday (no Fridays).

Cotuit   I16

Salty Dog B&B Inn

451 Main St, Cotuit, MA 02635-3114
(508)428-5228

A 300-year-old oak rests in front of this seaside Victorian inn, which was owned originally by a sea captain. Guest rooms offer four-poster beds surrounded by country decor. The home features wide floor boards, antique moldings and Oriental rugs. Breakfasts of freshly baked muffins and breads are served in the fireplaced common room. Cotuit, known for its picturesque main street, as well as the surrounding Cape Cod, offers plenty of antiquing, shopping and restaurants.

Innkeeper(s): Gerald Goldstein. $65-105. MC VISA. 5 rooms. Breakfast included in rates. Type of meal: continental-plus breakfast.

Certificate may be used: April through December, Sunday through Thursday.

Deerfield   C6

Deerfield Inn

81 Old Main St, Deerfield, MA 01342
(413)774-5587 (800)926-3865
Fax:(413)773-8712

Circa 1884. Deerfield was settled in 1670. Farmers in the area still unearth bones and ax heads from an ancient Indian massacre. Now 50 beautifully restored colonial and Federal homes line mile-long The Street, considered by many to be the loveliest street in New England. Twelve of these houses are museums open to the public. The inn is situated at the center of this peaceful village and is filled with antiques from historic Deerfield's remarkable collection. The village has been designated a National Historic Landmark.

Innkeeper(s): Jane Sabo. $99-141. MC VISA AX. 23 rooms with PB. 1 conference room. Breakfast and afternoon tea included in rates. Type of meal: full breakfast. Dinner and lunch available. Beds: QT. Fax and copier on premises. Handicap access. Antiques, fishing, cross-country skiing and theater nearby.

Location: Middle of historic village.

Seen in: Travel Today, Country Accents, Colonial Homes, Country Living.

"We've stayed at many New England inns, but the Deerfield Inn ranks among the best."

Certificate may be used: Sunday-Thursday, based on availability, excluding May, September, October.

Dennis   I18

Isaiah Hall B&B Inn

152 Whig St, Dennis, MA 02638-1917
(508)385-9928 (800)736-0160
Fax:(508)385-5879

Circa 1857. Adjacent to the Cape's oldest cranberry bog is this Greek Revival farmhouse built by Isaiah Hall, a cooper. His brother was the first cultivator of cranberries in America and Isaiah designed and patented the original barrel for shipping cranberries. In 1948, Dorothy Gripp, an artist, established the inn. Many examples of her artwork remain.

Innkeeper(s): Marie Brophy. $78-112. MC VISA AX TC. 11 rooms, 10 with PB, 1 with FP. Breakfast included in rates. Types of meals: continental-plus breakfast and early coffee/tea. Beds: QDT. Air conditioning in room. Cable TV and fax on premises. Antiques, fishing, parks, shopping, theater and watersports nearby.

Location: Cape Cod.

Seen in: Cape Cod Life, New York Times, Golf.

"Your place is so lovely and relaxing."

Certificate may be used: April & May, Sunday-Thursday, holidays excluded

Dennisport I18

Rose Petal B&B
152 Sea St, PO Box 974,
Dennisport, MA 02639
(508)398-8470

Circa 1872. This Cape Cod-style home was built for Almond Wixon, whose seafaring family was among the original settlers of Dennisport. In 1918,

Almond was lost at sea with all on board. The Wixon homestead was completely restored in 1986. Surrounded by a white picket fence and attractively landscaped yard, the Rose Petal is situated in the heart of Cape Cod, a short walk from the beach. Home-baked pastries highlight a full breakfast in the dining room.

Innkeeper(s): Gayle & Dan Kelly. $52-92. MC VISA AX. 3 rooms, 2 with PB. Breakfast included in rates. Types of meals: gourmet breakfast and early coffee/tea. Beds: QT. Air conditioning in room. Cable TV on premises. Antiques, fishing, parks, theater and watersports nearby.

"Perfect. Every detail was appreciated."

Certificate may be used: January, February, March anytime; April, May, November, Monday, Tuesday, Wednesday, Thursday only.

East Orleans H19

Ship's Knees Inn
186 Beach Rd, PO Box 756,
East Orleans, MA 02643
(508)255-1312 Fax:(508)240-1351

Circa 1820. This 175-year-old restored sea captain's home is a three-minute walk from the ocean. Rooms are decorated in a nautical style with antiques. Several rooms feature authentic ship's knees, hand-painted trunks, old clipper ship models and four-poster beds. Some rooms boast ocean views and the

Master Suite has a working fireplace. The inn offers swimming and tennis facilities on the grounds. About three miles away, the innkeepers also offer a one-bedroom efficiency apartment and two heated cottages on the Cove. Head into town or spend the day basking in the beauty of Nauset Beach with its picturesque sand dunes.

Innkeeper(s): Jean & Ken Pitchford. $45-100. MC VISA. 11 rooms with PB, 3 with FP. Breakfast included in rates. Type of meal: continental breakfast. Beds: KQDT. Amusement parks, antiques, fishing, parks, shopping, theater and watersports nearby.

Location: One-and-a-half hours from Boston.

Seen in: Boston Globe.

"Warm, homey and very friendly atmosphere. Very impressed with the beamed ceilings."

Certificate may be used: All year, except July, August & holidays excluded.

East Sandwich I17

The Azariah Snow House
529 Rt 6A, East Sandwich, MA 02537
(508)888-6677

Circa 1917. Innkeeper Dia Bacon takes pride in her hospitality and gourmet breakfasts, which might include lobster quiche and hazelnut French toast. Afternoon teas are given, especially on rainy days. Bacon will cook dinner on occasion at the request of guests. The bedrooms are uniquely decorated with fresh cut flowers and handmade quilts. There are plenty of scenic areas for walking and bicycling, and Hyannis, with its shopping and fine restaurants, is nearby.

Innkeeper(s): Dia Bacon. $45-65. TC. 3 rooms. Breakfast and afternoon tea included in rates. Types of meals: full breakfast, gourmet breakfast and early coffee/tea. Picnic lunch available. Beds: Q. VCR and bicycles on premises. Antiques, fishing, theater and watersports nearby.

Certificate may be used: Year-round, Sunday-Thursday.

Wingscorton Farm Inn
Rt 6A, Olde Kings Hwy,
East Sandwich, MA 02537
(508)888-0534

Circa 1763. Wingscorton is a working farm on seven acres of lawns, gardens and orchards. It adjoins a short walk to a private ocean beach. This Cape Cod manse, built by a Quaker family, is a historical landmark on what once was known as the King's Highway, the oldest historical district in the United States. All the rooms are furnished with antiques and working fireplaces (one with a secret compartment where runaway slaves hid). Breakfast features fresh produce with eggs, meats and vegetables from the farm's livestock and gardens. Pets and children welcome.

Innkeeper(s): Sheila Weyers & Richard Loring. $115-150. MC VISA AX PC TC. 7 rooms, 7 with FP. 4 suites. 2 cottages. Breakfast included in rates. Types of meals: full breakfast and gourmet breakfast. Beds: QDT. Swimming, library and child care on premises. Antiques, fishing, parks, shopping, downhill skiing, cross-country skiing, sporting events, theater and watersports nearby.

Location: North Side of Cape Cod, off Route 6A.

Seen in: Boston Globe, New York Times.

"Absolutely wonderful. We will always remember the wonderful time."

Certificate may be used: Nov. 1-May 1.

Edgartown   K16

Ashley Inn
129 Main St, PO Box 650,
Edgartown, MA 02539
(508)627-9655 (800)477-9655

Circa 1860. A retired whaling captain built this gracious Georgian inn on Martha's Vineyard. Guest rooms are furnished in period antiques, brass and wicker. The inn is just four blocks from the beach, and its Main Street location offers easy access to Edgartown's many fine restaurants and shops. Breakfasts are served in the English tea room, and guests find the inn's grounds perfect for an after-meal stroll. Others like to relax in the hammock or

in the comfortable sitting room. A special honeymoon package is available.

Innkeeper(s): Fred Hurley. $60-150. MC VISA AX. 8 rooms. 1 suite. Breakfast included in rates. Type of meal: continental breakfast. Air conditioning and cable TV in room. Antiques and shopping nearby.

Certificate may be used: Oct. 23-April 1, Nov. 1-Dec. 31.

Falmouth   J16

Village Green Inn
40 Main St, Falmouth, MA 02540-2667
(508)548-5621 (800)237-1119
Fax:(508)457-5051

Circa 1804. The inn was originally built in the Federal style for Braddock Dimmick, son of Revolutionary War General Joseph Dimmick. Later, "cranberry king" John Crocker moved the house onto a granite slab foundation, remodeling it in the Victorian style. There are inlaid floors, large porches and gingerbread trim.

Innkeeper(s): Diane & Don Crosby. $85-135. MC VISA AX PC TC. 5 rooms with PB, 2 with FP. 1 suite. Breakfast and afternoon tea included in rates. Types of meals: full breakfast and early coffee/tea. Beds: Q. Ceiling fan and cable TV in room. Bicycles on premises. Antiques, fishing, parks, shopping, sporting events, theater and watersports nearby.

Location: Falmouth's historic village green.

Seen in: Country Inns, Cape Cod Life, Yankee.

"Like we've always said, it's the innkeepers that make the inn!"

Certificate may be used: March-May, November-December, Monday-Thursday.

Great Barrington   F2

Wainwright Inn
518 Main St,
Great Barrington, MA 01230
(413)528-2062

Circa 1766. This pre-Revolutionary War home opened for guests in 1766 as Tory Tavern and Inn, and during the war served as a fort and Colonial armory. The home was also used to lay the groundwork for the commercial use of AC current, when it was owned by Franklin Pope. Pope worked with Thomas Edison and General Electric founder William Stanley. If the history of this inn fails to impress, the rich interior should do the trick. Snuggle up in front of a roaring fire or relax on one of the wraparound porches. Muffins and fresh coffee are delivered to guests each morning. A full breakfast is served later in the fire-lit dining room. Each season brings new activity to the Great Barrington area, which is full of antique shops, orchards to visit, ski slopes and beautiful scenery. The nearby Hancock Shaker Village is a popular attraction.

Innkeeper(s): David Rolland. $50-125. MC VISA AX. 8 rooms. Breakfast included in rates. Type of meal: full breakfast.

Certificate may be used: November-June, Sunday-Thursday.

Windflower Inn

684 S Egremont Rd,
Great Barrington, MA 01230-1932
(413)528-2720 (800)992-1993
Fax:(413)528-5147

Circa 1870. This country manor is situated on 10 acres shaded by giant oaks and maples. Early American and English antiques fill the spacious guest rooms. There is a piano room with shelves of books, and a clock collection is featured throughout. The inn's dinners have received excellent reviews and feature herbs, vegetables and berries from the garden. Guests may cross the street for tennis and golf at the country club.

Innkeeper(s): Barbara & Gerald Liebert, Claudia & John Ryan. $170-220. MAP. AX PC TC. 13 rooms with PB, 6 with FP. Breakfast, afternoon tea and dinner included in rates. Types of meals: full breakfast and early coffee/tea. Beds: KQT. Air conditioning in room. Fax, copier, swimming and library on premises. Antiques, parks, shopping, downhill skiing, cross-country skiing, theater and watersports nearby.

Seen in: Los Angeles Times, Boulevard, Redbook, Country Inns, Countryside, Road Best Traveled, Discerning Traveler.

"Every creative comfort imaginable, great for heart, soul and stomach."

Certificate may be used: Nov. 1-June 30, Sunday-Thursday non-

holiday. Monday-Wednesday, July 1-Oct. 31 non-holiday, non-fireplace September and October. B&B style only. Not to be used with any other promotion.

Greenfield   C6

The Brandt House

29 Highland Ave, Greenfield, MA 01301
(413)774-3329 (800)235-3329
Fax:(413)772-2908

Circa 1890. Three-and-a-half-acre lawns surround this impressive three-story Colonial Revival house, situated hilltop. The library and pool room are popular for lounging. A full breakfast often includes

homemade scones. There is a clay tennis court, nature trails, badminton, horseshoes and in winter, lighted ice skating at a nearby pond. Historic Deerfield is within five minutes.

Innkeeper(s): Phoebe Compton. $85-160. MC VISA AX DS TC. 8 rooms, 6 with PB, 2 with FP. 1 suite. 1 conference room. Breakfast included in rates. Types of meals: continental-plus breakfast, full breakfast and early coffee/tea. Gourmet lunch available. Beds: KQT. Air conditioning, ceiling fan and cable TV in room. VCR, fax, copier, tennis and library on premises. Antiques, fishing, parks, shopping, downhill skiing, cross-country skiing, sporting events, theater and watersports nearby.

"Ensconced deep in a featherbed under mounds of snow eiderdown, surrounded by a rich tapestry of childhood yesteryear, is like a foretaste of heaven...."

Certificate may be used: November through April.

Hamilton
C14

Miles River Country Inn
823 Bay Rd, Box 149,
Hamilton, MA 01936
(508)468-7206 Fax:(508)468-3999

Circa 1789. This rambling colonial inn sits on more than 30 acres of magnificent curving lawns bordered by trees and formal gardens that lead to the Miles River. There are meadows, woodlands and wetlands surrounding the property and available for

exploring. The river flows through the property, which is a haven for a wide variety of wildlife. Many of the inn's 12 fireplaces are in the guest rooms. Family heirloom antiques compliment the interior.
Innkeeper(s): Gretel & Peter Clark. $84-155. MC VISA AX PC TC. 8 rooms, 5 with PB, 4 with FP. 1 suite. 2 conference rooms. Breakfast and afternoon tea included in rates. Types of meals: full breakfast and early coffee/tea. Beds: QDT. Turn-down service and VCR in room. Cable TV, fax, copier, bicycles and library on premises. Antiques, fishing, parks, shopping, downhill skiing, cross-country skiing, sporting events, theater and watersports nearby.
Seen in: Boston Globe, Beverly Times.
Certificate may be used: Most weekdays, weekends November-April.

Harwich Port
I18

Augustus Snow House
528 Main St, Harwich Port, MA 02646
(508)430-0528 (800)320-0528
Fax:(508)432-7995

Circa 1901. This gracious, Queen Anne Victorian is a turn-of-the-century gem, complete with a wide, wraparound veranda, gabled windows and a distinctive turret. Victorian wallpapers, stained glass and rich woodwork complement the interior, which is appropriately decorated in period style. Each of the romantic guest quarters offers something special. One room has a canopy bed and a fireplace, while another includes a relaxing clawfoot tub. Three rooms have Jacuzzi tubs. The king-size beds are dressed in fine linens. As is the Victorian way,

afternoon tea is served each day. The breakfasts include delectables such as banana chip muffins, baked pears in raspberry cream sauce or, possibly, baked French toast with layers of homemade cinnamon bread, bacon and cheese.
Innkeeper(s): Joyce & Steve Roth. $105-160. MC VISA AX DS PC TC. 5 rooms with PB, 1 with FP. Breakfast and afternoon tea included in rates. Types of meals: gourmet breakfast and early coffee/tea. Beds: KQ. Air conditioning, ceiling fan and cable TV in room. Fax, copier and bicycles on premises. Antiques, fishing, parks, shopping and watersports nearby.
Certificate may be used: Dec. 1-April 15, Sunday-Friday.

Captain's Quarters
85 Bank St, Harwich Port, MA 02646
(508)432-1991 (800)992-6550

Circa 1850. This Victorian house features a classic wraparound porch, gingerbread trim, an authentic turret room and a graceful, curving front stairway. It is situated on an acre of sunny lawns, broad shade trees and colorful gardens. The inn is a five-minute walk to sandy Bank Street Beach and is close to town.
Innkeeper(s): Edward Kenney. $69-95. MC VISA AX DS. 6 rooms with PB. Breakfast included in rates. Type of meal: continental-plus breakfast. Beds: QT. Cable TV in room. Antiques, shopping, theater nearby.
Location: One-and-a-half hours from Boston.

"Accommodations are very comfortable and attractive. This is our favorite inn."
Certificate may be used: All days of the week, March through June 21 and post-Labor Day September through Oct. 31.

Dunscroft By The Sea Inn & Cottage
24 Pilgrim Rd, Harwich Port, MA 02646
(508)432-0810 (800)432-4345
Fax:(508)432-5134

Circa 1920. This gambrel-roofed house sits behind a split-rail fence at the end of a winding brick driveway. Inside the handsome columned entrance is an extensive library and a living room with a piano. Best of all is the candlelit bed chamber with turned-down bed and the music of ocean waves rolling onto the private beach on Nantucket Sound, 300 feet from the inn.

Innkeeper(s): Alyce & Wally Cunningham. $95-225. MAP. MC VISA AX PC. 9 rooms with PB, 2 with FP. 1 suite. 1 cottage. 1 conference room. Breakfast included in rates. Types of meals: full breakfast and gourmet breakfast. Catering service available. Beds: KQ. Air conditioning, turn-down service, ceiling fan and cable TV in room. Fax, copier, swimming, tennis and library on premises. Handicap access. Amusement parks, antiques, fishing, parks, shopping, cross-country skiing, sporting events, theater and watersports nearby.

Location: One-and-a-half hours from Providence, R.I., and Boston on Cape Cod.

Seen in: Cape Codder.

"A quaint and delightful slice of New England. Your generous hospitality is greatly appreciated. Your place is beautiful."

Certificate may be used: Nov. 1 to Memorial Day and Memorial Day to June 20, Sunday-Thursday.

Harbor Breeze

326 Lower County Rd,
Harwich Port, MA 02646-1625
(508)432-0337 (800)272-4343
Fax:(508)432-1276

Circa 1945. Ideally located across the street from picturesque Allens Harbor and only a short walk from the Brooks Road beach, this inn is a classic Cape Cod home. A rambling connection of cedar shake additions, nestled in an attractive pine setting, surround a garden courtyard to form a guest wing. Flowered walkways lead to nine guest rooms, which are furnished in wicker, woods and country floral. There are restful sitting areas amid the pines and a swimming pool where you can enjoy the ocean breezes. A short walk down a shady tree-lined street brings you to a sandy beach on Nantucket Sound.
Innkeeper(s): Kathleen & David Van Gelder. $75-120. MC VISA AX DS PC TC. 9 rooms with PB, 1 with FP. 1 suite. Breakfast included in rates. Types of meals: continental-plus breakfast and early coffee/tea. Beds: KQT. Cable TV in room. Fax and swimming on premises. Antiques, fishing, parks, shopping, theater and watersports nearby.

Certificate may be used: April 1 to June 15 and Sept. 5 to Oct. 31, Sunday through Friday. Not valid holidays or holiday weekends.

Hyannis Port   I17

The Simmons Homestead Inn

288 Scudder Ave,
Hyannis Port, MA 02647
(508)778-4999 (800)637-1649
Fax:(508)790-1342

Circa 1820. This former sea captain's home features period decor and includes huge needlepoint displays and lifelike ceramic and papiermache animals that give the inn a country feel. Some rooms boast canopy beds and each is individually decorated. Traditional full breakfasts are served in the formal

dining room. Evening wine helps guests relax after a day of touring the Cape.
Innkeeper(s): Bill Putman. $80-150. MC VISA AX DS TC. 10 rooms with PB. Breakfast included in rates. Type of meal: full breakfast. Beds: KQT. Ceiling fan in room. Cable TV, fax, copier and bicycles on premises. Antiques, fishing, parks, shopping and watersports nearby.

Location: In heart of Cape Cod.

Seen in: Bon Appetit, Cape Code Life, Yankee.

"This is not your average quaint inn, it's lots of fun and much more."

Certificate may be used: Oct. 1 to May 1, Sunday-Friday.

Lanesboro   C3

Whippletree B&B

10 Bailey Rd, Lanesboro, MA 01237-9600
(413)443-9874

Circa 1753. Decades before the first shots of the Revolutionary War were fired, this Federal Post & Beam farmhouse sat in its tranquil country setting. Today, after weathering the centuries, it still stands surrounded by five restful acres and offering views of the Berkshire Hills. Guest rooms are located either in the main house or in an adjacent renovated barn. There is a swimming pool on the premises, and guests are welcome to relax and enjoy the view from the inn's wraparound porch. The breakfasts are continental, but never ordinary, with items such as spicy mandarin muffins or carrot-pineapple squares.
Innkeeper(s): Chuck Lynch. $60-95. PC. 5 rooms, 2 with PB. 1 suite. Breakfast included in rates. Type of meal: continental-plus breakfast. Beds: Q. Air conditioning and cable TV in room. Swimming on premises. Amusement parks, antiques, fishing, parks, shopping, downhill skiing, cross-country skiing, sporting events, theater and watersports nearby.

Certificate may be used: Nov. 1 through June 30, Sunday-Thursday.

Lee   E2

Morgan House Inn

33 Main St, Lee, MA 01238-1611
(413)243-0181

Circa 1817. This classic Colonial inn reflects the stagecoach era with its stenciled wall coverings, comfortable antique-filled rooms and country prints. The innkeepers, Lenora and Stuart, are former owners of a Berkshire inn, a Cambridge fine dining restaurant, a wine and specialty food store and have years of experience in corporate dining. Lenora prepares contemporary and traditional New England cuisine. Her favorites include warm popovers, barbecue glazed pork tenderloin with Boston baked beans and sweet potato chips, duckling with cinnamon-spiced orange sauce, plum conserve, and wild rice pancakes.

Innkeeper(s): Lenora & Stuart Bowen. $48-145. EP. MC VISA AX DC DS TC. 13 rooms, 3 with PB. 1 conference room.

Breakfast included in rates. Types of meals: full breakfast and early coffee/tea. Dinner, evening snack, picnic lunch, lunch, catering service and catered breakfast available. Beds: KQDT. Air conditioning in room. Cable TV on premises. Antiques, fishing, parks, shopping, downhill skiing, cross-country skiing and theater nearby.

Seen in: Berkshire Book, Union News, Golden Ages, Restaurants of New England.

"Charming and friendly—5-star rating."

Certificate may be used: Nov. 1, 1996 to June 5, 1997; Nov. 3 to Dec. 31, 1997.

Lenox   E2

Brook Farm Inn

15 Hawthorne St, Lenox, MA 01240-2404
(413)637-3013 (800)285-7638
Fax:(413)637-4751

Circa 1870. Brook Farm Inn is named after the original Brook Farm, a literary commune that sought to combine thinker and worker through a society of intelligent, cultivated members. In keeping with that theme, this gracious Victorian inn offers poetry and writing seminars and has a 650-volume poetry library. Canopy beds, Mozart and a swimming pool tend to the spirit.

Innkeeper(s): Joe & Anne Miller. $75-185. MC VISA DS PC TC. 12 rooms with PB, 6 with FP. Breakfast and afternoon tea included in rates. Types of meals: full breakfast and early coffee/tea. Beds: KQDT. Air conditioning and ceiling fan in room. Fax, copier and swimming on premises. Antiques, fishing, parks, shopping, downhill skiing, cross-country skiing, sporting events, theater and watersports nearby.

Location: In the heart of Berkshire County.

Seen in: Berkshire Eagle, Country Inns, Travel & Leisure, Boston.

"We've been traveling all our lives and never have we felt more at home."

Certificate may be used: Midweek - Nov. 1 to June 15; Midweek - September.

The Gables Inn

81 Walker St, Rt 183, Lenox, MA 01240
(413)637-3416 (800)382-9401

Circa 1885. At one time, this was the home of Pulitzer Prize-winning novelist, Edith Wharton. The Queen Anne-style Berkshire cottage features a handsome eight-sided library and Mrs. Wharton's own four-poster bed. An unusual indoor swimming pool with spa is available in warm weather.

Innkeeper(s): Mary & Frank Newton. $80-195. MC VISA DS PC TC. 18 rooms with PB, 15 with FP. 3 suites. Breakfast included in rates. Beds: Q. Air conditioning, cable TV and VCR in room. Fax, swimming and tennis on premises. Antiques, fishing, parks, shopping, downhill skiing, cross-country skiing, sporting events, theater and watersports nearby.

Location: Within walking distance to Tanglewood, summer home of the Boston Symphony Orchestra.

Seen in: P.M., New York Times.

"You made us feel like old friends and that good feeling enhanced our pleasure. In essence it was the best part of our trip."

Certificate may be used: Nov. 1 to May 20, Sunday through Thursday only.

Seven Hills Country Inn

40 Plunkett St, Lenox, MA 01240-2704
(413)637-0060 (800)869-6518
Fax:(413)637-3651

Circa 1911. Descendants of those who sailed on the Mayflower built this rambling, Tudor-style mansion. The inn's 27 acres often serve as the site for weddings and receptions. The grounds include two tennis courts and a swimming pool. Guest rooms are elegantly appointed with antiques, and the mansion still maintains its hand-carved fireplaces and leaded glass windows. In addition to the original elements, some rooms contain the modern amenity of a whirlpool tub. The inn's chef, whose cuisine has been featured in Gourmet magazine, prepares creative, continental specialties. Seven Hills offers close access to many attractions in the Berkshires.

Innkeeper(s): Patricia & Jim Eder. $65-250. MAP. MC VISA AX DC CB DS PC TC. 52 rooms with PB, 5 with FP. 2 suites. 4 conference rooms. Breakfast included in rates. Type of meal: early coffee/tea. Beds: KQDT. Air conditioning in room. Cable TV, VCR, fax, copier, swimming, tennis, library and child care on premises. Handicap access. Antiques, fishing, parks, shopping, downhill skiing, cross-country skiing, theater and watersports nearby.

Certificate may be used: Jan. 1-April 30, all nights; May 1-June 30, Sunday-Friday; July 1-Aug. 31, Monday-Wednesday; Sept. 1-Oct. 26, Sunday-Friday; Oct. 27-Dec. 15, all nights; Dec. 16-31, Sunday-Friday.

Walker House

64 Walker St, Lenox, MA 01240-2718
(413)637-1271 (800)235-3098
Fax:(413)637-2387

Circa 1804. This beautiful Federal-style house sits in the center of the village on three acres of graceful woods and restored gardens. Guest rooms have fireplaces and private baths. Each is named for a favorite composer such as Beethoven, Mozart, or

Handel. The innkeepers' musical backgrounds include associations with the San Francisco Opera, the New York City Opera, and the Los Angeles Philharmonic. Walker House concerts are scheduled from time to time.

Innkeeper(s): Peggy & Richard Houdek. $60-180. PC. 8 rooms with PB, 5 with FP. 1 conference room. Breakfast and afternoon tea included in rates. Types of meals: continental-plus breakfast and early coffee/tea. Beds: QDT. Air conditioning in room. Cable TV, VCR, fax, copier, bicycles and library on premises. Handicap access. Antiques, fishing, parks, shopping, downhill skiing, cross-country skiing, theater and watersports nearby.

Location: Route 183 & 7A.

Seen in: Boston Globe, PBS, Los Angeles Times, New York Times.

"We had a grand time staying with fellow music and opera lovers! Breakfasts were lovely."

Certificate may be used: November-May, Sunday through Thursday, excluding holidays.

Leverett D6

Hannah Dudley House Inn

114 Dudleyville Rd, Leverett, MA 01054
(413)367-2323

Circa 1797. Each season brings with it a new reason to visit this 18th-century Colonial, which is named for a member of the first family to inhabit this home. In autumn, the home's 110 acres explode in color. In winter, snowcapped pines adds to the festive atmosphere, and guests snuggle up in front of a roaring fire. Two guest rooms include fireplaces, and the house offers four others. The guest room refrigerators are always stocked with drinks. During warm months, guests enjoy use of a barbecue grill and swimming pool. Stroll the grounds and you'll find plenty of wildlife, including two ponds inhabited by ducks, goldfish, trout and bullfrogs. During the winter months, the pond transforms into the inn's skating rink.

Innkeeper(s): Erni & Daryl Johnson. $125-188. MC VISA PC TC. 4 rooms with PB, 2 with FP. 1 suite. Breakfast, evening snack and picnic lunch included in rates. Types of meals: full breakfast and early coffee/tea. Dinner available. Beds: QD. Turn-down service in room. Swimming and library on premises. Antiques, fishing, parks, shopping, skiing, sporting events and theater nearby.

Certificate may be used: January, February, March, April, July, August, December. Advanced reservations required.

Lexington D12

Pacem

62 Sherburne Rd S,
Lexington, MA 02173-7059
(617)862-3337

Circa 1964. This contemporary inn and its grounds, which were designed by Royal Barry Wills, offers modern amenities in an area renowned for its historic significance. Guests enjoy relaxing in the family room and music room, both of which boast fireplaces, in addition to the library and patio. Visitors may borrow three-speed bicycles if they wish. The Hancock Clarke House, Minute Man National Historic Park, Munroe Tavern and the Museum of Our National Heritage are nearby.

Innkeeper(s): Carroll Ann Bottino. $55-85. PC TC. 3 rooms, 1 with PB. Breakfast included in rates. Type of meal: continental breakfast. Beds: DT. Ceiling fan in room. Bicycles and library on premises. Antiques, fishing, parks, shopping, cross-country skiing, sporting events, theater and watersports nearby.

Certificate may be used: Monday-Thursday nights, Nov. 1-March 30.

Lynn D14

Diamond District Breakfast Inn
142 Ocean St, Lynn, MA 01902-2007
(617)599-4470 (800)666-3076
Fax:(617)595-2200

Circa 1911. This 17-room Georgian house was built for shoe manufacturer P.J. Harney-Lynn. The Charles Pinkham family (son of Lydia Pinkham, a health tonic producer) later purchased it. Many of the original fixtures remain, and the inn is suitably

furnished with Oriental rugs and antiques. The parlor features a collection of antique musical instruments. There are several views of the ocean from the house, but the porch is the most popular spot for sea gazing. Breakfast is served in the dining room or on the porch. Fresh fruits, homemade breads and hot coffee, tea or cider start off the meal, followed by a special entree.

Innkeeper(s): Sandra & Jerry Caron. $61-110. MC VISA AX DC CB DS PC TC. 8 rooms, 4 with PB. 1 conference room. Breakfast included in rates. Type of meal: full breakfast. Beds: QDT. Air conditioning and ceiling fan in room. Fax, copier and computer on premises. Antiques, fishing, cross-country skiing and watersports nearby.

Seen in: Lynn Historic Home Tour

"The room was spectacular and breakfast was served beautifully. Bed and breakfast were both outstanding! Thanks so much for your hospitality."

Certificate may be used: November-May, Sunday through Thursday, holidays excluded.

Marblehead D14

The Nesting Place B&B
16 Village St, Marblehead, MA 01945
(617)631-6655

Circa 1890. Conveniently located one-half hour away from Boston and Cape Ann, this Victorian inn offers as much privacy as you require. Discover the world of the early clipper ships as you walk the narrow winding streets and the beaches of Marblehead's renowned harbor, only minutes away. There's a relaxing hot tub to top off a day of browsing through art galleries, antique shops and quaint boutiques.

Innkeeper(s): Louise Hirshberg. $55-70. MC VISA TC. 6 rooms. Breakfast included in rates. Types of meals: continental-plus breakfast and early coffee/tea. Beds: KQT. VCR and spa on premises. Antiques, fishing, parks, shopping, cross-country skiing, sporting events, theater and watersports nearby.

Certificate may be used: Nov. 1-May 15. May 16-July 15, weekdays only.

Spray Cliff on The Ocean
25 Spray Ave, Marblehead, MA 01945
(617)631-6789 (800)626-1530
Fax:(617)639-4563

Circa 1910. Panoramic views stretch out in grand proportions from this romantic English Tudor mansion set high above the Atlantic. The inn provides a spacious and elegant atmosphere inside. The grounds of the inn include a brick terrace surrounded by lush flower gardens where eider ducks, black cormorants and seagulls gather. Spray Cliff is the only Marblehead B&B inn located directly on the ocean.

Innkeeper(s): Roger Plauche. $149-189. MC VISA AX. 7 rooms with PB, 3 with FP. Breakfast included in rates. Type of meal: continental-plus breakfast. Beds: KQ. Antiques, fishing, shopping, cross-country skiing, sporting events, theater and watersports nearby.

Location: Fifteen miles north of Boston.

Seen in: New York Times, Glamour.

"I prefer this atmosphere to a modern motel. It's more relaxed and love is everywhere!"

Certificate may be used: November through May (except holidays).

Martha's Vineyard K16

Breakfast at Tiasquam
RR 1 Box 296,
Martha's Vineyard, MA 02535-9705
(508)645-3685

Circa 1987. This unique farmhouse sits amid woodlands and rolling pastures. The multi-level decks look out to fields of wildflowers, oaks and evergreens. Relax in a hammock or in your comfortable guest room. The sinks in the bathrooms were hand-thrown by potter Robert Parrott. The breakfast, as one might expect from the name, is delightful and

varies season to season. Fresh corn-blueberry pancakes might be topped with Vermont maple syrup, or freshly-caught fish may be found as part of the breakfast fare. Vacationers who just want to relax will appreciate the private, rural setting of this inn.

Innkeeper(s): Ron Crowe. $70-195. 8 rooms, 2 with PB, 1 with FP. Breakfast included in rates. Type of meal: full breakfast. Beds: KQTD. Ceiling fan in room. Cable TV, VCR and bicycles on premises. Handicap access. Antiques, fishing, shopping, theater and watersports nearby.

Location: Martha's Vineyard.

"Best breakfast on the island, the perfect B&B."

Certificate may be used: Oct. 15-May 20, Sunday-Thursday nights.

Captain Dexter House of Edgartown

35 Pease's Point Way, Box 2798,
Martha's Vineyard, MA 02539
(508)693-6564 Fax:(508)693-8448

Circa 1843. Located just three blocks from Edgartown's harbor and historic district, this black-shuttered sea merchant's house has a graceful lawn and terraced flower gardens. A gentle Colonial atmosphere is enhanced by original wooden beams, exposed floorboards, working fireplaces, old-fashioned dormers and a collection of period antiques. Luxurious canopy beds are featured, and some rooms include fireplaces.

Innkeeper(s): Rick Fenstemaker. $85-175. MC VISA AX PC TC. 8 rooms with PB, 2 with FP. 1 suite. Breakfast included in rates. Type of meal: continental-plus breakfast. Afternoon tea available. Beds: QD. Air conditioning and ceiling fan in room. Fax on premises. Antiques, fishing, parks, theater and watersports nearby.

Location: On a tree-lined residential street in downtown Edgartown on the island of Martha's Vineyard.

Seen in: Island Getaways, Vineyard Gazette, Martha's Vineyard Times, Cape Cod Life.

"Since we were on our honeymoon, we were hoping for a quiet, relaxing stay, and the Captain Dexter House was perfect!"

Certificate may be used: May 1 through June 15; Sept. 5 through Oct. 31; holidays and weekends excluded.

Captain Dexter House of Vineyard Haven

100 Main St, PO Box 2457,
Martha's Vineyard, MA 02568
(508)627-7289 Fax:(508)627-3382

Circa 1840. Captain Dexter House was the home of sea captain Rodolphus Dexter. Authentic 18th-century antiques and reproductions are among the inn's appointments. There are Count Rumford fireplaces and hand-stencilled walls in several rooms. Located on a street of historic homes, the inn is a short stroll to the beach, town and harbor. The innkeepers offer an evening aperitif and in the summer, lemonade is served.

Innkeeper(s): Rick Fenstemaker. $95-195. MC VISA AX PC TC. 11 rooms with PB, 4 with FP. Breakfast included in rates. Type of meal: continental-plus breakfast. Afternoon tea available. Beds: QD. Air conditioning and ceiling fan in room. Fax on premises. Antiques, fishing, parks, shopping, theater and watersports nearby.

Location: Martha's Vineyard.

Seen in: Martha's Vineyard Times, Cape Cod Life.

"The house is sensational. Your hospitality was all one could expect. You've made us permanent bed & breakfast fans."

Certificate may be used: May 1 through June 15, Sept. 5 through Oct. 31, holidays and weekends excluded.

Nancy's Auberge

102 Main St, PO Box 4433,
Martha's Vineyard, MA 02568
(508)693-4434

Circa 1840. This 1840 Greek Revival home affords harbor views from its spot in a historic neighborhood once home to early settlers and whaling captains. Three of the antique-filled rooms include fireplaces, and one of the bedchambers boasts a harbor view. The inn is just a few blocks from the local ferry. Bicycle paths and beaches are nearby, as well as restaurants and a variety of shops.

Innkeeper(s): Nancy Hurd. $68-108. MC VISA. 3 rooms. Breakfast included in rates. Type of meal: continental-plus breakfast. VCR on premises. Antiques, shopping and theater nearby.

Certificate may be used: Monday through Thursday, except during July and August.

Twin Oaks Inn

8 Edgartown Rd, PO Box 1767,
Martha's Vineyard, MA 02568
(508)693-8633 (800)696-8633
Fax:(508)693-5833

Circa 1906. Pastels and floral prints provide a relaxing atmosphere at this Dutch Colonial inn on Martha's Vineyard, which offers four guest rooms and an apartment with its own kitchen. The break-

fast specialty is applecrisp, and guests also enjoy afternoon tea on the enclosed wraparound front porch. The inn is within walking distance of the bicycle path, downtown businesses and the ferry, but its location off the main road affords a more relaxed and sedate feeling for visitors. The family-oriented inn accommodates family reunions, meetings and weddings, and its fireplace room is popular with honeymooners.

Innkeeper(s): Doris Clark. $55-180. MC VISA. 5 rooms, 3 with PB. 2 suites. 1 conference room. Breakfast included in rates. Types of meals: continental-plus breakfast and early coffee/tea. Afternoon tea available. Beds: QDT. Ceiling fan and cable TV in room. VCR on premises. Antiques, fishing, shopping, theater and watersports nearby.

Seen in: Detroit Free Press.

"We appreciated the wonderful welcome and kind hospitality shown us for our week's stay on your lovely island."

Certificate may be used: Jan. 1 through May 15.

☐ **For Martha's Vineyard, see also:** Edgartown and Oaks Bluff.

Middleboro H14

On Cranberry Pond B&B

43 Fuller St, Middleboro, MA 02346-1706
(508)946-0768 Fax:(508)947-8221

Circa 1989. Nestled in the historic "cranberry capital of the world," this modern farmhouse rests on a working berry bog by the shores of its namesake tarn. There are two miles of trails to meander, and during berry picking season, guests can watch as buckets of the fruit are collected. The rooms are decorated with knickknacks and flowers, the Master Suite includes a working fireplace. Innkeeper Jeannine LaBossiere creates the breakfasts, which begin with fresh coffee, muffins, cookies and scones.

Innkeeper(s): Jeannine LaBossiere & Tim Dombrowski. $65-125. MC VISA AX DC CB PC TC. 6 rooms, 3 with PB, 2 with FP. 2 suites. 1 conference room. Breakfast and evening snack included in rates. Types of meals: full breakfast, gourmet breakfast and early coffee/tea. Afternoon tea and banquet service available. Beds: QDT. Air conditioning, turn-

down service, ceiling fan, cable TV and VCR in room. Fax, copier, stables, bicycles, library and pet boarding on premises. Amusement parks, antiques, fishing, parks, shopping, downhill skiing, theater and watersports nearby.

Certificate may be used: All year, except holidays.

Nantucket L18

House of The Seven Gables

32 Cliff Rd, Nantucket, MA 02554-3644
(508)228-4706

Circa 1865. Originally the annex of the Sea Cliff Inn, one of the island's oldest hotels, this three-story Queen Anne Victorian inn offers 10 guest rooms. Beaches, bike rentals, museums, restaurants, shops and tennis courts are all found nearby. The guest rooms are furnished with king or queen beds and period antiques. Breakfast is served each morning in the guest rooms, and often include homemade coffee cake, muffins or Portuguese rolls.

Innkeeper(s): Suzanne Walton. $65-175. MC VISA AX. 10 rooms, 8 with PB. Breakfast included in rates. Type of meal: continental breakfast. Beds: KQF. Cable TV on premises. Antiques, fishing, shopping, theater and watersports nearby.

"You have a beautiful home and one that makes everyone feel relaxed and at home."

Certificate may be used: Oct. 15-May 22.

Ivy Lodge

2 Chester St, Nantucket, MA 02554-3505
(508)228-7755 Fax:(508)228-0305

Circa 1790. This 18th-century Colonial has spent much of its life serving the needs of travelers. In the 1800s, the home was used both as an inn and a museum. Today the home serves as a living museum of American history. The home still includes its classic, center chimney, pine floors and fireplaces. Guest rooms are decorated with antiques and beds topped with ornate bedspreads and lacy canopies. Vases filled with flowers add extra color. The Brant Point lighthouse is within walking distance of the inn, and the beach is nearby.

Innkeeper(s): Tuge Roseatra. $75-160. 6 rooms. Breakfast included in rates. Type of meal: continental-plus breakfast.

Certificate may be used: Nov. 1 to April 30; Oct. 1-30 and May 1 to June 15. Excluding holidays and all local festival days and weekends.

Stumble Inne

109 Orange St, Nantucket, MA 02554
(508)228-4482 Fax:(508)228-4752

Circa 1704. This Nantucket Island inn is appointed with fine antiques. Six of the inn's rooms are across the street from the Stumble Inne at the Starbuck House, an early 19th-century Nantucket

"half-house." Rooms feature wide pine floors, antique beds, ceiling fans and Laura Ashley decor. Innkeeper(s): Mary Kay & Mal Condon. $45-190. MC VISA AX TC. 15 rooms, 10 with PB. 2 suites. Breakfast and afternoon tea included in rates. Types of meals: continental-plus breakfast, full breakfast and early coffee/tea. Beds: Q. Air conditioning, ceiling fan, cable TV and VCR in room. Fax on premises. Antiques, fishing, shopping, theater and watersports nearby.

Seen in: Innsider.

"We realize much of our happiness was due to the warm hospitality that was a part of every day."

Certificate may be used: Oct. 1-May 15, Sunday-Thursday, excluding holiday periods.

The White House

48 Center St, Nantucket, MA 02554-3664
(508)228-4677

Circa 1800. For more than 40 years a favorite hostelry of visitors to Nantucket, The White House is situated ideally in the heart of the historic district and a short walk to the beach and ferry terminal. The first floor houses an antique shop. Guests stay in rooms on the second floor or a housekeeping apartment. Afternoon wine and cheese is served in the garden.
Innkeeper(s): Nina Hellman. $70-120. MC VISA AX. 4 rooms, 3 with PB. 1 suite. Breakfast included in rates. Type of meal: continental breakfast. Beds: Q. Antiques, fishing, theater and watersports nearby.

Certificate may be used: Weekdays, mid-April to mid-June and mid-September to mid-October. Anytime mid-October through December. Excludes holidays and special island events.

The Woodbox Inn

29 Fair St, Nantucket, MA 02554-3798
(508)228-0587

Circa 1709. Nantucket's oldest inn was built by Captain George Bunker. In 1711, the captain constructed an adjoining house. Eventually, the two

houses were made into one by cutting into the sides of both. Guest rooms are furnished with period antiques. The inn's gourmet dining room features an Early American atmosphere with low-beamed ceilings and pine-paneled walls.

Innkeeper(s): Dexter Tutein. $130-220. PC TC. 9 rooms with PB, 6 with FP. 6 suites. Type of meal: full breakfast. Beds: KQDT. Antiques, fishing, parks, shopping, theater and watersports nearby.

Location: Historic district.

Seen in: Wharton Alumni, Cape Cod Life, Boston.

"Best breakfast on the island, Yesterday's Island."

Certificate may be used: Midweek, from mid-October to Jan. 1 and May 1 to Memorial Day, holidays excluded.

Newburyport B14

Clark Currier Inn

45 Green St, Newburyport, MA 01950
(508)465-8363 (800)360-6582

Circa 1803. Once the home of shipbuilder Thomas March Clark, this three-story Federal-style inn provides gracious accommodations to visitors in the Northeast Massachusetts area. Visitors will enjoy the inn's details added by Samuel McEntire, one of the nation's most celebrated home builders and woodcarvers. Breakfast is served in the garden room, with an afternoon tea offered in the parlor. The

inn's grounds also boast a picturesque garden and gazebo. Parker River National Wildlife Refuge and Maudslay State Park are nearby.

Innkeeper(s): Mary & Bob Nolan. $65-145. MC VISA AX DS PC TC. 8 rooms with PB. Breakfast and afternoon tea included in rates. Type of meal: continental-plus breakfast. Beds: QDT. Air conditioning, cable TV and VCR in room. Bicycles, library and child care on premises. Handicap access. Amusement parks, antiques, fishing, parks, shopping, downhill skiing, cross-country skiing, sporting events, theater and watersports nearby.

"We had a lovely stay in your B&B! We appreciated your hospitality!"

Certificate may be used: Space available, January-May.

Windsor House

38 Federal St, Newburyport, MA 01950
(508)462-3778 Fax:(508)465-3443

Circa 1786. This brick Federal-style mansion was designed as a combination home and chandlery (a ship's outfitter and brokerage company for cargo). The third floor served as a warehouse and the Merchant Suite was once the main office. This suite

features a 14-foot ceiling with hand-hewn, beveled beams. It is appointed with a wing-back chair from the Old Boston Opera, a sleigh bed and an antique hope chest. The English innkeeper serves a hearty English country breakfast and a full English tea in the afternoon. Children are welcome.

Innkeeper(s): Judith & John Harris. $85-125. MC VISA AX DS. 5 rooms, 3 with PB. Breakfast and afternoon tea included in rates. Types of meals: full breakfast and gourmet breakfast. Beds: KQDT. Cable TV and VCR on premises. Amusement parks, antiques, fishing, parks, shopping, cross-country skiing, theater and watersports nearby.

Location: Thirty-eight miles north of Boston.

Seen in: New York Times, Boston, Boston Herald Sunday.

"You will find what you look for and be met by the unexpected too. A good time!"

Certificate may be used: Jan. 1-Feb. 15-open-no restriction; Feb. 15-Dec. 31, Monday, Tuesday, Wednesday only.

Oak Bluffs   K16

The Beach Rose

PO Box 2352, Oak Bluffs, MA 02557
(508)693-6135

This Martha's Vineyard inn offers three guest rooms, all decorated in antique country style. The skylit guest rooms of the Cape Cod-style inn share two baths. Breakfasts may be enjoyed in the inn's country kitchen, an outdoor deck or in front of the fireplace. Help yourself to iced tea and lemonade throughout the day. Within walking distance of the inn is a lagoon pond where guests may enjoy fishing, sailing, sunbathing and windsurfing. The State Lobster Hatchery is a short distance from the inn.

Innkeeper(s): Gloria Everett. $50-95. 3 rooms. Breakfast included in rates. Type of meal: full breakfast. Ceiling fan in room. Cable TV and VCR on premises. Antiques, shopping and theater nearby.

Certificate may be used: Sunday through Thursday, May 15 through June 30 and Sept. 10 through Oct. 9, excluding holidays and special events.

The Oak Bluffs Inn

Circuit and Pequot Ave,
Oak Bluffs, MA 02557
(508)693-7171 (800)955-6235

A widow's walk and gingerbread touches were added to this graceful home to enhance the Victorian atmosphere already prevalent throughout the inn. Rooms are decorated in Victorian style with antiques. Home-baked breads and fresh fruits start off the day. After enjoying the many activities Martha's Vineyard has to offer, return for a scrumptious afternoon tea with scones, tea sandwiches and pastries. Oak Bluffs originally was named Cottage City, and is full of quaint, gingerbread homes to view. Nearby Circuit Avenue offers shopping, ice cream parlors, eateries and the nation's oldest carousel.

Innkeeper(s): Maryann Mattera. $60-150. MC VISA AX DC DS. 9 rooms. Breakfast included in rates. Type of meal: continental breakfast.

Certificate may be used: Weekdays: Oct.1-June 15. Anytime: Oct. 15-April 30.

The Tucker Inn

46 Massasoit Ave, PO Box 2680,
Oak Bluffs, MA 02557
(508)693-1045

Circa 1872. Located on a quiet residential park within walking distance of retail establishments and the town beach, this two-story Victorian Stick/Shingle inn offers visitors to Martha's Vineyard a choice of suites and guest rooms with shared and private baths. The former doctor's

residence boasts an attractive veranda that is ideal for reading or relaxing after a busy day exploring the island's many attractions, or a trip to nearby Chappaquiddick. Public transportation and boat lines are a five-minute walk from the inn.

Innkeeper(s): William Reagan. $55-135. MC VISA. 8 rooms, 5 with PB. 2 suites. Breakfast included in rates. Type of meal: continental breakfast. Beds: QDT. Ceiling fan in room. Cable TV and VCR on premises. Antiques, fishing, shopping, theater and watersports nearby.

Certificate may be used: Oct. 1-June 15.

Onset   I15

Onset Pointe Inn
9 Eagle Way, PO Box 1450,
Onset, MA 02558
(508)295-8442 (800)356-6738
Fax:(508)295-5241

Circa 1880. This restored Victorian mansion is surrounded by the ocean on a sandy part of Onset Point. Its casually elegant decor is enhanced by sea views, sunlight, bright colors and florals. Spacious verandas, an enclosed circular sun porch and a bayside gazebo are available to guests. Accommodations are divided among the main house and two cottages. A full breakfast is served in a waterfront dining room. The inn received the National Trust first prize for preservation in their B&B category.

Innkeeper(s): Debi & Joe Lopes. $45-150. MC VISA AX DS PC TC. 15 rooms with PB. 6 suites. 2 cottages. 1 conference room. Breakfast included in rates. Beds: QDT. Cable TV, fax, copier and swimming on premises. Handicap access. Antiques, fishing, parks, shopping, theater and watersports nearby.

Location: Village of Onset, at the gateway to Cape Cod.

"We've found the B&B we've been looking for!"

Certificate may be used: Anytime, Oct. 15-May 1. Sunday-Thursday, May 1-Oct. 15.

Orleans   H19

The Farmhouse at Nauset Beach
163 Beach Rd, Orleans, MA 02653-2732
(508)255-6654

Circa 1870. Feel the intimacy of Orleans and capture the flavor of Cape Cod at this quiet country inn resting in a seashore setting. Rooms in this Greek Revival-style inn are comfortably furnished to depict their 19th-century past. Guests enjoy the "at home" feeling with morning coffee and freshly baked muffins or coffee cake. Nauset Beach is a short walk away. Spend a day charter fishing in Cape Cod Bay or the Atlantic. To make your stay complete, your itinerary can include antiquing, shopping, exploring quiet country lanes or a day at the beach.

Innkeeper(s): Dorothy Standish. $42-105. MC VISA PC. 8 rooms with PB, 1 with FP. Breakfast included in rates. Type of meal: continental-plus breakfast. Beds: KD. Ceiling fan and cable TV in room. Antiques, fishing, shopping, theater and watersports nearby.

Certificate may be used: October to April.

Provincetown   G18

Lamplighter Guest House
26 Bradford St, Provincetown, MA 02657
(508)487-2529 (800)263-6574

Circa 1800. From the top of a hill, this former sea captain's home affords a panoramic view of Cape Cod Bay. Two suites offer views of the bay, and two other rooms boast harbor views. The innkeepers also offer accommodations in a small cottage adjacent to the main house. A concierge service is available, and guests also can be shuttled to and from the airport or nearby docks.

Innkeeper(s): Steve Vittum & Brent Lawyer. $45-149. MC VISA AX TC. 11 rooms, 6 with PB. 1 suite. Breakfast and evening snack included in rates. Types of meals: continental breakfast and early coffee/tea. Beds: KQD. Air conditioning, turn-down service, ceiling fan and cable TV in room. Copier on premises. Antiques, fishing, parks, shopping, theater and watersports nearby.

Certificate may be used: Sept. 15 to June 30, holidays and special events excluded, on availability basis only. Advanced reservations required.

Watership Inn
7 Winthrop St, Provincetown, MA 02657
(508)487-0094 (800)330-9413
Fax:(508)487-2797

Circa 1820. This stately manor was built as a home port for a Provincetown sea captain. During the past 10 years, it has been renovated and the original beamed ceilings and polished plank floors provide a

background for the inn's antiques and simple decor. Guests enjoy the inn's sun decks and large yard, which offers volleyball and croquet sets.

Innkeeper(s): Roger Haas. $36-154. MC VISA AX DS. 16 rooms, 14 with PB. Breakfast included in rates. Type of meal: continental-plus breakfast. Beds: QDT. Bicycles on premises. Antiques and parks nearby.

Location: One-half block from Provincetown Harbor.

Seen in: Boston "In".

"We found your hospitality and charming inn perfect for our brief yet wonderful escape from Boston."

Certificate may be used: Oct. 1 through April 30.

Rehoboth   H12

Gilbert's Tree Farm B&B

30 Spring St, Rehoboth, MA 02769-2408
(508)252-6416

Circa 1835. This country farmhouse sits on 100 acres of woodland that includes an award-winning tree farm. Cross-country skiing, hiking, and pony-cart rides are found right outside the door. If they choose to, guests can even help with the farm chores, caring for horses and gardening. A swimming pool is open during summer. Three antique-filled bedrooms share a second-floor sitting room. The nearby town of Rehoboth is 350 years old.

Innkeeper(s): Jeanne & Martin Gilbert. $45-50. PC TC. 3 rooms. Breakfast, afternoon tea and evening snack included in rates. Types of meals: full breakfast and early coffee/tea. Beds: KDT. VCR, copier, swimming, stables, bicycles, library and pet boarding on premises. Antiques, fishing, parks, shopping, cross-country skiing, sporting events, theater and watersports nearby.

Location: Twelve miles east of Providence.

Seen in: Attleboro Sun Chronicle, Country, Somerset Spectator, Country Gazette, Pawtucket Times.

"This place has become my second home. Thank you for the family atmosphere of relaxation, fun, spontaneity and natural surroundings."

Certificate may be used: Nov. 1 through April 30, anytime.

Rockport   C15

Sally Webster Inn

34 Mount Pleasant St,
Rockport, MA 01966-1713
(508)546-9251

Circa 1832. William Choate left this pre-Civil War home to be divided by his nine children. Sally Choate Webster, the ninth child, was to receive several first-floor rooms and the attic chamber, but ended up owning the entire home. Innkeepers Tiffany and David Muhlenberg have filled the gracious home with antiques and reproductions, which

complement the original pine floors, antique door moldings and six fireplaces. The grounds boast Colonial herb and flower gardens. Shops, restaurants and the beach are all nearby.

Innkeeper(s): Tiffany Traynor-Muhlenberg. $55-90. MC VISA DS. 8 rooms, 7 with PB, 4 with FP. Breakfast included in rates. Type of meal: full breakfast. Beds: DT.

"All that a bed and breakfast should be."

Certificate may be used: December-March.

Tuck Inn

17 High St, Rockport, MA 01966-1644
(508)546-7260 (800)789-7260

Circa 1790. Two recent renovations have served to make this charming Colonial inn all the more enticing. Period antiques and paintings by local artists are featured throughout the spacious inn. A favorite gathering spot is the living room with its fireplace, wide pine floors, tasteful furnishings and a piano available for guest use. Buffet breakfasts feature homemade breads, muffins, cakes and scones, granola accompanied by fresh fruit and yogurt. Guests may take a dip in the swimming pool or at local beaches. Within easy walking distance are the many art galleries, restaurants and shops of Bearskin Neck. A nearby train station offers convenient access to Boston.

Innkeeper(s): Liz & Scott Wood. $47-107. MC VISA PC TC. 11 rooms with PB. 1 suite. Breakfast included in rates. Types of meals: continental-plus breakfast and early coffee/tea. Afternoon tea available. Beds: KQDT. Air conditioning, ceiling fan and cable TV in room. VCR, swimming, bicycles and library on premises. Antiques, fishing, parks, shopping, downhill skiing, cross-country skiing, sporting events, theater and watersports nearby.

Seen in: Fall River Herald News, North Shore News, Cape Ann Weekly.

"Wonderful people, lovely scenery, and great food, all good for the soul! Your hospitality and service was wonderful and we look forward to returning very soon!"

Certificate may be used: Nov. 1-April 30, Sunday through Thursday.

Salem D14

The Salem Inn

7 Summer St, Salem, MA 01970-3315
(508)741-0680 (800)446-2995
Fax:(508)744-8924

Circa 1834. This picturesque Federal-style inn is located in the heart of Salem's historic district, which features galleries, antiques, museums and the wharf and harbor. Many of the spacious guest rooms feature Jacuzzi tubs, fireplaces and canopy beds. Families will appreciate the two-room suites, which include kitchenettes. The dining area, with its brick walls and cozy atmosphere, is the perfect place to enjoy a light breakfast.

Innkeeper(s): Richard & Diane Pabich. $99-175. MC VISA AX DC CB DS TC. 31 rooms with PB, 14 with FP. 5 suites. 1 conference room. Breakfast included in rates. Type of meal: early coffee/tea. Picnic lunch, lunch, banquet service and catered breakfast available. Beds: KQT. Air conditioning and cable TV in room. Fax on premises. Antiques, fishing, parks, shopping, sporting events, theater and watersports nearby.

Location: Historic downtown.

Seen in: New York Times, Boston Sunday Globe.

"Delightful, charming. Our cup of tea."

Certificate may be used: Jan. 2 through April 1.

Sandwich I16

Captain Ezra Nye House

152 Main St, Sandwich, MA 02563-2232
(508)888-6142 (800)388-2278
Fax:(508)833-2897

Circa 1829. Captain Ezra Nye built this house after a record-shattering Halifax to Boston run, and the stately Federal-style house reflects the opulence and romance of the clipper ship era. Hand-stenciled walls and museum-quality antiques decorate the interior. Within walking distance are the Doll Museum, the Glass Museum, restaurants, shops, the famous Heritage Plantation, the beach and marina.

Innkeeper(s): Elaine & Harry Dickson. $75-100. MC VISA AX DS PC TC. 6 rooms with PB, 1 with FP. 1 suite. Breakfast included in rates. Types of meals: full breakfast, gourmet breakfast and early coffee/tea. Beds: QDT. Cable TV, VCR, fax and library on premises. Antiques, fishing, parks, shopping, theater and watersports nearby.

Location: In the heart of Sandwich Village, oldest town on Cape Cod.

Seen in: Glamour, Innsider, Cape Cod Life, Toronto Life, Yankee.

"The prettiest room and most beautiful home we have been to. We had a wonderful time."

Certificate may be used: Sunday through Thursday, Nov. 1 through April 30.

The Summer House

158 Main St, Sandwich, MA 02563-2232
(508)888-4991

Circa 1835. The Summer House is a handsome Greek Revival in a setting of historic homes and public buildings. (Hiram Dillaway, one of the owners, was a famous mold maker for the Boston & Sandwich Glass Company.) The house is fully restored and decorated with antiques and hand-stitched quilts. Four of the guest rooms have black marble fireplaces. The porch overlooks an old-fashioned perennial garden, antique rose bushes, and a 70-year-old rhododendron hedge.

Innkeeper(s): David & Kay Merrell. $65-85. MC VISA AX DS PC TC. 5 rooms, 1 with PB, 4 with FP. Breakfast and afternoon tea included in rates. Types of meals: full breakfast, gourmet breakfast and early coffee/tea. Beds: KQT. Library on premises. Antiques, fishing, parks, shopping, cross-country skiing, theater and watersports nearby.

Location: Center of village, Cape Cod.

Seen in: Country Living, Boston, Cape Cod Times.

"An absolutely gorgeous house and a super breakfast. I wish I could've stayed longer! Came for one night, stayed for three! Marvelous welcome."

Certificate may be used: Sunday-Thursday, November-March.

Sheffield   F2

Staveleigh House
59 Main St, PO 608,
Sheffield, MA 01257
(413)229-2129

Circa 1821. The Reverend Bradford, minister of Old Parish Congregational Church, the oldest church in the Berkshires, built this home for his family. Afternoon tea is served and the inn is especially favored for its four-course breakfasts and gracious hospitality. Located next to the town green, the house is in a historic district in the midst of several fine antique shops. It is also near Tanglewood, skiing and all Berkshire attractions.

Innkeeper(s): Dorothy Marosy & Marion Whitman. $70-95. TC. 5 rooms, 2 with PB. Breakfast and afternoon tea included in rates. Types of meals: full breakfast and early coffee/tea. Beds: KQDT. Turn-down service and ceiling fan in room. Handicap access. Antiques, fishing, parks, shopping, downhill skiing, cross-country skiing, theater and watersports nearby.

Seen in: Los Angeles Times, Boston Globe.

"Exceptionally good."

Certificate may be used: Sunday-Thursday, year-round; any day November-March, except holidays.

South Deerfield   D6

Deerfield B&B -
The Yellow Gabled House
111 N Main St,
South Deerfield, MA 01373-1026
(413)665-4922

Circa 1800. Huge maple trees shade the yard of this historic house, four miles from historic Deerfield and one mile from Route 91. Decorated with antiques and old lace, two of the guest rooms have their own cozy sofa. The battle of Bloody Brook Massacre in 1675 occurred at this site, now landscaped with perennial English gardens.

Innkeeper(s): Edna Stahelek. $70-105. 3 rooms, 1 with PB. Breakfast included in rates. Types of meals: full breakfast, gourmet breakfast and early coffee/tea. Beds: QDT. Air conditioning, ceiling fan and cable TV in room. VCR on premises. Antiques, fishing, shopping, downhill skiing, cross-country skiing, sporting events and theater nearby.

Location: One mile from crossroads of I-91, Rt 116 & Rts 5 & 10.

Seen in: Recorder, Boston Globe.

"We are still speaking of that wonderful weekend and our good fortune in finding you."

Certificate may be used: December, January and February.

South Dennis   I18

Captain Nickerson Inn
333 Main St, South Dennis, MA 02660
(508)398-5966 (800)282-1619

Circa 1828. This Queen Anne Victorian inn originally was built by a sea captain. Guests can relax on the front porch with white wicker rockers and tables. The guest rooms are decorated with period four-poster or white iron queen beds and 'Oriental' or hand-woven rugs. The dining room has a fireplace and a stained-glass picture window. The Cape Cod bike Rail Trail, which is more than 20 miles long, is less than a mile away.

Innkeeper(s): Pat & Dave York. $60-90. MC VISA DS PC. 5 rooms, 3 with PB. Breakfast included in rates. Type of meal: full breakfast. Beds: QDT. Air conditioning and ceiling fan in room. Cable TV, VCR, fax and

bicycles on premises. Antiques, fishing, parks, shopping, theater and watersports nearby.

"Your inn is great!"

Certificate may be used: Nov. 15 to May 15.

South Yarmouth I18

Captain Farris House B&B

308 Main St,
South Yarmouth, MA 02664-4530
(508)760-2818 (800)350-9477
Fax:(508)398-1262

Circa 1845. Listed in the National Register, this inn offers accommodations at both the Captain Allen Farris House and the adjacent Elisha Jenkins House. Eight rooms are found at the Captain's house, with two suites next door. The architectural stylings are Greek Revival and French Second Empire. Breakfasts are served either in the dining room, on the terrace or in the inn's courtyard. Be sure to inquire about picnic lunches, ideal for an afternoon of exploring the Cape's many attractions. Two blocks away is the Bass River.

Innkeeper(s): Scott Toney. $75-225. MC VISA AX. 10 rooms with PB. 4 suites. Breakfast included in rates. Type of meal: full breakfast. Afternoon tea, dinner, picnic lunch, lunch, gourmet lunch and catering service available. Beds: KQT. Turn-down service and cable TV in room. Antiques, fishing, shopping, theater and watersports nearby.

Seen in: Register.

"As always, a wonderful, relaxing stay! Thanks for your warmth and hospitality."

Certificate may be used: Nov. 15-April 15. Holiday weekends with purchase of two nights. Limited number of rooms available.

Stockbridge E2

Arbor Rose B&B

8 Yale Hill, Box 114,
Stockbridge, MA 01262
(413)298-4744

Circa 1810. This large, white farmhouse overlooks an 1800s mill, millpond and gardens with the mountains as a backdrop. Floral wallpapers, paintings and antiques occupy sunny rooms. After a day on the slopes or on cross-country paths, skiers can warm themselves next to the fireplace in the front parlor. Guests can walk to the Berkshire Theatre and Stockbridge Center. The Norman Rockwell Museum, Tanglewood Music Festival, ski areas, antique and other shops are all within a seven-mile radius.

Innkeeper(s): Christina Alsop. $60-150. MC VISA AX PC TC. 5 rooms, 2 with PB. 1 conference room. Breakfast included in rates. Types of meals: full breakfast, gourmet breakfast and early coffee/tea. Beds:

KQT. Ceiling fan in room. Cable TV and VCR on premises. Antiques, parks, shopping, skiing and theater nearby.

Location: One-half mile from center of Stockbridge.

Seen in: Yankee Traveler.

"If houses really do exude the spirit of events and feelings stored from their history, it explains why a visitor feels warmth and joy from the first turn up the driveway."

Certificate may be used: November-May, midweek.

The Inn at Stockbridge

PO Box 618, Stockbridge, MA 01262
(413)298-3337 Fax:(413)298-3406

Circa 1906. Giant maples shade the drive leading to this Southern-style Georgian Colonial with its impressive pillared entrance. Located on 12 acres, the grounds include a reflecting pool, a fountain, meadows and woodland as well as wide vistas of the rolling hillsides. The guest rooms feature antiques and handsome 18th-century reproductions. Breakfast is graciously presented with fine china, silver and linens.

Innkeeper(s): Alice & Lenny Schiller. $85-235. MC VISA AX PC TC. 8 rooms with PB. 2 suites. Breakfast and evening snack included in rates. Types of meals: full breakfast, gourmet breakfast and early coffee/tea. Beds: DT. Air conditioning in room. Cable TV, VCR, fax, copier, swimming and library on premises. Antiques, fishing, parks, shopping, downhill skiing, cross-country skiing, theater and watersports nearby.

Seen in: Vogue, New York Magazine, New York Daily News, Country Inns Northeast, Arts & Antiques.

"Classy & comfortable."

Certificate may be used: Sunday-Thursday, Nov. 1-May 15 excluding holidays.

Sturbridge
F8

Commonwealth Cottage
11 Summit Ave,
Sturbridge, MA 01566-1225
(508)347-7708

Circa 1873. This 16-room Queen Anne Victorian house, on an acre near the Quinebaug River, is just a few minutes from Old Sturbridge Village. Both the dining room and parlor have fireplaces. The Baroque theme of the Sal Raciti room makes it one of the guest favorites and it features a queen mahogany bed. Breakfast may be offered on the gazebo porch or in the formal dining room. It includes a variety of homemade specialties, such as freshly baked breads and cakes.

Innkeeper(s): Robert & Wiebke Gilbert. $85-145. PC TC. 5 rooms, 2 with PB. Types of meals: full breakfast and early coffee/tea. Evening snack available. Beds: QDT. Ceiling fan in room. Library on premises. Antiques, fishing, parks, shopping, theater and watersports nearby.
Seen in: Long Island Newsday, Villager.

"Your home is so warm and welcoming we feel as though we've stepped back in time. Our stay here has helped to make the wedding experience extra special!"

Certificate may be used: December-April, Sunday-Thursday, holiday weekends excluded.

Sturbridge Country Inn
PO Box 60, 530 Main St,
Sturbridge, MA 01566-0060
(508)347-5503 Fax:(508)347-5319

Circa 1840. Shaded by an old silver maple, this classic Greek Revival house boasts a two-story columned entrance. The attached carriage house now serves as the lobby and displays the original post-and-beam construction and exposed rafters. All guest rooms have individual fireplaces and whirlpool tubs. They are gracefully appointed in reproduction colonial furnishings, including queen-size, four-posters. A patio and gazebo are favorite summertime retreats.
Innkeeper(s): Patricia Affenito. $59-159. MC VISA AX DS PC TC. 9 rooms with PB, 9 with FP. 1 suite. 1 conference room. Breakfast included in rates. Types of meals: continental breakfast and early coffee/tea.

Room service available. Beds: KQ. Air conditioning, ceiling fan, cable TV and VCR in room. Fax, copier and spa on premises. Antiques, fishing, parks, shopping, downhill skiing, cross-country skiing, theater and watersports nearby.
Location: Near Old Sturbridge Village.
Seen in: Southbridge Evening News, Worcester Telegram & Gazette.

"Best lodging I've ever seen."

Certificate may be used: January-April, Sunday-Thursday.

Ware
E7

The Wildwood Inn
121 Church St, Ware, MA 01082-1203
(413)967-7798 (800)860-8098

Circa 1880. This yellow Victorian has a wraparound porch and a beveled-glass front door. American primitive antiques include a collection of New England cradles and heirloom quilts, a saddle-maker's bench, and a spinning wheel. The inn's two acres are dotted with maple, chestnut and apple trees. Through the woods you'll find a river.

Innkeeper(s): Fraidell Fenster & Richard Watson. $50-85. MC VISA AX PC TC. 9 rooms, 7 with PB. 1 suite. 2 conference rooms. Breakfast and afternoon tea included in rates. Types of meals: full breakfast and early coffee/tea. Banquet service, catering service and catered breakfast available. Beds: KQDT. Air conditioning, turn-down service and ceiling fan in room. Bicycles, tennis and library on premises. Handicap access. Amusement parks, antiques, fishing, parks, shopping, downhill skiing, cross-country skiing, sporting events and theater nearby.
Seen in: Boston Globe, National Geographic Traveler, Country, Worcester Transcript-Telegram.

"Excellent accommodations, not only in rooms, but in the kind and thoughtful way you treat your guests. We'll be back!"

Certificate may be used: Nov. 1 through June 30, excluding Brimfield Flea Market weeks. Sunday through Thursday.

Wareham 115

The Cranberry Rose B&B
105 High St, Wareham, MA 02571-2053
(508)295-5665 (800)269-5665

Circa 1903. Innkeeper Chris Makepeace's family built this sturdy, New England home. The house eventually was sold to another family, but Chris and wife, Sue, bought the home several years ago and renovated it into a bed & breakfast. Chris and Sue also have continued the Makepeace tradition as cranberry farmers. During the harvest, the two will prepare picnics and tours of their cranberry bogs. Sue has created several cranberry recipes, some of which she serves in the afternoon along with wine and sherry. Her recipe for Cranberry Bars was featured in Bon Appetit. The home is decorated in a cozy, country style with quilts, ceiling fans and antiques from an 18th-century boarding house.
Innkeeper(s): Sue & Chris Makepeace. $60-75. MC VISA PC TC. 3 rooms with PB. Breakfast and afternoon tea included in rates. Type of meal: early coffee/tea. Beds: KQDT. Air conditioning and ceiling fan in room. Cable TV, VCR, fax, copier and bicycles on premises. Antiques, fishing, parks, shopping, cross-country skiing, sporting events, theater and watersports nearby.
Certificate may be used: April 1-Dec. 31, Sunday-Friday.

Mulberry B&B
257 High St, Wareham, MA 02571-1407
(508)295-0684 Fax:(508)291-2909

Circa 1847. This former blacksmith's house is in the historic district of town and has been featured on the local garden club house tour. Frances, a former school teacher, has decorated the guest rooms in a country style with antiques. A deck, shaded by a tall mulberry tree, looks out to the back garden.

Innkeeper(s): Frances Murphy. $50-65. MC VISA AX DS PC TC. 3 rooms. Breakfast included in rates. Type of meal: full breakfast. Afternoon tea available. Beds: KDT. Air conditioning and turn-down service in room. Cable TV and VCR on premises. Antiques, fishing, parks, shopping, cross-country skiing, sporting events, theater and watersports nearby.
Seen in: Brockton Enterprise, Wareham Courier.
Certificate may be used: Sunday through Thursday, May through October, anytime November through April.

West Harwich 118

The Gingerbread House
141 Division St,
West Harwich, MA 02671-1005
(508)432-1901 (800)788-1901

Circa 1883. This rambling Queen Anne Victorian is decked with ornate, gingerbread trim and gables. The innkeepers, of Polish descent, have added European flavor to their inn with a collection of Polish art, crystal and crafts. Aside from the scrumptious breakfasts, the innkeepers offer dinner service at the inn's restaurant. Proper afternoon teas are served in the Tea Room, which is located in the Carriage House. Sandwiches, freshly baked goods and scones are accompanied by Devon clotted cream and a selection of teas. The inn is near many of Cape Cod's shops and restaurants.
Innkeeper(s): Stacia & Les Kostecki. $45-105. MC VISA TC. 5 suites, 1 with FP. 1 conference room. Breakfast and afternoon tea included in rates. Types of meals: continental breakfast, continental-plus breakfast, full breakfast, gourmet breakfast and early coffee/tea. Dinner, evening snack, picnic lunch, gourmet lunch and room service available. Beds: Q. Ceiling fan and cable TV in room. VCR and child care on premises. Handicap access. Antiques, fishing, parks, and theater nearby.
Certificate may be used: Sept. 17 to Dec. 10, Sunday-Saturday; May 1-Sept. 15, Sunday-Thursday, except for holidays.

West Stockbridge E2

Card Lake Inn
PO Box 38, West Stockbridge, MA 01266
(413)232-0272 Fax:(413)232-0272

Circa 1880. Located in the center of town, this Colonial Revival inn features a popular local restaurant on the premises. Norman Rockwell is said to have frequented its tavern. Stroll around historic West Stockbridge then enjoy the inn's deck cafe with its flower boxes and view of the sculpture garden of an art gallery across the street. Original lighting, hardwood floors and antiques are features of the inn. Chesterwood and Tanglewood are within easy driving distance.
Innkeeper(s): Edward Robbins. $60-140. MC VISA AX DS. 8 rooms. Breakfast included in rates. Types of meals: continental breakfast and early coffee/tea. Restaurant on premises. Beds: KQ. Air conditioning and ceiling fan in room. Cable TV and VCR on premises. Amusement parks, antiques, shopping and sporting events nearby.
Certificate may be used: Anytime excluding weekends in June, July, August and October.

Marble Inn

4 Stockbridge Rd,
West Stockbridge, MA 01266-0268
(413)232-7092

Circa 1835. Gourmet breakfasts, close access to area activities and cheerful, country guest rooms are some of the reasons to visit Marble Inn. The history of the early 19th-century home is another. The inn was built during the town's heyday as a center for marble trading and shipping. Egg nog French toast, a variety of omelets, herbed asparagus crepes, savory meats and freshly baked breads ensure guests will wake up on the right side of the bed. For an extra charge, the innkeepers may be able to prepare picnic lunches, with names such as The Yankee or The Gourmet. The Yankee, for example, is a basket filled with corn quiche, fried chicken, cole slaw, Parker House rolls and chocolate chip cookies. Guests can take these lunches along with them on trips to nearby museums, Tanglewood, the Shaker Village, antique shops and more.

Innkeeper(s): Yvonne & Joe Kopper. $85-135. MC VISA AX DS PC TC. 5 rooms with PB, 1 with FP. Breakfast included in rates. Type of meal: gourmet breakfast. Picnic lunch available. Beds: QD. Air conditioning in room. Antiques, fishing, downhill skiing, cross-country skiing, theater and watersports nearby.

Certificate may be used: Nov. 1-May 25, excluding holidays.

West Yarmouth   I17

Manor House

57 Maine Ave,
West Yarmouth, MA 02673-5816
(508)771-3433 (800)962-6679

Circa 1920. This bed & breakfast is located on Cape Cod's south shore overlooking Lewis Bay. The beach and a boat ramp are within walking distance. The quiet neighborhood also is near whale watching, golf and fine dining. Take a ferry to one of the islands or just relax in the comfort of your own room. The fireplaced sitting room is a great place to finish a book.

Innkeeper(s): Rick & Liz Latshaw. $58-108. MC VISA AX PC TC. 6 rooms with PB. Breakfast and afternoon tea included in rates. Types of meals: continental-plus breakfast and early coffee/tea. Beds: QD. Air conditioning and turn-down service in room. Cable TV, VCR and library on premises. Antiques, fishing, parks, shopping, theater and watersports nearby.

"An experience I am anxious to repeat."

Certificate may be used: Anytime between Nov. 1 and May 14.

Woods Hole   J15

The Marlborough B&B

PO Box 238, Woods Hole, MA 02543
(508)548-6218 (800)320-2322
Fax:(508)457-7519

Circa 1942. This is a faithful reproduction of a Cape-style cottage complete with picket fence and rambling roses. Although the inn is beautifully decorated, well-traveled children over two are welcome. An English paddle-tennis court and a swim-

ming pool are popular spots in summer. In winter, breakfast is served beside a roaring fire. The inn is the closest bed & breakfast to the ferries to Martha's Vineyard and Nantucket.

Innkeeper(s): Diana Smith. $65-125. MC VISA AX PC. 5 rooms, 6 with PB. 1 cottage. Breakfast included in rates. Types of meals: gourmet breakfast and early coffee/tea. Beds: QD. Air conditioning in room. Cable TV, fax, swimming and tennis on premises. Antiques, fishing, shopping, theater and watersports nearby.

Location: Near Falmouth historic district.

Seen in: Cape Cod Life.

"Our stay at the Marlborough was a little bit of heaven."

Certificate may be used: Nov. 1-May 15, Sunday-Thursday.

Worcester-Rutland   E9

The General Rufus Putnam House

344 Main St,
Worcester-Rutland, MA 01543-1303
(508)886-4864

Circa 1750. This restored Federal house, listed in the National Register, was the home of General Rufus Putnam, founder of Marietta, Ohio. A memorial tablet on the house states that "to him it is owing..that the United States is not now a great slaveholding empire." Surrounded by tall maples and a rambling stone fence, the inn rests on seven acres of woodlands and meadows. There are eight fireplaces, blue Delft tiles and a beehive oven. Afternoon tea and breakfast are served fireside in the keeping room.

Innkeeper(s): Chris & Marcia Warrington. $100-125. MAP. TC. 2 rooms, 1 with PB, 2 with FP. Breakfast, afternoon tea and evening snack included in rates. Types of meals: full breakfast and early coffee/tea. Picnic lunch available. Beds: KT. Turn-down service in room. Amusement parks, antiques, fishing, parks, shopping, downhill skiing, cross-country skiing, sporting events, theater and watersports nearby.

Location: Rural/Central Massachusetts.

Seen in: Sunday Telegram, The Land Mark, Washusett People.

"We were thrilled with the beauty and luxury of this B&B and especially the wonderful hospitality."

Certificate may be used: January-March, Sunday-Friday.

Yarmouth Port
117

Liberty Hill Inn
77 Main St, Rt 6A,
Yarmouth Port, MA 02675-1709
(508)362-3976 (800)821-3977

Circa 1825. Just back from historic Old King's Highway, this country inn is a restored Greek Revival mansion. It is located on the site of the original Liberty Pole dating from Revolutionary times. A romantic decor includes fine antiques and

thick carpets, enhancing the tall windows and high ceilings. Stroll past the inn's flower-edged lawns for a brief walk to antique shops, auctions and restaurants. The house was built by shipwrights.

Innkeeper(s): Jack & Beth Flanagan. $75-135. MC VISA AX PC TC. 5 rooms with PB. Types of meals: gourmet breakfast and early coffee/tea. Beds: KQDT. Air conditioning and ceiling fan in room. Computer on premises. Antiques, fishing, parks, shopping, theater and watersports nearby.

Location: On Cape Cod, 10 minutes north of Hyannis.

Seen in: Cape Cod Life, Colonial Homes.

"Your homey hospitality makes us want to return. We enjoyed our stay very much and your New England hospitality was as gracious as I heard. The place is wonderful."

Certificate may be used: March-June, November-February, any night except holiday weekends.

Olde Captain's Inn on The Cape
101 Main St Rt 6A,
Yarmouth Port, MA 02675-1709
(508)362-4496

Circa 1835. Located in the historic district and on Captain's Mile, this house is in the National Register. It is decorated in a traditional style, with coordinated wallpapers and carpets, and there are two suites that include kitchens and living rooms. Apple trees, blackberries and raspberries grow on the acre of grounds and often contribute to the breakfast menus. There is a summer veranda overlooking the property. Good restaurants are within walking distance.

Innkeeper(s): Sven Tilly. $35-100. 3 rooms, 1 with PB. 2 suites. Breakfast included in rates. Type of meal: continental-plus breakfast. Beds: KQD. Cable TV in room. Antiques, fishing, shopping, sporting events, theater and watersports nearby.

Location: Cape Cod.

Certificate may be used: Anytime, Nov. 1 to June 1. Sunday through Thursday, June 1 to Nov. 1. Excludes holidays.

Michigan

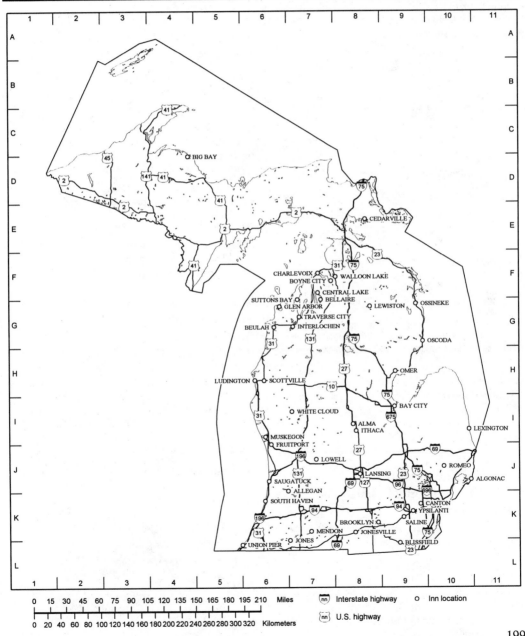

	Miles
0 15 30 45 60 75 90 105 120 135 150 165 180 195 210	
0 20 40 60 80 100 120 140 160 180 200 220 240 260 280 300 320	Kilometers

(nn) Interstate highway   o Inn location

(nn) U.S. highway

199

Algonac   *J10*

Linda's Lighthouse Inn
5965 Pointe Tremble Rd Box 828,
Algonac, MI 48001-4229
(810)794-2992

Circa 1920. Overlooking Dickerson Island, on the
north branch of the St. Clair River, is this two-story
Colonial inn, once used to aid bootleggers bringing
in liquor from Canada during Prohibition. Guests
who arrive by boat and use the inn's 100 feet of

dockage will have transportation to restaurants, provided for them. Guests choose from the Jacuzzi,
Lighthouse, Rose and Duck rooms, all featuring
feather pillows. St. John's Marsh is less than a
half-mile away.
Innkeeper(s): Ron & Linda (Russell) Yetsko. $75-100. MC VISA AX TC.
4 rooms with PB. Breakfast and evening snack included in rates. Types
of meals: gourmet breakfast and early coffee/tea. Picnic lunch available.
Beds: KQD. Air conditioning, turn-down service and ceiling fan in room.
Cable TV, VCR, copier and bicycles on premises. Antiques, fishing,
parks, shopping, cross-country skiing and watersports nearby.
Certificate may be used: May 1 to Oct. 31, Monday-Thursday, no
holidays.

Allegan   *J6*

Castle In The Country
340 M 40 S, Allegan, MI 49010-9609
(616)673-8054

Enjoy refreshing country views from every window
at this three-story Victorian, which was built by a
Civil War captain. Each of the guest quarters offers
something special. The Bittersweet, which has a
chandelier and private sitting area, boasts a view of
Bittersweet Mountain. The Rose Gazebo is located
in the home's turret. This unique, round room
includes white, wicker furnishings and flowery

linens. Each guest room is decorated with candles
and fresh flowers. Homemade breads and pastries
accompany the full, gourmet breakfasts, which can
be enjoyed in the privacy of your bedchamber or in
the formal dining room. The innkeepers host special
events such as murder-mystery weekends and
multi-day bicycle tours.
Innkeeper(s): Ruth Boren. $65-95. MC VISA. 4 rooms. Breakfast includ-
ed in rates. Type of meal: full breakfast.
Certificate may be used: Sunday-Thursday, Nov. 1-April 20 (excluding
holiday weekends).

Delano Inn
302 Cutler St, Allegan, MI 49010-1210
(616)673-2609

Circa 1863. This Italian Provincial mansion, surrounded by a wrought-iron fence, is listed in the
National Register of Historic Places. The inn offers
cozy sitting rooms and a summer porch. There are
stenciled floors, lace curtains, marble fireplaces,
crystal chandeliers, a spiral staircase, antique furnishings and European feather beds.
Innkeeper(s): Robert Ashley. $55-85. MC VISA. 5 rooms. 1 conference
room. Breakfast included in rates. Type of meal: continental-plus breakfast. Beds: QDT. Air conditioning and ceiling fan in room. Cable TV and
VCR on premises. Amusement parks, antiques, shopping, downhill skiing, cross-country skiing and theater nearby.
Seen in: Allegan County News & Gazette.

*"The world would be a much more peaceful place if we
all celebrated hospitality the way you folks do."*
Certificate may be used: Jan. 2 through March 30.

Winchester Inn
524 Marshall St M-89,
Allegan, MI 49010-1632
(616)673-3621 (800)582-5694

Circa 1864. This neo-Italian Renaissance mansion
was built of double-layer brick and has been restored
to its original beauty. Surrounded by a unique,
hand-poured iron fence, the inn is decorated with
period antiques and romantically furnished
bedchambers.
Innkeeper(s): Denise Ferber. $67-85. MC VISA AX. 4 rooms with PB. 1
conference room. Breakfast included in rates. Types of meals: continental breakfast, full breakfast and early coffee/tea. Beds: KQD. Ceiling fan

in room. Cable TV on premises. Handicap access. Antiques, fishing, shopping, downhill skiing, cross-country skiing, theater and watersports nearby.

Location: Near Grand Rapids, Kalamazoo, Holland, Saugatuck and Lake Michigan State Forest.

Seen in: Architectural Digest, Home and Away, Midwest Living, Detroit Free Press, Cleveland Plain Dealer, Grand Rapids Press.

"This is one of Michigan's loveliest country inns."

Certificate may be used: Sunday through Thursday, April through October. Any day November through March. Not during local festivals.

Alma 18

Saravilla
633 N State St, Alma, MI 48801-1640
(517)463-4078

Circa 1894. This Dutch Colonial home with its Queen Anne influences was built as a magnificent wedding gift for lumber baron Ammi W. Wright's only surviving child, Sara. Wright spared no expense building this mansion for his daughter, and the innkeepers have spared nothing in restoring the home to its former prominence. The foyer and dining room boast imported English oak woodwork. The foyer's hand-painted canvas wallcoverings come from France and complement the embossed, Italian wallpaper. The home still features original leaded glass windows, built-in bookcases, window seats and light fixtures. In 1993, the innkeepers added a sunroom with a hot tub that overlooks a formal garden. The full, formal breakfast includes such treats as homemade granola, freshly made coffeecakes, breads, muffins and a mix of entrees.

Innkeeper(s): Linda Darrow. $55-75. MC VISA DS. 6 rooms with PB. 1 suite. Breakfast and afternoon tea included in rates. Type of meal: full breakfast. Room service available. Beds: QDT. Antiques, fishing, cross-country skiing and theater nearby.

Seen in: Morning Sun, Saginaw News, Sault Sunday.

Certificate may be used: Sunday-Thursday, year-round.

Bay City 19

Clements Inn
1712 Center Ave M-25,
Bay City, MI 48708-6122
(517)894-4600 (800)442-4605
Fax:(517)895-8535

Circa 1886. The amber-paned windows and oak ceilings of this three-story Queen Anne Victorian inn are just a few of its impressive features. Built by William Clements, the home joined a number of other impressive estates on Center Avenue, most of which were owned by lumber barons. The inn's

well-appointed guest rooms are named for famous authors or fictional characters, continuing a strong tradition started by Clements, a collector of rare books. A winding staircase, original gas lighting fixtures and hand-carved woodwork have impressed many visitors.

Innkeeper(s): Brian & Karen Hepp. $70-140. MC VISA AX DC DS TC. 7 rooms, 2 with PB. 3 suites. 5 conference rooms. Breakfast and evening snack included in rates. Types of meals: continental-plus breakfast and early coffee/tea. Beds: KQDT. Air conditioning, cable TV and VCR in room. Fax on premises. Handicap access. Antiques, fishing, parks, shopping, downhill skiing, cross-country skiing and theater nearby.

Certificate may be used: Sunday-Thursday, Nov. 1-April 30.

Stonehedge Inn
924 Center Ave M-25,
Bay City, MI 48708-6118
(517)894-4342

Circa 1889. An exquisite oak staircase greets guests as they enter this 19th-century Tudor-style home. Marble fireplaces and original brass light fixtures add an elegant flair to the common rooms. The home was built by a lumber baron and many of the original features are still in operation including speaking tubes and a dumb-waiter. Spend an afternoon cruising the riverwalk or take a look at the historic district and museum.

Innkeeper(s): Ruth Koerber. $75-85. MC VISA AX DS PC TC. 7 rooms. 1 conference room. Breakfast included in rates. Types of meals: continental breakfast, continental-plus breakfast, full breakfast and early coffee/tea. Beds: QDT. Air conditioning in room. Cable TV on premises. Antiques, fishing, parks, shopping, downhill skiing and theater nearby.

Location: Downtown.

Seen in: Bay City Times, Midwest Living, Great Lakes Getaway, Michigan Tourist Monthly, Saginaw News .

"Your facilities provided a unique and warm atmosphere, and your friendly hospitality added a very personal touch."

Certificate may be used: Nov. 1-May. 15

Bellaire G7

Grand Victorian B&B Inn
402 N Bridge St, Bellaire, MI 49615-9591
(616)533-6111 (800)336-3860
Fax:(616)533-8197

Circa 1895. It's hard to believe that anything but joy has ever been associated with this beautiful Queen Anne Victorian inn, but its original owner, who built it in anticipation of his upcoming nuptials, left town broken-hearted when his wedding plans fell through. The eye-pleasing inn, with its gables, square corner towers, bays and overhangs, is listed in the National Register of Historic Places. There is much to do in this popular area of

Northern Michigan, with its famous nearby skiing and fishing spots, but the inn's impressive interior may entice guests to stay on the premises. Guest rooms are well-appointed with period antiques and lavish touches. Visitors may borrow a bicycle built for two for a relaxing tour of town.

Innkeeper(s): Jill Watson. $75-95. MC VISA AX. 4 rooms with PB. Breakfast and afternoon tea included in rates. Types of meals: full breakfast and early coffee/tea. Picnic lunch available. Beds: QDT. Air conditioning and VCR in room. Cable TV on premises. Antiques, fishing, shopping, downhill skiing, cross-country skiing and watersports nearby.

Seen in: Featured on Nabisco Crackers/Cookies Boxes Promotion.

"We certainly enjoyed our visit to the Grand Victorian. It has been our pleasure to stay in B&Bs in several countries, but never one more beautiful and almost never with such genial hosts."

Certificate may be used: Sunday through Thursday, Sept. 15-June 15.

Beulah   G6

Windermere Inn
7723 Crystal Dr, Beulah, MI 49617-9608
(616)882-9000

Circa 1894. This farmhouse is just across the road from Crystal Lake. The interior is furnished in country decor. Two fireplaces in the common area create a cozy atmosphere. Afternoon refreshments and turn-down service are included.

Innkeeper(s): Anne and Cameron Clark. $69. MC VISA. 4 rooms with PB. Type of meal: continental breakfast. Beds: QDT. Fishing and parks nearby.

Seen in: Record Patriot.

Certificate may be used: Midweek from Labor Day to Memorial Day, excluding holidays; weekends, Nov. 1 to April 30.

Big Bay   D4

The Big Bay Point Lighthouse B&B
3 Lighthouse Rd, Big Bay, MI 49808
(906)345-9957

Circa 1896. With 4,500 feet of frontage on Lake Superior, this landmark lighthouse commands 534 acres of forests and a five-acre lawn. The interior of the lighthouse features a brick fireplace. Several guest rooms look out to the water. The tower room on the top floor offers truly unforgettable views. Breakfast is light, so pack some extra food.

Innkeeper(s): Linda & Jeff Gamble. $85-155. PC TC. 7 rooms with PB. 2 suites. Breakfast and evening snack included in rates. Types of meals: full breakfast and early coffee/tea. Beds: QD. Ceiling fan in room. VCR, fax, copier and sauna on premises. Antiques, fishing, parks, shopping, downhill skiing, cross-country skiing, sporting events, theater and watersports nearby.

Location: Four miles northeast of Big Bay.

Seen in: Los Angeles Times, USA Today.

Certificate may be used: Nov. 1 to May 15 excluding holidays & special promotions.

Blissfield   L9

415 W Adrian St, US Hwy 223,
Blissfield, MI 49228-1001
(517)486-3155

Circa 1883. This red brick Italianate house is in a village setting directly across from the 1851 Hathaway House, an elegant historic restaurant. Rooms at the Hiram D. Ellis Inn feature handsome antique bedsteads, armoires and floral wallpapers. Breakfast is served in the inn's common room, and the innkeeper receives rave reviews on her peach and apple dishes. (There are apple, peach and pear trees on the property.) Bicycles are available for riding around town, or you can walk to the train station and board the murder-mystery dinner train that runs on weekends.

Innkeeper(s): Christine Webster & Frank Seely. $75-95. MC VISA AX TC. 6 rooms, 4 with PB. Breakfast included in rates. Types of meals: continental-plus breakfast, full breakfast and early coffee/tea. Beds: QD. Air conditioning and cable TV in room. Bicycles on premises. Antiques, fishing, parks, shopping, cross-country skiing and theater nearby.

Seen in: Ann Arbor News, Michigan Living.

"I have now experienced what it is truly like to have been treated like a queen."

Certificate may be used: All year, Sunday through Thursday.

Boyne City   F7

Deer Lake B&B
00631 E Deer Lake Rd,
Boyne City, MI 49712-9614
(616)582-9039

Located in a comfortable, ranch-style home, this bed & breakfast offers guests water views and peaceful surroundings. Two rooms include private balconies overlooking the lake, and the other three guest quarters share a 40-foot balcony. The house is bright and airy with elegant, country furnishings, French doors and a few lacy touches. For those who enjoy the outdoors, the area offers golf, fishing, swimming, sailing, skiing and much more. For those more creatively inclined, the innkeepers, both former jewelers, offer ring-making classes.

Innkeeper(s): Glenn & Shirley Piepenburg. $80-95. MC VISA DS PC TC. 5 rooms with PB. Breakfast and evening snack included in rates. Types of meals: full breakfast and early coffee/tea. Beds: KQT. Air conditioning, turn-down service and ceiling fan in room. Cable TV, VCR, swimming and bicycles on premises. Antiques, fishing, parks, shopping, downhill skiing, cross-country skiing and watersports nearby.

Certificate may be used: Jan. 2-June 30, Sept. 1-Nov. 30, Friday & Saturday weekends. July 8-Aug. 29 weekdays, Monday-Thursday.

Brooklyn   K8

Dewey Lake Manor
11811 Laird Rd, Brooklyn, MI 49230-9035
(517)467-7122

Circa 1868. This Italianate house overlooks Dewey Lake and is situated on 18 acres in the Irish Hills. The house is furnished in a country Victorian style with antiques. An enclosed porch is a favorite spot to relax and take in the views of the lake while having breakfast. Favorite pastimes include lakeside bonfires in the summertime and ice skating or cross-country skiing in the winter.

Innkeeper(s): Barbara Phillips. $55-75. MC VISA AX. 5 rooms with PB. 1 conference room. Breakfast included in rates. Types of meals: continental-plus breakfast and early coffee/tea. Evening snack and picnic lunch available. Beds: DT. Air conditioning, ceiling fan and cable TV in room. VCR on premises. Antiques, fishing, shopping, cross-country skiing, sporting events, theater and watersports nearby.

Location: In Irish Hills of southern Michigan.

Seen in: Ann Arbor News.

"I came back and brought my friends. It was wonderful."

Certificate may be used: November through April, holidays and special events excluded.

Canton   K9

Willow Brook Inn
44255 Warren Rd,
Canton, MI 48187-2147
(313)454-0019 Fax:(313)451-1126

Circa 1929. Willow Brook winds its way through the backyard of this aptly named inn, situated on a lush, wooded acre. Innkeepers Bernadette and Michael Van Lenten filled their home with oak and pine country antiques and beds covered with soft quilts. They also added special toys and keepsakes from their own childhood to add a homey touch. After a peaceful rest, guests are invited to partake in the morning meal either in the "Teddy Bear" dining room, in the privacy of their rooms or in the sun room, which also boasts a hot tub. Breakfasts consist of luscious treats such as homemade breads, scones topped with devon cream and a rich, egg dish.

Innkeeper(s): Bernadette & Michael Van Lenten. $75-95. MC VISA DS. 4 rooms, 2 with PB. 1 suite. Breakfast and evening snack included in rates. Types of meals: full breakfast, gourmet breakfast and early coffee/tea. Afternoon tea, picnic lunch and catering service available. Beds: KQDT. Turn-down service, ceiling fan and VCR in room. Fax, copier, bicycles, pet boarding and child care on premises. Antiques, fishing, parks, shopping, cross-country skiing, sporting events, theater and watersports nearby.

Seen in: Canton Observer, Canton Eagle, Detroit News.

"I love the Dolls Dollhouse Room. Really enjoyed my visit. Wonderful, warm, family feeling. Great scones!"

Certificate may be used: From Nov. 1 to May 15, Sunday through Thursday, excluding Feb. 14.

Cedarville E8

Island View Resort
PO Box 277, Cedarville, MI 49719-0277
(906)484-2252

These comfortable cottages offer a convenient, unique way to enjoy Michigan's scenic Les Cheneaux area. Each of the cottages includes stocked kitchens and freshly made beds, but guests must provide their own towels and washcloths. All of the cottages sleep four comfortably. The waterfront log cabin will sleep eight and boasts a fireplace. Several cottages afford lake views, the honeymoon cottage is a secluded, lakefront cabin with a private deck.

Innkeeper(s): Larry Smith. $59-89. MC VISA DS. 9 rooms. Breakfast included in rates.

Certificate may be used: May 1-June 15, Sunday-Thursday; Sept. 15-Oct. 31, Sunday-Thursday.

Central Lake F7

Bridgewalk B&B
2287 S Main, PO Box 399,
Central Lake, MI 49622-0399
(616)544-8122

Circa 1895. Secluded on a wooded acre, this three-story Victorian is accessible by crossing a foot bridge over a stream. Guest rooms are simply decorated with Victorian touches, floral prints and fresh flowers. The Garden Suite includes a clawfoot tub. Much of the home's Victorian elements have been restored, including pocket doors and the polished woodwork. Breakfasts begin with such items as a cold fruit soup, freshly baked muffins or scones accompanied with homemade jams and butters. A main dish, perhaps stuffed French toast, tops off the meal.

Innkeeper(s): Janet & Tom Meteer. $75-85. MC VISA PC TC. 5 rooms with PB. 1 suite. Breakfast included in rates. Types of meals: full breakfast and early coffee/tea. Beds: KQT. Ceiling fan in room. Antiques, fishing, parks, shopping, downhill skiing, cross-country skiing and watersports nearby.

Certificate may be used: Sunday through Thursday nights.

Torchlight Resort
PO Box 267,
Central Lake, MI 49622-0267
(616)544-8263

Circa 1940. These one- and two-bedroom cottages are located on the edge of scenic Torch Lake. The cottages, which all boast lake views, include stocked kitchens and barbecue grills, but towels and linens

are not provided. The owners offer docking for private boats, and there is a beach and swimming area.
Innkeeper(s): Robert & Glenda Knott. $45-85. 6 rooms with PB. Beds: D. Fishing nearby.

Certificate may be used: First week of May through third week of June and last week of August through last week of October.

Charlevoix F7

Belvedere Inn
306 Belvedere Ave,
Charlevoix, MI 49720-1413
(616)547-2251 (800)280-4667
Fax:(616)547-2251

Circa 1887. Guests at this attractive two-story inn are just a short walk from a public beach. Visitors have their choice of seven rooms, including two suites. The Broqua Suite features a kitchen and private entrance, perfect for honeymooners or for those

enjoying a longer-than-usual stay. All of the rooms offer private baths and most have queen beds. Guests may opt to relax and enjoy the beautiful surroundings or take advantage of the many recreational activities available in the Charlevoix area, including Fisherman's Island State Park.
Innkeeper(s): Tom & Karen Watters. $60-115. MC VISA AX PC TC. 7 rooms, 5 with PB. 2 suites. Breakfast and evening snack included in rates. Type of meal: full breakfast. Beds: KQT. Ceiling fan in room. Cable TV, VCR, fax and bicycles on premises. Antiques, fishing, parks, shopping, downhill skiing, cross-country skiing and watersports nearby.

Certificate may be used: Oct. 1-May 24, anytime. Sunday-Thursday, June 1-30. Sunday-Thursday, Sept. 1-30.

MacDougall House B&B
109 Petoskey Ave,
Charlevoix, MI 49720-1161
(616)547-5788

Circa 1896. This turn-of-the-century Victorian served guests for many years as the Northern Guest House. Today the home is still a warm, comfortable place for visitors. The Victorian decor and country furnishings are inviting. The front porch beckons to guests who wish to simply relax and enjoy a good book while lounging in a rocking chair. As the inn's name suggests, there is a Scottish influence here, which is evident during the breakfast hour.

Innkeeper(s): Steven & Sandra Bennett. $58-98. MC VISA DS TC. 5 rooms with PB. Breakfast and afternoon tea included in rates. Types of meals: full breakfast and early coffee/tea. Beds: QD. Ceiling fan in room. Cable TV, VCR and child care on premises. Antiques, fishing, parks, shopping, downhill skiing, cross-country skiing and watersports nearby.

Certificate may be used: Sept. 1 to March 1, reservation required.

Fruitport   J6

Village Park B&B

60 Park St, Fruitport, MI 49415-9668
(616)865-6289 (800)469-1118

Circa 1873. Located in the midst of Western Michigan's Tri-Cities area, this inn's small-town village location offers comfort and relaxation to those busy partaking of the many nearby activities. This farmhouse-style inn overlooks Spring Lake and a park where guests may picnic, play tennis, use pedestrian/bike path and boat launch. The inn offers six guest rooms, all with private bath. A library is just across the street. P.J. Hoffmaster State Park, the Gillette Nature Center and Pleasure Island water park are nearby. Fishing charters and sightseeing cruises on Lake Michigan can be arranged. Be sure to inquire about the inn's Wellness Weekends with massage.

Innkeeper(s): John Hewett. $60-95. MC VISA PC TC. 6 rooms with PB, 1 with FP. Breakfast included in rates. Types of meals: continental breakfast, continental-plus breakfast, full breakfast and early coffee/tea. Beds: KDT. Air conditioning in room. Cable TV, VCR, fax, spa, sauna, bicycles and tennis on premises. Amusement parks, antiques, fishing, parks, shopping, cross-country skiing, theater and watersports nearby.

Certificate may be used: Sunday through Thursday excluding June, July, August and holidays, subject to availability. Excludes corporate rates and packages.

Glen Arbor   G6

White Gull Inn

PO Box 351, 5926 SW Manitou Tr,
Glen Arbor, MI 49636-9702
(616)334-4486 Fax:(616)334-3998

Circa 1900. One of Michigan's most scenic areas is home to the White Gull Inn. With the Sleeping Bear Dunes and alluring Lake Michigan just minutes away, visitors will find no shortage of sightseeing or recreational activities during a stay here. The inn's farmhouse setting, country decor and five comfortable guest rooms offer guests a relaxing haven no matter what the season. Glen Lake is a block away, and guests also will enjoy the area's fine dining and shopping opportunities.

Innkeeper(s): Bill & Dotti Thompson. $50-75. MC VISA AX DS TC. 6 rooms, 1 with FP. Breakfast included in rates. Type of meal: continental-plus breakfast. Beds: QDT. Air conditioning, cable TV and VCR in room. Antiques, fishing, parks, shopping, downhill skiing, cross-country skiing, theater and watersports nearby.

Certificate may be used: Nov. 1-May 15

Interlochen   G7

Between The Lakes B&B

4570 Case Blvd Box 280,
Interlochen, MI 49643-9534
(616)276-7751 Fax:(616)276-7752

After more than two decades globetrotting as part of the foreign service, the owners of this bed & breakfast decided to become hosts instead of guests. Art, artifacts and furnishings from their world travels decorate the home. Two wooded acres offer privacy, and guests also may use the B&B's heated, indoor swimming pool. The home is within walking distance to Duck and Green lakes as well as the Interlochen Center for the Arts.

Innkeeper(s): Barbara & Gordon Evans. $65-75. MC VISA PC. 4 rooms with PB. Breakfast included in rates. Type of meal: continental-plus breakfast. Beds: KQT. VCR, fax and swimming on premises. Handicap access. Fishing, parks, shopping, cross-country skiing and watersports nearby.

Location: Within walking distance of Interlochen Center for the Arts.

Certificate may be used: Sunday through Thursday throughout the year, weekends from Sept. 30 to May 31 or whenever space is available during June, July, August and September.

Ithaca   I8

Chaffin Farms B&B

1245 W Washington Rd,
Ithaca, MI 48847-9782
(517)875-3410

Circa 1892. Located in central Michigan between Mount Pleasant and Lansing, this inn was once a large dairy farm with 12 barns housing various farm animals. Guests will be impressed with the inn's colorful stone wall, built with rocks hauled in from the surrounding area. The inn is furnished with antiques, and visitors will marvel at the inn's impressive kitchen, which was featured in Country Woman magazine. Antiquing is popular in the area and Alma College is nearby.

Innkeeper(s): Susan Chaffin. $45-55. PC. 2 rooms, 1 with PB. Breakfast included in rates. Types of meals: continental-plus breakfast, full breakfast and early coffee/tea. Beds: QT. Air conditioning in room. Antiques, parks, shopping and sporting events nearby.

Certificate may be used: April 15 to Nov. 15.

Jones   L7

The Sanctuary at Wildwood

58138 M-40, Jones, MI 49061-9713
(616)244-5910 (800)249-5910
Fax:(616)496-8403

Circa 1972. Travelers in search of relaxation and a little solitude will enjoy the serenity of this estate, surrounded by 93 forested acres. A stroll down the hiking trails introduces guests to a variety of wildlife, but even inside, guests are pampered by the inn's natural setting. One room, named Medicine Hawk, is adorned with a mural depicting a woodland scene. A mural of a pine forest graces the Quiet Solace room. The Keeper of the Wild Room includes a rustic birch headboard. Each of the rooms includes a fireplace, Jacuzzi and refrigerator. From the dining and great rooms, guests can watch birds and squirrels. The innkeeper offers a variety of interesting packages.

Innkeeper(s): Dusti Campbell. $129-179. MC VISA AX DS PC TC. 5 suites, 5 with FP. 1 conference room. Breakfast included in rates. Types of meals: full breakfast and early coffee/tea. Catering service available. Beds: Q. Air conditioning in room. VCR, swimming, bicycles and library on premises. Handicap access. Antiques, fishing, shopping, downhill skiing, cross-country skiing, sporting events and watersports nearby.

Certificate may be used: Nov. 1 to April 15, Sunday through Thursday only, excluding holidays periods.

Jonesville   K8

Horse & Carriage B&B

7020 Brown Rd,
Jonesville, MI 49250-9720
(517)849-2732 Fax:(517)849-2732

Circa 1898. Families are treated to a winter horse-drawn sleigh ride at this early 18th-century home, which is surrounded by a 700-acre dairy farm. In the warmer months, horse drawn carriage rides pass down an old country lane past Buck Lake. The innkeepers' family has lived on the property for more than 150 years. The home itself was built as a one-room schoolhouse. A mix of contemporary and country furnishings decorate the interior. The Rainbow Room, a perfect place for children, offers twin beds and a playroom. Guests are treated to hearty breakfasts made with farm-fresh eggs and cream from the farm's cows.

Innkeeper(s): Keith L. Brown & family. $50-75. PC. 3 rooms, 1 with PB. 1 suite. Breakfast and evening snack included in rates. Types of meals: continental breakfast, continental-plus breakfast, full breakfast, gourmet breakfast and early coffee/tea. Picnic lunch and catered breakfast available. Beds: QT. Air conditioning in room. Fax and copier on premises. Antiques, fishing, parks, shopping, cross-country skiing, sporting events, theater and watersports nearby.

Certificate may be used: All year subject to availability and suitable weather.

Munro House B&B

202 Maumee St,
Jonesville, MI 49250-1247
(517)849-9292

Circa 1840. Ten fireplaces are found at the historic Munro House, named for George C. Munro, a Civil War brigadier general. The Greek Revival structure, Hillsdale County's first brick house, also served as a safe haven for slaves on the Underground Railroad. Visitors can still see a secret room, used for hiding slaves, above the bath area of the downstairs bedroom. Many guests enjoy reading one of the library's special-interest books. Breakfast is eaten overlooking the inn's gardens. Hillsdale College is just five miles away.

Innkeeper(s): Joyce Yarde. $47-70. MC VISA. 5 rooms with PB. Breakfast included in rates. Type of meal: full breakfast. Evening snack available. Air conditioning, ceiling fan and cable TV in room. VCR on premises. Antiques, shopping, cross-country skiing, sporting events and theater nearby.

Certificate may be used: Any Sunday through Friday.

Lansing   J8

Ask Me House

1027 Seymour Ave,
Lansing, MI 48906-4836
(517)484-3127 (800)275-6341
Fax:(517)484-4193

Circa 1991. This early 20th-century home still includes its original hardwood floors and pocket doors. A hand-painted mural was added to the dining room in the 1940s. Guests can enjoy the unique art during the breakfasts, which are served on antique Limoges china and Depression glass. The innkeepers offer a quaint honeymoon cottage along with the guest rooms. The home is near a variety of museums, theaters, a historical village and Michigan State University.

Innkeeper(s): Mary Elaine Kiener & Alex Kruzel. $65-95. MC VISA PC TC. 4 rooms. 1 cottage. Breakfast included in rates. Types of meals: full breakfast, gourmet breakfast and early coffee/tea. Beds: DT. Ceiling fan in room. Cable TV, VCR and fax on premises. Antiques, parks, sporting events and theater nearby.

Certificate may be used: Anytime subject to availability.

Lewiston   G8

Gorton House
HCR 3 Box 3738, Wolflake Dr,
Lewiston, MI 49756-8948
(517)786-2764 Fax:(517)786-2764

Wolf Lake sits beside this comfortable bed & breakfast. Rooms are filed with antiques and lace. The innkeepers offer a variety of activities including use of a fishing boat and putting green. The grounds boast a lakeside beach and hot tub under a gazebo. Inside guests can relax near one of three fireplaces or take in a game of pool on the innkeepers' antique pool table. A hearty breakfast with entrees such as omelets or German pancakes are served along with fruits, juices and baked goods. In the summer, morning coffee can be enjoyed in the paddle boat. Freshly baked cookies are always available for a light snack. Antique shopping and golfing are some of the area's offerings.

Innkeeper(s): Lois Gorton. $55-75. 6 rooms. Breakfast included in rates. Type of meal: full breakfast.

Certificate may be used: September-December, Sunday-Sunday; January and February, Sunday-Thursday; March-June, Sunday-Sunday; July and August not available. Holidays excluded.

Lexington   I10

Governor's Inn
7277 Simons St, Lexington, MI 48450
(810)359-5770

Circa 1859. Former Michigan governor Albert Sleeper and his wife, Mary, made this Victorian their summer home. Mary's parents built the home, and she and Albert were married here. Wicker furnishings and antiques add to the Victorian charm. The wraparound porch is a wonderful place to relax. The dining room is warmed by a potbellied stove. An ornate, hand-carved staircase leads to the three guest rooms. One room includes an old chest that innkeeper Jim Boyda's grandparents brought with them when they sailed to America.

Innkeeper(s): Marlene & Jim Boyda. $45-55. MC VISA. 5 rooms, 3 with PB. Breakfast included in rates. Type of meal: continental-plus breakfast. Beds: D. Air conditioning in room. Antiques, fishing, parks, shopping, cross-country skiing, theater and watersports nearby.

Certificate may be used: Oct. 1 to May 1, anyday.

Lowell   J7

McGee Homestead B&B
2534 Alden Nash NE, Lowell, MI 49331
(616)897-8142

Circa 1880. Just 18 miles from Grand Rapids, travelers will find the McGee Homestead B&B, an Italianate farmhouse with four charming, antique-filled guest rooms. Surrounded by orchards, it is one of the largest farmhouses in the area. Breakfasts feature the inn's own fresh eggs. Guests may golf at an adjacent course, or enjoy nearby fishing and boating. Lowell is home to Michigan's largest antique mall, and many historic covered bridges are found in the surrounding countryside. Travelers who remain on the farm may relax in a hammock or visit a barnful of petting animals.

Innkeeper(s): Bill & Ardie Barber. $35-52. MC VISA PC TC. 4 rooms with PB. 1 conference room. Breakfast, afternoon tea and evening snack included in rates. Types of meals: full breakfast and early coffee/tea. Beds: KDT. Air conditioning, turn-down service, ceiling fan and VCR in room. Library and child care on premises. Antiques, fishing, parks, shopping, downhill skiing and cross-country skiing nearby.

Certificate may be used: Sunday-Saturday, March-December. Anytime available.

Ludington   H6

The Doll House Inn
709 E Ludington Ave,
Ludington, MI 49431-2224
(616)843-2286 (800)275-4616

Circa 1900. Antique dolls are among the special family heirlooms found throughout this Victorian inn. Seven rooms, decorated in lace curtains and brass or antique beds, include a bridal suite with a canopy bed and whirlpool tub for two. Guests can enjoy a full "heart-smart" breakfast on the wicker-filled porch. The beach is a short stroll from the inn.

Innkeeper(s): Barbara Gerovac. $65-110. MC VISA. 7 rooms, 5 with PB. 1 suite. Breakfast included in rates. Types of meals: full breakfast and early coffee/tea. Picnic lunch available. Beds: QTD. Air conditioning, turn-down service and cable TV in room. VCR on premises. Antiques, shopping, downhill skiing, cross-country skiing, sporting events and theater nearby.

Location: Four blocks to business area and six blocks to Lake Michigan car ferry.

Certificate may be used: Closed January, no holidays, Sunday through Thursday (September through December), anytime February through April.

Lamplighter B&B

602 E Ludington Ave,
Ludington, MI 49431-2223
(616)843-9792 Fax:(616)845-6070

This Queen Anne home offers convenient access to Lake Michigan's beaches, the Badger Carferry to Wisconsin and one of Michigan's state parks. A collection of European antiques and original paintings and lithographs by artists such as Chagall and Dali decorate the inn. The home's centerpiece, a golden oak curved staircase, leads guests up to their rooms. The innkeepers have created a mix of hospitality and convenience that draws both vacationers and business travelers. A full, gourmet breakfast is served each morning. Freddy, the inn's resident cocker spaniel, is always available for a tour of the area. The innkeepers are fluent in German.

Innkeeper(s): Judy & Heinz Bertram. $75-125. MC VISA AX DS. 4 rooms with PB. Breakfast included in rates. Types of meals: gourmet breakfast and early coffee/tea. Beds: Q. Air conditioning, turn-down service and cable TV in room. VCR on premises. Antiques, shopping and cross-country skiing nearby.

Certificate may be used: November through April, holidays excluded.

The Inn at Ludington

701 E Ludington Ave,
Ludington, MI 49431-2224
(616)845-7055 (800)845-9170

Circa 1890. This Queen Anne Victorian was built during the heyday of Ludington's lumbering era by a local dentist. Despite its elegant exterior with its three-story turret, the innkeepers stress relaxation at their inn. The rooms are filled with comfortable,

vintage furnishings. Guests can snuggle up with a book in front of a warming fireplace or enjoy a soak in a clawfoot tub. A hearty, buffet-style breakfast is served each morning. The innkeepers take great pride in their cuisine and are always happy to share some of their award-winning recipes with guests. After a day of beachcombing, antiquing, cross-

country skiing or perhaps a bike ride, guests return to the inn to find a chocolate atop their pillow.

Innkeeper(s): Diane Shields, David Nemitz. $65-85. MC VISA AX PC TC. 6 rooms with PB, 2 with FP. 1 suite. Breakfast included in rates. Types of meals: full breakfast and early coffee/tea. Picnic lunch available. Beds: QD. Air conditioning, turn-down service and ceiling fan in room. Cable TV, copier and library on premises. Amusement parks, antiques, fishing, parks, shopping, downhill skiing, cross-country skiing, theater and watersports nearby.

Location: Near Lake Michigan.

Seen in: Ludington Daily News, Detroit Free Press, Chicago Tribune, Country Accents.

"Loved the room and everything else about the house."

Certificate may be used: November-April, anytime; May, June, September, October, weekdays (or weekends as available at last minute).

The Ludington House

501 E Ludington Ave,
Ludington, MI 49431-2220
(616)845-7769

Enjoy the opulence of the Victorian Era at this 19th-century home, which was built by a lumber baron. Grand rooms with high ceilings, stained glass and polished oak floors are enhanced by a country collection of period antiques. A showpiece carved, winding staircase and Italian mantels are other notable architectural features. An antique wedding gown decorates the Bridal Suite. The innkeepers will prepare a picnic lunch, and there are bicycles for guest use. The innkeepers also offer murder-mystery packages.

Innkeeper(s): Patricia Cunningham. $80-90. MC VISA. 9 rooms. Breakfast included in rates. Type of meal: full breakfast.

Certificate may be used: Anytime except July and August and weekends in September and October.

Mendon   K7

The Mendon Country Inn

PO Box 98, Mendon, MI 49072-9502
(616)496-8132 (800)304-3366
Fax:(616)496-8403

Circa 1873. This two-story stagecoach inn was constructed with St. Joseph River clay bricks fired on the property. There are eight-foot windows, high ceilings and a walnut staircase. Country antiques are accentuated with woven rugs, collectibles and bright quilts. A creek runs by the property, and a romantic courting canoe is available to guests. Depending on the season, guests may also borrow a tandem bike or arrange for an Amish buggy ride. During the summer months, romantic canoe trips are available.

Innkeeper(s): Dick & Dolly Buerkle. $69-159. MC VISA AX DS PC TC. 18 rooms with PB, 14 with FP. 9 suites. 2 cottages. 2 conference rooms. Breakfast and evening snack included in rates. Types of meals: continental-plus breakfast and early coffee/tea. Picnic lunch available. Beds: QD. Air conditioning and ceiling fan in room. Fax, sauna, bicycles and library on premises. Handicap access. Antiques, fishing, parks, shopping, downhill skiing, cross-country skiing, sporting events and watersports nearby.

Location: Halfway between Chicago and Detroit.

Seen in: Innsider, Country Home.

"A great experience. Good food and great hosts. Thank you."

Certificate may be used: Nov. 1 to April 15, Sunday-Thursday only, excluding holiday periods.

Muskegon 16

Blue Country B&B

1415 Holton Rd,
Muskegon, MI 49445-1446
(616)744-2555

Once known as the Brookside Tea House during Prohibition, this Craftsman home now is known for its family-oriented atmosphere and woodsy setting. Four guest rooms include the Blue Tea Rose Room, with a hand-carved sycamore bed and vanity, and

the Whispering Woods Room, featuring wood furnishings and an attractive antique wall print. Guests will enjoy the teapot collection, and they are welcome to try the electronic organ and hammered dulcimer. The inn is just 10 minutes from Lake Michigan. There are numerous area attractions, including Muskegon and Duck Lake state parks.
Innkeeper(s): Barbara Stevens. $61. 3 rooms. Breakfast included in rates. Types of meals: full breakfast and early coffee/tea. Evening snack and room service available. Air conditioning and turn-down service in room. Cable TV, VCR and child care on premises. Amusement parks, antiques, shopping, cross-country skiing, sporting events and theater nearby.

Certificate may be used: All year, January-December, Sunday through Thursday.

Port City Victorian Inn

1259 Lakeshore Dr,
Muskegon, MI 49441-1659
(616)759-0205 (800)274-3574
Fax:(616)759-0205

Circa 1877. Among its proper Victorian features, the curved, leaded-glass windows of this Queen Anne-style home look out to Muskegon Lake and the harbor. A natural wood fireplace, high ceilings and ornate moldings are apparent as well. Walls are decorated with flowery papers, some in deep, rich colors, while others are bright and airy. Some rooms offer water views or whirlpool tubs. Guests can enjoy the full breakfasts on the sun porch, in the dining room or in the privacy of their own room. The innkeepers have created several packages, such as a Lake Michigan Adventure, Romantic Getaway for Two, and Snowflake Bed & Breakfast Holiday.
Innkeeper(s): Fred & Barbara Schossau. $65-125. MC VISA AX. 5 rooms, 2 with PB. 2 suites. Breakfast included in rates. Types of meals: continental-plus breakfast, full breakfast, gourmet breakfast and early coffee/tea. Evening snack and catering service available. Beds: QD. Air conditioning, turn-down service and ceiling fan in room. Cable TV, VCR, fax, copier and bicycles on premises. Amusement parks, antiques, fishing, parks, shopping, cross-country skiing, sporting events, theater and watersports nearby.

"The Inn offers only comfort, good food and total peace of mind."

Certificate may be used: Oct. 1 through May 31, Sunday-Friday.

Omer H9

Rifle River B&B

500 Center Ave, Omer, MI 48749
(517)653-2543

A gathering of maple trees shades this historic home, located in the heart of Omer. The town, which was founded just after the Civil War, has seen a multitude of disasters, and this sturdy home has stood through its fair share of floods, tornadoes and fires. The innkeepers offer four rooms decorated with antiques. Waterbeds and Jacuzzi tubs are relaxing amenities. The home, as its name might suggest, is only two blocks from the Rifle River, which offers fishing and canoeing.
Innkeeper(s): Joan Brock. $38-49. 4 rooms. Breakfast included in rates. Type of meal: continental breakfast.

Certificate may be used: September through April, anytime. May through August, Sunday through Thursday.

Oscoda
G9

Huron House
3124 N US-23, Oscoda, MI 48750
(517)739-9255

This is a great place to take long walks on the sandy beaches of Lake Huron and follow-up with a relaxing soak in the hot tub, or if you book the Jacuzzi Suite, enjoy your own private whirlpool. Another favorite room overlooks the lake. Homemade Belgium waffles, crepes, muffins and quiche are some of the delicious breakfasts that await you, served in the privacy of your room, in the spacious second floor breakfast room overlooking Lake Huron or on the outdoor decks. The inn is near the River Road National Forest Scenic Byway. The 22-mile route along the AuSable River provides some of the most breathtaking scenery in Michigan.

Innkeeper(s): Dennis & Martie Lorenz. $85-135. MC VISA. 12 rooms with PB, 5 with FP. 5 suites. Breakfast included in rates. Types of meals: continental-plus breakfast and early coffee/tea. Beds: KQ. Air conditioning, ceiling fan and cable TV in room. Spa and swimming on premises. Antiques, fishing, parks, shopping, cross-country skiing and watersports nearby.

Certificate may be used: Sept. 15 to May 15 Sunday-Thursday occupancy limited to two people per room.

Ossineke
G9

Fernwood B&B
10189 Ossineke Rd,
Ossineke, MI 49766-9629
(517)471-5176

Circa 1932. Originally built as a tearoom, Fernwood was the first building on the beach to have electricity. The sandy beaches of Thunder Bay are just a few yards away, visible from the sun porch where guests often sit and enjoy the view. The homestay bed & breakfast has two comfortable rooms decorated in a country style with stenciled walls and handmade quilts. With such close access to the beach, many watersports are available, but perhaps the most unusual is diving to view shipwrecks at the Thunder Bay Underwater Preserve.

Innkeeper(s): Jay & Susan Anders. $55. PC TC. 2 rooms. Breakfast included in rates. Type of meal: full breakfast. Beds: D. Ceiling fan in room. Cable TV, VCR, copier, spa and swimming on premises. Antiques, fishing, parks, shopping, cross-country skiing, theater and watersports nearby.

Certificate may be used: Sept. 8-Nov. 30 and Jan. 2-May 24, anyday.

Romeo
J10

Hess Manor B&B
186 S Main St, Romeo, MI 48065-5128
(810)752-4726

Circa 1854. This pre-Civil War home is located in a town which is listed in the National Register. The inn boasts a fireplace and Victorian decor.

The innkeepers also renovated the inn's 110-year-old carriage house into an antique and gift shop. Much of Romeo's historic sites are within walking distance of Hess Manor, including galleries, antique shops, bookstores and restaurants. Frontier Town, a collection of Old West-style buildings, is a popular attraction.

Innkeeper(s): John & Ilene Hess. $59-75. MC VISA PC. 4 rooms, 2 with PB. Breakfast and evening snack included in rates. Types of meals: full breakfast, gourmet breakfast and early coffee/tea. Beds: Q. Air conditioning in room. Cable TV, VCR and copier on premises. Antiques, fishing, parks, shopping, sporting events, theater and watersports nearby.

Certificate may be used: Nov. 1-April 30, all days.

Saline
K9

The Homestead B&B
9279 Macon Rd, Saline, MI 48176-9305
(313)429-9625

Circa 1851. The Homestead is a two-story brick farmhouse situated on 50 acres of fields, woods and river. The house has 15-inch-thick walls and is furnished with Victorian antiques and family heirlooms. This was a favorite camping spot for Indians while they salted their fish, and many arrowheads have been found on the farm. Activities include long walks through meadows of wildflowers and cross-country skiing in season. It is 40 minutes from Detroit and Toledo and ten minutes from Ann Arbor.

Innkeeper(s): Shirley Grossman. $60-70. MC VISA AX DC CB DS TC. 12 rooms, 1 with PB. 1 conference room. Breakfast and evening snack included in rates. Types of meals: full breakfast and early coffee/tea. Beds: DT. Air conditioning in room. VCR on premises. Antiques, parks, shopping, cross-country skiing and sporting events nearby.

Location: Southeastern Michigan, within six miles of I-94 & US 23.

Seen in: Ann Arbor News, Country Focus, Saline Reporter.

"It is so nice to be back after three years and from 5,000 miles away!"

Certificate may be used: Jan. 2 to June 1, Sunday to Friday & Sept. 1 to Dec. 30, Sunday to Friday.

Saugatuck J6

Bayside Inn
618 Water St Box 1001,
Saugatuck, MI 49453
(616)857-4321 (800)548-0077
Fax:(616)857-1870

Circa 1926. Located on the edge of the Kalamazoo River and across from the nature observation tower, this downtown inn was once a boathouse. The common room now has a fireplace and view of the

water. Each guest room has its own deck. The inn is near several restaurants, shops and beaches. Fishing for salmon, perch and trout is popular.

Innkeeper(s): Kathy Wilson. $60-225. MC VISA AX DS. 10 rooms with PB, 4 with FP. 4 suites. 1 conference room. Breakfast included in rates. Type of meal: continental-plus breakfast. Beds: KQD. Air conditioning, cable TV and VCR in room. Fax, copier and spa on premises. Antiques, fishing, shopping, cross-country skiing, theater and watersports nearby.

Location: On the water in downtown Saugatuck.

"Our stay was wonderful, more pleasant than anticipated, we were so pleased. As for breakfast, it gets our A 1 rating."

Certificate may be used: November through March, Monday through Thursday excluding holidays.

Kemah Guest House
633 Allegan St,
Saugatuck, MI 49453-9719
(616)857-2919 (800)445-3624

Circa 1906. Stained-glass windows, beamed ceilings, and stone and tile fireplaces are trademarks of this house. There is a billiard room, and a Bavarian rathskeller has German inscriptions on the wall and

original wine kegs. Deco Dormer, a guest room with a mahogany bedroom suite, was featured in a 1926 Architectural Digest. That same year, a Frank Lloyd Wright-style solarium with its own waterfall was added to the house. Kemah is situated on two hilltop acres with a view of the water. Spelunkers will want to explore the cave found on the property.

Innkeeper(s): Dan Osborn. $85-140. MC VISA AX DS TC. 6 rooms, 4 with PB. 1 conference room. Breakfast included in rates. Type of meal: continental-plus breakfast. Beds: KQD. Air conditioning and ceiling fan in room. Cable TV and VCR on premises. Antiques, fishing, parks, shopping, cross-country skiing, theater and watersports nearby.

Seen in: Innsider, West Michigan, Grand Rapids Press.

"What a wonderful time we had at Kemah. Thank you for a delightful stay. Your home is very special."

Certificate may be used: Oct. 1-April 30, Sunday-Thursday.

The Red Dog B&B
132 Mason St, Saugatuck, MI 49453
(616)857-8851

Circa 1879. This comfortable, two-story farmhouse is located in the heart of downtown Saugatuck and is just a short walk away from shopping, restaurants and many of the town's seasonal activities. Rooms are furnished with a combination of contemporary and antique furnishings. One room includes a fireplace and Jacuzzi tub for two. Guests can relax and enjoy views of the garden from the B&B's second-story porch, or warm up next to the fireplace in the living room. The full breakfast, which is served in the formal dining room, includes treats such as baked apple cinnamon French toast or a ham and cheese strata. The innkeepers offer special golf and off-season packages.

Innkeeper(s): Daniel Indurante. $60-110. MC VISA AX DC DS PC TC. 7 rooms, 5 with PB, 1 with FP. 1 suite. Breakfast included in rates. Types of meals: full breakfast and early coffee/tea. Beds: QD. Air conditioning, ceiling fan and cable TV in room. VCR, fax and copier on premises. Antiques, fishing, parks, shopping, cross-country skiing, theater and watersports nearby.

Seen in: South Bend Trio, Michigan Cyclist, Restaurant and Institutions.

Certificate may be used: November through April.

Sherwood Forest B&B
938 Center St, PO Box 315,
Saugatuck, MI 49453
(616)857-1246 (800)838-1246
Fax:(616)857-1996

Circa 1904. As the name suggests, this gracious Victorian is surrounded by woods and flanked with a large wraparound porch. Each guest room features antiques, one room offers a Jacuzzi and another an oak-manteled fireplace with a unique mural that transforms the room into a tree-top loft. A breakfast of delicious coffees or teas and homemade treats can be enjoyed either in the dining room or on the porch. The heated pool includes a mural of dolphins riding on ocean waves. White-sand beaches and the eastern shore of Lake Michigan are only a half block away.

Innkeeper(s): Keith & Susan Charak. $60-140. MC VISA DS PC. 4 rooms with PB, 1 with FP. 1 cottage. 1 conference room. Breakfast and afternoon tea included in rates. Types of meals: continental-plus breakfast and early coffee/tea. Catering service available. Beds: Q. Air conditioning and ceiling fan in room. Cable TV, VCR, fax, swimming and bicycles on premises. Antiques, fishing, parks, shopping, cross-country skiing, theater and watersports nearby.

Seen in: Commercial Record.

"Staying at Sherwood Forest was like staying at my best friend's house. The house itself is quaint and beautiful."

Certificate may be used: Nov. 1-April 30. Holidays and gourmet dinner weekends excluded.

Twin Oaks Inn

PO Box 867, 226 Griffith St,
Saugatuck, MI 49453-0867
(616)857-1600

Circa 1860. This large Queen Anne Victorian inn was a boarding house for lumbermen at the turn of the century. Now an old-English-style inn, it offers a variety of lodging choices, including three suites. Guests also may stay in the inn's cozy cottage, which boasts an outdoor hot tub. There are many diversions at the Twin Oaks, including a collection of videotaped movies numbering more than 600. An English garden with a pond and fountain provides a relaxing setting, and guests also may borrow bicycles or play horseshoes on the inn's grounds.

Innkeeper(s): Jerry & Nancy Horney. $65-105. MC VISA DS TC. 7 rooms with PB. 3 suites. 1 conference room. Breakfast and evening snack included in rates. Types of meals: continental-plus breakfast, full breakfast and early coffee/tea. Afternoon tea available. Beds: KQ. Air conditioning, cable TV and VCR in room. Spa, bicycles and child care on premises. Antiques, fishing, parks, shopping, cross-country skiing, theater and watersports nearby.

Location: On the Kalamazoo River.

Seen in: Home & Away, Cleveland Plain Dealer, South Bend Tribune.

Certificate may be used: Nov. 1-April 30, Sunday-Thursday.

Scottville   H6

Eden Hill B&B

1483 E Chauvez Rd,
Scottville, MI 49454-9758
(616)757-2023

Descendants of John Adams have owned this home for more than 120 years, and a special family tree is available for viewing. This farmhouse is decorated in cheerful, country decor with comfortable furnishings and antiques. Each of the guest rooms is named after relatives who once resided in the house. The full country breakfasts offer a great start to a busy day exploring the Michigan countryside.

Innkeeper(s): Carla Craven. $60-77. MC VISA. 3 rooms. Breakfast included in rates. Type of meal: full breakfast.

Certificate may be used: All year, (summer, Sunday-Thursday only. Winter, fall and spring anytime). No holidays.

South Haven   K6

The Seymour House

1248 Blue Star Hwy,
South Haven, MI 49090-9696
(616)227-3918 Fax:(616)227-3918

Circa 1862. Less than a mile from the shores of Lake Michigan, this pre-Civil War, Italianate-style home rests upon 11 acres of grounds, complete with nature trails and a stocked, fishing pond. Each of the guest rooms is named for a state significant in the innkeepers' lives. The Arizona Suite, popular with honeymooners, includes a Jacuzzi tub. Poached pears with raspberry sauce, buttermilk blueberry pancakes and locally made sausages are a few of the items that might appear on the breakfast menu. The inn is midway between Saugatuck and South Haven, which offer plenty of activities. Beaches, Kal-Haven Trail, shopping, horseback riding and winery tours are among the fun destination choices.

Innkeeper(s): Tom & Gwen Paton. $79-130. MC VISA PC TC. 5 rooms with PB, 2 with FP. 1 cottage. Breakfast, evening snack and picnic lunch included in rates. Types of meals: gourmet breakfast and early coffee/tea. Beds: KQD. Air conditioning, ceiling fan and VCR in room. Cable TV, fax, copier and swimming on premises. Antiques, fishing, parks, shopping, downhill skiing, cross-country skiing, theater and watersports nearby.

"Enjoyed our stay and the wonderful hospitality. Beware! We shall return."

Certificate may be used: Nov. 1-May 1, Sunday-Friday

Victoria Resort B&B

241 Oak St, South Haven, MI 49090-2302
(616)637-6414 (800)637-5793
Fax:(616)637-6127

Circa 1925. Less than two blocks from a sandy beach, this Classical Revival inn offers many recreational opportunities for its guests, who may choose from bicycling, beach and pool swimming, basketball and tennis, among others. The inn's rooms and suites provide visitors several options, including cable TV, fireplaces, whirlpool tubs and ceiling fans. Cottages with maid service, for families or groups traveling together, also are available. A 10-minute stroll down tree-lined streets leads visitors to South Haven's quaint downtown, with its riverfront restaurants and shops.

Innkeeper(s): Bob & Jan Leksich. $39-130. MC VISA DS PC TC. 11 rooms with PB, 2 with FP. 4 suites. 6 cottages. Breakfast included in rates. Type of meal: continental-plus breakfast. Beds: QD. Air conditioning, ceiling fan, cable TV and VCR in room. Fax, swimming, bicycles, tennis and library on premises. Antiques, fishing, parks, shopping, downhill skiing, cross-country skiing and watersports nearby.

Certificate may be used: From Sept. 3 to May 15, Sunday through Thursday excluding some holidays.

Suttons Bay   G7

Open Windows

PO Box 698, 613 St. Marys Ave,
Suttons Bay, MI 49682-0698
(616)271-4300 (800)520-3722

Circa 1893. The bay is just two blocks away for guests staying at this bed & breakfast, and those opting for the home's Rose Garden Room enjoy the water view from their quarters. The home's half-acre of grounds is dotted with flower gardens. Adirondack-style chairs, created by the innkeeper, line the front porch. Guests may borrow snowshoes in winter or use the home's grill and picnic table during the warmer months. Locally produced fresh fruits, entrees such as spinach and cheese crepes and homemade breads are among the breakfast fare, which is often served in a room with bay views.

Innkeeper(s): Don & Norma Blumenschine. $85-105. PC TC. 3 rooms with PB. Breakfast and evening snack included in rates. Types of meals: full breakfast, gourmet breakfast and early coffee/tea. Picnic lunch available. Beds: KQDT. Air conditioning and ceiling fan in room. Cable TV, VCR, bicycles and library on premises. Antiques, fishing, parks,

shopping, downhill skiing, cross-country skiing, theater and watersports nearby.

Certificate may be used: Jan. 15-May 15, Sunday-Thursday.

Traverse City   G7

Victoriana 1898

622 Washington St,
Traverse City, MI 49686-2646
(616)929-1009

Circa 1898. Egbert Ferris, a partner in the European Horse Hotel, built this Italianate Victorian manor and a two-story carriage house. Later, the bell tower from the old Central School was moved onto the property and now serves as a

handsome Greek Revival gazebo. The house has three parlors, all framed in fretwork. Etched and stained glass is found throughout. Guest rooms are furnished with family heirlooms. The house speciality is Belgian waffles topped with homemade cherry sauce.

Innkeeper(s): Flo & Bob Schermerhorn. $60-80. PC. 3 rooms with PB, 1 with FP. 1 suite. Breakfast and afternoon tea included in rates. Types of meals: gourmet breakfast and early coffee/tea. Beds: QD. Air conditioning and turn-down service in room. Cable TV, VCR, fax and library on premises. Antiques, fishing, parks, shopping, downhill skiing, cross-country skiing, theater and watersports nearby.

Seen in: Midwest Living, Oakland Press.

"In all our B&B experiences, no one can compare with the Victoriana 1898. You're 100% in every category!"

Certificate may be used: Sunday through Thursday, November through April.

Union Pier L6

Pine Garth B&B
15790 Lakeshore Rd,
Union Pier, MI 49129-9340
(616)469-1642 Fax:(616)469-1642

Circa 1905. The seven rooms and five guest cottages at this charming bed & breakfast inn are individually decorated in a country style and each boasts something special. Some rooms have a private deck and a wall of windows that look out to Lake Michigan. Other rooms feature Ralph Lauren linens, a fireplace and Laura Ashley decor. The deluxe cottages offer two queen-size beds, a woodburning fireplace, VCR, cable TV and an outdoor tub on a private deck with a gas grill.
Innkeeper(s): Paula & Russ Bulin. $80-145. MC VISA AX DS PC TC. 7 rooms with PB, 1 with FP. 5 cottages. 1 conference room. Breakfast included in rates. Types of meals: full breakfast and gourmet breakfast. Afternoon tea, evening snack and banquet service available. Beds: Q. Air conditioning, ceiling fan and VCR in room. Cable TV, fax, copier, swimming, bicycles and library on premises. Amusement parks, antiques, fishing, parks, shopping, sporting events, theater and watersports nearby.
Location: On the shores of Lake Michigan with private beach.

"Your warm and courteous reception, attentiveness and helpfulness will never be forgotten."

Certificate may be used: Nov. 1 to May 25, Sunday through Thursday, excluding holidays.

The Inn at Union Pier
9708 Berrien, Union Pier, MI 49129-0222
(616)469-4700 Fax:(616)469-4720

Circa 1920. Set on a shady acre across a country road from Lake Michigan, this inn features unique Swedish ceramic fireplaces, a hot tub and sauna, a veranda ringing the house and a large common room with comfortable overstuffed furniture and a grand piano. Rooms offer such amenities as private balconies and porches, whirlpools, views of the English garden and furniture dating from the early

1900s. Breakfast includes fresh fruit and homemade jams made of fruit from surrounding farms.
Innkeeper(s): Joyce & Mark Pitts. $110-185. MC VISA DS PC TC. 16 rooms with PB, 12 with FP. 2 suites. 1 conference room. Breakfast and evening snack included in rates. Types of meals: continental breakfast, full breakfast, gourmet breakfast and early coffee/tea. Catering service available. Beds: KQT. Air conditioning and ceiling fan in room. Cable TV, fax, copier, spa, swimming, sauna, bicycles and library on premises. Handicap access. Antiques, fishing, parks, cross-country skiing, sporting events, theater and watersports nearby.
Seen in: Chicago Tribune, USA Today, Detroit News, Chicago, Midwest Living, Chicago Sun Times.

"The food, the atmosphere, the accommodations, and of course, the entire staff made this the most relaxing weekend ever."

Certificate may be used: Oct. 1-May 25, Sunday through Thursday only, no holidays.

Garden Grove B&B
9549 Union Pier Rd,
Union Pier, MI 49129-9411
(616)469-6346 (800)613-2872
Fax:(616)469-3419

Circa 1925. This restored home originally was built using plans from a Sears-Roebuck catalog. The innkeepers have constructed an addition, keeping the home's cottage style in mind. Two guest rooms include fireplaces and whirlpool tubs, while the others have clawfoot tubs. Rooms have a garden theme with names such as The Sunflower or The Violet. The home is secluded on an acre of woods just a mile from Lake Michigan. The breakfasts here are hearty, and in keeping with the romance of the place, the innkeepers serve the morning meal on tables for two.
Innkeeper(s): Mary Ellen & Ric Postlewaite. $80-140. MC VISA TC. 4 rooms with PB, 2 with FP. Breakfast and evening snack included in rates. Types of meals: full breakfast and early coffee/tea. Beds: KQT. Air conditioning, ceiling fan, cable TV and VCR in room. Fax, copier, spa, bicycles and library on premises. Antiques, fishing, parks, shopping, cross-country skiing and watersports nearby.
Certificate may be used: Nov. 1 to May 1, Sunday-Friday, no holidays

White Cloud I7

Crow's Nest B&B
1440 N Luce Ave,
White Cloud, MI 49349-9712
(616)689-0088 (800)354-0850

Circa 1900. On the banks of the White River, under the shade of century-old beech and maple trees, the Crow's Nest is decorated in a gracious country decor with early 19th-century antiques. There is a formal dining room where full breakfasts are served. Pumpkin pancakes is a specialty. A

glass-enclosed porch features floor-to-ceiling views. The inn is located on five acres with formal gardens and clumps of raspberries and blueberries. Inner tubing and trout fishing are popular activities in the summer.

Innkeeper(s): Joyce & Dick Billingsley. $45-65. PC TC. 3 rooms, 1 with PB. Breakfast and evening snack included in rates. Type of meal: full breakfast. Beds: Q. Ceiling fan in room. VCR on premises. Fishing and cross-country skiing nearby.

"Great view! Breakfast was a delight."

Certificate may be used: Sept. 1 through April 30.

Ypsilanti   *K9*

Parish House Inn

103 S Huron St, Ypsilanti, MI 48197-5421
(313)480-4800 (800)480-4866
Fax:(313)480-7472

Circa 1893. This Queen Anne Victorian was named in honor of its service as a parsonage for the First Congregational Church. The home remained a parsonage for more than 50 years after its construction and then served as a church office and Sunday school building. It was moved to its present site in Ypsilanti's historic district in the late 1980s. The rooms are individually decorated with Victorian-style wallpapers and antiques. One guest room includes a two-person Jacuzzi tub. Those in search of a late-night snack need only venture into the kitchen to find drinks and the cookie jar. For special occasions, the innkeepers can arrange trays with flowers, non-alcoholic champagne, chocolates, fruit or cheese. The terrace overlooks the Huron River.

Innkeeper(s): Mrs. Chris Mason. $85-115. MC VISA AX PC TC. 9 rooms with PB, 2 with FP. 1 conference room. Breakfast and evening snack included in rates. Types of meals: continental breakfast, full breakfast, gourmet breakfast and early coffee/tea. Afternoon tea, picnic lunch, catering service and catered breakfast available. Beds: DT. Air conditioning, ceiling fan, cable TV and VCR in room. Fax and library on premises. Handicap access. Amusement parks, antiques, fishing, parks, shopping, cross-country skiing, sporting events, theater and watersports nearby.

Certificate may be used: December through May, Sunday through Thursday.

Minnesota

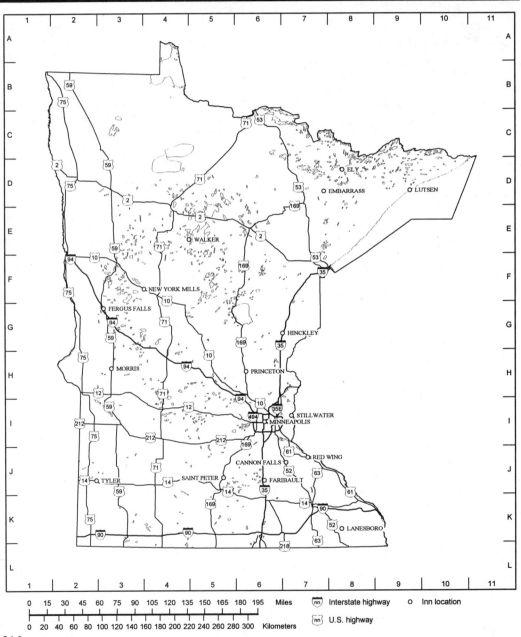

0 15 30 45 60 75 90 105 120 135 150 165 180 195 Miles

0 20 40 60 80 100 120 140 160 180 200 220 240 260 280 300 Kilometers

nn Interstate highway   O Inn location

nn U.S. highway

Cannon Falls   J7

Quill & Quilt
615 Hoffman St W,
Cannon Falls, MN 55009-1923
(507)263-5507 (800)488-3849
Fax:(507)263-4599

Circa 1897. This three-story, gabled Colonial Revival house has six bay windows and several porches and decks. The inn features a well-stocked

library, a front parlor with a fireplace, and handsomely decorated guest rooms. A favorite is the room with a double whirlpool tub, two bay windows, a king-size oak canopy bed and Victorian chairs.
Innkeeper(s): Marcia Flom. $55-130. AP. MC VISA. 4 rooms with PB. 1 suite. Breakfast included in rates. Types of meals: continental breakfast and full breakfast. Beds: KQD. Spa on premises. Antiques, fishing, downhill skiing, cross-country skiing and watersports nearby.
Location: Forty-five miles from Minneapolis/St. Paul and Rochester.
Seen in: Minneapolis Tribune, Country Quilts.

"What a pleasure to find the charm and hospitality of an English country home while on holiday in the United States."
Certificate may be used: Sunday - Thursday, Nov. 1 through April 30.

Ely   D8

Burntside Lodge
2755 Burntside Lodge Rd,
Ely, MN 55731-8402
(218)365-3894

Circa 1913. "Staying here is like taking a vacation 60 years ago," states innkeeper Lou LaMontagne. Families have come here for more than 70 years to enjoy the waterfront and woodside setting. The lodge and its cabins are in the National Register and much of the original hand-carved furnishings remain from the jazz age. Fishing, listening to the

cry of the loon and boating around the lake's 125 islands are popular activities. Breakfast and dinner are available in the waterside dining room.
Innkeeper(s): Lou & Lonnie LaMontagne. $90. MAP, EP. MC VISA AX DS PC TC. 24 cottages. Types of meals: full breakfast and early coffee/tea. Dinner and lunch available. Beds: KDT. VCR, fax, copier, swimming, sauna and library on premises. Antiques, fishing, parks, shopping and watersports nearby.
Location: Six miles southwest of Ely.

"Unforgettable."
Certificate may be used: May 15-June 24, Aug. 18-Sept 28.

Embarrass   D7

Finnish Heritage Homestead
4776 Waisanen Rd,
Embarrass, MN 55732-8347
(218)984-3318 (800)863-6545

Circa 1901. This turn-of-the-century Finnish-American log house offers outdoor recreation and family-style full breakfasts to visitors, who receive many personal touches, such as bath robes, slipper socks and turndown service in their guest rooms. Guests also may utilize the inn's relaxing sauna and enjoy badminton, bocce ball, croquet and horseshoes on its spacious grounds. Terrific fishing and skiing are found nearby, and be sure to inquire about the availability of picnic lunches to take along. A gazebo and gift shop also are on the premises.
Innkeeper(s): Elaine Bragenton & Buzz Schultz. $50-58. PC TC. 4 rooms. Breakfast included in rates. Types of meals: full breakfast and early coffee/tea. Afternoon tea, evening snack, picnic lunch and room service available. Beds: QT. Turn-down service and ceiling fan in room. VCR and sauna on premises. Antiques, fishing, parks, shopping, downhill skiing, cross-country skiing and watersports nearby.
Certificate may be used: Sunday to Thursday only.

Faribault J6

Cherub Hill B&B Inn
105 1st Ave NW,
Faribault, MN 55021-5102
(507)332-2024 (800)332-7254

Circa 1896. Midway between the Twin Cities and
Albert Lea, this Queen Anne Victorian inn offers
romantic accommodations to its guests, many of
whom are honeymooners. Guests are treated to early

coffee or tea before their full breakfasts are served.
The three air-conditioned guest rooms, which all
feature private baths and turndown service, also
include one suite. Other available guest room
amenities include a fireplace and whirlpool bath.
The charming town features many historic buildings, fine restaurants and shops. Nerstrand-Big
Woods and Sakatah Lake state parks are nearby.
Innkeeper(s): Jean Cummings. $80-95. MC VISA. 4 rooms, 3 with PB,
1 with FP. 1 suite. Breakfast included in rates. Types of meals: full
breakfast and early coffee/tea. Beds: QD. Air conditioning, turn-down
service and ceiling fan in room. Antiques, fishing, shopping, cross-
country skiing and sporting events nearby.
Certificate may be used: Sunday through Thursday, November-May.

Fergus Falls G3

Nims Bakketopp Hus
RR 2 Box 187A,
Fergus Falls, MN 56537-9802
(218)739-2915 (800)739-2915

Circa 1976. From the decks of this wooded home,
guests can enjoy the scenery of Long Lake and catch
glimpses of wildlife. Antiques, handmade quilts and
down comforters decorate the cozy guest rooms.
One room includes a private spa and draped canopy
bed. Another room includes a fireplace. A bounty of
nearby outdoor activities are sure to please nature
lovers, and antique shops and restaurants are nearby.
Innkeeper(s): Dennis & Judy Nims. $65-95. MC VISA DS PC TC. 3
suites. Breakfast, afternoon tea and evening snack included in rates.

Types of meals: gourmet breakfast and early coffee/tea. Beds: Q. Air
conditioning, ceiling fan and cable TV in room. VCR and swimming on
premises. Amusement parks, antiques, fishing, parks, shopping, downhill skiing, cross-country skiing, theater and watersports nearby.
Seen in: Minneapolis Tribune.
Certificate may be used: Sunday through Thursday for months of
March, November, December, January, February.

Hinckley G7

Dakota Lodge B&B
Rt 3 Box 178, Hinckley, MN 55037-9418
(320)384-6052 Fax:(320)384-6052

Circa 1976. Although this inn is situated between
Minneapolis and Duluth on six scenic acres, the
innkeepers named their B&B in honor of their birthplace: North Dakota. The guest rooms are named
after little known Dakota towns. The Medora and
Kathryn rooms include whirlpools and fireplaces.
Other rooms include lacy curtains, quilts and special
furnishings. The country breakfasts are expansive
with egg and meat dishes, fruit and a daily entree.
Hinckley offers a variety of activities, including a 32-
mile bike trail, a casino and antique shops.
Innkeeper(s): Mike Schmitz, Tad Hilborn. $58-135. MC VISA DS PC TC.
5 rooms with PB, 4 with FP. 1 cottage. Breakfast included in rates. Types
of meals: full breakfast and early coffee/tea. Beds: KQ. Air conditioning
and ceiling fan in room. VCR, fax, copier and library on premises.
Antiques, fishing, parks, cross-country skiing and watersports nearby.
Certificate may be used: All year, Sunday-Thursday.

Lanesboro K8

Historic Scanlan House
708 Parkway Ave S,
Lanesboro, MN 55949-9733
(507)467-2158 (800)944-2158

Circa 1889. This gracious Victorian, a National
Register house, was built by the Scanlans, successful merchants and bankers. Since then, more
recent owners have added window boxes and garden areas. There are stained-glass windows
throughout, and carved-oak woodwork adorns the
dining room and staircase.
Innkeeper(s): Mary, Gene & Kirsten Mensing. $65-130. MC VISA AX. 5
rooms with PB. Type of meal: full breakfast. Beds: QD.
Seen in: Post-Bulletin, Lacrosse Tribune.

*"We were refreshed and inspired and when the sun was
out, wanted not to budge from the balcony."*

Certificate may be used: Nov. 15-May 1, Monday through Thursday
only; excludes all holidays and special events, no exceptions.

Lutsen
D9

Lindgren's B&B on Lake Superior
County Rd 35, PO Box 56,
Lutsen, MN 55612-0056
(218)663-7450

Circa 1926. This '20s log home is in the Superior
National Forest on the north shore of Lake
Superior. The inn features massive stone fireplaces,
a baby grand piano, wildlife decor and a Finnish-
style sauna. The living room has tongue-and-groove,
Western knotty cedar wood paneling and seven-foot
windows offering a view of the lake.

Innkeeper(s): Shirley Lindgren. $85-125. MC VISA PC. 4 rooms with
PB, 1 with FP. Breakfast included in rates. Types of meals: full breakfast
and early coffee/tea. Afternoon tea, evening snack and picnic lunch
available. Beds: KDT. VCR, sauna and library on premises. Antiques,
fishing, parks, shopping, downhill skiing, cross-country skiing, theater
and watersports nearby.

Location: On the Lake Superior Circle Tour.

Seen in: Brainerd Daily Dispatch, Duluth News-Tribune, Tempo, Midwest
Living, Minnesota Monthly, Lake Superior.

*"Thanks so much for providing a home base for us as
we explored the North Country."*

Certificate may be used: Midweek (Monday-Thursday) April 1 to June
1 and Nov. 1 to Dec. 15, holidays excluded.

Minneapolis
I6

The LeBlanc House
302 University Ave NE,
Minneapolis, MN 55413-2052
(612)379-2570

Circa 1896. Visitors to the University of Minnesota
area should look no further than the LeBlanc
House. The restored Queen Anne Victorian offers
guests a historical perspective of life in the 1800s.
The inn's convenient location also provides easy
access to the Metrodome and downtown
Minneapolis, while giving its guests a chance to

relax in style after exploring the area. Amelia's
Room has a view of the city lights and visitors may
be treated to gourmet specialties such as pistachio
quiche or rum raisin French toast.

Innkeeper(s): Barb Zahasky & Bob Shulstad. $85-105. MC VISA AX PC.
3 rooms, 1 with PB. Breakfast included in rates. Type of meal: full
breakfast. Beds: Q. Air conditioning, turn-down service and ceiling fan
in room. Amusement parks, antiques, fishing, parks, shopping, downhill
skiing, cross-country skiing, sporting events, theater and watersports
nearby.

Certificate may be used: Anytime Sunday through Thursday only.

Morris
H3

The American House
410 E 3rd St, Morris, MN 56267-1426
(320)589-4054

Circa 1900. One block from the Morris campus of
the University of Minnesota, this is a two-story
house with a wide veranda. It is decorated in a country style with original stencil designs, stained glass
and family heirlooms. The Elizabeth Room holds a
Jenny Lind bed with a hand-crocheted bedcover.

Innkeeper(s): Karen Berget. $35-50. MC VISA PC TC. 3 rooms.
Breakfast included in rates. Type of meal: full breakfast. Beds: D. Air
conditioning and ceiling fan in room. Cable TV and bicycles on premises. Fishing, shopping and cross-country skiing nearby.

Seen in: Forum, Hancock Record.

"It was most delightful!"

Certificate may be used: Anytime, subject to availability.

New York Mills   F4

Whistle Stop Inn B&B
RR 1 Box 85,
New York Mills, MN 56567-9704
(218)385-2223

Circa 1903. A choo-choo theme permeates the atmosphere at this signature Victorian home. Antiques and railroad memorabilia decorate guest rooms with names such as Great Northern or Burlington Northern. The Northern Pacific room includes a bath with a clawfoot tub. For something unusual, try a night in the Cozy Caboose, which is exactly that, a restored 19th-century caboose. Despite the rustic nature, the caboose offers a double whirlpool tub. Freshly baked breads and seasonal fruit accompany the mouth-watering, homemade breakfasts.

Innkeeper(s): Roger & Jann Lee. $39-69. MC VISA AX DS PC. 4 rooms with PB. 1 suite. 1 cottage. 1 conference room. Breakfast and afternoon tea included in rates. Types of meals: continental breakfast, continental-plus breakfast, full breakfast and early coffee/tea. Lunch and catered breakfast available. Beds: QD. Turn-down service, ceiling fan and cable TV in room. VCR, spa, sauna and bicycles on premises. Antiques, fishing, parks, shopping, cross-country skiing, theater and watersports nearby.

Certificate may be used: All year, Sunday-Friday.

Princeton   H6

Oakhurst Inn B&B
212 8th Ave S, Princeton, MN 55371
(612)389-3553 (800)443-2258

Circa 1906. The Spain family occupies the third floor of their handsomely restored late Victorian bed & breakfast. Located in a small, quiet community of central Minnesota, Oakhurst was built originally for a local banker. Guests have access to a parlor where afternoon refreshments are served, a library room and three cheery guest rooms furnished in four-poster, iron and brass beds. Complimentary bicycles and horseshoes are also available.

Innkeeper(s): Suzie & Dave Spain. $70-85. MC VISA DS PC TC. 3 rooms with PB. 2 conference rooms. Breakfast, afternoon tea and evening snack included in rates. Types of meals: continental breakfast, continental-plus breakfast, full breakfast and early coffee/tea. Room service available. Beds: Q. Air conditioning in room. VCR and library on premises. Antiques, fishing, parks, shopping, cross-country skiing, theater and watersports nearby.

"It was like a dream to wake up in your lovely home."

Certificate may be used: Sunday through Thursday, year-round.

Red Wing   J7

St. James Hotel
406 Main St, Red Wing, MN 55066-2325
(612)388-2846 (800)252-1875
Fax:(612)388-5226

Circa 1875. The historic St. James provides a glimpse back to the exciting Mississippi riverboat era. The elegant Italianate structure, listed in the National Register, is filled with classy Victorian

touches. Just a block from the riverfront, the St. James has at its back door a city park, providing a restful setting for guests. The inn's rooms, some of which boast river views, sport names such as Samuel Clemens, LaCrosse Queen and Huck Finn, and a third of them carry non-smoking designations. Guests will appreciate the distinctive and period-authentic room furnishings and the detail-oriented staff.

Innkeeper(s): E.F. Foster. $100-155. EP. MC VISA AX DC CB DS TC. 60 rooms with PB. 13 conference rooms. Types of meals: continental breakfast, full breakfast and early coffee/tea. Dinner, lunch, banquet service and room service available. Beds: QT. Air conditioning, turn-down service and cable TV in room. VCR, fax, copier, spa and child care on premises. Handicap access. Antiques, fishing, parks, shopping, downhill skiing, cross-country skiing, theater and watersports nearby.

Seen in: Midwest Living.

Certificate may be used: Free night must be Sunday-Thursday except Sundays before a Monday holiday. Honored year-round. Guest is responsible for all taxes.

Saint Peter J5

Engesser House

1202 S Minnesota Ave, Saint Peter, MN
56082-2208
(507)931-9594 (800)688-2646
Fax:(507)931-9622

Circa 1880. This brick and stone home was built
by local brewer Joseph Engesser and features
Eastlake design with some Queen Anne
influences. Inside, the innkeepers
have decorated the
house with
artwork and
pieces collected on
their many
travels. Gourmet
breakfasts are
served in the
formal dining
room. Guest rooms
feature elegant
touches such as canopy beds, lace and quilts. The
innkeepers also offer plenty of amenities for the
business traveler, including fax and copy machines,
a typewriter and a Macintosh computer.

Innkeeper(s): Chuck & Julie Storm. $65-85. MC VISA AX DS PC TC. 4
rooms with PB. 1 suite. Breakfast included in rates. Types of meals:
gourmet breakfast and early coffee/tea. Evening snack and catering service available. Beds: KQT. Air conditioning, turn-down service, ceiling
fan, cable TV and VCR in room. Fax, copier, bicycles and library on
premises. Antiques, fishing, parks, shopping, downhill skiing, cross-
country skiing, sporting events, theater and watersports nearby.

Seen in: Saint Peter Herald, Mankato Free Press.

"The fine wines, interesting conversations, the wonder-
ful breakfast, the graciousness of you both made for a
memorable weekend."

Certificate may be used: Jan. 1 to Dec. 20, Sunday-Friday.

Stillwater I7

James A. Mulvey Residence Inn

622 W Churchill, Stillwater, MN 55082
(612)430-8008

Circa 1878. A charming river town is home to this
Italianate-style inn, just a short distance from the
Twin Cities, but far from the metro area in atmosphere. Visitors select from five guest rooms, including one suite. The rooms feature queen beds and
Victorian furnishings. The inn, just nine blocks
from the St. Croix River, is a popular stop with
couples celebrating anniversaries. Guests enjoy the
inn's convenient early coffee or tea service that

precedes the full breakfasts. Great antiquing, fishing and skiing are nearby, and there are many
picnic spots in the area.

Innkeeper(s): Truett & Jill Lawson. $99-149. MC VISA PC TC. 5 rooms
with PB, 3 with FP. 1 suite. Breakfast and afternoon tea included in
rates. Types of meals: gourmet breakfast and early coffee/tea. Beds:
QD. Air conditioning in room. Bicycles on premises. Antiques, fishing,
parks, shopping, downhill skiing, cross-country skiing, theater and
watersports nearby.

Certificate may be used: Sunday-Thursday only.

Rivertown Inn

306 Olive St W,
Stillwater, MN 55082-4932
(612)430-2955 (800)562-3632
Fax:(612)430-0034

Circa 1882. This three-story Victorian was built by
lumbermill owner John O'Brien. Framed by an iron
fence, the home has a wraparound veranda. Each
guest room has been decorated with care, but we
suggest the honeymoon suite or Patricia's Room
with its giant whirlpool and tall oak bedstead. A
burl-wood buffet in the dining room is laden each
morning with home-baked breads and cakes. The
St. Croix River is a short walk away.

Innkeeper(s): Chuck & Judy Dougherty. $79-179. MC VISA AX DC DS
PC TC. 12 rooms with PB, 9 with FP. 4 suites. 1 conference room.
Breakfast and evening snack included in rates. Types of meals: full
breakfast, gourmet breakfast and early coffee/tea. Beds: QD. Air conditioning, ceiling fan and cable TV in room. Fax, copier, library and child
care on premises. Handicap access. Antiques, fishing, parks, shopping,
downhill skiing, cross-country skiing and theater nearby.

Location: Four blocks from historic main street.

Seen in: Country Magazine.

"Fantastic place for a romantic getaway!"

Certificate may be used: Sunday-Thursday Nov. 1-May 1; holidays
excluded.

Tyler J2

Babette's Inn
308 S Tyler St, Tyler, MN 56178-9484
(507)247-3962 (800)466-7067

Circa 1914. Tyler's large Danish population inspired the name of this bed & breakfast, which was taken from Babette's Feast, Danish writer Isak Dinesen's novel about a French servant. A European influence is evident throughout the inn, not only because of the town's influence, but the innkeepers themselves lived on the continent for some time. Each of the large suites offers something unique. Babette's Suite affords a view of the garden and boasts a fireplace and canopy bed. The Isak Dinesen Suite, which features an adjoining study, includes all of the famed author's works. The Two Sister's Suite includes a balcony and private sitting area. The home's original parlor now houses a boutique featuring collectibles and specialty foods. Breakfasts are served in the eclectic dining room with specialties such as baked apple spice bread and cheese blintzes topped with Danish raspberry sauce.
Innkeeper(s): James & Alicia Johnson. $65-79. MC VISA TC. 3 suites, 2 with FP. Breakfast included in rates. Types of meals: full breakfast, gourmet breakfast and early coffee/tea. Beds: QDT. Air conditioning, ceiling fan and VCR in room. Bicycles on premises. Antiques, fishing, parks, shopping, cross-country skiing, sporting events, theater and watersports nearby.
Seen in: Sioux Falls Argus Leader, Minnesota Home and Away.

"Thank you for providing this place of peace. The breakfast was sumptuous — again! What a great value."
Certificate may be used: July 1-April 30 Sunday-Friday.

Walker E5

Peacecliff
HCR 73 Box 998D,
Walker, MN 56484-9579
(218)547-2832

Circa 1957. Innkeepers Dave and Kathy Laursen are Minnesota natives, and after years away, returned to their home state and opened this serene, waterfront B&B. The English Tudor affords views of Lake Leech from most of its rooms, which are decorated with a mix of traditional and Victorian furnishings. The Laursens are nature lovers, having trekked across miles of mountain trails and scenic areas. They are happy to point out nearby recreation sites, including the North Country Trail, a 68-mile journey through Chippewa National Forest.
Innkeeper(s): Dave & Kathy Laursen. $58-95. MC VISA AX DS TC. 5 rooms, 1 with PB, 1 with FP. 1 suite. Breakfast included in rates. Types of meals: full breakfast, gourmet breakfast and early coffee/tea. Beds: QDT. Cable TV and VCR on premises. Amusement parks, antiques, fishing, parks, shopping, cross-country skiing, theater and watersports nearby.
Certificate may be used: No holiday weekends.

Tianna Farms B&B
PO Box 968, Walker, MN 56484-0968
(218)547-1306 (800)842-6620

Circa 1922. Overlooking beautiful Leech Lake, this former dairy farm was started by the grandfather of the current owner, as was the 18-hole golf course, now named Tianna Country Club. Guests receive 50 percent off green fees. The inn's lakefront resort area lures many visitors, who may choose from five rooms, ranging from the Garden and Hunting rooms, with two twin beds, to the Suite, with a king and two twin beds. The innkeepers also offer a cabin which sleeps six. The family-oriented Tianna Farms also can be reserved at whole-house rates for weekends or full weeks. There are tennis facilities and a trampoline on the premises. The area boasts hiking, biking and snowmobile trails.
Innkeeper(s): Linda Wenzel. $45-125. MC VISA DS TC. 5 rooms with PB. Breakfast and evening snack included in rates. Type of meal: full breakfast. Beds: KQT. Cable TV and VCR on premises. Antiques, fishing, parks, shopping, cross-country skiing and watersports nearby.

"What a wonderful place!"
Certificate may be used: Oct. 16-May 14.

Mississippi

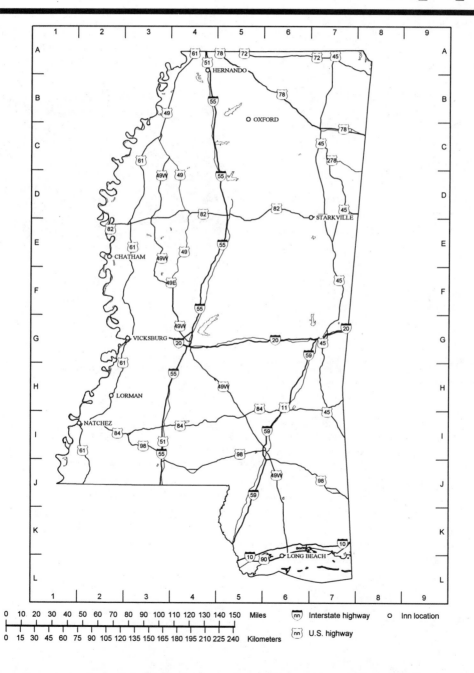

0 10 20 30 40 50 60 70 80 90 100 110 120 130 140 150   Miles

0 15 30 45 60 75 90 105 120 135 150 165 180 195 210 225 240   Kilometers

{nn} Interstate highway   o Inn location

{nn} U.S. highway

223

Chatham E2

Mount Holly Plantation Inn
HCR 63 Box 140,
Chatham, MS 38731-9601
(601)827-2652 Fax:(601)827-2652

Circa 1855. This 20-room mansion, on six acres fronting Lake Washington, is in the Italianate style. It has 24-inch-thick walls of brick. Most of the rooms are 25 by 25 feet. All bedrooms open off a large second-floor ballroom, including a room with a 12-foot-high canopy bed. Antique furnishings, bordered ceilings, and chandeliers decorate the interior.
Innkeeper(s): Ann Woods. $65-150. MC VISA DS PC TC. 7 rooms, 4 with PB, 4 with FP. 1 suite. 1 conference room. Breakfast included in rates. Types of meals: full breakfast and early coffee/tea. Beds: KQDT. Air conditioning and ceiling fan in room. Fax on premises. Antiques, fishing, parks and watersports nearby.

Location: On Lake Washington.

Seen in: Southern Living.

Certificate may be used: July 1-Aug. 31 & Nov. 1-Feb. 28, excluding weekends and holidays.

Hernando A4

Sassafras Inn
785 Highway 51 S,
Hernando, MS 38632-8149
(601)429-5864 (800)882-1897
Fax:(601)429-4591

Circa 1985. This modern inn offers guests to the state's Northwest corner a delightful respite from their travels or from the hustle and bustle of Memphis, 10 miles north. An impressive indoor swimming pool and spa are guest favorites and visitors also enjoy the cabana room for reading or lounging, or the recreation room with billiards, darts and ping pong. A romantic honeymoon cottage also is available. Arkabutla Lake is an easy drive from the inn.
Innkeeper(s): Dennis & Francee McClanahan. $80-175. MC VISA AX DS PC TC. 4 rooms, 3 with PB. 1 suite. 1 cottage. Breakfast, afternoon tea and evening snack included in rates. Types of meals: full breakfast and early coffee/tea. Beds: QD. Air conditioning, turn-down service, ceiling fan, cable TV and VCR in room. Fax, copier, spa, swimming and library on premises. Antiques, parks and watersports nearby.

Location: Near Graceland, 25 minutes from downtown Memphis.

Certificate may be used: All year, Sunday through Thursday, no holidays.

Long Beach L6

Red Creek Inn, Vineyard & Racing Stables
7416 Red Creek Rd,
Long Beach, MS 39560-8804
(601)452-3080 (800)729-9670
Fax:(601)452-4450

Circa 1899. This inn was built in the raised French cottage-style by a retired Italian sea captain, who wished to entice his bride to move from her parents' home in New Orleans. There are two swings on the

64-foot front porch and one swing that hangs from a 300-year-old oak tree. Magnolias and ancient live oaks, some registered with the Live Oak Society of the Louisiana Garden Club, dot 11 acres. The inn features a parlor, six fireplaces, ceiling fans and antiques, including a Victorian organ, wooden radios and a Victrola.
Innkeeper(s): Karl & "Toni" Mertz. $59-89. PC. 5 rooms, 3 with PB, 1 with FP. 1 suite. 1 conference room. Breakfast included in rates. Types of meals: continental-plus breakfast and early coffee/tea. Beds: DT. Air conditioning in room. Cable TV, VCR, fax, copier, stables and library on premises. Amusement parks, antiques, fishing, parks, shopping, theater and watersports nearby.

Seen in: Jackson Daily News, Innviews, TV Channel 13.

"We loved waking up here on these misty spring mornings. The Old South is here."

Certificate may be used: Sunday-Thursday, May-August and any time September-April (depending upon availability).

Lorman　　H2

Canemont Plantation
Rt 2 Box 45, Lorman, MS 39096-9602
(601)877-3784 (800)423-0684
Fax:(601)877-2010

Circa 1855. Guests traveling down the famed Natchez Trace will want to reserve a stay at this 6,000-acre working plantation. Among the many treasures found on the inn grounds, guest will discover the former quarters of Ben Coleman, a slave who hid the plantation silver away from the Yankees during the Civil War. Windsor Plantation, considered to be one of the grandest antebellum manors east of the Mississippi, is found within the immense grounds. Plantation guests stay in one of three guest cottages, which are sprinkled by the main house, an Italianate Revival structure peaked with three chimneys. Each of the cottages includes a wood-burning fireplace or stove. The hosts offer guided tours of the grounds, where encounters with deer and birds aren't uncommon, and guests may fish in the stocked ponds.

Innkeeper(s): Ray & Rachel Forrest. $145-165. MAP. MC VISA. 3 suites, 3 with FP. 2 conference rooms. Breakfast, dinner and evening snack included in rates. Types of meals: full breakfast and gourmet breakfast. Picnic lunch, lunch, banquet service and catering service available. Beds: KD. Air conditioning and ceiling fan in room. VCR, fax and copier on premises. Antiques, fishing, parks and shopping nearby.

Certificate may be used: June, July, August-Sunday through Thursday.

Natchez　　I2

Harper House
201 Arlington Ave,
Natchez, MS 39120-3548
(601)445-5557

Circa 1892. Located in the Arlington Heights section of Natchez, this Queen Anne Victorian inn is a fine example of the city's popular Victorian-style homes. The inn's convenient location, midway between Baton Rouge and Vicksburg, makes it an ideal stop for those exploring this beautiful and history-rich region. Breakfast is served in a charming gazebo. Natchez-Under-the-Hill and the

famous antebellum homes in the historic district are within easy walking distance. Natchez National Cemetery and Natchez State Park are nearby.

Innkeeper(s): Kay Warren. $90. MC VISA. 1 room. Breakfast included in rates. Types of meals: continental breakfast and full breakfast. Antiques, shopping and theater nearby.

Certificate may be used: November, December (excluding 23, 24, 25, 26). January-February.

Oxford　　B5

Oliver-Britt House
512 Van Buren Ave,
Oxford, MS 38655-3838
(601)234-8043

Circa 1905. White columns and a picturesque veranda highlight the exterior of this Greek Revival inn shaded by trees. English country comfort is the emphasis in the interior, which includes a collection of antiques. On weekends, guests are treated to a Southern-style breakfast with all the trimmings. A travel service is located on the premises.

Innkeeper(s): Glynn Oliver. $55-65. MC VISA AX DS TC. 5 rooms with PB. Breakfast included in rates. Types of meals: full breakfast and early coffee/tea. Banquet service and catering service available. Beds: KQ. Air conditioning, ceiling fan and cable TV in room. Antiques, parks, shopping and sporting events nearby.

Certificate may be used: Dec. 1 to Feb. 28, Sunday-Thursday.

Starkville　　D7

The Cedars B&B
2173 Oktoc Rd,
Starkville, MS 39759-9251
(601)324-7569

Circa 1836. This historic plantation offers a glimpse of life in the 19th-century South. The late Colonial/Greek Revival structure was built primarily

by slaves, with construction lasting two years. The inn's 183 acres boast fishing ponds, pasture and woods, and guests love to explore, hike and ride horses. Four guest rooms are available, two with private bath. Visitors enjoy the inn's collection of 19th- and early 20th-century horse and farm equipment. Noxubee Wildlife Refuge and the Tombigbee National Forest are within easy driving distance.

Innkeeper(s): Erin Scanlon. $50-65. TC. 4 rooms, 2 with PB, 4 with FP. 2 conference rooms. Breakfast and evening snack included in rates. Types of meals: continental breakfast, continental-plus breakfast, full breakfast and early coffee/tea. Picnic lunch available. Beds: FT. Air conditioning in room. Antiques, fishing, parks, shopping, sporting events, theater and watersports nearby.

Certificate may be used: Anytime based on availability.

Vicksburg G3

Balfour House

1002 Crawford Street,
Vicksburg, MS 39181-0781
(601)638-7113 (800)294-7113

Circa 1835. Writer and former resident Emma Balfour witnessed the Siege of Vicksburg from the window of this Greek Revival home. Until the Civil War, the home was the site of elegant balls attended by Southern belles in ornate gowns accompanied by Confederate beaus. Innkeepers Bob and Sharon Humble brought back these grand affairs during several re-enactment dances, in which guests dress up in period costume. The National Register home is a piece of history, with stunning architectural features, such as the home's showpiece, three-story elliptical spiral staircase.

Innkeeper(s): Bob & Sharon Humble. $85-150. MC VISA AX TC. 15 rooms, 4 with PB, 1 with FP. 1 conference room. Breakfast included in rates. Type of meal: gourmet breakfast. Catering service available. Beds: KQDT. Air conditioning and cable TV in room. Amusement parks, antiques, fishing, parks, shopping and theater nearby.

Certificate may be used: Jan. 30 to Sept. 30, Sunday-Friday.

Belle of The Bends

508 Klein St, Vicksburg, MS 39180-4004
(601)634-0737 (800)844-2308

Circa 1876. Located in Vicksburg's Historic Garden District, this Victorian, Italianate mansion was built by Mississippi State Senator Murray F. Smith and his wife, Kate, and is nestled on a bluff overlooking the Mississippi River. The decor includes period

antiques, Oriental rugs and memorabilia of the steamboats that plied the river waters in the 1880s and early 1900s. Two bedrooms and the first- and second-story wraparound verandas provide views of the river. A plantation breakfast is served and a tour of the house and history of the steamboats owned by the Morrissey Line is given. A tour of the Victorian Gardens also is available to guests.

Innkeeper(s): Wallace & Josephine Pratt. $75-105. MC VISA AX. 4 rooms. Breakfast and afternoon tea included in rates. Type of meal: full breakfast. Beds: QDT. Antiques and fishing nearby.

Seen in: Natchez Trace News Explorer, Victorian Style, America's Painted Ladies.

"Thank you for the personalized tour of the home and area. We greatly enjoyed our stay. This house got us into the spirit of the period."

Certificate may be used: January-February, September (one room in program-Riverview Room), Sunday-Thursday occupancy.

Missouri

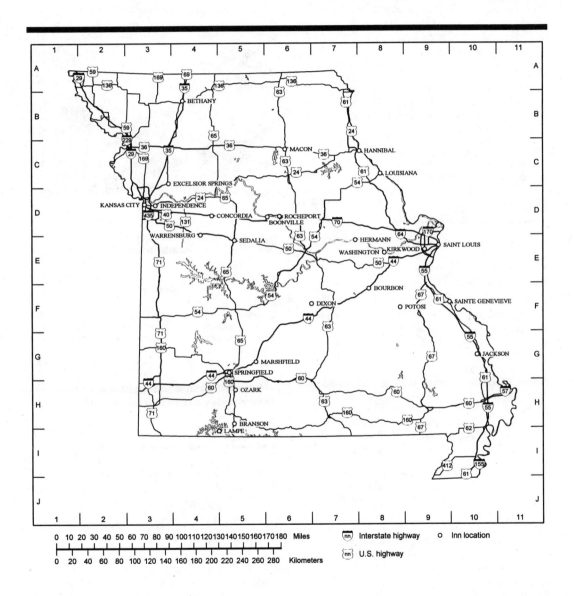

	Miles
0 10 20 30 40 50 60 70 80 90 100110120130140150160170180	
0 20 40 60 80 100 120 140 160 180 200 220 240 260 280	Kilometers

{nn} Interstate highway   o Inn location

{nn} U.S. highway

Bethany   B4

Unicorn Lodge B&B
119 S 15th St, Bethany, MO 64424-1925
(816)425-3676

Circa 1938. Midway between Kansas City and Des
Moines, this art deco brick hotel offers a pleasant
respite for Midwest travelers. Fifteen guest rooms are
available, and most feature king or queen accommodations. Guests may watch TV in the inn's sitting
room or take a relaxing stroll around the town
square, just a few steps away. The innkeepers chose
the Unicorn name for their establishment because it
symbolizes graciousness and tranquility, and visitors
will find its likeness throughout. There is a
restaurant on the premises.

Innkeeper(s): Wynn Walter Pollock. $35-60. 15 rooms, 14 with PB. 1
suite. 1 conference room. Breakfast included in rates. Beds: KQTD.
Antiques, parks and shopping nearby.

Certificate may be used: Anytime.

Boonville   D6

Morgan Street Repose B&B
611 E Morgan St,
Boonville, MO 65233-1221
(816)882-7195 (800)248-5061

Circa 1869. The historic Missouri River town of
Boonville is home to this inn, comprised of two
Italianate structures on the site of what once was a
hotel that served travelers on the Santa Fe Trail.
The inn is listed in the National Register of
Historic Places. More than 400 antebellum and
Victorian homes and buildings are found in town.
Visitors enjoy their gourmet breakfasts in one of
three dining rooms or in the Secret Garden.
Several state parks are within easy driving distance,
and the University of Missouri-Columbia is 20
miles to the east.

Innkeeper(s): Doris Shenk. $65-75. 3 rooms with PB. Breakfast and
afternoon tea included in rates. Types of meals: full breakfast and early
coffee/tea. Evening snack available. Beds: Q. Air conditioning and ceiling fan in room. Antiques and theater nearby.

*"We had a wonderful, romantic, relaxing honeymoon in
the Ashley Suite. The hospitality and atmosphere
exceeded our expectations by far. The memory of our
stay here will last a lifetime."*

Certificate may be used: February through December, Sunday through
Thursday.

Bourbon   F8

Meramec Farm Bed and Board
Star Route Box 50, Bourbon, MO 65441
(573)732-4765

Circa 1883. This farmhouse inn and cedar guest
cabin are found on a working cattle operation, little
more than an hour's drive from St. Louis. Seven
generations have lived and worked the farm, which

boasts 460 acres. Visitors stay in the 1880s farmhouse or the cabin, built from cedar cut on the
farm. The inn's proximity to the Meramec River
and Vilander Bluffs provides excellent views and
many outdoor activities. Spring visitors are treated
to the sight of baby calves. Meramec Caverns and
several state parks are nearby.

Innkeeper(s): Carol Springer. $70. 3 rooms. 1 cottage. Breakfast includ-
ed in rates. Types of meals: full breakfast and early coffee/tea. Picnic
lunch available. Beds: QDT. Air conditioning and ceiling fan in room.
Antiques and fishing nearby.

Location: Seventy-five miles southwest of St. Louis on scenic Meramec
River.

Seen in: Midwest Motorist, St. Louis Post-Dispatch, St. Louis.

Certificate may be used: Sunday-Thursday, year-round.

Branson   H5

The Inn at Fall Creek
391 Concord Ave,
Branson, MO 65616-8642
(417)336-3422 (800)280-3422
Fax:(417)336-5950

Circa 1980. Surrounded by 60 wooded acres, this
modern inn offers five guest rooms, two of them
suites. Less than two miles from Branson's "strip,"
the inn is ideally located for those taking advantage
of the area's many attractions, including nearby
Silver Dollar City and Talking Rocks. Guests are
treated to early coffee or tea and an evening snack
in addition to a full breakfast. The inn's guest rooms

are furnished in country decor. Rooms with fire-place, kitchenette or spa are available.

Innkeeper(s): J.C. McCracken. $70-95. MC VISA DS PC TC. 7 rooms, 4 with PB, 2 with FP. 2 suites. 1 conference room. Breakfast included in rates. Types of meals: full breakfast and early coffee/tea. Evening snack available. Beds: KQ. Air conditioning and ceiling fan in room. Fax and spa on premises. Amusement parks, antiques, fishing, shopping, theater and watersports nearby.

Certificate may be used: January-March.

Concordia   D4

Fannie Lee B&B Inn
902 Main St, Concordia, MO 64020
(816)463-7395

The main house on this property was built by German immigrants, who added many wonderful elements to their house, including a double oak stairway and front entrance flanked by windows of beveled-plate glass. An iron fence surrounds the home, and European-style lampposts are a charming addition. The bed & breakfast boasts one of the largest private rose gardens in Missouri. Spring guests will be amazed by the thousands of blooms that brighten the grounds. Rooms are filled with art collections and antiques, some of which date back 350 years.

Innkeeper(s): John Campbell. $65. MC VISA AX. 4 rooms. Breakfast included in rates. Type of meal: full breakfast.

Certificate may be used: Sunday through Thursday.

Dixon   F7

Rock Eddy Bluff
HCR 62 Box 241, Dixon, MO 65459-8403
(314)759-6081 (800)335-5921

Circa 1991. This inn's rural, off-the-beaten-path location is ideal for those seeking a secluded, country retreat. Visitors choose from two guest rooms or the three-bedroom Turkey Ridge Cottage. The East and West rooms offer antique furnishings, queen beds and TVs, not to mention magnificent views. Amid a rolling river valley and wooded ridges, the inn's setting is a nature lover's delight, complete with canoeing, fishing and hiking. Canoes are provided, and the innkeepers will take guests on horse-drawn wagon excursions. More than 75 species of birds have been sighted here, including bald eagles and great blue herons.

Innkeeper(s): Kathy & Tom Corey. $59-97. MC VISA PC. 4 rooms, 1 with PB. 5 cottages. Breakfast and evening snack included in rates. Type of meal: full breakfast. Beds: QDT. Air conditioning, ceiling fan and VCR in room. Spa, swimming and stables on premises. Antiques, fishing, parks and watersports nearby.

Location: On a bluff above Gasconade River.

Certificate may be used: Sunday through Thursday, April 1-Dec. 1. All weeks December-April 1.

Excelsior Springs   C3

Crescent Lake Manor
1261 Saint Louis Ave,
Excelsior Springs, MO 64024-2938
(816)637-2958 (800)897-2958

Circa 1900. Surrounded by a moat, this three-story Georgian-style house is just a half-hour drive from Kansas City. The three guest rooms are decorated with country and traditional touches, and a swimming pool and tennis court are found on the 21-acre grounds. Golfers will find a challenge at Excelsior Springs Golf Course, and many guests enjoy visiting the nearby Hall of Waters for a relaxing mineral bath and massage.

Innkeeper(s): Mary Elizabeth Leake. $55-65. MAP. MC VISA. 4 rooms, 1 with PB. 1 suite. Breakfast included in rates. Types of meals: full breakfast and early coffee/tea. Beds: KQD. Air conditioning, ceiling fan, cable TV and VCR in room. Amusement parks, antiques, fishing, parks and shopping nearby.

Certificate may be used: Jan. 1 to Nov. 1, Monday-Thursday.

Hannibal   C8

Fifth Street Mansion B&B
213 S 5th St, Hannibal, MO 63401-4421
(573)221-0445 (800)874-5661
Fax:(573)221-3335

Circa 1858. This 20-room Italianate house listed in the National Register displays extended eaves and heavy brackets, tall windows and decorated lintels. A cupola affords a view of the town. Mark Twain

was invited to dinner here by the Garth family and joined Laura Frazer (his Becky Thatcher) for the evening. An enormous stained-glass window lights the stairwell. The library features a stained-glass window with the family crest and is paneled with hand-grained walnut.

Innkeeper(s): Donalene & Mike Andreotti. $45-90. MC VISA AX DS TC. 7 rooms with PB. 1 conference room. Breakfast included in rates. Type of meal: full breakfast. Beds: Q. Air conditioning, cable TV and VCR in room. Fax on premises. Antiques, fishing and shopping nearby.

Location: North of St. Louis 100 miles.

Seen in: Innsider, Country Inns.

"We thoroughly enjoyed our visit. Terrific food and hospitality!"

Certificate may be used: Monday-Thursday - except holidays - October-March.

Garth Woodside Mansion

RR 1 Box 304, Hannibal, MO 63401-9634
(573)221-2789

Circa 1871. This Italian Renaissance mansion is set on 39 acres of meadow and woodland. Original Victorian antiques fill the house. An unusual flying staircase with no visible means of support vaults three stories. Best of all, is the Samuel Clemens

Room where Mark Twain slept. Afternoon beverages are served, and there are nightshirts tucked away in your room.

Innkeeper(s): Irv & Diane Feinberg. $65-105. MC VISA. 8 rooms with PB, 4 with FP. Breakfast and afternoon tea included in rates. Types of meals: gourmet breakfast and early coffee/tea. Beds: QD. Air conditioning and turn-down service in room. Amusement parks, antiques, fishing, parks and theater nearby.

Location: Along the Mississippi River just off highway 61.

Seen in: Country Inns, Chicago Sun-Times, Glamour, Victorian Homes, Midwest Living, Innsider, Country Living, Conde Nast Traveler, Bon Appetit.

"So beautiful and romantic and relaxing, we forgot we were here to work—Jeannie and Bob Ransom, Innsider."

Certificate may be used: Sunday-Thursday, November-April.

Hermann E7

Reiff House B&B

306 Market St,
Hermann, MO 65041-1058
(573)486-2994 (800)482-2994

Circa 1871. Hermann, once a busy Missouri River port city, now is home to a beautiful National Historic District, where the inn is found. A three-story former hotel, now the inn's first floor holds the Hermann visitor center. Guest rooms include the romantic Ivy Rose Suite. Breakfasts, which may feature freshly squeezed orange juice, German sausage, homemade muffins, quiche and sugar-free strawberry trifle, are enjoyed in the sitting room or courtyard, which turns into a German biergarten during Maifest and Oktoberfest weekends.

Innkeeper(s): Sue Scheiter. $65. MC VISA DS TC. 3 rooms with PB. Breakfast included in rates. Type of meal: full breakfast. Beds: KQD. Air conditioning and cable TV in room. Spa on premises. Antiques, fishing, parks, shopping and theater nearby.

Certificate may be used: Year round, except October.

Independence D3

Woodstock Inn

1212 W Lexington Ave,
Independence, MO 64050-3524
(816)833-2233

Circa 1900. This turn-of-the-century home is in the perfect location for sightseeing in historic Independence. Visit the home of Harry S Truman or the Truman Library and Museum. The Old Jail Museum is another popular attraction. A large country breakfast is served each morning. Independence is less than 30 minutes from Kansas City where you may spend the day browsing through the shops at Country Club Plaza or Halls' Crown Center.

Innkeeper(s): Ruth Harold. $45-70. MC VISA AX DS. 11 rooms with PB. 2 suites. Breakfast included in rates. Type of meal: full breakfast. Beds: KQTD. Air conditioning in room. Handicap access. Amusement parks, antiques, shopping, sporting events and theater nearby.

Location: Three miles from I-70 and I-435.

Seen in: Country, San Francisco Chronicle.

"Pleasant, accommodating people, a facility of good character."

Certificate may be used: September through November, Sunday-Thursday nights; December-May 1 anytime. May call at last minute, subject to availability.

Jackson   G10

Trisha's B&B
203 Bellevue, Jackson, MO 63755
(314)243-7427

Circa 1905. This inn offers a sitting room, library and spacious guest rooms. Some rooms have bay windows and are furnished with antiques and family heirlooms. Trisha provides fresh flowers and serves hand-picked fruits and homemade baked goods.

Innkeeper(s): Trisha Wischmann. $65-75. MC VISA AX. 4 rooms, 3 with PB. 1 conference room. Breakfast included in rates. Types of meals: full breakfast and gourmet breakfast. Beds: KQD. Fishing nearby. Seen in: Cash-Book Journal, Southeast Missourian.

"You have created a beautiful home so naturally. Your B&B is filled with love and care—a really special place."

Certificate may be used: Year-round, Sunday-Thursday, January-December.

Kansas City   D3

Dome Ridge
14360 Walker Rd,
Kansas City, MO 64163-1519
(816)532-4074

Circa 1985. The innkeeper custom-built this inn, a geodesic dome in a country setting just 10 minutes from the airport. One guest room boasts a king bed with a white iron and brass headboard, double spa and separate shower. In the inn's common areas, guests may enjoy a barbecue, CD player, fireplace, gazebo, library and pool table. The gourmet breakfasts, usually featuring Belgian waffles or California

omelets, are served in the dining room, but guests are advised that the inn's kitchen is well worth checking out.

Innkeeper(s): Roberta Faust. $60-95. 4 rooms, 3 with PB. Breakfast included in rates. Types of meals: full breakfast and early coffee/tea. Beds: KQDT. Air conditioning in room. Spa on premises. Amusement parks, antiques, fishing, shopping, downhill skiing, sporting events and theater nearby.

Certificate may be used: Sunday through Thursday, all-year.

Kirkwood   E9

Fissy's Place
500 N Kirkwood Rd, Kirkwood, MO
63122-3914
(314)821-4494

Circa 1939. The innkeeper's past is just about as interesting as the history of this bed & breakfast. A former Miss Missouri, the innkeeper has acted in movies with the likes of Burt Reynolds and Robert Redford, and pictures of many movie stars decorate the home's interior. A trained interior designer, she also shares this talent in the cheerfully decorated guest rooms. Historic downtown Kirkwood is within walking distance to the home, which also offers close access to St. Louis.

Innkeeper(s): Cheryl Bradley & Fay Haas. $69-76. MC VISA PC TC. 3 rooms with PB. 1 conference room. Breakfast and evening snack included in rates. Types of meals: continental-plus breakfast, full breakfast and early coffee/tea. Catering service available. Beds: QDT. Air conditioning, turn-down service, ceiling fan, cable TV and VCR in room. Copier on premises. Handicap access. Antiques, parks, shopping, sporting events and theater nearby.

Certificate may be used: Anytime.

Lampe   I5

Grandpa's Farm B&B
HCR 1, PO Box 476,
Lampe, MO 65681-0476
(417)779-5106 (800)280-5106

Circa 1891. This limestone farmhouse in the heart of the Ozarks offers guests a chance to experience country life in a relaxed farm setting. Midway between Silver Dollar City and Eureka Springs, Ark., the inn boasts several lodging options, including a duplex with suites and honeymoon suite. The innkeepers are known for their substantial country breakfast and say guests enjoy comparing how long the meal lasts before they eat again. Although the inn's 116 acres are not farmed extensively, domesticated farm animals are on the premises.

Innkeeper(s): Keith & Pat Lamb. $65-85. MC VISA DS PC TC. 4 rooms with PB. 3 suites. 1 conference room. Breakfast included in rates. Type of meal: full breakfast. Beds: KD. Air conditioning and ceiling fan in room. VCR, fax and spa on premises. Handicap access. Amusement parks, antiques, fishing, parks, shopping, theater and watersports nearby.

Certificate may be used: All months except June, July, August, October.

Louisiana
C8

Serando's House
918 Georgia St, PO Box 205,
Louisiana, MO 63353-1812
(314)754-4067 (800)754-4067

Circa 1876. Southerners traveling up the Mississippi River discovered this lush area in the early 19th century, founded it and named their little town Louisiana. The town still features many of the earliest structures in the downtown historic district. Serando's House still showcases much of its original woodwork and stained glass. The two guest rooms are comfortably furnished, and one includes a balcony. Guests select their breakfast from a variety of menu items.

Innkeeper(s): Tom & Jeannie Serandos. $65-85. AX PC TC. 2 rooms, 1 with PB. Breakfast included in rates. Types of meals: full breakfast and early coffee/tea. Dinner, picnic lunch and lunch available. Beds: Q. Air conditioning, ceiling fan, cable TV and VCR in room. Spa on premises. Antiques, fishing, parks, shopping, theater and watersports nearby.

Seen in: Discover Mid-America.

Certificate may be used: Feb. 15 to Nov. 20, weekdays, Monday through Thursday.

Macon
C6

St. Agnes Hall B&B
706 Jackson St, Macon, MO 63552-5106
(816)385-2774 Fax:(816)385-4436

Circa 1846. During the late 19th century, this home served as a boarding house and day school for young women. Rumor has it that a small room located beneath the house, but not connected to the basement, was used to hide slaves heading north to freedom. The home is filled with unique collectibles and antiques, all surrounded by Victorian decor. Breakfasts can be enjoyed in a variety of settings, on the veranda, in the garden, dining room or in the privacy of your guest room.

Innkeeper(s): Scott & Carol Phillips. $60-75. MC VISA AX TC. 4 rooms, 3 with PB, 2 with FP. 1 suite. Breakfast included in rates. Types of meals: full breakfast and early coffee/tea. Beds: KQ. Air conditioning, ceiling fan and cable TV in room. VCR, fax and copier on premises. Antiques, fishing, parks, shopping and watersports nearby.

Certificate may be used: Not honored for special events.

Marshfield
G5

Dickey House
331 S Clay St,
Marshfield, MO 65706-2114
(417)468-3000 Fax:(417)859-5478

Circa 1913. This Greek Revival mansion is framed by ancient oak trees and boasts eight massive two-story Ionic columns. Burled woodwork, beveled glass

and polished hardwood floors accentuate the gracious rooms. Interior columns soar in the parlor, creating a suitably elegant setting for the innkeeper's outstanding collection of antiques. A queen-size canopy bed, fireplace and balcony are featured in the Heritage Room.

Innkeeper(s): William & Dorothy Buesgen. $55-95. MC VISA DS PC TC. 6 rooms with PB, 2 with FP. 1 cottage. Breakfast included in rates. Types of meals: full breakfast and gourmet breakfast. Beds: KQD. Air conditioning, ceiling fan and VCR in room. Cable TV, fax, copier and library on premises. Handicap access.

"Thanks so much for all that you did to make our wedding special."

Certificate may be used: Anytime subject to availability.

Ozark
H5

Country Lane Cabin B&B
254 Carriage Ln, Ozark, MO 65721-7745
(417)581-7372 (800)866-5903

Located between Springfield and Branson, this contemporary log cabin offers old-fashioned country charm. The inn is a popular honeymoon destination, with many comforts provided for a romantic getaway. A fireplace, queen bed, refrigerator and a whirlpool bath are some of the amenities provided. Guests also enjoy early coffee and tea plus a full country breakfast and evening snack. A cozy front porch, pine floors and a handmade quilt add to the atmosphere. Fine antiquing is found nearby.

Innkeeper(s): Nancy Hughes. $85. 1 cottage. Breakfast included in rates. Types of meals: full breakfast and early coffee/tea. Evening snack available. Air conditioning and ceiling fan in room. Amusement parks, antiques, shopping, sporting events and theater nearby.

Certificate may be used: One Private Cabin. January through September, weeknights only.

Rocheport
D6

Roby River Run, A B&B

201 N Roby Farm Rd,
Rocheport, MO 65279-9315
(314)698-2173

Circa 1854. Moses Payne, known as Boone County's "Millionaire Minister," chose these wooded, 10-acre grounds nestled near the banks of the Missouri River, on which to build his home. The Federal-style manor offers three distinctive guest rooms. The Moses U. Payne room offers a cherry, Queen Anne poster bed and a fireplace. The Sarah Payne room, named for Moses' second wife, boasts a rice bed and antique wash-stand. The Hattie

McDaniel, named for the Academy Award-winning actress who portrayed Mammy in "Gone With the Wind," offers a peek at the inn's extensive collection of memorabilia from the movie. Homemade breakfasts include eggs, biscuits, country-cured ham and specialties such as marmalade-cream cheese stuffed French toast. Rocheport, a National Register town, offers several antique shops to explore, as well as the Katy Trail, a path for hikers and bikers that winds along the river. As the evening approaches, guests can head up to Les Bourgeois Vineyards and

purchase a picnic basket, a bottle of Missouri wine and watch the sun set over the river.

Innkeeper(s): Gary Smith & Randall Kilgore. $40-85. MC VISA AX DS PC. 3 rooms, 1 with PB, 1 with FP. Type of meal: full breakfast. Evening snack and picnic lunch available. Beds: Q. Air conditioning and turndown service in room. VCR and stables on premises. Antiques, shopping and theater nearby.

Certificate may be used: Monday-Thursday, Nov. 1-April 30.

School House B&B Inn

504 Third St, Rocheport, MO 65279
(573)698-2022

Circa 1914. This three-story brick building was once a schoolhouse. Now luxuriously appointed as a country inn, it features 13-foot-high ceilings, small print wallpapers and a bridal suite with Victorian furnishings and a private spa. Guests partake a delightful morning meal in the inn's dining

room/kitchen area which still features a schoolhouse chalkboard. The basement houses an antique shop. Be sure to visit the nearby winery. The Katy Trail, which runs along the river, provide many scenic miles for cyclists and hikers.

Innkeeper(s): Penny Province. $85-150. MC VISA. 10 rooms with PB. 1 suite. 1 conference room. Breakfast and evening snack included in rates. Types of meals: continental breakfast, continental-plus breakfast, full breakfast, gourmet breakfast and early coffee/tea. Afternoon tea available. Beds: KQDT. Air conditioning and ceiling fan in room. Cable TV, VCR, bicycles and library on premises. Antiques, fishing, parks, shopping, sporting events and theater nearby.

Seen in: Midwest Motorist, Missouri Wein Press, Successful Farming, Hallmark Greeting Cards.

"We are still talking about our great weekend in Rocheport. Thanks for the hospitality, the beautiful room and delicious breakfasts, they were really great."

Certificate may be used: January-April, June-September, November and December, Sunday through Thursday.

Sainte Genevieve F9

Main Street Inn
221 North Main St,
Sainte Genevieve, MO 63670
(573)883-9199 (800)918-9199

Circa 1883. This exquisite inn is one of Missouri's finest bed & breakfast establishments. Built as the Meyer Hotel, the inn has welcomed guests for almost a century. Each of the individually appointed rooms is stocked with amenities, such as bubble bath, lace and flowers. Many of the inn's antiques were used during the inn's days as the Meyer Hotel. One room features stencilled walls, while another includes a whirlpool tub. Beds are topped with vintage quilts, linens and bedspreads. The morning meal is served in a beautiful brick kitchen, which features an unusual blue cookstove. The menu changes from day to day, caramelized French toast is one of the inn's specialties.

Innkeeper(s): Ken & Karen Kulberg. $70-115. MC VISA AX DS PC TC. 7 rooms with PB. Breakfast and evening snack included in rates. Types of meals: full breakfast, gourmet breakfast and early coffee/tea. Beds: QDT. Air conditioning and ceiling fan in room. Cable TV, VCR, copier and library on premises. Antiques, parks and shopping nearby.

Certificate may be used: Jan. 15 to Dec. 15, Sunday-Thursday.

Inn St. Gemme Beauvais
78 N Main St,
Sainte Genevieve, MO 63670-1336
(573)883-5744 (800)818-5744
Fax:(573)883-3899

Circa 1848. This three-story, Federal-style inn is an impressive site on Ste. Genevieve's Main Street. The town is one of the oldest west of the Mississippi River, and the St. Gemme Beauvais is the oldest operating Missouri inn. The rooms are nicely appointed in period style, but there are modern amenities, too. The Jacuzzi tubs in some guest rooms are one relaxing example. There is also an outdoor hot tub. Guests are pampered with all sorts of cuisine, from full breakfasts to luncheons with sinfully rich desserts, and in the late afternoons, hors d'oeuvres and refreshments are served.

Innkeeper(s): Janet Joggerst. $69-125. AP. MC VISA PC TC. 7 rooms with PB, 1 with FP. 5 suites. 2 conference rooms. Breakfast, afternoon tea, dinner, evening snack and picnic lunch included in rates. Types of meals: full breakfast, gourmet breakfast and early coffee/tea. Lunch, gourmet lunch, banquet service, catering service, catered breakfast and room service available. Beds: QDT. Air conditioning, turn-down service, ceiling fan and cable TV in room. VCR, fax, copier, spa and bicycles on premises. Antiques, parks and shopping nearby.

Certificate may be used: Every day but Saturdays & holidays; based on availability.

Saint Louis E9

Doelling Haus
4817 Towne South Rd,
Saint Louis, MO 63128-2817
(314)894-6796

Circa 1965. This suburban, two-story Dutch Colonial serves as a home away from home for St. Louis-area visitors. Guests choose from the Blue Danube, Bavarian or Black Forest rooms. Central air ensures year-round comfort, and guests are welcome to park in the garage. A patio and sitting room also are popular places to relax. The innkeepers sometimes can accommodate visitors' pets if prior agreement is reached. The inn offers convenient access to interstate highways, and the historic towns of Hermann, St. Charles and St. Genevieve are within easy driving distance.

Innkeeper(s): Carol & David Doelling. $65. AP. 2 rooms, 1 with PB. Breakfast and evening snack included in rates. Types of meals: continental-plus breakfast, full breakfast and early coffee/tea. Afternoon tea available. Beds: QD. Air conditioning and turn-down service in room. Cable TV and VCR on premises. Amusement parks, antiques, fishing, parks, shopping, downhill skiing, sporting events, theater and watersports nearby.

Certificate may be used: Year-round, Sunday-Saturday.

The Eastlake Inn B&B
703 N Kirkwood Rd,
Saint Louis, MO 63122-2719
(314)965-0066

Circa 1920. Just minutes from St. Louis, in the town of Kirkwood, this inn features the turn-of-the-century style of decor made popular by furniture designer Charles Eastlake. These period antiques add elegance and charm to the Colonial Revival inn. A collection of antique dolls and bears, and the dining room's 1,129-piece chandelier also receive attention. The full breakfasts sometimes are enjoyed on the inn's sun porch. The Ulysses S. Grant National Historic Site, Hidden Valley Ski Area and Six Flags over Mid-America are nearby.

Innkeeper(s): Lori Ashdown. $62-72. MC VISA. 3 rooms with PB, 1 with FP. 1 conference room. Breakfast included in rates. Type of meal: full breakfast. Afternoon tea available. Beds: QD. Air conditioning, turn-down service and ceiling fan in room. Cable TV and VCR on premises. Amusement parks, antiques, shopping, downhill skiing, sporting events and theater nearby.

Certificate may be used: Oct. 31-April 1.

Lafayette House

2156 Lafayette Ave, Saint Louis, MO
63104-2543
(314)772-4429 Fax:(314)664-2156

Circa 1876. Captain James Eads, designer and builder of the first trussed bridge across the Mississippi River, built this Queen Anne mansion as a wedding present for his daughter Margaret. The rooms are furnished in antiques, and there is a suite with a kitchen on the third floor. The house over-looks Lafayette Park.

Innkeeper(s): Bill Duffield, Nancy Buhr, Anna Millet. $55-85. MC VISA AX DC CB DS PC TC. 5 rooms, 1 with PB. 1 suite. Breakfast included in rates. Types of meals: gourmet breakfast and early coffee/tea. Beds: QDT. Air conditioning and cable TV in room. VCR, fax and copier on premises. Antiques, parks, shopping, sporting events and theater nearby.

Location: In the center of St. Louis.

"We had a wonderful stay at your house and enjoyed the furnishings, delicious breakfasts and friendly pets."

Certificate may be used: September-December.

Lehmann House B&B

10 Benton Pl,
Saint Louis, MO 63104-2411
(314)231-6724

Circa 1893. This National Register manor's most prominent resident, former U.S. Attorney General Frederick Lehmann, hosted Presidents Taft, Theodore Roosevelt and Coolidge at this gracious home. Several key turn-of-the-century literary fig-ures also visited the Lehmann family. The inn's for-mal dining room, complete with oak paneling and a fireplace, is a stunning place to enjoy the formal breakfasts. Antiques and gracious furnishings dot

the well-appointed guest rooms. The home is locat-ed in St. Louis' oldest historic district.

Innkeeper(s): Marie & Michael Davies. $60-75. MC VISA AX DC DS PC TC. 4 rooms, 2 with PB, 3 with FP. 2 conference rooms. Breakfast included in rates. Types of meals: full breakfast and early coffee/tea. Catering service available. Beds: KQDT. Air conditioning, ceiling fan and VCR in room. Library on premises. Antiques, parks, shopping, sporting events and theater nearby.

Certificate may be used: April 1-Oct. 31, Sunday-Thursday; Nov. 1-March 31, anytime.

Sedalia   E5

Sedalia House

26097 Hwy HH, Sedalia, MO 65301
(816)826-6615

A working farm on 300 scenic acres is home to this spacious Colonial Revival inn, just two miles from town. Rolling hills, ponds and woods offer guests many outdoor recreational opportunities, including birdwatching and hiking. Guests enjoy a hearty coun-try breakfast before heading out to explore the area's many attractions, including Bothwell Lodge, Katy

Trail State Park and Whiteman Air Force Base, home of the stealth bomber. Sedalia also hosts the Missouri State Fair and the Scott Joplin ragtime music festival.

Innkeeper(s): Daniel Ice. $65. MC VISA. 6 rooms, 1 with PB. Antiques, shopping and sporting events nearby.

Certificate may be used: Sept. 15-May 15.

Springfield   G5

Virginia Rose B&B

317 E Glenwood St,
Springfield, MO 65807-3543
(417)883-0693 (800)345-1412

Circa 1906. Three generations of the Botts family, who raised chickens on the wooded property, lived in this home before it was sold to the current

innkeepers, Virginia and Jackie Buck. The grounds still include the rustic red barn. Comfortable, country rooms are named after Buck family members and feature beds covered with quilts. The innkeepers also offer a two-bedroom suite, the Ramblin' Rose, which is decorated in a sportsman theme in honor of the nearby Bass Pro. Hearty breakfasts are served in the dining room and the innkeepers will provide low-fat fare on request.

Innkeeper(s): Jackie & Virginia Buck. $50-90. MC VISA DS PC TC. 5 rooms, 3 with PB. 1 suite. Breakfast included in rates. Types of meals: full breakfast and early coffee/tea. Evening snack and picnic lunch available. Beds: QD. Air conditioning and turn-down service in room. Cable TV, VCR and fax on premises. Handicap access. Amusement parks, antiques, fishing, parks, shopping, sporting events, theater and watersports nearby.

Seen in: Auctions & Antiques.

"The accommodations are wonderful and the hospitality couldn't be warmer."

Certificate may be used: Any time, subject to availability.

Walnut Street Inn

900 E Walnut St,
Springfield, MO 65806-2603
(417)864-6346 (800)593-6346
Fax:(417)864-6184

Circa 1894. This three-story Queen Anne gabled house has cast-iron Corinthian columns and a veranda. Polished wood floors and antiques are featured throughout. Upstairs you'll find the gathering room with a fireplace. Ask for the McCann guest room with two bay windows. A full breakfast is

served, including items such as peach-stuffed French toast.

Innkeeper(s): Karol Brown. $65-150. MC VISA AX DC DS. 14 rooms with PB, 6 with FP. 2 suites. 1 conference room. Breakfast included in rates. Types of meals: continental breakfast, continental-plus breakfast, full breakfast, gourmet breakfast and early coffee/tea. Afternoon tea, evening snack and picnic lunch available. Beds: QD. Air conditioning, ceiling fan, cable TV and VCR in room. Fax and copier on premises. Handicap access. Amusement parks, antiques, fishing, parks, shopping, downhill skiing, sporting events, theater and watersports nearby.

Seen in: Midwest Living, Victoria, Country Inns, Innsider, Glamour, Midwest Motorist, Missouri, Saint Louis Post, KC Star, USA Today.

"Rest assured your establishment's qualities are unmatched and through your commitment to excellence you have won a life-long client."

Certificate may be used: Sunday-Thursday, excluding holidays and certain dates.

Warrensburg   D4

Cedarcroft Farm B&B

431 SE Y Hwy, Warrensburg, MO 64093
(816)747-5728 (800)368-4944

Circa 1867. John Adams, a Union army veteran, and Sandra's great grandfather, built this house. There are 80 acres of woodlands, meadows and creeks where deer, fox, coyotes and wild turkeys still roam. Two original barns remain. The house offers two upstairs rooms that share a downstairs bath. Bill participates in Civil War reenactments and is happy to demonstrate clothing, weapons and customs of the era. Sandra cares for her quarter horses and provides the homebaked, full country breakfasts.

Innkeeper(s): Sandra & Bill Wayne. $75-80. MC VISA AX DS PC TC. 1 room. Breakfast and evening snack included in rates. Type of meal: full breakfast. Beds: D. Air conditioning in room. Cable TV and VCR on premises. Antiques, fishing, parks, shopping and theater nearby.

Location: About six miles southeast of Warrensburg, Mo., 60 miles from Kansas City.

Seen in: Kansas City Star, Higginsville Advance, Midwest Motorist, KCTV, KMOS TV, Territorial Small Farm Today, Country America, Entrepreneur.

"We enjoyed the nostalgia and peacefulness very much. Enjoyed your wonderful hospitality and great food."

Certificate may be used: Sept. 1-June 30, Sunday-Thursday.

Washington   E8

Schwegmann House

438 W Front St, Washington, MO 63090
(314)239-5025 (800)949-2262

Circa 1861. John F. Schwegmann, a native of Germany, built a flour mill on the Missouri riverfront. This stately three-story home was built to provide extra lodging for overnight customers who

traveled long hours to the town. Today weary travelers enjoy the formal gardens and warm atmosphere
of this restful home. Patios overlook the river, and
the gracious rooms are decorated with antiques and
handmade quilts. The new Miller Suite boasts a tub
for two, and guests receive a bottle of Missouri wine

and breakfast in bed. In the old summer kitchen,
innkeepers have an old-time blacksmithing and
wood-working shop. Guests enjoy breakfasts complete with specialty teas, croissants, jams, fresh fruit,
ham and juice from local vineyards. Take a tour of a
local winery or visit one of the many galleries and
antique shops in the area.

Innkeeper(s): Catherine & Bill Nagel. $65-150. MC VISA AX PC TC. 9
rooms with PB, 2 with FP. 1 suite. Breakfast and evening snack included in rates. Types of meals: continental-plus breakfast, full breakfast,
gourmet breakfast and early coffee/tea. Beds: QD. Air conditioning and
ceiling fan in room. Cable TV and bicycles on premises. Antiques, fishing, parks, shopping and theater nearby.

Location: One hour west of St. Louis.

Seen in: St. Louis Post-Dispatch, West County Journal, Midwest Living,
Country Inns, Midwest Motorist, Ozark.

"Like Grandma's house many years ago."

Certificate may be used: Sunday through Thursday. No Friday or
Saturday to be included in stay. Not valid with any other specials.

Montana

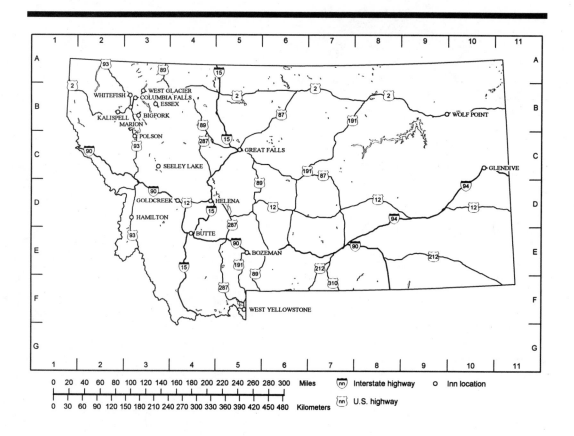

0 20 40 60 80 100 120 140 160 180 200 220 240 260 280 300   Miles

0 30 60 90 120 150 180 210 240 270 300 330 360 390 420 450 480   Kilometers

☐nn☐ Interstate highway   ○ Inn location

⌂nn⌂ U.S. highway

Bigfork B3

Burggraf's Countrylane
Rainbow Dr on Swan Lake,
Bigfork, MT 59911
(406)837-4608 (800)525-3344
Fax:(406)837-2468

Circa 1984. This contemporary log home on Swan Lake, minutes from Flathead Lake in the Rockies, offers fine accommodations in one of America's most beautiful settings. Upon arrival, visitors enjoy hors d'oeuvres, chilled wine, and fresh fruit. Ceiling fans, clock radios and turndown service are amenities. Picnic baskets are available and would be ideal for taking along on a paddle boat lake excursion. Excellent skiing and snowmobiling opportunities await winter visitors, and all will enjoy the inn's seven scenic acres.

Innkeeper(s): Natalie & RJ Burggraf. $85-100. AP. MC VISA PC TC. 6 rooms with PB. Breakfast and evening snack included in rates. Types of meals: full breakfast, gourmet breakfast and early coffee/tea. Picnic lunch available. Beds: KQT. Ceiling fan, cable TV and VCR in room. Fax, copier, swimming, library and pet boarding on premises. Handicap access. Antiques, fishing, parks, shopping, downhill skiing, cross-country skiing, sporting events, theater and watersports nearby.

Certificate may be used: Any time, unrestricted.

Bozeman E5

Lindley House
202 Lindley Pl, Bozeman, MT 59715-4833
(406)587-8403 (800)787-8404
Fax:(406)582-8112

Circa 1889. The beautiful Montana scenery is a perfect backdrop for this romantic bed & breakfast listed in the National Register. The pampering begins in the beautiful guest rooms, which offer plenty of soft, down comforters, feather pillows, fluffy robes and a collection of soaps and oils for a long soak in the tub. Each of the rooms is distinct and memorable. The
Marie Antoinette Suite boasts a fireplace, sitting room, clawfoot tub and balcony. The Garden Room offers French Provencal decor with a private garden entrance. Other rooms include items such

as wicker furnishings, bay windows, lacy curtains, a French bistro table or brass bed. The gourmet breakfasts, which feature special treats such as crepes, souffles and a variety of breads, yogurt and cereals, are a perfect start to the day.

Innkeeper(s): Stephanie Volz. $85-195. MC VISA. 5 rooms with PB. 2 suites. Breakfast and afternoon tea included in rates. Type of meal: full breakfast. Beds: KQT. Antiques, fishing, downhill skiing, cross-country skiing, theater and watersports nearby.

"Elegant, but comfortable. Beautifully restored, wonderful attention to detail."

Certificate may be used: Nov. 1 through April 30, Monday through Thursday.

Torch & Toes B&B
309 S 3rd Ave, Bozeman, MT 59715-4636
(406)586-7285 (800)446-2138

Circa 1906. This Colonial Revival home, three blocks from the center of town, boasts an old-fashioned front porch with porch swing and a carriage house. Antique furnishings in the dining room feature a Victrola and a pillared and carved oak

fireplace. Ron is a professor of architecture at nearby Montana State University and Judy is a weaver. Her loom and some of her colorful work are on display at this artisan's inn.

Innkeeper(s): Ron & Judy Hess. $80-90. MC VISA PC TC. 4 rooms with PB. Breakfast included in rates. Types of meals: full breakfast and gourmet breakfast. Beds: KQT. Ceiling fan in room. Cable TV and VCR on premises. Antiques, fishing, parks, shopping, downhill skiing, cross-country skiing, sporting events, theater and watersports nearby.

Location: North of Yellowstone National Park.

Seen in: Bozeman Chronicle, San Francisco Peninsula Parent, Northwest.

"Thanks for your warm hospitality."

Certificate may be used: Oct. 1-April 30, Sunday-Friday.

Voss Inn

319 S Willson Ave,
Bozeman, MT 59715-4632
(406)587-0982 Fax:(406)585-2964

Circa 1883. The Voss Inn is a restored two-story house with a large front porch and a Victorian parlor. Old-fashioned furnishings include an upright piano and chandelier. A full breakfast is served,

with fresh baked rolls kept in a unique warmer that's built into an ornate 1880s radiator. Day trips and overnight trips into Yellowstone Park are conducted by the owner, who has had extensive experience leading Safaris in Africa.

Innkeeper(s): Bruce & Frankee Muller. $85-95. MC VISA AX PC TC. 6 rooms with PB. Breakfast and afternoon tea included in rates. Types of meals: full breakfast and gourmet breakfast. Picnic lunch available. Beds: KQ. Air conditioning in room. Cable TV and fax on premises. Antiques, fishing, parks, shopping, downhill skiing, cross-country skiing and watersports nearby.

Location: Four blocks south of downtown.

Seen in: Sunset, Cosmopolitan, Gourmet, Countryside.

"First class all the way."

Certificate may be used: January through June, October-Dec. 15. July-September excluded.

Butte   E4

Copper King Mansion

219 W Granite St, Butte, MT 59701-9235
(406)782-7580

Circa 1884. This turn-of-the-century marvel was built, as the name indicates, by W.A. Clark, one of the nation's leading copper barons. In the early 1900s, Clark made millions each month hauling copper out of Butte's vast mines. Stained-glass windows, gold leafing on the ceilings and elaborate woodwork are just a few of the opulent touches. Clark commissioned artisans brought in from Germany to carve the intricate staircase, which graces the front hall. The mansion is decked floor to ceiling in antiques collected by the innkeeper's mother and grandmother, who purchased the home from Clark's relatives. A three-room master suite

includes two fireplaces, a lavish bedroom, a sitting room and a huge bathroom with a clawfoot tub.

Innkeeper(s): Maria Sigl. $55-95. MC VISA AX DS. 4 rooms. Breakfast included in rates. Type of meal: full breakfast.

Seen in: Sunset Magazine.

Certificate may be used: January, February, March, April, May, September, October, November, December.

Columbia Falls   B3

Plum Creek House

985 Vans Ave, Columbia Falls, MT 59912
(406)892-1816 (800)682-1429
Fax:(406)892-1876

Incredible views of the Flathead Valley's forests and mountains greet guests at this contemporary riverfront ranch inn. The inn offers something for everyone, even family pets who may stay in the sheltered outdoor kennel. Outdoor recreational opportunities are boundless, but guests who wish to put their feet up and relax also will find this inn to their liking. A heated pool and outdoor spa lure many guests. Glacier National Park can be seen from the inn and is just a short drive away.

Innkeeper(s): Caroline Stevens. $60-105. MC VISA AX DC DS. 5 rooms. 1 suite. Breakfast included in rates. Types of meals: full breakfast and early coffee/tea. Evening snack, lunch, banquet service, catering service and room service available. Air conditioning, turn-down service, ceiling fan, cable TV and VCR in room. Child care on premises. Antiques, shopping, downhill skiing, cross-country skiing and theater nearby.

Certificate may be used: Oct. 1 to June 1 excluding holidays.

Essex   B3

Izaak Walton Inn

123 Izaak Walton Rd, Essex, MT 59916
(406)888-5700 Fax:(406)888-5200

Circa 1939. The Izaak Walton Inn was built as an overnight lodging for Great Northern Railway workers. It is located now on the Burlington-Northern Mainline and is served twice daily by Amtrak. The inn is in a strategic location for enjoying Glacier National Park. You can take trails and rivers into the Rocky Mountain forests and meadows.

Innkeeper(s): Larry & Lynda Vielleux. $92-125. AP. MC VISA TC. 30 rooms with PB, 1 with FP. 3 suites. 2 conference rooms. Types of meals: full breakfast and early coffee/tea. Afternoon tea, dinner, evening snack, picnic lunch, lunch, banquet service and catering service available. Beds: QD. VCR, fax, copier, sauna and bicycles on premises. Handicap access. Fishing, parks and cross-country skiing nearby.

Seen in: Outdoor America-Summer, Seattle Times.

"The coziest cross-country ski resort in the Rockies."

Certificate may be used: March 15-June 15 and Sept. 15-Dec. 15, excluding all holidays.

Glendive C10

The Hostetler House B&B

113 N Douglas St,
Glendive, MT 59330-1619
(406)365-4505 Fax:(406)365-8456

Circa 1912. Casual country decor mixed with handmade and heirloom furnishings are highlights at this two-story inn. The inn features many comforting touches, such as a romantic hot tub and

gazebo, enclosed sun porch and sitting room filled with books. The two guest rooms share a bath, and are furnished by Dea, an interior decorator. The full breakfasts may be enjoyed on Grandma's china in the dining room or on the deck or sun porch. The Yellowstone River is one block from the inn and downtown shopping is two blocks away. Makoshika State Park, home of numerous fossil finds, is nearby.
Innkeeper(s): Craig & Dea Hostetler. $50. MC VISA DS PC TC. 2 rooms. Breakfast included in rates. Types of meals: full breakfast, gourmet breakfast and early coffee/tea. Beds: D. Air conditioning and ceiling fan in room. Cable TV, VCR, fax, copier, spa and library on premises. Antiques, fishing, parks, shopping, cross-country skiing, sporting events, theater and watersports nearby.

Seen in: Ranger Review.

"Warmth and loving care are evident throughout your exquisite home. Your attention to small details is uplifting. Thank you for a restful sojourn."

Certificate may be used: Anytime.

Gold Creek D4

LH Ranch B&B

471 Mullan Tr, Gold Creek, MT 59733
(406)288-3436

Circa 1851. Guests can take horseback riding lessons, pan for gold or roll up their sleeves and feed animals or bale hay at this 2,000-acre ranch. Relaxation is another option, and there are plenty of ideal spots. The home is furnished with a collection of family antiques. The LH Ranch is Montana's oldest operating bed & breakfast, open and run by the Lingenfelter family since 1955.
Innkeeper(s): Patti Lingenfelter-Hansen. $85. 2 rooms, 1 with FP. Breakfast included in rates. Types of meals: continental breakfast, continental-plus breakfast, full breakfast and early coffee/tea. Afternoon tea, dinner, evening snack, picnic lunch and lunch available. Beds: D. Amusement parks, antiques, fishing, parks, shopping, downhill skiing, cross-country skiing, theater and watersports nearby.

Certificate may be used: Jan.1 through Dec. 11.

Great Falls C5

The Chalet B&B Inn

1204 4th Ave N,
Great Falls, MT 59401-1414
(406)452-9001 (800)786-9002

Circa 1909. This simple stick-style Victorian chalet features handsomely decorated rooms highlighted by polished woodwork, French doors, beamed ceilings and leaded-glass windows. Marge is a noted San Francisco interior designer, now back in her hometown. David continues to carry on a family tradition as a violin maker. The C.M. Russell Museum is across the street on Old West Trail.
Innkeeper(s): Marge & David Anderson. $40-65. AX DS TC. 5 rooms, 3 with PB. 1 suite. Breakfast included in rates. Type of meal: early coffee/tea. Catered breakfast available. Beds: KQDT. Air conditioning and ceiling fan in room. Cable TV and VCR on premises. Antiques, fishing, parks, shopping, downhill skiing, cross-country skiing, theater and watersports nearby.

Seen in: Great Falls Tribune.

"Thanks for the royal treatment."

Certificate may be used: All year, based on availability.

Hamilton D3

The Bavarian Farmhouse B&B

163 Bowman Rd,
Hamilton, MT 59840-9638
(307)358-2033

Bavarian hospitality and flavor is found at this farmhouse inn, nestled amid a grove of large trees. Visitors are treated to a hearty German farm breakfast consisting of boiled eggs, breads, coffee, cereal, cheese, cold cuts, jam, juice, rolls and tea. The innkeepers, both experienced travelers, are happy to help arrange fishing, floating, horseback riding or hunting excursions if given advance notice. Efficiency cabins also are available. The Daly Mansion and Sleeping Child Hot Springs are within easy driving distance.
Innkeeper(s): Ann Reuthlinges. $45-55. 5 rooms.

Certificate may be used: Anytime other than over a Saturday night during July or August.

Deer Crossing B&B
396 Hayes Creek Rd,
Hamilton, MT 59840-9744
(406)363-2232 (800)763-2232

Circa 1980. The Homestead is a two-story brick farmhouse situated on 50 acres of fields, woods and river. The house has 15-inch-thick walls and is furnished with Victorian antiques and family heirlooms. This was a favorite camping spot for Indians while they salted their fish, and many arrowheads have been found on the farm. Activities include long walks through meadows of wildflowers and cross-country skiing in season.

Innkeeper(s): Mary Lynch. $40-100. MC VISA AX. 6 rooms with PB, 1 with FP. 2 suites. Breakfast and evening snack included in rates. Types of meals: full breakfast and early coffee/tea. Dinner, picnic lunch and lunch available. Beds: QDT. Turn-down service in room. VCR, bicycles and child care on premises. Handicap access. Antiques, parks, shopping, downhill skiing, cross-country skiing and watersports nearby.

Seen in: Country Focus, Saline Reporter.

"It is so nice to be back after three years and from 5,000 miles away!"

Certificate may be used: Oct. 1 to May 1 any day of the week.

Helena   D4

Appleton Inn B&B
1999 Euclid Ave, Helena, MT 59601-1908
(406)449-7492 (800)956-1999
Fax:(406)449-1261

Circa 1890. Montana's first resident dentist called this Victorian his home. It remained in his family until the 1970s when it was transformed into apartments. Fortunately, the innkeepers bought and restored the home, bringing back the original beauty. The innkeepers have their own furniture-making company and have created many of the pieces that decorate the guest rooms. Rooms range from the spacious Master Suite, with its oak, four-poster bed and bath with a clawfoot tub, to the quaint and cozy Attic Playroom. The inn is a convenient place to enjoy the Helena area, and there are mountain bikes on hand for those who wish to explore.

Innkeeper(s): Tom Woodall & Cheryl Boid. $50-105. AP. MC VISA AX DS PC TC. 5 rooms, 3 with PB. 2 suites. Breakfast included in rates. Afternoon tea and picnic lunch available. Beds: Q. Air conditioning in room. Cable TV, VCR, fax, copier and bicycles on premises. Antiques, fishing, parks, shopping, downhill skiing, cross-country skiing, sporting events, theater and watersports nearby.

Seen in: Philadelphia, Back Roads USA.

"For our first try at B&B lodgings, we've probably started at the top, and nothing else will ever measure up to this. Wonderful food, wonderful home, grounds and wonderful hostess!"

Certificate may be used: Sept. 15-May 15, Sunday-Saturday.

242

Kalispell   B3

Switzer House Inn
205 5th Ave E, Kalispell, MT 59901-4544
(406)257-5837 (800)257-5837

Circa 1910. Originally built for a lumberman from Minnesota, this Queen Anne Victorian is found on Kalispell's historic east side. Guests enjoy relaxing on the wraparound porch or by taking a stroll to Woodland Park, two blocks away. Downtown galleries, museums, restaurants, shops and theaters are

just five blocks from the inn. Visitors select from the Queen Anne, Blanche's Corner, Lew's Retreat or Twin's rooms, all found on the inn's second floor. The gourmet breakfast is served buffet style and guests also may help themselves to hot chocolate or lemonade in the library.

Innkeeper(s): Heather Brigham. $65-85. MC VISA. 4 rooms. Breakfast and afternoon tea included in rates. Types of meals: full breakfast and early coffee/tea. Beds: QT. Turn-down service in room. Cable TV and VCR on premises. Antiques, fishing, shopping, downhill skiing, cross-country skiing, theater and watersports nearby.

Seen in: Daily Interlake.

"Thanks so much for sharing such a beautiful place with us. You have created a very warm and welcoming atmosphere here."

Certificate may be used: Sept. 1 through May 31, Monday through Sunday.

Marion   B2

Hargrave Ranch
300 Thompson River Rd,
Marion, MT 59925-9710
(406)858-2284 (800)933-0696
Fax:(406)858-2284

Circa 1906. If you've ever wondered what it would be like to live on a working cattle ranch, a stay at this 86,000-acre spread will provide a glimpse into this Western lifestyle. Riding lessons, overnight camp-outs and lakeside picnics are just a few of the options available. Guests also may try their hand at cattle herding. Accommodations are unique and varied, and they include a log cabin (formerly a horse stable), the main house or two rustic cottages. The hosts prepare guests for their busy days with huge breakfasts with egg dishes, potatoes, yogurt, fruit, pancakes and other delectables. During the winter months, rates include cross-country skiing.

Innkeeper(s): Leo & Ellen Hargrave. $75-95. MC VISA TC. 10 rooms, 3 with PB, 2 with FP. 1 conference room. Breakfast, dinner, evening snack and picnic lunch included in rates. Types of meals: full breakfast and early coffee/tea. Lunch available. Beds: QDT. Ceiling fan in room. VCR, fax, copier, sauna and bicycles on premises. Antiques, fishing, parks, shopping, downhill skiing, cross-country skiing, theater and watersports nearby.

Certificate may be used: October-May 1.

Polson   C3

Hidden Pines
792 Lost Quartz Rd,
Polson, MT 59860-9428
(406)849-5612 (800)505-5612

Circa 1976. Relax on the porch of this secluded, quiet home and the only sounds you'll hear are birds chirping and the breezes that blow across the wooded grounds. Hidden Pines borders Flathead Lake, where guests will enjoy swimming and boating. The innkeepers offer picnic tables and lawn chairs for those who want to soak up the natural surroundings. The home's hot tub is a great place to end the day. The innkeepers prepare a hearty breakfast, but lighter fare is available. Each of the comfortable guest rooms features individual decor. The Deckside room has a private entrance onto the deck and hot tub area.

Innkeeper(s): Emy & Earl Atchley. $50-60. PC TC. 4 rooms, 2 with PB. Breakfast and picnic lunch included in rates. Types of meals: full breakfast and early coffee/tea. Beds: QD. Ceiling fan and VCR in room. Spa on premises. Antiques, fishing, parks, shopping, theater and watersports nearby.

Certificate may be used: June, July, August, Sunday through Thursday.

Seeley Lake   C3

The Emily A. B&B
Hwy 83, Box 350, Seeley Lake, MT 59868
(406)677-3474 (800)977-4639
Fax:(406)677-3474

Circa 1992. Nestled at the banks of the Columbia River, this rustic log home was fashioned from local timber. From the lodge, guests enjoy panoramic Rocky Mountain views. Stroll the inn's 158 acres

and you'll find hiking trails, wildlife and plenty of places to fish. The home is named for innkeeper Marilyn Shope Peterson's grandmother, a remarkable woman who helped found Montana's Boulder School for the Deaf Mute. Despite being widowed at a young age, Emily managed to support herself and seven children by running a boarding house. Marilyn inherited her grandmother's hospitable skills and she, and husband Keith, pamper their guests. Rooms are decorated with Western furnishings, beds are topped with feather duvets.

Innkeeper(s): Marilyn Shope Peterson. $95. MAP. MC VISA TC. 5 rooms, 2 with PB. 1 conference room. Types of meals: continental-plus breakfast, full breakfast and early coffee/tea. Afternoon tea, picnic lunch, banquet service and catered breakfast available. Beds: KQT. Cable TV, VCR, fax, copier, bicycles, pet boarding and child care on premises. Handicap access. Antiques, fishing, parks, shopping, downhill skiing, cross-country skiing, sporting events, theater and watersports nearby.

Certificate may be used: Oct. 1-May 1.

West Glacier   B3

Mountain Timbers Lodge
PO Box 94, West Glacier, MT 59936-0094
(406)387-5830 (800)841-3835
Fax:(406)387-5835

Circa 1973. With the wilderness of Glacier National Park as its backdrop, this rustic, log home is designed for nature lovers. The grounds include miles of professionally designed cross-country ski trails, and guests on a morning walk shouldn't be surprised if they encounter deer or elk sharing the countryside. The inviting interior complements the spectacular scenery. The huge living room is warmed by a rock and stone fireplace and decorated with Southwestern style furnishings. For those who prefer to simply relax and curl up with a good book, the innkeepers offer a well-stocked library. Beds are topped with down comforters, and guests are further pampered with an outdoor hot tub.

Innkeeper(s): Karen Schweitzer. $55-125. MC VISA. 7 rooms, 4 with PB. 1 conference room. Breakfast included in rates. Type of meal: full breakfast. Beds: QDT. Fax, copier and spa on premises. Fishing nearby.

Location: One mile outside Glacier National Park.

Certificate may be used: Jan. 1-June 15 and Sept. 1-Dec. 23.

West Yellowstone
F5

Sportsman's High B&B
750 Deer St,
West Yellowstone, MT 59758-9607
(406)646-7865 Fax:(406)646-9434

Circa 1984. Nature lovers will have a delightful time at this inn, a large contemporary home that blends Colonial, farm and rustic stylings. Four guest rooms and a log cabin are the lodging choices, all with private baths. Three resident collies enjoy showing visitors the inn's aspen- and pine-filled grounds. Hiking trails, lakes and trout streams are found nearby and cross-country skiing and snowmobiling are enjoyed in winter. The innkeepers are avid birdwatchers, fly-fishers and fly-tiers, and a fly-tying bench is available. Bring a camera to record some of the inn's plentiful wildlife, ranging in size from hummingbirds to moose.

Innkeeper(s): Diana & Gary Baxter. $65-95. MC VISA AX TC. 5 rooms with PB. Breakfast included in rates. Types of meals: full breakfast, gourmet breakfast and early coffee/tea. Afternoon tea available. Beds: KQ. Ceiling fan in room. Cable TV, VCR, fax and spa on premises. Antiques, fishing, parks, downhill skiing, cross-country skiing, theater and watersports nearby.

Location: Eight miles from Yellowstone National Park.

Seen in: Rocky Mountain Adventures, LA Times, West Yellowstone News.

Certificate may be used: Oct. 1 to May 31.

Whitefish
B3

Crenshaw House
5465 Hwy 93 S,
Whitefish, MT 59937-8410
(406)862-3496 (800)453-2863
Fax:(406)862-7640

Circa 1973. This contemporary farmhouse inn offers three guest rooms, all with private bath. Many amenities are found at the inn, including turndown service and a wake-up tray, which precedes the tasty gourmet breakfast prepared by innkeeper Anni Crenshaw-Rieker. Guests also enjoy afternoon tea and an evening snack. The inn also boasts a fireplace and spa, and child care can be arranged. Several state parks are found nearby.

Innkeeper(s): Anni Crenshaw-Rieker. $65-125. MAP. MC VISA AX DS PC TC. 3 rooms with PB. Breakfast included in rates. Types of meals: gourmet breakfast and early coffee/tea. Catering service available. Beds: KQDT. Turn-down service in room. Cable TV, VCR, fax, copier, spa, library, pet boarding and child care on premises. Antiques, fishing, parks, shopping, downhill skiing, cross-country skiing, theater and watersports nearby.

Certificate may be used: Sept. 15-Dec. 15, Jan. 5-June 15, depending on availability. Not Christmas, New Year's.

Garden Wall Inn B&B
504 Spokane Ave,
Whitefish, MT 59937-2781
(406)862-3440

Circa 1923. With its Colonial Revival architecture, this inn stands out among the area's homes and is one of the oldest in town. Rooms are decorated with period antiques and beds are dressed with luxurious linens and down duvets. Breakfast is a three-course affair. One might start off with freshly ground coffee, freshly squeezed juice and a poached pear in raspberry sauce. From there, home-baked breads or muffins are served, capped off by items such as a puff-pastry basket filled with herbed scrambled eggs with shrimp, pea-pods and mushrooms. The inn is less than half an hour from Glacier National Park and within walking distance to shops and restaurants. Guests may borrow bicycles for a trip around town or to nearby Whitefish Lake. The ski shuttle stop is a block from the house.

Innkeeper(s): Chris Schustrom. $95-115. MC VISA AX DS PC TC. 5 rooms, 3 with PB. 1 suite. Breakfast and evening snack included in rates. Types of meals: gourmet breakfast and early coffee/tea. Beds: KQDT. Turn-down service and ceiling fan in room. Bicycles on premises. Antiques, fishing, parks, shopping, downhill skiing, cross-country skiing and watersports nearby.

Certificate may be used: Jan. 5-June 15, Sunday-Thursday; Oct. 1-Dec. 20, Sunday-Thursday.

Wolf Point
B9

Forsness Farm B&B
HCR 33 Box 5035,
Wolf Point, MT 59201-9402
(406)653-2492

Circa 1926. A working farm/ranch is home to this Prairie-style inn, which was built by Indian traders and moved to its present location in 1975. Cattle, chickens, horses, milk cows, sheep and even a burro reside at the ranch, and guests are welcome to help with egg gathering or milking. Fishing for coho salmon, pike and prehistoric paddlefish is found in the Missouri River, less than two miles from the inn. Two upstairs guest rooms, one with king bed and the other with twin beds, share a bath with whirlpool tub. Summertime guests often enjoy Indian celebrations and the area also hosts an authentic Wild West rodeo.

Innkeeper(s): JoAnn & Dewey Forsness. $50. TC. 2 rooms. Breakfast and evening snack included in rates. Beds: KT. Fishing, shopping, theater and watersports nearby.

Certificate may be used: All year, Sunday-Friday.

Nebraska

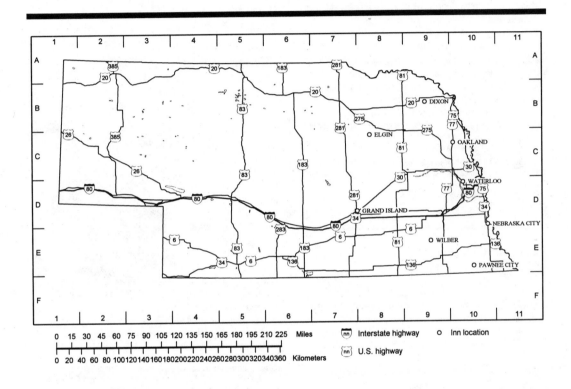

	Miles
0 15 30 45 60 75 90 105 120 135 150 165 180 195 210 225	

	Kilometers
0 20 40 60 80 100120140160180200220240260280300320340360	

nn Interstate highway   o Inn location

nn U.S. highway

Dixon
B9

The George Farm
Rt 1, Box 50, Dixon, NE 68732-9728
(402)584-2625

Circa 1926. Two miles south of Highway 20, west of Sioux City, lies this air-conditioned farmhouse furnished in country decor. Although in a rural setting, the farm offers a wide array of activities within easy driving distance. Wayne State College is nearby, as are an abundance of local crafts and antique establishments. Marie, an avid antiquer, can provide help for those searching the area for special items. Relax with a stroll through the farm's 640 acres, or just enjoy some peace and quiet in the library. The inn accepts children and pets, with prior arrangement.
Innkeeper(s): Marie George. $40-45. PC. 5 rooms. Breakfast included in rates. Type of meal: full breakfast. Beds: QD. Air conditioning in room. VCR, fax and copier on premises.

Certificate may be used: Year-round except second weekend in July and first weekend of pheasant hunting season (usually first weekend of November).

Elgin
C8

Plantation House
401 Plantation St, Elgin, NE 68636-9301
(402)843-2287 Fax:(402)843-2287

Circa 1916. This historic mansion sits adjacent to Elgin City Park, and guests will marvel at its beauty and size. Once a small Victorian farmhouse, the Plantation House has evolved into a 20-room Greek

Revival treasure. Visitors will be treated to a tour and a large family-style breakfast, and may venture to the park to play tennis or horseshoes. The antique-filled guest rooms include the Stained Glass Room, with a queen bed and available twin-bed anteroom, and the Old Master Bedroom, with clawfoot tub and pedestal sink.
Innkeeper(s): Merland & Barbara Clark. $35-60. PC. 5 rooms, 2 with PB. 1 cottage. 2 conference rooms. Breakfast included in rates. Types of meals: full breakfast and early coffee/tea. Banquet service available. Beds: QT. Air conditioning and ceiling fan in room. Cable TV, VCR, fax, copier and library on premises. Antiques, fishing, parks, shopping and watersports nearby.

Seen in: Omaha World Herald, Norfolk Daily News, Home & Away.

"Gorgeous house! Relaxing atmosphere. Just like going to Mom's house."

Certificate may be used: Sunday-Thursday, all year; anytime, Oct. 1-April 1 when available. Holidays excluded.

Grand Island
D8

Kirschke House B&B
1124 W 3rd St,
Grand Island, NE 68801-5834
(308)381-6851 (800)381-6851

Circa 1902. A steeply sloping roofline and a two-story tower mark this distinctive, vine-covered brick Victorian house. Meticulously restored, there are polished wood floors, fresh wallpapers and carefully chosen antiques. The Roses Roses Room is a spacious accommodation with a lace canopy bed, wicker rocking chair and decorating accents of roses and vines. In the old brick wash house is a wooden hot tub. In winter and spring, the area is popular for viewing the migration of sandhill cranes and whooping cranes.

Innkeeper(s): Lois Hank & Kiffani Smith. $55-70. MC VISA AX DS PC TC. 5 rooms, 2 with PB. 1 cottage. Breakfast included in rates. Types of meals: gourmet breakfast and early coffee/tea. Lunch and room service available. Beds: QDT. Air conditioning and ceiling fan in room. Cable TV, VCR, spa and library on premises. Antiques, fishing, parks, shopping and watersports nearby.

Location: In the historic district near downtown.
Seen in: Grand Island Daily Independent.

"We have been to many B&Bs in England, Canada and America. The Kirschke House ranks with the finest we've stayed in."

Certificate may be used: Anytime.

Nebraska City
D10

Whispering Pines
RR 2, Nebraska City, NE 68410-9802
(402)873-5850

Circa 1892. An easy getaway from Kansas City, Lincoln or Omaha, Nebraska City's Whispering Pines offers visitors a relaxing alternative from big-city life. Fresh flowers greet guests at this two-story brick Italianate, furnished with Victorian and country decor. Situated on more than six acres of trees, flowers and ponds, the inn is a birdwatcher's delight. Breakfast is served formally in the dining room, or guests may opt to eat on the deck with its view of garden and pines. The inn is within easy walking distance to Arbor Lodge, home of the founder of Arbor Day.

Innkeeper(s): W.B. Smulling. $45-65. MC VISA DS. 5 rooms, 1 with PB. Breakfast included in rates. Type of meal: full breakfast.

Certificate may be used: All year, Sunday through Thursday.

Oakland   C10

Benson B&B
402 N Oakland Ave,
Oakland, NE 68045-1135
(402)685-6051

Circa 1905. This inn is on the second floor of the Benson Building, a sturdy, turreted brick structure built of walls nearly 12 inches thick. Decorated throughout in mauve, blue and cream, the Benson B&B features three comfortable guest rooms, and a

restful, small-town atmosphere. Guests may visit the Swedish Heritage Center and a nearby city park. Breakfasts are served at a time which accommodates guests' needs, The meal is served on china and crystal and includes a variety of fruits, savory meats, a daily entree and fresh baked goods. An 18-hole golf course is a five-minute drive away. Check out the craft and gift store on the building's lower level, the inn's collection of soft drink memorabilia, and be sure to ask about the Troll Stroll.

Innkeeper(s): Stan & Norma Anderson. $47-55. PC TC. 3 rooms. Breakfast and evening snack included in rates. Types of meals: full breakfast and early coffee/tea. Beds: QD. Cable TV, VCR, spa and library on premises. Antiques, parks, shopping and sporting events nearby.

Certificate may be used: January, February, March, April, September, October, November and December, any night if space available.

Pawnee City   E10

My Blue Heaven B&B
1041 5th St, Pawnee City, NE 68420-2532
(402)852-3131

Circa 1920. Not many travelers know that just a shade north of the Kansas state line, in Nebraska's Southeast corner, they may find heaven, as in My Blue Heaven B&B. Legend says that Pawnee City, the county seat, once was the area's largest Pawnee Indian village. The hosts pride themselves on hospitality and the small-town feel of their history-laden community, which also features a barbed wire museum of 800 varieties. The inn's two guest rooms, one of which is known as the Blue Berry Hill Room, are filled with antiques.

Innkeeper(s): Duane & Yvonne Dalluge. $30-35. MC VISA TC. 2 rooms. Breakfast included in rates. Type of meal: full breakfast. Beds: D. Air conditioning and ceiling fan in room. Cable TV and VCR on premises. Antiques, fishing, parks, shopping and watersports nearby.

Certificate may be used: Nov. 15-April 15.

Waterloo   D10

J.C. Robinson House B&B
102 Lincoln St, PO Box 190, Waterloo,
NE 68069-2004
(402)779-2704

Circa 1905. A short drive from Omaha, the Journey's End is an elegant, Neoclassical Greek Revival home boasting two impressive Ionic columns. The inn, surrounded by large trees, is listed in the national and state historic registers. Antiques, including a stunning clock collection, are

found throughout the attractive interior, and the Gone With the Wind Room offers a garden and orchard view. The home, built by seed company founder J.C. Robinson, also features a guest room in his name. Fishing and canoeing are a short walk away or guests may decide to soak up the village's relaxed atmosphere.

Innkeeper(s): John Clark. $45-75. 4 rooms. 1 conference room. Breakfast included in rates. Types of meals: full breakfast and early coffee/tea. Dinner, evening snack, gourmet lunch and banquet service available.

Certificate may be used: Oct. 1 through April 30.

Wilber   E9

Hotel Wilber
203 S Wilson, PO Box 641,
Wilber, NE 68465
(402)821-2020 (800)609-4663

This historic, turn-of-the-century hotel includes a restaurant and a beer garden on its premises. The exterior is decidedly Victorian with grand verandas and ornate trim. Inside, the Victorian theme is combined with European influence, especially Czechoslovakian. The town of Wilber is know as the Czech Capital of the United States. This heritage is evident in the cuisine, a mix of American and Czech favorites. Each of the rooms features different decor. Several rooms have lavatories, but the shower facilities are located down the hall.

Innkeeper(s): Frances Erb. $42-65. MC VISA. 10 rooms. Breakfast included in rates. Type of meal: full breakfast.

Certificate may be used: Sept. 1 to June 30, Sunday through Saturday.

Nevada

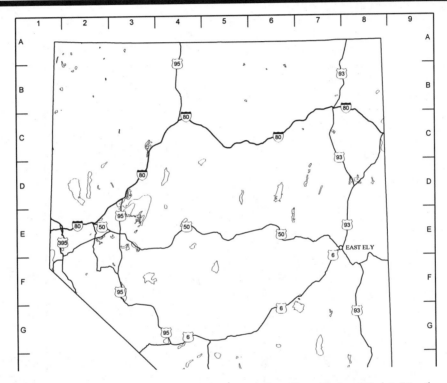

East Ely

E7

Steptoe Valley Inn
220 E 11th St, East Ely, NV 89315-1110
(702)289-8687

Circa 1907. Originally a grocery store at the turn of the century, this inn has been lovingly reconstructed to resemble a Victorian country cottage. Five uniquely decorated guest rooms are named for local pioneers. The rooms also have views of the inn's scenic surroundings, and three of them feature queen beds. A nearby railroad museum offers train rides

and Great Basin National Park is 70 miles away. Guests may rent a jeep at the inn for exploring the area's back country. This inn is open from June to October. During the off-season, guests may inquire about the inn at (702) 435-1196.

Innkeeper(s): Jane & Norman Lindley. $79-85. MC VISA AX PC TC. 5 rooms with PB. 1 conference room. Breakfast and evening snack included in rates. Type of meal: full breakfast. Beds: QT. Air conditioning, ceiling fan and cable TV in room. VCR and library on premises. Fishing and parks nearby.

Seen in: Las Vegas Review Journal, Great Getaways, Yellow Brick Road.

"Everything was so clean and first-rate."

Certificate may be used: Any time June through September, except 4th of July weekend, Labor Day weekend, Arts in the Park Week (1st weekend in August) & horse race weekends (usually last 2 weeks in August).

New Hampshire

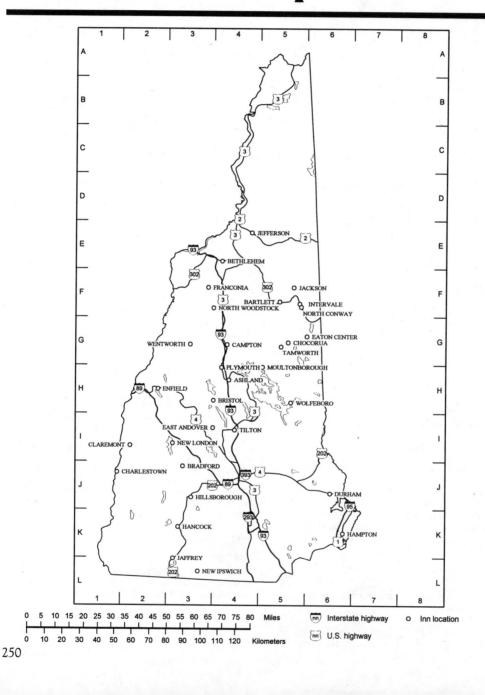

0 5 10 15 20 25 30 35 40 45 50 55 60 65 70 75 80 Miles

0 10 20 30 40 50 60 70 80 90 100 110 120 Kilometers

(nn) Interstate highway   o Inn location

(nn) U.S. highway

250

Ashland
H4

Glynn House Inn
43 Highland St, PO Box 719,
Ashland, NH 03217-0719
(603)968-3775 (800)637-9599
Fax:(603)968-3129

Circa 1895. A three-story turret, gables and verandas frosted with Queen Anne gingerbread come
together in an appealing mass of Victoriana in the
Glynn House. Carved-oak woodwork and pocket
doors accentuate the foyer.

Period furnishings and
ornate Oriental wall
coverings decorate the
parlor. The village of
Ashland is a few min-
utes from "On Golden
Pond" (Squam Lake)
and the White
Mountains.

Circa 1895

Innkeeper(s): Karol & Betsy
Paterman. $65-150. MC VISA AX
DC PC TC. 8 rooms with PB, 3 with FP. 2 suites. 1 conference room.
Breakfast included in rates. Types of meals: full breakfast, gourmet
breakfast and early coffee/tea. Banquet service available. Beds: KQDT.
Air conditioning, turn-down service, cable TV and VCR in room. Fax,
computer and tennis on premises. Amusement parks, antiques, fishing,
parks, shopping, downhill skiing, cross-country skiing, sporting events
and watersports nearby.

Location: Two hours from Boston.

*"Boston was fun, but the Glynn House is the place
we'll send our friends."*

Certificate may be used: Sunday-Thursday, November-June.

Bartlett
F5

The Country Inn at Bartlett
Rt 302, PO Box 327, Bartlett, NH 03812
(603)374-2353 (800)292-2353
Fax:(603)374-2547

Circa 1885. This New England farmhouse, built as
a summer home by a Portland sea captain, rests in a
stand of tall pines adjacent to national forest land.
For the last 50 years it has provided a homey atmosphere for families and friends coming to the White
Mountains. Accommodations are in the house or in
cottage rooms. An outdoor hot tub takes advantage
of the crisp, pine-scented air.

Innkeeper(s): Mark Dindorf. $58-128. MC VISA AX DS. 16 rooms, 11
with PB, 4 with FP. 10 cottages. Breakfast included in rates. Types of
meals: full breakfast and early coffee/tea. Beds: QDT. Air conditioning
and cable TV in room. VCR, fax and spa on premises. Antiques, fishing,
parks, shopping, skiing and theater nearby.

Location: White Mountains of New Hampshire.
Seen in: Outside.

"Walking through your door felt like stepping back in time."

Certificate may be used: Sunday-Thursday nights, excluding August,
October 1-15, Dec. 15-Jan. 1.

Bethlehem
E4

The Mulburn Inn
2370 Main St, Rt 302,
Bethlehem, NH 03574
(603)869-3389 (800)457-9440
Fax:(603)869-5633

Circa 1908. This summer cottage was known as the
Ivie Estate. Mrs. Ivie and Mrs. Frank Woolworth of
'Five and Dime' fame were sisters. Many of the Ivie
and Woolworth family members vacationed here in
summer. Cary Grant and Barbara Hutton spent their
honeymoon at the mansion. Polished oak staircases
and stained-glass windows add to the atmosphere.

Innkeeper(s): The Skeels Family. $55-80. MC VISA AX DS PC TC. 7
rooms with PB, 3 with FP. Breakfast and afternoon tea included in rates.
Types of meals: full breakfast and early coffee/tea. Beds: KQDT. Cable
TV, VCR and copier on premises. Amusement parks, antiques, fishing,
parks, downhill skiing, cross-country skiing and theater nearby.
Seen in: The Record, Yankee, Boston Globe.

*"You have put a lot of thought, charm, beauty and
warmth into the inn. Your breakfasts were oh, so
delicious!!"*

Certificate may be used: Except fall foliage season, President's week,
holiday weekends.

Bradford   J3

Candlelite Inn

5 Greenhouse Ln, Bradford, NH 03221
(603)938-5571

Nestled on more than three acres of countryside in
the valley of the Lake Sunapee region, this
Victorian inn has a gazebo porch perfect for sipping lemonade on a summer day. On winter days,
keep warm by the parlor's fireplace while relaxing
with a good book. All of the guest rooms have
mountain views and are decorated with fresh flowers and plants. Quilts on the beds and walls, cross
stitch pillows and pictures, and tole painting that
includes plaques to table-top decorations are the
innkeepers' creations.

Innkeeper(s): Marilyn Gordon. $65-75. MC VISA DS. 6 rooms. 1 suite.
Breakfast included in rates. Types of meals: full breakfast and early cof-
fee/tea. Evening snack available. Antiques, shopping, downhill skiing,
cross-country skiing, sporting events and theater nearby.

Certificate may be used: Nov. 1 to April 30.

The Rosewood Country Inn

RR 1 Box 225, Pleasant View Rd,
Bradford, NH 03221-9109
(603)938-5253 Fax:(603)938-5253

Circa 1850. This three-story country Victorian inn
in the White Mountains treats its guests to a candlelight and crystal breakfast and elegant accommodations that manage to avoid being stuffy. The inn
prides itself on special touches. The innkeepers like
to keep things interesting with ideas such as theme
weekends and special breakfast fare, including cinnamon apple pancakes with cider sauce. Mount
Sunapee Ski Area and Lake Sunapee are less than
20 minutes away.

Innkeeper(s): Lesley & Dick Marquis. $69-140. MC VISA PC TC. 7
rooms with PB. 1 suite. 1 conference room. Breakfast included in rates.
Types of meals: gourmet breakfast and early coffee/tea. Beds: QDT. Air
conditioning in room. Cable TV and fax on premises. Handicap access.
Antiques, fishing, shopping, downhill skiing, cross-country skiing,
sporting events, theater and watersports nearby.

Certificate may be used: January through June, September, November
and December; Sunday through Thursday.

Bridgewater

The Inn on Newfound Lake

1030 Mayhew Tpke,
Bridgewater, NH 03222-5108
(603)744-9111 Fax:(603)744-3894

Circa 1840. This inn was the mid-way stop on the
stage coach route from Boston to Montreal and

formerly was known as the Pasquaney Inn. A full
veranda overlooks the lake with its spectacular sunsets. Located in the foothills of the White
Mountains, the inn is situated on more than seven
acres of New Hampshire countryside.

Innkeeper(s): Phelps C. Boyce II. $55-105. MAP, AP. MC VISA AX DS.
31 rooms, 23 with PB. 2 suites. Breakfast and picnic lunch included in
rates. Type of meal: continental breakfast. Dinner and lunch available.
Beds: QT. Antiques, fishing, downhill skiing, cross-country skiing and
watersports nearby.

Seen in: Record Enterprise.

*"The rooms were quaint and cozy with just the right
personal touches, and always immaculate. The bed and
pillows were so comfortable, it was better than sleeping
at home! The inn itself is magnificent, elegance, never
felt so warm and homey."*

Certificate may be used: Oct. 15 through May 15.

Campton   G4

Campton Inn

RR 2, Box 12, Main & Owl Sts,
Campton, NH 03223-9411
(603)726-4449 Fax:(603)536-5610

Circa 1836. Three steep gables mark the roof line
of this historic country farmhouse. Simply but comfortably furnished rooms include a game room, a
large common room and a screened porch. A full
breakfast is served, a good time to tap into the
innkeepers' extensive knowledge of the area.

Innkeeper(s): Peter & Robbin Adams. $55-75. 6 rooms, 1 with PB.
Breakfast included in rates. Type of meal: full breakfast. Beds: QDT.

Antiques, fishing, parks, shopping, downhill skiing, cross-country skiing, sporting events, theater and watersports nearby.

Location: Heart of the White Mountain National Forest.

"What a great week. Excellent service!"

Certificate may be used: April 1 to July 31 and Oct. 15 to Dec. 23.

Mountain-Fare Inn
Mad River Rd, PO Box 553,
Campton, NH 03223
(603)726-4283

Circa 1820. This white farmhouse is surrounded by flower gardens in the summer and unparalleled foliage in the fall. Ski teams, family reunions and other groups often enjoy the outdoors here with

Mountain Fare as a base. In the winter everyone seems to be a skier, and in the summer there are boaters and hikers. The inn is decorated in a casual New Hampshire-style country decor. The hearty breakfast is a favorite of returning guests.

Innkeeper(s): Susan Preston. $65-90. MAP, EP. 10 rooms, 8 with PB, 1 with FP. 3 suites. Breakfast included in rates. Type of meal: full breakfast. Afternoon tea available. Beds: QDT. Air conditioning in room. Cable TV, VCR and child care on premises. Antiques, fishing, parks, skiing, sporting events, theater and watersports nearby.

Location: Two hours from Boston in the White Mountains.

Seen in: Ski, Skiing, Snow Country.

"Thank you for your unusually caring attitude toward your guests."

Certificate may be used: Sunday through Thursday nights except Dec. 15-Jan. 2 and Sept. 15-Oct 20.

Charlestown   J1

Maplehedge B&B
355 Main St, PO Box 638,
Charlestown, NH 03603-0638
(603)826-5237 (800)962-7539
Fax:(603)826-5237

Circa 1815. This elegantly restored home is set among acres of lawn and 200-year-old maple trees. The bed & breakfast boasts five distinctive bedrooms. The Beale Room is named for the innkeeper's

grandparents and is full of sentimental treasures such as milk bottles from her grandfather's dairy and family photos. The Butterfly Suite is filled with white wicker, including an antique, glass-topped hamper and Victorian butterfly trays. The rooms are furnished in antiques, including some of the linens. A delectable three-course breakfast is served and may include fresh fruit salads and scones. Evening refreshments include California wine with Vermont cheese. Guests can go on antiquing tours or attend country auctions.

Innkeeper(s): Joan & Dick DeBrine. $80-100. MC VISA PC. 5 rooms with PB. 1 suite. Breakfast and evening snack included in rates. Types of meals: gourmet breakfast and early coffee/tea. Beds: QT. Air conditioning and turn-down service in room. Fax, copier and library on premises. Antiques, fishing, parks, shopping, downhill skiing, cross-country skiing, theater and watersports nearby.

Location: Connecticut River Valley.

Seen in: Los Angeles Times, Buffalo News, Country Living, Yankee Traveler.

"The highlight of my two weeks in New England. A breakfast worth jumping out of bed for."

Certificate may be used: Upon availability and two week advance reservation, any time except Sept. 15-Oct. 25.

Chocorua   G5

Staffords-In-The-Field
PO Box 270, Chocorua, NH 03817-0270
(603)323-7766 Fax:(603)323-7531

Circa 1778. The main building of Stafford's, home to a prosperous farm family for more than 150 years, is Federal style. It became a guest house in the 1890s. An old apple orchard and sugar house remain, and there's a kitchen garden and a nine-hole golf course on the inn's 12 acres. A rocky brook still winds through the rolling fields, and in the adjacent woods, there's a natural swimming hole. Guest rooms are furnished in antiques. A canoe on nearby Lake Chocorua is available to guests.

Innkeeper(s): Ramona Stafford. $70-170. MAP. MC VISA. 14 rooms, 6 with PB, 1 with FP. Breakfast included in rates. Types of meals: full breakfast and gourmet breakfast. Beds: KQDT.

Location: White Mountains.

Seen in: Esquire, Boston Globe, Seattle Times, Los Angeles Times.

"Delicious food, delightful humor!"

Certificate may be used: Jan. 15 to Sept. 15 and November, subject to availability.

Claremont I2

Goddard Mansion B&B
25 Hillstead Rd, Claremont, NH 03743
(603)543-0603 Fax:(603)543-0001

Circa 1905. This mansion with its gazebo is set amid acres of lawn. The living room has a window seat, a large fireplace and a baby grand piano, while the dining room features a 1939 Wurlitzer jukebox. Many of the guest rooms have panoramic views of mountains in New Hampshire and Vermont. The airy French Country Room and the surreal Cloud

Room are favorites. Homemade muffins are served with preserves made from fruit grown on the property. There are historic sites, restaurants and plenty of antiquing nearby.

Innkeeper(s): Debbie Albee. $65-105. MC VISA AX DC CB DS PC TC. 10 rooms, 3 with PB. 1 suite. 2 conference rooms. Breakfast included in rates. Types of meals: continental-plus breakfast, full breakfast and gourmet breakfast. Beds: QDT. Air conditioning and turn-down service in room. Cable TV, VCR, fax, bicycles and library on premises. Antiques, fishing, parks, shopping, downhill skiing, cross-country skiing and theater nearby.

Seen in: Eagle Times.

"Our trip would not have been as enjoyable without having stayed at your inn."

Certificate may be used: Sunday through Thursday. One weekend night possible, November-mid-May.

Durham J6

University Guest House
47 Mill Rd, Durham, NH 03824-3006
(603)868-2728 Fax:(603)868-2744

Circa 1935. For the parents of college students, this B&B is a perfect choice, located within walking distance of the University of New Hampshire. But location isn't the only draw for guests at this Dutch Colonial home. The secluded grounds are covered

254

with trees and foliage, creating a peaceful, natural environment. The rooms are decorated like a country cottage. Walls are covered in bright, cheerful prints, and the comfortable furnishings are highlighted with a few antiques and collectibles.

Innkeeper(s): Elizabeth Fischer. $50-90. 4 rooms. Breakfast included in rates. Types of meals: continental-plus breakfast and early coffee/tea. Beds: QT. Antiques, fishing, parks, shopping, cross-country skiing, sporting events, theater and watersports nearby.

Certificate may be used: Year-round.

East Andover I4

Highland Lake Inn B&B
Maple St, East Andover, NH 03231-0164
(603)735-6426 Fax:(603)735-5355

Circa 1767. This early Victorian inn overlooks three mountains, and all the rooms have views of either the lake or the mountains. Many guest rooms feature handmade quilts and some have four-poster beds. Guests may relax with a book from the inn's library in front of the sitting room fireplace or walk the 12-acre grounds, and enjoy old apple and maple trees, as well as the shoreline. Adjacent to a 21-acre nature conservancy, there are scenic trails and a stream to explore. Highland Lake is stocked with bass and also has trout. Fresh fruit salads, hot entrees, and homemade breads are featured at breakfast.

Innkeeper(s): Mary Petras. $85-125. MC VISA AX. 10 rooms with PB. Breakfast included in rates. Type of meal: full breakfast. Beds: KQT. Ceiling fan in room. Cable TV and VCR on premises. Amusement parks, antiques, fishing, shopping, downhill skiing, cross-country skiing, sporting events, theater and watersports nearby.

Seen in: Andover Beacon.

"Place is very close to heaven."

Certificate may be used: Nov. 1 to May 1.

Eaton Center G6

Rockhouse Mountain Farm Inn
PO Box 90, Eaton Center, NH 03832
(603)447-2880

Circa 1900. This handsome old house is framed by maple trees on 450 acres of forests, streams, fields and wildflowers. Milking cows, pigs, geese, peacocks and llamas provide entertainment for city youngsters of all ages. Three generations of the Edges have operated this inn and some guests have been coming since 1946, the year it opened. A 250-year-old barn at times bulges with new-mown hay, and there is a nearby beach with swimming and boating for the exclusive use of guests.

Innkeeper(s): Johnny & Alana Edge. $50-58. MAP. PC TC. 18 rooms, 8 with PB, 1 with FP. 2 cottages. Breakfast included in rates. Types of

meals: full breakfast and gourmet breakfast. Dinner available. Beds: DT.
Ceiling fan in room. Swimming, sauna, stables, tennis and library on
premises. Handicap access. Antiques, fishing, parks, shopping, theater
and watersports nearby.

Location: Near the White Mountains.

Seen in: New York Times, Family Circle, Woman's Day, Boston Globe,
Country Vacations.

*"We have seen many lovely places, but Rockhouse
remains the real high spot, the one to which we most
want to return."*

Certificate may be used: Rate is MAP. June 15 to July 15, Labor Day
to Sept. 25, Oct. 15 to Nov. 1.

Enfield   H2

Boulder Cottage on Crystal Lake
RR 1 Box 257, Crystal Lake Rd, Enfield,
NH 03748-9326
(603)632-7355

Circa 1902. This simple Victorian home has been
in the innkeeper's family for more than 70 years and
affords a view of Crystal Lake. Guests can relax in
the home's living room, which offers a wood stove,
or stroll the 1.5-acre grounds. Swimming, hiking
and boating are among the area's many outdoor
attractions, and the surrounding area offers a variety
of sites, including the Hood Museum of Art and the
Billings Farm Museum.

Innkeeper(s): Barbara & Harry Reed. $55-65. 4 rooms, 2 with PB.
Breakfast and afternoon tea included in rates. Types of meals: continental breakfast, continental-plus breakfast, full breakfast and early
coffee/tea. Beds: DT. Cable TV and VCR on premises. Antiques, parks,
shopping, sporting events, theater and watersports nearby.

Certificate may be used: April 15 to Sept. 15, Sun. through Thurs.

Franconia   F3

Bungay Jar
PO Box 15, Easton Valley Rd,
Franconia, NH 03580-0015
(603)823-7775 Fax:(603)444-0110

Circa 1967. An 18th-century barn was taken down
and moved piece by piece to Easton Valley, six miles
from Franconia. A post-and-beam, barn-style-home
was constructed on 12 wooded acres with a stream
nearby and the White Mountains in view. The two-
story living room, reminiscent of a hay loft, is decorated with antique country furnishings, as are all the
guest rooms. Your host, a landscape architect, has
planted herb and perennial gardens, featured in
national magazines.

JANE STAUFFER

Innkeeper(s): Janet Engel. $65-130. MC VISA AX DS PC TC. 6 rooms,
4 with PB, 2 with FP. 2 suites. 1 cottage. Breakfast and afternoon tea
included in rates. Types of meals: full breakfast and early coffee/tea.
Beds: KQDT. Swimming and sauna on premises. Antiques, fishing,
parks, shopping, downhill skiing, cross-country skiing, theater and
watersports nearby.

Seen in: Country Accents, Discerning Traveler, Yankee, Brides,
American Homestyle.

"Such a perfect spot with such a great view."

Certificate may be used: November through June; Monday through
Thursday.

The Inn at Forest Hills
Rt 142, PO Box 783,
Franconia, NH 03580
(603)823-9550 Fax:(603)823-8701

Circa 1890. This Tudor-style inn in the White
Mountains offers a solarium, a living room with
fireplace and a large common room with fireplace
and cathedral ceilings. Breakfast is served with a
quiet background of classical music in the dining
room, where in the winter there's a blazing fireplace, and in summer the French doors open to the
scenery. Guest rooms feature a casual country decor
with quilts, flowered wall coverings and some

four-poster beds. Cross-country ski for free on the inn's property and on the 240 acres adjoining it. Downhill facilities are found at Bretton Woods, Cannon or Loon Mountain. Nearby Franconia Notch Park and the White Mountains offer trails designed for cycling and hiking.

Innkeeper(s): Gordon & Joanne Haym. $80-225. MC VISA AX DC PC TC. 6 rooms, 5 with PB. 1 suite. Breakfast included in rates. Type of meal: full breakfast. Evening snack available. Beds: KQ. Ceiling fan and cable TV in room. VCR, fax, tennis and library on premises. Antiques, fishing, parks, shopping, downhill skiing, cross-country skiing and watersports nearby.

"What a delightful inn! I loved the casual country elegance of your B&B and can understand why you are so popular with brides and grooms."

Certificate may be used: Sunday through Thursday, Nov. 1-April 30, except President, Christmas and New Years' weekends.

Franconia Inn

1300 Easton Rd, Franconia, NH 03580
(603)823-5542 (800)473-5299
Fax:(603)823-8078

Circa 1934. Beautifully situated on 117 acres below the White Mountain's famous Franconia Notch, this white clapboard inn is three stories high. An oak-paneled library, parlor, rathskeller lounge and

two verandas offer relaxing retreats. The inn's rooms are simply decorated in a pleasing style and there is a special honeymoon suite with private Jacuzzi. Bach, classic wines and an elegant American cuisine

are featured in the inn's unpretentious dining room. There's no shortage of activity here. The inn offers four clay tennis courts, horseback riding, a heated swimming pool, croquet, fishing, cross-country ski trails and glider rides among its outdoor amenities.

Innkeeper(s): Alec Morris. $75-135. MAP, EP. MC VISA AX. 34 rooms, 29 with PB, 3 with FP. 4 suites. 1 conference room. Breakfast included in rates. Types of meals: gourmet breakfast and early coffee/tea. Dinner, picnic lunch and catering service available. Beds: KQDT. VCR, copier, spa, swimming, bicycles, tennis and child care on premises. Amusement parks, antiques, fishing, parks, shopping, downhill skiing, cross-country skiing, sporting events and theater nearby.

Location: Exit 38 off I-93, two-and-a-half miles south on Route 116.

Seen in: Philadelphia Inquirer, Boston Globe, Travel & Leisure, Powder.

"The piece de resistance of the Franconia Notch is the Franconia Inn—Philadelphia Inquirer."

Certificate may be used: Midweek (Sunday-Thursday), non-holiday, from May 20 to June 22. Midweek Sept. 5-Sept. 21; any time from Oct. 29-Dec. 21; Midweek, non-holiday Jan. 1-April 1.

Hampton   K6

The Inn at Elmwood Corners

252 Winnacunnet Rd,
Hampton, NH 03842-2726
(603)929-0443 (800)253-5691

Circa 1870. This old sea captain's house boasts a wide wraparound porch, filled with wicker in the summer. The inn is decorated with stenciled walls, braided rugs and collections such as thimbles and dolls. Mary has stitched the quilts that top the beds. The library is jammed and guests may borrow a

book and finish reading it at home. A favorite breakfast is John's poached brook trout or Eggs Benedict. Dinner available upon request.

Innkeeper(s): John & Mary Hornberger. $65-85. MC VISA TC. 7 rooms, 2 with PB. 2 suites. Breakfast included in rates. Beds: QT. Air conditioning in room. Cable TV and library on premises. Amusement parks, antiques, fishing, parks, shopping, cross-country skiing, theater and watersports nearby.

Location: Three miles east of I-95, one mile west of the ocean.

Seen in: Hampton Union, Boston Globe, Country Magazine.

"Very hospitable, can't think of a thing you need to add."

Certificate may be used: Not valid weekends from Memorial Day through October.

Victoria Inn

430 High St, Hampton, NH 03842-2311
(603)929-1437

Circa 1865. Elegance and style are featured at this Queen Anne Victorian inn just a half-mile from the ocean. A romantic gazebo, spacious guest rooms and Victorian furnishings throughout the inn add to its considerable charm. The Honeymoon Suite and Victoria Room are popular with those seeking privacy and luxury. Guests may borrow the inn's bicycles for a relaxing ride or read a book in its deluxe morning room. Common areas include the living room and the sitting room, with its cozy fireplace.

Innkeeper(s): Bill & Ruth Muzzey. $75-95. MC VISA PC TC. 6 rooms, 3 with PB. Breakfast included in rates. Types of meals: full breakfast and early coffee/tea. Beds: KQDT. Air conditioning, turn-down service, ceiling fan and cable TV in room. VCR and library on premises. Antiques, fishing, parks, shopping, downhill skiing, cross-country skiing, sporting events, theater and watersports nearby.

Certificate may be used: Nov. 1-April 30.

Hancock
K3

The Hancock Inn

33 Main St, Hancock, NH 03449
(603)525-3318 (800)525-1789
Fax:(603)525-9301

Circa 1789. Travelers have enjoyed this old inn, now in the National Register of Historic Places, since the days it served as a stagecoach stop more than 200 years ago. The governor declared the building the oldest inn in New Hampshire. Canopied beds are found in some rooms and there are hooked rugs, wing-back chairs and rockers. The Mural Room boasts a pastoral mural painted in 1825. All rooms have hand-sewn quilts and antique appointments. The fireplaced common room has comfortable chairs and couches with a small bar. Dinner here is a must. The inn's restaurant has won several awards for its New England regional cuisine. The Shaker cranberry pot roast is a house specialty.

Innkeeper(s): Linda & Joe Johnston. $98-150. MAP, AP, EP. MC VISA AX DC CB DS PC TC. 11 rooms with PB. 1 conference room. Breakfast included in rates. Types of meals: full breakfast and early coffee/tea. Afternoon tea, dinner, picnic lunch and banquet service available. Beds: QDT. Air conditioning in room. Cable TV, fax and library on premises. Antiques, fishing, parks, shopping, downhill skiing, cross-country skiing, theater and watersports nearby.

Seen in: Country Inns, Boston Globe, Keene Sentinel, Yankee Homes.

"The warmth you extended was the most meaningful part of our visit."

Certificate may be used: November-July, not including holidays or holiday weekends.

Hillsborough
J3

The Inn at Maplewood Farm

447 Center Rd PO Box 1478,
Hillsborough, NH 03244-4825
(603)464-4242 (800)644-6695
Fax:(603)464-5401

Circa 1794. Antique-lovers will enjoy this historic inn, which not only features attractive American and European pieces, but a location in the heart of antique and auction country. The inn borders scenic Fox State Forest and historic Hillsborough Center is just up the road. Pats Peak Ski Area is nearby.

Innkeeper(s): Laura & Jayme Simoes. $75-115. EP. MC VISA AX DS PC TC. 4 suites. 1 conference room. Breakfast included in rates. Types of meals: full breakfast and early coffee/tea. Picnic lunch available. Beds: KQDT. Air conditioning, turn-down service and ceiling fan in room. VCR, fax and library on premises. Antiques, fishing, parks, shopping, downhill skiing, cross-country skiing and watersports nearby.

Seen in: New York Times, Boston Globe

"Your house is charming and you are both very hospitable."

Certificate may be used: Off-season, Nov. 1-April 30, midweek only (Sunday-Thursday).

Stonebridge Inn

365 W Main St, Hillsborough, NH 03244
(603)464-3155

Circa 1830. The innkeepers of this Federal-style farmhouse spent several years restoring and redecorating their country inn. Two acres laced with trees surround the early 19th-century home. Each of the guest rooms is decorated individually with antiques here and there. The home is directly across from a river, and Franklin Pierce Lake is less than two miles away.

Innkeeper(s): George & Clara Adame. $49-59. MAP. MC VISA TC. 5 rooms with PB. Breakfast included in rates. Types of meals: continental breakfast and early coffee/tea. Beds: D. Air conditioning in room. Cable TV and VCR on premises. Antiques, fishing, downhill skiing, cross-country skiing and watersports nearby.

Certificate may be used: May 1-Sept. 15, Sunday-Thursday.

Jackson   F5

Dana Place Inn
RR 16, Pinkham Notch Rd,
Jackson, NH 03846
(603)383-6822 (800)537-9276
Fax:(603)383-6022

Circa 1860. The original owners received this Colonial farmhouse as a wedding present. The warm, cozy atmosphere of the inn is surpassed only by the spectacular mountain views. During autumn,

the fall leaves explode with color, and guests can enjoy the surroundings while taking a hike or bike ride through the area. The beautiful Ellis River is the perfect place for an afternoon of fly-fishing or a picnic. After a scrumptious country breakfast, winter guests can step out the door and into skis for a day of cross-country skiing.

Innkeeper(s): The Levine Family. $75-135. MAP, AP. MC VISA AX DC CB DS PC TC. 31 rooms with PB. 4 suites. Breakfast and afternoon tea included in rates. Types of meals: continental-plus breakfast and full breakfast. Dinner and picnic lunch available. Beds: KQDT. Cable TV in room. VCR, fax, copier, spa, swimming, tennis and library on premises. Antiques, parks, shopping, downhill skiing, cross-country skiing and watersports nearby.

Location: At the base of Mt. Washington, White Mountain National Forest.

Seen in: Travel & Leisure, Inn Spots, Bon Appetit, Country Journal.

Certificate may be used: Midweek, excluding February; August; foliage (Sept. 20-Oct. 20) & holiday periods.

Ellis River House
Rt 16, Box 656, Jackson, NH 03846
(603)383-9339 (800)233-8309
Fax:(603)383-4142

Circa 1893. Andrew Harriman built this farmhouse, as well as the village town hall and three-room schoolhouse where the innkeepers' children

attended school. Classic antiques and Laura Ashley prints decorate the guest rooms and riverfront "honeymoon" cottage and each window reveals views of magnificent mountains, the vineyard, or spectacular Ellis River. In 1993, the innkeepers added 18 rooms, 13 of which feature fireplaces and three offer two-person Jacuzzis. They also added four family suites, a heated, outdoor pool, an indoor Jacuzzi and a sauna.

Innkeeper(s): Barry & Barbara Lubao. $79-229. MAP. MC VISA AX DC CB DS PC TC. 20 rooms with PB, 13 with FP. 4 suites. 1 cottage. 1 conference room. Breakfast included in rates. Types of meals: full breakfast and early coffee/tea. Afternoon tea, dinner and picnic lunch available. Beds: KQDT. Air conditioning and cable TV in room. Fax, spa, swimming and sauna on premises. Handicap access. Amusement parks, antiques, fishing, parks, shopping, downhill skiing, cross-country skiing, sporting events, theater and watersports nearby.

Location: White Mountain area.

Seen in: Philadelphia Inquirer.

"We have stayed at many B&Bs all over the world and are in agreement that the beauty and hospitality of Ellis River House is that of a world-class bed & breakfast."

Certificate may be used: All year, except holidays, fall foliage and ski weekends.

Whitneys' Inn
Rt 16B, PO Box 822, Jackson, NH 03846
(603)383-8916 (800)677-5737
Fax:(603)383-6886

Circa 1842. This country inn offers romance, family recreation and a lovely setting at the base of the Black Mountain Ski Area. The inn specializes in recreation, as guests enjoy cookouts, cross-country and downhill skiing, hiking, lawn games, skating, sledding, sleigh rides, swimming and tennis. Homemade corned beef hash is one of the breakfast specialties. Popular nearby activities include trying out Jackson's two golf courses and picnicking at Jackson Falls.

Innkeeper(s): Kevin Martin. $64-166. MAP. MC VISA AX DS PC TC. 29 rooms with PB, 3 with FP. 9 suites. 2 cottages. 1 conference room. Breakfast and dinner included in rates. Type of meal: full breakfast. Afternoon tea, picnic lunch and banquet service available. Beds: KQDT. Air conditioning, ceiling fan and cable TV in room. VCR, swimming, tennis and library on premises. Amusement parks, antiques, fishing, parks, downhill skiing, cross-country skiing, theater and watersports nearby.

Certificate may be used: Oct. 20-Nov. 20, Nov. 20-Dec. 20, all nights; Jan. 2-Feb. 10, March 16-Sept. 15, Sunday-Thursday.

Jaffrey   L3

The Benjamin Prescott Inn
Rt 124 E, 433 Turnpike Rd,
Jaffrey, NH 03452
(603)532-6637 Fax:(603)532-6637

Circa 1853. Colonel Prescott arrived on foot in
Jaffrey in 1775, with an ax in his hand and a bag of
beans on his back. The family built this classic Greek

Revival many years later. Now, candles light the windows, seen from the stonewall-lined lane adjacent to
the inn. Each room bears the name of a Prescott family member and is furnished with antiques.
Innkeeper(s): Jan & Barry Miller. $65-140. EP. MC VISA AX PC TC. 9
rooms with PB. 2 suites. 1 conference room. Breakfast included in
rates. Type of meal: full breakfast. Beds: KQDT. Air conditioning and
ceiling fan in room. VCR, fax and library on premises. Antiques, fishing,
parks, shopping, downhill skiing, cross-country skiing, sporting events,
theater and watersports nearby.

*"The coffee and breakfasts were delicious and the hospi-
tality overwhelming."*

Certificate may be used: Jan. 2-March 31, excluding holidays.

Jefferson   E4

Applebrook
Rt 115A, PO Box 178,
Jefferson, NH 03583
(603)586-7713 (800)545-6504

Circa 1797. Panoramic views surround this large
Victorian farmhouse nestled in the middle of New
Hampshire's White Mountains. Guests can awake to
the smell of freshly baked muffins made with locally
picked berries. A comfortable, fire-lit sitting room

boasts stained glass, a goldfish pool and a beautiful
view of Mt. Washington. Test your golfing skills at
the nearby 18-hole championship course, or spend
the day antique hunting. A trout stream and spring-
fed rock pool are nearby. Wintertime guests can ice
skate or race through the powder at nearby ski
resorts or by way of snowmobile, finish off the day
with a moonlight toboggan ride. After a full day,
guests can enjoy a soak in the hot tub under the
stars, where they might see shooting stars or the
Northern Lights.
Innkeeper(s): Sandra Conley. $45-75. MC VISA. 12 rooms, 5 with PB.
Breakfast and afternoon tea included in rates. Types of meals: full
breakfast and early coffee/tea. Beds: KQDT. Spa and bicycles on
premises. Amusement parks, antiques, fishing, shopping, downhill skiing, cross-country skiing, theater and watersports nearby.
Seen in: PriceCostco Connection, New Hampshire Outdoor Companion.

"We came for a night and stayed for a week."

Certificate may be used: Anytime except weekends July 1-Oct. 15 or
Dec. 15-March 15.

Moultonborough   H5

Olde Orchard Inn
RR 1 Box 256, Lees Rd & Lees Mill,
Moultonborough, NH 03254-9502
(603)476-5004 (800)598-5845
Fax:(603)476-5419

Circa 1790. This farmhouse rests next to a mountain brook and pond in the midst of an apple
orchard. Five guest rooms and one family suite are
available, all with private baths. After enjoying a
large country breakfast, guests may borrow a bicycle
for a ride to Lake Winnipesaukee, just a mile away.
The inn is within an hour's drive of five downhill
skiing areas, and guests also may cross-country ski
on the inn's own trails. Visitors are encouraged to
notify the innkeepers if bringing along a pet;
arrangements usually can be made. The Castle in
the Clouds and the Ossipee Ski Area are nearby.
Innkeeper(s): Jim & Mary Senner. $70-125. MC VISA PC TC. 9 rooms
with PB, 3 with FP. 1 suite. 1 cottage. Breakfast included in rates. Type
of meal: full breakfast. Beds: KQTD. Air conditioning in room. Cable TV,
VCR, fax and child care on premises. Antiques, fishing, parks, shopping, skiing, theater and watersports nearby.

Certificate may be used: Nov. 1-May 15, Friday and Saturday excluded.

New Ipswich   L3

The Inn at New Ipswich
11 Porter Hill Rd, Box 208,
New Ipswich, NH 03071-3732
(603)878-3711

Circa 1790. A classic red barn gives this inn a country feel. The grounds are bordered with stone walls, gardens and fruit trees. Two of the bedrooms have working fireplaces and all feature antiques. The front porch offers rockers for relaxing and the screened porch is an excellent place to take in the

evening breezes. The Monadnock region offers mountain climbing and hiking as well as a summer theater, antiquing and incredible fall foliage. In cool months, homemade breakfasts are served in the keeping room in front of a crackling fire.

Innkeeper(s): Virginia Bankuti. $45-65. MC VISA. 6 rooms, 5 with PB, 2 with FP. 1 suite. Breakfast included in rates. Type of meal: full breakfast. Evening snack available. Beds: QT. VCR on premises. Antiques, shopping, downhill skiing, cross-country skiing and theater nearby.

Location: In the Monadnock region.

"Breakfast alone is worth the trip."

Certificate may be used: Nov. 1 through May 31. Weekdays only: June 1 through Oct. 31. Excludes holidays and holiday weekends.

New London   I3

Colonial Farm Inn
Rt 11, PO Box 1053,
New London, NH 03257
(603)526-6121 (800)805-8504
Fax:(603)641-0314

Circa 1836. The village of New London holds what should be the world's most popular festival, the Chocolate Fest. The innkeepers at Colonial Farm won the award for top confection, a tangy chocolate-almond pate. The historic home, an example of a center-chimney Colonial, is decorated in a tasteful, period style with a mix of antiques and pieces such as four-poster beds. A memorable breakfast is served, and guests would be wise to save at least one night for dinner at the inn. The dining rooms, with exposed beams and plank floorboards, are cozy and

romantic, and the food has drawn many compliments. Specialties include crostini with chicken liver pate and prosciutto, roasted red and green peppers with goat cheese, tenderloin of beef with a burgundy-shallot sauce or, perhaps, chicken stuffed with homemade boursin cheese and walnuts.

Innkeeper(s): Robert & Kathryn Joseph. $85-95. MC VISA AX PC TC. 5 rooms with PB. 1 conference room. Breakfast included in rates. Type of meal: full breakfast. Beds: QDT. Air conditioning in room. Cable TV, VCR, bicycles and library on premises. Handicap access. Antiques, fishing, parks, shopping, downhill skiing, cross-country skiing, sporting events, theater and watersports nearby.

Certificate may be used: Jan. 1 through Dec. 31 except weekends in the summer

North Conway   F5

The 1785 Inn
3582 White Mountain Hwy,
North Conway, NH 03860-1785
(603)356-9025 (800)421-1785
Fax:(603)356-6081

Circa 1785. The main section of this center-chimney house was built by Captain Elijah Dinsmore of the New Hampshire Rangers. He was granted the land for service in the American Revolution. Original hand-hewn beams, corner posts, fireplaces, and a brick oven are still visible and operating.

Innkeeper(s): Becky & Charles Mallar. $69-169. MC VISA AX DC CB DS PC TC. 17 rooms, 12 with PB. 1 suite. 2 conference rooms. Breakfast included in rates. Types of meals: full breakfast, gourmet breakfast and early coffee/tea. Dinner, evening snack, banquet service and room service available. Beds: KQD. Air conditioning in room. Cable TV, VCR, fax, copier, swimming, library and child care on premises. Amusement parks, antiques, fishing, parks, shopping, downhill skiing, cross-country skiing, theater and watersports nearby.

Location: Two miles North of North Conway in the White Mountains.
Seen in: New England Getaways, Valley Visitor, Bon Appetit, Ski, Travel Holiday, Connecticut.

"Occasionally in our lifetimes is a moment so unexpectedly perfect that we use it as our measure for our unforgettable moments. We just had such an experience at The 1785 Inn."

Certificate may be used: January, March-June, November-December, excluding holidays.

Buttonwood Inn
PO Box 1817, North Conway, NH 03860
(603)356-2625 (800)258-2625
Fax:(603)356-3140

Circa 1820. This center-chimney, New England-style inn was once a working farm of more than 100 acres on the mountain. Of the original outbuildings, only the granite barn foundation remains. Through the years, the house has been extended to a total of 20 rooms.

Innkeeper(s): Claudia & Peter Needham. $70-150. MC VISA AX DS PC TC. 9 rooms, 5 with PB, 1 with FP. 2 suites. 1 conference room. Breakfast and afternoon tea included in rates. Types of meals: full breakfast, gourmet breakfast and early coffee/tea. Beds: KQDT. Cable TV, VCR, fax, swimming, bicycles and library on premises. Amusement parks, antiques, fishing, parks, shopping, downhill skiing, cross-country skiing, theater and watersports nearby.

Location: Tucked away on Mt. Surprise, two miles from town.

Seen in: Northeast Bound, Skiing, Boston Globe, Yankee Travel, The Mountain Ear.

"The very moment we spotted your lovely inn nestled midway on the mountainside in the moonlight, we knew we had found a winner."

Certificate may be used: Jan. 1 to June 20, Nov. 1 to Dec. 23, Sunday through Thursday, holiday weekends excluded.

Cranmore Mt Lodge

859 Kearsarge Rd, PO Box 1194,
North Conway, NH 03860-5344
(603)356-2044 (800)356-3596
Fax:(603)356-8963

Circa 1860. Babe Ruth was a frequent guest at this old New England farmhouse when his daughter was the owner. There are many rare Babe Ruth photos displayed in the inn and one guest room is still decorated with his furnishings. The barn on the property is held together with wooden pegs and contains dorm rooms.

Innkeeper(s): Judy & Dennis Helfand. $69-125. MC VISA AX DC DS PC TC. 21 rooms, 15 with PB. 1 suite. Breakfast included in rates. Types of meals: full breakfast and early coffee/tea. Beds: KQDT. Air conditioning, ceiling fan and cable TV in room. VCR, fax, copier, spa, swimming and tennis on premises. Amusement parks, antiques, fishing, parks, shopping, skiing, theater and watersports nearby.

Location: Village of Kearsarge.

Seen in: New England Getaways, Ski Magazine, Snow Country, Montreal Gazette, Newsday.

"Your accommodations are lovely, your breakfasts delicious."

Certificate may be used: April 1-Sept. 15.

The Forest - A Country Inn

PO Box 1376,
North Conway (Intervale), NH 03845
(603)356-9772 (800)448-3534
Fax:(603)356-5652

Circa 1830. This spacious Second Empire Victorian offers easy access to the many attractions of the Mt. Washington Valley. The inn's 11 guest rooms are uniquely decorated with country antique furnishings. Honeymooners often enjoy the privacy of the inn's turn-of-the-century stone cottage. A stream runs through the inn's 25 wooded acres, and guests may cross-country ski right on the property. The inn also boasts a built-in swimming pool. Breakfast fare could include apple pancakes, rum raisin French toast or spiced Belgian waffles. Heritage New Hampshire and Story Land are nearby.

Innkeeper(s): Bill & Lisa Guppy. $60-169. MC VISA AX DS PC TC. 12 rooms, 10 with PB, 5 with FP. 2 suites. 3 cottages. Breakfast and evening snack included in rates. Type of meal: full breakfast. Beds: QDT. Ceiling fan in room. Cable TV, fax, swimming and tennis on premises. Amusement parks, antiques, fishing, parks, shopping, downhill skiing, cross-country skiing, sporting events, theater and watersports nearby.

Certificate may be used: Anytime May, June, November-Dec. 23, holidays excluded.

Victorian Harvest Inn

28 Locust Ln, Box 1763,
North Conway, NH 03860
(603)356-3548 (800)642-0749
Fax:(603)356-8450

Circa 1883. Perched atop a hill in the Mt. Washington Valley, this Folk Victorian inn features comfortable surroundings and attention to detail. The country Victorian furnishings are highlighted by homemade quilts and teddy bears that visitors may adopt during their stay. The Victoria Station Room boasts its own carousel horse, and the Nook & Cranny Room offers a view of the entire Moat Range. Guests also enjoy strolling the grounds, which include a footbridge, gardens and a Victorian decorated pool.

Innkeeper(s): Linda & Robert Dahlberg. $65-90. MC VISA AX DS TC. 6 rooms, 4 with PB. Breakfast and afternoon tea included in rates. Type of meal: full breakfast. Air conditioning and ceiling fan in room. Cable TV, VCR, fax and copier on premises. Amusement parks, antiques, fishing, parks, shopping, downhill skiing, cross-country skiing, theater and watersports nearby.

Certificate may be used: Exempt September-October (foliage season).

Wyatt House Country Inn
PO Box 777, North Conway, NH 03860
(603)356-7977 (800)527-7978

Circa 1880. This rambling Victorian is surrounded by three acres of manicured grounds and trees on the banks of the Saco River. The private location is an inspiration for romance. Rooms are decorated with antiques in country Victorian style, and guests are pampered with in-room sherry, canopy beds and views of the river and mountains. The delightful, multi-course breakfasts are served on fine English Wedgwood and lace. Everything is fresh and home-made, including granola, muffins and squeezed orange juice. Apple cobbler with vanilla ice cream, cheese souffles, shirred eggs, spinach and Vermont cheese quiche, chocolate chip pancakes and New England breakfast pie are among the memorable treats.

Innkeeper(s): Arlene & Bill Strickland. $50-175. MC VISA AX DS PC TC. 6 rooms, 4 with PB. 3 suites. Breakfast, afternoon tea and picnic lunch included in rates. Types of meals: full breakfast, gourmet breakfast and early coffee/tea. Room service available. Beds: QDT. Air conditioning, ceiling fan and cable TV in room. Swimming, bicycles and library on premises. Amusement parks, antiques, fishing, parks, shopping, downhill skiing, cross-country skiing, sporting events, theater and water-sports nearby.

Certificate may be used: April 1 through and including June 15, Nov. 1 through Dec. 15, Monday through Sunday, excluding holidays and holiday weekends.

North Woodstock F4

Wilderness Inn
Rfd 1, Box 69, Rts 3 & 112,
North Woodstock, NH 03262-9710
(603)745-3890

Circa 1912. Surrounded by the White Mountain National Forest, this charming shingled home offers a picturesque getaway for every season. Guest rooms

262

are furnished with antiques and Oriental rugs, and the innkeepers also offer two suites and a private cottage with a view of Lost River. Breakfast is a delightful affair with choices ranging from fresh muffins to brie cheese omelets, French toast topped with homemade apple syrup, crepes or specialty pancakes. For the children, the innkeepers create teddy bear pancakes or French toast. If you have room, an afternoon tea also is prepared.

Innkeeper(s): Michael Yarnell. $40-90. MAP. MC VISA AX. 8 rooms, 5 with PB. 1 conference room. Breakfast included in rates. Types of meals: full breakfast and gourmet breakfast. Beds: QDT.

"It's nice to know that the next time we want to have a meeting up north, I won't have to search for a nice place to go."

Certificate may be used: All midweek except holidays and July-October.

Plymouth H4

Colonel Spencer Inn
RR 1, Box 206, Plymouth, NH 03264
(603)536-3438

Circa 1764. This pre-Revolutionary Colonial boasts Indian shutters, gleaming plank floors and secret passageways. Benjamin Baker, one of the house's early owners, fought at Bunker Hill and

with General Washington. Within view of the river and the mountains, the inn is now a cozy retreat with warm Colonial decor. Afternoon tea and evening coffee and dessert are served. A suite with kitchen is also available.

Innkeeper(s): Carolyn & Alan Hill. $45-65. PC TC. 7 rooms, 6 with PB. 1 suite. Breakfast and evening snack included in rates. Type of meal: full breakfast. Beds: D. Cable TV and tennis on premises. Amusement parks, antiques, fishing, parks, shopping, downhill skiing, cross-country skiing, sporting events, theater and watersports nearby.

Location: Near lake and mountain district.

"You have something very special here and we very much enjoyed a little piece of it!"

Certificate may be used: November through July.

Crab Apple Inn

PO Box 188, Rt 25, Plymouth, NH 03264
(603)536-4476

Circa 1835. Behind an immaculate, white picket fence is a brick Federal house beside a small brook at the foot of Tenney Mountain. There are fireplaces on the second floor and panoramic vistas from the third floor. Rooms are furnished with canopy beds and clawfoot tubs. The grounds include an English garden and meandering wooded paths.

Innkeeper(s): Christine DeCamp. $50-85. MC VISA PC TC. 5 rooms, 3 with PB. Breakfast and afternoon tea included in rates. Types of meals: gourmet breakfast and early coffee/tea. Beds: QDT. Air conditioning in room. Library on premises. Amusement parks, antiques, fishing, parks, shopping, downhill skiing, cross-country skiing, sporting events, theater and watersports nearby.

Location: Gateway to White Mountains in the Baker River Valley.

Seen in: Bon Appetit.

"We are still excited about our trip. The Crab Apple Inn was the unanimous choice for our favorite place to stay."

Certificate may be used: Year-round, midweek only (Tuesday and Wednesday or Wednesday and Thursday).

Tamworth   G5

Whispering Pines B&B

Rt 113A & Hemenway Road,
Tamworth, NH 03886
(603)323-7337

Circa 1901. Bordered on one edge by Hemenway State Forest, Whispering Pines is set upon 22 acres of woods. The guest rooms are decorated with antiques, and each is individually appointed with themes such as Woodlands and Memories. Items such as baked apple puffs and homemade muffins accompany the morning's breakfast entree. Shops and restaurants are nearby. There is an abundance of seasonal activities in the area, including berry picking, hay rides, summer theater, nature trails, bicycling, a popular farm festival and plenty of antiquing.

Innkeeper(s): Karen & Kim Erickson. $65-80. MC VISA DS PC TC. 4 rooms, 1 with PB. Breakfast and evening snack included in rates. Types of meals: full breakfast and early coffee/tea. Beds: KQD. Library on premises. Antiques, fishing, parks, shopping, downhill skiing, cross-country skiing, theater and watersports nearby.

Certificate may be used: From July 1 to Oct. 1, excluding Saturdays.

Thornton (Campton)   G4

Amber Lights Inn B&B

Rt 3, Thornton (Campton), NH 03223
(603)726-4077

Circa 1815. A breakfast to remember will delight this inn's guests, who are served a six-course, homemade meal in the Hannah Adams dining room. The Colonial inn offers five antique-filled guest rooms, all with queen beds and handmade quilts. Guests enjoy the inn's copper collection, on display in its country kitchen. They also like to relax in the sunny garden room, or quiet library, where wintertime visitors can watch other guests as they cross-country ski on the inn's grounds. Be sure to inquire about the inn's murder-mystery weekend packages. Fine downhill skiing is found within easy driving distance of the inn.

Innkeeper(s): Paul Sears & Carola Warnsman. $60-75. MC VISA AX DS PC TC. 5 rooms, 1 with PB. 2 suites. Breakfast included in rates. Types of meals: continental breakfast, full breakfast and gourmet breakfast. Beds: QT. Turn-down service in room. Library on premises. Antiques, fishing, shopping, downhill skiing, cross-country skiing, sporting events, theater and watersports nearby.

Location: In the White Mountains.

Seen in: NY NEX Update for Retirees, Union Leader.

"Another wonderful stay at Amber Lights. The food is, without question, the best, the surroundings always lovely and comfortable, however, there are no words for the wonderful hospitality!"

Certificate may be used: Anytime, April 1 through July 31, also Nov. 1 through Dec. 24, and weekdays only from Dec. 26 through March 30.

Tilton   I4

Tilton Manor

40 Chestnut St, Tilton, NH 03276-5546
(603)286-3457

Circa 1884. This turn-of-the-century Folk Victorian inn is just two blocks from downtown Tilton. The inn's comfortable guest rooms are furnished with antiques and sport handmade afghans. Guests are treated to a hearty country breakfast featuring freshly baked muffins, and dinner is available with advance reservations. Visitors enjoy relaxing in the sitting room, where they may play games, read or watch TV after a busy day exploring the historic area. Gunstock and Highland ski resorts are nearby and the Daniel Webster Birthplace and Shaker Village are within easy driving distance. Shoppers will enjoy Tilton's latest addition — an outlet center.

Innkeeper(s): Chip & Diane. $60-70. MC VISA AX DS PC TC. 4 rooms, 2 with PB, 1 with FP. 2 suites. Breakfast included in rates. Type of meal: full breakfast. Beds: KDT. Cable TV, library and child care on premises.

Antiques, fishing, shopping, downhill skiing, cross-country skiing and watersports nearby.

"A home away from home."

Certificate may be used: All year, except holidays and holiday weekends.

Wentworth G3

Wentworth Inn & Art Gallery
Ellsworth Hill Rd, Off Rt 25,
Wentworth, NH 03282
(603)764-9923

Circa 1800. This Federal Colonial-style inn is located on Baker Pond Brook in the foothills of the White Mountains. The guest rooms are elegantly decorated. A full country breakfast and afternoon snacks are offered. Gourmet candlelight dining is

available in the evening. The New Hampshire Vacations Tourist Information is located on the property and there is an art gallery and gift shop. A double-tiered veranda overlooks Mount Stinson.
Innkeeper(s): James Moffat. $60-80. MC VISA AX. 7 rooms, 4 with PB. 1 suite. 1 conference room. Breakfast included in rates. Types of meals: full breakfast and gourmet breakfast. Dinner, picnic lunch and lunch available. Beds: Q. Cable TV and copier on premises. Antiques, fishing, shopping, downhill skiing, cross-country skiing, sporting events, theater and watersports nearby.
Location: In the foothills of the White Mountains.
Seen in: Eagle-Tribune, Union Leader, Yankee, Manchester Union Leader, WMUR-TV.

Certificate may be used: Anytime Sunday through Saturday.

Wolfeboro H5

Tuc' Me Inn B&B
118 N Main St, PO Box 657, Rt 109 N,
Wolfeboro, NH 03894-4310
(603)569-5702

Circa 1850. This Federal Colonial-style house features a music room, parlor and screen porches. Afternoon tea with home-baked scones is served in the Victorian garden room. Chocolate chip or strawberry pancakes are often presented for breakfast in the dining room. The inn is a short walk to the quaint village of Wolfeboro and the shores of Lake Winnipesaukee.

Innkeeper(s): Terrille Foutz. $60-80. MC VISA. 7 rooms, 3 with PB. Breakfast included in rates. Types of meals: full breakfast and early coffee/tea. Afternoon tea available. Beds: QT. Air conditioning, ceiling fan and VCR in room. Cable TV on premises. Antiques, fishing, shopping, downhill skiing, cross-country skiing and theater nearby.
Seen in: Granite State News, Wolfeboro Times.

"Super in every detail."

Certificate may be used: April 15 to Oct. 20, Monday through Thursday; Oct. 21 to April 14, anytime.

New Jersey

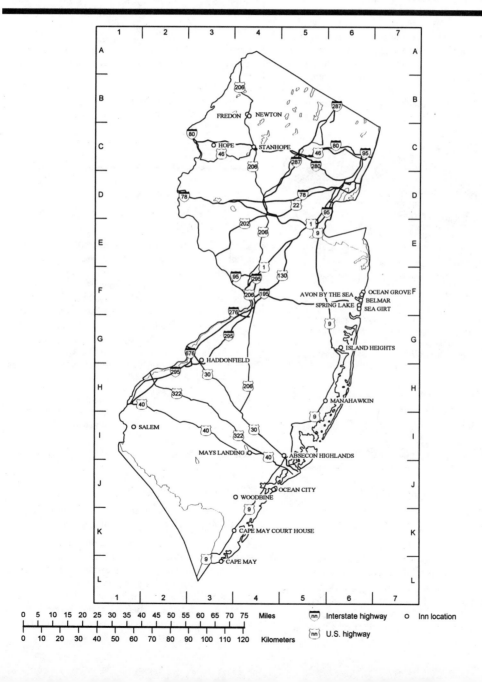

	Miles
0 5 10 15 20 25 30 35 40 45 50 55 60 65 70 75	Miles
0 10 20 30 40 50 60 70 80 90 100 110 120	Kilometers

nn Interstate highway   o Inn location

nn U.S. highway

Absecon Highlands   I5

White Manor Inn
739 S 2nd Ave,
Absecon Highlands, NJ 08201-9542
(609)748-3996 Fax:(609)652-0073

Circa 1932. This quiet country inn was built by the innkeeper's father and includes unique touches throughout, many created by innkeeper Howard Bensel himself, who became a master craftsman from his father's teachings and renovated the home extensively. Beautiful flowers and plants adorn both the lush grounds and the interior of the home. Everything is comfortable and cozy at this charming B&B, a relaxing contrast to the glitz of nearby Atlantic City.

Innkeeper(s): Anna Mae & Howard R. Bensel Jr. $48-85. PC TC. 7 rooms, 5 with PB, 5 with FP. 1 suite. 1 conference room. Breakfast and evening snack included in rates. Types of meals: continental breakfast, continental-plus breakfast and early coffee/tea. Beds: QDT. Air conditioning and ceiling fan in room. VCR on premises. Amusement parks, antiques, fishing, parks, shopping, sporting events, theater and watersports nearby.

"We felt more like relatives than total strangers. By far the most clean inn that I have seen — spotless!"

Certificate may be used: Monday through Thursday, Nov. 1 to April 1.

Avon By The Sea   F6

The Avon Manor B&B Inn
109 Sylvania Ave,
Avon By The Sea, NJ 07717-1338
(908)774-0110

Circa 1907. The Avon Manor was built as a private summer residence in the Colonial Revival style. The handsome facade is graced by a 100-foot wrap-around veranda. Light, airy bedrooms are decorated with antiques, wicker and period pieces. Guests breakfast in a sunny dining room or on the veranda.

Innkeeper(s): Kathleen Curley. $80-110. 8 rooms, 6 with PB. Breakfast and afternoon tea included in rates. Type of meal: full breakfast. Beds: QDT. Air conditioning in room. Cable TV and child care on premises. Amusement parks, antiques, fishing, shopping, sporting events, theater and watersports nearby.

Location: A block from the beach.

Certificate may be used: Sunday to Thursday, June through September. Weekends, October through May. Not valid holidays, special event weekends or with other promotions.

Belmar   F6

The Seaflower B&B
110 9th Ave, Belmar, NJ 07719-2302
(908)681-6006

Circa 1907. This comfortable Dutch Colonial inn is a half-block from the beach and boardwalk. Guest rooms feature the sound of ocean waves and the scent of fresh flowers. Wallpapers set off an eclectic mixture of antiques, new four-poster and canopy beds, and an abundance of paintings. Guests enjoy the ocean views from the porch's teak Adirondack chairs. One of the major deep-sea fishing ports on the Northeast Coast is nearby at the mouth of the Shark River, and your hosts can help set up charters.
Innkeeper(s): Knute Iwaszko. $65-98. AX. 7 rooms, 6 with PB. 1 suite. Breakfast included in rates. Type of meal: full breakfast. Beds: QDT. Ceiling fan in room. Cable TV, VCR and pet boarding on premises. Amusement parks, antiques, fishing, shopping and theater nearby.

Location: One-half block from beach and boardwalk.

Seen in: New Jersey Monthly.

Certificate may be used: Anytime except July, August and weekends in June.

The Inn at The Shore
301 4th Ave, Belmar, NJ 07719-2104
(908)681-3762 Fax:(201)945-2944

Circa 1880. This country Victorian actually is near two different shores. Both the ocean and Silver Lake are within easy walking distance of the inn. From the inn's windows, guests can view swans on the lake or people perusing Belmar's boardwalk. The innkeepers decorated their Victorian home in period style. The inn's patio is set up for barbecues.

Innkeeper(s): Rosemary & Tom Volker. $40-95. MC VISA AX. 12 rooms, 3 with PB. 1 conference room. Breakfast included in rates. Type of meal: continental-plus breakfast. Ceiling fan and cable TV in room. VCR and bicycles on premises. Amusement parks, antiques, fishing, parks, shopping, sporting events, theater and watersports nearby.

Certificate may be used: Monday to Thursday, Memorial Day to Labor Day, Monday to Sunday, Sept. 15 to May 15.

Cape May
L3

The Abbey
34 Gurney St at Columbia Ave,
Cape May, NJ 08204
(609)884-4506 Fax:(609)884-2379

Circa 1869. This inn consists of two buildings, one a Gothic Revival villa with a 60-foot tower, gothic arched windows and shaded verandas. Furnishings include floor-to-ceiling mirrors, ornate gas chandeliers, marble-topped dressers and beds of carved walnut, wrought iron and brass. The cottage adjacent to the villa is a Second Empire-style home with a mansard roof. A full breakfast is served in the dining room in spring and fall and on the veranda in the summer. Late afternoon refreshments and tea are served each day at 5 p.m.

Innkeeper(s): Jay & Marianne Schatz. $90-250. MC VISA PC TC. 14 rooms, 12 with PB. 2 suites. 2 conference rooms. Breakfast and afternoon tea included in rates. Types of meals: full breakfast and early coffee/tea. Beds: KQD. Antiques, fishing, parks, shopping, theater and watersports nearby.

Location: In the heart of Cape May's historic district, near the ocean.

Seen in: Richmond Times-Dispatch, New York Times, Glamour, Philadelphia Inquirer, National Geographic Traveler, Baltimore Sun

"Staying with you folks really makes the difference between a 'nice' vacation and a great one!"

Certificate may be used: Monday through Thursday, April, May and October (except Victorian week).

Abigail Adams B&B
12 Jackson St, Cape May, NJ 08204-1418
(609)884-1371

Circa 1888. The front porch of this Victorian, one of the Seven Sisters, is only 100 feet from the ocean. There is a free-standing circular staircase, as well as original fireplaces and woodwork throughout. The decor is highlighted with flowered chintz and antiques, and the dining room is hand-stenciled.

Innkeeper(s): Kate Emerson. $85-145. MC VISA AX. 5 rooms, 3 with PB, 2 with FP. Breakfast

included in rates. Type of meal: full breakfast. Afternoon tea available. Beds: QD. Air conditioning and ceiling fan in room. Amusement parks, antiques, fishing, theater and watersports nearby.

Location: In the primary historic district, 100 feet from the beach and a half block from the mall.

"What a wonderful time. Comfortable & homey."

Certificate may be used: Oct. 15-May 15, Sunday-Thursday.

Captain Mey's B&B Inn
202 Ocean St, Cape May, NJ 08204-2322
(609)884-7793

Circa 1890. Named after Dutch explorer Capt. Cornelius J. Mey, who named the area, the inn displays its Dutch heritage with table-top Persian rugs, Delft china and imported Dutch lace curtains. The

dining room features chestnut and oak Eastlake paneling and a fireplace. The charming exterior is painted in shades of lavender and cream. A hearty breakfast is served by candlelight, or on the wraparound veranda in the summertime.

Innkeeper(s): George & Kathleen Blinn. $75-210. MC VISA AX PC TC. 8 rooms with PB. 1 suite. Breakfast and afternoon tea included in rates. Type of meal: full breakfast. Beds: QDT. Air conditioning, ceiling fan and cable TV in room. Amusement parks, antiques, fishing, parks, shopping, theater and watersports nearby.

Seen in: Atlantic City, Americana, Country Living, New Jersey Monthly.

"The innkeepers pamper you so much you wish you could stay forever."

Certificate may be used: April to mid-May & mid-October to Dec. 20, excluding weekends, holidays and special events.

The Carroll Villa B&B
19 Jackson St, Cape May, NJ 08204-1417
(609)884-9619 Fax:(609)884-0264

Circa 1882. This Victorian hotel is located one-half block from the ocean on the oldest street in the historic district of Cape May. Breakfast at the Villa is a memorable event, featuring dishes acclaimed by the New York Times and Frommer's. Homemade fruit breads, Italian omelets and Crab Eggs Benedict are a few specialties. Meals are served in the Mad Batter Restaurant on a

European veranda, a secluded garden terrace or in the sky-lit Victorian dining room. The decor of this inn is decidedly Victorian with period antiques and wallpapers.

Innkeeper(s): Mark Kulkowitz. $75-135. MC VISA PC. 21 rooms with PB. 1 conference room. Breakfast included in rates. Type of meal: early coffee/tea. Lunch, banquet service, catering service and catered breakfast available. Beds: QD. Air conditioning and ceiling fan in room. Cable TV, VCR, fax, copier and computer on premises. Amusement parks, antiques, fishing, parks, shopping and theater nearby.

Location: One-half block from the ocean.

Seen in: Atlantic City Press, Asbury Press, Frommer's, New York Times, Washington Post.

"Mr. Kulkowitz is a superb host. He strives to accommodate the diverse needs of guests."

Certificate may be used: Sept. 26-May 25, Sunday-Thursday, only.

Fairthorne B&B

111 Ocean St, Cape May, NJ 08204-2319
(609)884-8791 (800)438-8742
Fax:(609)884-1902

Circa 1892. Antiques abound in this three-story Colonial Revival. Lace curtains and a light color scheme complete the charming decor. The signature

breakfasts include special daily entrees along with an assortment of home-baked breads and muffins. A light afternoon tea also is served with refreshments. The proximity to the beach will be much appreciated by guests, and the innkeepers offer the use of beach towels, bicycles and sand chairs. The nearby historic district is full of fun shops and restaurants.

Innkeeper(s): Diane & Ed Hutchinson. $90-185. MC VISA AX DC DS TC. 7 rooms. 1 suite. Breakfast and afternoon tea included in rates. Types of meals: full breakfast and early coffee/tea. Beds: KQ. Air conditioning and ceiling fan in room. Fax on premises. Amusement parks, antiques, fishing, parks, shopping, theater and watersports nearby.

Seen in: New Jersey Women's Magazine.

"What I found was one of the most relaxing and peaceful getaways we have ever been on. We absolutely loved our suite..."

Certificate may be used: Nov. 1 through June, Sunday-Thursday, holidays excluded.

Gingerbread House

28 Gurney St, Cape May, NJ 08204
(609)884-0211

Circa 1869. The Gingerbread is one of eight original Stockton Row Cottages, summer retreats built for families from Philadelphia and Virginia. It is a half-block from the ocean and breezes waft over the wicker-filled porch. The inn is listed in the National Register and is decorated with period antiques and a fine collection of paintings.

Innkeeper(s): Fred & Joan Echevarria. $65-190. MC VISA PC TC. 6 rooms, 2 with PB. 1 suite. Breakfast and afternoon tea included in rates. Type of meal: full breakfast. Beds: QD. Ceiling fan in room. Antiques, fishing, parks, shopping, theater and watersports nearby.

Location: Historic District, one-half block from the beach.

Seen in: Philadelphia Inquirer, New Jersey Monthly, Atlantic City Press Newspaper.

"The elegance, charm and authenticity of historic Cape May, but more than that, it appeals to us as `home'."

Certificate may be used: Monday through Thursday nights - April 1 to May 31 and Oct. 1 to Dec. 23

John Wesley Inn

30 Gurney St, Cape May, NJ 08204
(609)884-1012

Circa 1869. The innkeepers of this graciously restored Carpenter Gothic home have won awards for their captivating exterior Christmas decorations, and holidays at the inn are a seasonal delight. The interior decor preserves the Victorian Era so treasured in this seaside village. Antiques are set in rooms decorated with bright, patterned wallpapers and windows decked in lace. The innkeepers also offer a restored carriage house, featuring the same period decor, but the modern amenity of a stocked kitchen.

Innkeeper(s): John & Rita Tice. $75-165. PC TC. 6 rooms, 4 with PB. 2 apartments. 1 conference room. Breakfast included in rates. Type of meal: continental-plus breakfast. Beds: QD. Air conditioning and ceiling fan in room. Amusement parks, antiques, fishing, parks, shopping, theater and watersports nearby.

Certificate may be used: September to May, Sunday-Friday.

Mainstay Inn

635 Columbia Ave, Cape May, NJ 08204
(609)884-8690

Circa 1872. This was once the elegant and exclusive Jackson's Clubhouse popular with gamblers. Many of the guest rooms and the grand parlor look much as they did in the 1870s. Fourteen-foot-high ceilings, elaborate chandeliers, a sweeping veranda and a cupola add to the atmosphere. Tom and Sue Carroll received the annual American Historic Inns award in 1988 for their preservation efforts, and have been making unforgettable memories for guests

for 25 years. A writer for Conde Nast Traveler once wrote, "architecturally, no inn, anywhere, quite matches the Mainstay."

Innkeeper(s): Tom & Sue Carroll. $95-245. PC TC. 16 rooms with PB, 4 with FP. 7 suites. Breakfast and afternoon tea included in rates. Types of meals: continental breakfast, continental-plus breakfast, full breakfast, gourmet breakfast and early coffee/tea. Catered breakfast available. Beds: KQDT. Air conditioning, ceiling fan, cable TV and VCR in room. Library on premises. Handicap access. Amusement parks, antiques, fishing, parks, shopping, sporting events, theater and watersports nearby.

Location: Cape May National Landmark District.

Seen in: Washington Post, Good Housekeeping, New York Times, Conde Nast Traveler, Smithsonian, Americana, Travel & Leisure, National Geographic Traveler.

"By far the most lavishly and faithfully restored guesthouse...run by two arch-preservationists"—Travel & Leisure.

Certificate may be used: Jan. 1-April 27 and Oct. 23-April 25. Sunday-Thursday only.

The Mason Cottage

625 Columbia Ave, Cape May, NJ 08204
(609)884-3358 (800)716-2766

Circa 1871. Since 1946, this elegant seaside inn has been open to guests. The curved-mansard, wood-shingle roof was built by local shipyard carpenters. Much of the original furniture remains in the house, and it has endured both hurricanes and the 1878 Cape May fire.

Innkeeper(s): Dave & Joan Mason. $85-265. MC VISA AX TC. 9 rooms with PB. 4 suites. 1 conference room. Breakfast and afternoon tea included in rates. Type of meal: full breakfast. Beds: QD. Air conditioning and ceiling fan in room. Antiques, fishing, parks, shopping, theater and watersports nearby.

Location: In the historic district.

"We relaxed and enjoyed ourselves. You have a beautiful and elegant inn, and serve great breakfasts. We will be back on our next trip to Cape May."

Certificate may be used: April 1 to June 15 and Sept. 21-Dec. 15, Monday-Thursday.

The Mission Inn

1117 New Jersey Ave,
Cape May, NJ 08204-2638
(609)884-8380 (800)800-8380
Fax:(609)884-4191

Circa 1912. In a town filled with gingerbread trim and turrets, The Mission Inn is unusual. The Spanish Mission-style architecture and California decor are a departure from the town's notable Victorian flavor. Listed in the National Register, it is included among the 46 original historic structures of Cape May. In keeping with the more Western appearance, the innkeepers serve treats such as Santa Fe egg rolls for breakfast, along with fresh fruits and biscotti. The meal often is served on the veranda, where guests enjoy a view of the Jersey Shore. The innkeepers provide beach passes and can arrange trolley or house tours, carriage rides, boat cruises and more.

Innkeeper(s): Judith DeOrio & Diane Fischer. $105-175. MC VISA AX PC TC. 6 rooms with PB. 1 suite. 1 conference room. Breakfast and evening snack included in rates. Types of meals: full breakfast, gourmet breakfast and early coffee/tea. Beds: KQ. Air conditioning and ceiling fan in room. Cable TV, fax and copier on premises. Amusement parks, antiques, fishing, parks, shopping, theater and watersports nearby.

Certificate may be used: Monday through Thursday, May-June/September-October, holidays excluded

Poor Richard's Inn

17 Jackson St, Cape May, NJ 08204-1417
(609)884-3536

Circa 1882. The unusual design of this Second-Empire house has been accentuated with five colors of paint. Arched gingerbread porches tie together the distinctive bays of the house's facade. The combination of exterior friezes, balustrades and fretwork has earned the inn an individual listing in the National Register. Some rooms sport an eclectic country Victorian decor with patchwork quilts and pine furniture, while others tend toward a more traditional turn-of-the-century ambiance. A few apartment suites are available.

Innkeeper(s): Richard Samuelson. $59-135. EP. MC VISA. 9 rooms, 8 with PB. 2 suites. Breakfast included in rates. Types of meals: continental-plus breakfast and early coffee/tea. Beds: QDT. Air conditioning and cable TV in room. Copier on premises. Amusement parks, antiques, fishing, parks, theater and watersports nearby.

Seen in: Washington Post, New York Times, National Geographic Traveler, New Jersey Magazine.

Certificate may be used: Monday-Thursday, Sept. 20-June 15.

The Queen Victoria

102 Ocean St, Cape May, NJ 08204-2320
(609)884-8702

Circa 1881. Christmas is a special festival at these three beautifully restored Victorians. Special tours, Charles Dickens' feasts and costumed carolers crowd the calendar. The rest of the year, well-stocked libraries, and long porches lined with antique rocking chairs provide for more sedate entertainment. "Victorian Homes" featured 23 color photographs of The Queen Victoria. Amenities include afternoon

tea and mixers, a fleet of bicycles and evening turn-down service. Suites feature a whirlpool tub, fireplace or private porch. Guest rooms are spread among three, adjacent Victorian homes.

Innkeeper(s): Joan & Dane Wells. $75-225. EP. PC. 23 rooms with PB, 2 with FP. 7 suites. 2 cottages. Breakfast and afternoon tea included in rates. Types of meals: full breakfast and early coffee/tea. Room service available. Beds: QD. Air conditioning, turn-down service and ceiling fan in room. Cable TV, VCR, bicycles, library and child care on premises. Handicap access. Amusement parks, antiques, fishing, parks, shopping, theater and watersports nearby.

Location: In the heart of the historic district, one block from the beach.

Seen in: Discerning Traveler, New York Magazine, Cover Girl, Washington Post, Victorian.

"Especially impressed by the relaxed atmosphere and the excellent housekeeping."

Certificate may be used: November through March, Monday through Thursday, excluding holidays.

Rhythm of The Sea

1123 Beach Dr, Cape May, NJ 08204-2628
(609)884-7788 (800)498-6888

Circa 1915. Many of the features of a Craftsman home are incorporated in this seaside inn, which includes large, spacious rooms, adjoining dining and living areas with fireplaces and natural wood floors. Music lovers may want to check into the Symphonic Getaway packages that this inn has to offer. From September through May, a wide selection of classical performances are presented in

conjunction with the New Jersey Symphony Orchestra. Guests are given complimentary beach passes and towels and bicycles.

Innkeeper(s): Richard & Carol Macaluso. $99-210. MC VISA AX DC PC. 6 rooms with PB, 1 with FP. Breakfast and afternoon tea included in rates. Type of meal: full breakfast. Beds: Q. Air conditioning in room. VCR, copier and bicycles on premises. Amusement parks, antiques, fishing, shopping, theater and watersports nearby.

Seen in: Atlantic City Press.

"Your home is lovely, the atmosphere is soothing."

Certificate may be used: September-June, Sunday-Thursday, non-holiday periods.

Sea Holly B&B Inn

815 Stockton Ave, Cape May, NJ 08204
(609)884-6294 Fax:(609)884-5157

Circa 1875. The home-baked cuisine at this charming three-story Gothic cottage is an absolute delight. Innkeeper Christy Igoe began her love for baking in childhood and at 12, she created her own chocolate chip cookie recipe and now has her own cookbook. Her goodies are served at breakfast and in the afternoons with tea and sherry. The beautiful home is decorated with authentic Renaissance Revival and Eastlake antique pieces. Some rooms boast ocean views. The inn is a wonderful place for a special occasion as the Igoes offer honeymoon and anniversary specials.

circa 1875

Innkeeper(s): Christy Lacey-Igoe. $80-180. MC VISA AX TC. 8 rooms, 6 with PB. 2 suites. Breakfast and afternoon tea included in rates. Types of meals: full breakfast and early coffee/tea. Beds: KQ. Air conditioning and ceiling fan in room. Cable TV and fax on premises. Amusement parks, antiques, fishing, parks, shopping, theater and watersports nearby.

Seen in: Mid-Atlantic Newsletter, New Jersey Monthly.

"You have shown us what a real B&B is supposed to be like."

Certificate may be used: February, March, April, May, Sunday-Thursday; June, September, Monday-Thursday; October, November, December, Sunday-Thursday.

White Dove Cottage
619 Hughes St, Cape May, NJ 08204-2317
(609)884-0613 (800)321-3683

Circa 1866. The beautiful octagonal slate on the Mansard roof of this Second Empire house is just one of the inn's many handsome details. Bright sunny rooms are furnished in American and European antiques, period wallpapers, paintings, prints and handmade quilts. Breakfast is served to the soft music of an antique music box and boasts heirloom crystal, fine china and lace. Located on a

quiet gas-lit street, the inn is two blocks from the beach, restaurants and shops. Ask about mystery weekends and the inn's Honeymoon and Romantic Escape packages.

Innkeeper(s): Frank Smith. $80-190. 6 rooms with PB, 2 with FP. 2 suites. Breakfast and afternoon tea included in rates. Types of meals: full breakfast, gourmet breakfast and early coffee/tea. Beds: KQD. Air conditioning, turn-down service and cable TV in room. Antiques, fishing, shopping, theater and watersports nearby.

Location: Center of historic Cape May.

Certificate may be used: Weeknights after Labor Day, before Memorial Day, excluding holidays, Victorian week, Christmas week.

Cape May Courthouse K4

Doctors Inn
2 N Main St,
Cape May Courthouse, NJ 08210-2118
(609)463-9330 Fax:(609)463-9650

Circa 1854. Several doctors have lived in this pre-Civil War home, including current owner Carolyn Crawford, a neonatologist. Each of the romantic guest rooms is named after a doctor and includes a working fireplace and whirlpool tub. There is an emphasis on health here, and the inn includes a spa with lap Jacuzzi and exercise equipment. The inn features a posh restaurant, Bradbury's, and serves a variety of gourmet fare; the seafood is especially noteworthy. The inn also features The Gingerbread Giraffe, a Victorian giftshop.

Innkeeper(s): Jack Reber. $115-170. MC VISA AX DC DS TC. 6 rooms with PB, 6 with FP. 2 suites. 1 conference room. Breakfast and afternoon tea included in rates. Types of meals: full breakfast and early coffee/tea. Lunch, banquet service, catering service and room service available. Beds: KQF. Air conditioning and cable TV in room. Spa and sauna on premises. Handicap access. Amusement parks, antiques, fishing, parks, shopping, theater and watersports nearby.

Certificate may be used: Jan. 15 to April 30, Sunday-Thursday.

Fredon B4

Natalie's Country Inn
636 Rt 94, Fredon, NJ 07860
(201)383-9577

Circa 1790. The grounds on which this 200-year-old home rests were part of a land grant from the King of England. In the 1780s, race horses were raised on the farm, and the orchard served as a popular race course. Inside, hand-hewn beams and plank floors add to the nostalgic atmosphere. The innkeepers keep the fires crackling in the common rooms, where guests are invited to simply relax and enjoy the antique-filled environment. Factory outlets, Olde Lafayette Village and the Historic Village of Hope are just a few of the nearby attractions.

Innkeeper(s): Natalie Mine. $75-115. MC VISA DS. 3 rooms. Breakfast included in rates. Type of meal: full breakfast.

Certificate may be used: November through March.

Haddonfield G3

Queen Anne Inn
44 W End Ave, Haddonfield, NJ 08033
(609)428-2195 Fax:(609)354-1273

This National Trust home is located in historic Haddonfield, which has been praised as one of the top villages in the Delaware Valley. Historic homes, museums, antique shops and restaurants are just a short walk away from this Victorian treasure, which features a charming wraparound porch. Common rooms boast elegant decor and chandeliers, and bedchambers are decorated with antiques. The historic attractions of Philadelphia are less than 20 minutes away, and the train station is within walking distance of the inn.

Innkeeper(s): Nancy Lynn. $65-85. MC VISA AX DS. 7 rooms. Breakfast included in rates. Type of meal: continental-plus breakfast.

Certificate may be used: All times except Dec. 15-Jan. 1.

Hope C3

The Inn at Millrace Pond
PO Box 359, Rt. 59 at Millbrook Rd, Hope, NJ 07844
(908)459-4884 (800)786-4673
Fax:(908)459-5276

Circa 1769. The former grist mill buildings house an authentically restored Colonial inn, set in the rolling hills of Northwestern New Jersey. Decorated in the Colonial period, many of the rooms feature original wide-board floors, antiques and Oriental

rugs. Rooms in the limestone Grist Mill, a building listed in the National Register of Historic Places, boast hand-crafted American primitive reproductions and braided rugs. The inn's restaurant features the original millrace room, complete with running water. A former wheel chamber has a staircase that leads to the Tavern Room with its own walk-in fireplace and grain chute.

272

Innkeeper(s): Cordie & Charles Puttkammer. $85-165. MC VISA AX DC TC. 17 rooms with PB, 1 with FP. 1 suite. 1 conference room. Breakfast included in rates. Type of meal: continental-plus breakfast. Evening snack and banquet service available. Beds: Q. Air conditioning and cable TV in room. Fax, copier and bicycles on premises. Handicap access. Amusement parks, antiques, fishing, parks, shopping and cross-country skiing nearby.

"The most interesting thing of all is the way these buildings have been restored."

Certificate may be used: All year, Sunday through Thursday.

Island Heights G6

Studio of John F. Peto
102 Cedar Ave, PO Box 306, Island Heights, NJ 08732-0306
(908)270-6058

Circa 1889. This Victorian home is listed in the National Register of Historic Places and is of note because it was built by renowned artist John F. Peto. His granddaughter has opened the home for guests. Filled with artifacts, eclectic furnishings, memorabilia and reproductions of his art, the studio is decorated much as it was originally. There is a large screened porch with rocking chairs providing views down the hill to the river. A full breakfast is usually served.

Innkeeper(s): Joy Peto Smiley. $50-85. AX DS PC TC. 4 rooms. Breakfast included in rates. Type of meal: full breakfast. Beds: DT. Air conditioning and cable TV in room. Bicycles and library on premises. Amusement parks, antiques, fishing, parks, shopping and watersports nearby.

Location: Island Beach State Park.

Seen in: House and Gardens Magazine, Observer Entertainer.

"Breakfast is so great—we won't need any lunch."

Certificate may be used: Anytime except weekends in August.

Manahawkin H5

Goose N. Berry Inn
190 N Main St, Manahawkin, NJ 08050
(609)597-6350 Fax:(609)978-1155

Circa 1868. Blue and red trim adds a whimsical touch to this inn's simple Victorian exterior. The innkeepers provide plenty of places to relax, including a living room stocked with books, games (including an antique chess set) and a piano. Period antiques decorate the guest rooms, each of which has its own personal flair. One room features a nautical theme with paintings in honor of the area's seafaring tradition. Another room is decorated with antique needlepoint samplers. After regular check-in hours, wine, cheese and other light snacks are served, and a breakfast buffet is prepared each

morning. Guests enjoy sampling a variety of muffins, bagels, flavored cream cheeses, homemade preserves and fruits. For those who wish to tour the area, the innkeepers offer use of tandem bicycle. For an extra charge, picnic lunches can be prepared.
Innkeeper(s): Tom & Donna Smith. $79-89. TC. 11 rooms, 4 with PB. 1 suite. 1 conference room. Breakfast, afternoon tea and evening snack included in rates. Types of meals: continental-plus breakfast and early coffee/tea. Picnic lunch, gourmet lunch and catering service available. Beds: D. Air conditioning and turn-down service in room. Bicycles on premises. Amusement parks, antiques, fishing, parks, shopping, theater and watersports nearby.
Certificate may be used: Oct. 1 to May 20, Sunday to Thursday.

Mays Landing   I4

Abbott House
6056 Main St, Mays Landing, NJ 08330
(609)625-4400
Guests at this Victorian-style mansion can relax on the bluff overlooking the Great Egg Harbor River, read on the second-floor veranda with its intricate fretwork or take afternoon tea in the belvedere (cupola) with spectacular views of historic Mays Landing. The inn is within walking distance to Lake Lenape and its various summer attractions. Each room is individually decorated with antiques, wicker, handmade quilts and other special touches. The Victorian Parlor is a place for games, reading and conversation. Refreshments can be enjoyed on one of the many porches and verandas.
Innkeeper(s): Cliff Melder. $85-95. AX. 4 rooms. 1 suite. Breakfast included in rates. Type of meal: full breakfast. Air conditioning and turn-down service in room. Antiques and shopping nearby.
Certificate may be used: January to June and October to December, anytime. July through September, Sunday to Thursday.

Newton   B4

The Wooden Duck B&B
140 Goodale Rd, Andover Township,
Newton, NJ 07860-2788
(201)300-0395 Fax:(201)300-0141
Circa 1978. Guests enjoy exploring the 17 acres of wooded grounds and fields that surround this country farmhouse. The innkeepers keep their home filled with things to do. Guests can watch movies, play games or enjoy a good book as they snuggle up next to the huge, double hearth fireplace in the inn's game room. During warm months, guest can use the outdoor pool. Rooms are comfortable and cozy, decorated in country style. The innkeepers display their unique collectibles throughout the home.
Innkeeper(s): Bob & Barbara Hadden. $90-110. MC VISA AX DS PC TC. 5 rooms with PB. Breakfast and evening snack included in rates. Type

of meal: full breakfast. Beds: Q. Air conditioning, cable TV and VCR in room. Fax, copier, swimming and library on premises. Amusement parks, antiques, fishing, parks, shopping, downhill skiing, cross-country skiing, sporting events, theater and watersports nearby.
Certificate may be used: November through March, Sunday through Thursday.

Ocean City   J4

Serendipity B&B
712 E 9th St, Ocean City, NJ 08226-3554
(609)399-1554 (800)842-8544
Circa 1912. The beach and boardwalk are less than half a block from this renovated inn. Healthy full breakfasts are served, and the innkeepers offer dinners by reservation with a mix of interesting, vegetarian items. In the summer, breakfasts are served on a vine-shaded veranda. The guest rooms are decorated in pastels with wicker pieces.
Innkeeper(s): Clara & Bill Plowfield. $60-105. MC VISA AX DS PC TC. 6 rooms, 2 with PB. Breakfast and evening snack included in rates. Type of meal: full breakfast. Dinner available. Beds: KQDT. Air conditioning, ceiling fan and cable TV in room. Library on premises. Amusement parks, antiques, fishing, parks, theater and watersports nearby.
Certificate may be used: Nov. 1-May 31, Sunday-Thursday.

Ocean Grove   F6

The Cordova
26 Webb Ave, Ocean Grove, NJ 07756
(908)774-3084
Circa 1885. This Victorian community was founded as a Methodist retreat. Ocean-bathing and cars were not allowed until a few years ago, so there are no souvenir shops along the white sandy beach and wooden boardwalk. The inn has hosted Presidents Wilson, Cleveland and Roosevelt who were also speakers at the Great Auditorium with its 7,000 seats. The kitchen, lounge, picnic and barbecue areas make this a popular place for family reunions. Two cottage apartments also are available. The inn is open from mid-May to the end of September.

Innkeeper(s): Doris A. Chernik. $46-160. PC. 20 rooms, 5 with PB. 2 cottages. Breakfast included in rates. Type of meal: continental-plus breakfast. Beds: KQDT. Ceiling fan in room. VCR, bicycles and library on premises. Antiques and fishing nearby.

Seen in: New Jersey Magazine, Asbury Park Press, St. Martin's Press, "O'New Jersey" by Robert Heide and John Gilman.

"Warm, helpful and inviting, homey and lived-in atmosphere."

Certificate may be used: Memorial Day-October, Sunday-Thursday.

Pine Tree Inn
10 Main Ave, Ocean Grove, NJ 07756
(908)775-3264

Circa 1870. This small Victorian hotel is operated by long-standing residents of the area. Guest rooms are decorated in antiques and all the rooms are equipped with sinks. Bicycles and beach towels are available.
Innkeeper(s): Karen Mason. $45-100. MAP. MC VISA TC. 12 rooms, 4 with PB. 1 suite. Breakfast and afternoon tea included in rates. Types of meals: continental-plus breakfast and early coffee/tea. Beds: QD. Air conditioning, ceiling fan and cable TV in room. Bicycles on premises. Amusement parks, antiques, fishing, parks, shopping, theater and watersports nearby.

Seen in: Country Living.

Certificate may be used: All year, Sunday-Thursday only, except on holiday weekends. Must show certificate.

Salem   I1

Brown's Historic Home B&B
41-43 Market St, Salem, NJ 08079
(609)935-8595 Fax:(609)935-6573

Circa 1738. Brown's Historic Home originally was built as a Colonial house. About 1845 the house was modernized to the Victorian Era. The inn is fur-

nished with antiques and heirlooms, including a handmade chess set and quilt. The fireplaces are made of King of Prussia marble. The backyard garden features a lily pond, wildflowers and a waterfall.

Innkeeper(s): William & Margaret Brown. $55-100. MC VISA AX DS TC. 3 rooms, 2 with PB, 1 with FP. Breakfast included in rates. Types of meals: full breakfast and early coffee/tea. Beds: DT. Air conditioning, ceiling fan and cable TV in room. Fax on premises. Antiques, fishing, parks, shopping, theater and watersports nearby.

Location: Fifteen minutes from Delaware Memorial Bridge.

Seen in: Newsday, Mid-Atlantic Country, Early American Life, Today's Sunbeam.

"Down-home-on-the-farm breakfasts with great hospitality."

Certificate may be used: Monday to Friday, all year, excluding holidays.

Sea Girt   F6

Holly Harbor Guest House
112 Baltimore Blvd, Sea Girt, NJ 08750
(908)974-8389

Circa 1905. Holly trees border the lawn of this three-story shingled cottage located eight houses from the beach. A wide front porch is framed by a border of peonies. In the summer, a full buffet breakfast is served.
Innkeeper(s): Bill & Kim Walsh. $50-125. EP. MC VISA AX TC. 12 rooms, 1 with PB. Breakfast included in rates. Types of meals: full breakfast and early coffee/tea. Beds: KQT. Air conditioning, ceiling fan and cable TV in room. Fax on premises. Amusement parks, fishing and watersports nearby.

Seen in: New Jersey Monthly.

"Your hospitality and warmth are unequaled."

Certificate may be used: Jan. 1 to Dec. 31, Sunday-Thursday nights; Friday & Saturday, Sept. 30 to April 30.

Spring Lake   F6

Ashling Cottage
106 Sussex Ave, Spring Lake, NJ 07762
(908)449-3553 (800)237-1877

Circa 1877. Surrounded by shady sycamores on a quiet residential street, this three-story Victorian residence features a mansard-and-gambrel roof with hooded gambrel dormers. One of the two porches has a square, pyramid-roofed pavilion which has

been glass-enclosed and screened. Guests can watch the sun rise over the ocean one block away or set over Spring Lake. A full buffet breakfast can be enjoyed in the plant- and wicker-filled pavilion. Innkeeper(s): John Stewart. $70-165. PC TC. 10 rooms, 8 with PB. Breakfast and afternoon tea included in rates. Types of meals: full breakfast and early coffee/tea. Beds: Q. Air conditioning and ceiling fan in room. Cable TV, VCR, bicycles and library on premises. Amusement parks, antiques, fishing, parks, shopping, sporting events, theater and watersports nearby.

Location: Six miles from exit 98.

Seen in: New York Times, New Jersey Monthly, Town & Country, Country Living, New York, Harrods of London.

Certificate may be used: May 1 to June 15 and Sept. 17 to Oct. 31, Sunday through Thursday.

Stanhope   C4

Whistling Swan Inn
110 Main St, Stanhope, NJ 07874-2632
(201)347-6369 Fax:(201)347-3391

Circa 1905. This Queen Anne Victorian has a limestone wraparound veranda and a tall, steep-roofed turret. Family antiques fill the rooms and highlight the polished ornate woodwork, pocket doors and winding staircase. It is a little more than a mile from Waterloo Village and the International Trade Zone.

Innkeeper(s): Joe Mulay & Paula Williams. $85-135. MC VISA AX DS PC TC. 10 rooms with PB. 1 suite. 1 conference room. Breakfast included in rates. Type of meal: full breakfast. Beds: Q. Air conditioning and ceiling fan in room. Cable TV, VCR, fax, copier and bicycles on premises. Antiques, fishing, parks, shopping, sporting events, theater and watersports nearby.

Location: East of the Pocono Mountains. Forty-five miles west of New York City in the scenic Skylands tourism region.

Seen in: Sunday Herald, New York Times, New Jersey Monthly, Mid-Atlantic Country, Star Ledger, Daily Record, Philadelphia, Country, Chicago Sun Times.

"Thank you for your outstanding hospitality. We had a delightful time while we were with you and will not hesitate to recommend the inn to our listening audience,
friends and anyone else who will listen! — Joel H. Klein, Travel Editor, WOAI AM."

Certificate may be used: Sunday through Thursday, November through April.

Woodbine   J4

Henry Ludlam Inn
1336 Route 47, Woodbine, NJ 08270-3608
(609)861-5847

Circa 1740. This country inn borders picturesque Ludlam Lake. Canoeing, birding, biking and fishing are popular activities, and the innkeepers make sure you enjoy these at your peak by providing you with

a full country breakfast. Some of the bedrooms have fireplaces, and all feature antique double and queen beds topped with handmade quilts. Innkeeper(s): Chuck & Pat DeArros. $85-125. MC VISA AX DS PC TC. 5 rooms with PB, 3 with FP. Breakfast included in rates. Types of meals: full breakfast, gourmet breakfast and early coffee/tea. Picnic lunch and gourmet lunch available. Beds: QD. Air conditioning and ceiling fan in room. VCR and library on premises. Antiques, fishing, parks, shopping, cross-country skiing, theater and watersports nearby.

Location: Cape May County.

Seen in: Atlantic City Press, New Jersey Bride, Mid-Atlantic Country, New Jersey Outdoors, National Geographic Traveler.

"An unforgettable breakfast. Birding at its best."

Certificate may be used: Sunday-Thursday, no weekends, no holidays all year.

New Mexico

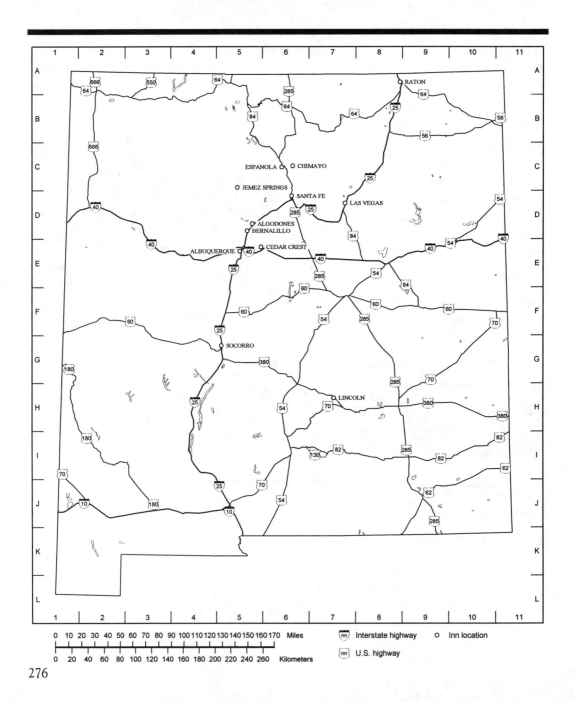

Albuquerque   E5

Bottger Mansion B&B

110 San Felipe NW, Old Town,
Albuquerque, NM 87104
(505)243-3639 Fax:(505)243-3639

Circa 1912. Just steps from the plaza in historic Old Town, this four-square Victorian mansion is a slight departure from the surrounding adobe architecture. The seven guest rooms feature brass, oak, cherry and mahogany four-poster beds. Evening wine and hors d'oeuvres are served. A soda fountain and coffee and tea bar are available at all times.

Innkeeper(s): Patsy Garcia. $79-109. MC VISA AX PC TC. 7 rooms with PB. 1 suite. Breakfast, afternoon tea and evening snack included in rates. Types of meals: continental breakfast, continental-plus breakfast, full breakfast, gourmet breakfast and early coffee/tea. Catered breakfast available. Beds: KQT. Air conditioning and ceiling fan in room. Cable TV, fax and copier on premises. Amusement parks, antiques, fishing, parks, shopping, downhill skiing, cross-country skiing, sporting events, theater and watersports nearby.

Location: In historic Old Town.

"Yours ranks with the best for ambiance and location."

Certificate may be used: January, February, June, November, December, Sunday through Friday, excludes Saturday nights.

Casa De Granjero

414 C De Baca Ln NW,
Albuquerque, NM 87114-1600
(505)897-4144 (800)701-4144
Fax:(505)897-9788

Circa 1890. Innkeepers Victoria and Butch Farmer, who appropriately named their home Casa de Granjero, or "the farmer's house," have designed their bed & breakfast to reflect Southwestern style with a hint old Spanish flair. The adobe's guest rooms all include a rustic, kiva fireplace. Cuarto Allegre is the largest suite, and includes a canopy bed covered in lace and French doors which open onto a small porch. Cuarto Del Rey affords a mountain view and includes Mexican furnishings and handmade quilts. Cuarto De Flores also has quilts,

Mexican tile and French doors leading to a private porch. The innkeepers have a hot tub room for guest use in a special garden area. A variety of baked goods, New Mexican-style recipes and fresh fruit are served each morning in the dining room or on the portal. Several recipes have been featured in a cookbook.

Innkeeper(s): Victoria Farmer. $79-149. MC VISA. 8 rooms, 7 with PB. 4 suites. Breakfast included in rates. Type of meal: full breakfast. Picnic lunch, catering service and room service available. Beds: KQT. Antiques, fishing, downhill skiing, cross-country skiing, theater and watersports nearby.

Seen in: Hidden SW.

"Wonderful place, wonderful people. Thanks so much."

Certificate may be used: January through August, Sunday through Thursday.

Las Palomas Inn

2303 Candelaria Rd NW,
Albuquerque, NM 87107-3055
(505)345-7228 (800)909-3683
Fax:(505)345-7328

Circa 1939. This adobe estate, built by a respected local journalist, features both Spanish-Pueblo Revival and Territorial Revival influences. The three-acre grounds boast beautiful gardens, orchards, an outdoor hot tub and tennis court. The home also includes five fireplaces and two courtyards. Guests can opt to stay in the adobe or in a restored, two-story boxcar. The home-baked breakfasts are served either in the dining room or in the courtyards or lawn. The inn is near many Albuquerque sites, and an excellent place to enjoy the city's famous annual balloon festival.

Innkeeper(s): Meg & Rick Stone. $85-125. MC VISA TC. 7 rooms with PB, 1 with FP. 4 suites. 1 conference room. Breakfast included in rates. Types of meals: full breakfast, gourmet breakfast and early coffee/tea. Afternoon tea available. Beds: KQD. Air conditioning and cable TV in room. Fax and spa on premises. Handicap access. Antiques, fishing, parks, shopping, downhill skiing, cross-country skiing, sporting events, theater and watersports nearby.

"What an oasis in a splendid city!"

Certificate may be used: Sunday-Thursday nights, all year (excluding Balloon Fiesta).

W.E. Mauger Estate

701 Roma Ave NW,
Albuquerque, NM 87102-2038
(505)242-8755 Fax:(505)842-8835

Circa 1897. This former boarding house is now an elegantly restored Victorian in the National Register. Rooms are done in Victorian style with views of downtown Albuquerque and the Sandia Mountains beyond. The second floor is decorated with antiques and lace. The inn is located six blocks from the convention center, which includes Civic

Plaza, an aquarium, botanical garden, museum and free trolley service.

Innkeeper(s): Charles Silver. $95-115. MC VISA AX. 8 rooms with PB. 4 suites. 1 conference room. Breakfast included in rates. Types of meals: full breakfast and early coffee/tea. Evening snack available. Beds: KQDT. Air conditioning and ceiling fan in room. VCR on premises. Amusement parks, antiques, shopping and theater nearby.

Location: Central Albuquerque between downtown and old town.

Seen in: Albuquerque Journal, Phoenix Home and Garden, Albuquerque Monthly, National Geographic Traveler, New Mexico Business Week, Golf Digest, Great Estates.

"Because of your hospitality, kindness and warmth, we will always compare the quality of our experience by the W.E. Mauger Estate."

Certificate may be used: Reservations taken ten days prior to stay, Nov. 15 to March 1, except Thanksgiving, Christmas, New Year periods, Saturday night only upon availability.

The W.J. Marsh House Victorian B&B
301 Edith Blvd SE,
Albuquerque, NM 87102-3532
(505)247-1001

Circa 1895. This three-story brick Queen Anne mansion is located in the Huning Highland Historic District. Original redwood doors and trim, porcelain fixtures and an ornate hand-carved fireplace are highlighted by high Victorian decor. A friendly ghost is said to inhabit the house, occasionally opening drawers and rearranging the furniture. The inn is listed in the national and state historic registers.

Innkeeper(s): Janice Lee Sperling, MD. $80-115. MC VISA TC. 6 rooms, 1 with FP. 1 cottage. Breakfast included in rates. Types of meals: full breakfast and gourmet breakfast. Picnic lunch available. Beds: QDT. Air conditioning in room. Library on premises. Amusement parks, antiques, fishing, parks, shopping, downhill skiing, cross-country skiing, sporting events, theater and watersports nearby.

Location: In one of Albuquerque's four historic districts, Huning Highland.

Seen in: Albuquerque Monthly.

Certificate may be used: Monday-Thursday except during Balloon Fiesta (first week in October) and major holidays. Certificate valid for Peach or Rose rooms only.

Algodones D5

Hacienda Vargas
PO Box 307, Algodones, NM 87001-0307
(505)867-9115 (800)261-0006
Fax:(505)867-1902

Circa 1900. Nestled among the cottonwoods and mesas of the middle Rio Grande Valley, Hacienda Vargas has seen two centuries of Old West history. It once served as a trading post for Native Americans as well as a 19th-century stagecoach stop between Santa Fe and Albuquerque. The grounds contain an adobe chapel, courtyard, and gardens. The main house features five kiva fireplaces, Southwest antiques, Spanish tile, a library, art gallery and suites with private Jacuzzis.

Innkeeper(s): Paul & Jule De Vargas. $79-149. MC VISA PC TC. 7 rooms with PB, 7 with FP. 4 suites. Breakfast included in rates. Type of meal: full breakfast. Beds: QT. Air conditioning and ceiling fan in room. Fax and library on premises. Antiques, fishing, shopping, downhill skiing, sporting events, theater and watersports nearby.

Location: Twenty-two miles north of Albuquerque, 22 miles south of Santa Fe.

Seen in: Vogue, San Francisco Chronicle, Albuquerque Journal.

"This is the best! Breakfast was the best we've ever had!"

Certificate may be used: Monday through Wednesday except Balloon Fiesta (Oct. 1-15).

Bernalillo D5

La Hacienda Grande
21 Baros Ln, Bernalillo, NM 87004
(505)867-1887 (800)353-1887
Fax:(505)867-4621

Circa 1711. The rooms in this historic adobe inn surround a central courtyard. The first European trekked across the grounds as early as 1540. The land was part of a 1711 land grant from Spain, and owned by descendants of the original family until the innkeepers purchased it. The decor is Southwestern, and each bedchamber is filled with beautiful, rustic furnishings. One includes an iron high-poster bed and Jacuzzi tub, others offer a kiva fireplace. Breakfasts are served in a dining room decorated with wood beams and a brick floor.

Innkeeper(s): Shoshana Zimmerman & Daniel Buol. $89-129. MC VISA AX DS TC. 6 rooms with PB, 5 with FP. 1 conference room. Breakfast included in rates. Types of meals: full breakfast and early coffee/tea. Beds: KQDT. Air conditioning in room. Cable TV, VCR, fax, copier and library on premises. Antiques, fishing, parks, shopping, downhill skiing, cross-country skiing, sporting events, theater and watersports nearby.

Certificate may be used: January-February, all seven days; remainder of year: Sunday-Wednesday based on availability.

Cedar Crest   E5

Elaine's, A B&B

PO Box 444, Cedar Crest, NM 87008
(505)281-2467 (800)821-3092

Circa 1979. This three-story log home is on four acres of evergreens in the forests of the Sandia Peaks. Rooms are furnished with European country antiques, and there are two fireplaces. Three varieties of hummingbirds visit the property. Guests enjoy views of the mountains from the inn's two balconies. Smoothies and raisin-cinnamon French toast are breakfast items.

Innkeeper(s): Elaine O'Neil. $80-90. MC VISA AX TC. 3 rooms with PB. Breakfast included in rates. Type of meal: full breakfast. Beds: KQ. Library on premises. Parks, shopping, skiing nearby.

Location: On four acres adjoining the Cibola National Forest in the Sandia Mountains.

Seen in: Fodor's, New Mexico Magazine.

Certificate may be used: Jan. 4-March 30.

Chimayo   C6

La Posada De Chimayo

279 CR 0101, Chimayo, NM 87522-0463
(505)351-4605 Fax:(505)351-4605

Circa 1891. The rustic charm of this adobe inn is matched only by the enthusiasm of innkeeper Sue Farrington, who built the original two-room guest house herself. Sturdy pine vigas, brick floors and a kiva fireplace offer guests an authentic New Mexico experience. A newly restored adobe farmhouse provides two additional rooms. The natural, no-frills setting of the inn is a treat for those weary of city life, and many guests make frequent return visits to relax and partake of the generous and delicious meals. Historic weaving and woodworking shops are nearby.

Innkeeper(s): Sue Farrington. $80-100. MC VISA DS. 4 rooms with PB, 4 with FP. 2 suites. Breakfast included in rates. Types of meals: full breakfast and early coffee/tea. Beds: QD. Fishing, shopping, downhill skiing and watersports nearby.

Location: Rural Chimayo, off the main road.

Seen in: Chicago Tribune, St. Louis Post-Dispatch, Albuquerque Journal.

"Thank you for this retreat and your thoughtfulness in all details."

Certificate may be used: Jan.5-March 9, all nights.

Espanola   C6

Casa Del Rio

PO Box 92, Hwy 84 #19946,
Espanola, NM 87532-0092
(505)753-2035

This authentic, adobe guest house is filled with local handmade crafts, rugs, bed coverings and furniture. Bathrooms boast handmade Mexican tile, and rooms are decorated in traditional New Mexico

style. The guest house also boasts a kiva fireplace. The patio window affords a view of cliffs above the Rio Chama, which is just a short walk from the home. The innkeepers also breed Arabian horses and sheep on this working ranch. Casa del Rio is nearby many attractions, including Indian pueblos, Ghost Ranch Living Museum, galleries and an abundance of outdoor activities. The adobe is halfway between both Taos and Santa Fe.

Innkeeper(s): Eileen Sopanen-Vigil. $85-105. MC VISA. 2 rooms. Breakfast included in rates. Type of meal: full breakfast.

Certificate may be used: Sunday through Thursday, December through March.

Jemez Springs   C5

Jemez River B&B Inn

16445 Highway 4,
Jemez Springs, NM 87025-9424
(505)829-3262

A little more than an hour outside of Albuquerque lies this rustic, adobe inn. For several years now, the home has been a welcoming haven for guests seeking

a natural setting, and also serves as a hummingbird sanctuary. The guest rooms surround the inn's courtyard, a striking outdoor garden with a flowing bird bath. The bath connects to a stream, which leads to the nearby Jemez River. Rooms are decorated in Southwestern style with artifacts honoring various Native American tribes. Beautiful pottery, baskets and many unique pieces decorate the guest rooms, which feature Mexican tile floors and wooden-beam ceilings. Each of the rooms is named for a different Native American nation. The inn, which affords views of the Jemez Mountains Virgin Mesa, also includes a gazebo, hot tub and exercise room.

Innkeeper(s): Larry Clutter. $70-159. MC VISA AX DC CB DS. 6 rooms. Breakfast included in rates. Type of meal: full breakfast.

Certificate may be used: September-April.

Las Vegas   D7

Plaza Hotel

230 Old Town Plaza,
Las Vegas, NM 87701
(505)425-3591 (800)328-1882
Fax:(505)425-9659

Circa 1882. This brick Italianate Victorian hotel, once frequented by the likes of Doc Holliday, Big Nose Katy and members of the James Gang, was renovated in 1982. A stencil pattern found in the dining room inspired the selection of Victorian wallpaper borders in the guest rooms, decorated with a combination of contemporary and period furnishings. Guests are still drawn to the warm, dry air and the hot springs north of town.

Innkeeper(s): Wid & Kak Slick. $55-130. MC VISA AX DC DS TC. 37 rooms with PB. 4 suites. 1 conference room. Types of meals: continental breakfast, continental-plus breakfast, full breakfast and gourmet breakfast. Dinner, picnic lunch, lunch, gourmet lunch, banquet service, catering service, catered breakfast and room service available. Beds: KQDT. Air conditioning and cable TV in room. VCR and copier on premises. Handicap access. Antiques, fishing, parks, shopping, cross-country skiing and watersports nearby.

Certificate may be used: Sunday-Thursday, Sept. 1-May 1.

Lincoln   H7

Casa De Patron B&B Inn

PO Box 27, Hwy 380 E,
Lincoln, NM 88338-0027
(505)653-4676 Fax:(505)653-4671

Circa 1860. This historic adobe once was used to imprison Billy the Kid and played an integral part in the colorful frontier days of Lincoln County. A shaded courtyard and walled garden add to the authentic

Old West atmosphere, and the comfortable rooms are supplemented by two contemporary adobe casitas. Cleis plays the inn's pipe organ and arranges soapmaking and quilting workshops for guests. Salon evenings feature classical music and Old World cookery. Dinner is available by advance reservation.

Innkeeper(s): Jeremy & Cleis Jordan. $79-107. MC VISA PC. 7 rooms with PB, 2 with FP. 2 cottages. 1 conference room. Breakfast included in rates. Types of meals: continental-plus breakfast and full breakfast. Dinner and catering service available. Beds: KQDT. Ceiling fan in room. VCR, fax and copier on premises. Handicap access. Antiques, fishing, parks, shopping and downhill skiing nearby.

Location: In the foothills of the Sacramento and Capitan mountain ranges, southeastern New Mexico. Located 185 miles southeast of Albuquerque and 160 miles northeast of El Paso, TX.

Seen in: Albuquerque Journal, Preservation News, Sunset, Travelin', Rocky Mountain News, Milwaukee Journal.

Certificate may be used: All year (Sunday through Thursday) with black-out dates: Memorial Day weekend, July 4th weekend, Thanksgiving week and Christmas-New Year's week, first weekend in August.

Raton   A8

Red Violet Inn

344 N 2nd St, Raton, NM 87740-3807
(505)445-9778 (800)624-9778

Circa 1902. Innkeepers Ruth and John Hanrahan have decorated their turn-of-the-century Victorian with a sense of whimsy. The home was built along the historic Santa Fe Trail for a minister and his wife. Rooms bear names such as The Yellow Hat or Handsome Jack. The furnishings are comfortable antiques surrounded by an eclectic mix of knick-knacks, including plate, pitcher and bowl collections. Breakfasts at the Red Violet are a treat, and the Hanrahans will provide a hearty lunch for an extra charge. Several of their tried-and-true recipes have been featured in a cookbook.

Innkeeper(s): Ruth & John Hanrahan. $50-75. MC VISA AX. 5 rooms, 3 with PB. Breakfast included in rates. Types of meals: full breakfast and gourmet breakfast. Afternoon tea, picnic lunch available. Beds: KQT. Ceiling fan in room. Cable TV, VCR, bicycles, pet boarding on premises. Antiques, fishing, parks, cross-country skiing and theater nearby.

Certificate may be used: October-January, all week, except holidays; March-May, all week.

Santa Fe

D6

Alexander's Inn

529 E Palace Ave, Santa Fe, NM 87501
(505)986-1431 Fax:(505)982-8572

Circa 1903. Twin gables and a massive front porch are prominent features of this Craftsman-style brick and wood inn. Eclectic decor, stained-glass windows and a selection of antiques create a light Victorian touch. Breakfast is often served in

the backyard garden. Home-baked treats are offered to guests in the afternoon, and the innkeepers keep a few bicycles on hand for those who wish to explore the neighborhood.

Innkeeper(s): Carolyn Lee. $75-150. EP. MC VISA PC TC. 8 rooms, 6 with PB, 4 with FP. 1 suite. 2 cottages. Breakfast and afternoon tea included in rates. Types of meals: continental-plus breakfast, gourmet breakfast and early coffee/tea. Beds: KQT. Cable TV and VCR in room. Fax, spa, bicycles, library and child care on premises. Antiques, fishing, parks, shopping, downhill skiing, cross-country skiing, theater and watersports nearby.

Seen in: New Mexican, Glamour, Southwest Art, San Diego Union Tribune.

"Thanks to the kindness and thoughtfulness of the staff, our three days in Santa Fe were magical."

Certificate may be used: November through February, Sunday through Thursday, no holidays.

Casa De La Cuma B&B

105 Paseo De La Cuma,
Santa Fe, NM 87501-1213
(505)983-1717 (888)366-1717
Fax:(505)988-2883

Circa 1940. These two locations offer different types of travel experiences. The Chapelle Street Casitas has private suites with fully equipped and furnished kitchens, living rooms and bedrooms with hand-crafted Southwestern-style furniture. The Casitas is located in the heart of the historic district and is four blocks from the Plaza, which is the center of activity in Santa Fe. Casa De La Cuma B&B has three unique rooms decorated with Navajo textiles, original artwork and Southwestern-period furniture. The inn offers views of the Sangre De Cristo Mountains and is also within walking distance of the Plaza.

Innkeeper(s): Arthur & Donna Bailey. $65-145. MC VISA PC TC. 8 rooms, 6 with PB. 5 suites. Breakfast and evening snack included in rates. Type of meal: continental-plus breakfast. Afternoon tea available. Beds: KQT. Air conditioning, ceiling fan and cable TV in room. Fax on premises. Antiques, parks and downhill skiing nearby.

Seen in: Denver Post.

"Their pleasant nature, helpful hints for visitors and genuine hospitality were memorable and valuable to us."

Certificate may be used: Jan. 5-Feb. 28 & Nov. 1-Dec. 15 (Sunday-Thursday only).

Don Gaspar Compound

623 Don Gaspar Ave,
Santa Fe, NM 87501-4427
(505)986-8664 Fax:(505)986-0696

Circa 1912. The suites that comprise this Mission, Adobe-style inn surround a lush courtyard garden, which also includes a fountain. The suites offer the opulence of a fireplace, whirlpool tubs and down comforters. The innkeepers pamper their guests by delivering the morning meal to each suite. Guests also can rent the Main House, which includes two fireplaces, three bedrooms, fully stocked kitchen and two bathrooms. Your hosts are full of knowledge about the area and happy to help plan the day's itinerary.

Innkeeper(s): Tom J. Crespin. $85-220. MC VISA AX DS. 6 cottages, 4 with FP. Breakfast included in rates. Types of meals: continental breakfast, continental-plus breakfast, full breakfast and early coffee/tea. Room service available. Beds: KQ. Air conditioning, turn-down service and ceiling fan in room. Fax and copier on premises. Antiques, fishing, parks, shopping, downhill skiing, cross-country skiing, sporting events, theater and watersports nearby.

Location: Near the plaza in Santa Fe.

"We had a fun get-away to Santa Fe."

Certificate may be used: $110-$150, 3 rooms, 3 with private baths, Monday-Thursday, November-June, Christmas & special events excluded.

El Paradero

220 W Manhattan Ave,
Santa Fe, NM 87501-2622
(505)988-1177

Circa 1820. This was originally a two-bedroom Spanish farmhouse that doubled in size to a Territorial style in 1860, was remodeled as a Victorian in 1912, and became a Pueblo Revival in 1920. All styles are present and provide a walk through many years of history.

Innkeeper(s): Ouida MacGregor & Thomas Allen. $60-130. MC VISA. 14 rooms, 10 with PB, 5 with FP. 2 suites. 1 conference room.

Breakfast and afternoon tea included in rates. Types of meals: gourmet breakfast and early coffee/tea. Beds: QT. Air conditioning in room. Cable TV on premises. Fishing, cross-country skiing and theater nearby.

Location: Downtown.

Seen in: Innsider, Country Inns, Outside, Sunset, New York Times, Los Angeles Times, Travel & Leisure, America West, Travel & Holiday.

"I'd like to LIVE here."

Certificate may be used: Sunday-Thursday, Nov. 28 to Dec. 18; Jan. 6 to Feb. 28.

Heart Seed B&B
Retreat Center and Spa

PO Box 6019, Santa Fe, NM 87502-6019
(505)471-7026

Circa 1991. Pinons and junipers cover the 100-acre grounds that surround this rustic retreat, which affords glorious mountain views. Pamper yourself at the center's spa with massages, herbal wraps and other decadent treats. The Desert Hearts Room is decorated in a '50s cowboy-cowgirl motif and includes two, queen-size beds. The Mountain-Sky Room boasts a wonderful view and a private deck. Studio-apartment rooms are available for guests planning a long stay in Santa Fe. The studios offer fully equipped kitchenettes and can sleep up to four guests. All rooms have mountain views. The hosts have designed special discount packages for those who wish to enjoy the spa along with their stay.

Innkeeper(s): Judith Polich. $79-89. VISA AX DS. 4 rooms with PB. 3 suites. 2 cottages. 1 conference room. Breakfast and evening snack included in rates. Types of meals: full breakfast, gourmet breakfast and early coffee/tea. Beds: Q. VCR, fax, copier, spa and library on premises. Antiques, fishing, shopping, downhill skiing, cross-country skiing, sporting events and theater nearby.

Certificate may be used: Monday-Thursday.

Preston House

106 E Faithway St, Santa Fe, NM 87501
(505)982-3465 Fax:(505)982-3465

Circa 1886. This gracious 19th-century home is the only authentic example of Queen Anne architecture in Santa Fe. Owner Signe Bergman is also a well-known artist and designer. Her skills have created a wonderful Victorian atmosphere with period furnishings, bright wallpapers and beds covered with down quilts. Afternoon tea is a must, as the innkeeper serves up a mouth-watering array of cakes, pies, cookies and tarts. There are seven additional rooms in a rustic, adobe home. Preston House, which is located in downtown Santa Fe, is within walking distance of the Plaza.

Innkeeper(s): Andrea Corcoran. $48-160. MC VISA AX PC TC. 15 rooms, 13 with PB, 5 with FP. 1 suite. 2 cottages. 1 conference room. Breakfast and afternoon tea included in rates. Types of meals: continental-plus breakfast and early coffee/tea. Beds: KQDT. Air conditioning and ceiling fan in room. Fax, copier and pet boarding on premises. Handicap access. Fishing, parks, downhill skiing and theater nearby.

Certificate may be used: Sunday-Thursday, Nov. 1-May 1, no holidays.

Socorro   G5

The Historic Eaton House

403 Eaton Ave, Socorro, NM 87801-4414
(505)835-1067 Fax:(505)835-3527

Circa 1881. Birdwatchers, prepare your binoculars. Within six miles of the Eaton House, bird lovers might discover 345 species throughout the year. For those who prefer other activities, this home, which was built from native materials, offers guests plenty of other reasons to stay. Rooms are filled with antiques, artwork and furnishings built by local artisans. The Colonel Eaton Room features Victorian decor, flowered tile, lace, needlework and wood furnishings. The quaint Daughter's Room features push button switches, a clawfoot tub and twin beds designed for twin daughters 80 years ago. The innkeepers also offer two casitas during the year. Each of these rooms boasts fireplaces, high ceilings and unique decor. The innkeepers serve up gourmet breakfasts, which may include entrees such as bluecorn pancakes with walnuts or French toast marinated overnight in Grand Marinier. A special basket of goodies can be arranged for those wishing to birdwatch before breakfast is served.

Innkeeper(s): Anna Appleby. $85-135. MC VISA AX. 5 rooms with PB, 2 with FP. Breakfast included in rates. Types of meals: gourmet breakfast and early coffee/tea. Picnic lunch available. Beds: KQDT. Air conditioning and ceiling fan in room. Fax on premises. Handicap access. Antiques, fishing, parks, shopping and theater nearby.

Seen in: American Way in Flight, Sunset, Atlanta Constitution, NY Times, Boston Globe, Portland Oregonian, Albuquerque

Certificate may be used: June 1 to Sept. 30, Sunday through Thursday.

New York

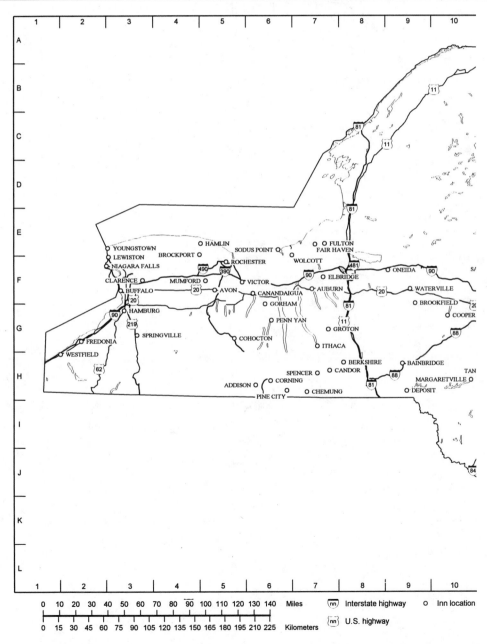

0 10 20 30 40 50 60 70 80 90 100 110 120 130 140 Miles

0 15 30 45 60 75 90 105 120 135 150 165 180 195 210 225 Kilometers

⌐nn⌐ Interstate highway   o Inn location

⌐nn⌐ U.S. highway

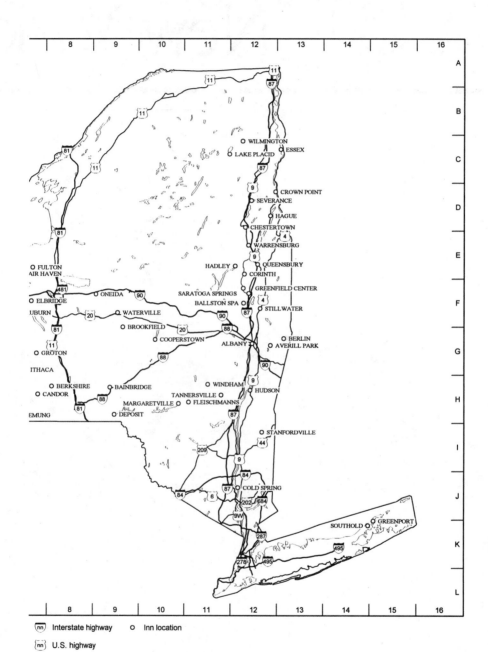

Addison H6

Addison Rose B&B

37 Maple St, Addison, NY 14801-1009
(607)359-4650

Circa 1892. Located on a scenic highway south of the Finger Lakes, this Queen Anne Victorian "painted lady" inn is an easy getaway from Corning or Elmira. The inn was built by a doctor for his bride and was presented to her on Christmas Eve, their wedding day. The three guest rooms offer authentic Victorian furnishings. Many fine examples of Victorian architecture exist in Addison. Pinnacle State Park is just east of town.
Innkeeper(s): William & Maryann Peters. $65-85. PC TC. 3 rooms with PB. Breakfast and afternoon tea included in rates. Types of meals: gourmet breakfast and early coffee/tea. Beds: DT. Ceiling fan in room. Library on premises. Antiques, fishing, parks, shopping and cross-country skiing nearby.
Certificate may be used: November-June, any day, subject to availability.

Albany G12

Mansion Hill Inn

115 Philip St, Albany, NY 12202-1731
(518)465-2038 Fax:(518)434-2313

Circa 1861. This Victorian houses guest rooms and apartment suites on the top two floors and a restaurant on the street level. Originally the home of brush maker Daniel Brown, it later served as a bulk grocery store. It is located in the historic district just around the corner from the Governor's Executive Mansion in the Mansion Neighborhood. It is a few minutes' walk to the State Capitol and the downtown Albany business district.
Innkeeper(s): Maryellen, Elizabeth & Steve Stofelano Jr. $95-155. MC VISA AX DC CB DS PC TC. 8 rooms with PB. 1 conference room. Breakfast included in rates. Types of meals: continental-plus breakfast, full breakfast and gourmet breakfast. Dinner, gourmet lunch and room service available. Beds: Q. Air conditioning and cable TV in room. VCR, fax, copier, pet boarding and child care on premises. Antiques, fishing, parks, shopping, sporting events and theater nearby.

"Rooms were beautiful and comfortable down to the shower curtain."

Certificate may be used: Entire year on Fridays, Saturdays and Sundays; subject to availability and reservation.

Pine Haven B&B

531 Western Ave, Albany, NY 12203
(518)482-1574

Circa 1896. This turn-of-the-century Victorian is located in Pine Hills, an Albany historic district. In keeping with this history, the innkeepers have tried to preserve the home's 19th-century charm. The

rooms offer old-fashioned comfort with Victorian influences. The Capitol Building and other historic sites are nearby.
Innkeeper(s): Janice Tricarico. $64-79. PC TC. 5 rooms, 2 with PB. Breakfast included in rates. Types of meals: continental-plus breakfast and early coffee/tea. Beds: DT. Air conditioning in room. Antiques, parks, shopping, cross-country skiing, sporting events and theater nearby.
Certificate may be used: Anytime, depending only on availability.

Auburn F7

The Irish Rose - A Victorian B&B

102 South St, Auburn, NY 13021-4836
(315)255-0196 (800)255-0196
Fax:(315)255-0988

Circa 1872. A Victorian setting and Irish hospitality are blended at this National Register Queen Anne Victorian. The inn features cherry hardwood floors, cherry fireplace mantels, and cherry doors. An uncluttered Victorian style includes some antiques. The innkeeper, once a head chef, provides a full gourmet buffet breakfast. On the grounds are a swimming pool and rose garden.

Innkeeper(s): Patricia Fitzpatrick. $65-105. MC VISA AX DS PC TC. 5 rooms, 3 with PB, 1 with FP. 1 suite. 1 conference room. Breakfast and picnic lunch included in rates. Type of meal: gourmet breakfast.
Catering service and room service available. Beds: KQT. Air conditioning and ceiling fan in room. Cable TV, VCR, fax and copier on premises. Antiques, fishing, shopping, downhill skiing, cross-country skiing, sporting events, theater and watersports nearby.
Location: Fingerlakes region.
Seen in: Auburn Citizen, Syracuse News Times, Fingerlakes, Central New York, Echo.

"My first B&B experience, won't be my last. Romantic."
Certificate may be used: January-May, Sunday-Saturday. September-December, based on availability, seven days.

Averill Park G12

Ananas Hus B&B

148 South Rd, Averill Park, NY 12018
(518)766-5035

Circa 1963. This ranch home in the mountains east of Albany offers stunning views of the Hudson River Valley. Visitors enjoy gourmet breakfasts and relaxing afternoon teas. There are 29 acres available to guests who wish to hike or play lawn games. The surrounding area offers antiquing, downhill skiing and shopping, and the inn's location provides convenient access to the recreation and sightseeing opportunities of three states. Cherry Plain State Park is nearby.

Innkeeper(s): Clyde & Thelma Olsen Tomlinson. $60. AX PC. 3 rooms. Breakfast included in rates. Types of meals: full breakfast, gourmet breakfast and early coffee/tea. Afternoon tea available. Beds: DT. VCR on premises. Antiques, fishing, downhill skiing, cross-country skiing, theater and watersports nearby.

Location: One mile off route 43.

Seen in: Discovery Press.

Certificate may be used: Nov. 1 to May 1, Monday through Thursday (excluding holidays).

The Gregory House
Country Inn & Restaurant
PO Box 401, Averill Park, NY 12018-0401
(518)674-3774 Fax:(518)674-8916

Circa 1837. This colonial house was built in the center of the village by stockbroker Elias Gregory. It became a restaurant in 1984. The historic section of the building now holds the restaurant, while a new portion accommodates overnight guests. It is decorated with Early American braided rugs and four-poster beds.

Innkeeper(s): Robert Jewell. $80-90. MC VISA AX DC CB DS. 12 rooms with PB. Breakfast included in rates. Types of meals: continental breakfast and gourmet breakfast. Beds: QDT. Fax and copier on premises. Fishing nearby.

Location: Minutes from Albany.

Seen in: Hudson Valley, Albany Times Union, Schenectady Gazette, Courier, Sunday Record.

"We experienced privacy and quiet, lovely surroundings indoors and out, excellent service, and as much friendliness as we were comfortable with, but no more."

Certificate may be used: Anytime Nov. 1 to April 30.

Avon   F5

Avon Inn
55 E Main St, Avon, NY 14414-1438
(716)226-8181 Fax:(716)226-8185

Circa 1820. This Greek Revival mansion, in both the state and national historic registers, has been providing lodging for more than a century. After 1866, the residence was turned into a health center that provided water cures from the local sulphur springs. The guest registry included the likes of Henry Ford, Thomas Edison and Eleanor Roosevelt. Though the inn is no longer a health spa, guests can still relax in the garden with its gazebo and fountain or on the Grecian-pillared

front porch. A full-service restaurant and conference facilities are on the premises.

Innkeeper(s): Linda Reusch. $50-85. MC VISA AX DC CB DS TC. 15 rooms with PB. Breakfast included in rates. Types of meals: continental breakfast and early coffee/tea. Picnic lunch available. Beds: KQD. Air conditioning in room. Cable TV, fax and copier on premises. Amusement parks, antiques, fishing, parks, shopping, downhill skiing and cross-country skiing nearby.

Location: Nestled in the Village of Avon, 20 minutes south of Rochester.

Certificate may be used: Not valid Saturdays May 1-Oct. 31. Minimum stay is two nights.

Bainbridge   H9

Berry Hill Farm B&B
PO Box 128, Bainbridge, NY 13733-0128
(607)967-8745 (800)497-8745
Fax:(607)967-8745

Circa 1820. Surrounded by flower and herb gardens, this farmhouse presides over 180 acres. Guest rooms are furnished in antiques and decorated with bunches of fresh and dried flowers. Organic gardens

provide 100 varieties of annuals and perennials. There are tulips, poppies, lilacs, sweet peas and in May, the fruit trees are in bloom. A full country breakfast is served. By advance reservation you can arrange for a sleigh ride or horse-drawn wagon to take you through the woods and meadows of the Berry Hill Farm, or you may stroll through the gardens and woods on your own.

Innkeeper(s): Jean Fowler & Cecilia Rios. $60-70. MC VISA AX PC TC. 4 rooms. Breakfast included in rates. Types of meals: full breakfast and early coffee/tea. Beds: QDT. Ceiling fan in room. VCR, fax, copier, swimming and library on premises. Antiques, fishing, parks, shopping, downhill skiing, cross-country skiing and sporting events nearby.

Seen in: Tri-Town News, Daily Star.

"The house is just wonderful and our rooms were exceptionally comfortable."

Certificate may be used: Jan. 2 to April 30, anytime. May 1 to Dec. 20, Sunday through Thursday only. Holidays and special events excluded.

Berkshire
H8

Kinship B&B
12724 Route 38, Berkshire, NY 13736
(607)657-4455 (800)493-2337

Circa 1809. An antique and collectible doll shop is found on the premises of this farmhouse-style inn. Post and beam construction, four fireplaces and plank floors reflect the inn's character. Kinship is centrally located for easy access to the Finger Lakes, upstate New York wineries and Ithaca, Cortland and Binghamton colleges. Four downhill ski areas and cross-country skiing are nearby. In the fall, visitors can enjoy the colors in Fillmore Glen, Treman and Watkins Glen.

Innkeeper(s): John & Carole Shipley. $45-85. TC. 4 rooms, 1 with FP. 1 suite. Breakfast and evening snack included in rates. Types of meals: full breakfast and gourmet breakfast. Picnic lunch available. Beds: KDT. Cable TV and VCR on premises. Antiques, fishing, parks, shopping, downhill skiing, cross-country skiing, sporting events, theater and watersports nearby.

Certificate may be used: April-December, Sunday-Saturday (excluding college weekends). Two-night minimum stay.

Berlin
G13

Sedgwick Inn
Rt 22, Box 250, Berlin, NY 12022
(518)658-2334 Fax:(518)658-3998

Circa 1791. The Sedgwick Inn sits on 12 acres in the Taconic Valley in the Berkshire Mountains. The main house features guest rooms, the low-ceilinged Coach Room Tavern and a glass-enclosed dining

porch facing an English garden. A Colonial-style motel behind the main house sits beside a rushing brook. A small antique shop, once a Civil War recruiting station, is designed in the Neoclassical style of the early 19th century. A converted carriage house with a hardwood dance floor and hand-hewn beams serves as a gift shop with prints, paintings, sculptures and a selection of unusual crafts and gourmet items.

Innkeeper(s): Edith Evans. $65-95. MC VISA AX DC CB DS TC. 11 rooms, 10 with PB. 1 suite. 1 conference room. Breakfast included in rates. Type of meal: full breakfast. Dinner, lunch and room service available. Beds: KQD. Ceiling fan and cable TV in room. VCR and fax on premises. Antiques, fishing, parks, downhill skiing, cross-country skiing and theater nearby.

Location: Berkshire Mountains.

Seen in: Berkshire Eagle, Hudson Valley, Albany Times Union, Good Housekeeping.

"We were absolutely enchanted. We found this to be a charming place, a rare and wonderful treat."

Certificate may be used: Sunday-Thursday, no holiday Sundays.

Brockport
E5

The Portico B&B
3741 Lake Rd N, Brockport, NY 14420
(716)637-0220

Named for its three porches, called porticos, this Greek Revival inn is situated amid blue spruce, maple and sycamore trees in a historic district. Tall columns and a cupola add to its charm. Three antique-filled guest rooms are available to visitors, who enjoy a full Victorian breakfast and kettledrum, also known as afternoon tea. The surrounding area offers many attractions, including the Cobblestone Museum, Darien Lake Amusement Park, George Eastman House and Strasenburgh Planetarium. Several colleges, golf courses and parks are nearby.

Innkeeper(s): Anne Klein. $60-70. 3 rooms. Breakfast included in rates. Types of meals: full breakfast and early coffee/tea. Turn-down service in room. VCR on premises. Amusement parks, antiques, shopping, downhill skiing, cross-country skiing, sporting events and theater nearby.

Certificate may be used: Midweek, Monday through Thursday except October.

The Victorian B&B
320 S Main St, Brockport, NY 14420
(716)637-7519 (800)836-1929
Fax:(716)637-2319

Circa 1890. Within walking distance of the historic Erie Canal, this Queen Anne Victorian inn is located on Brockport's Main Street. Visitors select from eight second-floor guest rooms, all with phones, private baths and TVs. Victorian furnishings are found throughout the inn. A favorite spot is the solarium, with its three walls of windows, perfect for curling up with a book or magazine. Two first-floor sitting areas also provide relaxing havens for guests. Lake Ontario is just 10 miles away, and visitors will find much to explore in nearby Rochester.

Innkeeper(s): Sharon Kehoe. $59-75. 5 rooms. Breakfast included in rates. Type of meal: full breakfast. Air conditioning in room. Cable TV and VCR on premises. Antiques, shopping, cross-country skiing, sporting events and theater nearby.

Certificate may be used: Jan. 1 through April 30; Nov. 1 through Dec. 31.

Brookfield
G9

Gates Hill Homestead

PO Box 96, Brookfield, NY 13314-0096
(315)899-5837

Circa 1976. This early American salt-box inn is found on 64 acres of forested farmland, and is home to a working farm and prize-winning Percheron horses. Early American furnishings highlight the inn's four guest rooms. The innkeepers also lead horse-drawn stagecoach tours of the history-rich area, complemented by a delicious, family-style dinner. Sleigh rides are available in winter, with or without dinner. Colgate University and the Upstate Auto Museum are within easy driving distance.
Innkeeper(s): Charlie & Donna Tanney. $64-79. VISA PC TC. 4 rooms, 2 with PB. Breakfast included in rates. Types of meals: full breakfast and early coffee/tea. Dinner available. Beds: DT. Air conditioning and ceiling fan in room. VCR and stables on premises. Antiques, cross-country skiing and theater nearby.
Certificate may be used: Monday through Thursday, inclusive April through November.

Buffalo
F3

Beau Fleuve B&B Inn

242 Linwood Ave, Buffalo, NY 14209
(716)882-6116

Circa 1881. With five different styles of rooms to choose from, visitors are sure to find accommodations to their liking in this Victorian mini-mansion. Artifacts accented by stunning stained-glass windows render homage to the Western New York Native American tribes in the Native American Common Area room. The French Room is dedicated to the memory of French explorer LaSalle, credited as the first European to travel through the Niagara Frontier. Absolute comfort is complete with every touch, from the Louis XIV chairs and queen-size antique brass bed to the curtains dressing the

windows. Set in the Linwood Historic District, this inn is in the middle of everything. Millionaires' Row is only one block away, in addition to nearby Niagara Falls, other historic neighborhoods, museums, art galleries and Allentown antiques. A friendly ambiance will remind guests why Buffalo is known as the "City of Good Neighbors."
Innkeeper(s): Ramona Pando Whitaker. $69-85. MC VISA DS. 5 rooms, 1 with PB. Breakfast included in rates. Type of meal: full breakfast. Beds: QDT. Antiques, fishing, downhill skiing, cross-country skiing, theater and watersports nearby.
Seen in: Buffalo News, WIVB-TV.

"Relaxing, comfortable hospitality in beautiful surroundings."

Certificate may be used: Anytime, except during May and October or on local festival weekends and holidays and holiday weekends.

Canandaigua
F6

The Acorn Inn

4508 Rt 64 S, Canandaigua, NY 14424
(716)229-2834 Fax:(716)229-5046

Circa 1795. Visitors to this Federal Stagecoach inn may enjoy afternoon tea before the blazing fire of a large colonial fireplace equipped with antique crane and hanging iron pots. Guest rooms are furnished

with period antiques, canopy beds, luxury linens and bedding, and each has a sitting area. Books are provided in each guest room as well as in the libraries. After a day of skiing and dinner at a local restaurant, guests will find a carafe of ice water and chocolates in their room. Beds are turned down nightly and in colder weather, warmed to await your return.
Innkeeper(s): Joan & Louis Clark. $60-140. MC VISA DS PC TC. 4 rooms with PB. Breakfast and afternoon tea included in rates. Types of meals: continental-plus breakfast, full breakfast, gourmet breakfast and early coffee/tea. Beds: Q. Air conditioning, turn-down service, cable TV and VCR in room. Fax, copier and library on premises. Antiques, fishing, parks, shopping, downhill skiing, cross-country skiing, theater and watersports nearby.
Seen in: New York/Mid-Atlantic.

Certificate may be used: Monday-Thursday, year-round, Bristol & Hotchkiss rooms.

Enchanted Rose Inn B&B

7479 Routes 5 & 20,
Canandaigua, NY 14424
(716)657-6003 Fax:(716)657-4405

Circa 1820. During the restoration of this early 19th-century home, the innkeepers uncovered many original features, including the wood floors that now glimmer. The chimney was taken from an 18th-century log cabin. The inn was built by the Toby family, who occupied the home for more than a century. The innkeepers are only the fourth owners and have returned the home to its original glory. Freshly cut flowers from the inn's gardens are placed in the guest rooms, which feature antiques and romantic decor. The dining room table is set with beautiful china, a perfect accompaniment to the gourmet breakfasts. Afternoon tea is served in the rose garden or in an inviting fireplaced parlor.
Innkeeper(s): Jan & Howard Buhlmann. $95-125. MC VISA DS PC TC. 3 rooms, 2 with PB. 1 suite. Breakfast included in rates. Types of meals: full breakfast, gourmet breakfast and early coffee/tea. Evening snack available. Beds: Q. Air conditioning, turn-down service and VCR in room. Fax and library on premises. Antiques, fishing, parks, shopping, downhill skiing, cross-country skiing, sporting events, theater and watersports nearby.
Certificate may be used: Sunday-Thursday, year-round.

Nottingham Lodge B&B

5741 Bristol Valley Rd, Rt 64,
Canandaigua, NY 14424
(716)374-5355

Circa 1825. South of Canandaigua Lake in the heart of the Bristol Mountain Ski Center area, this Tudor-style inn offers stunning views of the nearby mountain from its valley setting. Visitors select from the Michelle Room, with its canopy bed; Valerie Room, four-poster; and Katheryn, iron and brass. The inn's full breakfast features fresh fruit and homemade baked goods, and it is served in the dining room with its breathtaking view of Bristol Mountain. Guests enjoy gathering around the cobblestone fireplace or hiking along the stream behind the inn.
Innkeeper(s): Bonnie Robinson. $60-65. MC VISA AX DS. 3 rooms. Breakfast included in rates. Type of meal: full breakfast. Antiques, shopping, downhill skiing, cross-country skiing and theater nearby.
Certificate may be used: Jan. 1-Sept. 30, Nov. 1-Dec. 24, anytime; Oct. 1-31, Sunday-Thursday.

The Sutherland House B&B

5285 Bristol Rd, Canandaigua, NY 14424
(716)396-0375 (800)396-0375
Fax:(716)396-9281

Circa 1885. Innkeepers Cor and Diane Van Der Woude refurbished this gracious home, adding more than 40 new windows, but leaving original elements such as a winding cherry staircase and marble fireplaces. Their restoration effort has created a charming 19th-century atmosphere. Rooms feature elegant, Victorian decor, and some boast two-person whirlpool tubs. Diane serves up a bountiful breakfast each morning. The home is just a mile and a half from Main Street Canandaigua, and wineries, antique shopping and outdoor activities are nearby.
Innkeeper(s): Cor & Diane Van Der Woude. $85-145. MC VISA AX PC. 5 rooms with PB, 1 with FP. 1 suite. 1 conference room. Breakfast, afternoon tea, dinner and evening snack included in rates. Types of meals: continental breakfast, continental-plus breakfast, full breakfast, gourmet breakfast and early coffee/tea. Lunch, banquet service, catered breakfast and room service available. Beds: KQD. Air conditioning, ceiling fan and VCR in room. Fax, copier and spa on premises. Antiques, fishing, parks, shopping, downhill skiing, cross-country skiing, sporting events, theater and watersports nearby.
Certificate may be used: November, January, March, April.

Candor   H7

The Edge of Thyme, A B&B Inn

6 Main St, Candor, NY 13743-1615
(607)659-5155 (800)722-7365

Circa 1840. Originally the summer home of John D. Rockefeller's secretary, this two-story Georgian-style inn offers gracious accommodations a short drive from Ithaca. The inn sports many interesting features, including an impressive stairway, marble fireplaces, parquet floors, pergola (arbor) and windowed

porch with leaded glass. Guests may relax in front of the inn's fireplace, catch up with reading in its library or watch television in the sitting room. An authentic turn-of-the-century full breakfast is served, and guests also may arrange for special high teas.
Innkeeper(s): Prof. Frank & Eva Mae Musgrave. $65-80. MC VISA TC. 5 rooms, 2 with PB. 2 suites. Breakfast included in rates. Types of meals: full breakfast, gourmet breakfast and early coffee/tea. Afternoon tea available. Beds: KQDT. Cable TV and VCR on premises. Antiques, fishing, parks, shopping, downhill skiing, cross-country skiing, sporting events and theater nearby.
Certificate may be used: Sunday through Thursday (except May). Not valid in May.

Chemung   H7

Halcyon Place B&B
197 Washington St, PO Box 244,
Chemung, NY 14825
(607)529-3544

Circa 1820. The innkeepers chose the name "halcyon" because it signifies tranquility and a healing richness. The historic Greek Revival inn and its grounds offer just that to guests, who will appreciate the fine period antiques, paneled doors, six-over-six windows of hand-blown glass and wide plank floors. An herb garden and screen porch also beckon visitors. Full breakfasts may include omelets with garden ingredients, raspberry muffins, rum sticky buns or waffles. The inn's three guest rooms feature double beds, and one boasts a romantic fireplace. Fine antiquing and golfing are found nearby.

Innkeeper(s): Douglas & Yvonne Sloan. $55-70. PC TC. 3 rooms, 1 with PB, 1 with FP. Breakfast included in rates. Type of meal: gourmet breakfast. Afternoon tea available. Beds: D. Turn-down service in room. Antiques, parks, shopping, cross-country skiing, sporting events, theater and watersports nearby.

Seen in: Elmira Star Gazette, Chemung Valley Reporter, Evening Star.

"We appreciate all the little touches you attend to, to make our stay special."

Certificate may be used: May 1-Oct. 31, Sunday-Thursday; Nov. 1-April 30, anytime; Holidays excluded. Subject to availability.

Chestertown   D12

The Friends Lake Inn
Friends Lake Rd, Chestertown, NY 12817
(518)494-4751 Fax:(518)494-4616

Circa 1860. Formerly a boardinghouse for tanners who worked in the area, this Mission-style inn now offers its guests elegant accommodations and fine

dining. Overlooking Friends Lake, the inn provides easy access to many well-known skiing areas, including Gore Mountain. Guests are welcome to borrow a canoe for a lake outing and use the inn's private dock and beach. Guest rooms are well-appointed and include brass and iron beds. Many have breathtaking lake views. An outdoor hot tub is a favorite spot after a busy day of recreation. The new 30 km Nordic Ski Center is on site with groomed, wilderness trails, lessons and rentals.

Innkeeper(s): Sharon & Greg Taylor. $160-250. MAP. MC VISA AX PC TC. 14 rooms with PB. Breakfast and dinner included in rates. Type of meal: full breakfast. Picnic lunch, catering service and room service available. Beds: Q. Air conditioning and turn-down service in room. Cable TV, VCR, fax, copier, swimming and library on premises. Handicap access. Amusement parks, antiques, fishing, parks, shopping, downhill skiing, cross-country skiing, sporting events, theater and watersports nearby.

"Everyone here is so pleasant, you end up feeling like family!"

Certificate may be used: Any Sunday through Thursday, (Friday and Saturday are not applicable).

Clarence   F3

Asa Ransom House
10529 Main St, Clarence, NY 14031-1624
(716)759-2315 Fax:(716)759-2791

Circa 1853. Set on spacious lawns, behind a white picket fence, the Asa Ransom House rests on the site of the first grist mill built in Erie County. Silversmith Asa Ransom, constructed an inn and grist mill here in response to the Holland Land

Company's offering of free land to anyone who would start and operate a tavern. Specialties of the dining room are "Chicken & Leek Pie" and "Pistachio Banana Muffins."

Innkeeper(s): Robert & Judy Lenz. $85-145. MAP, EP. MC VISA DS PC TC. 9 rooms with PB, 7 with FP. 2 suites. 1 conference room. Breakfast included in rates. Types of meals: full breakfast and early coffee/tea. Dinner available. Beds: KQDT. Air conditioning and turn-down service in room. Fax, copier and library on premises. Handicap access. Amusement parks, antiques, parks, shopping, cross-country skiing and theater nearby.

Seen in: Country Living.

"Popular spot keeps getting better."

Certificate may be used: Feb. 16 to June 15, Nov. 1 to Dec. 20, Sunday-Thursday.

Cohocton   G5

Button's Creekside Farm B&B
9705 County Road 9,
Cohocton, NY 14826-9453
(607)566-2406

Circa 1810. Families are welcomed and encouraged at this country farmhouse, which offers something for everyone. Children are invited to help with the farm chores, which might include gathering eggs or feeding a calf. Heartier guests can milk cows or bale hay if they wish, but relaxation is always an option. Innkeepers Arlan and Carol Button have owned and operated this 350-acre sheep and dairy farm for more than 20 years, and are full of knowledge about the area. The Buttons serve traditional country fare with fresh fruit, pancakes, egg dishes, meats and

potatoes. This is a comfortable family home decorated in a simple, Early American style with antiques.

Innkeeper(s): Arlan & Carol Button. $50. TC. 4 rooms, 1 with PB. 1 suite. Breakfast and evening snack included in rates. Type of meal: full breakfast. Beds: DT. Turn-down service in room. Cable TV, VCR and bicycles on premises. Antiques, fishing, parks, shopping, downhill skiing, cross-country skiing and sporting events nearby.

Certificate may be used: Jan. 1-Dec. 31, Sunday-Friday.

Cold Spring   J12

Pig Hill
73 Main St, Cold Spring, NY 10516-3014
(914)265-9247 Fax:(914)265-2155

Circa 1808. The antiques at this stately three-story inn can be purchased and range from Chippendale to chinoiserie style. Rooms feature formal English and Adirondack decor, with special touches such as four-poster or brass beds, painted rockers and, of course, pigs. The lawn features a tri-level garden. The delicious breakfasts can be shared with guests in the dining room or garden, or you can take it in the privacy of your room. The inn is about an hour out of New York City, and the train station is only two blocks away.

Innkeeper(s): Wendy O'Brien. $100-150. MC VISA AX. 8 rooms, 5 with PB, 6 with FP. 1 conference room. Breakfast included in rates. Type of meal: full breakfast. Afternoon tea and catering service available. Beds: QDT. Air conditioning and ceiling fan in room. Antiques, fishing, shopping, sporting events and theater nearby.

Seen in: National Geographic, Woman's Home Journal, Country Inns, Getaways for Gourmets.

"Some of our fondest memories of New York were at Pig Hill."

Certificate may be used: Monday-Thursday, excluding holidays, May and October.

Cooperstown

G10

Litco Farms B&B

PO Box 1048, Cooperstown, NY 13326
(607)547-2501 Fax:(607)547-2067

The 70-acre grounds that surround this Greek
Revival farmhouse include 18 acres of mapped wetlands. The natural setting includes trails lined with
wildflowers and guests are sure to spot deer and a
variety of birds. On cold days, guests can snuggle up
to the wood-burning stove, and there are plenty of
ideal spots for picnics during the warmer months.
The scent of baking breads and fresh coffee entices
guests to the morning meal of country fare.

Innkeeper(s): Jim Wolff. $69-109. 4 rooms. Breakfast included in rates.
Type of meal: full breakfast.

Certificate may be used: April 1 to May 15 & Sept. 15 to Oct. 30,
Monday through Thursday.

Corinth

E12

Agape Farm B&B

4894 Route 9N, Corinth, NY 12822-1704
(518)654-7777

Circa 1870. Amid 33 acres of fields and woods, this
Adirondack farmhouse inn is home to chickens and
horses, as well as guests seeking a refreshing getaway.
Visitors have their choice of six guest rooms, all with
ceiling fans, phones, private baths and views of the
tranquil surroundings. The inn's wraparound porch
lures many visitors, who often enjoy a glass of icy
lemonade. Homemade breads, jams, jellies and
muffins are part of the full breakfast served here, and
guests are welcome to pick berries or gather a ripe
tomato from the garden. A trout-filled stream on the
grounds flows to the Hudson River, a mile away.

Innkeeper(s): Fred & Sigrid Koch. $60-125. MC VISA PC TC. 6 rooms
with PB. 1 cottage. Breakfast, afternoon tea and evening snack included
in rates. Types of meals: full breakfast and early coffee/tea. Beds:
KQDT. Ceiling fan in room. Cable TV, VCR, library and child care on
premises. Handicap access. Amusement parks, antiques, fishing,
parks, shopping, downhill skiing, cross-country skiing, sporting events,
theater and watersports nearby.

Location: Between Saratoga & Lake George attractions.

"Clean and impeccable, we were treated royally."

Certificate may be used: Sept. 15 to June 15.

Corning

H6

1865 White Birch B&B

69 E 1st St, Corning, NY 14830-2715
(607)962-6355

Circa 1865. This Victorian is a short walk from historic Market Street, the Corning Glass Museum and
many restaurants. Guests will appreciate the
detailed woodwork, hardwood floors, an impressive

winding staircase and many antiques. The rooms are
decorated in a cozy, country decor. Home-baked
breakfasts provide the perfect start for a day of visiting wineries, antique shops or museums.

Innkeeper(s): Kathy Donahue. $50-70. MC VISA AX. 4 rooms, 2 with
PB. Breakfast included in rates. Type of meal: full breakfast. Beds: QT.
Cable TV on premises. Antiques, fishing, shopping, cross-country ski-
ing, sporting events and theater nearby.

Location: In the heart of Finger Lakes.

*"This is a beautiful home, decorated to make us feel
warm and welcome."*

Certificate may be used: January-March, November-December,
Sunday through Thursday.

Delevan House

188 Delevan Ave, Corning, NY 14830
(607)962-2347

Circa 1933. Visitors to the Corning area will find a
touch of home at this comfortable Colonial Revival
house on a hill overlooking town. The inn's
screened porch offers the perfect spot for reading,
relaxing or sipping a cool drink. A full breakfast is
served before guests head out for a day of business,
sightseeing or travel. The Finger Lakes are 30 miles
away, and just two miles from the inn visitors will
find the city's historic district. The Mark Twain
Home and Pinnacle State Park are nearby.

Innkeeper(s): Mary DePumpo. $60-85. TC. 8 rooms, 1 with PB. Breakfast included in rates. Types of meals: full breakfast, gourmet breakfast and early coffee/tea. Beds: D. Cable TV in room. Antiques, fishing, parks, shopping, downhill skiing, cross-country skiing, sporting events and watersports nearby.

Certificate may be used: Oct. 29 to end of March, Monday-Sunday.

Crown Point D12

Crown Point B&B
Main St, Rt 9N, PO Box 490, Crown
Point, NY 12928-0490
(518)597-3651 Fax:(518)597-4451

Circa 1886. This Queen Anne Victorian inn north of Fort Ticonderoga offers a fascinating vantage point from which to view the historical area. Crown Point served as a fortress guarding Lake Champlain

during the Revolutionary War. The inn, originally owned by a local banker, boasts cherry, chestnut, mahogany, oak, pine and walnut woodwork. The spacious guest rooms, furnished with period antiques, all feature private baths. The Master Bedroom Suite includes a highback walnut bed and marble-topped dresser. Three parlors are available for relaxing and socializing.

Innkeeper(s): Al & Jan Hallock. $60-120. MC VISA PC TC. 5 rooms, 4 with PB. 1 suite. Breakfast included in rates. Type of meal: continental-plus breakfast. Beds: QDT. Turn-down service and ceiling fan in room. Cable TV, fax and copier on premises. Antiques, fishing, parks, shopping, cross-country skiing, theater and watersports nearby.

Certificate may be used: Nov. 1-April 30, any day; May 1-Oct. 31, Monday-Thursday.

Deposit H9

The White Pillars Inn
82 2nd St, Deposit, NY 13754-1122
(607)467-4191 Fax:(607)467-2264

Circa 1820. Guests are greeted with freshly baked cookies at this exquisite Greek Revival inn. This is only the beginning of a food adventure to remember. After a restful night's sleep on a hand-carved,

highboard bed, guests linger over a five-course breakfast, which might include an overstuffed omelette or a baked apple wrapped in pastry and topped with caramel sauce. Dinner is a gourmet's treat, and all meals are prepared by innkeeper Najla Aswad, whose recipes have been recommended by Gourmet magazine. The inn is decorated with beautiful antiques, rich Persian carpets and colorful floral arrangements.

Innkeeper(s): Najla Aswad. $85-125. MC VISA AX DC CB DS. 5 rooms, 3 with PB. 1 suite. 1 conference room. Breakfast included in rates. Types of meals: full breakfast and gourmet breakfast. Catering service and room service available. Beds: KDT. Air conditioning, turn-down service, cable TV and VCR in room. Fax and copier on premises. Antiques, fishing, shopping, downhill skiing, cross-country skiing and sporting events nearby.

Location: Foothills of the Catskills.

Seen in: Gourmet.

"The perfect place to do nothing but eat!"

Certificate may be used: November-April.

Elbridge F7

Fox Ridge Farm B&B
4786 Foster Rd, Elbridge, NY 13060-9770
(315)673-4881 Fax:(315)673-3691

Circa 1910. Guest shouldn't be surprised to encounter deer or other wildlife at this secluded country home surrounded by woods. The innkeepers have transformed the former farmhouse into a cozy inn with rooms boasting quilts, a mahogany sleigh bed or four-poster bed and views of the woods or flower garden. Enjoy breakfasts in front of a fire in the large country kitchen. The innkeepers are happy to accommodate dietary needs. Snacks and refreshments are always available for hungry guests in the evening. Nearby Skaneateles Lake offers swimming, boating and other outdoor activities. Dinner cruises, touring wineries and antique shopping are other popular activities.

Innkeeper(s): Marge Sykes. $55-65. MC VISA AX DS PC TC. 3 rooms, 1 with PB. Breakfast and evening snack included in rates. Types of meals: continental-plus breakfast, full breakfast, gourmet breakfast and early coffee/tea. Beds: QDT. VCR on premises. Antiques, fishing, parks, shopping, downhill skiing, cross-country skiing, sporting events, theater and watersports nearby.

Certificate may be used: Anytime as available, except Fridays and Saturdays during July, August.

Essex   C13

The Stone House
PO Box 43, Essex, NY 12936-0043
(518)963-7713 Fax:(518)963-7713

Circa 1826. Just a two-minute walk from the ferry that traverses Lake Champlain, this stately Georgian stonehouse offers a tranquil English country setting. Breakfast may be eaten in the elegant dining room or on the garden terrace, and guests also enjoy an evening snack and glass of wine by candlelight on the inn's porch. The charming hamlet of Essex, listed in the National Register, is waiting to be explored and visitors may do so by borrowing one of the inn's bicycles. Antiquing, fine dining and shopping are found in town, and Lake Champlain and nearby Lake George provide many recreational activities.

Innkeeper(s): Sylvia Hobbs. $55-95. 4 rooms, 2 with PB. 2 suites. Breakfast and afternoon tea included in rates. Types of meals: continental-plus breakfast and early coffee/tea. Evening snack available. Beds: QDT. Air conditioning and turn-down service in room. Cable TV and VCR on premises. Antiques, fishing, shopping, downhill skiing, cross-country skiing, theater and watersports nearby.

"Without a doubt, the highlight of our trip!"

Certificate may be used: May-October excluding long holiday weekends.

Fair Haven   E7

Black Creek Farm B&B
PO Box 390, Fair Haven, NY 13064-0390
(315)947-5282

Circa 1888. Pines and towering birch trees frame this Victorian farmhouse inn, filled with an incredible assortment of authentic antiques. Set on 20 acres in the countryside west of Fair Haven, this inn offers a refreshing escape from big-city life. The inn's impressive furnishings come as no real surprise since there is an antique shop on the premises. Guests enjoy relaxing in a hammock, on the porch, or by taking a stroll along the peaceful country roads. The inn is two miles from Lake Ontario's shoreline and within easy reach of Fair Haven Beach State Park and Thorpe Vineyard.

Innkeeper(s): Bob & Kathy Sarber. $50-75. MC VISA DS PC. 3 rooms, 1 with PB. Breakfast and afternoon tea included in rates. Types of meals: full breakfast and early coffee/tea. Evening snack available. Beds: DT. Air conditioning in room. VCR and bicycles on premises.

Antiques, fishing, parks, cross-country skiing and watersports nearby.

Certificate may be used: Anytime except weekends (Friday-Sunday) in July and August.

Frost Haven B&B Inn
14380 West Bay Rd, PO Box 241,
Fair Haven, NY 13064
(315)947-5331

This Federal-style inn near Lake Ontario offers a relaxing getaway for residents of nearby Rochester and Syracuse. Four guest rooms are available, all furnished with Victorian stylings and featuring bath robes and ceiling fans. Guests enjoy a full breakfast before beginning a busy day of antiquing, fishing, sightseeing, swimming or sunbathing. Fair Haven Beach State Park is nearby, and Fort Ontario is within easy driving distance.

Innkeeper(s): Brad & Chris Frost. $66. MC VISA AX. 7 rooms. Ceiling fan in room. VCR on premises. Antiques nearby.

Certificate may be used: Weekends July through Labor Day excluded.

Fleischmanns   H11

River Run
Main St, Box D4,
Fleischmanns, NY 12430
(914)254-4884

Circa 1887. The backyard of this large three-story Victorian slopes to the river where the Little Red Kill and the Bushkill trout streams join. Guests are invited to bring their well-behaved pets with them. (They are given a spot on the back porch where there are doggie towels for wiping dusty paws before entering the inn.) Kennel crates are provided when guests want to explore the area without their pets. Inside, stained-glass windows shine on the hardwood floors of the dining room, and there's a pleasant fireplace in the parlor. Adirondack chairs are situated comfortably on the front porch. The inn is two and a half hours out of New York City, 35 minutes west of Woodstock, and accessible by public transportation.

Innkeeper(s): Larry Miller. $60-95. MC VISA PC. 10 rooms, 6 with PB. 1 suite. Breakfast and afternoon tea included in rates. Types of meals: continental-plus breakfast and early coffee/tea. Beds: KQDT. Cable TV, VCR, bicycles and library on premises. Antiques, fishing, parks, shopping, downhill skiing, cross-country skiing, theater and watersports nearby.

Location: Country village in the high peaks of the Catskill Mountains.

Seen in: Catskill Mountain News, Kingston Freeman, New York Times, New York Daily News, Philadelphia Inquirer, Inn Country USA.

"We are really happy to know of a place that welcomes all of our family."

Certificate may be used: Weekends late March to mid-May and November-December; weekdays all year (all holiday periods excluded). Call for availability of other times.

Fredonia
G2

The White Inn
52 E Main St, Fredonia, NY 14063-1822
(716)672-2103 Fax:(716)672-2107

Circa 1868. Built on the homesite of the county's first physician, this elegant mansion features a 100-foot-long veranda where refreshments are served. Period antiques and reproductions are found in every bedroom. Guests enjoy gourmet meals at this inn, a charter member of the Duncan Hines "Family of Fine Restaurants." Local wineries offer tours and wine tastings. Specialty and antique shops are nearby. Chautauqua Institute is a short drive from the inn, and guests can arrange Chautauqua-White Inn packages. Fredonia is also the summer home of the Buffalo Bills. Lake Erie provides relaxation and an opportunity to enjoy a sail aboard the inn's 37-foot sloop.

Innkeeper(s): Robert Contiguglia & Kathleen Dennison. $59-159. EP. MC VISA AX DC DS PC TC. 23 rooms with PB, 2 with FP. 11 suites. 4 conference rooms. Breakfast included in rates. Type of meal: full breakfast. Dinner, lunch, banquet service and catering service available. Beds: KQD. Air conditioning and cable TV in room. VCR, fax, copier and bicycles on premises. Handicap access. Antiques, parks, shopping, cross-country skiing and theater nearby.

Seen in: Country Living, Innsider.

"Thanks again for another wonderful stay."

Certificate may be used: November-April, Sunday-Thursday, excluding holiday weekends.

Fulton
E7

Battle Island Inn
2167 State Route 48, Fulton, NY 13069
(315)593-3699

Circa 1840. Topped with a gothic cupola, this family farmhouse overlooks the Oswego River and a golf course. There are three antique-filled parlors. Guest accommodations are furnished in a variety of styles including Victorian and Renaissance Revival.

There are four wooded acres with lawns and gardens. Guests are often found relaxing on one of the inn's four porches and enjoying the views.

Innkeeper(s): Richard & Joyce Rice. $60-95. AP. MC VISA AX DS PC TC. 5 rooms with PB. 1 suite. Breakfast included in rates. Types of meals: full breakfast, gourmet breakfast and early coffee/tea. Beds: QDT. Ceiling fan and cable TV in room. VCR, fax and copier on premises. Handicap access. Fishing, parks, shopping, cross-country skiing, theater and watersports nearby.

Location: Seven miles south of Oswego on Lake Ontario.

Seen in: Lake Effect, Palladium Times, Travel, Journey, Oswego County Business, Valley News.

"We will certainly never forget our wonderful weeks at Battle Island Inn."

Certificate may be used: Sunday-Thursday.

Gorham
G6

The Gorham House
4752 E Swamp Rd, Gorham, NY 14461
(716)526-4402 Fax:(716)526-4402

Circa 1887. The Gorham House serves as a homey, country place to enjoy New York's Finger Lakes region. The five, secluded acres located between Canandaigua and Seneca lakes, include herb gardens, wildflowers and berry bushes. Part of the home dates back to the early 19th century, but it's the architecture of the 1887 expansion that accounts for the inn's Victorian touches. The interior is warm and cozy with comfortable, country furnishings. Some of the pieces are the innkeepers' family heirlooms. There are more than 50 wineries in the area, as well as a bounty of outdoor activities.

Innkeeper(s): Nancy & Al Rebmann. $60-80. PC TC. 3 rooms, 1 with PB. Breakfast included in rates. Types of meals: gourmet breakfast and early coffee/tea. Beds: QD. Air conditioning in room. Library on premises. Antiques, fishing, parks, shopping, downhill skiing, cross-country skiing, sporting events, theater and watersports nearby.

Certificate may be used: Jan. 1 to Aug. 31, Sunday-Friday.

Greenfield Center   F12

The Wayside Inn
104 Wilton Rd,
Greenfield Center, NY 12833-1705
(518)893-7249 Fax:(518)893-2884

Circa 1786. This Federal-style inn and arts center provides a unique atmosphere to visitors of the Saratoga Springs area. Situated on 10 acres amid a brook, herb gardens, pond, wildflowers and willows, the inn originally served as a stagecoach tavern. Many interesting pieces, gathered during the innkeepers' 10 years living abroad highlight the inn's interior. Visitors select from the Colonial American, European, Far East and Middle East rooms. The inn shares space with an arts center, located in the big, blue barn that serves as a local landmark. Migrating birds are known to frequent the inn's picturesque pond.

Innkeeper(s): Karen Shook. $60-150. MC VISA. 5 rooms with PB. 1 cottage. 2 conference rooms. Breakfast included in rates. Types of meals: full breakfast and early coffee/tea. Air conditioning and ceiling fan in room. Cable TV and VCR on premises. Amusement parks, antiques, shopping, downhill skiing, cross-country skiing, sporting events and theater nearby.

Certificate may be used: January-June, September, December; Sunday, Monday, Tuesday, Wednesday, Thursday. Space available.

Greenport   K15

The Bartlett House Inn
503 Front St, Greenport, NY 11944-1519
(516)477-0371

Circa 1908. A family residence for more than 60 years and then a convent for a nearby church, this large Victorian house became a bed & breakfast in 1982. Features include corinthian columns, stained-glass windows, two fireplaces and a large front porch. Period antiques complement the rich interior. The inn is within walking distance of shops, the harbor, the Shelter Island Ferry and train station.

Innkeeper(s): Bill May & Diane Natale. $65-110. MC VISA AX PC TC. 10 rooms with PB, 1 with FP. 1 suite. 1 conference room. Breakfast included in rates. Types of meals: continental-plus breakfast and early coffee/tea. Beds: QDT. Air conditioning in room. Amusement parks, antiques, fishing, parks, shopping and watersports nearby.

Certificate may be used: Monday-Thursday, year-round, excluding holidays.

White Lions B&B
433 Main St, Greenport, NY 11944-1427
(516)477-8819

Circa 1870. A mansard roof tops this Italianate-style home, which is graced by a covered porch and intricate, carved trim. The innkeepers have decorated the five guest rooms in a mix of Victorian and Art Deco styles. The full breakfasts include such items as homemade granola, seasonal fruit and a French souffle. Greenport, once a bustling whalers' village, offers a harbor, sailing, fishing, restaurants and plenty of shopping.

Innkeeper(s): Pat & Paul Kulsziski. $65-80. MC VISA DS PC TC. 5 rooms, 3 with PB. Breakfast included in rates. Type of meal: full breakfast. Beds: QD. Air conditioning and ceiling fan in room. VCR and library on premises. Antiques, fishing, parks, shopping, theater and watersports nearby.

Certificate may be used: Nov. 1 to April 30, Sunday-Thursday.

Groton   G7

Gale House B&B
114 Williams St, Groton, NY 13073-1136
(607)898-4904

Circa 1830. Old-fashioned lace, crystal, elegant woodwork and antiques fill this beautiful Queen Anne Victorian inn. Each bedroom has its own antique bed accentuated with beautiful blankets and

pillows. Wineries, lake cruises and ski slopes are nearby. The inn is only 20 minutes from Cornell University, Ithaca College and SUNY Cortland. If road trips aren't your style, relax in the parlor or browse through the inn's antique shop.

Innkeeper(s): Barbara Ingraham. $95-105. MC VISA DS. 4 rooms, 2 with PB. Breakfast included in rates. Type of meal: full breakfast. Beds: Q.

Location: Gateway to the eastern Finger Lakes.

"Everything about our stay was just perfect."

Certificate may be used: Monday through Thursday, year-round.

Hadley   E12

Saratoga Rose
4174 Rockwell St, Hadley, NY 12835
(518)696-2861 (800)942-5025
Fax:(518)696-5319

Circa 1885. This romantic Queen Anne Victorian offers a small, candlelit restaurant perfect for an evening for two. Breakfast specialties include Grand

Marnier French Toast and Eggs Anthony. Rooms are decorated in period style. The Queen Anne Room, decorated in blue, boasts a wood and tile fireplace and a quilt-covered bed. The Garden Room offers a private sunporch and an outside deck with a Jacuzzi spa. Each of the rooms features something special. Guests can take in the mountain view or relax on the veranda while sipping a cocktail.

Innkeeper(s): Nanz Merlino. $80-160. EP. MC VISA DS. 5 rooms, 4 with PB, 1 with FP. Breakfast included in rates. Types of meals: full breakfast and gourmet breakfast. Dinner, evening snack, picnic lunch, lunch, gourmet lunch, banquet service, catering service, catered breakfast and room service available. Beds: KD. Air conditioning and ceiling fan in room. Cable TV, VCR and spa on premises. Amusement parks, antiques, fishing, parks, shopping, downhill skiing, cross-country skiing, sporting events and theater nearby.

Seen in: Getaways for Gourmets.

"A must for the inn traveller."

Certificate may be used: November-May, Monday-Thursday, may exclude holidays, upon availability.

Hague D12

Trout House Village Resort
PO Box 510, Hague, NY 12836-0510
(518)543-6088 (800)368-6088

Circa 1934. On the shores of beautiful Lake George is this resort inn, offering accommodations in the lodge, authentic log cabins or cottages. Many of the guest rooms in the lodge boast lake views, while the log cabins offer jetted tubs and fireplaces. The guest quarters are furnished comfortably. The emphasis here is on the abundance of outdoor activities. Outstanding cross-country skiing, downhill skiing and snowmobiling are found nearby. The inn furnishes bicycles, canoes, kayaks, paddle boats, rowboats, sleds, skis and toboggans. Summertime evenings offer games of capture-the-flag and soccer. Other activities include basketball, horseshoes, ping pong, a putting green and volleyball.

Innkeeper(s): Scott & Alice Patchett. $46-94. AP. MC VISA AX DS PC TC. 13 rooms, 11 with PB, 15 with FP. 1 suite. 15 cottages. 2 conference rooms. Types of meals: continental-plus breakfast and early coffee/tea. Banquet service available. Beds: QDT. Cable TV and VCR in room. Spa, swimming, bicycles, tennis, library and child care on premises. Handicap access. Amusement parks, antiques, fishing, parks, shopping, skiing and watersports nearby.

"My wife and I felt the family warmth at this resort. There wasn't that coldness you get at larger resorts."

Certificate may be used: Weekdays except June 1 through Sept. 15.

Hamburg G3

Sharon's B&B Lake House
4862 Lake Shore Rd, Hamburg, NY 14075
(716)627-7561

Circa 1935. This historic lakefront house is located 10 miles from Buffalo and 45 minutes from Niagara Falls. Overlooking Lake Erie, the West Lake Room and the Upper Lake Room provide spectacular views. The home's beautiful furnishings offer additional delights.

Innkeeper(s): Sharon & Vince De Maria. $100-110. PC TC. 2 rooms, 1 with PB. Breakfast included in rates. Type of meal: gourmet breakfast. Afternoon tea available. Beds: D. Ceiling fan and cable TV in room. VCR and swimming on premises. Fishing, parks, shopping, downhill skiing, cross-country skiing, theater and watersports nearby.

Location: On the shore of Lake Erie.

"Spectacular view, exquisitely furnished."

Certificate may be used: Anytime, all year.

Hamlin E5

Sandy Creek Manor House
1960 Redman Rd, Hamlin, NY 14464
(716)964-7528 (800)594-0400

Circa 1910. Six acres of woods and perennial gardens provide the setting for this English Tudor house. Stained glass, polished woods and Amish quilts add warmth to the home. Breakfast is served on the open porch in summer. Fisherman's Landing, on the banks of Sandy Creek, is a stroll away. Bullhead, trout and salmon are popular catches. There is a gift shop on premises. Ask about murder-mystery and sweetheart dinner packages.

Innkeeper(s): Shirley Hollink & James Krempasky. $50-70. MC VISA AX DS PC TC. 4 rooms, 1 with PB. Breakfast, afternoon tea and evening snack included in rates. Types of meals: continental breakfast, continental-plus breakfast, gourmet breakfast and early coffee/tea. Beds: KQDT. Air conditioning in room. VCR, bicycles and library on premises. Antiques, fishing, parks, shopping, downhill skiing, cross-country skiing, sporting events and watersports nearby.

Location: Four miles north of Route 104; 25 miles northwest of Rochester; located near the Seaway Trail.

Seen in: Rochester Times Union.

"Delightful in every way."

Certificate may be used: Anytime.

Hudson H12

The Inn at Blue Stores
2323 Rt 9, Hudson, NY 12534-0099
(518)537-4277

Circa 1908. A rural Hudson Valley setting may seem an unusual place for a Spanish-style inn, but this former gentlemen's farm now provides a unique setting for those seeking a relaxing getaway. Visitors

will enjoy the inn's clay tile roof and stucco exterior, along with its impressive interior, featuring black oak woodwork, leaded-glass entry and stained glass. Visitors are treated to full breakfasts and refreshing afternoon teas. The spacious porch and swimming pool are favorite spots for relaxing and socializing.
Innkeeper(s): Linda & Robert Saulpaugh. $99-165. MC VISA. 5 rooms, 3 with PB. 1 suite. Breakfast included in rates. Types of meals: full breakfast and early coffee/tea. Afternoon tea available. Beds: KQT. Air conditioning and VCR in room. Fax and swimming on premises. Antiques, cross-country skiing, sporting events and theater nearby.
Certificate may be used: November-April, Monday-Thursday, except holidays.

Ithaca G7

A Slice of Home B&B
178 N Main St, Ithaca, NY 14883
(607)589-6073

Circa 1850. This Italianate inn's location, approximately equidistant from Ithaca and Elmira, offers a fine vantage point for exploring the Finger Lakes winery region. Although the area is well-known for its scenery, many recreational opportunities also are available. The innkeeper is happy to help guests plan tours, and has a special fondness for those traveling by bicycle. The inn offers five guest rooms, furnished in country decor. Guests may relax by taking a stroll on the inn's 12 acres, mountain hiking or having a cookout in the inn's back yard. Guests can begin a cross-country ski excursion right from the back porch.
Innkeeper(s): Bea Brownell. $35-120. PC. 5 rooms, 1 with PB. 1 suite. Breakfast and evening snack included in rates. Types of meals: full breakfast and early coffee/tea. Picnic lunch available. Beds: KQD. Air conditioning and cable TV in room. VCR, copier and bicycles on premises. Antiques, fishing, parks, shopping, downhill skiing, cross-country skiing, sporting events, theater and watersports nearby.
Certificate may be used: All year, some weekends excepted.

La Tourelle Country Inn
1150 Danby Rd, Rt 96B,
Ithaca, NY 14850-9406
(607)273-2734 (800)765-1492
Fax:(607)273-4821

Circa 1986. This white stucco European-style country inn is located on 70 acres three miles from town, allowing for wildflower walks, cross-country skiing and all-season hiking. Adjacent Buttermilk Falls State Park provides stone paths, waterfalls and streams. The inn is decorated with a hint of European decor and includes fireplace suites and tower suites. A continental breakfast arrives at your door in a basket, French Provincial style, and guests often tote it to the patio or gazebo to enjoy views of the rolling countryside. There is an indoor tennis court.

Innkeeper(s): Leslie Leonard. $75-125. EP. MC VISA AX TC. 34 rooms with PB, 1 with FP. 1 conference room. Breakfast included in rates. Types of meals: continental breakfast and early coffee/tea. Evening snack, banquet service and catering service available. Beds: KQ. Air conditioning, cable TV and VCR in room. Copier and tennis on premises. Handicap access. Antiques, fishing, parks, shopping, skiing, sporting events, theater and watersports nearby.
Certificate may be used: Sunday through Thursday only.

Log Country Inn - B&B
PO Box 581, Ithaca, NY 14851-0581
(607)589-4771 (800)274-4771
Fax:(607)589-6151

Circa 1969. As the name indicates, this bed & breakfast is indeed fashioned from logs and rests in a picturesque country setting surrounding by 15 wooded acres. The cozy rooms are rustic with exposed beams and country furnishings. The decor is dotted with a European influence, as is the morning meal. The innkeepers, who moved to the United States from Europe, offer plenty of relaxing amenities, including a Finnish dry sauna.
Innkeeper(s): Wanda Grunberg. $45-65. MC VISA TC. 3 rooms, 1 with PB. 1 suite. Breakfast and afternoon tea included in rates. Type of meal:

full breakfast. Beds: QDT. Cable TV in room. VCR, fax and sauna on premises. Parks, cross-country skiing and sporting events nearby.
Certificate may be used: Jan. 15-May 1, Sunday-Thursday.

Rose Inn

Rt 34 N, Box 6576, Ithaca, NY 14851
(607)533-7905 Fax:(607)533-7908

Circa 1848. This classic Italianate mansion has long been famous for its circular staircase of Honduran mahogany. It is owned by Sherry Rosemann, a noted interior designer specializing in mid-19th-century architecture and furniture, and her husband Charles, a hotelier from Germany. On 20 landscaped acres, it is 10 minutes from Cornell University. The inn has been the recipient of many awards for its lodging and dining.

Innkeeper(s): Charles & Sherry Rosemann. $100-275. MC VISA PC TC. 17 rooms with PB, 2 with FP. 5 suites. 1 cottage. 1 conference room. Breakfast included in rates. Type of meal: full breakfast. Banquet service, catering service and catered breakfast available. Beds: KQDT. Air conditioning, turn-down service and ceiling fan in room. Cable TV, VCR, fax, copier and library on premises. Antiques, fishing, parks, shopping, downhill skiing, cross-country skiing, sporting events, theater and watersports nearby.

Seen in: Country Inn, New York Times, Ithaca Times, New Woman, Toronto Globe & Mail, Newsday.

"The blending of two outstanding talents, which when combined with your warmth, produce the ultimate experience in being away from home. Like staying with friends in their beautiful home."

Certificate may be used: Dec. 1-March 31, Sunday through Friday; April 1-Nov. 30, Monday through Thursday.

Lake Placid   C11

Interlaken Inn

15 Interlaken Ave,
Lake Placid, NY 12946-1142
(518)523-3180 (800)428-4369
Fax:(518)523-0117

Circa 1906. The five-course dinner at this Victorian inn is prepared by owner Carol Johnson and her talented staff. The high-quality cuisine is rivaled only by the rich decor of this cozy inn. Walnut paneling covers the dining room walls, which are topped with a tin ceiling. Bedrooms are carefully decorated with wallpapers, fresh flowers and luxurious bed coverings. Spend the afternoon gazing at the mountains and lakes that surround this Adirondack hideaway, or visit the Olympic venues.

Innkeeper(s): Kathy & Jim Gonzales. $120-180. MAP. MC VISA AX. 11 rooms with PB. 1 suite. Breakfast, afternoon tea and dinner included in rates. Types of meals: full breakfast and early coffee/tea. Beds: KQD. Ceiling fan in room. Cable TV, VCR and fax on premises. Antiques, fishing, shopping, downhill skiing, cross-country skiing, sporting events, theater and watersports nearby.

Location: Quaint Olympic Village.
Seen in: Outside, Country Inns, Wine Trader.
Certificate may be used: Sunday through Thursday.

Lewiston   F3

The Cameo Inn

4710 Lower River Rd,
Lewiston, NY 14092-1053
(716)745-3034

Circa 1875. This classic Queen Anne Victorian inn offers a breathtaking view of the lower Niagara River. Located on the Seaway Trail, the inn offers convenient access to sightseeing in this popular region. The inn's interior features family heirlooms and period antiques, and visitors choose from four guest rooms, including a three-room suite overlooking the river. Breakfast is served buffet-style, and the entrees, which change daily, may include crepes Benedict, German oven pancakes or Grand Marnier French toast. Area attractions include Old Fort Niagara, outlet malls and several state parks.

Innkeeper(s): Gregory Fisher. $65-115. 4 rooms, 2 with PB. 1 suite. Breakfast included in rates. Type of meal: full breakfast. Beds: QDT. Ceiling fan and cable TV in room. Amusement parks, antiques, fishing, shopping, downhill skiing, cross-country skiing, sporting events, theater and watersports nearby.

Location: Five miles north of Niagara Falls.
Seen in: Country Folk Art, Esquire, Journey, Seaway Trail, Waterways, Buffalo News.

"I made the right choice when I selected Cameo."

Certificate may be used: Anytime Nov. 15-April 30; Sunday through Thursday May 1-Nov. 14. Holidays and special event periods excluded. All subject to availability.

The Little Blue House B&B

115 Center St, Lewiston, NY 14092-1537
(716)754-9425

Circa 1906. Located in the heart of the village's main street, this Colonial inn offers charming accommodations and convenient access to area activities. Three unique guest rooms are available, including a Chinese-themed room with a king bed and a Victorian-style room with a queen bed. The inn's decor includes antiques, collectibles and contemporary art. Ten minutes away are the American and Canadian Falls.

Innkeeper(s): Michael & Margot Kornfeld. $65-175. AX PC TC. 3 rooms, 1 with PB. 1 suite. Breakfast included in rates. Types of meals: continental-plus breakfast and gourmet breakfast. Beds: KQ. Air conditioning, ceiling fan and cable TV in room. VCR on premises. Amusement parks, antiques, fishing, parks, shopping, cross-country skiing, sporting events and theater nearby.

Certificate may be used: May through October-Sunday through Wednesday. November through April-seven days per week. Holidays and special events excluded.

Margaretville H10

Margaretville Mountain Inn B&B
Margaretville Mountain Rd,
Margaretville, NY 12455-9735
(914)586-3933

Circa 1886. Reminiscent of the Victorian Era, this home rests on the site of the nation's first cauliflower farm. The owners have restored the slate roof, elaborate exterior woodwork and decorative interior woodwork. A full breakfast is served in the formal dining room on English china, or guests can enjoy the morning meal on the veranda, which overlooks the Catskill Mountains. The surrounding area offers a variety of activities including antique shopping, ice skating and hiking.

Innkeeper(s): Carol Molnar. $50-85. MC VISA AX. 7 rooms, 2 with PB. Breakfast included in rates. Types of meals: full breakfast and gourmet breakfast. Beds: QDT. Fax and computer on premises. Fishing nearby.

Location: In the Catskill Mountains.

"Truly a step back in time to all that was charming, elegant and wholesome—right here in the 20th century."

Certificate may be used: Sunday-Thursday, non-holidays. Weekends only in March and April.

Mumford F5

Genesee Country Inn
948 George St, Mumford, NY 14511-0340
(716)538-2500 (800)697-8297
Fax:(716)538-4565

Circa 1833. This stone house with two-and-a-half-foot-thick limestone walls served as a plaster mill and later as a hub and wheel factory. Now it is an inn set on six acres with views of streams, woodlands and ponds. There is a deck adjacent to a 16-foot waterfall. Ask for a garden room and enjoy a fireplace and your own balcony overlooking the mill ponds.

Innkeeper(s): Kim Rasmussen. $85-130. MC VISA DC DS. 9 rooms with PB, 3 with FP. Breakfast and afternoon tea included in rates. Type of meal: full breakfast. Beds: Q. Air conditioning in room. Fax and copier on premises. Amusement parks, antiques, parks, downhill skiing and watersports nearby.

"You may never want to leave."

Certificate may be used: Dec. 1 to April 30, Sunday-Friday. No fireplace rooms eligible.

Niagara Falls F3

The Cameo Manor North
3881 Lower River Rd,
Niagara Falls, NY 14174
(716)745-3034

Circa 1860. This Colonial Revival inn offers a restful setting ideal for those seeking a peaceful getaway. The inn's three secluded acres add to its romantic setting, as does an interior that features several fireplaces. Visitors select from three suites, which feature private sun rooms, or two guest rooms that share a bath. Popular spots with guests include the library, outdoor deck and solarium. Fort Niagara and Wilson-Tuscarora state parks are nearby, and the American and Canadian Falls are within easy driving distance of the inn. The inn is actually located about six miles from Niagara Falls in the nearby village of Youngstown.

Innkeeper(s): Gregory Fisher. $75-175. 4 rooms. Breakfast included in rates. Type of meal: full breakfast.

Seen in: Country Folk Art, Esquire, Journey, Seaway Trail, Waterways, Buffalo News.

"I made the right choice when I selected Cameo."

Certificate may be used: Anytime Nov. 15-April 30, Sunday-Thursday; May 1-Nov. 14, holidays and special event periods excluded. All subject to availability.

Oneida F9

The Pollyanna
302 Main St, Oneida, NY 13421-2125
(315)363-0524

Circa 1862. Roses and iris grace the gardens of this Italian villa. Inside are special collections, antiques and three Italian-marble fireplaces. Of the two crystal chandeliers, one is still piped for gas. A hand-crafted white wool and mohair rug runs up the staircase to the rooms where guests are pampered with

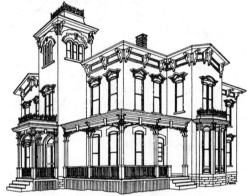

bed warmers and down quilts. The innkeeper teaches spinning, felting, bobbin lace and other crafts. The home is near the Oneida Indian Casino, Oneida silver outlet, and it's six miles to Vernon Downs Racetrack.

Innkeeper(s): Doloria & Ken Chapin. $55-125. MC VISA AX DS TC. 5 rooms with PB. 2 suites. 2 conference rooms. Breakfast included in rates. Types of meals: full breakfast, gourmet breakfast and early coffee/tea. Beds: QD. Air conditioning and cable TV in room. Antiques, fishing, parks, shopping, downhill skiing, cross-country skiing, sporting events, theater and watersports nearby.

Location: In historic district, between Syracuse and Utica.

Seen in: Oneida Daily Dispatch, Historical Chronicle.

"Don't miss the gardens. They are superb. We love your beds."

Certificate may be used: Monday-Thursday year-round, subject to availability.

Penn Yan G6

Finton's Landing
661 E Lake Rd, Penn Yan, NY 14527-9421
(315)536-3146

Circa 1861. This Victorian house is located on the east shore of Keuka Lake, with 165 feet of private beach. Wonderful views of green lawns, hills and the crystal-clear water may be enjoyed from the porch. The inn features a country decor. Nearby are Mennonite shops and craft stores to explore.

Innkeeper(s): Doug & Arianne Tepper. $79. MC VISA TC. 4 rooms. 4 conference rooms. Breakfast included in rates. Types of meals: continental-plus breakfast, full breakfast, gourmet breakfast and early coffee/tea. Beds: DT. Ceiling fan in room. Antiques, fishing, parks, shopping, downhill skiing, cross-country skiing and watersports nearby.

Certificate may be used: Sunday-Thursday.

Pine City H6

Rufus Tanner House
60 Sagetown Rd, Pine City, NY 14871
(607)732-0213

Circa 1864. This Greek Revival farmhouse sits among century-old sugar maple and dwarf fruit trees. Its spacious rooms are filled with antiques and other period furnishings that add greatly to the inn's ambiance. The four guest rooms include the first-floor Master Bedroom, with its marble-topped high Victorian furniture, and a bath with two-person shower, whirlpool and black marble floor. Guests are welcome to use the treadmill and weight machine in the basement. The Elmira-Corning area near the inn offers many attractions, including Mark Twain's Burial Site and the National Soaring Museum.

Innkeeper(s): Bill Knapp & John Gibson. $55-95. MC VISA TC. 4 rooms with PB. Breakfast included in rates. Types of meals: full breakfast and early coffee/tea. Dinner available. Beds: QD. Cable TV, VCR and spa on premises. Antiques, fishing, parks, shopping and theater nearby.

Certificate may be used: Sunday-Thursday.

Queensbury E12

The Crislip's B&B
693 Ridge Rd, Queensbury, NY 12804
(518)793-6869

Circa 1802. This Federal-style house was built by Quakers and was once owned by the area's first doctor, who used it as a training center for young interns. There's an acre of lawns and annual gardens and a Victorian Italianate veranda overlooks the Green Mountains. The inn is furnished with 18th-century antiques and reproductions, including four-poster canopy beds and highboys. There's a keeping room with a huge fireplace. Historic stone walls flank the property.

Innkeeper(s): Ned & Joyce Crislip. $45-75. MC VISA TC. 3 rooms with PB. Breakfast included in rates. Types of meals: full breakfast and early coffee/tea. Beds: KD. Air conditioning in room. Cable TV on premises. Amusement parks, antiques, fishing, parks, shopping, downhill skiing, cross-country skiing, sporting events, theater and watersports nearby.

Location: Lake George, Saratoga area.

Certificate may be used: November through May, Sunday-Thursday.

Sanford's Ridge B&B

749 Ridge Rd, Queensbury, NY 12804
(518)793-4923

Circa 1797. Visitors to the Adirondacks will find a bit of history and more than a little hospitality at this Federal-style inn, built by David Sanford after the Revolutionary War. The inn has retained its original elegance and added a few modern touches such as a slate billiard table in the carriage house, an in-ground swimming pool and a sunny outdoor deck. Visitors select from the Haviland, Sanford and Webster rooms, all with private baths and each with its special charms. The full breakfasts include a special entree of the day and grape jam from fruit grown on the premises. Lake George is a short drive away.
Innkeeper(s): Carolyn Rudolph. $65-95. MC VISA PC TC. 3 rooms with PB, 2 with FP. Breakfast included in rates. Type of meal: full breakfast. Beds: KQT. Air conditioning in room. Cable TV, swimming and library on premises. Amusement parks, antiques, fishing, parks, shopping, downhill skiing, cross-country skiing, theater and watersports nearby.

Certificate may be used: November-April except holiday weekends or holiday periods.

Rochester   F5

"428 Mt. Vernon" - A B&B Inn

428 Mount Vernon Ave,
Rochester, NY 14620-2710
(716)271-0792 (800)836-3159

Circa 1917. Victorian furnishings and decor grace the interior of this stately Irish manor house. Set on two lush acres of shade trees and foliage, guests will find this a relaxing, secluded spot. Guests can create their morning meals from a varied breakfast menu. The inn is adjacent to Highland Park, a perfect spot for a picnic or birdwatching.
Innkeeper(s): Philip & Claire Lanzatella. $99. MC VISA AX TC. 7 rooms with PB, 3 with FP. 1 conference room. Breakfast included in rates. Types of meals: full breakfast, gourmet breakfast and early coffee/tea. Catering service and room service available. Beds: QDT. Air conditioning, turn-down service, ceiling fan and cable TV in room. Amusement parks, antiques, parks, cross-country skiing and theater nearby.

"Everything was wonderful, they took care in every detail."

Certificate may be used: Jan. 15-April 1-Sunday-Thursday.

Dartmouth House B&B

215 Dartmouth St, Rochester, NY 14607
(716)271-7872 (800)724-6298
Fax:(716)473-0778

Circa 1905. The lavish, four-course breakfasts served daily at this beautiful turn-of-the-century Edwardian home are unforgettable. Innkeeper and gourmet cook Ellie Klein starts off the meal with

special fresh juice, which is served in the parlor. From this point, guests are seated at the dining table to enjoy a series of delectable dishes, such as pears poached in port wine, a mouth-watering entree, a light, lemon ice and a rich dessert. And each of the courses is served on a separate pattern of depression glass. If the breakfast isn't enough, Ellie and husband, Bill, have stocked the individually decorated guest rooms with flowers, fluffy towels, bathrobes and special bath amenities. Each of the bedchambers boast antique collectibles and guests can soak in inviting clawfoot tubs.
Innkeeper(s): Elinor & Bill Klein. $75-125. MC VISA AX PC TC. 4 rooms with PB. Breakfast, afternoon tea and evening snack included in rates. Types of meals: full breakfast, gourmet breakfast and early coffee/tea. Room service available. Beds: KQT. Air conditioning, turn-down service, ceiling fan and VCR in room. Cable TV, fax, bicycles and library on premises. Antiques, parks, theater and watersports nearby.

Seen in: Democrat & Chronicle, DAKA, Genesee Country, Seaway Trail, Oneida News, Travelers News.

"The food was fabulous, the company fascinating, and the personal attention beyond comparison. You made me feel at home instantly."

Certificate may be used: Jan. 1 to April 1, Monday through Thursday, excluding holidays and special events.

Strawberry Castle B&B

1883 Penfield Rd, Rt 441,
Rochester, NY 14526
(716)385-3266

Circa 1875. A rosy brick Italianate villa, Strawberry Castle was once known for the grapes and strawberries grown on the property. Ornate plaster ceilings and original inside shutters are special features. There are six roof levels, carved ornamental brackets, and columned porches topped by a white cupola.
Innkeeper(s): Anne Felker. $60-95. MC VISA AX. 3 rooms with PB. 1 suite. 1 conference room. Breakfast included in rates. Type of meal: full breakfast. Beds: D. Air conditioning in room. Cable TV on premises. Amusement parks, antiques, fishing, shopping, downhill skiing, sporting events and theater nearby.

Location: East of Rochester on Route 441.

Seen in: Upstate.

"You have a most unusual place. We applaud your restoration efforts and are thankful you've made it available to travelers."

Certificate may be used: Sunday-Thursday, November through April.

Saratoga Springs   F12

Apple Tree B&B

49 W High St, Saratoga Springs
(Ballston Spa), NY 12020
(518)885-1113

Circa 1878. A bird fountain and garden decorate the entrance to this Second Empire Victorian, which is located in the historic district of Ballston Spa, a village just a few minutes from Saratoga Springs. Guest rooms feature Victorian and country French decor and each has antiques and whirlpool tubs. Guests enjoy fresh fruit, homemade baked goods, a selection of beverages and a daily entree during the breakfast service.

Innkeeper(s): Dolores & Jim Taisey. $75-150. MC VISA AX PC TC. 4 rooms with PB. Breakfast included in rates. Types of meals: full breakfast and early coffee/tea. Beds: Q. Air conditioning, cable TV and VCR in room. Amusement parks, antiques, fishing, parks, shopping, skiing, sporting events, theater and watersports nearby.

Certificate may be used: January-December, excluding Saratoga Racing & special weekends.

Six Sisters B&B

149 Union Ave,
Saratoga Springs, NY 12866-3518
(518)583-1173 Fax:(518)587-2470

Circa 1880. The unique architecture of this charming Victorian home, features a large second-story bay window, a hardwood front door decked with stained glass and a veranda accentuated with plants and rocking chairs. Inside, the antiques, ceiling fans

and Oriental rugs create an elegant atmosphere. During racing season, guests can rise early and take a short walk to the local race track to watch the horses prepare. Upon their return, guests are greeted with the smells of a delicious breakfast. Visit Saratoga Springs' downtown area with its shops and many restaurants.

Innkeeper(s): Kate Benton. $70-250. MC VISA AX PC TC. 4 rooms with PB. 2 suites. Breakfast included in rates. Types of meals: gourmet breakfast and early coffee/tea. Beds: KQD. Air conditioning, ceiling fan and cable TV in room. Fax on premises. Amusement parks, antiques, fishing, parks, shopping, downhill skiing, cross-country skiing, sporting events, theater and watersports nearby.

Location: Thirty minutes north of Albany and thirty minutes south of Lake George.

Seen in: Gourmet, Country Inns, Country Folk Art, Country Victorian.

"The true definition of a bed & breakfast."

Certificate may be used: Sunday-Thursday except July, August and special events.

Westchester House B&B

102 Lincoln Ave,
Saratoga Springs, NY 12866-4536
(518)587-7613 (800)587-7613

Circa 1885. This gracious Queen Anne Victorian has been welcoming vacationers for more than 100 years. Antiques from four generations of the Melvin's family grace the high-ceilinged rooms. Oriental rugs top gleaming wood floors, while antique clocks and lace curtains set a graceful tone. Guests gather on the wraparound porch, in the parlors or gardens for an afternoon refreshment of old-fashioned lemonade. Racing season rates are quoted separately.

Innkeeper(s): Bob & Stephanie Melvin. $90-250. MC VISA AX CB PC TC. 7 rooms with PB. 1 conference room. Breakfast and afternoon tea included in rates. Types of meals: continental-plus breakfast and early coffee/tea. Beds: KQT. Air conditioning and ceiling fan in room. Library on premises. Antiques, fishing, parks, shopping, cross-country skiing, sporting events, theater and watersports nearby.

Location: Thirty miles north of Albany in the Adirondack foothills.

Seen in: Getaways for Gourmets, Albany Times Union, Saratogian, Capital, Country Inns, New York Daily News, WNYT, Newsday, Hudson Valley.

"I adored your B&B and have raved about it to all. One of the most beautiful and welcoming places we've ever visited."

Certificate may be used: Sunday-Thursday, April, May, June to 15th, September, November, excluding holiday weekends.

Severance
D12

The Red House
PO Box 125, Severance, NY 12872-0125
(518)532-7734

Circa 1850. Twenty feet from the banks of Paradox Brook, on the West end of Paradox Lake, is this two-story farmhouse inn that boasts a multitude of recreational offerings for its guests. In addition to the farmhouse, there are 11 guest houses on the grounds. The houses, which include fully equipped kitchens, have three to five bedrooms. The inn's full breakfasts include homemade breads and regional specialties. Be sure to plan a day trip to Fort Ticonderoga and ride the ferry across Lake Champlain to Vermont.

Innkeeper(s): Helen Wildman. $55-75. PC. 3 rooms, 1 with PB. Breakfast included in rates. Type of meal: full breakfast. Beds: QDT. Swimming, tennis and library on premises. Antiques, fishing, parks, shopping, downhill skiing and cross-country skiing nearby.

"Thanks for your wonderful hospitality."

Certificate may be used: Sunday through Thursday.

Sodus Point
E6

Carriage House Inn
8375 Wickham Blvd,
Sodus Point, NY 14555-9608
(315)483-2100 (800)292-2990

Circa 1870. Located on four acres in a quiet residential area, the Carriage House Inn overlooks Lake Ontario and a historic lighthouse. The main house is Victorian and the grounds feature a stone carriage house and barn. The inn caters to fishermen and couples looking for a cozy getaway.

Innkeeper(s): James Den Decker. $65. MC VISA. 4 rooms, 8 with PB. Breakfast and picnic lunch included in rates. Type of meal: full breakfast. Beds: KT. Handicap access. Antiques, fishing and watersports nearby.

Seen in: Finger Lakes Times, Democrat and Chronicle, WTVH.

"My wife and I have been telling everyone about the beautiful room we had and your courtesy."

Certificate may be used: Dec. 1 through April 15.

Southold
K14

Goose Creek Guesthouse
1475 Waterview Dr, PO Box 377,
Southold, NY 11971-2125
(516)765-3356

Circa 1862. Grover Pease left for the Civil War from this house, and after his death, his widow, Harriet, ran a summer boarding house here. The basement actually dates from the 1780s and is constructed of large rocks. The present house was moved here and put on the older foundation. Southold has many historic homes and a guidebook is provided for visitors. The inn is close to the ferry to New London and the ferries to the South Shore via Shelter Island.

Innkeeper(s): Mary Mooney-Getoff. $55-85. PC TC. 4 rooms. Breakfast and afternoon tea included in rates. Types of meals: full breakfast, gourmet breakfast and early coffee/tea. Picnic lunch available. Beds: KQDT. Air conditioning in room. VCR and library on premises. Amusement parks, antiques, fishing, parks, shopping, theater and watersports nearby.

Location: One-and-one-half miles south of Rt 25 on the north fork of Long Island.

Seen in: New York Times, Newsday.

"We will be repeat guests. Count on it!!"

Certificate may be used: Anytime, subject to availability.

Springville   G3

The Franklin House
432 Franklin St, Springville, NY 14141
(716)592-7877 Fax:(716)592-5388

Circa 1843. Once the home of a well-known area chicken farm, this Queen Anne Victorian inn now serves visitors to attraction-rich Western New York. An easy getaway from Buffalo, the inn offers three guest rooms, including a suite. Visitors will enjoy cross-country skiing on the inn's five acres or hot tubbing in the Hawaiian Room. An award-winning, homemade country-style breakfast is served before guests set out for their day's activities, which could include hitting the slopes at the Kissing Bridge Ski Area or a visit to Letchworth State Park, the Grand Canyon of the East.

Innkeeper(s): Paulette Timm. $60-110. MC VISA AX. 4 rooms. Breakfast included in rates. Types of meals: full breakfast and early coffee/tea. Evening snack available. Air conditioning, turn-down service, ceiling fan, cable TV and VCR in room. Antiques, shopping, downhill skiing, cross-country skiing and sporting events nearby.

Certificate may be used: Sunday-Thursday.

Stanfordville   I12

Lakehouse Inn on Golden Pond
Shelley Hill Rd, Stanfordville, NY 12581
(914)266-8093 (800)726-3323
Fax:(914)266-4051

Circa 1990. Romance abounds at this secluded contemporary home, which is surrounded by breathtaking vistas of woods and Golden Pond. Rest beneath a canopy flanked by lacy curtains as you gaze out the window. Enjoy a long, relaxing bath, or take a stroll around the 22-acre grounds. Each guest room includes a fireplace and whirlpool tub, and most include decks. The decor is a mix with a hint of Victorian, some Asian influences and modern touches that highlight the oak floors and vaulted pine ceilings. The innkeepers start off the day with a gourmet breakfast delivered to your room in a covered basket.

Innkeeper(s): Judy & Rich Kohler. $125-475. MC VISA PC. 9 rooms with PB, 7 with FP. 7 suites. 2 cottages. 1 conference room. Breakfast included in rates. Beds: KQ. Air conditioning, ceiling fan and VCR in room. Fax, copier and swimming on premises. Antiques, fishing, parks, cross-country skiing, sporting events, theater and watersports nearby.

Location: Ninety miles North of New York City.

Seen in: Newsday, New York Post.

Certificate may be used: Mon., Tues., Wed., excluding holidays.

Stillwater   F12

Lee's Deer Run B&B
411 County Rd 71, Stillwater, NY 12170
(518)584-7722

Circa 1981. In an idyllic countryside setting between Saratoga Lake and Saratoga National Historic Park, this inn, crafted from a 19th-century barn, now is home to four guest rooms, some with four-poster beds. The inn's full breakfasts are served in the dining room or on a deck with a view of the surrounding area. Bennington Battlefield and the Willard Mountain Ski Area are nearby.

Innkeeper(s): Rose & Donald Lee. $85-150. 8 rooms, 4 with PB. 3 suites. Breakfast included in rates. Types of meals: full breakfast and early coffee/tea. Beds: KQ. Air conditioning, turn-down service and ceiling fan in room. Copier on premises. Antiques, fishing, parks, shopping, cross-country skiing, sporting events, theater and watersports nearby.

Certificate may be used: Oct. 1 to May 1, Monday-Sunday.

Tannersville   H11

Kennedy House
PO Box 770, Tannersville, NY 12485
(518)589-6082

Circa 1890. The Kennedy House was built in the 1920s as a temporary Red Cross hospital serving those scattered among the Catskill Mountains. Since 1987, the home has welcomed bed & breakfast guests who come for the comfortable surroundings and beautiful views of Cortina Valley, Rip Van Winkle Lake and the Hunter Mountain ski areas. Rooms afford wonderful views and are decorated with antiques. The innkeepers operated an antique and gift shop on the premises. The Catskills, a popular resort area since the early 19th century, offers a bounty of activities with each season.

Innkeeper(s): Donna Kennedy. $50-90. PC. 6 rooms, 4 with PB. Breakfast included in rates. Type of meal: continental-plus breakfast. Beds: QT. Ceiling fan in room. Cable TV and VCR on premises. Antiques, fishing, parks, shopping, downhill skiing and cross-country skiing nearby.

Certificate may be used: Midweek, non-holiday.

Victor   F5

Golden Rule B&B
6934 Rice Rd, Victor, NY 14564-9355
(716)924-0610

Circa 1865. Although the exterior of this bed & breakfast might invoke images of children trudging to school for a day of reading, writing and arithmetic, the interior is nothing short of elegant. The building still maintains its original sign and red front door. The original school bell is still housed in the belfry. But, inside, hardwood floors are covered with oriental rugs and elegant furnishings. Stenciled walls grace the bedrooms filled with antiques. One guest room boasts a canopied bed, and both include ceiling fans. The gourmet breakfasts are served by candlelight.

Innkeeper(s): Richard de Maurias. $55-80. PC. 2 rooms. Breakfast included in rates. Types of meals: continental-plus breakfast, gourmet breakfast and early coffee/tea. Afternoon tea available. Beds: QD. Air conditioning, turn-down service and ceiling fan in room. Cable TV, VCR, fax and swimming on premises. Antiques, parks, shopping, downhill skiing and cross-country skiing nearby.

Certificate may be used: Weekdays, May to October; anytime, November to April.

Warrensburg   E12

Country Road Lodge B&B
HC 1 Box 227 Hickory Hill Rd,
Warrensburg, NY 12885-9801
(518)623-2207 Fax:(518)623-4363

Circa 1929. This simple farmhouse lodge is situated on 35 acres along the Hudson River at the end of a country road. Rooms are clean and comfortable. A full breakfast is provided with homemade breads and muffins. The sitting room reveals panoramic views of the river and Sugarloaf Mountain. Bird watching, hiking and skiing are popular activities. Groups often reserve all four guest rooms.

Innkeeper(s): Sandi & Steve Parisi. $55-58. PC. 4 rooms, 2 with PB. Breakfast included in rates. Types of meals: full breakfast and early coffee/tea. Beds: DT. Ceiling fan in room. Library on premises. Amusement parks, antiques, fishing, parks, shopping, downhill skiing, cross-country skiing, theater and watersports nearby.

Location: Adirondack Mountains near Lake George.

Seen in: North Jersey Herald & News.

"Homey, casual atmosphere. We really had a wonderful time. You're both wonderful hosts and the Lodge is definitely our kind of B&B! We will always feel very special about this place and will always be back."

Certificate may be used: Year-round excluding January and February winter weekend packages.

House on The Hill B&B
Rt 28 Box 248, Warrensburg, NY 12885
(518)623-9390 (800)221-9390
Fax:(518)623-9396

Circa 1750. This historic Federal-style inn on a hill in the Adirondacks offers five guest rooms. After they are treated to coffee and baked goods in their rooms, guests enjoy the inn's full breakfasts in the Sun Room, which offers wonderful views of the surrounding fields and woods from its many windows. Cross-country skiing and hiking may be enjoyed on the spacious grounds, covering 176 acres. Gore Mountain Ski Area is close and Lake George is a 10-minute drive.

Innkeeper(s): Joe & Lynn Rubino. $79-109. MC VISA AX DC CB DS PC TC. 5 rooms, 1 with PB. Breakfast included in rates. Types of meals: continental breakfast, full breakfast and early coffee/tea. Beds: KQD. Air conditioning in room. Cable TV, VCR, fax and copier on premises. Handicap access. Amusement parks, antiques, fishing, parks, shopping, downhill skiing, cross-country skiing, sporting events, theater and watersports nearby.

Seen in: Chronicle, Post Star, G.F. Business Journal, Country Victorian.

"Very favorable."

Certificate may be used: Sunday through Thursday, all year, subject to availability.

The Merrill Magee House
PO Box 391, Warrensburg, NY 12885
(518)623-2449

Circa 1839. This stately Greek Revival home offers beautiful antique fireplaces in every guest room. The Sage, Rosemary, Thyme and Coriander rooms feature sitting areas, and a family suite includes two bedrooms, a sitting room with a television, refrigerator and a bathroom with a clawfoot tub. The decor is romantic and distinctly Victorian. Romantic getaway packages include complimentary champagne and candlelight dinners. The local area hosts art and craft festivals, an antique car show, white-water rafting and Gore Mountain Oktoberfest. Tour the Adirondacks from the sky during September's balloon festival or browse through the world's largest garage sale in early October.

Innkeeper(s): Ken & Florence Carrington. $105-125. MAP, EP, MC VISA AX DS TC. 10 rooms with PB, 10 with FP. 1 cottage. 2 conference rooms. Breakfast included in rates. Types of meals: full breakfast and early coffee/tea. Dinner, lunch and banquet service available. Beds: KQDT. Air conditioning and turn-down service in room. Cable TV, spa, swimming and library on premises. Handicap access. Amusement parks, antiques, fishing, parks, shopping, downhill skiing, cross-country skiing, sporting events, theater and watersports nearby.

Location: In Adirondack State Park.

"A really classy and friendly operation—a real joy."

Certificate may be used: Sunday through Thursday, non-holiday or special events.

Waterville   F9

B&B of Waterville

211 White St, Waterville, NY 13480-1149
(315)841-8295

Circa 1871. This two-story Victorian is in the Waterville Historic Triangle District, one block from Rt. 12 and 20 minutes away from Hamilton College and Colgate University. The hostess is an avid quiltmaker and the house is filled with her handiwork. La Petite Maison, a fine French restaurant, is a few steps away. Thirty-five antique shops are within 10 miles.

Innkeeper(s): Stanley & Carol Sambora. $45-55. MC VISA PC TC. 3 rooms, 1 with PB. Breakfast included in rates. Type of meal: full breakfast. Beds: DT. Air conditioning in room. Cable TV and VCR on premises. Amusement parks, antiques, fishing, parks, shopping and cross-country skiing nearby.

Location: Near Utica.

Seen in: Observer Dispatch.

"Don't change a thing ever. As a hopeless romantic... I felt that your B&B was just what we needed. We have come away renewed and refreshed. It's so lovely here, love to stay forever!"

Certificate may be used: As available, all year.

Westfield   H2

Westfield House

E Main Rd, PO Box 505, Rt 20,
Westfield, NY 14787
(716)326-6262

Circa 1840. This brick home was built as a homestead on a large property of farmland and vineyards. The next owner constructed the impressive Greek-Revival addition. The home also served guests as a tea room and later as a family-style eatery. Modern guests will enjoy the elegance of the past, which has been wonderfully preserved at Westfield House. Breakfasts are served on fine china and silver in the home's formal dining room. Wintertime guests feast

on their morning meal in front of a warm fire. Each of the rooms offers something special. The Ruth Thomas Room offers a four-poster bed, high ceilings, antique quilts and a fireplace, while the Rowan Place boasts beautiful furnishings and Gothic crystal windows which look out to maple trees.

Innkeeper(s): Betty & Jud Wilson. $60-85. MC VISA PC TC. 7 rooms, 6 with PB, 1 with FP. 1 suite. 2 conference rooms. Breakfast and evening snack included in rates. Types of meals: full breakfast and early coffee/tea. Beds: KQD. Air conditioning, ceiling fan and cable TV in room. VCR on premises. Handicap access. Antiques, fishing, parks, downhill skiing, cross-country skiing, theater and watersports nearby.

Location: Southwestern New York state.

Seen in: Canadian Leisure Ways, Buffalo News, Innsider.

"Your accommodations and hospitality are wonderful! Simply outstanding. The living room changes its character by the hour."

Certificate may be used: When available.

The William Seward Inn

6645 S Portage Rd, Westfield, NY 14787
(716)326-4151 (800)338-4151
Fax:(716)326-4163

Circa 1821. This two-story Greek Revival estate stands on a knoll overlooking Lake Erie. Seward was a Holland Land Company agent before becoming governor of New York. He later served as Lincoln's Secretary of State and is known for the Alaska Purchase. George Patterson bought Seward's home and also became governor of New York. Most of the mansion's furnishings are dated 1790 to 1870 from the Sheraton-Victorian period.

Innkeeper(s): James & Debbie Dahlberg. $85-165. MC VISA DS. 14 rooms with PB, 1 with FP. Breakfast included in rates. Type of meal: full breakfast. Beds: KQD. Air conditioning in room. Cable TV, fax and library on premises. Handicap access. Amusement parks, antiques, fishing, parks, shopping, downhill skiing, cross-country skiing and watersports nearby.

Location: Three hours from Cleveland, Pittsburgh and Toronto.

Seen in: Intelligencer, Evening Observer, New York-Pennsylvania Collector, New York Times, Pittsburgh Post-Gazette, Toronto Globe & Mail.

"The breakfasts are delicious. The solitude and your hospitality are what the doctor ordered."

Certificate may be used: Anytime, except Friday-Saturday, June 20 through October, some holiday weekends.

Wilmington   C12

Willkommen Hof

Rt 86, PO Box 240, Wilmington, NY 12997
(518)946-7669 (800)541-9119
Fax:(518)946-7626

Circa 1925. This turn-of-the-century farmhouse served as an inn during the 1920s, but little else is known about its past. The innkeepers have created a cozy atmosphere, perfect for relaxation after a day exploring the Adirondack Mountain area. A large selection of books and roaring fire greet guests who choose to settle down in the reading room. The innkeepers also offer a large selection of movies. Relax in the outdoor sauna or spa or simply enjoy the comfort of your bedchamber.

Innkeeper(s): Heike & Bert Yost. $30-80. MAP. MC VISA PC TC. 9 rooms, 2 with PB. 1 suite. Breakfast and afternoon tea included in rates. Type of meal: full breakfast. Beds: KQDT. Ceiling fan in room. VCR, fax, spa, sauna, bicycles and pet boarding on premises. Antiques, fishing, parks, shopping, downhill skiing, cross-country skiing and watersports nearby.

Seen in: Adirondack Source Book.

"Thank you for a wonderful time, FIVE STARS!"

Certificate may be used: Midweek, non-holiday, year-round.

Windham H11

Albergo Allegria B&B

Rt 296, PO Box 267,
Windham, NY 12496-0267
(518)734-5560 (800)625-2374
Fax:(518)734-5570

Circa 1876. Two former boarding houses were joined to create this luxurious, Victorian bed & breakfast whose name means "the inn of happiness." Guest quarters, laced with a Victorian theme, are

decorated with period wallpapers and antique furnishings, two rooms boast whirlpool tubs. There are plenty of relaxing options at Albergo Allegria, including a rustic lounge with a large fireplace and overstuffed couches. A second-story library, decorated with plants and wicker furnishings, is still another location to relax with a good book. The innkeepers came to the area to open LaGriglia, a deluxe, gourmet restaurant just across the way from the bed & breakfast. Their command of cuisine is evident each morning as guests feast on a variety home-baked muffins and pastries, gourmet omelets, waffles and other tempting treats. Innkeeper Vito Radelich hosts cooking school packages during the year,

which aside from instruction, include a three-night stay, breakfasts and dinners at LaGriglia.

Innkeeper(s): Vito & Lenore Radelich. $55-195. MC VISA PC. 21 rooms with PB, 7 with FP. 9 suites. Breakfast included in rates. Types of meals: full breakfast and gourmet breakfast. Afternoon tea, picnic lunch and gourmet lunch available. Beds: KQT. Air conditioning, turn-down service, ceiling fan, cable TV and VCR in room. Fax, copier and bicycles on premises. Handicap access. Amusement parks, antiques, fishing, parks, shopping, downhill skiing, cross-country skiing and watersports nearby.

Seen in: Country Inns, Yankee.

"A jewel of an inn! The ambiance was elegant, yet relaxed; beautiful, yet comfortable, reflecting the nurturance of two generations of skillful, generous innkeepers."

Certificate may be used: Year-round (except Dec. 1-March 31). Midweek: Sunday-Thursday (non-holiday).

Country Suite B&B

Rt 23 W, PO Box 700,
Windham, NY 12496
(518)734-4079

This spacious country farmhouse in the Catskill Mountains offers easy access to the many scenic attractions of the region. Seven guest rooms, three with private baths, are available to visitors. The inn's country-style furnishings include antiques and family heirlooms. After a busy day of exploring the area, guests often gather in the inn's comfortable living room to relax. Ski Windham is just two miles from the inn and several other ski areas are within a 30-minute drive.

Innkeeper(s): Lorraine Seidel. $65-75. AX. 7 rooms. Breakfast included in rates. Type of meal: full breakfast. Antiques and downhill skiing nearby.

Certificate may be used: Year-round except holidays. May not be used in conjunction with any other discount.

Danske Hus

361 South St, Windham, NY 12496
(518)734-6335

Circa 1865. Located just across the road from Ski Windham, this farmhouse-style inn offers countryside and mountain views to its guests. Eclectic furnishings are found throughout the inn and its four guest rooms. Breakfast may be enjoyed in the dining room or outside on a picturesque deck. Guests also enjoy a large living room, piano, sauna, TV room and woodburning fireplace. Windham Golf Course is within walking distance. The Catskills provide many other tourist attractions, including caverns, fairs and ethnic festivals.

Innkeeper(s): Barbara Jensen. $40-85. AX DS. 4 rooms, 3 with PB. Breakfast and afternoon tea included in rates. Type of meal: full breakfast. Beds: KQDT. Cable TV, VCR, sauna, library, pet boarding and child care on premises. Amusement parks, antiques, fishing, parks, shopping, downhill skiing, cross-country skiing and watersports nearby.

Certificate may be used: Anytime, except holidays, holiday weekends, and Dec. 13-March 13.

Wolcott   E7

Bonnie Castle Farm B&B
PO Box 188, Wolcott, NY 14590-0188
(315)587-2273 (800)587-4006
Fax:(315)587-4003

Circa 1887. Bonnie Castle Farm is surrounded by expansive lawns and trees which overlook the east side of Great Sodus Bay, a popular resort at the turn of the century. Accommodations include a suite and large guest room with water views. Another room features wainscoting and cathedral ceilings. A full

gourmet breakfast includes cereal bar, fresh fruit and juices and an assortment of entrees such as Orange Blossom French toast, sausages, a creamy potato casserole and fresh-baked pastries topped off with teas and Irish creme coffee.

Innkeeper(s): Eric & Georgia Pendleton. $70-120. MC VISA AX PC TC. 8 rooms with PB. 1 suite. Breakfast included in rates. Types of meals: full breakfast and gourmet breakfast. Beds: KQDT. Air conditioning, ceiling fan, cable TV and VCR in room. Fax, copier, spa and swimming on premises. Antiques, fishing, parks, shopping, downhill skiing, cross-country skiing, sporting events, theater and watersports nearby.

Location: Located in Sodus Bay, N.Y., in the Finger Lakes District of upstate New York.

"We love Bonnie Castle. You have a magnificent establishment. We are just crazy about your place. Hope to see you soon."

Certificate may be used: Anytime except Friday and Saturday in June, July and August.

Youngstown   E3

The Mill Glen Inn
1102 Pletcher Rd,
Youngstown, NY 14174-9763
(716)754-4085

Circa 1880. This two-story, 19th-century farmhouse inn offers easy access to the many attractions found in the Niagara Falls area. Visitors select from three guest rooms that feature ceiling fans and turndown service. Breakfasts are served in the Wagner dining room or on the inn's covered porch. Fort Niagara State Park and the Artpark are nearby, and the American and Canadian Falls are just a short drive from the inn. Great fishing can be found on Lake Ontario and the lower Niagara River.

Innkeeper(s): Peter Brass. $40-65. 3 rooms. Breakfast included in rates. Types of meals: continental-plus breakfast and early coffee/tea. Turn-down service and ceiling fan in room. VCR on premises. Antiques, shopping, downhill skiing, cross-country skiing, sporting events and theater nearby.

Certificate may be used: Anytime, Oct. 1-April 30; Sunday-Thursday only May 1-Sept. 30. Holidays and special events excluded.

North Carolina

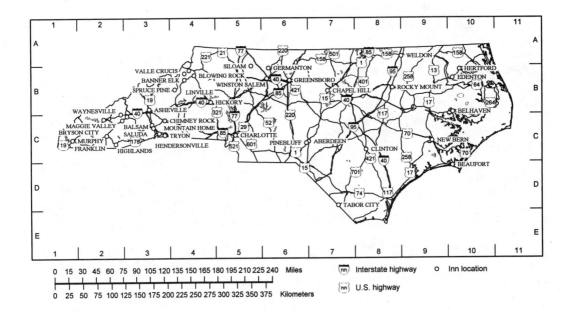

	Miles
0 15 30 45 60 75 90 105 120 135 150 165 180 195 210 225 240	
0 25 50 75 100 125 150 175 200 225 250 275 300 325 350 375	Kilometers

Interstate highway   o   Inn location

U.S. highway

Aberdeen
C7

The Inn at Bryant House
214 N Poplar St,
Aberdeen, NC 28315-2812
(910)944-3300 (800)453-4019
Fax:(910)944-8898

Circa 1913. This Colonial Revival inn has been completely restored to its original Southern splendor. Pastel colors flow through the entire house and the sitting, dining and living rooms open to one another for easy access. Breakfast is served buffet-style in the dining or garden room. With advance notice, lunches and dinners can be served for small business meetings, wedding parties, family gatherings, club activities and weekend retreats. The Pinehurst area is known for its quiet rolling hills and more than 30 championship-quality golf courses.

Innkeeper(s): Abbie Gregory. $45-70. MC VISA AX DS. 8 rooms, 6 with PB. Breakfast included in rates. Type of meal: continental-plus breakfast. Beds: QDT. Air conditioning in room. Cable TV and VCR on premises. Antiques, shopping, sporting events and theater nearby.

"Excellent!! Bill & Abbie Gregory are just wonderful hosts. Superb continental breakfast."

Certificate may be used: Anytime of the year, when available.

Asheville
B3

Acorn Cottage B&B
25 Saint Dunstans Cir,
Asheville, NC 28803-2618
(704)253-0609 (800)699-0609
Fax:(704)258-2129

Circa 1923. This home was designed by Ronald Green, a prominent, turn-of-the-century Asheville architect, who designed many of the area's historic buildings. This Arts & Crafts period, Craftsman-style granite bungelow is found in the heart of town. The inn, with its eclectic decor and beautiful gardens, is close to many nearby attractions, including the Biltmore Estate. Guests can enjoy a cool drink while resting on the porch swing during summer afternoons or warm themselves by the fire in the living room on cool evenings. Bedrooms feature fine linens and private baths with special soaps.

Innkeeper(s): Sharon Tabor. $70-95. MC VISA DS PC TC. 4 rooms with PB. Breakfast, afternoon tea and evening snack included in rates. Types of meals: full breakfast and early coffee/tea. Beds: Q. Air conditioning and cable TV in room. VCR and fax on premises. Antiques, parks, shopping, sporting events, theater and watersports nearby.

Certificate may be used: Jan. 15-Sept. 30; Nov. 1-30 Sunday-Thursday excluding holidays.

Corner Oak Manor
53 Saint Dunstans Rd,
Asheville, NC 28803-2620
(704)253-3525

Circa 1920. Surrounded by oak, maple and pine trees, this English Tudor inn is decorated with many fine oak antiques and handmade items. Innkeeper Karen Spradley has handstitched something special

for each room and the house features handmade items by local artisans. Breakfast delights include entrees such as Blueberry Ricotta Pancakes, Four Cheese and Herb Quiche and Orange French Toast. When you aren't enjoying local activities, you can sit on the shady deck, relax in the Jacuzzi, play a few songs on the piano or curl up with a good book.

Innkeeper(s): Karen & Andy Spradley. $90-150. MC VISA AX DS PC TC. 4 rooms with PB, 1 with FP. 1 suite. 1 cottage. Breakfast included in rates. Type of meal: gourmet breakfast. Beds: Q. Air conditioning and ceiling fan in room. Antiques, fishing, parks, shopping, downhill skiing and theater nearby.

"Great food, comfortable bed, quiet, restful atmosphere, you provided it all and we enjoyed it all!"

Certificate may be used: January, February, March anytime except holidays. April through December, Sunday-Thursday only (no holidays).

Dogwood Cottage
40 Canterbury Rd N,
Asheville, NC 28801-1560
(704)258-9725

Circa 1910. This Carolina mountain home is located a mile-and-a-half from downtown Asheville, on Sunset Mountain. The veranda, filled with white wicker and floral chintz prints, is the focal point of the inn during summer. It affords tree-top views to the Blue Ridge Mountains. Wing chairs and fresh country pieces accent the inn's gleaming hardwood floors. Breakfast is served in the formal dining room or on the covered porch.

Innkeeper(s): Joan & Don Tracy. $95-105. MC VISA AX PC. 4 rooms with PB, 3 with FP. Breakfast included in rates. Types of meals: full breakfast, gourmet breakfast and early coffee/tea. Beds: Q. Air conditioning and ceiling fan in room. Cable TV, swimming and pet boarding on premises. Handicap access. Antiques, fishing, parks, shopping, downhill skiing, sporting events, theater and watersports nearby.

"Cozy, warm and gracious."

Certificate may be used: Sunday through Thursday only, not in October and December.

The Lion & The Rose
276 Montford Ave,
Asheville, NC 28801-1660
(704)255-7673 (800)546-6988

Circa 1895. Asheville's Montford Historic District wouldn't be complete without this Queen Anne Victorian, listed in the National Register. Innkeepers Lisa and Rice Yordy preserve the history of this home with the Victorian decor and heavy English influences. The interior is gracious, showcasing the original leaded- and stained-glass windows and glossy woods. A wonderful afternoon tea is served each day, often on the inn's wraparound veranda. Lisa prepares the memorable breakfasts, which are served on English china with silver. Fresh flowers and chocolates welcome guests to their well-appointed rooms.

Innkeeper(s): Rice & Lisa Yordy. $115-175. MC VISA TC. 5 rooms with PB. 1 suite. Breakfast and afternoon tea included in rates. Type of meal: gourmet breakfast. Beds: QT. Air conditioning, turn-down service, ceiling fan and cable TV in room. Antiques, fishing, parks, shopping, theater and watersports nearby.

Certificate may be used: Jan. 30 to Sept. 30, Monday through Thursday.

Balsam   C2

Balsam Mountain Inn
Balsam Mountain Inn Rd,
Balsam, NC 28707-0040
(704)456-9498 (800)224-9498
Fax:(704)456-9298

Circa 1905. This mountain inn with Neoclassical architecture overlooks the scenic hamlet of Balsam. The inn is listed in the National Register of Historic Places and is designated a Jackson County Historic Site. It features a mansard roof and wraparound porches with mountain views.

Innkeeper(s): Merrily Teasley. $75-130. MC VISA DS TC. 34 rooms with PB. 3 suites. Breakfast included in rates. Types of meals: full breakfast, gourmet breakfast and early coffee/tea. Dinner, picnic lunch, gourmet lunch, banquet service and room service available. Beds: KD. Fax and copier on premises. Handicap access. Antiques, fishing, parks, shopping and downhill skiing nearby.

"What wonderful memories we have of this beautiful inn."

Certificate may be used: Sunday-Thursday, November-June & September, excluding holiday periods.

Banner Elk   B4

Beech Alpen Inn
700 Beech Mountain Pkwy,
Banner Elk, NC 28604-8015
(704)387-2252 Fax:(704)387-2229

Circa 1968. This rustic inn is a Bavarian delight affording scenic vistas of the Blue Ridge Mountains. The innkeepers offer accommodations at Top of the Beech, a Swiss-style ski chalet with views of nearby slopes. The interiors of both properties are inviting. At the Beech Alpen, several guest rooms have stone fireplaces or French doors that open onto a balcony. Top of the Beech's game room is a wonderful place to relax with a huge stone fireplace and comfortable furnishings. The Beech Alpen Restaurant serves a variety of dinner fare.

Innkeeper(s): Lisa & Taylor Rees. $44-135. MC VISA AX TC. 25 rooms with PB, 4 with FP. Breakfast included in rates. Types of meals: continental breakfast and early coffee/tea. Beds: KQD. Cable TV in room. Fax and copier on premises. Antiques, fishing, parks, shopping, downhill skiing, cross-country skiing, sporting events and theater nearby.

Certificate may be used: Sunday-Thursday, Jan. 3-Dec. 14.

Beaufort   D10

Pecan Tree Inn B&B
116 Queen St, Beaufort, NC 28516-2214
(919)728-6733

Circa 1866. Originally built as a Masonic lodge, this state historic landmark is in the heart of Beaufort's historic district. Gingerbread trim, Victorian porches, turrets, and two-century-old pecan trees grace the exterior. Guests can relax in the parlor, on the porches, or pay a visit to the flower and herb gardens. The Bridal Suite and WOW suite boast a king-size, canopied bed and two-person Jacuzzi.

Innkeeper(s): Susan & Joe Johnson. $85-125. MC VISA DS PC TC. 7 rooms with PB. 1 suite. Breakfast included in rates. Types of meals: continental-plus breakfast and early coffee/tea. Beds: KQ. Air conditioning and ceiling fan in room. Bicycles and library on premises.

Amusement parks, antiques, fishing, parks, shopping and watersports nearby.

Location: In the heart of the historic district, one-half block from the waterfront.

Seen in: Sunday Telegram, This Week, Conde Nast Traveler, State.

"After visiting B&Bs far and wide I give Pecan Tree Inn a Five-Star rating in all respects."

Certificate may be used: September to May, Sunday through Thursday.

Belhaven

River Forest Manor

600 E Main St, Belhaven, NC 27810-1622
(919)943-2151 (800)346-2151
Fax:(919)943-6628

Circa 1899. Both Twiggy and Walter Cronkite have passed through the two-story, pillared rotunda entrance of this white mansion located on the Atlantic Intracoastal Waterway. Ornate, carved ceilings, cut and leaded-glass windows and crystal chandeliers grace the inn. Antiques are found throughout. Each evening a smorgasbord buffet features more than 65 items from the inn's kitchen.

Innkeeper(s): Melba, Axson Jr. & Mark Smith. $65-85. MAP. MC VISA. 12 rooms with PB. Breakfast included in rates. Types of meals: continental breakfast and full breakfast. Dinner available. Beds: KQD. Air conditioning and cable TV in room. VCR, fax and copier on premises. Antiques, fishing and watersports nearby.

Seen in: Southern Living, National Geographic, North Carolina Accommodations, Country Inns, State, Historical Inns.

"River Forest Manor is our favorite place in east North Carolina."

Certificate may be used: April 1 through April 30, Sunday through Thursday.

Blowing Rock

Maple Lodge

PO Box 1236, 152 Sunset Dr,
Blowing Rock, NC 28605-1236
(704)295-3331 Fax:(704)295-9986

Circa 1943. Guests at this country B&B enjoy a 50-year tradition of innkeeping during their stay. The home was built to be a bed & breakfast, and the current innkeepers are aces at hospitality. Country antiques and family heirlooms fill the rooms. Lace, handmade quilts and down comforters create a warm, romantic atmosphere in the guest rooms, some of which include canopy beds. The buffet breakfasts are served in the unique Garden Room, which includes a wood-burning stove and stone floor.

Innkeeper(s): Marilyn & David Bateman. $78-128. MC VISA AX DC DS PC TC. 11 rooms with PB. 1 suite. 3 conference rooms. Breakfast included in rates. Types of meals: full breakfast and early coffee/tea. Beds: KQDT. Ceiling fan and cable TV in room. Fax and library on premises. Amusement parks, antiques, fishing, parks, shopping, down-hill skiing, cross-country skiing, sporting events, theater and watersports nearby.

Certificate may be used: Jan. 1-May 30, Monday-Thursday; Nov. 1-Dec. 20, Monday-Thursday.

Bryson City

Randolph House

PO Box 816, Bryson City, NC 28713-0816
(704)488-3472 (800)480-3472

Circa 1895. Randolph House is a mountain estate tucked among pine trees and dogwoods, near the entrance of Great Smoky Mountain National Park. Antiques, some original to the house, fill this National Register home. Each guest room is appointed in a different color scheme. The house provides an unforgettable experience, not the least of which is the gourmet dining provided on the terrace or in the dining room.

Innkeeper(s): Bill & Ruth Randolph Adams. $110-160. MAP. MC VISA AX DS PC TC. 7 rooms, 3 with PB, 2 with FP. 2 suites. 1 cottage. 1 conference room. Breakfast and dinner included in rates. Types of meals: full breakfast and early coffee/tea. Beds: KQDT. Air conditioning and cable TV in room. Library on premises. Handicap access. Antiques, fishing, parks, shopping and watersports nearby.

Seen in: Tourist News.

"Very enjoyable, great food."

Certificate may be used: May-June and September, weekdays only.

Chapel Hill

The Inn at Bingham School

PO Box 267, Chapel Hill, NC 27514-0267
(919)563-5583 (800)566-5583
Fax:(919)563-9826

Circa 1790. This inn served as one of the locations of the famed Bingham School. This particular campus was the site of a liberal arts preparatory school for those aspiring to attend the University at Chapel Hill. The inn is listed as a National Trust property and has garnered awards for its restoration. The property still includes many historic structures including a 1790s log home, an 1801 addition, an 1835 Greek Revival home, the headmaster's office, which was built in 1845, and a well house, smokehouse and milk house. The dining rooms and living rooms include the original pine flooring, wainscoting and milk-based paint on the ceilings. Guests can opt to stay in the Log Room, located in the log cabin, with a tightwinder staircase and fireplace. Other possibilities include Rusty's Room with two antique rope beds. Some rooms feature special mantels, an antique clawfoot tub and one offers a bedroom glassed in on three sides. A mix of breakfasts are served, from a Southern style with grits and ham to French with quiches and souffles. Gourmet coffee and tea complement each meal.

Innkeeper(s): Francois & Christina Deprez. $75-120. MC VISA AX PC TC. 5 rooms with PB, 1 with FP. 1 suite. 1 cottage. 1 conference room. Breakfast and evening snack included in rates. Types of meals: full breakfast, gourmet breakfast and early coffee/tea. Picnic lunch available. Beds: QD. Air conditioning in room. Cable TV, VCR, fax and library on premises. Antiques, fishing, parks, shopping, sporting events, theater and watersports nearby.

Seen in: Southern Inns, Mebane Enterprise, Burlington Times, Times News.

"Our stay at the inn was like a dream, another time, another place. Francois & Christina were the most hospitable, friendly hosts we've ever met..."

Certificate may be used: All year Sunday-Thursday (free night cannot fall on Friday or Saturday nights).

Charlotte C5

The Homeplace B&B
5901 Sardis Rd,
Charlotte, NC 28270-5369
(704)365-1936

Circa 1902. Situated on two-and-one-half wooded acres in Southeast Charlotte, this peaceful setting is an oasis in one of the South's fastest-growing cities. Bedrooms have 10-foot ceilings, heart-of-pine floors and blends of Country/Victorian decor. Special

touches include quilts, fine linens, handmade accessories, family antiques and original primitive paintings by innkeeper Peggy Dearien's father. Spend the afternoon or evening relaxing on the porches or walking the secluded gardens. While touring the grounds, you will see a 1930s log barn that was moved to the property in 1991. A "Garden Room" addition provides space for small meetings and special occasions.

Innkeeper(s): Margaret Dearien. $88-110. MC VISA AX. 4 rooms, 2 with PB. 1 suite. Breakfast included in rates. Types of meals: full breakfast and early coffee/tea. Beds: QT. Air conditioning and ceiling fan in room. Cable TV and VCR on premises. Antiques, shopping and sporting events nearby.

Seen in: Charlotte Observer, Birmingham News, Country, Southern Living's Weekend Vacations.

"Everything was perfect. The room was superb, the food excellent!"

Certificate may be used: January, February, March, July, and August, Sunday through Thursday only.

Chimney Rock C3

Esmeralda Inn
Hwy 74A PO Box 57,
Chimney Rock, NC 28720
(704)625-9105

Circa 1890. Nestled in the Blue Ridge Mountains, this rustic country lodge served as home base for production of several silent movies, and notables such as Mary Pickford, Gloria Swanson, Douglas Fairbanks, Clark Gable and many others used the

Esmeralda as a hideout. Lew Wallace, noted author, finished the script for "Ben Hur" in room No. 9. The lobby, constructed of natural trees and filled with local artifacts, is a favorite place for visitors to take refuge and relax.

Innkeeper(s): Ackie & Joanne Okpych. $45-70. MC VISA AX DS TC. 13 rooms, 7 with PB. 3 suites. 1 conference room. Breakfast included in rates. Picnic lunch and lunch available. Beds: KQD. Ceiling fan in room. Library on premises. Antiques, fishing, parks, shopping and watersports nearby.

Certificate may be used: Sunday through Thursday, except October. Season is from March 17 to Dec. 9.

Clinton   C8

The Shield House Inn

216 Sampson St, Clinton, NC 28328-3418
(910)592-2634 (800)462-9817
Fax:(910)592-2634

Circa 1916. This house was built for businessman
Robert Herring. The facade is dominated by four
colossal fluted columns rising 22 feet to support a

portico. The veranda, with 12 Ionic columns, wraps
around three sides. Intricately designed leaded glass
highlights the entrance, and inside are walnut and
mahogany antiques. A 22-foot-long mural of Orton
Plantation can be seen in the dining room. The
innkeepers are twin sisters who are also nurses.
Innkeeper(s): Añita Green. $50-100. MC VISA AX DC. 15 rooms, 17
with PB, 7 with FP. 7 suites. 1 conference room. Breakfast included in
rates. Type of meal: continental-plus breakfast. Beds: KQDT. Antiques
nearby.
Seen in: Country, Tasteful, State, Fayetteville, Observer, Sampson
Independent.

*"I have never been pampered so much. A beautiful
home and a beautiful spirit."*
Certificate may be used: Nov. 15 to March 31.

Edenton   B10

The Lords Proprietors' Inn

300 N Broad St, Edenton, NC 27932-1905
(919)482-3641 (800)348-8933
Fax:(919)482-2432

Circa 1801. On Albemarle Sound, Edenton was
one of the Colonial capitals of North Carolina.
The inn consists of
three houses, provid-
ing elegant accom-
modations in
Edenton's Historic
District. Breakfast
and dinner are
served in a separate
dining room on a
patio. A guided
walking tour from

the Visitor's Center provides an opportunity to see
museum homes.
Innkeeper(s): Arch & Jane Edwards. $185-235. MAP. PC TC. 20 rooms
with PB. 1 conference room. Breakfast, afternoon tea and dinner included in rates. Types of meals: gourmet breakfast and early coffee/tea.
Beds: KQT. Air conditioning, ceiling fan, cable TV and VCR in room. Fax
and child care on premises. Handicap access. Antiques, fishing and
shopping nearby.
Location: Main street of town.
Seen in: Southern Living, Mid-Atlantic Country, House Beautiful,
Washington Post.

*"One of the friendliest and best-managed inns I have
ever visited."*
Certificate may be used: Anytime, except holidays and special weekends (i.e. April Pilgrimage). Dinner may be included in rate.

Franklin   C2

Buttonwood Inn

50 Admiral Dr, Franklin, NC 28734-8474
(704)369-8985

Circa 1927. Tall pine trees surround this two-story
batten board house located adjacent to the Franklin
Golf Course. Local crafts and handmade family
quilts accent the country decor. Wonderful breakfasts are served here—often Eggs Benedict, baked
peaches and sausage and freshly baked scones with
homemade lemon butter. On a sunny morning
enjoy breakfast on the deck and savor the Smoky
Mountain vistas. Afterward, you'll be ready for
white-water rafting, hiking and fishing.
Innkeeper(s): Liz Oehser. $60-90. PC TC. 4 rooms with PB. Breakfast
and afternoon tea included in rates. Types of meals: full breakfast and
early coffee/tea. Beds: QDT. Ceiling fan in room. Cable TV on premises.
Antiques, fishing, parks and shopping nearby.
Certificate may be used: Sunday-Thursday, except October, no
holidays or weekends.

Greensboro   B6

Greenwood B&B

205 N Park Dr,
Greensboro, NC 27401-1535
(910)274-6350 (800)535-9363
Fax:(910)274-9943

Circa 1908. Greenwood is a fully renovated, stick-
style chalet on the park in the historic district.
President W. H. Taft was once a guest here. The inn
is decorated with fine western art, family heirlooms,
and antiques. Turndown service and Southern cooking will make your stay unforgettable. There are two
living rooms, each with a fireplace, and a swimming
pool is in the backyard.

Innkeeper(s): Mike & Vanda Terrell. $80-105. MC VISA AX DS PC TC. 4 rooms with PB. Breakfast and evening snack included in rates. Types of meals: continental breakfast, full breakfast and early coffee/tea. Beds: KQT. Air conditioning, turn-down service and ceiling fan in room. Cable TV, VCR, fax, copier, swimming and library on premises. Amusement parks, antiques, fishing, parks, shopping, sporting events, theater and watersports nearby.

Location: Central Greensboro in the historic district.

Seen in: Triad Style.

"Your house is lovely and comfortable but more than that it is your warmth and generous of spirit that will long be remembered."

Certificate may be used: Sunday-Friday, all year except during special events.

Hendersonville C3

Echo Mountain Inn
2849 Laurel Park Hwy,
Hendersonville, NC 28739-8925
(704)692-4008 Fax:(704)697-2047

Circa 1896. Sitting on top of Davis Mountain, this large stone and wood inn has spectacular views, especially from the dining room and many of the guest rooms. Rooms are decorated with antiques and reproductions and many include a fireplace. The historic town of Hendersonville is three miles

away. Gourmet dining includes an added touch of the city lights below. Guests may want to partake in refreshments of their choice served in the inn's fireside tavern.

Innkeeper(s): Karen Kovacik. $35-175. MC VISA AX DS. 31 rooms, 30 with PB. 2 suites. 1 conference room. Breakfast included in rates. Types of meals: continental breakfast and early coffee/tea. Dinner, picnic lunch, banquet service and room service available. Beds: KQDT. Air conditioning, turn-down service, cable TV and VCR in room. Child care on premises. Antiques, fishing, shopping, downhill skiing and theater nearby.

"It was quite fabulous and the food entirely too rich."

Certificate may be used: February-May, September, November-December, anyday; June-August on Sunday-Thursday. Holidays and holiday weeks excluded, special events excluded.

Waverly Inn
783 N Main St,
Hendersonville, NC 28792-5079
(704)693-9193 (800)537-8195
Fax:(704)692-1010

Circa 1898. In the National Register, this three-story Victorian and Colonial Revival house has a two-tiered, sawn work trimmed porch and widow's walk. A beautifully carved Eastlake staircase and an original registration desk grace the inn. There are four-poster canopy beds and clawfoot tubs. Breakfast is served in the handsome dining room. The Waverly is the oldest surviving inn in Hendersonville.

Innkeeper(s): John & Diane Sheiry, Darla Olmstead. $89-139. MC VISA AX DS PC. 14 rooms with PB. 1 suite. Breakfast and evening snack included in rates. Type of meal: full breakfast. Picnic lunch available. Beds: KQDT. Air conditioning and ceiling fan in room. Cable TV and fax on premises. Antiques, fishing, parks, shopping, cross-country skiing and theater nearby.

Location: Corner of 8th Avenue & Main Street (Rt. 25 North)

Seen in: New York Times, Country, Blue Ridge Country, Vogue, Southern Living, Travel South.

"Our main topic of conversation while driving back was what a great time we had at your place."

Certificate may be used: January, February, March anytime. November, December, April, May, September, Sunday-Thursday.

Hertford
B10

1812 on The Perquimans B&B Inn
Rt 3, Box 10, Hertford, NC 27944
(919)426-1812

William and Sarah Fletcher were the first residents of this Federal-style plantation home, and the house is still in the family today. The Fletchers were Quakers and the first North Carolina residents to free their slaves, and also offered to pay the way for workers who wished to return to Africa. The farm rests along the banks of the Perquimans River, and the grounds retain many original outbuildings, including a brick dairy, smokehouse and a 19th-century frame barn. Inside, the mantels, marble and woodwork have been restored.

Innkeeper(s): Nancy D. Rascoe. $75-90. MC VISA. 5 rooms. Breakfast included in rates. Type of meal: full breakfast.

Certificate may be used: During the week.

Hickory
B4

The Hickory B&B
464 7th St SW, Hickory, NC 28602-2743
(704)324-0548 (800)654-2961
Fax:(704)345-6163

Circa 1908. Bedrooms in this Georgian-style inn are decorated with antiques, collectibles, fresh flowers and a country flavor. There's a parlor to sit in and chat and a library to enjoy a good book or to play a game. Homemade tea and lemonade, with something from the oven are served to guests in the late afternoon. The inn is located in a city that has evolved from a furniture and textile mill town of yesteryear into a cultural arts mecca of mountain communities. From mountains to malls, Hickory satisfies the shopper as well as the sportsperson.

Innkeeper(s): Suzanne & Bob Ellis. $70-85. PC TC. 4 rooms with PB. 1 suite. 2 conference rooms. Breakfast and afternoon tea included in rates. Types of meals: full breakfast and early coffee/tea. Beds: QT. Air conditioning and ceiling fan in room. Cable TV, VCR, swimming and library on premises. Antiques, fishing, parks, shopping, sporting events, theater and watersports nearby.

Location: Located in the furniture capitol of the world.

Seen in: Mid-Atlantic Country, Hickory Daily News, Charlotte Observer.

"Now we know what Southern hospitality means. We had such a wonderful weekend with you."

Certificate may be used: Nov. 15-Aug. 31, holidays excluded, based upon availability and other promotions.

Highlands
C2

Morning Star Inn
480 Flat Mountain Estates Rd,
Highlands, NC 28741-8325
(704)526-1009 Fax:(704)526-4474

Circa 1962. For anyone hoping to enjoy the serenity and scenery of North Carolina, this inn is an ideal place for that and more. Hammocks and rockers are found here and there on the two-acre grounds, dotted with gardens and trees. There is a parlor with a stone fireplace and a wicker-filled sunporch. Rooms are decorated in a romantic, but uncluttered country style. Beds are dressed with fine linens and down comforters. To top off the amenities, one of the innkeepers is a culinary school graduate and prepares the mouthwatering cuisine guests enjoy at breakfast and when afternoon refreshments are served. The innkeeper also is working on a cookbook, which will no doubt include tidbits such as cheese grits and fresh fruit with amaretto cream sauce. For those interested in improving their culinary skills, cooking classes sometimes are available.

Innkeeper(s): Pat & Pat Allen. $105-130. MC VISA PC TC. 5 rooms with PB. 1 suite. Breakfast, afternoon tea and evening snack included in rates. Types of meals: gourmet breakfast and early coffee/tea. Beds: KQ. Air conditioning, turn-down service, ceiling fan and cable TV in room. Fax and copier on premises. Antiques, fishing, parks, shopping, downhill skiing, theater and watersports nearby.

Certificate may be used: January-May, Sunday through Thursday.

Linville
B4

Linville Cottage Bed & Breakfast
PO Box 508, Linville, NC 28646-0508
(704)733-6551

Circa 1910. Just two miles from North Carolina's Grandfather Mountain rests this Victorian cottage. The innkeepers emphasize country comfort, decorating their B&B with simple antiques and collectibles. English and herb gardens surround the inn. Visit the inn's shops or simply enjoy the mountain breezes from the front porch. The area is full of scenic sites, including the Blue Ridge Parkway and Linville Caverns.

Innkeeper(s): Fran Feely. $50-95. MC VISA PC TC. 4 rooms with PB. Breakfast and afternoon tea included in rates. Type of meal: continental-plus breakfast. Beds: QD. Cable TV, VCR, library and pet boarding on premises. Handicap access. Amusement parks, antiques, fishing, parks, shopping, downhill skiing, cross-country skiing, sporting events, theater and watersports nearby.

Certificate may be used: Monday to Thursday year-round, except on holidays or special local events.

Maggie Valley

C2

The Ketner Inn & Farm

190 Jonathan Creek Rd, Maggie Valley,
NC 28751
(704)926-1511 (800)714-1397

Circa 1898. The innkeepers, owners of two area
restaurants, bought this historic home from the
grandson of its original owners. There are more than
two dozen acres to explore, which include antique
farm equipment and the modern amenity of a hot
tub. The home is furnished with Victorian and
country-style antiques. Country breakfasts are prepared on a vintage, 1930s cookstove. The inn offers
close access to many popular sites, including the
Blue Ridge Parkway and Biltmore Estate.

Innkeeper(s): Randall & Sara McCrory. $50-60. MC VISA. 5 rooms with
PB. Breakfast included in rates. Type of meal: gourmet breakfast. Beds:
QD. Air conditioning and cable TV in room. Spa on premises.
Amusement parks, antiques, fishing, parks, shopping, downhill skiing,
cross-country skiing, sporting events and theater nearby.

Certificate may be used: Jan. 2 to May 15, Sunday to Saturday; Sept.
1-30 and Nov. 1 to Dec. 15, Monday to Thursday.

Mountain Home

C3

Mountain Home B&B

PO Box 234,
Mountain Home, NC 28758-0234
(704)697-9090 (800)397-0066

Circa 1915. Although technically built in 1941,
this bed & breakfast has a long history, dating back
to the early 1800s, when a plantation home and its
outbuildings stood here. The original 1915 structure
was used as an inn, and after burning down in the

1930s, a local dentist rebuilt the place, using the
same architecture on a smaller scale. Today, the
home is filled with elegant furnishings and country
Victorian decor. Canopied and four-poster beds
grace some rooms, and all are individually appointed. Guests partake of a morning feast that is both
romantic and hearty. Items such as raspberry stuffed
French toast are served by candlelight.

Innkeeper(s): Bob & Donna Marriott. $85-180. MC VISA AX PC. 8
rooms, 6 with PB, 1 with FP. 1 suite. 1 conference room. Breakfast and
evening snack included in rates. Types of meals: full breakfast, gourmet
breakfast and early coffee/tea. Banquet service available. Beds: KQD.
Air conditioning and cable TV in room. Handicap access. Antiques, fishing, parks, shopping and theater nearby.

Seen in: Arts & Entertainment.

*"Thanks for showing us what 'Southern hospitality'
is like."*

Certificate may be used: January, February, March.

Murphy

C1

Huntington Hall B&B

500 Valley River Ave,
Murphy, NC 28906-2829
(704)837-9567 (800)824-6189
Fax:(704)837-2527

Circa 1881. This two-story country Victorian home
was built by J.H. Dillard, the town mayor and twice
a member of the House of Representatives.

Clapboard siding
and tall columns
accent the large
front porch. An
English country
theme is highlight-
ed throughout.
Afternoon refresh-
ments and evening
turndown service
are included.
Breakfast is served
on the sun porch.
Murder-mystery,

summer-theater, and white-water-rafting packages
are available.

Innkeeper(s): Kate & Bob DeLong. $65-95. MAP. MC VISA AX DC CB
DS PC TC. 5 rooms with PB, 2 with FP. 1 conference room. Breakfast
included in rates. Types of meals: full breakfast, gourmet breakfast and
early coffee/tea. Beds: KQDT. Air conditioning, turn-down service, ceiling fan and cable TV in room. VCR, fax, copier, tennis and library on
premises. Antiques, fishing, parks, shopping, theater and watersports
nearby.

Location: One block from downtown.

Seen in: Atlanta Journal, Petersen's 4-Wheel, New York Times.

*"Your skill and attitude make it a pleasant experience to
stay and rest at HH."*

Certificate may be used: Sunday through Thursday any month.

New Bern C9

Harmony House Inn
215 Pollock St,
New Bern, NC 28560-4942
(919)636-3810 (800)636-3113
Fax:(919)636-3810

Circa 1850. Long ago, this two-story Greek Revival was sawed in half and the west side moved nine feet to accommodate new hallways, additional rooms and a staircase. A wall was then built to divide the house into two sections. The rooms are decorated with antiques, family heirlooms and collectibles. Offshore breezes sway blossoms in the lush garden. Cross the street to an excellent restaurant or take a picnic to the shore.
Innkeeper(s): Ed & Sooki Kirkpatrick. $85-120. MC VISA DS PC TC. 10 rooms with PB, 11 with FP. 1 suite. 2 conference rooms. Breakfast and evening snack included in rates. Types of meals: full breakfast and early coffee/tea. Beds: KQT. Air conditioning, ceiling fan and cable TV in room. Fax on premises. Antiques, parks, shopping and watersports nearby.
Location: In the historic district, four blocks to Tyron Palace.
Seen in: Americana.

"We feel nourished even now, six months after our visit to Harmony House."

Certificate may be used: Year-round, Sunday through Thursday night.

Pinebluff C6

Pine Cone Manor
450 E Philadelphia Ave,
Pinebluff, NC 28375
(910)281-5307

Circa 1912. The family that built this home lived here for more than 60 years, finally selling it in the 1970s. Today the house is a comfortable B&B set on private, wooded acres that include a variety of the namesake pines. The front porch is an ideal place to relax, offering a collection of rockers and a swing. The area is full of interesting sites, NASCAR and horse racing tracks are just a few. The area, which offers dozens of golf courses, also includes the World Golf Hall of Fame.
Innkeeper(s): Virginia H. Keith. $60-65. MC VISA PC TC. 3 rooms, 2 with PB, 1 with FP. 1 cottage. Breakfast included in rates. Types of meals: continental-plus breakfast and early coffee/tea. Beds: KQDT. Air conditioning, ceiling fan and cable TV in room. Library on premises. Antiques, parks, shopping and sporting events nearby.
Certificate may be used: Anytime subject to availability.

Rocky Mount B8

Sunset Inn B&B
1210 Sunset Ave, Rocky Mount, NC
27804-5126
(919)446-9524 (800)786-7386

Circa 1920. This Georgian inn is an impressive site from its spot on Sunset Avenue. The innkeepers filled the home with antiques and vast collections of art. Each of the guest rooms is appointed with Victorian furnishings and decor. With advance notice, the innkeepers can accommodate pets.
Innkeeper(s): Dale & Herbert Fuerst. $60-100. MC VISA AX DS TC. 5 rooms with PB. 2 conference rooms. Breakfast included in rates. Types of meals: full breakfast and early coffee/tea. Catered breakfast available. Beds: KQT. Air conditioning and cable TV in room. Copier on premises. Amusement parks, antiques and parks nearby.
Certificate may be used: All year.

Saluda C3

Ivy Terrace B&B Inn
PO Box 639, Saluda, NC 28773-0639
(704)749-9542 (800)749-9542
Fax:(704)749-2017

Circa 1890. Capt. W.G. Hinson built this two-story dwelling, surrounded by towering cedars, spruces and firs, as his summer home. The house later served as a boarding house, but today it has been lovingly transformed into an idyllic getaway. Comfortable furnishings create a homey, country atmosphere. Enjoy afternoon refreshments as you

take in the sounds of birds chirping away on the porches or patios. Breakfasts at Ivy Terrace won't be soon forgotten. Juices or fresh cider, made or pressed from locally grown apples, starts off an expansive meal with items such as hazelnut oatmeal pancakes with sauteed apples and sausage, or perhaps a cheddar French toast with maple syrup and a side of honey-marinated Canadian bacon. After the morning meal, guests can take in all the shops, outlets and craft stores in the area or head up scenic Blue

Ridge Parkway. Nature lovers will enjoy the hike to Pearsons Falls.

Innkeeper(s): Diane & Herbert McGuire & Walter Hoover. $95-140. MC VISA TC. 7 rooms with PB, 2 with FP. 1 conference room. Breakfast and evening snack included in rates. Types of meals: full breakfast and early coffee/tea. Beds: KQT. Cable TV, VCR, fax and copier on premises. Handicap access. Antiques, fishing, parks, theater and watersports nearby.

Seen in: SC CPA Newsletter.

"We had a wonderful weekend, due in large part to the wonderful accommodations and surroundings of the Ivy Terrace. Be sure you will see us again!"

Certificate may be used: Nov. 1-Sept. 30 Note: Rooms will be available any day for all months except October.

Spruce Pine   B4

Ansley Richmond Inn B&B
101 Pine St, Spruce Pine, NC 28777-2733
(704)765-6993

Circa 1939. The scent of freshly baked muffins and steaming coffee serves as a pleasing wake-up call for guests staying at this country mountain home. More than an acre of wooded grounds surround the inn, which overlooks the Toe River valley. Rooms are decorated with family heirlooms and antiques. Several guest chambers include four-poster beds. Crackling flames from the stone fireplace warm the living room, a perfect place to relax. The innkeepers keep a guest refrigerator in the butler's pantry.

Innkeeper(s): Bill Ansley & Lee Boucher. $45-70. MC VISA TC. 7 rooms with PB. Breakfast included in rates. Types of meals: full breakfast and early coffee/tea. Beds: QT. Ceiling fan in room. Cable TV, VCR and fax on premises. Antiques, parks, shopping, downhill skiing, cross-country skiing, theater and watersports nearby.

Certificate may be used: Sunday through Thursday, no holidays or special events. Nov. 1 to Sept. 30 (not in October).

Tabor City   D7

Four Rooster Inn
403 Pireway Rd,
Tabor City, NC 28463-2519
(910)653-3878

Circa 1949. This family home is situated on more than an acre of grounds featuring azaleas and camellias planted by the innkeeper's father. Guest rooms are decorated with antiques, elegant fabrics and fine linens. Guests are encouraged to return early for a spot of afternoon tea, served in the inn's parlor. Guests also are pampered with chocolate turn-down service. Sherried fruit compote, Tabor City yam bread and stuffed French toast are delectable examples of breakfast fare. Myrtle Beach's long stretch of

golf courses begins just four miles from the inn and outlet shopping, beaches and restaurants are nearby.

Innkeeper(s): Gloria & Bob Rogers. $45-75. MAP. MC VISA AX DC DS PC TC. 4 rooms, 2 with PB. Breakfast, afternoon tea and evening snack included in rates. Types of meals: gourmet breakfast and early coffee/tea. Beds: QD. Air conditioning and turn-down service in room. Cable TV and VCR on premises. Amusement parks, antiques, fishing, parks, shopping, sporting events, theater and watersports nearby.

Certificate may be used: Anytime - subject to availability.

Tryon   C3

Mimosa Inn
One Mimosa Inn Ln, Tryon, NC 28782
(704)859-7688

Circa 1903. The Mimosa is situated on the southern slope of the Blue Ridge Mountains. With its long rolling lawns and large columned veranda, the

inn has been a landmark and social gathering place for almost a century. There is a stone patio and outdoor fireplace. During fox hunting season there are two hunts a week in the area as well as two annual steeplechases.

Innkeeper(s): Jay & Sandi Franks. $65. MC VISA DS PC TC. 9 rooms with PB. 1 conference room. Breakfast included in rates. Types of meals: full breakfast and early coffee/tea. Beds: QT. Air conditioning in room. Cable TV and library on premises. Amusement parks, antiques, fishing, parks, shopping and theater nearby.

Certificate may be used: January-March, Sunday-Thursday. April-December, Monday-Thursday.

Tryon Old South B&B
107 Markham Rd, Tryon, NC 28782-3054
(704)859-6965 (800)288-7966
Fax:(704)859-2756

Circa 1910. This Colonial Revival inn is located just two blocks from downtown and Trade Street's antique and gift shops. Located in the Thermal Belt, Tryon is known for its pleasant, mild weather. Guests don't go away hungry from innkeeper Terry Cacioppo's large Southern-style breakfasts. Unique woodwork abounds in this inn and equally as impressive is a curving staircase. Behind the property is a large wooded area and several waterfalls are just a couple of miles away. The inn is close to Asheville attractions.

Innkeeper(s): Michael & Terry Cacioppo. $55-125. MC VISA DS PC TC. 6 rooms, 4 with PB. 2 cottages. Breakfast included in rates. Types of meals: full breakfast and early coffee/tea. Beds: QDT. Air conditioning in room. Cable TV, VCR, fax and copier on premises. Antiques, fishing, parks, shopping and theater nearby.

Certificate may be used: Weekdays, year-round.

Valle Crucis   B4

Mast Farm Inn
PO Box 704, Valle Crucis, NC 28691
(704)963-5857 Fax:(704)963-6404

Circa 1885. Listed in the National Register of Historic Places, this 18-acre farmstead includes a main house and seven outbuildings. The inn features a wraparound porch with rocking chairs, swings and a view of the mountain valley. Homemade breads and vegetables fresh from the garden are specialties. Rooms are furnished with antiques, quilts and mountain crafts.

Innkeeper(s): Sibyl & Francis Pressly. $85-175. MAP. MC VISA TC. 13 rooms, 11 with PB, 5 with FP. 4 suites. Breakfast and dinner included in rates. Types of meals: continental-plus breakfast and early coffee/tea. Beds: KQD. Ceiling fan in room. Fax on premises. Handicap access. Amusement parks, antiques, fishing, parks, shopping, downhill skiing, cross-country skiing, sporting events, theater and watersports nearby.
Seen in: Southern Bride, News & Observer, Blue Ridge Country, Country, Southern Living, Mid-Atlantic Country.

"Your warm hospitality is a rare find and one that we will remember for a long time."

Certificate may be used: January-May only, Sunday-Thursday. Not applicable Sundays on holiday weekends.

Waynesville   C3

Belle Meade Inn
5170 S Main St, PO Box 1319,
Waynesville, NC 28786
(704)456-3234

Circa 1908. Located near Asheville in the mountains of the Western part of the state, this Craftsman-style home was named Belle Meade, a French phrase meaning "beautiful meadow." Chestnut woodwork provides the background for

antiques and traditional furnishings. A fieldstone fireplace is featured in the living room. The Great Smoky Mountain Railroad ride is nearby. After a day exploring the area, guests return to enjoy light, afternoon refreshments.

Innkeeper(s): Gloria & Al DiNofa. $65-70. MC VISA DS PC TC. 4 rooms with PB, 2 with FP. Breakfast included in rates. Types of meals: full breakfast and early coffee/tea. Beds: QD. Air conditioning, ceiling fan and cable TV in room. VCR on premises. Amusement parks, antiques, fishing, parks, shopping, downhill skiing, sporting events and theater nearby.

Seen in: Blue Ridge, Asheville Citizen Times, St. Petersburg Times.

"Immaculately clean. Distinctively furnished. Friendly atmosphere."

Certificate may be used: Dec. 31 to April 1, no holidays.

Grandview Lodge
809 Valley View Cir Rd,
Waynesville, NC 28786
(704)456-5212 (800)255-7826
Fax:(704)452-5432

Circa 1890. Grandview Lodge is located on two-and-a-half acres in the Smoky Mountains. The land surrounding the lodge has an apple orchard, rhubarb patch, grape arbor and vegetable garden for

the inn's kitchen. Rooms are available in the main lodge and in a newer addition. The inn's dining room is known throughout the region and Linda, a home economist, has written "Recipes from Grandview Lodge."

Innkeeper(s): Stan & Linda Arnold. $100-110. MAP. PC TC. 11 rooms, 9 with PB, 3 with FP. 2 suites. Breakfast and dinner included in rates. Types of meals: full breakfast and early coffee/tea. Lunch available. Beds: KQDT. Air conditioning and cable TV in room. VCR, fax, computer and library on premises. Handicap access. Amusement parks, antiques, fishing, parks, shopping, downhill skiing, sporting events, theater and watersports nearby.

Seen in: Asheville Citizen, Winston-Salem Journal, Raleigh News & Observer.

"It's easy to see why family and friends have been enjoying trips to Grandview."

Certificate may be used: November through May, anytime; June, July-September, Sunday through Thursday; not participating August and October. Rates include dinner.

Mountain Creek Inn

100 Chestnut Walk,
Waynesville, NC 28786
(704)456-5509 Fax:(704)456-6728

Circa 1950. From its floor-to-ceiling windows, this hilltop lodge affords views of mountains and woods and is surrounded by more than five, peaceful acres. Meander through the gardens or take a leisurely stroll on a nature path. The innkeepers found their bed & breakfast while trekking through the Smoky Mountains on a tandem bicycle. If weather permits, the champagne continental breakfast is served on the deck. For an additional charge, picnic lunches and romantic getaway packages for two can be prepared.

Innkeeper(s): Guy & Hylah Smalley. $85-110. AP. MC VISA AX DS PC TC. 5 rooms with PB. Breakfast and afternoon tea included in rates. Types of meals: continental breakfast, full breakfast and early coffee/tea. Evening snack, picnic lunch and gourmet lunch available. Beds: KQ. Air conditioning and turn-down service in room. Cable TV, VCR, spa, swimming and library on premises. Handicap access. Amusement parks, antiques, fishing, parks, shopping, downhill skiing, cross-country skiing, theater and watersports nearby.

Certificate may be used: Nov. 1-June 30, Sunday-Friday.

Weldon   A9

Weldon Place Inn

500 Washington Ave,
Weldon, NC 27890-1644
(919)536-4582 (800)831-4470
Fax:(919)536-4708

Circa 1913. Homemade strawberry bread is a pleasant way to start your morning at this Colonial Revival home. Located in the historic area, it is two miles from I-95. Wedding showers and other celebrations are popular here. There are beveled-glass windows, canopy beds and Italian fireplaces. Most of the inn's antiques are original to the house, including a horse-hair stuffed couch with its original upholstery. Select the Romantic Retreat package and you'll enjoy flowers, sparkling cider, a whirlpool tub and breakfast in bed.

Innkeeper(s): Angel & Andy Whitby. $55-89. MC VISA AX. 4 rooms with PB. Breakfast included in rates. Type of meal: full breakfast. Beds: D. Air conditioning and cable TV in room. VCR on premises. Antiques, fishing, shopping and theater nearby.

Certificate may be used: Anytime.

Winston-Salem   B6

Augustus T. Zevely Inn

803 S Main St,
Winston-Salem, NC 27101-5332
(910)748-9299 (800)928-9299
Fax:(910)721-2211

Circa 1844. The Zevely Inn is the only lodging in Old Salem. Each of the rooms at this charming pre-Civil War inn boasts a view of historic Old Salem. Moravian decor permeates the decor of each of the guest quarters, some of which boast working fireplaces and whirlpool/steam baths. The home's architecture is reminiscent of many structures built in Old Salem during the second quarter of the 19th century. The formal dining room and parlor, often used for weddings and parties, offer woodburning fireplaces. Breakfasts and evening refreshments are served on the two-story covered porch. A line of Old Salem furniture has been created by Lexington Furniture Industries, and several pieces were created especially for the Zevely Inn.

Innkeeper(s): Linda Anderson. $80-185. MC VISA AX PC TC. 12 rooms with PB, 3 with FP. 1 suite. 2 conference rooms. Breakfast and evening snack included in rates. Types of meals: full breakfast, gourmet breakfast and early coffee/tea. Catering service available. Beds: KQDT. Air conditioning and cable TV in room. Fax, copier and bicycles on premises. Antiques, fishing, parks, shopping, sporting events, theater and watersports nearby.

"Wouldn't change one thing, service was absolutely wonderful."

Certificate may be used: November, December, January, February on Sundays, Mondays, excluding seasonal events.

Colonel Ludlow Inn

434 Summit at W 5th,
Winston-Salem, NC 27101
(910)777-1887 (800)301-1887
Fax:(910)777-1890

Circa 1887. The innkeepers at this Queen Anne house with its graceful wrap-around porches and hipped gable roof pamper guests with a bounty of amenities. Fluffy bath robes, bubble bath and fresh flowers are only a few of the offerings. More modern amenities include hair dryers and irons, small refrigerators and a stereo system with a selection of tapes. The home boasts an ornate entrance and several stained-glass windows bordering the stairway. The dining room has a gold-plated chandelier and reproduction wallpaper. The guest rooms feature

Victorian antiques, antique beds and more stained-glass windows. Some rooms include two-person whirlpool tubs and fireplaces. The innkeepers also offer an extensive collection of movies to enjoy.

Innkeeper(s): Constance Creasman. $99-179. MC VISA AX DS PC TC. 9 rooms with PB, 5 with FP. Breakfast included in rates. Types of meals: full breakfast and early coffee/tea. Beds: KQ. Air conditioning, ceiling fan, cable TV and VCR in room. Computer on premises. Antiques, fishing, parks, shopping, sporting events and theater nearby.

Location: Off highway I-40.

Seen in: Charlotte Observer, Mid-Atlantic Country, Southern Living, Southern Accents, USA Today, American Way.

"I have never seen anything like the meticulous and thorough attention to detail—Dannye Romine, The Charlotte Observer."

Certificate may be used: Sunday-Monday.

Meadowhaven B&B

PO Box 222, Winston-Salem
(Germanton), NC 27019-0222
(910)593-3996 Fax:(910)593-3138

Circa 1976. This contemporary retreat is secluded on 25 acres within the Blue Ridge foothills. Guest stay either in the main house, a log cabin with mountain views or in a two-bedroom, mountain-top cabin. Bathrobes and hairdryers are provided in the rooms, as are TVs, VCRs and a selection of movies. Oversize bathtubs for two (one heart-shaped, no less), a heated indoor swimming pool, sauna and spa are a few more amenities awaiting guests. The home is near Hanging Rock and Pilot Mountain state parks, as well as Old Salem.

Innkeeper(s): Samuel & Darlene Fain. $70-175. MC VISA AX DS PC TC. 6 rooms with PB, 2 with FP. 2 suites. 2 cottages. Breakfast and evening snack included in rates. Types of meals: full breakfast and early coffee/tea. Picnic lunch available. Beds: QD. Air conditioning, turn-down service, ceiling fan, cable TV and VCR in room. Fax, copier, spa, swimming and sauna on premises. Antiques, fishing, parks, shopping, sporting events, theater and watersports nearby.

"Heaven is a good name for Meadowhaven. I felt like I could relax in a home atmosphere."

Certificate may be used: Sunday-Thursday except April, August, October and holidays.

Wachovia B&B

513 Wachovia St,
Winston-Salem, NC 27101-5042
(910)777-0332

Circa 1907. This rose and white Victorian cottage with a wraparound porch is located on a quiet, tree-lined street. The inn is located only a few blocks from the Winston-Salem city center and the Old Salem Historic District. Guests may choose to eat their breakfast in the large dining room, in their rooms or on the porch. The innkeepers like to provide flexible check-in and check-out times and there is no rigid breakfast schedule. Within walking distance is the Stevens Center for performing arts, gourmet restaurants, antique and specialty shops and several exercise facilities and parks.

Innkeeper(s): Susan & Greg Pfaff. $55-65. MC VISA TC. 5 rooms, 2 with PB, 1 with FP. Breakfast included in rates. Types of meals: continental-plus breakfast, full breakfast and early coffee/tea. Beds: QDT. Air conditioning, turn-down service and ceiling fan in room. Cable TV on premises. Antiques, parks, shopping, sporting events and theater nearby.

Seen in: Parentips Magazine, Winston-Salem Magazine.

Certificate may be used: All year subject to availability.

North Dakota

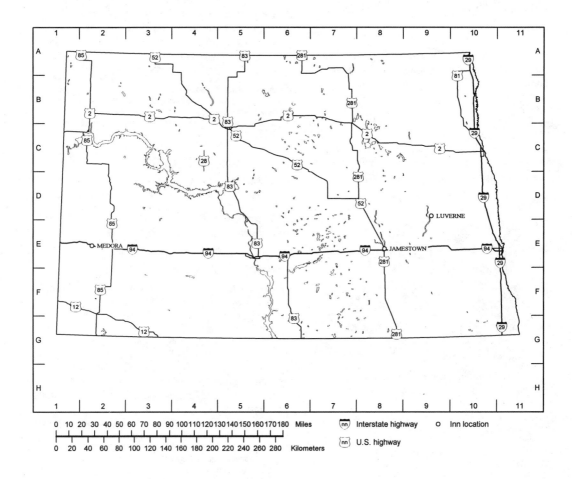

Jamestown E8

Country Charm B&B
RR 3 Box 71, Jamestown, ND 58401
(701)251-1372 (800)331-1372

Circa 1897. Jamestown not only offers convenience, centrally located at the intersection of the state's east-west interstate and main north-south highway, it features the Country Charm, a prairie farmhouse six miles from town and a short hop from I-94. The inn's tranquil setting is accented by the surrounding pines and cottonwood trees. The blue-dominated Patches and Lace Room features a multi-shaded patchwork quilt. Activities and places of interest abound in the Jamestown area, including Frontier Village and North Dakota's oldest courthouse.
Innkeeper(s): Ethel Oxtoby. $42-53. 4 rooms. Breakfast included in rates. Type of meal: full breakfast. Air conditioning and ceiling fan in room. VCR on premises. Antiques, fishing, shopping, cross-country skiing, sporting events and theater nearby.

Certificate may be used: Monday through Thursday, all year.

Luverne D9

Volden Farm
RR 2, Box 50, Luverne, ND 58056
(701)769-2275

Circa 1926. Perennial gardens and a hedge of lilacs surround this redwood house with its newer addition. A favorite room is the North Room with a lace canopy bed, an old pie safe and a Texas Star quilt made by the host's grandmother. Guests enjoy soaking in the clawfoot tub while looking out to the apple and plum orchard. There is a library, music room and game room. The innkeepers also offer accommodations in the Law Office, a private home ideal for couples or small families. The Law Office includes a king-size feather bed. A stream, bordered by old oaks and formed by a natural spring, meanders through the property. The chickens here lay green and blue eggs. Supper is available by advanced arrangement.
Innkeeper(s): Jim & JoAnne Wold. $50-75. PC. 4 rooms. 1 suite. 1 cottage. Breakfast and evening snack included in rates. Types of meals: full breakfast, gourmet breakfast and early coffee/tea. Dinner, picnic lunch, lunch, gourmet lunch, catering service and room service available. Beds: KDT. VCR, bicycles and library on premises. Antiques, fishing, parks, shopping, downhill skiing, cross-country skiing and watersports nearby.

Location: 80 miles northwest of Fargo.

Seen in: Fargo Forum, Horizons, Grand Forks Herald.

"Very pleasant indeed! Jim & JoAnne make you feel good. There's so much to do, and the hospitality is amazing!"

Certificate may be used: Anytime, holidays excluded.

Medora E2

The Rough Riders Hotel B&B
Medora, ND 58645
(701)623-4444 Fax:(701)623-4494

Circa 1865. This old hotel has the branding marks of Teddy Roosevelt's cattle ranch as well as other brands stamped into the rough-board facade out front. A wooden sidewalk helps to maintain the turn-of-the-century cow-town feeling. Rustic guest rooms are above the restaurant and are furnished with homesteader antiques original to the area. In the summer, an outdoor pageant is held complete with stagecoach and horses. In October deer hunters are accommodated. The hotel, along with two motels, is managed by the non-profit Theodore Roosevelt Medora Foundation.
Innkeeper(s): Randy Hatzenbuhler. $55. MC VISA AX. 9 rooms with PB. Breakfast included in rates.

Certificate may be used: Oct. 1 to May 1, excluding Friday and Saturday nights.

Ohio

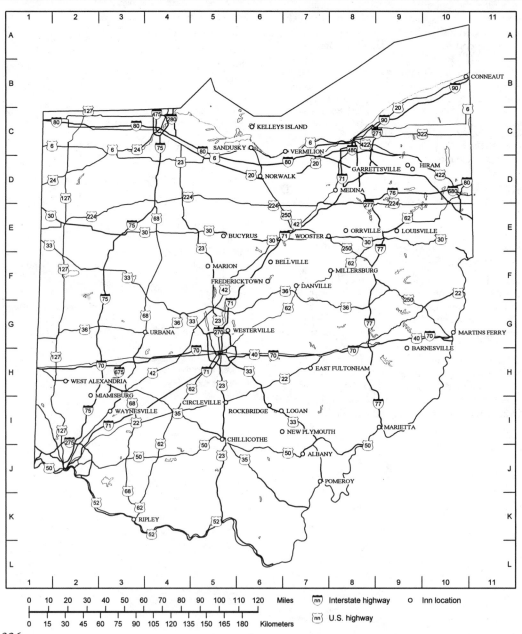

Albany J7

Albany House
9 Clinton St, Albany, OH 45710
(614)698-6311 (800)600-4941

Circa 1860. Located seven miles from Ohio University in a quaint village setting, this inn is filled with antiques, quilts, Oriental rugs and collectibles.

Because of four two-story columns, it is often referred to as "Tara North." A new addition includes an indoor pool, showers and changing room.
Innkeeper(s): Sarah & Ted Hutchins. $65-100. MC VISA AX DS. 6 rooms, 2 with PB. 1 conference room. Breakfast and evening snack included in rates. Types of meals: continental-plus breakfast, gourmet breakfast and early coffee/tea. Beds: QDT. Antiques, fishing, parks, shopping, theater and watersports nearby.
Seen in: Post.
Certificate may be used: Weekdays, Sunday-Thursday, weekends if available.

Barnesville H9

Georgian Pillars B&B
128 E Walnut St,
Barnesville, OH 43713-1237
(614)425-3741 (800)525-3741

Victorian charm permeates this Georgian Revival home, which boasts ornate woodwork and stained-glass windows. The decidedly Victorian parlors offer a refreshing change of pace from the rush of modern times, one of the parlors has a fireplace. Posh breakfasts are served in the elegant dining room on Royal Doulton pieces. Teal and mauve hues abound in the guest rooms, which feature unique, Victorian furnishings with flowery prints. The bed & breakfast also houses a small gift shop with a signed, numbered set of "Barnesville Collection of Historic Miniature Houses.".

Innkeeper(s): Janet Thompson. $45-55. MC VISA. 3 rooms. Breakfast included in rates. Type of meal: full breakfast.
Certificate may be used: Sunday through Thursday, June through Oct. 30; November through May, anytime.

Bellville F6

Frederick Fitting House
72 Fitting Ave, Bellville, OH 44813-1043
(419)886-2863 Fax:(419)886-2863

This blue and white Italianate Victorian house commands a corner of the town of Bellville, 10 minutes from Ohio University. Rooms include the Colonial Room with a queen canopy bed and the Shaker Room with twin beds that can be converted to a king. Breakfast is served in the Victorian dining room or garden gazebo, but you may wish to carry it to the front porch or to the library where you can settle down during the winter in front of a roaring fire. Malabar Farms is nearby as is the Mohican River.

Innkeeper(s): Suzanne Wilson. $48-72. 3 rooms. Breakfast included in rates. Types of meals: full breakfast and early coffee/tea. Evening snack and picnic lunch available. Ceiling fan in room. Cable TV and VCR on premises. Antiques, shopping, downhill skiing, cross-country skiing and sporting events nearby.
Certificate may be used: Sunday-Thursday, May-October. Anyday, November-April.

Bucyrus E5

Hide Away B&B
1601 State Route 4,
Bucyrus, OH 44820-9587
(419)562-3013 Fax:(419)562-3003

Circa 1938. This aptly named B&B sits on six acres, which afford views of the nearby Little Scioto River. The home was built by inventor S.H. Smith, who among his patents, was responsible for creating transistor radios used in World War II aircraft. Guest rooms are decorated in a comfortable country motif with special antiques and amenities such as a feathertick. The grounds include a swimming pool and relaxing Jacuzzi.

Innkeeper(s): Steve & Debbie Miller. $40-125. MC VISA AX DS TC. 4 rooms with PB. 2 conference rooms. Types of meals: continental breakfast, continental-plus breakfast, full breakfast, gourmet breakfast and early coffee/tea. Afternoon tea, dinner, evening snack, picnic lunch, lunch, gourmet lunch, banquet service, catering service and catered breakfast available. Beds: KQ. Air conditioning, turn-down service and VCR in room. Fax, copier, spa, bicycles and child care on premises. Amusement parks, antiques, parks, shopping, downhill skiing, theater and watersports nearby.
Certificate may be used: Jan. 2-Dec. 31, Sunday-Thursday. Corporate rates not applicable.

Chillicothe I5

Chillicothe B&B
202 S Paint St,
Chillicothe, OH 45601-3827
(614)772-6848

Circa 1867. This National Register home, which was constructed while the nation struggled with the Civil War, was built by the owner of the town's first paper mill. Innkeepers Katie and Jack Sullivan furnished the home with antiques and collectibles, including a collection of vintage clothing. Clothing is somewhat of a passion for Katie, who has created costumes for many local theatrical productions. Jack, an artist and photographer, will provide a tour of his studio to interested guests. Chillicothe, once the capital of Ohio, is full of many historic homes.
Innkeeper(s): Kathryn Sullivan. $35-50. MC VISA. 4 rooms. Breakfast included in rates. Type of meal: full breakfast.
Certificate may be used: Sunday through Thursday, year-round.

Circleville I5

Penguin Crossing B&B
3291 State Route 56 W,
Circleville, OH 43113-9622
(614)477-6222 Fax:(614)477-6222

Circa 1820. This farmhouse originally served as a stagecoach stop. Rooms include amenities such as a woodburning fireplace, clawfoot tub, brass bed or a heart-shaped whirlpool tub. As the name might suggest, the innkeepers have a collection of penguins on display. Breakfasts include a selection of natural foods, and the innkeeper is happy to cater to special dietary needs.

D. OSTER

Innkeeper(s): Ross & Tracey Irvin. $100-150. MC VISA DS PC TC. 4 rooms with PB, 1 with FP. Breakfast included in rates. Types of meals: continental breakfast, continental-plus breakfast, full breakfast, gourmet breakfast and early coffee/tea. Beds: KQDT. Air conditioning and turn-down service in room. VCR and fax on premises. Handicap access. Antiques, fishing, parks, shopping, theater and watersports nearby.
Certificate may be used: Year-round, Monday-Thursday.

Conneaut B10

Campbell Braemar
390 State St, Conneaut, OH 44030-2510
(216)599-7362

Circa 1927. This little Colonial Revival house is decorated in a Scottish style, and a Scottish breakfast is provided. Guests are invited to use the kitchen for light cooking as the hosts live next door. Wineries, golf, fishing, sandy beaches and hunting are nearby.

Innkeeper(s): Mary & Andrew Campbell. $58-68. TC. 3 rooms. Breakfast and afternoon tea included in rates. Types of meals: continental breakfast, continental-plus breakfast, full breakfast and early coffee/tea. Beds: KQD. Air conditioning and cable TV in room. Antiques, fishing, parks and watersports nearby.
Certificate may be used: Jan. 1-Dec. 31, Sunday-Thursday.

Danville F7

Red Fox Country Inn
26367 Danville Amity Rd,
Danville, OH 43014-9769
(614)599-7369

Circa 1830. This country inn was built originally to house those traveling on the Danville-Amity Wagon Road and later became a farm house. Amish woven rag rugs and antiques decorate the guest rooms. Three rooms include Amish-made oak beds and the other boasts an 1880s brass and iron double

bed. The renovated horse stable now serves as an antique shop with a variety of interesting pieces. Breakfasts include freshly baked pastries, fruits and coffee along with a variety of delectable entrees. For an additional charge and advance notice, guests are welcome to bring friends along for the morning meal. Special low-fat, low-cholesterol dishes are available on request. Golfing, canoeing on the Mohican River and horseback riding are a few of the area activities. Guests can visit local orchards and farm markets, and the area is host to festivals and fairs throughout the year.

Innkeeper(s): Ida & Mort Wolff. $65-85. MC VISA AX DS PC TC. 4 rooms with PB. Breakfast included in rates. Afternoon tea, dinner, banquet service and catering service available. Beds: QD. Air conditioning in room. Library on premises. Amusement parks, antiques, fishing, parks, shopping, cross-country skiing, sporting events, theater and watersports nearby.

Seen in: Columbus Dispatch, Mount Vernon News.

"You have indeed mastered the gift of Innkeeper! Your inn is wonderfully warm & instantly inviting. The food was absolutely 'delicious.'"

Certificate may be used: Weekdays all year round. Weekends Dec. 1 to March 31. Excludes holidays and events at area colleges

The White Oak Inn

29683 Walhonding Rd, SR 715,
Danville, OH 43014-9681
(614)599-6107

Circa 1915. Large oaks and ivy surround the wide front porch of this three-story farmhouse situated on 13 green acres. It is located on the former Indian trail and pioneer road that runs along the Kokosing

River, and an Indian mound has been discovered on the property. The inn's woodwork is all original white oak, and guest rooms are furnished in antiques. Visitors often shop for maple syrup, cheese and handicrafts at nearby Amish farms. Three cozy fireplace rooms provide the perfect setting for romantic evenings.

Innkeeper(s): Yvonne & Ian Martin. $75-140. MAP. MC VISA AX DS PC TC. 10 rooms with PB, 3 with FP. 1 conference room. Breakfast and evening snack included in rates. Types of meals: full breakfast and early coffee/tea. Catering service available. Beds: QDT. Air conditioning and ceiling fan in room. Bicycles and library on premises. Antiques, fishing, parks, shopping and watersports nearby.

Location: Holmes County Amish area, north central Ohio.

Seen in: Ladies Home Journal, Columbus Monthly, Cleveland Plain Dealer, Country, Glamour, Columbus Dispatch.

"The dinner was just fabulous and we enjoyed playing the antique grand piano."

Certificate may be used: Sunday to Thursday nights all year-round.

East Fultonham H7

Hill View Acres B&B

7320 Old Town Rd,
East Fultonham, OH 43735
(614)849-2728

Circa 1905. Hill View Acres was an apt description for this relaxing country home, which is surrounded by more than 20 acres of rolling hills. The large deck is a wonderful place to sit and soak up the atmosphere. The grounds also include a swimming pool and spa. Innkeeper Dawn Graham has won several local cooking contests and enjoys treating her guests to a hearty country breakfast each morning. Dawn and husband Jim work out the menu with guests the night before, taking in all dietary concerns. Dawn creates luscious items accompanied by homemade jams and jellies. The home is near many attractions, including wildlife preserves, museums, outlet shopping and the Ohio Ceramic Center.

Innkeeper(s): Jim & Dawn Graham. $40-45. MC VISA AX DS TC. 2 rooms. Breakfast and evening snack included in rates. Types of meals: full breakfast and early coffee/tea. Dinner, picnic lunch and lunch available. Beds: D. Air conditioning and ceiling fan in room. Cable TV, VCR and spa on premises. Antiques, fishing, parks and shopping nearby.

Certificate may be used: Jan. 1 to Dec. 31, excluding Dec. 25.

Fredericktown

F6

Heartland Country Resort

2994 Township Rd 190,
Fredericktown, OH 43019
(419)768-9300 (800)230-7030

Circa 1878. This restored farmhouse offers guests a serene country setting with hills, woods, pastures, fields, wooded trails, barns, horse stables and riding arenas. With full run of the huge house, guests also

have their choice of a wide variety of recreation. Horseback riding is the recreation of choice for most visitors. Innkeeper Dorene Henschen tells guests not to miss the beauty of the woods as seen on the guided trail rides.

Innkeeper(s): Dorene Henschen. $80-105. MC VISA. 4 rooms, 2 with PB. 1 suite. Breakfast and afternoon tea included in rates. Type of meal: continental-plus breakfast. Dinner, picnic lunch, lunch and room service available. Beds: KQT. Antiques, fishing, downhill skiing, cross-country skiing and watersports nearby.

Seen in: Columbus Dispatch.

Certificate may be used: Monday through Thursday.

Garrettsville

D9

Blueberry Hill B&B

11085 North St (Rt 88),
Garrettsville, OH 44231
(216)527-5068

Although this restored Victorian is just minutes from downtown Garrettsville, the landscaped grounds create a secluded, pastoral setting. Relax in front of a wood-burning fireplace or stroll through nearby woods. Rooms are decorated in Laura Ashley prints with Victorian touches and the innkeepers own impressive collection of artwork.

The home is located on the outskirts of one of the largest Amish towns in the United States, and near both Hiram College and Kent State University.

Innkeeper(s): Deborah Darling. $60. 2 rooms. Breakfast included in rates. Type of meal: continental breakfast.

Certificate may be used: All year Monday through Thursday, except holidays.

Hiram

D9

The Lily Ponds B&B

PO Box 322, 6720 Wakefield Rd,
Hiram, OH 44234-0322
(216)569-3222 (800)325-5087
Fax:(216)569-3223

Circa 1940. This homestay is located on 22 acres of woodland dotted with clumps of rhododendron and mountain laurel. There are two large ponds and an old stone bridge. Your hostess works with a tour company and has traveled around the world. The inn's decor includes her collections of Eskimo art and artifacts and a variety of antiques. Sea World is fifteen minutes away. Pecan waffles served with locally harvested maple syrup are a favorite breakfast. Guests enjoy borrowing the canoe or hiking the inn's trails.

Innkeeper(s): Marilane Spencer. $55-75. MC VISA. 3 rooms with PB. Breakfast included in rates. Types of meals: full breakfast, gourmet breakfast and early coffee/tea. Beds: KQT. Air conditioning and cable TV in room. VCR, bicycles, library and child care on premises. Amusement parks, antiques, fishing, parks, shopping, downhill skiing, cross-country skiing and watersports nearby.

Location: 15 minutes from Sea World.

Seen in: Record-Courier, Record-News.

"We felt like we were staying with friends from the very start."

Certificate may be used: Any day, year-round, except Friday and Saturday, June through September.

Kelleys Island

C6

Fly Inn B&B

PO Box 471, Dwelle Ln,
Kelleys Island, OH 43438-0471
(419)746-2525 (800)359-4661
Fax:(419)746-2525

Circa 1988. Kelleys Island, for those not familiar with Ohio, encompasses a 2,800-acre patch of land in Lake Erie, all designated a historic district in the National Register. One acre of this wooded island encircles this rustic B&B, adjacent to the airport. Guests can watch as light planes cruise by or visit the island's historic sites and winery. The guest rooms are comfortable and homey, with modern decor. During the summer, guests can dive into the inn's swimming pool, and the innkeepers offer bicycles for touring the area.

Innkeeper(s): Ken & Joann Neufer. $90-110. MC VISA DS TC. 4 rooms, 2 with PB. 1 conference room. Breakfast included in rates. Beds: KQ. Air conditioning in room. VCR, fax and bicycles on premises. Handicap access. Amusement parks, fishing, parks, shopping and watersports nearby.

Location: On Lake Erie.

Certificate may be used: Sunday through Thursday beginning Oct. 1 and ending April 30, no holidays included.

The Inn on Kelleys Island
PO Box 11,
Kelleys Island, OH 43438-0011
(419)746-2258

Circa 1876. With a private deck on the shore of Lake Erie, this waterfront Victorian offers an acre of grounds. Built by the innkeeper's ancestor, Captain Frank Hamilton, the house features a black marble

fireplace and a porch with a spectacular Lake Erie view. The Pilot House is a room with large windows looking out to the lake. The inn is close to the ferry and downtown with restaurants, taverns and shops.

Innkeeper(s): Lori Hayes. $65-85. 4 rooms. Breakfast included in rates. Types of meals: continental breakfast and early coffee/tea. Beds: D. Ceiling fan in room. VCR on premises. Amusement parks, antiques, fishing and shopping nearby.

Location: Lakefront on Kelleys Island.

Certificate may be used: Sunday-Thursday during months of April, May, September, October and November excluding holidays.

Logan
I6

The Inn at Cedar Falls
21190 State Rt 374, Logan, OH 43138
(614)385-7489 (800)653-2557
Fax:(614)385-0820

Circa 1987. This barn-style inn was constructed on 80 acres adjacent to Hocking State Park and a half

mile from the waterfalls. The kitchen and dining room is in a 19th-century log house with a wood-burning stove, and 18-inch-wide plank floor. Accommodations in the new barn building are simple and comfortable, each furnished with antiques. Verandas provide sweeping views of woodland and meadow. The grounds include organic gardens for the inn's gourmet dinners, and animals that have been spotted include bobcat, red fox, wild turkey and whitetail deer.

Innkeeper(s): Ellen Grinsfelder. $75-185. MC VISA PC. 14 rooms, 9 with PB, 5 with FP. 5 cottages. 1 conference room. Breakfast included in rates. Types of meals: full breakfast, gourmet breakfast and early coffee/tea. Dinner, picnic lunch, lunch and gourmet lunch available. Beds: QT. Air conditioning in room. Fax, copier and library on premises. Handicap access. Antiques, fishing, parks, shopping, cross-country skiing and theater nearby.

Seen in: Post.

"Very peaceful, relaxing and friendly. Couldn't be nicer."

Certificate may be used: Sunday through Thursday beginning Nov. 15 and ending April 15, no holidays included, rooms only.

Louisville
E9

The Mainstay B&B
1320 E Main St, Louisville, OH 44641
(216)875-1021

Circa 1886. Built by a Civil War veteran, this Victorian still has the original fish scale on its gables, and inside, it features carved-oak woodwork and oak doors. Guests are treated to a complimentary basket of fruit and cheese in their air-conditioned rooms. Outside are flower gardens with birdbaths and a water fountain. This is a great stop in the middle of a long trip because laundry facilities are available

to guests. Nearby colleges are Malone, Walsh, Mount Union and Kent State University.

Innkeeper(s): Mary & Joe Shurilla. $50-60. AP. MC VISA PC. 3 rooms with PB. Breakfast and evening snack included in rates. Types of meals: full breakfast and early coffee/tea. Beds: QDT. Air conditioning in room. Cable TV and VCR on premises. Antiques, parks and downhill skiing nearby.

Certificate may be used: Sunday through Thursday, not holidays.

Marietta I9

The Buckley House

332 Front St, Marietta, OH 45750-2913
(614)373-3080 Fax:(614)373-8000

Circa 1879. A double veranda accents this gable-front Greek Revival house and provides views of Muskingum Park and river as well as Lookout Point and the "Valley Gem," a traditional Mississippi river boat. Guests are served tea, evening aperitifs and breakfast from the inn's parlor, porches and dining room. Within a five-block area are museums, a mound cemetery, the W.P. Snyder Jr. Sternwheeler, boat rides, trolley tours and shops and restaurants.

Innkeeper(s): Dell & Alf Nicholas. $70-80. MC VISA DS PC TC. 3 rooms with PB, 1 with FP. 1 suite. Breakfast included in rates. Types of meals: full breakfast and early coffee/tea. Beds: KDT. Air conditioning and ceiling fan in room. Cable TV, VCR, fax, spa and library on premises. Antiques, fishing, parks, shopping, theater and watersports nearby.

Certificate may be used: Nov. 15-March 31, Monday-Thursday.

Marion F5

Olde Towne Manor

245 Saint James St,
Marion, OH 43302-5134
(614)382-2402 (800)341-6163

Circa 1920. This beautiful stone house, located in the heart of Marion's historic district, won Marion's most attractive building award in 1990. The home offers bookworms the chance to browse through a

1,000-volume library. A gazebo or sauna are ideal settings for relaxation. The nearby home of President Warren G. Harding and the Harding Memorial will attract history buffs. In August, the town hosts the U.S. Open Drum and Bugle Corps National Championships, and the Marion Popcorn Festival is a unique attraction the weekend after Labor Day.

Innkeeper(s): Mary Louisa Rimbach. $55-65. MC VISA AX. 4 rooms with PB. Breakfast included in rates. Type of meal: full breakfast. Beds: QDT. Air conditioning in room. Cable TV, VCR and sauna on premises. Antiques, fishing, shopping and theater nearby.

Seen in: Marion Star, News Life, Ohio Week.

"Thanks for a warm and intimate home away from home! Lovely place with great hostess!"

Certificate may be used: Anytime, except Dec. 24 & 25.

Martins Ferry G10

Mulberry Inn B&B

53 N 4th St,
Martins Ferry, OH 43935-1523
(614)633-6058 Fax:(614)633-5923

Circa 1868. The Roosevelt Room in this Victorian inn once housed Eleanor Roosevelt during a "Bond Drive." Mrs. Blackford, goddaughter of Jefferson Davis, was the hostess during that time and was well-known for her hospitality during the Depression. The inn is decorated with country antiques and quilts.

Innkeeper(s): Charles & Shirley Probst. $45-55. MC VISA AX DS. 3 rooms, 1 with PB. Breakfast and evening snack included in rates. Types of meals: continental-plus breakfast and early coffee/tea. Beds: QD. Air conditioning, turn-down service and ceiling fan in room. Cable TV on premises. Antiques, fishing, parks, shopping, downhill skiing, sporting events, theater and watersports nearby.

Location: Southeast Ohio along the Ohio River.

Seen in: Times Leader, Herald Star.

"I really loved this place! It felt so private, yet (as most B&B's are), it was personal. It smells so good here!"

Certificate may be used: Jan. 4 to March 31, Sunday-Saturday.

Medina D8

Livery Building

254 E Smith Rd, Medina, OH 44256-2623
(216)722-1332

This three-story Queen Anne, which once housed a local livery horse business, offers one immense suite featuring antique furnishings, small parlor and kitchenette with a wet bar. The wood-burning stove adds country charm. The innkeepers offer a full breakfast made from organic ingredients. The bed &

breakfast is within walking distance of Medina's restored Victorian town square and historic district.
Innkeeper(s): Candace Hutton. $65. 1 room. Breakfast included in rates. Type of meal: full breakfast.

Certificate may be used: Anytime, June 1 through Sept. 30.

Miamisburg   H2

English Manor B&B
505 E Linden Ave,
Miamisburg, OH 45342-2850
(513)866-2288 (800)676-9456

This is a beautiful English Tudor mansion situated on a tree-lined street of Victorian homes. Well-chosen antiques combined with the innkeepers' personal heirlooms added to the inn's polished floors, sparkling leaded- and stained-glass windows and shining silver, make this an elegant retreat. Breakfast is served in the formal dining room or by the fireplace in your room, and in the afternoon, tea is served. Fine restaurants, a waterpark, baseball and theater are close by, as is The River Corridor bikeway on the banks of the Great Miami River.
Innkeeper(s): Jack DiDrichson. $62-75. MC VISA AX DC CB DS. 5 rooms. 1 conference room. Breakfast included in rates. Type of meal: full breakfast. Air conditioning and turn-down service in room. Cable TV and VCR on premises. Amusement parks, antiques, shopping, sporting events and theater nearby.

Certificate may be used: Sunday through Thursday.

Millersburg   F8

Bigham House
151 S Washington St,
Millersburg, OH 44654-1315
(330)674-2337 (800)689-6950

Circa 1869. Bigham House is a two-story Victorian located in the world's largest Amish settlement. Antiques and Victorian reproductions decorate the rooms. Ask for Dr. Bigham's Room and you'll enjoy stained-glass windows, a fireplace and brass ceiling fan. Nearby activities include buggy rides and the restored Ohio Central Railway.
Innkeeper(s): John Henry Ellis. $70-80. MC VISA. 4 rooms, 3 with PB, 1 with FP. Breakfast included in rates. Types of meals: full breakfast and gourmet breakfast. Afternoon tea available. Beds: Q.

Location: In the heart of the largest Amish settlement in the world, Holmes County, Ohio.

Seen in: Holmes County Traveler.

Certificate may be used: November-May, Sunday-Thursday.

New Plymouth   I6

Ravenwood Castle
Rt 1 Box 52-B,
New Plymouth, OH 45654-9707
(614)596-2606 (800)477-1541
Fax:(614)596-5818

Circa 1995. Although this is a newer construction, the architect modeled the inn after a 12th-century, Norman-style castle, offering a glimpse back at Medieval England. A Great Hall with massive stone fireplace, an English Pub, dramatic rooms and suites with antique stained-glass windows and gas fireplaces make for a unique getaway. The castle, which

Castle Inn - Circleville, Ohio

overlooks Vinton County's Swan township, is surrounded by 50 acres of forest and large rock formations and is reached by a half-mile private road.
Innkeeper(s): Jim & Sue Maxwell. $85-150. MC VISA DS. 8 rooms with PB. Breakfast included in rates. Types of meals: full breakfast and early coffee/tea. Afternoon tea, dinner, evening snack, picnic lunch and room service available. Beds: KQD. Air conditioning and ceiling fan in room. VCR, fax and copier on premises. Handicap access. Antiques, fishing, shopping and watersports nearby.

Seen in: Columbus Dispatch, Cincinnati Enquirer, Athens Messenger, Southeast Ohio Traveler, Vinton County Courier, Hocking Hills Travel News, A Taste for Columbus, Country Register.

"The atmosphere is romantic, the food excellent, the hospitality super!"

Certificate may be used: Nov. 1-March 31, Sunday-Thursday, except holidays.

Norwalk

D6

Boos Family Inn B&B

5054 State Route 601,
Norwalk, OH 44857-9729
(419)668-6257 Fax:(419)668-7722

Circa 1860. To see the modern additions to this former farm home, you would not at first realize that parts of this home date back to the mid-1800s. There are two acres of flowers, lawns and trees. Five minutes away is Thomas Edison's home, Ohio's largest outlet mall and Cedar Point.

Innkeeper(s): Don & Mary Boos. $45-85. MC VISA AX DS PC TC. 3 rooms with PB. 1 suite. Breakfast included in rates. Type of meal: continental breakfast. Beds: QD. Air conditioning and cable TV in room. Fax and copier on premises. Amusement parks, antiques, fishing, parks, shopping, downhill skiing, cross-country skiing, sporting events, theater and watersports nearby.

Certificate may be used: September through June; Monday through Thursday in July and August.

Orrville

E8

Grandma's House B&B

5598 Chippewa Rd,
Orrville, OH 44667-9750
(330)682-5112

Circa 1860. Wheat and corn fields surround this friendly brick farmhouse. It has been in the same family for the last 60 years. The inn is furnished with antique bedsteads, homemade quilts and a

collection of old rolling pins. An old-fashioned porch entices guests to relax, and behind the house is a 16-acre wooded hillside with walking paths. Marilyn specializes in hot cinnamon rolls and home-baked breads.

Innkeeper(s): Marilyn & Dave Farver. $55-90. PC TC. 5 rooms, 3 with PB. Breakfast included in rates. Types of meals: continental-plus

breakfast and early coffee/tea. Beds: QDT. Ceiling fan in room. Handicap access. Antiques, parks, shopping, cross-country skiing and theater nearby.

Seen in: Wooster Daily Record, Northeast Ohio Avenues.

"What a delight. We will definitely be back. Perfect."

Certificate may be used: Sunday through Thursday, all year. Anytime from November through April.

Pomeroy

J7

Holly Hill Inn

114 Butternut Ave,
Pomeroy, OH 45769-1295
(614)992-5657 Fax:(614)992-2319

Circa 1836. This gracious clapboard inn with its many shuttered windows is shaded by giant holly trees. Original window panes of blown glass remain, as well as wide-board floors, mantels and fireplaces. The family's antique collection includes a crocheted canopy bed in the Honeymoon Room overlooking a working fireplace. Dozens of antique quilts are displayed and for sale. Guests are invited to borrow an antique bike to ride through the countryside.

Innkeeper(s): John Fultz. $59-89. MC VISA DS. 4 rooms, 2 with FP. 1 conference room. Breakfast included in rates. Type of meal: full breakfast. Catering service available. Beds: DT. Cable TV and VCR in room. Antiques, shopping and sporting events nearby.

Seen in: Sunday Times-Sentinel.

"Your inn is so beautiful, and it has so much historic charm."

Certificate may be used: Sunday through Thursday, some weekends. Not special weekends and holidays.

Ripley

K3

Baird House B&B

201 N 2nd St, Ripley, OH 45167-1002
(513)392-4918

Circa 1825. A lacy wrought-iron porch and balcony decorate the front facade of this historic house, while the second-floor porch at the rear offers views of the Ohio River, 500 feet away. There are nine marble fireplaces and an enormous chandelier in the parlor. A full breakfast is served.

Innkeeper(s): Patricia Kittle. $75-95. 2 rooms, 1 with PB, 3 with FP. Breakfast included in rates. Types of meals: full breakfast and early coffee/tea. Afternoon tea and evening snack available. Beds: KDT. Air conditioning, turn-down service and ceiling fan in room. Antiques, shopping and sporting events nearby.

Location: Fifty miles east of Cincinnati.

Seen in: Ohio Magazine, Country Inn Cookbook.

"Anxious to return."

Certificate may be used: November through May, Monday through Thursday or anytime available.

The Signal House

234 N Front St, Ripley, OH 45167-1015
(513)392-1640

Circa 1830. This Greek Italianate home is said to have been used to aid the Underground Railroad. A light in the attic told Rev. John Rankin, a dedicated abolitionist, that it was safe to transport slaves to freedom. Located within a 55-acre historical district, guests can take a glance back in time, exploring

museums and antique shops. Twelve-foot ceilings with ornate plaster-work graces the parlor, and guests can sit on any of three porches watching paddlewheelers traverse the Ohio River.

Innkeeper(s): Vic & Betsy Billingsley. $65-75. MC VISA DS PC TC. 2 rooms, 2 with FP. Breakfast included in rates. Types of meals: full breakfast and early coffee/tea. Beds: QD. Air conditioning and ceiling fan in room. Cable TV, VCR, copier and library on premises. Antiques, fishing, parks, shopping and watersports nearby.

Seen in: Cincinnati Enquirer, Ohio Columbus Dispatch, Ohio Off the Beaten Path, Cincinnati.

Certificate may be used: Monday-Thursday, no holidays.

Rockbridge   I6

Glenlaurel Inn

15042 Mount Olive Rd,
Rockbridge, OH 43149-9738
(614)385-4070 (800)809-7378
Fax:(614)385-9669

Circa 1994. This rustic, Old World-style manor house is secluded on more than 100 acres, which include trails, gardens and a gorge. Take a walk through the woods and you half expect to see King Arthur riding along. In addition to the manor and carriage house, there are four cottages tucked on a

place called Thistle Ridge. The carriage house and cottages sport a Scotish country look, and each cottage has an outdoor hot tub. Several main house guest rooms include a stone fireplace or whirlpool tub.

Innkeeper(s): Michael Daniels. $105-235. MC VISA AX DS PC TC. 10 rooms with PB, 8 with FP. 2 suites. 4 cottages. 1 conference room. Breakfast and afternoon tea included in rates. Types of meals: full breakfast and early coffee/tea. Picnic lunch, banquet service and room service available. Beds: Q. Air conditioning and turn-down service in room. Cable TV, VCR, fax, copier, spa and library on premises. Handicap access. Antiques, parks, shopping, cross-country skiing and watersports nearby.

Seen in: Los Angeles Times.

"The warm feelings that we felt as guests only made it more difficult to leave. The laughter, the warmth, the friendship will be with us through the years."

Certificate may be used: Dec. 1 to March 31 Sunday night-Thursday night.

Sandusky   C6

Wagner's 1844 Inn

230 E Washington St,
Sandusky, OH 44870-2611
(419)626-1726 Fax:(419)626-8465

Circa 1844. This inn originally was constructed as a log cabin. Additions and renovations were made, and the house evolved into an Italianate-style accented with brackets under the eaves and black shutters on the second-story windows. A wrought-iron fence frames the house, and there are ornate wrought-iron porch rails. A billiard room and screened-in porch are available to guests. The ferry to Cedar Point and Kelleys Island is within walking distance.

Innkeeper(s): Walt & Barb Wagner. $70-90. MC VISA DS TC. 3 rooms with PB, 2 with FP. Breakfast included in rates. Type of meal: continental breakfast. Beds: Q. Air conditioning and ceiling fan in room. Cable TV, copier and library on premises. Handicap access. Amusement parks, antiques, fishing, parks and shopping nearby.

Seen in: Lorain Journal.

"This B&B rates in our Top 10."

Certificate may be used: Nov. 1 to May 1.

Urbana   G4

Northern Plantation B&B

3421 E RR 296, Urbana, OH 43078
(513)652-1782 (800)652-1782

Circa 1913. This Victorian farmhouse, located on 100 acres, is occupied by fourth-generation family members. (Marsha's father was born in the downstairs bedroom in 1914.) The Homestead Library is decorated traditionally and has a handsome fireplace, while the dining room features a dining set and a china cabinet made by the innkeeper's great-grandfather. Most of the guest rooms have canopy beds. A large country breakfast is served. On the property is a fishing pond, corn fields, soybeans and woods with a creek. Nearby are Ohio Caverns and Indian Lake.

Innkeeper(s): Marsha J. Martin. $65-95. MC VISA DS. 4 rooms, 1 with PB. Breakfast included in rates. Types of meals: continental-plus breakfast and full breakfast. Evening snack available. Beds: KD. Air conditioning in room. Cable TV, VCR and library on premises. Antiques, parks, shopping and cross-country skiing nearby.

Certificate may be used: Any day except holidays.

Vermilion   C7

Captain Gilchrist
5662 Huron St,
Vermilion, OH 44089-1000
(216)967-1237

Captain J.C. Gilchrist, owner of the largest fleet of ships on the Great Lakes, built this charming 1885 Victorian, which is listed in the National Register. From the wraparound porch, guests can relax and enjoy the view. The grounds, nestled near Lake Erie's southern shore, are surrounded by gracious old buckeye trees. Guest rooms are filled with antiques. The innkeepers transformed the second-story ballroom into a comfortable common room filled with games and a TV. The large, continental breakfasts feature sweet rolls and muffins from Vermilion's century-old family bakery. The innkeepers also offer kitchen suites for those planning longer stays. The home is only 400 feet from city docks and the beach, and a two-block walk takes guests into the downtown area with its many shops and restaurants. A maritime museum and historic lighthouse are next door.

Innkeeper(s): Dan Roth. $65-89. MC VISA AX. 4 rooms. Breakfast included in rates. Type of meal: continental-plus breakfast.

Certificate may be used: Sunday through Thursday, September through May.

Waynesville   I3

Lakewood Farm B&B
8495 Rt 48, Waynesville, OH 45068
(513)885-9850 Fax:(513)885-9874

Circa 1834. The earliest portion of this home served as a gristmill. When mill operations ceased, it became a residence and subsequent sections were added. Each of the guest rooms is unique. For instance, The Loft, located in a early portion of the home was once accessible only by ladder. It now has its own porch and a unique square bathtub. The 25-acre grounds are decorated with gardens, some started more than a half-century ago. There is a five-acre lake, hiking trails, tennis facilities and in the winter, guests can enjoy sledding and ice skating on the premises.

Innkeeper(s): Liz & Jay Jorling. $60-125. MC VISA PC TC. 5 rooms with PB, 1 with FP. 1 suite. 1 cottage. 1 conference room. Breakfast and evening snack included in rates. Type of meal: full breakfast. Afternoon tea, catered breakfast and room service available. Beds: QT. Air conditioning and ceiling fan in room. Cable TV, VCR, fax, copier, swimming, stables, tennis and library on premises. Handicap access. Amusement parks, antiques, fishing, parks, shopping, cross-country skiing, sporting events, theater and watersports nearby.

Seen in: Los Angeles Times.

"The warm feelings that we felt as guests only made it more difficult to leave. The laughter, the warmth, the friendship will be with us through the years."

Certificate may be used: From March 1 to Dec. 31, Sunday-Friday.

West Alexandria   H2

Twin Creek Country B&B
5353 Enterprise Rd,
West Alexandria, OH 45381-9518
(513)787-3990

Circa 1835. This brick farmhouse is the oldest house in the township, and the 170 acres surrounding the home was part of a land grant signed by Thomas Jefferson. Beautiful rich woodwork highlights the interior, which has an old-fashioned, country appeal. Innkeepers Mark and Carolyn Ulrich live in an adjacent home, providing their guests with extra privacy. The grounds offer more than 70 acres of woods to hike through. The innkeepers also own Twin Creek Townehouse B&B, an Italianate-style home that includes a tea room and catering business. The two upstairs guest rooms are decorated with local antiques. The tea room is an impressive feature, with a carved ceiling, marble fireplace and walls painted in a deep teal hue with rose trim.

Innkeeper(s): Dr. Mark & Carolyn Ulrich. $69-89. MC VISA AX DS PC TC. 2 rooms with PB. 1 suite. Breakfast and evening snack included in rates. Type of meal: full breakfast. Beds: DT. Air conditioning in room. Amusement parks, antiques, fishing, parks, shopping, sporting events, theater and watersports nearby.

Certificate may be used: No holidays; good Monday through Thursday, subject to availability.

Westerville G5

Cornelia's Corner B&B
93 W College Ave,
Westerville, OH 43081-2031
(614)882-2678 (800)745-2678
Fax:(614)523-0008

Circa 1851. This handsome mid-19th-century house is located just across the street from Otterbein College. The front entryway displays a staircase with a gleaming cherry banister. Oak floors, 10-foot ceilings, lace curtains and a front porch furnished with

white wicker add to the old-fashioned cozy feeling. The magical sound of chimes ringing at Towers Hall can be heard often. Sally is a former president of the Ohio Education Association and has visited countries around the world as a delegate.

Innkeeper(s): Sally Savage. $50-75. 3 rooms with PB. Breakfast included in rates. Type of meal: full breakfast. Beds: KQT. Bicycles on premises. Handicap access. Antiques, theater and watersports nearby.

Location: Fifteen minutes from Columbus airport, two blocks from antique shops.

Seen in: Westerville News, Columbus News Channel 10, Columbus Monthly.

"Terrific!"

Certificate may be used: Sunday through Thursday, open all year.

Wooster E7

Historic Overholt House B&B
1473 Beall Ave, Wooster, OH 44691-2303
(330)263-6300 (800)992-0643
Fax:(330)263-6300

Circa 1874. This burgundy Victorian with its peaked roofs and colorful trim literally was saved from the wrecking ball. Several concerned locals fought to have the home moved to another location rather than face demolition in order to make way for a parking lot. The current owners later purchased the historic home and furnished it with beautiful wall coverings, antiques and Victorian touches. The focal point of the interior is a magnificent walnut "flying staircase" that rises three stories. The innkeepers provide plenty of ways to spend a comfortable evening. The common room is stocked with games, a television and reading material. Autumn and winter guests are invited to snuggle up in front of a roaring fire while sipping a hot drink and munching on homemade cookies. The area boasts many craft, antique and gift shops, as well as activities at the College of Wooster, which is adjacent to the Overholt House.

Innkeeper(s): Sandy Pohalski & Bobbie Walton. $63-70. MC VISA DS PC. 3 rooms with PB. 1 suite. Breakfast and evening snack included in rates. Types of meals: continental breakfast, continental-plus breakfast, full breakfast and early coffee/tea. Dinner available. Beds: QD. Air conditioning, ceiling fan and cable TV in room. VCR, fax and spa on premises. Amusement parks, antiques, parks, shopping and theater nearby.

Seen in: Exchange, Daily Record, Pathways.

"A real retreat. So quiet, clean and friendly. I feel pampered! An old penny always returns."

Certificate may be used: December to April, any time. Sunday through Thursday, all year.

Oklahoma

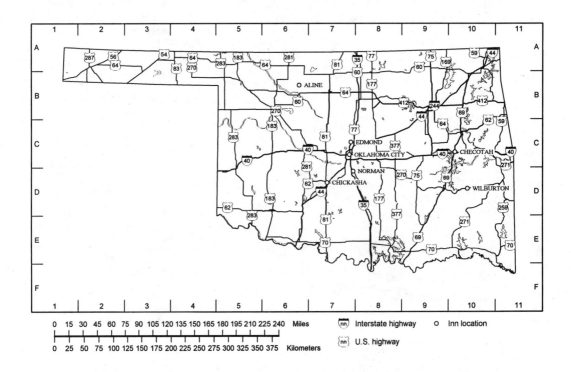

0 15 30 45 60 75 90 105 120 135 150 165 180 195 210 225 240   **Miles**

0 25 50 75 100 125 150 175 200 225 250 275 300 325 350 375   **Kilometers**

Interstate highway   O Inn location

U.S. highway

Aline   B6

Heritage Manor

RR 3 Box 33, Aline, OK 73716-9118
(405)463-2563 (800)295-2563

Circa 1903. A wonderful way to experience
Oklahoma history is to stay at the Heritage Manor,
two turn-of-the-century restored homes. One is an
American four-square house and the other, a glori-
fied Arts-and-Crafts-style home. Antiques were
gathered from area pioneer homes and include an
Edison Victrola Morning Glory Horn and a cathedral pump organ. Antique sofas and English leather
chairs fill the sitting room. Mannequins dressed in
pioneer clothing add to the decor. There are several
fireplaces, and a widow's walk tops the main house.
Innkeeper(s): A.J. & Carolyn Rexroat. $55-150. PC TC. 4 rooms. 2
suites. 2 conference rooms. Breakfast and evening snack included in
rates. Types of meals: full breakfast and early coffee/tea. Afternoon tea,
dinner, picnic lunch, lunch, gourmet lunch and banquet service available. Beds: D. Air conditioning and cable TV in room. VCR, spa and
library on premises. Handicap access. Antiques, fishing, parks, shopping, sporting events, theater and watersports nearby.
Seen in: Country, Enid Morning News, Daily Oklahoman.
Certificate may be used: Year-round, Monday-Saturday.

Checotah   C10

Sharpe House

301 NW 2nd St,
Checotah, OK 74426-2240
(918)473-2832

Circa 1911. Built on land originally bought from a
Creek Indian, this Southern plantation-style inn
was a teacherage—the rooming house for single
female teachers. It is furnished with heirlooms from
the innkeepers' families and hand-crafted accessories. The look of the house is antebellum, but the
specialty of the kitchen is Mexican cuisine. Family-
style evening meals are available upon request.
Checotah is located at the junction of I-40 and U.S.
69. This makes it the ideal base for your day trips of
exploration or recreation in Green Country.
Innkeeper(s): Kay Kindt. $35-50. PC TC. 3 rooms, 2 with PB. 1 suite.
Breakfast included in rates. Types of meals: continental breakfast, continental-plus breakfast, full breakfast and early coffee/tea. Catered breakfast available. Beds: D. Air conditioning, ceiling fan and cable TV in
room. Library and child care on premises. Amusement parks, antiques,
fishing, parks, shopping and watersports nearby.
Certificate may be used: Anytime.

Chickasha   D7

Campbell-Richison House B&B

1428 Kansas, Chickasha, OK 73018
(405)222-1754

Circa 1909. Upon entering this prairie-style home,
guests will notice a spacious entryway with a gracious stairway ascending to the second-floor guest
rooms. The front parlor is a wonderful spot for
relaxing, reading or just soaking up the history of
the home. The dining room has a stained-glass window that gives off a kaleidoscope of beautiful colors
when the morning sun shines through. A spacious
yard encompasses one-quarter of a city block and
has large shade trees that can be enjoyed on a swing
or from the wicker-lined porch.
Innkeeper(s): David Ratcliff. $35-55. 3 rooms, 1 with PB. Breakfast
included in rates. Types of meals: continental-plus breakfast and early
coffee/tea. Beds: D. Air conditioning in room. Cable TV and VCR on
premises. Antiques, shopping and sporting events nearby.
Seen in: Oklahoma Today, Chickasha Express, Cache Times Weekly.

*"We enjoyed our stay at your lovely B&B! It was just
the getaway we needed to unwind from a stressful few
weeks. Your hospitality fellowship and food were just
wonderful."*

Certificate may be used: Anytime, except December weekends and
swap meet weekends.

Edmond   C7

The Arcadian Inn B&B

328 E 1st St, Edmond, OK 73034-4543
(405)348-6347 (800)299-6347
Fax:(405)348-6347

Circa 1908. Unwind in the garden spa of this
Victorian inn or on the wraparound porch to enjoy
the Oklahoma breeze. Breakfast may be served privately in your suite or in the dining room flooded
with morning sunlight, beneath the ceiling paintings

C. 1908

of angels and Christ done by a local artisan. Located next to the University of Central Oklahoma, the inn is four blocks from downtown antique shopping. Guests will enjoy the private baths with Jacuzzis and clawfoot tubs.

Innkeeper(s): Martha & Gary Hall. $65-195. AP. MC VISA AX DS TC. 6 rooms with PB. 4 suites. Breakfast included in rates. Type of meal: full breakfast. Beds: KQ. Air conditioning, ceiling fan and cable TV in room. Fax and spa on premises. Amusement parks, antiques, fishing, parks, shopping, sporting events, theater and watersports nearby.

Seen in: Daily Oklahoman, Antique Traveler.

Certificate may be used: Sunday through Thursday, excluding holidays.

Norman D7

Holmberg House B&B

766 Debarr Ave, Norman, OK 73069-4908
(405)321-6221 (800)646-6221
Fax:(405)321-6221

Circa 1914. Professor Fredrik Holmberg and his wife Signy built this Craftsman-style home across the street from the University of Oklahoma. Each of the antique-filled rooms has its own individual decor and style. For instance, the Blue Danube Room is a romantic retreat filled with wicker, a

wrought iron bed and floral accents throughout. The Bed and Bath Room boasts an old-fashioned tub next to a window seat. The parlor and front porch are perfect places to relax with friends, the lush grounds include a lovely garden. Aside from close access to the university, Holmberg House is within walking distance to more than a dozen restaurants.

Innkeeper(s): Maryjo Meacham. $75-85. MC VISA AX DS PC TC. 4 rooms with PB. Breakfast included in rates. Types of meals: gourmet breakfast and early coffee/tea. Beds: QDT. Air conditioning, ceiling fan and cable TV in room. Fax, copier and library on premises. Antiques, parks, shopping, sporting events and theater nearby.

Seen in: Metro Norman, Oklahoma City Journal Record, Norman Transcript.

"Your hospitality and the delicious food were just super."

Certificate may be used: Anytime.

Oklahoma City C7

The Grandison

1841 NW 15th St,
Oklahoma City, OK 73106-2023
(405)232-8778 (800)240-4667
Fax:(405)521-0011

Circa 1904. This brick and shingled three-story house is shaded by pecan, apple and fig trees. You'll find a pond and gazebo among the lawns and gardens. The building's original Belgian stained glass remains, and the decor is an airy country Victorian. The bridal suite includes a working fireplace, white-lace curtains and a clawfoot tub, with Jacuzzi.

Innkeeper(s): Claudia & Bob Wright. $75-150. MC VISA AX DS PC TC. 9 rooms with PB, 4 with FP. 3 suites. 1 conference room. Breakfast and evening snack included in rates. Types of meals: continental-plus breakfast, full breakfast and early coffee/tea. Banquet service, catering service and room service available. Beds: KQT. Air conditioning, ceiling fan, cable TV and VCR in room. Fax, copier, sauna and library on premises. Handicap access. Antiques, parks, sporting events and theater nearby.

Seen in: Daily Oklahoman, Oklahoma Pride, Oklahoma Gazette, Discover Oklahoma.

"Like going home to Grandma's!"

Certificate may be used: Anytime.

Wilburton D10

The Dome House

315 E Main St,
Wilburton, OK 74578-4411
(918)465-0092

Circa 1908. An area landmark since it was built, the Victorian inn's unique feature is its distinctive dome-topped, two-story turret. A sitting area in the turret and wide porches invite guests to relax and remember a simpler time. A parlor where guests can meet and enjoy conversation includes a fireplace. Situated in the heart of the beautiful Kiamichi Mountains, the inn is centrally located to a wide variety of outdoor activities. The Court House, Federal Building, post office and restaurants are all within walking distance.

Innkeeper(s): LaVerne McFerran. $45-75. DS PC TC. 5 rooms with PB. 3 suites. 1 cottage. Breakfast included in rates. Types of meals: continental-plus breakfast and early coffee/tea. Beds: QDT. Air conditioning, turn-down service, ceiling fan and cable TV in room. VCR and library on premises. Fishing, parks, shopping and sporting events nearby.

Certificate may be used: Anytime during the week from Sunday night to Friday morning and when available on weekends.

Oregon

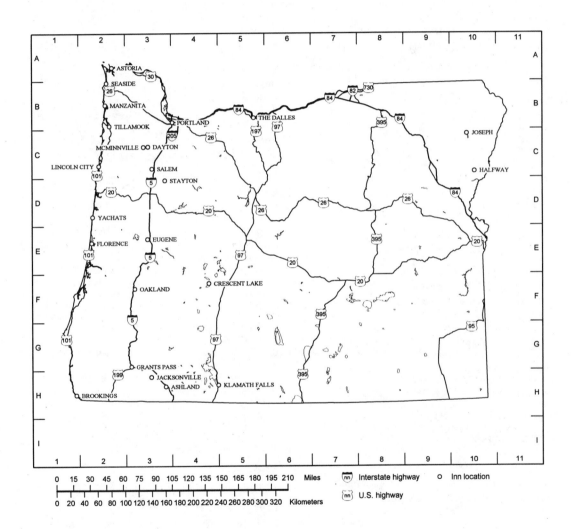

| 0 | 15 | 30 | 45 | 60 | 75 | 90 | 105 | 120 | 135 | 150 | 165 | 180 | 195 | 210 | Miles |
| 0 | 20 | 40 | 60 | 80 | 100 | 120 | 140 | 160 | 180 | 200 | 220 | 240 | 260 | 280 | 300 | 320 | Kilometers |

Interstate highway   Inn location

U.S. highway

341

Ashland
H3

Chanticleer B&B Inn

120 Gresham St,
Ashland, OR 97520-2807
(503)482-1919 (800)898-1950
Fax:(503)482-1919

Circa 1920. This gray clapboard, Craftsman-style
house has been totally renovated and several rooms
added. The inn is light and airy and decorated with
antiques. Special features include the open hearth
fireplace and bricked patio garden.

Innkeeper(s): Pebby Kuan. $90-160. MC VISA. 6 rooms with PB, 1 with
FP. Breakfast included in rates. Types of meals: full breakfast, gourmet
breakfast and early coffee/tea. Beds: QT. Air conditioning in room. Cable
TV on premises. Antiques, shopping, downhill skiing, cross-country
skiing, sporting events and theater nearby.

Seen in: Country Home, Pacific Northwest.

*"Chanticleer has set the standard by which all others will
be judged."*

Certificate may be used: Nov. 1-March 31, excluding weekends and
holidays.

Iris Inn

59 Manzanita St,
Ashland, OR 97520-2615
(541)488-2286 (800)460-7650
Fax:(541)488-3709

Circa 1905. The Iris Inn is a restored Victorian set
on a large flower-filled yard. It features simple
American country antiques. The upstairs guest
rooms have views of the valley and mountains.
Evening sips of wine often are taken out on the large
deck overlooking a rose garden. Breakfast boasts an
elegant presentation with dishes such as buttermilk
scones and peaches and cream French toast.

Innkeeper(s): Vickie Lamb. $60-98. MC VISA. 5 rooms with PB.
Breakfast included in rates. Type of meal: full breakfast. Beds: QDT. Air
conditioning, turn-down service and ceiling fan in room. Fax on premises. Antiques, fishing, shopping, downhill skiing, cross-country skiing,
sporting events, theater and watersports nearby.

Location: Southern Oregon.

Seen in: Sunset, Oregonian.

"It's like returning to home to be at the Iris Inn."

Certificate may be used: October, Sunday-Thursday only; any night
November-February; March-May, Sunday-Thursday, only.

Mt. Ashland Inn

550 Mt Ashland Ski Rd,
Ashland, OR 97520-9745
(541)482-8707 (800)830-8707
Fax:(541)482-8707

Circa 1987. This handcrafted log lodge is surrounded by a pine forest. During chilly months, a fire
crackles in the front room's magnificent stone fireplace. Guests trample in after a day on the slopes
ready to enjoy a cup of hot
chocolate. Guest rooms
and suites are
appointed with
elegant, yet com-
fortable furnish-
ings. Quilts,
antiques, won-
derful views or
a two-person
Jacuzzi are just
some of the sur-
prises guests will
discover. Winter isn't
the only season to visit the
inn, the area offers hiking, fishing, shopping, galleries, museums and more. No matter what time of
year, guests are treated to a hearty breakfast. A typical three-course breakfast might include watermelon
and kiwi with lemon sorbet, freshly baked scones
and French bananas tucked in whole wheat crepes.

Innkeeper(s): Chuck & Laurel Biegert. $76-180. MC VISA AX DS PC. 5
rooms with PB, 3 with FP. 3 suites. 1 conference room. Breakfast
included in rates. Type of meal: gourmet breakfast. Beds: KQT. VCR in
room. Fax, copier, spa, sauna and bicycles on premises. Antiques, fishing, parks, shopping, downhill skiing, cross-country skiing, theater and
watersports nearby.

Location: Sixteen miles from Ashland. Six miles west of I-5 on Mount
Ashland Road.

Seen in: Pacific Northwest, Edward Carter's Travels, Snow Country,
Oregon, Glamour, Travel & Leisure.

*"The romantic atmosphere and special personal touches
you've provided made our stay doubly enjoyable."*

Certificate may be used: Sunday through Thursday, Oct. 15 to May
31, excluding holiday periods.

Mousetrap Inn

312 Helman St, Ashland, OR 97520-1138
(541)482-9228 (800)460-5453

Circa 1895. The century-old farmhouse is furnished
with antiques and decorated with modern art and
pottery created by the innkeepers. Breakfasts often
feature organically grown foods and include treats
such as juice smoothies, fresh fruit, baked goods and
frittatas. The grounds are dotted with gardens and
there is a swing on the inn's porch. The inn is located in Ashland's historic Railroad District.

Innkeeper(s): Robert, Linda & Tessah Joseph. $70-95. MC VISA PC. 6 rooms with PB. Breakfast included in rates. Types of meals: full breakfast and early coffee/tea. Beds: Q. Air conditioning and ceiling fan in room. Fishing, parks, shopping, theater and watersports nearby.

Certificate may be used: May & October 1996; June, July, August, September Monday-Thursday only.

Oak Hill Country B&B

2190 Siskiyou Blvd,
Ashland, OR 97520-2531
(503)482-1554

Circa 1910. Decorated with hints of French country, this Craftsman farmhouse has a fine front porch that creates a relaxing spot for enjoying the less crowded South end of town. A hearty country gourmet breakfast is served family style in the dining room. There are bicycles for exploring the area.

Innkeeper(s): Ron Bass. $60-90. MC VISA. 5 rooms. Breakfast included in rates. Air conditioning, turn-down service, ceiling fan and cable TV in room. VCR on premises. Antiques, shopping, downhill skiing, cross-country skiing, sporting events and theater nearby.

Certificate may be used: November-May, Monday-Thursday, excluding holidays.

Pinehurst Inn at Jenny Creek

17250 Highway 66,
Ashland, OR 97520-9406
(503)488-1002

Circa 1923. This lodge, built from logs harvested on the property, once accommodated travelers along the new state highway 66, which was built to replace the Southern Oregon Wagon Road. As the name suggests, the inn is situated by the banks of Jenny Creek, and guest enjoy stunning canyon views from the upstairs sunroom. The lobby, with its huge stone fireplace, is a welcoming site. The inn

also includes a full service restaurant open for guests and the public. The inn is less than a half hour from Ashland, and Klamath Falls is 39 miles away.

Innkeeper(s): Mary Jo & Mike Moloney. $75-105. MC VISA DS. 6 rooms with PB. 2 suites. Breakfast and dinner included in rates. Types of meals: full breakfast and early coffee/tea. Lunch available. Beds: KQD. Ceiling fan in room. Antiques, fishing, shopping, downhill skiing, cross-country skiing and theater nearby.

Seen in: Sunset, Travel & Leisure.

"Romantic and peaceful. A favorite inn. Wonderful dinner and accommodations."

Certificate may be used: January-December, Sunday-Thursday excluding holidays.

The Woods House B&B

333 N Main St, Ashland, OR 97520-1703
(503)488-1598 (800)435-8260
Fax:(503)482-7912

Circa 1908. Built and occupied for almost 40 years by a prominent Ashland physician, each room of this Craftsman-style inn boasts special detail. Many guest rooms offer canopied beds and skylights. Full breakfasts are served either in the sunny dining room or in the garden under a spreading walnut tree. After breakfast, take a stroll through the half-acre of terraced, English gardens. Located in the historic district, the inn is four blocks from Ashland's Shakespearean theaters.

Innkeeper(s): Francoise Roddy. $65-112. MC VISA. 6 rooms with PB. Breakfast included in rates. Types of meals: full breakfast and early coffee/tea. Room service available. Beds: KQT. Air conditioning in room. Cable TV, VCR, fax, copier and bicycles on premises. Antiques, shopping, downhill skiing, cross-country skiing and theater nearby.

Seen in: The Times.

"Within this house lies much hospitality, friendship and laughter. What more could a home ask to be?"

Certificate may be used: October-March, any nights.

Astoria   A2

Grandview B&B
1574 Grand Ave, Astoria, OR 97103-3733
(503)325-5555 (800)488-3250

Circa 1896. To fully enjoy its views of the
Columbia River, this Victorian house has both a
tower and a turret. Antiques and white wicker furnishings contribute to the inn's casual, homey feeling. The Meadow Room is particularly appealing to

bird lovers with its bird cage, bird books and bird
wallpaper. Breakfast, served in the main-floor turret,
frequently includes smoked salmon with bagels and
cream cheese.

Innkeeper(s): Charleen Maxwell. $39-92. MC VISA DS PC TC. 9 rooms,
7 with PB, 3 with FP. 2 suites. Breakfast and evening snack included in
rates. Type of meal: continental-plus breakfast. Beds: QT. Antiques,
fishing, parks, shopping, theater and watersports nearby.
Seen in: Pacific Northwest, Northwest Discoveries, Los Angeles Times,
Oregonian, Daily Astorian.

*"We're still talking about our visit and the wonderful
breakfast you served."*

Certificate may be used: Nov. 1 to May 17 holidays OK except two
weekends in February may be excluded.

Inn-Chanted B&B
708 8th St, Astoria, OR 97103-4725
(503)325-5223 (800)455-7018

Circa 1883. This four-square Victorian was presented to Maude Hobson as a wedding present from her
father, John, an Astoria pioneer. Guest rooms afford
views of the Columbia River. Silk brocade wallcoverings and crystal chandeliers are elegant touches to
the interior of this home. Guests design their own
breakfast, choosing from entrees such as puffed pancakes, almond creme crepes or quiches. Astoria is
the oldest United States settlement west of the
Mississippi River, and offers a walking tour of historic homes and buildings.

Innkeeper(s): Richard & Dixie Swart. $50-110. EP. MC VISA AX DS TC.
3 rooms with PB, 1 with FP. 1 suite. Breakfast and afternoon tea included in rates. Types of meals: gourmet breakfast and early coffee/tea.
Beds: QT. Ceiling fan, cable TV and VCR in room. Antiques, fishing,
parks, theater and watersports nearby.
Certificate may be used: November-February.

Brookings   H1

Chetco River Inn
21202 High Prairie Rd,
Brookings, OR 97415-8200
(541)469-8128 Fax:(541)469-4341

Circa 1987. Situated on 35 wooded acres and the
Chetco River, this modern B&B offers a cedar lodge
exterior and a marble- and antique-filled interior. A
collection of crafts, Oriental rugs and leather sofas
add to your enjoyment. Because it's 18 miles from
Brookings, you may wish to arrange ahead for a dinner. Then you can enjoy the sounds of the rushing
river without interruption.

Innkeeper(s): Sandra Brugger. $95. MC VISA PC TC. 4 rooms, 3 with
PB. 1 conference room. Breakfast and evening snack included in rates.
Types of meals: full breakfast and early coffee/tea. Dinner available.
Beds: KQT. Cable TV, VCR, swimming and library on premises.
Antiques, fishing, parks, shopping, theater and watersports nearby.
Location: Kalmiopsis Wilderness Area close by.
Certificate may be used: No holidays, all year, Monday-Thursday. May
have to share bathroom.

South Coast Inn B&B
516 Redwood St,
Brookings, OR 97415-9672
(541)469-5557 (800)525-9273
Fax:(541)469-6615

Circa 1917. Enjoy panoramic views of the Pacific
Ocean from two guest rooms at this Craftsman-style
inn built by San Francisco architect Bernard
Maybeck. All rooms are furnished with antiques,

ceiling fans, VCRs and TVs. A floor-to-ceiling stone fireplace and beamed ceilings make the parlor a great place to gather with friends. There are sun decks, a strolling garden and an indoor hot tub and sauna. Brookings is in the warm "Banana Belt" of the South Coast.

Innkeeper(s): Ken Raith & Keith Pepper. $74-84. MC VISA AX DS PC TC. 4 rooms with PB. 1 cottage. Breakfast included in rates. Types of meals: full breakfast, gourmet breakfast and early coffee/tea. Beds: Q. Ceiling fan, cable TV and VCR in room. Fax, spa, sauna and library on premises. Antiques, fishing, parks, shopping, theater and watersports nearby.

Certificate may be used: November-May.

Crescent Lake F4

Willamette Pass Inn

PO Box 35,
Crescent Lake, OR 97425-0035
(541)433-2211 (800)301-2218
Fax:(541)433-2855

Circa 1984. Each of the guest rooms at this rustic, comfortable lodge includes a fireplace and pine furnishings. Beds are topped with flannel sheets. Turndown service is a real treat, guests return from dinner to find cookies and muffins waiting. The inn is located in a national forest, ancient Indian grounds and more than one dozen lakes are nearby.

Innkeeper(s): George & Alicia Prigmore. $44-58. MC VISA DS PC TC. 12 rooms with PB, 10 with FP. Evening snack included in rates. Beds: Q. Turn-down service, cable TV and VCR in room. Fax and library on premises. Handicap access. Antiques, fishing, parks, shopping, downhill skiing, cross-country skiing and watersports nearby.

Certificate may be used: All year, except holidays and Saturday nights.

Dayton C3

Wine Country Farm

6855 NE Breyman Orchards Rd,
Dayton, OR 97114-7220
(503)864-3446 (800)261-3446
Fax:(503)864-3446

Circa 1910. Surrounded by vineyards and orchards, Wine Country Farm is an eclectic French house sitting on a hill overlooking the Cascade Mountain Range. Arabian horses are raised here and five varieties of grapes are grown. Request the master bedroom and you'll enjoy a fireplace. The innkeepers can arrange for a horse-drawn buggy ride and picnic, wedding facilities outdoors or in new wine tasting room. Downtown Portland and the Oregon coast are each an hour away.

Innkeeper(s): Joan Davenport. $65-125. MC VISA PC. 5 rooms with PB, 1 with FP. 1 suite. 1 conference room. Breakfast included in rates.

Types of meals: full breakfast, gourmet breakfast and early coffee/tea. Picnic lunch, banquet service, catering service and room service available. Beds: KQDT. Air conditioning, ceiling fan and VCR in room. Fax, copier, stables, library and pet boarding on premises. Antiques, fishing, parks, shopping, downhill skiing, cross-country skiing, sporting events, theater and watersports nearby.

Seen in: Wine Spectator.

Certificate may be used: January through April, Monday-Thursday.

Eugene E3

Atherton Place, A B&B Inn

690 W Broadway, Eugene, OR 97402-5216
(541)683-2674 (800)507-1354

Circa 1925. Within a few minutes' walk of the City Center Mall, Hult Center and the University of Oregon is Atherton Place, a Dutch Colonial-style home. A library, sun room and sitting room offer cozy places to read. Crown moldings, polished oak floors and built-in cabinets attest to a craftsmanship of former days. Guest rooms have new queen beds and a casual country decor.

Innkeeper(s): Marne Krozek. $60-95. PC TC. 3 rooms, 2 with PB. Breakfast and evening snack included in rates. Types of meals: gourmet breakfast and early coffee/tea. Beds: QDT. Turn-down service and ceiling fan in room. Cable TV on premises. Antiques, fishing, parks, shopping, sporting events, theater and watersports nearby.

Certificate may be used: Nov. 15-April 15.

Campbell House, A City Inn

252 Pearl St, Eugene, OR 97401-2366
(541)343-1119 (800)264-2519
Fax:(541)343-2258

Circa 1892. An acre of grounds surrounds this Victorian inn, built by a local timber owner and gold miner. The rooms range from a ground-level room featuring fly-fishing paraphernalia and knotty-pine paneling to an elegant two-room honeymoon

suite on the second floor, complete with fireplace, jetted bathtub for two and a view of the mountains. The Campbell House, located in Eugene's historic Skinner Butte District, is within walking distance of restaurants, the Hult Center for the Performing Arts, the 5th Street Public Market and antique shops. Outdoor activities include jogging or biking along riverside paths.

Innkeeper(s): Myra Plant. $72-235. MC VISA AX DS TC. 14 rooms with PB, 3 with FP. 1 suite. 3 conference rooms. Breakfast included in rates. Types of meals: full breakfast and early coffee/tea. Afternoon tea, evening snack, picnic lunch and room service available. Beds: KQDT. Air conditioning, turn-down service, ceiling fan, cable TV and VCR in room. Fax, copier and library on premises. Handicap access. Antiques, fishing, parks, shopping, sporting events, theater and watersports nearby.

Seen in: KVAL & KAUW T.V. News, Eugene Register Guard, Country Inns, Oregonian, Sunset, B&B Innkeepers Journal.

"I guess we've never felt so pampered! Thank you so much. The room is beautiful! We had a wonderful getaway."

Certificate may be used: November through April (not valid during events, holidays or conferences).

Kjaer's House In Woods

814 Lorane Hwy, Eugene, OR 97405-2321
(541)343-3234 (800)437-4501

Circa 1910. This handsome Craftsman house on two landscaped acres was built by a Minnesota lawyer. It was originally accessible by streetcar. Antiques include a square grand piano of rosewood

and a collection of antique wedding photos. The house is attractively furnished and surrounded by flower gardens.

Innkeeper(s): George & Eunice Kjaer. $55-75. PC TC. 2 rooms with PB. 1 conference room. Breakfast included in rates. Types of meals: continental breakfast, full breakfast, gourmet breakfast and early coffee/tea. Beds: Q. Turn-down service in room. Cable TV, VCR and library on premises. Antiques, fishing, parks, shopping, sporting events and theater nearby.

Seen in: Register-Guard, Oregonian.

"Lovely ambiance and greatest sleep ever. Delicious and beautiful food presentation."

Certificate may be used: October through April.

The Oval Door

988 Lawrence St, Eugene, OR 97401-2827
(541)683-3160 (800)882-3160

Circa 1990. This is a New England farm-style house, complete with wraparound porch. It is located in a residential neighborhood 15 blocks from the University of Oregon. Guest rooms feature ceiling fans and antiques. There is a whirlpool room, library and parlor. Breakfast can be catered to your dietary needs.

Innkeeper(s): Judith McLane. $70-93. MC VISA AX. 4 rooms with PB. Beds: QT. Turn-down service and ceiling fan in room. Cable TV, VCR, fax and library on premises.

Certificate may be used: Anytime except special event weekends.

Pookie's B&B on College Hill

2013 Charnelton St,
Eugene, OR 97405-2819
(541)343-0383 (800)558-0383
Fax:(541)343-0383

Circa 1918. Pookie's is a charming Craftsman house with an English influence. Surrounded by maple and fir trees, the B&B is located in the College Hill neighborhood. Mahogany and oak antiques decorate the rooms. In addition to the two guest rooms, the innkeepers offer a larger suite as well. The innkeeper worked for many years in the area as a concierge and can offer you expert help with excursion planning or business needs.

Innkeeper(s): Pookie & Doug Walling. $65-90. AP. PC TC. 3 rooms, 2 with PB. 1 suite. Breakfast included in rates. Types of meals: continental breakfast, continental-plus breakfast, full breakfast and early coffee/tea. Beds: KQT. Ceiling fan and cable TV in room. VCR, fax and copier on premises. Antiques, fishing, parks, shopping, sporting events, theater and watersports nearby.

Seen in: Oregon Wine.

"I love the attention to detail. The welcoming touches: flowers, the 'convenience basket' of necessary items... I'm happy to have discovered your lovely home."

Certificate may be used: November-April, Sunday-Wednesday nights, private bath suite, only.

Florence

E2

The Johnson House

216 Maple St, PO Box 1892,
Florence, OR 97439-9657
(503)997-8000 (800)768-9488

Circa 1892. This late Victorian is a favorite site in
Florence's Old Town, surrounded by a white picket
fence. The home is just blocks from the Siuslaw
River. Rooms are decorated with period antiques,
including beds topped with fluffy, down comforters.
Fresh flowers and lacy touches add romance. The
hearty breakfasts are the perfect way to start the day.
Enjoy gourmet fare such as fresh berries with cream,
heavenly crepes or omelets, prepared with herbs
from the inn's garden.

Innkeeper(s): Jayne & Ron Fraese. $95-105. MC VISA DS TC. 6 rooms,
3 with PB. Breakfast included in rates. Types of meals: full breakfast
and early coffee/tea. Afternoon tea available. Beds: Q. Fax, copier and
pet boarding on premises. Handicap access. Antiques, fishing, parks
and shopping nearby.

Certificate may be used: Sunday-Wednesday, October-June.

Grants Pass

G3

Martha's House

764 NW 4th St,
Grants Pass, OR 97526-1517
(503)476-4330 (800)261-0167

Circa 1910. If you pass by this inn in the morning,
you may hear the happy chatter of guests on the
veranda enjoying a breakfast of freshly baked breads,
farm fresh eggs and local produce. And Felix the cat

may be nearby. This Victorian farmhouse is close to
the center of town. Antique toys are a feature in
Rachel's Room, which also harbors a Jacuzzi tub,
queen brass bed and antiques. Enjoy the area's river
rafting and nearby Shakespearean Festival.

Innkeeper(s): Evelyn & Glenn Hawkins. $50-85. EP. MC VISA. 3 rooms
with PB. Breakfast and evening snack included in rates. Types of meals:
full breakfast and early coffee/tea. Afternoon tea available. Beds: KQ.

Air conditioning, turn-down service, ceiling fan and cable TV in room.
Fax on premises. Antiques, fishing, parks, shopping, theater and watersports nearby.

Certificate may be used: Sunday through Thursday.

Pine Meadow Inn

1000 Crow Rd, Grants Pass, OR 97532
(541)471-6277 (800)554-0806
Fax:(541)471-6277

Circa 1991. Built on a wooded knoll, this handsome yellow farmhouse looks out on a four-acre
meadow, which the innkeepers call their front yard.
Five, private acres feature walking paths, gardens
and sitting areas. The wraparound porch is filled

offers wicker furnishings for those who wish to relax.
There is a deck and hot tub under the pines, as well
as a koi pond and waterfall where one can relax and
contemplate. The inn is easily accessible from I-5,
yet feels worlds away.

Innkeeper(s): Nancy & Maloy Murdock. $80-110. PC. 4 rooms with PB.
Breakfast included in rates. Types of meals: gourmet breakfast and
early coffee/tea. Beds: Q. Air conditioning, turn-down service and ceiling fan in room. Fax, copier, spa and library on premises. Antiques,
fishing, parks, shopping, theater and watersports nearby.

Certificate may be used: October through April, consecutive Friday and
Saturday nights only.

Halfway

C10

Birch Leaf Farm

Rt 1, Box 91, Halfway, OR 97834-9704
(503)742-2990

Circa 1905. Nestled in the middle of a 42-acre
farm near the Oregon Trail and halfway between
the Eagle Cap Wilderness and Hells Canyon, this
National Register farmhouse boasts original woodwork and hardwood floors. Each guest room has a
view of the Wallowa Mountains. A country-style
breakfast is served complete with locally made jams
and honey. Nearby activities include white-water
rafting, jet-boat trips, pack trips and skiing through
local mountains.

Innkeeper(s): Maryellen Olson. $65-70. VISA. 4 rooms, 1 with PB. 1 conference room. Breakfast included in rates. Types of meals: full breakfast and early coffee/tea. Afternoon tea and catering service available. Beds: KQDT. Antiques, fishing, shopping, downhill skiing and cross-country skiing nearby.

Location: Wallowa-Eagle Camp Wilderness & NRA-Hells Canyon area.

Seen in: Hells Canyon Journal.

"I will always remember the warmth and quiet comfort of your place."

Certificate may be used: Anytime, except holidays.

Jacksonville H3

Colonial House B&B
1845 Old Stage Rd, PO Box 1298,
Jacksonville, OR 97530
(503)770-2783

Circa 1916. This expansive Georgian Colonial Revival Manor rests on five acres of wooded grounds, complete with a pond, huge black oaks and wonderful views of the mountains and Rogue River

COLONIAL HOUSE

Valley. Inside, each room features something unique, including beautiful woodwork and seven fireplaces. A grand staircase leads up to the guest rooms, boasting antiques and sitting areas. Afternoon tea and gourmet breakfasts are served in the garden room or on the Roman-style terrace during warm weather.

Innkeeper(s): Philip Sadlier. $95-110. AX. 2 suites. Breakfast and afternoon tea included in rates. Type of meal: full breakfast. Beds: KQT. Antiques, fishing, downhill skiing, cross-country skiing, theater and watersports nearby.

Seen in: Medford Mail Tribune Lifestyles.

"The best! We are overwhelmed by your talents! Your house is absolutely breathtaking. The breakfast was delicious and the offerings unbelievable. A pleasure!"

Certificate may be used: November through April excluding holiday weeks.

Reames House
540 E California St,
Jacksonville, OR 97530-9404
(541)899-1868

Circa 1868. This white frame house, in the National Register of Historic Places, was built for Thomas Reames, Wells Fargo banker and town sheriff. Perennial gardens bloom throughout the yard and climbing roses frame the front veranda. The plant-filled, white-wicker sitting room is brightened by hand-stenciled pink roses. The Colonial Room features a canopy bed, while The Victoria boasts a carved walnut bed and clawfoot tub. In spring and summer, guests enjoy boarding the horse-drawn wagon that passes nearby and meanders through Jacksonville. Bicycles, tennis rackets and gold-panning equipment may be borrowed.

Innkeeper(s): George & Charlotte Winsley. $80-90. 4 rooms, 2 with PB. Breakfast included in rates. Type of meal: full breakfast. Beds: QT. Air conditioning and ceiling fan in room. Bicycles on premises. Antiques, fishing, parks, shopping, downhill skiing, cross-country skiing, theater and watersports nearby.

Location: Southwestern Oregon.

Seen in: Oregonian, Mail Tribune.

"Such a beautiful house and location."

Certificate may be used: Oct. 1-May 31, anytime. June 1-Sept.30, Monday-Thursday

Touvelle House
455 N Oregon St,
Jacksonville, OR 97530-1891
(503)899-8938 (800)846-8422
Fax:(503)899-3992

Circa 1916. This Craftsman inn is two blocks away from the main street of this old Gold Rush town. The common areas of this Craftsman inn include The Library, which has a TV and VCR; The Great Room, featuring a large-stoned fireplace; The Sunroom, which consists of many windows; and The Dining Room, featuring an intricate built-in buffet. Guests can relax on either of two spacious covered verandas.

Innkeeper(s): Carolee Casey. $80-95. 6 rooms with PB. 1 suite. Breakfast included in rates. Type of meal: full breakfast. Beds: QDT. Antiques, fishing, downhill skiing, cross-country skiing, theater and watersports nearby.

Seen in: Mail Tribune.

"The accommodations are beautiful, the atmosphere superb, the breakfast and other goodies delightful, but it is the warmth and caring of the host and hostess that will make the difference in this B&B!! Thank you, special people for adding a place in our world."

Certificate may be used: Sunday-Thursday (except holidays) November-April.

Joseph
C10

Chandler's Inn
PO Box 639, 700 S Main St,
Joseph, OR 97846-0639
(541)432-9765 (800)452-3781

Circa 1981. From the gazebo, guests can gaze at vistas of the Wallowa Mountains. A sunroom in the post-and-beam home also affords a similar view. The innkeepers honor Oregon's hearty pioneer spirit with old photographs and memorabilia. The inn's suite includes a sitting area and private deck with a mountain view. The beds are cozy, but the scent of freshly ground coffee and the innkeepers' home-made breakfast will lure even the sleepiest of guests to the morning table.

Innkeeper(s): Jim & Ethel Chandler. $50-80. MC VISA PC. 5 rooms, 3 with PB. Breakfast included in rates. Type of meal: full breakfast. Afternoon tea available. Beds: KQT. Ceiling fan, cable TV and VCR in room. Bicycles on premises. Antiques, fishing, parks, shopping, downhill skiing, cross-country skiing, theater and watersports nearby.

Certificate may be used: January-May, any time.

Klamath Falls
H4

Thompsons' B&B
1420 Wild Plum Ct,
Klamath Falls, OR 97601-1983
(541)882-7938

Circa 1987. The huge picture windows in this comfortable retreat look out to a spectacular view of Klamath Lake and nearby mountains. Popular Moore Park is practically next door, providing a day of hiking, picnicking or relaxing at the marina. The inn is a perfect site to just relax and enjoy the view. Bird watching is a must, as the inn is home to pelicans, snow geese and many varieties of wild ducks.

Innkeeper(s): Mary & Bill Pohll. $55-75. PC. 4 rooms with PB. Breakfast included in rates. Types of meals: full breakfast and early coffee/tea. Air conditioning and cable TV in room. Antiques, parks and watersports nearby.

"Hospitality as glorious as your surroundings."

Certificate may be used: November through March.

Lincoln City
C2

The Enchanted Cottage
4507 SW Coast Ave,
Lincoln City, OR 97367-1528
(503)996-4101 Fax:(503)996-2682

Circa 1945. This 4,000-square-foot house is 300 feet from the beach and a short walk from Siletz Bay

with its herd of sea lions. Victoria's Secret is a favorite romantic guest room that features a queen canopy bed, antique furnishings and, best of all, the sounds of the Pacific surf. Ask for Natalie's Garden Room if you must see and hear the ocean. But everyone takes in the view in the morning when homemade biscuits and breakfast casseroles are specialties served in the dining room.

Innkeeper(s): Cynthia Gale Fitton. $100-175. MC VISA. 3 rooms, 2 with PB. Breakfast included in rates. Types of meals: full breakfast and early coffee/tea. Evening snack available. Beds: KQ. Cable TV in room. VCR, fax, copier and pet boarding on premises. Handicap access. Antiques, fishing and shopping nearby.

Seen in: Oregonian.

Certificate may be used: October through April, except Saturday night. May and September, except Friday and Saturday night

Manzanita
B2

The Arbors at Manzanita
78 Idaho Ave, PO Box 68,
Manzanita, OR 97130
(503)368-7566

Circa 1920. This old-English-style cottage is a half block from the wide sandy beaches for which the area is known. The Neakahnie Mountains are in view as well as the panoramic stretches of the Pacific coastline. Ask for the Waves View room to enjoy the largest view. Enjoy the library, garden and the innkeeper's evening snacks.

Innkeeper(s): H.L. Burrow. $90-105. 2 rooms. Breakfast included in rates. Types of meals: full breakfast and gourmet breakfast. Beds: QT. Cable TV and VCR on premises. Antiques, fishing and shopping nearby.

Location: Two hundred feet from Pacific Ocean.

Certificate may be used: October through June 15, Sunday through Thursday.

McMinnville
C3

Baker Street B&B
129 S Baker St, McMinnville, OR 97128
(503)472-5575 (800)870-5575

Circa 1914. The natural wood that graces the interior of this Craftsman inn has been restored to its original luster. Vintage Victorian antiques and memorabilia decorate the rooms. Several guest rooms include clawfoot tubs, each features a different color scheme. Couples traveling together or those planning longer visits, might consider the Carnation Cottage, which includes two bedrooms, a bathroom, living room, kitchen and laundry facilities. The breakfast table is set with china and silver.

Innkeeper(s): John & Cheryl Collins. $65-95. MC VISA AX DS PC TC. 5 rooms, 4 with PB. 1 cottage. Type of meal: full breakfast. Beds:

KQDT. Air conditioning, turn-down service, ceiling fan and VCR in room. Cable TV on premises. Antiques, parks, shopping, downhill skiing and theater nearby.

Certificate may be used: All year.

Oakland   F3

The Beckley House
PO Box 198, Oakland, OR 97462-0198
(503)459-9320

Local merchant Charles Beckley built this two-story home, a historic example of late 19th-century Classic Revival architecture. Rooms are furnished in Victorian style with period antiques, including a rare Victrola. One of the guest rooms boasts a white, iron bed. Fresh flowers brighten the rooms and add to the home's garden setting. Breakfasts are a treat, featuring entrees such as apple dumpings with cheese or Grand Marinier French Toast. Enjoy a glass of wine or iced tea on the canopied swing or on the plant-filled patio. Walking tours of the historic town are available, as are romantic carriage rides.
Innkeeper(s): Karene Biedermann. $63-80. 2 rooms. Breakfast included in rates. Type of meal: continental breakfast.

Certificate may be used: October-April.

Portland   B4

John Palmer House Bed & Breakfast
4314 N Mississippi Ave,
Portland, OR 97217-3135
(503)284-5893 (800)518-5893
Fax:(503)284-1239

Circa 1890. This stunning Victorian has been restored to the height of grandeur. The interior boasts beautifully restored and preserved woodwork, pressed tin ceilings and walls, gracious chandeliers and stained glass. Rooms are decorated in ornate, Victorian style. The grounds are picturesque as well, decorated with gardens and plants. On Sundays, the innkeepers offer public tours of the home, which is listed in the National Register, followed by high tea. The inn is located in an urban, Portland redevelopment area, convenient to many downtown sites.
Innkeeper(s): Richard & Mary Sauter. $75-96. MC VISA AX DS PC TC. 3 rooms. 1 suite. 1 conference room. Breakfast included in rates. Types of meals: continental breakfast, full breakfast and gourmet breakfast. Afternoon tea available. Beds: QD. Air conditioning in room. Cable TV, VCR, fax, copier and spa on premises. Antiques, fishing, parks, shopping, sporting events, theater and watersports nearby.

"Your collection of Victorian furniture is exquisite, the hospitality grand, and the food is delicious."

Certificate may be used: Oct. 30 through March 30, Monday-Thursday; Excluding holidays and large city convention dates with more than 4,000 participants.

Salem   C3

State House B&B
2146 State St, Salem, OR 97301-4350
(503)588-1340

Circa 1920. This three-story house sits on the banks of Mill Creek where ducks and geese meander past a huge old red maple down to the water. (A baby was abandoned here because the house looked "just right" and "surely had nice people there." The 12-year-old boy who found the baby on the side porch grew up to become a Supreme Court judge and legal counsel to Governor Mark Hatfield.) The inn is close to everything in Salem.
Innkeeper(s): Judy Uselman. $50-75. MC VISA DS. 6 rooms, 5 with PB, 1 with FP. Breakfast included in rates. Type of meal: full breakfast. Beds: QD. Copier and spa on premises.
Location: One mile from the I-5 Santiam turn-off.
Seen in: Statesman-Journal.

"You do a wonderful job making people feel welcome and relaxed."

Certificate may be used: Sept. 15-May 15.

Seaside   B2

The Anderson's Boarding House
208 N Holladay Dr, Seaside, OR 97138
(503)738-9055 (800)995-4013

Situated by the Necanicum River, two blocks from the convention center, is this Victorian with beamed ceilings, paneling and tongue-and-groove walls. Rooms offer down quilts, wicker pieces and family heirlooms. The Cottage is a small Victorian on the river bank with a kitchen, two sleeping areas and deck with river views that include ducks, seals and cranes. Breakfast is served in the dining room or on the wraparound porch. The innkeepers will help you find the best places to dig for clams, explore tide pools, dine, discover shipwrecks and picnic.
Innkeeper(s): Barbara Harlan Edwards. $70-110. MC VISA. 6 rooms with PB. 1 cottage. Cable TV in room. Amusement parks, antiques, shopping and theater nearby.

Certificate may be used: Oct. 1-June 1, Sunday-Thursday, Holidays and special events excluded.

Chateau on The River
486 Necanicum Dr,
Seaside, OR 97138-6039
(503)738-8800 (800)789-7287

Lewis and Clark once treaded the soil near this inn, and Indians once called the banks of the adjacent Necanicum River home. The Chateau affords mountain and river views, and guests will enjoy watching as the abundant water fowl pass by. Individually decorated rooms include special features such as four-poster beds, hand-crafted quilts, private decks, antique brass beds or lacy curtains. Innkeeper Barbara Kennedy serves a lavish breakfast with fresh fruit, juices, coffee and a daily entree in the Great Blue Heron Room on a family heirloom dining table. Guests are treated to breakfast as well as a panoramic view. The beach is just a few minutes away, as are the sites and sounds of charming Seaside.

Innkeeper(s): Barbara Kennedy. $55-99. MC VISA. 4 rooms. Breakfast included in rates. Type of meal: full breakfast.

Certificate may be used: November-March 31.

Custer House B&B

811 1st Ave, Seaside, OR 97138-6803
(503)738-7825

Circa 1900. Wicker furnishings and a clawfoot tub are features of one of the rooms in this farmhouse-style B&B. It is located four blocks from the ocean and two blocks from the Seaside Convention Center. Your host is retired from the Air Force. Enjoy exploring the area's historic forts and beaches.

Innkeeper(s): Skip & Helen Custer. $55-75. MC VISA AX DC CB DS TC. 3 rooms, 1 with PB. 1 conference room. Breakfast included in rates. Type of meal: full breakfast. Beds: QT. Cable TV, VCR and bicycles on premises. Antiques, fishing, parks, shopping, theater and watersports nearby.

Seen in: Oregon Adventures Magazine.

Certificate may be used: Oct. 15 through May 15.

Sand Dollar B&B

606 N Holladay Dr,
Seaside, OR 97138-6926
(503)738-3491 (800)738-3491

Circa 1920. This Craftsman-style home looks a bit like a seashell, painted in light pink with pale blue trim. In fact, one of the guest rooms bears the name Sea Shell, filled with bright quilts and wicker. The Driftwood Room can be a two-bedroom suite for families. As the room names suggest, the house is decorated in a beach theme, graced by innkeeper Nita Hempfling's stained glasswork. The innkeepers also offer a cottage on the banks of the Necanicum River. The cottage includes a fully equipped kitchen and living room. Before breakfast is served, coffee or tea is delivered to the rooms.

Innkeeper(s): Robert & Nita Hempfling. $55-100. MC VISA AX DS TC. 3 rooms with PB. 1 suite. 1 conference room. Breakfast and evening snack included in rates. Beds: KQT. Ceiling fan, cable TV and VCR in room. Bicycles on premises. Antiques, fishing, parks, shopping and watersports nearby.

Certificate may be used: Sept. 15 through May 15, Sunday-Thursday.

Stayton
D3

The Inn at Gardner House Bed & Breakfast

633 N 3rd Ave, Stayton, OR 97383-1731
(503)769-6331

Circa 1893. A former Stayton postmaster and city councilman built this home, which features a wraparound veranda. Accommodations include a suite with a small kitchen and dining room. Each guest room is comfortably furnished, with some antiques. The innkeeper prepares creative breakfasts with homemade breads, fresh fruit and entrees such as asparagus quiche or breakfast burritos topped with salsa.

Innkeeper(s): Dick Jungwirth. $55-65. MC VISA AX DC CB DS PC TC. 4 rooms, 2 with PB. 1 suite. Breakfast included in rates. Types of meals: full breakfast, gourmet breakfast and early coffee/tea. Afternoon tea, dinner, evening snack, picnic lunch, lunch and gourmet lunch available. Beds: QT. Air conditioning, cable TV and VCR in room. Copier and library on premises. Antiques, fishing, parks, shopping, downhill skiing, cross-country skiing, sporting events, theater and watersports nearby.

Certificate may be used: Jan. 1 to Dec. 31.

The Dalles
B5

Williams House Inn

608 W 6th St,
The Dalles, OR 97058-1314
(503)296-2889

Circa 1899. This large Victorian inn occupies its own wooded hilltop in historic The Dalles, located in the Columbia River Gorge. A natural arboretum extends to Mill Creek on the west. Georgian and Victorian antiques decorate the interior. The innkeepers are happy to share their knowledge of this historic home and surrounding area and will help with excursions to landmarks, special events, recreation opportunities and fine restaurants. If weather permits, breakfast is served in the secluded gazebo.

Innkeeper(s): Don & Barbara Williams. $65-75. MC VISA AX DS. 3 rooms with PB. Breakfast included in rates. Type of meal: full breakfast. Beds: D. Air conditioning, turn-down service and cable TV in room. Copier on premises. Antiques, fishing, shopping, downhill skiing, cross-country skiing and watersports nearby.

Location: Downtown.

Seen in: Oregonian, New York Times, Glamour.

"A fantasy come true, including the most gracious, delightful company in conversation, Barb and Don Williams!"

Certificate may be used: Oct. 1 through April 30

351

Tillamook
B2

Yachats
D2

Blue Haven Inn
3025 Gienger Rd,
Tillamook, OR 97141-8258
(503)842-2265

Circa 1916. This Craftsman-style home has been refurbished and filled with antiques and collectibles. Guest rooms feature limited-edition plate series as themes. Tall evergreens, lawns and flower gardens add to the setting.

Innkeeper(s): Joy Still. $60-75. PC TC. 3 rooms, 1 with PB. Breakfast included in rates. Beds: QD. Cable TV, VCR, bicycles and library on premises.

Seen in: Oakland Tribune.

"Your home is like a present to the eyes."

Certificate may be used: Sunday-Thursday, November & December, January-June.

Sea Quest
95354 Highway 101 S,
Yachats, OR 97498-9713
(541)547-3782 Fax:(541)547-3719

Circa 1990. This 6,000-square-foot cedar and glass house is only 100 feet from the ocean, located on two-and-one-half acres. Each guest room has a Jacuzzi tub and outside entrance. The second-floor breakfast room is distinguished by wide views of the ocean, forest and Ten Mile Creek. Oregon Coast Aquarium is among the nearby attractions.

Innkeeper(s): George & Elaine Rozsa. $125-245. MC VISA DS PC. 5 rooms with PB. Breakfast included in rates. Types of meals: full breakfast and early coffee/tea. Beds: Q. Air conditioning and ceiling fan in room. Fax, spa, sauna and library on premises. Antiques, fishing, parks, shopping and watersports nearby.

Location: One hundred feet from the water, where the forest meets the sea.

Certificate may be used: Jan. 5 to May 15, Sunday to Thursday only, no holidays.

Pennsylvania

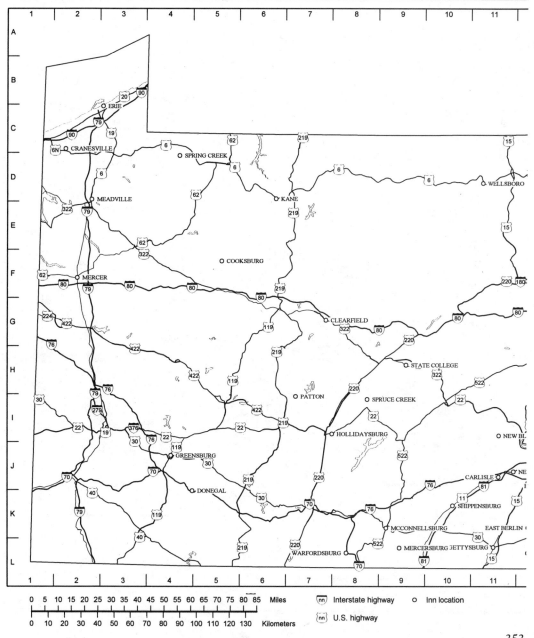

0 5 10 15 20 25 30 35 40 45 50 55 60 65 70 75 80 85 Miles

0 10 20 30 40 50 60 70 80 90 100 110 120 130 Kilometers

nn Interstate highway   o Inn location

nn U.S. highway

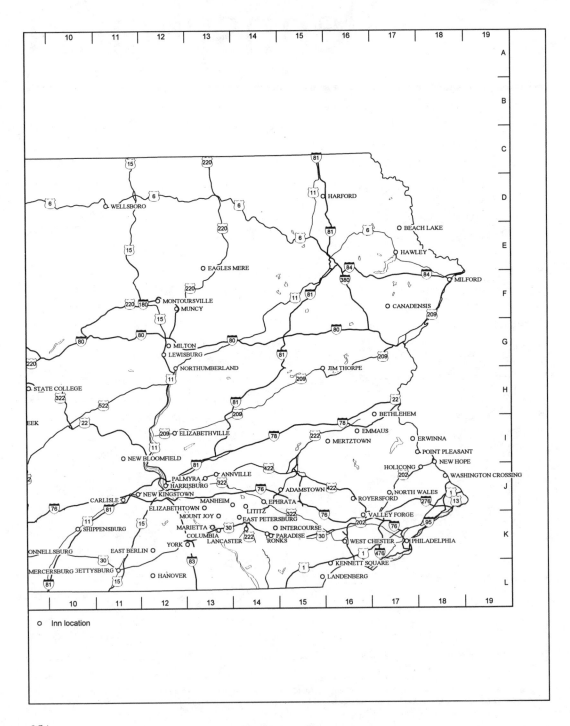

○ Inn location

Adamstown

J15

Adamstown Inn
62 W Main St, Adamstown, PA 19501
(717)484-0800 (800)594-4808

Circa 1830. This square brick house, with its 1850s
pump organ found in the large parlor and other
local folk art, fits right into this community (2,500
antique dealers) known as one of the antique capi-
tols of America. Other decorations include family

heirlooms, Victorian wallpaper, handmade quilts
and lace curtains. Before breakfast, coffee, tea or hot
chocolate is brought to your room. For outlet mall
fans, Adamstown is 10 miles from Reading, which
offers a vast assortment of top quality merchandise.
Innkeeper(s): Tom & Wanda Berman. $65-105. MC VISA DS PC TC. 4
rooms with PB, 2 with FP. 1 suite. Breakfast, afternoon tea and evening
snack included in rates. Types of meals: continental-plus breakfast and
early coffee/tea. Beds: KQD. Air conditioning, ceiling fan and cable TV
in room. Copier and library on premises. Amusement parks, antiques,
fishing, parks, shopping and theater nearby.

Seen in: Lancaster Intelligencer, Reading Eagle, Travel & Leisure,
Country Almanac.

*"Your warm hospitality and lovely home left us with
such pleasant memories."*

Certificate may be used: Sunday through Thursday, Nov. 1 to March 31.

Annville

J13

Swatara Creek Inn
Box 692, Rd 2, Annville, PA 17003
(717)865-3259

Circa 1860. A former boys' home, this bed & breakfast now boasts canopy beds and lacy curtains. The
first floor of this Victorian mansion provides a sitting
room, dining room and gift shop. A full breakfast is
served in the dining room, but honeymooners can
request their meal in the comfort of their rooms. For

chocolate lovers, nearby Hershey is a treat. Several
shopping outlets are about an hour away or visit the
Mount Hope Estate and Winery. For an unusual day
trip, tour the Seltzer and Weaver Bologna plant in
Lebanon. Each September, the town hosts a popular
bologna festival. Nearby Lancaster County is the
home of Amish communities.
Innkeeper(s): Jeanette Hess. $45-80. MC VISA AX DC DS. 10 rooms
with PB. 1 suite. Breakfast included in rates. Types of meals: full breakfast and early coffee/tea. Beds: QT. Air conditioning in room. Handicap
access. Amusement parks, antiques, fishing, parks, shopping, sporting
events and theater nearby.

Seen in: Daily News, Patriot-News.

"Peaceful."

Certificate may be used: Sunday through Thursday. All year.

Beach Lake

E17

East Shore House B&B
PO Box 250, Beach Lake, PA 18405-0250
(717)729-8523 Fax:(717)729-8080

Circa 1901. This Victorian-style home boasts a
wraparound porch perfect for rest and relaxation.
The gazebo, which sits on top of a bubbling brook,
offers another enchanting rest spot. Rooms feature
decor typical of turn-of-the-century boardinghouse
rooms. Each season brings a host of new activities.
In warm months, enjoy canoeing and hiking at
nearby Delaware River. The "Fall Foliage Express"
takes tourists on a train excursion through the local
countryside. In winter, guests can snuggle up by the
woodstove after a day of skiing or ice skating.
Innkeeper(s): Amy Wood. $45-65. MC VISA. 6 rooms, 4 with PB.
Breakfast included in rates. Type of meal: full breakfast. Beds: D. Ceiling
fan in room. Amusement parks, antiques, fishing, shopping and downhill skiing nearby.

Certificate may be used: Sunday through Thursday, year-round.

Bethlehem H17

Wydnor Hall

3612 Old Philadelphia Pike,
Bethlehem, PA 18015-5320
(610)867-6851 (800)839-0020
Fax:(610)866-2062

Circa 1810. On the Old Philadelphia Pike, this Georgian fieldstone mansion is close to Lehigh University and the historic district. Tall trees shade

the acre of grounds. Meticulously restored, the house is appointed with an English decor. Amenities include pressed linens, down comforters and terry cloth robes. The breakfast table is set with fine china and silver. Homemade pastries, breads and cakes are served at tea time.
Innkeeper(s): Kristina & Charles Taylor. $110-140. MC VISA AX DC CB DS PC TC. 5 rooms with PB. 2 suites. 1 conference room. Breakfast included in rates. Type of meal: early coffee/tea. Afternoon tea available. Beds: KQD. Air conditioning, turn-down service, ceiling fan and cable TV in room. Fax on premises. Amusement parks, antiques and sporting events nearby.
Seen in: Express Times, Morning Call.

"Wydnor Hall is warm, clean, charming, and comfortable. Your staff is cheerful, delightful and makes your guests feel graciously welcomed."
Certificate may be used: Weekends January, February & March.

Canadensis F17

Brookview Manor B&B Inn

RR 1 Box 365,
Canadensis, PA 18325-9740
(717)595-2451 (800)585-7974
Fax:(717)595-2065

Circa 1911. By the side of the road, hanging from a tall evergreen, is the welcoming sign to this forest retreat. There are brightly decorated common rooms and four fireplaces. The carriage house has three

bedrooms and is suitable for small groups. The innkeepers like to share a "secret waterfall" within a 30-minute walk from the inn.
Innkeeper(s): Mary Anne Buckley. $100-150. MC VISA AX DS PC TC. 10 rooms, 9 with PB, 1 with FP. 1 suite. Breakfast and afternoon tea included in rates. Types of meals: full breakfast and early coffee/tea. Picnic lunch available. Beds: QD. Air conditioning in room. Cable TV, VCR and fax on premises. Amusement parks, antiques, fishing, parks, shopping, downhill skiing, cross-country skiing, theater and watersports nearby.
Location: On scenic route 447, Pocono Mountains.
Seen in: Mid-Atlantic Country, Bridal Guide.

"Thanks for a great wedding weekend. Everything was perfect."
Certificate may be used: Year-round Sunday-Friday

The Merry Inn

PO Box 757, Rt 390,
Canadensis, PA 18325-0757
(717)595-2011 (800)858-4182

Circa 1942. Set in the picturesque Pocono Mountains, this inn is a 90-minute drive from the metropolitan New York and Philadelphia areas. The turn-of-the-century, mountainside home was built by two sisters and at one time was used as a boarding house. Current owners and innkeepers Meredyth and Chris Huggard have decorated their B&B using an eclectic mix of styles. Each guest room is individually appointed, with styles ranging from Victorian to country. Guests enjoy use of an outdoor Jacuzzi set into the mountainside.
Innkeeper(s): Meredyth & Christopher Huggard. $65-95. MC VISA PC TC. 6 rooms, 4 with PB. Breakfast included in rates. Type of meal: full breakfast. Beds: KQDT. Cable TV in room. VCR, copier, spa and library on premises. Amusement parks, antiques, fishing, parks, shopping, downhill skiing, cross-country skiing, theater and watersports nearby.
Certificate may be used: Anytime midweek, weekends November - April 15.

Carlisle
J11

Clearfield
G7

Line Limousin Farm House B&B
2070 Ritner Hwy,
Carlisle, PA 17013-9303
(717)243-1281

Circa 1864. The grandchildren of Bob and Joan are the ninth generation of Lines to enjoy this 200-year-old homestead. A stone and brick exterior accents the farmhouse's graceful style, while inside, family heirlooms attest to the home's longevity. This is a breeding stock farm of 110 acres and the cattle raised here, Limousin, originate from the Limoges area of France. Giant maples shade the lawn and there are woods and stone fences.

Innkeeper(s): Bob & Joan Line. $55-75. PC. 4 rooms, 2 with PB. Breakfast included in rates. Type of meal: full breakfast. Beds: KQDT. Air conditioning and cable TV in room. VCR and library on premises. Amusement parks, antiques, fishing, parks, shopping, cross-country skiing, sporting events and theater nearby.

Certificate may be used: Monday through Thursday, except special events. Non-smokers only.

Pheasant Field B&B
150 Hickorytown Rd,
Carlisle, PA 17013-9732
(717)258-0717 Fax:(717)258-0717

Circa 1800. Located on eight acres of central Pennsylvania farmland, this brick, two-story Federal-style farmhouse features wooden shutters and a covered front porch. An early 17th-century stone barn is on the property, and horse boarding often is available. The Appalachian Trail is less than a mile away. Fly-fishing is popular at Yellow

Breeches and Letort Spring. Dickinson College and Carlisle Fairgrounds are other points of interest.

Innkeeper(s): Denise Fegan. $65-95. MC VISA AX. 4 rooms, 2 with PB. Breakfast included in rates. Types of meals: full breakfast and early coffee/tea. Beds: KQ. Air conditioning and turn-down service in room. Cable TV and VCR on premises. Amusement parks, antiques, fishing, downhill skiing, cross-country skiing and theater nearby.

Seen in: Outdoor Traveler.

"You have an outstanding, charming and warm house. I felt for the first time as being home."

Certificate may be used: November through March.

Christopher Kratzer House
101 E Cherry St,
Clearfield, PA 16830-2315
(814)765-5024

Circa 1840. This inn is the oldest home in town, built by a carpenter and architect who also started Clearfield's first newspaper. The innkeepers keep a book of history about the house and town for interested guests. The interior is a mix of antiques from different eras, many are family pieces. There are collections of art and musical instruments. Several guest rooms afford views of the Susquehanna River. Refreshments and a glass of wine are served in the afternoons. Bridal suite special offers complimentary champagne, fruit and snacks.

Innkeeper(s): Bruce & Ginny Baggett. $55-70. MC VISA DS PC TC. 4 rooms, 1 with PB. Breakfast, afternoon tea and evening snack included in rates. Types of meals: gourmet breakfast and early coffee/tea. Beds: KQT. Ceiling fan and cable TV in room. Library on premises. Antiques, fishing, parks, shopping, downhill skiing, cross-country skiing, sporting events and theater nearby.

Certificate may be used: January-August, anytime; September-November, anytime excepting Penn State home football weekends.

Victorian Loft B&B
216 S Front St, Clearfield, PA 16830-2218
(814)765-4805 (800)798-0456
Fax:(814)765-9596

Circa 1894. Accommodations at this bed & breakfast are available in either a historic Victorian home on the riverfront or in a private, three-bedroom cabin. The white brick home is dressed with colorful, gingerbread trim and inside, a grand staircase, stained glass and antique furnishings add to the Victorian charm. The suite is ideal for families as it contains two bedrooms, a living room, dining room, kitchen and a bath with a whirlpool tub. The cabin, Cedarwood Lodge is located on eight, wooded acres near Elliot State Park. This is a perfect setting for small groups. The cabin sleeps six comfortably, and it's stocked with amenities.

Innkeeper(s): Tim & Peggy Durant. $45-100. MC VISA AX DS PC TC. 3 rooms, 1 with PB. 1 suite. 1 cottage. Breakfast included in rates. Types of meals: full breakfast and early coffee/tea. Beds: QD. Air conditioning, cable TV and VCR in room. Antiques, fishing, parks, shopping, cross-country skiing, sporting events, theater and watersports nearby.

Certificate may be used: Sunday-Thursday nights based on availability.

Columbia K13

The Columbian
360 Chestnut St,
Columbia, PA 17512-1156
(717)684-5869 (800)422-5869

Circa 1897. This stately three-story mansion is a fine example of Colonial Revival architecture.

Antique beds, a stained-glass window and home-baked breads are among its charms. Guests may relax on the wraparound sun porches.
Innkeeper(s): Chris & Becky Will. $70-89. MC VISA PC TC. 6 rooms with PB, 1 with FP. 1 suite. Breakfast included in rates. Type of meal: full breakfast. Beds: QT. Air conditioning, ceiling fan and cable TV in room. Amusement parks, antiques, fishing, parks, shopping, downhill skiing, cross-country skiing, sporting events, theater and watersports nearby.
Seen in: Philadelphia Inquirer, Lancaster Intelligencer Journal, Columbia News, Washington Post, Potomac.

"In a word, extraordinary! Truly a home away from home. First B&B experience but will definitely not be my last."

Certificate may be used: Sunday through Thursday, December through April.

Cooksburg F5

Clarion River Lodge
HC 1 Box 22D,
Cooksburg, PA 16217-9704
(814)744-8171 (800)648-6743
Fax:(814)744-8553

Circa 1964. The Clarion River Lodge is a rustic retreat above the Clarion River surrounded by Cook Forest. Its pegged-oak flooring, oak beams, pine ceiling, wild cherry and butternut paneling and field-stone fireplace add to the lodge's natural character. A distinctive glassed-in breezeway leads from the

main building to the guest wing. Rooms are decorated with modern Scandinavian decor.
Innkeeper(s): Ellen O'Day. $72-129. MC VISA AX TC. 20 rooms with PB. 1 conference room. Breakfast and dinner included in rates. Types of meals: continental breakfast, continental-plus breakfast, full breakfast, gourmet breakfast and early coffee/tea. Afternoon tea, evening snack, lunch, gourmet lunch, banquet service and room service available. Beds: KQ. Air conditioning and cable TV in room. VCR, fax and bicycles on premises. Handicap access. Antiques, fishing, parks, shopping and theater nearby.
Location: Adjacent to Cook Forest State Park and on the Clarion River.
Seen in: Pittsburgh Press, Pittsburgh Women's Journal.

"If your idea of Paradise is a secluded rustic retreat surrounded by the most beautiful country this side of the Rockies, search no more."

Certificate may be used: November-April, Sunday-Thursday, no holidays.

Cranesville C2

Historic Zion's Hill B&B
8951 Miller Rd,
Cranesville, PA 16410-9618
(814)774-2971

Circa 1830. Dan Rice, the man whose face has been immortalized as Uncle Sam, once lived in this historic home. Rice was also a famed American circus clown and the first person to erect a monument in honor of U.S. soldiers who died in battle. The Colonial home is decorated with antiques and a mix of Colonial and Victorian styles. The home is surrounded by 100 acres of farmland. Lake Erie, which offers boating, swimming and fishing, is just a few miles away.
Innkeeper(s): John & Kathy Byrne. $55-65. TC. 5 rooms, 3 with PB. Breakfast included in rates. Types of meals: continental-plus breakfast and early coffee/tea. Beds: QD. Air conditioning and ceiling fan in room. Handicap access. Amusement parks, antiques, fishing, parks, shopping, downhill skiing, cross-country skiing, sporting events and watersports nearby.
Certificate may be used: Sept. 15-April 30.

Donegal K4

Mountain View B&B & Antiques
Mountain View Rd, Donegal, PA 15628
(412)593-6349

Circa 1855. Six wooded acres surround this Georgian-style farmhouse, a county historic landmark. The innkeepers own Donegal antiques and have selected many fine 18th- and 19th-century pieces to furnish the inn. There is a large barn on the property. Guests enjoy the rural setting for its outstanding views of the Laurel Mountains.

Fallingwater, a famous Frank Lloyd Wright house, is 20 minutes away.

Innkeeper(s): Lesley O'Leary. $95-150. MC VISA AX DC DS. 7 rooms, 3 with PB. Breakfast included in rates. Types of meals: full breakfast and early coffee/tea. Evening snack available. Beds: QD. Air conditioning in room. Amusement parks, antiques, fishing, shopping, downhill skiing, cross-country skiing and theater nearby.

Certificate may be used: Anytime except holiday weekends and month of October.

Eagles Mere   E13

Crestmont Inn

Crestmont Dr, Eagles Mere, PA 17731
(717)525-3519 (800)522-8767

Eagles Mere has been a vacation site since the late 19th century and still abounds with Victorian charm. The Crestmont Inn is no exception. The rooms are tastefully decorated with Oriental rugs, flowers and elegant furnishings. A hearty country breakfast is served each morning, and guests also are treated to a five-course dinner in the candlelit dining room. Savor a variety of mouth-watering entrees and finish off the evening with scrumptious desserts such as fresh fruit pies, English trifle or Orange Charlotte. The cocktail lounge is a perfect place to mingle and enjoy hors d'oeuvres, wines and spirits. The inn grounds offer a large swimming pool, tennis and shuffleboard courts. The Wyoming State Forest borders the property, and golfing is just minutes away.

Innkeeper(s): Kathleen Oliver. $89-125. MC VISA. 19 rooms. Breakfast included in rates. Type of meal: full breakfast.

Certificate may be used: All year, Sunday through Thursday.

Shady Lane B&B

Allegheny Ave, PO Box 314,
Eagles Mere, PA 17731
(717)525-3394 (800)524-1248

Circa 1947. This ranch-style house rests on two mountaintop acres. Eagles Mere is a Victorian town with gaslights and old-fashioned village shops.

Crystal clear Eagles Mere Lake is surrounded by Laurel Path, a popular scenic walk. The Endless Mountains provide cross-country skiing, fishing and hiking. Tobogganing is popular on the Eagles Mere Toboggan Slide.

Innkeeper(s): Pat & Dennis Dougherty. $75. TC. 8 rooms, 7 with PB. 1 suite. Breakfast and afternoon tea included in rates. Types of meals: full breakfast and gourmet breakfast. Beds: KQDT. Ceiling fan in room. Cable TV on premises. Antiques, fishing, parks, shopping and cross-country skiing nearby.

Certificate may be used: Sunday through Thursday from Sept. 1 to June 30 (not in July or August).

East Berlin   K12

Bechtel Mansion Inn

400 W King St, East Berlin, PA 17316
(717)259-7760 (800)331-1108

Circa 1897. The town of East Berlin, near Lancaster and Gettysburg, was settled by Pennsylvania Germans prior to the American Revolution. William Leas, a wealthy banker, built this many-gabled romantic Queen Anne mansion,

now listed in the National Register. The inn is furnished with an abundance of museum-quality antiques and collections. Mennonite quilts top many of the handsome bedsteads.

Innkeeper(s): Ruth Spangler. $80-145. MC VISA AX DC DS PC TC. 9 rooms, 7 with PB. 2 suites. 1 conference room. Breakfast included in rates. Types of meals: full breakfast and early coffee/tea. Beds: KQD. Air conditioning in room. Library on premises. Antiques, shopping, downhill skiing, cross-country skiing and theater nearby.

Seen in: Washington Post, Richmond Times.

"Ruth was a most gracious hostess and took time to describe the history of your handsome museum-quality antiques and the special architectural details."

Certificate may be used: May 1, 1996 through May 1, 1997, excluding holiday weekends and weekends during October, 1996.

East Petersburg   K14

The George Zahm House
6070 Main St,
East Petersburg, PA 17520-1266
(717)569-6026

Circa 1856. The bright red exterior of this Federal-style inn is a landmark along this village road. The home is named for its builder and first resident, who constructed his study dwelling with 18-inch-thick brick walls. Innkeeping is a family affair for owners Robyn Kemple-Keeports and husband, Jeff Keeports, who run the inn along with Robyn's mother Daneen. The rooms are inviting and comfortable, yet elegant. Beautiful drapery, rich wallpapers and a collection of early American furniture combine to give the house an opulent feel. Many of the pieces are family heirlooms. Breakfasts with homemade breads, muffins and pastries are served in the dining room on a table set with Blue Willow china.
Innkeeper(s): Robyn & Jeff Keeports. $65-85. MC VISA TC. 4 rooms, 3 with PB. 1 suite. Breakfast and afternoon tea included in rates. Types of meals: continental-plus breakfast and early coffee/tea. Evening snack and room service available. Beds: KQT. Air conditioning and ceiling fan in room. Handicap access. Amusement parks, antiques, parks, shopping, sporting events and theater nearby.
Certificate may be used: Year-round, Sunday-Thursday.

Elizabethtown   J13

Apples Abound Inn B&B
518 S Market St,
Elizabethtown, PA 17022-2530
(717)367-3018 Fax:(717)367-9788

Circa 1907. As the name suggests, apples do abound at this early 20th-century home, which features a unique apple collection. In the local historic register, this three-story Victorian has a turret and a wide, wraparound veranda. Other features include

cranberry-colored glass transoms, bay windows, a stained-glass window, chestnut wood trim and doors and built-in china cabinets. Rooms are decorated with antiques and a traditional country decor. Lancaster, Harrisburg and Hershey are nearby.
Innkeeper(s): Jennifer & Jon Sheppard. $70-80. MC VISA PC TC. 4 rooms, 2 with PB. Breakfast included in rates. Types of meals: full breakfast and early coffee/tea. Beds: QD. Air conditioning, turn-down service and ceiling fan in room. Amusement parks, antiques, fishing, parks, shopping, downhill skiing, cross-country skiing and sporting events nearby.
Certificate may be used: Jan. 1 to March 31, Sunday-Saturday.

West Ridge Guest House
1285 W Ridge Rd,
Elizabethtown, PA 17022-9739
(717)367-7783 (800)367-7783
Fax:(717)367-8468

Circa 1890. Guests at this country home have many choices. They may opt to relax and enjoy the view from the gazebo, or perhaps work out in the inn's exercise room. The hot tub provides yet another soothing possibility. The 20-acre grounds also include two fishing ponds. The innkeepers pass out a breakfast menu to their guests, allowing them to choose the time they prefer to eat and a choice of entrees. Along with the traditional fruit, muffins or coffeecake and meats, guests choose items such as omelets, waffles or pancakes.
Innkeeper(s): Alice P. Heisey. $60-100. MC VISA AX. 9 rooms, 7 with PB, 3 with FP. 2 suites. Breakfast included in rates. Type of meal: full breakfast. Beds: KQ. Air conditioning, ceiling fan, cable TV and VCR in room. Fax, copier and spa on premises. Antiques, fishing, parks and shopping nearby.
Certificate may be used: All year when available except holiday weekends.

Elizabethville   I12

The Inn at Elizabethville
30 W Main St, Box V,
Elizabethville, PA 17023
(717)362-3476 Fax:(717)362-4571

Circa 1883. This comfortable, two-story house was owned by a Civil War veteran and founder of a local wagon company. The innkeepers decided to buy and fix up the house to help support their other business, renovating old houses. The conference room features an unusual fireplace with cabinets and painted decorations. Rooms are filled with antiques and Mission oak-style furniture. County auctions, local craft fairs and outdoor activities entice guests. Comfortable living rooms, porches and a sun parlor are available for relaxation.

Innkeeper(s): James S. Facinelli. $55-65. AP. MC VISA TC. 7 rooms with PB. 1 suite. 1 conference room. Breakfast included in rates. Type of meal: continental breakfast. Beds: DT. Air conditioning and ceiling fan in room. Cable TV, VCR, fax and copier on premises. Antiques, fishing, parks, shopping and watersports nearby.

Seen in: Harrisburg Patriot-News, Upper Dauphin Sentinel.

Certificate may be used: Anytime with prior notice.

Emmaus   I16

Leibert Gap Manor

4502 S Mountain Dr, PO Box 623,
Emmaus, PA 18049-4503
(215)967-1242 (800)964-1242

This three-story Williamsburg-style house is on 17 acres. Random-width pine floors, open-beam ceilings and a Colonial fireplace are on the main floor. Primitive and cottage pieces, along with canopy beds and antiques, are found in the guest rooms. A solarium overlooks the Leibert Gap flyway and you may watch hawks and other birds pass by. In the afternoon, enjoy tea and scones on the long brick porch. Nearby are 10 colleges as well as many antique shops and factory outlets.

Innkeeper(s): Pauline & Wayne Sheffer. $75-125. MC VISA AX DC CB. 4 rooms. 2 suites. 1 conference room. Breakfast included in rates. Type of meal: full breakfast. Catering service available. Air conditioning, turn-down service and VCR in room. Cable TV on premises. Amusement parks, antiques, shopping, downhill skiing, sporting events and theater nearby.

Certificate may be used: Sunday through Thursday, January through March, space available. August-December excluded. April, May and June, space available.

Ephrata   J14

The 1777 House at Doneckers

301 W Main St, Ephrata, PA 17522-1713
(717)738-9502 Fax:(717)738-9552

Circa 1777. Jacob Gorgas, a devout member of the Ephrata Cloister and a clock maker, noted for crafting 150 eight-day Gorgas grandfather clocks, built this stately Dutch Colonial-style home. Guests can

opt to stay in one of four antique-filled homes. The 1777 House, which includes 12 rooms, features hand-stenciled walls, suites with whirlpool baths, fireplaces, original stone masonry and an antique tiled floor. The home served as a tavern in the 1800s and an elegant inn in the early 1900s. The Homestead includes four suites all with fireplaces and amenities such as Jacuzzis, sitting areas and four-poster beds. The Guesthouse features a variety of beautifully decorated rooms each named and themed in honor of local landmarks or significant citizens. The Gerhart House memorializes prominent innkeepers or hotel owners in Ephrata's history. All guests enjoy an expansive breakfast with freshly squeezed juice, fruits, breakfast cheeses, sausage, fresh pastries and other delicacies. The homes are part of the Donecker Community, which features upscale fashion stores, art galleries and a restaurant within walking distance of the 1777 House.

Innkeeper(s): Jill Brown. $89-185. MC VISA AX DC CB DS. 40 rooms, 12 with PB, 4 with FP. 6 suites. 1 conference room. Breakfast included in rates. Types of meals: continental-plus breakfast and gourmet breakfast. Beds: KQDT. Air conditioning in room. Cable TV, fax, copier and spa on premises. Antiques, shopping and theater nearby.

Location: Junction of Routes 222 & 322 in Lancaster County.

Seen in: Daily News, Country Inns.

"A peaceful refuge."

Certificate may be used: Sunday through Thursday, except holidays, year-round.

Erie
C3

Spencer House B&B

519 W 6th St, Erie, PA 16507-1128
(814)454-5984 (800)890-7263
Fax:(814)456-5091

Circa 1876. This three-story Victorian Stick house features gabled windows and a wraparound porch. Original woodwork, much of it carved with scrolls and scripture, is one of the inn's most outstanding features. Twelve-foot ceilings, interior folding shutters and a well-stocked library with black walnut bookshelves are other highlights. The Tree Top Room offers a ceiling-to-floor canopy and a reading nook.

Innkeeper(s): Pat & Keith Hagenbuch. $65-95. MC VISA AX DS TC. 5 rooms with PB, 5 with FP. 1 suite. Breakfast and afternoon tea included in rates. Types of meals: continental breakfast, continental-plus breakfast, full breakfast and early coffee/tea. Dinner and picnic lunch available. Beds: Q. Air conditioning, ceiling fan, cable TV and VCR in room. Fax and copier on premises. Amusement parks, antiques, fishing, parks, shopping, downhill skiing, cross-country skiing, sporting events, theater and watersports nearby.

Certificate may be used: Sept. 30 to April 30, Sunday-Thursday.

Erwinna
I17

Evermay-On-The-Delaware

River Rd, Erwinna, PA 18920
(610)294-9100 Fax:(610)294-8249

Circa 1700. Twenty-five acres of Bucks County at its best — rolling green meadows, lawns, stately maples and the silvery Delaware River — surround this three-story manor. Serving as an inn since 1871, it has hosted such guests as the Barrymore family. Rich walnut wainscoting, a grandfather clock and twin fireplaces warm the parlor, scented by vases of roses or gladiolus. Antique-filled guest rooms overlook the river or gardens.

Innkeeper(s): Dawn Smigo. $85-180. MC VISA PC TC. 16 rooms with PB. 1 suite. 2 cottages. 2 conference rooms. Breakfast and afternoon tea included in rates. Type of meal: continental-plus breakfast. Dinner and picnic lunch available. Beds: QD. Air conditioning and turn-down service in room. VCR, fax, copier, computer, swimming and library on premises. Handicap access. Antiques, fishing, parks, shopping, cross-country skiing, sporting events, theater and watersports nearby.

Seen in: New York Times, Philadelphia, Travel & Leisure, Food and Wine, Child.

"It was pure perfection. Everything from the flowers to the wonderful food."

Certificate may be used: Sunday through Thursday, excluding holidays.

Gettysburg
L11

Keystone Inn B&B

231 Hanover St,
Gettysburg, PA 17325-1913
(717)337-3888

Circa 1913. Furniture maker Clayton Reaser constructed this three-story brick Victorian with a wide-columned porch hugging the north and west sides. Cut stone graces every door and window sill,

each with a keystone. A chestnut staircase ascends the full three stories, and the interior is decorated with comfortable furnishings, ruffles and lace.

Innkeeper(s): Wilmer & Doris Martin. $59-100. MC VISA DS TC. 5 rooms, 3 with PB. 1 suite. Breakfast and afternoon tea included in rates. Types of meals: full breakfast and early coffee/tea. Beds: KQDT. Air conditioning and ceiling fan in room. Library on premises. Amusement parks, antiques, fishing, parks, shopping, downhill skiing, cross-country skiing and theater nearby.

Location: Route 116 - East Gettysburg.

Seen in: Gettysburg Times, Hanover Sun, York Sunday News, Pennsylvania, Lancaster Sunday News, Los Angeles Times.

"We slept like lambs. This home has a warmth that is soothing."

Certificate may be used: November-April Monday-Thursday.

The Old Appleford Inn

218 Carlisle St,
Gettysburg, PA 17325-1305
(717)337-1711 (800)275-3373
Fax:(717)334-6228

Circa 1867. Located in the historic district, this Italianate-style brick mansion offers a taste of 19th-century charm and comfort. Among its inviting features are a plant-filled sunroom and a parlor with a baby grand piano. As the inn was built just following the Civil War, the innkeepers have tried to keep a sense of turbulent history present. Most of the guest rooms are named for Civil War generals, another for Abraham Lincoln. Breakfasts are a

fashionable affair served on fine china in the inn's Victorian dining room.

Innkeeper(s): John & Jane Wiley. $73-118. MC VISA AX DS. 10 rooms with PB, 2 with FP. 1 suite. Breakfast and afternoon tea included in rates. Types of meals: full breakfast and early coffee/tea. Catering service available. Beds: QD. Air conditioning in room. Fax and library on premises. Amusement parks, antiques, parks, shopping, downhill skiing and theater nearby.

Location: Two blocks from downtown.

Seen in: Innsider, Gettysburg Times, Baltimore Sun, Philadelphia.

"Everything in your place invites us back."

Certificate may be used: Sunday-Thursday, except July and August excluding holidays or special events.

Greensburg   J4

Huntland Farm B&B
Road 9, Box 21,
Greensburg, PA 15601-9232
(412)834-8483 Fax:(412)838-8253

Circa 1848. Porches and flower gardens surround the three-story, columned, brick Georgian manor that presides over the inn's 100 acres. Corner bedrooms are furnished with English antiques. Fallingwater, the Frank Lloyd Wright house, is nearby. Other attractions include Hidden Valley, Ohiopyle water rafting, Bushy Run and Fort Ligonier.

Innkeeper(s): Robert & Elizabeth Weidlein. $75. AX PC TC. 4 rooms, 2 with FP. Breakfast included in rates. Type of meal: full breakfast. Beds: KQDT. Ceiling fan in room. Cable TV, VCR, fax, copier and library on premises. Antiques, parks, shopping and theater nearby.

Certificate may be used: All year. Nov. 1 to May 1, any day; May 1-Oct. 31, weekdays only.

Hanover   L12

Beechmont B&B Inn
315 Broadway, Hanover, PA 17331-2505
(717)632-3013 (800)553-7009

Circa 1834. This gracious Georgian inn was a witness to the Civil War's first major battle on free soil, the Battle of Hanover. Decorated in Federal-period

antiques, several guest rooms are named for the battle's commanders. The romantic Diller Suite contains a marble fireplace and queen canopy bed. The inn is noted for elegant breakfasts.

Innkeeper(s): William & Susan Day. $80-135. MC VISA AX DS PC TC. 7 rooms with PB, 3 with FP. 3 suites. 1 conference room. Breakfast, afternoon tea and evening snack included in rates. Types of meals: full breakfast, gourmet breakfast and early coffee/tea. Picnic lunch and room service available. Beds: QD. Air conditioning, ceiling fan and cable TV in room. Copier and library on premises. Amusement parks, antiques, fishing, parks, shopping, downhill skiing, cross-country skiing, sporting events, theater and watersports nearby.

Location: Three miles from Lake Marburg.

Seen in: Evening Sun, York Daily Record.

"I had a marvelous time at your charming, lovely inn."

Certificate may be used: Sunday-Thursday, except holidays.

Harford   D15

9 Partners Inn
1 N Harmony Rd, PO Box 300,
Harford, PA 18823
(717)434-2233 Fax:(717)434-1233

Circa 1794. A bright red door welcomes guests to this white three-story, salt-box New England house. There are several fireplaces, original to the building, and the rooms are furnished with a mix of antiques and maple pieces. A large deck to the side of the house overlooks 24 acres of rolling meadows and the mountains beyond. Breakfast is offered in the dining room.

Innkeeper(s): Rudy Sumpter & Jim DeCoe. $55-85. MC VISA AX DS. 3 rooms with PB, 3 with FP. Breakfast and evening snack included in rates. Types of meals: full breakfast, gourmet breakfast and early coffee/tea. Picnic lunch and catering service available. Beds: KQT. Antiques, fishing, parks, shopping, downhill skiing and cross-country skiing nearby.

Certificate may be used: April 1 to June 20 & Aug. 28 to Nov. 20, Sunday-Friday except holiday weekends.

Harrisburg

J12

Abide With Me B&B

2601 Walnut St,
Harrisburg, PA 17103-1952
(717)236-5873

Circa 1870. A city historical site, this B&B is a brick Second Empire Victorian. There are three stories with shuttered windows, a large bay and a rounded front veranda. Oak, parquet and wide-plank floors and fireplaces add to the interest inside. Modestly furnished, the B&B offers some antiques and country pieces. The Harrisburg State Capital is a mile-and-a-half away.

Innkeeper(s): Don & Joyce Adams. $56. PC. 3 rooms. Breakfast included in rates. Types of meals: gourmet breakfast and early coffee/tea. Beds: QDT. Air conditioning in room. Cable TV and VCR on premises. Amusement parks, antiques, fishing, parks, shopping, sporting events, theater and watersports nearby.

Certificate may be used: Upon availability, excluding first week of October.

Hawley

E17

Academy Street B&B

528 Academy St, Hawley, PA 18428-1434
(717)226-3430 Fax:(201)335-5051

Circa 1863. This restored Civil War Victorian home boasts a mahogany front door with the original glass paneling, two large fireplaces (one in mosaic, the other in fine polished marble) and a living room with oak sideboard, polished marble mantel and yellow pine floor. The airy guest rooms have canopied brass beds. Guests are welcome to afternoon tea, which includes an array of cakes and pastries.

Innkeeper(s): Judith Lazan. $65-80. MC VISA. 7 rooms, 4 with PB. Breakfast and afternoon tea included in rates. Type of meal: early coffee/tea. Beds: QDT. Air conditioning, ceiling fan and cable TV in room. VCR on premises. Amusement parks, antiques, fishing, parks, shopping, theater and watersports nearby.

Seen in: Wayne Independent, Citizens' Voice.

"Truly wonderful everything!"

Certificate may be used: Monday through Friday.

Holicong

J18

Barley Sheaf Farm

5281 York Rd, Rt 202 Box 10,
Holicong, PA 18928
(215)794-5104 Fax:(215)794-5332

Circa 1740. Situated on part of the original William Penn land grant, this beautiful stone house with white shuttered windows and mansard roof is set on 30 acres of farmland. Once owned by noted playwright George Kaufman, it was the gathering place for the Marx Brothers, Lillian Hellman and S. J. Perlman. The bank barn, pond and majestic old trees round out a beautiful setting.

Innkeeper(s): Peter Suess. $105-255. MC VISA AX PC TC. 12 rooms with PB, 3 with FP. 4 suites. 3 conference rooms. Breakfast and afternoon tea included in rates. Types of meals: full breakfast and early coffee/tea. Catering service available. Beds: KQD. Air conditioning in room. Cable TV, VCR, fax, copier and swimming on premises. Handicap access. Amusement parks, antiques, fishing, parks, shopping, downhill skiing, cross-country skiing, theater and watersports nearby.

Location: Fifty miles north of Philadelphia in Bucks County.

Seen in: Country Living.

Certificate may be used: Sunday through Thursday, no holidays.

Hollidaysburg

I8

Hoenstine's B&B

418 N Montgomery St,
Hollidaysburg, PA 16648-1432
(814)695-0632

Circa 1839. This inn is an antique lover's dream, as it boasts many pieces of original furniture. Stained-glass windows and the 10-foot-high ceilings add to the atmosphere. Breakfast is served in the home's formal dining room. Guests will sleep well in the comfortable and beautifully decorated rooms, especially knowing that the house is being protected by innkeeper Barbara Hoenstine's black standard poodle, Dickens, who is a happy guide and escort around the canal-era town. The inn is within walking distance of shops, restaurants, the downtown historic district and an antique shop.

Innkeeper(s): Barbara Hoenstine. $50-80. MC VISA. 4 rooms, 1 with PB. Breakfast included in rates. Type of meal: full breakfast. Beds: QDT. Ceiling fan, cable TV and VCR in room. Copier on premises. Amusement parks, antiques, fishing, parks, shopping, downhill skiing, cross-country skiing and theater nearby.

"Thank you for a truly calm and quiet week. This was our first B&B experience and it won't be our last."

Certificate may be used: Sunday-Friday, November-March, last minute anytime.

Intercourse

K14

Carriage Corner

3705 E Newport Rd, PO Box 371,
Intercourse, PA 17534-0371
(717)768-3059

Circa 1981. Located on two acres, this is a two-story, white Colonial house. The inn is decorated with folk art and country furnishings. Homemade

breads and hot cereals are served in the dining room. Walk five minutes to the village and explore shops displaying local crafts, pottery and hand-made furniture. The inn is located in the hub of Amish farmland.

Innkeeper(s): Gordon & Gwen Schuit. $48-68. MC VISA PC. 5 rooms with PB. Breakfast included in rates. Type of meal: full breakfast. Beds: QD. Air conditioning and cable TV in room. Child care on premises. Amusement parks, antiques, parks, shopping and theater nearby.

Certificate may be used: December-February, excluding holiday weekends.

Jim Thorpe

H15

Harry Packer Mansion

Packer Hill, Jim Thorpe, PA 18229
(717)325-8566

Circa 1874. This extravagant Second Empire mansion was constructed of New England sandstone, and local brick and stone trimmed in cast iron. Past ornately carved columns on the front veranda, guests enter 400-pound, solid walnut doors. The opulent interior includes marble mantels, hand-painted ceilings, and elegant antiques.

Innkeeper(s): Robert & Patricia Handwerk. $85-135. MC VISA TC. 13 rooms, 10 with PB. 3 suites. 3 conference rooms. Breakfast included in rates. Types of meals: full breakfast, gourmet breakfast and early coffee/tea. Beds: QD. Air conditioning, turn-down service and ceiling fan in room. Cable TV and VCR on premises. Antiques, fishing, parks, shopping, downhill skiing, cross-country skiing and watersports nearby.

Location: Six miles south of Exit 34.

Seen in: Philadelphia Inquirer, New York, Victorian Homes.

"The best B&B we have ever stayed at! We'll be back."

Certificate may be used: Sunday through Thursday night except for holidays.

The Inn at Jim Thorpe

24 Broadway, Jim Thorpe, PA 18229-2028
(717)325-2599 (800)329-2599
Fax:(717)325-9145

Circa 1848. This massive New Orleans-style structure, now restored, hosted some colorful 19th-century guests, including Thomas Edison, John D. Rockefeller and Buffalo Bill. All rooms are appointed with Victorian furnishings and have private baths with pedestal sinks and marble floors. Also on the premises are a Victorian dining room, Irish pub and a conference center. The inn is situated in

the heart of Jim Thorpe, a quaint Victorian town that was known at the turn of the century as the "Switzerland of America."

Innkeeper(s): David Drury. $65-250. MAP. MC VISA AX DC DS TC. 30 rooms, 26 with PB, 3 with FP. 4 suites. 2 conference rooms. Breakfast included in rates. Type of meal: continental-plus breakfast. Dinner, lunch and room service available. Beds: KQD. Air conditioning and cable TV in room. Fax and copier on premises. Handicap access. Antiques, fishing, parks, shopping, downhill skiing, cross-country skiing, theater and watersports nearby.

Location: In the western part of the Pocono Mountains.

Seen in: Philadelphia Inquirer, Pennsylvania, Allentown Morning Call.

"Thank you for having provided us a relaxing getaway."

Certificate may be used: Sunday-Thursday nights, excluding holidays.

Kane

D6

Kane Manor Country Inn

230 Clay St, Kane, PA 16735-1410
(814)837-6522 Fax:(814)837-6664

Circa 1896. This Georgian Revival inn, on 250 acres of woods and trails, was built for Dr. Elizabeth Kane, the first female doctor to practice in the area. Many of the family's possessions dating back to the American Revolution and the Civil War remain. (Ask to see the attic.) Decor is a mixture of old family items in an unpretentious country style. There is a pub, popular with locals, on the premises. The building is in the National Register. Dinner is available on request.

Innkeeper(s): Helen Johnson & Cheri Manfredo. $89-99. MC VISA AX DS PC TC. 10 rooms, 7 with PB. Breakfast and afternoon tea included in rates. Types of meals: continental breakfast, continental-plus breakfast, full breakfast and early coffee/tea. Beds: DT. Cable TV in room. VCR, fax, copier and library on premises. Handicap access. Amusement parks, antiques, fishing, parks, shopping, downhill skiing, cross-country skiing and watersports nearby.

Seen in: Pittsburgh Press, News Herald, Cleveland Plain Dealer, Youngstown Indicator.

"It's a place I want to return to often, for rest and relaxation."

Certificate may be used: Jan. 1 through Sept. 15 and Dec. 1-29.

Kennett Square L16

Scarlett House
503 W State St,
Kennett Square, PA 19348-3028
(610)444-9592 (800)820-9592

Circa 1910. This stone four-square home features an extensive wraparound porch and front door surrounded by leaded-glass windows. Beyond the foyer are two downstairs parlors, while a second-floor parlor provides a sunny setting for afternoon tea. Rooms are furnished in romantic Victorian decor. Beds are turned down with a flower and chocolate at night. When served in the dining room, breakfast is by candlelight with fine china and lace linens. Mushroom-shaped chocolate chip scones are a novel breakfast specialty at the inn—a reminder that this is the acclaimed mushroom capital of the world.

Innkeeper(s): Jane & Sam Snyder. $75-110. VISA TC. 4 rooms, 2 with PB. 1 suite. 1 conference room. Breakfast, afternoon tea and evening snack included in rates. Types of meals: gourmet breakfast and early coffee/tea. Beds: QD. Air conditioning and ceiling fan in room. Cable TV on premises. Antiques, fishing, parks, shopping, theater and watersports nearby.

Location: Located in the heart of Brandywine Valley in the town of Kennett Square. Just 15 minutes to Wilmington, Del., and 45 minutes to Philadelphia.

"Truly an enchanting place."

Certificate may be used: From Jan. 1 to March 31 Sunday-Saturday, July 1-Aug. 31 Sunday-Thursday, Nov. 1 to Dec. 31 Sunday-Saturday. No holidays or holiday weekends.

Lancaster K14

Flowers & Thyme B&B
238 Strasburg Pike,
Lancaster, PA 17602-1326
(717)393-1460

Circa 1941. This home was built by an Amishman for a Mennonite minister and his family. The innkeepers grew up among Amish and Mennonite communities and are full of knowledge about the area and its history. Fresh flowers from the inn's beautiful gardens are placed in the guest rooms in season. A country breakfast is served in the breakfast room overlooking the herb garden. The inn is only minutes away from outlet stores and plenty of outdoor activities.

Innkeeper(s): Don & Ruth Harnish. $70-100. PC TC. 3 rooms with PB. 1 suite. Breakfast included in rates. Types of meals: full breakfast and gourmet breakfast. Beds: QD. Air conditioning and ceiling fan in room. Cable TV and library on premises. Amusement parks, antiques, parks, shopping, sporting events, theater and watersports nearby.

Seen in: Lancaster newspapers

"Your home is beautiful, perfectly decorated, warm and inviting and we felt so welcome. Your breakfast was delicious and served so elegantly."

Certificate may be used: Sunday through Thursday, May 1 to Nov. 30; anytime Jan. 1 to April 30.

Hollinger House
2336 Hollinger Rd,
Lancaster, PA 17602-4728
(717)464-3050

Circa 1876. A peach bottom slate roof tops this large Adams-style brick house, and there is a wraparound veranda and a double balcony. Several fireplaces and original hardwood floors have been

restored. Adding to the setting's pastoral beauty, sheep meander over the meadow and woodland stream. The innkeepers serve hors d'oeuvres upon arrival, tea in the afternoon, and additional goodies at bedtime. In the morning, a bountiful breakfast is provided.

Innkeeper(s): Gina & Jeff Trost. $90-95. 5 rooms with PB. Evening snack, picnic lunch and catering service available. Air conditioning and turn-down service in room. Cable TV and VCR on premises. Amusement parks, antiques, shopping, cross-country skiing, sporting events and theater nearby.
Certificate may be used: November-March.

The King's Cottage, A B&B Inn
1049 E King St, Lancaster, PA 17602-3231
(717)397-1017 (800)747-8717
Fax:(717)397-3447

Circa 1913. This Mission Revival house features a red-tile roof and stucco walls, common in many stately turn-of-the-century houses in California and

New Mexico. Its elegant interiors include a sweeping staircase, a library with marble fireplace, stained-glass windows, and a solarium. The inn is appointed with Oriental rugs and antiques and fine 18th-century English reproductions. The formal dining room provides the location for gourmet morning meals.
Innkeeper(s): Karen Owens. $80-175. MC VISA DS. 9 rooms with PB. 1 conference room. Breakfast and afternoon tea included in rates. Type of meal: full breakfast. Beds: KQ. Air conditioning and turn-down service in room. Cable TV on premises. Amusement parks, antiques, fishing, shopping, cross-country skiing, sporting events and theater nearby.
Location: Pennsylvania Dutch country.
Seen in: Country, USA Weekend, Bon Appetit, Intelligencer Journal, Times.

"I appreciate your attention to all our needs and look forward to recommending your inn to friends."
Certificate may be used: Monday-Thursday, November-August.

New Life Homestead B&B
1400 E King St, Rt 462,
Lancaster, PA 17602-3240
(717)396-8928

Circa 1912. This two-story brick home is situated within six miles of the Amish farms. Innkeepers Carol and Bill Giersch often host evening discussions about the culture and history of the surrounding Pennsylvania Dutch Country, and they will, with advance notice, arrange tours and meals in Amish homes. Their full country breakfasts are made from produce purchased at local Amish markets.

Innkeeper(s): Carol Giersch. $50-75. 3 rooms, 2 with PB. 1 suite. Breakfast included in rates. Type of meal: full breakfast. Evening snack available. Beds: KQDT. Amusement parks, antiques, fishing, shopping, sporting events and theater nearby.
Location: In the heart of Pennsylvania Dutch country.
Seen in: Keystone Gazette, Pennsylvania Dutch Traveler.

"Reminded me of my childhood at home."
Certificate may be used: Anytime: December-March. Monday-Thursday: April-June, September, November, only.

O'Flaherty's Dingeldein House B&B
1105 E King St, Lancaster, PA 17602-3233
(717)293-1723 (800)779-7765
Fax:(717)293-1947

Circa 1910. This Dutch Colonial home was once residence to the Armstrong family, who acquired fame and fortune in the tile floor industry. Springtime guests will brighten at the sight of this home's beautiful flowers. During winter months, innkeepers Jack and Sue Flatley deck the halls with plenty of seasonal decorations. The hearty country breakfast might include fresh-baked muffins, fruits, the innkeepers' special blend of coffee and mouth-watering omelets, pancakes or French toast. Cozy rooms include comfortable furnishings and cheery wall coverings. The innkeepers can arrange for guests to enjoy dinner at the home of one of their Amish friends.
Innkeeper(s): Jack & Sue Flatley. $70-80. MC VISA DS PC TC. 4 rooms, 2 with PB. 1 suite. Breakfast included in rates. Types of meals: full breakfast, gourmet breakfast and early coffee/tea. Beds: KQDT. Air conditioning and ceiling fan in room. Cable TV, VCR, fax, copier and library on premises. Amusement parks, antiques, fishing, parks, shopping, sporting events and theater nearby.
Location: Downtown, 15 minutes from heart of Amish Country.
Seen in: Gourmet.

"You made our visit here very pleasant, your hospitality is what makes the stay here so wonderful."
Certificate may be used: January through June, November-December.

Witmer's Tavern - Historic 1725 Inn
2014 Old Philadelphia Pike,
Lancaster, PA 17602-3413
(717)299-5305

Circa 1725. This pre-Revolutionary War inn is the sole survivor of 62 inns that once lined the old Lancaster-to-Philadelphia turnpike. Immigrant Conestoga wagon trains were made up here for the Western and Southern journeys to wilderness homesteads. Designated as a National Landmark, the property is restored to its original rustic, pioneer style. There are sagging wide-board floors and antiques with original finish. History buffs will enjoy seeing the Indian escape tunnel entrance and knowing Lafayette, Benjamin Franklin and

presidents Washington, Jefferson and Adams stayed here. Guest rooms feature antiques, old quilts, fresh flowers and original working fireplaces.

Innkeeper(s): Brant Hartung. $60-90. PC. 7 rooms, 2 with PB, 7 with FP. 3 cottages. 1 conference room. Breakfast included in rates. Type of meal: continental-plus breakfast. Beds: D. Air conditioning in room. Amusement parks, antiques, fishing, parks, shopping, downhill skiing, cross-country skiing, sporting events, theater and watersports nearby.

Location: One mile east of Lancaster on Route 340.

Seen in: Stuart News, Pennsylvania, Antique, Travel & Leisure, Mid-Atlantic, Country Living, Early American Life, Colonial Homes, USA Today.

"Your personal attention and enthusiastic knowledge of the area and Witmer's history made it come alive and gave us the good feelings we came looking for."

Certificate may be used: December-April, Sunday through Thursday only, excluding all holidays.

Landenberg   L15

Cornerstone B&B Inn
300 Buttonwood Rd,
Landenberg, PA 19350-9398
(610)274-2143 Fax:(610)274-0734

Circa 1704. The Cornerstone is a fine 18th-century country manor house filled with antique furnishings. Two fireplaces make the parlor inviting. Wing chairs, fresh flowers and working fireplaces add enjoyment to the guest rooms. A water garden and swimming pool with hot tub are additional amenities. Stay in one of five guest cottages with kitchen, fireplace and living room.

Innkeeper(s): Linda Chamberlin & Marty Mulligan. $75-150. MC VISA DS PC TC. 7 rooms with PB, 5 with FP. 1 suite. 6 cottages. Breakfast included in rates. Types of meals: continental-plus breakfast, full breakfast and early coffee/tea. Beds: KQT. Air conditioning and cable TV in room. VCR, fax, spa and swimming on premises. Amusement parks, antiques, parks, shopping, sporting events and theater nearby.

Certificate may be used: Sunday-Thursday, Jan. 2-Dec. 15.

Lewisburg   G12

Brookpark Farm B&B
100 Reitz Rd, Lewisburg, PA 17837-9653
(717)523-0220

Circa 1914. Twenty-five acres surround this three-story brick house. The innkeepers operate the Pennsylvania House Gallery in their enormous barn on the property. The inn, therefore, includes traditional, transitional and country designs from these furniture collections including cherry, pine and mahogany woods.

Innkeeper(s): Crystale & Todd Moyer. $63-68. MC VISA. 7 rooms. 3 suites. 2 conference rooms. Breakfast and afternoon tea included in rates. Types of meals: full breakfast, gourmet breakfast and early coffee/tea. Lunch and banquet service available. Beds: Q. Air conditioning in room. Cable TV on premises. Amusement parks, antiques, fishing, parks, shopping, sporting events and theater nearby.

Certificate may be used: No restrictions, year-round.

Lititz   J14

Alden House
62 E Main St, Lititz, PA 17543-1947
(717)627-3363 (800)584-0753

Circa 1850. For more than 200 years, breezes have carried the sound of church bells to the stately brick homes lining Main Street. The Alden House is a brick Victorian in the center of this historic district and within walking distance of the Pretzel House (first in the country) and the chocolate factory. A favorite room is the suite with a loft dressing room and private bath. A full breakfast is served, often carried to one of the inn's three porches.

Innkeeper(s): Fletcher & Joy Coleman. $75-125. MC VISA PC. 6 rooms with PB, 2 with FP. 3 suites. Breakfast included in rates. Types of meals: full breakfast and early coffee/tea. Beds: QD. Air conditioning, ceiling fan and cable TV in room. Amusement parks, antiques, fishing, parks, shopping and theater nearby.

Location: Seven miles North of Lancaster.

Seen in: Early American Life, Travel, Lititz Record Express, Penn Dutch Traveler, Now in Lancaster County, Philadelphia Inquirer.

"Truly represents what bed & breakfast hospitality is all about. You are special innkeepers. Thanks for caring so much about your guests. It's like being home."

Certificate may be used: May-November, Sunday-Thursday; December-April, seven days.

Manheim J14

Herr Farmhouse Inn

2256 Huber Dr, Manheim, PA 17545-9130
(717)653-9852 (800)584-0743

Circa 1750. This pre-Revolutionary War stone farmhouse is one of the oldest buildings in Lancaster County. The woodwork, including the moldings, cabinets and doors is original. Early American antiques and reproductions set the scene for a truly

Colonial vacation. Two rooms include fireplaces. The kitchen, where a hearty continental breakfast is served, boasts a walk-in fireplace. Antique shopping, historic attractions and Amish dining are nearby.

Innkeeper(s): Barry Herr. $75-95. MC VISA PC TC. 4 rooms, 2 with PB, 2 with FP. 1 suite. Breakfast included in rates. Types of meals: full breakfast and early coffee/tea. Beds: KQDT. Air conditioning, turn-down service and ceiling fan in room. Copier and library on premises. Amusement parks, antiques, fishing, parks, shopping and sporting events nearby.

Location: Nine miles west of Lancaster off Route 283 (Mt. Joy 230 exit).

Seen in: Country Inns.

"Your home is lovely. You've done a beautiful job of restoring and remodeling."

Certificate may be used: Monday through Thursday, holidays and special events excluded.

Marietta K13

The Noble House

113 W Market St,
Marietta, PA 17547-1411
(717)426-4389

Circa 1810. A 12-foot-high ceiling and charming stenciled front hallway greet guests at this restored Federal-style brick home. A collection of beautiful antiques and knickknacks fills each of the rooms. Carved fireplaces, flower arrangements and candles add to the charm. One of the guest rooms features a unique collection of dolls, another offers a four-poster brass bed. Guest rooms are individually decorated, one includes the theme of a 1950s railroad sleeper car. Breakfasts are served in the candlelit dining room with a combination of fruits, fresh breads, egg dishes, French toast and potatoes. The living room with its fireplace and piano is a wonderful location to relax with a good book.

Innkeeper(s): Elissa Noble. $75-95. 3 rooms with PB. 2 suites. Breakfast included in rates. Type of meal: full breakfast. Picnic lunch, catering service and room service available. Beds: KQDT.

Seen in: Early American Life, Pennsylvania Dutch Hollydays, Elizabethtown Mount Joy Merchandiser.

"Thank you for your hospitality. We felt like royalty, and enjoyed the detail in your beautiful home."

Certificate may be used: November-March, Sunday-Thursday.

Railroad House Restaurant B&B

280 W Front St, Marietta, PA 17547-1405
(717)426-4141

Circa 1820. The Railroad House, a sprawling old hotel, conjures up memories of the days when riding the rail was the way to travel. The house was built as a refuge for weary men who were working along the Susquehanna River. When the railroad finally made its way through Marietta, the rail station's waiting room and ticket office were located in what's now known as the Railroad House. The restored rooms feature antiques, Oriental rugs, Victorian decor and rustic touches such as exposed brick walls. The chefs at the inn's restaurant create a menu of American and continental dishes using spices and produce from the beautifully restored gardens. The innovative recipes have been featured in Bon Appetit. The innkeepers also host a variety of special events and weekends, including murder mysteries and clambakes serenaded by jazz bands. Carriage rides and special walking tours of Marietta can be arranged.

Innkeeper(s): Richard & Donna Chambers. $79-99. MC VISA PC TC. 10 rooms, 8 with PB, 6 with FP. 1 cottage. 1 conference room. Breakfast included in rates. Types of meals: full breakfast, gourmet breakfast and early coffee/tea. Afternoon tea, dinner, evening snack, picnic lunch, lunch, gourmet lunch, banquet service, catering service and catered breakfast available. Beds: QDT. Air conditioning in room. Copier and bicycles on premises. Amusement parks, antiques, fishing, parks, shopping, downhill skiing, sporting events, theater and watersports nearby.

Certificate may be used: Anytime.

River Inn
258 W Front St, Marietta, PA 17547-1405
(717)426-2290 Fax:(717)426-2966

Circa 1790. This Colonial has more than 200 years of history within its walls. The home is listed in the National Register and located in Marietta's historic district. Herb and flower gardens decorate the grounds. Relaxing in front of a fireplace is an easy task since the inn offers six, one of which resides in a guest room. Colonial decor and antiques permeate the interior. The inn is within walking distance to the Susquhana River.

Innkeeper(s): Joyce & Bob Heiserman. $60-75. MC VISA DC CB DS PC TC. 3 rooms with PB, 1 with FP. Breakfast included in rates. Types of meals: full breakfast and early coffee/tea. Picnic lunch available. Beds: QT. Air conditioning in room. Cable TV, bicycles and library on premises. Amusement parks, antiques, fishing, parks, shopping, sporting events, theater and watersports nearby.

Certificate may be used: Year-round, Sunday-Friday.

Vogt Farm B&B
1225 Colebrook Rd,
Marietta, PA 17547-9101
(717)653-4810 (800)854-0399

Circa 1868. Twenty-eight acres surround this farmhouse. There are three porches from which to enjoy the pastoral scene of cattle and sheep. Keith offers a

walking tour of the farm, including the grain elevator. The innkeepers have hosted guests for 20 years and have created a comfortable setting for overnight stays. Desks, private phones and a copier are available to business travelers.

Innkeeper(s): Keith & Kathy Vogt. $60-100. MC VISA AX DC DS PC TC. 3 rooms. 1 suite. Breakfast and evening snack included in rates. Types

of meals: full breakfast and early coffee/tea. Beds: KQT. Air conditioning in room. Cable TV, VCR, copier and library on premises. Amusement parks, antiques, fishing, parks, shopping, sporting events and theater nearby.

"Thank you for your hospitality. Your warmth and friendliness made our stay pleasant. You have a lovely place. "

Certificate may be used: Dec. 31-March 31 & Sunday-Thursday April 1-June 30 Sunday-Thursday September & November

McConnellsburg   K9

Market Street Inn
131 W Market St,
McConnellsburg, PA 17233-1007
(717)485-5495

Circa 1903. This turn-of-the-century home exemplifies American Four-Square design. The home was built by a retired Union officer of the Civil War. The three guest rooms include four-poster, canopy beds and lace curtains. Locally smoked hickory sausage, homemade apple butter, lemon poppy seed muffins, herbed potatoes and a ham and egg roll topped with cheddar dill sauce are among the breakfast specialties. Cowans Gap State Park and Buchanan State Forest are nearby, as is Whitetail Ski Resort.

Innkeeper(s): Tim & Margie Taylor. $60. MC VISA AX PC TC. 3 rooms with PB. Breakfast included in rates. Type of meal: gourmet breakfast. Beds: QD. Air conditioning and cable TV in room. Fax, copier and library on premises. Antiques, fishing, parks, downhill skiing, cross-country skiing and watersports nearby.

Certificate may be used: March through August, Sunday through Thursday

Meadville   D2

Fountainside B&B
628 Highland Ave,
Meadville, PA 16335-1938
(814)337-7447

Circa 1855. A long front porch extends across the front of this farmhouse-style B&B. A full breakfast is served on the weekends, a continental breakfast during the week. Both Victorian and modern pieces are combined to furnish the rooms. Allegheny College is next door.

Innkeeper(s): Maureen Boyle. $50-65. MC VISA AX DS. 5 rooms. 1 conference room. Breakfast included in rates. Types of meals: continental breakfast, full breakfast and early coffee/tea. Evening snack and room service available. Turn-down service and ceiling fan in room. Cable TV on premises. Amusement parks, antiques, shopping, cross-country skiing, sporting events and theater nearby.

Certificate may be used: Anytime room is available.

Mercer
F2

The Magoffin Inn

129 S Pitt St, Mercer, PA 16137-1211
(412)662-4611 (800)841-0824

Circa 1884. Dr. Magoffin built this house for his
Pittsburgh bride, Henrietta Bouvard. The Queen
Anne style is characterized by patterned brick
masonry, gable detailing, bay windows and a wraparound porch. The technique of marbleizing was
used on six of the nine fireplaces. Magoffin Muffins
are featured each morning. Lunch is available
Monday through Saturday, and dinner, Tuesday
through Saturday.

Innkeeper(s): Jacque McClelland. $60-115. MC VISA AX PC TC. 12
rooms, 10 with PB, 8 with FP. 4 suites. 3 cottages. 3 conference
rooms. Breakfast and evening snack included in rates. Types of meals:
full breakfast and early coffee/tea. Dinner available. Beds: QD. Air conditioning and cable TV in room. Antiques, parks and shopping nearby.
Location: Near I-79 and I-80.
Seen in: Western Reserve, Youngstown Vindicator.

*"While in Arizona we met a family from Africa who
had stopped at the Magoffin House. After crossing the
United States they said the Magoffin House was quite
the nicest place they had stayed."*

Certificate may be used: Sunday through Thursday nights.

Mercersburg
L9

The Mercersburg Inn

405 S Main St,
Mercersburg, PA 17236-9517
(717)328-5231 Fax:(717)328-3403

Circa 1909. Situated on a hill overlooking the Blue
Ridge Mountains, the valley and village, this
20,000-square-foot Georgian Revival mansion was
built for industrialist Harry Byron. Six massive
columns mark the entrance, which opens to a
majestic hall featuring chestnut wainscoting and an
elegant double stairway and rare scagliola (mar-
bleized) columns. All the rooms are furnished with
antiques and reproductions. A local craftsman built
the inn's four-poster, canopied king-size beds. Many
of the rooms have their own balconies and a few
have fireplaces. During the weekends, the inn's chef
prepares noteworthy, elegant six-course dinners,
which feature an array of seasonal specialties.

Innkeeper(s): John Mohr. $110-180. MC VISA DS. 15 rooms with PB, 6
with FP. 1 conference room. Breakfast included in rates. Types of
meals: full breakfast and gourmet breakfast. Picnic lunch and banquet
service available. Beds: KQT. Air conditioning in room. Cable TV and
VCR on premises. Antiques, fishing, shopping, downhill skiing, cross-
country skiing, theater and watersports nearby.

Seen in: Mid-Atlantic Country, Washington Post, The Herald-Mail,
Richmond News Leader, Washingtonian, Philadelphia Inquirer,
Pittsburgh.

*"Elegance personified! Outstanding ambiance and warm
hospitality."*

Certificate may be used: Sunday-Thursday, non-holidays. Not in combination with any other package or promotion.

Mertztown
I16

Longswamp B&B

1605 State St, Mertztown, PA 19539-8912
(610)682-6197 Fax:(610)682-4854

Circa 1789. Country gentleman Colonel Trexler
added a mansard roof to this stately Federal mansion
in 1860. Inside is a magnificent walnut staircase and
pegged wood floors. As the story goes, the colonel
discovered his unmarried daughter having an affair
and shot her lover. He escaped hanging, but it was
said that after his death his ghost could be seen in
the upstairs bedroom watching the road. In 1905, an
exorcism was reported to have sent his spirit to a
nearby mountaintop.

Innkeeper(s): Elsa Dimick. $70-75. MC VISA AX. 10 rooms, 6 with PB,
2 with FP. 2 suites. Breakfast and afternoon tea included in rates. Types
of meals: full breakfast, gourmet breakfast and early coffee/tea. Picnic
lunch and catering service available. Beds: QT. Air conditioning and
ceiling fan in room. Cable TV, VCR and bicycles on premises. Antiques,
fishing, shopping, cross-country skiing and sporting events nearby.
Seen in: Washingtonian, Weekend Travel, The Sun.

*"The warm country atmosphere turns strangers into
friends."*

Certificate may be used: November-April.

Milford
F18

Cliff Park Inn & Golf Course

RR 4 Box 7200, Milford, PA 18337-9708
(717)296-6491 (800)225-6535
Fax:(717)296-3982

Circa 1820. This historic country inn is located on
a 600-acre family estate, bordering the Delaware
River. It has been in the Buchanan family since
1820. Rooms are spacious with individual climate
control, telephone and Victorian-style furnishings.
Cliff Park features both a full-service restaurant and
golf school. The inn's golf course, established in
1913, is one of the oldest in the United States. Cliff
Park's picturesque setting is popular for country
weddings and private business conferences. Both
B&B or MAP plans are offered.

Innkeeper(s): Harry W. Buchanan III. $93-160. MAP, AP, EP. MC VISA
AX DC CB DS. 18 rooms with PB. 1 conference room. Breakfast included in rates. Types of meals: full breakfast and gourmet breakfast.

Dinner, picnic lunch and lunch available. Beds: KQDT. Fax on premises. Handicap access. Cross-country skiing and watersports nearby.

Location: In the foothills of the Pocono Mountains on the Delaware River.

"Cliff Park Inn is the sort of inn I look for in the English countryside. It has that authentic charm that comes from History."

Certificate may be used: Nov. 1-May 20, Sunday-Thursday

Milton   G12

Pau-Lyn's Country B&B
RR 3 Box 676, Milton, PA 17847-9506
(717)742-4110

Circa 1850. This three-story Victorian brick home offers a formal dining room with a fireplace and antique musical instruments. A porch and patio overlook the large lawn. Nearby are working farms and dairies, covered bridges, mountains, hills and valleys.
Innkeeper(s): Evelyn Landis. $45-55. 7 rooms. 2 suites. Breakfast included in rates. Type of meal: full breakfast. Air conditioning in room. Cable TV on premises. Amusement parks, antiques, shopping, downhill skiing, cross-country skiing, sporting events and theater nearby.

Certificate may be used: Year-round, Sunday through Thursday, some weekends. All depend on availability.

Teneriff Farm B&B
Rd 1 Box 314, Milton, PA 17847-9402
(717)742-9061

Acres of farmland create a relaxing, natural environment at this turn-of-the-century Victorian. The home includes the detailed woodwork, French pocket doors and carved staircase one might expect from Victorian Era design, and these wonderful elements are complements to the comfortable, country decor. Although a working farm, this is a place for relaxing. Stroll the grounds or simply sip a cup of tea on the veranda. Breakfasts are created to fit the guests' needs.
Innkeeper(s): Christa Haseloff. $40-45. 3 rooms. Breakfast included in rates. Types of meals: continental breakfast, continental-plus breakfast and full breakfast.

Certificate may be used: Subject to availability.

Tomlinson Manor B&B
250 Broadway St, Milton, PA 17847-1706
(717)742-3657

Circa 1927. In the Georgian style, this appealing three-story stone manor was designed by Dr. Charles Tomlinson, a local physician and amateur architect. Shutters border the small-paned windows, and there are gardens all around. All the rooms, including the library, are furnished with antiques. Next door to the B&B is a dinner theater.

Innkeeper(s): Nancy Slease. $55. MC VISA. 3 rooms. Breakfast included in rates. Type of meal: full breakfast. Air conditioning in room. Cable TV and VCR on premises. Antiques, shopping, sporting events and theater nearby.

Certificate may be used: Anytime except college weekends.

Montoursville   F12

The Carriage House at Stonegate
RR 1 Box 11A, Montoursville, PA 17754
(717)433-4340 Fax:(717)433-4653

Circa 1850. President Herbert Hoover was a descendant of the original settlers of this old homestead in the Loyalsock Creek Valley. Indians burned the original house, but the present farmhouse and numerous outbuildings date from the early 1800s. The Carriage House is set next to a lovely brook.
Innkeeper(s): Harold & Dena Mesaris. $50-70. PC. 2 rooms. Breakfast included in rates. Type of meal: continental-plus breakfast. Beds: QD. Cable TV in room. Fax, library, pet boarding and child care on premises. Amusement parks, antiques, fishing, parks, shopping, downhill skiing, cross-country skiing, sporting events, theater and watersports nearby.

Location: Six miles off I-180, north of Montoursville.

"A very fine B&B — the best that can be found. Gracious hosts."

Certificate may be used: Monday through Thursday nights, all months.

Mount Joy   K13

Cedar Hill Farm
305 Longenecker Rd,
Mount Joy, PA 17552
(717)653-4655

Circa 1817. Situated on 51 acres overlooking Chiques Creek, this stone farmhouse boasts a two-tiered front veranda affording pastoral views of the surrounding fields. The host was born in the house and is the third generation to have lived here since the Swarr family first purchased it in 1878. Family heirlooms and antiques include an elaborately carved walnut bedstead, a marble-topped wash-

stand and a "tumbling block" quilt. One guest room has a whirlpool tub. In the kitchen, a copper kettle, bread paddle and baskets of dried herbs accentuate the walk-in fireplace, where guests often linger over breakfast. Cedar Hill is a working poultry and grain farm.

Innkeeper(s): Russel & Gladys Swarr. $65-75. MC VISA AX DS TC. 5 rooms with PB. Breakfast included in rates. Types of meals: continental-plus breakfast and early coffee/tea. Beds: KQDT. Air conditioning in room. VCR and computer on premises. Amusement parks, antiques, fishing, parks, shopping, cross-country skiing, sporting events, theater and watersports nearby.

Location: Midway between Lancaster and Hershey.

Seen in: Women's World, Lancaster Farming, Philadelphia, New York Times, Ladies Home Journal.

"Dorothy can have Kansas, Scarlett can take Tara, Rick can keep Paris — I've stayed at Cedar Hill Farm."

Certificate may be used: Nov. 1 to April 1, Sunday through Thursday, holidays excluded.

Hillside Farm B&B

607 Eby Chiques Rd,
Mount Joy, PA 17552-8819
(717)653-6697 Fax:(717)653-5233

Circa 1863. This comfortable farm has a relaxing homey feel to it. Rooms are simply decorated and special extras such as handmade quilts and antiques add an elegant country touch. The home is a true monument to the cow. Dairy antiques, cow knick-knacks and antique milk bottles abound. Some of

the bottles were found during the renovation of the home and its grounds. Spend the day hunting for bargains in nearby antique shops, malls and factory outlets, or tour local Amish and Pennsylvania Dutch attractions. The farm is a good vacation spot for families with children above the age of 10.

Innkeeper(s): Gary & Deborah Lintner. $55-70. PC TC. 5 rooms, 3 with PB. Breakfast, afternoon tea and evening snack included in rates. Types of meals: full breakfast and early coffee/tea. Beds: KQDT. Air conditioning and ceiling fan in room. VCR, fax, spa and library on premises. Amusement parks, antiques, fishing, parks, shopping, downhill skiing, cross-country skiing, theater and watersports nearby.

Location: In the heart of Dutch/Amish country.

"Warm, friendly, comfortable ... feels like home."

Certificate may be used: Anytime except Fridays and Saturdays in September and October

The Olde Square Inn

127 E Main St, Mount Joy, PA 17552
(717)653-4525 (800)742-3533
Fax:(717)653-0976

Circa 1917. Located on the town square, this Neoclassical house features a handsome columned fireplace and leaded-glass windows. Items such as baked oatmeal, cherry cobbler, sausage, pancakes and freshly baked muffins or breads get the day off to the right start. The inn is within walking distance of restaurants, shops and parks. Amish farms and marketplaces are nearby.

Innkeeper(s): Fran & Dave Hand. $65-105. MC VISA PC TC. 4 rooms with PB. Breakfast included in rates. Types of meals: full breakfast and early coffee/tea. Beds: KQDT. Air conditioning, cable TV and VCR in room. Fax on premises. Amusement parks, antiques, fishing, parks, shopping, sporting events and theater nearby.

Certificate may be used: Anytime, except weekends in September and October. Last minute if available.

Muncy   F12

The Bodine House B&B

307 S Main St, Muncy, PA 17756-1507
(717)546-8949 Fax:(717)546-8949

Circa 1805. This Federal-style townhouse, framed by a white picket fence, is in the National Register. Antique and reproduction furnishings highlight the inn's four fireplaces, the parlor, study and library. A favorite guest room features a walnut canopy bed, hand-stenciled and bordered walls, and a framed sampler by the innkeeper's great-great-great-grandmother. Candlelight breakfasts are served beside the fireplace in a gracious Colonial dining room. Also available is a guest cottage with kitchenette.

Innkeeper(s): David & Marie Louise Smith. $50-125. MC VISA AX DS PC TC. 5 rooms with PB, 1 with FP. 1 cottage. Breakfast included in rates. Types of meals: full breakfast and early coffee/tea. Afternoon tea available. Beds: QDT. Air conditioning, turn-down service and cable TV in room. VCR, fax, bicycles and library on premises. Antiques, fishing, parks, shopping, cross-country skiing and sporting events nearby.

Seen in: Colonial Homes, Philadelphia Inquirer.

"What an experience, made special by your wonderful hospitality."

Certificate may be used: Sunday through Thursday, year-round, subject to availability.

New Bloomfield I11

Tressler House B&B
PO Box 38, 41 W Main St, New
Bloomfield, PA 17068-0038
(717)582-2914

Circa 1830. A white picket fence frames the acre
of lawn surrounding this Federal-period home. A
spider web window transom marks the front
entrance. Oriental rugs, coordinated fabrics and
wallcoverings fill the 22 rooms. Old mill stones, collected by the former owner, are woven into the
brick patio and sidewalk. There is a covered porch
filled with antique wicker, and a walled duck pond.
Smoked turkey sausages and blueberry pancakes
often are featured at breakfast.

Innkeeper(s): David & Carol Ulsh. $55-65. 4 rooms, 2 with PB. Types
of meals: full breakfast and early coffee/tea. Beds: DT. Air conditioning
and cable TV in room.

Seen in: Perry County Times, Perry County Shopper, Antiques &
Auction News.

Certificate may be used: Sunday-Thursday, upon availability, all year.

New Hope I18

Hollileif B&B
677 Durham Rd (Rt 413),
New Hope, PA 18940
(215)598-3100

Circa 1700. This handsome former farmhouse sits
on more than five rolling acres of scenic Bucks
County countryside. The name "hollileif," which
means "beloved tree," refers to the 40-foot holly
trees that grace the entrance. Bedrooms are appointed with lace and fresh flowers. Afternoon refreshments in the parlor or patio are provided, as well as
evening turndown service.

Innkeeper(s): Ellen & Richard Butkus. $85-155. MC VISA AX DS PC TC.
5 rooms with PB, 2 with FP. Breakfast and afternoon tea included in
rates. Types of meals: gourmet breakfast and early coffee/tea. Beds:
QD. Air conditioning, turn-down service and ceiling fan in room. VCR,

fax, copier and library on premises. Antiques, fishing, parks, shopping,
downhill skiing, cross-country skiing, theater and watersports nearby.

Location: Midway between Newtown and Buckingham.

Seen in: Trentonian, Bucks County Courier Times.

*"The accommodations were lovely and the breakfasts
delicious and unusual, but it is really the graciousness of
our hosts that made the weekend memorable."*

Certificate may be used: Sunday through Thursday except (1) during
month of October, (2) holidays and holiday periods, (3) Dec. 26-31.

The Wedgwood Collection of Historic Inns
111 W Bridge St, New Hope, PA 18938
(215)862-2570 Fax:(215)862-2570

Circa 1870. A Victorian and a Classic Revival
house sit side by side and comprise the Wedgwood
Inn. Twenty-six-inch walls are in the stone house.
Lofty windows, hardwood floors and antique furnishings add to the warmth and style. Pennsylvania
Dutch surreys arrive and depart from the inn for
nostalgic carriage rides.

Innkeeper(s): Carl Glassman & Nadine Silnutzer. $95-195. MC VISA. 18
rooms with PB, 6 with FP. 6 suites. 1 conference room. Breakfast and
afternoon tea included in rates. Types of meals: continental-plus breakfast and full breakfast. Catering service and room service available.
Beds: KQT. Bicycles on premises. Handicap access. Antiques, fishing,
cross-country skiing and theater nearby.

Location: In the historic district, one block from the heart of New Hope.

Seen in: National Geographic Traveler, Women's Day, Inc., Innsider,
New York Times, Philadelphia Inquirer.

*"The Wedgwood has all the comforts of a highly profes-
sional accommodation yet with all the warmth a personal friend would extend."*

Certificate may be used: Monday-Thursday, December-April, Holidays
excluded.

The Whitehall Inn
1370 Pineville Rd, New Hope, PA 18938
(215)598-7945

Circa 1794. This white-plastered stone farmhouse
is located on 13 country acres studded with stately
maple and chestnut trees. Inside, a winding walnut
staircase leads to antique-furnished guest rooms that
offer wide pine floors, wavy-glass windows, high
ceilings and some fireplaces. An antique clock collection, Oriental rugs and late Victorian furnishings
are found throughout. Afternoon tea, evening
chocolates and candlelight breakfasts served with
heirloom china and sterling reflect the inn's many
amenities. There are stables on the property and
horseback riding may be arranged.

Innkeeper(s): Mike Wass. $130-190. MC VISA AX DC CB DS. 6 rooms.
Breakfast included in rates. Types of meals: full breakfast and early cof-
fee/tea. Air conditioning and turn-down service in room. Amusement
parks, antiques, shopping, cross-country skiing and theater nearby.

Certificate may be used: January through September, Monday through
Thursday.

New Kingstown · J11

Kanaga House B&B
Us Rt 11/Carlisle Pike,
New Kingstown, PA 17072-0092
(717)697-2714

Circa 1775. This gracious three-story German stonehouse is built of limestone. The innkeepers have gathered historic information that links the builder of the home, Joseph Junkin, with the Revolutionary War, the Puritans and the first Covenater's Communion. A Joseph Junkin letter to his son, commander of the Battle of Brandywine, is in the parlor. The Elizabeth Junkin Room features a hope chest dated 1796, while the Eleanor Junkin Room offers a canopy bed with rose and blue bed hangings. Outside, an enormous gazebo creates a focal point for garden weddings.
Innkeeper(s): Mary Jane Kretzing. $60-85. MC VISA. 5 rooms with PB, 1 with FP. 1 conference room. Breakfast included in rates. Types of meals: full breakfast and early coffee/tea. Afternoon tea and picnic lunch available. Beds: Q. Air conditioning in room. Cable TV, VCR and copier on premises. Amusement parks, antiques, shopping, downhill skiing and theater nearby.
Location: Dutch Country.

Certificate may be used: Sunday through Thursday, all year.

North Wales · J17

Joseph Ambler Inn
1005 Horsham Rd, North Wales, PA
19454-1413
(215)362-7500 Fax:(215)362-7500

Circa 1734. This beautiful fieldstone-and-wood house was built over a period of three centuries. Originally, it was part of a grant that Joseph Ambler, a Quaker wheelwright, obtained from William Penn in 1688. A large stone bank barn and tenant cottage on 12 acres constitute the remainder of the property. Guests enjoy the cherry wainscoting and walk-in fireplace in the schoolroom.
Innkeeper(s): Wendy Hammel. $95-140. MC VISA AX DC CB DS. 28 rooms with PB. 1 suite. 1 conference room. Breakfast included in rates. Type of meal: full breakfast. Dinner and banquet service available. Beds: QD. Air conditioning and cable TV in room. Handicap access. Antiques, shopping, downhill skiing, cross-country skiing, sporting events and theater nearby.
Seen in: Colonial Homes, Country Living.

"What a wonderful night my husband and I spent. We are already planning to come back to your wonderful getaway."
Certificate may be used: Anytime.

Northumberland · H12

Campbell's B&B
707 Duke St, Northumberland, PA 17857
(717)473-3276

Circa 1859. This old farmhouse has three stories and there are porches overlooking the well-planted grounds and rose gardens. A few antiques and reproductions add to the country decor. Lake Augusta is a mile away for fishing and boating.
Innkeeper(s): Bob & Millie Campbell. $55-65. 3 rooms, 2 with PB. 1 suite. 1 conference room. Breakfast, afternoon tea and evening snack included in rates. Types of meals: full breakfast and early coffee/tea. Beds: QT. Air conditioning, turn-down service, ceiling fan and cable TV in room. VCR and swimming on premises. Amusement parks, antiques, fishing, parks, cross-country skiing, theater and watersports nearby.
Certificate may be used: Anytime except local college weekends. Monday through Thursday.

Paradise · K14

Creekside Inn
44 Leacock Rd, Paradise, PA 17562-0435
(717)687-0333 Fax:(717)687-8200

Circa 1781. This 18th-century Georgian home was built by David Witmer, a prominent citizen and member of one of the first families to settle in the area. The stone exterior features a gable roof with five bay windows. Relaxing guest quarters feature special amenities such as four-poster or Windsor

beds. The Cameo and Creekside rooms boast fireplaces. A hearty, full breakfast is served each morning, and Amish dinners sometimes can be prepared. Antique and outlet shopping, as well as a variety of sporting activities are nearby.
Innkeeper(s): Catherine & Dennis Zimmermann. $70-120. MC VISA. 6 rooms, 4 with PB. Breakfast included in rates. Type of meal: gourmet breakfast. Afternoon tea available. Beds: QDT. Antiques, fishing and theater nearby.

Certificate may be used: November through March; Sunday through Thursday, excluding holidays.

Pine Grove Mills

The Chatelaine at Split-Pine Farmhouse
347 W Pine Grove Rd,
Pine Grove Mills, PA 16868
(814)238-2028 (800)251-2028

Circa 1830. Filled with generations of antiques layered into an English Country look, this Federal farmhouse is located a few minutes away from State College. Belleek china is used during both tea time and the candlelight breakfast, which is served in the elegantly appointed dining room. The breakfast menu features dishes such as Mushroom Charlottes with Currant Sauce, Santa Fe Strata and Champagne Granita.
Innkeeper(s): Mae McQuade. $70-125. MC VISA AX DS PC TC. 4 rooms, 2 with PB. Breakfast and afternoon tea included in rates. Types of meals: full breakfast and early coffee/tea. Picnic lunch available. Beds: KQT. Air conditioning and turn-down service in room. Amusement parks, antiques, fishing, shopping, downhill skiing, cross-country skiing, sporting events, theater and watersports nearby.

Certificate may be used: Monday-Thursday, all year, excluding holidays and Arts Fest.

Palmyra   J13

The Hen-Apple B&B
409 S Lingle Ave, Palmyra, PA 17078
(717)838-8282

Circa 1825. Located at the edge of town, this Georgian farmhouse is surrounded by an acre of lawns and gardens. There are antiques and country pieces, along with a collection of wicker in the Wicker Room. Breakfast is provided in the dining room or the screened porch. Hershey is two miles away.
Innkeeper(s): Flo & Harold Echert. $55-75. MC VISA AX PC TC. 6 rooms with PB. Breakfast included in rates. Type of meal: full breakfast. Beds: QDT. Air conditioning and ceiling fan in room. Cable TV on premises. Amusement parks, antiques, fishing, parks, shopping, sporting events, theater and watersports nearby.

Certificate may be used: Jan. 9-April 30, Friday, Saturday, Sunday; Sunday-Thursday, year-round excluding holidays and first week in October.

Patton   I7

Nationality House
209 Magee Ave, Patton, PA 16668-1013
(814)674-2225

One room is like stepping into the captain's quarters of a tall ship. Another room evokes images of pyramids, pharaohs and ancient Egypt. Innkeeper and

376

world traveler Loretta Albright has appointed each room of her inn to reflect a different culture or style, down to the smallest detail. The French parlor is decorated with Monet prints, and even the linens in each bedchamber reflect the room's theme. Loretta likes to keep life interesting, varying not only the breakfast menu each day, but also the style of china it's served on. Whatever the meal, guests won't leave hungry, as Loretta prepares a feast.
Innkeeper(s): Loretta Albright. $50-90. 7 rooms. Breakfast included in rates. Type of meal: full breakfast.

Certificate may be used: May 1 to Oct. 31, all days of the week.

Philadelphia   K17

Shippen Way Inn
416-18 Bainbridge St,
Philadelphia, PA 19147
(215)627-7266 (800)245-4873

Circa 1750. In the National Register of Historic Places, Shippen Way is located close to Independence Hall. Working fireplaces, timbered walls and ceiling beams create an authentic Colonial decor. This era is reinforced with a cobbler's bench, pencil-post beds, a stenciled kitchen floor and a flax wheel. Old-fashioned roses and herbs are set in a walled garden where breakfast is often served.
Innkeeper(s): Ann Foringer & Raymond Rhule. $75-105. EP. MC VISA AX TC. 9 rooms with PB, 1 with FP. Breakfast and evening snack included in rates. Type of meal: continental-plus breakfast. Beds: QDT. Air conditioning and cable TV in room. Handicap access. Antiques, parks, shopping, sporting events and theater nearby.
Seen in: Life Today, Mid-Atlantic Country.

Certificate may be used: January, February, March, Sunday-Thursday.

Point Pleasant   I17

Tattersall Inn
16 Cafferty Rd, Point Pleasant, PA 18950
(215)297-8233 (800)297-4988

Circa 1740. This plastered fieldstone house with its broad porches and wainscoted entry hall was the home of local mill owners for 150 years. The walls are 18 inches thick. Breakfast is usually served in the dining room where a vintage phonograph collection is on display. Breakfast can also be brought to your room. The Colonial-style common room features a beamed ceiling and walk-in fireplace. Guests gather here for apple cider, cheese and crackers and tea or coffee in the late afternoon.
Innkeeper(s): Herbert & Geraldine Moss. $70-115. MC VISA AX DS PC. 6 rooms with PB. 2 suites. 1 conference room. Breakfast, afternoon tea and evening snack included in rates. Types of meals: continental-plus

breakfast and early coffee/tea. Room service available. Beds: QT. Air conditioning in room. Fax, copier and library on premises. Antiques, fishing, parks, shopping, cross-country skiing, theater and watersports nearby.

Location: Bucks County, New Hope area.

Seen in: Courier Times, Philadelphia, New York Times, WYOU.

"Thank you for your hospitality and warm welcome. The inn is charming and has a wonderful ambiance."

Certificate may be used: All year, Sunday-Thursday, holidays excluded.

Ronks
K14

Candlelight Inn B&B
2574 Lincoln Hwy E, Ronks, PA 17572
(717)299-6005 (800)772-2635
Fax:(717)299-6397

Circa 1920. Located in the Pennsylvania Dutch area, this Federal-style house offers a side porch for enjoying the home's acre and a half of tall trees and surrounding Amish farmland. Guest rooms are individually decorated with Victorian style. Guests are pampered with a candlelight breakfast featuring items such as creme caramel French toast. Lancaster is five miles to the west.

Innkeeper(s): Tim & Heidi Soberick. $65-105. MC VISA DS PC TC. 6 rooms, 4 with PB. 1 suite. Breakfast and afternoon tea included in rates. Types of meals: full breakfast and gourmet breakfast. Beds: KQT. Air conditioning in room. Cable TV and fax on premises. Amusement parks, antiques, fishing, parks, shopping, downhill skiing, cross-country skiing, sporting events, theater and watersports nearby.

Certificate may be used: December through June, Sunday to Thursday.

Shippensburg
K10

Field & Pine B&B
2155 Ritner Hwy,
Shippensburg, PA 17257-9756
(717)776-7179

Circa 1790. Local limestone was used to build this stone house, located on the main wagon road to Baltimore and Washington. Originally, it was a tav-

ern and weigh station, and the scales are still attached to the stagecoach barn on the property. The house is surrounded by stately pines, and sheep graze on the inn's 80 acres. The bedrooms are hand-stenciled and furnished with quilts and antiques.

Innkeeper(s): Mary Ellen & Allan Williams. $65-75. MC VISA PC TC. 3 rooms, 1 with PB, 1 with FP. 1 suite. Breakfast and evening snack included in rates. Types of meals: gourmet breakfast and early coffee/tea. Banquet service available. Beds: QDT. Air conditioning and turn-down service in room. VCR on premises. Antiques, fishing, parks and shopping nearby.

Location: Twelve miles south of Carlisle, on U.S. Route 11.

Seen in: Valley Times-Star.

"Our visit in this lovely country home has been most delightful. The ambiance of antiques and tasteful decorating exemplifies real country living."

Certificate may be used: Sunday through Thursday, year-round.

Spring Creek
D4

Spring Valley B&B
RR 1 Box 117, Spring Creek, PA 16436
(814)489-3000 (800)382-1324
Fax:(814)489-7333

Circa 1820. Although located on Pennsylvania's Allegheny Plateau, this 105-acre spread feels more like a Western-style ranch. Deer and other wildlife roam the grounds, and there are hiking and cross-country ski trails on the premises. The land is adjacent to more than 8,000 acres of state game lands. There are two suites available in the main house as well as a log and cedar cottage. The cottage sleeps six and includes a fireplace and deck overlooking the woods. Four guests can stay comfortably in the Parlor Suite, which includes a corn-burning stove and clawfoot tub. For an additional fee, guests can enjoy guided, horseback trail rides.

Innkeeper(s): Jim Bird & Debora Regis. $68-130. MC VISA DS PC TC. 3 rooms. Breakfast and evening snack included in rates. Types of meals: continental breakfast, continental-plus breakfast, full breakfast, gourmet breakfast and early coffee/tea. Picnic lunch, lunch, gourmet lunch, catering service, catered breakfast and room service available. Beds: QD. Ceiling fan and cable TV in room. VCR, fax, copier, stables, bicycles, library and child care on premises. Handicap access. Antiques, fishing, parks, shopping, downhill skiing, cross-country skiing, theater and watersports nearby.

Certificate may be used: Weekdays only, except holiday weekends, upon availability and excluding first 2 weeks in October.

Spruce Creek
I8

The Dell's B&B at Cedar Hill Farm
HC-01 Box 26 Rt 45,
Spruce Creek, PA 16683-9707
(814)632-8319

Circa 1810. The original stone section of this house
is joined by a later addition. The area overlooks
Spruce Creek, famous for fly-fishing. Ask for the
room with the brass bed and fireplace. If you have

children you'll want to bring them in the spring
when the newborn calves, pigs, chickens and beagle
dogs arrive. Vegetables, pumpkins, corn and hay are
grown on the farm's 100 acres. Nearby, a working
dairy farm allows visitors during milking hours. A
hearty Pennsylvania Dutch breakfast is served.
Innkeeper(s): Sharon Dell. $35-50. MC VISA AX DC DS. 4 rooms, 1
with FP. Breakfast included in rates. Type of meal: full breakfast. Beds:
DT. Ceiling fan in room. Cable TV and VCR on premises. Amusement
parks, antiques, shopping, downhill skiing and sporting events nearby.

"Lovely surroundings, delightful hosts."
Certificate may be used: December until May.

Valley Forge
K16

The Great Valley House of Valley Forge
110 Swedesford Rd, Rd 3, Valley Forge
(Malvern), PA 19355
(610)644-6759 Fax:(610)644-7019

Circa 1691. This 300-year-old Colonial stone farmhouse sits on four acres just two miles from Valley
Forge Park. Boxwoods line the walkway and ancient
trees surround the house. Each of the three guest
rooms are hand-stenciled and feature canopied or
brass beds topped with handmade quilts. Guests
enjoy a full breakfast before a 14-foot fireplace in
the "summer kitchen," the oldest part of the house.

On the grounds are a swimming pool, walking and
hiking trails, and the home's original smokehouse.
Innkeeper(s): Pattye Benson. $75-90. AP. MC VISA DS PC TC. 3 rooms,
2 with PB. Breakfast included in rates. Types of meals: gourmet breakfast and early coffee/tea. Picnic lunch available. Beds: QDT. Air conditioning, turn-down service and cable TV in room. Fax and swimming on
premises. Antiques, fishing, parks, shopping, cross-country skiing,
sporting events, theater and watersports nearby.
Location: Two miles from Valley Forge National Park.
Seen in: Main Line Philadelphia, Philadelphia Inquirer, Washington Post,
New York Times, Suburban Newspaper, Phoenixville Sun.

*"Our favorite, an excellent breakfast in an enchanting
old stone kitchen."*
Certificate may be used: Year-round-Sunday-Thursday.

Shearer Elegance
154 Main St,
Valley Forge (Linfield), PA 19468-1139
(610)495-7429 (800)861-0308
Fax:(610)495-7814

This stone Queen Anne mansion is the height of
Victorian opulence and style. Peaked roofs, intricate
trim and a stenciled wraparound porch grace the
exterior. Guests enter the home via a marble entry
which boasts a three-story staircase. Stained-glass
windows and carved mantels are other notable features. The Victorian furnishings and decor complement the ornate workmanship, and lacy curtains are
a romantic touch. The bedrooms feature hand-
carved, built-in wardrobes. The grounds are dotted
with gardens. The inn is located in the village of
Linfield, about 15 minutes from Valley Forge.
Innkeeper(s): Shirley Shearer. $65-85. MC VISA DS. 7 rooms. Breakfast
included in rates. Type of meal: full breakfast.
Certificate may be used: Anytime, excluding holidays.

Warfordsburg
L8

Buck Valley Ranch
Rt 2 Box 1170, Warfordsburg, PA 17267
(717)294-3759 (800)294-3759
Fax:(717)294-3759

Circa 1930. Trail riding is a popular activity on the
ranch's 64 acres in the Appalachian Mountains of
South Central Pennsylvania. State game lands and
forests border the ranch. The guest house, decorated
in a ranch/cowboy style, is a private farmhouse that
can accommodate eight people. Meals are prepared
using homegrown vegetables and locally raised
meats. Rates include horseback riding.
Innkeeper(s): Nadine & Leon Fox. $60. MC VISA DS PC TC. 4 rooms.
Breakfast, dinner, evening snack and picnic lunch included in rates.
Types of meals: full breakfast, gourmet breakfast and early coffee/tea.
Lunch and gourmet lunch available. Beds: DT. Air conditioning in room.
Fax, copier, swimming, sauna and stables on premises. Amusement

378

parks, antiques, fishing, parks, shopping, downhill skiing, cross-country skiing and watersports nearby.

Certificate may be used: March 1 through Nov. 30, Sunday-Thursday (no weekends).

Washington Crossing J18

Inn to The Woods
150 Glenwood Dr,
Washington Crossing, PA 18977-1518
(215)493-1974 (800)982-7619
Fax:(215)493-7592

Circa 1978. Located on 10 forested acres, this chalet offers seclusion and trails for hiking. Victorian furnishings and framed art add to the pleasingly appointed guest rooms. There is an indoor garden and fishpond. The chalet has beamed ceilings and parquet floors. On weekdays a continental breakfast is served, while on Saturday a full breakfast is provided. The fare for Sunday is a champagne brunch.

Innkeeper(s): Barry & Rosemary Rein. $85-175. MC VISA AX PC TC. 6 rooms with PB. 1 suite. 1 conference room. Breakfast, afternoon tea and evening snack included in rates. Types of meals: continental breakfast, continental-plus breakfast, full breakfast, gourmet breakfast and early coffee/tea. Dinner, picnic lunch, lunch, gourmet lunch, banquet service, catered breakfast and room service available. Beds: KQD. Air conditioning, ceiling fan and cable TV in room. VCR, fax, copier, bicycles and library on premises. Amusement parks, antiques, fishing, parks, shopping, cross-country skiing, theater and watersports nearby.

Certificate may be used: All seasons, Sunday-Thursday.

Wellsboro D11

Waln Street B&B
54 Waln St, Wellsboro, PA 16901-1936
(717)724-3543

Circa 1886. This three-story Dutch Colonial Revival Home is decorated with lace and walnut period pieces. Guests are invited to rock away the

afternoon on a sweeping wraparound porch. Evenings often are spent enjoying the sounds from a Grand piano in the drawing room. Soft beds are flanked with overstuffed pillows and after a restful night's sleep, guests enjoy a lavish breakfast served on fine china and crystal. The bed & breakfast is located only two blocks from the quaint gaslights which decorate Wellsboro's main street.

Innkeeper(s): Catherine Casiello. $40-60. MC VISA. 4 rooms, 1 with PB. Breakfast included in rates. Type of meal: full breakfast. Beds: QD. Antiques, fishing, downhill skiing, cross-country skiing, theater and watersports nearby.

Seen in: Wellsboro Gazette, Williamsport Sun Gazette.

"You have a beautiful presentation. Splendid."

Certificate may be used: Winter, Spring, Summer, anytime. Fall weekdays.

West Chester K16

Bankhouse B&B
875 Hillsdale Rd,
West Chester, PA 19382-1975
(610)344-7388

Circa 1765. Built into the bank of a quiet country road, this 18th-century house overlooks a 10-acre horse farm and pond. The interior is decorated with country antiques, stenciling and folk art. Guests

have a private entrance and porch. Two bedrooms share a common sitting room library. Hearty country breakfasts include German apple souffle pancakes, custard French toast and nearly 100 other recipes. West Chester and the Brandywine Valley attractions are conveniently close.

Innkeeper(s): Diana & Michael Bove. $65-85. TC. 2 rooms. 1 suite. Breakfast and evening snack included in rates. Types of meals: full breakfast, gourmet breakfast and early coffee/tea. Beds: DT. Air conditioning and ceiling fan in room. Antiques, parks, shopping, cross-country skiing, sporting events and theater nearby.

Location: In Brandywine Valley.

Seen in: Philadelphia Inquirer, Mercury, Bucks County Town & Country Living, Chester County Living, Washington Post.

"Everything was so warm and inviting. One of my favorite places to keep coming back to."

Certificate may be used: Nov. 1-April 30, Sunday-Thursday.

York

K13

Friendship House B&B

728 E Philadelphia St, York, PA 17403
(717)843-8299

Circa 1897. A walk down East Philadelphia Street
takes visitors past an unassuming row of 19th-centu-
ry townhouses. The Friendship House is a welcoming site with its light blue shutters and pink trim.
Innkeepers Becky Detwiler and Karen Maust have
added a shot of Victorian influence to their charming townhouse B&B, decorating with lacy curtains
and cherry wallcoverings. A country feast is prepared each morning with choices ranging from
quiche to French toast accompanied with items
such as baked apples, smoked sausage and homemade breads. All the items are selected carefully
from a nearby farmer's market. Becky and Karen
make sure guests never leave their friendly home
empty-handed, offering a bottle of Pennsylvania's
finest maple syrup upon departure.

Innkeeper(s): Becky Detwiler & Karen Maust. $50-60. 3 rooms, 2 with
PB. 1 suite. Breakfast and evening snack included in rates. Types of
meals: continental-plus breakfast and full breakfast. Beds: Q. Air conditioning in room. VCR on premises. Antiques, fishing, parks, shopping
and theater nearby.

Certificate may be used: November-March.

Rhode Island

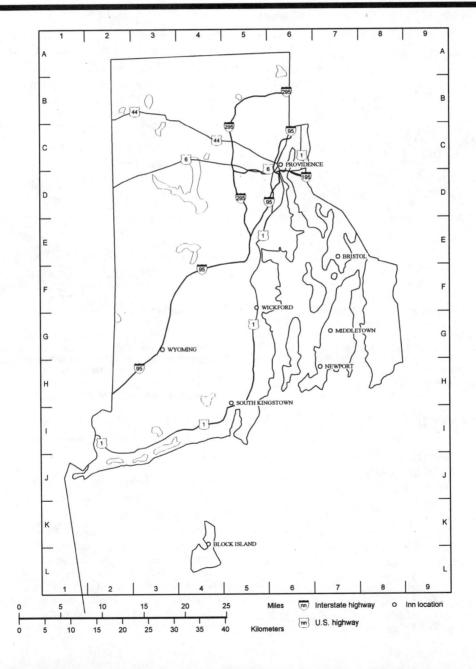

🛡 Interstate highway	○ Inn location	
🛡 U.S. highway		

Miles

Kilometers

Block Island
K4

The Bellevue House

PO Box 1198, High St,
Block Island, RI 02807-1198
(401)466-2912

Offering a hilltop perch, meadow-like setting and ocean views, this Colonial Revival farmhouse inn in the Block Island Historic District has served guests for more than a century. In addition to the inn's five bed & breakfast rooms and two cottages, there are five apartments available. Breakfast is included for bed & breakfast guests only. The Old Harbor Ferry, restaurants and shops are just a five-minute walk

from the inn. Guests may use ferries from New London, Conn., Montauk Point, N.Y., and Newport, Point Judith and Providence, R.I., to reach the island. Beaches, Block Island National Wildlife Reserve and Rodmans Hollow Nature Area are nearby. Children are welcome.

Innkeeper(s): Neva Flaherty. $65-160. MC VISA PC TC. 5 rooms. 2 cottages. Breakfast included in rates. Type of meal: continental breakfast. Beds: KQD. Library on premises. Fishing, parks, shopping and watersports nearby.

Certificate may be used: Sunday through Thursday, May 14-June 22, Sept. 10-Oct. 5. B&B rooms available for this offer.

Blue Dory Inn

PO Box 488, Dodge St,
Block Island, RI 02807-0488
(401)466-5891 (800)992-7290
Fax:(401)466-9910

Circa 1887. This Shingle Victorian inn on Crescent Beach offers many guest rooms with ocean views. The Cottage, The Doll House and The Tea House are separate structures for those desiring more room or privacy. Antiques and Victorian touches are featured throughout. Year-round car ferry service, taking approximately one hour, is found at Point Judith, R.I. The island also may be reached by air on New England Airlines or by charter. Mohegan Bluffs Scenic Natural Area is nearby.

Innkeeper(s): Ann Loedy. $65-195. MC VISA AX DS PC TC. 14 rooms with PB. 3 suites. 4 cottages. 1 conference room. Breakfast and afternoon tea included in rates. Types of meals: continental-plus breakfast and early coffee/tea. Catered breakfast available. Beds: KQDT. Cable TV, VCR, fax, copier, swimming and child care on premises. Antiques, fishing, parks, shopping, theater and watersports nearby.

"The Blue Dory is a wonderful place to stay. The room was lovely, the view spectacular and the sound of surf was both restful and tranquil."

Certificate may be used: Midweek Sept. 15 through June 15, Sunday through Thursday.

Sheffield House

High St, Box C-2, Block Island, RI 02807
(401)466-2494 Fax:(401)466-5067

Circa 1888. Step off the ferry and step into a bygone era at this charming Queen Anne Victorian, which overlooks the Old Harbor district and scenic ocean vistas. Relax on the front porch or enjoy the fragrance as you stroll through the private garden. The cookie jar is always full of home-baked treats. Breakfasts are served in the quaint day room, which features a collection of milk bottles from around the world. Guests also can enjoy the morning meal in the garden surrounded by beautiful flowers and herbs. Guest rooms feature international touches, antiques and family pieces.

Innkeeper(s): Steve & Claire McQueeny. $50-150. VISA. 7 rooms, 5 with PB. Breakfast, afternoon tea and evening snack included in rates. Types of meals: continental-plus breakfast and early coffee/tea. Beds: Q. Ceiling fan in room. Cable TV, VCR and copier on premises. Antiques, fishing, parks, shopping and watersports nearby.

Certificate may be used: Sept. 10 through May 25, Sunday-Thursday.

Bristol
E7

The Joseph Reynolds House

956 Hope St, Bristol, RI 02809-1113
(401)254-0230 (800)754-0230
Fax:(401)254-2610

Circa 1684. The Joseph Reynolds House is a National Historic Landmark and the oldest known 17th-century, three-story wooden structure in New England. It was the military headquarters of General Lafayette in 1778. Gradually being restored to its original elegance, guest rooms are on the second and third floors. Most of the common rooms have high ceilings and were painted to look like marble. There is a Jacobean staircase, a keeping room and a great room.

Innkeeper(s): Wendy & Richard Anderson. $49-95. PC TC. 5 rooms, 3 with PB. 2 suites. Breakfast and afternoon tea included in rates. Type of meal: gourmet breakfast. Beds: KQDT. Cable TV, VCR, fax, copier and library on premises. Antiques, fishing, parks, shopping, sporting events and theater nearby.

Location: Twenty-five minutes from Newport.

Seen in: American Design, New England Colonial, Early Houses of Rhode Island, New York Travel, Providence Journal, New England.

"Wonderful, restful week after chaos."

Certificate may be used: November to April (not on holiday weeks); midweek year-round, subject to availability.

William's Grant Inn
154 High St, Bristol, RI 02809-2123
(401)253-4222 (800)596-4222

Circa 1808. This handsome Federal Colonial home was built by Governor William Bradford for his son. There are two beehive ovens and seven fireplaces as well as original wide-board pine floors and paired interior chimneys. Antique furnishings and folk art make the guest rooms inviting. A hearty continental breakfast is served in the country kitchen.

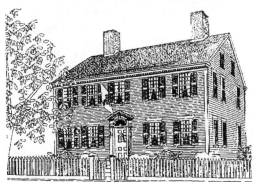

Innkeeper(s): Michael Rose. $65-95. MC VISA AX DS PC TC. 5 rooms, 3 with PB, 5 with FP. Breakfast included in rates. Types of meals: full breakfast and gourmet breakfast. Afternoon tea available. Beds: QD. Turn-down service and ceiling fan in room. Bicycles on premises. Antiques, fishing, parks, sporting events and watersports nearby.

Location: Located in the heart of Bristol's historic waterfront district.

Seen in: New York Times, Sun Sentinal, Providence Journal, Bristol Phoenix.

"We felt better than at home with the wonderful treats (the breakfasts were fabulous), the lovely rooms, the inn is full of inspiration and innovation..."

Certificate may be used: November-May, Sunday-Thursday, based on availability.

Middletown
G7

Lindsey's Guest House
6 James St, Middletown, RI 02842-5932
(401)846-9386

Circa 1955. This contemporary split-level home in a residential area features three guest rooms, including one on the ground level that has a private entrance and is handicap-accessible. Breakfast is served in the dining room and usually includes cereal, coffee cake, fruit, juice, muffins and jam, and coffee or beverage of choice. The innkeeper has worked in the hospitality industry for more than 30 years and is happy to offer sightseeing tips. The Norman Bird Sanctuary and Sachuest Point National Wildlife Reserve are nearby.

Innkeeper(s): Anne T. Lindsey. $40-75. MC VISA AX PC TC. 2 rooms with PB. Breakfast included in rates. Type of meal: continental-plus breakfast. Beds: KD. Ceiling fan in room. VCR on premises. Handicap access. Antiques, fishing, parks, theater and watersports nearby.

Certificate may be used: Oct. 15 to April 15.

The Inn at Shadow Lawn
120 Miantonomi Ave,
Middletown, RI 02842-5450
(401)849-1298 (800)828-0000
Fax:(401)849-1306

Circa 1853. This elegant, three-story Stick Victorian inn offers a glimpse of fine living in an earlier age. The innkeepers' attention to detail is evident throughout, with French crystal chandeliers, stained-glass windows and Tiffany lighting in the library as a few of the highlights. Parlors are found on each of the inn's floors. Newport's many attractions, including the Art Museum, the Artillery Museum and Belcourt Castle, are just a short drive from the inn, which also offers a daily shuttle to the city.

Innkeeper(s): Randy & Selma Fabricant. $65-135. MC VISA TC. 8 rooms with PB, 6 with FP. 2 conference rooms. Breakfast included in rates. Type of meal: continental-plus breakfast. Beds: KQT. Air conditioning in room. Fax, copier and library on premises. Antiques nearby.

Certificate may be used: Jan. 11- April 1, Monday-Sunday, excluding holidays.

Newport
H7

The Burbank Rose B&B
111 Memorial Blvd W,
Newport, RI 02840-3469
(401)849-9457

Circa 1850. The innkeepers of this cheery, yellow home named their B&B in honor of famed horticulturist Luther Burbank. As a guest, he probably would be taken by the bright, flowery hues that adorn the interior of this Federal-style home. Rooms, some of which afford harbor views, are light and airy with simple decor. The innkeepers serve afternoon wine and refreshments and a substantial breakfast buffet. The home is located in Newport's Historic Hill district and within walking distance of shops, restaurants and many of the seaside village's popular attractions.

Innkeeper(s): John & Bonnie McNeely. $49-129. AX TC. 6 rooms, 3 with PB. Breakfast and afternoon tea included in rates. Types of meals: full breakfast and early coffee/tea. Beds: QDT. Air conditioning in room. Cable TV, VCR and copier on premises. Antiques, fishing, shopping, theater and watersports nearby.

Certificate may be used: Oct. 1-May 1 Sunday-Thursday.

Halidon Hill Guest House

Halidon Ave, Newport, RI 02840
(401)847-8318 (800)227-2130

Circa 1968. This contemporary, two-story Georgian-style inn offers a convenient location and comfortable accommodations for those exploring the Newport area. The two spacious suites both boast kitchenettes. The inn is just a 10-minute walk to Hammersmith Farm and provides easy access to the area's mansions, restaurants and shopping. Guests will enjoy lounging on the roomy deck near the in-ground pool, or in front of the fireplace in cooler weather. Newport Harbor and the Tennis Hall of Fame are nearby.

Innkeeper(s): Helen Burke. $55-150. AX DC DS. 2 suites. Breakfast included in rates. Type of meal: full breakfast. VCR on premises. Shopping and sporting events nearby.

Certificate may be used: Anytime, between November-May and during the week between May through October.

Hammett House Inn

505 Thames St, Newport, RI 02840-6723
(401)848-0593 (800)548-9417
Fax:(401)848-2258

Circa 1758. This three-story Georgian Federal-style home has watched the nation grow and prosper from its little nook on Thames Street. The rooms are decorated with romance in mind. Especially picturesque are the Rose and Windward rooms, which afford views of Newport's harbor. The Pewter Room includes a unique metal canopy bed. The inn is a short walk from shops, restaurants and the waterfront.

Innkeeper(s): Marianne Spaziano. $95-195. MC VISA AX DS TC. 5 rooms with PB. Breakfast included in rates. Type of meal: continental-plus breakfast. Beds: Q. Air conditioning and cable TV in room. Fax on premises. Antiques, fishing, parks, shopping, downhill skiing, theater and watersports nearby.

Certificate may be used: Anytime Nov. 16-April 1; April-June, Tuesday-Thursday only.

Hydrangea House

16 Bellevue Ave, Newport, RI 02840-3206
(401)846-4435 (800)945-4667
Fax:(401)846-6602

The scent of fresh flowers welcomes guests into their cheery rooms at this B&B, which once housed a school of music. After abdicating his throne, King Edward was guest at this home. Romance is emphasized by the decor in each of the individually appointed guest rooms, which feature wicker and antique furnishings. Breakfasts are served on the veranda, with its view of the gardens. In cooler weather, the breakfast buffet is set up in the art gallery, which features many original works.

Innkeeper(s): Grant Edmondson. $55-139. MC VISA. 6 rooms. Breakfast included in rates. Type of meal: full breakfast.

Certificate may be used: Nov. 1-April 30, Sunday-Wednesday.

The Melville House

39 Clarke St, Newport, RI 02840-3023
(401)847-0640 Fax:(401)847-0956

Circa 1750. This attractive, National Register two-story Colonial inn once housed aides to General Rochambeau during the American Revolution. Early American furnishings decorate the interior. There is also an unusual collection of old appliances, including a cherry-pitter, mincer and dough maker. A full breakfast includes Portuguese Quiche, Jonnycakes, homemade bread and Portuguese egg sandwiches. The inn is a pleasant walk from the waterfront and historic sites.

Innkeeper(s): Vincent DeRico & David Horan. $85-135. MC VISA AX DS PC TC. 7 rooms, 5 with PB, 1 with FP. 1 suite. Breakfast and afternoon tea included in rates. Types of meals: full breakfast, gourmet breakfast and early coffee/tea. Picnic lunch available. Beds: KDT. Air conditioning in room. Fax and bicycles on premises. Antiques, fishing, parks, shopping, theater and watersports nearby.

Location: In the heart of Newport's Historic Hill.

Seen in: Country Inns, "Lodging Pick" for Newport, Good Housekeeping.

"Comfortable with a quiet elegance."

Certificate may be used: November-April; Sunday-Thursday.

Providence   C6

State House Inn

43 Jewett St, Providence, RI 02908-4904
(401)351-6111 Fax:(401)351-4261

Circa 1889. Shaker and Colonial furniture fill this turn-of-the-century home, located in the midst of a quaint and peaceful Providence neighborhood. The rooms provide amenities that will please any business traveler and have the country comfort and elegance of days gone by. The common room contains a small library for guest use. A famed historic district, featuring restored homes and buildings, is three blocks away, and the capitol is a five-minute walk.

Innkeeper(s): Frank & Monica Hopton. $79-119. EP. MC VISA AX PC TC. 10 rooms with PB, 2 with FP. Breakfast included in rates. Type of meal: full breakfast. Afternoon tea available. Beds: KQ. Air conditioning and cable TV in room. Fax, copier and computer on premises. Antiques and parks nearby.
Location: Forty minutes from Newport.
Seen in: Providence.

"Thank you again for the warm, comfortable and very attractive accommodations."

Certificate may be used: Weekdays, year-round. Weekends in November-April.

South Kingstown   H5

Admiral Dewey Inn

668 Matunuck Beach Rd, South
Kingstown, RI 02879-7021
(401)783-2090 (800)457-2090
Fax:(401)783-0680

Circa 1898. Although the prices have risen a bit since this inn's days as a boarding house (the rate was 50 cents per night), this stick-style home still offers hospitality and comfort. The National Register inn is within walking distance of Matunuck Beach. Guests can enjoy the sea breeze from the inn's wraparound porch. Period antiques decorate the guest rooms, some of which offer ocean views.

Innkeeper(s): Joan Lebel. $40-120. MC VISA PC. 10 rooms, 8 with PB. Breakfast included in rates. Types of meals: continental-plus breakfast and early coffee/tea. Picnic lunch available. Beds: QDT. Cable TV, VCR, fax, copier and swimming on premises. Antiques, fishing, parks, shopping, theater and watersports nearby.
Certificate may be used: Oct. 15 to May 15 Sunday to Friday.

Wickford   F5

Meadowland

765 Old Baptist Rd, Wickford, RI 02852
(401)294-4168

Circa 1853. Situated on a half-acre of land surrounded by fruit trees, Meadowland was once the site of a Victorian Era celery farm. Bedrooms are furnished in wicker, and each of the three floors has a sitting room. A formal breakfast is served by candlelight. The innkeeper can arrange a half-day sail or sunset dinner cruise on the 46-foot Morning Star.
Innkeeper(s): Linda Iavarone. $69-74. 5 rooms. 1 suite. Breakfast included in rates. Type of meal: continental-plus breakfast. Beds: DT. Air conditioning in room. VCR on premises. Antiques, fishing, shopping and theater nearby.
Location: Minutes from historic Wickford Village.
Seen in: Ocean State Traveler.

"Serenity at its best."

Certificate may be used: Oct. 20 to May 15 subject to availability.

Wyoming   G3

The Cookie Jar B&B

64 Kingstown Rd Rt 138,
Wyoming, RI 02898-1103
(401)539-2680 (800)767-4262

Circa 1732. The living room of this historic farmhouse inn once served as a blacksmith shop. The inn's original stone walls and wood ceiling remain, along with a granite fireplace built by an Indian stonemason after the forge, was removed. Years later, as rooms were added, the building became the Cookie Jar tea room, a name the innkeepers judged worth keeping. Visitors select their full breakfast fare from a menu listing the night before. The inn's grounds boast more than 60 fruit trees, a flower garden, a barn and a swimming pool. Those who love the beach or fishing will find both fresh and salt water within a 20-minute drive.
Innkeeper(s): Charles Sohl. $60-75. PC TC. 3 suites. Breakfast included in rates. Type of meal: full breakfast. Beds: KQDT. Air conditioning and cable TV in room. VCR on premises. Amusement parks, antiques, fishing, shopping, downhill skiing, cross-country skiing, sporting events, theater and watersports nearby.
Location: Boston is slightly more than an hour from the inn.
Certificate may be used: Anytime except Friday and Saturday during months of May through October. Not valid on holidays or special events.

South Carolina

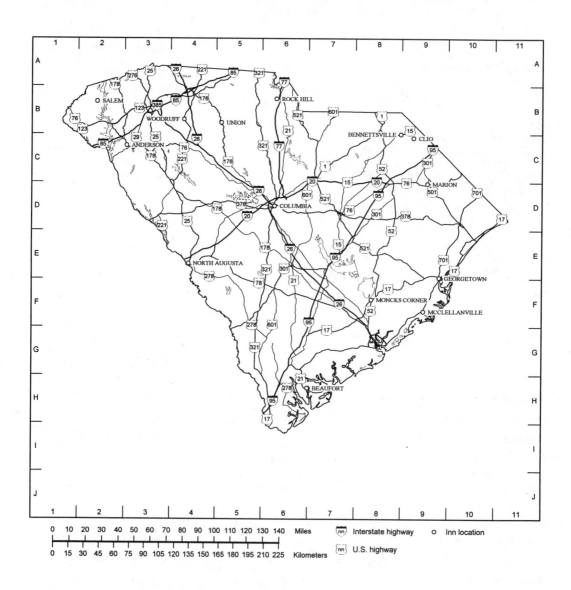

0 10 20 30 40 50 60 70 80 90 100 110 120 130 140   Miles
0 15 30 45 60 75 90 105 120 135 150 165 180 195 210 225   Kilometers

[nn] Interstate highway   o Inn location
[nn] U.S. highway

Anderson   C3

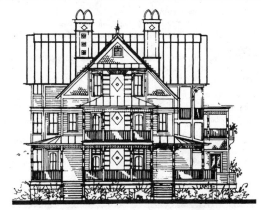

Evergreen Inn
1103 S Main St, Anderson, SC 29624
(803)225-1109

Circa 1834. This gracious Greek Revival house features tall columns rising to the third-story pediment and a wraparound veranda. It is located on two-and-a-half acres, next to another fine National Register mansion, which houses the inn's restaurant. Scarlet's Room features a tall four-poster bed and burgundy velvet drapes. Another guest room boasts an exotic navy satin canopy bed. Antique shops and the downtown area are within walking distance.

Innkeeper(s): Myrna Ryter. $56-70. MC VISA AX DC. 7 rooms, 6 with PB. 2 suites. 1 conference room. Breakfast included in rates. Types of meals: continental breakfast and gourmet breakfast. Dinner available. Beds: KQ. Handicap access. Antiques nearby.

Location: Historical district.

Seen in: Travel Host Magazine, Greenville News.

"Fantastic! Very imaginative & fun."

Certificate may be used: All times.

River Inn
PO Box 2093, 612 E River St,
Anderson, SC 29622-2093
(864)226-1431 Fax:(864)231-9847

Circa 1914. This three-story, dormered Georgian Plantation house borders the historic district of Anderson. Leaded glass, 10-foot beamed ceilings and working coal fireplaces mark this country manor. An eclectic collection of antiques include a mahogany dining set and leaded china cabinets. Each room has its own fireplace and bath. Mounds of azaleas, 70-year-old fragrant camellia sasanqua trees, roses and crepe myrtles add grace to the inn's five acres. Dinner sometimes is available for guests with a reservation.

Innkeeper(s): Patricia Clark. $60-85. 4 rooms with PB, 4 with FP. 1 conference room. Breakfast and evening snack included in rates. Type of meal: full breakfast. Beds: KQDT. Air conditioning, ceiling fan and cable TV in room. VCR and spa on premises. Antiques, fishing, parks, shopping, sporting events, theater and watersports nearby.

Certificate may be used: January through July.

Beaufort   H6

The Beaufort Inn
809 Port Republic St, Beaufort, SC 29901
(803)521-9000 Fax:(803)521-9500

Circa 1907. Every inch of this breathtaking inn offers something special. The interior is decorated to the hilt with lovely furnishings, plants, beautiful rugs and warm, inviting tones. Rooms include four-poster and canopy beds combined with the modern amenities such as two-person Jacuzzi tubs, fireplaces, wet bars and stocked refrigerators. Enjoy a complimentary full breakfast at the inn's gourmet restaurant. The chef offers everything from a light breakfast of fresh fruit, cereal and a bagel to heartier treats such as whole grain French toast stuffed with Brie and sun-dried peaches served with fresh fruit and crisp bacon.

Innkeeper(s): Russell & Debbie Fielden. $125-185. MC VISA AX DS PC TC. 13 rooms with PB, 4 with FP. 1 suite. 1 conference room. Breakfast and afternoon tea included in rates. Types of meals: full breakfast, gourmet breakfast and early coffee/tea. Dinner, picnic lunch, gourmet lunch, banquet service, catering service and room service available. Beds: KQ. Air conditioning, turn-down service, ceiling fan and cable TV in room. VCR, fax, copier and bicycles on premises. Handicap access. Antiques, fishing, parks, shopping, theater and watersports nearby.

Seen in: Beaufort, Southern Living, Country Inns, Carolina Style, U.S. Air.

Certificate may be used: December, January and February, Sunday through Wednesday night only. Good only for rooms which have a rate of $175.

The Rhett House Inn
1009 Craven St, Beaufort, SC 29902-5577
(803)524-9030 Fax:(803)524-1310

Circa 1820. Most people cannot pass this stunning two-story clapboard house without wanting to step up to the long veranda and try the hammock. Guest rooms are furnished in antiques, with quilts and fresh flowers. Many guest rooms have fireplaces. Handsome gardens feature a fountain and are often the site for romantic weddings. Bicycles are available.

Innkeeper(s): Stephen Harrison. $125-175. MC VISA AX. 10 rooms with PB, 2 with FP. 1 suite. 1 conference room. Breakfast and afternoon tea included in rates. Types of meals: full breakfast and early coffee/tea. Dinner, evening snack, picnic lunch, catering service and room service available. Beds: KQ. Air conditioning, turn-down service, ceiling fan and cable TV in room. Fax on premises. Handicap access. Antiques, fishing, theater and watersports nearby.

Location: In historic downtown.

Seen in: Innsider, Family Business, Lowcountry Ledger, New York Times, Vogue, Elle, Conde Nast Traveler, Travel & Leisure.

"A dream come true!"

Certificate may be used: January, February, June through September and December, Sunday through Thursday.

Bennettsville C8

The Breeden Inn & Carriage House
404 E Main St, Bennettsville, SC 29512
(803)479-3665

Circa 1886. One especially bountiful cotton crop paid for the construction of this mansion, which local attorney Thomas Bouchier presented to his bride as a wedding gift. The exterior is graced with more than two dozens columns and the interior boasts a carved oak archway in the center hall. Stained and beveled glass are found throughout the home, along with original light fixtures. Breakfasts can be served in the formal dining room, in the garden or on the veranda. The innkeepers also offer accommodations in a restored guest house, which includes a sitting room, kitchen and front porch lined with rocking chairs.

Innkeeper(s): Wesley & Bonnie Park. $55-65. MC VISA PC TC. 7 rooms with PB, 6 with FP. 1 suite. 1 cottage. 1 conference room. Breakfast included in rates. Types of meals: full breakfast and early coffee/tea. Beds: DT. Air conditioning, ceiling fan, cable TV and VCR in room. Fax, copier and swimming on premises. Antiques, fishing, theater nearby.

"You have truly given 'Southern Hospitality' a higher meaning."

Certificate may be used: Year-round. Not honored on special event dates or holidays.

Clio C9

Henry Bennett House
301 Red Bluff St, Clio, SC 29525-3009
(803)586-2701

A huge veranda, decorated with whimsical gingerbread trim, rambles around the exterior of this Victorian, which was built by a cotton farmer. A turret and widow's walk also grace the home. Clawfoot tubs and working fireplaces are some of the amenities found in the comfortable guest rooms. The area offers several golf courses and antiquing.

Innkeeper(s): Connie Hodgkinson. $50. MC VISA. 3 rooms. Breakfast included in rates. Type of meal: full breakfast.

Certificate may be used: March-December.

Columbia D6

Chesnut Cottage B&B
1718 Hampton St, Columbia, SC 29201
(803)256-1718

Circa 1850. This inn was originally the home of Confederate General James Chesnut and his wife, writer Mary Boykin Miller Chesnut. She authored "A Diary From Dixie," written during the Civil War but published posthumously in 1905. The white frame one-and-a-half-story house has a central dormer with an arched window above the main entrance. The small porch has four octagonal columns and an ironwork balustrade. Hearty breakfasts are served in the privacy of your room, on the porch or in the main dining room. The innkeepers can provide you with sightseeing information, make advance dinner reservations, as well as cater to any other special interests you might have.

Innkeeper(s): Diane & Gale Garrett. $65-150. MC VISA AX DC DS TC. 4 rooms with PB. 1 suite. Breakfast and evening snack included in rates. Types of meals: continental-plus breakfast, full breakfast, gourmet breakfast and early coffee/tea. Picnic lunch and room service available. Beds: KQ. Air conditioning, turn-down service, ceiling fan and VCR in room. Fax and bicycles on premises. Antiques, fishing, parks, shopping, sporting events, theater and watersports nearby.

Seen in: TV show "Breakfast with Christie," Sandlapper, London Financial Times.

"You really know how to pamper and spoil. Chesnut Cottage is a great place to stay."

Certificate may be used: Jan. 1 through May 1 & July 1 through Aug. 31, Sunday through Thursday.

Georgetown E9

1790 House B&B Inn
630 Highmarket St,
Georgetown, SC 29440-3652
(803)546-4821 (800)890-7432

Circa 1790. Located in the heart of a historic district, this beautifully restored West Indies Colonial just celebrated its 200th birthday. The spacious rooms feature 11-foot ceilings and seven fireplaces, three in the guest bedrooms. The inn decor reflects the plantations of a bygone era. Guests can stay in former slave quarters, renovated to include a queen bedroom and sitting area. Each of the romantic rooms feature special touches, such as the red and deep blue decor of the Indigo Room, and the antique white iron and brass bed in the Prince

George Suite. The Dependency Cottage is a perfect honeymoon hideaway with a private entrance enhanced with gardens and a patio, and the room also includes a Jacuzzi tub.

Innkeeper(s): John & Patricia Wiley. $65-125. MC VISA AX DS PC TC. 6 rooms with PB, 1 with FP. 1 cottage. Breakfast and evening snack included in rates. Type of meal: gourmet breakfast. Picnic lunch available. Beds: QT. Air conditioning, ceiling fan and cable TV in room. VCR and bicycles on premises. Antiques, fishing, parks, shopping and theater nearby.

Seen in: Georgetown Times.

"The 1790 House always amazes me with its beauty."

Certificate may be used: Anytime in December-February. Sunday-Thursday for March-November.

Ashfield Manor

3030 S Island Rd, Georgetown, SC 29440
(803)546-0464

Circa 1960. Breakfast with many homemade items is served in guests' rooms, the parlor or on the inn's long, screened porch. Georgetown is conveniently located 30 miles from Myrtle Beach and 60 miles from Charleston. A beautiful public beach is 15 minutes away at Pawleys Island. Located on Winyah Bay, the town's seaport offers area restaurants with abundant fresh seafood. Many homes and churches date back to the 1700s and can be seen on a walking tour or by carriage or tour train. Also available are harbor tours that allow you to see Georgetown and its plantations from the water.

Innkeeper(s): Carol Ashenfelder. $50-65. MC VISA AX DC CB DS. 4 rooms. Breakfast included in rates. Type of meal: continental breakfast. Beds: Q. Air conditioning, ceiling fan and cable TV in room. Amusement parks, antiques, fishing, shopping and theater nearby.

Certificate may be used: Based upon availability.

Du Pre House

921 Prince St, Georgetown, SC 29442
(803)546-0298 (800)921-3877
Fax:(803)546-0298

Circa 1740. The lot upon which this pre-Revolutionary War gem stands was partitioned off in 1734, and the home built six years later. Three guest rooms have fireplaces, and all are decorated with a poster bed. On the weekends, a full breakfast is prepared featuring such items as egg or grit

casseroles, fresh fruit and home-baked muffins. For those who love history, Georgetown, South Carolina's third oldest city, offers more than 60 registered National Historic Landmarks.

Innkeeper(s): Marshall Wile. $60-95. MC VISA PC TC. 5 rooms with PB. Breakfast, afternoon tea and evening snack included in rates. Types of meals: continental-plus breakfast and early coffee/tea. Picnic lunch available. Beds: Q. Air conditioning, turn-down service and ceiling fan in room. Cable TV, fax, copier, spa, swimming and library on premises. Amusement parks, antiques, fishing, parks, shopping, theater and watersports nearby.

Certificate may be used: Sunday-Thursday, January 1-July 1.

King's Inn at Georgetown

230 Broad St, Georgetown, SC 29440
(803)527-6937 (800)251-8805
Fax:(803)527-6937

Circa 1825. During the Civil War, Union troops seized this Federal-style manor and used it for headquarters. The house is named for its first resident, Benjamin King. The well-appointed surroundings are full of regal touches. The parlors, which feature ornate carved woodwork, are wonderful locations to relax and soak up the 19th-century ambiance. Each of the guest rooms offers a different color scheme and several offer amenities such as Jacuzzi tubs, poster or canopy beds, fireplaces and chandeliers. Antiques and reproductions are found throughout the home. Gourmet breakfasts are served on fine china, and guests have the option of dining at a table for two or with other guests in the dining room. Nightly turndown service, afternoon tea and coffee placed by your door in the morning are just a few of the thoughtful amenities. The inn was ranked as one of the nation's best by Country Inns magazine. Walking tours of the historic district and boat tours of nearby plantations are some of the popular activities in the area.

Innkeeper(s): Marilyn & Jerry Burkhardt. $75-115. MC VISA AX. 7 rooms with PB. Breakfast and afternoon tea included in rates. Types of meals: continental breakfast, continental-plus breakfast, full breakfast and early coffee/tea. Picnic lunch available. Beds: KQDT. Air conditioning and turn-down service in room. Cable TV, VCR, bicycles and child care on premises. Antiques, fishing, parks, shopping, sporting events, theater and watersports nearby.

Certificate may be used: Sunday-Friday, all year.

The Shaw House B&B

613 Cypress Ct, Georgetown, SC 29440
(803)546-9663

Circa 1985. Near Georgetown's historical district is the Shaw House. It features a beautiful view of the Willowbank marsh, which stretches out for more than 100 acres. Sometimes giant turtles come up and lay eggs on the lawn. Guests enjoy rocking on the inn's front and back porches and identifying the large variety of birds that live here. A Southern

home-cooked breakfast often includes grits, quiche and Mary's heart-shaped biscuits.

Innkeeper(s): Mary & Joe Shaw. $55-70. PC TC. 3 rooms with PB. Breakfast included in rates. Types of meals: full breakfast and early coffee/tea. Evening snack available. Beds: KQT. Air conditioning, turn-down service, ceiling fan and cable TV in room. Bicycles and library on premises. Amusement parks, antiques, fishing, parks, shopping, theater and watersports nearby.

Seen in: Charlotte Observer, Country.

"Your home speaks of abundance and comfort and joy."

Certificate may be used: Anytime available.

Winyah Bay B&B
403 Helena St, Georgetown, SC 29440
(803)546-9051 (800)681-6176

Circa 1984. Enjoy the breezes from the bay as you stroll down the longest private dock in South Carolina. Winyah Bay also offers access to a small private island. The innkeepers have decorated the rooms in bold, vibrant colors, and each room boasts a view overlooking the bay and a bathroom with skylights. The cupboards are stocked with breakfast goodies and guests have access to a refrigerator, microwave and coffeemaker.

Innkeeper(s): Peggy Wheeler. $50-65. MC VISA TC. 2 suites. 1 cottage. Breakfast and evening snack included in rates. Type of meal: continental-plus breakfast. Picnic lunch available. Beds: KD. Air conditioning, ceiling fan, cable TV and VCR in room. Amusement parks, antiques, fishing, shopping and theater nearby.

Certificate may be used: January, February and March.

Marion
D9

Montgomery's Grove
408 Harlee St, Marion, SC 29571-3144
(803)423-5220 Fax:(803)423-5220

Circa 1893. The stunning rooms of this majestic Eastlake-style manor are adorned in Victorian tradition with Oriental rugs, polished hardwood floors, chandeliers and gracious furnishings. High ceilings and fireplaces in each room complete the elegant look. Guest rooms are filled with antiques and magazines or books from the 1890s. Hearty full breakfasts and afternoon teas are served each day on the wraparound porches, and candlelit dinner packages can be arranged. Guests will appreciate this inn's secluded location, surrounded by trees and gardens. The inn is about a half-hour drive to famous Myrtle Beach.

Innkeeper(s): Richard Roberts. $60-80. 4 rooms, 3 with PB. 1 suite. Breakfast included in rates. Type of meal: full breakfast. Afternoon tea, dinner, picnic lunch, lunch and catering service available. Beds: KQ. Antiques, fishing, theater and watersports nearby.

Seen in: Pee Dee Magazine, Sandlapper, Marion Star.

Certificate may be used: Anytime.

McClellanville
F9

Laurel Hill Plantation
8913 N Highway 17,
McClellanville, SC 29458-9423
(803)887-3708

Circa 1850. From the large wraparound porch of this plantation house is a view of salt marshes, islands and the Atlantic Ocean. A nearby creek is the perfect location for crabbing, and there is a fresh-water pond for fishing. The home was destroyed by Hurricane Hugo, but has been totally reconstructed in its original Low Country style. It is furnished with antiques, local crafts and folk art. The inn has a gift shop that features books, antiques and decorative items.

Innkeeper(s): Jackie & Lee Morrison. $65-95. MC VISA PC TC. 4 rooms with PB. Breakfast and evening snack included in rates. Types of meals: full breakfast and early coffee/tea. Beds: QT. Air conditioning and ceiling fan in room. Cable TV and VCR on premises. Antiques, fishing, parks, shopping and watersports nearby.

Location: Thirty minutes north of Charleston on Hwy 17.

Seen in: Country Living, Seabreeze, Pee Dee, State.

"The total privacy yet friendliness was very much appreciated."

Certificate may be used: November, December, January, February; Sunday-Thursday.

Moncks Corner

F8

Rice Hope Plantation Inn

206 Rice Hope Dr,
Moncks Corner, SC 29461-9781
(803)761-4832 (800)569-4038
Fax:(803)884-0223

Circa 1929. Resting on 11 acres of natural beauty, the inn is set among live oaks on a bluff overlooking the Cooper River. On the property are formal gardens that boast 200-year-old camellias and many old varieties of azaleas and other trees and plants. Nearby attractions include the Trappist Monastery at Mepkin Plantation, Francis Marion National Forest, Cypress Gardens and historic Charleston. Outdoor occasions are great because of the inn's formal gardens and the Cooper River backdrop.

Innkeeper(s): Doris Kasprak. $60-80. MC VISA AX. 5 rooms, 3 with PB. 1 conference room. Breakfast included in rates. Types of meals: continental-plus breakfast, full breakfast, gourmet breakfast and early coffee/tea. Afternoon tea, lunch, gourmet lunch, banquet service and catering service available. Beds: QD. Air conditioning and ceiling fan in room. Cable TV, VCR and child care on premises. Antiques and fishing nearby.

Location: Forty-five miles from Historic Charleston.

Certificate may be used: Monday-Thursday, all year, when rooms available.

North Augusta

E4

Rosemary & Lookaway Halls

804 Carolina Ave,
North Augusta, SC 29841-3436
(803)278-6222 (800)531-5578
Fax:(803)278-4877

Circa 1902. The magnificent historic homes are gracious examples of Southern elegance and charm. Manicured lawns adorn the exterior of both homes, which appear almost as a vision out of "Gone With the Wind." The Rosemary Hall boasts a spectacular heart-of-pine staircase. The homes stand as living museums, filled to the brim with beautiful furnishings and elegant decor, all highlighted by stained-glass windows, chandeliers and lacy touches. Some guest rooms include Jacuzzis, while others offer verandas. A proper afternoon tea is served each afternoon at Rosemary Hall. The Southern hospitality begins during the morning meal. The opulent gourmet fare might include baked orange-pecan English muffins served with Canadian bacon, or perhaps a Southern strata with cheese and bacon. The catering menu is even more tasteful, and many weddings, showers and parties are hosted at these inns.

Innkeeper(s): Mr. N. Wago & Geneva Robinson. $125-250. MC VISA AX DC CB DS PC TC. 23 rooms with PB. 2 conference rooms. Breakfast and evening snack included in rates. Types of meals: continental-plus breakfast, full breakfast and early coffee/tea. Beds: KQDT. Air conditioning, turn-down service, cable TV and VCR in room. Fax and copier on premises. Handicap access. Antiques, fishing, parks, shopping, sporting events and watersports nearby.

Certificate may be used: Jan. 3-April 1, April 20-Sept. 1, Sunday-Tuesday.

Rock Hill

B6

East Main Guest House

600 E Main St, Rock Hill, SC 29730-5325
(803)366-1161

Circa 1919. Although this Craftsman-style home was built in the early 20th century, its second floor remained unfurnished until the innkeepers acquired the home in 1990. Today the upstairs offers three individually decorated guest quarters, including the Bridal Suite, which boasts a canopy bed and whirlpool garden tub. The East Bedroom offers a fireplace, and the charming Garden Room affords a view of the back garden. The innkeepers serve a bounty of freshly baked breads and muffins for breakfast, and wine and cheese is offered in the evenings. The home is within walking distance of downtown Rock Hill.

Innkeeper(s): Jerry Peterson. $59-79. MC VISA. 3 rooms with PB, 2 with FP. Breakfast included in rates. Type of meal: continental-plus breakfast. Fax and copier on premises. Fishing nearby.

Certificate may be used: Sunday through Thursday (not Friday or Saturday nights).

Salem

B2

Sunrise Farm B&B

PO Box 164, 325 Sunrise Dr,
Salem, SC 29676-0164
(864)944-0121

Circa 1890. Situated on the remaining part of a 1,000-acre cotton plantation, this country Victorian features large porches with rockers and wicker. Guest rooms are furnished with period antiques, thick comforters, extra pillows and family heirlooms. The "corn crib" cottage is located in the original farm structure used for storing corn. It has a fully equipped kitchen, sitting area and bedroom with tub and shower. The June Rose Garden cottage includes a river rock fireplace, full kitchen and views of pastures and mountains. A continental breakfast is available for cottage guests. Bed & breakfast guests are treated to a full breakfast.

Innkeeper(s): Jean Webb. $55-95. MC VISA AX TC. 3 rooms. 2 cottages. Breakfast and evening snack included in rates. Types of meals:

continental-plus breakfast and full breakfast. Beds: QD. Air conditioning and ceiling fan in room. Antiques, fishing, parks, sporting events and watersports nearby.

"Saying thank you doesn't do our gratitude justice."

Certificate may be used: Weekdays except October. Any day during winter.

Union
B5

The Inn at Merridun
100 Merridun Pl, Union, SC 29379-2200
(864)427-7052 Fax:(864)427-7052

Circa 1855. Nestled on nine acres of wooded ground, this Greek Revival inn is in a small Southern college town. During spring, see the South in its colorful splendor-blooming azaleas, magnolias and wisteria. Sip an iced drink on the inn's marble verandas and relive memories of a bygone era. Soft strains of Mozart and Beethoven, as well as the smell of freshly baked cookies and country suppers, fill the air of this antebellum country inn.

Innkeeper(s): Jim & Peggy Waller. $85-105. MC VISA PC TC. 5 rooms with PB. 3 conference rooms. Breakfast included in rates. Types of meals: full breakfast, gourmet breakfast and early coffee/tea. Afternoon tea, dinner, evening snack, picnic lunch, lunch, gourmet lunch, banquet service, catering service, catered breakfast and room service available. Beds: KQT. Air conditioning, ceiling fan and cable TV in room. VCR, fax, copier and library on premises. Amusement parks, antiques, fishing, parks, shopping, sporting events and watersports nearby.

Certificate may be used: Anytime Jan. 1-Nov. 30.

Woodruff
B4

The Nicholls-Crook Plantation House
120 Plantation Dr, Woodruff, SC 29388
(803)476-8820

Circa 1793. The innkeepers at this 18th-century home have restored the historic house with warmth and charm in mind. Period antiques, original mantels and the widest chimney in the state create a

charming, rustic environment. The grounds boast 18th-century flowers, a white-rock courtyard and a pecan grove with one of the largest pecan trees in South Carolina. Innkeepers Jim and Suzanne are full of information about the home's family history and the residents' ties to Revolutionary War heroes. A rich, plentiful breakfast is the perfect way to start off a day full of sightseeing and shopping or enjoying the area's many outdoor activities.

Innkeeper(s): Suzanne & Jim Brown. $85. AX TC. 3 rooms, 2 with PB. 1 suite. Breakfast included in rates. Type of meal: continental breakfast. Beds: QD. Air conditioning and turn-down service in room. Antiques nearby.

Seen in: Herald Journal News, Country, Sandlapper.

"A beautiful, restful experience. "

Certificate may be used: From April 1-March 31, Monday-Thursday.

South Dakota

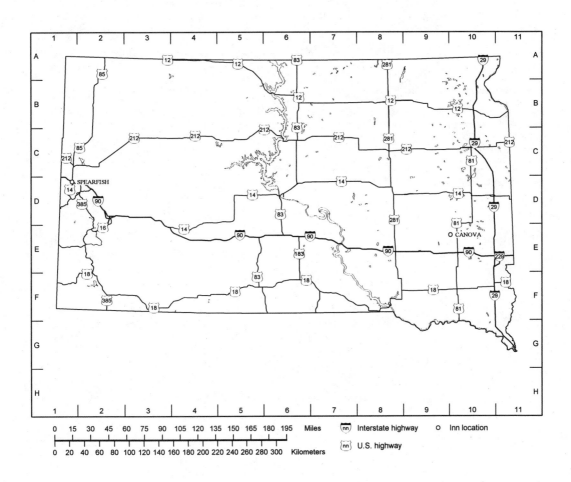

| | 0 | 15 | 30 | 45 | 60 | 75 | 90 | 105 | 120 | 135 | 150 | 165 | 180 | 195 | Miles |
| 0 | 20 | 40 | 60 | 80 | 100 | 120 | 140 | 160 | 180 | 200 | 220 | 240 | 260 | 280 | 300 | Kilometers |

Interstate highway   O   Inn location

U.S. highway

Canova
E10

B&B at Skoglund Farm

Rt 1 Box 45, Canova, SD 57321-9726
(605)247-3445

Circa 1917. This is a working farm on the South
Dakota prairie. Peacocks stroll around the farm along
with cattle, chickens
and other fowl.
Guests can enjoy an
evening meal with
the family. The
innkeepers offer spe-
cial rates for families
with children.

Innkeeper(s): Alden &
Delores Skoglund. $60. PC.
4 rooms. Breakfast and dinner included in rates. Types
of meals: full breakfast and early coffee/tea. Evening snack available.
Beds: QDT. VCR and library on premises. Antiques, fishing, parks,
shopping, sporting events and watersports nearby.

Location: Southeast South Dakota.

"Thanks for the down-home hospitality and good food."

Certificate may be used: Anytime.

Spearfish
D1

Eighth Street Inn

735 N 8th St, Spearfish, SD 57783-2147
(605)642-9812 (800)642-9812

Circa 1900. A mix of country furnishings and
antiques, some of which are family heirlooms, create
the warm, welcoming environment prevalent at this
National Register home. Beds are covered with
quilts and rooms showcase the innkeepers' old family photos. Guest rooms are named in honor of the
innkeepers' grandparents. Breakfast are hearty, but
include healthy offerings such as lean meats, fresh
fruits and homemade breads.

Innkeeper(s): Brad & Sandy Young. $55-85. MC VISA TC. 5 rooms, 1
with PB. 1 suite. Breakfast included in rates. Type of meal: full breakfast. Beds: QD. VCR and spa on premises. Amusement parks, antiques,
fishing, parks, shopping, downhill skiing, cross-country skiing, theater
and watersports nearby.

Certificate may be used: Oct. 1-May 25, Sunday-Saturday.

Tennessee

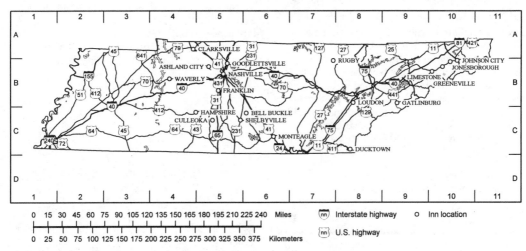

| | 1 | 2 | 3 | 4 | 5 | 6 | 7 | 8 | 9 | 10 | 11 |

0 15 30 45 60 75 90 105 120 135 150 165 180 195 210 225 240   Miles
0 25 50 75 100 125 150 175 200 225 250 275 300 325 350 375   Kilometers

{nn} Interstate highway   o Inn location
{nn} U.S. highway

Ashland City   B5

Bird Song Country Inn B&B
1306 Highway 49 E,
Ashland City, TN 37015-2848
(615)792-4005 Fax:(615)792-4005

Circa 1910. This rambling lodge-style house, in
the National Register of Historic Places, was built
with cedar logs by the Cheek family of Maxwell
House coffee fame. Handsome furnishings and an
art collection set off the chinked walls and beamed
ceilings. The inn boasts a screened-in front porch,
English gardens and green lawns. Hammocks swing
underneath walnut and cedar trees, and there are
peach and pear trees on the 10 acres. Hike or pic-

nic along Sycamore Creek, visit the barn or soak
in the heated spa.

Innkeeper(s): Anne & Brooks Parker. $90-100. MC VISA AX DS PC TC.
4 rooms, 3 with PB. 1 suite. Breakfast included in rates. Types of
meals: full breakfast, gourmet breakfast and early coffee/tea. Evening
snack, picnic lunch and catering service available. Beds: QD. Air conditioning and ceiling fan in room. Cable TV, VCR, fax, copier, spa and stables on premises. Antiques, fishing, parks, and watersports nearby.

"Hands down, the best B&B we have ever stayed in!
Wish we could come back every weekend."

Certificate may be used: Year-round except for holidays and weekends
(Friday/Saturday) on a space available basis.

Bell Buckle   C6

Spindle House B&B
201 Hinkle Hill, Bell Buckle, TN 37020
(615)389-6766

Circa 1920. This country home was built as a
boarding house, and the innkeepers have hosted
several of the former boarders as guests. Guests are
encouraged to relax at this comfortable house. From
the front porch, guests can rock away the hours and
watch as rail cars pass. Each of the rooms has a different theme. The Sewing Room contains a dress
form, while the Western Room commemorates the
Native American and Cowboy traditions.

Innkeeper(s): Sue Thelen. $55-65. AX. 4 rooms. Breakfast included in rates. Types of meals: full breakfast and gourmet breakfast. Afternoon tea available. Beds: QDT. Fishing nearby.

Seen in: Tullahoma News and Guardian.

Certificate may be used: All months except August.

Clarksville   A4

Hachland Hill Inn
1601 Madison St, Clarksville, TN 37043
(615)647-4084 Fax:(615)552-3454

Circa 1795. This log cabin contains a dining room and, in a stone-walled chamber, a place where pioneers sought refuge during Indian attacks. Three of Clarksville's oldest log houses have been reconstructed in the garden where old-fashioned barbeque suppers and square dances are held. Newly built rooms are available in the brick building, so request the log cabin if you want authentic historic atmosphere.
Innkeeper(s): Phila Hach. $65. MC VISA AX. 20 rooms, 10 with PB, 3 with FP. 1 conference room. Type of meal: full breakfast. Beds: D. Fax on premises. Handicap access.

Location: Near Nashville.

Certificate may be used: Anytime if rooms available.

Culleoka   C5

Sweetwater Inn B&B
2436 Campbells Station Rd,
Culleoka, TN 38451-2304
(615)987-3077

This gracious, turn-of-the-century home, adorned by wraparound porches on the first and second stories, is one of the few remaining relics from Culleoka's heyday as a thriving agricultural community. The innkeepers have restored the home's original beauty. Each of the bedchambers has a private entrance to the porch where guests can admire the view of Tennessee's rolling hills. A lavish, Southern breakfast is prepared each morning and served in fancy, formal style.
Innkeeper(s): Sandy Shotwell. $90-110. MC VISA. 4 rooms. Breakfast included in rates. Type of meal: full breakfast.

Certificate may be used: Sunday through Thursday, April 1 to Sept. 30; Oct. 1 to March 30, anytime.

Ducktown   C8

White House B&B
104 Main St, PO Box 668,
Ducktown, TN 37326
(423)496-4166 (800)775-4166
Fax:(423)496-4166

Circa 1898. This Queen Anne Victorian boasts a wraparound porch with a swing. Rooms are decorated in traditional style with family antiques. Innkeepers pamper their guests with Tennessee hospitality, a hearty country breakfast and a mouthwatering sundae bar in the evenings. The innkeepers also help guests plan daily activities, and the area is

bursting with possibilities. Hiking, horseback riding, panning for gold and driving tours are only a few choices. The Ocoee River is the perfect place for a river float trip or take on the challenge of roaring rapids. The river has been selected as the site of the 1996 Summer Olympic Whitewater Slalom events.
Innkeeper(s): Dan & Mardee Kauffman. $60-65. MC VISA DS PC TC. 3 rooms, 1 with PB. Breakfast, afternoon tea and evening snack included in rates. Types of meals: full breakfast and early coffee/tea. Catering service and catered breakfast available. Beds: QT. Air conditioning and ceiling fan in room. Cable TV, VCR, fax and library on premises. Antiques, fishing, parks, shopping and watersports nearby.

Seen in: Mountaineer Times.

"Thank you so very much for your hospitality. We were very comfortable and felt very much at home. And I better not forget to mention a most delicious breakfast."

Certificate may be used: Sunday through Thursday, April-November. Everyday, December through March. Holidays and special events excluded.

Franklin B5

Magnolia House B&B

1317 Columbia Ave, Franklin, TN 37064
(615)794-8178

In summer, a blooming Magnolia tree shades the wicker-filled front porch of this gabled Craftsman cottage. The land is where the Battle of Franklin was fought. Furnishings range from 19th-century Victorian and Empire pieces to an Eastlake bedroom

suite. The most popular breakfast here is Tennessee country ham, biscuits, cheese grits casserole and fresh fruit. An English flower garden and herb garden are in the back. Walk five blocks through a maple shaded neighborhood of historic houses to downtown Franklin, 15 blocks of which are in the National Register of Historic Places.
Innkeeper(s): Betty Blankenship. $60-70. 3 rooms. Breakfast included in rates. Types of meals: full breakfast and early coffee/tea. Air conditioning, turn-down service and ceiling fan in room. Cable TV and VCR on premises. Amusement parks, antiques, shopping and theater nearby.
Certificate may be used: Sunday through Thursday.

Namaste Acres Barn B&B

5436 Leipers Creek Rd,
Franklin, TN 37064-9208
(615)791-0333

This handsome Dutch Colonial is directly across the street from the original Natchez Trace. As the B&B is within walking distance of miles of hiking and horseback riding trails, the innkeepers offer free horse boarding for their guests. Each of the suites includes private entrances and feature individual themes. One room boasts rustic, cowboy decor with a clawfoot tub, hand-crafted furnishings, log and rope beds, and rough sawn lumber walls. The Franklin Quarters offers a sitting area where guests can settle down with a book from the large collection of historical material. The innkeepers chose the name Namaste from an Indian word, and carry an Indian theme in one of the guest rooms. Each of the quarters sleeps four comfortably. Namaste Acres is just 12 miles outside of historic Franklin, which

offers plenty of shops, a self-guided walking tour, Civil War sites and the largest assortment of antique dealers in the United States.
Innkeeper(s): Lisa Winters. $65-80. MC VISA AX. 3 rooms. Breakfast included in rates. Type of meal: full breakfast.
Certificate may be used: Year-round, Sunday-Thursday.

Gatlinburg B9

7th Heaven Log Inn on The Golf Resort

3944 Castle Rd, Gatlinburg, TN 37738
(423)430-5000 (800)248-2923
Fax:(423)436-7748

Circa 1991. Wake up to Eggs Benedict Mountain Style served on the deck among the tree tops and you'll start to understand the inn's name. There are views of the golf course, dogwood trees, wild ducks and hummingbirds. Decks stretch for two stories all around the inn. Across the road is the Smoky Mountain National Park. Ride America's largest aerial tram, try the 1,800-foot Alpine Slide or hike and picnic in the Smoky Mountain National Park.
Innkeeper(s): Cheryl & Donald Roese. $87-137. MC VISA DS PC TC. 4 rooms with PB. 1 suite. Breakfast and evening snack included in rates. Types of meals: full breakfast and early coffee/tea. Beds: KQD. Air conditioning and ceiling fan in room. Cable TV, VCR, fax, copier and sauna on premises. Amusement parks, antiques, fishing, parks, shopping, downhill skiing, sporting events, theater and watersports nearby.
Location: A short putt from the 7th green of Bent Creek Golf Resort.

"Five days was not enough. We'll be back."

Certificate may be used: Nov. 1-June 1, Sun.- Thurs. not on holidays.

Goodlettsville B5

Woodshire B&B

600 Woodshire Dr,
Goodlettsville, TN 37072-2931
(615)859-7369

Circa 1850. A gentle gray and white salt-box house, the Woodshire also includes a reconstructed mid-19th-century log cabin. John's woodcrafts and Beverly's weavings and paintings add to the home's antiques to provide a warm and personal decor. Homemade breads and biscuits are offered at breakfast. Opryland is eight miles away.
Innkeeper(s): Beverly Grayson. $40-70. 3 rooms. Breakfast included in rates. Type of meal: continental breakfast. Air conditioning and cable TV in room. Amusement parks, antiques, shopping, sporting events and theater nearby.
Certificate may be used: Any Monday through Thursday nights, no weekends.

Greeneville   B10

Hilltop House B&B
6 Sanford Cir, Greeneville, TN 37743
(423)639-8202

Circa 1920. Situated on a bluff overlooking the Nolichuckey River valley, this manor home boasts mountain views from each of the guest rooms. The Elizabeth Noel room, named for the original owner, includes among its treasures a canopy bed, sitting room and a private veranda, a perfect spot to watch the sunsets. After a hearty breakfast, take a stroll across the beautifully landscaped grounds. Innkeeper Denise Ashworth is a landscape architect and guests will marvel at her wonderful gardens. Ashworth sponsors several gardening workshops each year at the inn, covering topics such as flower arranging, Christmas decorations and landscaping your home grounds.

Innkeeper(s): Denise Ashworth. $70-75. MC VISA AX PC TC. 3 rooms with PB. Breakfast and afternoon tea included in rates. Types of meals: full breakfast, gourmet breakfast and early coffee/tea. Dinner, gourmet lunch and catering service available. Beds: KQD. Air conditioning, turn-down service, cable TV and VCR in room. Library on premises. Antiques, fishing, parks, shopping, theater and watersports nearby.

Seen in: Country Inns.

"Peaceful and comfortable, great change of pace."

Certificate may be used: January-April.

Hampshire   C4

Ridgetop B&B
Hwy 412 W, PO Box 193,
Hampshire, TN 38461-0193
(615)285-2777 (800)377-2770

Circa 1979. This contemporary Western cedar house rests on 20 cleared acres along the top of the ridge. A quarter-mile below is a waterfall. Blueberries grow in abundance on the property and guests may pick them in summer. These provide the filling for luscious breakfast muffins, waffles and pancakes year-round. There are 170 acres in all, mostly wooded. Picture windows and a deck provide views of the trees and wildlife: flying squirrels, birds, raccoons and deer. The inn is handicap-accessible. The innkeepers will help guests plan excursions on the Natchez Trace, including biking trips.

Innkeeper(s): Bill & Kay Jones. $65-85. MC VISA PC TC. 1 room with PB, 1 with FP. 2 cottages. Breakfast included in rates. Types of meals: full breakfast and early coffee/tea. Beds: DT. Air conditioning and ceiling fan in room. Handicap access. Antiques, fishing, parks, shopping and watersports nearby.

Seen in: Columbia Daily Herald.

Certificate may be used: Nov. 15-March 15; July 6-Aug. 31.

Johnson City   B10

Hart House B&B
207 E Holston Ave,
Johnson City, TN 37601-4612
(423)926-3147

Circa 1910. Antique shopping is a hobby of innkeepers Frank and Vanessa Gingras and this is evident in every nook and cranny of Hart House. The Dutch Colonial home is flanked by a wicker-filled porch complete with a swing, a perfect place to enjoy summer breezes. The cozy parlor and dining room each include a fireplace, as does one of the guest rooms. Breakfast treats such as quiche, pecan pancakes or Belgian waffles are served up each morning along with a variety of fresh fruit and breads. Johnson City is near a variety of antique shops, an outlet mall and the Appalachian Trail.

Innkeeper(s): Francis Gingras. $60. MC VISA AX DS. 3 rooms with PB. Breakfast included in rates. Type of meal: full breakfast. Beds: Q. Antiques, fishing, downhill skiing, cross-country skiing, theater and watersports nearby.

Seen in: Loafer.

"Impressive and charming throughout."

Certificate may be used: Anytime except first week in October.

Jonesborough   B10

Aiken-Brow House
104 S 3rd Ave, Jonesborough, TN 37659
(615)753-9440

Circa 1850. There's a beautiful gazebo on the grounds of this historic Greek Revival home, located a half-block from Main Street. There are porches for rocking and Victorian furnishings prevail. The inn is located in the Jonesborough Historic District.

Innkeeper(s): Calvin & Ann Brow. $65-100. TC. 3 rooms, 2 with PB. Breakfast included in rates. Types of meals: continental-plus breakfast, full breakfast and early coffee/tea. Beds: DT. Air conditioning in room. Cable TV on premises. Amusement parks, antiques, fishing, parks, shopping, downhill skiing, cross-country skiing, sporting events, theater and watersports nearby.

Seen in: Blue Ridge, East Tennessee.

Certificate may be used: All year, except Oct. 1-5, April 7-10 & Aug. 25 & 26, Monday, Tuesday, Wednesday & Thursday.

Bowling Green Inn B&B
901 W College St, Jonesborough, TN 37659-5253
(423)753-6356

Circa 1772. Eleven acres surround this recently restored farmhouse that once was a stagecoach stop on the Old Stage Road between Bristol and

Leesburg. Antique furnishings and country items decorate the inn. Jonesborough is Tennessee's oldest town and has retained its beautiful historic houses. Special events include Civil War reenactment weekend with its Confederate Memorial Ball, quilting festivals, historic days and the National Storytelling Festival.

Innkeeper(s): Donna & Perry Cleveland. $50-60. MC VISA PC. 7 rooms, 1 with PB. 3 suites. Breakfast included in rates. Type of meal: full breakfast. Beds: QDT. Air conditioning, cable TV and VCR in room. Handicap access. Amusement parks, antiques, fishing, parks, shopping, sporting events, theater and watersports nearby.

Certificate may be used: Depending on availability, anytime except Aug. 25-26, Oct. 6-7, April 26-27.

Limestone   B10

Snapp Inn B&B
1990 Davy Crockett Park Rd, Limestone,
TN 37681-6026
(423)257-2482

Circa 1815. From the second-story porch of this brick Federal, guests enjoy views of local farmland as well as the sounds of Big Limestone Creek. The Smoky Mountains are seen from the back porch. Decorated with locally gathered antiques, the home is within walking distance of Davy Crockett Birthplace State Park. A full country breakfast often includes Ruth's homemade biscuits.

Innkeeper(s): Ruth & Dan Dorgan. $50. PC TC. 2 rooms with PB. Breakfast included in rates. Types of meals: full breakfast and early coffee/tea. Beds: D. Air conditioning in room. Cable TV, VCR and library on premises. Antiques, fishing, parks, theater and watersports nearby.

Seen in: Greenville Sun.

Certificate may be used: Anytime, subject to availability.

Loudon   B8

The Mason Place B&B
600 Commerce St, Loudon, TN 37774
(423)458-3921

Circa 1865. In the National Register, Mason Place received an award for its outstanding restoration. In the Greek Revival style, the inn has a red slate roof,

graceful columns and a handsome double-tiered balcony overlooking three acres of lawns, trees and gardens. There are 10 working fireplaces, a Grecian swimming pool, gazebo and wisteria-covered arbor. A grand entrance hall, fine antiques and tasteful furnishings make for an elegant decor, suitable for the mansion's 7,000 square feet.

Innkeeper(s): Bob & Donna Siewert. $96-120. PC TC. 5 rooms with PB, 5 with FP. Breakfast included in rates. Types of meals: gourmet breakfast and early coffee/tea. Afternoon tea and picnic lunch available. Beds: QD. Air conditioning in room. Cable TV, VCR, swimming, bicycles, tennis and library on premises. Antiques, fishing, parks, shopping, sporting events, theater and watersports nearby.

Location: Smoky Mountains Cherokee National Forest.

Seen in: Country Inn, Country Side, Country Travels, Antiquing in Tennessee, Knox-Chattanooga, Oak Ridge, Detroit.

"Absolutely wonderful in every way. You are in for a treat! The best getaway ever!"

Certificate may be used: February & March, Tuesday, Wednesday only.

Monteagle   C6

Adams Edgeworth Inn
Monteagle Assembly,
Monteagle, TN 37356
(615)924-4000 Fax:(615)924-3236

Circa 1896. This National Register Victorian inn recently has been refurbished in an English-manor style. Original paintings, sculptures and fine English antiques are found throughout. Wide verandas are filled with white wicker furnishings and breezy

hammocks, and there's a prize-winning rose garden. You can stroll through the 96-acre Victorian village that surrounds the inn and enjoy rolling hills, creeks and Victorian cottages. Waterfalls, natural caves and scenic overlooks are along the 150 miles of hiking trails of nearby South Cumberland State Park.

Innkeeper(s): Wendy Adams. $70-195. MAP, EP. MC VISA AX. 12 rooms with PB, 4 with FP. 1 suite. 1 conference room. Breakfast included in rates. Types of meals: continental breakfast, gourmet breakfast and early coffee/tea. Dinner, picnic lunch, lunch and gourmet lunch available. Beds: KQDT. Air conditioning, turn-down service, ceiling fan and cable TV in room. VCR, fax, copier and spa on premises. Handicap access. Antiques, fishing, parks, sporting events and theater nearby.

Location: On top of the Cumberland Mountains between Nashville & Chattanooga on I-24.

Seen in: Country Inns, Chattanooga News Free Press, Tempo, Gourmet, Victorian Homes, Brides, Tennessean, Southern Living, PBS Crossroads, ABC TV, CBS TV.

"Leaving totally rejuvenated. Incredibly beautiful accommodations, welcome and gracious hosts, awesome food."

Certificate may be used: January and February, Monday-Thursday.

Nashville   B5

The Hillsboro House
1933 20th Ave S, Nashville, TN 37212
(615)292-5501

Circa 1904. The Hillsboro House is a cozy home base for guests wanting to experience the sites and sounds of Nashville. Vanderbilt University and famed Music Row are within walking distance from this Victorian home. After a dreamy night's sleep snuggled in a feather bed, guests are served a hearty homemade breakfast and head out for a day in Nashville, which offers a multitude of shops, outdoor activities and restaurants to explore.

Innkeeper(s): Andrea Beaudet. $75-85. MC VISA AX DS. 4 rooms, 3 with PB. Breakfast included in rates. Type of meal: continental breakfast. Beds: Q. Antiques and theater nearby.

"This is the real thing, as fresh and welcoming as the ingredients in your fabulous breakfasts. "

Certificate may be used: Sunday-Thursday, except during holidays and special events.

Rugby   B7

Newbury House at Historic Rugby
Hwy 52, PO Box 8, Rugby, TN 37733
(423)628-2430 Fax:(423)628-2266

Circa 1880. Mansard-roofed Newbury House first lodged visitors to this English village when author and social reformer Thomas Hughes founded Rugby. Filled with authentic Victorian antiques, the inn includes some furnishings that are original to the colony. There are also several restored cottages on the property.

Innkeeper(s): Historic Rugby. $62-72. MC VISA PC TC. 5 rooms, 3 with PB. 2 cottages. Breakfast and afternoon tea included in rates. Types of meals: full breakfast and early coffee/tea. Dinner, picnic lunch, lunch and banquet service available. Beds: D. Air conditioning and ceiling fan in room. Library on premises. Antiques, fishing, parks, shopping and watersports nearby.

Seen in: New York Times, Americana, USA Weekend, Tennessean, Southern Living, Atlanta Journal Constitution, Victorian Homes, Los Angeles Times

"I love the peaceful atmosphere here and the beauty of nature surrounding Rugby."

Certificate may be used: Nov. 1 through March 31, excluding Friday and Saturday nights.

Shelbyville   C5

Cinnamon Ridge B&B
799 Whitthorne St,
Shelbyville, TN 37160-3501
(615)685-9200 Fax:(615)684-0978

Circa 1927. Tennessee offers many reasons to visit, not the least of which is this hospitable home. The light scent of cinnamon permeates the home, which is decorated with antiques in a mix of Colonial and Traditional styles. Innkeeper Pat Sherrill loves to pamper guests, especially with food. The full breakfasts are accompanied by candlelight and soft, soothing music. Pat serves afternoon teas and has created a few special events, including her Chocolate Lovers' Paradise, where guests enjoy a variety of cocoa-laden delicacies.

Innkeeper(s): Bill & Pat Sherrill. $55-65. MC VISA AX TC. 5 rooms with PB. 1 conference room. Breakfast, afternoon tea and evening snack included in rates. Types of meals: full breakfast and early coffee/tea. Beds: KQT. Air conditioning, ceiling fan and cable TV in room. VCR, fax and bicycles on premises. Amusement parks, antiques, fishing, parks, shopping, theater and watersports nearby.

Certificate may be used: Jan. 7 to Nov. 13, Sunday through Wednesday.

Waverly
B4

Nolan House Inn
375 Hwy 13 N, Waverly, TN 37185
(615)296-2511

Circa 1870. This National Register home was built by prominent businessman James Nolan, who among his many occupations ran the Nolan House Hotel. The innkeepers have maintained Nolan's reputation for excellent hospitality at their Victorian-style inn, which features 19th-century furnishings throughout the home. The grounds boast walking trails, an old-fashioned stone fountain, gazebo and flower gardens. The inn also houses a gift shop where guests can find handmade gifts, antique collectibles and original artwork created by innkeeper Laverne Turner.

Innkeeper(s): Linda & Patrick O'Lee. $60-75. TC. 3 rooms with PB, 1 with FP. 1 conference room. Breakfast and afternoon tea included in rates. Types of meals: continental-plus breakfast, full breakfast and early coffee/tea. Beds: QD. Air conditioning in room. Cable TV and VCR on premises. Antiques, parks and shopping nearby.

Certificate may be used: March through June (Spring).

Texas

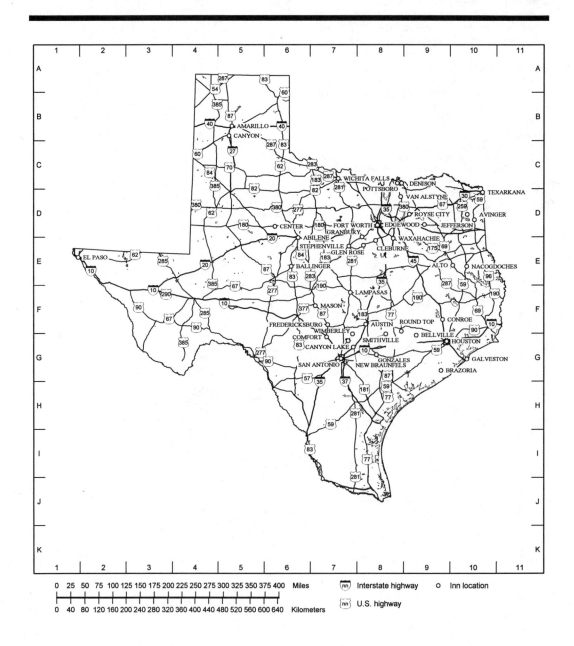

0 25 50 75 100 125 150 175 200 225 250 275 300 325 350 375 400 Miles

0 40 80 120 160 200 240 280 320 360 400 440 480 520 560 600 640 Kilometers

{nn} Interstate highway   o Inn location

{nn} U.S. highway

Abilene   E6

Bolin's Prairie House B&B
508 Mulberry St, Abilene, TX 79601-4908
(915)675-5855 (800)673-5855

Circa 1902. This B&B was completely redesigned in 1920, omitting all references to the previous Victorian architecture and transforming into a prairie-style home. The home is filled with country antiques and knickknacks. Rooms bear the names Love, Joy, Peace and Patience, all clues to the relaxing, hospitable atmosphere. Peace includes a huge clawfoot tub.

Innkeeper(s): Sam & Ginny Bolin. $50-65. MC VISA AX TC. 4 rooms, 2 with PB. Breakfast included in rates. Type of meal: full breakfast. Beds: KQFT. Ceiling fan in room. Cable TV and VCR on premises. Antiques, fishing, parks, shopping, sporting events, theater and watersports nearby.

Certificate may be used: Sunday through Thursday.

Alto   E10

Lincrest Lodge
Hwy 21 E, PO Box 799, Alto, TX 75925
(409)858-2223 Fax:(409)858-2232

The lush 16 acres surrounding this expansive Dutch Colonial Home overlook the Angelina River Valley. Many of the suites offer views of the beautiful valley. Hearty breakfasts are served each morning, and the porch cafe is a perfect place to enjoy the scenery

and a variety of deli treats. Box lunches can be prepared. The innkeepers serve an afternoon tea, which is followed on most nights by a country buffet dinner. The Alto area is an important historic area for Indian, Spanish and Texan colonization. Davy Crocket National Forest and Nacogdoches, the oldest town in Texas, are nearby attractions.

Innkeeper(s): Chester Woj. $75. MC VISA AX. 6 rooms. Breakfast included in rates. Type of meal: full breakfast.

Certificate may be used: All year, anytime, except Valentine weekend, Thanksgiving and Christmas weekends.

Amarillo   B5

Parkview House B&B
1311 S Jefferson St,
Amarillo, TX 79101-4029
(806)373-9464

Circa 1908. Ionic columns support the wraparound wicker-filled front porch of this gabled grandma's Victorian. Herb and rose gardens surround the property and the back garden has a Victorian gazing ball. Antique mahogany, walnut and oak pieces are found throughout. The French, Colonial, Dutch and Victorian Rose rooms all feature draped bedsteads and romantic decor. Sticky buns, homemade granola and fruits are served in kitchen or dining room. Guests can enjoy a soak under the stars in the inn's hot tub or borrow a bicycle for a tour of the historic neighborhood. Dinners are available with advance reservations.

Innkeeper(s): Carol & Nabil Dia. $65-105. MC VISA AX PC TC. 5 rooms, 3 with PB. 1 suite. 1 cottage. Breakfast and evening snack included in rates. Types of meals: continental breakfast, continental-plus breakfast, gourmet breakfast and early coffee/tea. Beds: QD. Air conditioning in room. Cable TV, VCR, fax, computer and bicycles on premises. Amusement parks, antiques, parks, shopping, theater and watersports nearby.

Seen in: Lubbock Avalanche, Amarillo Globe News, Accent West, Sunday Telegraph Review.

"You are what give B&B's such a wonderful reputation. Thanks very much for the wonderful stay! The hospitality was warm and the ambiance incredible."

Certificate may be used: Anytime, excluding holidays or weekends, Christmas, New Year's, Valentine's, Memorial Day, Mother's and Father's Day, etc.

Austin   F8

Carrington's Bluff
1900 David St, Austin, TX 78705-5312
(512)479-0638 (800)871-8908
Fax:(512)476-4769

Circa 1877. Situated on a tree-covered bluff in the heart of Austin, this inn sits next to a 500-year-old oak tree. The innkeepers, one a Texan, the other British, combine down-home hospitality with English charm. The house is filled with English and American antiques and handmade quilts. Rooms are carefully decorated with dried flowers, inviting colors and antique beds, such as the oak barley twist bed in the Martha Hill Carrington Room. After a hearty breakfast, relax on a 35-foot-long porch that overlooks the bluff. The Austin area is booming with things to do.

Innkeeper(s): Lisa & Edward Mugford. $69-99. MC VISA AX DC CB DS PC TC. 8 rooms, 6 with PB. 1 suite. 1 cottage. 1 conference room. Breakfast and evening snack included in rates. Types of meals: full breakfast, gourmet breakfast and early coffee/tea. Beds: KQDT. Air conditioning, ceiling fan and cable TV in room. VCR, fax, copier, library and child care on premises. Amusement parks, antiques, fishing, parks, shopping, sporting events, theater and watersports nearby.

Location: Downtown.

Seen in: PBS Special.

"Victorian writer's dream place."

Certificate may be used: Jan. 2 to Dec. 24, Sunday-Thursday.

Governors' Inn

611 W 22nd St, Austin, TX 78705-5115
(512)479-0638 Fax:(512)479-0638

Circa 1897. This Neo-Classical Victorian is just a few blocks from the University of Texas campus, and once served as a fraternity. Guests can enjoy the view of two acres of trees and foliage from the porches which decorate each story of the inn. The innkeepers have decorated the guest rooms with antiques and named them after former Texas governors. Several of the bathrooms include clawfoot tubs.
Innkeeper(s): Lisa & Edward Mugford. $69-99. MC VISA AX DC CB DS TC. 10 rooms with PB, 5 with FP. 1 conference room. Breakfast, afternoon tea and evening snack included in rates. Types of meals: full breakfast, gourmet breakfast and early coffee/tea. Picnic lunch, banquet service and catering service available. Beds: KQF. Air conditioning, turndown service, ceiling fan and cable TV in room. VCR, fax and copier on premises. Handicap access. Amusement parks, antiques, fishing, parks, shopping, sporting events, theater and watersports nearby.

Certificate may be used: January 2 to Dec. 24, Sunday-Thursday.

Woodburn House B&B

4401 Avenue D, Austin, TX 78751-3714
(512)458-4335 Fax:(512)458-4319

Circa 1909. This stately home was named for Bettie Hamilton Woodburn, who bought the house in 1920. Hamilton's father was once the provisional governor of Texas and a friend of Abraham Lincoln. The home once was slated for demolition and saved in 1978 when George Boutwell bought the home for $10 and moved it to its present location. A friendly

dog greets guests who will be taken immediately by the warmth of the home surrounded by old trees. The home is furnished with family antiques. Breakfasts are served on the wraparound verandas.
Innkeeper(s): Herb & Sandra Dickson. $79-89. MC VISA AX PC TC. 4 rooms with PB. Breakfast included in rates. Types of meals: gourmet breakfast and early coffee/tea. Beds: KQ. Air conditioning and ceiling fan in room. Cable TV, VCR and fax on premises. Antiques, fishing, parks, shopping, sporting events and theater nearby.

Seen in: Austin Chronicle.

"The comfort, the breakfasts and the hospitality were excellent and greatly appreciated."

Certificate may be used: Sunday-Thursday, no holidays, excluding February, March, April, October & November.

Ballinger E6

Miz Virginia's B&B

107 S 6th St, Ballinger, TX 76821-5714
(915)365-2453 (800)344-0781

Circa 1886. Serving the community as a hotel and boarding house since before the turn of the century, this inn stands as one of the oldest buildings in town. An antique store and restaurant are now on the premises of the B&B. Guests can browse through collectibles. After getting a taste of shopping, there's more to be found in town with quaint shops of antiques, pottery, woodworking, arts and crafts. Courthouse Square hosts many festivities, including an annual Ethnic Festival and Christmas in Olde Ballinger.
Innkeeper(s): Juanita Chrisco. $45-65. MC VISA AX DS PC TC. 7 rooms, 2 with PB. 2 suites. Breakfast included in rates. Types of meals: full breakfast and early coffee/tea. Dinner available. Beds: D. Air conditioning in room. Cable TV, VCR and spa on premises. Amusement parks, antiques, parks, shopping, sporting events and watersports nearby.

Certificate may be used: Year-round.

Bellville G9

High Cotton Inn

214 S Live Oak St,
Bellville, TX 77418-2340
(409)865-9796 (800)321-9796
Fax:(409)865-5588

Use of the downstairs parlor, fenced swimming pool and bottomless cookie jar is encouraged at this Victorian B&B. Porch swings are strategically located on the balcony and front porch. There's a cozy upstairs sitting room for reading, television or conversation. Around 9 a.m. each morning, guests gather in the old family dining room for a full Southern-style breakfast. Innkeepers can provide information on excursions to Blue Bell Creamery, Winedale, Round Top and Festival Hill.

Innkeeper(s): Anna Horton. $50-60. 5 rooms. Breakfast included in rates. Type of meal: full breakfast. Air conditioning and ceiling fan in room. Cable TV on premises. Antiques nearby.

Certificate may be used: Sunday through Thursday.

Brazoria   G9

Roses and The River
7074 CR 506, Brazoria, TX 77422
(409)798-1070 (800)610-1070
Fax:(409)798-1070

Circa 1982. The San Bernard River provides the scenery at this farmhouse. Aside from the view from the home's wraparound veranda, lined with rockers, a path leads to a riverside deck. A swing also hangs nearby from one of the many trees that grace the two acres. Bright, cheery rooms boast such names as New Dawn or Rise 'n' Shine, all rose varieties that grow in the area. Rainbow's End features window seats and a clawfooted, whirlpool tub. The breakfasts include anything from orange coolers to baked Alaska grapefruit to savory egg dishes. A historical museum, Varner-Hogg State Historical Park and a marine center all are nearby.

Innkeeper(s): Mary Jo & Dick Hosack. $94. MC VISA PC. 3 rooms with PB. Breakfast and evening snack included in rates. Types of meals: full breakfast and early coffee/tea. Beds: Q. Air conditioning, turn-down service, ceiling fan, cable TV and VCR in room. Fax and copier on premises. Antiques, fishing, parks, shopping, theater and watersports nearby.

Certificate may be used: Sunday through Thursday nights.

Canyon   B5

Country Home B&B
RR 1 Box 447, Canyon, TX 79015-9743
(806)655-7636 (800)664-7636

Circa 1989. This bed & breakfast is, as the title suggests, a quaint country home located on an acre of ground that offers a restful porch swing and a gazebo. Each of the two guest rooms share a bath with a clawfoot tub. Flowered prints, iron beds, candles, family heirlooms and antiques add to the country ambiance. Guests enjoy use of an outdoor hot tub. Homemade muffins, fresh fruit and specialties such as quiche often appear at the breakfast table.

Innkeeper(s): Tammy & Dennis Brooks. $70-85. MC VISA AX DS PC TC. 2 rooms. 1 cottage. Breakfast and evening snack included in rates. Types of meals: continental-plus breakfast, full breakfast and early coffee/tea. Beds: D. Air conditioning in room. VCR, spa and bicycles on premises. Amusement parks, antiques, parks, shopping and theater nearby.

Certificate may be used: October-April, Sunday-Thursday.

Historical Hudspeth House
1905 4th Ave, Canyon, TX 79015-4023
(806)655-9800 (800)655-9809
Fax:(806)655-7457

Circa 1909. Artist Georgia O'Keefe was once a guest at this three-story prairie home, which serves as a bed & breakfast and health spa. Guests can take exercise classes, learn about diet and skin-care issues or enjoy a relaxing massage. A cosmetologist and fashion consultant are on staff, so guests can leave refreshed and with a new look at the same time. The home boasts many impressive architectural features, including an expansive entry with stained glass and a grandfather clock. The parlor boasts 12-foot ceilings and antiques, other rooms include chandeliers and huge fireplaces. Breakfasts are served by candlelight in the guest's room, and guests also can arrange candlelit dinners.

Innkeeper(s): Mark & Mary Clark. $55-110. MC VISA AX DS PC TC. 8 rooms with PB, 5 with FP. 2 suites. 2 conference rooms. Breakfast included in rates. Type of meal: early coffee/tea. Beds: KQ. Air conditioning, ceiling fan and cable TV in room. Fax, copier and spa on premises. Amusement parks, antiques, parks, sporting events and theater nearby.

Certificate may be used: Sunday-Thursday, September-April, holidays excluded.

Canyon Lake   G7

Aunt Nora's B&B
120 Naked Indian Tr, New Braunfels, Canyon Lake, TX 78132
(210)905-3989 (800)687-2887

Circa 1983. Nestled on four acres, amid oak, cedar and Indian trees, this Texas country inn has many nearby scenic areas that include a walk to the top of the hill to view Canyon Lake. The sitting room is a perfect place to relax among handmade furnishings, antiques, paintings, lacy crafts, a wood stove and natural wood floors. Enjoy the private collection of Pigtails & Lace hand-crafted dolls. The guest rooms are decorated with country curtains, natural woodwork, handmade maple and cherry wood furnishings, ceiling fans and quilts.

Innkeeper(s): J. Haley. $75-150. 4 rooms. Breakfast included in rates. Types of meals: continental breakfast and full breakfast. Air conditioning and ceiling fan in room. Spa on premises. Amusement parks, shopping and sporting events nearby.

Certificate may be used: November through March, Sunday through Thursday, excluding special events and holidays.

Holiday Lodge
537 Skyline Dr,
Canyon Lake, TX 78133-4894
(210)964-3693

This lodge was one of the first buildings to be constructed on this lakeside land, which was part of a colony of German settlers. The German influence still permeates the area, and many of the colonists' ancestors live in the area, the site of a heavily attended German festival. The innkeepers have turned this country motel into a special place. The comfortable rooms are decorated with oak dressers, antiques and each guest room includes a kitchenette. The grounds include picnic areas and barbecue grills.

Innkeeper(s): Doyle Patton. $85-95. MC VISA AX. 8 rooms. Breakfast included in rates.

Certificate may be used: Oct. 1 through March 1.

Center   D6

Pine Colony Inn
500 Shelbyville St,
Center, TX 75935-3732
(409)598-7700

Circa 1940. This inn is a restored hotel with more than 8,000 square feet of antique-filled rooms. Artwork from local artist Woodrow Foster adorns

the walls. These limited-edition prints are framed and sold by the innkeepers. The town is located between Toledo Bend, which has one of the largest man-made lakes in the United States, and Lake Pinkston, where the state record bass (just under 17 pounds) was caught in 1986. Ask the innkeepers about all the little-out-of-the-way places to see either by foot, bicycle or car.

Innkeeper(s): Marcille Hughes. $55-75. MC VISA. 10 rooms with PB. 4 suites. Breakfast included in rates. Types of meals: full breakfast and early coffee/tea. Air conditioning, turn-down service, ceiling fan, cable

TV and VCR in room. Amusement parks, antiques, fishing, parks, shopping, sporting events and watersports nearby.

Location: Near Louisiana border.

Certificate may be used: All days except Thanksgiving Day, Christmas Eve. All other days are acceptable.

Cleburne   E8

Anglin Queen Anne B&B
723 N Anglin St,
Cleburne, TX 76031-3905
(817)645-5555

Circa 1892. This home, which was once owned by a cattle baron, is dominated by a three-story cupola set between two second-story porches. The first story includes a large round veranda with porch posts and gingerbread fretwork. The mansion's interior is embellished with wood paneling, molding and fancy carvings. Two main staircases have elaborate grillwork, paneling and stained glass. The dining rooms include a Northwind dining set, Oriental warlord's chair and a carved chair set from a European guest house.

Innkeeper(s): Billie Anne Leach. $49-149. 5 rooms. 1 suite. 1 conference room. Breakfast included in rates. Types of meals: continental-plus breakfast and early coffee/tea. Dinner, evening snack, picnic lunch, lunch, gourmet lunch, banquet service, catering service, catered breakfast and room service available. Air conditioning, ceiling fan and VCR in room. Amusement parks, antiques, shopping, sporting events and theater nearby.

Certificate may be used: Yearly.

Comfort   G7

Idlewilde
115 Hwy 473, Comfort, TX 78013
(210)995-3844

Circa 1902. This Western-style farmhouse and cottages has come to be known as "Haven in the Hills." The home and surrounding grounds were a girls' summer camp for more than 60 years. The inn has no set check-in or check-out times. The innkeepers offer breakfast either in the main house dining area or at your specified spot (which could be breakfast in bed). The large, unique hallways and

center rooms are open and airy with lots of windows. Antiques and country French furniture decorate the entire lodge.

Innkeeper(s): Hank Engel & Connie Cazel. $77-93. MC VISA. 2 cottages, 1 with FP. 1 suite. 1 conference room. Breakfast included in rates. Type of meal: full breakfast. Picnic lunch available. Beds: Q. Amusement parks, antiques, fishing, shopping, sporting events and watersports nearby.

Location: Forty-five miles West of San Antonio.

Seen in: Austin Chronicle, Hill Country Recorder.

"Everyone should make a hobby of visiting B&Bs. Idlewilde should be at the top of their list."

Certificate may be used: Sunday through Thursday night, year-round, except holidays.

Conroe   F9

Heather's Glen . . . A B&B

200 E Phillips St, Conroe, TX 77301-2646
(409)441-6611 (800)665-2643
Fax:(409)441-6603

Circa 1900. This turn-of-the-century mansion still maintains many of its original features, such as heart-of-pine flooring, gracious staircases and antique glass windows. Verandas and covered porches decorate the exterior, creating ideal places to relax. Guest rooms are decorated in a romantic, country flavor. One room has a bed draped with a lacy canopy, and two rooms include double Jacuzzi tubs. Antique shops, an outlet mall and Lake Conroe are nearby, and the home is within an hour of Houston.

Innkeeper(s): Ed & Jamie George. $65-95. MC VISA AX DS PC TC. 6 rooms, 5 with PB, 3 with FP. 1 suite. 3 conference rooms. Breakfast, afternoon tea and evening snack included in rates. Types of meals: full breakfast and early coffee/tea. Beds: QD. Air conditioning, turn-down service, ceiling fan and cable TV in room. Fax, copier, sauna, library and pet boarding on premises. Handicap access. Amusement parks, antiques, fishing, parks, shopping, downhill skiing, sporting events, theater and watersports nearby.

Certificate may be used: Anytime except weekends & holidays.

Denison   C8

Ivy Blue B&B

1100 W Sears St,
Denison, TX 75020-3326
(903)463-2479 (888)489-2583
Fax:(903)465-6773

Circa 1899. This Victorian charmer is set on a manicured lawn and shaded by several large trees. Guest rooms are named in honor of previous owners. Some of the furnishings and antiques that decorate the rooms are original to the home. Old newspaper

clippings, antique dress patterns, historical documents and a time capsule are among the unique surprises guests might discover in their rooms. Fresh flowers, fragrant soaps and sachets add a touch of romance. Breakfasts are served on tables set with lace and antique china. Such items as banana almond waffles or bread pudding topped with berry sauce get the morning off to a great start. The inn's carriage house, which contains Lois' Cottage and the Feild Suite, is an ideal spot for children or for those who prefer a bit more privacy. Carriage house guests may opt to enjoy breakfast in their room.

Innkeeper(s): Lane & Tammy Segerstrom. $65-145. MC VISA AX PC TC. 6 rooms with PB. 4 suites. 2 cottages. Breakfast and evening snack included in rates. Types of meals: gourmet breakfast and early coffee/tea. Afternoon tea, picnic lunch, lunch and room service available. Beds: KDT. Air conditioning, turn-down service, ceiling fan and cable TV in room. VCR, fax, swimming and library on premises. Handicap access. Antiques, fishing, parks, shopping and watersports nearby.

Certificate may be used: Anytime.

Edgewood   D9

Crooked Creek Farm B&B

RR 1 Box 180, Edgewood, TX 75117-9709
(903)896-1284 (800)766-0790

Circa 1977. This traditional brick farmhouse, which is found in a rural community of 1,300, is nestled on the edge of the East Texas timberline. The farm covers more than 100 acres. Cattle are raised here and there are trees, creeks, a nature trail, ponds and four fishing tanks on the property. A hearty breakfast may feature country ham and bacon, eggs, biscuits and gravy and a fruit dish. In town, an ongoing bicentennial project includes a museum and 14 authentically restored and furnished structures representing rural life in 1900.

Innkeeper(s): Dorthy Thornton. $65-75. 6 rooms. Breakfast included in rates. Types of meals: full breakfast and early coffee/tea. Air conditioning and ceiling fan in room. Cable TV and VCR on premises. Antiques and shopping nearby.

Certificate may be used: All year, except "Canton Texas," first Monday weekend each month.

El Paso   E1

Sunset Heights B&B

717 W Yandell Dr, El Paso, TX 79902
(915)544-1743 (800)767-8513
Fax:(915)544-5119

Circa 1905. This luxurious inn is accentuated by palm trees and Spanish-style arches. Inside, bedrooms are filled with antiques and boast brass and four-poster beds. Breakfast is a five- to eight-course

feast prepared by innkeeper Richard Barnett. On any morning, a guest might awake to sample a breakfast with Southwestern flair, including Eggs Chillquillas and pit-smoked Machakas, a combination of smoked beef, avocado and onion. Juice, fresh coffee, tea, dessert and fresh fruits top off the meal, which might begin with caviar and quiche. Enjoy the morning meal in the dining room or have breakfast in bed.

Innkeeper(s): R. Barnett & Ms. R. Martinez, M.D. $75-200. MC VISA AX DS PC TC. 5 rooms with PB, 1 with FP. 1 suite. 1 cottage. 1 conference room. Breakfast included in rates. Types of meals: full breakfast and gourmet breakfast. Dinner and picnic lunch available. Beds: KQD. Air conditioning, turn-down service, ceiling fan, cable TV and VCR in room. Fax, copier, spa and swimming on premises. Amusement parks, antiques, parks, shopping and sporting events nearby.

Location: Near downtown and the university.

Seen in: Southwest Profile.

Certificate may be used: Year-round, except holidays, Sun Bowl week, Christmas or New Year's week.

Fort Worth   D8

Miss Molly's Hotel
109 1/2 W Exchange Ave,
Fort Worth, TX 76106-8508
(817)626-1522 (800)996-6559
Fax:(817)625-2723

Circa 1910. An Old West flair adds charm to this hotel, which once was a house of ill repute. Miss Josie's Room, named for the former madame, is decked with elaborate wall and ceiling coverings and carved oak furniture. The Gunslinger Room is filled with pictures of famous and infamous gunsmen. Rodeo memorabilia decorates the Rodeo Room, and twin iron beds and a pot belly stove add flair to the Cowboy's Room. Telephones and TV sets are the only things missing from the rooms, as the innkeeper hopes to preserve the flavor of the past.

Innkeeper(s): Mark Hancock & Alice Williams. $85-150. MC VISA AX DC CB DS PC TC. 8 rooms, 1 with PB. Breakfast included in rates. Types of meals: continental-plus breakfast and early coffee/tea. Restaurant on premises. Beds: TD. Air conditioning and ceiling fan in room. Fax and copier on premises. Amusement parks, antiques, shopping, sporting events and theater nearby.

Seen in: British Bulldog, Arkansas Gazette, Dallas Morning News, Fort Worth Star-Telegram, Continental Profiles.

Certificate may be used: Year-round, Monday through Thursday, excluding holidays and Stockyards annual special event dates.

Fredericksburg   F7

Allegani's Little Horse Inn
307 S Creek St,
Fredericksburg, TX 78624-4652
(210)997-7448

Circa 1917. This historic ranch house is an ideal way to travel with a family. The home offers two bedrooms and a sleeping porch, as well as a fireplace kitchen, living room and dining area. The front porch includes a swing, and there's also a Jacuzzi tub. Children and pets are welcome in this unit, which is owned by Jani Schofield, the artist who runs the Allegani's Sunday Haus. The Little Horse Inn is just a few blocks from shops and restaurants.

Innkeeper(s): Jani Schofield. $85-150. 3 rooms. Breakfast included in rates. Type of meal: continental breakfast.

Certificate may be used: Weekdays of January, February, May, August and December, no event weekends.

Allegani's Sunday Haus
418 W Creek St,
Fredericksburg, TX 78624-3114
(210)997-7448

Nearly a century ago, German ranchers and farmers used a "Sunday house" as a place in town where they could go and visit with their neighbors. Allegani's Sunday House was used by Alfred Mohr and his family, and the neighborhood is full of German and Victorian flair. Innkeeper Jani Schofield is a folk artist and created some of the furniture seen in the house. Lacy curtains, folk art, antiques and hand-painted pieces add to the charming country decor.

Innkeeper(s): Jani Schofield. $65-95. 2 rooms. Breakfast included in rates. Type of meal: continental breakfast.

Certificate may be used: January, February, May, August, September, December. Not on event weekends.

Country Cottage Inn Nimitz Birthplace
249 E Main St,
Fredericksburg, TX 78624-4114
(210)997-8549 Fax:(210)997-8549

Circa 1850. This beautifully preserved house was built by blacksmith and cutler Frederick Kiehne. With two-foot-thick walls, it was the first two-story limestone house in town. The Country Cottage holds a collection of Texas primitives and German country antiques, accentuated by Laura Ashley linens. Some of the baths include whirlpool tubs. The innkeepers have restored a second historic house, a block away, which is also available. Full regional-style breakfasts are brought to each room.

Innkeeper(s): Mary Lou Rodriquez. $80-120. MC VISA PC. 11 rooms with PB, 7 with FP. 9 suites. 1 conference room. Breakfast included in rates. Types of meals: full breakfast and early coffee/tea. Beds: KQD. Air conditioning, ceiling fan and cable TV in room. VCR and fax on premises. Handicap access. Antiques, fishing, parks and watersports nearby.

Seen in: Weekend Getaway, Dallas Morning News, Glamour, Texas B&B.

"A step back in time in 1850 style."

Certificate may be used: Year-round, Monday-Wednesday, excluding holiday periods, spring breaks & local special events.

East of The Sun-West of The Moon

512 W Austin St,
Fredericksburg, TX 78624-3210
(210)997-4981 (800)865-9668

Circa 1903. Having been recently remodeled to restore its charm and pioneer spirit, this yellow house has furnishings and decor that include an eclectic mix of Western, country antiques and a few contemporary pieces. Upon arrival, guests join the innkeepers for wine and cheese during a "get-acquainted time." Located one block north of Main Street, the inn is within walking distance of shopping, restaurants and entertainment. The living room has a wood-burning fireplace for cool, hill country evenings.

Innkeeper(s): Mark & Teresa Ray. $85. MC VISA TC. 2 rooms. Breakfast included in rates. Beds: QT. Air conditioning and ceiling fan in room. Cable TV on premises.

Certificate may be used: Sunday-Thursday, excluding holidays.

Magnolia House

101 E Hackberry St,
Fredericksburg, TX 78624-3915
(210)997-0306 (800)880-4374
Fax:(210)997-0766

Circa 1923. This Craftsman-style home is listed as a Texas Historic Landmark and was built by the same man who designed the Gillespie County Courthouse as well as many other local buildings. There are porches filled with wicker furnishings for those who wish to relax. Guest rooms are decorated with antiques and reproductions. The Bluebonnet Suite includes a wood-burning fireplace, antique clawfoot tub and a vintage refrigerator in the small kitchen. Southern-style breakfasts are served on tables set with antique china and silver. Guests enjoy privileges at a nearby fitness club. The home is located about seven blocks from the main shopping area, and museums, wineries and the Lyndon Johnson State and National Park is 16 miles away.

Innkeeper(s): Joyce & Patrick Kennard. $75-125. MC VISA PC TC. 6 rooms, 4 with PB, 2 with FP. 2 suites. Breakfast and evening snack included in rates. Types of meals: full breakfast, gourmet breakfast and early coffee/tea. Beds: KQ. Air conditioning, ceiling fan and cable TV in room. VCR on premises. Antiques, fishing, parks and shopping nearby.

Certificate may be used: April 1-Dec. 31, Sunday-Thursday, excluding holidays & special events.

Galveston G10

Carousel Inn

712 Tenth St, Galveston, TX 77550-5116
(409)762-2166

Circa 1886. The Carousel Inn stands as a testament to Texas stamina. The home, located in a historic Galveston neighborhood, was one of few left standing after a fierce storm ripped through the Gulf in 1900. The inn's namesake, a hand-carved carousel horse, decorates the parlor. The guest rooms are inviting with special touches such as leaf pine walls, a private porch swing or a roomy pineapple bed. The carriage house offers the added amenity of a sitting area, private entrance and antique walnut bed. The innkeepers offer a variety of home-baked treats each morning, served up in the cheerful breakfast room. The home is near many Galveston attractions including a rail museum, a tall ship and many shops and restaurants.

Innkeeper(s): Jim & Kathleen Hughes. $80-95. MC VISA AX DS PC TC. 4 rooms, 3 with PB. 1 suite. Breakfast included in rates. Types of meals: continental-plus breakfast and early coffee/tea. Afternoon tea and picnic lunch available. Beds: KQD. Air conditioning and ceiling fan in room. Bicycles and library on premises. Amusement parks, antiques, fishing, shopping, theater and watersports nearby.

Certificate may be used: Sept. 5-March 31, Sunday-Thursday.

Hazelwood House B&B Inn

PO Box 1326, Galveston, TX 77553-1326
(409)762-1668

Circa 1877. Charles Cleveland, a young lawyer, built this romantic Victorian for his bride and presented it to her as a wedding gift. The second owner also presented the home to his young wife as a present, gift-wrapped with gingerbread trim and all the whimsical touches typical of Victorian Era design. Guests enjoy almost complete privacy. The innkeeper keeps the refrigerator stocked with breakfast goodies and a tray of wine and cheese awaits guests upon arrival. Instructions and directions concerning the home are provided for guests and then it's up to them to relax and enjoy.

Innkeeper(s): Pat Hazlewood. $55-150. EP. 3 rooms with PB. 1 suite. Breakfast and evening snack included in rates. Types of meals: continental-plus breakfast and early coffee/tea. Beds: KQD. Air conditioning, ceiling fan and cable TV in room. Antiques, fishing, parks, shopping, sporting events, theater and watersports nearby.

Certificate may be used: Sunday through Thursday.

Michael's B&B

1715 35th St, Galveston, TX 77550-6717
(409)763-3760 (800)776-8302

Circa 1916. Built by Hans Guldman, Galveston's one-time vice-consul for Denmark, the massive red brick home sits on an acre of gardens that include Mrs. Guldman's greenhouse and fish pond. Guests

can have breakfast in the formal dining room or in the sunroom overlooking the garden. The house holds a cache of family antiques with contemporary pieces and original art. Common rooms include a large dining room, parlor, sunroom and study.

Innkeeper(s): Mikey Isbell. $85. MC VISA. 4 rooms. Breakfast included in rates. Type of meal: full breakfast. Air conditioning and ceiling fan in room. Antiques and theater nearby.

Certificate may be used: Sunday-Thursday anytime rooms are available (April-September); anytime available during October-March.

Glen Rose E8

Ye Ole' Maple Inn

PO Box 1141, Glen Rose, TX 76043-1141
(817)897-3456

Circa 1950. Pecan trees shade this comfortable home, which overlooks the Paluxy River. The interior is decorated with a variety of antiques, including a grandfather clock imported from Germany. The innkeepers also keep on display a Santa Claus collection. The fireplaced den offers a large selection of reading material. One of the bedrooms, decked in pink and gray hues, includes an iron and brass bed and wicker furnishings. The other features Victorian decor and a four-poster bed. Breakfasts feature specialties such as oatmeal waffles with pecan sauce or an egg, sausage and apple casserole. Innkeeper Roberta Maple also serves up a mouth-watering selection of evening desserts including peanut butter pie and Texas brownies.

Innkeeper(s): Roberta Maple. $65-80. MC VISA AX PC TC. 2 rooms with PB. Breakfast and evening snack included in rates. Type of meal: full breakfast. Beds: Q. Ceiling fan in room. Cable TV, VCR and library on premises. Handicap access. Antiques, fishing, shopping, theater and watersports nearby.

Certificate may be used: All year, Monday through Thursday; on weekends, January through March.

Gonzales G8

St. James Inn

723 Saint James St,
Gonzales, TX 78629-3411
(210)672-7066

Circa 1914. Ann and J.R. Covert spent three years restoring this massive Texas Hill Country mansion, once owned by a cattle baron. On the main floor is a tiled solarium and living room. The second-floor guest rooms all have working fireplaces. On the third and top level is a unique wind tunnel—a long crawl space with windows on either end—which provides

natural air conditioning. Gourmet candlelight dinners are available in addition to the full breakfasts. Innkeeper(s): Ann & J.R. Covert. $75-100. MC VISA AX PC TC. 5 rooms, 4 with PB, 1 with FP. 2 suites. 1 conference room. Breakfast and afternoon tea included in rates. Types of meals: full breakfast, gourmet breakfast and early coffee/tea. Dinner, picnic lunch, lunch, gourmet lunch and banquet service available. Beds: KQ. Air conditioning, turn-down service, ceiling fan and cable TV in room. Antiques, fishing, parks, shopping, theater and watersports nearby.

Location: One hour east of San Antonio, one hour south of Austin.

Seen in: Gonzales Inquirer, Houston Chronicle, Victoria Advocate.

"We had a wonderful weekend. It's a marvelous home and your hospitality is superb. We'll be back."

Certificate may be used: January-August.

Granbury
E8

Dabney House B&B

106 S Jones St, Granbury, TX 76048-1905
(817)579-1260 Fax:(817)579-0426

Circa 1907. Built during the Mission Period, this Craftsman-style country manor boasts original hardwood floors, stained-glass windows and some of the original light fixtures. The parlor and dining rooms have large, exposed, wooden beams and the ceilings

throughout are 10-feet high. The Dabney Suite has a private entrance into an enclosed sun porch with rattan table and chairs that allow for a private breakfast. The bedroom of this suite is furnished with a four-post tester bed with drapes and an 1800 dresser. Innkeeper(s): John & Gwen Hurley. $60-105. MC VISA AX PC TC. 4 rooms with PB. 1 suite. Breakfast and evening snack included in rates. Type of meal: full breakfast. Dinner available. Beds: QD. Air conditioning and ceiling fan in room. VCR, spa and library on premises. Antiques, fishing, parks, shopping, theater and watersports nearby.

Seen in: Fort Worth Star Telegram, Dallas Morning News.

"Very enjoyable and certainly up among the very best of the B&Bs you are likely to find in the United Kingdom. It reminded me of staying at grandma's house. Thanks for bringing back such warm memories."

Certificate may be used: Sunday through Thursday, all year, does not apply on major holidays or special events.

Pearl Street Inn B&B

319 W Pearl St,
Granbury, TX 76048-2437
(817)279-PINK (888)732-7578

Circa 1912. Known historically as the B. M. Estes House, the inn is decorated with a mix of English, French and American antiques. The English Garden Suite is fashioned in a green, peach and ivy

motif and features a king-size iron and brass bed, English antique furniture, airy sitting room and full bath accented by a cast iron tub and 1912 wall sink. Other guest rooms include clawfoot tubs, crystal lamps and lace. Innkeeper(s): Danette D. Hebda. $59-98. TC. 5 rooms with PB. 1 suite. Breakfast included in rates. Types of meals: full breakfast, gourmet breakfast and early coffee/tea. Beds: KD. Air conditioning and ceiling fan in room. VCR and copier on premises. Antiques, fishing, parks, shopping, theater and watersports nearby.

Seen in: Dallas Morning News.

"Needless to say, we want to stay forever! We had a grand time and highly enjoyed conversations and hospitality."

Certificate may be used: Sunday-Thursday, excluding special events.

Houston
G9

Durham House B&B

921 Heights Blvd,
Houston, TX 77008-6911
(713)868-4654 (800)722-8788
Fax:(713)868-7965

Circa 1902. Located 10 minutes from downtown Houston, this Victorian house, listed in the National Register of Historic Places, was built by the area's first fire chief. Antique furniture, a gazebo, player piano, tandem bicycle and tapes of old radio programs create an atmosphere reminiscent of the early 1900s. Breakfast in bed and romantic dining locations are available for guests, and innkeeper Marguerite Swanson offers escorted tours of the city. Innkeeper(s): Marguerite & Dean Swanson. $65-95. MC VISA AX DS PC TC. 7 rooms, 6 with PB. 1 suite. 1 conference room. Breakfast included in rates. Types of meals: continental-plus breakfast, full breakfast and early coffee/tea. Afternoon tea and evening snack available. Beds: QD. Air conditioning, turn-down service, ceiling fan and VCR in room. Fax and library on premises. Amusement parks, antiques, fishing, parks, shopping, sporting events, theater and watersports nearby.

Seen in: Victorian Homes, Houston Chronicle.

"Another comfortable, wonderful stay."

Certificate may be used: Sunday through Thursday.

The Highlander

607 Highland St,
Houston, TX 77009-6628
(713)861-6110 (800)807-6110
Fax:(713)861-6110

Circa 1922. Nestled among stately pecan trees, this four-square-style home is conveniently close to downtown Houston, yet removed from the city hustle and bustle. The four guestrooms are filled with lace and family heirlooms.

Innkeeper(s): Georgie McIrvin. $80-95. MC VISA AX DS PC TC. 3 rooms with PB. Breakfast included in rates. Types of meals: full breakfast and early coffee/tea. Beds: KQ. Air conditioning, turn-down service, ceiling fan and VCR in room. Fax and library on premises. Antiques, parks, sporting events and theater nearby.

Location: Downtown.

"Best night's sleep in years."

Certificate may be used: All year, Sunday through Thursday.

Robin's Nest

4104 Greeley St,
Houston, TX 77006-5609
(713)528-5821 (800)622-8343
Fax:(713)942-8297

Circa 1895. Legend denotes this former dairy farm as one of the oldest homes in Houston. The inn features elegant, tall windows and ceiling fans. Beautiful flowers decorate the front lawn of this home. Guests will appreciate the inn's proximity to downtown Houston, theaters and gourmet restaurants. Located in the Montrose area of the city, the inn is less than an hour from popular attractions such as NASA and Galveston.

Innkeeper(s): Robin Smith. $80-95. MC VISA AX CB DS. 4 rooms with PB. 1 conference room. Breakfast included in rates. Type of meal: full breakfast. Beds: QDT. Air conditioning, ceiling fan and cable TV in room. Amusement parks, antiques, fishing, shopping, sporting events, theater and watersports nearby.

Location: Inside 610 Loop very near downtown, Brown Convention Center and Texas Medical Center. The inn is in the Museum District.

Seen in: Houston Home and Garden, Houston Business Journal, Woman's Day, Houston Metropolitan, Houston Post, Southern Living, Texas Monthly.

"Fanciful and beautiful, comfortable and happy. We saw a whole new side of Houston, thanks to you."

Certificate may be used: Sunday-Thursday.

Jefferson
D10

McKay House

306 E Delta St, Jefferson, TX 75657-2026
(903)665-7322 (800)468-2627

Circa 1851. Both Lady Bird Johnson and Alex Haley have enjoyed the gracious Southern hospitality offered at the McKay House. Accented by a Williamsburg-style picket fence, the Greek Revival cottage features a pillared front porch. Heart-of-pine floors, 14-foot ceilings and documented wallpapers complement antique furnishings. Orange and pecan French toast or home-baked muffins and shirred eggs are served on vintage china. Victorian nightshirts and gowns await guests in each of the bedchambers. A "gentleman's" style breakfast is served.

Innkeeper(s): Peggy Taylor. $80-145. MC VISA AX. 7 rooms with PB, 5 with FP. 3 suites. 1 conference room. Breakfast included in rates. Types of meals: full breakfast, gourmet breakfast and early coffee/tea. Beds: QD. Air conditioning and ceiling fan in room. Antiques and theater nearby.

Seen in: Southern Accents, Dallas Morning News, Country Home, Southern Bride.

"The facilities of the McKay House are exceeded only by the service and dedication of the owners."

Certificate may be used: Sunday through Thursday, not including Spring Break or festivals/holidays, space available reserve one week in advance please.

Pride House

409 Broadway, Jefferson, TX 75657
(903)665-2675 (800)894-3526
Fax:(541)488-0091

Circa 1889. Mr. Brown, a sawmill owner, built this Victorian house using fine hardwoods, sometimes three layers deep. The windows are nine-feet tall on both the lower level and upstairs. The rooms include amenities such as fireplaces, balconies, canopy beds and private entrances. Most boast original stained-glass windows. The West Room is decorated in crimson reds and features a gigantic clawfoot tub that has received an award from Houston Style Magazine for "best tub in Texas." A wide veranda stretches around two sides of the house.

Innkeeper(s): Carol Abernathy & Christel Frederick. $75-110. MC VISA PC TC. 10 rooms with PB, 3 with FP. 1 suite. 1 cottage. Breakfast and

Air conditioning and ceiling fan in room. Cable TV, swimming and library on premises. Handicap access. Antiques, fishing, shopping, theater and watersports nearby.

Certificate may be used: Jan. 10 through Dec. 20.

Lampasas F7

Historic Moses Hughes B&B
RR 2 Box 31, Lampasas, TX 76550-9601
(512)556-5923

Circa 1856. Nestled among ancient oaks in the heart of the Texas Hill Country, this native stone ranch house rests on 45 acres that include springs, a creek, wildlife and other natural beauty. The ranch was built by Moses Hughes, the first white settler

and founder of Lampasas. He and his wife decided to stay in the area after her health dramatically improved after visiting the springs. Guests can join the innkeepers on the stone patio or upstairs wooden porch for a taste of Texas Hill Country life.
Innkeeper(s): Al & Beverly Solomon. $75-85. PC. 2 rooms with PB. Breakfast included in rates. Types of meals: full breakfast and gourmet breakfast. Beds: D. Air conditioning in room. VCR and library on premises. Antiques, fishing, parks and watersports nearby.
Seen in: Dallas Morning News, Spiegal Catalog, Discover.

"What a delightful respite! Thank you for sharing your very interesting philosophies and personalities with us at this very special B&B. We hate to leave."

Certificate may be used: Year-round, Sunday-Thursday, no holidays.

Mason F7

Hasse House and Ranch
1221 Ischar St, PO Box 58,
Mason, TX 76856
(915)347-6463

Circa 1883. Guests may explore the 320-acre Hasse ranch, which is a working ranch where deer, wild turkey, feral hogs and quail are common sights.

---

evening snack included in rates. Types of meals: gourmet breakfast and early coffee/tea. Afternoon tea available. Beds: KQDT. Air conditioning and ceiling fan in room. Handicap access. Antiques, fishing, parks, theater and watersports nearby.
Seen in: Woman's Day, Country Home, Texas Highways, Texas Homes.

"Like Goldilock's porridge—just right."

Certificate may be used: Weekdays (Sunday-Thursday) and some Fridays.

Lake O' The Pines

Mckenzie Manor
Woodland Shore, Hwy 729,
Lake O' The Pines, TX 75630
(903)755-2240

Circa 1964. Nature trails with private ponds are right outside the door of this rustic, rock lodge set on the shore of Lake O' The Pines. Guests can sit on wide decks and watch eagles soar, beavers build dams and deer graze. Relax in the gazebo or by the large rock fireplace with a good book from the private library of the innkeeper, historian and author Fred

McKenzie. This four-generation family home is designed with a large meeting room, vaulted ceilings and stained-glass windows. All rooms are adjacent to sitting areas and each room is decorated in its own unique style with antiques and family possessions.
Innkeeper(s): Paul & Carol Harrell. $65-95. MC VISA PC TC. 7 rooms, 5 with PB, 1 with FP. 1 suite. 1 conference room. Breakfast and afternoon tea included in rates. Types of meals: continental-plus breakfast, full breakfast and early coffee/tea. Catering service available. Beds: KQD.

After purchasing the land, Henry Hasse and his wife lived in a log cabin on the property before building the sandstone home 23 years later. Three generations of Hasses have lived here, and today it is owned by a great-granddaughter who restored the home in 1980. The inn is located in the small German village of Art, Texas, which is located six

miles east of Mason. The innkeepers rent the two-bedroom National Register home out to only one group or guest at a time. The home is filled with period furniture and accessories, yet offers the modern convenience of an on-site washer and dryer and a fully stocked kitchen. The ranch grounds include a two-mile hiking trail perfect for nature lovers.
Innkeeper(s): Laverne Lee. $95. MC VISA PC TC. 2 rooms with PB. Breakfast included in rates. Type of meal: continental-plus breakfast. Beds: D. Air conditioning, ceiling fan and VCR in room. Library on premises. Handicap access. Antiques, fishing, parks, shopping and watersports nearby.

"We enjoyed every aspect of our stay; the atmosphere, sense of history, rustic setting with a touch of class. We would love to return the same time next year!"

Certificate may be used: Anytime except holidays.

Mason Square B&B

134 Ft. McKavett, PO Box 298,
Mason, TX 76856
(915)347-6398 (800)369-0405
Fax:(915)347-6398

Circa 1901. A fine collection of framed, historically significant maps of Texas and the Southwest that span centuries of discovery and settlement are throughout the guest rooms and hallway of this inn. Located on the second floor of a historic commercial building, the B&B has original pressed-tin ceilings, Victorian woodwork and doors, stained-glass transoms and oak floors. Guests can step outside for a stroll down memory lane as the inn is part of the courthouse square with buildings dating from 1879. Several antique shops, galleries and some local businesses have occupied the same buildings for generations.
Innkeeper(s): Brent Hinckley. $45-60. 3 rooms. Breakfast included in rates. Type of meal: continental-plus breakfast. Air conditioning and ceiling fan in room. VCR on premises. Antiques nearby.

Certificate may be used: All times, except holidays.

Nacogdoches E10

Llano Grande Plantation

RR 4 Box 9400,
Nacogdoches, TX 75964-9276
(409)569-1249

Circa 1840. A collection of three lodgings sits on this 600-acre property of rivers and pine forest. The land was home to Native Americans for many centuries, and in 1867 La Salle's expedition passed through. One of the first Spanish missions in this huge region, north of the Rio Grande, was established here 30 years later. Carefully chosen period antiques resemble those of the original owners. A farmhouse is from the Texas Republic period and another building is Southern Country Georgian.
Innkeeper(s): Captain Charles & Ann Phillips. $60-70. TC. 3 suites. Breakfast included in rates. Types of meals: continental breakfast, continental-plus breakfast and full breakfast. Afternoon tea and catering service available. Air conditioning in room. Antiques, fishing, parks, shopping, sporting events, theater and watersports nearby.

Certificate may be used: April to Feb. 28, Sunday-Thursday, except local college (SFASU) events (homecoming, parents weekend, etc.).

New Braunfels G7

The Rose Garden B&B

195 S Academy Ave,
New Braunfels, TX 78130-5607
(210)629-3296

Circa 1930. In a town full of rich German heritage, this Colonial Revival inn features designer bedrooms, fluffy towels, scented soaps and potpourri-filled rooms. Take a stroll along the cool, Comal Springs or browse antique shops, which are all within walking distance. Relax in the parlor by the fireplace or in the rose garden. Breakfast is served in the formal dining room, garden or brought to your room on a specially prepared tray. The inn is only one block from downtown.
Innkeeper(s): Dawn Mann. $75-105. 2 rooms with PB. Breakfast included in rates. Types of meals: full breakfast and early coffee/tea. Beds: Q. Turn-down service and ceiling fan in room. Antiques, fishing, shopping, theater and watersports nearby.
Seen in: Herald-Zeitung.

"A get-away to a B&B like yours truly revitalizes the spirit and was just what we were looking for. The food was delicious and beautifully presented."

Certificate may be used: Monday-Thursday (year-round), excluding holidays and special events.

Pottsboro   C8

Yacht-O-Fun

PO Box 1480, Pottsboro, TX 75076-1480
(903)786-8188 Fax:(214)669-1550

Guests can stay in a nearby condo or in the cabin of this 51-foot yacht. Tours on Lake Texoma are included in this unusual bed & breakfast experience. Guests first embark on a moonlight cruise, then the next morning brunch and another trip around the lake. The vessel includes two staterooms, and guests can relax and catch some rays on the sundeck or take in the view from the salon.

Innkeeper(s): Diana Greer. $225. 2 rooms. Breakfast included in rates. Type of meal: full breakfast.

Certificate may be used: April 1 through Nov. 30. Rate includes two cruises.

Round Top   F8

Heart of My Heart Ranch B&B

PO Box 106, Round Top, TX 78954-0106
(800)327-1242 Fax:(409)249-3171

Circa 1825. This log frontier home was built by Jared Groce, known as the father of Texas agriculture. Groce planted the state's first cotton, and built the first cotton gin in Texas. Well-appointed rooms feature antiques such as a cannonball or canopy bed. The Lone Star and Brookfield rooms boast fireplaces. The Lone Star has a unique staircase that leads up to the second-story Harwood Room. The innkeepers also offer accommodations in the charming carriage house, and a rustic setting in the 170-year-old log cabin. The cabin boasts a sleeping loft, stone fireplace, clawfoot tub and a complete kitchen. Rockers have been set up on the expansive front porch, perfect for relaxing. The lush grounds offer a swimming pool, Jacuzzi, fruit tree orchard and gardens. A hearty, country breakfast is served each morning, and for an extra charge, the innkeepers will prepare a picnic lunch.

Innkeeper(s): Frances Harris. $65-135. MC VISA AX DS. 17 rooms. Breakfast included in rates. Type of meal: full breakfast.

Certificate may be used: Sunday-Thursday.

Royse City   D9

Country Lane B&B

RR 2 Box 94B,
Royse City, TX 75189-9802
(214)636-2600 (800)240-8757
Fax:(214)635-2300

Circa 1992. Each of the guest rooms at this Texas-style farmhouse has a different movie theme, with names such as the Happy Trails suite. The Mae West room is a provocative place with lace and velvet touches. Some rooms have whirlpool tubs for two. Relax on the rocker-lined veranda and you'll enjoy views of the catfish pond, sunsets and starry skies. The breakfast table is set with china, crystal and linen napkins, and guests partake of gourmet coffees, freshly squeezed juice, homemade muffins, frittatas and fresh fruit.

Innkeeper(s): James & Annie Cornelius. $45-85. MC VISA AX. 5 rooms, 4 with PB. Breakfast included in rates. Types of meals: full breakfast and early coffee/tea. Evening snack, banquet service, catered breakfast and room service available. Beds: QDT. Air conditioning, ceiling fan and VCR in room. Fax and library on premises. Handicap access. Antiques, fishing, parks and watersports nearby.

Certificate may be used: Jan. 15 through Oct. 31 Sunday-Thursday

San Antonio   G7

The Ogé House on The River Walk

209 Washington,
San Antonio, TX 78204-1336
(210)223-2353 (800)242-2770
Fax:(210)226-5812

Circa 1857. This impressive antebellum mansion is a Texas Historic Landmark. It rests on the banks of the beautiful San Antonio Riverwalk on an acre-and-a-half of gardens. Shaded by graceful oak and pecan trees, the inn has a gazebo and double-tiered veranda. There are nine fireplaces. Queen- and king-size beds are provided and all the rooms are distinguished with period antiques, handsomely upholstered sofas and chairs and Oriental carpets. The trolley, convention center and the Alamo are steps away.

Innkeeper(s): Sharrie & Patrick Magatagan. $135-195. MC VISA AX DC CB DS TC. 10 rooms with PB, 7 with FP. 1 conference room. Breakfast included in rates. Types of meals: continental-plus breakfast, full breakfast, gourmet breakfast and early coffee/tea. Beds: KQ. Air conditioning, ceiling fan, cable TV and VCR in room. Fax and library on premises. Amusement parks, antiques, parks, shopping, sporting events, theater and watersports nearby.

Location: Five blocks from the Alamo on the Riverwalk.

Seen in: San Antonio Express News, New York Times, Glamour, Texas Times, Fiesta.

"Wonderfully relaxing weekend in an elegant home with pure Southern hospitality."

Certificate may be used: Year-round, Monday-Thursday, King rooms only, no holidays or Fiesta.

Smithville
G8

The Katy House
201 Ramona St, PO Box 803,
Smithville, TX 78957-0803
(512)237-4262 (800)843-5289
Fax:(512)237-2239

Circa 1909. The Italianate exterior is graced by an arched portico over the bay-windowed living room. The Georgian columns reflect the inn's turn-of-the-century origin. Cypress floors, pocket doors and a graceful stairway accent the completely refurbished interior. The inn is decorated almost exclusively in American antique oak. A leisurely 10-minute bicycle ride (innkeepers provide bikes) will take you to the banks of the Colorado River. Also available are maps that outline walking or biking tours with lists of some of the historical and interesting information of the area.

Innkeeper(s): Bruce & Sallie Blalock. $56-85. MC VISA PC TC. 4 rooms with PB. 1 suite. 2 cottages. Breakfast included in rates. Types of meals: full breakfast and early coffee/tea. Beds: Q. Air conditioning, ceiling fan and cable TV in room. VCR, fax, bicycles and pet boarding on premises. Antiques, fishing, parks, shopping and watersports nearby.

Certificate may be used: Sunday through Thursday

Stephenville
E7

Oxford House
563 N Graham St,
Stephenville, TX 76401-3548
(817)965-6885 Fax:(817)965-7555

Circa 1898. A $3,000 lawyer's fee provided funds for construction of The Oxford House, and the silver was brought to town in a buckboard by W. J.

Oxford, Esq. The house was built of cypress with porches three-quarters of the way around. Hand-turned, gingerbread trim and a carved wooden ridgerow are special features.

Innkeeper(s): Bill & Paula Oxford. $65-75. MC VISA AX PC. 4 rooms with PB. Breakfast included in rates. Types of meals: full breakfast and early coffee/tea. Afternoon tea and catering service available. Beds: QD. Air conditioning in room. Amusement parks, antiques, parks and theater nearby.

Seen in: Glamour, Dallas Morning News.

"A perfect evening of serenity sitting on the front porch with such kind hosts."

Certificate may be used: All year.

Texarkana
D10

Mansion on Main B&B
802 Main St, Texarkana, TX 75501-5104
(903)792-1835

Circa 1895. Spectacular two-story columns salvaged from the St. Louis World's Fair accent the exterior of this Neoclassical-style inn. Victorian nightgowns and sleepshirts are provided, and whether you are on a business trip or your honeymoon, expect to be pampered. Six bedchambers

vary from the Butler's Garret to the Governor's Suite and are all furnished with antiques and period appointments. The inn is located in the downtown historic area. Enjoy a fireside cup of coffee or a lemonade on the veranda.

Innkeeper(s): Lee & Inez Hayden. $60-109. MC VISA AX PC TC. 6 rooms with PB. 1 suite. Breakfast included in rates. Types of meals: full breakfast, gourmet breakfast and early coffee/tea. Afternoon tea available. Beds: KD. Air conditioning, ceiling fan and cable TV in room. Handicap access. Antiques, fishing, shopping and theater nearby.

Certificate may be used: Anytime, space available, reserved at least one week in advance.

Van Alstyne D8

Durning House B&B
205 W Stephens, PO Box 1173,
Van Alstyne, TX 75495
(903)482-5188

Circa 1900. Decorated with American oak and antiques, the inn has been host to many events, including weddings, office parties, Christmas parties, club meetings and murder mystery dinners. Three life-size pigs grace the east garden. The innkeepers have published a cookbook titled "Hog Heaven" that includes more than 400 recipes featured at the inn. Your hosts also appear regularly on a TV show preparing recipes from "Hog Heaven."

Innkeeper(s): Brenda Hix & Sherry Heath. $75-95. MC VISA TC. 2 rooms. Type of meal: continental breakfast. Dinner available. Beds: QD. Air conditioning and ceiling fan in room. Handicap access. Antiques, fishing, shopping, sporting events, theater and watersports nearby.

Certificate may be used: Year-round, Sunday-Friday.

Waxahachie E8

Bonnynook Inn
414 W Main St,
Waxahachie, TX 75165-3234
(214)938-7207 (800)486-5936
Fax:(214)937-7700

Circa 1887. Each of the five guest rooms at this gingerbread Victorian is filled with plants and antiques from around the world. The Sterling Room, a large octagon-shaped chamber, features a French Country Belgian bedroom set dating back to the 1880s. The Morrow Room boasts a 100-year-old sleigh bed and antique clawfoot bathtub. Three of the guest baths offer whirlpool tubs. Bon Appetit featured BonnyNook as part of an article on bed & breakfasts. The hearty breakfasts feature such notable items as blueberry pudding coffeecake or Bohemian double wedding ring bread filled with raisins and almonds. Innkeeper Bonnie Franks keeps a special Coffee Nook filled with teas, coffee, hot cocoa and a refrigerator for her guests. Don't forget to ask about the inn's special cookies. BonnyNook is only two blocks from antique shops, boutiques and restaurants. The inn features a restaurant on the premises and gourmet, six-course meals are available by reservation.

Innkeeper(s): Vaughn & Bonnie Franks. $70-105. MC VISA AX DC DS TC. 5 rooms with PB. 1 conference room. Breakfast and evening snack included in rates. Types of meals: continental breakfast, continental-plus breakfast, full breakfast and early coffee/tea. Picnic lunch, banquet service, catering service and room service available. Beds: KQDT. Air conditioning and ceiling fan in room. VCR, fax, copier and pet boarding on premises. Handicap access. Antiques, parks, shopping and sporting events nearby.

Location: Thirty miles south of downtown Dallas on I-35.

Seen in: Texas Highways, Dallas Morning News, Forbes, Texas People & Places, Bon Appetit.

"This was a wonderful retreat from the everyday hustle and bustle and we didn't hear a phone ring once!"

Certificate may be used: Sunday-Thursday, September-December.

Wichita Falls   C7

Harrison House B&B
2014 11th St,
Wichita Falls, TX 76301-4905
(817)322-2299 (800)327-2299

This prairie-style inn features 10-foot ceilings, narrow-board oak floors, a hand-carved mantelpiece, gumwood paneling and detailed molding. The home was built by oilman, developer and philanthropist N.H. Martin. After the discovery of oil on the family

ranch in nearby Jolly, Martin and his partner went on to build the Country Club Estates. They donated the land on which Hardin Junior College (now Midwestern State University) was built. The inn also caters to special occasions and as many as 200 guests can be accommodated for a stand-up buffet. Innkeeper(s): Suzanne Staha. $55-125. MC VISA AX. 4 rooms. 1 suite. Breakfast included in rates. Type of meal: full breakfast. Air conditioning and ceiling fan in room. Cable TV and VCR on premises. Antiques and shopping nearby.

Certificate may be used: Anytime with advance notice.

Wimberley   G7

Southwind
2701 FM 3237,
Wimberley, TX 78676-5511
(512)847-5277 (800)508-5277

Circa 1985. Located three miles east of the quaint village of Wimberly, this early Texas-style inn sits on 25 wooded acres. Roam the unspoiled acres and discover deer crossing your path and armadillos, raccoons and foxes skittering just beyond your footsteps. During the wet season, enjoy clear natural springs with access to swimming hole. There's a porch outside guest rooms and secluded cabins where one can sit in a rocking chair, feel gentle breezes and listen to birds sing. The parlor is a cool retreat in the summer and provides a warm fireplace in winter weather.

Innkeeper(s): Carrie Watson. $75-85. MC VISA AX DS PC TC. 5 rooms with PB, 3 with FP. 2 cottages. Breakfast included in rates. Types of meals: full breakfast and early coffee/tea. Beds: KQ. Air conditioning and ceiling fan in room. Library on premises. Handicap access. Amusement parks, antiques, fishing, parks, shopping, sporting events, theater and watersports nearby.

Certificate may be used: Sunday through Thursday nights only.

Utah

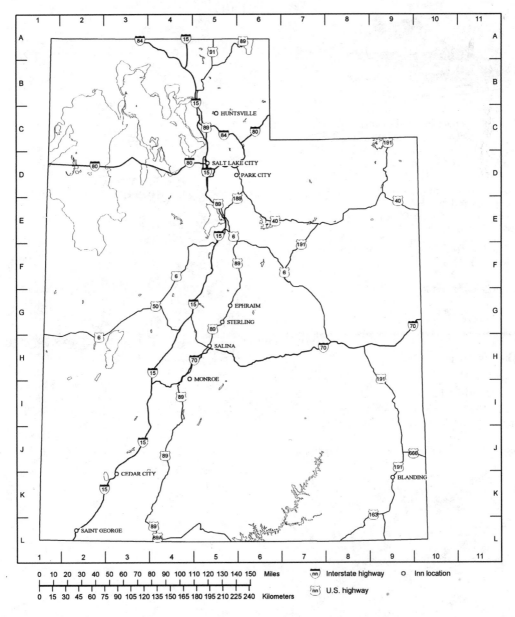

Miles: 0 10 20 30 40 50 60 70 80 90 100 110 120 130 140 150

Kilometers: 0 15 30 45 60 75 90 105 120 135 150 165 180 195 210 225 240

Interstate highway   O Inn location

U.S. highway

Blanding K9

The Grayson Country Inn B&B
118 E 300 S, Blanding, UT 84511-2908
(801)678-2388 (800)365-0868

Circa 1908. Over the years, The Grayson Country Inn has served a number of purposes, including a small hotel and boarding house for Native American girls who attended a local school. The

inn is the perfect location to enjoy the many sites in the area, and is within walking distance from a pottery factory and gift shops. The area abounds with outdoor activities, as many national parks are nearby. Edge of the Cedars State Park is only a mile from the inn. A three-bedroom cottage is available for groups and/or families.
Innkeeper(s): Dennis & Lurlene Gutke. $42-52. MC VISA AX. 11 rooms with PB, 1 with FP. 1 cottage. Breakfast included in rates. Type of meal: full breakfast. Beds: Q. Air conditioning, ceiling fan and cable TV in room. Library on premises. Fishing, parks, shopping and watersports nearby.
Seen in: Salt Lake Tribune.
Certificate may be used: Nov. 1 to March 31.

Cedar City K3

Bard's Inn
150 S 100 W, Cedar City, UT 84720-3276
(801)586-6612

Circa 1910. This handsome bungalow features stained-glass windows, a wide front porch and a second-story porch. The Katharina Room has an antique, high-back queen bed and a twin-size

walnut sleigh bed. Homemade pastries and fruit are served on the porch or in the formal dining room.
Innkeeper(s): Jack & Audrey Whipple. $75. MC VISA. 7 rooms, 5 with PB. Breakfast included in rates. Type of meal: continental-plus breakfast. Beds: QT. Air conditioning in room. Antiques, parks, shopping, downhill skiing, cross-country skiing, sporting events and theater nearby.
Certificate may be used: Anytime Oct. 1 to May 31.

Paxman's House B&B
170 N 400 W,
Cedar City, UT 84720-2421
(801)586-3755

Circa 1900. This steeply-gabled, turn-of-the-century Victorian offers a small veranda overlooking a residential street, two blocks from the Shakespearean Festival. Early Mormon pioneer pieces furnish the Pine Room, while walnut and marble Victorian

furnishings fill the Master bedroom on the downstairs level. Breakfast includes fruit, cheese and homemade bread. Brian Head Ski Resort and Zion National Park are a short drive away.
Innkeeper(s): Karlene Paxman. $55-77. MC VISA. 3 rooms. Breakfast included in rates. Air conditioning in room. VCR on premises. Antiques, shopping, downhill skiing, cross-country skiing, sporting events and theater nearby.
Certificate may be used: Sept. 15 to May 15, Sunday to Thursday.

Ephraim
G5

Ephraim Homestead
135 W 100 N (43-2),
Ephraim, UT 84627-1131
(801)283-6367

Circa 1880. Three buildings comprise this Mormon pioneer homestead. The Granary, circa 1860, is furnished in Mormon pioneer items and resembles a museum reproduction with its fireplace, cast-iron cookstove, rustic kitchen, antique beds and cradle. The barn offers two rustic rooms on the top floor, while the Victorian Gothic house, fashioned of adobe, is furnished in Eastlake antiques. It features Scandinavian/Victorian stenciling in its two tiny guest rooms located up steep stairs off the kitchen. Apple muffins and French toast are prepared on the wood stove for guests.
Innkeeper(s): Sherron Andreasen. $45-75. 3 suites. 1 cottage. Breakfast included in rates. Type of meal: full breakfast. Evening snack available. Air conditioning in room. Antiques, shopping, cross-country skiing, sporting events and theater nearby.
Certificate may be used: All year, excluding second and third weeks of July, Christmas, Thanksgiving eves and days.

Huntsville
C5

Jackson Fork Inn
7345 E 900 S, Huntsville, UT 84317-9778
(801)745-0051 (800)255-0672

Circa 1938. This former dairy barn was named after the hay fork that was used to transport hay into the barn. The romantic inn now includes eight guest rooms and a restaurant. Four rooms include two-person Jacuzzi tubs, and all are cozy and comfortable. A self-serve continental breakfast is prepared each day with muffins and fresh coffee. The inn is ideal for skiers and located near Powder Mountain, Nordic Valley and Snowbasin ski resorts.
Innkeeper(s): Vicki Petersen. $40-110. MC VISA AX DS PC TC. 8 rooms with PB. Breakfast included in rates. Dinner and lunch available.

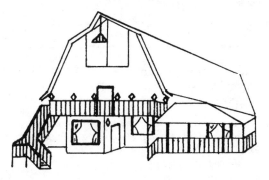

Beds: Q. Ceiling fan in room. Fishing, parks, shopping, downhill skiing, cross-country skiing and watersports nearby.
Certificate may be used: Monday through Thursday excluding holidays.

Monroe
H4

Peterson's B&B
PO Box 142, Monroe, UT 84754-0142
(801)527-4830

Circa 1895. Although it appears to be a modern ranch house, this home has sections more than 100 years old. For 20 years Mary Ann has hosted bed & breakfast guests here. A former cooking teacher, she

offers breakfasts of Hawaiian French toast, Pannokoken with applesauce and eggs benedict. The fenced yard is shaded by an ancient apple tree. Visit Fremont Indian State Park and discover petroglyphs and pictographs carved into the cliffs, as well as pit dwellings of the Fremonts. The waters of Mystic Hot Springs, seven blocks away, have the color of lemonade and are non-sulfurous. Monroe is halfway between Denver and Los Angeles.
Innkeeper(s): Mary Ann Peterson. $70-75. 3 rooms, 2 with PB. Breakfast included in rates. Types of meals: gourmet breakfast and early coffee/tea. Beds: K. Air conditioning and turn-down service in room. Cable TV and VCR on premises. Fishing, parks, shopping, cross-country skiing and theater nearby.
Certificate may be used: April 1-Oct. 31

Park City
D5

The Imperial Hotel
221 Main St, PO Box 1628,
Park City, UT 84060
(801)649-1904 (800)669-8824
Fax:(801)645-7421

Circa 1904. The Imperial, a historic turn-of-the-century hotel, is decorated to look like an Old West-style lodging complete with Victorian furnishings and antiques. Several guest rooms include amenities like clawfoot or Roman tubs and sitting areas. A few overlook Park City's historic Main Street. The inn's largest suite includes a bedroom and a spiral staircase leading up to a cozy loft area. Ski lockers, a Jacuzzi and transportation to area ski lifts are some of the amenities offered to guests. Innkeeper(s): Paulette Anderson. $65-230. MC VISA AX DS TC. 10 rooms, 9 with PB. 1 suite. Breakfast included in rates. Types of meals: full breakfast and early coffee/tea. Evening snack available. Beds: KQT. Cable TV in room. Fax and spa on premises. Antiques, fishing, parks, shopping, downhill skiing, cross-country skiing, sporting events, theater and watersports nearby.

Certificate may be used: April 15-June 15 & Sept. 15-Nov. 15, space available.

The Old Miners' Lodge - A B&B Inn

615 Woodside Ave, PO Box 2639,
Park City, UT 84060-2639
(801)645-8068 (800)648-8068
Fax:(801)645-7420

Circa 1889. This originally was established as a miners' boarding house by E. P. Ferry, owner of the Woodside-Norfolk silver mines. A two-story Victorian with Western flavor, the lodge is a significant structure in the Park City National Historic District. Just on the edge of the woods is a deck and a steaming hot tub.

Innkeeper(s): Susan Wynne. $55-245. MC VISA AX DS PC TC. 12 rooms with PB, 1 with FP. 4 suites. 2 conference rooms. Breakfast and evening snack included in rates. Types of meals: full breakfast and early coffee/tea. Banquet service and catering service available. Beds: KQDT. Turn-down service and ceiling fan in room. Fax, copier, spa and library on premises. Antiques, fishing, parks, shopping, downhill skiing, cross-country skiing and theater nearby.

Location: In the Park City Historic District.

Seen in: Boston Herald, Los Angeles Times, Detroit Free Press, Washington Post, Ski, Bon Appetit.

"This is the creme de la creme. The most wonderful place I have stayed at bar none, including ski country in the U.S. and Europe."

Certificate may be used: April 15-June 15, Sept. 15-Nov. 15, subject to availability.

Saint George   L2

Greene Gate Village Historic B&B Inn

76 W Tabernacle St,
Saint George, UT 84770-3420
(801)628-6999 (800)350-6999
Fax:(801)628-5068

Circa 1872. This is a cluster of six restored pioneer homes all located within one block. The Bentley House has comfortable Victorian decor, while the Supply Depot is decorated in a style reflective of its

origin as a shop for wagoners on their way to California. The Orson Pratt House and the Carriage House are other choices, all carefully restored. The fifth house contains three bedrooms each with private bath, a kitchen, living room and two fireplaces. One of the bedrooms has a large whirlpool tub. Innkeeper(s): Barbara Greene. $45-110. MC VISA AX DS. 16 rooms with PB, 9 with FP. 4 suites. 1 conference room. Breakfast included in rates. Types of meals: full breakfast and early coffee/tea. Dinner, picnic lunch, catering service and room service available. Beds: KQT. Air conditioning, cable TV and VCR in room. Handicap access. Antiques, fishing, shopping, downhill skiing, cross-country skiing, sporting events, theater and watersports nearby.

Seen in: Deseret News, Spectrum, Better Homes & Garden, Sunset, Country.

"You not only provided me with rest, comfort and wonderful food, but you fed my soul."

Certificate may be used: Sunday-Thursday.

Salina   H5

The Victorian Inn

190 W Main St, Salina, UT 84654-1153
(801)529-7342 (800)972-7183

A courtyard filled with a rose garden, stained-glass windows and fine wood floors and moldings set the tone for this Victorian experience. The inn has down comforters, king beds and antique clawfoot

tubs. Abundant Grandmother-type servings are offered at breakfast. The valley, surrounded by mountains as high as 12,000 feet, offers close spots for fishing, hunting and snowmobiling.
Innkeeper(s): Debbie Van Horn. $75-90. MC VISA. 3 rooms. Breakfast included in rates. Type of meal: full breakfast. Air conditioning in room. Cross-country skiing nearby.

Certificate may be used: Mid-June through mid-August, Sunday-Thursday only.

Salt Lake City   D5

The Anton Boxrud B&B
57 S 600 E, Salt Lake City, UT 84102
(801)363-8035 (800)524-5511
Fax:(801)596-1316

Circa 1901. One of Salt Lake City's "grand old homes," this Victorian home with eclectic style is on the register of the Salt Lake City Historical Society. The interior is furnished with antiques from around the country and Old World details. In the sitting and dining rooms guests will find chairs with intricate carvings, a table with carved swans for support, embossed brass door knobs and stained and beveled glass. The inn is located just a half-block south of the Utah Governor's Mansion.
Innkeeper(s): Mark Brown. $59-119. MC VISA AX DC CB DS. 7 rooms, 3 with PB. 1 suite. Breakfast included in rates. Types of meals: full breakfast and early coffee/tea. Evening snack available. Beds: KQT. Cable TV on premises. Amusement parks, antiques, fishing, shopping, downhill skiing, cross-country skiing, sporting events, theater and watersports nearby.
Seen in: Salt Lake Tribune.
Certificate may be used: Oct. 15 to Jan. 15.

Saltair B&B
164 S 900 E, Salt Lake City, UT 84102
(801)533-8184 (800)733-8184
Fax:(801)595-0332

Circa 1903. The Saltair is the oldest continuously operating bed & breakfast in Utah and a offers a prime location to enjoy Salt Lake City. The simply decorated rooms include light, airy window dresses, charming furnishings and special touches. One room includes a wood-burning stove and exposed brick. Breakfasts, especially the delicious breads, are memorable. The inn is within walking distance to four historic districts and only one block from Temple Square and the Governor's Mansion. Day trips include treks to several national and state parks and the Wasatch Front ski areas.
Innkeeper(s): Michael Harr & Karen Morrell. $79-135. MC VISA AX DC CB DS TC. 5 rooms, 2 with PB. Breakfast and evening snack included in rates. Types of meals: continental breakfast, continental-plus breakfast, full breakfast, gourmet breakfast and early coffee/tea. Beds: QT. Air conditioning in room. Cable TV, VCR, fax and spa on premises. Amusement parks, antiques, fishing, parks, shopping, downhill skiing, cross-country skiing, sporting events, theater and watersports nearby.
Seen in: Mobil, Logan Sun.

"Your swing and Saltair McMuffins were fabulous."
Certificate may be used: Oct. 1-30, Nov. 1-30, Dec. 1-15.

Wildflowers B&B
936 E 1700 S, Salt Lake City, UT 84105
(801)466-0600 (800)569-0009
Fax:(801)484-7832

Circa 1891. Holding true to its name, the grounds surrounding this Victorian home are covered with all sorts of flowers ranging from wild geraniums to coreopsis to meadow rue. The outside beauty only serves to complement the magnificence on the inside of this historic residence. Hand-carved staircases, stained-glass windows, clawfoot bathtubs and original chandeliers make up just some of the touches that will make a stay here memorable. Situated in the heart of Salt Lake City, this home offers all the comfort one could ask for and the convenience of being just a few minutes away from skiing or a trip downtown. Like this classic residence, 10 nearby homes are also listed in the National Register of Historic Places.
Innkeeper(s): Jeri Parker & Cill Sparks. $70-125. MC VISA AX. 5 rooms with PB. 2 suites. 1 conference room. Breakfast included in rates. Type of meal: gourmet breakfast. Beds: KQD. Air conditioning, ceiling fan, cable TV and VCR in room. Fax, copier and bicycles on premises. Amusement parks, antiques, fishing, parks, shopping, downhill skiing, cross-country skiing, sporting events, theater and watersports nearby.

"Service above and beyond my expectations with people that I'll remember."
Certificate may be used: Not February, March, holidays. All other times depending on availability.

Sterling G5

Cedar Crest Inn

819 Palisade Rd, Sterling, UT 84665

(801)835-6352

Circa 1903. Several structures comprise the Cedar Crest Inn, including the Swiss-style Lindenhaus, named for a giant linden tree adjacent to the home. The tree was brought to America from Germany as a seedling. Guests also can opt to stay in Linderhof, which offers three beautiful suites. The third structure on this 18-acre property is the popular Cedar Crest Restaurant, which serves a variety of gourmet entrees, including lobster, chicken Cordon Bleu and Filet Mignon. The grounds are beautiful, and on cold nights, guests can stay indoors and watch a favorite movie. The innkeepers have a selection of more than 300.

Innkeeper(s): Ron & Don Kelsch. $52-100. MC VISA AX DS. 12 rooms, 9 with PB. 2 suites. 1 conference room. Breakfast included in rates. Types of meals: full breakfast, gourmet breakfast and early coffee/tea. Banquet service and catered breakfast available. Beds: KQD. Air conditioning, cable TV and VCR in room. Spa and bicycles on premises. Antiques, parks, shopping, cross-country skiing and watersports nearby.

Certificate may be used: August through December, holidays excluded.

Vermont

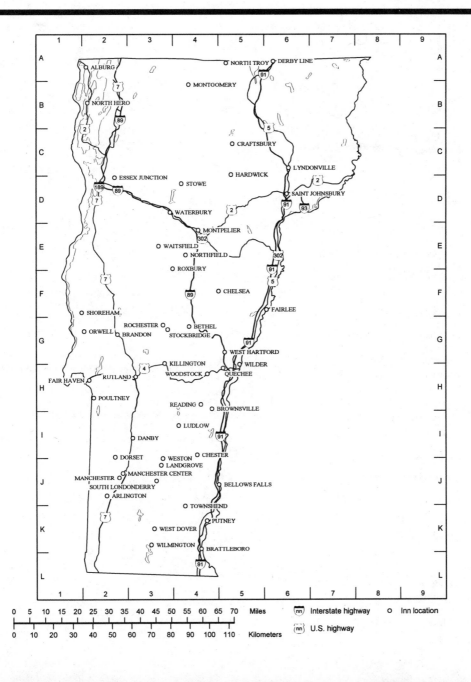

	1	2	3	4	5	6	7	8	9	

A
ALBURG
NORTH TROY DERBY LINE
MONTGOMERY
91

B
NORTH HERO
7
2
89

C
CRAFTSBURY
5
LYNDONVILLE

D
ESSEX JUNCTION STOWE HARDWICK SAINT JOHNSBURY
189 89 WATERBURY 2 91 93
7

E
MONTPELIER
WAITSFIELD 302
NORTHFIELD
ROXBURY 302
91
5

F
CHELSEA
7
89
FAIRLEE

G
SHOREHAM
ROCHESTER BETHEL
ORWELL BRANDON STOCKBRIDGE
WEST HARTFORD

H
KILLINGTON WILDER
FAIR HAVEN RUTLAND 4 WOODSTOCK QUECHEE
POULTNEY

I
READING BROWNSVILLE
LUDLOW
DANBY 91

J
DORSET WESTON CHESTER
LANDGROVE
MANCHESTER MANCHESTER CENTER
SOUTH LONDONDERRY BELLOWS FALLS
ARLINGTON

K
TOWNSHEND
7 PUTNEY
WEST DOVER
WILMINGTON BRATTLEBORO
91

L

0	5	10	15	20	25	30	35	40	45	50	55	60	65	70	Miles

0	10	20	30	40	50	60	70	80	90	100	110	Kilometers

(nn) Interstate highway   ○ Inn location

(nn) U.S. highway

Alburg
A2

Thomas Mott Homestead
Blue Rock Rd, Rt 2 Box 149-B,
Alburg, VT 05440-9620
(802)796-3736 (800)348-0843
Fax:(802)796-3736

Circa 1838. Each room in this restored farmhouse provides a special view of Lake Champlain, yet guests often may be found enjoying the view from the sitting room as they warm by the fireplace. There are

also full views of Mt. Mansfield and nearby Jay Peak. Montreal Island is one hour away. Full gourmet dinners may be arranged by advance reservations. Patrick is a noted wine consultant, and holds Master's Degrees in criminology, sociology and the classical arts. A boat dock recently has been added to the property which extends 75 ft. into the lake.

Innkeeper(s): Patrick Schallert. $65-85. MC VISA AX DC CB DS PC TC. 5 rooms with PB, 1 with FP. 2 suites. 3 conference rooms. Breakfast and evening snack included in rates. Types of meals: full breakfast, gourmet breakfast and early coffee/tea. Beds: KQ. Turn-down service and ceiling fan in room. Cable TV, fax, copier and library on premises. Amusement parks, antiques, fishing, parks, shopping, downhill skiing, cross-country skiing, sporting events, theater and watersports nearby.

Location: Northwest corner of Vermont.

Seen in: Los Angeles Times, St. Alban's Messenger, Yankee Traveler, Boston Globe, Elle, Outside, Prime Time, Vermont.

"Hospitality reigns. I loved the beautiful pressed maple leaf—it is perfect and so personal."

Certificate may be used: Nov. 1 through April 30.

Arlington
J2

The Arlington Inn
Historic Rt 7A, PO Box 369,
Arlington, VT 05250
(802)375-6532 (800)443-9442

Circa 1848. The Arlington Inn is one of Vermont's finest examples of Greek Revival architecture. Set on lushly landscaped grounds, the inn boasts elegantly appointed guest rooms filled with period antiques. Norman Rockwell once used the carriage house as a studio.

Innkeeper(s): Mark Gagnon. $70-160. MAP. MC VISA AX DC DS. 13 rooms with PB, 2 with FP. 5 suites. 1 conference room. Breakfast included in rates. Types of meals: full breakfast and gourmet breakfast. Dinner and picnic lunch available. Beds: KQDT. Air conditioning in room. Cable TV, VCR, fax, copier and bicycles on premises. Antiques, fishing, shopping, downhill skiing, cross-country skiing, sporting events, theater and watersports nearby.

Location: Intersection of Route 313.

Seen in: San Diego Times, Bon Appetit, Country Inns, Vermont Life, Gourmet, New York Magazine.

"What a romantic place and such outrageous food!"

Certificate may be used: Weekdays, excluding Sept. 15-Oct. 23.

Arlington Manor House B&B
Buck Hill Rd, RR 2 - 420,
Arlington, VT 05250
(802)375-6784

Circa 1908. A view of Mt. Equinox is enjoyed from the spacious terrace of this Dutch Colonial inn in the Battenkill River Valley. The inn also sports its own lighted tennis courts and is within easy walking distance of the Battenkill River, where canoeing, fishing and river tubing are popular activities. A variety of accommodations is offered, and two of the inn's guest rooms have romantic fireplaces. A bikers' workshop and bench stand are on the premises.

Innkeeper(s): Al & Kit McAllister. $45-130. MC VISA PC TC. 5 rooms, 3 with PB, 2 with FP. 1 suite. 2 conference rooms. Breakfast and afternoon tea included in rates. Types of meals: full breakfast, gourmet breakfast and early coffee/tea. Room service available. Beds: QDT. Air conditioning, turn-down service and VCR in room. Tennis and library on premises. Antiques, fishing, parks, shopping, downhill skiing, cross-country skiing, theater and watersports nearby.

Certificate may be used: Sunday-Thursday non-holiday except Sept. 15-Oct. 22.

Hill Farm Inn
RR 2 Box 2015,
Arlington, VT 05250-9311
(802)375-2269 (800)882-2545
Fax:(802)375-9918

Circa 1790. One of Vermont's original land grant farmsteads, Hill Farm Inn has welcomed guests since 1905 when the widow Mettie Hill opened her home to summer vacationers. The farm is surrounded by 50 peaceful acres that border the Battenkill River. Guests can relax and enjoy the simple life and 360-

degree views of the mountains. Guest rooms are charming and cozy. Summer guests have the option of staying in one of four cabins. A large, country breakfast of homemade fare starts off each day.

Innkeeper(s): George & Joanne Hardy, Kelly Stork. $105-140. MAP. MC VISA AX DS. 17 rooms, 10 with PB. 2 suites. Breakfast, afternoon tea and dinner included in rates. Types of meals: full breakfast and early coffee/tea. Beds: KQTD. Cable TV, fax and copier on premises. Antiques, fishing, parks, shopping, downhill skiing and cross-country skiing nearby.

Location: One-half mile from Historic Route 7A.

Seen in: Providence Journal, Boston Globe, Innsider.

"A superb location with lots to do indoors and out. Beautifully kept rooms and excellent home cooking."

Certificate may be used: Nov. 1-Sept. 15, Sunday-Thursday; Excluding holiday periods

Ira Allen House
Rural Delivery 2, Box 2485,
Arlington, VT 05250
(802)362-2284 Fax:(802)362-0928

Built by Ethan Allen's brother, this historic Colonial Revival inn is a state historic site. Hand-blown glass panes, hand-hewn beams, handmade bricks and wide-board floors provide evidence of the inn's longevity. Surrounded by farms and forest, the inn's setting is perfect for those searching for some peace and quiet. Plenty of recreational activities also are found nearby, including fine trout fishing in the

Battenkill River just across the street. Saturday-night dinners are available in winter, and guests are welcome to raid the living room fridge, where they will find complimentary soda and non-alcoholic beer.

Innkeeper(s): Rowland Bryant. $55-70. MC VISA AX. 9 rooms. 2 suites. Breakfast included in rates. Type of meal: full breakfast. Dinner

available. Ceiling fan in room. VCR on premises. Antiques, shopping, downhill skiing, cross-country skiing and theater nearby.

Certificate may be used: Year-round except foliage season (last week September-last week October) and holidays.

Bellows Falls   J5

River Mist B&B
7 Burt St, Bellows Falls, VT 05101-1401
(802)463-9023

The scenic village of Bellows Falls is home to this turn-of-the-century Queen Anne Victorian inn, with its inviting wraparound porch and charming country Victorian interior. Guests may relax in any of three sitting rooms or in front of its fireplace. Enjoy a day of antiquing, skiing or just wandering around the picturesque environs. Be sure to take a ride on the Green Mountain Flyer before leaving town.

Innkeeper(s): Linda Maresca. $35-75. 3 rooms. Breakfast included in rates. Type of meal: full breakfast. Cable TV on premises. Amusement parks, antiques, shopping, downhill skiing, cross-country skiing and theater nearby.

Certificate may be used: Anytime except foliage season weekends Sept. 1-Oct. 31 and holiday weekends.

Bethel   G4

Greenhurst Inn
River St, Rd 2, Box 60,
Bethel, VT 05032-9404
(802)234-9474

Circa 1890. In the National Register of Historic Places, Greenhurst is a gracious Victorian mansion built for the Harringtons of Philadelphia. Overlooking the White River, the inn's opulent interiors include etched windows once featured on the cover of Vermont Life. There are eight masterpiece fireplaces and a north and south parlor.

Innkeeper(s): Lyle & Claire Wolf. $50-100. EP. MC VISA DS PC TC. 13 rooms, 7 with PB, 4 with FP. Breakfast included in rates. Types of meals: continental breakfast, continental-plus breakfast and early

coffee/tea. Beds: QDT. Air conditioning in room. Cable TV, VCR and library on premises. Antiques, fishing, parks, shopping, downhill skiing, cross-country skiing, theater and watersports nearby.

Location: Midway between Boston and Montreal.

Seen in: Los Angeles Times, Time, New York Times, Vermont Life.

"The inn is magnificent! The hospitality unforgettable."

Certificate may be used: Sunday-Thursday except Sept. 15-Oct. 15.

Brandon

G2

The Gazebo Inn
On Rt 7 (25 Grove St),
Brandon, VT 05733
(802)247-3235

Circa 1865. This National Register home is like a little museum with antique tools, toys, glass, bottles, musical instruments and other collectibles placed throughout the rooms. In the summer and fall months, the innkeepers open an antique shop on the premises, and the area is bursting with places to hunt for antiques and crafts. A variety of dishes, from traditional pancakes with locally produced maple syrup to huevos rancheros, are served each morning in the dining room. Guests are invited to simply sit and relax in the gazebo, on the porch or in front of a wood-burning stove.

Innkeeper(s): Janet & Joel Mondlak. $55-75. MC VISA AX DS TC. 4 rooms with PB. Breakfast included in rates. Type of meal: full breakfast. Beds: DT. Cable TV, copier and bicycles on premises. Antiques, fishing, parks, shopping, downhill skiing, cross-country skiing, sporting events, theater and watersports nearby.

"Thank you for your hospitality. We had a wonderful time. We will try to make this an annual event."

Certificate may be used: Always except fall foliage and holiday weekends.

Hivue B&B Tree Farm
RR 1, Box 1023, High Pond Rd.,
Brandon, VT 05733-9704
(802)247-3042 (800)880-3042

Circa 1960. There are meadows and woods to meander through, and a stream stocked with trout winds its way through the 76-acre grounds at this raised ranch-style home. Accommodations are comfortable, a bit like an old country farmhouse. Guests

enjoy views of the surrounding White Mountains. Brandon, a historic little village, is just a few miles down the road.

Innkeeper(s): William & Winifred Reuschle. $50. 3 rooms with PB. 1 conference room. Breakfast included in rates. Type of meal: full breakfast. Picnic lunch available. Beds: KD. Ceiling fan and VCR in room. Antiques, fishing, parks, shopping, downhill skiing, cross-country skiing and watersports nearby.

Certificate may be used: Jan. 1-May 23, Monday-Thursday; June 17-July 3, Monday-Wednesday; July 10-Aug. 30, Wednesday-Friday; Sept. 4-Sept. 24, Wednesday-Tuesday; Oct. 22-Dec. 23, Tuesday-Monday.

Moffett House
69 Park St, Brandon, VT 05733-1121
(802)247-3843 (800)752-5794

Circa 1856. This graceful French Second Empire house has a mansard roof and a Queen Anne Victorian veranda that was added in 1880. Widow walks top the roof, and gingerbread trim adds to the streetside appeal of Moffett House. The inn was named after Hugh Moffett, Time-Life editor and Vermont legislator. A country breakfast is served in the dining room. The Kellington-Pico ski area is nearby.

Innkeeper(s): Mary Bowers, Doug Flanagan. $65-125. MAP, AP, EP. MC VISA. 7 rooms, 3 with PB. 1 suite. Breakfast included in rates. Types of meals: full breakfast and early coffee/tea. Dinner and picnic lunch available. Beds: KQTD. Ceiling fan and cable TV in room. Antiques, fishing, parks, shopping, downhill skiing, cross-country skiing, theater and watersports nearby.

Seen in: Rutland Business Journal.

"My mother, aunt, cousin and I were all delighted with the lovely accommodations and the delicious breakfasts."

Certificate may be used: Sunday-Friday.

Rosebelle's Victorian Inn
PO Box 370, Rt 7,
Brandon, VT 05733-0370
(802)247-0098 (888)767-3235

Circa 1839. This elegant Second Empire Victorian inn with mansard roof is listed in the National Register of Historic Places. Impressive both inside and out, the inn and its six guest rooms have been

lovingly furnished with authentic Victorian pieces by the innkeepers. Favorite gathering spots include the comfortable common rooms and the wicker-filled porch. Guests also enjoy strolling the lush grounds where they often experience close encounters with butterflies and hummingbirds. The innkeepers, who speak French, offer gift certificates and special packages. The inn is near Middlebury College and minutes from major ski areas.

Innkeeper(s): Ginette & Norm Milot. $75-95. MC VISA AX PC TC. 6 rooms, 4 with PB. Breakfast included in rates. Types of meals: full breakfast and early coffee/tea. Afternoon tea and evening snack available. Beds: QDT. Ceiling fan in room. Cable TV and VCR on premises. Antiques, fishing, parks, shopping, downhill skiing, cross-country skiing, sporting events, theater and watersports nearby.

Location: Heart of Vermont and only a short drive to all of Vermonts special interests.

"You have captured a beautiful part of our history."

Certificate may be used: November-June, Sunday to Thursday, excluding holidays and special events. Call for possible weekend availability.

Brattleboro   K4

"40 Putney Road" B&B
40 Putney Rd,
Brattleboro, VT 05301-2944
(802)254-6268 Fax:(802)258-2673

The West River runs alongside this French Baronial estate. The inn's well-manicured lawn includes gardens and two fountains. The home, considered a town landmark, was built by the superintendent of the Brattleboro Retreat, which was a psychiatric hospital. Antiques and Oriental rugs grace the interior. Guests are pampered with chocolates, turn-down service, fresh flowers and complimentary port wine.

Innkeeper(s): Joan Broderick. $80-95. MC VISA DS. 4 rooms. Breakfast included in rates. Type of meal: full breakfast. Beds: QDT.

Certificate may be used: Sunday through Thursday, Nov. 1-May 31.

Brownsville   H4

Mill Brook B&B
PO Box 410, Brownsville, VT 05037-0410
(802)484-7283

Circa 1860. Once known as the House of Seven Gables, Mill Brook has been in constant use as a family home and for a while, a boarding house for mill loggers. Old German Fraktur paintings decorate the woodwork and there are three sitting rooms for guests. Antique furnishings are found throughout. Popular activities in the area include hang gliding, bike tours and canoeing.

Innkeeper(s): K. Carriere. $65-105. MC VISA. 5 rooms, 3 with PB. 3 suites. Breakfast included in rates. Types of meals: full breakfast and

early coffee/tea. Evening snack and catering service available. Beds: QDT. Ceiling fan in room. VCR on premises. Antiques, shopping, downhill skiing, cross-country skiing, sporting events and theater nearby.

Location: Fourteen miles from Woodstock, seven from Windsor.

"Splendid hospitality. Your B&B was beyond our expectation."

Certificate may be used: Sunday - Thursday. January, March, April, May, June, July, August, November.

Chelsea   F5

Shire Inn
8 Main St, PO Box 37,
Chelsea, VT 05038
(802)685-3031 (800)441-6908
Fax:(802)685-3871

Circa 1832. Granite lintels over the windows and a sunburst light over the entry highlight this Adams-style brick home. The inn, which is located in a 210-year-old historic village, has a grand spiral staircase ascending from wide-plank pumpkin pine floors

in the entryway. Guestrooms include antique canopied beds and wood-burning fireplaces, tall windows and 10 foot ceilings. Included on the property's 23 acres are granite post fencing, perennial gardens dating from the 19th century, and a broad, rocky stream spanned by a farm bridge.

Innkeeper(s): Jay & Karen Keller. $86-210. MAP. MC VISA DS PC TC. 6 rooms with PB, 4 with FP. Breakfast and dinner included in rates. Types of meals: full breakfast and early coffee/tea. Afternoon tea available. Beds: KQD. Fax, copier, bicycles and library on premises. Antiques, fishing, parks, shopping, downhill skiing, cross-country skiing, theater and watersports nearby.

Seen in: Country Inn Review, Vermont Life.

"What an inn should be! Absolutely delicious food - great hospitality! The rooms are filled with romance."

Certificate may be used: Anytime except Sept. 10-Oct. 20.

Chester
14

Henry Farm Inn
PO Box 646, Chester, VT 05143-0646
(802)875-2674 (800)723-8213
Fax:(802)875-2674

Circa 1760. Fifty acres of scenic woodlands provide the setting for this handsomely restored stagecoach stop in the Green Mountains. There are original wide pine floors and carefully selected early American furnishings. A pond and river are nearby.

Innkeeper(s): Barbara Bowman. $55-85. MC VISA AX PC TC. 7 rooms with PB. Types of meals: full breakfast and early coffee/tea. Afternoon tea available. Beds: KQT. VCR, fax and copier on premises.

Location: Ten miles from I-91.

"Very comfortable and pleasant."

Certificate may be used: Dec. 1 to Sept. 1, Sunday to Friday.

Inn Victoria and Tea Pot Shoppe
On The Green, PO Box 788,
Chester, VT 05143
(802)875-4288 (800)732-4288
Fax:(802)875-4323

Circa 1820. High tea is one of the highlights for guests, who can keep the memory alive by purchasing from the innkeeper's Tea Pot Shoppe. This Second Empire Victorian is among several historic houses and seven churches found in Chester's On the Green area. Many weekends include Victorian fairs and festivals. Overture to Christmas is a festive time for townspeople and visitors dressing Victorian and caroling door-to-door. Two summer theater groups are nearby.

Innkeeper(s): Tom & KC Lanagan. $75-125. MC VISA AX DC CB TC. 7 rooms with PB, 1 with FP. Breakfast and afternoon tea included in rates. Types of meals: full breakfast, gourmet breakfast and early coffee/tea. Beds: Q. Air conditioning, cable TV and VCR in room. Fax and spa on premises. Antiques, fishing, parks, shopping, downhill skiing, cross-country skiing, sporting events, theater and watersports nearby.

Certificate may be used: Year-round, Sunday-Thursday.

The Inn at Long Last
PO Box 589, Chester, VT 05143-0589
(802)875-2444

Circa 1923. Located on the town green, this renovated inn reflects the personality of owner Jack Coleman, a former college professor and author. Fulfilling a dream, he created an inn for all seasons featuring fine cuisine and gracious surroundings. The home boasts a 3,000-book library, a historic collection of miniature marching bands, quilts, fine art and unusual antiques. A private court is available for guests to try out their tennis skills.

Innkeeper(s): Jack Coleman, Leo Graham. $160. MAP, EP. MC VISA TC. 30 rooms, 26 with PB. 4 suites. 1 conference room. Breakfast and dinner included in rates. Types of meals: full breakfast and early coffee/tea. Banquet service available. Beds: QD. Cable TV, VCR and copier on premises. Antiques, fishing, parks, shopping, downhill skiing, cross-country skiing and theater nearby.

Seen in: New York Times, Philadelphia Inquirer, Gourmet.

"An inn of character where character has real meaning."

Certificate may be used: Year-round, Sunday through Thursday, except Sept. 15-Oct. 20 and Dec. 20-Jan. 2.

Craftsbury
C5

Craftsbury Inn
Main St, Box 36, Craftsbury, VT 05826
(802)586-2848 (800)336-2848

Circa 1850. Bird's-eye maple woodwork and embossed tin ceilings testify to the history of this Greek Revival inn, which also features random-width floors with square nails. The foundation and porch steps were made of bullseye granite, quarried in town. The living room fireplace once graced the first post office in Montpelier. Guest rooms sport country antiques and handmade quilts. The dining room is open to the public by advance reservation and features four dinner seatings.

Innkeeper(s): Blake & Rebecca Gleason. $60-110. MAP, AP. MC VISA TC. 10 rooms, 6 with PB. 1 conference room. Breakfast included in rates. Type of meal: full breakfast. Dinner, picnic lunch, banquet service, catering service and catered breakfast available. Beds: KQDT. VCR on premises. Antiques, fishing, shopping, downhill skiing, cross-country skiing and watersports nearby.

Certificate may be used: Valid Sunday through Thursday, January-December, except during foliage season.

Danby

I3

Quail's Nest B&B

PO Box 221, Danby, VT 05739-0221
(802)293-5099 Fax:(802)293-6300

Circa 1835. Located in the village, this Greek Revival inn features six guest rooms, and on each bed is found a handmade quilt. Full breakfasts are made to order by your innkeepers, who also provide early morning coffee or tea, afternoon tea and an evening snack. The Green Mountain National Forest is just to the east of the inn, providing many outstanding recreational opportunities. Outlet shopping is found just a few miles south in Manchester, and Alpine skiing is enjoyed at Bromley, Killington, Okemo, Pico and Stratton ski areas, all within easy driving distance.

Innkeeper(s): Greg & Nancy Diaz. $60-85. MC VISA AX PC TC. 6 rooms, 4 with PB. 1 conference room. Breakfast and afternoon tea included in rates. Types of meals: full breakfast and early coffee/tea. Beds: KDT. Turn-down service in room. Cable TV and VCR on premises. Antiques, fishing, shopping, downhill skiing, cross-country skiing, sporting events, theater and watersports nearby.

Certificate may be used: Sunday-Thursday, January, February, March, April, May, June, July, August, November, December, excluding our own special promotions.

Silas Griffith Inn

South Main St, Danby, VT 05739
(802)293-5567 (800)545-1509

Circa 1891. Originally on 55,000 acres, this stately Queen Anne Victorian mansion features solid cherry, oak and bird's-eye maple woodwork. Considered an architectural marvel, an eight-foot, round, solid-cherry pocket door separates the original music room from the front parlor.

Innkeeper(s): Paul & Lois Dansereau. $70-100. MC VISA PC TC. 17 rooms, 14 with PB. Breakfast and afternoon tea included in rates. Types of meals: full breakfast, gourmet breakfast and early coffee/tea. Picnic lunch available. Beds: QT. Cable TV, VCR, swimming and library on premises. Antiques, fishing, parks, shopping, downhill skiing, cross-country skiing, theater and watersports nearby.

Seen in: Vermont Weathervane, Rutland Business Journal, Vermont, Country Magazine.

"Never have I stayed at a B&B where the innkeepers were so friendly, sociable and helpful. They truly enjoyed their job."

Certificate may be used: Sunday-Thursday, January-March, May 1-Sept. 20, Oct. 20-Dec. 31.

Derby Line

A6

Derby Village Inn

46 Main St, Derby Line, VT 05830-9203
(802)873-3604

Circa 1900. This stately Victorian manor is more formal than whimsical, without the abundance of gingerbread trim common to the colorful "Painted Ladies." The interior is elegant, boasting intricate wainscoting and original light fixtures. Antique-filled bedchambers are decorated with lovely wallpapers, Victorian sinks and vintage wall fixtures. The parlors are wonderful places to relax, one includes a baby grand piano and a fireplace. The inn's library also includes a fireplace. Innkeeper Phyllis Moreau's vast collection of Norman Rockwell plates decorates the high shelves that surround the kitchen. Phyllis also has designed many of the quilts and crafts found throughout the home.

Innkeeper(s): Tom & Phyllis Moreau. $60-70. MC VISA DS PC TC. 8 rooms, 5 with PB. Breakfast included in rates. Types of meals: full breakfast and early coffee/tea. Beds: KQDT. Air conditioning in room. Cable TV, VCR and library on premises. Antiques, fishing, parks, shopping, downhill skiing, cross-country skiing, theater and watersports nearby.

Certificate may be used: Anytime except Saturdays and Sept. 1 to Oct. 31.

Dorset

I2

Marble West Inn

PO Box 847, Dorset West Rd,
Dorset, VT 05251-0847
(802)867-4155 (800)453-7629

Circa 1840. This historic Greek Revival inn boasts many elegant touches, including stenciling in its entrance hallways done by one of the nation's top artisans. Guests also will enjoy Oriental rugs, handsome marble fireplaces, stenciled walls and polished dark oak floors. A grand piano and antiques also decorate the home. Visitors delight at the many stunning views enjoyed at the inn, including Green Peak and Owl's Head mountains, flower-filled gardens and meadows and two trout-stocked ponds. Outlet shopping, galleries, theater, Emerald Lake State Park and a host of outdoor activities are nearby.

Innkeeper(s): June & Wayne Erla. $90-135. MC VISA AX PC. 8 rooms with PB, 1 with FP. 1 suite. Breakfast and afternoon tea included in rates. Type of meal: full breakfast. Beds: KQDT. Turn-down service in room. Library on premises. Antiques, fishing, parks, shopping, downhill skiing, cross-country skiing, theater and watersports nearby.

"A charming inn with wonderful hospitality. The room was comfortable, immaculate, and furnished with every imaginable need and comfort."

Certificate may be used: Anytime except fall foliage and holidays.

Essex Junction   D2

The Inn at Essex Junction
70 Essex Way,
Essex Junction, VT 05452-3383
(802)878-1100 Fax:(802)878-0063

Elegant furnishings and decor, each in a different style, grace the guest rooms at this luxurious Colonial inn, which carries a four-diamond rating. Several guest suites include whirlpool tubs, and 30 of the rooms include woodburning fireplaces. The two restaurants are run by the New England Culinary Institute, one a gourmet bistro and the other a more casual cafe. The inn also includes a swimming pool, library, art gallery and a bakery. Innkeeper(s): Linda Seville. $109-170. MC VISA AX DC CB DS. 97 rooms. Breakfast included in rates. Type of meal: continental breakfast.

Certificate may be used: November-July.

Fair Haven   H2

Maplewood Inn
Rt 22A S, Fair Haven, VT 05743-9802
(802)265-8039 (800)253-7729
Fax:(802)265-8210

Circa 1843. This beautifully restored Greek Revival house was once the family home of the founder of Maplewood Dairy, Isaac Wood. Period antiques and reproductions grace the inn's spacious rooms and suites. Some rooms boast fireplaces and all have sitting areas. A collection of antique spinning wheels and yarn winders is displayed. A porch wing, built around 1795, was a tavern formerly located down the road. Overlooking three acres of

lawn, the inn offers an idyllic setting. The parlor's cordial bar and evening turndown service are among the many amenities offered by the innkeepers. Innkeeper(s): Cindy & Doug Baird. $75-115. MC VISA AX DC CB DS PC TC. 5 rooms with PB, 4 with FP. 2 suites. 1 conference room. Breakfast, afternoon tea and evening snack included in rates. Beds: QD. Air conditioning, turn-down service, cable TV and VCR in room. Fax, copier, bicycles and library on premises. Amusement parks, antiques, fishing, parks, shopping, downhill skiing, cross-country skiing, sporting events, theater and watersports nearby.

Location: One mile south of Fair Haven village and 18 miles west of Rutland.

Seen in: Country, Innsider, Americana, New England Getaways.

"Your inn is perfection. Leaving under protest."

Certificate may be used: Jan. 2-June 30, anytime; July 1-Sept. 14, Sunday-Thursday; Nov.1-Dec. 23, anytime.

Fairlee   F6

Silver Maple Lodge & Cottages
S Main St, RR 1, Box 8,
Fairlee, VT 05045
(802)333-4326 (800)666-1946

Circa 1790. This old Cape farmhouse was expanded in the 1850s and became an inn in the '20s when Elmer & Della Batchelder opened their home to guests. It became so successful that several cottages, built from lumber on the property, were added. For 60 years, the Batchelder family continued the operation. They misnamed the lodge, however, mistaking

silver poplar trees on the property for what they thought were silver maples. Guest rooms are decorated with many of the inn's original furnishings and the new innkeepers have carefully restored the rooms and added several bathrooms. A screened-in porch surrounds two sides of the house. Three of the cottages include working fireplaces and one is handicap accessible.

Innkeeper(s): Scott & Sharon Wright. $49-74. MC VISA AX DS PC TC. 16 rooms, 14 with PB, 3 with FP. 8 cottages. Breakfast included in rates. Type of meal: continental breakfast. Beds: KQDT. VCR, copier and bicycles on premises. Handicap access. Antiques, fishing, parks, shopping, downhill skiing, cross-country skiing, theater and watersports nearby.

Location: East central Vermont.

Seen in: Boston Globe, Vermont Country Sampler, Travel Holiday.

"Your gracious hospitality and attractive home all add up to a pleasant experience."

Certificate may be used: Sunday-Thursday, Nov. 1-Sept. 15.

Hardwick   C5

Carolyn's Victorian Inn
15 Church St, PO Box 1087,
Hardwick, VT 05843-1087
(802)472-6338

Guests are treated to English tea and sweets upon arrival at this historic home, which boasts natural hardwood floors, original cherry woodwork and porches decorated with wicker. A cypress staircase leads up to the guest rooms, which have feather beds and quilts. The home's antiques are steeped in Vermont history. Carolyn serves up luscious breakfasts in the dining room on tables set with lacy tablecloths and fine linens. The special entrees include delectables such as banana-walnut pancakes, souffles or Yorkshire pudding with raspberry sauce.

Innkeeper(s): Carolyn Richter. $75-150. MC VISA. 5 rooms. Breakfast included in rates. Type of meal: full breakfast.

Certificate may be used: January, April, May, November, December.

Somerset House B&B
24 Highland Ave, PO Box 1098,
Hardwick, VT 05843
(802)472-5484 (800)838-8074

Circa 1880. After having been away for two years in England, the innkeepers returned home to Vermont and settled in this gracious Victorian house to provide lodging for those visiting this beautiful part of the country. The home is located in the heart of the village and set amid lawns and flower gardens. Breakfast is served in the dining room.

Innkeeper(s): Ruth & David Gaillard. $65-80. EP. MC VISA PC TC. 4 rooms. Breakfast and afternoon tea included in rates. Types of meals: full breakfast and gourmet breakfast. Beds: QT. Library on premises. Antiques, fishing, shopping, downhill skiing, cross-country skiing, theater and watersports nearby.

"We found a treasure. C'est super fun."

Certificate may be used: Anytime except August-October.

Killington   G3

The Cascades Lodge & Restaurant
RR 1 Box 2848,
Killington, VT 05751-9710
(802)422-3731 (800)345-0113
Fax:(802)422-3351

Circa 1980. Breathtaking views and modern amenities are found at this contemporary three-story country lodge in the heart of the Green Mountains. Guests enjoy an exercise area, indoor pool with sundeck, sauna and whirlpool. A bar and restaurant are on the premises, and the inn's amenities make it an ideal spot for meetings, reunions or weddings. Within walking distance is an 18-hole golf course and the Killington Summer Theater.

Innkeeper(s): Bob, Vickie & Andrew MacKenzie. $50-159. MAP, EP. MC VISA AX DS TC. 46 rooms, 45 with PB. 6 suites. Breakfast included in rates. Types of meals: full breakfast and early coffee/tea. Dinner, picnic lunch, catering service and room service available. Beds: KQD. Cable TV in room. VCR, fax, copier, spa and sauna on premises. Handicap access. Antiques, fishing, parks, shopping, downhill skiing, cross-country skiing and theater nearby.

Certificate may be used: May 15 to Oct. 15.

The Peak Chalet
PO Box 511, Southview Path,
Killington, VT 05751-0511
(802)422-4278

Circa 1978. This contemporary chalet-style inn is located in the heart of the Killington Ski Resort. That convenience is matched by the inn's elegant accommodations and attention to detail. Guest rooms feature either a four-poster, iron, panel or sleigh bed, all queen-size. The living room, with its impressive stone fireplace and view of the Green Mountains, is a favorite gathering spot for those not on the slopes.

Innkeeper(s): Greg & Diane Becker. $50-110. MC VISA AX DC PC TC. 4 rooms with PB. Breakfast and afternoon tea included in rates. Type of meal: continental-plus breakfast. Beds: QT. Cable TV and VCR on premises. Antiques, fishing, parks, shopping, downhill skiing, cross-country skiing, theater and watersports nearby.

Certificate may be used: Jan. 1 to Sept. 21 and Oct. 15 to Dec. 21, Sunday-Thursday, holidays excluded.

The Vermont Inn
Rt 4, Killington, VT 05751
(802)775-0708 (800)541-7795
Fax:(802)773-2440

Circa 1840. Surrounded by mountain views, this rambling red and white farmhouse has provided lodging and superb cuisine for many years. Exposed beams add to the atmosphere in the living and game

rooms. The award-winning dining room provides candlelight tables beside a huge fieldstone fireplace. Innkeeper(s): Megan & Greg Smith. $50-185. MAP, EP. MC VISA AX DC PC TC. 18 rooms with PB, 4 with FP. Breakfast and afternoon tea included in rates. Types of meals: full breakfast and early coffee/tea. Banquet service available. Beds: QDT. Air conditioning and ceiling fan in room. Cable TV, VCR, fax, copier, spa, swimming, sauna, tennis and library on premises. Handicap access. Antiques, fishing, parks, shopping, downhill skiing, cross-country skiing, theater and watersports nearby.

Seen in: New York Daily News, New Jersey Star Leader, Rutland Business Journal, Bridgeport Post Telegram, New York Times, Boston, Vermont.

"We had a wonderful time. The inn is breathtaking. Hope to be back."

Certificate may be used: Midweek, except during foliage season.

Landgrove   J3

The Landgrove Inn
Rd Box 215, Landgrove Rd,
Landgrove, VT 05148
(802)824-6673 (800)669-8466
Fax:(802)824-3055

Circa 1820. This rambling inn is located along a country lane in the valley of Landgrove in the Green Mountain National Forest. The Rafter Room is a game room with a fireside sofa for 12. Breakfast and dinner are served in the timbered dining room. Evening sleigh or hay rides are sometimes arranged. Rooms vary from dorm style to newly decorated rooms with country decor, so inquire when making your reservation. Innkeeper(s): Kathy & Jay Snyder. $65-115. MC VISA AX DS TC. 18 rooms, 16 with PB. 1 conference room. Breakfast included in rates. Type of meal: full breakfast. Afternoon tea and dinner available. Beds: QD. Cable TV, VCR, fax, copier and spa on premises. Antiques, fishing, parks, shopping, downhill skiing, cross-country skiing and theater nearby.

"A superb example of a country inn."

Certificate may be used: May 20-Sept. 20 and Dec. 20- April 1, Sunday through Thursday, non-holiday weeks.

Ludlow   I4

Black River Inn
100 Main St, Ludlow, VT 05149-1050
(802)228-5585

Circa 1835. This inn is located on the banks of the Black River, across from the gazebo at the village green. One guest room features an original copper-lined bathtub, and Abraham Lincoln is said to have slept in the 1794 walnut four-poster featured in another room. There is a two-bedroom suite available for families. A full country breakfast is served. Dinner and cocktails are available by reservation in the inn's dining room. Innkeeper(s): Nancy & Darwin Thomas. $79-125. MAP. MC VISA AX DS PC. 10 rooms, 8 with PB. Breakfast included in rates. Type of meal: full breakfast. Dinner available. Beds: KQD. Cable TV, VCR and library on premises. Antiques, fishing, shopping, downhill skiing, cross-country skiing and theater nearby.

Location: At the base of Okemo Mountain.

Certificate may be used: Fall and winter, Sunday through Thursday (non-holiday); spring and summer, anytime.

Echo Lake Inn
PO Box 154, Ludlow, VT 05149-0154
(802)228-8602 (800)356-6844
Fax:(802)228-3075

Circa 1840. Just minutes from Killington and Okemo ski areas, this New England country-style inn offers gourmet candlelight dining and a full country breakfast, a library and parlor. Guests also

may borrow canoes and are allowed to pick wild-flowers and berries in season. Within easy driving distance, guests will find golf, horseback riding, waterfalls and wineries. The inn is located in Tyson, five miles north of Ludlow. Innkeeper(s): John & Yvonne Pardieu, Chip Connelly. $58-168. MAP. MC VISA AX DS. 25 rooms, 10 with PB. 1 suite. Breakfast and dinner included in rates. Types of meals: full breakfast and early coffee/tea. Room service available. Beds: QDT. Ceiling fan in room. Cable TV, fax, spa, swimming, sauna, tennis and library on premises. Antiques, fishing, shopping, downhill skiing, cross-country skiing, theater and watersports nearby.

Seen in: Bon Appetit, Gourmet.

"Very special! We've decided to make the Echo Lake Inn a yearly tradition for our family."

Certificate may be used: All year except April, November and holidays. Sunday through Thursday.

Lyndonville   C6

Wheelock Inn B&B
RR 2 Box 160, Wheelock Rd,
Lyndonville, VT 05851-9101
(802)626-8503 Fax:(802)626-3403

Circa 1809. This 19th-century farmhouse features handhewn beams and wide pine flooring. Renovations have added to the charm and attractiveness. Spacious grounds and a quiet setting make it ideal for both the outdoor enthusiast and those seeking an escape. A guest lounge provides a place for games or reading. Bean Pond and Branch Brook offer boating, fishing and swimming opportunities. The inn's gardens furnish flowers, fruit and vegetables. Burke Mountain is nearby.

Innkeeper(s): John Ayers. $45-75. MC VISA. 3 rooms. Breakfast included in rates. Types of meals: full breakfast and early coffee/tea. Evening snack and picnic lunch available. Cable TV and VCR on premises. Antiques, shopping, downhill skiing, cross-country skiing and theater nearby.

Certificate may be used: Anytime except Sept. 15-Oct. 15.

Manchester   J2

The Battenkill Inn
PO Box 948, Manchester, VT 05254-0948
(802)362-4213 (800)441-1628
Fax:(802)362-0975

Circa 1840. There is something for everyone at this Victorian farmhouse inn. Guest rooms are filled with antiques, and four of them boast working fireplaces. Fine fishing is found in the Battenkill River

on the inn's grounds, and guests also are welcome to stroll down to the pond to feed the ducks or play croquet on the lush lawns. Two sitting rooms with fireplaces are popular gathering areas. Dining and shopping experiences await visitors in Manchester Village and Emerald Lake State Park is a short drive from the inn.

Innkeeper(s): Mary Jo & Ramsay Gourd. $75-140. MC VISA AX TC. 11 rooms with PB, 4 with FP. Breakfast and evening snack included in rates. Types of meals: full breakfast and early coffee/tea. Beds: KQDT. Air conditioning, turn-down service and ceiling fan in room. VCR, fax, copier and library on premises. Handicap access. Antiques, fishing, parks, shopping, downhill skiing, cross-country skiing, theater and watersports nearby.

"The inn is beautiful and the atmosphere soothing. "

Certificate may be used: November-June, Sunday-Thursday, no holidays.

The Inn at Manchester
PO Box 41, Historic Route 7A,
Manchester, VT 05254-0041
(802)362-1793 (800)273-1793
Fax:(802)362-3218

Circa 1880. This restored Victorian and its carriage house are in the National Register. In a setting of beautiful gardens and meadows of wildflowers with a meandering brook, the inn offers an extensive art collection of old prints and paintings. Guest rooms have French doors, bay windows and antiques. The inn was restored by the innkeepers. The guest pool is set in a secluded meadow.

Innkeeper(s): Stan & Harriet Rosenberg. $95-160. MC VISA AX DS PC TC. 18 rooms with PB, 2 with FP. 4 suites. 1 conference room. Breakfast and afternoon tea included in rates. Types of meals: full breakfast, gourmet breakfast and early coffee/tea. Beds: KQDT. Air conditioning in room. Cable TV, fax, copier, swimming and library on premises. Antiques, fishing, shopping, downhill skiing, cross-country skiing and theater nearby.

Seen in: New York Times, Boston Globe, Travel & Leisure, Gourmet, Newsday.

"Spectacular! Bob Newhart — eat your heart out. Thank you for being here. Very friendly, great retreat."

Certificate may be used: Monday through Thursday except foliage season and holidays.

Village Country Inn
PO Box 408, Rt 7A,
Manchester, VT 05254-0408
(802)362-1792 (800)370-0300
Fax:(802)362-7238

Circa 1889. Townsfolk refer to the Village Country Inn as the old summer house of the Kellogg cereal family. A Grecian-columned porch spans 100 feet across the front of the house and is filled with chintz-covered rockers and pots of flowers. Decorated in a French Country style, rooms feature

French lace and antiques. Dinner is served in a garden dining room, which overlooks marble terraces and fountains.

Innkeeper(s): Anne Degen. $140-225. MAP. MC VISA AX DS. 31 rooms, 30 with PB. 12 suites. Breakfast and dinner included in rates. Types of meals: full breakfast, gourmet breakfast and early coffee/tea. Picnic lunch available. Beds: KQD. Air conditioning, turn-down service, ceiling fan and cable TV in room. Fax on premises. Antiques, fishing, shopping, downhill skiing, cross-country skiing and theater nearby.

Location: Historic route 7A.

Seen in: Country Inns, Albany Times Union, Gourmet, Vacations, USA Today, ABC-TV, Country Decorating Ideas, Victorian.

"Absolutely charming. So much attention to detail. We loved it."

Certificate may be used: Sunday through Thursday, non-holiday, non-foliage, second night B&B only.

Manchester Center J2

Manchester Highlands Inn
Highland Ave, Box 1754A, Manchester Center, VT 05255
(802)362-4565 (800)743-4565
Fax:(802)362-4028

Circa 1898. This Queen Anne Victorian mansion sits proudly on the crest of a hill overlooking the village. From the three-story turret, guests can look out over Mt. Equinox, the Green Mountains and the valley below. Feather beds and down comforters adorn the beds in the guest rooms. A game room with billiards and a stone fireplace are

popular in winter, while summertime guests enjoy the outdoor pool, croquet lawn and veranda. Gourmet country breakfasts and home-baked afternoon snacks are served.

Innkeeper(s): Patricia & Robert Eichorn. $105-135. MC VISA AX PC TC. 15 rooms with PB. Breakfast and afternoon tea included in rates. Types of meals: full breakfast and gourmet breakfast. Beds: QDT. Cable TV, VCR, fax, swimming and library on premises. Antiques, fishing, parks, shopping, downhill skiing, cross-country skiing and theater nearby.

Seen in: Toronto Sun, Vermont, Asbury Park Press, Vermont Weathervane, Yankee Traveler.

"We couldn't believe such a place existed. Now we can't wait to come again."

Certificate may be used: Sunday through Thursday anytime except during holiday periods and from Sept. 15-Oct. 30.

Montgomery B4

Black Lantern Inn
Route 118, Montgomery, VT 05470
(802)326-4507 (800)255-8661
Fax:(802)326-4077

Circa 1803. This brick inn and restaurant originally served as a stagecoach stop. There is a taproom with beamed ceilings, and two downstairs lounges. A large three-bedroom suite has its own spa. Vermont antiques fill all the guest rooms. A few minutes from the inn, skiers (novice and expert) can ride the tramway to the top of Jay Peak.

Innkeeper(s): Rita & Allen Kalsmith. $60-125. MAP. EP. MC VISA AX DS PC TC. 16 rooms, 10 with PB. 6 suites. Breakfast included in rates. Type of meal: full breakfast. Beds: KQDT. Ceiling fan and VCR in room. Fax on premises. Antiques, fishing, downhill skiing and cross-country skiing nearby.

Seen in: Burlington Free Press, Los Angeles Times, Bon Appetit, Ottawa Citizen.

"...one of the four or five great meals of your life—Jay Stone, Ottawa Citizen."

Certificate may be used: Anytime except holiday (Christmas) and fall foliage.

Montpelier E4

Betsy's B&B
74 E State St, Montpelier, VT 05602-3112
(802)229-0466 Fax:(802)229-5412

Circa 1895. Within walking distance of downtown and located in the state's largest historic preservation district, this Queen Anne Victorian with romantic turret and carriage house features lavish Victorian antiques throughout its interior. Bay windows, carved woodwork, high ceilings, lace curtains and wood floors add to the authenticity. An exercise room, hot tub and porch tempt many visitors. The

full breakfast varies in content but not quality, and guest favorites include chocolate chip waffles and sourdough banana pancakes.

Innkeeper(s): Jon & Betsy Anderson. $50-110. MC VISA PC TC. 8 rooms, 7 with PB. 1 suite. Breakfast included in rates. Type of meal: full breakfast. Beds: QDT. Cable TV in room. VCR, fax, spa and library on premises. Antiques, fishing, parks, shopping, downhill skiing, cross-country skiing, theater and watersports nearby.

Certificate may be used: Nov.1 to April 30, holiday weekends excluded.

North Hero   B2

North Hero House
Rt 2 Box 106, Champlain Islands,
North Hero, VT 05474
(802)372-8237

Circa 1891. This three-story inn stands on a slight rise overlooking Lake Champlain and Vermont's highest peak, Mt. Mansfield. Three other houses, including the Wadsworth store located at the City Dock, also provide accommodations for the inn's guests. Rooms hang over the water's edge and feature waterfront porches.

Innkeeper(s): Ann Marie Sherlock. $65-140. EP. MC VISA AX DS. 23 rooms, 21 with PB. Breakfast included in rates. Type of meal: continental-plus breakfast. Beds: T. Sauna on premises. Handicap access.

Seen in: Gourmet.

"We have visited many inns and this house was by far the best, due mostly to the staff!"

Certificate may be used: All of May and June; Sunday, Monday, Tuesday, Wednesday - July, August, September and October.

North Troy   A5

Rose Apple Acres Farm
RR 2, Box 300, East Hill Rd,
North Troy, VT 05859
(802)988-4300

Circa 1900. Surrounded by panoramic views, this 52-acre working farm is the perfect place for relaxing vacations. Rest on the porch and take in the view or tour the grounds, lush with gardens, woods and ponds. The innkeepers house sheep, goats, cows and Belgian horses on the farm. Homemade goodies abound on the breakfast table, and guests can purchase farm-made maple syrup, jams, jellies and honey. Home-spun yarn also is available. The surrounding area boasts a number of factories, including the Cabot Cheese Factory and Ben & Jerry's Ice Cream Factory. Tour the Bread and Puppet Museum or the Haskell Free Library and Opera House. In winter, skiing the slopes at Jay Peak is a must.

Innkeeper(s): Jay & Camilla Mead. $50-60. TC. 3 rooms, 1 with PB. Breakfast included in rates. Types of meals: continental-plus breakfast and full breakfast. Beds: TD. VCR on premises. Antiques, fishing, parks, shopping, downhill skiing, cross-country skiing and watersports nearby.

Location: On the Canadian border.

Seen in: Washington Times, Vermont Life, Montreal Gazette.

"So relaxing, non-stress here."

Certificate may be used: Jan. 10-Sept. 10 and Oct. 15-Dec. 15, all days.

Northfield   E4

Northfield Inn
27 Highland Ave,
Northfield, VT 05663-1448
(802)485-8558

Circa 1901. A view of the Green Mountains can be seen from this Victorian inn, which is set on a hillside surrounded by gardens. The picturesque inn also affords a view of the village of Northfield and historic Norwich University. Rooms are decorated with antiques and Oriental rugs, and bedrooms feature European feather bedding and brass and carved-wood beds. Many outdoor activities are available on the three-acre property, including croquet, horseshoes and sledding. Visitors may want to take a climb uphill to visit the Old Slate Quarry or just relax on one of the porches overlooking the garden with bird songs, wind chimes and gentle breezes.

Innkeeper(s): Aglaia Stalb. $75-85. MC VISA PC TC. 8 rooms with PB. 2 suites. Breakfast and evening snack included in rates. Type of meal: full breakfast. Beds: QDT. Turn-down service, ceiling fan and cable TV in room. VCR, bicycles and library on premises. Antiques, fishing, parks, shopping, downhill skiing, cross-country skiing, sporting events, theater and watersports nearby.

Location: Overlooking the village.

"A treasure of sweet delights. Thank you."

Certificate may be used: November-June, Monday-Thursday, as available, holidays excluded.

Orwell
G2

Historic Brookside Farms

PO Box 36, Route 22A,
Orwell, VT 05760-9615
(802)948-2727 Fax:(802)948-2015

Circa 1789. Nineteen stately Ionic columns grace the front of this Neoclassical Greek Revival farmhouse, which was designed by James Lamb. This is a working farm with Hereford cattle, Hampshire sheep, maple syrup production and poultry. There are 300

acres of lush country landscape with several miles of cross-country skiing and a 26-acre pond for boating and fishing. Innkeeper Murray Korda is an orchestra leader/concert violinist and speaks nine languages. Innkeeper(s): Joan Korda. $85-150. MAP, AP. 7 rooms, 2 with PB. 1 suite. 1 conference room. Breakfast and afternoon tea included in rates. Types of meals: full breakfast, gourmet breakfast and early coffee/tea. Dinner, evening snack, picnic lunch, lunch and banquet service available. Beds: DT. VCR, fax, copier, computer and child care on premises. Handicap access. Antiques, fishing, shopping, downhill skiing, cross-country skiing, sporting events and theater nearby.

Seen in: New York Times, Burlington Free Press, Los Angeles Times, Preservation Magazine Antiques.

"A wonderful piece of living history."

Certificate may be used: Jan. 1-May 15, June 1-Aug. 31, Nov. 1-Dec. 15.

Poultney
H2

Tower Hall B&B

2 Bentley Ave, Poultney, VT 05764-1134
(802)287-4004 (800)894-4004

Circa 1895. A three-story peaked turret lends its name to this Queen Anne inn located next to Green Mountain College. Stained glass, polished woodwork and original fireplace mantels add to the Victorian atmosphere, and the guest rooms are furnished with antiques of the period. A sitting room adjacent to the guest rooms has its own fireplace. Kathy's cranberry nut and date nut breads are especially popular breakfast items.

Innkeeper(s): Kathy & Ed Kann. $55-75. MC VISA TC. 3 rooms, 1 with PB. Breakfast included in rates. Types of meals: continental-plus breakfast and early coffee/tea. Beds: D. Cable TV in room. Bicycles on premises. Antiques, fishing, parks, shopping, cross-country skiing and watersports nearby.

Location: Adjacent to Green Mountain College, near lakes region.

Seen in: Rutland Herald, Rutland Business Journal.

"Your beautiful home was delightful and just the best place to stay!"

Certificate may be used: Nov. 1-April 30, Sunday-Saturday.

Putney
K4

Misty Meadows B&B

Rr 1 Box 458, Putney, VT 05346-9601
(802)722-9517 (800)566-4789

Circa 1986. Herb and flower gardens and a gazebo overlooking a mountainous valley are two of the reasons why guests enjoy Misty Meadows. There are 10 acres to explore, dotted with wildflowers and a stream. Many guests are drawn to the living room, which offers a fireplace, books and games. The innkeepers' four friendly cats often entertain guests as well. There is plenty to do in the area, including berry picking, historic tours, flea markets, canoeing and skiing.

Innkeeper(s): Jane & Dave Savage. $65-85. PC. 3 rooms with PB. Breakfast included in rates. Type of meal: full breakfast. Beds: KQD. Ceiling fan in room. Library on premises. Handicap access. Amusement parks, antiques, fishing, shopping, downhill skiing, cross-country skiing, theater and watersports nearby.

Certificate may be used: Jan. 1-Sept. 15, Nov. 1-December, no holiday weekends.

Quechee
H5

Parker House Inn

16 Main St, Box 0780,
Quechee, VT 05059
(802)295-6077

Circa 1857. State Sen. Joseph C. Parker built this riverside manor in 1857, and three of the guest rooms are named in honor of his family. Mornings at the inn begin with a delicious country breakfast served in the Parker House Restaurant's cozy dining rooms. The chefs are justifiably proud of their "comfort food" cuisine. Airy guest rooms feature furnishings and unique decor. Guests can stroll next door to watch the art of glass blowing, or take a walk along the Ottauquechee River. The surroundings of this historic town provide hours of activity for nature lovers and shutterbugs. Fall foliage, of course, is an autumnal delight.

Innkeeper(s): Barbara & Walt Forrester. $100-135. MAP. MC VISA AX PC TC. 7 rooms with PB. Breakfast included in rates. Types of meals: full breakfast and gourmet breakfast. Dinner and banquet service available. Beds: KQ. Air conditioning and ceiling fan in room. Cable TV, VCR, fax and bicycles on premises. Antiques, fishing, downhill skiing, cross-country skiing, theater and watersports nearby.

Seen in: Quechee Times.

"The inn is lovely, the innkeepers are the greatest, excellent food and heavenly bed!"

Certificate may be used: Anytime, Nov. 1 through April 30; Sunday through Thursday, May 1 through July 30.

Rochester   G3

Liberty Hill Farm
RR 1 Box 158, Liberty Hill Rd,
Rochester, VT 05767-9501
(802)767-3926

Circa 1825. A working dairy farm with a herd of registered Holsteins, this farmhouse offers a country setting and easy access to recreational activities. The inn's location, between the White River and the Green Mountains, is ideal for outdoor enthusiasts and animal lovers. Barn cats, chickens, a dog, ducks, horses and turkeys are found on the grounds, not to mention the Holstein herd. Fishing, hiking, skiing and swimming are popular pastimes of guests, who are treated to a family-style dinner and full breakfast, both featuring many delicious homemade specialties.

Innkeeper(s): Robert & Beth Kennett. $120. MAP. PC TC. 7 rooms. Breakfast and dinner included in rates. Types of meals: full breakfast and early coffee/tea. Beds: QDT. VCR, fax, swimming, library and child care on premises. Antiques, fishing, parks, shopping, downhill skiing, cross-country skiing, sporting events, theater and watersports nearby.

Seen in: New York Times, Boston Globe, Vermont Life, Family Circle, Family Fun, Woman's Day, Country Home.

Certificate may be used: January-May, except holidays, Sunday-Thursday nights only.

Roxbury   E3

The Inn at Johnnycake Flats
RR1, Carrie Howe Road,
Roxbury, VT 05669
(802)485-8961

Circa 1806. The guest rooms in this registered historical site include family antiques, Shaker baskets and handmade quilts. The innkeepers can help you identify local wildflowers and birds. In winter, enjoy cross-country skiing and come home to sip hot cider beside the fire. Ask Debra and Jim about their hobby, cold climate gardening. A popular toboggan ride is down the lane in front of the inn. An old swimming hole known to locals for many years is popular.

Innkeeper(s): Debra & Jim Rogler. $65-75. DS PC TC. 4 rooms, 1 with PB. Breakfast and afternoon tea included in rates. Types of meals: continental breakfast, continental-plus breakfast, full breakfast and early coffee/tea. Beds: DT. Ceiling fan in room. VCR, bicycles and library on premises. Antiques, fishing, parks, shopping, downhill skiing, cross-country skiing, sporting events, theater and watersports nearby.

"You've nurtured a bit of paradise here, thanks for the lovely stay."

Certificate may be used: January-April, May (except 1st & 2nd week), June, July (except 2nd week), August, September (except 3rd & 4th week), October (except 1st & 2nd week), November and December, except holidays. Sunday-Thursday.

Rutland   H3

The Inn at Rutland
70 N Main St, Rutland, VT 05701-3249
(802)773-0575 (800)808-0575

Circa 1890. This distinctive Victorian mansion is filled with many period details, from high, plaster-worked ceilings to leather wainscotting in the dining room. Leaded windows and interesting woodwork are found throughout. Guest rooms have been decorated to maintain Victorian charm without a loss of modern comforts. A wicker-filled porch and

common rooms are available to guests. Located in central Vermont, The Inn at Rutland is only 15 minutes from the Killington and Pico ski areas.

Innkeeper(s): Bob & Tanya Liberman. $49-195. MC VISA DC CB DS TC. 10 rooms with PB. 1 suite. 2 conference rooms. Breakfast included in rates. Types of meals: full breakfast and gourmet breakfast. Beds: KQD. Air conditioning, ceiling fan and cable TV in room. VCR, fax, copier and bicycles on premises. Antiques, fishing, parks, shopping, downhill skiing, cross-country skiing, sporting events, theater and watersports nearby.

Location: In central Vermont.

"A lovely page in the 'memory album' of our minds."

Certificate may be used: April 1-Aug. 31 & Nov. 1-Dec. 15, Sunday-Thursday, excluding holidays,

Saint Johnsbury   D6

Looking Glass Inn
Rt 18 Box 199,
Saint Johnsbury, VT 05819
(802)748-3052 (800)579-3644

Circa 1850. This historic Second Empire Victorian once served travelers in the early 19th century. Visitors today enjoy the same Northeast Vermont setting and old-time hospitality, including special romantic candlelight dinners that can be arranged by reservation. Visitors start their day with a large country breakfast served in the mauve-accented dining room. Later in the day, guests are welcome to relax with a cup of tea or glass of sherry. Idyllic country roads are found throughout the surrounding area, perfect for exploring year-round.

Innkeeper(s): Barbara & Perry Viles. $60-85. MC VISA PC TC. 6 rooms, 2 with PB. 1 conference room. Breakfast and afternoon tea included in rates. Types of meals: continental breakfast, continental-plus breakfast, full breakfast and early coffee/tea. Beds: DT. Library on premises. Antiques, fishing, parks, shopping, downhill skiing, cross-country skiing and watersports nearby.

Certificate may be used: All year except holidays and period between Sept. 20 and Oct. 15.

Shoreham   F1

Shoreham Inn & Country Store
On The Green, Main St,
Shoreham, VT 05770
(802)897-5081 (800)255-5081

Circa 1790. Located just five miles east of Fort Ticonderoga, this Federal-style inn is a favorite of nature-lovers. Fascinating antique shops and many

Circa 1790

covered bridges are found in the area. The inn's dining room, with its large open fire, is a popular gathering spot, and guests also are drawn to the restored 19th-century sitting rooms. Guest rooms are furnished with country antiques. A country store is on the premises.

Innkeeper(s): Cleo & Fred Alter. $85. AP. MC VISA PC TC. 11 rooms, 1 with PB. Breakfast included in rates. Types of meals: full breakfast and early coffee/tea. Dinner available. Beds: QDT. Fax, copier and library on premises. Antiques, fishing, parks, shopping, downhill skiing, cross-country skiing, sporting events, theater and watersports nearby.

Certificate may be used: Anytime on space available basis.

South Londonderry   J3

Londonderry Inn
PO Box 301-931, Rt 100,
South Londonderry, VT 05155
(802)824-5226 Fax:(802)824-3146

Circa 1826. For almost 100 years, the Melendy Homestead, overlooking the West River and the village, was a dairy farm. In 1940, it became an inn. A tourist brochure promoting the area in 1881 said, "Are you overworked in the office, counting room or workshop and need invigorating influences? Come ramble over these hills and mountains and try the revivifying effects of Green Mountain oxygen." Dinner is available weekends and holiday periods, in season.

Innkeeper(s): Esther Fishman. $39-105. EP. 25 rooms, 20 with PB. 1 conference room. Breakfast included in rates. Dinner available. Beds: KQDT. Ceiling fan in room. Cable TV, VCR, fax and copier on premises. Antiques, fishing, shopping, downhill skiing, cross-country skiing, sporting events, theater and watersports nearby.

Location: Route 100 between Manchester and Springfield.
Seen in: New England Monthly, Ski, McCall's.

"A weekend in a good country inn, such as the Londonderry, is on a par with a weekend on the ocean in Southern Maine, which is to say that it's as good as a full week nearly anyplace else — The Hornet."

Certificate may be used: All times subject to availability, excludes holiday periods, fall foliage, Christmas week, President's week and winter weekends.

Stockbridge G3

Stockbridge Inn B&B

PO Box 45, Stockbridge, VT 05772-0045
(802)746-8165 (800)588-8165

This Italianate inn has a history involving Justin Morgan, who was instrumental in developing the Morgan horse breed. The inn's location in the countryside outside of Stockbridge and provides easy access to the nearby White River, famed for its canoeing, trout fishing and white-water rafting. Killington Mountain skiing is within easy driving distance, and autumn colors in the surrounding area are hard to beat.

Innkeeper(s): Janice Hughes. $40-90. MC VISA. 6 rooms. Breakfast included in rates. Type of meal: full breakfast. Cable TV and VCR on premises. Antiques, shopping, downhill skiing, cross-country skiing and theater nearby.

Certificate may be used: Anytime except holiday weeks/weekends and fall foliage.

Stowe D4

Brass Lantern Inn

717 Maple St, Stowe, VT 05672-4250
(802)253-2229 (800)729-2980
Fax:(802)253-7425

Circa 1810. This rambling farmhouse and carriage barn rests at the foot of Mt. Mansfield. A recent award-winning renovation has brought a new shine to the inn from the gleaming plank floors to the polished woodwork and crackling fireplaces. Quilts and antiques fill the guest rooms and some, like the Honeymoon Room, have their own fireplace and mountain view. A complimentary afternoon and evening tea is provided along with a full Vermont-style breakfast. 1995 and 1996 winner of the Golden Fork Award from the Gourmet Dinners Society of North America.

Innkeeper(s): Andy Aldrich. $75-175. MC VISA AX. 9 rooms with PB, 3 with FP. Breakfast and afternoon tea included in rates. Types of meals: full breakfast and early coffee/tea. Beds: QDT. Air conditioning in room. VCR, fax, copier and library on premises. Antiques, fishing, parks, shopping, downhill skiing, cross-country skiing, sporting events, theater and watersports nearby.

Location: One-half mile from village center.
Seen in: Vermont, Vermont Life, Innsider, Discerning Traveler, Ski.

"The little things made us glad we stopped."

Certificate may be used: Midweek April, May, and to mid-June, late October, November, and to early December, excluding holidays.

Plum Door

PO Box 606, School St,
Stowe, VT 05672-0606
(802)253-9995 (800)258-7586

Circa 1890. The Plum Door is a relaxing place to enjoy a ski vacation. The innkeepers offer secure equipment lockers for each guest, and the inn is near many of Stowe's celebrated slopes. The cozy guest rooms include ceiling fans. The Dunbar and Spaulding rooms afford mountain views, and the Dunbar room also includes a fireplace. During the warmer months, the homemade continental breakfasts are served on the balcony. For an extra charge, guests enjoy privileges at a nearby athletic club.

Innkeeper(s): Herb & Fran Greenhalgh. $50-90. MC VISA TC. 3 rooms with PB, 1 with FP. Breakfast included in rates. Type of meal: continental-plus breakfast. Beds: Q. Ceiling fan in room. Cable TV and VCR on premises. Antiques, fishing, parks, shopping, downhill skiing, cross-country skiing and theater nearby.

Certificate may be used: May 1-Sept. 15 & Oct. 15-Dec. 15, Sunday-Friday.

The Siebeness Inn

3681 Mountain Rd,
Stowe, VT 05672-4764
(802)253-8942 (800)426-9001
Fax:(802)253-9232

Circa 1952. A multi-course full breakfast enjoyed with a view of majestic Mt. Mansfield is a highlight of this New England Colonial inn. The charming village of Stowe is just a few miles away, and a free trolley shuttle takes visitors there to partake of the town's many attractions. The inn offers bicycles, an exercise room, hot tub and pool for relaxing and recreation. A fireplace, library and television are available in the inn's common areas. Favorite guest activities include tours of Ben & Jerry's Ice Cream Factory, Green Mountain Chocolate Factory and the Shelburne Museum. During the winter months, breakfast and dinner may be included in the price of the room.

Innkeeper(s): Sue & Nils Andersen. $65-135. MAP. MC VISA AX DS PC TC. 11 rooms with PB. 1 cottage. Breakfast included in rates. Types of meals: full breakfast and early coffee/tea. Afternoon tea, dinner, evening snack and picnic lunch available. Beds: KQDT. Air conditioning in room. Cable TV, VCR, fax, copier, swimming, bicycles and library on premises. Antiques, fishing, parks, shopping, downhill skiing, cross-country skiing, sporting events, theater and watersports nearby.
Certificate may be used: January, April 1-June 30 (all days), Aug. 20-Sept. 15 (Sunday-Friday), Oct. 22-Dec. 15 (all days).

Ye Olde England Inne

433 Mountain Rd, Stowe, VT 05672-4628
(802)253-7558 (800)477-3771
Fax:(802)253-8944

Circa 1890. Originally a farmhouse, Ye Olde England Inne has acquired a Tudor facade, interior beams and stone work. Brass and copper pieces, Laura Ashley decor and English antiques add to the atmosphere. The inn sponsors polo events and features a polo package. Gliding, golf and ski packages are also available. A popular honeymoon package includes champagne sleigh rides. Nightly entertainment is provided at Mr. Pickwick's Polo Pub and romantic dining is available at Copperfields.
Innkeeper(s): Christopher Francis. $98-375. MAP. MC VISA AX. 30 rooms, 20 with PB, 4 with FP. 12 suites. 1 conference room. Breakfast included in rates. Types of meals: full breakfast and gourmet breakfast.

Afternoon tea and gourmet lunch available. Beds: QDT. Air conditioning, ceiling fan and cable TV in room. Fax, copier and spa on premises. Antiques, parks, shopping, downhill skiing, cross-country skiing, sporting events and theater nearby.
Location: In the village.
Seen in: National Geographic Traveler, Channel 5 TV in Boston.

"Even more perfect than we anticipated."

Certificate may be used: Midweek, non-holiday, subject to advance reservations and availability.

Townshend   K4

Boardman House

PO Box 112, On the Green,
Townshend, VT 05353-0112
(802)365-4086

Circa 1840. This stately Greek Revival is located on the village green of Townshend in Southeast Vermont. Guests enjoy a full breakfast before beginning their day, which could include antiquing, canoeing or kayaking in the West River or skiing at Bromley, Magic Mountain or Stratton ski areas, all

within easy driving distance. The inn boasts a large, lush lawn and pretty gardens, a parlor with a library and a refreshing sauna. Early coffee or tea is served and picnic lunches are available.
Innkeeper(s): Paul Weber & Sarah Messenger. $70-75. PC TC. 6 rooms, 5 with PB. 1 suite. Breakfast included in rates. Types of meals: full breakfast, gourmet breakfast and early coffee/tea. Picnic lunch available. Beds: QT. Air conditioning in room. Cable TV, VCR, sauna and

library on premises. Antiques, fishing, parks, shopping, downhill skiing, cross-country skiing and watersports nearby.

Location: On Village Green at crossroads of Rte 35 and 30.

Certificate may be used: Nov. 1-Dec. 15, Feb. 28-Aug. 31

Townshend Country Inn

RR 1 Box 3100,
Townshend, VT 05353-9705
(802)365-4141 (800)569-1907

Circa 1980. Perennial gardens grace the front and back of this Colonial farmhouse, situated on four riverfront acres. The inn is decorated with quilts, stenciling, antiques and reproductions. The innkeeper serves homemade muffins and fruit breads at breakfast.

Innkeeper(s): Joseph & Donna Peters. $65-85. MC VISA DS TC. 3 rooms. Breakfast included in rates. Type of meal: continental-plus breakfast. Dinner, banquet service and catering service available. Beds: D. Ceiling fan in room. Cable TV on premises. Amusement parks, antiques, fishing, parks, shopping, downhill skiing, cross-country skiing, sporting events, theater and watersports nearby.

Certificate may be used: May 10-March 31, Sunday-Thursday.

Waitsfield E3

Lareau Farm Country Inn

PO Box 563, Rt 100, Waitsfield, VT
05673-0563
(802)496-4949 (800)833-0766

Circa 1794. This Greek Revival house was built by Simeon Stoddard, the town's first physician. Old-fashioned roses, lilacs, delphiniums, iris and peonies fill the gardens. The inn sits in a wide meadow next to the crystal-clear Mad River. A canoe trip or a refreshing swim are possibilities here.

Innkeeper(s): Dan & Susan Easley. $60-125. MC VISA DS PC TC. 13 rooms, 11 with PB. 1 suite. 1 conference room. Breakfast included in rates. Types of meals: full breakfast, gourmet breakfast and early coffee/tea. Dinner available. Beds: QD. Swimming and library on premises. Antiques, fishing, shopping, downhill skiing, cross-country skiing and theater nearby.

Location: Central Vermont, Sugarbush Valley.

Seen in: Pittsburgh Press, Philadelphia Inquirer, Los Angeles Times.

"Hospitality is a gift. Thank you for sharing your gift so freely with us."

Certificate may be used: Dec. 15-April 1 and May 1-June 29, holiday weeks excluded.

Mad River Inn

Tremblay Rd, PO Box 75,
Waitsfield, VT 05673
(802)496-7900 (800)832-8278
Fax:(802)496-5390

Circa 1860. Surrounded by the Green Mountains, this Queen Anne Victorian sits on seven scenic acres along the Mad River. The charming inn boasts attractive woodwork throughout, highlighted by ash, bird's-eye maple and cherry. Guest rooms feature European featherbeds and include the Hayden

Breeze Room, with a king brass bed, large windows and sea relics, and the Abner Doubleday Room, with a queen ash bed and mementos of baseball's glory days. The inn sports a billiard table, gazebo, organic gardens and a Jacuzzi overlooking the mountains. Autumn visitors are free to take home a pumpkin from the inn's prolific patch.

Innkeeper(s): Rita & Luc Maranda. $69-125. MC VISA AX. 10 rooms with PB. Breakfast and afternoon tea included in rates. Type of meal: gourmet breakfast. Beds: KQ. Turn-down service and ceiling fan in room. Cable TV, VCR, fax, spa, stables and child care on premises. Antiques, fishing, shopping, downhill skiing, cross-country skiing, sporting events, theater and watersports nearby.

Seen in: Innsider, Victorian Homes, Let's Live, Skiing, AAA Home & Away, Tea Time at the Inn, Travel & Leisure.

"Your hospitality was appreciated, beautiful house and accommodations, great food & friendly people, just to name a few things. We plan to return and we recommend the Mad River Inn to friends & family."

Certificate may be used: Sunday-Thursday, except Dec. 21-31, Sept. 21-Oct 15.

Millbrook Inn

RFD Box 62, Waitsfield, VT 05673
(802)496-2405 (800)477-2809

Circa 1855. Guests enter Millbrook through the warming room, where an antique Glenwood parlor stove usually is roaring. This classic Cape-style farmhouse is known for its individually stenciled guest rooms, Green Mountain views and one of the valley's best dining rooms.

Innkeeper(s): Joan Gorman. $92-140. MAP. MC VISA AX. 7 rooms, 4 with PB. Breakfast included in rates. Type of meal: full breakfast. Beds: DT. Ceiling fan in room. Bicycles on premises. Antiques, fishing, shopping, downhill skiing and cross-country skiing nearby.

Seen in: Daily News, Los Angeles Times, Boston Globe, Travel Today, Gourmet.

"A weekend at your place is just what the doctor had in mind."

Certificate may be used: Rate includes dinner also. Subject to availability winter weekdays-does not include Christmas week or February vacation week.

The Valley Inn

Rt 1 Box 8 Rt 100, Waitsfield, VT 05673
(802)496-3450 (800)638-8466

Circa 1949. The exterior of this Colonial home is a deep, rich oak, an inviting site down this country road. The decor is comfortable with quilts and old-fashioned furnishings. The inn includes a pub and restaurant, and guests are treated to a country breakfast. The grounds offer an outdoor spa, and seasonal activities abound in the area. For the truly adventures, guests can learn how to use a glider and soar around the countryside.

Innkeeper(s): Bill & Millie Stinson. $59-99. MAP. MC VISA AX TC. 20 rooms with PB. 1 conference room. Breakfast included in rates. Type of meal: full breakfast. Dinner available. Beds: QDT. Cable TV, VCR, copier, sauna and bicycles on premises. Handicap access. Antiques, fishing, parks, shopping, downhill skiing, cross-country skiing, theater and watersports nearby.

Certificate may be used: May 15-Sept. 15, Sunday-Friday; Jan. 2-Feb. 2, Sunday-Thursday. Dinner is included in the price in winter.

Waitsfield Inn

Rt 100, PO Box 969,
Waitsfield, VT 05673
(802)496-3979 (800)758-3801

Circa 1825. This Federal-style home once served as a parsonage and was home to a state senator. Surrounded by a picket fence, the home's grounds boast a large garden. The old barn is now the common room and includes the original wood-planked flooring and a fireplace. Guest quarters are filled with period antiques. The inn is close to all the sites in Waitsfield, and the area offers an abundance of outdoor activities throughout the year.

Innkeeper(s): Ruth Lacey. $69-119. MC VISA AX DS. 14 rooms with PB. Breakfast included in rates. Type of meal: full breakfast. Evening snack available. Beds: DT. Bicycles on premises. Antiques, fishing, shopping, downhill skiing, cross-country skiing, theater and watersports nearby.

Location: Near Sugarbush and Mad River Glen ski areas.

Certificate may be used: Sunday-Thursday, March, July, August, Sept.1-15, anytime (excluding holidays) in January, April, May, June, November, December.

Waterbury D3

The Inn at Blush Hill

Blush Hill Rd, Box 1266,
Waterbury, VT 05676
(802)244-7529 (800)736-7522
Fax:(802)244-7314

Circa 1790. This shingled Cape-style house was once a stagecoach stop en route to Stowe and is the oldest Inn in Waterbury. A 12-foot-long pine farmhand's table is set near the double fireplace and the kitchen bay window, revealing views of the Worcester Mountains. A favorite summertime breakfast is pancakes with fresh blueberries, topped with ice cream and maple syrup.

Innkeeper(s): Gary & Pam Gosselin. $69-130. MC VISA AX DS PC TC. 5 rooms with PB, 1 with FP. Breakfast, afternoon tea and evening snack included in rates. Types of meals: full breakfast, gourmet breakfast and early coffee/tea. Beds: QDT. Air conditioning, turn-down service and ceiling fan in room. Cable TV, fax and library on premises. Antiques, fishing, parks, shopping, downhill skiing, cross-country skiing, theater and watersports nearby.

Location: Three-quarter mile off scenic Rte 100 at I-89.

Seen in: Vermont, Charlotte Observer, Yankee, New York Times, Ski.

"Our room was wonderful — especially the fireplace. Everything was so cozy and warm."

Certificate may be used: Sunday through Thursday, January to June; November-December (excluding holidays).

Grunberg Haus B&B and Cabins

RR 2 Box 1595-No,
Waterbury, VT 05676-9621
(802)244-7726 (800)800-7760

Circa 1972. This hillside Tyrolean chalet was hand-built by George and Irene Ballschneider. The Grunberg Haus captures the rustic charm of country guest homes in Austria with its wall of windows overlooking the Green Mountains, a massive fieldstone fireplace and a self-service Austrian pub. Rooms are furnished with antique furniture and cozy quilts. All rooms open onto the second-floor balcony that surrounds the chalet. Attractions in Stowe, the Mad River Valley, Montpelier and the Lake Champlain region are close at hand.

Innkeepers regularly entertain their guests at the Steinway Grand piano.

Innkeeper(s): Chris Sellers & Mark Frohman. $55-125. MAP. MC VISA AX DS PC TC. 15 rooms, 10 with PB, 3 with FP. 1 suite. 4 cottages. 1 conference room. Breakfast and afternoon tea included in rates. Types of meals: full breakfast, gourmet breakfast and early coffee/tea. Beds: QDT. Spa, sauna, tennis and library on premises. Antiques, fishing, parks, shopping, downhill skiing, cross-country skiing, theater and watersports nearby.

Location: South of Waterbury on scenic route 100, between Stowe and Waitsfield.

Seen in: Hudson Dispatch, Innsider, Ski, Toronto Globe, Vermont, Washington Times, Yankee.

"You made an ordinary overnight stay extraordinary."

Certificate may be used: March 20-June 20 (daily), Oct. 20-Dec. 20 (daily), January, February and March (Monday-Thursday).

Thatcher Brook Inn

PO Box 490, Rt 100 N, Waterbury, VT
05676-0490
(802)244-5911 (800)292-5911
Fax:(802)244-1294

Circa 1899. Listed in the Vermont Register of Historic Buildings, this restored Victorian mansion features a porch with twin gazebos. A covered walkway leads to the historic Wheeler House. Guest rooms are decorated in Laura Ashley-style. The inn specializes in Country French cuisine and Bailey's Fireside Tavern is on the premises.

Innkeeper(s): Kelly & Peter Varty. $75-185. MAP. MC VISA AX DC DS PC TC. 22 rooms with PB, 4 with FP. 1 suite. 1 conference room. Breakfast included in rates. Type of meal: full breakfast. Evening snack and banquet service available. Beds: KQDT. Ceiling fan in room. Cable TV, VCR, fax, copier and library on premises. Handicap access. Antiques, fishing, parks, shopping, downhill skiing, cross-country skiing, sporting events, theater and watersports nearby.

"I'd have to put on a black tie in Long Island to find food as good as this and best of all it's in a relaxed country atmosphere. Meals are underpriced."

Certificate may be used: November through August, Sunday through Thursday.

West Dover   K3

Austin Hill Inn

Rt 100, Box 859, West Dover, VT 05356
(802)464-5281 (800)332-7352
Fax:(802)464-1229

Circa 1930. Situated outside the historic village of West Dover, at the edge of a mountain, this completely renovated inn has walls decorated with old barn board and floral Victorian wallpapers.

Old antiques and family heirlooms include family photographs dating from 1845. Most rooms have balconies and four-poster or brass beds. A full country breakfast in the fireplaced dining room is offered, as well as afternoon tea, complimentary wine and cheese.

Innkeeper(s): Robbie Sweeney. $90-125. MC VISA AX DS. 12 rooms with PB. 1 conference room. Breakfast and afternoon tea included in rates. Type of meal: full breakfast. Catering service available. Beds: KQDT. Fax, copier and computer on premises. Antiques, fishing, parks, downhill skiing, cross-country skiing and theater nearby.

Location: Mount Snow Valley.

Seen in: Garden City Life, Newsday, Greenwich Times.

"Another repeat of perfection."

Certificate may be used: Sunday through Thursday, non-holidays excluding Sept. 15 to Oct. 20.

West Hartford
G5

The Half Penney Inn B&B
PO Box 84,
West Hartford, VT 05084-0084
(802)295-6082

Circa 1775. This brick Federal-style home was one of the first farms in Vermont and still features the original walk-in fireplace and bake ovens. Original wideboard floors, woodwork and old window panes along with an assortment of antiques create a homey atmosphere. Guests enjoy roaming the 40 acres of meadows and woods. The Appalachian Trail is just behind the inn and the White River is around the corner. Despite its secluded country location, the towns of Quechee, Woodstock and Hanover are close by. Golfing, horseback riding and an abundance of hiking and skiing are in the area.
Innkeeper(s): Gretchen Fairweather, Bonny Hooper. $85-130. MC VISA AX. 5 rooms with PB, 1 with FP. Breakfast included in rates. Types of meals: full breakfast and early coffee/tea. Afternoon tea, picnic lunch and banquet service available. Beds: KQDT. Turn-down service in room. Child care on premises. Antiques, fishing, parks, shopping, downhill skiing, cross-country skiing, sporting events, theater and watersports nearby.
Seen in: NBC-TV, BBC-TV, Valley News.

"Wonderful breakfast. Your hospitality was warm and friendly, I felt right at home!"

Certificate may be used: Nov. 1 to Sept. 15, Sunday-Thursday.

Weston
J3

Darling Family Inn
Rt 100, Weston, VT 05161
(802)824-3223

This two-story inn also features two cottages. Located in the Green Mountains, just minutes from Bromley, Okemo and Stratton ski areas, the inn provides a taste of life from the early Colonial days. Guest rooms feature handmade quilts crafted locally. The cottages include kitchenettes, and pets are welcome in the cottages if prior arrangements are made.
Innkeeper(s): Chapin Darling. $65-95. 7 rooms. 2 suites. Breakfast included in rates. Type of meal: full breakfast. Turn-down service in room. VCR on premises. Antiques, shopping, downhill skiing, cross-country skiing and theater nearby.

Certificate may be used: Sundays through Thursday (excluding Sundays of holiday weekends); January through June; Sept. 1 through 15; Oct. 15 through Dec. 23.

Wilder Homestead Inn
25 Lawrence Hill Rd,
Weston, VT 05161-5600
(802)824-8172

Circa 1827. Within walking distance of the Green Mountain National Forest, this inn with both Federal and Greek Revival stylings features seven guest rooms, all with private baths and views. Five of the rooms have log-burning fireplaces. Large

country breakfasts may include eggs, homemade biscuits with jam, hotcakes with genuine Vermont maple syrup, Lumberjack mush or sausage. Spring visitors enjoy an abundance of wildflowers. A craft shop is on the premises.
Innkeeper(s): Peggy Varner. $65-105. MC VISA. 7 rooms, 5 with PB. Breakfast included in rates. Type of meal: full breakfast. Beds: KQDT. Ceiling fan in room. Cable TV and VCR on premises. Antiques, fishing, shopping, downhill skiing, cross-country skiing, sporting events and theater nearby.
Seen in: Gourmet, Country, Boston Globe, San Paulo, Brazil.

"Like coming home to Grandma's house. Lovely setting in quaint village. Nice to be back."

Certificate may be used: Sunday through Thursday, non-holiday days. January-March; May through July; November and December.

Wilder
H5

Stonecrest Farm B&B
PO Box 504, 119 Christian St,
Wilder, VT 05088-0504
(802)296-2425 (800)730-2425
Fax:(802)295-1135

Circa 1810. Two acres of grounds and a charming red barn create a secluded, country atmosphere at Stonecrest Farm. The former dairy farm was owned by a prominent Vermont family and hosted notable guests such as Calvin Coolidge and Amelia Earhart. Guest rooms are decorated with antiques, and beds are topped with down comforters. The abundant breakfasts feature a different entree each morning. Orange French toast and vegetable frittatas are some of the possibilities.

Innkeeper(s): Gail L. Sanderson. $95-120. MC VISA AX PC TC. 6 rooms with PB. Breakfast and afternoon tea included in rates. Types of meals: full breakfast and early coffee/tea. Beds: QDT. Cable TV, VCR, fax, copier and library on premises. Antiques, fishing, parks, shopping, downhill skiing, cross-country skiing, sporting events, theater and watersports nearby.

Certificate may be used: From Jan. 2 to Sept. 15 and Nov. 1 to Dec. 15 excluding certain Dartmouth College weekends for parents not available because previously booked.

Wilmington K3

The Inn at Quail Run

HCR 63 Box 28, 106 Smith Rd,
Wilmington, VT 05363-7905
(802)464-3362 (800)343-7227
Fax:(802)464-3362

Circa 1968. Enjoy the serenity of the Vermont countryside at this inn surrounded by 12 private acres and mountain views. Brass and antique beds are covered with comforters perfect for snuggling. A hearty country breakfast is served each morning. Murder-mystery and Christmas Inn Vermont packages add an extra flair to vacations. Relax in the sauna after working out in the exercise room or solar-heated pool. Skiing and sleigh rides make good use of the Vermont winter. Country Theatre, flea markets and the Marlboro Music Festival are nearby attractions.

Innkeeper(s): Tom, Marie & Molly Martin. $75-125. MC VISA AX DS TC. 13 rooms with PB, 4 with FP. 1 suite. 1 cottage. Type of meal: full breakfast. Beds: KQT. Cable TV, VCR, fax, copier, swimming, sauna and library on premises. Antiques, fishing, parks, shopping, downhill skiing, cross-country skiing, theater and watersports nearby.

Certificate may be used: Anytime space available.

Woodstock H4

Bailey's Mills B&B

PO Box 117, Bailey's Mills Rd,
Woodstock (Reading), VT 05062
(802)484-7809 (800)639-3437

Circa 1820. This historic Federal-style inn features the architectural stylings of a Southern manor and boasts a ballroom and 11 fireplaces, with two original beehive ovens. The suite has a king bed and private sun porch. Two rooms have working fireplaces. The inn's sun porch overlooks the ruins of the old mill dam of the original house. The quiet country setting is perfect for bike rides and relaxing strolls, and terrific photo opportunities are found at Jenne Farm, just a few minutes away.

Innkeeper(s): Barbara Thaeder & Don Whitaker. $70-105. MC VISA AX PC TC. 3 rooms with PB, 2 with FP. 1 suite. Breakfast included in rates.

Types of meals: continental-plus breakfast and early coffee/tea. Beds: KQ. Swimming and library on premises. Antiques, fishing, parks, shopping, downhill skiing, cross-country skiing and theater nearby.

"If words could encapsulate what a wonderful weekend would be, it would have to be 'Bailey's Mills B&B.' Your home is beautiful. It is elegant yet homey."

Certificate may be used: November-May, Sunday-Thursday or call anytime for last minute openings.

Canterbury House

43 Pleasant St,
Woodstock, VT 05091-1129
(802)457-3077 (800)390-3077

Circa 1880. National Geographic tabbed Woodstock as one of America's most beautiful villages, and this Victorian inn offers a lovely stopping place for those exploring the area. Visitors find themselves within easy walking distance of antique stores, art galleries, museums, restaurants and shopping. The inn has bicycles available for guest use, perfect for an outing on the area's scenic country roads. Ski lifts at Killington, Pico and Okemo are only minutes away.

Innkeeper(s): Fred & Celeste Holden. $85-150. MC VISA AX PC. 8 rooms with PB, 1 with FP. Breakfast included in rates. Type of meal: gourmet breakfast. Dinner, evening snack and picnic lunch available. Beds: KQDT. Air conditioning and cable TV in room. VCR and bicycles on premises. Antiques, fishing, parks, shopping, downhill skiing, cross-country skiing, sporting events, theater and watersports nearby.

Seen in: Philadelphia Inquirer.

Certificate may be used: Jan. 1-Sept. 15, Nov. 1-Dec. 31.

Carriage House of Woodstock

15 Route 4 W,
Woodstock, VT 05091-1253
(802)457-4322

Circa 1850. This century-old home has been generously refurbished and features rooms filled with period antiques and individual decor. Those in search of relaxation will find plenty of possibilities, from a hammock tucked underneath a shade tree to a porch offering a view of trees and fields. Antique shopping, the historic Billings Farm Museum and plenty of outdoor activities are found in the Woodstock area. Fall and spring bring an explosion of color, and scenic drives will take you under covered bridges.

Innkeeper(s): Dennis Wagner. $95-125. MC VISA. 7 rooms, 5 with PB. Breakfast included in rates. Type of meal: full breakfast. Beds: KQT. Fishing nearby.

Certificate may be used: Sunday-Thursday, Nov. 1-Aug. 1 except holidays and holiday weekends.

Charleston House

21 Pleasant St,
Woodstock, VT 05091-1131
(802)457-3843

Circa 1810. This authentically restored brick Greek Revival town house is furnished with antiques, an art collection and Oriental rugs. Most of the rooms boast four-poster beds. The Summer Kitchen room also offers a private entrance. A hearty full breakfast starts off the day, and the innkeepers serve afternoon refreshments as well.

Innkeeper(s): Bill Hough. $90-150. MC VISA AX. 7 rooms with PB. Breakfast included in rates. Type of meal: full breakfast. Beds: QT. Antiques, fishing, downhill skiing, cross-country skiing and theater nearby.

Seen in: Harbor News, Boston Business Journal, Weekend Getaway, Inn Spots, Special Places.

"I felt like I was a king, elegant but extremely comfortable."

Certificate may be used: January-September, November-January.

Woodstocker B&B

61 River St, Woodstock, VT 05091-1227
(802)457-3896 (800)457-3896

Circa 1830. Enjoy the sites of historic Woodstock at this inn. The innkeepers recently completed an extensive redecorating of their farmhouse. Each room is unique and cozy, and the suites feature

kitchens and living rooms. Woodstock boasts many quaint shops and art galleries. Watch glass being made at a local glass factory, or try out the Alpine slide at Pico.

Innkeeper(s): Jerry Lowe. $95-130. MC VISA. 9 rooms with PB. 2 suites. Breakfast included in rates. Types of meals: full breakfast and early coffee/tea. Afternoon tea available. Beds: QD. Air conditioning, ceiling fan and cable TV in room. VCR, fax and copier on premises. Antiques, shopping, downhill skiing, cross-country skiing, sporting events, theater and watersports nearby.

"Thank you for a wonderful stay and delicious breakfast at The Woodstocker. We (the five Midwest women) found it to be the cleanest and nicest inn we stayed in on our journey through Vermont and New Hampshire."

Certificate may be used: Sunday through Thursday, except July 1-Oct. 20 and Dec. 20-Jan. 1.

Virginia

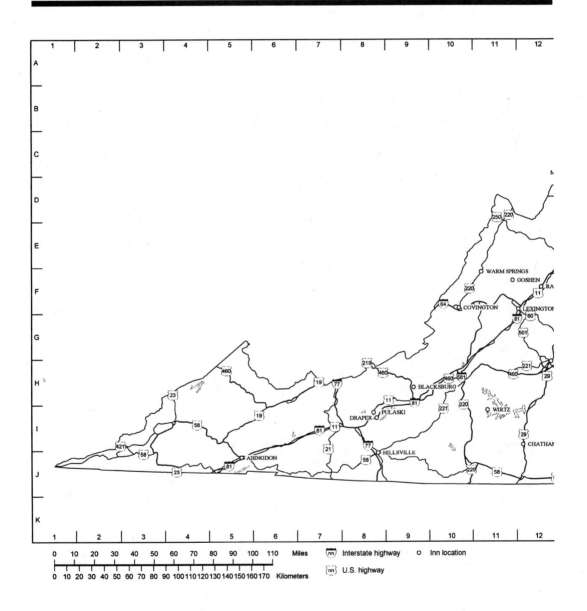

0 10 20 30 40 50 60 70 80 90 100 110 Miles

0 10 20 30 40 50 60 70 80 90 100 110 120 130 140 150 160 170 Kilometers

(nn) Interstate highway   o Inn location

(nn) U.S. highway

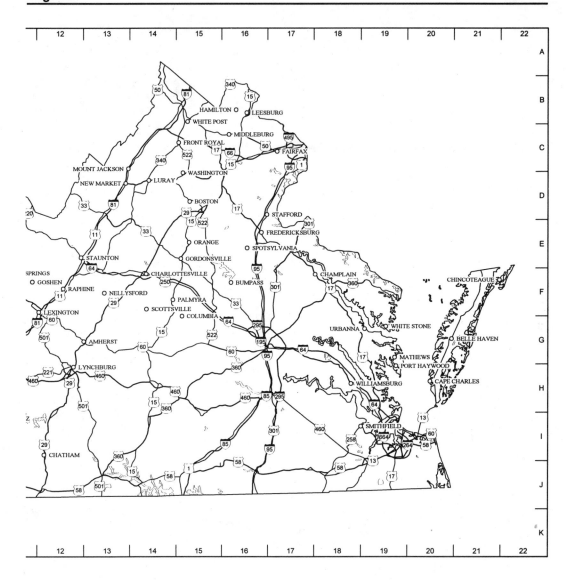

Abingdon   J5

Maplewood Farm B&B
20004 Cleveland Rd,
Abingdon, VA 24211-5836
(540)628-2640

Circa 1880. From the arched windows of this farmhouse, an example of Virginia Vernacular design, guests can gaze out at the wooded countryside. This site is especially picturesque during the fall foliage season. There are more than 60 acres to wander, or guests can simply take in the view of trees and a lake from the deck. The decor is elegant, but not too posh, decorated with French influences. The home rests on a working horse farm, and guests can arrange to board their own horses on the property. Innkeeper(s): Doris Placak. $75. TC. 3 rooms with PB. 1 conference room. Breakfast and afternoon tea included in rates. Types of meals: full breakfast, gourmet breakfast and early coffee/tea. Evening snack and picnic lunch available. Beds: QDT. Turn-down service in room. Child care on premises. Handicap access. Antiques, fishing, parks, shopping, downhill skiing, cross-country skiing, sporting events, theater and watersports nearby.

Certificate may be used: Year-round except certain weekends in April, August and October.

White Birches

268 White Mills Rd,
Abingdon, VA 24210
(540)676-2140 (800)BIRCHES

Circa 1910. This Cape Cod-style home, painted in creamy blue hues, is decorated with an assortment of English and American antiques. Oriental rugs decorate the floors. The covered porches, complete with plants, wicker and paddle fans, are an idyllic spot for the morning meal. A koi pond completes the lush look. The meal is a formal affair, served with silver, crystal and antique china. The innkeepers often choose this spot to serve afternoon refreshments. Outlet shopping, the popular Barter Theatre and a variety of restaurants are nearby.

Innkeeper(s): Michael & Paulette Wartella. $75. MC VISA AX PC. 3 rooms with PB. Breakfast and evening snack included in rates. Type of meal: full breakfast. Beds: Q. Air conditioning, turn-down service, ceiling fan and cable TV in room. VCR on premises. Antiques, parks, shopping, downhill skiing and theater nearby.

Certificate may be used: Jan. 2 to March 15.

Amherst   G13

Dulwich Manor B&B Inn

Rt 5, Box 173A, Rt 60E,
Amherst, VA 24521
(804)946-7207

Circa 1912. This red Flemish brick and white columned English Manor sits on five secluded acres at the end of a country lane and in the midst of 85 acres of woodland and meadow. The Blue Ridge Mountains may be enjoyed from the veranda. The entry features a large center hall and a wide oak staircase. Walls are 14 inches thick. The 18 rooms include a 50-foot-long ballroom on the third floor. The inn is decorated with a creative mix of antiques, reproductions and modern art. Your host is a professional singer and actor and your hostess was in public relations and a costumer for the theater.

Innkeeper(s): Bob & Judy Reilly. $69-89. PC TC. 6 rooms, 4 with PB, 2 with FP. Breakfast included in rates. Types of meals: full breakfast and early coffee/tea. Afternoon tea available. Beds: QD. Air conditioning and ceiling fan in room. Spa on premises. Antiques, fishing, parks, shopping, downhill skiing, sporting events, theater and watersports nearby.
Seen in: Country Inn.

"Our experience at Dulwich Manor surpassed all of our inn visits. A truly delightful stay!"

Certificate may be used: Sunday-Thursday except May, October, holidays and holiday eves. Anytime, December-February, except holidays and holiday eves.

Belle Haven   G20

Bay View Waterfront B&B

35350 Copes Dr,
Belle Haven, VA 23306-1952
(804)442-6963 (800)442-6966

Circa 1800. This rambling inn stretches more than 100 feet across and has five roof levels. There are heart-pine floors, high ceilings and several fireplaces. The hillside location affords bay breezes and

wide views of the Chesapeake, Occohannock Creek and the inn's surrounding 140 acres. The innkeepers are descendants of several generations who have owned and operated Bay View. If you come by water to the inn's deep water dock, look behind Channel Marker 16.

Innkeeper(s): Wayne & Mary Will Browning. $95. PC TC. 3 rooms, 1 with PB, 1 with FP. Breakfast included in rates. Type of meal: full breakfast. Beds: D. Air conditioning in room. VCR, swimming, bicycles and library on premises. Antiques, fishing, parks, shopping, theater and watersports nearby.
Seen in: Rural Living, City.

"We loved staying in your home, and especially in the room with a beautiful view of the bay. You have a lovely home and a beautiful location. Thank you so much for your hospitality."

Certificate may be used: Nov. 15 to March 30, Sunday-Thursday, excluding holidays.

Blacksburg
H9

Sycamore Tree B&B
PO Box 10937,
Blacksburg, VA 24062-0937
(703)381-1597

Circa 1990. This inn sits on 126 acres at the foot of Hightop Mountain. Decorated in a traditional style, all the guest rooms have private baths. The innkeepers enjoy offering advice on local activities such as nearby hiking on the Appalachian Trail and the walk to a 60-foot waterfall at the Cascades.

Innkeeper(s): Charles & Gilda Caines. $75-110. MC VISA. 6 rooms with PB. Breakfast included in rates. Types of meals: full breakfast and early coffee/tea. Beds: KQD. Air conditioning in room. VCR and fax on premises. Handicap access. Antiques, fishing, parks, shopping, sporting events, theater and watersports nearby.

Certificate may be used: Jan. 1 to April 30, Sunday-Thursday. June 1-July 30, Sunday-Thursday.

Boston
D15

Thistle Hill B&B
5541 Sperryville Pike, Boston, VA 22713
(703)987-9142 Fax:(703)987-9122

The inn, an antique shop and restaurant combine to create this restful bed & breakfast. The rambling home rests alongside a former military turnpike used during the Civil War. There are 10 acres of woods to stroll through, a stream, hot tub and a gazebo. Rooms are furnished with antiques and reproductions. The Little Thistle House, a romantic, cozy cottage, offers a sleigh bed, fireplace and sitting room for those seeking solitude. Breakfasts are huge—freshly baked muffins, fruit and coffee accompany the day's entree. Dinners are served by candlelight, and guests can arrange a private dinner for two.

Innkeeper(s): Marianne Topjian-Wilson. $95-145. MAP. MC VISA AX DS. 5 rooms, 4 with PB, 1 with FP. 1 conference room. Breakfast included in rates. Types of meals: full breakfast and gourmet breakfast. Afternoon tea available. Beds: Q. Fax and spa on premises. Handicap access.

Seen in: Washington Post.

Certificate may be used: Sunday through Thursday, excluding holidays.

Bumpass
F16

Rockland Farm Retreat
3609 Lewiston Rd,
Bumpass, VA 23024-9659
(540)895-5098

Circa 1820. The 75 acres of Rockland Farm includes pasture land, livestock, vineyards, crops and a farm pond for fishing. The grounds here are said to have spawned Alex Haley's "Roots." Guests can study documents and explore local cemeteries describing life under slavery in the area surrounding this historic home and 272-year-old farm.

Innkeeper(s): Roy E. Mixon. $60-65. MAP. AX PC. 4 rooms, 3 with PB, 8 with FP. 1 suite. 2 conference rooms. Breakfast included in rates. Type of meal: full breakfast. Dinner, lunch, banquet service and catering service available. Beds: DT. Air conditioning in room. VCR on premises. Amusement parks, antiques, fishing, parks, shopping and watersports nearby.

Location: Thirty minutes south of Fredericksburg, Route 601 at Lake Anna.

Seen in: Washington Post, Free Lance-Star.

Certificate may be used: Jan. 1 to Dec. 30, Sunday-Thursday. No national holidays. No Friday & Saturday nights.

Cape Charles
H20

Bay Avenue Sunset B&B
108 Bay Ave,
Cape Charles, VA 23310-3102
(804)331-2424 (888)422-9283
Fax:(804)331-4877

Circa 1915. Located on waterfront Chesapeake Bay property, this inn offers delightful breezes from its Victorian porch. Newly renovated guest rooms include eclectic decor and Hunter fans. The Victoria Room offers a window seat, queen and day bed and period wallpaper. Awake to the scent of freshly brewed coffee. After a hearty breakfast of cereals, fruits, home-baked breads and delicious entrees, explore the secluded beach or take in a day of birdwatching, fishing or cycling.

Innkeeper(s): Albert Longo & Joyce Tribble. $65-85. MC VISA AX DS TC. 4 rooms with PB. Breakfast included in rates. Types of meals: full breakfast and early coffee/tea. Beds: Q. Air conditioning, ceiling fan, cable TV and VCR in room. Fax, spa and bicycles on premises. Antiques, fishing, parks, shopping, theater and watersports nearby.
Seen in: Port Folio Magazine.

"Your house is beautiful, the meals were wonderful and you really made us feel at home."

Certificate may be used: November through March, Sunday through Thursday.

Champlain F18

Linden House B&B & Plantation
PO Box 23, Champlain, VA 22438-0023
(804)443-1170 (800)622-1202

Circa 1750. This restored planters home is designated a state landmark and listed in the National Register. Cattle and horses graze on the pastures of this 204-acre estate. The lush grounds include walking trails, a garden and a gazebo, where guests can relax and enjoy the wooded surroundings. Guest rooms are decorated with 18th-century reproductions and antiques. Some rooms offer fireplaces, others have sitting areas. The plantation breakfasts are a rich mix of cuisine, from Belgian waffles to specialty omelets, all accompanied by bacon, sausage, fresh fruits, home-baked breads and freshly ground coffee. There is a gift store on the premises. The home is located on the Tidewater Trail and is close to many historic sites.
Innkeeper(s): Ken & Sandra Pounsberry. $85-135. MC VISA AX PC TC. 8 rooms, 4 with PB. 3 with FP. 1 suite. 1 conference room. Breakfast included in rates. Types of meals: full breakfast and early coffee/tea. Afternoon tea, evening snack, banquet service, catering service and catered breakfast available. Beds: Q. Air conditioning, turn-down service, ceiling fan and VCR in room. Stables and bicycles on premises. Handicap access. Amusement parks, antiques, fishing, parks, shopping, theater and watersports nearby.

Certificate may be used: February through December, Sunday through Thursday.

Charlottesville F14

The 1817 Antique Inn
1211 W Main St,
Charlottesville, VA 22903-2823
(804)979-7353 (800)730-7443

Circa 1817. This historic bed & breakfast was built by Thomas Jefferson's own craftsman, James Dinsmore. The innkeeper is a published interior designer, a talent evident in each of the guest rooms decked with bright colors and fashionable furnishings. Elegant rooms are appointed with a variety of

unique antiques, and many of the beautiful pieces are available for purchase. The inn is within walking distance to the University of Virginia and a few blocks from the rotunda, restaurants and shops.
Innkeeper(s): Candace DeLoach Wilson. $89-195. MC VISA TC. 5 rooms with PB, 3 with FP. 2 suites. Breakfast and afternoon tea included in rates. Types of meals: continental-plus breakfast and early coffee/tea. Lunch, gourmet lunch, catering service and catered breakfast available. Beds: KQD. Air conditioning, turn-down service, ceiling fan and cable TV in room. VCR and bicycles on premises. Antiques, fishing, shopping, sporting events and theater nearby.
Seen in: Charlottesville Observer, Cavalier Daily, Virginia Alumni News.

"Felt right at home, slept like a baby, ate like a king, dreamed beautiful dreams, couldn't have been better!"

Certificate may be used: June & July, Sunday-Thursday, December & January, Sunday-Thursday, excluding holidays.

Palmer Country Manor
Rr 1 Box 1390,
Charlottesville (Palmyra), VA 22963-9801
(804)589-1300 (800)253-4306
Fax:(804)589-1300

Circa 1830. Each season brings a special beauty to this farmhouse surrounded by 180 wooded acres. The home and grounds originally belonged to a 2,500-acre ranch which was named Solitude, an apt title for this secluded property. Guests can opt to stay in the historic house or in one of several little cottages. Each cheery guest room is individually appointed and includes a fireplace. The hearty country breakfasts are served in a rustic room with exposed beams and brick walls. Gourmet, candlelight dinners are another romantic option available for guests. The area is full of unique activities, including white-water rafting down the James River or taking in the view on a balloon ride.
Innkeeper(s): Gregory & Kathleen Palmer. $85-125. MAP, AP. MC VISA AX DC DS TC. 12 rooms, 10 with PB, 10 with FP. 10 suites. 2 conference rooms. Breakfast included in rates. Type of meal: full breakfast. Afternoon tea, dinner, picnic lunch, lunch, catering service and room service available. Beds: KQ. Air conditioning in room. Fax and bicycles on premises. Antiques, fishing, parks, shopping, sporting events and watersports nearby.

Certificate may be used: All year, Monday through Thursday

Chatham I12

Eldon, The Inn at Chatham

State Rd 685, Rt 1, Box 254-B,
Chatham, VA 24531
(804)432-0935

Circa 1835. Beautiful gardens and white oaks surround this former tobacco plantation home set among the backdrop of the Blue Ridge Mountains. Stroll the grounds and discover sculptures and an array of flowers and plants. Southern hospitality reigns at this charming home filled with Empire antiques. Guests rooms are light and airy and tastefully decorated with beautiful linens and traditional

knickknacks. Fresh flowers accentuate the bright, cheerful rooms. A lavish, Southern-style breakfast is served up each morning, and dinners at Eldon feature the gourmet creations of Chef Joel Wesley, a graduate of the Culinary Institute of America. Eldon is a popular location for weddings and parties.

Innkeeper(s): Joy & Bob Lemm. $65-80. MC VISA PC TC. 4 rooms, 3 with PB. 1 suite. Breakfast included in rates. Types of meals: continental-plus breakfast, full breakfast, gourmet breakfast and early coffee/tea. Dinner available. Beds: QDT. Air conditioning and turn-down service in room. Swimming and library on premises. Handicap access. Antiques, fishing, parks, shopping and watersports nearby.

Seen in: Richmond Times, Chatham Star Tribune.

"The food, the ambiance, your wonderful hospitality made for a most charming weekend."

Certificate may be used: January, February, March-anytime; April, May, June, July, August, Sunday-Thursday; Friday and Saturday as available.

Sims-Mitchell House B&B

PO Box 429, Chatham, VA 24531-0429
(804)432-0595 (800)967-2867
Fax:(804)432-0596

Circa 1870. This Italianate house has 11 fireplaces, original horsehair-based plaster, furnishings from several generations of Mitchells and original art by Southern artists. (Art created by your host also is displayed.) There is a two-bedroom suite and a separate two-bedroom cottage at the side yard offering pastoral views. Hargrave Military Academy and

Chatham Hall are within a five-block walk. Henry operates the local planetarium and Patricia is the author of several cookbooks and specializes in health-conscious Southern cuisine.

Innkeeper(s): Patricia & Henry Mitchell. $60-70. MC VISA. 2 suites. Breakfast included in rates. Type of meal: continental-plus breakfast. Air conditioning in room. Antiques nearby.

Certificate may be used: Monday through Thursday nights, except April-May and October-November.

Chincoteague F21

The Watson House

4240 Main St,
Chincoteague, VA 23336-2801
(804)336-1564 (800)336-6787
Fax:(804)336-5776

Circa 1898. Situated in town, this white Queen Anne Victorian has a large front porch overlooking Main Street. The porch is a favorite spot of guests and often the location for afternoon tea and refreshments. Beach towels, chairs and bicycles are complimentary, and there is an outdoor shower for cleaning up after sunning.

Innkeeper(s): Tom & Jacque Derrickson, David & Jo Anne Snead. $65-115. MC VISA PC TC. 6 rooms with PB. 2 cottages. Breakfast and afternoon tea included in rates. Beds: QD. Air conditioning and ceiling fan in room. Fax and bicycles on premises. Antiques, fishing, parks, shopping and watersports nearby.

Certificate may be used: March, April and October, Monday through Thursday.

Columbia G15

Upper Byrd Farm B&B

6452 River Rd W,
Columbia, VA 23038-2002
(804)842-2240

Circa 1890. This 26-acre farm rests on top of a hill overlooking the James River. The scenic location is dotted with trees and wildflowers. Innkeeper Ivona Kaz-Jepsen, a native of Lithuania, had her work cut out for her when she began renovation of the house, which was inhabited by college students. She transformed the home into an artist's retreat, filling it with antiques and her own artwork. The breakfast table is set with a beautiful mix of china, and the meal is served by candlelight.

Innkeeper(s): Ivona Kaz-Jepsen. $70. 3 rooms, 2 with FP. Breakfast included in rates. Types of meals: full breakfast, gourmet breakfast and early coffee/tea. Beds: KT. Air conditioning in room. VCR on premises. Antiques, fishing and watersports nearby.

Certificate may be used: June 15 to Aug. 20.

Covington
F10

Milton Hall B&B Inn
207 Thorny Ln,
Covington, VA 24426-5401
(540)965-0196

Circa 1874. This historic 44-acre estate adjoins the George Washington National Forest, and the inn appears as an exquisite English country manor with its buttressed porch towers, gables and Gothic trimmings. The home was built for the Viscountess of

Milton, Maria Theresa Fitzwilliam, whose brother found the site while living in America and serving in the Union Army. Each spacious, romantic room boasts its own fireplace and is decorated in a different color scheme. The rooms reflect the styles of the late 1800s. A full English breakfast is served each morning and a proper afternoon tea also is offered.

Innkeeper(s): John & Vera Eckert. $75-140. MC VISA PC TC. 6 rooms with PB, 6 with FP. 1 suite. Breakfast included in rates. Picnic lunch available. Beds: Q. Air conditioning, turn-down service, cable TV and VCR in room. Antiques, fishing, parks, downhill skiing and theater nearby.

Location: Adjoins George Washington National Forest.

Seen in: Alleghany Highlander, Washington Post, Country Inns.

"A lovely place, a relaxing atmosphere, delicious breakfasts, gracious hospitality. We thank you."

Certificate may be used: Anytime.

Draper
I8

Claytor Lake Homestead Inn
Rt 1, Box 184E-5, SR 651,
Draper, VA 24324
(540)980-6777 (800)676-5253

Circa 1800. This inn was once a two-story log cabin built by slaves for the Ross family. It has been enlarged several times over the past century. The dining room's bay window overlooks Claytor Lake and a private beach. There is also a spectacular view of the lake from the brick-and-stone wraparound porch, which has rocking chairs and a swing. Furnishings include early American and country antiques, many collected from the historic Hotel Roanoke.

Innkeeper(s): Doug & Linda Eads. $85. MC VISA AX DC DS PC TC. 5 rooms, 1 with PB. 2 suites. 1 conference room. Breakfast included in rates. Type of meal: early coffee/tea. Afternoon tea, dinner and catering service available. Beds: KQD. Air conditioning, turn-down service, ceiling fan and VCR in room. Fax, copier, swimming, bicycles and library on premises. Antiques, fishing, shopping, sporting events, theater and watersports nearby.

Seen in: Roanoke Times, Smyth County News, Southwest Times, Blue Ridge Country, Blue Ridge Digest.

"The total environment, including innkeepers, is first-class."

Certificate may be used: Sept. 15 through May 15, Sunday-Thursday only. Holidays and college graduation dates subject to availability.

Fairfax
C17

Bailiwick Inn
4023 Chain Bridge Rd,
Fairfax, VA 22030-4101
(703)691-2266 (800)366-7666
Fax:(703)934-2112

Circa 1800. Located across from the county courthouse where George Washington's will is filed, this distinguished three-story Federal brick house has recently been renovated. The first Civil War casualty occurred on what is now the inn's lawn. The elegant, early-Virginia decor is reminiscent of the state's fine plantation mansions. Ask to stay in the Thomas Jefferson Room, a replica of Mr. Jefferson's bedroom at Monticello.

Innkeeper(s): Bob & Annette Bradley. $130-295. MC VISA AX. 14 rooms with PB, 4 with FP. 1 suite. 1 conference room. Breakfast and afternoon tea included in rates. Types of meals: full breakfast, gourmet breakfast and early coffee/tea. Beds: KQT. Air conditioning and turn-down service in room. VCR, fax and copier on premises. Antiques, parks, shopping, sporting events and theater nearby.

Seen in: Washington Post, Journal, Fairfax Connection, Inn Times, Mid-Atlantic Country, Victoria, Country Inns.

"A visit to your establishment clearly transcends any lodging experience that I can recall."

Certificate may be used: All year, Sunday-Thursday only.

Fredericksburg E16

La Vista Plantation
4420 Guinea Station Rd,
Fredericksburg, VA 22408-8850
(540)898-8444 (800)529-2823
Fax:(540)898-1041

Circa 1838. La Vista has a long and unusual past, rich in Civil War history. Both Confederate and Union armies camped here, and this is where the Ninth Cavalry was sworn in. The house, a Classical Revival structure with high ceilings and pine floors, sits on 10 acres of pasture and woods. The grounds include a pond stocked with bass. Guest quarters include a spacious room with a four-poster bed and Empire furniture or a four-room apartment that can accommodate up to six guests and includes a fireplace. Breakfasts include homemade egg dishes from chickens raised on the property.

Innkeeper(s): Michele & Edward Schiesser. $95. MC VISA PC TC. 2 rooms with PB, 2 with FP. 1 suite. 1 cottage. 1 conference room. Breakfast included in rates. Types of meals: full breakfast and early coffee/tea. Beds: KQDT. Air conditioning in room. Copier and library on premises. Amusement parks, antiques, fishing, parks, shopping, sporting events, theater and watersports nearby.
Location: Just outside historic Fredericksburg.
Seen in: Free Lance Star, Mid Atlantic Country.

"Coming here was an excellent choice. La Vista is charming, quiet and restful, all qualities we were seeking. Breakfast was delicious."
Certificate may be used: January and February, Monday-Thursday.

Front Royal C15

Chester House Inn
43 Chester St, Front Royal, VA 22630
(540)635-3937 (800)621-0441
Fax:(540)636-8695

Circa 1905. This stately Georgian-style estate rests on two acres of terraced gardens, which include vast plantings of boxwood, wisteria arbors, a fountain and brick walkways and walls. Elaborately carved

marble mantels from London remain, and an original speaker tube extends from the second-floor bedroom to the kitchen. Just down the street is the renovated village commons, the Confederate Museum and the Belle Boyd Cottage.

Innkeeper(s): Bill & Ann Wilson. $65-180. MC VISA AX PC TC. 7 rooms, 5 with PB, 4 with FP. 1 suite. 1 cottage. Breakfast, afternoon tea and evening snack included in rates. Types of meals: continental-plus breakfast and early coffee/tea. Beds: KQDT. Air conditioning and turn-down service in room. Cable TV, VCR and fax on premises. Antiques, fishing, parks, shopping, cross-country skiing, theater and watersports nearby.
Seen in: Winchester Star, Northern Virginia Daily, Blue Ridge Country.

"A home of greater charm would be hard to find."
Certificate may be used: Jan. 1 to March 30 and June 1 to Aug. 30, Sunday through Thursday.

Gordonsville E15

Sleepy Hollow Farm B&B
16280 Blue Ridge Tpke,
Gordonsville, VA 22942-8214
(703)832-5555 (800)215-4804
Fax:(703)832-2515

Circa 1785. Many generations have added to this brick farmhouse with its 18th-century dining room and bedrooms. The pink and white room was

frequently visited by a friendly ghost from Civil War days, according to local stories. She hasn't been seen for several years since the innkeeper, a former missionary, had the house blessed. The grounds include an herb garden, a pond with gazebo, a chestnut slave cabin, terraces and abundant wildlife. Innkeeper(s): Beverley Allison & Dorsey Allison Comer. $65-95. MC VISA. 6 rooms with PB, 2 with FP. 3 suites. Breakfast and afternoon tea included in rates. Types of meals: full breakfast and early coffee/tea. Beds: QDT. Air conditioning in room. VCR, fax, copier and child care on premises. Antiques, fishing, parks, shopping, downhill skiing, sporting events and theater nearby.

Location: Between Gordonsville & Somerset on Rt 231.

Seen in: Orange County Review, City, Town & County.

"This house is truly blessed."

Certificate may be used: Sunday-Thursday. Call last minute Thursday/Friday, excludes all holidays.

Tivoli

9171 Tivoli Dr,
Gordonsville, VA 22942-8115
(703)832-2225 (800)840-2225

Innkeeper Phil Audibert's family has owned this gracious mansion since the 1950s, but it wasn't until 1990 that he and wife Susie renovated the home and opened for guests. The commanding home, which is surrounded by a 235-acre cattle farm, affords views of the Blue Ridge Mountains.

Tastefully decorated rooms are filled with antiques that span four centuries, and each guest room boasts a working fireplace. Phil and Susie offer champagne to guests upon arrival. The home is near plenty of historic attractions, including Montpelier, the home of James Madison, and several Civil War sites. Innkeeper(s): Philip Audibert. $75-125. MC VISA. 4 rooms. Breakfast included in rates. Type of meal: full breakfast.

Certificate may be used: Anytime, January through March; Monday through Thursday, April through December.

Goshen

The Hummingbird Inn

PO Box 147, Wood Ln,
Goshen, VA 24439-0147
(540)997-9065 (800)397-3214
Fax:(540)997-0289

Circa 1780. This early Victorian villa is located in the Shenandoah Valley against the backdrop of the Allegheny Mountains. Both the first and second floors offer wraparound verandas. Furnished with

antiques, the inn features a library and sitting room with fireplaces. The rustic den and one guest room comprise the oldest portions of the inn, built around 1780. Four-course dinners, which include wine, are available by advance reservation. An old barn and babbling creek are on the grounds. Lexington, the Virginia Horse Center, Natural Bridge, the Blue Ridge Parkway and antiquing are all nearby. Innkeeper(s): Diana & Jeremy Robinson. $70-155. MAP. MC VISA AX DS PC TC. 5 rooms with PB, 2 with FP. Breakfast included in rates. Types of meals: full breakfast and early coffee/tea. Afternoon tea and dinner available. Beds: Q. Air conditioning and ceiling fan in room. Cable TV, VCR, fax, computer and library on premises. Handicap access. Antiques, fishing, shopping, downhill skiing, cross-country skiing and theater nearby.

Seen in: Blue Ridge Country, Mid-Atlantic Getaways, Inn Spots and Special Places.

"We enjoyed our stay so much that we returned two weeks later on our way back ... for a delicious home-cooked dinner, comfortable attractive atmosphere, and familiar faces to welcome us after a long journey."

Certificate may be used: Sunday-Thursday, November-May 15, holidays excluded.

Hamilton
B16

Stonegate B&B

PO Box 100, Hamilton, VA 22068-0100
(703)338-9519

A country doctor built this stone home for his new bride. The bed & breakfast is surrounded by two lush acres of gardens and trees. The guest rooms are filled with antiques, and named for Generals Grant and Lee. The Lee Room includes a bath with whirlpool tub. Breakfasts are served on a screened-in veranda. Civil War battlefields are a short distance, as is shopping, horse racing and restaurants.
Innkeeper(s): Vicki Gallant. $65-75. 2 rooms. Breakfast included in rates. Type of meal: continental breakfast.

Certificate may be used: Sunday through Thursday, April through November.

Hillsville
J8

Bray's Manor B&B Inn

PO Box 385, Hillsville, VA 24343-0385
(703)728-7901 (800)753-2729

Circa 1991. This farmhouse was newly built to accommodate guests and now has private baths and a two-room apartment with its own Jacuzzi. The front porch overlooks the valley where Hereford cattle are usually found grazing. You can play croquet or badminton on the five acres or simply enjoy the view from the porch. Country breakfasts are served.
Innkeeper(s): Helen Bray. $69. MC VISA DS. 3 rooms. 1 suite. Breakfast included in rates. Types of meals: full breakfast and early coffee/tea. Air conditioning, turn-down service and ceiling fan in room. VCR on premises. Antiques and shopping nearby.

Certificate may be used: March, April, May, June, July, November and December.

Leesburg
B16

The Norris House Inn

108 Loudoun St SW, Leesburg, VA 20175
(703)777-1806 (800)644-1806
Fax:(703)771-8051

Circa 1760. The Norris brothers, Northern Virginia's foremost architects and builders, purchased this building in 1850 and began extensive renovations several years later. They used the finest wood and brick available, remodeling the exterior to an Eastlake style. Beautifully restored, the inn features built-in bookcases in the library and a cherry fireplace mantel.

Innkeeper(s): Pamela & Don McMurray. $65-125. MC VISA AX DC CB DS PC TC. 6 rooms, 3 with FP. 1 conference room. Breakfast and evening snack included in rates. Types of meals: full breakfast and early coffee/tea. Afternoon tea available. Beds: QD. Air conditioning and turn-down service in room. Fax and library on premises. Antiques, fishing, parks, shopping and watersports nearby.

Location: Less than one hour from Washington, D.C.

Seen in: New York Times, Better Homes and Gardens, Washingtonian, Country Home.

"Thank you for your gracious hospitality. We enjoyed everything about your lovely home, especially the extra little touches that really make the difference."

Certificate may be used: Sunday through Friday only.

Lexington
F12

Brierley Hill B&B Inn

RR 2 Box 21A, Lexington, VA 24450
(540)464-8421 (800)422-4925
Fax:(540)464-8925

Circa 1993. Visitors to this inn on eight acres enjoy a spectacular view of the Shenandoah Valley and Blue Ridge Mountains. The natural setting aside, the interior is reason enough for a stay. The rooms are decorated in light, romantic colors, reminiscent of a field of wildflowers. Antiques and poster beds blend with flowery prints, light wallpapers and knickknacks. Breakfasts, weather permitting, are served on the veranda, which offers a wonderful view.
Innkeeper(s): Barry & Carole Speton. $75-140. MC VISA TC. 6 rooms with PB, 2 with FP. 1 suite. Breakfast and afternoon tea included in rates. Types of meals: full breakfast, gourmet breakfast and early coffee/tea. Beds: KQ. Air conditioning and ceiling fan in room. Cable TV, fax, copier and library on premises. Antiques, fishing, parks, shopping, downhill skiing, cross-country skiing, sporting events, theater and watersports nearby.

Certificate may be used: Nov. 1-March 31, Sunday-Thursday. Holidays not included.

Maple Hall

RR 5 Box 223,
Lexington, VA 24450-8842
(540)463-2044 Fax:(540)463-6693

Circa 1850. Maple Hall is one of the Historic
Country Inns of Lexington, an elegant ensemble of
some of Virginia's notable mansions and homes.
The red brick manor, flanked by stately columns,
remained in the original owners' family until the
mid-1980s. Many of the rooms include working fireplaces and all are individually decorated with
antiques. A restored guest house, dating prior to the
1850 main house, includes three bedrooms, a
kitchen and living room. Secluded accommodations
also are available at Pond House, which includes
four mini-suites and a back veranda with a view of
the pond and surrounding countryside. The home
rests on a 56-acre estate with boxwoods, walking
trails, a fishing pond, swimming pool and tennis
courts. Breakfast and evening wine is included, and
gourmet dining is available at the inn's restaurant,
serving specialties such as lobster bisque, prime rib
or poached Alaskan salmon.

Innkeeper(s): Don Gredenburg. $95-160. MC VISA PC. 21 rooms with
PB, 16 with FP. 5 suites. 2 cottages. 1 conference room. Breakfast
included in rates. Type of meal: continental-plus breakfast. Banquet service available. Beds: QDT. Air conditioning in room. VCR, fax, copier,
swimming and tennis on premises. Antiques, fishing, parks, shopping,
sporting events and theater nearby.

*"The view from the back balcony was so peaceful and
serene. What a perfect weekend!"*

Certificate may be used: July and August, November and December
(except first week), January-March.

Seven Hills Inn

408 S Main St,
Lexington, VA 24450-2346
(540)463-4715 Fax:(540)463-6526

Circa 1929. This Colonial Revival house stands in
the heart of the Shenandoah Valley. Carefully renovated, the inn's white columns and brick exterior are
reminiscent of a Southern plantation. The guest
rooms, named after area homesteads, are furnished
with antiques and reproductions, and the Fruit Hill
room offers a Jacuzzi tub. Within a 10-minute walk is
Washington and Lee University, the Virginia
Military Institute and the Lexington Visitors Center.

Innkeeper(s): Shirley Ducommun. $75-125. MC VISA AX PC TC. 7
rooms, 6 with PB. 1 suite. Breakfast included in rates. Types of meals:
continental-plus breakfast and early coffee/tea. Afternoon tea and catering service available. Beds: QDT. Air conditioning in room. Cable TV,
VCR, fax, copier and library on premises. Antiques, fishing, parks,
shopping, sporting events, theater and watersports nearby.

Certificate may be used: Any time except May & October depending
upon availability.

The Inn at Union Run

Union Run Rd, Lexington, VA 24450
(703)463-9715 (800)528-6466
Fax:(703)463-3526

Circa 1883. This inn was named for the spring-fed
creek that meanders in front of this restored farmhouse. Union troops, specifically the 2nd and 4th
Michigan Calvary, camped on the grounds during
the Civil War. The home is surrounded by 10 acres
with a fishing pond and brook. The innkeepers have
traveled extensively throughout Europe and have
brought the influence into their inn. The furnishings, many of which were fashioned out of oak, are a
mix of American and Victorian styles.

Innkeeper(s): Roger & Jeanette Serens. $75-125. MAP. MC VISA AX
TC. 8 rooms with PB, 1 with FP. 3 suites. 1 conference room. Breakfast
and afternoon tea included in rates. Types of meals: full breakfast and
early coffee/tea. Evening snack, picnic lunch, lunch, banquet service
and room service available. Beds: Q. Air conditioning, turn-down service and ceiling fan in room. Fax, copier and pet boarding on premises.
Handicap access. Antiques, fishing, parks, shopping, cross-country
skiing, theater and watersports nearby.

Certificate may be used: January to December, excludes holidays,
Sundays to Thursdays.

Luray D14

The Ruffner House

RR 4 Box 620, Luray, VA 22835-9704
(540)743-7855

Circa 1840. Situated on a farm nestled in the heart
of the Shenandoah Valley, this stately manor was
built by Peter Ruffner, the first settler of Page Valley
and Luray. Ruffner family members discovered a
cavern opposite the entrance to the Luray Caverns,
which were found later. Purebred Arabian horses
graze in the pasture on this 18-acre estate.

Innkeeper(s): Stephen Hand & John Gerace. $70-150. TC. 8 rooms, 6
with PB, 1 with FP. 2 suites. Breakfast included in rates. Types of meals:
full breakfast and early coffee/tea. Evening snack and picnic lunch
available. Beds: QD. Air conditioning and ceiling fan in room. Cable TV,
VCR and spa on premises. Antiques, fishing, parks, shopping, downhill
skiing, cross-country skiing, sporting events and watersports nearby.

Location: Shenandoah Valley, South of Hwys. 211 and 340.

Seen in: Page News & Courier, Virginian Pilot.

*"This is the loveliest inn we have ever stayed in. We
were made to feel very welcome and at ease."*

Certificate may be used: Jan. 15-Sept. 15, Monday-Thursday. Nov. 1-
Dec. 15, Monday-Thursday.

Spring Farm B&B
13 Wallace Ave, Luray, VA 22835-9067
(540)743-4701 (800)203-2814
Fax:(540)743-7851

Circa 1795. Spring Farm is on 10 acres two miles from Luray Caverns. Hite's Springs run through the land. The Greek Revival home has double front and back verandas. Rooms feature a mix of antique and

new furnishings, and there is a fireplace in the living room. Ask the innkeepers for advice on shopping, dining and activities in the Shenandoah and they'll be happy to help you plan a getaway you'll long remember.

Innkeeper(s): Thelma Mayes & Susan Murphy. $75-150. MC VISA DC DS PC TC. 4 rooms, 2 with PB. 1 cottage. Breakfast, afternoon tea and evening snack included in rates. Types of meals: full breakfast and early coffee/tea. Picnic lunch available. Beds: QD. Air conditioning in room. Cable TV, VCR and fax on premises. Antiques, fishing, parks, shopping, downhill skiing and watersports nearby.

Certificate may be used: Weekdays only during April through December (Tuesday-Thursday).

Lynchburg   H12

Lynchburg Mansion Inn B&B
405 Madison St,
Lynchburg, VA 24504-2455
(804)528-5400 (800)352-1199

Circa 1914. This regal, Georgian mansion, with its majestic Greek Revival columns, is located on a brick-paved street in the Garland Hill Historic District. The grand hall showcases an oak and cherry staircase which leads up to the solarium. Breakfasts are served in the formal dining room on antique china. Romantic rooms feature inviting touches such as a four-poster beds, Laura Ashley and Ralph Lauren linens, Battenburg lace pillows and some include fireplaces. The Veranda Suite, as the name suggests, opens onto a romantic circular veranda and a treetop sunroom. The Garden Suite, with its private garden entrance includes an original

clawfoot tub. Lynchburg offers many exciting activities, including the unique Community Market and plenty of galleries, antique shops and boutiques.

Innkeeper(s): Mauranna Sherman. $89-119. MC VISA AX DC. 5 rooms with PB, 2 with FP. 2 suites. 1 conference room. Breakfast included in rates. Types of meals: full breakfast, gourmet breakfast and early coffee/tea. Beds: KQ. Air conditioning, turn-down service and cable TV in room. Handicap access. Antiques, shopping, downhill skiing, sporting events and theater nearby.

Location: Lynchburg is three hours from Washington, D.C.

Seen in: News & Advance, Roanoker.

"The Lynchburg Mansion Inn is the creme de la creme. You have earned all sorts of pats on the back for the restoration and hospitality you offer. It is truly elegant"

Certificate may be used: Year-round excluding holidays and eves of holidays; excluding weekends around holidays; excluding weekends in April, May, June, August and October.

Mathews   G19

Ravenswood Inn
PO Box 1430, Mathews, VA 23109-1430
(804)725-7272

Circa 1913. This intimate waterfront home is located on five acres along the banks of the East River, where passing boats still harvest crabs and oysters. A long screened porch captures river breezes. Most rooms feature a river view and are decorated in Victorian, country, nautical or wicker. The inn's speciality is its noted French and Mediterranean cuisine. Williamsburg, Jamestown and Yorktown are within an hour.

Innkeeper(s): Sally Preston & Ricky Durham. $75. TC. 3 rooms with PB. Breakfast included in rates. Types of meals: gourmet breakfast and early coffee/tea. Beds: KQT. Air conditioning and ceiling fan in room. Cable TV, VCR and spa on premises. Amusement parks, antiques, shopping, sporting events, theater and watersports nearby.

Seen in: Virginian Pilot, Daily Press.

"While Ravenswood is one of the most beautiful places we've ever been, it is your love, caring and friendship that has made it such a special place for us."

Certificate may be used: April-November, Sunday-Thursday.

Middleburg
C16

Red Fox Inn & Mosby's Tavern
2 E Washington St,
Middleburg, VA 2117-0385
(703)687-6301 (800)223-1728
Fax:(703)687-6187

Circa 1728. Originally Chinn's Ordinary, the inn was a popular stopping place for travelers between Winchester and Alexandria. During the Civil War, Colonel John Mosby and General Jeb Stuart met here. Guest rooms are furnished in 18th-century decor and most feature four-poster canopy beds.
Innkeeper(s): F. Turner Reuter, Jr. $135-225. MC VISA AX DS TC. 24 rooms with PB, 3 with FP. 4 conference rooms. Breakfast included in rates. Types of meals: continental breakfast, continental-plus breakfast, full breakfast, gourmet breakfast and early coffee/tea. Afternoon tea, dinner, evening snack, picnic lunch, lunch, gourmet lunch, banquet service, catering service, catered breakfast and room service available. Beds: KQ. Air conditioning, turn-down service and cable TV in room. VCR, fax, copier, pet boarding and child care on premises. Handicap access. Antiques nearby.

Location: Thirty miles west of Washington on Route 50.

Seen in: Washingtonian.

Certificate may be used: Sunday-Thursday, all year.

Welbourne
22314 Welbourne Farm Ln,
Middleburg, VA 22117-3939
(703)687-3201

Circa 1775. This seventh-generation mansion once presided over 3,000 acres. With family members starting their own estates, Welbourne now stands at 600 acres. Furnishings and carpets were collected during world travels over the past 200 years and display a faded elegance of the past. Civil War stories fill the family history book, shared with guests. In the 1930s, F. Scott Fitzgerald and Thomas Wolfe and their literary friends used the house as a setting for their writings.
Innkeeper(s): Nathaniel Morison III. $85-96. 7 rooms with PB, 7 with FP. 2 suites. 1 conference room. Breakfast included in rates. Type of meal: full breakfast. Beds: QT.

Location: Fifty miles west of Washington, DC.

"Furnishings portray a house and home that's been around for a long, long time. And none of it is held back from guests. Life today at Welbourne is quiet and unobtrusive. It's genteel, Philip Hayward, Country Magazine."

Certificate may be used: All year (Sunday-Thursday).

Mount Jackson
C13

Widow Kip's Country Inn
355 Orchard Dr,
Mount Jackson, VA 22842-9753
(540)477-2400 (800)478-8714

Circa 1830. This restored farmhouse with its sweeping view of the Massanutten Mountains is situated on seven acres. It's a stone's throw from a fork of the Shenandoah River. Locally crafted quilts enhance the four-poster, sleigh and hand-carved Victorian beds. Two restored cottages (the Silk Purse and Sow's Ear) as well as a gift shop, create a Williamsburg-style courtyard. Cows graze unexpectedly a few feet away from the swimming pool.
Innkeeper(s): Betty & Bob Luse. $65-85. MC VISA PC TC. 5 rooms with PB, 5 with FP. 1 suite. 2 cottages. Breakfast included in rates. Type of meal: early coffee/tea. Beds: QD. Air conditioning, ceiling fan and cable TV in room. Swimming, bicycles and pet boarding on premises. Antiques, fishing, parks, shopping, downhill skiing, sporting events, theater and watersports nearby.

Location: I-81 to Mt. Jackson. Exit 69 to Route 11, south to 263.

Seen in: Country Inns, Mid-Atlantic Country, Americana, Sojourner, Washington Post, Country.

"Everything sparkled. The rooms were decorated with flair and imagination."

Certificate may be used: December-March, anytime. April-November, Sunday-Thursday. Holiday weekends excluded.

Nellysford
F13

The Mark Addy
Rt 151 at Rt 613W, Box 375,
Nellysford, VA 22958-9526
(804)361-1101 (800)278-2154

Circa 1837. It's not hard to understand why Dr. John Everett, the son of Thomas Jefferson's physician, chose this picturesque, Blue Mountain setting for his home. Everett expanded the simple, four-room farmhouse already present into a gracious manor. The well-appointed guest rooms feature double whirlpool baths, double showers or a clawfoot tub. Beds are covered with vintage linens, feather pillows and cozy, down comforters. There are plenty of relaxing possibilities, including five porches and a hammock set among the trees.
Innkeeper(s): John Storck Maddox & Saverio Anselmo. $90-125. EP. MC VISA PC TC. 9 rooms with PB. 1 suite. Types of meals: continental breakfast, full breakfast, gourmet breakfast and early coffee/tea. Afternoon tea, dinner, picnic lunch, lunch, gourmet lunch, banquet service, catering service and catered breakfast available. Beds: KQDT. Air conditioning and ceiling fan in room. Cable TV, VCR and library on premises. Handicap access. Antiques, fishing, parks, shopping, downhill skiing, sporting events and theater nearby.

Certificate may be used: January, March, June-September, December, Sunday to Thursday.

New Market

A Touch of Country B&B

9329 N Congress St,
New Market, VA 22844-9508
(540)740-8030

Circa 1870. This white clapboard Shenandoah Valley I-frame house has a second-story pediment centered above the veranda entrance. It was built by Captain William Rice, commander of the New Market Cavalry, and the house sits on what was once a battleground of the Civil War. Rice's unit was highly praised by General Lee. Guest chambers are in the main house and in the handsome carriage house.

Innkeeper(s): Jean Schoellig/Dawn Kasow. $60-75. MC VISA AX DS PC TC. 6 rooms with PB. Breakfast included in rates. Types of meals: full breakfast and early coffee/tea. Beds: QDT. Air conditioning in room. Cable TV and VCR on premises. Antiques, fishing, parks, shopping, downhill skiing, sporting events and watersports nearby.
Seen in: USA Today Weekend, Country.

"Every morning should start with sunshine, bird song and Dawn's strawberry pancakes."

Certificate may be used: Sunday through Thursday, April through November; anytime, December through March; no holiday weekends.

Cross Roads Inn B&B

9222 John Sevier Rd,
New Market, VA 22844-9649
(540)740-4157

Circa 1925. This Victorian is full of Southern hospitality and European charm. The innkeepers serve imported Austrian coffee alongside the homemade breakfasts, and strudel is served as an afternoon refreshment. The home is decorated like an English garden, laced with antiques, some of which are family pieces. Four-poster and canopy beds are topped with fluffy, down comforters. The historic downtown area is within walking distance.
Innkeeper(s): Mary Lloyd & Roland Freisitzer. $55-95. MC VISA TC. 6 rooms with PB, 1 with FP. 1 conference room. Breakfast, afternoon tea and evening snack included in rates. Types of meals: full breakfast, gourmet breakfast and early coffee/tea. Beds: KQDT. Air conditioning and turn-down service in room. Cable TV, VCR, fax and copier on

premises. Handicap access. Antiques, fishing, parks, shopping, downhill skiing, sporting events, theater and watersports nearby.
Certificate may be used: November to September, Sunday-Friday.

Red Shutter Farmhouse B&B

RR 1 Box 376,
New Market, VA 22844-9306
(540)740-4281 (800)738-8262
Fax:(540)740-4281

Circa 1790. For generations, the veranda at the Red Shutter has been the location of choice during summer to view the valley and mountains. Located on 20 acres, the inn offers large rooms and suites and a library/conference room. Breakfast is in the dining room. Enjoy drives to the many area caverns, New Market Battlefield and Skyline Drive.
Innkeeper(s): Juanita Miller. $55-70. MC VISA PC TC. 5 rooms, 3 with PB, 3 with FP. 1 suite. 1 conference room. Breakfast included in rates. Types of meals: full breakfast and early coffee/tea. Beds: KQDT. Ceiling fan in room. VCR, fax and library on premises. Antiques, fishing, parks, shopping, downhill skiing, cross-country skiing, sporting events and theater nearby.
Certificate may be used: Dec. 1 through Feb. 29 anytime; March 1 through Nov. 30, Monday through Thursday.

Orange

Hidden Inn

249 Caroline St, Orange, VA 22960-1529
(540)672-3625 Fax:(540)672-5029

Circa 1880. Acres of huge old trees can be seen from the wraparound veranda of this Victorian inn nestled in the Virginia countryside. Guests are pampered with romantic decor and encouraged to arrive in time for a spot of afternoon tea. Monticello, Blue Ridge, Montpelier, wineries, shops and antiquing are located nearby. Gourmet, candlelight dinners also are available and guests can order candlelight picnics as well.
Innkeeper(s): Barbara & Ray Lonick, Chrys Dermody. $79-159. MC VISA AX PC TC. 10 rooms with PB, 2 with FP. 2 cottages. 1 conference room. Breakfast and afternoon tea included in rates. Types of meals: full breakfast and early coffee/tea. Beds: KQDT. Air conditioning, ceiling fan and cable TV in room. VCR, fax, copier, computer and library on premises. Antiques, fishing, shopping, sporting events, theater and watersports nearby.
Location: Intersection of Rte 15 & Rte 20.
Seen in: Forbes, Washington Post, Country Inns, Learning Channel, Inn Country USA.

"It just doesn't get any better than this!"

Certificate may be used: Monday-Thursday, except May and October.

Willow Grove Inn

14079 Plantation Way, Orange, VA 22960
(703)672-5982 (800)349-1778
Fax:(703)672-3674

Circa 1778. The exterior of this inn is Classical Revival style, while the interior retains Federal simplicity. Located in Orange County, Virginia, the inn is listed in the National Register of Historic Places and has been designated a Virginia Historic Landmark. The mansion, nestled on 37 acres, has survived two wars. Generals Wayne and Muhlenberg camped here during the Revolution and the mansion was under siege during the Civil War. Trenches and breastworks are visible near the manor house, and a cannonball was removed from the eaves not too long ago.

Innkeeper(s): Angela Malloy. $115-255. 7 rooms, 5 with PB. 2 suites. Breakfast included in rates. Type of meal: full breakfast. Picnic lunch available. Beds: QDT. Antiques, fishing, theater and watersports nearby.
Seen in: Southern Living, Country Inns, Victorian Homes, Countryside, Virginia, Washington Post, Washington Times, Country Accents, Baltimore Sun, Washingtonian.

"Your congenial staff, excellent food, elegant and historical ambiance ... meticulous attention to detail, and of course your gracious hospitality, overwhelmingly delighted our senses and contributed to an experience we will never forget."

Certificate may be used: Tuesday, Wednesday, Thursday, MAP only, breakfast and dinner included. Four-course dinner off menu.

Port Haywood
H19

Tabb's Creek Inn

PO Box 219 Rt 14 Matthews Co, Port Haywood, VA 23138-0219
(804)725-5136 Fax:(804)725-5136

Circa 1820. Surrounded by 30 acres of woods and located on the banks of Tabb's Creek, this post-Colonial farm features a detached guest cottage. There are maple, elm, magnolia trees and 150 rose bushes on the property. The suites and guest rooms feature fireplaces and antiques. Boats for rowing and canoeing, docks, a swimming pool, and private waterview porches make this an especially attractive getaway for those seeking a dose of seclusion.

Innkeeper(s): Cabell & Catherine Venable. $125. PC TC. 4 rooms with PB, 1 with FP. 2 suites. Breakfast included in rates. Types of meals: full breakfast and early coffee/tea. Beds: KQD. Air conditioning, turn-down service, ceiling fan and VCR in room. Cable TV, fax, copier, swimming, bicycles and library on premises. Antiques and fishing nearby.
Location: Mobjack Bay/Chesapeake Bay, near Yorktown/Williamsburg, Va.

"A spot of tea with a bit of heaven. Truly exceptional hosts. The best B&Bs I've happened across!"

Certificate may be used: All year.

Pulaski
I8

The Count Pulaski B&B and Garden

821 Jefferson Ave N,
Pulaski, VA 24301-3609
(540)980-1163 (800)980-1163

Circa 1910. The innkeeper's many travels to Europe and Asia form the core of the inn's furnishings, which are combined with family antiques. The Colonial Revival house is located in the historic district on a half-acre of lawn and gardens. This inn is located in a quiet, easy-to-find neighborhood and if time permits, the home offers close access to lakes, mountains, national and state parks, museums, art galleries and antique shops. Ask about the dinner cruise on the Pioneer Maid.

Innkeeper(s): Flo Stevenson. $75. MC VISA. 3 rooms with PB. 1 suite. Breakfast included in rates. Types of meals: full breakfast and early coffee/tea. Evening snack available. Beds: KQT. Air conditioning and ceiling fan in room. Cable TV on premises. Antiques, fishing, shopping and sporting events nearby.
Seen in: Roanoke Times, Southwest Times.

"I'm back again! Even better than my first visit. Thanks for making me feel so at home."

Certificate may be used: December, January, February, Monday through Thursday.

Raphine
F12

Oak Spring Farm B&B

5895 Borden Grant Tr,
Raphine, VA 24472-9717
(540)377-2398 (800)841-8813

Circa 1826. A willow tree droops gracefully over a pond at Oak Spring Farm, a working gentlemen's farm that includes a five-acre vineyard on 40 acres of woods, creeks, lawns and orchards. The historic plantation house features porch views of the Blue Ridge Mountains and has been pristinely renovated.

Filled with fine antiques, the inn offers bouquets of fresh flowers in all the guest rooms. A herd of friendly burros belonging to the Natural Bridge Petting Zoo live here.

Innkeeper(s): Celeste & John Wood. $85-95. MC VISA PC TC. 3 rooms with PB. 1 suite. Breakfast and afternoon tea included in rates. Types of meals: gourmet breakfast and early coffee/tea. Dinner available. Beds: Q. Air conditioning in room. Antiques, fishing, shopping, downhill skiing, sporting events and theater nearby.

Location: Halfway between historic Lexington and Staunton.

Seen in: News-Gazette, News and County Press, Mid-Atlantic Country.

"The good taste, the privacy, the decor and the hosts were unbeatable!"

Certificate may be used: Sunday-Thursday Jan. 1-Dec. 1.

Scottsville   F14

High Meadows Vineyard & Mtn Sunset Inn

Rt 4 Box 6, Scottsville, VA 24590-9706
(804)286-2218 (800)232-1832
Fax:(804)286-2124

Circa 1832. Minutes from Charlottesville on the Constitution Highway (Route 20), High Meadows stands on 50 acres of gardens, forests, ponds, a creek and a vineyard. Listed in the National Register, it is actually two historic homes joined by a breezeway as well as a turn-of-the-century Queen Anne manor

house. The inn is furnished in Federal and Victorian styles. Guests are treated to gracious Virginia hospitality in an elegant and peaceful setting with wine tasting and a romantic candlelight dinner every evening.

Innkeeper(s): Peter Sushka. $95-155. MAP. MC VISA. 12 rooms with PB, 6 with FP. 5 suites. 1 conference room. Breakfast included in rates. Types of meals: full breakfast and gourmet breakfast. Dinner available. Beds: KQDT. Air conditioning, turn-down service and ceiling fan in room. Handicap access. Antiques, fishing, shopping, downhill skiing, cross-country skiing, sporting events, theater and watersports nearby.

Seen in: Washington Times, Cavalier Daily, Daily Progress, Washington Post, Richmond Times Dispatch, Mid-Atlantic, Washingtonian.

"We have rarely encountered such a smooth blend of hospitality and expertise in a totally relaxed environment."

Certificate may be used: All year Sunday-Thursday, non-holidays; Sunday-Friday, Dec.1-March 1, non-holidays.

Smith Mountain Lake

The Manor at Taylor's Store B&B Country Inn

RR 1 Box 533,
Smith Mountain Lake, VA 24184-9725
(540)721-3951 (800)248-6267
Fax:(540)721-5243

Circa 1820. Situated on 120 acres of rolling countryside, this two-story, columned manor was built on the site of Taylor's Store, a trading post just off the old Warwick Road. It served as the plantation house for a prosperous tobacco farmer, Moses Greer Booth. Guest rooms feature a variety of antiques and styles including traditional colonial and English Country. From the solarium, a wildflower trail winds through the inn's colonial garden and green meadows where a canoe awaits those who wish to paddle across one of six ponds on the property.

Innkeeper(s): Lee & Mary Lynn Tucker. $85-185. MC VISA PC TC. 9 rooms, 8 with PB, 6 with FP. 4 suites. 1 cottage. 3 conference rooms. Breakfast included in rates. Types of meals: full breakfast, gourmet breakfast and early coffee/tea. Afternoon tea, dinner, picnic lunch, gourmet lunch, banquet service and catering service available. Beds: QD. Air conditioning and turn-down service in room. Cable TV, VCR, fax, copier, spa, swimming, stables and library on premises. Antiques, fishing, parks, sporting events, theater and watersports nearby.

Seen in: Smith Mountain Eagle, Lake Country, Blue Ridge Country, Franklin News-Post, Southern Living, Brides.

"This B&B experience is a delightful one!"

Certificate may be used: Jan. 1-June 1 and Nov. 1-Dec. 29 Monday-Thursday only, excludes holidays and holiday weekends.

Smithfield   I19

Isle of Wight Inn

1607 S Church St, Smithfield, VA 23430
(804)357-3176 (800)357-3245

Circa 1980. This Colonial inn is located in a historic seaside town, boasting more than 60 homes which date back to the mid-18th century. St. Luke's Church, the oldest in the United States, dating back to 1632, is located near the inn. Antiques and reproductions fill the rooms, the suites offer the added amenities of fireplaces and whirlpool tubs. The inn also houses a gift boutique

and one of the area's finest antique shops, featuring old clocks and period furniture.

Innkeeper(s): Jackie Madrigel & Bob Hart. $59-119. MC VISA AX DS TC. 9 rooms with PB, 3 with FP. 2 suites. 1 conference room. Breakfast and evening snack included in rates. Types of meals: full breakfast and early coffee/tea. Beds: QDT. Air conditioning, turn-down service and cable TV in room. VCR, stables and library on premises. Handicap access. Amusement parks, antiques, fishing, parks, shopping, theater and watersports nearby.

Certificate may be used: Sunday through Thursday, space available.

Spotsylvania   E16

Roxbury Mill B&B

6908 S Roxbury Mill Rd,
Spotsylvania, VA 22553-2438
(703)582-6611

Circa 1723. Once a working mill for the Roxbury Plantation, this early 18th-century home has seen the formation of a nation and the wars that would follow. Civil War relics have been found on the property, which includes a dam and millpond. The innkeepers strive to maintain a sense of history at their B&B, keeping the decor in Colonial to pre-Civil War styles. The large master suite affords a view of the river from its private deck, and the bed is an 18th-century antique. The small guest room also offers a view, a private porch and a four-poster bed. Traditional Southern-Colonial fare, from family recipes fill the breakfast menu. Cornpone topped with slab bacon or country ham and biscuits are some of the appetizing choices. For late risers, the innkeepers also offer brunch.

Innkeeper(s): Joyce B. Ackerman. $75-150. MC VISA TC. 3 rooms, 2 with PB. 1 suite. Breakfast and afternoon tea included in rates. Types of meals: full breakfast, gourmet breakfast and early coffee/tea. Dinner and catering service available. Beds: QD. Air conditioning, turn-down service, ceiling fan and cable TV in room. VCR on premises. Amusement parks, antiques, fishing, parks, and watersports nearby.

Certificate may be used: Nov. 1 through March 15, Sunday through Thursday.

Stafford   D16

Renaissance Manor B&B Inn & Art Gallery

2247 Courthouse Rd, Stafford, VA 22554
(540)720-3785 (800)720-3784
Fax:(540)720-3785

Circa 1990. Although this elegant manor is a recent construction, it closely resembles Mount Vernon, the home of George Washington, which is just 20 miles away. Stroll the winding brick walkway and enjoy the site of gardens, a gazebo, fountain and

rose arbors. Each of the rooms is named for a historical figure, including Martha's Retreat, in honor of America's original first lady. The room features a huge, four-poster bed and Jacuzzi tub. The breakfasts and afternoon tea are served on fine china, crystal and silver. The area offers several Civil War battlefields, national monuments and other historic sites.

Innkeeper(s): JoAnn Houser & Deneen Bernard. $55-150. MC VISA AX PC TC. 6 rooms, 4 with PB, 1 with FP. 2 suites. 1 conference room. Breakfast and afternoon tea included in rates. Types of meals: continental-plus breakfast and gourmet breakfast. Banquet service and catering service available. Beds: KQDT. Air conditioning, turn-down service and ceiling fan in room. Cable TV, VCR, fax, copier and library on premises. Amusement parks, antiques, fishing, parks and shopping nearby.

Certificate may be used: Anytime.

Staunton   E12

Ashton Country House

1205 Middlebrook Ave,
Staunton, VA 24401-4546
(540)885-7819 (800)296-7819

Circa 1860. This Greek Revival home is surrounded by 25 explorable acres where cows roam and birds frolic in the trees. A mix of traditional and Victorian antiques grace the interior. Four of the guest rooms include a fireplace, and each is appointed individually. The inn's porches, where afternoon tea often is served, are lined with chairs for those who seek relaxation and the scenery of rolling hills. Woodrow Wilson's birthplace is among the town's notable attractions.

Innkeeper(s): Dorie & Vince Di Stefano. $90-125. MC VISA PC TC. 5 rooms with PB, 4 with FP. 1 suite. Breakfast, afternoon tea and evening snack included in rates. Types of meals: full breakfast, gourmet breakfast and early coffee/tea. Picnic lunch available. Beds: QD. Air conditioning and ceiling fan in room. Cable TV and VCR on premises. Handicap access. Antiques, fishing, parks, and watersports nearby.

Certificate may be used: Feb. 1 to March 31, Monday-Thursday.

Frederick House

28 N New St, Staunton, VA 24401-4306
(540)885-4220 (800)334-5575

Circa 1810. Across from Mary Baldwin College, this inn consists of five renovated town houses, the oldest of which is believed to be a copy of a home designed by Thomas Jefferson. A full breakfast is served in

Chumley's Tea Room. Guest rooms are furnished with antiques and feature robes, ceiling fans, some with fireplaces. Original staircases and woodwork are highlighted throughout. Suites are available.

Innkeeper(s): Joe & Evy Harman. $65-125. MC VISA AX DC DS PC TC. 20 rooms with PB, 6 with FP. 12 suites. 1 cottage. 2 conference rooms. Breakfast and afternoon tea included in rates. Types of meals: full breakfast and early coffee/tea. Picnic lunch available. Beds: KQDT. Air conditioning, ceiling fan and cable TV in room. Sauna, library and child care on premises. Antiques, fishing, parks, shopping, downhill skiing, cross-country skiing, sporting events, theater and watersports nearby.

Location: Downtown.

Seen in: Richmond Times-Dispatch, News Journal, Washington Post, Blue Ridge Country.

"Thanks for making the room so squeaky-clean and comfortable! I enjoyed the Virginia hospitality. The furnishings and decor are beautiful."

Certificate may be used: Weekdays, Sunday-Thursday, except May, August & October.

Thornrose House at Gypsy Hill
531 Thornrose Ave, Staunton, VA 24401
(540)885-7026 (800)861-4338

Circa 1912. A columned veranda wraps around two sides of this gracious red brick Georgian-style house. Two sets of Greek pergolas grace the lawns and there are gardens of azalea, rhododendron and hydrangea. The inn is furnished with a mix of

antique oak and walnut period pieces and overstuffed English country chairs. Bircher muesli, and hot-off-the-griddle whole grain banana pecan pancakes are popular breakfast items, served in the dining room (fireside on cool days). Across the street is a 300-acre park with lighted tennis courts, an 18-hole golf course and swimming pool.

Innkeeper(s): Otis Huston. $55-75. 5 rooms with PB. Breakfast and afternoon tea included in rates. Type of meal: full breakfast. Beds: KQDT. Air conditioning, turn-down service and ceiling fan in room. Cable TV on premises. Antiques, fishing, and theater nearby.

"We enjoyed ourselves beyond measure, the accommodations, the food, your helpfulness, but most of all your gracious spirits."

Certificate may be used: Dec. 1 through March 31, Sunday through Thursday, no holidays.

Urbanna   G19

Hewick Plantation
VSH 602/615, Box 82,
Urbanna, VA 23175
(804)758-4214 (800)484-7514
Fax:(804)758-4080

Circa 1678. A driveway lined with large oak trees leads to this two-story brick Colonial located on 66 acres. There is an ancient family cemetery on the

grounds, and at the rear of the house is an archaeological dig conducted by the College of William and Mary. A cross-stitch kit of Hewick Plantation, made by the Heirloom Needlecraft company, is available at the inn. The historic "Urbanna" coverlet is another unique item on display. The innkeeper is a tenth-generation descendant of Christopher Robinson, builder of Hewick Plantation and an original trustee of the College of William and Mary.

Innkeeper(s): Helen & Ed Battleson. $95-135. MC VISA AX DS PC TC. 2 rooms with PB, 2 with FP. Breakfast included in rates. Type of meal: continental-plus breakfast. Beds: QDT. Air conditioning and cable TV in room. Fax and stables on premises. Amusement parks, antiques, fishing, parks, shopping and watersports nearby.

Seen in: Richmond Times Dispatch, Daily Press, Pleasant Living, WRIC-TV.

Certificate may be used: November through June, Monday through Thursday, no holidays.

Warm Springs   F11

Three Hills Inn
PO Box 9, Warm Springs, VA 24484-0009
(540)839-5381 (888)234-4557
Fax:(540)839-5199

Circa 1913. Mary Johnston, who wrote the book "To Have and to Hold," built this inn, which rests on 38 mountainous acres. In 1917, Mary and her sisters opened the home to guests, earning a reputation for the home's view of the Allegheny Mountains and

Warm Springs Gap. The innkeepers now offer lodging in the antique-filled main house or adjacent cottages. Some rooms include private decks, while others have fireplaces or clawfoot tubs. Each of the cottages include a kitchen, one has a working fireplace, another offers a woodburning stove.

Innkeeper(s): Doug & Charlene Fike. $49-149. MC VISA DS PC TC. 15 rooms with PB, 4 with FP. 7 suites. 2 cottages. 1 conference room. Breakfast and afternoon tea included in rates. Types of meals: continental breakfast, gourmet breakfast and early coffee/tea. Picnic lunch, gourmet lunch, banquet service and catering service available. Beds: KQDT. Ceiling fan and cable TV in room. VCR, fax, copier, pet boarding and child care on premises. Antiques, fishing, parks, shopping, downhill skiing, cross-country skiing and theater nearby.

Certificate may be used: Anytime, except weekends in October and major (legal) holidays.

Washington D15

Caledonia Farm - 1812
47 Dearing Rd (Flint Hill),
Washington, VA 22627
(540)675-3693 (800)262-1812
Fax:(540)675-3693

Circa 1812. This gracious Federal-style stone house in the National Register is beautifully situated on 52 acres adjacent to Shenandoah National Park. It was built by a Revolutionary War officer, and his musket

is displayed over a mantel. The house, a Virginia Historic Landmark, has been restored with the original Colonial color scheme retained. All rooms have working fireplaces and provide views of Skyline Drive and the Blue Ridge Mountains. The innkeeper is a retired broadcaster.

Innkeeper(s): Phil Irwin. $80-140. MC VISA DS PC TC. 3 rooms, 2 with PB, 3 with FP. 2 suites. 1 cottage. 1 conference room. Breakfast and evening snack included in rates. Types of meals: gourmet breakfast and early coffee/tea. Beds: D. Air conditioning, turn-down service and VCR in room. Fax, copier, spa, bicycles and library on premises. Antiques, fishing, parks, shopping, downhill skiing, cross-country skiing, theater and watersports nearby.

Location: Four miles north of Washington, Va. 68 miles from Washington, DC.

Seen in: Country, Country Almanac, Country Living, Blue Ridge Country, Discovery, Washington Post, Baltimore Sun.

"We've stayed at many, many B&Bs. This is by far the best!"

Certificate may be used: Non-holiday Sunday-Wednesday, Jan. 2-Sept. 15.

Fairlea Farm Bed & Breakfast
636 Mt Salem Ave, PO Box 124,
Washington, VA 22747
(540)675-3679 Fax:(540)675-1064

Circa 1960. View acres of rolling hills, farmland and the Blue Ridge Mountains from this fieldstone house. Rooms are decorated with crocheted canopies and four-poster beds. Plants and floral bedcovers add a homey feel. The stone terrace is set up for relaxing with chairs lined along the edge. As a young surveyor, George Washington inspected the boundaries of this historic village, which is just a short walk from the home. Fairlea Farm is a working sheep and cattle farm.

Innkeeper(s): Susan & Walt Longyear. $75-125. PC TC. 3 rooms, 1 with FP. 1 suite. Breakfast and afternoon tea included in rates. Types of meals: full breakfast, gourmet breakfast and early coffee/tea. Beds: QT. Air conditioning and turn-down service in room. VCR, fax and copier on premises. Antiques, fishing, parks, shopping, downhill skiing and theater nearby.

Certificate may be used: Jan. 2 through March, Sunday through Friday.

The Foster-Harris House
PO Box 333, Washington, VA 22747
(540)675-3757 (800)666-0153

Circa 1900. This Victorian farmhouse stands on a lot laid out by George Washington and is situated at the edge of the village. The streets of the town are exactly as surveyed 225 years ago, and the town is the first of the 28 Washingtons in the United States. The village has galleries and craft shops as well as the Inn at Little Washington's five-star restaurant.

Innkeeper(s): Phyllis Marriott. $95-135. MC VISA AX DS. 4 rooms with PB, 1 with FP. 1 suite. Breakfast and afternoon tea included in rates. Type of meal: full breakfast. Dinner, picnic lunch and catering service available. Beds: QD. Air conditioning and ceiling fan in room. Computer on premises. Antiques, fishing, shopping, cross-country skiing and theater nearby.

Location: Sixty-five miles west of Washington, D.C.

Seen in: Culpeper News, Richmond Times-Dispatch.

"The View Room is charming, as are the hosts."

Certificate may be used: November-April, Sunday through Thursday.

Gay Street Inn
PO Box 237, Gay St,
Washington, VA 22747
(540)675-3288

Circa 1855. After a day of Skyline Drive, Shenandoah National Park and the caverns of Luray and Front Royal, come home to this stucco, gabled farmhouse. If you've booked the fireplace

room, a canopy bed will await you. Furnishings include period Shaker pieces. The innkeepers will be happy to steer you to the most interesting vineyards, "pick-your-own" fruit and vegetable farms and Made-In-Virginia food and craft shops. Five-star dining is within walking distance of the inn.

Innkeeper(s): Robin & Donna Kevis. $95-115. MC VISA AX PC TC. 3 rooms with PB, 1 with FP. Breakfast and afternoon tea included in rates. Types of meals: continental-plus breakfast, full breakfast, gourmet breakfast and early coffee/tea. Picnic lunch available. Beds: QD. Air conditioning in room. Child care on premises. Handicap access. Antiques, fishing, parks, shopping, theater and watersports nearby.

"Thank you for a wonderful visit. Your hospitality was superb."

Certificate may be used: Any Sunday through Friday.

White Post   B15

L'Auberge Provencale

PO Box 119, White Post, VA 22663-0119
(540)837-1375 (800)638-1702
Fax:(540)837-2004

Circa 1753. This farmhouse was built with fieldstones gathered from the area. Hessian soldiers crafted the woodwork of the main house, Mt. Airy. As the name suggests, a French influence is prominent throughout the inn. Victorian and European antiques fill the elegant guest rooms, several of which include fireplaces. Innkeeper Alain Borel hails from a long line of master chefs, his expertise creates many happy culinary memories guests cherish. Many of the French-influenced items include ingredients from the inn's gardens, and Alain has been hailed by James Beard as a Great Country Inn Chef.

Innkeeper(s): Alain & Celeste Borel. $145-195. MC VISA AX DC DS PC TC. 10 rooms with PB, 5 with FP. 1 suite. 1 conference room. Breakfast included in rates. Type of meal: gourmet breakfast. Dinner, evening snack, picnic lunch, banquet service and room service available. Beds: QD. Air conditioning, turn-down service and ceiling fan in room. Fax, copier and bicycles on premises. Handicap access. Antiques, fishing, parks, shopping and theater nearby.

Location: One mile south of Route 50 on Route 340.

Seen in: Bon Appetit, Glamour, Washington Dossier, Washington Post, Baltimore, Richmond Times.

"Peaceful view and atmosphere, extraordinary food and wines. Honeymoon and heaven all in one!"

Certificate may be used: Wednesday through Friday, no May or October or holidays.

White Stone   G19

Flowering Fields B&B

RR 2 Box 1600, White Stone, VA 22578
(804)435-6238 Fax:(804)435-6238

Circa 1790. Guests will find plenty to do at this Victorian bed & breakfast. The game room is stocked with a pool table, games, darts and a fireplace. The grounds are shared by the innkeepers friendly dogs, cat and several horses. The parlor is a bit more formal,and the music room includes a baby grand piano. Guests are pampered with a selection of appetizers and beverages after check-in. Cookies and chocolates are available later in the evening, and the morning begins with a huge breakfast. Omelets, fried apples and unique items such as oyster frittatas are served, and the innkeepers will plan the meal around guests' dietary restrictions. Guest rooms include items such as a four-poster rice bed, antiques, Queen Anne chairs and Oriental rugs.

Innkeeper(s): Lloyd Niziol & Susan Moenssens. $75-120. PC TC. 5 rooms, 2 with PB. 1 suite. 1 conference room. Breakfast, afternoon tea and evening snack included in rates. Types of meals: full breakfast, gourmet breakfast and early coffee/tea. Beds: KQDT. Air conditioning and ceiling fan in room. Cable TV, VCR, fax, copier, bicycles and library on premises. Antiques, fishing, parks, and watersports nearby.

Certificate may be used: Jan. 1-Dec. 31, Sunday-Saturday, excluding holiday weekends (Thanksgiving, Fourth of July, Memorial, Labor Day, Christmas).

Williamsburg   H18

Cedars

616 Jamestown Rd,
Williamsburg, VA 23185-3945
(757)229-3591 (800)296-3591

Circa 1930. This three-story brick Georgian home is an eight-minute walk from Colonial Williamsburg and is located across from the College of William and Mary. Rooms are decorated with Traditional antiques, Colonial reproductions, fireplaces and four-poster or canopy beds. The bountiful breakfasts include a hearty entree, fresh fruits, breads, muffins and cereals.

Innkeeper(s): Carol, Jim & Brona Malecha. $76-165. MC VISA PC TC. 8 rooms with PB, 2 with FP. 2 suites. 1 cottage. Breakfast included in rates. Types of meals: full breakfast and early coffee/tea. Beds: KQT. Air conditioning and ceiling fan in room. Library on premises. Amusement parks, parks and shopping nearby.

Certificate may be used: Jan. 2 through March 15, excluding Martin Luther King and President's Day holidays.

Homestay B&B

517 Richmond Rd,
Williamsburg, VA 23185-3537
(804)229-7468 (800)836-7468

Circa 1933. This Colonial Revival house is decorated with Victorian pieces inherited from the innkeeper's family. A screened back porch and fireplace in the living room are gathering spots. Collections of hand-crafted Noah's arks may be found throughout the house. The College of William and Mary is adjacent, and Colonial Williamsburg's is four blocks away.

Innkeeper(s): James Thomassen. $75-85. MC VISA. 3 rooms with PB. Breakfast included in rates. Type of meal: full breakfast. Beds: KT. Air conditioning and ceiling fan in room. Cable TV and VCR on premises. Amusement parks, antiques, sporting events and theater nearby.

"Our stay at your inn has been wonderful. Thank you so much for your warm and gracious welcome."

Certificate may be used: All year except holidays and holiday weekends.

Williamsburg Manor B&B

600 Richmond Rd,
Williamsburg, VA 23185-3540
(804)220-8011 (800)422-8011
Fax:(804)220-8011

Circa 1927. Built during the reconstruction of Colonial Williamsburg, this Georgian brick Colonial is just three blocks from the historic village. Notable interior features include arched doorways, a grand staircase, brick study and a fireplace in the living room. Waverly fabrics, Oriental rugs and antiques decorate the guest rooms. Breakfasts begin

with fresh fruits and home-baked breads, followed by a special daily entree. For instance, guests might start off with a freshly baked poppy seed muffins and then a warm apple cobbler topped with raspberry coulis. From there a specialty quiche and stone-ground grits are served. Gourmet regional Virginia

dinners also are available, and the innkeeper offers a full catering service.

Innkeeper(s): Laura Sisane. $75-150. MC VISA PC TC. 5 rooms with PB. Breakfast included in rates. Types of meals: gourmet breakfast and early coffee/tea. Picnic lunch, lunch, gourmet lunch, catering service and catered breakfast available. Beds: QT. Air conditioning, ceiling fan and cable TV in room. VCR and fax on premises. Amusement parks, antiques, fishing, parks, shopping, sporting events, theater and watersports nearby.

Location: Three blocks from colonial Williamsburg.

Seen in: Williamsburg.

"Lovely accommodations - Scrumptious breakfast."

Certificate may be used: January, February, March, July, August, November. Midweek, Monday-Thursday.

Williamsburg Sampler B&B

922 Jamestown Rd,
Williamsburg, VA 23185-3917
(757)253-0398 (800)722-1169
Fax:(757)253-2669

Circa 1976. Although this 18th-century-style home was built in the year of the bicentennial, it captures the early American spirit of Colonial Williamsburg. In fact, the home impressed Virginia's governor enough to state, "I call its significant to the attention of all our citizens." The rooms serve as wonderful replicas of an elegant Colonial home, with antiques, pewter and framed American and English samplers found throughout the inn. Bedchambers and roof-top, garden suites are cozy with rice-carved, four-poster beds and paddle fans. The innkeepers term the morning meal a "skip-lunch breakfast," an apt description of the colossal menu. Guests start off with a choice of juices, followed by fresh fruit, homemade muffins and Danishes. From there, a selection of entrees are offered, including quiche, waffles, pancakes, egg dishes or the like, accompanied with meats, potatoes and biscuits. If they can move after this wonderful meal, guests head out for a day exploring historic Williamsburg.

Innkeeper(s): Helen & Ike Sisane. $90-130. MC VISA PC. 4 rooms, 2 with PB, 2 with FP. 2 suites. Breakfast included in rates. Types of meals: full breakfast and early coffee/tea. Beds: KQT. Air conditioning, ceiling fan, cable TV and VCR in room. Fax, copier and library on premises. Amusement parks, antiques, fishing, parks, shopping, sporting events, theater and watersports nearby.

Certificate may be used: Jan. 2-March 31.

Washington

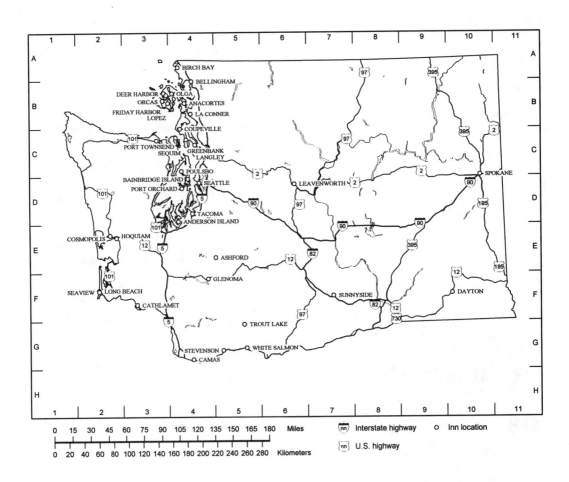

BIRCH BAY
BELLINGHAM
DEER HARBOR
OLGA
ORCAS
ANACORTES
FRIDAY HARBOR
LA CONNER
LOPEZ
COUPEVILLE
PORT TOWNSEND
GREENBANK
SEQUIM
LANGLEY
POULSBO
BAINBRIDGE ISLAND
SEATTLE
PORT ORCHARD
TACOMA
ANDERSON ISLAND
COSMOPOLIS
HOQUIAM
ASHFORD
GLENOMA
SEAVIEW
LONG BEACH
CATHLAMET
TROUT LAKE
STEVENSON
WHITE SALMON
CAMAS
LEAVENWORTH
SPOKANE
SUNNYSIDE
DAYTON

| 0 | 15 | 30 | 45 | 60 | 75 | 90 | 105 | 120 | 135 | 150 | 165 | 180 | Miles |

| 0 | 20 | 40 | 60 | 80 | 100 | 120 | 140 | 160 | 180 | 200 | 220 | 240 | 260 | 280 | Kilometers |

(nn) Interstate highway   ○ Inn location

(nn) U.S. highway

Aberdeen (Cosmopolis) *E2*

Cooney Mansion B&B

PO Box 54, 1705 Fifth St., Aberdeen
(Cosmopolis), WA 98537-0054
(360)533-0602 (800)977-7823

Circa 1908. This former lumber magnate's home,
in a wooded setting, boasts 37 rooms. In the
National Register, it was built with a ballroom in
the basement, nine bedrooms and eight bathrooms.

There is an intercom system with the original
script still visible. Mission furnishings, original to
the house, include the dining room set, sofas, desks
and library tables. Weddings and corporate retreats
are popular here.
Innkeeper(s): Judi & Jim Lohr. $60-135. MC VISA AX DC DS TC. 8
rooms, 5 with PB, 1 with FP. 1 suite. 1 conference room. Breakfast and
afternoon tea included in rates. Types of meals: full breakfast and early
coffee/tea. Banquet service and catering service available. Beds: KQDT.
Cable TV, VCR, fax, spa and sauna on premises. Antiques, fishing,
parks, shopping, sporting events, theater and watersports nearby.
Seen in: Daily World.

*"Rooms are beautiful and the food was delicious—on a
scale of 1 to 10, I would say 11!"*

Certificate may be used: September through June 15, holidays
excluded.

Anacortes *B4*

Channel House

2902 Oakes Ave, Anacortes, WA 98221
(360)293-9382 (800)238-4353
Fax:(360)299-9208

Circa 1902. Built by an Italian count, the Channel
House is designated the Krebs House by the
Historical Home Tour. Guest rooms view Puget
Sound and the San Juan Islands, and the ferry is
minutes away. The inn has a Victorian flavor, with a
library, three fireplaces, and a dining room with
French doors leading out to the garden.

Innkeeper(s): Dennis & Pat McIntyre. $69-95. MC VISA AX DS PC TC.
6 rooms with PB, 2 with FP. 1 cottage. Breakfast and afternoon tea
included in rates. Types of meals: full breakfast and early coffee/tea.
Beds: KQ. Fax and spa on premises. Antiques, fishing, parks, shopping,
theater and watersports nearby.

Location: 85 miles north of Seattle.

Seen in: Skagit Valley Herald.

*"The house is spectacular and your friendly thoughtful-
ness is the icing on the cake."*

Certificate may be used: Oct . 1 through April 30, Sunday through
Thursday.

Old Brook Inn

530 Old Brook Ln, Anacortes, WA 98221
(360)293-4768 (800)503-4768

Circa 1983. A traditional, New England decor complements this home's Cape Cod appearance. The
three guest rooms are simply furnished in an uncluttered style, and one includes a fireplace. The bed &
breakfast is close to horseback riding facilities, and
there is an orchard on the 10-acre grounds. An
ample breakfast with items such as fruit, blueberry
pancakes, baked egg dishes and potatoes is served.
Innkeeper(s): Richard M. Ash. $70-80. MC VISA DS PC TC. 3 rooms
with PB. Breakfast included in rates. Types of meals: continental breakfast and continental-plus breakfast. Beds: QT. Turn-down service in
room. VCR, stables, library and pet boarding on premises. Antiques,
fishing, parks and shopping nearby.

Certificate may be used: Jan. 1-March 30, April 15-June 15, Sept. 1-
Dec. 31, Sunday-Thursday.

Anderson Island *D4*

The Inn at Burg's Landing

8808 Villa Beach Rd,
Anderson Island, WA 98303-9785
(206)884-9185 Fax:(206)488-8682

Circa 1987. A short ferry trip from Steilacoom and
Tacoma, this log homestead boasts beautiful views of
Mt. Rainier, Puget Sound and the Cascade
Mountains. The master bedroom features a skylight
and a private whirlpool bath. After a full breakfast,
guests can spend the day at the inn's private beach.

Golf, hiking and freshwater lakes are nearby, and the area has many seasonal activities, including Fourth of July fireworks, the Anderson Island fair and parade in September and a February Sweetheart Dance and Dinner.

Innkeeper(s): Ken & Annie Burg. $75-110. MC VISA PC TC. 4 rooms, 2 with PB. Breakfast included in rates. Type of meal: full breakfast. Beds: Q. VCR in room. Spa on premises. Amusement parks, fishing, parks, shopping and downhill skiing nearby.

Seen in: Sunset, Tacoma News Tribune, Portland Oregonian.

Certificate may be used: Sunday-Thursday, May 1 to Sept. 30, Oct. 1 to April 30, anytime.

Ashford   E5

Mountain Meadows Inn B&B
28912 St Rt 706 E, Ashford, WA 98304
(360)569-2788

Circa 1910. Originally built for the superintendent of the Pacific National Lumber Company, the house boasts hanging baskets of fuchsias which accentuate the veranda. Comfortable guest rooms feature a view of the woodland setting, occasionally visited by deer and elk. An unusual collection of railroad artifacts, including museum-quality model trains, is found throughout the inn. Breakfasts are prepared on an 1889 wood cooking stove. The innkeeper also operates the Hobo Inn, six miles away, which features guest rooms in renovated railroad cabooses, one with its own Jacuzzi.

Innkeeper(s): Chad Darrah. $65-95. MC VISA. 5 rooms with PB, 1 with FP. 1 suite. 1 conference room. Breakfast included in rates. Type of meal: full breakfast. Beds: KQDT. VCR on premises.

Location: One-half mile west of Ashford.

Seen in: Seattle Times, Pacific Northwest, Eastside Weekly, Prime Times.

"Our stay here will be one of the nicest memories of our vacation."

Certificate may be used: October-May, Sunday-Thursday.

Bainbridge Island   D4

Bombay House
8490 NE Beck Rd,
Bainbridge Island, WA 98110-2251
(206)842-3926 (800)598-3926

Circa 1907. A ferry ride will transport guests out of busy Seattle and onto quiet, secluded Bainbridge Island and the Bombay House. The home, built by a master shipbuilder, affords beautiful views. Grounds are lush with gardens and have a charming gazebo. Inside, innkeepers Bunny and Roger have created a relaxing environment filled with country antiques. Curl up with a book in front of the open-hearth

fireplace or watch as ferries scurry across Puget Sound. Breakfasts are served in the large country kitchen and feature a variety of breads, muffins, breakfast cakes, pastries, fruit and cereals. The innkeepers are happy to accommodate special dietary needs or early risers with advance notice. The home is just a few blocks from the beach, a country theater, shopping and restaurants.

Innkeeper(s): Bunny Cameron & Roger Kanchuk. $59-149. AP. MC VISA AX DS PC. 5 rooms, 3 with PB. 1 conference room. Breakfast included in rates. Beds: KQDT. Cable TV and VCR on premises. Antiques, fishing, parks, shopping, sporting events and theater nearby.

Location: A ferry ride from downtown Seattle.

Seen in: Bainbridge Review.

"We had a great time, thanks to you and your husband for your hospitality."

Certificate may be used: All year Sunday-Thursday, excluding any holiday.

Bellingham   B4

The Castle B&B
1103 15th St, Bellingham, WA 98225
(360)676-0974

Circa 1889. All the guest rooms of this mauve Victorian mansion look out to Bellingham Bay and the San Juan Islands. Statuary, fountains and ponds accent the inn's gables, steeply-pitched turret and bays. The Bayview Room, with its panoramic water view, is the inn's honeymoon suite, complete with private veranda and fireplace. Ornate castle-appropriate antiques mingle with your hosts' extensive lamp and clock collection sprinkled throughout the 21 rooms. There is also a waterfront cottage available.

Innkeeper(s): Gloria & Larry Harriman. $45-95. PC TC. 4 rooms, 3 with PB, 1 with FP. 2 suites. 1 conference room. Breakfast included in rates. Types of meals: continental-plus breakfast and early coffee/tea. Beds: KQDT. Cable TV and VCR on premises. Antiques, fishing, parks, shopping, downhill skiing, cross-country skiing, sporting events, theater and watersports nearby.

Location: Historic Fairhaven.

Seen in: Sunset Magazine.

"Never have I seen a B&B with so many museum-quality pieces of furniture."

Certificate may be used: Nov. 1 through April 30, Wednesday & Thursday only.

Birch Bay   A4

Birch Bay B&B
8068 Birch Bay Dr, Birch Bay, WA 98230
(206)325-3500 Fax:(206)325-3500

This private, beachcomber cottage features a sun deck perfect for enjoying a summer day. The cottage offers comfortable, county decor and includes a bedroom, bathroom and kitchenette. The hosts keep the refrigerator stocked with juice, fresh eggs and bacon. During crabbing season, you'll find fresh crabmeat in the refrigerator. Guests are welcome to use the hosts' tandem bicycle, a perfect way to enjoy the scenic area. Birch Bay and nearby Semiahmoo offer plenty of restaurants, a dance hall and outlet shopping.

Innkeeper(s): Ronald Walken. $70. 1 room. Breakfast included in rates. Type of meal: continental breakfast.

Certificate may be used: Cottage, Monday through Thursday.

Cathlamet   F3

The Gallery B&B at Little Cape Horn
4 Little Cape Horn Rd,
Cathlamet, WA 98612-9544
(360)425-7395 Fax:(360)425-1351

Circa 1959. This unique modern home affords a view of the Columbia River and the surrounding valley. From the inn's redwood hot tub, guests can watch as ships traverse the river channel. The home is furnished with antiques, but the decor is contemporary, enhanced by a collection of artwork. Some of the guest rooms include Jacuzzi tubs. A gallery and gift shop are located on the premises.

Innkeeper(s): Eric & Carolyn Feasey. $80-135. 4 rooms, 3 with PB. 1 suite. 1 conference room. Breakfast included in rates. Types of meals: continental breakfast, full breakfast, gourmet breakfast and early coffee/tea. Beds: QT. Air conditioning and ceiling fan in room. VCR, fax, copier and spa on premises. Fishing, parks, shopping and watersports nearby.

Location: On the banks of the Lower Columbia River.

Seen in: Portland Oregonian, Seattle Post Intelligencer.

Certificate may be used: Jan. 1 to Dec. 31, subject to availability.

Coupeville   C4

Captain Whidbey Inn
2072 W Captain Whidbey Inn Rd,
Coupeville, WA 98239
(360)678-4097 (800)366-4097
Fax:(360)678-4110

Circa 1907. Overlooking Whidbey Island's Penn Cove, this log house inn has comfortable rooms featuring down comforters, feather beds and views of lagoons and gardens. The dining room also has a magnificent view and guests can enjoy their meals by the fireplace. The chef utilizes local catches like steelhead fish, salmon, Dungeness crab, spot prawns and Penn Cove mussels. The innkeeper is also a sailing captain and guests often book an afternoon on his 52-foot ketch, Cutty Sark. The innkeeper's family has run the inn for more than 30 years.

Innkeeper(s): Dennis Argent. $85-195. EP. MC VISA AX DC DS. 32 rooms, 20 with PB, 7 with FP. 1 conference room. Breakfast included in rates. Type of meal: full breakfast. Dinner, evening snack, picnic lunch and lunch available. Beds: KQD. Cable TV, VCR, fax and copier on premises. Antiques, shopping and theater nearby.

Location: Central Whidbey Island.

Seen in: Gourmet Magazine, USA-Weekend.

"I visit and stay here once a year and love it."

Certificate may be used: October-May, Sunday-Thursday, excluding special events/holidays.

Colonel Crockett Farm
1012 S Fort Casey Rd,
Coupeville, WA 98239-9753
(360)678-3711

Circa 1855. In the National Register, this Victorian farmhouse presides over 40 island acres of lawns, meadows and country gardens. Sweeping views of Crockett Lake and Admiralty Inlet may be enjoyed from the inn and its grounds. The Crockett

Room, a favorite of newlyweds, has a blue chintz canopied bed and fainting couch. Danny DeVito and Michael Douglas stayed at the inn during the Coupeville filming of War of the Roses.

Innkeeper(s): Beulah Whitlow. $65-95. MC VISA. 5 rooms with PB. Breakfast included in rates. Type of meal: full breakfast. Beds: KQD. Antiques, shopping and theater nearby.

Location: On Whidbey Island near the Port Townsend ferry terminal at

Keystone, near Fort Casey State Park.

Seen in: Peninsula, Portland Oregonian, Country Inns, Glamour.

"Everyone felt quite at home...such a beautiful spot."

Certificate may be used: October through April, Sunday (except on three-day holiday weekends) through Thursday (except Thanksgiving and Christmas).

The Victorian B&B

602 N Main, Coupeville, WA 98239-0761
(360)678-5305

Circa 1889. This graceful Italianate Victorian sits in the heart of one of the nation's few historic reserves. It was built for German immigrant Jacob Jenne, who became the proprietor of the Central Hotel on Front Street. Noted for having the first running water on the island, the house's old wooden water tower stands in the back garden. An old-fashioned storefront, once the local dentist's office, sits demurely behind a picket fence, now a private hideaway for guests.

Innkeeper(s): Alfred Sasso. $65-100. MC VISA. 3 rooms with PB. 1 suite. Breakfast included in rates. Type of meal: full breakfast. Beds: Q. Cable TV and VCR on premises. Antiques, fishing, and theater nearby.

Seen in: Seattle Times, Country Inns.

"If kindness and generosity are the precursors to success (and I certainly hope they are!), your success is assured."

Certificate may be used: October through May, Sunday through Friday.

Dayton   F10

The Purple House

415 E Clay St, Dayton, WA 99328-1348
(509)382-3159 (800)486-2574

Circa 1882. History buffs will adore this aptly named bed & breakfast, colored in deep purple tones with white, gingerbread trim. The home, which is listed in the National Register, is the perfect place to enjoy Dayton, which boasts two historic districts and a multitude of preserved Victorian homes. Innkeeper Christine Williscroft has filled the home with antiques and artwork. A highly praised cook, Christine prepares the European-style

full breakfasts, as well as mouthwatering afternoon refreshments. Guests can relax in the richly appointed parlor or library, and the grounds also include a swimming pool.

Innkeeper(s): D. Christine Williscroft. $85-125. EP. MC VISA. 4 rooms, 2 with PB, 1 with FP. 1 suite. Breakfast and afternoon tea included in rates. Types of meals: full breakfast, gourmet breakfast and early coffee/tea. Dinner and picnic lunch available. Beds: QD. Air conditioning and ceiling fan in room. Cable TV, VCR, swimming, library and pet boarding on premises. Handicap access. Antiques, fishing, parks, shopping, downhill skiing, cross-country skiing, sporting events, theater and watersports nearby.

Seen in: Sunset.

"You have accomplished so very much with your bed & breakfast to make it a very special place to stay."

Certificate may be used: By arrangement only.

Weinhard Hotel

235 E Main St, Dayton, WA 99328-1352
(509)382-4032 Fax:(509)382-2640

Circa 1890. This luxurious Victorian hotel, tucked at the base of the scenic Blue Mountains, originally served up spirits as the Weinhard Saloon and Lodge Hall. Guests are transported back to the genteel Victorian Era during their stay. After a restful sleep among period pieces, ornate carpeting and ceilings fans, guests might imagine the days when horses and buggies road through town. While the innkeepers have worked to preserve the history of the hotel, they didn't forget such modern luxuries as Jacuzzi tubs in each of the guest baths. The hotel boasts a beautiful Victorian roof garden, a perfect place to relax with a cup of tea or gourmet coffee. For a unique weekend, try the hotel's special Romantic Getaway package. Guests are presented with sparkling wine or champagne and a dozen roses. The package also includes a five-course meal served in the privacy of your own room.

Innkeeper(s): Virginia Butler. $65-115. MC VISA. 15 rooms with PB. Breakfast included in rates. Afternoon tea, lunch and catering service available. Beds: Q.

Seen in: Seattle, Daily Journal of Commerce, Sunset, Lewiston Morning Tribune.

"It's spectacular! Thank you so much for all your kindness and caring hospitality."

Certificate may be used: Sunday-Thursday, year-round except May 26-29, July 14-17, Sept.1-5, holidays.

Deer Harbor   B3

Deep Meadow Farm B&B

PO Box 321, Deer Harbor, WA 98243
(360)376-5866

Circa 1939. Located on 40 acres, this homestead is one of the few family farms still remaining on Orcas Island. It served for many years as the local dairy

farm. Now, with an added wing and new front porch it serves as a handsome B&B. Midwestern farm furniture and Civil War memorabilia furnish the inn, including a certificate from President Lincoln signed to the innkeeper's great-great-great Grandfather. There are two horses, a border collie and two cats. Kayaking and whale watching are popular pastimes.

Innkeeper(s): Anna Elisa Tejada-Boyle. $85-95. 2 rooms with PB. Breakfast and afternoon tea included in rates. Types of meals: full breakfast and early coffee/tea. Beds: D. VCR on premises. Antiques, fishing, shopping, theater and watersports nearby.

"Outstanding hospitality. The best of Orcas!"

Certificate may be used: Oct. 1 through April 30.

Friday Harbor   B3

San Juan Inn B&B

50 Spring St, Box 776,
Friday Harbor, WA 98250-0776
(360)378-2070 (800)742-8210
Fax:(360)378-6437

Circa 1873. In the National Register, this old European-style hotel is filled with stained glass, old photographs and flowers picked from the inn's garden. A Victorian settee is situated under a cherry tree within sniffing distance of the lilacs and roses. It's a half-block to the ferry landing. The innkeeper speaks Danish, German, Norwegian, French, Swedish and English.

Innkeeper(s): Annette & Skip Metzger. $70-175. MC VISA AX DS PC TC. 10 rooms, 4 with PB. 1 suite. Breakfast included in rates. Type of meal: continental-plus breakfast. Beds: KQDT. Ceiling fan, cable TV and VCR in room. Fax and spa on premises. Fishing, parks, shopping, theater and watersports nearby.

Certificate may be used: Oct. 1-April 30.

States Inn

2039 W Valley Rd,
Friday Harbor, WA 98250-9211
(360)378-6240 Fax:(360)378-6241

Circa 1910. This sprawling ranch home has nine guest rooms, each named and themed for a particular state. The Arizona and New Mexico rooms,

often booked by families or couples traveling together, can be combined to create a private suite with two bedrooms, a bathroom and a sitting area. The oldest part of the house was built as a country school and later used as a dance hall, before it was relocated to its current 60-acre spread. Baked French toast, accompanied by fresh fruit topped with yogurt sauce and homemade muffins are typical breakfast fare.

Innkeeper(s): Garreth Jeffers. $64-110. MC VISA PC TC. 9 rooms, 8 with PB, 1 with FP. 1 suite. Breakfast and afternoon tea included in rates. Types of meals: full breakfast and early coffee/tea. Beds: KQDT. Fax and stables on premises. Handicap access. Antiques, fishing, parks, shopping, theater and watersports nearby.

Location: On San Juan Island.

Seen in: Glamour.

Certificate may be used: Nov. 1 to March 31, all days.

Tucker House B&B With Cottages

260 B St, Friday Harbor, WA 98250-8074
(360)378-2783 (800)965-0123
Fax:(360)378-6437

Circa 1898. Only two blocks from the ferry landing, the white picket fence bordering Tucker House is a welcome sight for guests. The spindled entrance leads to the parlor and the simply furnished five guest rooms in the house. A separate cottage next to the hot tub is popular with honeymooners.

Innkeeper(s): Skip & Annette Metzger. $75-135. MC VISA AX DS PC TC. 5 rooms, 3 with PB. 3 cottages. Breakfast included in rates. Types of meals: full breakfast and gourmet breakfast. Beds: QD. Cable TV and VCR in room. Fax and spa on premises. Antiques, fishing, parks, shopping, theater and watersports nearby.

Location: San Juan Island.

Seen in: Sunset, Pacific Northwest, Western Boatman.

"A lovely place, the perfect getaway. We'll be back."

Certificate may be used: Oct. 16-April 1, excluding holidays or holiday periods.

Glenoma   F4

St. Helens Manor House

7476 US Hwy 12, Glenoma, WA 98336
(360)497-2090 (800)551-3290

This restored farmhouse maintains all of its original stained, etched and beveled glass, as well as the woodwork. Rooms are decorated with period pieces and decor. The well-groomed grounds include a unique arch made from thin tree branches. Hikers can trek up nearly to the point of where Mt. St. Helens erupted several years ago. Be sure to ask innkeeper Susyn Dragness about the inn's ghost.

Innkeeper(s): Susyn Dragness. $59-89. 4 rooms. Breakfast included in rates. Type of meal: full breakfast.

Certificate may be used: Sunday-Thursday, January-July and September-December.

Greenbank C4

Guest House Cottages, A B&B Inn

3366 S Hwy 525, Whidbey Island,
Greenbank, WA 98253-6400
(360)678-3115 Fax:(360)321-0631

Circa 1922. These storybook cottages and log
home are nestled within a peaceful forest on 25
acres. The Hansel and Gretel cottage features
stained-glass and criss-cross pared windows that give
it the feel of a gingerbread house. Ask for the Lodge
and you'll enjoy a private setting with a pond just
beyond your deck. Inside is a Jacuzzi tub, stone fireplace, king bed, antiques and an intimate hunting
lodge atmosphere.

Innkeeper(s): Don & Mary Jane Creger. $110-285. MC VISA AX DS PC
TC. 6 cottages. Breakfast included in rates. Type of meal: full breakfast.
Beds: KQDT. Air conditioning, turn-down service and VCR in room.
Cable TV, fax, copier, spa, swimming and library on premises. Antiques,
fishing, parks, shopping, theater and watersports nearby.

Location: On Whidbey Island.

Seen in: Los Angeles Times, Woman's Day, Sunset, Country Inns,
Bride's.

*"The wonderful thing is to be by yourselves and redis-
cover what's important."*

Certificate may be used: Nov. 15 through March 15. Monday through
Thursday, holidays and holiday weeks excluded.

Hoquiam E2

Lytle House

509 Chenault Ave,
Hoquiam, WA 98550-1821
(360)533-2320 (800)677-2320
Fax:(360)533-4025

Circa 1900. Set high on a hill overlooking the harbor, this massive three-story Queen Anne Victorian
was built by a lumberman. There are graceful sun
porches, arches and gingerbread trim. The

Treehouse Room is
shaded by a 100-foot
copper beech tree,
while the Rose
Room offers a view
of the harbor.
Afternoon tea is
available. The
innkeepers will host
a murder-mystery
dinner party or ele-
gant high tea by
prior arrangement.
Innkeeper(s): Robert
Bencala. $65-105. MC VISA
AX. 8 rooms. 1 suite.
Breakfast included in rates. Types of meals: full breakfast and early cof-
fee/tea. Evening snack, banquet service and catering service available.
Cable TV and VCR on premises. Antiques, shopping and theater nearby.

Certificate may be used: Sept. 15-May 1, excluding holidays. Some
restrictions may apply.

La Conner B4

Katy's Inn

503 S Third, La Conner, WA 98257-0869
(360)466-3366 (800)914-7767

Circa 1876. This pristinely renovated farmhouse is
framed by flower gardens and graceful oak trees.
Victorian wallpapers enhance a collection of
antique furnishings. Each guest room opens to the
veranda or balcony, providing a view of the countryside. Bicycles and boats can be rented from the village three blocks away.
Innkeeper(s): Bruce & Kathie Hubbard. $69-95. MC VISA AX DS. 4
rooms, 2 with PB. Breakfast and evening snack included in rates. Types
of meals: full breakfast and early coffee/tea. Room service available.
Beds: QD. Spa on premises. Antiques, fishing, parks, shopping and
watersports nearby.

Location: Heart of town.

*"The most charming and warmest of the B&Bs in which
we stayed."*

Certificate may be used: January & February, Sunday-Thursday.

Langley C4

Island Tyme, Bed & Breakfast Inn

4940 S Bayview Rd, Langley, WA 98260
(360)221-5078 (800)898-8963

Circa 1993. Located on Whidbey Island, this
Victorian is a whimsical mix of colors topped with
gingerbread trim and a turret. The inn's 10 acres
ensure solitude, and romantic amenities abound. The
Heirloom Suite boasts both a fireplace and a Jacuzzi

tub for two. The Turret room is tucked into the inn's tower and offers a Jacuzzi tub for two. Quilts, antiques and collectibles are found throughout the guest rooms. The dining room, where the country breakfasts are served, is located in the inn's turret.

Innkeeper(s): Lyn & Phil Fauth. $75-135. MC VISA AX PC TC. 5 rooms with PB, 2 with FP. 1 suite. Breakfast and evening snack included in rates. Types of meals: gourmet breakfast and early coffee/tea. Beds: KQ. Turn-down service, ceiling fan, cable TV and VCR in room. Library, pet boarding and child care on premises. Handicap access. Antiques, fishing, parks, shopping, theater and watersports nearby.

Certificate may be used: Oct. 15 through April 30, except third weekend of February.

Twickenham House B&B Inn
5023 S Langley Rd, Langley, WA 98260
(360)221-2334

Circa 1990. If the beauty of Puget Sound isn't enough, this island inn will be sure to satisfy. Innkeepers Maureen and Ray Cooke take the idea of bed & breakfast seriously. They offer comfortable rooms with French Canadian and European pine furniture, and a gourmet, three-course breakfast each morning. The home offers three living rooms with fireplaces and a British pub area. The inn shares the expansive 10-acre grounds with Northwest evergreens, ducks, sheep, hens and roosters. The island has many restaurants, boutiques and shops. Langley holds several seasonal events, including a country fair and a mystery weekend.

Innkeeper(s): Pat & Cece Egging. $85-120. MC VISA. 6 rooms, 4 with PB. 2 suites. 1 conference room. Breakfast included in rates. Types of meals: gourmet breakfast and early coffee/tea. Banquet service and catering service available. Beds: Q. VCR on premises. Antiques, fishing, shopping, theater and watersports nearby.

Location: The south end of Whidbey Island.

Seen in: Sunset, Country Living, Oregonian, Odyssey.

"Gracious and friendly hosts."

Certificate may be used: Monday-Thursday, excluding holiday periods.

Leavenworth
D6

Haus Rohrbach Pension
12882 Ranger Rd,
Leavenworth, WA 98826-9503
(509)548-7024 (800)548-4477
Fax:(509)548-5038

Circa 1975. This inn is located two minutes away from the village. Private fireplaces and whirlpools for two are features of each of three suites. Sourdough pancakes and cinnamon rolls are specialties of the house. Guests often take breakfast out to the deck to enjoy pastoral views that include grazing sheep and a pleasant pond. In the evening, return from white-water rafting, tobogganning, skiing or

sleigh rides to soak in the hot tub or indulge in the inn's complimentary desserts served in front of the wood stove.

Innkeeper(s): Kathryn Harrild. $75-160. MC VISA AX DS. 10 rooms, 8 with PB, 3 with FP. 3 suites. 2 conference rooms. Breakfast included in rates. Types of meals: full breakfast and early coffee/tea. Dinner, evening snack, picnic lunch, lunch, catering service and catered breakfast available. Beds: KQD. Air conditioning in room. Handicap access. Antiques, fishing, shopping, downhill skiing and cross-country skiing nearby.

Location: Two minutes from the Bavarian village of Leavenworth.

Certificate may be used: March, April, November-all days. January, February, May, June, September, October-Sunday through Thursday.

Old Blewett Pass B&B
3470 Hwy 97, Leavenworth, WA 98826
(509)548-4475

Circa 1908. Turn-of-the-century travelers stopped at this inn before crossing the mountain passes in search of their destiny. Today, weary travelers still will find this rustic inn a refreshing place for rest and relaxation. A traditional breakfast with bacon, eggs, sausages, waffles or perhaps omelettes, cereals and muffins are sure to satisfy. Innkeepers Dave and Laura Wagner are happy to show guests the secrets of  gold panning, and you can try your luck in Peshastin Creek, which runs through the property. Leavenworth is 15 minutes away.

Innkeeper(s): Sandy Jingling. $75-85. MC VISA. 4 rooms with PB. Breakfast included in rates. Types of meals: full breakfast and early coffee/tea. Beds: QD. Cable TV, VCR and bicycles on premises. Antiques, fishing, shopping, downhill skiing and cross-country skiing nearby.

"So glad we were sent this way."

Certificate may be used: Anytime, except holidays and festival weekends. No December dates.

Long Beach
F2

Boreas B&B
607 N Boulevard, Long Beach, WA 98631
(360)642-8069 (888)642-8069
Fax:(360)642-8069

Circa 1920. This inn started as a beach house and was remodeled eclectically with decks and a massive stone fireplace. There are two living rooms that offer views of the beach. Guest rooms all have ocean or mountain views (depending on the weather). Guests can enjoy the hot tub on the sun deck, take the path that winds through the dunes to the surf, or walk to the boardwalk, restaurants and shopping.

Innkeeper(s): Susie Goldsmith & Bill Verner. $75-105. MC VISA AX DC DS PC TC. 4 rooms. 2 suites. 1 cottage. Breakfast included in rates. Type of meal: full breakfast. Beds: QDT. VCR, fax, spa, bicycles and library on premises. Antiques, fishing, parks, and watersports nearby.

Certificate may be used: Sept. 15-May 15, Sunday-Thursday.

Scandinavian Gardens Inn
1610 S California St,
Long Beach, WA 98631-9801
(360)642-8877 (800)988-9277
Fax:(360)642-8763

You are asked to honor a Scandinavian custom of removing your shoes upon entering this B&B. White wool carpeting and blond-wood pieces decorate the living room. A recreation room offers a hot tub and Finnish sauna. The Icelandic Room has an antique armoire and hand-painted cabinets, while the Swedish Suite features a two-person soaking tub tucked into a private nook. Breakfast items such as creamed rice, shrimp au gratin and Danish pastries are served smorgasbord-style with the hosts in costume.

Innkeeper(s): Marilyn Dakan. $75-125. MC VISA. 5 rooms. 1 suite. Breakfast included in rates. Type of meal: full breakfast. Turn-down service in room. Antiques and shopping nearby.

Certificate may be used: Anytime except holidays and festivals.

Lopez
B3

MacKaye Harbor Inn
RR 1 Box 1940, Lopez, WA 98261-9801
(360)468-2253 Fax:(360)468-2253

Circa 1927. This seaside home was the first house on the island to have electric lights, and it was also the island's first inn. Several guest rooms have views of the harbor or bay. The waterfront parlor is a perfect place to relax, and the eight-acre grounds include a quarter mile of beach. The innkeepers also

offer accommodations in two carriage house units. The studio unit includes a kitchenette and can sleep up to three people. Studio guests may enjoy a full breakfast with the main house guests or can opt to have continental fare delivered to their door. The master unit includes a larger, stocked kitchen area and living room. The innkeepers also offer mountain bike and kayak rentals.

Innkeeper(s): Christy & Ingrid. $69-139. MC VISA PC TC. 5 rooms, 2 with PB, 1 with FP. 1 suite. 1 conference room. Breakfast included in rates. Types of meals: full breakfast, gourmet breakfast and early coffee/tea. Afternoon tea and picnic lunch available. Beds: KQDT. Turn-down service in room. Fax, copier and bicycles on premises. Antiques, fishing, parks and watersports nearby.

Location: San Juan Islands.
Seen in: Los Angeles Times, Sunset, Northwest.
Certificate may be used: Oct. 20-March 30.

The Inn at Swifts Bay
Rt 2, Box 3402, Lopez, WA 98261-9563
(360)468-3636 Fax:(360)468-3637

Circa 1975. This renovated country house is situated in a grove of fir trees, not too far from the ferry boats and a bike ride away from the village. Request the Attic Room for its skylights and queen-size sleigh bed topped with a lamb's wool comforter. Three guest rooms have fireplaces. A secluded hot tub is available for private star-gazing and soaking. Breakfasts delight gourmet palates.

Innkeeper(s): Robert Herrmann, Chris Brandmeir. $75-155. MC VISA AX DC DS TC. 5 rooms, 3 with PB, 3 with FP. 3 suites. 1 cottage. Breakfast and evening snack included in rates. Types of meals: full breakfast and early coffee/tea. Beds: Q. VCR, fax, spa and sauna on premises. Antiques, fishing, parks and watersports nearby.

Seen in: Brides, Vogue, San Francisco Examiner.
"Don't know how any future B&Bs at which we stay can top your home."
Certificate may be used: Nov. 1 to April 1, Sunday-Thursday

Olga
B4

Buck Bay Farm
Star Route Box 45, Olga, WA 98279
(360)376-2908

Before its reconstruction, this home was the spot for the town's community ball. The farmhouse is secluded on five acres and is decorated in country style. Down pillows and comforters are a few homey touches. Homemade breakfasts include items like freshly baked muffins, scones and biscuits still steaming from the oven.

Innkeeper(s): Rick & Janet Bronkey. $70-95. MC VISA AX DS PC TC. 5 rooms, 3 with PB. 1 suite. Breakfast and evening snack included in rates. Types of meals: full breakfast and early coffee/tea. Beds: Q. Cable TV and spa on premises. Handicap access. Antiques, fishing, parks, shopping, theater and watersports nearby.

Certificate may be used: Oct. 15 to May 15, everyday except holiday weekends.

Orcas   B3

Chestnut Hill Inn B&B

PO Box 213, Orcas, WA 98280-0213
(360)376-5157 Fax:(360)376-5283

Circa 1970. Guests enjoying an early morning walk
through the 15 acres of majestic countryside that
surround this inn are sure to see a variety of wildlife,
including an occasional deer. Four-poster or canopy
feather beds create an inviting atmosphere in the
bedchambers, all of which boast fireplaces.
Homemade breads and muffins accompany the
morning entree, which changes from day to day.

The grounds are a perfect place to enjoy a picnic,
and the innkeepers will fix up a basket for those
seeking a romantic outing. In the chilly months, a
cup of afternoon tea is served alongside refreshments. The gazebo adds character to the inn's garden. From November to April, the innkeepers provide special dinner "Inn," featuring a variety of
Pacific Northwest cuisine.

Innkeeper(s): Daniel & Marilyn Loewke. $95-145. MC VISA AX DS PC
TC. 4 rooms with PB, 4 with FP. Breakfast included in rates. Types of
meals: gourmet breakfast and early coffee/tea. Afternoon tea and picnic
lunch available. Beds: Q. Ceiling fan in room. VCR, fax, stables and
bicycles on premises. Fishing, parks, shopping, theater and watersports nearby.

Certificate may be used: Sunday-Thursday, Oct. 1-May 1, no holidays.

Port Orchard   D4

Northwest Interlude

3377 Sarann Ave E,
Port Orchard, WA 98366-8109
(360)871-4676

Antiques such as Grandma's four-poster bed fill
this contemporary Northwest home, overlooking
Puget Sound and the Olympic Mountain range.
Snacks are offered when you check in, and visitor's

enjoy evening turndown service and gourmet
breakfasts. Pike Street Market in Seattle is a short
ferry ride away.

Innkeeper(s): Barbara Cozad. $45-75. MC VISA. 3 rooms. Breakfast
included in rates. Types of meals: full breakfast and early coffee/tea.
Turn-down service, cable TV and VCR in room. Antiques, shopping,
cross-country skiing, sporting events and theater nearby.

*"It was appropriate that we had a king-sized bed, since
the moment we met Frances & Barbara we were treated
royally."*

Certificate may be used: October through March except Thanksgiving
and Christmas.

Port Townsend   C4

Ann Starrett Mansion

744 Clay St, Port Townsend, WA 98368
(360)385-3205 (800)321-0644
Fax:(360)385-2976

Circa 1889. George Starrett came from Maine to
Port Townsend and became the major residential
builder. By 1889, he had constructed one house a
week, totaling more than 350 houses. The
Smithsonian believes the Ann Starrett's elaborate
free-hung spiral staircase is the only one of its type
in the United States. A frescoed dome atop the
octagonal tower depicts four seasons and four
virtues. On the first day of each season, the sun
causes a ruby red light to point toward the appropriate painting.

Innkeeper(s): Bob & Edel Sokol. $65-225. MC VISA AX DS PC TC. 11
rooms with PB, 2 with FP. 2 suites. 2 cottages. 2 conference rooms.
Breakfast and afternoon tea included in rates. Types of meals: full
breakfast, gourmet breakfast and early coffee/tea. Beds: KQDT. Cable
TV in room. VCR, fax, copier and spa on premises. Antiques, fishing,
parks, shopping, cross-country skiing, theater and watersports nearby.

Location: Three blocks from the business district.

Seen in: Peninsula, New York Times, Vancouver Sun, San Francisco
Examiner, London Times, Colonial Homes, Elle, Leader, Japanese
Travel, National Geographic Traveller.

"A wonderful experience for aspiring time travelers."

Certificate may be used: November-March.

The English Inn

718 F St, Port Townsend, WA 98368-5211
(360)385-5302 (800)254-5302
Fax:(360)385-5302

Circa 1885. This Italianate Victorian was built during Port Townsend's 19th-century heyday, when the
town served the railroad and shipping industries.
The home overlooks the Olympic Mountains, and
several guest rooms offer mountain views. The rooms
are named in honor of English poets. There is a four-
person Jacuzzi tub secluded in the garden. Guests

often enjoy sunsets and scenic vistas from the gazebo, and many weddings take place at this picturesque spot. Breakfasts are seasonal and creative, offering such items as raspberry strudel muffins, herbed poached eggs on crumpets, artichoke frittatas or broiled grapefruit with brandy sauce.

Innkeeper(s): Nancy Borino. $65-95. MC VISA AX DC DS PC TC. 5 rooms with PB. 2 conference rooms. Breakfast included in rates. Types of meals: gourmet breakfast and early coffee/tea. Afternoon tea available. Beds: KQ. Ceiling fan in room. Cable TV, VCR, fax, copier, spa and bicycles on premises. Antiques, fishing, parks, shopping, theater and watersports nearby.

Certificate may be used: Jan. 1-June 30 & Oct. 1-Dec. 31, Sunday-Friday.

Holly Hill House B&B
611 Polk St, Port Townsend, WA 98368
(360)385-5619 (800)435-1454

Circa 1872. A unique "upside-down" 100-year-old Camperdown elm and several holly trees surround this aptly named bed & breakfast, built by Robert C. Hill, the co-founder of the First National Bank of Port Townsend. The cozy, romantic rooms are decorated with florals and lace. Billie's Room affords a view of Admiralty Inlet and Mt. Baker, while Lizette's Room offers Victorian decor and a view of the garden. The Skyview Room includes a wonderful skylight. The spacious Colonel's Room features a picture window with water and mountain views, and the Morning Glory Room is a cozy retreat with lace-trimmed quilts. Expansive breakfasts are served in the dining room, and coffee and tea are always available for a thirsty guest.

Innkeeper(s): Lynne Sterling. $78-145. 5 rooms with PB. 1 suite. Breakfast included in rates. Type of meal: early coffee/tea. Afternoon tea, evening snack and picnic lunch available. Beds: KQT. Turn-down service in room. Cable TV and library on premises. Antiques, parks, shopping and theater nearby.

Location: Two miles from Fort Worden State Park and in the heart of historic district.

Certificate may be used: Oct. 31 to April 30, Sunday to Thursday.

Lizzie's
731 Pierce St, Port Townsend, WA 98368
(360)385-4168 (800)700-4168

Circa 1887. Named for Lizzie Grant, a sea captain's wife, this Italianate Victorian is elegant and airy. In addition to the gracious interiors, some rooms command an outstanding view of Port Townsend Bay, Puget Sound, and the Olympic and Cascade mountain ranges. Each room is filled with antiques dating from 1840 to the turn-of-the-century. The dog's house in the garden is a one-quarter scale replica of the original house. Lizzie's is known for its elaborate breakfasts, where guests are encouraged to help themselves to seconds.

Innkeeper(s): Patricia Wickline. $63-126. MC VISA DS PC TC. 7 rooms, 7 with PB. Breakfast, evening snack included in rates. Type of meal: full breakfast. Beds: KQ.

Location: In uptown historic district.

Seen in: Travel & Leisure.

"As they say in show biz, you're a hard act to follow."

Certificate may be used: October through May, Sunday through Thursday.

Manresa Castle
PO Box 564, 7th & Sheridan, Port Townsend, WA 98368-0564
(360)385-5750 (800)732-1281
Fax:(360)385-5883

Circa 1892. When businessman Charles Eisenbeis built the largest private residence in Port Townsend, locals dubbed it "Eisenbeis Castle," because it resembled the castles in Eisenbeis' native Prussia. The home is a truly royal delight to behold, both inside and out. Luxurious European antiques and

hand-painted wall coverings decorate the dining room and many of the castle's stately guest rooms. The turret suites are unique and many of the rooms have mountain and water views, but beware of the third floor. Rumors of ghosts in the upper floor have frightened some, but others seek out the "haunted" rooms for a spooky stay. Port Townsend offers a variety of galleries, gift shops and antiquing.

Innkeeper(s): Roger O'Connor. $65-175. MC VISA DS. 40 rooms with PB. 1 conference room. Breakfast included in rates. Type of meal: continental breakfast. Dinner, banquet service and catered breakfast available. Beds: KQDT. Cable TV in room. Spa on premises. Antiques, fishing, shopping, theater and watersports nearby.

Seen in: Island Independent, Leader News, Province Showcase.

Certificate may be used: Sunday through Friday, October through May.

Palace Hotel
1004 Water St,
Port Townsend, WA 98368-6706
(360)946-5176 Fax:(360)946-5287

Circa 1889. This old brick hotel has been restored and refurbished in a Victorian style. The Miss Rose Room has a six-foot Jacuzzi tub and is on the third floor. Some rooms have kitchenettes, such as Miss Kitty's Room, with its velvet settee, antique bed and wood stove.

Innkeeper(s): Paul Jinneman. $59-119. MC VISA AX DS. 15 rooms. Breakfast included in rates. Type of meal: continental-plus breakfast. Beds: KQD. Spa on premises.

Certificate may be used: January to May, October to December, except Saturday nights.

Ravenscroft Inn
533 Quincy St,
Port Townsend, WA 98368-5839
(360)385-2784 (800)782-2691
Fax:(360)385-6724

Circa 1987. A second suite has been added to this relaxing inn, which includes a fireplace, six-foot soaking tub. From the suite's large window seat, guests can enjoy the view of Mt. Baker. The room has an Impressionist touch, decorated in Monet colors. Other rooms are equally interesting, all individually decorated with Colonial influences. The inn is just three blocks from the water.

Innkeeper(s): Leah Hammer. $65-165. MC VISA AX DS PC TC. 8 rooms with PB, 3 with FP. 2 suites. 1 conference room. Breakfast included in rates. Types of meals: full breakfast, gourmet breakfast and early coffee/tea. Afternoon tea and catering service available. Beds: KQT. Cable TV, VCR, fax and library on premises. Antiques, fishing, parks, shopping, cross-country skiing, theater and watersports nearby.

Certificate may be used: Oct. 15-May 15, Sunday-Thursday.

Poulsbo   C4

Foxbridge B&B
30680 Hwy 3 NE, Poulsbo, WA 98370
(360)598-5599 Fax:(360)598-3588

Circa 1993. The innkeepers at this Georgian-style home have taken the words bed & breakfast to heart. Each of the comfortable rooms has an individual theme. The Country Garden room is a floral delight with a canopy bed. The Old World room includes a sleigh bed and down comforter. The Foxhunt room is done up in masculine hues with a

four-poster bed. Antiques are placed throughout the home. As for the breakfast, each morning brings a new menu. Heart-shaped waffles topped with blueberries and cream might be the fare one morning, while another day could bring eggs Benedict or a smoked-salmon quiche. All are served with cereals and a special starter, perhaps baked nectarines with cream Ambrose.

Innkeeper(s): Beverly & Chuck Higgins. $75. MC VISA PC. 3 rooms with PB. Breakfast and afternoon tea included in rates. Types of meals: gourmet breakfast and early coffee/tea. Beds: Q. Turn-down service in room. Fax and library on premises. Antiques, fishing, parks, shopping, cross-country skiing, theater and watersports nearby.

Certificate may be used: Nov. 1 to May 15.

Seattle   D4

Prince of Wales
133 13th Ave E, Seattle, WA 98102-5809
(206)325-9692 (800)327-9692
Fax:(206)322-6402

Circa 1903. This friendly Victorian home is ideal for walks to shops, parks and local restaurants. The Prince's Retreat guest room offers a private rooftop deck, complete with telescope for viewing the Seattle skyline. There is a clawfoot tub. Early breakfasts may be accommodated by advance arrangement. Downtown is a mile and a half away.

Innkeeper(s): Carol Norton. $75-110. MC VISA AX DS PC TC. 4 rooms with PB. 2 suites. Breakfast included in rates. Types of meals: full breakfast and early coffee/tea. Beds: QT. Fax on premises. Amusement parks, antiques, fishing, parks, shopping, sporting events, theater and watersports nearby.

Location: Capitol Hill in Seattle.

Certificate may be used: Nov. 15-March 15 (no holidays), Sunday-Thursday nights, weekends if available, if stay is for more than four days.

Seaview   F2

Gumm's B&B Inn
PO Box 447,
Seaview, WA 98644-0447
(360)642-8887
(800)662-1046

Circa 1900. This gracefully restored Northwest Craftsman home and its yard take up one city block a mile from the ocean. It offers a massive stone fireplace in the living room, a sun porch and outdoor hot tub. Ask for Barbara's Room to enjoy a

four-poster rice bed, TV and armoire. Special accommodations for families make the inn popular for small weddings, family reunions and anniversaries. Walk a half block to the cranberry bogs or come to the cranberry festival in the fall. Other local celebrations include sandcastle building, whale watching, antique auto parades and a water music festival.
Innkeeper(s): Esther M. Slack. $70-85. MC VISA PC TC. 4 rooms, 2 with PB. Breakfast and evening snack included in rates. Types of meals: full breakfast and early coffee/tea. Afternoon tea available. Beds: QD. Cable TV in room. Spa on premises. Antiques, fishing, parks, shopping and theater nearby.

Certificate may be used: Jan. 1 to May 31 and Sept. 15 to Dec. 15.

Sequim   C3

Greywolf Inn
395 Keeler Rd, Sequim, WA 98382-9024
(360)683-5889 Fax:(360)683-1487

Built in a farmhouse style, this house is located on five acres. If you prefer a canopy bed, request the Pamela Room and enjoy Bavarian decor. Salmon and egg dishes are presented at breakfast. Decks surround the house, affording views of an occasional

eagle, ducks in the pond and Mount Baker. A nature trail provides a pleasant walk through the fields, tall fir trees and over a small stream. Visit the buffalo that come up to the road at the Olympic Game Farm. Birdwatching and beachcombing are popular on the Dungeness Spit.
Innkeeper(s): Peggy Melang. $80-120. MC VISA AX. 5 rooms. 1 suite. Breakfast included in rates. Type of meal: full breakfast. Ceiling fan and VCR in room. Antiques, shopping, downhill skiing, cross-country skiing and theater nearby.

Certificate may be used: Anytime from Oct. 15 to May 30. Offer limited to three rooms.

Spokane   C10

Fotheringham House
2128 W 2nd Ave, Spokane, WA 99204
(509)838-1891 Fax:(509)838-1807

A vintage Victorian in the National Register, this inn was built by the first mayor of Spokane, David Fotheringham. There are tin ceilings, a carved

staircase, gabled porches and polished woodwork. Victorian furnishings and stained-glass pieces are featured. Across the street is Coeur d'Alene Park and the Patsy Clark Mansion, a favorite Spokane restaurant. Walk two blocks to the Elk Drug Store to enjoy sitting at the old-fashioned soda fountain.
Innkeeper(s): Jacquelin Johnson. $70-85. MC VISA. 3 rooms. Breakfast included in rates. Types of meals: full breakfast and early coffee/tea. Ceiling fan in room. Cable TV and VCR on premises. Antiques, shopping, sporting events and theater nearby.

Certificate may be used: Consecutive nights Sunday through Thursday, November through April.

Marianna Stoltz House
427 E Indiana Ave, Spokane, WA 99207
(509)483-4316 (800)978-6587
Fax:(509)483-6773

Circa 1908. Located on a tree-lined street, two miles from downtown Spokane, is this American four-square Victorian. It is in the local historic register and features a wraparound porch, high ceilings and leaded-glass windows. Furnishings include Oriental rugs and period pieces.

Peach Melba Parfait and Stoltz House Strada are breakfast specialties.
Innkeeper(s): Phyllis & Jim Maguire. $65-85. MC VISA AX DC DS PC TC. 4 rooms, 2 with PB. 1 suite. Breakfast included in rates. Types of meals: full breakfast and early coffee/tea. Beds: KQT. Air conditioning and cable TV in room. Fax and copier on premises. Amusement parks, fishing, parks, shopping, downhill skiing, cross-country skiing, sporting events and theater nearby.

Certificate may be used: Nov. 1-March 31.

Stevenson G5

Sojourner Inn
142 Lyons Rd, Stevenson, WA 98648
(509)427-7070 Fax:(509)427-4229

A contemporary tri-level cedar house, the Sojourner is set on a ridge with unparalleled views of the confluence of the Columbia and Wind Rivers. National forests surround the inn's four acres, and a pair of bald eagles reside on the property. In addition to the stunning river views, the inn offers an excellent library, back deck and patio. The innkeeper is a Cordon Bleu chef and can provide dinners and receptions for special occasions.
Innkeeper(s): Judith Yeckel. $40-115. MC VISA. 5 rooms. Breakfast included in rates. Types of meals: full breakfast and early coffee/tea. Dinner, evening snack, picnic lunch, gourmet lunch, catering service and room service available. Air conditioning in room. Cable TV and VCR on premises. Antiques, downhill skiing, cross-country skiing, sporting events and theater nearby.
Certificate may be used: Year-round, Sunday through Thursday nights.

Sunnyside F7

Sunnyside Inn B&B
800 E Edison Ave, Sunnyside, WA 98944
(509)839-5557 (800)221-4195

Circa 1919. This wine country inn offers spacious rooms, decorated in a comfortable, country style. Most of the rooms include baths with Jacuzzi tubs. The one bedroom without a Jacuzzi, includes the home's original early 20th-century fixtures. Two rooms offer fireplaces. Breakfasts are served in the inn's restaurant, which also offers dinner service.
Innkeeper(s): Jim & Geri Graves. $42-85. MC VISA AX DS TC. 10 rooms with PB, 2 with FP. Breakfast and evening snack included in rates. Types of meals: continental breakfast and full breakfast. Dinner and room service available. Beds: KQ. Air conditioning, ceiling fan and cable TV in room. Spa on premises. Antiques, fishing, parks, shopping, cross-country skiing and theater nearby.
Certificate may be used: Jan. 30 to Nov. 10, Sunday-Thursday.

Tacoma D4

Commencement Bay B&B
3312 N Union Ave, Tacoma, WA 98407
(206)752-8175 Fax:(206)759-4025

Circa 1937. Watch boats sail across the bay while enjoying breakfast served with gourmet coffee at this Colonial Revival inn. Guest rooms feature bay or garden views and are uniquely decorated. The surrounding area includes historic sites, antique shops, restaurants, waterfront parks, wooded nature trails and Pt. Defiance Zoo and Aquarium. Relax in

a secluded hot tub and deck area or in the fireside room for reading and the romantic view.
Innkeeper(s): Sharon & Bill Kaufmann. $75-105. AP. MC VISA AX DS PC TC. 3 rooms with PB. 1 conference room. Breakfast and evening snack included in rates. Types of meals: full breakfast and early coffee/tea. Beds: Q. Cable TV and VCR in room. Fax, spa, bicycles and library on premises. Amusement parks, antiques, fishing, parks, shopping, sporting events, theater and watersports nearby.
Seen in: Tacoma Weekly, News Tribune.
Certificate may be used: January, February, March; Sunday through Thursday.

Trout Lake G5

The Farm Bed & Breakfast
490 Sunnyside Rd,
Trout Lake, WA 98650-9715
(509)395-2488

Circa 1890. Four acres surround this three-story yellow farmhouse, 25 miles north of the Columbia Gorge and Hood River. The old rail fence, meadow and forested foothills of Mount Adams create a pastoral scene appropriate for the inn's herd of Cashmere goats. A big farm breakfast is served. Inside, entertainment centers around the player piano, wood stove and satellite dish. Outdoors, take a flight from Trout Lake into Mount St. Helens, or gear up for huckleberry picking, trout fishing and hiking at nearby Gifford Pinchot National Forest. Ask the innkeepers about the fairs, rodeos and Saturday markets.
Innkeeper(s): Rosie & Dean Hostetter. $55-85. PC. 2 rooms. Breakfast included in rates. Types of meals: full breakfast and early coffee/tea. Lunch available. Beds: QD. Cable TV, VCR and bicycles on premises. Antiques, fishing, shopping, downhill skiing, cross-country skiing and watersports nearby.
Certificate may be used: Oct. 15-May 31.

White Salmon G5

Llama Ranch B&B
1980 Highway 141,
White Salmon, WA 98672-8032
(509)395-2786 (800)800-5262

Llamas abound at this unique, picturesque ranch, which affords views of Mt. Adams. Innkeepers Jerry and Rebeka Stone offer nature walks through the woods accompanied by some of their friendly llamas. The Stones also offer the unusual amenity of llama boarding. The White Salmon area, located in between the Mt. Adams Wilderness Area and Columbia Gorge, is full of interesting activities, including whitewater rafting, horseback riding and berry picking.
Innkeeper(s): Jerry & Rebeka Stone. $55-75. MC VISA DS. 7 rooms. Breakfast included in rates. Type of meal: full breakfast.
Certificate may be used: Oct. 15 through April 15.

Washington, D.C.

The Embassy Inn
1627 16th St NW,
Washington, D.C. 20009-3063
(202)234-7800 (800)423-9111
Fax:(202)234-3309

Circa 1913. This restored inn is furnished in a Federalist style. The comfortable lobby offers books and evening sherry. Conveniently located, the inn is seven blocks from the Adams Morgan area of ethnic restaurants. The Embassy's philosophy of innkeeping includes providing personal attention and cheerful hospitality. Concierge services are available.

Innkeeper(s): Jennifer Schroeder & Susan Stiles. $69-110. MC VISA AX DC CB TC. 38 rooms with PB. Breakfast included in rates. Type of meal: continental-plus breakfast. Beds: DT. Air conditioning and cable TV in room. Fax and copier on premises. Antiques, parks and theater nearby.

Location: Downtown Washington, D.C., 10 blocks north of the White House.

Seen in: Los Angeles Times, Inn Times, Business Review.

"When I return to D.C., I'll be back at the Embassy."

Certificate may be used: Year-round except April 3-8 and May 25-27, based on availability.

Reeds B&B
PO Box 12011, Washington, D.C. 20005
(202)328-3510 Fax:(202)332-3885

Circa 1887. This three-story Victorian townhouse was built by John Shipman, who owned one of the first construction companies in the city. The turn-of-the-century revitalization of Washington began in Logan Circle, considered to be the city's first truly residential area. During the house's restoration, flower gardens, terraces and fountains were added. Victorian antiques, original wood paneling, stained glass,

chandeliers, as well as practical amenities, such as air conditioning and laundry facilities, make this a comfortable stay.

Innkeeper(s): Charles & Jackie Reed. $55-90. MC VISA AX DC TC. 6 rooms, 2 with FP. 1 suite. 1 cottage. Breakfast included in rates. Type of meal: continental-plus breakfast. Beds: QD. Air conditioning and cable TV in room. Computer on premises. Antiques, parks, shopping, sporting events and theater nearby.

Location: Downtown, 10 blocks from White House.

Seen in: Philadelphia Inquirer, Washington Gardner, Washington Post, 101 Great Choices, Washington, D.C.

"This home was the highlight of our stay in Washington! This was a superb home and location. The Reeds' treated us better than family."

Certificate may be used: January, February, March 1-15 except inauguration week of January, 1997.

The Windsor Inn
1842 16th St NW,
Washington, D.C. 20009-3316
(202)667-0300 (800)423-9111
Fax:(202)667-4503

Circa 1910. Recently renovated and situated in a neighborhood of renovated townhouses, the Windsor Inn is the sister property to the Embassy Inn. It is larger and offers suites as well as a small meeting room. The lobby is in an art deco style. Carved, marble-top antiques are in abundance, and a private club atmosphere prevails. It is five blocks to the Metro station at Dupont Circle. There are no elevators.

Innkeeper(s): Jennifer Schroeder & Susan Stiles. $69-125. MC VISA AX DC CB TC. 46 rooms with PB. 2 suites. 1 conference room. Breakfast included in rates. Type of meal: continental-plus breakfast. Beds: QDT. Air conditioning and cable TV in room. Fax, copier and library on premises. Antiques, parks, shopping and theater nearby.

Location: Twelve blocks north of the White House.

Seen in: Los Angeles Times, Inn Times, Sunday Telegram, WCUA Press Release.

"Being here was like being home. Excellent service, would recommend."

Certificate may be used: Year-round, based on availability, with the exception of Cherry Blossom Week, April 3-8 and May 25-28.

West Virginia

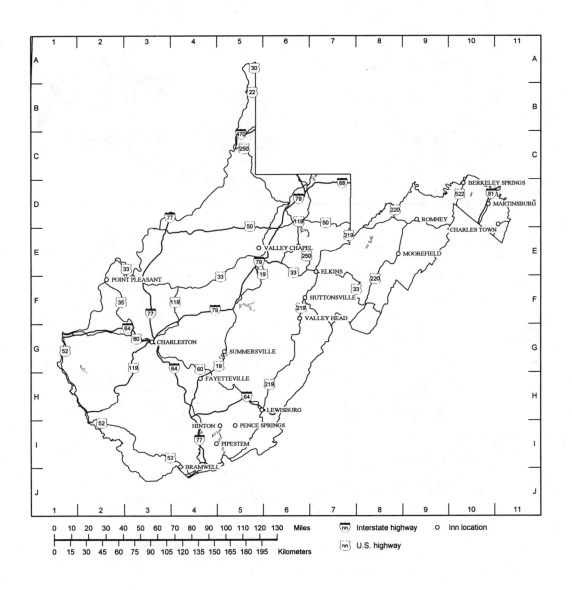

Berkeley Springs
D10

The Manor Inn

415 Fairfax St,
Berkeley Springs, WV 25411-1607
(304)258-1552 (800)225-5982

Circa 1878. In the National Register, this Second Empire Victorian features 12-foot ceilings, a mansard roof, large porch and French doors. The innkeeper collects antique quilts and is herself a quilter. George Washington is said to have bathed in the warm mineral springs in town where he owned a property a block from the Manor Inn. Roman and Turkish baths are featured in The Baths, a West Virginia State Park.

Innkeeper(s): Don & Dot Trask. $75-95. MC VISA PC TC. 4 rooms, 2 with PB. 1 suite. Breakfast included in rates. Types of meals: full breakfast, gourmet breakfast and early coffee/tea. Beds: QD. Air conditioning, ceiling fan and cable TV in room. VCR on premises. Antiques, fishing, parks, shopping, downhill skiing, cross-country skiing, theater and watersports nearby.

Certificate may be used: All year.

Bramwell
I4

Perry House B&B

Main St, PO Box 248,
Bramwell, WV 24715-0248
(304)248-8145 (800)328-0248
Fax:(304)248-8145

Circa 1902. This brick Victorian was built by a bank cashier and remained in the family for 80 years, when the current innkeepers purchased it. The rooms are decorated in period style with antiques. The innkeepers offer a private cottage with three bedrooms, a kitchen, living room and laundry facilities. Although a small village, Bramwell once was home to more than a dozen millionaires, and some of these families' homes are located on the town walking tour.

Innkeeper(s): Charlie & Charlotte Sacre. $40-55. MC VISA PC TC. 4 rooms, 1 with PB. 1 cottage. Breakfast included in rates. Types of meals: continental breakfast and early coffee/tea. Beds: KDT. Air conditioning and ceiling fan in room. Cable TV, fax, copier and library on premises. Antiques, fishing, parks, shopping, downhill skiing, theater and watersports nearby.

Certificate may be used: January-May, September-December, all days.

Charles Town
D11

Gilbert House B&B of Middleway

PO Box 1104, Charles Town, WV 25414
(304)725-0637

Circa 1760. A magnificent graystone of early Georgian design, the Gilbert House boasts the state's oldest flagstone sidewalk. During restoration, graffiti found on the upstairs bedroom walls included a drawing of President James Polk and a child's

growth chart from the 1800s. Elegant appointments include fine Oriental rugs, tasteful art and antique furnishings. The inn is located in the 18th-century village of Middleway, which contains one of the country's most well-preserved collections of log houses. The village was a mill site on the original settlers' trail into Shenandoah Valley. Middleway was also the site of "wizard clip" hauntings through most of the last decade of the 1700s. The region was home to members of "Virginia Blues," commanded by Daniel Morgan during the American Revolutionary War.

Innkeeper(s): Bernard F. Heiler. $80-140. MC VISA AX PC. 3 rooms, 2 with PB, 2 with FP. 1 suite. 1 conference room. Breakfast included in rates. Types of meals: full breakfast and gourmet breakfast. Beds: QT. Air conditioning in room. VCR and library on premises. Antiques, parks, shopping and theater nearby.

Location: Middleway historic district.

"We have stayed at inns for fifteen years, and yours is at the top of the list as best ever!"

Certificate may be used: December through May.

The Washington House Inn

216 S George St,
Charles Town, WV 25414-1632
(304)725-7923 (800)297-6957
Fax:(304)728-5150

Circa 1899. This three-story brick Victorian is said to have been built by the descendants of President Washington's brothers, John Augustine and Samuel.

Carved oak mantels, fireplaces, spacious guest rooms, antique furnishings and refreshments served on the wraparound porch make the inn memorable. Harpers Ferry National Historic Park, Antietam, and the Shenandoah and Potomac rivers are all within a 15-minute drive, as is Martinsburg outlet shopping.

Innkeeper(s): Mel & Nina Vogel. $70-125. MC VISA AX DS PC TC. 6 rooms with PB. 1 suite. 1 conference room. Breakfast, afternoon tea and evening snack included in rates. Types of meals: continental breakfast, continental-plus breakfast, full breakfast and early coffee/tea. Beds: QT. Air conditioning, turn-down service and ceiling fan in room. Cable TV, VCR, fax, copier and bicycles on premises. Antiques, fishing, parks, shopping, theater and watersports nearby.

Certificate may be used: November through May, Sunday through Thursday.

Charleston G3

Benedict Haid Farm
8 Hale St, Charleston, WV 25301-2806
(304)346-1054

Circa 1869. Although no breakfast is served, we couldn't help including this farm on 350-mountaintop acres because it specializes in raising exotic animals that include llamas, guanacos and black mountain sheep, as well as donkeys and cows. There are two rustic cabins for those looking for an economical stay. Most will prefer the main German-built, hand-hewn log lodge, which features antique furnishings and a large screened-in deck with fireplace and hot tub. There is a stocked pond. Bring your own breakfast. The farm is located about 23 miles outside of Charleston.

Innkeeper(s): Steve Jones. $100. MC VISA TC. 3 rooms. 1 cottage. Beds: D. Air conditioning in room. Cable TV, VCR and bicycles on premises. Fishing and cross-country skiing nearby.

Location: Twenty-three miles northeast of Charleston.

Seen in: Television Travel Show, One Tank Trips.

"Like stepping back in time."

Certificate may be used: Anytime, based on availability.

Brass Pineapple B&B
1611 Virginia St E,
Charleston, WV 25311-2113
(304)344-0748 (800)225-5982
Fax:(304)344-0748

Circa 1910. Located in Charleston's historic district, the Brass Pineapple is a cozy, yet elegant retreat. The home's original stained glass and oak woodwork has been restored, adding to the ambiance of rooms decorated with Victorian or Laura Ashley patterns. Hair dryers and terry robes are few touches guests will appreciate. There are many amenities for the business traveler as well, including data ports, fax machine and copier. Guests choose between an ample, full breakfast or low-fat continental fare, and a snack basket and beverages always are available. The inn half a block from the Capitol Complex.

Innkeeper(s): Cheryl Tincher. $75-100. MC VISA AX DC PC TC. 6 rooms with PB, 3 with FP. 1 suite. Breakfast, afternoon tea and evening snack included in rates. Types of meals: continental breakfast, full breakfast and early coffee/tea. Room service available. Beds: KQT. Air conditioning, turn-down service, ceiling fan, cable TV and VCR in room. Fax, copier and bicycles on premises. Antiques, fishing, parks, shopping, sporting events, theater and watersports nearby.

Seen in: Mid-Atlantic Country, Charlestonian, News 8 TV news, Charleston Daily Mail.

"Many thanks for a wonderful stay. We felt like a part of a family in this dear old house.

Certificate may be used: Anytime, based on availability.

Elkins E7

Tunnel Mountain B&B
Rt 1, Box 59-1, Elkins, WV 26241-9711
(304)636-1684

Circa 1938. Nestled on five acres of wooded land, this three-story Fieldstone home offers privacy in a peaceful setting. Rooms are tastefully decorated with antiques, collectibles and crafts. Each bedroom boasts a view of the surrounding mountains. The

chestnut and knotty pine woodwork accentuate the decor. The fireplace in the large common room is a great place for warming up after a day of touring or skiing. The area is home to a number of interesting events, including a Dulcimer festival.
Innkeeper(s): Anne & Paul Beardslee. $65-75. PC TC. 3 rooms with PB, 1 with FP. Breakfast included in rates. Type of meal: full breakfast. Beds: QD. Air conditioning and cable TV in room. Antiques, fishing, parks, shopping, downhill skiing, cross-country skiing, theater and watersports nearby.

Seen in: Blue Ridge Country.

Certificate may be used: November to May, Sunday-Thursday.

Fayetteville   H4

Morris Harvey House
201 W Maple Ave,
Fayetteville, WV 25840-1435
(304)574-1179 (800)225-5982

Circa 1902. The first thing guests notice at this Queen Anne Victorian is its incredible garden, which is shaped like a flower. But this home, built for banker and Confederate veteran Morris Harvey, offers many more unique features. The second story includes an 800-gallon tank built to gather rain, and the floorboards are a mix of colors. Each of the guest rooms includes a fireplace. The Rosa Suite, named to honor Mrs. Harvey, includes a clawfoot tub and bay window. The wraparound porch is lined with rocking chairs, enticing guests to just sit and relax.
Innkeeper(s): George & Elizabeth Soros. $75-85. MC VISA TC. 4 rooms with PB. Breakfast and afternoon tea included in rates. Types of meals: continental breakfast, full breakfast and gourmet breakfast. Beds: QD. Turn-down service and ceiling fan in room. Antiques, fishing, parks, shopping, theater and watersports nearby.

Certificate may be used: March 1 to Dec. 1, Sunday through Thursday, and upon vacancy.

Hinton   I5

Historic Hinton Manor
PO Box 1645, Hinton, WV 25951-1645
(304)466-3930

Local teacher, banker and salesman Joseph Roles drew up the blueprints for this manor, calling the place his dream home. The home was filled with fine furniture and decorated with woodwork imported from Bavaria. The current innkeepers found the home in disarray with a few furnishings and collectibles here and there. They polished up the woodwork, furnished the home with antiques and restored the original family's grand piano and other pieces. Several rooms showcase  lace dresses worn by the Roles' wife and sister. Breakfast is served by candlelight, and in the evenings, tea and dessert are served. The home is located in a National Historic District.
Innkeeper(s): Carla Leslie. $80. 2 rooms. Breakfast included in rates. Type of meal: continental breakfast.

Certificate may be used: April-December.

Huttonsville   F6

Hutton House
Route 250/219, PO Box 88,
Huttonsville, WV 26273
(304)335-6701

Circa 1898. This rambling Queen Anne Victorian in the National Register sits above the village, providing views of Tygart River Valley and the Laurel Mountains. Ornate windows, a three-story turret, pocket doors, wraparound porch and gingerbread trim are features. The inn is comfortably decorated with antiques and suitable Victorian touches. A full breakfast is served with antique Depression glass collected by the innkeeper.
Innkeeper(s): Loretta Murray. $60-70. MC VISA. 6 rooms. Breakfast included in rates. Type of meal: full breakfast. Evening snack available. Cable TV and VCR on premises. Shopping nearby.

Location: Near Showshoe Ski Resort, Cass Railroad, City of Elkins, state and national parks.

Certificate may be used: Sunday-Thursday, all year, excluding festival or holiday (three-day) weekends, and Dec. 25-Jan. 1.

Lewisburg H5

The General Lewis
301 E Washington St,
Lewisburg, WV 24901-1425
(304)645-2600 (800)628-4454
Fax:(304)645-2600

Circa 1834. This gracious Federal-style inn boasts a columned veranda, flower gardens and long lawns. Patrick Henry and Thomas Jefferson registered at the inn's walnut desk, which was retrieved from an old hot springs resort in the area. A stagecoach that

once delivered travelers to springs on the James River and Kanawha Turnpike, rests under an arbor. American antiques are featured throughout the inn, and Memory Hall displays household items and tools once used by local pioneers. Nearby are state parks, national forests, streams and rivers, as well as sites of the Revolutionary and Civil wars.

Innkeeper(s): Nan Morgan. $64-92. EP. MC VISA AX DS. 26 rooms with PB. 2 suites. Beds: QD. Air conditioning and cable TV in room. Fax and copier on premises. Handicap access. Antiques, shopping and theater nearby.

Seen in: Southern Living, New York Times.

"The staff is wonderful at making us feel at home, and we can be as much a part of the inn as we want."

Certificate may be used: Sunday-Thursday year-round, any day Dec. 1 through March 31.

Martinsburg D10

Pulpit & Palette Inn
516 W John St, Martinsburg, WV 25401
(304)263-7012

Circa 1870. Listed in the National Register, this Victorian inn is set off by a handsome iron fence. The interior is filled with a mix of American antiques, Tibetan rugs and art, setting off moldings and other architectural details in the library, drawing room and upstairs veranda. Your British-born

innkeeper prepares afternoon tea for guests. The Blue Ridge Outlet Center is two blocks away.

Innkeeper(s): Bill & Janet Starr. $75. MC VISA DS TC. 2 rooms. Breakfast, afternoon tea and evening snack included in rates. Types of meals: full breakfast, gourmet breakfast and early coffee/tea. Beds: Q. Air conditioning and turn-down service in room. Cable TV on premises. Antiques, parks, and theater nearby.

Seen in: Morning Herald, Antique Traveler, Journal.

"You have set an ideal standard for comfort and company."

Certificate may be used: March 1 to May 31, Sunday-Thursday; Nov. 1 to Dec. 31, Sunday-Thursday.

Moorefield E8

McMechen House Inn
109 N Main St, Moorefield, WV 26836
(304)538-7173 (800)298-2466
Fax:(304)538-7841

Circa 1853. This handsomely restored three-story brick Greek Revival townhouse is in the National Register. There are polished pine floors, a spectacular cherry staircase winding up to the third floor, walnut doors and woodwork, cranberry glass light fixtures and indoor folding shutters. Two parlors and a library add to the gracious dining room that houses the inn's restaurant. From May through September, guests can enjoy meals outdoors Green Shutters Garden Cafe. There is an antique book and gift shop on premises. Small weddings and receptions often are held at this inn.

Innkeeper(s): Linda & Bob Curtis. $60-85. MC VISA AX DC PC TC. 7 rooms, 4 with PB. 1 suite. Breakfast, afternoon tea and evening snack included in rates. Types of meals: full breakfast and early coffee/tea. Dinner, lunch, banquet service, catering service, catered breakfast and room service available. Beds: D. Air conditioning in room. VCR, fax, copier and library on premises. Antiques, fishing, parks, downhill skiing and theater nearby.

Certificate may be used: November-August. Exempt months: September and October.

Pence Springs I5

The Pence Springs Hotel
Rt 3, PO Box 90,
Pence Springs, WV 24962
(304)445-2606 (800)826-1829
Fax:(304)445-2204

Circa 1918. This elegant brick structure has served several purposes through the years. The hotel first gained prominence as a mineral spa frequented by many wealthy guests. From there, The Pence Springs was transformed into a women's prison. But it was again refurbished into a grand getaway. Guest

rooms are furnished in the art deco style, reminiscent of the hotel's heyday in the '20s. Guests enjoy full breakfasts each morning, and during the summer months, a lavish Sunday brunch is served, including vegetables grown on the hotel's 400 acres. The hotel's restaurant, The Riverside, serves English and Colonial specialties, and has been named as one of the top restaurants in the state. Spend the day strolling the lush grounds or relaxing in the Cider Press lounge or on the sunporch. The area boasts many outdoor activities and plenty of antique shopping. The innkeepers are happy to help guests plan tours of the area.

Innkeeper(s): D. Ashby Berkley & Rosa Lee Berkley Miller. $70-100. MC VISA AX DC CB DS PC TC. 25 rooms, 15 with PB. 3 suites. 4 conference rooms. Breakfast included in rates. Type of meal: gourmet breakfast. Dinner, picnic lunch, banquet service, catering service and room service available. Beds: KDT. Air conditioning in room. Cable TV, VCR, fax, copier, swimming, stables, bicycles and child care on premises. Handicap access. Antiques, fishing, parks, shopping, downhill skiing, theater and watersports nearby.

Seen in: Mid-Atlantic Country, Charleston Gazette, Beckley Register-Herald, Richmond, Goldenseal, Wonderful West Virginia, Travel Host.

"As always, I left your place rejuvenated. The property grows even more beautiful year after year."

Certificate may be used: April through December, Sunday through Thursday, non-holiday.

Pipestem I4

Walnut Grove Inn
HC 78 Box 260, Pipestem, WV 25979
(304)466-6119 (800)701-1237

Circa 1850. Located on 38 acres, this red shingled country farmhouse also has a century-old log barn and ancient cemetery with graves of Confederate soldiers and others prior to the Civil War. The farmhouse is decorated eclectically and the front porch is furnished with rocking chairs and a swing. Swimming, basketball, badminton and horseshoes are available. A country breakfast of biscuits and gravy, fresh eggs and homemade preserves is served in the dining room or screen room.

Innkeeper(s): Bonnie & Larry Graham. $65. MC VISA AX DC. 5 rooms, 3 with PB. 1 suite. Breakfast, afternoon tea and evening snack included in rates. Types of meals: gourmet breakfast and early coffee/tea. Beds: KQDT. Air conditioning in room. Cable TV and swimming on premises. Fishing, parks, shopping, downhill skiing, cross-country skiing, theater and watersports nearby.

Certificate may be used: Weekdays Monday through Thursday, all year; weekdays and weekends, Nov. 1 through May 1.

Point Pleasant F2

Stone Manor
12 Main St, Point Pleasant, WV 25550
(304)675-3442

Circa 1887. This stone Victorian sits on the banks of the Kanawha River with a front porch that faces the river. Point Pleasant Battle Monument Park, adjacent to the inn, was built to commemorate the location of the first battle of the Revolutionary War. In the National Register, the inn was once the home of a family who ran a ferry boat crossing for the Ohio and Kanawha rivers. Now restored, the house is decorated with Victorian antiques and offers a pleasant garden with a Victorian fish pond and fountain.

Innkeeper(s): Janice & Tom Vance. $50. PC. 3 rooms, 3 with FP. Breakfast included in rates. Type of meal: full breakfast. Beds: QD. Air conditioning and VCR in room. Cable TV on premises.

Certificate may be used: Anytime except Oct. 12-15.

Romney D9

Hampshire House 1884
165 N Grafton St, Romney, WV 26757
(304)822-7171

Circa 1884. Located near the south branch of the Potomac River, the garden here has old boxwoods and walnut trees. The inn features ornate brickwork, tall, narrow windows, and fireplaces with

handsome period mantels. A sitting room with a well-stocked library, a cozy patio and a music room with an antique pump organ are favorite places.
Innkeeper(s): Jane & Scott Simmons. $65-80. MC VISA AX DC DS PC TC. 5 rooms with PB, 3 with FP. 1 conference room. Breakfast included in rates. Types of meals: full breakfast and early coffee/tea. Evening snack available. Beds: QDT. Air conditioning, cable TV and VCR in room. Bicycles on premises. Antiques, fishing, shopping and watersports nearby.
Seen in: Hampshire Review, Mid-Atlantic Country, Weekend Journal.

"Your personal attention made us feel at home immediately."

Certificate may be used: November-May 1; weekdays only May 2-Sept. 30 (not honored in October).

Summersville G5

Historic Brock House B&B Inn

1400 Webster Rd,
Summersville, WV 26651-1524
(304)872-4887

Circa 1890. This Queen Anne farmhouse is the second venture into the bed & breakfast business for innkeepers Margie and Jim Martin. The exterior looks friendly and inviting, perhaps because of its long history of welcoming guests. The National Register inn originally served as a hotel and later as a boarding house. Margie has a degree in design, her skills are evident in the cheerful, country rooms. Each of the guest rooms has a different color scheme and decor. One is decked in deep blue, another is appointed with flowery bedspreads and pastel curtains.
Innkeeper(s): Margie N. Martin. $70-90. MC VISA PC TC. 6 rooms, 4 with PB. 1 suite. 1 conference room. Breakfast, afternoon tea and evening snack included in rates. Types of meals: continental breakfast, full breakfast, gourmet breakfast and early coffee/tea. Dinner, gourmet lunch, banquet service, catering service and catered breakfast available. Beds: QT. Air conditioning and turn-down service in room. Cable TV, VCR, fax and library on premises. Antiques, fishing, parks, shopping, theater and watersports nearby.
Certificate may be used: February until Dec. 22 and upon vacancy.

Valley Chapel, Weston E5

Ingeberg Acres

Millstone Rd, PO Box 199, Valley
Chapel, Weston, WV 26446-0199
(304)269-2834 Fax:(304)269-2834

Circa 1981. Enjoy the privilege of hunting turkey, grouse and deer on private, posted land on the 450 acres of this horse and cattle farm. Wildflowers, blackberries and raspberries may be gathered as well. A pond on the property is stocked with game fish

for anglers. Breakfast is served family-style and you are invited to participate in or observe everyday farm chores.
Innkeeper(s): Ingeborg & John Mann. $59. PC TC. 3 rooms. 1 cottage. Breakfast and evening snack included in rates. Type of meal: full breakfast. Beds: KDT. Air conditioning in room. Cable TV, VCR, fax, copier, swimming, stables and library on premises. Antiques, fishing, parks and shopping nearby.
Location: Fifteen minutes from I-79 near Weston.
Certificate may be used: Anytime, except two days before and two days after holidays.

Valley Head F6

Nakiska Chalet B&B

HC 73 Box 24, Valley Head, WV 26294
(304)339-6309 (800)225-5982

Circa 1982. On the way to this bed & breakfast, you'll be traveling the mountainous roads of West Virginia, and the hosts remind you to slow down and enjoy the scenery. Their A-frame house on 11 acres is surrounded by forests of sugar maples that display the best of foliage in autumn. Breakfast, served buffet-style, often includes local maple syrup atop blueberry pancakes. Wild turkey, deer, fox and grouse have been spotted from the deck.
Innkeeper(s): Joyce & Doug Cooper. $60-70. MC VISA DS PC. 4 rooms, 1 with PB. Breakfast and evening snack included in rates. Type of meal: full breakfast. Dinner available. Beds: KQT. Ceiling fan in room. Spa, sauna and library on premises. Fishing, downhill skiing and cross-country skiing nearby.
Certificate may be used: Sunday through Thursday nights, excluding holidays, subject to availability.

Wisconsin

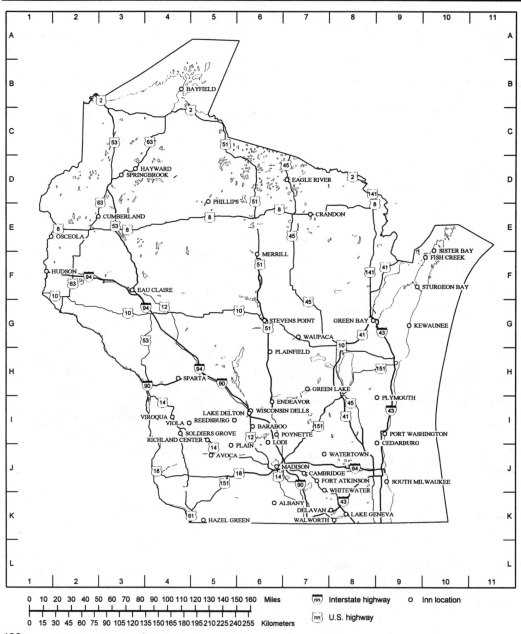

{nn} Interstate highway	O Inn location
{nn} U.S. highway	

0 10 20 30 40 50 60 70 80 90 100 110 120 130 140 150 160 Miles

0 15 30 45 60 75 90 105 120 135 150 165 180 195 210 225 240 255 Kilometers

Albany K6

Albany Guest House
405 S Mill St, Albany, WI 53502-9502
(608)862-3636

Circa 1908. The brick walkway, red-tiled foyer, lace curtains and abundance of flowers set the comfortable tone for this three-story inn. An upright piano in the large foyer and fireplace in the living room also add to the pleasant atmosphere. The guest rooms have picture windows and hand-carved antiques. Outside, maple and black walnut trees and various gardens grace the inn's eight-acre property. Guests can tour New Glarus, a village known as America's Little Switzerland, which is a short drive away. Also, not too far away is a cheese factory that is available for tours. Bicycle on the Sugar River Trail.

Innkeeper(s): Bob & Sally Braem. $55-75. MC VISA PC. 6 rooms, 4 with PB, 1 with FP. Breakfast included in rates. Types of meals: full breakfast and early coffee/tea. Beds: KQD. Air conditioning and ceiling fan in room. VCR and library on premises. Antiques, fishing, parks and cross-country skiing nearby.

Seen in: Silent Sports, Madison, Monroe Evening Times.

"Was even more than I expected."

Certificate may be used: Monday-Thursday, May-October. Anytime, November-April.

Oak Hill Manor
401 E Main St, Albany, WI 53502-9797
(608)862-1400 Fax:(608)862-1403

Circa 1908. The state's scenic Hidden Valley region is home to this American four-square inn, just 30 minutes south of Madison. Sylvia's Room boasts a five-foot iron and brass headboard on its queen bed, a view of the garden and a fireplace. The romantic Judith's Room features a heart-shaped queen canopy bed. Guests enjoy a three-course gourmet breakfast, including a sample of some of the area's outstanding cheeses. Nearby recreational activities include canoeing the Sugar River, hiking the Ice Age Trail or riding the inn's bikes on the Sugar River Trail.

Innkeeper(s): Donna & Glen Rothe. $50-75. MC VISA PC TC. 4 rooms with PB, 1 with FP. Breakfast, afternoon tea and evening snack included in rates. Types of meals: gourmet breakfast and early coffee/tea. Beds: Q. Air conditioning in room. Cable TV, bicycles and library on premises. Antiques, fishing, parks, shopping, cross-country skiing and watersports nearby.

Certificate may be used: Sunday-Thursday, subject to availability.

Avoca J5

Prairie Rose
107 S 2nd St, Avoca, WI 53506
(608)532-6878 (800)409-7673

Circa 1915. This comfortable home is filled with antiques and decorated in quaint, country style. The Rose Room boasts a fireplace, four-poster bed and private sitting area. The home is less than half an hour to many area sites, including the Wisconsin River, The House on the Rock, and Frank Lloyd Wright's buildings.

Innkeeper(s): Barbara & Terry Struble. $45-55. PC TC. 3 rooms, 1 with PB, 1 with FP. Breakfast included in rates. Type of meal: full breakfast. Beds: D. Cable TV and VCR on premises. Antiques, fishing, parks, cross-country skiing and theater nearby.

Certificate may be used: Sunday through Thursday, all year.

Baraboo I6

Victorian Rose B&B
423 3rd Ave, Baraboo, WI 53913-2408
(608)356-7828

Circa 1893. Victorian charm can be found in this classic inn with its wraparound front porch, beveled mirror oak fireplace, sliding pocket doors and intricate woodwork. The decor includes period antiques and heirloom collectibles. The innkeepers are proud to show off their Wisconsin hospitality. The Queen Victoria room is ideal for enjoying honeymoons and anniversaries. The inn is within walking distance to historic downtown Baraboo, the Al Ringling Theater and Ochsner Park, with a zoo and picnic area overlooking the Baraboo River.

Innkeeper(s): Bob & Carolyn Stearns. $65-80. DS PC TC. 3 rooms with PB. 1 conference room. Breakfast and afternoon tea included in rates. Types of meals: gourmet breakfast and early coffee/tea. Beds: D. Air conditioning and ceiling fan in room. Cable TV, VCR and library on premises. Amusement parks, antiques, fishing, parks, shopping, skiing, sporting events and watersports nearby.

Seen in: Baraboo News Republic.

"This has been so relaxing, stepping back in time. I always felt I was born too late. This period is the era I love."

Certificate may be used: All year, Sunday through Thursday (except holidays).

Bayfield   B4

Apple Tree Inn

Rt 1, Box 251, Hwy 135,
Bayfield, WI 54814-9767
(715)779-5572

Circa 1911. The Apple Tree Inn is a fully restored farmhouse overlooking Lake Superior. It was once owned by a dairy farmer/landscape artist. A rustic old barn on the grounds now serves as an antique store. Breakfast is served on the porch before the lake. Guest rooms are furnished in early Americana style and three have lake views.

Innkeeper(s): Joanna Barningham. $49-84. MC VISA PC TC. 4 rooms with PB. Breakfast included in rates. Types of meals: full breakfast, gourmet breakfast and early coffee/tea. Picnic lunch available. Beds: KQD. Air conditioning and ceiling fan in room. Cable TV, VCR, pet boarding and child care on premises. Antiques, fishing, parks, shopping, downhill skiing, cross-country skiing, theater and watersports nearby.

Seen in: Lake Superior.

"You made us feel like old friends rather than guests."

Certificate may be used: Weekdays; Sunday-Thursday, Sept. 20-May 15.

Thimbleberry Inn B&B

15021 Pagent Rd, PO Box 1007,
Bayfield, WI 54814
(715)779-5757

Circa 1992. The waters of Lake Superior sparkle beside the 400-foot shoreline adjacent to this natural wood home. The peaceful forest setting adds to the romance of the rooms, which include fireplaces. Innkeeper Sharon Locey writes a food column and currently is writing her first cookbook. Her culinary expertise makes breakfast a gourmet treat. While enjoying your morning meal, watch for wildlife and

bald eagles as they soar over the Loceys' 40 acres. The deck features a cedar hot tub perfect for relaxing after skiing, hiking or just spending the day by the lake's side.

Innkeeper(s): Sharon Locey. $75-115. 3 rooms with PB, 3 with FP. 1 suite. Breakfast included in rates. Types of meals: full breakfast and early coffee/tea. Beds: KQ. Antiques, fishing, shopping, downhill skiing and cross-country skiing nearby.

Location: On Lake Superior looking at five of the Apostle Islands.

Certificate may be used: January-May 15, November-Dec. 15, Sunday-Thursday.

Cambridge   J7

The Night Heron B&B

315 E Water St, Cambridge, WI 53523
(608)423-4141

Circa 1866. This brick Italianate home is covered with ivy and the grounds are dotted with flowers. The home originally served as a tavern, dance hall and saloon. The Koshkonong River and a 300-acre nature park are across the way. Innkeeper Pamela Schorr is an interior designer and has decorated each of the three bedchambers with something unique. The Knotty Pine Room includes a skylight, ceiling and walls fashioned from pine, creating a cabin-like environment. The Rockdale Room features a metal ceiling, and the Indigo Bunting Room is full artwork and includes a sitting area. Guests are presented with a bottle of champagne and enjoy use of a hot tub. The substantial breakfasts are served on the terrace under umbrella-covered tables.

Innkeeper(s): Pam Schorr & John Lehman. $70-75. TC. 3 rooms, 1 with PB. Breakfast included in rates. Types of meals: full breakfast and early coffee/tea. Beds: KQ. Air conditioning, ceiling fan and VCR in room. Fax, copier, spa and bicycles on premises. Antiques, fishing, parks, cross-country skiing, sporting events and theater nearby.

Certificate may be used: Nov. 1 to June 30, Sunday-Thursday, no holidays.

Cedarburg   I9

The Washington House Inn

W 62 N 573 Washington Ave,
Cedarburg, WI 53012
(414)375-3550 (800)554-4717
Fax:(414)375-9422

Circa 1886. Completely renovated, this brick building is decorated in a light-hearted country Victorian style, featuring antiques, whirlpool baths and fireplaces. The original guest registry, more than 100 years old, is displayed proudly in the lobby. Innkeeper(s): Wendy Porterfield. $59-179. MAP. MC VISA AX DC DS TC. 34 rooms with PB. 3 suites. 1 conference room. Breakfast included in rates. Types of meals: continental-plus breakfast and early coffee/tea. Beds: KQD. Air conditioning, ceiling fan, cable TV and VCR in room. Fax, copier and sauna on premises. Antiques, fishing, parks, shopping, cross-country skiing, sporting events and theater nearby.

Location: In the heart of downtown Cedarburg.

Seen in: Country Home, Chicago Sun-Times.

"A piece of time lost to all but a fortunate few who will experience it. Please save it for my children."

Certificate may be used: Valid entire promotion, Sunday-Thursday on $99-$179 rooms.

Crandon   E7

Courthouse Square B&B

210 E Polk St, Crandon, WI 54520-1436
(715)478-2549

Circa 1905. Situated on the shores of Surprise Lake, this Victorian Shingle also manages to provide the conveniences of town with its location. The inn features antique and country furnishings, and each of its guest rooms offers a lake or park view. The area provides excellent antiquing and shopping opportunities, in addition to cross-country and downhill skiing. Visitors also enjoy borrowing a bike to explore the town, relaxing on the inn's porch or venturing across the street to a city park. Innkeeper(s): Les & Bess Aho. $50-60. AX. 3 rooms, 1 with PB. Breakfast included in rates. Types of meals: gourmet breakfast and early coffee/tea. Afternoon tea and evening snack available. Beds: QDT. Ceiling fan in room. Cable TV and VCR on premises. Antiques, fishing, parks, shopping, skiing and watersports nearby.

Certificate may be used: Sunday to Thursday, except holidays & special events.

Cumberland   E2

The Rectory

1575 Second Ave, Box 1042,
Cumberland, WI 54829
(715)822-3151

Circa 1905. This city's unique island setting makes it an ideal stopping point for those exploring the state's lake-rich Northwest. The German Gothic inn, once home to the parish priest, features charming guest rooms, all filled with antiques, heirlooms and items of interest. The Mae Jenet Room, with its striking corner turret, features a doll collection and other unique toys. Breakfasts, served in the roomy parlor, often feature the inn's famous Breakfast Pie. A gaming casino is nearby, and 50 lakes are found within a 10-mile radius of Cumberland.

Innkeeper(s): Gerald & Ethel Anderson. $60-65. MC VISA. 4 rooms, 2 with PB. Ceiling fan in room. VCR on premises. Antiques, shopping, cross-country skiing and theater nearby.

Certificate may be used: Sunday-Thursday, excluding holidays and special events.

Delavan   K8

Lakeside Manor Inn

1809 S Shore Dr, Delavan, WI 53115
(414)728-5354 Fax:(414)728-2043

Circa 1897. This manor is, as the name suggests, situated next to a lake. The home was one of the first estates to grace the shore, built by a manufacturer of sewing machines and automobiles. Most of the guest rooms offer views of the lake, and each is named for a literary character. The Lakeside Bridal Suite, the home's former ballroom, includes a wood-burning fireplace, original light fixtures and a four-poster bed. This suite also includes a kitchenette. For those seeking complete privacy, the innkeepers offer the Silver Sands Cottage, which is just a few yards from shore. This cottage has two bedrooms and a glass-enclosed sleeping porch and kitchen. Innkeeper(s): Patricia K. McCauley. $79-159. MC VISA PC TC. 7 rooms, 4 with PB, 1 with FP. 1 suite. 1 cottage. Breakfast included in rates. Types of meals: continental-plus breakfast, full breakfast and early coffee/tea. Beds: KQDT. Air conditioning, ceiling fan, cable TV and VCR in room. Fax and swimming on premises. Amusement parks, antiques, fishing, parks, shopping, downhill skiing, cross-country skiing, theater and watersports nearby.

Certificate may be used: Sunday through Thursday, four rooms included.

Eagle River   D7

Brennan Manor

1079 Everett Rd, Eagle River, WI 54521
(715)479-7353

Circa 1928. This Tudor-style manor evokes images of a baronial hunting lodge with its 35-foot ceilings, timber rafters and suit of armor at the entry.

Hand-carved woodwork, arched windows, and a 30-foot stone fireplace in the Great Room completes the Old World ambiance. On the grounds are two stone patios, expansive lawns leading to the lake, a private swimming beach, wet boat house and two piers. A lake-view guest house is available, as well as four lavishly decorated bedrooms that lead to an open balcony overlooking the Great Room.

Innkeeper(s): Robert Lawton. $69-99. MC VISA. 4 rooms with PB. Breakfast included in rates. Type of meal: full breakfast. Afternoon tea available. Beds: Q. VCR and bicycles on premises. Handicap access. Amusement parks, antiques, fishing, parks, shopping, downhill skiing, cross-country skiing, theater and watersports nearby.

Location: On the famed Eagle River Chain of Lakes.

Seen in: Wisconsin Trails, Country Extra, Silent Sports, Northern Action, Best of the Northwoods.

Certificate may be used: September-June, Sunday-Thursday.

Eau Claire   F3

Otter Creek Inn
2536 Hwy 12, Eau Claire, WI 54701
(715)832-2945

Circa 1950. On a hillside overlooking a creek is this Tudor-style inn, surrounded by oaks and pines. Visitors immediately feel welcome as they make their way up the inn's curved pebblestone walk to the front door. The Palm Room has an antique sleigh bed, romantic loveseat and sunken whirlpool

tub. The Rose Room, often the choice of honeymooners, features a cloverleaf-shaped whirlpool tub that overlooks the gardens and gazebo. The spacious inn provides many spots for relaxation, including a gazebo, the great room with its inviting fireplace and a roomy patio.

Innkeeper(s): Shelley Hansen. $79-139. MC VISA AX DC CB DS. 5 rooms, 4 with PB. 1 suite. 1 conference room. Breakfast included in rates. Types of meals: continental-plus breakfast and early coffee/tea. Beds: QD. Air conditioning and cable TV in room. Spa on premises. Antiques, shopping, cross-country skiing, sporting events and theater nearby.

Location: Two hours to St. Paul.

Seen in: Country Magazine.

Certificate may be used: Monday through Thursday, November through April, except holiday weeks.

Endeavor   I6

Neenah Creek Inn & Pottery
W7956 Neenah Rd, Endeavor, WI 53930
(608)587-2229 Fax:(608)587-2229

Circa 1900. Wildlife lovers will enjoy the creek-front setting of this turn-of-the-century Portage brick farmhouse. The Circus Room honors nearby Baraboo, and features a brass queen bed. Country furnishings are found throughout the inn. Guests enjoy relaxing in the common room, on the outdoor porch, in the solarium and in the spacious dining-living room. The inn's 11 acres are filled with walking paths. Don't be shy about asking for a demonstration of the potter's wheel. Wisconsin Dells is an easy drive away.

Innkeeper(s): Pat & Doug Cook. $65-105. MC VISA DS TC. 4 rooms with PB. 1 suite. Breakfast and evening snack included in rates. Type of meal: gourmet breakfast. Beds: QT. Air conditioning in room. VCR, fax and copier on premises. Amusement parks, antiques, fishing, parks, shopping, skiing and watersports nearby.

Certificate may be used: Dec. 1-May 1 (not Valentine's weekend), all days of the week.

Fish Creek   F10

Thorp House Inn & Cottages
4135 Bluff Rd, PO Box 490,
Fish Creek, WI 54212
(414)868-2444

Circa 1902. Freeman Thorp picked the site for this home because of its view of Green Bay and the village. Before his house was finished, however, he perished in the bay when the Erie L. Hackley sank. His wife completed it as a guest house. Each room has a view of the harbor, cedar forest or village. A stone fireplace is the focal point of the parlor, and four of the cottages on the property have fireplaces. Some cottages have whirlpools. Everything upon which the eye might rest must be "of the era."

Innkeeper(s): Christine & Sverre Falck-Pedersen. $75-135. PC TC. 4 rooms with PB, 4 with FP. 6 cottages. Breakfast included in rates. Types of meals: continental-plus breakfast and early coffee/tea. Beds: KQDT. Air conditioning, ceiling fan, cable TV and VCR in room. Bicycles and library on premises. Amusement parks, antiques, fishing, parks, shopping, cross-country skiing, theater and watersports nearby.

Location: Heart of Door County, in the village of Fish Creek.

Seen in: Madison PM, Green Bay Press-Gazette, Milwaukee Journal/Sentinel, McCall's, Minnesota Monthly.

"Amazing attention to detail from restoration to the furnishings. A very first-class experience."

Certificate may be used: Sunday through Thursday nights, Nov. 6 through May, holidays excluded.

Fort Atkinson   J7

Lamp Post Inn

408 S Main St, Fort Atkinson, WI 53538
(414)563-6561

Circa 1878. Prepare to enjoy an authentic Victorian experience at this charming, restored home. Innkeepers Debra and Mike Rusch get into the spirit of things donning Victorian ware. Each of the guest rooms includes a working Victrola, which guests are encourage to use and enjoy. Debra and Mike pamper guests with fresh flowers and chocolates. Rooms are furnished completely with antiques. Breakfasts include specialties such as jelly-filled muffins, scones, Swedish puff pancakes and strawberry sorbet.

Innkeeper(s): Debra & Mike Rusch. $60-95. PC TC. 3 rooms, 2 with PB. Breakfast included in rates. Types of meals: gourmet breakfast and early coffee/tea. Afternoon tea, evening snack, picnic lunch and catering service available. Beds: D. Air conditioning and VCR in room.

Certificate may be used: Sunday through Thursday.

Green Bay   G8

The Astor House B&B

637 S Monroe Ave, Green Bay, WI 54301
(414)432-3585

Circa 1888. Located in the Astor Historic District, the Astor House is completely surrounded by Victorian homes. Guests have their choice of five rooms, each uniquely decorated for a range of ambiance, from The Vienna Balconies to the Marseilles Garden to the Hong Kong Retreat. The parlor, veranda and many suites feature a grand view of City Centre's lighted church towers. This home is also the first and only B&B in Green Bay and recently received the Mayor's Award for Remodeling and Restoration. Business travelers should take notice of the private phone lines in each room, as well as the ability to hook up a modem.

Innkeeper(s): Doug Landwehr. $79-149. MC VISA AX DS. 5 rooms with PB, 4 with FP. 3 suites. 1 conference room. Breakfast included in rates. Type of meal: continental-plus breakfast. Beds: KQDT. Air conditioning, turn-down service, cable TV and VCR in room. Amusement parks, antiques, fishing, parks, shopping, cross-country skiing, sporting events, theater and watersports nearby.

Certificate may be used: Monday-Thursday.

Green Lake   H7

McConnell Inn

497 S Lawson Dr, Green Lake, WI 54941
(414)294-6430

Circa 1901. This stately home retains many of its original features, including leaded windows, woodwork, leather wainscoting and parquet floors. Each of the guest rooms includes beds covered with handmade quilts and clawfoot tubs. The grand, master suite comprises the entire third floor and boasts 14-foot vaulted beam ceilings, Victorian walnut furnishings, a Jacuzzi and six-foot oak buffet now converted into a unique bathroom vanity. Innkeeper Mary Jo Johnson, a pastry chef, creates the wonderful pastries that accompany an expansive breakfast with fresh fruit, granola and delectable entrees.

Innkeeper(s): Mary Jo Johnson. $80-130. MC VISA. 5 rooms. Breakfast included in rates. Type of meal: full breakfast.

Certificate may be used: November-April.

Hayward   D3

Lumberman's Mansion Inn

204 E Fourth St, Hayward, WI 54843
(715)634-3012 Fax:(715)634-5724

Circa 1887. This Queen Anne Victorian, once the home of a local lumber baron, sits on a hill overlooking the city, park and pond. An oak staircase, maple floors, tiled fireplaces, pocket doors and a carriage stoop are among the finely restored details. Antique furnishings blend with modern amenities

such as whirlpool tubs and a video library. Wild rice pancakes, Wisconsin sausages and fresh-squeezed cranberry juice are some of the regional specialties featured for breakfast. The innkeepers host many seasonal events and evening lectures. Plays are sometimes performed on the front porch.

Innkeeper(s): Jan Blaedel. $70-100. MC VISA. 5 rooms with PB. 2 suites. 1 conference room. Breakfast and afternoon tea included in rates. Type of meal: full breakfast. Beds: Q. Spa and bicycles on premises. Antiques, fishing, downhill skiing, cross-country skiing and watersports nearby.

Location: One block from main street.

Seen in: Sawyer County Record, Chicago Sun Times, Wisconsin Trails, Minneapolis Star Tribune, Wisconsin Country Life.

"The food was excellent. And the extra personal touches (chocolate on the pillow, cookies & pie at night, muffins in the morning, etc.) were especially nice. This is definitely the best B&B we've ever been to."

Certificate may be used: Sunday-Thursday.

Mustard Seed

205 California, PO Box 262,
Hayward, WI 54843
(715)634-2908

Circa 1895. Situated in a quiet neighborhood within easy walking distance of downtown Hayward, this inn offers guests a cozy mix of country antique and Scandinavian decor. The inn's enclosed yard helps afford privacy to guests, who may opt for the spacious Governor's Suite with its two-sided fireplace. (Wisconsin Governor Tommy Thompson was a recent visitor.) Breakfasts may be enjoyed in the formal dining area, country-style kitchen or on the patio in summer. Nearby attractions include Historyland, Telemark Ski Area and the National Fresh Water Fishing Hall of Fame.

Innkeeper(s): Mary Gervais. $45-85. MC VISA DS. 6 rooms, 4 with PB, 1 with FP. Breakfast included in rates. Type of meal: full bkfst. Beds: QDT.

Seen in: Sawyer County Record.

"We cannot believe our good fortune in finding you and your marvelous home."

Certificate may be used: Monday-Thursday, October through May, excluding last week in December and February.

Hazel Green K5

De Winters of Hazel Green

2225 Main St, PO Box 384,
Hazel Green, WI 53811
(608)854-2768

Circa 1847. This Federal and Greek Revival home dates back to pre-Civil War times. Innkeeper Don Simison was born in the home and his family heirlooms fill the house. A hearty homemade breakfast is served each morning. Explore Hazel Green or just relax at the inn. The city hosts some interesting attractions including a parade and open house of historic homes early in December.

Innkeeper(s): Don & Cari Simison. $45-75. TC. 3 rooms, 1 with PB. Breakfast included in rates. Type of meal: full breakfast. Beds: D. Air conditioning in room. Library on premises. Antiques, fishing, parks, shopping, downhill skiing and theater nearby.

"Good food and fun."

Certificate may be used: Any with reservation, only will take one certificate couple at a time on a busy weekend.

Wisconsin House Stagecoach Inn

2105 Main, PO Box 71,
Hazel Green, WI 53811
(608)854-2233

Circa 1846. Located in southwest Wisconsin's historic lead mining region, this one-time stagecoach stop will delight antique-lovers. The innkeepers, who also deal in antiques, enjoy helping guests in their search for that special piece. The spacious two-story inn once hosted Ulysses S. Grant, whose home is just across the border in Illinois. One of the inn's guest rooms bears his name and features a walnut four-poster bed. Don't miss the chance to join the Dischs on a Friday or Saturday evening for one of their famous country inn dinners. The meals are served, by reservation only, at a handsome 16-footlong dining table.

Innkeeper(s): Ken & Pat Disch. $55-110. MC VISA DS PC. 8 rooms, 6 with PB. 2 suites. Breakfast included in rates. Types of meals: full breakfast, gourmet breakfast and early coffee/tea. Dinner available. Beds: KQDT. Air conditioning in room. Cable TV, copier, bicycles and library on premises. Antiques, fishing, parks, downhill skiing, cross-country skiing and theater nearby.

Seen in: Chicago Tribune, Milwaukee Journal, Country Living, Midwest Living.

"Your ears should be burning because we are telling so many about you."

Certificate may be used: Anytime, except weekends Labor Day to Oct. 31.

Hudson
F1

Grapevine Inn B&B
702 Vine St, Hudson, WI 54016-1725
(715)386-1989

Guests at this Queen Anne Victorian/Greek Revival inn enjoy a wake-up tray of coffee and baked breads before sitting down to a three-course breakfast. Three elegant, antique-filled guest rooms will delight visitors. The St. Croix River and the scenic riverway are within walking distance, and tubing excursions down the Apple River are popular. Willow River State Park is nearby, and the impressive Mall of America is just a 30-minute drive from the inn.

Innkeeper(s): Barbara Dahl. $89-129. 3 rooms. 1 conference room. Breakfast included in rates. Types of meals: full breakfast and early coffee/tea. Evening snack available. Air conditioning, turn-down service and ceiling fan in room. VCR and library on premises. Amusement parks, antiques, shopping, downhill skiing, cross-country skiing, sporting events and theater nearby.

Certificate may be used: Sunday through Thursday, year-round, excluding holidays and special events.

Lake Delton
I6

The Swallow's Nest B&B
141 Sarrington, PO Box 418,
Lake Delton, WI 53940
(608)254-6900

Circa 1988. This inn has a picturesque view of the Wisconsin Dells and Lake Delton. The Swallow's Nest features a two-story atrium with skylights, and cathedral windows and ceiling. Guests may relax on the screened deck, in the library by the fireplace or in the gazebo by the waterfall. The inn is furnished with English period furniture, rocking chairs, lace curtains, handmade quilts and goose-down comforters.

Innkeeper(s): Mary Ann Stemo. $65-70. MC VISA. 4 rooms with PB, 2 with FP. Breakfast included in rates. Type of meal: full breakfast. Beds: QDT. Air conditioning in room. Cable TV on premises. Amusement parks, antiques, shopping, downhill skiing, cross-country skiing, sporting events and theater nearby.

Seen in: Milwaukee Journal, Wisconsin Trails.

"Your home is beautiful, and the breakfasts were wonderful!"

Certificate may be used: Monday through Thursday, no holidays or holiday weekends.

Lake Geneva
K8

T.C. Smith Inn B&B
865 W Main St, Lake Geneva, WI 53147
(414)248-1097 (800)423-0233
Fax:(414)248-1672

Circa 1845. Listed in the National Register of Historic Places, this High Victorian-style inn blends elements of Greek-Revival and Italianate architecture. The inn has massive carved wooden doors, hand-painted moldings and woodwork, a high-ceilinged foyer, an original parquet floor, Oriental carpets, museum-quality period antiques and European oil paintings. Guests may enjoy tea in the Grand Parlor by a marble fireplace or enjoy breakfast on an open veranda.

Innkeeper(s): The Marks Family. $95-350. MC VISA AX DC DS PC TC. 8 rooms with PB, 5 with FP. 2 suites. 1 conference room. Breakfast, afternoon tea and evening snack included in rates. Types of meals: full breakfast, gourmet breakfast and early coffee/tea. Room service available. Beds: QD. Air conditioning, ceiling fan and VCR in room. Fax, copier, bicycles and child care on premises. Handicap access. Antiques, fishing, parks, downhill skiing, cross-country skiing, theater and watersports nearby.

Location: Forty miles from Milwaukee.

Seen in: Keystone Country Peddler, Pioneer Press Publication.

"As much as we wanted to be on the beach, we found it impossible to leave the house. It's so beautiful and relaxing."

Certificate may be used: Nov. 15 to May 15, no holidays, Sunday-Thursday.

Lodi
I6

Victorian Treasure B&B Inn
115 Prairie St, Lodi, WI 53555-7147
(608)592-5199 (800)859-5199
Fax:(608)592-7147

Circa 1893. The Victorian Treasure is a combination of two charming, 19th-century Queen Anne Victorians, built by Carl Menes, a Norwegian immigrant who constructed many of the area's

Victorian homes. The interior boasts beautiful oak and birch pocket doors, leaded-glass windows and restored woods. Cozy guest rooms offer fluffy pillows, down comforters, bathrobes and soft towels. Formal, full breakfasts are served in the well-appointed dining room with treats such as eggs Florentine or whole wheat pancakes topped with homemade strawberry-rhubarb sauce.

Innkeeper(s): Todd & Kimberly Seidl. $79-169. MC VISA PC TC. 8 rooms with PB, 4 with FP. 4 suites. Breakfast and evening snack included in rates. Types of meals: gourmet breakfast and early coffee/tea. Beds: Q. Air conditioning in room. Fax, copier and library on premises. Antiques, parks, shopping, downhill skiing, cross-country skiing, sporting events, theater and watersports nearby.

Seen in: Wisconsin, Catholic Knight, Milwaukee Sentinel, Portage Daily Register, Baraboo News Republic, Lodi Enterprise, State Journal.

"Your home is so incredibly beautiful. Thank you so much for a very memorable stay and your wonderful hospitality."

Certificate may be used: Monday through Thursday; April-May, November-December.

Madison   J6

Arbor House, An Environmental Inn
3402 Monroe St, Madison, WI 53711
(608)238-2981 Fax:(608)238-1175

Circa 1853. Nature lovers not only will enjoy the inn's close access to a 1,280-acre nature preserve, they also will appreciate the innkeepers' ecological theme. Organic sheets and towels are offered for guests as well as environmentally safe bath products. Arbor House is one of Madison's oldest existing homes and features plenty of historic features, such as reading chairs and antiques, mixed with modern amenities and unique touches. The Studio Room features a skylit whirlpool tub, and the Tap Room, with its nautical theme, includes a fish tank. The innkeepers provide a computer system for business travelers. Lake Wingra is within walking distance as are biking and nature trails, bird watching and a host of other outdoor activities.

Innkeeper(s): John & Cathie Imes. $74-180. MC VISA AX PC TC. 8 rooms with PB, 2 with FP. 1 suite. 1 conference room. Breakfast included in rates. Types of meals: continental-plus breakfast and full

breakfast. Beds: Q. Air conditioning, ceiling fan, cable TV and VCR in room. Fax and copier on premises. Handicap access. Antiques, fishing, parks, cross-country skiing, sporting events and watersports nearby. Seen in: E.

"What a delightful treat in the middle of Madison. Absolutely, unquestionably, the best time I spent in a hotel or otherwise. B&Bs are the only way to go! Thank you!"

Certificate may be used: January-March, Sunday-Thursday, excluding holidays.

Mansion Hill Inn
424 N Pinckney St, Madison, WI 53703
(608)255-3999 (800)798-9070
Fax:(608)255-2217

Circa 1895. The facade of this Romanesque Revival sandstone mansion boasts magnificent arched windows, Swedish railings, verandas and a belvedere. There are marble floors, ornate moldings and a magnificent mahogany and walnut staircase

that winds up four stories. Recently restored and lavishly decorated, the inn easily rivals rooms at the Ritz for opulence. A special occasion warrants requesting the suite with the secret passageway behind a swinging bookcase.

Innkeeper(s): Janna Wojtal. $100-270. MC VISA AX PC TC. 11 rooms with PB, 4 with FP. 2 suites. 1 conference room. Breakfast and evening snack included in rates. Types of meals: continental-plus breakfast and early coffee/tea. Room service available. Beds: KQ. Air conditioning, turn-down service, cable TV and VCR in room. Fax, copier and library on premises. Fishing, parks, sporting events and theater nearby.

Seen in: Chicago Tribune, New York Times, Country Inns, Americana, Glamour.

"The elegance, charm and superb services made it a delightful experience."

Certificate may be used: Dec. 1 to April 30, Sunday-Thursday, no holidays.

Osceola E1

Pleasant Lake Inn

2238 60th Ave, Osceola, WI 54020-4509
(715)294-2545 (800)294-2545

Circa 1990. This country-style home commands a view of Pleasant Lake from its picturesque forest setting. All the rooms have their own sun room or private deck and two have double whirlpools. The original farm, a quarter of a mile from the inn, has been in the Berg family for more than 130 years. Maintained trails wind along the lake and through the woods, and an apple orchard is a favorite spot for picture-taking in the spring and apple-gathering in the fall. A full breakfast often includes Dutch pancakes made from freshly ground flour and served with honey from the innkeepers' beehives.

Innkeeper(s): Richard & Charlene Berg. $40-100. MC VISA DS. 4 rooms with PB. Breakfast and evening snack included in rates. Types of meals: full breakfast and early coffee/tea. Beds: Q. Air conditioning and ceiling fan in room. VCR on premises. Antiques, fishing, parks, shopping, skiing, theater and watersports nearby.

Location: Located just one hour from the Twin Cities and 10 minutes from Osceola.

Seen in: Sun.

"We enjoyed sharing our mornings with the hummingbirds and the evenings by the bonfire."

Certificate may be used: Monday-Thursday, Nov. 1-March 1, excluding holidays.

St. Croix River Inn

305 River St, PO Box 356,
Osceola, WI 54020
(715)294-4248

Circa 1910. This stone house is poised on a bluff overlooking the St. Croix River. The sitting room overlooks the river. All guest rooms have whirlpool baths. Rooms feature such amenities as four-poster canopy beds, a tile fireplace, a Palladian window that stretches from floor to ceiling, stenciling, bull's-eye moldings and private balconies. Breakfast is served in bed.

Innkeeper(s): Bev Johnson. $85-200. MC VISA AX. 7 rooms with PB, 1 with FP. Breakfast included in rates. Type of meal: full breakfast. Beds:

Q. Spa on premises. Fishing and parks nearby.

Location: St. Croix River Valley.

Seen in: Chicago Sun-Times, Skyway News, St. Paul Pioneer Press.

Certificate may be used: Sunday-Thursday all year.

Phillips D5

East Highland School House B&B

West 4342, Hwy D, Phillips, WI 54555
(715)339-3492

Guests are invited to ring the bell at this restored one-room schoolhouse. Additions were made to the building in the 1920s, and rooms feature rustic exposed beams, brick walls and original light fixtures. Innkeepers Jeanne and Russ Kirchmeyer filled the home with family antiques and turn-of-the-century pieces. Lacy curtains, doilies and hand-hooked rugs lend to the romantic, country atmosphere. The kitchen, which once served as a stage for the school, is now where Jeanne prepares the expansive morning meals.

Innkeeper(s): Jeanne Kirchmeyer. $45-60. 4 rooms. Breakfast included in rates. Type of meal: full breakfast.

Certificate may be used: Year-round, weekends if available.

Plain J5

Bettinger House B&B

855 Wachter Ave, Hwy 23,
Plain, WI 53577
(608)546-2951 Fax:(608)546-2951

Circa 1904. This two-story brick inn once was home to the town's midwife, (and the innkeeper's grandmother) who delivered more than 300 babies here. The current innkeepers are just as eager to bring new guests into their home. The Elizabeth Room, named for the midwife, boasts a round king-size bed and private bath. Lavish country breakfasts often include potatoes dug from the innkeeper's off-site farm, sour cream cucumbers, breakfast pie with eggs and sausage, rhubarb coffeecake, and sorbet. Area attractions are plentiful, including the House on the Rock, St. Anne's Shrine and the Wisconsin River. Be sure to visit the nearby Cedar Grove Cheese Factory.

Innkeeper(s): Marie Neider. $50-65. MC VISA. 5 rooms, 3 with PB. Breakfast included in rates. Type of meal: full breakfast. Afternoon tea available. Beds: KQ. Air conditioning and ceiling fan in room. Cable TV, VCR, fax and copier on premises. Antiques, fishing, parks, shopping, cross-country skiing, theater and watersports nearby.

Certificate may be used: Sunday through Thursday, except holidays.

Plainfield   H6

Johnson Inn
231 W North St, Box 487,
Plainfield, WI 54966-9704
(715)335-4383

Circa 1870. Located in a scenic region of Central Wisconsin known for its antiques, flea markets, lakes and hunting, this inn offers a fine stopping point for those exploring the area's attractions. Antiques, birch flooring, carved oak paneling and tall ceilings highlight the interior. The lacy Rathermel Room features a pink, blue and white color scheme, with wicker furnishings, queen bed and private bath, while the Sherman Safari Room boasts a unique jungle print decor and a queen bed. The innkeepers' well-tended garden helps furnish some of the inn's foodstuffs.

Innkeeper(s): Burrell & Nancy Johnson. $35-75. TC. 4 rooms, 2 with PB. Breakfast, afternoon tea and evening snack included in rates. Types of meals: full breakfast, gourmet breakfast and early coffee/tea. Beds: Q. Ceiling fan in room. Antiques, fishing, parks, shopping, downhill skiing, cross-country skiing, sporting events and watersports nearby.

Certificate may be used: Year-round, Monday through Thursday, except first week in August.

Plymouth   I9

Yankee Hill Inn B&B
405 Collins St, Plymouth, WI 53073-2361
(414)892-2222

Circa 1870. Two outstanding examples of 19th-century architecture comprise this inn, one a striking Italianate Gothic listed in the National Register, and the other a Queen Anne Victorian with many custom touches. Between the two impressive structures, visitors will choose from 11 spacious guest rooms, all featuring antique furnishings and handmade quilts. Visitors can walk to downtown, where they will find an antique mall, shopping and fine dining.

Innkeeper(s): Peg Stahlman. $72-96. MC VISA. 12 rooms with PB. Breakfast included in rates. Types of meals: continental-plus breakfast, full breakfast and early coffee/tea. Beds: QD. VCR on premises. Antiques, fishing, shopping, cross-country skiing and theater nearby.

Seen in: Wisconsin Country Life.

"You have mastered the art of comfort. All the perfect little touches make this a dream come true. I only regret that we cannot stay forever."

Certificate may be used: Nov. 1 through April 30, anytime except holidays or holiday weekends. May 1 through Oct. 31, Monday through Thursday only.

Port Washington   I9

The Inn at Old Twelve Hundred
806 W Grand Ave, Port
Washington, WI 53074-2032
(414)268-1200 Fax:(414)284-6885

Circa 1890. There's plenty of room to relax at this Queen Anne Victorian inn, which features three enclosed, wicker-filled porches. Guests can sit in the parlor surrounded by natural woodwork and stained glass. A private sitting room with a fireplace is the main feature of the original Master Suite. Two of the guest rooms offer large whirlpool tubs. The outside area includes a large, private yard with croquet available and a gazebo. Ambitious guests may want to take a ride on the inn's tandem bicycles.

Innkeeper(s): Stephanie & Ellie Bresette. $95-155. MC VISA AX. 7 rooms with PB. Breakfast included in rates. Types of meals: continental-plus breakfast and early coffee/tea. Beds: KQD. Air conditioning,

ceiling fan and cable TV in room. Bicycles on premises. Antiques, fishing, shopping, cross-country skiing, sporting events, theater and watersports nearby.

Location: On Lake Michigan.

"I can't think of a more romantic or relaxing place to be."

Certificate may be used: Sunday-Thursday, year-round.

Poynette I6

Jamieson House
407 N Franklin St, Poynette, WI 53955
(608)635-4100 Fax:(608)635-2292

Circa 1879. Victorian elegance and proximity to recreational activities and sightseeing attractions help bring enthusiastic guests to this inn, which consists of three different structures. A main house, guest house and schoolhouse all are furnished with antiques gathered statewide and from the entire Midwest. Four of the rooms have whirlpool tubs, and the inn's breakfast fare is noteworthy. Water sports are just a few miles away on Lake Wisconsin, and Baraboo's Circus World Museum, Madison and the Wisconsin Dells are within easy driving distance.

Innkeeper(s): Heidemarie Hutchison. $65-130. MC VISA AX DS. 11 rooms with PB, 1 with FP. 1 conference room. Breakfast included in rates. Type of meal: full breakfast. Beds: KQDT.

Location: Between Madison & Wisconsin Dells.

Seen in: Capital Times, North West News, Poynette Press.

Certificate may be used: Sunday-Thursday, anytime.

Reedsburg I5

Parkview B&B
211 N Park St, Reedsburg, WI 53959-1652
(608)524-4333

Circa 1895. Tantalizingly close to Baraboo and Wisconsin Dells, this central Wisconsin inn overlooks a city park in the historic district. The gracious innkeepers delight in tending to their guest's desires and offer wake-up coffee and a morning paper. The home's first owners were in the hardware business, so there are many original, unique fixtures, in addition to hardwood floors, intricate woodwork, leaded and etched windows and a suitors' window. The downtown business district is just a block away.

Innkeeper(s): Tom & Donna Hofmann. $60-75. MC VISA AX. 4 rooms, 2 with PB. Breakfast included in rates. Types of meals: gourmet breakfast and early coffee/tea. Evening snack available. Beds: KQT. Air conditioning and ceiling fan in room. Cable TV on premises. Antiques, fishing, parks, shopping, downhill skiing and cross-country skiing nearby.

Seen in: Reedsburg Times Press.

"Your hospitality was great! You all made us feel right at home."

Certificate may be used: Sunday-Thursday, May 15-Oct. 15; anytime rest of the year.

Richland Center I5

Lambs Inn B&B
Rt 2, Box 144,
Richland Center, WI 53581-9626
(608)585-4301

Circa 1800. An old-fashioned family farm in a scenic hidden valley is the setting for this inn, with four guest rooms and an adjacent cottage. Ann's Room, with its cream walls, lace curtains and rose carpet, is highlighted by a quilt hand-pieced by

Donna's grandmother. Marie's Room, with its yellow and blue tones, offers a stunning view of the valley. The country kitchen is a favorite gathering place. Breakfast fare sometimes features bread pudding or kringle.

Innkeeper(s): Donna & Dick Messerschmidt. $60-105. MC VISA. 6 rooms, 4 with PB. Breakfast and evening snack included in rates. Types of meals: continental-plus breakfast, full breakfast and early coffee/tea. Beds: KQT. Air conditioning and ceiling fan in room. VCR on premises. Antiques, fishing, parks, shopping, downhill skiing, cross-country skiing, theater and watersports nearby.

Certificate may be used: Jan. 1-Dec. 31.

Sister Bay E10

The Wooden Heart Inn
11086 Highway 42, Sister Bay, WI 54234
(414)854-9097

This contemporary log home in the woods of beautiful Door County offers antique furnishings, ceiling fans and queen beds. An adjoining loft is available to read, relax or watch television. Guests also are welcome to join the innkeepers on the main floor to enjoy the fireplace and refreshments, which are served each evening. The full country

breakfasts are served in the great room. A gift shop, specializing in Christmas, country and Scandinavian items, is on the premises.

Innkeeper(s): Mike Hagerman. $85-95. MC VISA. 3 rooms. Breakfast included in rates. Types of meals: full breakfast and early coffee/tea. Air conditioning and ceiling fan in room. Cable TV and VCR on premises. Amusement parks, antiques, shopping, cross-country skiing and the-ater nearby.

Certificate may be used: Nov. 1 to April 30, Sunday through Thursday.

Soldiers Grove   I4

Old Oak Inn & Acorn Pub
Rt 1, Box 1500, Hwy 131 S, Soldiers
Grove, WI 54655-9777
(608)624-5217

Circa 1900. Guests will find lodging and dining at this spacious Queen Anne Victorian turreted inn, a mile from town. Beautiful etched and stained glass and woodcarving dominate the interior, while the guest rooms boast antique-style furnishings and imported woodwork. The area is well-known for its antiquing, cross-country skiing and fishing, and many visitors just enjoy soaking up the abundant local scenery. The inn's facilities make it a natural location for meetings and receptions, and it also is popular with those celebrating anniversaries.

Innkeeper(s): Karen Norbert. $48-62. AP. MC VISA. 7 rooms. Types of meals: continental breakfast, continental-plus breakfast, full breakfast, gourmet breakfast and early coffee/tea. Afternoon tea, dinner, evening snack, picnic lunch, lunch, gourmet lunch, banquet service, catering service and catered breakfast available. Restaurant on premises. Beds: KDT. Air conditioning and cable TV in room. VCR on premises. Antiques, fishing, parks, shopping, downhill skiing, cross-country skiing and watersports nearby.

Certificate may be used: Nov. 1 through March 1, anytime; March 1 through Oct. 31, Sunday through Thursday with reservations.

South Milwaukee   J9

Riley House B&B
727 Hawthorne Ave,
South Milwaukee, WI 53172-1733
(414)764-2521

Circa 1903. The Riley House boasts antique furni-ture, stained glass, Victorian reproduction wallpaper (as well as some 1903 original wallpaper), hard-rock maple floors and intricate patterning on the banister of the oak staircase. The ladies' parlor features old photographs, a bird cage and lace curtains. The gen-tlemen's parlor has a fireplace, ceiling fan, upright piano and antique books. The inn offers homemade truffles at bedtime.

Innkeeper(s): Mark & Roberta (Bert) Tyborski. $65-95. MC VISA TC. 3 rooms, 1 with PB. 1 suite. Breakfast included in rates. Types of meals: full breakfast and early coffee/tea. Room service available. Beds: QDT. Turn-down service and ceiling fan in room. Antiques, fishing, parks, shopping, cross-country skiing, sporting events, theater and water-sports nearby.

Seen in: Milwaukee Journal.

"The house is beautiful, the food delicious and the hosts thoughtful and charming."

Certificate may be used: May 1 to June 15, Oct. 15 to Jan. 31.

Sparta   H4

Briar Patch B&B
307 N Water St, Sparta, WI 54656-1742
(608)269-1026

This century-old home features original hardwood floors, country furnishings, antiques and collectibles. Early risers are offered coffee in the sun porch, which is decorated with wicker furnishings and a variety of plants. The aroma of freshly baked breads and other treats will lure even the deepest sleeper to the breakfast table where a hearty, country meal is served. Downtown Sparta and the popular Elroy-Sparta Bike Trail are nearby, along with antique shops and a bicycle/space museum.

Innkeeper(s): Nancy Holdeman. $75. MC VISA. 3 rooms. Breakfast included in rates. Type of meal: full breakfast.

Certificate may be used: November through April, other major dates avail-able according to availability and midweek vacancy. By reservation only.

The Franklin Victorian
220 E Franklin St, Sparta, WI 54656-1804
(608)269-3894 (800)845-8767

Circa 1800. Built for a banker when Sparta was the hub of social life, this house still boasts of such splendid woods as black ash, curly birch, quarter-cut

white oak and red birch. Features include leaded windows in the library and dining room, many of the original filigreed brass light fixtures, and a magnificent sunset stained-glass window. Sparta is nestled among the hills of Wisconsin's Coulee Region. Area attractions include rivers, trout streams, craft and antique shops.

Innkeeper(s): Lloyd & Jane Larson. $70-92. MC VISA. 4 rooms, 2 with PB, 1 with FP. 1 conference room. Breakfast included in rates. Types of meals: gourmet breakfast and early coffee/tea. Beds: KQ. Ceiling fan in room. Antiques, fishing, parks, shopping, downhill skiing, cross-country skiing and sporting events nearby.

Certificate may be used: Year-round, Sunday-Thursday.

Just-N-Trails B&B/Nordic Ski Center
Rt 1, Box 274, Sparta, WI 54656-9729
(608)269-4522 (800)488-4521
Fax:(608)269-3280

Circa 1920. Nestled in a scenic valley sits this 200-acre dairy farm. Guests are welcome to share in the dairy operations and encouraged to explore the hiking and cross-country ski trails. In addition to delightfully decorated rooms in the farmhouse, there are a Scandinavian log house and plush restored granary for those desiring more privacy. The well-cared-for grounds and buildings reflect the innkeepers' pride in their home, which was built by Don's grandfather.

Innkeeper(s): Don & Donna Justin. $70-250. MC VISA AX DS PC TC. 8 rooms, 6 with PB, 3 with FP. 3 cottages. 1 conference room. Breakfast included in rates. Type of meal: full breakfast. Beds: KQDT. Air conditioning and ceiling fan in room. Antiques, fishing, parks, shopping, downhill skiing and cross-country skiing nearby.

Location: Elroy-Sparta bike trail.

Seen in: Milwaukee Journal, Country, Wisconsin Woman, Wisconsin Trails.

"Everything was perfect, but our favorite part was calling in the cows."

Certificate may be used: Monday-Thursday except holidays.

Springbrook   D3

The Stout Trout B&B
Rt 1, Box 1630, Springbrook, WI 54875
(715)466-2790

Circa 1900. Located on 40 acres of rolling, wooded countryside, The Stout Trout overlooks a lily-ringed

bay on Gull Lake. The lake can be viewed from the living room, dining areas and second-floor guest rooms. The inn features wood-plank floors, folk art, classic prints and country-style furniture. Homemade jams and maple syrup are served.

Innkeeper(s): Kathleen Fredricks. $65. 4 rooms with PB. Breakfast included in rates. Type of meal: full breakfast. Beds: QD. Antiques, fishing, shopping, cross-country skiing and sporting events nearby.

Location: Northwest Wisconsin.

Seen in: Chicago Tribune, Wisconsin West.

"Thank you again for the comfortable setting, great food and gracious hospitality!"

Certificate may be used: Nov. 1 through May 30, Sunday through Thursday.

Stevens Point   G6

Dreams of Yesteryear B&B
1100 Brawley St,
Stevens Point, WI 54481-3536
(715)341-4525 Fax:(715)344-3047

Circa 1901. This elegant, three-story Queen Anne home is within walking distance of downtown, the Wisconsin River and the University of Wisconsin. The inn features golden oak woodwork, hardwood floors and leaded glass. Each guest room offers exquisite decor, the third-floor Ballroom Suite boasts a whirlpool. Gourmet breakfasts are served in the inn's formal dining room. An excellent hiking trail is just a block from the inn.

Innkeeper(s): Bonnie & Bill Maher. $55-129. MC VISA AX DS PC TC. 6 rooms, 4 with PB. 2 suites. Breakfast, afternoon tea and evening snack included in rates. Types of meals: full breakfast, gourmet breakfast and early coffee/tea. Beds: KQDT. Air conditioning and cable TV in room. VCR, bicycles and library on premises. Amusement parks, antiques, fishing, parks, shopping, downhill skiing, cross-country skiing, sporting events, theater and watersports nearby.

Seen in: Victorian Homes, Reach, Stevens Point Journal.

"Something from a Hans Christian Anderson fairy tale."

Certificate may be used: Nov. 15-March 15, Monday-Thursday.

Sturgeon Bay

The Inn at Cedar Crossing
336 Louisiana St,
Sturgeon Bay, WI 54235-2422
(414)743-4200

Circa 1884. This historic hotel, in the National Register, is a downtown two-story brick building that once housed street-level shops with second-floor apartments for the tailors, shopkeepers and pharmacists who worked below. The upstairs, now guest rooms, is decorated with floral wallpapers, stenciling and antiques. The Anniversary Room has a mahogany bed, fireplace and whirlpool tub. The Victorian Era dining room and pub, both with fireplaces, are on the lower level. The waterfront is three blocks away.

Innkeeper(s): Terry Wulf. $85-145. MC VISA DS PC TC. 9 rooms with PB, 6 with FP. Breakfast and evening snack included in rates. Types of meals: continental breakfast, continental-plus breakfast, full breakfast, gourmet breakfast and early coffee/tea. Dinner, picnic lunch, lunch, gourmet lunch, catering service, catered breakfast and room service available. Beds: KQ. Air conditioning, cable TV and VCR in room. Fax, copier and library on premises. Antiques, fishing, parks, shopping, downhill skiing, cross-country skiing, theater and watersports nearby.
Seen in: New Month, Milwaukee Sentinel, Chicago Sun-Times, Green Bay Press Gazette, Midwest Living, Milwaukee Journal.

"The second year stay at the inn was even better than the first. I couldn't have found a more romantic place."
Certificate may be used: Nov. 15 through May 1, Sunday through Thursday (excludes holiday stays).

Gray Goose B&B
4258 Bay Shore Dr,
Sturgeon Bay, WI 54235-2358
(414)743-9100

Circa 1862. Civil War veteran Alexander Templeton would have been proud of the transformation of his homestead to an intimate country inn. Surrounded by trees and an apple orchard, the Gray Goose overlooks Green Bay. Jessie, an inveterate antique collector, has decorated the inn to reflect this passion. All shapes and sizes of old cookie cutters form a unique ceiling border in the Pewter Room, where there is a sunset view of the bay.
Innkeeper(s): John Bruzenas & Sandy Hoffa. $65-80. MC VISA AX. 4 rooms. Type of meal: full breakfast. Beds: QDT. Bicycles on premises. Fishing nearby.
Location: In Door County.
Seen in: Door County Advocate, New Month, Wisconsin Country Life.

"Thanks for such charming and comfortable accommodations! It has been a delightful experience. Everything was just great."
Certificate may be used: November-April, Sunday-Thursday.

Scofield House B&B
908 Michigan St,
Sturgeon Bay, WI 54235-1849
(414)743-7727 Fax:(414)743-7727

Circa 1902. Mayor Herbert Scofield, prominent locally in the lumber and hardware business, built this late-Victorian house with a sturdy square tower and inlaid floors that feature intricate borders patterned in cherry, birch, maple, walnut, and red and white oak. Oak moldings throughout the house boast raised designs of bows, ribbons, swags and

flowers. Equally lavish decor is featured in the guest rooms with fluffy flowered comforters and cabbage rose wallpapers highlighting romantic antique bedsteads. Door County cherry muffins are a house specialty. Modern amenities include many suites with fireplaces and double whirlpools. "Room at the Top" is a skylit 900-square-foot suite occupying the whole third floor and furnished with Victorian antiques.
Innkeeper(s): Bill & Fran Cecil. $89-190. PC TC. 6 rooms with PB, 5 with FP. 3 cottages. Breakfast and afternoon tea included in rates. Types of meals: full breakfast and gourmet breakfast. Beds: Q. Air conditioning, ceiling fan, cable TV and VCR in room. Fax, copier and library on premises. Amusement parks, antiques, fishing, parks, shopping, downhill skiing, cross-country skiing, sporting events, theater and watersports nearby.
Seen in: Innsider, Glamour, Country, Wisconsin Trails, Green Bay Press Gazette, Chicago Tribune, Milwaukee Sentinel-Journal, Midwest Living,

Victorian Decorating & Lifestyle, Country Inns, National Geographic Traveler.

"You've introduced us to the fabulous world of B&Bs. I loved the porch swing and would have been content on it for the entire weekend."

Certificate may be used: Nov. 15-April 30, Monday through Thursday only.

White Lace Inn

16 N 5th Ave, Sturgeon Bay, WI 54235
(414)743-1105

Circa 1903. White Lace Inn is three Victorian houses, one an ornate Queen Anne. It is adjacent to two districts listed in the National Register. Often the site for romantic anniversary celebrations, a favorite suite has a two-sided fireplace, magnificent walnut Eastlake bed, English country fabrics and a two-person whirlpool tub. Enjoy the landscaped gardens and gazebo.

Innkeeper(s): Dennis Statz. $80-165. MC VISA AX DS. 15 rooms with PB. 1 suite. Breakfast included in rates. Type of meal: continental-plus breakfast. Beds: QD. Spa on premises. Handicap access. Antiques, fishing, cross-country skiing, theater and watersports nearby.

Location: Door County, Lake Michigan on one side, Green Bay on the other.

Seen in: Milwaukee Sentinel, Brides, National Geographic Traveler, Wisconsin Trails, Milwaukee, Country Home, Midwest Living.

"Each guest room is an overwhelming visual feast, a dazzling fusion of colors, textures and beautiful objects. It is one of these rare gems that established a tradition the day it opened — Wisconsin Trails."

Certificate may be used: November-April, Sunday through Thursday, holidays excluded.

Viola   I4

The Inn at Elk Run

S 4125 County Hwy SS, Viola, WI 54664
(608)625-2062 (800)729-7313
Fax:(608)625-4310

Circa 1905. This Dutch Colonial farmhouse in the scenic Mississippi River Valley region offers a relaxing getaway from city life. Visitors select from the Sarah, Simplicity or Sunrise rooms, all featuring ceiling fans, clock radios, desks, phone and turndown service. Guests are treated to full country breakfasts and afternoon teas. The area is well-known for its antiquing, apple orchards, bike trails and cross-country skiing. In addition, many guests enjoy exploring the local Amish settlement and shops or taking a canoe trip on the nearby Kickapoo River.

Innkeeper(s): Janet & Roger Hugg. $40-55. MC VISA. 3 rooms. Breakfast, afternoon tea and evening snack included in rates. Types of meals: full breakfast and early coffee/tea. Beds: QD. Fax and copier on premises. Antiques, fishing, shopping, downhill skiing, cross-country skiing and watersports nearby.

Certificate may be used: Dec. 1-April 30, any day of week.

Viroqua   I4

Viroqua Heritage Inn B&B

217 & 220 E Jefferson St,
Viroqua, WI 54665
(608)637-3306

Circa 1890. The three-story turret of this gabled Queen Anne mansion houses the sitting rooms of two guest chambers and the formal first-floor parlor. Columns, spindles and assorted gingerbread spice the exterior, while beveled glass, ornate fireplaces and crystal chandeliers grace the interior. An antique baby grand piano, a violin and Victrola reside in the music room. Breakfast is served on the original carved-oak buffet and dining table.

Innkeeper(s): Nancy Rhodes. $50-80. MC VISA DS PC TC. 9 rooms, 5 with PB, 1 with FP. 1 suite. Breakfast included in rates. Types of meals: full breakfast and early coffee/tea. Beds: KQD. Air conditioning and VCR in room. Bicycles, library and child care on premises. Antiques, fishing, parks, shopping, downhill skiing, cross-country skiing, theater and watersports nearby.

Seen in: Milwaukee, Lax.

"Wonderful house, great hosts."

Certificate may be used: Weekdays, all year, except September-October. All week, November-March, except holidays.

Walworth   K8

Arscott House B&B

PO Box 875, 241 S Main,
Walworth, WI 53184-0875
(414)275-3233

Circa 1903. Built by a master carpenter at the turn of the century, this turreted Queen Anne Victorian has been lovingly restored to its original stylings. A new addition is the inn's Arizona Suite, with Southwestern decor, a spacious sitting room and a private, outside entrance. A roomy front porch and two outside decks are favorite relaxing spots, and guests may breakfast in their rooms if

they wish. The inn is just minutes from Lake Geneva's many attractions.

Innkeeper(s): Valerie C. Dudek. $45-145. MC VISA DS PC TC. 4 rooms, 1 with PB. Breakfast and afternoon tea included in rates. Types of meals: full breakfast and early coffee/tea. Room service available. Beds: QDT. Air conditioning, turn-down service, ceiling fan, cable TV and VCR in room. Child care on premises. Antiques, fishing, parks, shopping, downhill skiing, cross-country skiing, theater and watersports nearby.

"Enjoyed your gracious hospitality. Loved the breakfast. Loved your house. We'll be back again. Thank you for making our first anniversary such an enjoyable one."

Certificate may be used: November, December, January, February and March-Monday through Thursday.

Watertown   J7

Brandt Quirk B&B

410 S 4th St, Watertown, WI 53094-4526
(414)261-7917

Circa 1875. This Greek Revival manor is named for its second owner, whose family owned the house for more than 70 years. Marble fireplaces and stained-glass windows add ambiance to the Victorian decor. Many of the antiques and crafts are also available for purchase. One suite includes a brass bed and Battenburg lace, while another features a pine cannonball bed set.

Innkeeper(s): Wayne & Elda Zuleger. $55-75. MC VISA TC. 5 rooms, 3 with PB. 3 suites. 1 conference room. Breakfast included in rates. Types of meals: full breakfast and early coffee/tea. Beds: Q. Air conditioning and cable TV in room. Antiques, fishing, parks, shopping, downhill skiing and cross-country skiing nearby.

Certificate may be used: Jan. 1 to Feb. 29 (two-night minimum).

Waupaca   G7

Crystal River B&B

E1369 Rural Rd, Waupaca, WI 54981
(715)258-5333

Circa 1853. The stately beauty of this historic Greek Revival farmhouse is rivaled only by its riverside setting. Each room features a view of the water, garden, woods or all three. A Victorian gazebo, down comforters and delicious breakfasts, with pecan sticky buns, a special favorite, add to guests' enjoyment. Exploring the village of Rural, which is in the National Register, will delight those interested in bygone days. Recreational activities abound, with the Chain O'Lakes and a state park nearby.

Innkeeper(s): Lois Sorenson. $55-95. MC VISA. 7 rooms, 2 with PB. Breakfast included in rates. Type of meal: full breakfast. Beds: Q. Air conditioning and ceiling fan in room. Cable TV on premises. Antiques, shopping, skiing and sporting events nearby.

Location: Historic district.

Seen in: Resorter, Stevens Point Journal, Wisconsin Trail Magazine.

"It was like being king for a day."

Certificate may be used: Sunday through Thursday, excluding Memorial and Labor day weekends, excluding June, July, August.

Thomas Pipe Inn

11032 Pipe Rd, Waupaca, WI 54981-8604
(715)824-3161

Circa 1854. A former stagecoach stop in the pre-railroad days, this historic Greek Revival inn offers four elegant guest rooms to visitors, many who have come to explore the Chain O'Lakes and its many attractions. Elizabeth's Room boasts a clawfoot tub and canopy bed, while the Florence Pipe Room features a brass bed loaded with pillows. The Thomas Pipe Room has a beautiful view of the woods and Marjorie's Suite has an antique bed and sitting room with sleeper sofa and fireplace. Hartman's Creek State Park is a 10-minute drive from the inn.

Innkeeper(s): Marcella Windisch. $65-125. MC VISA. 4 rooms. 1 suite. Breakfast included in rates. Type of meal: full breakfast. Air conditioning in room. VCR on premises. Antiques, shopping and cross-country skiing nearby.

Certificate may be used: December through April, seven days a week.

Whitewater   J7

Victoria-On-Main B&B

622 W Main St, Whitewater, WI 53190
(414)473-8400

Circa 1895. This Queen Anne Victorian is located in the heart of Whitewater National Historic District, adjacent to the University of Wisconsin. It was built for Edward Engebretson, mayor of Whitewater. Each guest room is named for a

1895

Wisconsin hardwood. The Red Oak Room, Cherry Room and Bird's Eye Maple Room all feature antiques, Laura Ashley prints and down comforters. A hearty breakfast is served and there are kitchen facilities available for light meal preparation. Whitewater Lake and Kettle Moraine State Forest are five minutes away.

Innkeeper(s): Nancy Wendt. $65-75. MC VISA. 3 rooms, 1 with PB, 1 with FP. Breakfast included in rates. Types of meals: full breakfast and early coffee/tea. Beds: D. Ceiling fan in room. Cable TV on premises. Antiques, fishing, parks, shopping, cross-country skiing, theater and watersports nearby.

Location: Between Madison and Milwaukee.

"We loved it. Wonderful hospitality."

Certificate may be used: June through September and January, Sunday through Thursday

Wisconsin Dells 16

Historic Bennett House

825 Oak St, Wisconsin Dells, WI 53965
(608)254-2500

Circa 1863. This handsomely restored Greek Revival-style home, framed by a white picket fence, housed the Henry Bennetts, whose family still operates the Bennett photographic studio, the oldest continuously operating studio in the country. Noted for the first stop-action photography, Mr. Bennett's work is displayed in the Smithsonian. The inn, which is listed in the National Register, is decorated in a romantic, elegant style with European touches, candles, lace and flowers. The grounds offer both sun and shade gardens.

Innkeeper(s): Gail & Rich Obermeyer. $70-90. PC TC. 3 rooms, 1 with PB. 1 suite. Breakfast included in rates. Types of meals: gourmet breakfast and early coffee/tea. Beds: QD. Air conditioning, ceiling fan, cable TV and VCR in room. Library on premises. Amusement parks, antiques, parks, shopping, theater and watersports nearby.

Seen in: Midwest Living, Travel & Leisure, Country Life.

"We have told everyone of your little paradise and we hope to visit again very soon."

Certificate may be used: October through May, Sunday through Thursday.

Terrace Hill B&B

922 River Rd, Wisconsin Dells, WI 53965
(608)253-9363

Circa 1900. With a park bordering one edge and the Wisconsin River just across the street, Terrace Hill guests are treated to pleasant surroundings both inside and out. The interior is a cheerful mix of Victorian and country decor. The Park View suite includes a canopy bed and a clawfoot tub, while other rooms offer views and cozy surroundings. There are barbecue grills and picnic tables available for guest use. The inn is just a block and a half from downtown Wisconsin Dells.

Innkeeper(s): Len, Cookie, Lenard & Lynn Novak. $45-110. PC TC. 4 rooms, 3 with PB. 1 suite. Breakfast, afternoon tea and evening snack included in rates. Types of meals: full breakfast and early coffee/tea. Beds: Q. Air conditioning in room. Cable TV, VCR and library on premises. Amusement parks, antiques, fishing, parks, shopping, downhill skiing, cross-country skiing, theater and watersports nearby.

Certificate may be used: Sept. 20 to June 30.

Thunder Valley B&B

W15344 Waubeek Rd, Wisconsin Dells,
WI 53965-9005
(608)254-4145

As the area is full of both Scandinavian and Native American heritage, the innkeeper of this country inn has tried to honor the traditions. Chief Yellow Thunder, for whom this inn is named, often camped out on the grounds and surrounding area. The inn's restaurant is highly acclaimed, and the breakfasts are hard to beat. Everything is fresh, the innkeepers grind the wheat for the morning pancakes and rolls. Guests can stay in the farmhouse, which offers a microwave and refrigerator for guest use, or spend the night in one of two cottages. The Guest Hus features gable ceilings and a knotty pine interior. The Wee Hus, is a smaller unit, but includes a refrigerator.

Innkeeper(s): Anita M. Nelson. $40-80. MC VISA. 12 rooms. Breakfast included in rates. Type of meal: full breakfast.

Certificate may be used: November through May on Sunday to Friday, upon availability.

Wyoming

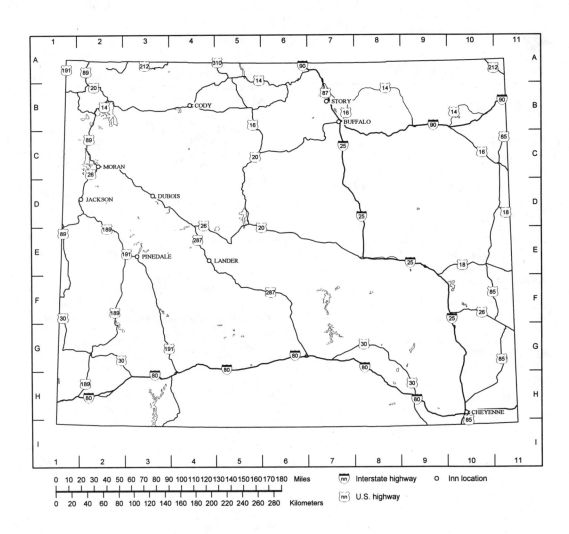

0 10 20 30 40 50 60 70 80 90 100 110 120 130 140 150 160 170 180 Miles

0 20 40 60 80 100 120 140 160 180 200 220 240 260 280 Kilometers

(nn) Interstate highway   o Inn location

(nn) U.S. highway

Buffalo B7

Cloud Peak Inn
590 N Burritt Ave, Buffalo, WY 82834
(307)684-5794 (800)715-5794
Fax:(307)684-7653

Circa 1906. Built at the turn of the century by a wealthy rancher, this inn features a graceful staircase, elegant parlor and spacious bedrooms. At the end of the day, guests can relax in front of the "fossilized" fireplace, soak in the Jacuzzi or unwind on the porch or balcony. Arrangements can be made

for dinner although there are some excellent restaurants in the area. A fine golf course is only two blocks from the inn. The innkeepers will tell you about the secret fishing spots in the mountains that are sure bets. Geologic tours of the area can be arranged with prior notice.

Innkeeper(s): Rick & Kathy Brus. $45-75. MC VISA AX PC TC. 5 rooms, 3 with PB. 1 conference room. Breakfast and evening snack included in rates. Types of meals: full breakfast, gourmet breakfast and early coffee/tea. Banquet service and catering service available. Beds: KQDT. Ceiling fan in room. Cable TV, VCR, fax, copier, spa and library on premises. Amusement parks, antiques, fishing, parks, shopping, downhill skiing, cross-country skiing and watersports nearby.

Seen in: Billings Gazette, Sheridan Press, Los Angeles Times.

Certificate may be used: All year.

Cheyenne H10

A. Drummonds Ranch B&B
399 Happy Jack Rd, Hwy 210,
Cheyenne, WY 82007
(307)634-6042 Fax:(307)634-6042

Circa 1990. With 120 acres of Wyoming wilderness and a nearby National Forest and State Park, this Old English farmhouse offers a quiet retreat. An outside hot tub, adjacent to the house, provides a view of the surrounding area and for evening soakers, an unmatched night sky. Boarding is available for those traveling with horses and pets. A. Drummonds Ranch is located half way between Cheyenne and Laramie.

Innkeeper(s): Taydie Drummond. $60-150. MC VISA PC TC. 4 rooms, 2 with PB, 1 with FP. 1 suite. Breakfast, afternoon tea and evening snack included in rates. Types of meals: full breakfast, gourmet breakfast and early coffee/tea. Dinner, picnic lunch and lunch available. Beds: QDT. Turn-down service and VCR in room. Fax, copier, sauna, bicycles, library, pet boarding and child care on premises. Fishing, parks, cross-country skiing, sporting events, theater and watersports nearby.

Certificate may be used: January-April, October-December, Sunday nights-Thursday nights.

Adventurers' Country B&B
Raven Cry Ranch
3803 I-80 Service Rd, Cheyenne, WY 82001-9118
(307)632-4087 Fax:(307)635-6744

Circa 1985. Situated behind an adobe fence, this Southwestern-style inn rests on a knoll overlooking 102 acres of prairie. Guests enjoy the tree-lined adobe courtyard, flower gardens and a front veranda filled with rocking chairs and swings. The inn offers murder-mystery weekends and a Western Adventure package. Weekly rodeos, a scenic rail excursion and crystal and granite lakes are nearby.

Innkeeper(s): Fern White. $50-140. 5 rooms, 4 with PB, 1 with FP. 1 suite. Breakfast included in rates. Types of meals: full breakfast and early coffee/tea. Afternoon tea, dinner, evening snack, picnic lunch, lunch and room service available. Beds: KQ. Turn-down service in room. Cable TV and VCR on premises. Antiques, parks, shopping, skiing, sporting events and theater nearby.

"The service was superbly personalized with great attention to detail and a great down-home cowboy atmosphere."

Certificate may be used: All year (except for July 18-31), availability. Any months, any day of week.

Porch Swing
712 E 20th St, Cheyenne, WY 82001
(307)778-7182 Fax:(307)778-7182

At this Victorian inn, breakfast is served on the back porch in summer and by the dining room fire in cold weather. Guests can enjoy items like yeast waffles

with maple syrup and fresh strawberries, orange pecan French toast and German pancakes with Swiss honey butter. All these recipes and more are found in the innkeepers' cookbook available for sale. The property's summer gardens are colorful and fragrant with a variety of perennials, aromatic and culinary herbs, wildflowers and annuals. The innkeepers would be happy to send you home with a cutting or seeds of something that's taken your fancy.

Innkeeper(s): Carole Eppler. $39-66. MC VISA. 3 rooms. Breakfast included in rates. Types of meals: full breakfast and early coffee/tea. Evening snack available. Cable TV and VCR on premises. Antiques, shopping, downhill skiing and sporting events nearby.

Certificate may be used: Anytime except last 10 days of July.

Cody   B4

The Lockhart B&B Inn

109 W Yellowstone Ave,
Cody, WY 82414-8723
(307)587-6074 (800)377-7255
Fax:(307)587-8644

Circa 1890. Once the home of author and journalist Caroline Lockhart, this Victorian inn has beautiful mountain views from its veranda. The deck affords a view of the Shoshone River. Rooms are decorated with antiques, old-fashioned beds and a clawfoot tub. Breakfast is served on fine china at your private table in the dining room. Airport pick-up service is offered, as well as making reservations for dining, river rafting, golfing, rodeo events and more.

Innkeeper(s): Cindy Baldwin. $78-95. MC VISA DS. 7 rooms with PB. Breakfast included in rates. Type of meal: full breakfast. Picnic lunch available. Beds: QT. Air conditioning, ceiling fan and cable TV in room. Antiques, fishing, shopping, downhill skiing, cross-country skiing, sporting events, theater and watersports nearby.

Seen in: Glamour, National Geographic Traveler, Windsurf, New York Times, Houston Post, Los Angeles Times.

"Just like going to grandma's house, like coming home to family — home away from home."

Certificate may be used: January-May, September-December.

Dubois   D3

Jakey's Fork Homestead

PO Box 635, Dubois, WY 82513-0635
(307)455-2769

Circa 1896. Nestled on a hillside, this farmhouse-style inn overlooks the original turn-of-the-century log buildings and Jakey's Fork Creek, an unspoiled trout stream. This rustic home is heated by a wood stove and large brick fireplace. The rooms are decorated with mountain artwork and photography.

Through the gardens and down the boardwalk are the original sod-covered homestead buildings. One of the buildings has been converted to a workshop where the innkeeper crafts unique handmade knives.

Innkeeper(s): Irene & Justin Bridges. $48-65. EP. MC VISA. 3 rooms, 1 with PB. Breakfast included in rates. Types of meals: full breakfast and early coffee/tea. Dinner, picnic lunch, lunch and catered breakfast available. Beds: QD. VCR and sauna on premises. Fishing, parks, shopping, downhill skiing and cross-country skiing nearby.

Certificate may be used: Sept. 1 to June 30, Sunday-Saturday.

Jackson   D2

H.C. Richards B&B

160 W Deloney, Jackson, WY 83001
(307)733-6704 Fax:(307)733-0930

Circa 1969. Many afternoons at this ranch-style stone home are filled with the smells of baking scones, eccles cakes, crumpets or other special items from the large kitchen. Located just one-and-a-half blocks west of the town square, the inn is within walking distance to many museums, art galleries, restaurants, theaters and shops. A tennis court, basketball court and park are just out the back door and skiing is a short six blocks away. The area is a paradise for outdoor enthusiasts, as the Grand Teton and Yellowstone national parks are nearby.

Innkeeper(s): Jackie Williams. $81-97. MC VISA PC TC. 3 rooms with PB. Breakfast and afternoon tea included in rates. Types of meals: full breakfast, gourmet breakfast and early coffee/tea. Room service available. Beds: QD. Turn-down service and cable TV in room. VCR and fax on premises. Antiques, fishing, parks, shopping, downhill skiing, cross-country skiing, theater and watersports nearby.

Certificate may be used: April-May (excluding Memorial weekend), October and November.

Sassy Moose Inn
HC 362, Teton Village Rd,
Jackson, WY 83001
(307)733-1277 (800)356-1277
Fax:(307)739-0793

Circa 1992. All of the rooms at this log-house-style inn have spectacular Teton views. The Mountain Room has a rock fireplace, queen bed and mountain cabin decor. The River Room's decor is dominated by the colors of the Snake River and accented with antiques. The inn is five minutes from Teton Village and the Jackson Hole Ski Resort. Teton Pines Golf Course and Nordic Trails are just across the road. After a day of activities, enjoy sharing your experiences over tea or relaxing in the large hot tub.

Innkeeper(s): Polly Englant. $109-154. MC VISA AX DS. 5 rooms with PB. Breakfast included in rates. Types of meals: full breakfast and early coffee/tea. Afternoon tea available. Beds: KQT. Cable TV, VCR, fax, copier, spa, pet boarding and child care on premises. Fishing, parks, shopping, downhill skiing, cross-country skiing, theater and watersports nearby.

Certificate may be used: Anytime except January-February and June-September.

Lander   E4

Piece of Cake B&B
PO Box 866, 2343 Baldwin Creek Rd,
Lander, WY 82520-0866
(307)332-7608 (800)251-6080

Circa 1991. View roaming wildlife and the breathtaking Wind River mountains from more than 1,000 square feet of deck attached to this lodge-style log home. Guest rooms include a Jacuzzi tub in a private bath. The inn is open year-round and winter guests can enjoy the Continental Divide Snowmobile Trail and the inn's 10,000 acres. In the summer, mountain bikes are available.

Innkeeper(s): Ed & Betty Lewis. $65-85. PC TC. 5 rooms with PB. 1 suite. 2 conference rooms. Breakfast and evening snack included in rates. Types of meals: full breakfast, gourmet breakfast and early coffee/tea. Afternoon tea, dinner, picnic lunch, lunch, gourmet lunch, banquet service, catering service and room service available. Beds: QDT. Turn-down service in room. VCR, fax, spa and pet boarding on premises. Antiques, fishing, parks, shopping, downhill skiing, cross-country skiing and watersports nearby.

Certificate may be used: March, April, October, November.

Moran   C2

The Inn at Buffalo Fork
18200 E Hwy 287, PO Box 311,
Moran, WY 83013
(307)543-2010 (800)260-2010
Fax:(307)543-2010

This farmhouse with covered porch, shutters and gables has the incredible Teton Range as its backdrop. Herds of elk pass by and sandhill cranes visit this five-acre property, located in the heart of the Buffalo Valley ranch lands. Breakfast is served beside a rustic, river-rock hearth. The host has more than 25 years of experience guiding Snake River scenic tours and fishing expeditions. He is also the grandson of one of the original Jackson Hole homesteaders and a lifelong resident who is well-versed in the history and geography of the area.

Innkeeper(s): Jeannie Ferrin. $100-150. MC VISA AX. 5 rooms. 1 suite. Breakfast included in rates. Types of meals: full breakfast and early coffee/tea. Evening snack and picnic lunch available. Turn-down service in room. Pet boarding and child care on premises. Downhill skiing, cross-country skiing and theater nearby.

Certificate may be used: Oct. 15-May 1, excluding holiday periods.

Diamond D Ranch-Outfitters
Buffalo Valley Rd, Box 211,
Moran, WY 83013
(307)543-2479

Located on the scenic Buffalo Valley Road, this log house inn serves many purposes including being an old hunting lodge, guest ranch, pack trip outfitter, cross-country skiing lodge and snowmobile and base lodge for touring Yellowstone and Grand Teton national parks. There's a relaxed atmosphere with a flexible schedule. The main lodge has two units each with private baths and the cabins have two units also with private baths. The staff teaches Western horsemanship and has horses for each guest's ability.

Innkeeper(s): Rod Doty. $99. 16 rooms. 2 suites. Breakfast included in rates. Type of meal: full breakfast. Dinner and lunch available. Cable TV in room. Cross-country skiing nearby.

Certificate may be used: Days of the week.

Pinedale   E3

Window on The Winds
10151 Hwy 191, PO Box 135,
Pinedale, WY 82941
(307)367-2600 Fax:(307)367-2395

Circa 1968. At the base of the Wind River Mountains, this log house inn has lodgepole pine queen beds, down comforters and rustic furnishings. A grand room with a breathtaking view of the mountains offers a hearth for warmth and comfort. There is a sun room with a hot tub. Pinedale was the location for the Green River Rendezvous. In the early 1800s, trappers, traders, Indians and others in the area would gather to trade goods. The Mountain Men and and Indians of Pinedale re-enact The Rendezvous every year.

Innkeeper(s): Leanne McClain. $50-68. MC VISA PC TC. 4 rooms. 1 conference room. Breakfast and afternoon tea included in rates. Types of meals: full breakfast and early coffee/tea. Evening snack and picnic lunch available. Beds: QT. Cable TV, VCR, fax, copier, spa, stables and pet boarding on premises. Fishing, shopping, downhill skiing, cross-country skiing and watersports nearby.

Location: Wind River Mountains.

Certificate may be used: Sept. 1 through May 31, all days of the week.

Story   B7

Piney Creek Inn B&B
11 Skylark Ln, PO Box 456,
Story, WY 82842
(307)683-2911

Circa 1956. There's an abundance of wildlife on the property of this secluded log-house-style inn nestled in the Big Horn Mountains. For the Old West buff, historic sites that are only minutes away include Fort Phil Kearny, Bozeman Trail, Little Big Horn Battlefield, numerous Indian battle sites and

museums and galleries. Ranch experiences and trail ride packages are favorites. At the end of the day, relax on the deck or in the common area, where visitors will find a television, books, magazines and games. Guests also can relax by the campfire for conversation and viewing the stars.

Innkeeper(s): Vicky Hoff. $50-85. MAP. PC TC. 5 rooms, 2 with PB. 1 cottage. Breakfast and evening snack included in rates. Types of meals: continental breakfast, full breakfast and early coffee/tea. Dinner, picnic lunch and lunch available. Beds: KQDT. Ceiling fan in room. Cable TV, VCR and library on premises. Handicap access. Antiques, fishing, shopping, cross-country skiing and theater nearby.

Certificate may be used: Nov. 1 to April 30, excluding holidays.

U. S. Territories

Puerto Rico

Ceiba

Ceiba Country Inn
PO Box 1067, Ceiba, PR 00735-1067
(809)885-0471 Fax:(809)885-0471
A large Spanish patio is available at this tropical country inn perched on rolling, green hills. Situated 500 feet above the valley floor, the inn affords a view of the ocean with the isle of Culebra on the horizon. A continental buffet is served in the warm and sunny breakfast room. The inn is four miles from Puerto Del Rey, the largest marina in the Caribbean, and 10 miles from Luquillo Beach, which is a mile of white sand, dotted with coconut palms.
Innkeeper(s): Nicki Treat. $60. 9 rooms. Breakfast included in rates. Type of meal: continental-plus breakfast. Air conditioning in room.
Certificate may be used: May-November.

Maricao

Parador La Hacienda Juanita
Road 105, PO Box 777,
Maricao, PR 00606
(809)838-2550 (800)981-7575
Fax:(809)838-2551
Circa 1976. This hacienda-style building once served as the main lodge for a coffee plantation. There are 24 acres situated 1600 feet above sea level in the mountains. Antique coffee-making implements decorate the lobby and bunches of bananas usually hang from the ceiling of the veranda. Breakfast usually includes grapefruit, oranges and guavas grown on the farm. The Rain Forest Reserve and Maricao Fish Hatchery are five miles away.
Innkeeper(s): Victoria E. Martinez Rivera. $72. MAP, EP. MC VISA AX TC. 22 rooms, 21 with PB. 1 conference room. Type of meal: full breakfast. Dinner, lunch, catering service and catered breakfast available. Beds: KDT. Ceiling fan in room. Fax and copier on premises. Handicap access.
". . .This is the most beautiful place I've ever seen. We fell in love with your hacienda and Maricao and want to live there."
Certificate may be used: November-March, Sundays to Thursdays.

Virgin Islands

Saint Croix

Pink Fancy
27 Prince St, Saint Croix, VI 00820-5032
(809)773-8460 (800)524-2045
Fax:(809)773-6448
Circa 1780. Innkeepers George and Cindy Tyler strive to help guests enjoy their island visit. For those arriving in late afternoon or early evening, the Tylers can arrange to have a light snack or dinner waiting so guests can simply relax. Rental car pickup and daily itineraries also can be arranged here. The inn was built in Dutch Colonial style and has been decorated in a tropical motif with ceiling fans. The rooms also include kitchenettes. There is a poolside happy hour each evening, and the innkeepers offer packages for honeymooners or those who wish to dive or snorkel.
Innkeeper(s): George & Cindy Tyler. $75-120. AP. MC VISA AX TC. 13 rooms with PB. Breakfast included in rates. Type of meal: continental-plus breakfast. Beds: KQT. Air conditioning, ceiling fan and cable TV in room. Fax and copier on premises. Antiques, fishing, parks, shopping and watersports nearby.
Certificate may be used: April 15 through Dec. 15.

Canada

British Columbia

North Vancouver

Laburnum Cottage B&B
1388 Terrace Ave,
North Vancouver, BC V7R 1B4
(604)988-4877 Fax:(604)988-4877

Set in a half-acre of beautifully kept English gardens, this country-style inn is surrounded by virgin forest, yet is only 15 minutes from downtown Vancouver. Afternoon tea is offered on the covered porch overlooking the award-winning gardens and meandering creek. Besides the guest rooms, there are two self-contained cottages. Both cottages include a fireplace, kitchen facilities and a private bath. Check-in time is flexible and two major bus routes are only two blocks away.

Innkeeper(s): Delphine Masterton. $80-125. MC VISA. 6 rooms. 2 suites. Breakfast included in rates. Type of meal: full breakfast. Cable TV and VCR on premises. Shopping, downhill skiing and cross-country skiing nearby.

Certificate may be used: November to April (low season) and non-legal holidays.

Sooke

Ocean Wilderness Country Inn
109 W Coast Rd, RR 2,
Sooke, BC V0S 1N0
(604)646-2116 (800)323-2116
Fax:(604)646-2317

Circa 1940. The hot tub of this log house inn is in a Japanese gazebo overlooking the ocean. Reserve your time for a private soak, and terry bathrobes are supplied. The innkeepers are pleased to prepare picnic lunches and arrange fishing charters, nature walks and beachcombing. Guests can enjoy wonderful seafood cookouts on Ocean Wilderness beach. Coffee is delivered to your room a half hour before breakfast is served. Rooms include antiques, sitting areas and canopy beds. Two of the rooms have hot tubs for two with spectacular ocean and Olympic Mountain views.

Innkeeper(s): Marion J. Rolston. $85-175. MC VISA TC. 9 rooms with PB. Breakfast included in rates. Types of meals: full breakfast and early coffee/tea. Picnic lunch and catered breakfast available. Beds: KQT. Fax and copier on premises. Handicap access. Amusement parks, antiques, fishing, parks, shopping and theater nearby.

Seen in: Puget Sound Business Journal, Getaways from Vancouver.

"Thank you for the most wonderful hospitality and accommodations of our entire vacation."

Certificate may be used: Oct. 1 to June 30.

Valemount

Rainbow Retreat B&B
PO Box 138, Valemount, BC V0E 2Z0
(604)566-9747

This authentically-fashioned log cabin home rests beside an old fur-trader's route nestled in the Canadian Rockies and surrounded by woods. Guests are sure to see plenty of birds and wildlife, including the occasional deer that march across the grounds. The innkeepers have kept the rustic touch, but added Victorian touches such as stained glass and a grand piano. Hearty breakfasts start off the day and gourmet dinners are made-to-order. The secluded retreat is just a few minutes from Mount Robson Provincial Park and its just a short walk to Fraser River, especially popular during the annual salmon spawning run.

Innkeeper(s): Keith Burchnall. $50-70. 2 rooms. Breakfast included in rates. Type of meal: full breakfast.

Certificate may be used: Anytime, except July and August.

Vancouver

The Inn at Manor Guest House
345 W 13th Ave,
Vancouver, BC V5Y 1W2
(604)876-8494 Fax:(604)876-5763

Circa 1902. This turn-of-the-century Edwardian still features many original elements, including carved banisters, polished wood floors and ornate wainscoting. The home is one of the city's oldest. The innkeeper has decorated the home with a collection of English antiques. The penthouse suite, which includes a bedroom, loft, deck and kitchen, boasts a view of the city. Fresh fruits, home-baked breads and specialties such as a cheese and mushroom souffle or blueberry cobbler highlight the breakfast menu.

Innkeeper(s): Brenda Yablon. $65-160. MC VISA TC. 10 rooms, 6 with PB, 1 with FP. 1 suite. 1 conference room. Types of meals: full breakfast and gourmet breakfast. Beds: KQDT. Cable TV in room. VCR, fax and copier on premises. Antiques, parks, shopping, downhill skiing, sporting events, theater and watersports nearby.

Certificate may be used: Nov. 1-March 31, Sunday-Wednesday.

Vernon

Pleasant Valley B&B
4008 Pleasant Valley Rd,
Vernon, BC V1T 4M2
(604)545-9504

Because of its central location, outdoor enthusiasts can make this Victorian inn their home base for daily activities. The ski area of Silverstar Mountain is a 30-minute drive and two major lakes (Okanagan and Kalamalka) are 10 minutes from the inn. A fireplace in the living room brings warmth in the winter months, and an outdoor deck and hot tub are enjoyed year-round. The innkeeper can direct you to adventure travel packages and local wineries. Breakfasts can include a variety of quiche or stuffed French toast with peach sauce.

Innkeeper(s): Christine Somerville. $45-55. VISA. 3 rooms. Breakfast included in rates. Type of meal: full breakfast. Ceiling fan in room. Antiques, shopping, downhill skiing and cross-country skiing nearby.

Certificate may be used: Anytime, except for Canadian holiday weekends.

Victoria

Gregory's Guest House
5373 Patricia Bay Hwy,
Victoria, BC V8Y 1S9
(250)658-8404 Fax:(250)658-4604

Circa 1927. The two acres of this historic hobby farm are just across the street from Elk Lake, six miles from Victoria. All the rooms are decorated in antiques and lace, and they feature garden views. Lake activities include swimming, canoeing and waterskiing. A country breakfast is served. There is a veranda for guest use.

Innkeeper(s): Paul & Elizabeth Gregory. $55-80. MC VISA PC TC. 3 rooms, 2 with PB. Breakfast included in rates. Type of meal: full breakfast. Beds: DT. Fax, library and child care on premises. Amusement parks, antiques, fishing, parks, shopping, sporting events, theater and watersports nearby.

Location: On the east side of the highway, across from Elk Lake.

"Our family felt very welcome, loved the house and especially liked the super breakfasts."

Certificate may be used: October through March.

Rose Cottage B&B
3059 Washington Ave,
Victoria, BC V9A 1P7
(604)381-5985 Fax:(604)592-5221

The well-traveled hosts of this Folk-Victorian inn know the value their visitors place on a warm welcome. The innkeepers have plenty of inside information about Victoria to make your visit as adventurous or as relaxing as you want. The inn sits on a peaceful street close to downtown and a short distance from the Gorge Park Waterway. The decor includes large, high ceilings, period furniture, a guest parlor that boasts a nautical theme and a large dining room with library.

Innkeeper(s): Robert Bishop. $65-80. MC VISA. 3 rooms. Breakfast included in rates. Type of meal: full breakfast. Turn-down service in room. Cable TV and VCR on premises. Antiques and shopping nearby.

Certificate may be used: Sept. 15 through May 31.

Whistler

Golden Dreams B&B
6412 Easy St, Whistler, BC V0N 1B6
(604)932-2667 (800)668-7055
Fax:(604)932-7055

Circa 1986. This private homestay boasts hearty vegetarian breakfasts that include homemade jam. The Victorian, Oriental and Aztec guest rooms feature duvets, sherry and slippers. Enjoy views of the mountains and the herb and flower gardens. One of the innkeepers is a coach for the National Ski Team and you may arrange for your own private coaching. Innkeeper(s): Ann & Terry Spence. $65-105. MAP. MC VISA PC TC. 3 rooms, 1 with PB. Breakfast included in rates. Beds: QD. Cable TV, VCR, spa, bicycles, library and child care on premises. Fishing, parks, shopping, skiing and watersports nearby.

"Great house, great food, terrific people."

Certificate may be used: April 15-June 15 and Sept. 15-Nov. 15, except holidays.

Nova Scotia

Liverpool

Lane's Privateer Inn & B&B
27-33 Bristol Ave, PO Box 509,
Liverpool, NS B0T 1K0
(902)354-3456 (800)794-3332
Fax:(902)354-7220

Circa 1798. For more than 30 years, three generations of the Lane family have run this historic lodge nestled among Nova Scotia's scenic coast and forests. The inn is a participant in "A Taste of Nova Scotia," which features a group of fine eateries that meet strict government standards. Lane's hosts a "Sip and Savour" series throughout the year, featuring wine tasting and gourmet meals. Breakfast at the inn is a treat with specialty menus featuring such items as haddock cakes and Eggs Benedict. Nearby Kejimkujik National Park offers plenty of outdoor activities, and beaches are only a few miles away. Liverpool offers many fine shops and restaurants to enjoy.
Innkeeper(s): The Lane Family, Ron, Carol, Susan & Terry. $40-60. MC VISA AX DC DS. 30 rooms, 27 with PB. Breakfast included in rates. Afternoon tea, dinner, picnic lunch, lunch, catering service and room service available. Beds: QDT. Antiques, fishing, cross-country skiing, theater and watersports nearby.
Seen in: Encore Travel, Providence, Rhode Island News.

"Warm and relaxed atmosphere!"

Certificate may be used: Oct. 15-May 15 (inclusive).

Ontario

Alymer

Ye Olde Apple Yard B&B
RR 4, Alymer, ON N5H 2R2
(519)765-2708

This Italianate farmhouse is set on acres of secluded countryside. Guests can stroll through the apple orchard or simply relax with a picnic under the trees. Romantic dinners for two can be arranged. Guests can also enjoy the company of the resident farm animals, or simply sit and relax by the fireplace. The area offers many interesting shops and Amish farms.
Innkeeper(s): Tino Smiaris. $60. 2 rooms. Breakfast included in rates. Type of meal: full breakfast.

Certificate may be used: Monday to Thursday, Nov. 1 to April 30.

Elora

Cedarbrook Farm B&B
RR 2, Elora, ON N0B 1S0
(519)843-3481

Circa 1876. A 100-acre working farm surrounds this simple stone farm house where guests enjoy eating breakfast overlooking fields of cattle and Arabian horses. A stream and trails on the property may be explored or visit the nearby Mennonite communities of Elmira and St. Jacobs. Elora Gorge is a few minutes away. Select a full or continental breakfast or choose a vegetarian repast.
Innkeeper(s): M.I. Elste. $50. 2 rooms. Breakfast included in rates. Types of meals: continental breakfast and full breakfast.

"Very comfortable house, lovely countryside, thank you for all of your hospitality."

Certificate may be used: Nov. 1 to April 30 all week; Sunday to Wednesday balance of year.

Lakefield

Windmere

Selwyn, RR 3, Lakefield, ON K0L 2H0
(705)652-6292 (800)465-6327
Fax:(705)652-6949

Circa 1840. Windmere is a 100-acre working farm set in the heart of the Kawartha Lakes. Joan and Wally Wilkins' restored stone home, one of Peterborough County's original homesteads, overlooks shaded grounds and a deep-water swimming pond. Scottish stone masons, brought to Canada after the War of 1812 to help build the Rideau Canal, built the home. The Wilkins' livestock consists of Rob, the resident horse.

Innkeeper(s): Wallace Wilkins. $45-70. 3 rooms, 1 with PB. 1 suite. Breakfast included in rates. Type of meal: full breakfast. Afternoon tea, evening snack and picnic lunch available. Beds: DT. Air conditioning and turn-down service in room. Cable TV, VCR, fax and copier on premises. Amusement parks, antiques, fishing, shopping, downhill skiing, cross-country skiing, theater and watersports nearby.

"Beautiful house and lovely people."

Certificate may be used: April-July, September-October, Monday to Thursday.

London

Idlewyld Inn

36 Grand Ave, London, ON N6C 1K8
(519)433-2891

A wealthy London businessman and member of Parliament constructed this manor, which still features the original woodwork, fireplace and stained-glass windows. A huge staircase graces the center hall. Several rooms include fireplaces or whirlpool tubs. Unique, hand-painted wallcoverings grace the conference room walls. For a romantic occasion, the hosts will provide a candlelit dinner for two in the guests' room.

Innkeeper(s): C. Mariawad. $69-165. MC VISA AX DC. 27 rooms. Breakfast included in rates. Type of meal: continental-plus breakfast.

Certificate may be used: January through December based on availability.

Ottawa

Auberge McGee's Inn

185 Daly Ave, Ottawa, ON K1N 6E8
(613)237-6089 (800)262-4337
Fax:(613)237-6201

Circa 1886. The portico of this restored Victorian mansion is reminiscent of the McGee's Irish roots featuring pillars that were common in Dublin architecture. The home was built for John McGee, Canada's first Clerk of the Privy Council. Rooms are comfortable and decorated in soft, pleasing colors. Amenities such as stocked mini-bars and mounted hair dryers add a touch of modern convenience. For extended stays, the inn provides the use of laundry facilities and a guest kitchenette. The innkeepers celebrate ten plus years of Award Winning Hospitality. There is no end to what guests can see and do in Ottawa. Visit the Byward Market, the many museums or 230-store Rideau center.

Innkeeper(s): Anne Schutte & Mary Unger. $58-150. MC VISA. 14 rooms, 10 with PB, 2 with FP. 2 suites. Breakfast included in rates. Type of meal: full breakfast. Beds: KQDT. Air conditioning and cable TV in room. Fax on premises. Antiques, parks, shopping, downhill skiing, cross-country skiing, sporting events, theater and watersports nearby.

Seen in: Country Inns, Ottawa Citizen, LaPressee, Ottawa.

"All we could ask for."

Certificate may be used: January, March, April, June, July, September to December; Monday-Thursday. Friday to Sunday, space permitting.

Rideau View Inn

177 Frank St, Ottawa, ON K2P 0X4
(613)236-9309 (800)658-3564
Fax:(613)237-6842

Circa 1907. This large Edwardian home is located on a quiet residential street near the Rideau Canal. A hearty breakfast is served in the dining room. Guests are encouraged to relax in front of the fireplace in the living room.

Innkeeper(s): George Hartsgrove, Richard Brouse & Charles Young. $65-80. AP. MC VISA AX DC TC. 7 rooms, 2 with PB, 1 with FP. Breakfast included in rates. Type of meal: full breakfast. Beds: QDT. Air conditioning in room. Cable TV, VCR, fax and copier on premises. Antiques, parks, shopping, downhill skiing, cross-country skiing, sporting events and theater nearby.

Location: In the center of Ottawa.

Seen in: Toronto Star.

Certificate may be used: Nov. 1 to April 30, Sunday-Saturday.

Prince Edward Island

Charlottetown

Anne's Ocean View Haven B&B Inn
Box 2044, Kinloch Rd,
Charlottetown, PE C1A 7N7
(902)569-4644 (800)665-4644
Fax:(902)569-4456

Circa 1986. Situated in a countryside setting with a panoramic view of Northumberland strait, this B&B offers quiet surroundings while being close to downtown. With both traditional and modern decor, the inn's guest rooms have sitting areas, refrigerators and four-piece baths. The island boasts beautiful, white sandy beaches and fertile red fields of potatoes. The beauty of the island attracts photographers from around the world and the many summer festivals provide much to do.
Innkeeper(s): R. Anne Olson. $70-120. TC. 5 rooms with PB. 1 suite. Breakfast and picnic lunch included in rates. Type of meal: full breakfast. Dinner available. Beds: KQDT. Turn-down service, cable TV and VCR in room. Fax, copier and child care on premises. Handicap access. Amusement parks, fishing, parks, shopping, cross-country skiing, sporting events, theater and watersports nearby.

Certificate may be used: Nov. 15-April 30. Also provide stay-Saturday & Sunday, get Friday & Monday free.

Quebec

North Hatley

Cedar Gables
Box 355, 4080 Magog Rd,
North Hatley, PQ J0B 2C0
(819)842-4120

Circa 1896. Bordering Lake Massiwippi, this gabled home boasts a wooded country setting. The inn's dock, canoes, and rowboat are available to guests. Some bedrooms have lake views. Breakfast is served out on the veranda, weather permitting. The village is a five-minute walk from the inn.
Innkeeper(s): Ann & Don Fleischer. $80-104. MC VISA AX PC TC. 5 rooms with PB, 1 with FP. 1 suite. Breakfast and afternoon tea included in rates. Types of meals: continental-plus breakfast, gourmet breakfast and early coffee/tea. Catered breakfast available. Beds: K. Cable TV and VCR in room. Swimming and library on premises. Handicap access. Antiques, fishing, parks, downhill skiing, cross-country skiing, sporting events, theater and watersports nearby.

Location: At lakeside on Lake Massiwippi in Quebec's eastern townships, 100 miles east of Montreal, 20 miles north of the Vermont-Quebec border.

Seen in: Montreal Gazette.

"We felt comfortable and at home the minute we stepped in the door."

Certificate may be used: Sunday-Thursday nights, generally mid-October through mid-May with holiday exceptions.

Inns of Interest

African American History

Wingscorton Farm Inn . . . . .East Sandwich, Mass.
Munro House B&B . . . . .Jonesville, Mich.
Sleepy Hollow Farm . . . . .Gordonsville, Va.

Associated with Literary Figures

Ralph Waldo Emerson, Louisa May Alcott, Nathaniel Hawthorne
Hawthorne Inn . . . . .Concord, Mass..
F. Scott Fitzgerald, Thomas Wolfe
Welbourne . . . . .Middleburg, Va.
Jack London
Vichy Hot Springs Resort Inn . . . . . .Ukiah, Calif.
Becky Thatcher
Fifth Street Mansion B&B . . . . . .Hannibal, Mo.
Mark Twain/Samuel Clemens
Vichy Hot Springs Resort & Inn . . . .Ukiah, Calif.
Fifth Street Mansion B&B . . . . . .Hannibal, Mo.
Garth Woodside Mansion . . . . . . .Hannibal, Mo.
Edith Wharton
The Gables Inn . . . . .Lenox, Mass.

Barns

Cornerstone B&B Inn . . . . .Landenberg, Pa.
Waitsfield Inn . . . . .Waitsfield, Vt.
Old Church House Inn . . . . .Mossville, Ill.

Civil War

The Mansion B&B . . . . .Bardstown, Ky.
La Vista Plantation . . . . .Fredericksburg, Va..
The Sedgwick Inn . . . . .Berlin, N.Y.
Welbourne . . . . .Middleburg, Va.
A Touch of Country B&B . . . . .New Market, Va.

Cookbooks

Dairy Hollow House . . . . . . .Eureka Springs, Ark.
"Dairy Hollow House Cookbook"
"Dairy Hollow House Soup & Bread Cookbook"
The Old Yacht Club Inn . . . .Santa Barbara, Calif.
"The Old Yacht Club Inn Cookbook"
Sea Holly Inn . . . . .Cape May, N.J.
"Sea Holly Bed and Breakfast, A Sharing of Secrets"
Grandview Lodge . . . . .Waynesville, N.C.
"Recipes from Grandview Lodge"
The Durning House B&B and Tea Room
. . . . .Van Alstyme, Texas
"Hog Heaven"
Hill Farm Inn . . . . .Arlington, Vt.
"Recipes from the Kitchen of"
Sims-Mitchell House B&B . . . . . . .Chatham, Va.
"Waking Up Down South"
"Well Bless Your Heart,"Vols. I & II
"Butter'em While They're Hot"
Bombay House . . . . .Bainbridge Island, Wash.
"Breakfast with Bunny"
Ravenscroft Inn . . . . .Port Townsend, Wash
"Something's CookInn"

Farms and Orchards

Apple Blossom Inn B&B . . . . . .Ahwahnee, Calif.
Apple Lane Inn . . . . .Aptos, Calif.
Rockin' A B&B . . . . .Julian, Calif.
The Inn at Shallow Creek Farm . . . .Orland, Calif.
Living Spring Farm & Guest Ranch
. . . . .Platina, Calif.
Howard Creek Ranch . . . . .Westport, Calif.
Black Forest B&B . . . . . .Colorado Springs, Colo.
Maple Hill Farm . . . . .Coventry, Conn.
Kingston 5 Ranch B&B . . . . .Kingston, Id.

521

The Shaw House . . . . .Anamosa, Iowa	
Lear Acres B&B . . . . .Bern, Kan.	
Peaceful Acres B&B . . . . .Great Bend, Kan.	
Canaan Land Farm B&B . . . . . .Harrodsburg, KY	
Gilbert's B&B . . . . .Rehoboth, Mass.	
Wingscorton Farm Inn . . . . . . .Sandwich, Mass.	
Liberty Hill Inn . . . . .Yarmouth Port, Mass.	
Ellis River B&B . . . . .Jackson, N.H.	
Vogt Farm B&B . . . . .Marietta, Pa.	
Cedar Hill Farm . . . . .Mount Joy, Pa.	
Field & Pine B&B . . . . .Shippensburg, Pa.	
Dells B&B at Cedar Hill Farm . . . . .Spruce Creek, Pa.	
B&B at Skogland Farm . . . . .Canova, S.D.	
Llano Grande Plantation . . . .Nacogdoches, Texas	
Hill Farm Inn . . . . .Arlington, Vt.	
Historic Brookside Farms . . . . .Orwell, Vt.	
Liberty Hill Farm . . . . .Rochester, Vt.	
The Foster-Harris House . . . . . . .Washington, Va.	
Deep Meadow Farm B&B . . . .Deer Harbor, Wash.	

Gold Mines & Gold Panning

Pearson's Pond Luxury Inn . . . . . .Juneau, Alaska.
Julian Gold Rush Hotel . . . . .Julian, Calif.
Dunbar House 1880 . . . . .Murphys, Calif.
Old Blewett Pass B&B . . . . .Leavenworth, Wash.

Hot Springs

Vichy Hot Springs Resort & Inn . . . .Ukiah, Calif.

Inns Built Prior to 1799

1678 Hewick Plantation . . . . .Urbanna, Va.
1690 The Great Valley House of Valley Forge
. . . . .Malvern, Pa.
1700 Hacienda Vargas . . . . . .Algodones, N.M.
1700 Hollileif B&B . . . . .Newtown, Pa.
1704 Stumble Inne . . . . .Nantucket Island, Mass.
1709 The Woodbox Inn
. . . . .Nantucket Island, Mass.
1714 Hartwell House . . . . . . .Ogunquit, Maine
1720 Butternut Farm . . . . . . .Glastonbury, Conn.
1725 Witmer's Tavern - Historic 1725 Inn
. . . . .Lancaster, Pa.
1731 Maple Hill Farm B&B . . . .Coventry, Conn.

1732 The Cookie Jar B&B . . . . . .Wyoming, R.I.
1734 Joseph Ambler Inn . . . . .North Wales, Pa.
1738 Brown's Historic Home B&B . . .Salem, N.J.
1738 Herr Farmhouse Inn . . . . . .Manheim, Pa.
1739 The Ruffner House . . . . .Luray, Va.
1740 Red Brook Inn . . . . .Mystic, Conn.
1740 Henry Ludlam Inn . . . . . . .Woodbine, N.J.
1740 Evermay-on-the-Delaware . . . .Erwinna, Pa.
1740 Barley Sheaf Farm . . . . .Holicong, Pa.
1743 The Inn at Mitchell House
. . . . .Chestertown, Mary.
1750 House on the Hill B&B
. . . . .Lake George/Warrensburg, N.Y.
1750 Shippen Way Inn . . . . . . .Philadelphia, Pa.
1750 Melville House . . . . .Newport, R.I.
1750 Henry Farm Inn . . . . .Chester, Vt.

1753 Maplehedge B&B . . . . . .Charlestown, N.H.
1753 L'Auberge Provencale . . . . .White Post, Va.
1754 Crocker Tavern B&B . . . .Barnstable, Mass.
1756 Bee and Thistle Inn . . . . .Old Lyme, Conn.
1759 Ira Allen House . . . . .Arlington, Vt.
1760 The Winchester Country Inn
. . . . .Westminster, Mary.
1760 Henry Ludlam Inn . . . . . . .Woodbine, N.J.
1760 Gilbert House B&B of Middleburn
. . . . .Charles Town, W.V.
1763 Colonel Spencer Inn . . . . .Plymouth, N.H.
1765 Bankhouse B&B . . . . . . .West Chester, Pa.
1767 Highland Lake Inn B&B
. . . . .East Andover, N.H.
1770 Silvermine Tavern . . . . . . .Norwalk, Conn.
1772 The Bagley House . . . . . . .Durham, Maine
1775 Colonel Roger Brown House
. . . . .Concord, Mass.
1775 Kanaga House B&B
. . . . .Harrisburg/N. Kingston, Pa.
1775 Welbourne . . . . .Middleburg, Va.
1776 The Inn at Chester . . . . . .Chester, Conn.
1776 Townshend Country . . . . .Townshend, Vt.
1778 Staffords-in-the-Field . . . . .Chocorua, N.H.
1779 Miles River Country Inn . .Hamilton, Mass.
1780 The 1780 Egremont Inn
. . . . .South Egremont, Mass.
1785 The 1785 Inn . . . . . . .North Conway, N.H.
1786 Silvermine Tavern . . . . . . .Norwalk, Conn.
1786 Kenniston Hill Inn . . . . . .Boothbay, Maine

1786 Windsor House . . . . . . .Newburyport, Mass.

1786 The Wayside Inn
. . . . .Greenfield Center, N.Y.

1787 The Lords Proprietors' Inn
. . . . .Edenton, N.C.

1788 Sleepy Hollow Farm B&B
. . . . .Gordonsville, Va.

1789 The Hancock Inn . . . . .Hancock, N.H.

1789 Longswamp B&B . . . . .Mertztown, Pa.

1789 Historic Brookside Farms . . . . .Orwell, Vt.

1790 Fairhaven Inn . . . . .Bath, Maine

1790 Crown 'N' Anchor . . . .Newcastle, Maine

1790 Tuck Inn . . . . .Rockport, Mass.

1790 Olde Orchard Inn . . . . .Moultonboro, N.H.

1790 The Inn at New Ipswich
. . . . .New Ipswich, N.H.

1790 Pheasant Field B&B . . . . .Carlisle, Pa.

1790 Field & Pine B&B . . . . .Shippensburg, Pa.

1790 1790 House . . . . .Georgetown, S.C.

1790 Hill Farm Inn . . . . .Arlington, Vt.

1790 Silver Maple Lodge & Cottages
. . . . .Fairlee, Vt.

1790 Shoreham Inn & Country Store
. . . . .Shoreham Village, Vt.

1790 Lareau Farm Country Inn
. . . . .Waitsfield, Vt.

1790 Red Shutter Farmhouse B&B
. . . . .New Market, Va.

1791 St. Francis Inn . . . . . .Saint Augustine, Fla.

1791 The Sedgwick Inn . . . . .Berlin, N.Y.

1793 Cove House . . . . . . .Kennebunkport, Maine

1794 The Inn at Maplewood Farm
. . . . .Hillsboro, N.H.

1795 Canaan Land Farm B&B
. . . . .Harrodsburg, Ky.

1795 The Acorn Inn . . . . .Canadaigua, N.Y.

1795 Maplewood Inn . . . . .Fair Haven, Vt.

1795 Spring Farm B&B . . . . .Luray, Va.

1796 National Pike Inn . . . . .New Market, Mary.

1797 Sanford's Ridge B&B . . . .Queensbury, N.Y.

1797 Bay View Waterfront B&B
. . . . .Belle Haven, Va.

Jail House

Casa de Patron . . . . .Lincoln, N.M.

Lighthouses

The Keeper's House . . . . . .Isle Au Haut, Maine

Big Bay Point Lighthouse B&B
. . . . .Big Bay, Mich.

Llama Ranches

Canaan Land Farm B&B . . . . . .Harrodsburg, Ky.

Liberty Hill Inn . . . . .Yarmouth Port, Mass.

Rockhouse Mountain Farm Inn
. . . . .Eaton Center, N.H.

Log Houses/Cabins

Ocean Wilderness Country Inn
. . . . .Sooke, British Columbia

Old Carson Inn . . . . .Lake City, Colo.

The Log House . . . . .Russellville, Ky.

Lindgren's B&B . . . . .Lutsen, Minn.

Trout House Village Resort . . . . .Hague, N.Y.

Inn at Cedar Falls . . . . .Logan, Oh.

Claytor Lake Homestead Inn . . . . . .Draper, Va.

The Inn at Burg's Landing
. . . . .Anderson Island, Wash.

Old Mills

Lodge at Manuel Mill . . . . .Arnold, Calif.

Silvermine Tavern . . . . .Norwalk, Conn.

Arbor Rose B&B . . . . .Stockbridge, Mass.

Asa Ransom House . . . . .Clarence, N.Y.

The Inn at Gristmill Square
. . . . .Warm Springs, Va.

Old Taverns

Red Brook Inn . . . . .Old Mystic, Conn.

Silvermine Tavern . . . . .Norwalk, Conn.

Witmer's Tavern-Historic 1725 Inn
. . . . .Lancaster, Pa.

Oldest Continuously ‧ Operated Inns

Historic National Hotel B&B
. . . . .Jamestown, Calif.

Julian Gold Rush Hotel . . . . .Julian, Calif.

Florida House Inn . . . . .Amelia Island, Fla.

The Bellevue House . . . . .Block Island, R.I.

Ranches

Random Oaks Ranch . . . . .Julian, Calif.
Howard Creek Ranch . . . . .Westport, Calif.
The Lazy Ranch B&B . . . . .Edwards, Colo.
Pinehurst Inn at Jenny Creek . . . . .Ashland, Ore.
Wine Country Farm . . . . .Dayton, Ore.

Revolutionary War

Crocker Tavern B&B . . . . .Barnstable, Mass.
Colonial Roger Brown House . . . .Concord, Mass.
Village Green Inn . . . . .Falmouth, Mass.
The Melville House . . . . .Newport, R.I.
Willow Grove Inn . . . . .Orange, Va.

Schoolhouses

Ridgeview B&B . . . . .Elizabeth, Ill.
The Bagley House . . . . .Durham, Maine
Old Sea Pines Inn . . . . .Brewster, Mass.
School House B&B . . . . .Rocheport, Mo.

Space Shuttle Launches

The Higgins House . . . . .Sanford, Fla.

Stagecoach Stops

Melitta Station Inn . . . . .Santa Rosa, Calif.
Maple Hill Farm B&B Inn . . . . .Hallowell, Maine
Morgan House Inn . . . . .Lee, Mass.
The Inn at Bingham School . . .Chapel Hill, N.C.
Mountain Home B&B . . . .Mountain Home, N.C.
Bowling Green Inn B&B . . . .Jonesborough, Tenn.
Inn at Blush Hill . . . . .Waterbury, Vt.
The General Lewis . . . . .Lewisburg, W.V.

Still in the family

Crystle's B&B . . . . .Concordia, Kan.
The Sherwood Inn . . . . .New Haven, Ky.
Cedarcroft Farm B&B . . . . .Warrensburg, Mo.
Line Limousin Farmhouse B&B . . . . .Carlisle, Pa.
Hasse House and Ranch . . . . .Mason, Texas
Bay View Waterfront B&B . . . . .Belle Haven, Va.
Welbourne . . . . .Middleburg, Va.
Hewick Plantation . . . . .Urbanna, Va.

Three-seat Outhouse

Maple Hill Farm B&B . . . . . . .Coventry, Conn.

Train Stations & Renovated Rail Cars

The Inn at Depot Hill . .Capitola-by-the-Sea, Calif.
Trout City Inn . . . . .Buena Vista, Colo.
Mountain Meadows Inn B&B . . . .Ashford, Wash.

Tunnels, Secret Passageways, Caves

Wingscorton Farm . . . . . . .East Sandwich, Mass.
Munro House B&B . . . . .Jonesville, Mich.
Kemah Guest House . . . . .Saugatuck, Mich.
Colonel Spencer Inn . . . . .Plymouth, N.H.
Witmer's Tavern-Historic 1725 Inn
. . . . .Lancaster, Pa.
Lynchburg Mansion Inn . . . . . . .Lynchburg, Va.

Unusual Architecture

The Oscar Swan Country Inn . . . . . .Geneva, Ill.

Unusual Sleeping Places

In a winery
Cavender Castle Winery . . . . .Dahlonega, Georgia
50 yards from reversing whitewater rapids
The Weskeag Inn . . . . . .South Tomaston, Maine
On or next to an archaelogical dig site
The White Oak Inn . . . . .Danville, Ohio
Hewick Plantation . . . . .Urbanna, Va.

Waterfalls

Sycamore Tree B&B . . . . .Blacksburg, Va.

Who Slept/Visited Here

John Adams
Witmer's Tavern-Historic 1725 Inn
. . . . .Lancaster, Pa.
John James Audubon
Weston House . . . . .Eastport, Maine
The Barrymore family
Evermay-on-the-Delaware . . . . .Erwinna, Pa.

Henry Bennett, photographer
Historic Bennett House . . . .Wisconsin Dells, Wis.
Sarah Bernhardt, Lillie Langtry
"An Elegant Victorian Mansion" . . .Eureka, Calif.
Billy the Kid
Casa de Patron . . . . .Lincoln, N.M.
Billy the Kid, Doc Holliday, Big Nose Katy
Plaza Hotel . . . . .Las Vegas, N.M.
Clark Gable
The Gable House . . . . .Tucson, Ariz.
Clark Gable, Carole Lombard
Gold Mountain Manor Historic B&B
. . . . .Big Bear, Calif.
Herbert Hoover
The Carriage House at Stonegate
. . . . .Montoursville, Pa.
Thomas Jefferson, Patrick Henry
The General Lewis . . . . .Lewisburg, W.V.
Kellogg family
Village Country Inn . . . . .Manchester Village, Vt.
Abraham Lincoln
Black River Inn . . . . .Ludlow, Vt.
Jack London, Mark Twain, Theodore Roosevelt

Vichy Hot Springs Resort & Inn . . . .Ukiah, Calif.
Mary Pickford, Gloria Swanson, Douglas Fairbanks, Clark Gable
Esmeralda Inn . . . . .Chimney Rock, N.C.
Eleanor Roosevelt
Mulberry Inn B&B . . . . .Martins Ferry, Ohio
Theodore Roosevelt
Vichy Hot Springs Resort & Inn . . . .Ukiah, Calif.
Lillian Russell
Bayview Hotel B&B Inn . . . . .Aptos, Calif.
Babe Ruth
Cranmore Mt. Lodge . . . . . .North Conway, N.H.
William Seward
The William Seward Inn . . . . . . .Westfield, N.Y.
Martin Van Buren
Old Hoosier House . . . . .Knightstown, Ind.
Woodrow Wilson, Grover Cleveland
The Cordova . . . . .Ocean Grove, N.J.
Woolworth family, Barbara Hutton, Cary Grant
The Mulburn Inn . . . . .Bethlehem, N.H.

Additional Publications
From American Historic Inns

Bed & Breakfast and Country Inns, Eighth Edition

By Deborah Sakach

Imagine the thrill of receiving this unique book with its FREE night certificate as a gift. Now you can let someone else experience the magic of America's Country Inns with this

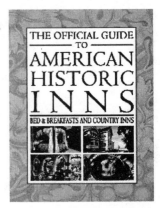

unmatched offer. *Bed & Breakfasts and Country Inns* is the most talked about guide among inngoers.

This fabulous guide features more than 1,600 Inns from across the United States and Canada. Best of all, no other "bookstore" guide offers a FREE night certificate.* This certificate can be used at any one of the Inns featured in the guide.

American Historic Inns, Inc. has been publishing books about Bed & Breakfasts since 1981. Its books and the FREE night offer have been recommended by many travel writers and editors, and featured in: *The New York Times, Washington Post, Boston Globe, Chicago Sun Times, USA Today, Good Housekeeping, Cosmopolitan, Consumer Reports* and more.

*With purchase of one night at the regular rate required. Subject to limitations.

539 pages, paperback, 500 illustrations.   **Price $21.95**

The Official Guide to American Historic Inns
Completely Revised and Updated, Fifth Edition

By Deborah Sakach

Open the door to America's past with this fascinating guide to Historic Inns that reflect our colorful heritage. From Dutch Colonials to Queen Anne Victorians, these Bed & Breakfasts and Country Inns offer experiences of a lifetime.

This special edition guide includes certified American Historic Inns that provide the utmost in hospitality, beauty, authentic restoration and preservation. Inns have been carefully selected so as to provide readers with the opportunity to visit genuine masterpieces.

With Inns dating back to as early as 1637, this guide is filled with treasures waiting to be discovered. Full descriptions, illustrations, guest comments and recommendations are all included to let you know what's in store for you before choosing to stay at America's Historic Inns.

528 pages, paperback, 800 illustrations.   **Price $15.95**

526

the Road Best Traveled – Monthly Newsletter

Here's the only way to make sure you don't get left out of the latest Bed & Breakfast and Country Inn promotions. This travel newsletter is packed with information about more FREE night offers, huge discounts on lodgings and family vacation opportunities.

And that's not all! *The Road Best Traveled* is your one-stop travel shopping source to help you plan your next vacation. This outstanding publication includes the latest hotel bargains, methods to get the cheapest air fare, unbelievable cruise deals and affordable excursion packages to exotic and far off places.

Wait, there's more! As a special offer to readers of this book, you'll receive a special edition of *Bed & Breakfasts and Country Inns* FREE with your subscription. This book includes a FREE night certificate! A great gift for a friend or another FREE night for you!

One-year subscription (12 issues) (Reg. $48.00)   Special price $39.95
Special two-year subscription (Reg. $96.00)   Special price $69.95

Bed & Breakfast and Country Inn Travel Club
Membership From American Historic Inns, Inc.

SAVE! SAVE! SAVE! We offer an exclusive discount club that lets you enjoy the excitement of Bed & Breakfast and Country Inn travel again and again. As a member of this once-in-a-lifetime offer you'll receive benefits that include savings of 25% to 50% off every night's stay!

Your membership card will entitle you to tremendous savings at some of the finest Inns in America. Members receive a guide with more than 1,100 Bed & Breakfasts and Country Inns to choose from. Plan affordable getaways to Inns nearby or visit an area of the country you've always wanted to experience.

The best part of being an American Historic Inns Travel Club Member is that the card can be used as many times as you like.

In addition to your card, you will get a FREE night's stay certificate—truly a club membership that's hard to pass up!

That's not all! Sign up for a charter membership now and receive a sample issue of *The Road Best Traveled*, the only monthly newsletter that keeps you up to date on all of the latest Bed & Breakfast and Country Inn promotions. Not only will you find out about saving on inn stays, but you will also find travel bargains on air fares, car rentals, cruises, vacation packages and more.

All travel club members receive:

- Travel club card entitling holder to 25% to 50% off lodging.
- FREE night's stay certificate.
- Guide to more than 1,100 participating Inns across America.
- Sample issue of *The Road Best Traveled*, a monthly newsletter with discount updates.

Membership is good for one year. Free night's stay with purchase of one night at the regular rate. Discount and certificate cannot be combined.

Introductory price with full benefits (Reg. $59.95) $49.95

How To Start & Run Your Own Bed & Breakfast Inn

By Ripley Hotch & Carl Glassman

In this book you'll discover the secrets of the best Inns. Learn how to decide whether owning or leasing an Inn is right for you. Find out what business strategies characterize a successful Inn and learn how to incorporate them in your own business.

If you've always dreamed of owning a Bed & Breakfast, then this book is for you!

182 pages, paperback.   Price $14.95

AMERICAN HISTORIC I N N S
INCORPORATED

PO Box 669
Dana Point
California
92629-0669
(714) 499-8070
Fax (714) 499-4022

Order Form

Date: __ __ / __ __ / __ __   Shipped: __ __ / __ __ / __ __

Name: _____

Street: _____

City/State/Zip: _____

Phone: (__ __ __) __ __ __ - __ __ __ __

QTY.	Prod. No.	Description	Amount	Total
_____	AHI8	Bed & Breakfasts and Country Inns	$21.95	_____
_____	AHIH5	The Official Guide to American Historic Inns	$15.95	_____
_____	AHIN1	The Road Best Traveled Newsletter (one year; includes free-night guide and Shipping)	$39.95	_____
_____	AHIN2	The Road Best Traveled Newsletter (two years; includes free-night guide and Shipping)	$69.95	_____
_____	AHIC2	Bed & Breakfast and Country Inn Travel Club (Includes sample issue of The Road Best Traveled)	$49.95	_____
_____	CB03	How to Start Your Own B&B	$14.95	_____

Subtotal _____

California buyers add 7.75% sales tax _____

Shipping and Handling on Book and Travel Club Orders
4th Class Book Rate (10-20 days): $2.25 for the first book. 75¢ each additional copy.
Priority Mail (2-4 days): $3.75 for one copy. $5.50 – two copies. $6.50 – three copies.

_____

TOTAL _____

❏ Check/Money Order   ❏ Mastercard   ❏ Visa   ❏ American Express

Account Number __ __ __ __ __ __ __ __ __ __ __ __ __ __ __ __   Exp. Date __ __ / __ __

Name on card _____

Signature _____

INN EVALUATION FORM

Please copy and complete this form for each stay and mail to the address shown. Since 1981 we have maintained files that include thousands of evaluations from inngoers who have sent this form to us. This information helps us evaluate and update the inns listed in this guide.

Name of Inn: _____

City and State: _____

Date of Stay: _____

Your Name: _____

Address: _____

City/State/Zip: _____

Phone: (_ _ _) _ _ _ _ – _ _ _ _

Please use the following rating scale for the next items.
1: Outstanding. 2: Good. 3: Average. 4: Fair. 5: Poor.

Location	1	2	3	4	5
Cleanliness	1	2	3	4	5
Food Service	1	2	3	4	5
Privacy	1	2	3	4	5
Beds	1	2	3	4	5
Bathrooms	1	2	3	4	5
Parking	1	2	3	4	5
Handling of reservations	1	2	3	4	5
Attitude of staff	1	2	3	4	5
Overall rating	1	2	3	4	5

Comments on Above: _____

_____

_____

_____

_____

MAIL THE COMPLETED FORM TO:
American Historic Inns, Inc.
PO Box 669
Dana Point, CA 92629-0669
(714) 499-8070

Finally, a card for Bed & Breakfast and Country Inn travelers!

Take a good look at what the American Historic Inns™ MasterCard® card has to offer:

No Annual Fee

❖❖

A Buy-One-Night-Get-One-Night-Free Certificate worth up to $200 or more, valid when you stay at a participating Bed & Breakfast.

❖❖

A complimentary 96-page edition of *Bed & Breakfast and Country Inns.*

❖❖

A complimentary copy of *The Road Best Traveled™*, a monthly travel newsletter featuring the best Bed & Breakfast bargains, special events and packages.

❖❖

An option to join the American Historic Inn Bed & Breakfast and Country Inn Travel Club™ as a charter member at a discounted fee of only $20. (Annual travel club price is $59.95.) This club offers members up to 50% off at participating inns.

❖❖

Additional travel benefits through GoldPassage® Travel Service.*

❖❖

Issued through MBNA America Bank, N.A., the MasterCard is welcome at more than 11 million locations worldwide, including country inns, B&Bs, restaurants and retail shops.

Inn-dulge yourself, request the American Historic Inns MasterCard, today! To apply call MBNA at

1-800-847-7378
and mention code SAST.